D1073564

Hubert Harrison (c. 1920s). *Source:* Schomburg Center for Research in Black Culture, Photographs and Prints Division, the New York Public Library Digital Collections.

Hubert Harrison

The Struggle for Equality, 1918–1927

Jeffrey B. Perry

Columbia University Press
New York

COLUMBIA
UNIVERSITY
PRESS

Columbia University Press gratefully acknowledges the generous support for this book provided by donors and Publishers Circle members. Their names appear on page 773.

Columbia University Press
Publishers Since 1893
New York Chichester, West Sussex
cup.columbia.edu
Copyright © 2021 Jeffrey B. Perry
All rights reserved

Library of Congress Cataloging-in-Publication Data

Names: Perry, Jeffrey Babcock, author.
Title: Hubert Harrison: the struggle for equality, 1918–1927 / Jeffrey B. Perry.
Description: New York : Columbia University Press, [2021] |
Includes bibliographical references and index.
Identifiers: LCCN 2020001982 (print) | LCCN 2020001983 (ebook) | ISBN 9780231182621
(hardback) | ISBN 9780231182638 (paperback) | ISBN 9780231552424 (ebook)
Subjects: LCSH: Harrison, Hubert H. | Harrison, Hubert H.—Political and social views. |
African Americans—Civil rights—History. | Harlem Renaissance—Social aspects. |
United States—Social conditions—1865-1918. | United States—Race relations. |
African American authors—New York (State)—New York—Biography.
Classification: LCC E185.97.H367 P465 2021 (print) | LCC E185.97.H367 (ebook) |
DDC 323.1196/073—dc23
LC record available at https://lccn.loc.gov/2020001982
LC ebook record available at https://lccn.loc.gov/2020001983

Cover image: Hubert Harrison teaching, Harlem, September 9, 1926. Courtesy of the Hubert
H. Harrison Papers, Rare Book and Manuscript Library, Columbia University Library.
Cover design: Milenda Nan Ok Lee

To the memory of
Aida Harrison Richardson, William Harrison,
Charles Richardson, Ray Richardson,
Theodore W. Allen, and Yuri Kochiyama
and to Ilva Harrison, Yvette N. Richardson-Hudson,
Becky Hom, Perri Lin Hom, and Joyce Moore Turner.

Contents

A Note on Usage

Hubert Harrison used the word "Negro" with a capital N (as opposed to such words as "colored" and "negro"), and he struggled to have others do the same. This usage is evident in his work in the "New Negro Movement"; in the organization that he founded, the Liberty League of Negro-Americans; and in his daily activities. It is also evident in the publications that he edited including *The Voice*—"A Newspaper for the New Negro," the *New Negro* monthly, the *Negro World*, the *Embryo of the Voice of the Negro*, and the *Voice of the Negro*. Results of the capitalization struggles that he and others waged included the change to the capital N by the *International Socialist Review* in 1912 and by the *New York Times* in 1930 (after his death).

In the 1960s, however, there was a shift from that usage, and today the word "Negro" is often replaced in the United States by "Black," "African American," "African-American," "Afro-American," "Afro-Caribbean," "Afro-Latino," "Afro-Asian," "African," or "Afrikan."

In this text, "Negro" is retained in titles, names, and quoted passages. When Harrison used the term it is capitalized, since that is how he wrote it. In other cases, capitalization depends on the policy of the source document. When the term is contextually appropriate, it is often enclosed in quotation marks. In general discussions "Negro," African American, or Black are often used.

Because Harrison and others struggled to capitalize the N in "Negro" as both a statement of pride in the face of racial oppression *and* as a challenge to white supremacy, when the word Black is used as its equivalent it is used with a capital B. There is no similarly compelling basis for capitalizing the w in "white."

Harrison also spoke of "the so-called white race." Based on over forty years of work related to Theodore W. Allen's seminal, two-volume *The Invention of the White Race,* this author understands the "white race" to be not merely a social construct but a ruling-class social-control formation and sees nothing progressive in "white" identity. For these reasons, the word "white" and the phrase "white race," when not used in quotations or in context, are lowercased and at times placed in quotation marks.

Introduction

Hubert Harrison: The Struggle for Equality, 1918–1927 follows the Columbia University Press publication of *Hubert Harrison: The Voice of Harlem Radicalism, 1883–1918*. This two-volume biography is based on more than thirty-nine years of research and extensive use of the Hubert H. Harrison Papers and diary, which this author preserved and inventoried before placing them with Columbia University's Rare Book and Manuscript Library. It is believed to be the first full-life, multivolume biography of an Afro-Caribbean and only the fourth of an African American after those of Booker T. Washington, W. E. B. Du Bois, and Langston Hughes.

St. Croix, Virgin Islands–born, Harlem-based Hubert Harrison (April 27, 1883–December 17, 1927) merits such attention. He was a brilliant, autodidactic, working-class, race- and class-conscious writer, orator, editor, educator, book reviewer, political activist, and radical internationalist.[1] The historian Joel A. Rogers in *World's Great Men of Color* described him as an "Intellectual Giant and Free-Lance Educator" who was "perhaps the foremost Aframerican intellect of his time" and "one of America's greatest minds." Rogers added that "no one worked more seriously and indefatigably to enlighten his fellow men" and that "none of the Aframerican leaders of his time had a saner and more effective program."[2] The labor and civil rights activist A. Philip Randolph, referring to a period when Harlem was considered an international "Negro Mecca" and the "center of radical black thought," described him as "the father of Harlem radicalism."[3] Richard B. Moore, a major activist and bibliophile who worked with the Socialist Party, African Blood Brotherhood, Communist Party, and movements for Caribbean independence and federation, described him as "above all" his contemporaries in his steady emphasis that "a vital aim" was "the liberation of the oppressed African and other colonial peoples."[4]

Harrison played unique, signal roles in the largest class radical movement (socialism) and the largest race radical movement (the "New Negro"/Garvey movement) of his era. He was a major influence on the class radical Randolph, the race radical Marcus Garvey, and other militant "New Negroes" and "common people" in the period around World War I. W. A. Domingo, a socialist and the first editor of the *Negro World*, Garvey's newspaper, explained that "Garvey like the rest of us [Randolph, Moore, Grace Campbell, Chandler Owen, Cyril Briggs and other militant 'New Negroes'] followed Hubert Harrison." The historian and Garvey expert Robert A. Hill refers to Harrison as "the New Negro ideological mentor."[5] Considered the most class conscious of the race radicals and the most race conscious of the class radicals in those years, Harrison is a key link in two great trends of the Civil Rights/Black Liberation struggle—the labor and civil rights trend associated with Randolph and Martin Luther King Jr. and the race and nationalist trend associated with Garvey and Malcolm X. (King marched on Washington with Randolph at his side, and Malcolm's father was a Garveyite preacher and his mother a reporter for Garvey's *Negro World*, the newspaper for which Harrison had been principal editor.) Harrison's lectures and writings were prolific and wide-ranging; he was a pioneering and unrivalled soapbox orator and brilliant editor; and he authored "the first . . . regular book-review section known to Negro newspaperdom."[6]

This second volume details the extraordinary last nine and one-half years of Harrison's life, which were lived at the edge of poverty in a United States shaped by capitalism, imperialism, and white supremacy. He had been a leader in the struggle against those forces, but he had found that the Left and labor movements in the United States put the "white" race first, before class. In that context, he deemed it a priority to work at developing an enlightened race consciousness, racial solidarity, and radical internationalism among "Negro" people—especially the "common people" in struggles for "political equality," against white supremacy, and for radical social change.

This volume is presented in roughly chronological order and has four broad sections:

Part 1 (1918–1919) covers his pioneering, seminal, and long-ignored writings and work that gave direction to the militant "New Negro Movement" he had founded and led since 1916–1917. Part 2 (1920–1922) details his outstanding contributions and influence as a writer for and editor of the *Negro World*, discusses his differences with Marcus Garvey as well as his differences with Black socialists publishing *The Emancipator*, and makes clear that Harrison's writings and literary influence (including his "Book Review" and "Poetry for the People" columns) contributed significantly to the climate leading up to Alain

Locke's 1925 publication *The New Negro*. Part 3 (1922–1924) focuses on his pro-
lific and wide-ranging writing and speaking efforts as an independent "Free-
Lance Educator," including his work as a public lecturer with the New York
City Board of Education and as a regular columnist for the *Boston Chronicle*.
And Part 4 (1924–1927) examines his innovative and more broadly unitary
efforts in his last years, including the founding of the International Colored
Unity League and its organ *The Voice of the Negro*.

———

In telling the important story of his life between 1918 and 1927, this second volume seeks to contribute to the growing appreciation of Harrison and his work.
Drawing from his writings, talks, diary, scrapbooks (over forty of which remain),
personal correspondence, and many other primary and secondary sources, it
offers valuable insights on the period in which he lived, on prominent contemporaries and other key figures, and on a wide array of political and literary subjects as well as struggles that were waged.

Harrison's most personally revealing document is his diary (which has
recently been made available online). He first started it shortly after arriving
in the United States, but that copy has not been located. When he restarted a
new diary on September 18, 1907, at age twenty-four, he wrote down his thoughts
on why he made that decision:

> It must surely be instructive to look back after long years on one's past
> thoughts and deeds and form new estimates of ourselves and others. Seen
> from another perspective large things grow small, small ones large and the
> lives of relative importance are bound to change position. At any rate it must
> be instructive to compare the impression of the moment, laden as it may be
> with the bias of feeling and clouded by partisan or personal prejudice, with
> the more broad and impartial review which distance in time or space makes
> possible.
>
> This may serve me in some sort as a history of myself twisted of two
> threads—what I do, and what I think. I hope I shall not make any conscious
> effort to impress upon it a character of any sort. So far as life is concerned as
> it comes so must it be set down. And if I omit any one phase of my life's expe-
> rience I do so for judicial reasons and not for the sake of seeming better in
> my own eyes when memory has ceased to testify.[7]

While Harrison wrote his diary for himself, there is no doubt from its content
and occasional marginal comments that it was also written for those who would
come after him to read and learn from. It seems clear that even as a young man
he had a strong sense of self-worth, he was aware of the significance of the work

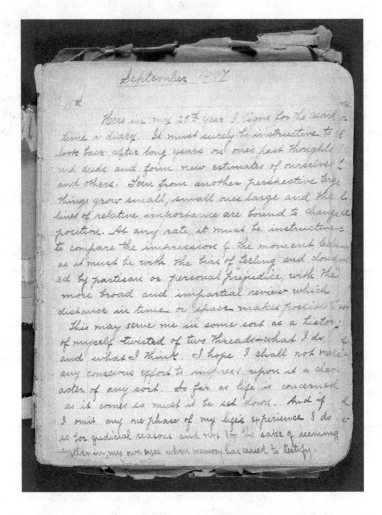

Figure 0.1. Hubert Harrison on restarting his diary, September 18, 1907. In his diary entry of September 18, 1907, Hubert Harrison, at age twenty-four, wrote, "It must surely be instructive to look back after long years on one's past thoughts and deeds and form new estimates of ourselves and others. Seen from another perspective large things grow small, small ones large and the lives of relative importance are bound to change position. At any rate it must be instructive to compare the impression of the moment, laden as it may be with the bias of feeling and clouded by partisan or personal prejudice, with the more broad and impartial review which distance in time or space makes possible." He added: "I hope I shall not make any conscious effort to impress upon it [the diary] a character of any sort. So far as life is concerned as it comes so must it be set down. And if I omit any one phase of my life's experience I do so for judicial reasons and not for the sake of seeming better in my own eyes when memory has ceased to testify." While Harrison wrote his diary for himself, there is no doubt that even as a young man he had a strong sense of self-worth, he was aware of the importance of the work he undertook, and he thought it important that a more complete record of his thinking and actions, as well as the period in which he lived, be recorded. *Source:* Hubert H. Harrison Papers, Box 9, Folder 1, Rare Book and Manuscript Library, Columbia University Library. See https://dlc.library.columbia.edu/catalog/cul:mpg4f4qt3x.

Figure 0.2. Aida M. Harrison Richardson. The third daughter of Hubert Harrison and Irene Louise Horton Harrison was Aida M. Harrison Richardson (July 4, 1912–June 28, 2001). In 1942 she married Virgil J. Richardson, a founder of the American Negro Theatre and a Tuskegee Airman. They had two children—Charles Richardson (March 2, 1944–February 20, 2017) and Ray Richardson (March 31, 1946–c. January 25, 1971). Aida and her brother William were instrumental in preserving the Hubert H. Harrison Papers until they were entrusted to Jeffrey B. Perry in the 1980s. Aida's son Charles was similarly instrumental in helping (along with Perry) to place the papers at Columbia University's Rare Book and Manuscript Library in 2005. Aida's son Ray was a militant Black TV producer of *Say Brother* (1968–1970) on Boston Public Television (WGBH). Ray died of drowning under suspicious conditions in Mexico. *Source:* Charles Richardson.

he undertook, and he thought it important that a more complete record of his thinking and actions, as well as the period in which he lived, be recorded—"as it comes so must it be set down."[8]

This volume, reinforcing the value of Harrison's approach, and in an effort to allow him to speak to current and future audiences, frequently cites his diary, papers, writings, and talks.

Figure 0.3. Joel A. Rogers, 1936. Joel Augustus Rogers (September 6, 1880—March 26, 1966) was born in Negril, Jamaica. After coming to the United States in 1906 he worked as a Pullman porter while pursuing a career as a domestic and international journalist and historian of people of African descent, biography, and "race relations." In his *World's Great Men of Color* Rogers described Harrison (following chapters on Booker T. Washington, William Monroe Trotter, W. E. B. Du Bois, and Marcus Garvey) as an "Intellectual Giant and Free-Lance Educator" who was "perhaps the foremost Aframerican intellect of his time" and "one of America's greatest minds." Rogers added that "no one worked more seriously and indefatigably to enlighten his fellow men" and that "none of the Aframerican leaders of his time had a saner and more effective program." Rogers, one of the most perceptive writers on Harrison's life and a man who knew Harrison and his family well, insightfully added: "Harrison was not without his faults. The life of any leader, scrutinized detail for detail, does not look like the handsome image presented by ecstatic admirers after flaws have been removed and bits retouched. As the saying goes—'No man is a hero to his valet.'" In Harrison's case, however, as Rogers emphasizes, this is no reason to "deny" his "essential greatness." *Source:* Courtesy of Thabiti Asukile.

In its approach it draws insight from Harrison's "Meditation" entitled "A Soul in Search of Itself" (offered in the October 1920 *Negro World*), where he wrote, "No man was ever as good as his creed."[9]

In a similar vein, this volume's approach also draws from comments by two of Harrison's contemporaries—Eugene O'Neill and J. A. Rogers. O'Neill, a future recipient of the Nobel Prize in Literature, in a June 9, 1921, letter to Harrison, wrote, "The only propaganda that ever strikes home is the truth about the human soul, black or white. Intentional uplift . . . never amount[s] to a damn—especially as uplift. To portray a human being, that is all that counts.[10] Rogers, a historian and one of the most perceptive writers on Harrison's life, and a man who knew Harrison and his family well, offered: "Harrison was not without his faults. The life of any leader, scrutinized detail for detail, does not look like the handsome image presented by ecstatic admirers after flaws have been removed and bits retouched. As the saying goes—'No man is a hero to his valet.'" In Harrison's case, however, as Rogers emphasizes, this is no reason to "deny" his "essential greatness."[11]

Finally, this volume keeps in mind words uttered at Harrison's funeral by the extraordinary bibliophile of the Black experience Arturo Alfonso Schomburg—words that partly inspired the writing of this biography. Puerto Rico–born Schomburg, with great historical perspective and knowing how immensely popular and significant Harrison was in his day, stated simply, "He came ahead of his time." With these words Schomburg correctly points to Hubert Harrison's importance for current and future generations.[12]

"New Negro Movement"
Editor and Activist

1

Return to Harlem and Resurrection of *The Voice*
(July–December 1918)

In July 1918, thirty-five-year-old Hubert Harrison returned home from the Liberty Congress in Washington, DC, to the fifth-floor walk-up apartment at 231 West 134th Street in Harlem that he shared with his wife, Lin, and their four young daughters—Frances (eight), Alice (seven), Aida (almost six), and Ilva (almost four). Also sharing the apartment was a widowed, fifty-plus-years-old lodger, Laura Forrester, who in 1910 had shared an apartment with Harrison's close friends, the activists Charles and Williana Jones Burroughs. These living conditions were crowded and made it difficult for Harrison to read, study, and write at home.[1]

The Harrison family had lived near the edge of poverty since Hubert's firing from the Post Office Department in September 1911. After losing his postal employment, Harrison, a working-class intellectual and activist, had largely survived on tutoring, ad hoc teaching, public speaking, bookselling, work with the Socialist Party (until his departure in 1914), work as an instructor at the Freethought- and anarchist-influenced Modern School, and journalism.[2] Upon his return to Manhattan in the summer of 1918, although a Black leader of national prominence, he had no regular employment or source of income, and he faced serious financial pressures.

In the period from his postal firing through the completion of the Liberty Congress (June 24–28, 1918), Harrison had made an indelible mark. He had been the leading Black activist, organizer, and theoretician in the Socialist Party; an extremely popular soapbox orator; an officer (along with Arthur Schomburg and John E. Bruce) in the Negro Society for Historical Research; an Industrial Workers of the World supporter (and the only Black speaker) at the historic Paterson, NJ, silk workers strike of 1913; a pioneering Black participant in the Freethought and birth control movements; a journalist and labor-organizing activist; and a founder of the Radical Forum lecture series in Manhattan.[3] Perhaps most importantly for his future work, in 1917 he had been the founder of the first organization (the Liberty League) and the first newspaper (*The Voice*) of the New Negro Movement.[4] These efforts were followed in June 1918 by his co-chairing of the Liberty Congress—the major national Black protest effort during World War I.[5] Harrison's seminal work profoundly influenced New Negro political and literary activism,[6] paved the way for the development of the Garvey movement,[7] foreshadowed aspects of the Civil Rights and Black Power movements of the 1960s,[8] and earned him the title "the father of Harlem radicalism."[9]

The 1918 Liberty Congress included 115 male and female delegates, from thirty-five states and the District of Columbia, and it stands as an important though much ignored component of the long Civil Rights Movement. It demanded an end to lynching, segregation, and disfranchisement and called for basic civil rights, including enforcement of the Thirteenth, Fourteenth, and Fifteenth Amendments. It also petitioned the U.S. Congress for federal anti-lynching legislation, which was a demand that the National Association for the Advancement of Colored People (NAACP), headed by its "white" chairman of the board, Joel E. Spingarn, refused to make at that time. During World War I Spingarn was a pro-war major in Military Intelligence (MI) and monitored "Negroes" for the War Department. He supported the creation of segregated officer training camps (which Harrison and much of the Black press had opposed), led efforts to undermine the Black-led Liberty Congress, and, beginning in 1914, funded the NAACP's eponymous "Spingarn Medal," which, from 1915 was awarded "for the highest or noblest achievement by a living American Negro during the preceding year or years."[10]

Around the time of the Liberty Congress Harrison became one of the first Black activists to come under surveillance by the Bureau of Investigation (BI), which had been founded in 1908 and in 1935 would be renamed the Federal Bureau of Investigation (FBI). The Bureau agent who initially investigated him was J. G. C. Corcoran, in Washington, DC. Corcoran used the services of Special Officer C. E. Addison, a "colored plain clothes man," and Dr. Arthur Ulysses Craig, an undercover "high class colored informant" who was a high school teacher. Bureau surveillance of Harrison would continue after he left Washington, and Corcoran would also seek to use John E. Bowles, an informant at American University.[11]

On his return to Harlem in July 1918 Harrison's public speaking and writing were increasingly circumscribed by the Espionage Act of June 15, 1917, as amended and broadened by the Sedition Act of May 16, 1918. In addition, like other "Negroes" who were born in St. Croix before the Woodrow Wilson–signed cession of the Virgin Islands from Denmark to the United States of January 16,

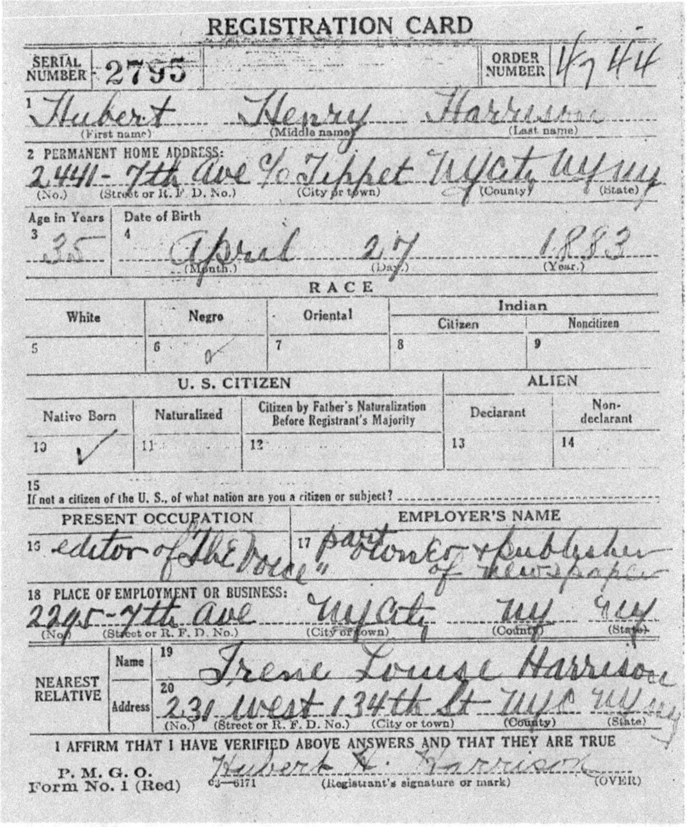

REGISTRATION CARD

SERIAL NUMBER 2795 — ORDER NUMBER 1/7 44

1 Hubert Henry Harrison
(First name) (Middle name) (Last name)

2 PERMANENT HOME ADDRESS:
2441 - 7th ave c/o Tippet NY City NY NY
(No.) (Street or R. F. D. No.) (City or town) (County) (State)

Age in Years	Date of Birth		
3 35	4 April	27	1883
	(Month.)	(Day.)	(Year.)

RACE

White	Negro	Oriental	Indian: Citizen	Indian: Noncitizen
5	6 ✓	7	8	9

U. S. CITIZEN: Native Born	U. S. CITIZEN: Naturalized	U. S. CITIZEN: Citizen by Father's Naturalization Before Registrant's Majority	ALIEN: Declarant	ALIEN: Non-declarant
10 ✓	11	12	13	14

15
If not a citizen of the U. S., of what nation are you a citizen or subject?

PRESENT OCCUPATION	EMPLOYER'S NAME
16 editor of "The Voice"	17 part owner & publisher of newspaper

18 PLACE OF EMPLOYMENT OR BUSINESS:
2295 - 7th ave NY City NY NY
(No.) (Street or R. F. D. No.) (City or town) (County) (State)

NEAREST RELATIVE
Name 19 Irene Louise Harrison
Address 20 231 West 134th St NYC NY NY
(No.) (Street or R. F. D. No.) (City or town) (County) (State)

I AFFIRM THAT I HAVE VERIFIED ABOVE ANSWERS AND THAT THEY ARE TRUE

P. M. G. O.
Form No. 1 (Red) 3—6171 Hubert H. Harrison (Registrant's signature or mark) (OVER)

Figure 1.1. Hubert H. Harrison Draft Registration, September 12, 1918, page 1.

In 1918 Hubert Harrison's public speaking and writing were increasingly circumscribed by the Espionage Act of June 15, 1917, as amended and broadened by the Sedition Act of May 16, 1918. In addition, like other "Negroes" who were born in St. Croix before the Woodrow Wilson–signed January 16, 1917, cession of the Virgin Islands from Denmark to the United States, his citizenship status in the United States was not clear. Harrison had the confusing status described by the historian William W. Boyer as "citizenship in the United States" but not "citizenship of the United States." Whether he was officially recognized as a U.S. citizen (he was listed as a citizen in the 1915 New York State Census, though he was not naturalized until 1922), or as an alien who had applied for citizenship (which he had done in 1915), he was, as a male between the ages of eighteen and forty-five (pursuant to the Selective Service Act of May 18, 1917) required to register for the draft on the third draft registration day of September 12, 1918. That signup deadline came several days after New York City witnessed a series of intense "slacker raids" that saw thousands of people "suspected" of not signing up for the draft improperly seized by private armies of the American Protective League, local police, and federal authorities. It also came in the wake of what the *Chicago Defender* described as numerous lawless outbreaks and near riots that had recently occurred in Harlem. These factors may have been related to the "U.S. Citizen: Native Born" box being checked and the address listing for Harrison being different than that for his wife. (Hubert and his wife, Lin, may also have been living separately at the time, since Harrison at times during their marriage moved to a different apartment.) The lawless outbreaks led to the formation of a vigilance committee headed by Harlem community leaders, including Harrison, who sought to exercise their influence against mob violence. After his registration Harrison was classified as 1-A. *Source:* Mary Ann Hawkins, Regional Archives Branch, General Services Administration, East Point, Georgia, to Jeffrey Perry, July 15, 1984.

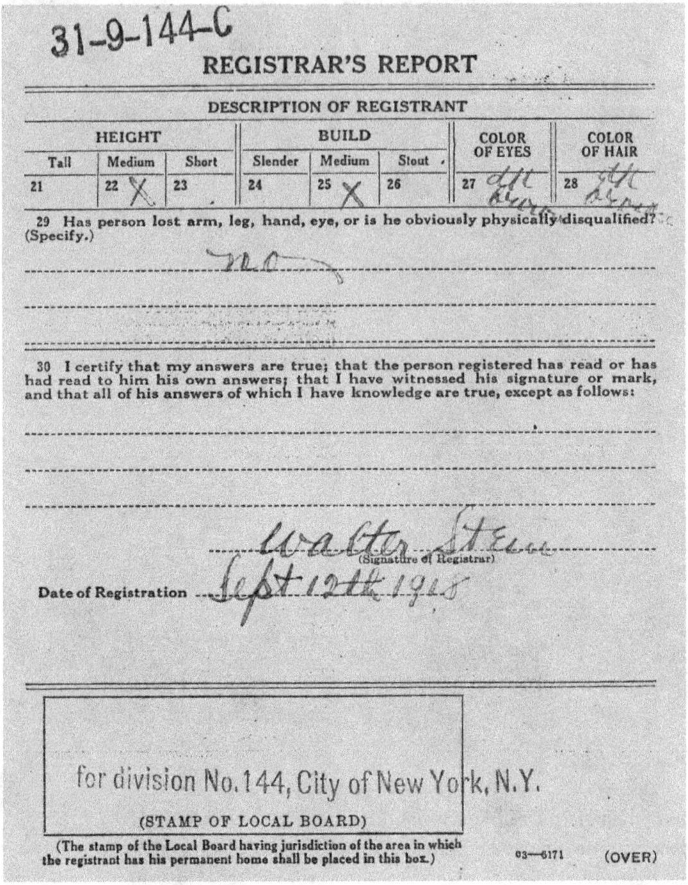

31-9-144-C

REGISTRAR'S REPORT

DESCRIPTION OF REGISTRANT

HEIGHT			BUILD			COLOR OF EYES		COLOR OF HAIR
Tall	Medium	Short	Slender	Medium	Stout			
21	22 X	23	24	25 X	26	27	28	

29 Has person lost arm, leg, hand, eye, or is he obviously physically disqualified? (Specify.)

no

30 I certify that my answers are true; that the person registered has read or has had read to him his own answers; that I have witnessed his signature or mark, and that all of his answers of which I have knowledge are true, except as follows:

Walter Stein
(Signature of Registrar)

Date of Registration ....*Sept 12th 1918*

for division No.144, City of New York, N.Y.

(STAMP OF LOCAL BOARD)

(The stamp of the Local Board having jurisdiction of the area in which the registrant has his permanent home shall be placed in this box.)

03—6171   (OVER)

Figure 1.2. Hubert H. Harrison Draft Registration, September 12, 1918, page 2. *Source:* Mary Ann Hawkins, Regional Archives Branch, General Services Administration, East Point, Georgia, to Jeffrey Perry, July 15, 1984.

1917, his citizenship status in the United States was not clear. Harrison had the confusing status described by the historian William W. Boyer as "citizenship in the United States" but not "citizenship of the United States." Whether he was officially recognized as a U.S. citizen (he was listed as a citizen in the 1915 New York State census, though he was not naturalized until 1922) or as an alien who had applied for citizenship (which he had done in 1915), he was, as a male between the ages of eighteen and forty-five (pursuant to the Selective Service Act of May 18, 1917), required to register for the draft on the third draft registration day of September 12, 1918. That sign-up deadline came several days after

New York City witnessed a series of intense "slacker raids," wherein thousands of people "suspected" of not signing up for the draft were improperly seized by private armies of the American Protective League, local police, and federal authorities. It also came in the wake of what the *Chicago Defender* described as numerous lawless outbreaks and near riots that had recently occurred in Harlem—incidents that led to the formation of a vigilance committee headed by Harlem community leaders, including Harrison, who sought to exercise their influence against mob violence. It was in this context that Harrison registered for the draft on September 12 and checked the "Native Born" box in the "U.S. Citizen" category.[12]

———

Despite the financial and political pressures he faced, and in a United States sharply divided by class and shaped by white supremacy, Harrison was undaunted. He had a vision of the political and educational work he thought was needed, and upon his return to Harlem he quickly restarted *The Voice*, which was described on its masthead as "A Newspaper for the New Negro." Over the remainder of the year he tried unsuccessfully to establish it on a regular basis in New York City and Washington, DC, and to take it into the South. By March–April 1919, however, it would cease publication after leaving what he described as "an indelible impression."[13]

From the lead-up to the "rejuvenated and resurrected" *Voice* of July 11, 1918, through December 1918, Harrison participated in labor-organizing efforts among hotel workers and Pullman porters, and he lectured in New York City, Washington, DC, and Virginia. In addition to these mass outreach efforts, as editor of *The Voice*, he honed skills and shaped perspectives that would be used in his next two major publication efforts—as the editor of the *New Negro* monthly in the latter part of 1919 and as the principal editor of the *Negro World*, the newspaper of the Marcus Garvey–led Universal Negro Improvement Association (UNIA) and African Communities League, in 1920.[14]

Harrison had originally founded *The Voice* in Harlem on July 4, 1917. When it temporarily halted publication on November 14 of that year, he was determined to push forward. In July 1918 he enacted plans to resurrect the newspaper on a grander scale. It was to be headquartered in Harlem (at 2295 Seventh Avenue, just south of 135th Street), and he announced that it would have a branch in Washington, DC. From there the paper could be taken into the South, the home of 80 to 90 percent of the country's Black population and the center of white supremacist reaction, legal segregation, disfranchisement, peonage, and lynching. The size of the Black population and the intensity of the racial and class oppression in the South gave Harrison's plan an audacious logic. That plan, which centered around reaching the Black masses with a militant call for developing "race-consciousness" and "racial solidarity," while struggling for democracy and equality, sensed the mobilizing potential among African Americans, particularly in the South, and foreshadowed the organizational growth that the Garvey-led UNIA would soon realize in that region.[15]

The Voice, now resurrected, was owned by the Race Publishing Company, which had been incorporated in December 1917. Its original incorporators included Harrison (president); Clayton Dowdy of the Elevator and Switch-Board Operators Union (secretary); Julius A. Thomas of the Alpha Physical Culture Club; Charles T. Magill, who would later be active with the Republican Party; and Charles Burroughs, Harrison's old friend from the post office and from a postal workers' study group of a decade earlier. Burroughs was also an actor who would occasionally lecture for the Board of Education. In addition, the incorporators included Cornelius A. Hughes, a local Democratic Party political activist, who had been involved in internal party struggles and was formerly active with the Equity Congress (which sought to get "Negroes" into the police and fire departments in New York City and to establish a Black National Guard regiment in New York State). The all-Black leadership of the Race Publishing Company, which also listed Charles Flourney of the Pullman Porters' Union as treasurer, was noticeably worker influenced and pledged to "run and own the paper."[16]

Harrison informed readers of *The Voice* in July 1918 that "one white man in Harlem" had offered to put up ten thousand dollars in December 1917 to own the paper in partnership with the editor. This was not the direction Harrison wanted to go, however, and the offer was rejected. Instead, $25,000 in stock in *The Voice* was to be sold at $10 a share, and "every friend of freedom" who believed in the paper's "policy and spirit" and that it couldn't "be bought off" was urged to support it financially. The editorial policy was to be shaped by the stockholders, who could help make it "the greatest Negro paper in America." In addition to Thomas, Dowdy, Hughes, and Burroughs, *The Voice*'s board of directors included the attorney Rufus L. Perry Jr. (son of the Brooklyn pastor and lay historian Rufus L. Perry); the socialist reverend Dr. George Frazier Miller, of St. Augustine's Church in Brooklyn; the businesswoman Bernia L. Smith, of the Indol System of Hair Culture; St. Croix–born James Cornelius Lionel Canegata, an organizer of the Pullman Porters' Union (whose son would later become the well-known actor Canada Lee); and the journalist John E. Bruce (a friend of Harrison from both St. Benedict's Lyceum a decade earlier and from the Negro Society for Historical Research in 1911). Readers were told that under able business management, investments in the paper would be "earning money every week."[17]

In early July 1918 Harrison announced in a leaflet that the "Manhood Movement" was now needed more than ever and that *The Voice* was "Coming Out to

Stay!" He invited all who were striving for justice in war time and working for democracy at home "while our Brave Boys are fighting for Democracy Abroad" to come to a July 4 mass meeting at Bethel AME Church, at 60 West 132nd Street (the site of the movement's "birth" a year earlier), where the first issue of volume 2 of *The Voice* would appear. The attorney James D. Carr, a Black Democratic politician, would deliver the opening address, followed by Hughes. Toney would have the paper's finance books at the meeting and answer questions. At the same time, the corporation's attorney, Rufus Perry, would be at *The Voice*'s office with the corporation's stock certificates, stock book, transfer book, and seal. Harrison planned to address rumors about previous financial mismanagement of *The Voice* directly, and he would disclose "sensational correspondence" between him and Emmett J. Scott, the current special assistant secretary of war for Negro affairs (who had been involved in Harrison's firing by the U.S. Post Office in 1911). The correspondence would tell "The Whole Story of the Paper," suggesting that Scott may have been linked to earlier difficulties with *The Voice*.[18]

A rare complete edition—possibly the only one—of the resurrected *Voice* is that of July 11, 1918. It contained four pages, sold for two cents, and indicated that future issues were scheduled to come out on Thursdays. In it Harrison thanked the thousands of "common people" who, in the paper's absence, kept asking news dealers for it, and he claimed that never before in Black journalism had there been so many calls for a paper that had suspended publication. He described how readers in many states requested bundles, particularly after the December 11, 1917, hanging of thirteen Black soldiers stationed in Houston, Texas, who were "executed while the 'colored' papers and magazines kept silent and licked the foot that kicked them." It was especially during the period of suffering in the wake of those hangings, he explained, that cries for *The Voice* came from those who wanted "the one paper which could be trusted to shoot the point-blank truth into the bull's-eye of oppression."[19]

Harrison aimed to make sure that there was "at least one Negro paper" buttressed by the love and devotion of "the masses of *our own race*." But the paper needed money. Supporters were urged to buy *The Voice* and its stock, and volunteers were solicited as news gatherers, advertising agents, and distributors. The paper would offer tips on advertising and publish a "Guaranteed List" of advertisers whose merit it could conscientiously commend. Harrison, however, warned of "sinister forces at work" that sought "to choke the voice of protest and dam the flood of our just demands." He urged that the only way to meet such forces effectively was by "the creation of a national organ of the new Spirit of Negro Manhood; an organ whose policy is shaped by ourselves alone."[20]

A little over ten months earlier, in *The Voice* of September 4, 1917, Harrison, an outstanding internationalist, had offered additional insight on his use of the "ourselves alone" concept. In the article "The New Policies for the New Negro" he explained, "Negroes" in the United States "were realizing that 'our first duty is to ourselves,'" and he emphasized that the "Negro of the Western world must follow the path of the Swadesha [Swadeshi] movement of India and the Sinn Fein movement of Ireland. The meaning of both these terms is 'ourselves first.'" This was "the mental background of the new politics of the New Negro," and "the new Negro race in America will not achieve political self-respect until it is in a position to organize itself as a politically independent party and follow the example of the Irish Home Rulers."[21]

The front page of the July 11, 1918, issue of *The Voice* was dominated by race-conscious articles—on international, national, and local themes. The international coverage featured an article about Blaise Diagne, the "full blooded Negro" representing Senegal in the French Chamber of Deputies. National coverage included two articles on the Liberty Congress. One article reprinted the Liberty Congress's "Petition to the House of Representatives" of June 29, 1918, which demanded that lynching be made a federal crime, that "all distinctions, discriminations, and segregations based upon our race and color" be abolished, that the powers of the Thirteenth, Fourteenth, and Fifteenth Amendments of the U.S. Constitution be exercised, and that "Negroes" be granted suffrage in states that deprive them "of their right." A second article, quoting from Harrison's Liberty Congress talk on the "Vision of the Future," explained that *The Voice* was the "organ by which the spirit of that [New Negro] movement" would be "nurtured and made strong." It added that when *The Voice*'s circulation reached two thousand, a branch of the paper would be established in Washington, DC. One domestic article, "The Negro Will Win His Rights," reprinted from the *Brooklyn Standard Union*, discussed "the Negro's fighting mettle" and implicitly contrasted it with the actions of "white" draft dodgers in the Arkansas National Guard, who were the subject of an adjacent article. Another domestic piece described how ("white") "Crackers Steal $200,000 from Negro Children," and smaller national news briefs focused on membership increases in the "Negro church" and unity efforts of "Negro Methodist leaders."[22]

Local agitation pieces included one that described "a Harlem first"—a "white" detective inspector who was arrested on a charge of oppression brought by a West Indian rooming house owner, Joseph Gordon, who claimed the inspector had stationed a uniformed policeman outside his building for two months. Another local agitation piece called for "A Negro Intern at Bellevue Hospital" and expressed the hope that both Harlem Hospital and Lincoln Hospital in the Bronx would soon break the color barrier and hire Black doctors. The existing policy, *The Voice* explained, was one that allowed Black women nurses to work alongside "white" doctors but did not allow for Black male doctors.[23]

The front page also highlighted organizing activities including a scheduled Jubilation meeting for the publication of the resurrected *Voice* at St. Marks Hall, 57 West 138th Street, on July 11. It noted that Harrison lectured for free every Sunday evening at 8:30 p.m. at the Lafayette Lodge Rooms, 165 West 131st Street, for the Harlem People's Forum and that on Sunday the fourteenth he would speak on "Our Professional Friends, The 'N.A.A.C.P.': National Association for the Acceptance of Color Proscription." The talk was likely an updated version of his November 7, 1917, *Voice* article on "Our Professional Friends." In that article he criticized "good white friends of the colored people," including the NAACP leaders Mary White Ovington and Oswald Garrison Villard; emphasized that "we need no benevolent dictators"; and stressed that "it is we, not they, who must shape Negro policies." He added: "If they want to help in carrying them out we will appreciate their help," and he stressed that "it was the realization of the need for a more radical policy than that of the N. A. A. C. P. that called into being the Liberty League of Negro Americans." The July 11 issue of *The Voice* described the Harlem People's Forum as a place where "men and women who have the spirit of the New Negro assemble to hear lectures and to discuss among themselves the big problems with which human society finds itself confronted." Fittingly, the front page also featured a poem entitled "The Voice," by the leading poet of the militant New Negro Movement, Andrea Razaf-keriefo. "Raz" (whose father was from Madagascar and whose mother was the daughter of John Waller, the U.S. consul at Madagascar) would later (as Andy Razaf) became a prominent songwriter for Fats Waller and Eubie Blake. He wrote:

> Yeah Negro, let your heart rejoice
> For in this sheet you have a Voice
> That will speak out and dare all laws;
> The greatest champion of your cause.[24]

As with every paper that Harrison would edit, *The Voice* was neatly laid out and excellently written, and it carried pithy and militant editorials. The July 11 issue had four editorials, including two on the reappearance of the paper, one calling for "Negro Policemen," and one entitled "Is Democracy Unpatriotic?" which discussed the importance of struggle for democracy in wartime America.[25]

"Negro Policemen" argued that, unlike the larger-circulation Black weekly *Amsterdam News*, *The Voice* did not believe that the new mayor of New York City, the Democrat John F. Hylan, was a secret traitor or secret German sympathizer but rather viewed him as a representative mayor of an American city and "a jewel" alongside of John Purroy Mitchel. The *Amsterdam News* had favored

Mitchel, the Republican former mayor, who was now a pro-war Fusion candidate and who had long been identified with the Police Department's get-tough attitude toward "Negroes." *The Voice* called on Hylan to "make good" and "realize that Negro Harlem pins its faith to Negro policemen" and wants "many more" as "quick as we can get them." (In 1916 there were only fifteen Black police officers in the entire five-borough New York City police force.) The reason was that "with white policemen we are forced to take a chance and their conduct depends entirely on the goodwill of the Police Commissioner," but "with Negro policemen . . . the chances of police brutality to Negro citizens is reduced." *The Voice* suggested that the Black community would remember the Democrats if they delivered Black police officers.[26]

In the next issue of *The Voice* a week later Harrison added more on police brutality, on provocations by "white policemen" against Black men and women, and on the need for "Negro policemen." He wrote:

> Recent disturbances in this community have revealed that Negroes do not receive the amount of police protection to which they are entitled. Policemen, seemingly, are of the opinion that they have license to insult and brutalize Negroes whenever it suits their whims [and] . . . the same notable disregard of the rights of Negroes which has been manifested elsewhere, is shown by them in dealing with Negro citizens, [thus, they] unnecessarily provoke and foment disturbances by their threatening attitude and brutal tactics.
>
> Every case of injustice and persecution deprives the white policemen of confidence and respect, and makes Negroes more insistent in demanding that Negro communities shall be policed by Negro policemen.[27]

The Voice frequently criticized discrimination against "Negroes," and the July 11 issue pointed out that there was not a single Black Red Cross nurse overseas serving in a capacity equal to that of "whites." It discussed a recent Red Cross mass meeting, which aimed at eliminating the color barrier, and also reprinted an article from the *New York World* about one hundred trained Black nurses in New York who were not being accepted for overseas service, even as the nation was putting out a call that twenty-five thousand nurses were needed.[28]

In 1920 Harrison would explain that "while the war lasted," rather than to "go to jail," he would at times "camouflage the truth" as a "safer and more effective" way to counter discrimination, struggle for racial equality, and reach people in politically repressive wartime America. Such "camouflage, however, was never of that truckling quality which was accepted by the average American editor to such a nauseating degree."[29]

One example that he cited was the July 11, 1918, *Voice* editorial entitled "Is Democracy Unpatriotic?" in which he argued against those who said it was "disloyalty" for "Negroes" to put forth demands for justice during wartime. On the contrary, he countered, to demand justice was "the fullest loyalty to the letter and spirit of the President's war-aims." Any other view would "presume to accuse the President of having war-aims other than those which he has set forth." Further, "freedom from lynching and disfranchisement and the ending of discrimination—by the Red Cross for instance"—would "strengthen the hand of the administration," thereby "strengthening its hold on the hearts of the Negro masses." It would "make all Negroes—soldiers as well as civilians— more competent to give effective aid in winning the war."[30]

This demand for justice was "a patriotic request," and anyone who thought otherwise must also be "prepared to maintain that lynching, Jim-crow and disfranchisement are consistent with patriotism and ought to be preserved." *The Voice* asserted, with tongue fully in cheek, "that we have on our side the President of America, the world's foremost champion of democracy who defined it as 'the right of all those who submit to authority to have a VOICE in their own government'" (to which Harrison added, "—whether it be in Germany or in Georgia"). The portion of the quotation about "the right of all those who submit to authority to have a VOICE in their own government" was from President Woodrow Wilson's April 2, 1917, speech to a joint session of Congress seeking a declaration of war against Germany (it came on April 6), and Harrison ran it, without attribution, on the masthead of *The Voice*.[31]

Harrison also offered a profound look at his thinking in this 1918 period and his use of "camouflage." In a clear allusion to that Wilson speech of April 2, in which the president stressed that "the world must be made safe for democracy," Harrison, in 1920, offered:

I was well aware that Woodrow Wilson's protestations of democracy were lying protestations, consciously and deliberately designed to deceive. What, then, was my duty in the face of that fact? I chose to pretend that Woodrow Wilson meant what he said, because by so doing I could safely hold up to contempt and ridicule the undemocratic practices of his administration and the actions of his white countrymen in regard to the Negro.[32]

There was considerable basis for Harrison's approach. During the "Great War" broad legal attacks on the general population intensified, and Harrison, as a critic of U.S. policy and as a noncitizen, was particularly vulnerable. The first Espionage Act, passed by Congress on June 15, 1917, forbade obstruction of the draft and insubordination in the services and provided for penalties of up to twenty years and fines of up to $10,000. The May 16, 1918, Sedition Act

(40 stat. 533 [1918])—passed shortly before his July 11 "Is Democracy Unpatri-otic?" article—amended section 3 of the first Espionage Act. It called for a $5,000 fine, up to twelve years imprisonment, or both, for those who "willfully utter, print, write, or publish any disloyal, profane, scurrilous, or abusive lan-guage about the form of government of the United States" or in "support or favor [of] the cause of any country with which the United States is at war." The act made it a crime to bring "into contempt, scorn, contumely, or disrepute" the United States or its Constitution, armed forces, or flag. Overall, prosecutions under these legislations totaled 988 from June 15, 1917, to July 1, 1918. Some 2,168 people were ultimately prosecuted and 1,055 convicted under the Espio-nage Act including, on June 30, 1918, Eugene V. Debs, the former and future Socialist Party presidential candidate for whom Harrison had campaigned in 1912.[33]

As was his custom in the newspapers he edited, Harrison published smaller (sometimes chatty and satirical) pieces in the July 11 *Voice*. These included "In the Crow's Nest," which was written under the pseudonym "Gunga Din" with the help of his eight-year-old daughter Frances. "Gunga Din" (a pseudonym Har-rison had used as early as 1915) noted that Morris Hillquit, the Socialist Par-ty's New York City mayoral candidate, received 25 percent of the Black vote in 1917. Harrison, as "Our Panama Correspondent," wrote on high rents in "News from Panama." A year earlier in *The Voice* he had written similarly and pseud-onymously in the article "Real Estate News from Siam," which was attributed to a Southeast Asian correspondent named "Yung Chen." *The Voice* also included a sports section with an article on the outstanding Black boxer Sam McVey and a standard Harrison "Poetry for the People" section that included poems by Olive Bruce Miller (the daughter of John E. Bruce) and Raz. Harrison would later establish a similar, and very influential, "Poetry for the People" section in the *Negro World*.[34]

A James Weldon Johnson article, reprinted from the June 1918 *Liberator* mag-azine, edited by Max Eastman, Crystal Eastman, and Floyd Dell, noted that "the Negro" has been "counseled to refrain 'at this time' from pressing his claim to the full rights of American citizenship." Such counsel was not being heeded, however, and Johnson argued, "in pressing the claim for a larger degree of democracy for the black people within the borders of the United States, we are not only not hindering the war, but acting in fullest harmony with its ultimate aims." This sentiment was closer to Harrison's position than that of Joel E. Spin-garn and the NAACP, and Harrison duly noted the fact. He included a pointed dig at Spingarn and his leadership position with the NAACP in his headline to the article—referring to Johnson as the "'Well-Known' Colored Editor, [and] Field Secretary of Major [Joel A.] Spingarn's National Association."[35]

On the same page as the Johnson reprint was a powerful article by a fellow Virgin Islander, the St. Croix–born Anselmo R. Jackson, on "The Awakening of the Masses." It was a strong critique of the roles being played by Spingarn, Du Bois, the NAACP, and others and offered sentiments similar to Harrison's. Jackson discussed the "growing spirit of unrest among the masses of Negroes" dissatisfied with "the hypocrisy of hand-picked leaders" and "the iniquitous intrusion of white 'professional friends' who contributed their dollars to Negro organizations for the purpose of being in a position to dictate the attitude of Negroes on matters affecting themselves." He warned of these "masked enemies of the race, supporting the policy of segregation" and urged the "race-traitors, return to your masters and tell them the truth—that you can no longer deceive the masses of Negroes, that you cannot deliver them into the hands of their enemies." "Take heed!" Jackson warned. "The masses are awakening."[36]

Other articles in *The Voice* of July 11 included a letter brought by New Haven delegates to the Liberty Congress that protested racial proscriptions and emphasized contributions made by Black army volunteers (even though segregated at the Des Moines, Iowa, training camp and in fighting units in France). Special mention was made of wide support from "Negroes" for efforts such as "Liberty Bonds, War Saving Stamps and Certificates, Red Cross and Y. M. C. A. Funds, food conservation, munitions manufacturing, and the knitting of wearing apparel."[37]

Elsewhere *The Voice* reported on the War Department's public position that it would not tolerate discrimination against colored draftees by local draft boards and on Secretary of War Newton D. Baker's commitment to correct improper draft board actions. Mention was made of an appeal from Herbert Hoover and the Food Administration that African Americans save food, grow crops, and substitute other foods for those that most easily could be shipped to soldiers. A poem, "To the Patriotic Lady Across the Way," reprinted from the Socialist Party paper the *New York Call*, concerned a "white" woman on a train disdainfully moving away from a Black youth while simultaneously wearing a Liberty button and apparently thinking she was doing her share to make the world safe for democracy. Another article cautiously warned of a huckster pretending to be the war hero and Croix de Guerre recipient Henry Johnson, who had ripped off a congregation of the Bridge Street African Methodist Episcopal Church in Brooklyn.[38]

In the resurrected *Voice*, as he had done in the past, Harrison continued to address the issues of "Negro leadership" and education of the masses. The July 18 issue included "Read! Read! Read!" one of his classic editorials, written directly for the Black masses. Harrison began by observing, "as a people our bent for books is not encouraging" and "we mostly read trash." This was true, he said, "not only of our rank and file but even of our leaders." As an example he cited Kelly Miller, dean of the College of Arts and Sciences of Howard University, as a leader who exhibited ignorance of modern science and thought and added that Miller's biology "ignored Charles Darwin, Herbert Spencer, and Jacques Loeb" and showed little knowledge of astronomy and geology. According to Harrison, such ignorance was typical of most Black leaders, and he reasoned that little could be expected from the Black reading masses unless they took the issue of education into their own hands. He urged self-education through books and reading as a principal means to obtain "that education which we get out of school for ourselves—the only one that is really worth while." He also stressed that the "New Negro" needed "New Knowledge" from books, that "the masses must be taught to love good books," and that "every Negro of the new model" should be determined "to get the essentials of modern science and modern thought."[39]

He then appended his recommended list of essential books, which, if mastered, would provide a "better 'education' than is found in nine-tenths of the graduates of the average American college." Among the books he listed were: *Modern Science and Modern Thought*, by Samuel Laing; *The Origin of Species* and *The Descent of Man*, by Charles Darwin; *The Principles of Sociology* and *First Principles*, by Herbert Spencer; *The Childhood of the World* and *The Childhood of Religion*, by Edward Clodd; *Anthropology*, by E. B. Tylor; *History of Civilization*, by Henry Thomas Buckle; *Decline and Fall of the Roman Empire*, by Edward Gibbon; *The Martyrdom of Man*, by Winwood Reade; books on Africa by David Livingstone (*Missionary Travels and Researches in South Africa*) and Mungo Park (*Travels in the Interior of Africa*); and *The Mind of Primitive Man*, by Franz Boas. In order to stimulate interest in such books Harrison planned to start a bookshop at *The Voice*'s office. He would sell secondhand books cheaply and new books cheaper than any bookstore in Harlem. His message to *The Voice*'s audience was a repeated "Read! Read! Read!"[40]

This emphasis on education and self-education was a central concern of the autodidactic Harrison, who, two years later in "Education and the Race," wrote that "it behooves my race as well as the other subject races to learn the wisdom of the weak and to develop to the fullest that organ whereby weakness has been able to overcome strength; namely, the intellect." That being the case, "we Negroes must take to reading, study and the development of intelligence as we have never done before." As an example, he cited the Japanese, who had "gone to school to Europe but have never used Europe's education to make them the apes of Europe's culture." They had "absorbed, adopted, transformed and utilized," and he reasoned that "we Negroes must do the same."[41]

Regarding leadership, Harrison, in his 1920 book *When Africa Awakes: The "Inside Story" of the Stirrings and Strivings of the New Negro in the Western World*, offered some comments on what he considered to be key issues regarding the problems of leadership faced by the "new Negro" in mid-1918. He explained that for the "new Negro" a "strikingly new element" in the leadership issue had emerged—the "problem of outside interference." The question was whether "the leading of our group" should "be the product of our group's consciousness or of a consciousness originating from outside that group." A second issue meriting attention was the need for that leadership to be unimpeachable.[42]

He addressed the topic of unimpeachable leadership in his forthright criticism, "The Descent of Du Bois," which appeared in *The Voice* of July 25, 1918. The editorial took Du Bois to task for his "Close Ranks" editorial in *The Crisis*—an editorial written at Joel E. Spingarn's request. In that editorial Du Bois urged: "Let us, while this war lasts, *forget our special grievances* and close our ranks, shoulder to shoulder with our white fellow-citizens and the allied nations that are fighting for democracy." Harrison pointed out that the phrase "special grievances" was well understood to refer to "lynching, segregation, and disfranchisement" and that Du Bois wrote his editorial while he was applying for a captaincy in Military Intelligence (the branch of the government that monitored the Black and the radical communities).[43]

Harrison provided some background on the political importance of the issue:

> Dr. Du Bois first palpably sinned in his editorial "Close Ranks" in the July number of the *Crisis*. But this offense (apart from the trend and general tenor of the brief editorial) lies in a single sentence: "Let us, while this war lasts, *forget our special grievances* and close our ranks, shoulder to shoulder with our white fellow-citizens and the allied nations that are fighting for democracy." From the latter part of the sentence there is no dissent, so far as we know. The offense lies in that part of the sentence which ends with the italicized words. It is felt by all his critics, that Du Bois, of all Negroes, knows best that our "special grievances" which the War Department Bulletin describes as "justifiable" consist of lynching, segregation and disfranchisement, and that the Negroes of America can not preserve either their lives, their manhood or their vote (which is their political life and liberties) with these things in existence. The doctor's critics feel that America can not use the Negro people to any good effect unless they have life, liberty and manhood assured and guaranteed to them. Therefore, instead of the war for democracy making these things less necessary, it makes them more so.[44]

Figure 1.3. Raz (Andrea Razafkeriefo) at the piano, undated. Madagascar-born Andrea Razaf[in] keriefo (December 16, 1895–February 3, 1973), known as Andy Razaf and called "Raz," was the leading poet of the militant New Negro Movement and, later, an extremely popular lyricist. He wrote poems for the Harrison-edited *Voice* (1917 and 1918) and *New Negro* (1919) and was a member of the *Crusader* staff (1919) and contributor to the *Negro World* (c. 1920). He also wrote popular songs with the pianist and jazz composer Fats Waller, the pianist-composer Eubie Blake, and others. Raz wrote poems about Hubert Harrison and about *The Voice* in 1918 and about Harrison after his death in 1927. *Source:* Hubert H. Harrison Papers, Box 15, Folder 25, Rare Book and Manuscript Library, Columbia University Library. See https://dlc.library.columbia.edu/catalog/cul:zkh18933m1.

This editorial and events surrounding it cast grave doubt on Du Bois's leadership and marked Harrison as a spearhead of the opposition to "close ranks" and as a spokesperson for the New Negro Movement. Some nineteen years after Du Bois's death in 1963, and almost sixty-four years after his 1918 editorial, the historian Herbert Aptheker, the editor of Du Bois's writings and correspondence, offered a revealing comment on this subject. Aptheker wrote that the "Close Ranks" statement "produced a flood of discussion, pro and con with much of it

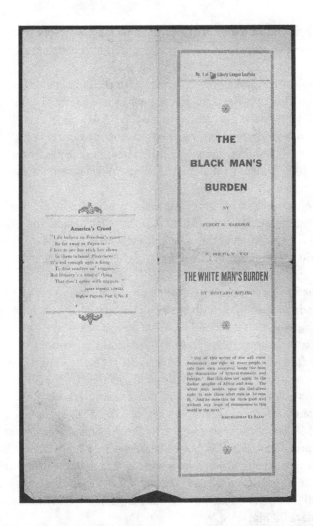

Figure 1.4. Hubert Harrison, "The Black Man's Burden [1915] and Rudyard Kipling, White Man's Burden [1899]," c. 1918, Liberty League Leaflet no. 1, Cover. Hubert Harrison's "The Black Man's Burden: A Reply to Rudyard Kipling," written under the pseudonym "Gunga Din," first appeared in the December 1915 *Colored American Review*. Rudyard Kipling's "The White Man's Burden: The United States and the Philippine Islands" had first appeared in *The Times* (London) on February 4, 1899, and the *New York Sun* on February 5, 1899. Harrison reprinted his poem in the October 1919 *New Negro* and in his *When Africa Awakes* (1920). He also published (on the leaflet) words from James Russell Lowell's "America's Creed" (from his *Biglow Papers*). *Source:* Hubert H. Harrison Papers, Box 4, Folder 14, Rare Book and Manuscript Library, Columbia University Library. See https://dlc.library.columbia.edu/catalog/cul:2bvq83bmtw.

printed in subsequent issues of *The Crisis*. It took some twenty years before Du Bois came to the conclusion that those opposed to the statement were in the right."[45]

Harrison was also concerned not only with Du Bois's editorial and leadership but also with "outside interference" such as that exerted by Du Bois's close friend Joel E. Spingarn. Spingarn had led the NAACP as it, according to Harrison, "urged Negroes to compromise our manhood by begging eagerly for 'Jim Crow' [officers'] training camps" in 1917. Then, in June 1918, while functioning as a major in Military Intelligence, Spingarn had sought to undermine the Liberty Congress.[46]

Harrison commented on "outside interference" in August 1920 in "The Problems of Leadership." His assessment was that Black leadership should come from within the group and bring Black grievances to the fore.[47] In reference to the scenario of events around the Liberty Congress, he explained:

> The time has long passed when white people, however benevolent, could safely and successfully, limit the range and determine the scope and pattern of the Negro people's aspirations—as Dr. Spingarn tried to do in 1918 when as a major in the Intelligence Dept. of the Army he presumed to tell the promoters of the First National Race Congress [the Liberty Congress] that they must not convene that gathering as that was no time for Negroes to present their grievances, their objections to a continuance of lynching, disfranchisement and the ghetto. . . . And it was because Dr. W. E. B. Du Bois followed the lead of such white sponsors in the subservient and acquiescent tone of the wartime editorials in *The Crisis* and wanted to secure a position as semicivilian captain under Major Spingarn to carry on in that spirit of such a policy that he stumbled and fell from the pinnacle of racial leadership, a point to which all the strenuous pulling and handling of his white friends has never been able to lift him since.[48]

The series of "Close Ranks"–related events would also elicit insightful comments from Harrison on the question of Black leadership and on Du Bois as a Black leader in his editorial "When the Blind Lead" (c. 1920). Harrison, who repeatedly saw the "future in the distance," wrote:

> In 1918 the lynchings were still going on while Dr. Du Bois was solemnly advising us to "forget our grievances." Any one who insisted then on putting such grievances as lynchings, disfranchisement and segregation in the foreground was described by the *Crisis'* editor as seeking "to turn his country's tragic predicament to his own personal gain." At that time he either believed or pretended to believe every one of the empty words that flowed from

Woodrow Wilson's lips, and on the basis of this belief he was willing to act as a brilliant bellwether to the rest of the flock. Unfortunately, the flock refused to follow the lost leader.

"If the blind lead the blind they will both fall into the ditch." But in this case those being led were not quite so blind as those who wanted to lead them by way of captaincies in the army. Which was why some captaincies were not forthcoming. The test of vision in a leader is the ability to foresee the immediate future, the necessary consequences of a course of conduct and the dependable sentiments of those whom he assumes to lead. In all these things Dr. Du Bois has failed.

Harrison pointedly stated: "The Negro leaders of the future will be expected . . . to stand by us in war as well as in peace," and he emphasized, "while it is as easy as eggs for a leader to fall off the fence, it is devilishly difficult to boost him up again."[49]

The August 1, 1918, issue of *The Voice* included reprints of Harrison's earlier "Close Ranks" editorial from July 25 and of President's Wilson's statement against "Mob Action" from July 26, 1918. Harrison's "Close Ranks" editorial argued that "America is in this war to win" and that it should brook no attempt "to compromise its declared principles"; "the whole world, Tennessee as well as Turkey—must be made safe for democracy," and "we must fight on until this is accomplished." He emphasized, in clear distinction from Du Bois, that "no true American can say that we must defer the accomplishment of any part of our aims 'while this war lasts,'" and that the president's watchword "is not to make Europe [alone] safe for democracy, but to make the world safe for democracy." Wilson's statement had criticized "the mob spirit" in the land, denounced "many lynchings," and mentioned the importance that U.S. "laws be kept inviolate." Spingarn, who advocated temporary wartime antilynching measures, used it in an effort to minimize the impact of the Liberty Congress. This effort did not, however, appease militant activists like Harrison, who considered it to be too little, too late. After Wilson's statement was published the War Department decided that even a temporary wartime antilynching bill was irrelevant, and at the end of July it decided against a Spingarn-proposed advisory committee to the General Staff of the War Department that was to be headed by Du Bois and was to carry out "counter espionage" activities among Black Americans. It also rejected Du Bois's application for a captaincy in Military Intelligence.[50]

Harrison's *Voice* editorial of August 1, 1918, "A Note on the Foregoing," accompanied the reprints of "Close Ranks" and Wilson's statement. It suggested that "perhaps now 'Dr. W. E. B. Du Bois, editor of The Crisis' and other fearful or foolish patriots who asked us not to insist on these same things [federal antilynching legislation and enforcement of the Thirteenth, Fourteenth, and

Fifteenth Amendments] 'while this war lasts' will now feel ashamed of their cowardice and stupidity." *The Voice* would neither "gloat" nor "comment"; it simply "knew what was coming—and said so." Harrison bitingly added that *The Voice* "correctly understood and rightly interpreted the temper of the times" and the president's "democratic purpose" and cited the previous *Voice* editorials ("Is Democracy Unpatriotic?" and "Close Ranks" of July 11 and July 25, 1918).[51]

In the same August 1 issue *The Voice* reported that the July 25 issue with Harrison's "Descent of Du Bois" editorial had quickly sold out and that the paper would be expanded. Though copies of articles from later issues remain, no complete subsequent issues have been located. Harrison later reported that *The Voice* last published in February 1919 and failed in March or April 1919.[52]

While editing *The Voice* Harrison lectured for the Harlem People's Forum at 154 West 131st Street. On Sunday evening, July 28, he spoke on "Negro History and Its Place in Negro Education" and put out a call for the study of "Negro History," particularly in "Negro colleges." His talk centered on the history and customs of Africans based on anthropology and sociology and included discussion of sacred traditions, the evolutionary stages of African society, the psychology of the native African, family habits, the great love for mothers and respect for all women exhibited by Africans, and the African understanding that "maternity is a matter of fact and paternity is a matter of faith." He also offered observations on the temperament of West Indians and West Africans rooted in their different forms of society. The talk, according to Sinclair Wilberforce in *The Voice*, was very popular and was to continue the following Sunday.[53]

In the second half of 1918 Harrison was also briefly involved with the Socialist Party. He had been readmitted to SP membership on March 27, 1918, and terminated his membership less than six months later. In his September 16, 1918, diary entry he wrote: "Just finished writing my resignation from membership in the Socialist Party."[54] In a parenthetical statement that may have been added later, he explained: "I had dropped out [of the SP] in the spring of 1914, but went back . . . because I admired their first stand on the war. But when I observed the dirty deal which Randolph & Owen had made with [Julius] Gerber, the Party's Secretary [for Local New York], I saw that the party was still hopelessly in the control of petty-bourgeois reactionaries and therefore I dropped out for ever. H.H."

Regarding "the first stand on the war" Harrison was presumably referring to the "Proclamation and Program" adopted at the SP's Special Convention in St. Louis from April 7–14, 1917, only days after the United States' declaration of war. At St. Louis the party reaffirmed "allegiance to the principle of internationalism and working class solidarity the world-over" and proclaimed "its unalterable opposition to the war just declared by the government of the United States."[55] Later in the year, in October, pro-war socialists met in Chicago, called themselves the National Party, and developed a pro-war position, which gained support in New York, especially after German attacks on the new revolutionary Russian government. Many New York socialists, including the city's socialist alderman, supported the Third Liberty Loan Drive and spoke at war-bond rallies.[56]

It appears that Harrison, who was critical of the war as both a product of imperialism and an effort by capitalists to block and blunt efforts at social change[57] and who saw Wilson's pronouncements about making the world safe for democracy as a wedge for pushing Black demands for equality, publicly supported the Black troops (in part to minimize legal pressure on himself). His papers include a ribbon from the "Mayor's Committee of Welcome to Home-Coming Troops" and a "Certificate of Membership on the Mayor's Committee of Welcome to Home Coming Troops." These were for serving on the reviewing stand at a Harlem parade honoring the highly decorated 369th Regiment, 93rd Infantry Division (the old 15th New York National Guard), the Black volunteer unit known as the "Harlem Hellfighters."[58] His papers also include a token of appreciation from the "National War Savings Committee of the United States Government . . . Committee of Greater New York."[59]

In all probability Harrison's socialist connections and short stay in the party in 1918 helped him land union speaking engagements with both the Pullman workers and the hotel workers and helped him obtain an SP advertisement for his paper later in the year. There is little indication that he did other work for the SP during this period. He submitted his resignation on September 16, and the Executive Committee referred it to the Central Committee on September 18. His diary reference to "the dirty deal" was probably a reference to the SP's plan to run Randolph and Owen as candidates in New York's nineteenth and twenty-first assembly districts, respectively, in moves that directly pitted the two Black Socialists against two Black Republicans with good chances for victory, Edward Austin Johnson in the nineteenth and John C. Hawkins in the twenty-first. This was the first time that New York City Republicans had ever officially backed Black candidates in these Harlem assembly districts. It may have also been related to the SP's decision to give Randolph and Owen money at a time when Harrison was looking for some for his paper.[60]

In his letter to the Executive Committee Harrison explained that he tendered his resignation not "as a prelude to any public attacks upon my former comrades" and added, "I shall hold myself free, on grounds of private friendship as well as of public policy, to work for the election of the Rev. Geo. Frazier Miller to Congress as a member of your party." Miller was running for Congress as a Socialist, and although he was running against another Black politician with socialist leanings, the Rev. Reverdy C. Ransom, editor of the *AME Review*, support of Miller did not threaten to snatch victory from Ransom. Ransom had twice before run as an independent Republican after having been defeated in Republican primaries, and this time he was again running as an independent. Harrison's opposition to Randolph and Owen was distinguished from the "anti-Bolshevist" stance of the *New York Age*. It was also distinguished from the support given to Owen and Randolph over Johnson and Hawkins by Cyril V. Briggs, editor of *The Crusader*. Harrison, who supported Johnson and Hawkins as well as the socialist Miller, took a stand that called for the need to break the white monopoly of office (in his support of Johnson and Hawkins) and for class and "race" solidarity (in his support for Miller).[61]

Toward the latter part of 1918 Harrison took some time to promote *The Crusader*, the new magazine edited by Briggs, a former editor of the *Colored American Review* (which had published Harrison's poem "The Black Man's Burden: A Reply to Rudyard Kipling" in 1915) and the *Amsterdam News. The Crusader* began publication in September 1918, and in its very first issue it quoted from "Hubert Harrison in the rejuvenated and resurrected 'Voice'" that "the principle of 'Justice' in wartime be applied to Negroes," and it placed Harrison on its "Roll of Honor," citing "many favorable mentions in his lectures and addresses as well as in his paper."[62] Briggs also reprinted the laudatory poem by Andrea Razafkeriefo entitled "Hubert H. Harrison" in the December 1918 *Crusader*. That poem began with the following four lines:

> Speaker, editor and sage,
> Thou who wrote a brighter page
> In the Negro's Book of thought—
> What a change thy work has wrought!

A variant of these words appears on the tombstone, which in 2014 (some eighty-seven years after his death), was placed on Harrison's formerly unmarked gravesite in Woodlawn Cemetery in the Bronx.[63]

———

On the same day that Harrison's resurrected *Voice* was first published, the BI agent Corcoran asked a "colored messenger" to ascertain "all details regarding who drew the resolutions, who were the men behind the [Liberty] *Congress* and who were the white men associated with *Harrison*." Five days later Corcoran interviewed the informant John E. Bowles and instructed him to use a letter of introduction that he had obtained and present it to Harrison in New York.[64]

On July 20 Corcoran met Arthur Ulysses Craig, a "colored" Justice Department informant and Liberty League delegate. Corcoran gave him "very valuable" information regarding Harrison, who, according to a Corcoran report, "seems to be the leading figure regarding the German activities at the Liberty Congress." (No substantiation of this claim has been found.) Craig added that Herman Bernelot Moens, a Dutchman whom he (incorrectly) believed to be "a German agent and a Master spy," had been in the city for three years and had "been constantly associated with this man Harrison."[65]

Interestingly, Joel E. Spingarn may have played a role in initiating MI's discussion of Moens as a spy. According to a report by MI major Herbert Parsons, at a time when Spingarn was "energetic about a [segregated instead of an integrated] camp for negro officers," Spingarn said that Moens had asked him for "the names of radical negro leaders" and that "there was a rumor that he was instigating the negroes to stand up for their rights and make trouble." (Parsons noted that Spingarn was careful not to say that Moens "was a spy, but merely stated these facts in the course of conversation.")[66]

In his report of August 30 Corcoran commented that Craig was willing to do anything asked by the department to assist in their investigation. At one meeting of the Liberty Congress, Craig claimed to have seen Harrison "flush" at the podium and become "greatly excited at his [Moens's] entrance." Corcoran suspected there was "a direct connection between Moens and Harrison," and he thought that Craig might be able to "get to the point where the german [*sic*] interests are working." Corcoran also indicated he had received a letter from the informant Bowles, and the Washington, DC, lawyer Joseph H. Stewart was to give Bowles "a strong letter of introduction to Harrison" if he could get someone to vouch for him.[67]

Corcoran additionally worked at entrapping Moens. He planned to speak with Charlotte Hunter, a public school teacher at Dunbar High School in Washington, DC, who had been associated with Moens for three years, in order to get her to work as an informant. He similarly attempted to secure government employment for another "colored co-informant in this case," the school teacher Helen Saunders.[68]

Corcoran soon finalized plans, involving Saunders, to entrap Moens. On September 13 he met with Craig and then went to the MI bureau, where he met with a Captain Manning and a Mr. Adams regarding their progress with a "plant they are alleged to have installed in the residence of *Prof. Moens* in his connection with *german propaganda.*"[69]

On October 18 Corcoran obtained a warrant to search Moens's residence. At 8 p.m. Corcoran and Saunders went there and split up; she entered the house while he met Special Agent Murphy and went into the house next door. Corcoran and others involved in this operation heard Moens and Saunders talking and awaited the signal from her that they were in bed. She then opened the back door leading to the porch and left it unlocked, looked out on the porch, and gave a signal that everything was all right. Corcoran's group stayed on the porch half an hour as the light went out in the bedroom and Moens and Saunders prepared to go to bed. At about 9:10 p.m. Moens noticed that the door was open, and when he went to the porch to close it he discovered the agents there. Moens slammed the door with an awful jolt, ran back into his room, and almost instantly returned "with a *german gun and bayonet attached*." He was about to use his bayonet on the agents when Corcoran hit him with his blackjack and took his gun, getting cut by Moens's bayonet in the process. The agent's group entered the room where Saunders was "partly undressed having her coat, bar [bra] and over-skirt off," with the light out. Moens said he was a scientist studying colored mixtures, and Corcoran maintained that Moens had spoiled their plans to detect a radio outfit across the street. Later that night Corcoran met Saunders, who said that Moens believed the subterfuge and thought everything was all right. According to Corcoran, Saunders was "willing to work further in this case" and was "interested to get the subject in an embarrassing position." Corcoran summed up that though "there was not a mistake made by anyone," they did have "a bad break of luck."[70]

Moens's arrest finally came on October 25, 1918. Justice Department officials, who believed he was an Austrian citizen and "a German spy and agent," searched his belongings and took what he claimed were "two scientific photographs," which were later used in charges against him. Though treated as a spy, Moens was actually arrested on the pretext of having and exhibiting "obscene prints and pictures in obscene, impudent and indecent positions, too filthy, obscene and disgusting to be further described." Since the Justice Department kept all his papers and bank drafts, he could not post bail until October 31. After several days in jail he was released after depositing a cash bond of $5,000 (which on March 10, 1919, would be reduced to $3,000).[71]

The obscenity charge against Moens soon led to a heated controversy involving the DC school system. Background to the matter involved the fact that the Washington superintendent of schools, Roscoe Conkling Bruce, acting upon the Dutch Embassy's recommendation, had granted Moens permission to photograph public school girls, some in the nude, to obtain comparative anthropological data. Harrison would be drawn into this matter in 1919.[72]

Of particular importance is that from the Liberty Congress through the end of 1918 Harrison was the subject of government surveillance; that the government considered entrapping him; and that the government made an effort to entrap Moens, who was being treated as a spy and with whom Harrison was identified. Whether Harrison had any indication of the government surveillance is not clear, although it is possible that Walter H. Loving of Military Intelligence kept him abreast of the Justice Department's monitoring and cautioned him on how to couch his pronouncements. This is indicated by a Harrison diary entry of February 4, 1919, made after Loving visited him at the Washington, DC, YMCA. Harrison described Loving as "an agent of the War Dept. but [a man who] has often given me much friendly advice as to keeping the substance of my criticism of the government on the safe side of hostility."[73]

––––––––

Toward the end of 1918, as the "Great War" drew to a close, Harrison manifested increased interest in the Armistice (of November 11) and the terms of the peace. On that day he described in his diary how, "amid the shrieking of steam whistles the din of horns and pans and the shouting of many millions, New York City celebrated the great event—The Coming of Peace." This was after the city "heard that the German military authorities had signed the armistice at the headquarters of [French] Marshal [Ferdinand] Foch," the commander in chief of the allied armies.[74]

Two days later, in a more contemplative mood, he commented in his diary on the "two main points of interest" in the West: "the German Emperor's flight to Holland and the problem of the Socialistic Republic of Germany." He noted how the New York papers, particularly the *Globe, Evening Standard*, and *Evening Mail*, were "thirsting" for the kaiser's blood and "yapping about trying him before a court for his crimes." Only the week before, Kaiser Wilhelm II, emperor of Germany and king of Prussia, had abdicated and gone into exile in Holland in response to revolutionary unrest from below. In the allied countries there was considerable sentiment to deport him as a war criminal. Harrison observed that, based on the rage against the Kaiser, one would think "the Kaiser had personally led his armies and set fire to houses, and sunk the Lusitania." "To be sensible and consistent," he wrote, "they should demand the trial of [the German chief of staff, Paul von] Hindenburg, [his deputy, General Erich] Ludendorff and [Field Marshall August von] Mackensen." Then, in a pensive commentary on twentieth-century monarchy, Harrison added:

These same papers would have demanded in 1913 the extradition of any German revolutionist who had attempted to shoot the Kaiser for his only crime, the one which involved his official participation in the events of the last four years, viz: the crime of being the autocratic official of the German State. Now they want to "try" [Kaiser] Wilhelm Hohenzollern for having been the ruler of Germany, a position to which he was as truly and unavoidably born as was the half-imbecile King [George V] of England. What a silly world it is!

This ex-ruler of Germany (granting both his temperamental idiosyncrasies and the inexcusable brutality with which the German forces waged war) was the most efficient European monarch of the present age. Personally, I am opposed to the existence of *all* monarchs *as such*; but we must give the devil his due. The former Kaiser did not and does not deserve the asinine personal execration with which our newspapers and play-houses teemed and still teem. A Napoleon might have deserved it, because he planned and declared wars on his sole personal initiative; but in our day, no single monarch—not the late Czar of Russia, nor the Sultan of Turkey—has had any such power.[75]

Harrison also questioned "whether the Anglo-Saxons will endeavor to live up to their boasted declarations about 'making the world safe for democracy.'" He noted that "their attitude toward the first attempt to establish real democracy in Russia does not impress one favorably." Then he speculated on how far their hatred of socialism might take them and on what the response might be:

I think it will be found that they hate and fear Socialism, whether in Russia, Germany or Austria, more than they hated and feared the Kaiser; and I shouldn't be at all surprised if they were to play up the unavoidable "excesses" of the Revolution as an excuse to try to put the Kaiser back on the throne in a ring of reactionary bayonets buttressed by the international "combine" of Plutocracy and Militarism. And if they do, there will be hell let loose for a period. The Revolution may then spread to their own lands. *Il reste à savoir* [it remains to be known].[76]

After the November Armistice the victors quickly made plans for a peace conference scheduled to begin in Paris in January 1919. When the first plenary session was eventually held on January 18, delegates from twenty-seven countries attended, and Germany was excluded. The Paris Peace Conference lasted almost a year and would end with the formation of the League of Nations on January 10, 1920.[77]

Harrison's article "The Negro at the Peace Congress" was written as preparations for the conference were underway. He explained that while the world "expected the Peace Congress . . . to settle *the questions about which the war was fought*," "Negroes" wanted "to know if the Peace Congress will settle such questions as those of lynching, disfranchisement and segregation." He did not think so "because the war was not fought over these." Nevertheless, he warned, "various bodies of Negroes, who do not seem to understand the modern system of political government under which they live, are seeking to get money from the unsuspecting masses of our people 'for the purpose of sending delegates.'" This reference was apparently to Du Bois, Trotter, Garvey, and Eliezer Cadet, each of whom was either planning to go to or planning to send someone to Paris. Harrison termed such projects "sublimely silly" because the Peace

Congress was "not open to any body who chooses to be sent" and only the U.S. president had the power to designate American delegates. Of course, anyone could send a visitor to Versailles or Paris at their own expense, but such a visitor could not get within a block of the Peace Congress. To prevent a useless waste of the money of poor people, who could ill afford it, Harrison suggested that readers simply send to France for copies of *Le Temps* or *Le Matin*.[78]

Harrison pointedly responded to the argument that such visitors to Paris could "make propaganda" in France that would "force the Peace Conference to consider American lynching, disfranchisement and segregation." He countered that if such propaganda "could rise to the height of embarrassing them, the French authorities would sternly put it down and banish the troublesome persons" as they had previously done to "Karl Marx, [the anarchist theoretician] Prince [Piotro Alekseyevich] Kropotkin, [the anarchist Errico] Malatesta and [Vladimir Ilich Ulianov] Lenine [*sic*]" under "less provoking circumstances." Advising his readers not "to play the part of silly fools," he stressed:

> Lynching, disfranchisement and segregation are evils HERE; and the place in which we must fight them is HERE. If foolish would-be leaders have no plan to lay before our people for the fighting HERE, in God's name, let them say so, and stand out of the way! Let us gird up our loins for the stern tasks which lie before us HERE and address ourselves to them with courage and intelligence.[79]

In *The Voice* of December 26, 1918, Harrison offered a probing editorial on "Africa at the Peace Table" and emphasized that the war was really "fought over African questions." He explained:

> When Nations go to war, they never openly declare what they WANT. They must camouflage their sordid greed behind some [high-]sounding phrase like "freedom of the seas," "self-determination," "liberty" or "democracy." But only the ignorant millions ever think that those are the real objects of their bloody rivalries. When the war is over, the mask is dropped, and then they seek "how best to scramble at the shearers' feast." It is then that they disclose their real war aims.

As a striking case in point he explained that at the peace conference the responsible heads of the allied governments would make clear that "freedom of the seas" meant "a benevolent naval despotism maintained by them" and that "democracy" meant simply "the transfer of Germany's African lands to England and the others." The reason was that Africa was "the real stakes at the peace table," and although occasional headlines might read "'Negroes Ask For

German Colonies,'" Harrison advised that "Negroes of sense should not be deluded" because these colonies would not pass to their hands. Lacking battleships, guns, and finances, they were simply "not a POWER." This was so, because "the King-word of modern nations is POWER" and "the secret of England's greatness" is "not bibles but bayonets—bayonets, business and brains," and "as long as white nations have a preponderance of these, so long will they rule."[80]

Harrison considered agitation among African Americans for the liberation of Africa to be "a healthy sign" but little else, since Africa's hands were currently tied. He recommended that "American Negroes" study how to unloose her bonds later and advised, with noteworthy humility and with confidence in African peoples, that instead of elaborating plans on how to liberate Africa, it would be better to learn from Africa. He suggested:

Let us American Negroes go to Africa, live among the natives and LEARN WHAT THEY HAVE TO TEACH US (for they have much to teach us). Let us go there—not in the coastlands,—but in the interior, in Nigeria and Nyassaland [Nyasaland]; let us study engineering and physics, chemistry and commerce, agriculture and industry; let us learn more of nitrates, of copper, rubber and electricity; so we will know why Belgium, France, England and Germany want to be in Africa. Let us begin by studying the scientific work of the African explorers and stop reading and believing the silly slush which ignorant missionaries put into our heads about the alleged degradation of our people in Africa. Let us learn to know Africa and Africans so well that every educated Negro will be able at a glance to put his hands on the map of Africa and tell where to find the Jolofs, Ekois, Mandingoes, Yorubas, Bechuanas or Basutos and can tell something of their marriage customs, their property laws, their agriculture and systems of worship. For, not until we can do this will it be seemly for us to pretend to be anxious about their political welfare.

Indeed, it would be well now for us to establish friendly relations and correspondence with our brothers at home. For we don't know enough about them to be able to do them any good at THIS peace congress (even if we were graciously granted seats there); but fifty years from now—WHO KNOWS?[81]

In the same December 26, 1918, issue of *The Voice*, the Freethought-influenced Harrison wrote the editorial "Goodwill Toward Men." He observed that "peace and goodwill" were "always in the forefront of the doctrine of Christ" though "'Christian' nations of today don't seem to care much about the doctrine of

Christ." The "centers of 'white Christianity'" were "the centers of organized bloodshed and permanent preparation for perpetual war." In China "five hundred million Chinese" were "driven from their calm" and "compelled to arm themselves . . . to stand off the followers of the Prince of Peace!" As for goodwill, Harrison, in full literary passion and in an apparent allusion to the horrific killings of Mary Turner and her unborn baby in May 1918 in Valdosta, Georgia, explained how "in our own land, the hook-wormed helots of the Anglo-Saxon south drop into Africa to mark their belief in the brotherhood of man, and then go out to roast a gravid Negro woman, to chop off her fingers and toes to serve as souvenirs, to rip her body open and trample the unborn babe beneath their cow-hide boots by way of proving how well the religion of Christ has sweetened their soul." He added, in contrast to the "meek and lowly Nazarene" who "loved even those who murdered Him," his followers of the "Anglo-Saxon race in this country" demonstrate "neither love nor goodwill for its fellow-citizens—when they are Negro blood."[82]

To Harrison, Christmas clearly helped show "the great gulf fixed between Christianity and Christ, between the all-embracing charity of the carpenter of Nazareth and the cruel, stubborn pride, the vicious race-prejudice, the hatred and intolerance of the white savages who take His name in vain in the twentieth century of the 'Christian' era." With an insightful ironic touch, Harrison pointed out how Jesus "was despised and rejected of men" and that, in this, Christ was "nearer this Christmas Day to the despised and down-trodden Negro then [*sic*] to his haughty Anglo-Saxon oppressor." He then optimistically predicted that "Ethiopia shall stretch forth her hands, and the Negro, stolen from his Fatherland, degraded by his oppressors, may (when the wheel of fortune turns) be again the companion of the gods and the chief of Heaven's favorites."[83]

In *The Voice* of January 30, 1919, Harrison explained how the French phrase "they shall not pass" had been used against the German military to heroically hold back the kaiser's legions but was now being used by "white statesmen who run our government in Washington" to prohibit travel to France of the seventy-odd Black "delegates" who were "elected" at mass meetings and concerts. He claimed that the U.S. government, with the backing of Emmett Scott (former assistant to the late Booker T. Washington), who had been named special assistant for Negro affairs to the secretary of war, Newton D. Baker, was refusing to issue passports by telling Madame C. J. Walker, Trotter, and Judge (Henry?) Harrison they would have to wait. While *The Voice* held no brief for these people and had "taken the trouble to tell them just how silly their project was," it was nevertheless proper to inquire publicly as to why the government would not let them go. Harrison thought he knew the answer—the government's conscience was not clear, and this was why they ordered "that ludicrous lackey, Mr. R. R. Moton, to go."[84] (After Booker T. Washington's death in November 1915 Moton succeeded him as principal of Tuskegee Institute.) The government had created "sinecures for Mr. [Emmett] Scott and the other barnacles" because of its guilty conscience. It didn't want to have African Americans telling Europe "that the land which is to make the world 'safe for democracy' is rotten with race-prejudice"; that Jim Crow, lynching, and disfranchisement hold sway "in that part of the country in which nine-tenths of them live." Regarding Harrison's editorial, the historian Mark Ellis insightfully writes: "As usual, Harrison had captured the essence of what was going on."[85]

Instead of going to France, Harrison again stressed that work needed to be done here, and he asked, "Are these *Negro emigres* afraid to face the white men here in the Republican Party or any other and raise Hades until the Constitution is enforced?" Probing further, he asked if "cowardice" was "the real reason for their running to France to uncork their mouths." It appeared so. He then advised, "don't run," for "the fight is here, and here you will be compelled to face it, or report to us on the reason why."[86]

Harrison also sharply criticized the old-style Black leaders who had decided that "we Negroes must make every sacrifice to help win the war and lay aside our just demands for the present that we may win a shining place on the pages of history." One of his most pointed commentaries came after the appearance of the first postwar schoolbook of American history, by Reuben Gold Thwaites and Calvin Noyes Kendall. Their book devoted thirty-one pages to the war and America's part in it, and *"not one word is said of the Negro's part therein,"* noted Harrison. While this was similar to the treatment of the role of "the Negro in the Civil War," it nevertheless led him to pointedly write: "If there is a spark of manhood left in the bosoms of our 'white men's niggers' who sold us out during the war they must feel pained and humiliated when the flood of after-the-war school histories, of which this is the first, quietly sink the Negro's contributions (as chronicled by Mr. Emmett Scott and others) into the back waters of forgetfulness."[87]

By the end of 1918 Harrison was clearly critical of the war and of the peace aims of the imperial nations and their leaders. In addition, while he condemned the leadership offered by old-style Black leaders, he did praise the sacrifices and valor of African American soldiers.

In this eventful latter part of 1918 Harrison had ascended to the pinnacle of national prominence as a protest leader at the Liberty Congress; he then resurrected *The Voice* as a "Newspaper for the New Negro." The overall strategy of protest for equal rights during wartime was logical, timely, and sound. A similar strategic approach would lead to gains a quarter of a century later when applied by A. Philip Randolph and others during World War II and again in the

1960s with Civil Rights/Black Liberation protests during the Vietnam War era. In 1918, however, the militant and autonomous Liberty Congress effort, in which Harrison played a leading role, was undermined by government action and by the efforts of Spingarn, Du Bois, and others. Harrison's efforts also led to government surveillance of him a full year before the Red Summer of 1919. In this setting he continued with his political work.

2

Political Activities in Washington and Virginia
(January–July 1919)

On December 23, 1918, as Christmas drew near, Major Walter Howard Loving, who was doing intelligence work, wrote his superior, Director of Military Intelligence Brigadier General Marlborough Churchill, on the "Spirit of Unrest Among Negroes." He explained that since the signing of the November 11 armistice there was "a growing feeling of unrest among the negroes all over the United States," who were asking, "What will be the negro's reward for helping to win the war for democracy?" He added that "Negroes" had not been so "worked up" since the attacks of July 1917 on the Black community of East St. Louis, Illinois (attacks that Harrison had militantly protested and described as a "pogrom") and that mass meetings were being organized in many large cities.[1]

During the last week of December 1918, while Loving's letter was circulating among government officials, Harrison traveled from Harlem to Washington, DC, to implement a major new work plan. He aimed to develop circulation of *The Voice* in Washington and to use that city as a base to move newspaper distribution into the South. Over the next seven months he spent much of his time in Washington and Virginia delivering lectures, making contacts, playing an active role in meetings and conferences, and, for a short time, stumping for *The Voice.* January 1919, in particular, was a busy month for meetings in Washington, and Harrison, who appeared to Loving to be "active in all the meetings and conferences," delivered at least eight public talks, beginning with one at the Thrift Race of the World's Race and Labor Consolidation Conference, January 1–3, at the Washington YMCA. This was followed by other talks on January 4 and 30 at the John Wesley (AME Zion) Church (at 1615 Fourteenth Street, NW), January 7 and 28 at the Bethel Literary Society, January 14 and 29 at the Florida Avenue Church, and January 24 at the "Y."[2]

The Thrift Race of the World (Incorporated) was founded in Washington, DC, in 1906 by Henry E. Bryant. The "Thrift Race" was a substitute name "for [the] existing Name of [the] Darker Races of the World." Its aim was "to plan the industrial, commercial, financial and manufacturing of Thrift Products of the Thrift Race of the World" and "to plan for a complete organization of Labor forces and interests of Thrift American Citizen's Unions for the promotion and protection of their interests in the Thrift Races of the World." The journalist and activist T. Thomas Fortune presided over the January 1919 conference, and included in the list of speakers were Harrison; Bryant; the attorney Joseph H. Stewart, from DC; the Richmond attorney and businessman Giles B. Jackson; the NAACP's James Weldon Johnson; the AME Church financial secretary John R. Hawkins; Dr. M. A. N. Shaw of Boston; the educator Nannie H. Burroughs; I. S. Levy, from Columbia, South Carolina; and J. Finley Wilson, editor of the *Washington Eagle*. Jeanette Carter of Washington, DC, founder of the Women's Wage Earners Association, served as a registrar. Loving wrote to Churchill that "nothing of importance was transacted, and the speeches of the radicals were very tame." He added that Harrison spoke on the "Necessity for Race and Labor Consolidation," discussed "labor conditions the world over," and "made no reference to the war."[3]

At the Bethel Literary Society on January 28 Harrison delivered a militant speech in which he reportedly "offered to put the first dollar into a fund to buy guns and ammunition to be furnished [to] the colored people of the south for their protection." This was similar to speeches supporting armed self-defense that he had delivered in 1917 at the June 12 founding meeting of the Liberty League, at a June 13 meeting in Boston, and at a July 4 meeting in the wake of the July 1–3 attacks on the Black community in East St. Louis. At the same activity Rev. George Frazier Miller of Brooklyn reportedly declared Bolshevism would be the salvation of America, praised the radical IWW, and advised colored people to join labor unions.[4]

It is probable that in his January 28 speech Harrison, who was planning to go into the South, drew on an article he was preparing, "A Cure for the Ku-Klux," which appeared in *The Voice* of January 30. The modern KKK was growing rapidly and would add an estimated two million new members in the next seven years. Its program included white supremacy, Protestant fundamentalism, "Americanism," and opposition to "Negroes," Catholics, Jews, and immigrants.[5]

In his article Harrison detailed the formation of the original Klan in Pulaski, Tennessee, in late 1865 and described how "cowardly 'crackers' who couldn't lick the Yankees began organizing to take it out on the Negroes." He analyzed two laws: one that declared that any Black man who couldn't produce three hundred dollars was a vagrant (and subject to work on a chain gang on public works in the cities) and a second that prohibited three "Negroes" from gathering unless a "white" man was present. He explained that these laws were passed in order "to maintain white supremacy." Harrison also depicted attempts by the U.S. Congress "to counter such Southern efforts," including its December 1865 decision to keep these states out of the Union until they agreed to do better. Despite such actions, Southern "white" resistance persisted, and Congress responded by passing the Fourteenth and Fifteenth Amendments and "put the 'cracker' states under military rule until they accepted the amendments." The struggle continued, and over half a century later, after "the Negro has been stripped of the ballot's protection by the connivance of white Republicans in Washington and white Democrats at the South," the KKK again dared "to raise its ugly head in its ancestral state of Tennessee." Given "this crisis," Harrison wondered what "the Negro 'leaders'" had to say. He asked: "where are Emmett Scott, Moton and Dr. Du Bois? What will the N.A.A.C.P. do besides writing frantic letters? We fear that they can never rise above the level of appeals."[6]

Harrison then suggested a more militant approach—a cure for the KKK. If "the common Negro in Tennessee" let it be known that "for the life of every Negro soldier or civilian, two 'crackers' will die" and "that it will be as costly to kill Negroes as it would be to kill real people," then "the Ku-Klux would be met upon its own ground." He noted that "all our laws" declare "lynching and white-capping are crimes . . . [and that] people singly or in groups, have the right to kill in defense of their lives." Thus, "if the Ku-Klux prevents the officers of the law from enforcing the law then it is up to Negroes to help the officers by enforcing the law on their own account." He reasoned that "Lead and steel" are just as potent against "crackers" as they were against Germans and that "democracy is as well worth fighting for in Tennessee as ever it was on the plains of France." He added, "Not until the Negroes of the south recognize this truth will anybody else recognize it for them." He then closed the *Voice* article with an oratorical invocation from the narrative poem *Childe Harold's Pilgrimage*, by the early-nineteenth-century English poet George Gordon (Lord) Byron:

> Hereditary bondmen, know ye not
> Who would be free themselves must strike the blow?[7]

While Harrison was in Washington, other New York "soap box orators" descended upon the city. In addition to Rev. Miller's talk at the Bethel Literary Society, Chandler Owen and Randolph arranged a conference for the third week of January, and Garvey spoke at a mass meeting at the Metropolitan Church. Major Loving, writing to Churchill, observed, "all of these New York 'soap box orators' are beginning to invade this city, and their presence must carry some significance." This comment was more portentous than he realized—later in the summer, when Washington's African American community came under white supremacist attack—it armed and fought back."[8]

Around January 1919 the autodidactic Harrison, reflecting his concern for the "common people," wrote an article (probably for *The Voice*), which sought to help point the way forward. Entitled "To the Young Men of My Race," it offered a scorching critique of the old "Negro leadership." He argued that in a vastly changing world "millions of Negroes" could not "render effective aid to the world without understanding something of how the world, or society, is arranged, how it runs, and how it is run." He attributed the existing lack of understanding to "the burdens put on them by the White Lords of subjection and repression" typified by the 39 cents worth of education a year in Alabama; the "deep race hatred of the Christian Church, the Y.M.C.A. and the Associated Press"; the "lynching in the land of 'liberty'"; the "disfranchisement in 'democratic' America"; and the "segregation on the Federal trains and in the Federal departments." To overcome these obstacles and to achieve happiness and freedom from this oppression required a new and different "Negro leadership." He described the old leaders as

the old men whose minds are always retrospecting and reminiscing to the past, who are "trained" to read a few dry and dead books which they still fondly believe are hard to get—these do not know anything of the modern world, its power of change and travel, and the mighty range of its ideas. Its labor problems and their relation to wars and alliances and diplomacy are not even suspected by these quaint fossils. They think that they are "leading" Negro thought, but they could serve us better if they were . . . laid aside in lavender as mementos of a dead past.[9]

In contrast to this older leadership, Harrison argued that young "men" must prepare for the task of leadership, its "stern and necessary duties" of training, irreverence, and courage. Just as it took Christ thirty years to make his great sacrifice, so must "young Negro men of America" prepare and "get education not only in school and college, but in books and newspapers, in market-places, institutions, and movements." He advised them to "prepare by knowing; and never think you know until you have listened to ten others who know differently— and have survived the shock." Regarding "irreverence," he explained that respect for the antiquated because it was antiquated was the old way and that "oldsters love ruts because they help them to 'rub along,' they are easy to understand; they require the minimum of exertion and brains, they give the maximum of ease." In contrast, Harrison advised to get the very best out of yourself shun a rut as you would shun the plague! Never bow the knee to Baal because Baal is in power; never respect wrong and injustice because they are enshrined in "the sacred institutions of our glorious land"; never have patience with either Cowardice or Stupidity because they happen to wear venerable whiskers. Read, reason, and think on all sides of all subjects. Don't compare yourself with the runner behind you on the road; always compare yourself with the one ahead; so only will you go faster and farther. And set it before you, as a sacred duty always to surpass the teachers that taught you—and this is the essence of irreverence.[10]

He then stressed that "courage" was crucial and that if all else failed, one should "never let *that* fail." Even more than preparation, courage was needed for "a downtrodden race" that "must learn the lesson of Gideon and his band" (who, in the Bible's book of Judges, opposed the Baal cult). Harrison then quoted from Paul Laurence Dunbar's poem "Right's Security," on the courage to be in a minority:

> Minorities since time began
> Have shown the better side of man;
> And often, in the lists of time,
> One man has made a cause sublime.[11]

In conclusion Harrison offered that "a people under the heel of oppression has more need of heroic souls than one for whom the world is bright." "Negroes" needed leadership with "courage, fortitude, heroism."[12]

———

Harrison maintained an active social life while in Washington. Away from his family for over a month, he wrote in his diary that on Saturday, February 1, 1919, he spent "a most enjoyable evening" at the T Street apartment of Miss Marie James, the former sweetheart of his (postal worker) friend Charles Burroughs. Marie and Hubert chatted, she spoke of her aspirations and artistic strivings, and she sang for him "O Mia Fernando," from *La Favorita*, by the nineteenth-century Italian composer Gaetano Donizetti. Hubert was impressed by the "splendid technical training and rare original fineness of expression" of her voice but felt that she suffered from "artist's—soul" and was oversensitive. He considered her "a singing genius" wasting "in an unfavorable atmosphere." After a second visit to her apartment, on the evening of Sunday, February 9, Hubert noted in his diary, "she forces the pace a bit." After a third visit on the evening of Monday, March 3, he wrote, "after some interesting philandering, *je lui tenais dans une embras passionelle* [I gave her a passionate embrace]."[13]

On Sunday, February 2, Harrison went to Lincoln Temple at Eleventh and R Streets, where he heard a layman, Prof. John R. Hawkins of the AME Church, preach a sermon he described as "uplifting but superficial in its intellectual quality." He then went to "Poli's Theater downtown" and heard Louise Bryant and Albert Rhys Williams, both of whom had taken part in the Bolshevik Revolution, speak on "The Truth About Russia." He described Williams, the author of a biography of Lenin (*Lenin: The Man and His Work*), as "eloquent; a tall vigorous, capable, American-looking man, splendidly equipped, physically and mentally." Bryant, a fine journalist who was also the wife of John Reed (a famed author on the Bolshevik Revolution and soon to be a founding leader of the Communist Labor Party of America), was described as "slight and nervous" and an orator who "walked back and forth on the platform as she spoke." He bought her book, *Six Red Months in Russia: An Observer's Account of Russia Before and During the Proletarian Dictatorship*, with his last two dollars.[14]

Then, on the afternoon of February 4, after almost ten years of marriage, Harrison mailed the "first love-letter" in his life to his wife, Lin. In his papers there is very little Hubert-to-Lin correspondence and no letters from Lin to Hubert. (Any additional correspondence that existed was either lost, destroyed, or possibly pulled from his papers by Lin, their daughter Aida, or son William.) Hubert's diary has few mentions of Lin.[15]

On February 5, around 12:30 a.m., Harrison met for the first time the man who had been so instrumental in his postal firing, Emmett Scott, at an Eleventh Street restaurant near U Street. Harrison commented in his diary that "another mulatto who was dining with him had the nerve to introduce us," and "naturally I did not take the gentleman's hand nor give him any greeting except my 'Good night gentlemen', on going out."[16]

The following week, on Thursday, February 13, Harrison spoke to the children of the Garnett School, on U Street near Tenth Street, NW, after being invited by Miss Chase, the supervising head of a three-school group. He told the youngsters that he awoke early because "children were the most important things in life for us human beings." The "thought" he then tried to impart was that "the intellect shown by Sherlock Holmes was not as worth while to average humanity as the intellect shown by Robinson Crusoe." He suggested, "the best way to test a way of thinking or doing is to ask one's self what would happen if everybody thought or did the same." The students were told that "if our race were turned adrift with only thinkers and writers and speakers millions would starve to death" and that they "should aim to become makers of things that were necessary for life; of things to eat, to wear, to shelter instead of nourishing the pitiful ambition to become clerks, typewriters and scriveners." Harrison emphasized that the "boy who could make a girl's doll-carriage or a bench was a more valuable kind of brain than the boy who could say the

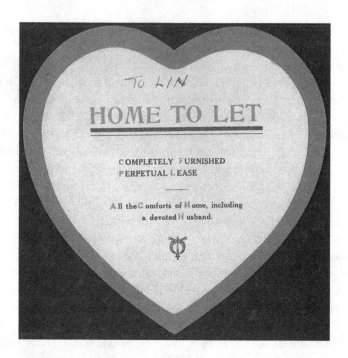

Figure 2.1. Hubert Harrison, "To Lin," Valentine card, n.d. This card is one of only a few items of correspondence between Hubert Harrison and his wife, Lin, in the Hubert H. Harrison Papers at Columbia University. Whether there was more correspondence between Hubert and Lin than that currently in the papers is not known. *Source:* Hubert H. Harrison Papers, Box 2, Folder 18, Rare Book and Manuscript Library, Columbia University Library. See https://dlc.library.columbia .edu/catalog/cul:37pvmcvg90.

multiplication table backwards." The local supervisor and several teachers thanked him, and he then visited a few classrooms with Miss Nellie Quander, a public school teacher, who was interested in his lecture work and who had helped him in the past. Quander, who had a BA from Howard University and a MA from Columbia University, was the First Supreme Basileus, or president, of the Alpha Kappa Alpha Sorority, which had been established by African American women, and she had organized and presided at its first two Boules, or regulating meetings.[17]

While in Washington, Harrison roomed at the "Colored" YMCA on Twelfth Street, NW. On Friday, February 14, Mr. Davis, the "Y" secretary, handed him a typed piece of paper with the question: "What to your mind would [should? —bracket insert by HH] be the program of a man whose work was the social and economic reconstruction of the returning soldiers and sailors?"

Harrison took the sheet and worked on a thoughtful reply. He assumed that Davis was referring to Black soldiers and sailors and advised to "help them to insist on getting, in their own land, that same democracy for which they went 3,000 miles to make the world safe." He advocated:

1. Help them to get, in our industrial system, a chance to earn their living that bears the same relation to the returned white soldiers' chance that their fighting in France bore to the white soldiers' fighting.

2. Help them to voice their demand for the right to vote in such parts of the country as they may have fought to protect; and help them to secure this demand.

If these two core elements of equality were achieved, Harrison thought that the returned Black soldiers and sailors would be in a position to remove the other obstacles themselves. It was a brief, yet profound, response.[18]

On February 17, 1919, Major Loving again wrote to the director of MID to discuss the mass meetings held in January 1919; he also mentioned Harrison's talks over the past six weeks. Loving's letter was circulated among MID officials, along with comments from the acting director, John M. Dunn, who called "special attention to the increased activity in radical propaganda among the colored people since the signing of the armistice." Harrison had particularly impressed Loving, who in his report wrote that

all of the speakers named on inclosed [sic] lists [Harrison, Garvey, Trotter, Rev. Miller, Owen, and Randolph] are radicals and frequently advocate Bolshevism in their speeches. This is especially true of Mr. Hubert Harrison, who claims that "Bolshevism is the salvation of America." The conservative colored population of Washington has never been accustomed to radical addresses of this nature and when Mr. Harrison first appeared before Washington audiences the people list[e]ned at him in awed silence. Now that he has been delivering addresses there for the past six weeks, the people have not only become accustomed to his philosophy but are applauding it. During this brief stay of six weeks Mr. Harrison has developed a very large following in the city of Washington, just as he did in New York.[19]

While concentrating his energies in Washington Harrison did periodically return to New York. One such trip, on Sunday, February 23, included an attendance at an afternoon mass meeting at the packed headquarters of the Virgin Islands Protective Association (VIPA) at 45 West 133rd Street. VIPA's vice president and cofounder, Miss Elizabeth Hendrickson, chaired and explained that the meeting aimed "to devise ways and means of alleviating the present intolerable conditions existing in the islands, due to maladministration in its worst form." Hendrickson castigated the Southern-cracker-style rule by the U.S. Navy under Rear Admiral James Harrison Oliver, the naval governor of the islands, who had issued a proclamation putting an end to free speech. She also introduced Reverend Paul, a former St. Croix schoolmaster who offered a prayer, and VIPA's president and cofounder, Ashley L. Totten, who spoke of civil disturbances on the islands, the oppressive behavior of the armed U.S. Marines (the native police and civilians were disarmed), and the consequent spread of immorality and disease. Totten introduced a former St. Croix police-man named (Cornelius?) Richardson, who was discharged from his duties and driven from the island because he demanded respect for island women and protested the degraded activities of the Marines. Totten also read letters from the St. Thomas attorney Octavius Granady and from Rev. William E. Hen-dricks of St. Paul's Church in Philadelphia. Another St. Croix native, Reverend Jensen, spoke along with the Reverend Charles Martin of Beth Tphilllah Mora-vian Church at 124 West 136th Street in Manhattan.[20] Martin, a former curate on St. Thomas, urged people to band together and stand up like men and women.[21]

After these speakers, Harrison spoke broadly on disarmament and explained that "they are disarming the black man, the brown man, the yellow man and all the darker races" because they know that the darker races will "defend them-selves when it comes to their rights and integrity." He added that might is right for a smaller people against a bigger people and that the task was now to kick off might with might. He then contributed two dollars, which, in his opinion, triggered the financial success of the afternoon. After Anselmo Jackson (the organization's corresponding secretary) spoke, discussion followed, and Mrs. McKenith, a permanent resident of New York (recently returned from St. Croix) offered to provide an affidavit on the excesses of the U.S. Marines.[22]

On the following Thursday evening, February 27, Harrison was back in Washington to speak on "The Religion of West Africa" before the Woman's Home and Foreign Missionary Society of Washington, DC, at Galbraith AME Zion Church. Publicity for the event described him as "the great African trav-eler" (though he had never been to Africa), editor of *The Voice*, and author of *The Negro and the Nation*.[23]

He was now working on plans to develop a magazine that would replace *The Voice*, whose final issue was that of February 1919. His "first full day of work on the magazine project" was Saturday, March 1; he described the results as "encouraging." He broached the subject with J. P. Bond of the Mutual Life

Figure 2.2. Hubert Harrison standing in Washington, DC, March 1919.

During the last week of December 1918, Hubert Harrison traveled from Harlem to Washington, DC, to implement a major new work plan. He aimed to develop circulation of *The Voice* and to use that city as a base to move newspaper distribution into the South. Over the next seven months he spent much of his time in Washington and Virginia delivering lectures, making contacts, playing an active role in meetings and conferences, and, for a short time, stumping for *The Voice*. Of note in this photo is the fact that Harrison was not yet wearing glasses and that he is smoking. He would soon begin wearing glasses and would periodically struggle to stop smoking over his remaining years. This photo was sent to Hubert's wife, Lin, with a message on the back addressed: "To My Wife and Sweetheart From Her Husband & Lover March 1919." *Source:* Hubert H. Harrison Papers, Box 15, Folder 14, Rare Book and Manuscript Library, Columbia University Library. See https://dlc.library.columbia.edu/catalog/cul:ffbg79cq92.

Insurance Company, Prof. Charles Wesley, Prof. Charles Thomas, and a printer named (Daniel?) Murray. Harrison was "to draw up a prospective" and Thomas was to see about "interesting a certain gentleman to become the treasurer of the venture." Thomas's interest soon waned, however, and he "seemed to shy off" the matter.[24]

On Sunday, March 2, Rev. T. J. Moppins delivered a sermon at Union Wesley Church in Washington, DC, and then introduced Harrison, who explained to the congregation that he was in DC "'projecking [projecting] with *The Voice*." After his talk, members of various church organizations scrambled to book his services. The Christian Endeavor Society signed him up for March 25, and he was to accompany Miss Williams, the chorister, and her party to address Black soldiers in camp at Alexandria, Virginia. After dinner on the evening of March 2, Harrison, Moppins, and another church official went to the Pythian Temple for a meeting of the Secular League. It was Harrison's first such visit—though scheduled the previous Sunday, he had been unable to leave New York in time. He apologized for his absence, and Dr. J. J. Shirley offered to step off the program the following Sunday to enable him to speak.[25]

Harrison next lectured on "The League of Nations and the Darker Races" for an hour on March 6 in the auditorium of the library at Howard University before the Social Science Club. Professor Kelly Miller chaired, and Harrison, who saw the League as "the effort of [a weakened] white Europe to achieve a racial solidarity," expressed doubt regarding the sincerity of the League's desire to prevent war. He pointed out that the League was similar to a gigantic trust or "plunderbund" (a league of financial, political, or commercial interests that exploits the public) and was implicitly organized to exploit the darker races of the world. As an alternative to the present constitution of the League of Nations he proposed that the German African colonies be internationalized. The *Howard University Record* stated that it had no doubt that his "inspiring" talk would "lead to much Pan African thought in the University."[26]

On Tuesday, March 18, 1919, Harrison wrote to Dr. James L. Gordon, pastor of Washington's First Congregational Church, seeking a speaking engagement at his church. Gordon requested that Harrison stop by his office on Thursday. When they met Gordon imposed "the difficult condition of first securing not only the endorsement of Dr. [J. Stanley] Durkee, the [last] white head of Howard, but his agreement to present me to the audience in the name, and in behalf, of Howard University." Harrison assumed that Dr. Gordon "had already been 'reached' and 'tampered' with" but nevertheless "cheerfully accepted this condition," as he explained, "reasoning somewhat after the manner of the

Bolsheviki in the Prinkipo [Princess Island Conference] matter: that if the condition was set in the hope that I wouldn't comply with it, then my move was to defeat that hope."[27]

Harrison went home "thinking hard" and wrote out a "skeleton-outline" of his intended lecture on "The New Covenant of Peace." As he described it in his diary:

> It certainly is a fairly conservative thing—from the standpoint of the New Negro. It stresses the need for a new compromise, starting from farther forward than Booker Washington's Atlanta Compromise of 1896; it makes clear that this compromise must be a real give-and-take, not all the "give" on one side and all the "take" on the other; it insists that [Robert Russa] Moton, [Emmett] Scott, [George Edmund] Haynes and Du Bois cannot put through such a program because they have lost their grip on the people, and that, inasmuch as it must be put through by Negro leaders who have a grip on the masses, those white men of leadership who wish to see peace established in the sphere of race-relationship must perforce deal with the radical compromise or else face the responsibility for a disquieting future.[28]

Harrison intended to take the outline with him to give to Durkee to study. If he refused to endorse it, Harrison reasoned that he "would be putting himself in the position not of a conservative but of a reactionary who wished us to be lynched, disfranchised, and educationally starved without making even a mild effort at changing these things." If such were the case, Harrison "naturally" planned "to give the widest and most permanent publicity to such a conclusion."[29]

Dr. Johnson, Dr. Gordon's curate, telephoned Mr. Davis of the "Y" on March 21 "to find out what manner of man" Harrison was and whether he "might be trusted to be 'safe' and 'sound.'" Davis told Johnson that Harrison "was preeminently safe and sound," by which he meant that he demonstrated "reliability of statement, knowledge of the facts, and correctness in the conclusions drawn from them." Davis also assured Johnson that "they *needed*" Harrison's talk because "we Christians" seem "to be the only ones who are afraid of the truth.'" After hearing of these conversations from Davis, Harrison changed his tactics and decided to send the lecture outline directly to Gordon, "furnishing him with the opportunity of judging the matters and spirit" of the "message." Harrison also felt this would undercut "influences that may have 'got to' him," thereby "shaming him into deciding the case for himself." This would also allow Harrison to "dodge Durkee," whom he didn't "trust," and would put "the burden of rejecting an effort at mediation squarely on his shoulders." Harrison sent the letter on March 22; in the last paragraph, which accompanied the outline, he wrote:

> If our white friends themselves refuse the gesture of welcome to such a compromise program, presented by Liberals and acquiescing Radicals of statesmanlike intelligence on our side, then there will be no other conclusion left for those who are not slaves except this: that their friends' friendship is only a cloak for covering sentiments and intentions indistinguishable from those which characterize their so-called enemies.[30]

On March 20, while dealing with the Howard University situation, Harrison briefly met George Edmund Haynes (of the National League on Conditions Among Urban Negroes, which in 1920 would become the National Urban League), on the steps of the "Y" and told him that he would soon be going south. In 1918 Woodrow Wilson had appointed Haynes to head the newly formed Division of Negro Economics of the War Labor Administration, which, since that time, had established some 225 local committees to build "racial harmony." Haynes "positively trembled" and recommended that Harrison not go because he doubted his "presence there would be productive of good." Haynes then added, "in certain sections both sides were literally armed to the teeth and a mere spark might bring on another Atlanta" (a reference to the vicious, white supremacist mob attacks on Atlanta's African American community in 1906). Harrison felt he had genuinely scared Haynes and commented, "Naturally, the poor fool thinks that I intend to furnish that spark!" Harrison then "analyzed his [Haynes's] fears, the weakness of his position and the strength of mine" and decided to make "bold moves on the board rather than cautious ones, attacking rather than defending."[31]

On the evening of Friday, March 21, Harrison dictated a letter to Major Loving that was intended as a letter "to his superiors in the 'Bureau of Intelligence,' War Dept." In the letter Harrison apprised Loving of his "forthcoming lecture 'before a large, white congregation' in Washington," without mentioning the congregation by name. He also enclosed a copy of his lecture outline on "The New Covenant of Peace" and told Loving that he "was going south to make friends for such a covenant on both sides of the color-line." Harrison also enclosed the summary of his positions in a letter "to a friend in Tennessee." The "radicals, of vision," he explained, "would heartily cooperate in the give-and-take compromise," allowing the government to save money currently being spent on surveillance of Negro activities. In this way they would also be "serviceable in allaying friction and promoting goodwill." "But," he concluded, "we absolutely demand, as the price of our aid, the head of John the Baptist on a charger, viz: that [Emmett] Scott, [George] Haynes and their ilk be dumped once and for all." Harrison was willing to compromise, but the old leadership had to go.[32]

Harrison made plans for his upcoming lecture tour of the South. He contacted the attorney James M. Harrison (no relation) of Norfolk, who provided a list of prominent ministers and leaders. He established relations with two leaders of the Richmond African American community, John Mitchell Jr. of the *Richmond Planet* and the Mechanics' Savings Bank, and Giles B. Jackson, a leading lawyer, businessman, and journalist. He also intended to write others in that circle of cities to complete his arrangements. In March and April he obtained recommendations from Rev. W. C. Brown, pastor of John Wesley AME Zion Church in Washington; William Gordon, of the Howard University School of Theology; Dr. John Alex Morgan of Yonkers, New York; W. E. Lew, of Miles Memorial College in Birmingham and formerly of Lane College in Jackson, Tennessee; B. T. Johnson, president of the Social Science Club of Howard University; and J. P. Bond, the District of Columbia director of the Standard Life Insurance Company of Atlanta.[33]

Overall the recommendations were laudatory, although the one from Bond was not very accurate. Bond described Harrison as a "native of Denmark" (he was from the Danish West Indies) who was "educated in England [which he was not] and the United States," and he recommended him as "a lecturer to schools, colleges, churches and societies." Lew emphasized that Harrison was "a student of science, an author, a lecturer of rare ability and an editor without fear." Rev. Brown stressed Harrison's "sense of fairness, moral courage and humanitarian spirit," which never fails "to win the respect of his audience." He added that Harrison's "discussion of the most important questions before the peoples of today" were "masterly done."[34]

On Tuesday, March 25, Harrison lectured on "Negro History You Should Know" at Union Wesley AME Zion Church on Twenty-third Street, NW, in Washington. In publicity for the event sponsored by the Christian Endeavor Society he was described as an "Author, African and Oriental Traveler, Humorist and Race Advocate." (He had not traveled to Africa or Asia.) A *Washington Post* article about the talk was headlined "Negroes Urged to Strive: Dr. Hubert Harrison Warns Against Imitating White People." This appears to be the first of many times that Harrison was incorrectly described as "Dr." In his diary Harrison described the lecture as "fairly successful," noting that 169 people attended. His 50 percent share of the fifteen-cent tickets came to $12.65. He also sold fifty-two books (probably *The Negro and the Nation*); his total net income from the lecture came to $24.09, of which he was sending $15 to his wife, Lin, by telegraph in the morning. In his talk, according to the *Post*, Harrison reportedly urged that the Negroes of America must cease whining and complaining . . . must cease looking up to others for that which is within their own grasp. They should learn the history of their race and the contributions which it has made to civilization. On this rock of racial self-knowledge they must build their house of racial self-respect before they can gain the respect and friendship of the white race.[35]

That night Harrison noted in his diary, "I have been fighting back another nervous break-down during the past four days. I can't see what can be the cause of nerve troubles at this time. Guess I'd better 'lay-off' for a while." These health problems, which may have been a factor in the previous cessation of *The Voice*, were probably the final blow to any plans to continue publishing the resurrected *Voice*. The newspaper last published in February and terminated in March–April 1919. The nervousness may have been related to his heavy workload, financial and political pressures, and to what he later, in his diary of July 6, 1919, self-diagnosed as "malarial fever."[36]

On Friday, March 28, Harrison was scheduled to speak in Washington, DC, at the John Wesley AME Zion Church on "A Race in Search of Its Soul." Three days later, on March 31, he sent a photo of himself, a friend, and a Black policeman "To My Wife and Sweetheart From her Husband and Lover." Harrison, who had been pushing for more Black police officers in Harlem, added: "the policeman is a friend of ours, a Mr. Lester." He also attended a chicken supper at John Wesley Church on April 2 and met with Dr. Durkee of Howard on April 5. Then on April 6 he went to Union Wesley, and, after speaking with Rev. Moppins and going to John Wesley Church to speak with Rev. W. C. Brown, he called on Miss Pearl Brooks and Mrs. Eula Daniels—for which he "got properly 'bawled out' afterwards by Mrs. Daniels." After going to an evening activity on Tuesday, April 8, at the John Wesley Church, Harrison and the poet Walter Everette Hawkins called on Professor Alain Leroy Locke and his mother (Mary Ishmael Locke) on F Street. There they met "the real object of our visit, Mr. Plenyono Ngbe [Gbe] Wolo, a young Kru graduate of Harvard," who was studying at Union Theological Seminary. Also present was another Liberian, Miss Anna E. Cooper, who had attended Howard University and would later become the first dean of the College of Liberia. Harrison was particularly excited about the evening and in his diary reported that Wolo "thinks the thoughts about Africa which I have been thinking for many years and we had a most enjoyable conversation." In his diary Harrison also noted that at noon on April 9 he met Major Loving at F Street.[37]

———

Harrison's major spring 1919 activity was his planned tour of the South, which, because of difficulties, wound up being limited to the state of Virginia. On

Sunday morning, April 13, he spoke in Richmond at a Sunday sing of the Army and Navy Club. Later that afternoon he lectured at True Believers' Hall in the Moore Street Baptist Church, and in the evening he addressed an audience at the Second Baptist Church. The *Richmond News Leader* noted that Harrison had "the distinguished patronage of some of the best people of both races in Richmond," described him as a "sensation," and claimed that he was a "Noted African Traveler" and "African Scholar, who has travelled and studied in four continents." It added that "Dr. Harrison" held "the degree of Ph. D. from the University of Copenhagen, Denmark" (this was not true).[38]

Major Loving met again with Harrison the following Saturday, April 19, and they had "a heart-to-heart talk" about Harrison's planned trip into the South. Loving had reviewed Harrison's previous letter to him, including the enclosures, with his chief, Colonel Churchill. Harrison believed his "ferment" was "working" and predicted, "I shall live to see Emmett Scott paid off for what was done to me in 1911 and Geo. Haynes for—other things." (Scott was instrumental in having Harrison fired from the Post Office in 1911, and Haynes may have been involved in preventing Harrison from becoming editor of an Urban League–related publication around 1915.) Later in the year, in his diary entry of November 13, 1919, Harrison added, "Read today in a newspaper that Geo. E. Haynes has lost his job as Secretary of the National Urban League."[39]

In Richmond, on Wednesday, April 30, Harrison was scheduled to speak on "Negro History and Negro Education" before the Spartan Literary and Athletic Association at the Reformers' Hall and at a community sing for colored soldiers. In publicity for the event, "Dr. Harrison" was described as "the only Negro of our time who has held the chair of Comparative Religion in a white institution of learning, taught Economics in another and been the black leader of a white lecture forum in New York." It added that he had a "Ph.D. from the University of Copenhagen," that he had "traveled extensively in Europe and Africa," and that he was famous all over the East as a lecturer and teacher.[40]

On Sunday, July 6, 1919, while staying in Norfolk, Hubert, thinking about his family, noted in his diary that his daughter Aida was seven years old (on July 4) but that he "was unable to go back to New York to give them [his family] an outing as I had promised, because last Monday's audience failed to appear. There were about 40 present." He had spent the Fourth of July in his room, except for an appointment with Plummer B. Young, editor of the Norfolk *Journal and Guide,* and the president of the new bank on Church Street. On July 5 and 6, Hubert took sick with what he diagnosed as "a touch of malaria or the grip." Nevertheless, on Wednesday evening, July 9, he left Norfolk by boat for Washington, commenting, "I certainly have had some hard luck in this town." He had been sick for the previous five days with what he diagnosed as "malarial fever" but hoped "to have better luck in Washington and Alexandria." He was also due in New York on Saturday (July 12) where, as he noted, "my little Sweetheart-Wife will be waiting for me." This last comment and his March 31 postcard suggest that Hubert and Lin may have significantly improved their matrimonial relationship. On his return home he again turned to soapbox oratory, and the August 2 *Chicago Defender* reported that "Hubert Harrison, editor and lecturer, has been speaking on Lenox avenue during the week."[41]

Major Loving was clearly impressed by Harrison, and on August 6, 1919, as he was about to be relieved of his duties with the Office of Intelligence, he wrote his "Final Report on Negro Subversion" to Brigadier General Marlborough Churchill, the MID director in Washington. Loving explained that "until about four years ago radical sentiment among negroes was of a moderate character and confined to denunciations of lynching, disfranchisement, Jim Crow-ism, etc." Since "early in 1915, however, a number of the younger and more intellectual negroes abandoned the attitude of the older men and boldly adopted socialism," and "many negroes, especially of the younger generation, flocked to meeting halls and street corners to hear men of their own race expound a new philosophy and attack the Government to which they attributed all the social and economic evils suffered by black and white races alike." The report, unequivocally pointing to the interrelatedness of racial oppression to class rule in the United States, added that "the present negro situation of the U.S.A. would thus appear to be due to the growing race-consciousness of the educated negro and to the use made of the colour question by revolutionary agitators to stimulate a sympathetic unrest among the coloured races in order to make the breakdown of the Capitalist system universal."[42]

In his report Loving paid special attention to Harrison, who had just returned to Harlem after his lecture tour in Washington and Virginia. Loving's description of Harrison is noteworthy:

Mr. Harrison is a Negro of West Indian birth. He is a scholar of broad-learning and a radical propagandist. Most of his time is spent in lecture tours in cities having large Negro populations. He is not affiliated with any political party and freely criticizes all of them. He differs from other Negro radicals, in that his methods are purely scholastic. He typifies the professor lecturing to his classes rather than a soap box orator appealing to popular clamor. One of his favorite themes is to review the history of exploitation of Africa, India and other countries by the Caucasian races. His lectures on the subject are always interspersed with sarcastic and ironical references to what he terms "the brazen hypocricy" of the white races, especially the Anglo-Saxon. He also makes frequent attacks upon the church, asserting that its influence has been inimical to the progress of humanity by enslaving the minds of the people with foolish dogmas and theories that will not bear the light of reason. He pictures the heads of the church as being in league with the master capitalists in a pact to plunder the proletariat of all nations. Thoroughly versed in history and sociology, Mr. Harrison is a very convincing speaker. I consider his influence to be more far reaching than that of any other individual radical because his subtle propaganda, delivered in such scholastic language and backed by the facts of history, carries an appeal to reason that reaches the more thoughtful and conservative class of Negroes who could not be reached by the "cyclone" methods of the more extreme radicals. As a matter of fact, Mr. Harrison's lectures might well be considered a preparatory school for radical thought in that they prepare the minds of conservative Negroes to receive and accept the more extreme doctrines of Socialism. Without any deliberate intent to serve in such a capacity, he is the drill master training recruits for the Socialist army led by the extreme radicals, Messrs. Owen and Randolph. Mr. Harrison's lectures are always well attended and he ranks as one of the very important factors in the dissemination of radical thought among Negroes. Mr. Harrison has recently returned to this city after an extended lecture tour through the South and is now engaged in addressing street meetings in Harlem.[43]

———————

Another aspect of Harrison's stay in Washington was his reinvolvement in matters concerning the Dutch anthropologist Herbert Marie Bernelot Moens. On the evening of April 9, 1919, Harrison attended a meeting at the YMCA of the Washington branch of the NAACP. The topic was the Moens case, which the historian Constance McLaughlin Green has described as "trivial in itself" but that "fanned the smoldering embers of racial antagonisms" in Washington. It remained an emotionally charged topic at meetings of the board of trustees of the Board of Education and in the pages of the *Washington Bee* into 1920.[44]

According to the strongly critical *Messenger*, Moens used "only light complexioned and beautiful colored girls" in his studies, which involved examination of genital areas and kissing all over the body as a means of intensifying passions. He was accused of taking advantage of innocent students and indulging in indecent behavior with a teacher. Leading the attack was the Parents League, a group of six to seven hundred Black families that organized protests at the Franklin School and at Dunbar High and called for the removal of Roscoe C. Bruce, assistant superintendent of the Franklin School, and Charlotte Hunter, his chief assistant at Dunbar. Bruce, who was African American, was accused of incompetence, favoritism, and "lack of vigilance," though he received support from "white" members of the Washington school board and from Mrs. Coralie Cook, an African American member, who characterized stories about him as exaggerations and lies. After pickets were set up at Dunbar, Miss Hunter resigned. A clamor also arose over deeper causes of the problem. The Black community was divided, while many "whites" belittled Black agitation as alleged evidence of emotional instability and poor judgment.[45]

There had been an attempt at a settlement in March 1919. The legation of the Netherlands was asked to find out if Moens would be willing to plead guilty, pay a fine of $2,500, and leave the country. Moens said he was ready to pay the fine and leave the country, but he would refuse to plead guilty to a charge he considered "absurd, unjust and malicious." His trial began on March 24, 1919, and lasted until April 1. Moens was found guilty by a jury in criminal court "on charges of having improper photographs in his possession" and was sentenced to one year in prison and a fine of $500.[46]

The evidence and decision were widely disputed. R. W. Shufeldt, a former major and official of the Army Medical Museum and a staunch defender of Moens, said the photographic samples he was shown "were not lewd . . . except in the minds of those who habitually confuse the lewd." He considered his examination at the trial to be "a farce," since those who interrogated him "were coarsely ignorant of every factor entering into the matter under consideration." In submitted documents Simon Flexner, president of the Rockefeller Institute, and Professor Franz Boas, of Columbia University, attested to the anthropological value of the pictures. On the other side, Mr. Ales Hrdlicka, of the Smithsonian Institute, succeeded in persuading the jury that the pictures were without any scientific value.[47]

The same day that the verdict was rendered the case was appealed, and Moens was released on a $5,000 bond. The judgment would subsequently be reversed and the case remanded for further proceedings. When the Department of Justice later filed a motion for a rehearing in the Court of Appeals, the motion would be denied, the judgment condemning Moens to one year of jail arrested, the indictments quashed, and the bail returned, less $79 for "keeping the money."[48]

Harrison became involved in the Moens case shortly after Moens's conviction but before the rulings in his favor. At the April 9, 1919, meeting of the DC chapter of the NAACP, the attorney James A. Cobb, whom Harrison described as "the official Galahad," spoke on "the trial and its social effects." According to Harrison, Cobb deprecated the attempts of the *Washington Bee* and of Parents League indignation meetings "to besmirch the moral reputation of Washington Negro school teachers." Harrison felt that he (Harrison) personally "helped the meeting out of a hole when the sentiment against Cobb was sputtering to the explosion point" by offering what he described as "a thrilling three minute argument" that ended with a move to table the resolution then before the house. The motion carried.[49]

In late 1919 Harrison again became involved. He ghostwrote an article for Moens entitled "Three Black Bands," which appeared in the December 1919 *Medical Review of Reviews*. It aimed to counter censorship and "erotic bashfulness" and to set the record straight on Moens. Harrison began by describing Moens's arrival and background in the United States. He explained how Moens's intellectual interest was aroused by "chance contact in Los Angeles with that highly mixed race described here [in the United States] as colored people" and how, because of race prejudice, they "had not been considered fit subjects for study by any American scientist," not even at the Smithsonian Institution, which had "not deigned to make studies of these colored people . . . in their midst." When Moens showed the Smithsonian director a series of five photographs of the heads of Washington schoolgirls, the director asked, "From what part of the world did you collect these interesting types?" Moens replied, "From right here in Washington, but you couldn't see them because they are colored." Moens then set about studying the stigma of racial intermixture.[50]

The subject matter aroused opposition on many sides, and Moens's photos were given to the Department of Justice, after which, according to Harrison, on pornographic grounds and under Comstockian censors (a reference to Anthony Comstock and associates at the Society for the Suppression of Vice), Moens was indicted and convicted. He was defended by a host of influential people, including Dr. Shufeldt, who described Moens's nude photography as "exceptionally fine anthropological photographs, mainly of crosses between a number of races—undertaken in the usual anthropological poses, anterior, posterior, lateral, etc." As "works of art" they were "most tasteful and valuable." The photos "seized" as "obscene, disgusting and filthy" were viewed as not being pornographic but of having high scientific, artistic, and social standing in statements signed by R. S. Woodward, president of the Carnegie Institution; Flexner, of the Rockefeller Institute of Medical Research; Boas, of the Department of Anthropology at Columbia; William Crawford Gorgas, a former surgeon general of the U.S. Army; George Julian Zolany, president of the Society of Washington Artists; P. Bryant Baker, of the Royal Society of British Sculptors; Congressman W. W. Hastings; Congressman T. A. Chandler; Louise Tayler-Jones, MD; the artist Mathilde M. Leisenring; Charlotte Brooks, superintendent of nurses of the Emergency Hospital; Mabel T. Boardman, on the Central Committee of the Red Cross; and others.[51]

Harrison defended Moens both on scientific grounds and because much of the attack against him, in the name of antipornography, reflected a much narrower mental viewpoint. He began by referring to Moens's article "The Intermixture of Races," in the September 1919 *Medical Review of Reviews*. He described how that article contained illustrated photos, including six of nude females, three with broad black bands across their pelvic regions. Harrison used the issue of censorship as an opening to discuss the question of "erotic bashfulness" and asserted he was doing so "from the viewpoint of the scientific men of Europe." He described the American mind's erotic bashfulness as "a disturbance of consciousness based on a perturbed propriety" centered on primary erotic areas of the body and stated that it was "a well known fact outside of the United States that an excess of erotic bashfulness, instead of being a proof of purity is one of the surest signs of mental nastiness." He argued, "a perfectly nude figure of either sex is less suggestive and inciting to a normal mind than the studied indecencies of the half-draped."[52]

Harrison, who Richard Bruce Nugent in *Gay Rebel of the Harlem Renaissance* would later point out had a "superlative collection of erotic literature, second to none in New York," next reviewed two relatively recent cases of "American official bashfulness." First was the case of "Bull Durham," the trade name of a popular tobacco brand whose trademark was a full-sized Durham bull standing before a pasture gate. According to Harrison, "some filthy-minded 'purists' observed with shrinking horror that the bull was pictured with the characteristic genitalia of bulls and at once took up the issue with the psychologic experts of the police department with the result that an army of pot-painters were set to work painting bars across the bull's genitalia." It seemed that "the angry angels of Art and Morality were both appeased and America was once more made safe for morality."[53]

The second case cited was that of "September Morn," a painting (actually entitled *September Morning*) by the French artist Paul Chabas. Anthony Comstock and associates at the Society for the Suppression of Vice had seized reproductions of the picture in 1913 and declared there was a figure of a nude woman in the stream. All the attention on the picture led to hundreds of thousands of reproductions being sold, and "the people took it up and the mental attitude of the Comstockians was lampooned on the stage, in the newspapers and in general conversation." Harrison saw similarities between the erotic bashfulness around the tobacco trademark and *September Morning* and that around the Moens case. He felt science and art should not be stifled and that there was "scientific value and significance of the nude pictures which were therein Bull Durhamed."[54]

Later, in the *Negro World* of May 8, 1920, Harrison would discuss the Moens matter again, this time in the midst of a debate with Randolph, Owen, and others. His article was entitled "Scientific Radical Liars: What Randolph and Owen Know (?) About Anthropology and Sociology: Prof Boas and Col. Snyder vs.

the Editors of the *Messenger*; The Evidence in the Case"; it was part of a larger piece he wrote in the *Chicago Enterprise*. Harrison explained that in June 1919 the editors of the *Messenger*, "who modestly describe their magazine as 'the only journal of scientific radicalism in the world published by Negroes' promised for their next issue a 'scientific' exposition of the Moens case." In July they stated, "When we met him (Prof. Moens) we talked to him for about five minutes and then we immediately stepped aside and stated that Moens was a fraud. He knew nothing of sociology or economics of biology or anthropology." Harrison asked, "Upon what facts did they base this 'scientific' conclusion which they so confidently passed on to their readers who depend on them for reliable information?" Harrison didn't know, though he did "know some facts bearing on this point," which he offered, "permitting the readers to draw their own conclusion and compare with those of Messrs. Randolph and Owen."[55]

First Harrison cited a copy of a letter from H. D. Snyder, Colonel Medical Corps, U.S. Army and Chief Medical Officer in Panama, dated December 20, 1918, which bore the seal of the Department of State and the War Department and stated: "I have known the bearer, Mr. Herbert M. Benelot Moens, since early in the year 1915," when he was in Panama "making a study of the atavistic characteristics appearing in mixed races." He lectured "on this subject before the Canal Zone Medical Association," and we "had frequent discussions on scientific subjects" during the following months. Snyder regarded "his learning and special knowledge in these matters of the very highest, and his studies of great importance, much of his work being original."[56]

Next, Harrison cited a January 16, 1920, letter to R. P. Evans, a Washington, DC, attorney, written by Boas, whom he described as "the highest authority on anthropology in the two Americas." Harrison compared Boas's letter "with the bumptious cocksureness of the two ignoramuses [Randolph and Owen] who have bluffed themselves (and others) into believing that they know something of 'sociology or economics, of biology or anthropology,'" and, he added, "five-minute scholars are the curse of our race." Boas wrote that he had "known Professor Moens since he first came here about five years ago." At that time Moens called on him, and Boas then "introduced him to the American Ethnological Society." They met again in 1919. Boas said he was "thoroughly impressed with the deep interest which professor Moens takes in scientific work, his publications, as well as the way in which he discusses the problems in question" and how he shows "that his interest centers around the facts of race mixture, the probable occurrence of atavistic traits and the significance that these data have in relation to modern social problems."[57]

Whether one agreed with Moens's fundamental ideas, reasoned Boas, "the fact remains that all his discussions show a thorough understanding of certain fundamental biological theories and that his effort is directed toward an application of these theories to the phenomena of race mixture." Studies of this kind required investigation of the body as a whole, just as an examination of enlisted men required examining a nude, and a scientist would be "entirely unaffected by the prudery which prevents an examination of any part of the body, provided scientific reasons should make this necessary." Body examination was "particularly unavoidable" in "the case of the mixture between Negroes and whites," explained Boas, "because there are certain peculiar formations in the sexual organs of certain African races which set them off very clearly from other human races and which in any investigation of race mixture should be taken into account." Boas added that he would consider "any inquiry into Negro mixture inadequate if these particular points should not be taken into consideration," and he emphasized that "it is necessary to record any data of this kind by photographic reproduction."[58]

Boas went further. He felt that the photographs selected by Professor Moens, "some of which have been reproduced in medical journals," were "of the greatest value, because they show the effect of race mixture in such a way as to illuminate: for instance, the problem of the development of Polynesian races." He emphasized that a few of the photographs, designated as obscene in court, were "of the very highest scientific value" and that the attitude that held such pictures obscene was based on a "complete lack of comprehension of what is needed for scientific work." Boas pointed out that the "anthropological and medical journals abound in illustrations," which would come under the same category, if looked at unscientifically, and cited in particular the *Journal of the Royal Anthropological Institution of Great Britain and Ireland*. Finally, Boas told Moens's attorney R. P. Evans that he was "at liberty" to use his statements "in the interest of your client in any way you may see fit." Harrison concluded, in a stingingly sarcastic response to Randolph and Owen, "most of us ordinary mortals feel it necessary to have facts to back up the opinions that we scatter broadcast, but 'scientific radicals' are able to dispense with them."[59]

A new indictment was filed against Moens in May 1920, in which he was charged with "having 'knowingly' exhibited obscene pictures." He was forced to post a new bond and to remain against his will in the United States. In the face of the approaching elections in 1920, there was little effort either to try him again or drop the case altogether and return his bail. The new Warren G. Harding administration had little interest in pushing the new case. In 1922 the periodical *Issues of To-Day* reviewed the entire case and concluded "through the combined force of war hysteria, professional jealousy, and officious zeal of a bureaucracy anxious to establish a reason for its continued existence at the end of the war, a great injustice has been inflicted upon a scientist of established international reputation." On November 19, 1923, a nolle prosequi (do not prosecute) was entered in the court, and the charges against Moens were dropped, although he was not notified he was no longer under indictment until May 1924.[60]

The Moens matter would extend from 1919 into 1920 and beyond. For Harrison, however, the second half of 1919 proved to be one of the most eventful periods of his life. The United States would be torn by class struggle and racial strife, Marcus Garvey would begin his meteoric rise, and Harrison would undertake one of his most formidable journalistic efforts, editing the magazine the *New Negro*. As he edited that monthly he displayed a wide range of literary skills and further solidified his roles as the radical driving force of the militant New Negro Movement and as the "Father of Harlem Radicalism."

3

New Negro Editor and Agitator
(July–December 1919)

Hubert Harrison returned to Harlem during the violent summer of 1919 and soon began editing the monthly *New Negro*, which, as he explained in the August issue, was "intended as an organ of the international consciousness of the darker races—especially of the Negro race." Its presentation and interpretation columns were modeled after those of Oswald Garrison Villard's politically left, fifty-four-year-old weekly magazine *The Nation*. Harrison emphasized, "*The New Negro* must be for Negro-America what *The Nation* is for white America."[1]

The year 1919 was one of the most violent peacetime years in the history of the United States. The Great War was over, and the cost of living had almost doubled since 1914. Workers were demanding higher wages, shorter hours, unions, and collective bargaining, and they faced rigid opposition from employers. Class conflict between labor and capital was intense. Over four million workers, 20 percent of the nation's workforce, took part in some 3,600 strikes. This was the largest strike wave in U.S. history. New York City was a center of labor conflict: in January its harbor was closed by a strike of 17,000 tugboat workers; in May 50,000 cloak and suit makers struck; in July 25,000 shirt makers and 40,000 tobacco workers downed tools; and in August there were work stoppages involving 14,000 painters and 15,000 streetcar workers. Similar struggles occurred across the nation. From February 6–11, some 60,000 Seattle workers staged the first citywide general strike in the history of the country, and this sparked a similar action in nearby Tacoma; on September 22 the "Great Steel Strike" of 365,000 workers against "the strongest capitalist aggregation in the world"— the "Steel Trust"—started. The steel battle lasted two and a half months and resulted in a deployment of state troops in Pittsburgh and imposition of martial law under General Leonard Wood and the National Guard in Gary, Indiana. While the steel workers struck, over half a million miners walked out on November 1 in a national coal strike that lasted eight days and resulted in the use of federal troops in Pennsylvania, Oklahoma, New Mexico, Utah, and Washington.[2]

Though such class struggle was at times ferocious, these battles were not the most intense on the domestic scene that year. There were numerous instances in which "white" bosses and workers turned their venom not on each other but on Black workers and Black communities. The historian Arthur I. Waskow found that despite the fierce class struggle, "less actual violence occurred during 1919 in connection with struggles between labor and capital than in connection with conflicts between Negroes and whites." Seventy-six "Negroes" were reported lynched, the most in a decade, and the year witnessed a series of the bloodiest attacks on Black communities in U.S. history, including some sparked by attacks by "white" labor and others prompted by white supremacist police brutality. It seemed, according to the historian William Tuttle, that though there had been racial violence during the war, "the first year of peace after World War I was even more conducive to racial violence than during the war itself." Seven of the twenty-six attacks on Black communities were "major," beginning with Charleston on May 10; Longview, Texas, on July 11–12; Washington, DC, on July 19–21; Chicago, on July 27–August 2; Knoxville, Tennessee, on August, 30; Omaha, Nebraska, on September 28; and Phillips County, Arkansas, around Elaine, on September 30–October 1.[3]

These attacks were part of what the NAACP's James Weldon Johnson aptly described as "the red summer," and those in Washington and Chicago in particular were marked by a militant armed resistance.[4] The historian John Hope Franklin characterized the summer of 1919 as "the greatest period of interracial strife the nation ever witnessed."[5]

The attacks in Washington, where Harrison had recently spent considerable time, were in the nation's "largest and most prosperous Black community." They began with a "rampage by about 400 whites" on "Negroes" on Saturday, July 19. The "whites" were reportedly inflamed by "sensational newspaper accounts of alleged sex crimes by a 'negro fiend.'" Their attacks continued on July 20 and were further inflamed by the press when the *Washington Post* printed on July 21 that "a mobilization of every available service man stationed in or near Washington or on leave" was "ordered for tomorrow evening near the Knights of Columbus hut on Pennsylvania Avenue between Seventh and Eighth Streets." The *Post* added that at nine o'clock a "clean up" was scheduled that would cause the events of the previous two evenings "to pale into insignificance." Though it offered no explanation of where the "orders" came from, the fact that it chose to run such inflammatory material was strongly criticized in the Black community. On the night of July 21, after the *Post*'s mobilization notice, Blacks began to arm. During the fighting that ensued, over thirty people were reported killed and police and National Guardsman were shot. The militancy and willingness to fight back of the Black community was pronounced.[6]

On Sunday, July 27, a week after Washington, violence erupted in Chicago, provoked in large part, as the *Chicago Defender* explained, by the hostility of "white" workers. In the week of pitched battles that followed, at least fifteen "whites" (Harrison said that "more than 30 white policemen were killed in the Negro district alone") and twenty-three "Negroes" were reported killed and 537 people were reported injured. In Chicago, as in Washington, the postwar spirit of militancy, particularly among returning Black soldiers, was unmistakable.[7]

The domestic turmoil, the growth of the Bolshevik Revolution in Russia, and attempts to establish Soviet governments elsewhere in Europe seemed to many people to herald the onset of revolution. In addition, from late April through early June there was a nationwide series of bombings and attempted bombings of high-level government officials, including the new attorney general, A. Mitchell Palmer, a leader in government attacks on radicals. The Justice Department was asked to reply to Congress on domestic radicalism, and shortly after the June 2 bombing of Palmer's home in Washington, DC, Congress appropriated $500,000 to aid the Justice Department in apprehending the radicals allegedly involved. Justice subsequently announced the formation of a special radical-hunting team. On August 1 the Justice Department's Bureau of Investigation formed a General Investigation Division (GID) headed by J. Edgar Hoover, a young career worker who had joined the department in July 1917. Hoover had been placed in charge of arrests and deportations in July 1919 and was now assigned as special assistant to the attorney general. At his disposal were the eighty agents of the BI, and he was empowered to select targets of government investigation.[8]

Harrison was attentive to the revolutionary climate. His personal scrapbook copy of the article "Danger Peace Conference May Fail, Mr. [Frank H.] Simond Says," in the March 29, 1919, *Literary Digest*, reads in part: "The almost inescapable certainty that when the people of England and France and Italy discover that after six months of promises, following four and a half years of sacrifice, they have to bear the burden of another war, and are not to enjoy the blessings of peace and the fruits of victory, they will turn on their own governments, and eastern and western economic and political unrest will meet at the Rhine." To this, Harrison handwrote in the margin, "My own prophecy." This article was grouped with others he had on the Bolshevik and Bulgarian revolutions and the Spartacan uprising.[9]

As one of his first tasks as special assistant to the attorney general, Hoover submitted a twenty-six-page report on Black radicalism. The report was actually prepared by Robert Adger Bowen, of the translation department of the Post Office; his name was removed from the report by Hoover. This so-called Hoover Report was then officially submitted by Attorney General Palmer to the Senate Committee on the Judiciary as part of a 187-page report on radicalism, sedition, and anarchy entitled *Investigation Activities of the Department of Justice.*[10]

The section of the Bowen/Hoover/Palmer report on "Radicalism and Sedition Among the Negroes as Reflected in Their Publications," written after the race riots, found African Americans "rapidly being made strongly race conscious and class conscious" and spoke of a "well-concerted movement among a certain class of Negro leaders of thought and action to constitute themselves a determined and persistent source of radical opposition to the Government, and to the established rule of law and order." This was manifest in the Black press by "the ill-governed reaction toward race rioting"; the "threat of retaliatory measures in connection with lynching"; the "more openly expressed demand for social equality"; the "identification of the Negro with such radical organizations as the I.W.W. and an outspoken advocacy of the Bolshevik or Soviet doctrine"; and the "political stand assumed toward the present Federal administration, the South in general . . . the peace treaty and the league of nations." Underlying all, according to Bowen/Hoover/Palmer, was the "increasingly emphasized feeling of a race consciousness," which seemed "always antagonistic to the white race and openly, defiantly assertive of its own equality and even superiority." The report claimed that every discussion of the recent "race riots" noticeably "reflected the note of pride that the Negro has found" because they "fought back" and "never again" will "tamely submit to violence or intimidation." Such "defiance and . . . condemnation of the white race" appeared "in every issue of the more radical publications." According to the report, "The Negro is 'seeing red.'"[11]

The government report drew materials from various publications, including the Harrison-edited *New Negro* of September 1919. It quoted from the article "A Prophetic 'Voice': The Cause of the Negro's New Attitude Towards Race Riots," which contained a reprint of Harrison's 1917 *Voice* editorial on "The East St. Louis Horror." It also quoted from Andrea Razafkeriefo's "The Village Lynch-Smith (with Apologies to Longfellow)" in the same September *New Negro*. Importantly, while Harrison agreed with many of the Bowen/Hoover/Palmer examples of the "Negro's New Attitude," and though he had been a leader in such agitation, he criticized the report's analysis on the important ground that it failed to give proper emphasis to the "justifiable grievances" of Negro Americans and to the "indifference" of the U.S. government. It relied far too much on

"Beneath the Rule of Men Entirely Great, The Pen is Mightier Than The Sword"

A Magazine for the New Negro

Published Fortnightly in the Interest of The New Negro Manhood Movement, Advocating Race Solidarity by The Clarion Publishing Association

Unity is Strength.　Liberty is Life.　Liberty is Progress.　Liberty is Prosperity

VOL. III.　　　　New York City, August, 1919.　　　　No. 7

AS THE CURRENTS FLOW

ANNOUNCEMENT

With this issue of "The Clarion" we announce the reappearance of THE NEW NEGRO on September 1, 1919. The man who first coined that phrase "the New Negro"—and chiselled the path which "the new crowd" has taken—Mr. Hubert H. Harrison—assumes (with Mr. Bernier) the editorship of this magazine. The resulting change of policy may be summed up in the simple statement that "THE NEW NEGRO is intended as an organ of the international consciousness of the darker races—especially of the Negro race. Some of the reasons which justify such an aim will be found in Mr. Harrison's Editorial: "Our Larger Duty" in this issue of "The Clarion". In the September issue of THE NEW NEGRO our readers will find a fuller editorial statement of its purpose and scope.

During the past fortnight great events have taken place. The race battles in Washington and Chicago, although tragical, are nevertheless to be recorded as brilliant events in the history of the Negro race in America. It is most gratifying for us to note that the New Negro spirit is a fait accompli. It has found an abode in the hearts of all the truly liberty-loving and progressive Negroes. It has been too long the practice of the Southern Negro victims to beg and plead for mercy at the hands of a sordid mob. We have often wondered why these men, at the first sign of trouble, do not arm themselves preparatory for self-defence. If they are to die at the hands of a "legalized" mob, then it is up to them to sell their lives as dearly as possible. The white man must be made to take his own medicine so that he may learn to appreciate its disagreeable and disgusting flavor.

The white press of this country has noted that the Negro American has entered a new epoch in the history of his country. The baneful effects of the lessons forced upon him during his period as a chattel slave is wearing off. The New Negro—unlike the Negro of the "old conservative crowd" who is ever willing to compromise everything that is held dear to his race in order to obtain for himself a miserable pittance and some sympathy from his former master—is identifying himself with every progressive and radical movement: he is uncompromising and non-partisan, as the New York World stated in an editorial a part of which we reproduce here:

There are enough points of friction between the races without introducing party. The Negro owes nothing to any party. He has been abandoned by all of them, most notably by the Republicans, who in 1877 TRADED HIS RIGHTS AT THE SOUTH TO PERFECT THE TITLE OF A STOLEN PRESIDENCY. Colored men assuming to lead their people should know this by this time that the political and incidentally the legal privileges conferred upon them can never be enjoyed so long as they are the mere chattels of a party."

The New Negro is Negro first, Negro last, and Negro always. He needs not the white man's sympathy; all he is asking for is equal justice before the law and equal opportunity in the battle of life. He needs and asks for no special privileges that are not

Figure 3.1. The New Negro, "A Magazine for the New Negro," 3, no. 7 (August 1919), page 3. Hubert Harrison began editing the *New Negro* shortly after his scheduled July 12, 1919, return to New York from Washington, DC. Though the magazine had appeared in March 1918 under the editorship of the Liberty Leaguer August Valentine Bernier, its twenty-page advance copy for August 1919 was printed on the forms of *The Clarion* (which had been published by Liberty League members) but proclaimed that it was now published under a different policy and under the editorship of Bernier and Harrison. Harrison was described as the man who "chiselled the path which 'the new crowd' has taken." In the "As the Currents Flow" article on page 3 Harrison proclaimed the "New Negro" a *"fait accompli"* and described the recent "royal racial battles" in Washington and Chicago as "great events" that, though "tragical," deserved to be "recorded as brilliant events in the history of the Negro race in America." They demonstrated that the spirit of the "New Negro" was "in the hearts of all the truly liberty-loving and progressive Negroes" and that the baneful effects of slavery were wearing off. "Negroes" were rejecting "unmanly teaching," and Harrison declared that the "New Negro" was "unlike the Negro of the 'old conservative crowd'" who was "ever willing to compromise everything that is held dear to his race in order to obtain for himself a miserable pittance and some sympathy from his former master." This "New Negro" was "identifying himself with every progressive and radical movement," was "uncompromising and non-partisan," and "owed nothing to any political party." Harrison militantly concluded that "the New Negro is Negro first, Negro last, and Negro always [and seeks] . . . equal justice before the law and equal opportunity in the battle of life" and is willing to sacrifice "an eye for an eye, a tooth for a tooth." *Source:* Hubert H. Harrison Papers, Box 17, Folder 8, Rare Book and Manuscript Library, Columbia University Library. See https://dlc.library.columbia.edu/catalog/cul:qv9s4mw886.

what the historian Theodore Kornweibel Jr. describes as "the widespread perception among worried whites that black militancy could be inspired only by renegade whites" and "not by domestic social, economic, or political conditions."[12]

Overall, however, the vision that Harrison was articulating was taking shape as the militant "New Negro" emerged. The Bowen/Hoover/Palmer statements accurately described the fact that "Negroes" were "rapidly being made strongly race conscious and class conscious." The historian Waskow emphasized that "Negroes would from 1919 on be prepared to fight back against attack" and that the "first thaw had come in the long bleak winter of 'the nadir,' the capitulation to racism." It was "Negroes themselves, turning passionately and violently against the white mobs that attacked them," and "the police forces that sided with their attackers" who "broke the winter."[13]

Harrison described the new reality in the August 1919 *New Negro*:

> The New Negro is Negro first, Negro last, and Negro always. He needs not the white man's sympathy; all he is asking for is equal justice before the law and equal opportunity in the battle of life. He needs and asks for no special privileges that are not granted to the other races; he is not a weakling. He has proven his physical strength as well as his intellectual equality which enables him to live both as a savage among savages and as the most cultured and civilized being among those who profess to have reached that stage of life. . . . "An eye for an eye, a tooth for a tooth," and sometimes two eyes or a half dozen teeth for one is the aim of the New Negro.[14]

This increased race consciousness and militancy among "New Negroes" posed problems for old-time leaders and opened up new organizational opportunities. The historian Judith Stein describes how "race leaders discovered that their hegemony dissolved as former white allies withdrew and they adopted new agendas and methods." The NAACP was pushed from below as working-class African Americans flooded headquarters with their requests for aid and charters. In 1919 some eighty-five new branches were established, almost 35,000 new members joined, and the NAACP developed an organizational presence in the Deep South. The racial violence seemed to produce "a new urgency" and "a new opportunity" for modern, mass organizing in labor unions, civil rights organizations, and "organizations seeking 'racial independence in business.'" The militancy of the race-conscious "New Negro" was growing.[15]

———

The growing emergence of the militant "New Negro" was clearly articulated in the short-lived, Harrison-edited, monthly magazine of that name.[16] His influence is apparent in each of the three issues that he edited in 1919, and the articles and editorials show the range and depth of his race- and class-conscious, radical internationalist journalism. They also reveal much about his role in the growth of the militant New Negro Movement.[17]

Harrison began editing the *New Negro*, "A Magazine of General Information for the New Negro," shortly after his scheduled July 12, 1919, return to New York. Though the magazine had appeared in March 1918 under the editorship of the Liberty Leaguer August Valentine Bernier, its twenty-page advance copy for August 1919, selling for ten cents and printed on the forms of *The Clarion* (which had been published by Liberty League members), proclaimed that it was now published under a different policy and under the editorship of Bernier and Harrison. Harrison was described as the man who "chiselled the path which 'the new crowd' has taken."[18]

The sixteen-page September issue provided a fuller editorial statement of the magazine's "purpose and scope." The lead article by Harrison, entitled "The Need for It," discussed why "Negro-Americans" needed to develop "racial consciousness," understand world events, and have a publication that served their interests. It also emphasized that the "meeting and mingling of the darker peoples on the plains of France under stress of war" had "served to bring more clearly before the minds of Negro-Americans" three things:

> (1) The need and value of extending racial consciousness beyond the bounds of the white countries in which we find ourselves.
>
> (2) That the basis of such extension must be found in a common current knowledge of the facts and happenings of the international world, especially in so far as they affect the status and welfare of the darker races and of subject peoples everywhere.
>
> (3) That, as a people, we Negro Americans need to know and understand events and their trend; we need a publication which will not only chronicle events of world-importance, but will also interpret them for us in the light of our own race's intents and aims, and keeps us at the same time in touch with the interpretations put on these world events by the controlling culture of the white world.[19]

In the *New Negro* Harrison sought to develop a monthly that would be in touch with Black writers in Asia, South Africa, West Africa, Egypt, Europe, America, and the West Indies; would "render effective aid in molding international consciousness of the darker races"; would promote race consciousness by interpreting events in light of the "race's interests and aims"; and would be internationalist, anti-imperialist, and pro-labor. A typical issue included news and commentary; major editorials; international articles (particularly on Africa,

African peoples, and on people of color worldwide); articles on women, labor, and radicalism; satiric pieces; poems for the people; book reviews; letters; and reprints from assorted publications. Many of these features had appeared in *The Voice*, and Harrison would include them in the *Negro World* and *The Voice of the Negro*, two papers he later edited.[20]

In the September issue Harrison explained that the *New Negro* would contain, "first and foremost N E W S," which would "not [be] a mere reprint of newspaper articles and items" but instead "well-digested summaries of the world's news of the month" insofar as they have "special significance for the darker races." The magazine would carry "special articles" written "mainly by colored" authors that gave information and furnished "simple, clear and enlightening" interpretation. Readers would receive "all the different currents of ideas that flow into the sea of racial consciousness," and the "presentation and interpretation" columns would be like those of *The Nation*.[21]

The *New Negro* contained two news commentary columns of presentation and interpretation, "As the Currents Flow" and "The World This Month." The first focused on domestic matters, the second on international matters.

In his August 1919 "As the Currents Flow" column Harrison proclaimed the "New Negro" a "*fait accompli*" and described the recent "royal racial battles" in Washington and Chicago as "great events" that, though "tragical," deserved to be "recorded as brilliant events in the history of the Negro race in America." They demonstrated that the spirit of the "New Negro" was "in the hearts of all the truly liberty-loving and progressive Negroes" and that the baneful effects of slavery were wearing off. "Negroes" were rejecting "unmanly teaching," and Harrison declared that the "New Negro" was "unlike the Negro of the 'old conservative crowd'" who was "ever willing to compromise everything that is held dear to his race in order to obtain for himself a miserable pittance and some sympathy from his former master." This "New Negro" was "identifying himself with every progressive and radical movement," was "uncompromising and non-partisan," and "owed nothing to any political party," as the "'Colored' men assuming to lead the race should know." Harrison militantly concluded (as the Department of Justice would later cite) that "The New Negro is Negro first, Negro last, and Negro always [seeking] . . . equal justice before the law and equal opportunity in the battle of life" and willing to sacrifice "'an eye for an eye, a tooth for a tooth.'"[22]

"The World This Month" column first appeared in the September issue, where it discussed the fact that the Senate Foreign Relations Committee had agreed to hear from Black organizations on the issue of the final disposal of the German colonies in Africa. This was viewed as a great opportunity for the organizations to go on record and an appropriate place for "the eminent 'delegates' who were chosen to go to the Peace Congress in France" to "now go to

Washington and present their arguments to the Foreign Relations Committee."
No one would have to wait for the State Department to grant a passport, and
the Senate was going to amend the Wilson peace treaty.[23]

There was no mistaking the references to the efforts by Du Bois, Trotter,
and Garvey to go as (or to send, in Garvey's case) delegates to Paris for the
peace conference. Harrison's position, as previously mentioned, was that "lynching, disfranchisement and segregation are evils HERE; and the place in which
we must fight them is HERE." He added:

> Since Africa will not be given over to the Africans this trip, the committee of
> Negroes will offer such practical suggestions to the Senate's committee as
> will result in an amendment to the League covenant which should give to the
> natives of former German territory a qualified vote at the start, to be later
> expanded to full and equal suffrage. Such an amendment would, at least,
> begin a promise with a performance; and in the face of British rulership in
> Africa, performances, not professions, are what the African natives need.
> True, Britain rules them (and the "League" would rule) purely from high
> altruistic motives. Just the same, Britain does not advance them, even locally,
> to a share in the government which their taxes support. Here is a handle for
> the Negroes of America to grasp.[24]

In the October 1919 "The World This Month" Harrison discussed the proposal brought before the Foreign Relations Committee by Reverend Jernagin,
of the National Baptist Convention in Washington, DC, and a Mr. Thompson of
Ohio "that the former German colonies in Africa be turned over to the United
States under a mandate from the League of Nations!" He considered this an
especially "green" notion, the kind that would "cause the New Negro to insist
that his leaders should be equipped, among other things, with wide international knowledge of Africa and African problems." Harrison was especially critical of the idea as the experience of the United States "in governing darker
peoples both at home and abroad" had been "neither happy nor successful."[25]

As far as Mr. Thompson's proposal to send "Negro-American" schoolteach-
ers to the Cameroons, Harrison felt this, too, showed "an unfortunate lack of
knowledge . . . of the school situation there and here." He noted that the secretary of the American Board of Commissioners for Foreign Missions had recently
testified that in the Cameroons and Togoland, under German control, the school
facilities "surpassed" those of Nigeria, the neighboring British colony. This was
so in spite of the fact that both the French and British governments "encourage education and make sizable appropriations for this purpose."[26]

Harrison reasoned that only when our national government and the southern states begin to "encourage education" of the sort that exists under Germany

Figure 3.2. New Negro 4, no. 1 (September 1919), front cover. The front cover article "The Need For It" discusses "the need and value of extending racial consciousness" and stresses that "we Negro Americans need . . . a publication which will not only chronicle events of world-importance, but will also interpret them for us in the light of our own race's intents and aims." The front cover also, expressing Hubert Harrison's radical internationalism, discusses the need to develop a monthly that would be in touch with "writers in Asia, South Africa, West Africa, Egypt, Europe, America and the West Indies" and would "render effective aid in molding international consciousness of the darker races." *Source:* Hubert H. Harrison Papers, Box 17, Folder 8, Rare Book and Manuscript Library, Columbia University Library. See https://dlc.library.columbia.edu/catalog/cul:s4mw 6m91v3.

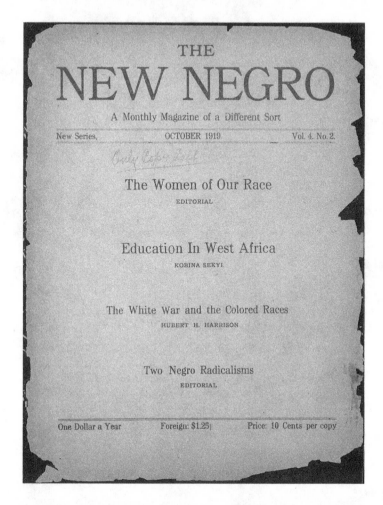

Figure 3.3. New Negro 4, no. 2 (October 1919), front cover. This striking front page suggests the broad range of subjects ("The Women of Our Race," "Education in West Africa," "The White War and the Colored Races," and "Two Negro Radicalisms") Harrison sought to address in the *New Negro. Source:* Hubert H. Harrison Papers, Box 17, Folder 8, Rare Book and Manuscript Library, Columbia University Library. See https://dlc.library.columbia.edu/catalog/cul:2fqz612m86.

in the Cameroons would it "be time to talk of sending thousands of Negro-American school teachers there." Until then, he advised that Thompson consider statistics on public school spending in South Carolina and Georgia. Based on these figures, he suggested that it "would be well if we Negro-Americans, before seeking to legislate directly or indirectly for Africa, would first deign to get some little knowledge of Africa—to say nothing of our own country."[27]

In the October "The World This Month" Harrison also expressed opposition to the "present process of transforming our republic into an empire" over "weak and 'inferior' peoples." He referred particularly to the U.S. Navy's recent activities in Turkey and the Caribbean. In Turkey the United States was "shaking the big stick over the heads of the Sultan's subjects" while it usurped the functions of Congress and the State Department and maintained a high commissioner at Constantinople. This action pleased England, which was "eager to have our soldiers and sailors relieve her of the trouble and expense of policing Turkey while she dismembers her." In the Virgin Islands, Haiti, and Santo Domingo, the imposition of a "Naval Administration" was "new to the average American mind" and seemed to ignore George Washington's farewell address warning "against 'entangling alliances.'"[28]

In the same commentary Harrison provocatively asked, "Will the white race destroy itself?" He described how, at the peace conference in Paris, the European powers were at one another's throats: Britain grabbed Persia, France sought to build up "a balance of power in Eastern Europe" to threaten England and destroy Germany's dominance, and Germany and Austria were "driven by the spoliation of their lands and the starvation of their people to pile up a mountainous mass of hatred against England, France and the United States." All this suggested that "the white man's burden is himself" and that "the inherent restlessness and greed of the dominant white race will in the end destroy it politically and culturally." Though the white race had "been on the stage of human history for the short period of 2,500 years," in that time it engaged in "more wars than any other," with "most [being] against each other," which "proved [them] absolutely incapable of living in peace." It thus seemed likely that "their great technical inventions," which "surpassed [those of] all other races," would "help to hasten their doom."[29]

A perceptive critic of Christianity, Harrison also used his column to discuss the visit to America of Cardinal Désiré Joseph Mercier of Belgium, a cleric who had recently been quoted as saying that "socialism, militarism and government politics are interfering with the normal exercise of spirituality." Harrison thought it unfortunate that "when the brutalities of Belgium in the Congo were being revealed to a horror-struck world this eminent prelate, far from seeing any menace to religion therein, denied the facts." In fact, Mercier maintained that position "until the photographs of Consul-General Roger Casement showed the heaps of severed limbs and the swollen bodies of Negroes." Casement, a supporter of the Irish National Volunteers against England, had visited Germany in 1914 to gain assistance in the fight for Irish independence. He obtained and published anti-British pamphlets documenting atrocities, and for such "treason" he was subsequently tried and hanged by the British in London on August 3, 1916. The atrocities he exposed were the kind that had "helped to reduce the Congo population from 20 millions to 12 millions" and "brought fat tribute to Belgium." Harrison concluded that "Cardinal Mercier's brave defense of his country from foreign tyrants; [and] his ringing protests against the atrocities perpetrated on his people, deserve and should receive the approval of the civilized world." By "the same token," however, "his support of similar atrocities in 'the Congo Free State' must detract equally from his credit and his Christianity."[30]

Finally, in the October "The World This Month" column Harrison described how England, having robbed Egypt of her independence, sought now "to rob her of the credit due her for the part she played in the world war." He labeled a recent letter by the chargé d'affaires Donald Lindsay claiming that the British government had "carefully avoided destroying Egyptian sovereignty" as "a plain blunt lie." Clearly, Harrison's news commentary columns in the *New Negro* did what was intended—they offered both presentation and interpretation of "special significance for the darker races."[31]

––––––––––

In the scrapbooks that he maintained, in part for organizing articles that he wrote, Harrison divided his editorials into "major" and "minor." The major editorials were a principal feature of the *New Negro*, as they would be in the *Negro World* and every publication he edited. They were consciously not "literary essays," and in them he strove, as he wrote in his diary, for "terseness, point, pungency and force." In general, they put forth the main messages he was trying to deliver and are articulate statements of his views. They offer important public statements on his thinking on aspects of the militant New Negro Movement.[32]

In the August issue the major editorial, entitled "Our Larger Duty," described the principal task of the "New Negro" as the development of the "international consciousness of the darker races—especially of the Negro race." Harrison began by echoing Du Bois's turn-of-the-century dictum that "the problem of the twentieth century is the problem of the Color Line." He then explained that the color line was "the practice of the theory that the colored and 'weaker' races of the earth shall not be free to follow 'their own way of life and allegiance,' but shall live, work and be governed after such fashion as the dominant white race may decide." The editorial called attention to the fact that the "so-called white race" was "on top by virtue of its control of the physical force of the world—ships, guns, soldiers, money and other resources," despite the fact that "twelve hundred million of the seventeen hundred million people of the earth were colored" ("black and brown and yellow"). It was through physical force that England ruled and robbed India, Egypt, Africa and the West Indies; that the United States told Haitians, Hawaiians, and Filipinos how much they would get for their labor and what would be done in their lands; and that Belgium told the Congo-lese whether they would "have their hands hacked off or their eyes gouged out." All of this was done "without any reference to what Africans, Asiatics or other inferior members of the world's majority may want."[33]

To Harrison, this color line revealed the hypocrisy of "democracy":

As long as the Color Line exists all the perfumed protestations of Democ-racy on the part of the white race must be simply downright lying. The cant of "Democracy" is intended as dust in the eyes of white voters, incense on the altar of their own self-love. It furnishes bait for the clever statesmen who hold the destinies of their people in their hands when they go fishing for suckers in the waters of public discussion. But it becomes more and more apparent that Hindus, Egyptians, Africans, Chinese and Haytians have taken the measure of this cant and hypocrisy. And, whatever the white world may think, it will have these peoples to deal with during the twentieth century.[34]

Times were changing, and Harrison predicted that the "white" man would no longer be able to "listen to his own voice alone in determining what colored peoples should have." Such a "God role" had resulted in two methods of treat-ment. The first and simplest was to kill people of color off "either by slaughter pure and simple," as with "the American Indians and the Congo natives," or "by forcibly changing their mode of life," as with the Tasmanians. An alterna-tive treatment involved the importation of "rum, guns, whiskey and consump-tion," as was done with "Negroes" of Africa and North America. This last method bred resistance, however, and, argued Harrison, "most of these subject peoples have refused to be killed off. Their vitality is too strong." Accordingly, a "more recent method," composed of both "internal and external" treatment, was devel-oped. Under the internal treatment people of color worked "to develop the resources of their ancestral lands, not for themselves, but for their white over-lords," so that "national and imperial coffers" could "be filled to overflowing, while the Hindu ryot [peasant or tenant famer], on six cents a day, lives down to the imperialist formula." Under the external treatment people were girdled "with forts and battleships" and "armies in readiness to fly at their throats upon the least sign of 'uppishness' or 'impudence.'" All of these various methods cre-ated a "similarity of suffering" for the oppressed and, as Harrison explained:

This similarity of suffering on the part of colored folk has given, and is giv-ing, rise to a certain similarity of sentiment. Egypt has produced the Young Egypt movement; India, the Swadesha, the All-India Congress, and the pres-ent revolutionary movement which has lit the fuse of the powder-keg on which

Britain sits in India today; Africa has her Ethiopian Movement which ranges from the Zulus and Hottentots of the Cape to the Ekoi of Nigeria; in short, the darker races, chafing under the domination of the alien whites, are every-where showing a disposition to take Democracy at its word and to win some measure of it—for themselves.[35]

The part in this great drama to be played by "Negroes of the Western world" was yet to be decided, but he believed that developing an international perspective was a necessary first step. Before playing "any effective part" in African liberation "they must first acquaint themselves with what is taking place in the larger world whose millions are in motion." They had to keep well informed of "the trend of that motion and of its range and possibilities," and, wrote Harrison, "if our problem here is really a part of a great world-wide problem," then "we must make our attempts to solve our part [in order to] link up with the attempts being made elsewhere to solve the other parts." In this way, "Negroes of the Western world" would "profit by a wider experience and perhaps be able to lend some assistance to that ancient Mother Land of ours."[36]

The major editorial in September's *New Negro* was on "Negro Culture and the Negro College," and it called for "Negro colleges" to develop "courses in Negro history and the culture of West African peoples" and to become general "institution[s] of Negro learning." Harrison described education as "the pro-cess by which the ripened generation brings to bear upon the rising genera-tion any stored-up knowledge and experience of the past and present genera-tions to fit it for the business of life." The modern line of discussion on the subject focused on aim, intent, and object, but shaping our youth was a problem because "we are muddled as to what the young are to be made into" and therefore "mud-dled in our methods." Harrison thought Black youth should be shaped for liv-ing in a world in which they are currently at bottom, and the task ahead was how, under those circumstances, to prepare them for struggle against that infe-rior status.[37]

Harrison then discussed how in the United States and the West Indies the educational system "was shaped by white people for white youth." The "white boy and girl draw exclusively from the stored-up knowledge and experience of the past and present generations of white people to fit them for the business of being dominant whites in a world full of colored folk." They are fed "exclusively white examples," and therefore they think that "only white men are valorous and fit to rule and only white women are virtuous and entitled to chivalry, respect and protection." They also think "almost instinctively, that the Negro's proper place, nationally and internationally, is that of an inferior." The other, ignored, side of this matter was that the Negro boy and girl, getting the same (though worse) instruction, also get from it the same notion of the Negro's place and part in life which the white children get . . . they so readily accept the status of inferiors; that they tend to disparage themselves, and think themselves worthwhile only to the extent to which they look and act and think like the whites. . . . They know nothing of the stored-up knowledge and experience of the past and present generations of Negroes in their ancestral lands, and conclude there is no such store of knowledge and experience. They readily accept the assumption that Negroes have never been anything but slaves and that they have never had a glorious past as other fallen peoples like the Greeks and Persians have.

Unfortunately, he commented, these views were frequently accepted, "despite the mass of collected testimony in the works of [Heinrich] Barth, [Georg August] Schweinfurth, Mary Kingsley, Lady [Flora Luisa (Shaw)] Lugard, [Edmund D.] Morel, [Job] Ludolphus, [Edward Wilmot] Blyden, [George Washington] Ellis, [Friedrich] Ratzel,[38] [Dudley] Kidd, [Abd al-Rahman al] Es-Saadi, [Joseph Ephraim] Casely Hayford[39] and a host of others, Negro and white."[40]

Harrison added, "logic, educational ideas and ideals spread from above downwards." Therefore, "a large part of the blame for this deplorable condition must be put upon the Negro colleges like Howard, Fisk, Livingstone [in Salisbury, North Carolina] and Lincoln [in Chester County, Pennsylvania] in the United States, and Codrington [in St. John, Barbados], Harrison [in Bridgetown, Barbados], and Mico [in Kingston, Jamaica] in the West Indies." These institutions, not the common schools, were where "cultural ideals and educational systems" were "fashioned for the shaping of the minds of the future generations of Negroes." Thus, he argued:

If we are ever to enter into the confraternity of colored peoples it should seem the duty of our Negro colleges to drop their silly smatterings of "little Latin and less Greek" and establish modern courses in Hausa and Arabic, for these are the living languages of millions of our brethren in modern Africa. Courses in Negro history and the culture of West African peoples, at least, should be given in every college that claims to be an institution of learning for Negroes. Surely an institution of learning for Negroes should not fail to be also an institution of Negro learning.

Harrison noted that "up to the present the only Negro college which has even planned such courses" was the Baptist Seminary and College at Lynchburg, Virginia (under Dr. R. C. Woods), which, quite fittingly, was "owned and controlled entirely by Negroes and has a Negro president responsible to a Negro board of trustees."[41]

––––––––

Harrison's third, powerful *New Negro* editorial was his "Two Negro Radical-isms," in the October 1919 issue. It was a plea for developing race-conscious radicalism and in it, for the first time, Harrison publicly stated that Marcus Gar-vey was effectively publicizing "racialism, race-consciousness, [and] racial solidarity" as had been advocated by *The Voice*. The editorial set the stage for the joint work that would take place between Garvey and Harrison beginning in January 1920.[42]

In describing the growth of radicalism among "Negroes," Harrison explained that twenty years ago "all Negroes known to the white publicists of America could be classed as conservatives on all the great questions on which thinkers differ" and "could be trusted to take the backward view" in "matters of indus-try, commerce, politics, [or] religion." The only exception was on "the question of the Negro's 'rights,'" where there were "a small handful" of "radicals" who "were howled down by both the white and colored adherents of the conserva-tive point of view." Conditions had dramatically changed, however, and now "Negroes differ[ed] on all those great questions on which white thinkers dif-fer," and there were "Negro radicals of every imaginable stripe—agnostics, atheists, I.W.W.'s, Socialists, Single Taxers, and even Bolshevists."[43]

While this radicalism grew, so, too, did the white world's continued inability to comprehend it. In "the good old days," he explained, "white people derived their knowledge of what Negroes were doing from those Negroes who were nearest to them, generally their own selected exponents of Negro activity or of their white point of view." The "classic illustration of this" was "the Republican Party; but the Episcopal Church, the Urban League, or the U.S. Government would serve as well." Though "the white world" was "vaguely, but disquietingly, aware that Negroes are awake," it still retained "its traditional method of inter-preting the mass by the Negro nearest to themselves in affiliation or contact." A clear example was the Socialist Party, which "thinks that the 'unrest' now apparent in the Negro masses is due to the propaganda which its adherents support, and believes that it will function largely along the lines of socialist political thought." Other examples were the "great dailies," which "scream 'Bolshevist propaganda' and flatter themselves that they have found the true cause; while the government's unreliable agents envisage it as 'disloyalty.'"[44]

To Harrison, the "truth" was, as usual, to be "found in the depths." These "white" organizations were "all prevented" from understanding this "by men-tal laziness and that traditional off-handed, easy contempt with which white men in America, from scholars like Lester Ward to scavengers like [Archibald E.]

Stevenson [the driving force of the government's Lusk Committee, investigating 'seditious activities'],[45] deign to consider the colored population of twelve millions." Harrison emphasized that the "prime cause of racial unrest" and radicalism among Negroes was not socialism or Bolshevism; it was the "similarity of suffering" that produced a "similarity of sentiment" in "all lands where whites rule colored races":

> In the first place the cause of the "radicalism" among American Negroes is international. . . . The international Fact to which Negroes in America are now reacting is not the exploitation of laborers by capitalists; but the social, political and economic subjection of colored peoples by white. It is not the Class Line, but the Color Line, which is the incorrect but accepted expression for the Dead Line of racial inferiority. This fact is a fact of Negro consciousness as well as a fact of externals. The international Color Line is the practice and theory of that doctrine which holds that the best stocks of Africa, China, Egypt and the West Indies are inferior to the worst stocks of Belgium, England, and Italy, and must hold their lives, lands and liberties upon such terms and conditions as the white races may choose to grant them.[46]

The motive for this oppression, according to Harrison, "was originally economic; but it is no longer purely so." The available facts proved that whether in the United States or in Africa or China, "the economic subjection is without exception keener and more brutal when the exploited are black, brown and yellow." People of color "begin to feel and realize that they are so subjected because they are members of races condemned as 'inferior' by their Caucasian overlords." Thus, the "fact presented to their minds is one of race, and in terms of race do they react to it. Put the case to any Negro by way of test and the answer will make this clear."[47]

It was, he wrote, the "great World War, by virtue of its great advertising campaign for democracy and the promises which were held out to subject peoples," that "fertilized the Race Consciousness of the Negro people into the stage of conflict with the dominant white idea of the Color Line." The Negro people "took democracy at its face value—which is—equality," but "the hypocritical advertisers of democracy had not bargained for [this]." The "American Negroes, like the other darker peoples," attempted to present "their checques" and "to 'cash in,'" and delays in that process, however unavoidable to the paying tellers," caused "a plentiful lack of belief in either their intention or their ability to pay" and resulted in a "run on Democracy's bank," described in the press as "Negro unrest."[48]

Harrison concluded "Two Negro Radicalisms" with three important paragraphs—the first two of which did not appear in later reprints of this editorial. In the first of these three paragraphs he explained two forms of the growing race consciousness and argued that Marcus Garvey's mass appeal was thanks to his Liberty League–like call to "racialism, race consciousness, and race solidarity," as opposed to the radicalism of Black socialists (such as A. Philip Randolph and Chandler Owen). Harrison elaborated:

> This Race Consciousness takes many forms, some negative, others positive. On the one hand we balk at Jim Crow, object to educational starvation, refuse to accept goodwill for good deeds, and scornfully reject our conservative leaders. On the other hand, we are seeking racial independence in business and reaching out into new fields of endeavor. One of the most striking enterprises at present is the Black Star Line, a steamship enterprise being floated by Mr. Marcus Garvey of New York. Garvey's project (whatever may be its ultimate fate) has attracted tens of thousands of Negroes. Where Negro "radicals" of the type known to white radicals can scarce get a handful of people, Garvey fills the largest halls and the Negro people rain money on him. This is not to be explained by the argument of "superior brains," for this man's education and intelligence are markedly inferior to those of the brilliant "radicals" whose "internationalism" is drawn from other than racial sources. But this man holds up to the Negro masses those things which bloom in their hearts—racialism, race-consciousness, racial solidarity—things taught first in 1917 by *THE VOICE* and The Liberty League. That is the secret of his success so far.[49]

The next paragraph explained that in the United States and the West Indies "Negroes" were "responding to the call of battle against the white man's Color Line," and "so long as this ['Color Line'] remains, the international dogma of the white race, so long will the new Negro war against it." "This," Harrison added, "is the very Ethiopianism which England has been combatting from Cairo to the Cape."[50]

Finally, in his last paragraph, Harrison concluded by explaining that, at least some (including socialists) who advocated "Class-Consciousness" and "Race-Consciousness" accepted biology as fact and that race superseded class:

> Undoubtedly some of these newly-awakened Negroes will take to Socialism and Bolshevism. But here again the reason is racial. Since they suffer racially from the world as at present organized by the white race, some of their ablest hold that it is "good play" to encourage and give aid to every subversive movement within that white world which makes for its destruction "as it is." For by its subversion they have much to gain and nothing to lose. Yet they build on their own foundations. Parallel with the dogma of Class-Consciousness they

run the dogma of Race-Consciousness. And they dig deeper. For the roots of Class-Consciousness inhere in a temporary economic order; whereas the roots of Race-Consciousness must of necessity survive any and all changes in the economic order. Accepting biology as a fact, their view is the more fundamental. At any rate, it is that view with which the white world will have to deal.[51]

The two penultimate sentences were likely an indirect reference to the "Majority Report on Immigration" of the Socialist Party of America's 1912 Convention, which stated, "Class-consciousness must be learned, but race consciousness is inborn and cannot be wholly unlearned," a position of which Harrison was critical. Harrison had previously written a probing analysis of "Race Prejudice" on December 4, 1911, in the socialist newspaper *New York Call*. In that article he argued that "race prejudice is not innate" and that, at their core, all arguments defending race prejudice ultimately distill to the argument "that race prejudice is innate." He also maintained that "race prejudice" has economic causes, that it is in "the interests of the capitalists" to foster and to maintain "race prejudice" and to "pit the workers white against black," and that capitalists benefit and workers lose from "race prejudice." By maintaining that "race prejudice" arose from socioeconomic causes Harrison was suggesting that it could be subjected to eliminative social action. In 1924 he would offer additional insight on this topic when he wrote that a "race-problem," such as the "Negro problem," "is not insoluble: no human social problem ever was. There is work to be done on it; and while it is primarily of the white man's making, the colored man must do most of the work." The last three sentences in "Two Negro Radicalisms" appear, in part, to be Harrison throwing the position of some leading socialists of 1912 at the socialists in 1919.[52]

In the October 1919 *New Negro* Harrison published "The White War and the Colored Races," an extraordinarily powerful statement based on his indoors and outdoors talks of 1915 and 1916. It was his major article on World War I, and he wrote it in 1918 ("when the Great War still raged") for "a certain well known radical magazine," which found it "to be 'too radical' for publication at that time." Harrison was possibly referring to the *International Socialist Review*, which ceased publishing in February 1918, or, more likely, to *The Messenger*, edited by Randolph and Owen, which received considerable coverage in the "white" press for its "radical" antiwar stand.[53] Interestingly, a Harrison article entitled "The White Man's War," with a "radical indictment," though included in the original publication plan, similarly did not make it into the publication of the March 1925, Alain Locke–edited *Survey Graphic* issue, entitled "Harlem:

Mecca of the New Negro," which was later expanded into the 1925 Locke-edited anthology *The New Negro: An Interpretation*.[54]

This possible labeling of Harrison's "The White War and the Colored Races" article as "too radical," as well as other differences with Randolph and Owen (who had supported Woodrow Wilson in 1916), is instructive background to Harrison's position in 1920 in what he considered to be a dispute between the "radical" socialists and "not Mr. Garvey personally, but the principles of the New Negro Manhood Movement, a portion of which had been incorporated by him and his followers of the U.N.I.A. and A.C.L."[55]

When Harrison reprinted "The White War and the Colored Races" in *When Africa Awakes* in August 1920, he explained that he did so "partly because the underlying explanation which it offers of the root-cause of the war has not yet received treatment (even among socialist radicals) and partly because recent events in China, India, Africa and the United States have proved the accuracy of its forecasts." Harrison began "The White War and the Colored Races" with a description of "the international expansion of capitalism—the economic system of the white peoples of Western Europe and America—and its establishment by force and fraud over the lands of the colored races, black and brown and yellow" in the nineteenth century. He then described how the twentieth century provided "the sorry spectacle of these same white nations cutting each other's throats to determine which of them shall enjoy the property which has been acquired." This was "the real sum and substance of the original 'war aims' of the belligerents," though, because of "Christian cunning," this was "never frankly avowed." Instead, people were fed with the "camouflage" that "they are fighting for 'Kultur' and 'on behalf of small nationalities.'"[56]

In looking more carefully at this camouflage Harrison examined what he referred to (in a subheading in his 1920 reprint of this article) as "The Sham of 'Democracy.'" He pointed out that while the United States was "waging war to establish democracy three thousand miles away, millions of Negroes" were "disfranchised in our own land by the 'cracker' democracies of the Southern States," which were "more intent upon making slaves of their black fellow-citizens than upon rescuing the French and Belgians from the similar brutalities of the German Junkers." East St. Louis was "the climax of a long series of butcheries perpetrated on defenseless Negroes" that had "made the murder rate of Christian America higher than that of heathen Africa and of every other civilized land." Harrison postulated that a "horrible holocaust" like East St. Louis was "possible only in three modern states—Russia of the Romanoffs, Turkey and the United States." In Russia there had been repeated pogroms against the Jews, and Turkey had implemented genocidal attacks on Armenians in 1915 and 1916. He also compared the government-ordered execution of thirteen Black soldiers at Houston "for resenting the wholesale insults to the uniform of the United States and defending their lives from civilian aggressors" to the fact that "not one of the murderers of black men, women and children has been executed or even ferreted out" and that Congress had not "seen fit as yet to make lynching a Federal crime." In light of such treatment and disparity, there was little wonder "the Negro masses" were now "insisting that before they can be expected to enthuse over the vague formula of making the world 'safe for democracy' they must receive some assurance that their corner of the world—the South—shall first be made 'safe for democracy!'" Harrison also made the insightful point that sham democracy ironically may have caused and prolonged U.S. involvement in the war. He reasoned "that perhaps the situation and treatment of the American Negro by our own government and people may have kept the Central Powers from believing that we mean to fight for democracy in Europe." Perhaps also, he added, it "caused them to persist in a course which has driven us into this war."[57]

To Harrison, "'democracy,' like 'Kultur,'" was "more valuable as a battle-cry than as a real belief to be practised by those who profess it." This was evidenced by the experiences of "Ireland, Greece, and Egypt." Harrison was convinced that the war was "waged to determine who shall dictate the destinies of the darker peoples and enjoy the usufruct of their labor and their lands." To support this view he quoted Sir Henry Hamilton (Harry) Johnston, the English explorer, colonial administrator, and writer on Africa who, in the London-based periodical *The Sphere*, described the European powers' "imperial aims" and declared that "the war, deny it who may, was really fought over African questions." This, to Harrison, was "the sum and substance of what [Arthur] Schopenhauer would have called 'the sufficient reason' for this war," and there was "no word of 'democracy' there, but instead the easy assumption that, as a matter of course, the lands of black Africa belong to white Europe and must be apportioned" by those who held power.[58]

Harrison then went on to describe "The Economics of War" and offered his profound description of the roots of modern war in the capitalist system and its expansion:

It is the same economic motive that has been back of every modern war since the merchant and trading classes secured control of the powers of the modern state from the battle of Plassy to the present world war. This is the natural and inevitable effect of the capitalist system, of what (for want of a worse name) we call "Christendom." For that system is based upon the wage relationship between those who own and those who operate the gigantic forces of land and machinery. Under this system no capitalist employs a worker for two dollars a day unless that worker creates more than two dollars worth of wealth for him. Only out of this surplus can profits come. If ten million workers should thus create one hundred million dollars' worth of wealth each day and get twenty five of fifty million in wages, it is obvious that they can expend only what they have received, and that, therefore, every nation whose industrial system is organized on a capitalist basis must produce a mass of surplus products over and above, not the need, but the purchasing power of the nation's producers. Before these products can return to their owners as profits they must be sold somewhere. Hence the need for foreign markets, for fields of exploitation and "spheres of influence" in "undeveloped" countries whose virgin resources are exploited in their turn after the capitalist fashion. But, since every industrial nation is seeking the same outlet for its products, clashes are inevitable and in these clashes beaks and claws—armies and navies—must come into play. Hence beaks and claws must be provided beforehand against the day of conflict, and hence the exploitation of white men in Europe and America becomes the reason for the exploitation of black and brown and yellow men in Africa and Asia. And, therefore, it is hypocritical and absurd to pretend that the capitalist nations can ever intend to abolish wars. For, as long as black men are exploited by white men in Africa, so long must white men cut each other's throats over that exploitation. And thus, the selfish and ignorant white worker's destiny is determined by the hundreds of millions of those whom he calls "niggers."[59]

Harrison realized, however, that "economic motives have always their social side" and that the "exploitation of the lands and labor of colored folk expresses itself in the social theory of white domination; the theory that the worst human stocks of Montmarte, Seven Dials and the Bowery are superior to the best human stocks of Rajputana or Khartoum." Whenever "these colored folk who make up the overwhelming majority of this world demand decent treatment for themselves," then "the proponents of this theory accuse them of seeking social equality." There was a stark contrast between "white" efforts to manage their own ancestral lands, free from domination, which were "variously described as 'democracy' and 'self-determination,'" and similar efforts by "Negroes, Egyptians and Hindus," which were declared to be "impudence." Because of this color line, there existed "a seething volcano whose slumbering fires are made up of the hundreds of millions of Chinese, Japanese, Hindus, and Africans!" and this fact reaffirmed "'the problem of the 20th Century is the problem of the Color Line.'" Harrison predicted that "wars are not likely to end; in fact, they are likely to be wider and more terrible—so long as this theory of white domination seeks to hold down the majority of the world's people under the iron heel of racial repression."[60]

He also described what he considered to be the "pivotal fact of the war":

The white race is superior—its will goes—because it has invented and amassed greater means for the subjugation of nature and of man than any other race. It is the top dog by virtue of its soldiers, guns, ships, money, resources and brains. Yet there in Europe it is deliberately burning up, consuming and destroying these very soldiers, guns, ships, money, resources and brains, the very things upon which its supremacy rests. When this war is over, it will be less able to enforce its sovereign will upon the darker races of the world.

It would be depleted in numbers, and "its quality, physical and mental," would "be considerably lowered for a time," since war first destroys "the strongest and the bravest, the best stocks, the young men who were to father the next generation." This, he noted, "was the thought back of Mr. [William Randolph] Hearst's objection to our entering the war. He wanted the United States to stand as the white race's reserve of man-power when Europe had been bled white."[61]

Harrison felt that as "the iron hand of 'discipline'" was "relaxed," pressure would be lifted off the colored majority, and they would "first ask, then demand, and finally secure, the right of self-determination." They would "insist that, not only the white world, but the whole world, be made 'safe for democracy.'" This would mean "a self-governing Egypt, a self-governing India, and independent African states as large as Germany and France—and larger." This analysis was based on the information that he received from the newspapers and books written and published "by colored men in Africa and Asia during the past three years." Yet, though this thought was "inflaming the international underworld, not a word appear[ed] in the parochial press of America," which seemed to think that "if it can keep its own Negroes down to servile lip-service, it need not face the world-wide problem of the 'Conflict of Color.'"[62]

The "more intelligent portions of the white world," however, were "becoming distressingly conscious" of these developments, as evidenced by "the first great manifesto of the Russian Bolsheviki" in 1917, which asked about "Britain's subject peoples." Similarly, the British workingmen had recently issued declarations that seemingly recognized "the ultimate necessity of compelling their own aristocrats to forgo . . . imperial aspirations" and to extend "the principle of self-determination even to the black people of Africa." "But," he added, "eyes which for centuries have been behind the blinders of race prejudice cannot but blink and water when compelled to face the full sunlight." Thus "Britain's workers [could still] insist that 'No one will maintain that the Africans are fit for self-government.'" Of course, it was "the same principle (of excluding the opinion of those who are most vitally concerned)" by which Britain's ruling class could, in turn, tell them "that 'No one maintains that the laboring classes of Britain are fit for self-government.'" Nevertheless, the fact that these workers had made a "half-hearted demand that an international committee shall take over the British, German, French and Portuguese possessions in Africa and manage them as independent nationalities" showed some improvement.[63]

Harrison concluded that the war in Europe was "the result of the desire of the white governments of Europe to exploit for their own benefit the lands and labor of the darker races." He predicted it would "decrease the white man's stock of ability to do this successfully against the wishes of the inhabitants of those lands." It would also "result in their freedom from thralldom and the extension of political, social and industrial democracy to the twelve hundred million black and brown and yellow peoples of the world." This, he declared, was "the idea which dominates today the thought of those darker millions."[64]

––––––––

The *New Negro* paid noteworthy attention to Black women, as exemplified by Harrison's October 1919 piece on "The Women of Our Race." He opened by noting that "America owes much to the foreigner" and that "the Negro in America owes even more." One reason for this was that it was the "white foreigner" who "first proclaimed that the only music which America had produced that was worthy of the name was Negro music." It took time for this truth to sink in, and, in the meantime, "the younger element of Negroes, in their weird worship of everything that was white, neglected and despised their own race-music." This attitude was demonstrated by college classes that were "highly insulted when their white teacher had asked them to sing 'Swing Low Sweet Chariot' and 'My Lord, What a Morning.'"[65]

Harrison used this introduction to suggest that any foreigner coming to America to review the nation's women "would pick out as the superior of them all—the Negro woman." It would be "a great pity," however, if the foreigner was "to 'discover' the Negro-American woman," since "her own mankind" had seen her "for centuries." Yet, "outside of the vague rhetoric of the brethren in church and lodge" who seek "to turn their functions into financial successes," and "outside of Paul Laurence Dunbar and perhaps two other poets," there had been "no proper amount of esthetic appreciation" that came "from their side." Although the "white" women of America were "charming to look at—in the upper social classes," Harrison argued that the "Negro laundress, cook or elevator girl far surpasses her mistress in the matter of feminine charms." "No white woman" had "a color as beautiful as the dark brown[s], light-brown[s], peach-browns, or gold and bronze of the Negro girl," and it was this reality that made "a walk through any Negro section of New York or Washington" a "feast of delight." In the matter of form—the "bodies and limbs of our Negro women" were, "on the whole, better built and better shaped than those of any other women on earth—except perhaps, the Egyptian women's," and "their gait and movement" were artistic and "inimitable." To Harrison, however, the "most striking characteristic" was "the way in which they carry their clothes." They dressed "well." From "shoes and stockings to shirtwaists and hats, they choose their clothes with fine taste and show them off to the best advantage when they put them on." That was "why a man may walk down any avenue with a Negro cook or factory girl without anyone's being able to guess that she has to work for a living." Black women were similarly "far ahead of all others in America" regarding "charm" and had "more native grace, more winsomeness, greater beauty and more fire and passion." Harrison observed that "these facts have already begun to attract [a]ttention, here and elsewhere," and he predicted that "eventually, the Negro woman will come into her own." He concluded, "What say you, brothers! Shall we not love her while she is among us? Shall we not bend the knee in worship and thank high heaven for the great good fortune which has given us such sisters and sweethearts, mothers and wives?"[66]

Before the publication of "The Women of Our Race," the September 1919 issue of the *New Negro* included an article, "The West African Woman (part I)," attributed to "Itambo Asong." Asong was described as a schoolmaster in the Oban district of northern Nigeria, educated in the Cameroons, who planned to come to the United States in 1920. It is probable that the article, which discusses both polygamy and eugenics, was actually written by Harrison, since it appears in one of his personal writings scrapbooks and is consistent with his style.[67]

Asong commented that "not only white Westerners, but black ones also seem to think that Africa is a land of jungles and swamps and that African 'natives' wear rings in their noses and cook and eat each other." He observed that "the source of these notions" was "not easy for an outsider to trace," since the books on Africa he had diligently examined over the past year, including Frederick Starr's *Liberia* and George W. Ellis's *Negro Culture in West Africa* (books read by Harrison), did not contain "the roots of such misinformation." Nevertheless, "these misconceptions hurt both the African and the Western Negro" and effectively prevented the "active goodwill and mutual help which grows out of mutual understanding." Since the "educated leaders of Negro American thought" seemed "neither to know Africa and Africans, nor to be taking any steps toward such mutual understanding," it appeared that "the duty of leading off devolves upon the African Negro himself."[68]

Asong began by discussing the position of West African women. He reasoned that the status of women was "a fair index to the culture of a people" and that some information on the "Negro women of West Africa" might "serve as the starting point of the circle of sympathy in which the Negro in Africa and the Negro in the western world must meet if they are to help each other in days to come." The article focused on the Ekoi people of Nigeria "because their condi-tion fairly represents that of the women of various tribes between the Gambia and Calabar coast." Asong discussed the polygamy practiced among the Ekoi and argued that women were basically treated equally in that society. Though "European writers generally assume that where polygamy exists women are mere serfs," this was "not so in Nigeria," where "a man's first wife is the head of the house" and the "younger wives obey her." He claimed that the women "generally get on peacefully together" and that the "first wife, far from object-ing to her husband's marrying other wives, insists on his doing so, because it lightens her household duties, some of which she can delegate to others." There were even "many cases" where wives brought husbands "before the Native Court on charges of cruelty for refusing to get other wives." Asong argued that a "woman's Rights Movement would be unthinkable in Nigeria, because wom-an's rights are so strictly guarded by the native law that it is not unusual for a woman to summon her husband before the court for having made use of some of her property (perhaps a pot or pan) without her permission." In addition, it was "native custom" that a man wishing to marry an Ekoi maiden "must first render service to her people," particularly in the case of the first wife, although often for latter ones also. The husband-to-be would help clear the bush for the next season's farms and do other work while marriage arrangements were made "with the parents of the girl." Then, while the husband-to-be rendered service, the "engaged girl of free-born well-to-do parents" would spend time between her engagement and marriage in "the Fatting House, an institution similar to that of the Gree-Gree Bush of the Gold Coast," where she was "trained for the duties of motherhood and household management." When the woman left the Fatting House it was "to become the mistress of her own establishment."[69]

According to Asong, the system of polygamy afforded certain protections to the mother and child. The "native custom" freed the mother of the newborn from marital duties for two to three years, and this helped ensure that there were "no sickly bottle-fed babies." The child received full attention from the mother "during the period when it needs it most" and could grow "strong and sturdy," while the mother avoided "the strain of too frequent child bearing." This, Asong claimed, was "the main reason why they can rear large families of healthy children." In West Africa a "eugenic movement could hardly develop," since "the people have practiced eugenics for thousands of years and stand in no need of advice from the developed decadence of Christian countries, where a falling birth-rate sounds its knell of doom over the closing coffin-lid of the white man's civilization." Another "advantage of African polygamy," said Asong, was "the absence of the surplus woman," and, consequently, the absence of the "social evil" of prostitution, which existed in the Western countries. In West Africa the prostitute existed "only in the coast regions where the African tribal system" was "disrupted and supplanted by the invading capitalistic system of white christian civilization." This absence of prostitution was admitted even by missionaries.[70]

Asong cited other practices as examples of equality. There was the "division of work between the sexes" that existed "from time immemorial." Men hunted, cleared brush for new farms, cut timber, and built houses, while women tended and owned livestock, planted yams and plantains, and weeded. The women had "their own club-organizations and native secret societies like the Ikkpai club" and the Ekkpa. The "clearest indication of the equality of women in Nigeria," however, was "the fact that God is conceived as two persons: Obassi Osaw, the male God of the sky and Obassi Nsi, the female god of the earth, vegetation and fertility." Asong added that to "the simple pagan of Nigeria, a god, who is entirely male, implies the subjection of women in the social life of a people."[71]

———

One of Harrison's important contributions to the New Negro Movement was his radical internationalist perspective. He believed that in order to extend racial consciousness "Negroes" needed "a common current knowledge of the facts and happenings of the international world, especially in so far as they affect the status and welfare of the darker races and of subject peoples everywhere."[72] Every issue of the *New Negro* featured articles and editorials on international subjects, particularly on people of color, and every issue had a special emphasis on Africa and/or people of African descent, such as the article on "The West African Woman."

The August *New Negro* had international pieces including "The Labor Unions in British Guiana," by G. McLean Ogle, which referred to the labor union efforts of Georgetown-born Hubert Critchlow, reprinted from the June 1919 first issue of the *Trinidad Literary Magazine*. It also included "Anxious Over Morocco in Africa!" on the growth of revolt in Morocco, which suggested that the Spanish zone should be described as "a mandatory" (a territory guided by a larger European state in a relationship recognized by the League of Nations) and expressed the hope that the Moroccan rebel leader, Ahmad ibn Muhammad Raisuli, would have a long reign.[73]

The September issue contained the article "John Bull's Judge Lynch," which reported that the Society of Peoples of African Origin, in London, had issued a circular referring to 1919 racial riots in England and put out a call to "work out our own salvation." In "Black Men's White Wives," a British author reprinted a 1913 circular of the Australian Government warning white women not to marry Afghans and Pathans. The article added that "in London one frequently sees white women in the company of coloured men in public places" and warned "English girls" that "the association of white women with coloured men is to normal healthy people unthinkable." In the September issue Harrison also wrote a brief introduction, "The Fruits of Civilization: A Comparison," to an Arnold White article, "West Ham and West Africa," reprinted from *The Referee*. He noted "the serious doubts in the minds of many of the most thoughtful leaders in West Africa as to the so-called 'benefits' of civilization, and the suitability of the European social system to their people." This served as an appropriate lead-in to the White article, which described how "the benighted tribes in the centre of Darkest Africa are better off than the men and women of West Ham" (in East London) and how "knowledge which is carefully concealed from the young people of West Ham is imparted to ebony youngsters in central and West Africa."[74]

In the *New Negro* for October Harrison reprinted "Education in West Africa" by Kobina Sekyi, who was described as a Gold Coast "exponent of traditional polity." The article, which challenged the notion that the "unlettered, were uneducated," was to be continued in the November issue. It may have come from Duse Muhammad Ali's *African Times and Orient Review*, and it subsequently drew considerable attention when it was read before the 1922 UNIA convention in New York.[75]

A major concern of Harrison, personally and politically, was the land of his birth. He regularly kept abreast of developments in the Virgin Islands, and this was reflected in the *New Negro*. In September he discussed the islands' "unique position" of being governed by the U.S. Navy Department and noted that both the head of the department, Sumner Kittelle, and Rear Admiral James H. Oliver, the first governor of the islands, were "southerners." Past experience had proved, he added, "that southerners can not be trusted to give good government to Negroes." He charged that Governor Oliver permitted U.S. Marines "to commit all kinds of outrages, physical and sexual, on the inoffensive people of the islands" and that when "Negroes" there organized effective protests, Oliver was replaced and sent home in disgrace. U.S. Marines were similarly replaced, primarily by "Negro policemen." Though Rear Admiral Joseph Wallace Oman, the new governor, had attempted to correct the most flagrant abuses, Harrison emphasized that "the government of an American colony under Danish laws" was "shameful and stupid, and the condition of the people in regards to legal process, work and wages, suffrage, land-holding and education" was "a standing disgrace to the government of an enlightened country."[76]

In the October *New Negro* Harrison explained that Oman had received orders "to remove all aliens from office, to appoint qualified natives in their place, and to transmit to Washington all records of court proceedings since 1917." Harrison felt that this would help the Islands' Council at an upcoming October 9 meeting and that this, along with the ferment of the mass of working people and the "organization of an 'industrial' union" two weeks previous, were all good signs.

The union was led by D. Hamilton Jackson, Harrison's boyhood friend in St. Croix.[77]

Interestingly, Harrison had helped Jackson's efforts as far back as October 1915, when he chaired the founding meeting of the Danish West Indies Committee at St. Mark's Hall on West 138th Street. Jackson had passed through New York on his way to Denmark to present concerns of the Danish Islanders to the king and parliament, and the DWIC came together to support Jackson's efforts. At the meeting other speakers included the activists Ashley Totten, James A. Glasgow, Karl Hendricks, Victor Murphy, and Sylvanie Smith. The DWIC created a Jackson Fund, and committees of correspondence proposed to purchase a newspaper plant and publish a newspaper in St. Croix "to express the viewpoint of the Negro population there" and to offer a Mutual Improvement Society to offer educational assistance and services to young people as well as Danish language classes.[78]

The October 1919 *New Negro* discussed how in St. Thomas "the black working people" had elected Rothschild Francis, "one of their own class to the legislature of the island" and contributed money "to send him to Washington as their spokesman to press their grievances and present a bill of reforms." Then, when Francis appeared before a Senate committee, he succeeded in getting a joint commission of three members of each house, who were to be sent to the islands in November to take testimony and to present their findings and recommendations before January 1.[79] Other coverage from the period indicates that Francis's efforts were supported by the Virgin Islands Protective League (VIPL) in New York City, which was organized by its president, Ashley L. Totten and Elizabeth Hendrickson. Though the 1920 census would show only 1,431 Virgin Islanders in all of New York State, there was a core of outstanding activists in and around the VIPL, which aimed to serve as a watchdog for the islands and, according to Charles Evans, a member of its executive board, sought "ultimate liberation from the white man." The VIPL raised money, conducted mass meetings on Francis's behalf, and planned to send Totten and Hendrickson to the islands in December to fact find and build unity between islanders and mainlanders.[80]

Harrison was one of the most thoughtful and insightful U.S. writers of his era on India, and the September *New Negro* contained two India-related pieces. The first, a letter by Sir Rabindranath Tagore, the Hindu poet and Nobel Prize winner for literature in 1913, maintained that the disturbances "in all three countries where the British have their sway—Ireland, Egypt and India" were not attributable to the "system of government or the law" but to "the men entrusted with the carrying on of the Government." These men had "not the imagination or sympathy truly to know the people whom they rule," and they seemed to imagine that "their material power" was permanent. Tagore stressed that those with such "blind pride" would continue "seeking the source of mischief outside themselves."[81]

A second September piece, "Britain in India," was written by Harrison under the pseudonym "Sayid Muhammad Berghash." Berghash discussed a familiar Harrison theme, the press, and argued that the "international control of news" was "in the hands of England's imperial Englishmen," who used this "to create current myths." Britain's international arm had gone into France, Switzerland, and the United States to arrest and deport Hindu exiles who "dared to tell the whole world the awful facts of Britain's bloody rule in India," had taken "native newspapers" from the mails so that they didn't leave India, and had removed "American books and pamphlets . . . touching on the condition of India's peoples." Berghash added that Tagore had "resigned his knighthood as a protest against the awful orgy of brutality" that the British government of India was "indulging against a people whom they disarmed long ago."[82]

Berghash then noted that Britain took $200 to $500 million from India in taxes each year; that India's people had so little to eat that over five million died of starvation in 1918; and that in the territory of the Gaekwar of Baroda, which had "an enlightened ruler of an Indian 'native state,'" some 85 percent of the population was literate, while in British India 94 percent were illiterate after 160 years of British rule. Berghash cited the budget, which allotted $206 million for the military machine that held India by its throat, $121 million for the railways "owned by British capitalists and operated by the government for them," but only $2.5 million for agriculture and irrigation, $.8 million for education, and "nothing for Indian industries!" He explained that out of taxes "wrung from the starving ryots" some 40 percent (four times the amount spent by Japan on her army and navy) was taken for the upkeep of an army "in which no Indian is permitted to command even a regiment of infantry." While thousands of English troops were trained in India, it was India that had to pay their passage and purchase all their military supplies from England. Noting that the viceroy of India had "officially declared that open rebellion exists and half of India's vast territory is under martial law," Berghash saw "small wonder that the natives revolt." The "all-India Congress" had been "insidiously suppressed"; the Swadeshi Movement, "which was breaking down the walls of caste, race and sect, and drawing the Indians together in the work of self-regeneration" was outlawed; and the English in India, by their own declarations, were "ruling by sheer brute force." In the previous three months "Delhi, Lucknow and other Indian cities were 'raided (in the native quarters) by huge bombing aeroplanes.'" These raids were of such ferocity that "every barbarity which the British and American press denounced when done by Germany in time of war, has been perpetrated on these unarmed Hindus in time of peace." Then there were the recently enacted Rowlatt Bills, which provided that an accused could "be arrested on one charge and tried on another," could "neither be represented by counsel nor have the right to be confronted with his alleged accusers," and could not have the proceedings published in any native paper "on pain of instant suppression" of that publication. Harrison would refer to these Rowlatt Bills as the "rottenest legal terrorism that the modern world has yet seen."[83]

"The result of all this," wrote Berghash, was "that Rebellion stalks stealthily through the length and breadth of British India." In the north, secret missions were dispatched to Russia, while in the south and east it was rumored that communications had been opened with Japan. This "spectre" of trade with Japan "forced the British at the Peace Congress to grant Shantung to Japan which thereupon withdrew its 'commercial agents' from British India." In addition, "the most significant result of all" was the consolidation of the Indian patriotic parties." Lines had been drawn, and there were now "no moderates, conservatives and liberals" but "only patriots and traitors," the latter being "restricted to the Rajahs and their circles, the decorated decoys." In concluding, Berghash emphasized that there was "a consolidation of anti-British and anti-European sentiment all over Asia, from Persia to Peking."[84]

In October, the *New Negro* followed with some statistics on India under British rule. The illiteracy rate of 94 percent meant that 295 million people out of 315 million could neither read nor write. Taxes of $1.60 were approximately twenty percent on average yearly earnings of $9.50, while in the United States $12 in taxes on $372 average yearly earnings was only about 3 percent. Finally, in India the death rate of thirty-two per thousand was over double that of the United States' fourteen per thousand.[85]

————

On the domestic scene, Harrison used the August issue of the *New Negro*[86] to focus attention on the summer's "race war" in Washington (July 19–23) and the "outbreak on the streets of Chicago" (July 27–August 3) that resulted "in a score of deaths." He wondered when the country would understand the significance of these outbreaks and suggested that it would be better to "talk a great deal less about Bolshevism in Russia and a great deal more about anarchy in America." He added that some "blind editors, like those of the *New York Times*," were "proceeding precisely as the Russian newspapers did in regard to the Jewish pogroms." They saw "in these two outbreaks the result of Bolshevist propaganda, or pro-German propaganda," but then "place the blame on the Negroes." Harrison maintained that "the blame lies elsewhere, as *The Nation* has so constantly pointed out." The world war "left the colored people of America inflamed to the highest degree because of the denial of their fundamental rights as American citizens," and *The Nation* correctly "prophesied these riots" and "more and more bloodshed until this question is settled right."

Harrison then focused criticism on the *Washington Post* for encouraging law-lessness. "On the morning of the worst day in Washington, when mobs led by men in United States uniforms were dragging innocent Negroes from street-cars and brutally beating them," the *Post* announced "a mobilization of every available service man stationed in or near Washington or on leave" to meet "near the Knights of Columbus hut on Pennsylvania Avenue between Seventh and Eighth Streets" at 9:00 p.m. in order to "'clean-up.'"[87]

In the wake of the bloody summer of 1919, the September *New Negro* reprinted Harrison's editorial on the East St. Louis "pogrom" from the first issue of *The Voice* (July 4, 1917), under the title "A Prophetic 'Voice': The Cause of the Negro's New Attitude Toward Race Riots." The *New Negro* emphasized, "In the genesis of the new spirit, *The Voice* was both pioneer and prophet." It added that "at that time no other Negro paper ventured to say what *The Voice* then said, and many of them," including some that at that time "condemned our attitude of 'fighting back,'" were "now anxious to take the lead in fostering that attitude."[88]

In "'Suppressing' Race Riots," in the October *New Negro*, Harrison again criticized the "white" press, arguing that one striking aspect of the recent race riots was "the enormous amount of suppression and lying which the Associ-ated Press and other white news distributing agencies have done." He felt that "only those who have inner first-hand knowledge of what happened in Wash-ington and Chicago can form an adequate idea of the volume of suppressed information." As an example he cited the fact that during the Washington riots "a certain southern Congressman [probably J. Willard Ragsdale, Democrat from South Carolina, who died on July 23, 1919] took part in the attack upon Negroes, informing the white hoodlums that they didn't know how to handle niggers and that he would show them." Twenty minutes later "he was shot under the eye while leading a mob and died shortly in a doctor's office." Though his colleagues in Congress "did not pay him the usual official courtesy of follow-ing his body at the funeral," reports indicated "he died of disease."[89]

Harrison added: "In Chicago, as in Washington, the number of casualties was treated by the newspapers according to the same formula employed in our war casualty lists." Thus, "after the armistice had been signed the 'reliable' newspapers were printing even longer casualty-lists than usual every day for two months to catch up with their previous suppressions." He stated that "more than 30 white policemen were killed in the Negro district alone and the Negro newspapermen were threatened with penalties if they should tell the truth." He scorned how "'the great dailies' in their summaries of the event give us 35 per-sons, black and white, as the total number killed." He also commented how, "out of the Eighth armory the Negroes took over 700 rifles and 100,000 rounds of ammunition for the defense of their lives when the policemen proved either unable or unwilling to defend them." They also "captured a machine-gun on State St. after sending south two policemen who were engaged in assembling it for use against them." But "these facts and many more of a similar nature" were "kept out of the tide of public information" for "the same reason that prompted the Congressional committee which investigated the East St. Louis riot to suppress the publication of their report." The reason was that "the stark truth, if published, would tend to discourage race-rioting."[90]

In the October *New Negro* Harrison described two standard methods of the "white" press "in explanation of the new spirit . . . shown by Negroes." One method was "to take the thought of certain Negro persons, and to assume that, somehow, this was a fair index of the thought of the masses." A second method was "to catch the current phrases of condemnation and apply them unchanged to the Negro situation." Thus, while "last year it was 'pro-German propaganda,'" it was now "'Bolshevik propaganda,'" and in both cases, he concluded, "ignorance perched on high places prescribes remedies for a situation whose causes are unknown."[91]

Harrison was a particularly vociferous critic of the *New York Times* and described it as an "out-and-out southern paper . . . which deserves the prize 'for ways that are dark and for tricks that are vain.'" In the September issue of the *New Negro* he described how the *Times* "buys copies of Negro newspapers and magazines of a radical turn of mind, reprints portions of their contents under Washington date-lines, pretends to forget their names, and constructs a Bolshevik bogey to account for the new spirit of the New Negro." He suggested that if the paper looked around "it could find a sufficient explanation in the continuance of lynching, disfranchisement and peonage side by side with our wartime assertions of democracy and the Negro's experiences in France" with "both 'crackers' and 'Huns.'" Harrison also commented critically on the *Times'* "brainless explanation of current events," its claim that the government had "a mass of evidence showing activities of agitators among the Negro population," and its attribution of "most of the unrest among the Negro population" to "incendiary writings and speeches of the agitators."[92]

In opposition to the *Times* analysis, Harrison emphasized that the "cause of 'most of the unrest among the Negro population'" had "already been officially determined by the United States government." He paraphrased from the June 1918 Editors' Conference's *Official Bulletin* of Saturday, June 29, 1918: "We believe to-day that Justifiable grievances of the colored people are producing, not disloyalty, but an amount of bitterness which even the best efforts of the leaders may not be able always to guide. . . . Bolshevik propaganda among us is powerless, but the apparent indifference of our own government may be dangerous." Harrison noted he had "merely substituted 'Bolshevik' for 'German'—as every body does these days."[93]

In the September *New Negro* Harrison described the National Negro Race Congress scheduled for the first week in October 1919 in Washington as a "significant gathering" that would "map out the political and industrial policy of the New Negro on a comprehensive scale." Bankers, lawyers, doctors, teachers, businessmen and -women, and working people were to be represented by delegates from every state in the union, and "all the different points of view, radical, liberal, conservative," would "be aired and assessed" at the six-day conference. He also wrote about the August issue of *Current Opinion*, which asserted that in one year the U.S. Army lost $2.5 million through the incapacitation of soldiers by venereal disease and that from September 1917 to 1918 the army had 190,000 such cases. He wryly commented that in the past year "Congress voted $4,100,000 to fight this characteristic curse of Christian civilization."[94]

Harrison commented, in the *New Negro* of September, on Alain Locke, the "young and promising professor" trained at Harvard, Oxford, and the University of Pennsylvania, who worked in "cloistered seclusion" at Howard University, in Washington. Though only in his early thirties, Harrison judged that "he stands upon the heights, side by side with Ernest Just and Kelly Miller" and carried "his wealth of learning with becoming modesty." Three years earlier Locke had developed a syllabus for an extension course of lectures on "Race Contacts and Inter-Racial Relations." The five lectures were "The Theoretical and Scientific Conception of Race," "The Political and Practical Conception of Race," "The Phenomena and Laws of Race Contacts," "Modern Race Creeds and Their Fallacies," and "Racial Progress and Race Adjustment." According to Harrison the lectures "swept the whole circle of the social sciences in a competent and scholarly way" and touched on sociology, economics, political science, ethnology, biology, and social psychology and "yielded up their treasures under his magic touch."[95]

Referring to himself by one of his pen names, "The Taster," Harrison wrote of visiting Locke and witnessing at first hand "the burden of academic and other duties under which he labored effectively." He expressed the hope that Professor Locke "give[s] to the world A BOOK which would not only shed lustre on his name, but would be a much-need Gift of Enlightenment to America and the Negro race. There never was a time when both were in such dire need of such a book." He commented, "If Professor Locke fails to write that book he will have disappointed the friends of his genius."[96]

In the September *New Negro* Harrison also used the example of Native Americans in an effort to point out the illogic of white supremacist thought. He began by commenting on a bill by the Democratic congressman Charles David Carter (who was of Cherokee and Chickasaw descent and had been born near Boggy Depot, Choctaw Nation Indian Territory, later Oklahoma). Carter's bill aimed to give full citizenship rights to the Indians of the United States. Harrison thought the Democrats "ought to find it easy to vote for such a bill," since they had already "shown their friendship for the Indian by taking from the Negro race the office of Registrar of the Treasury" and giving it to "Houston B. Teehee, a full-blooded Cherokee Indian." He also noted that a Southern paper "proudly blazoned the story of Mrs. Woodrow Wilson's reputed descent from Pocahontas, an Indian girl." Harrison found this all very interesting because current anthropology, "which ranks the races of mankind according to their utensils, weapons, arts and inventions," maintained "that the Negro races of West Africa, from whom we are descended, are superior to the American Indians"; because Friedrich Ratzel, in *History of Mankind*, praised West Africans as "the best and keenest tillers of the soil"; because Augustin Hecquard, H. J. Baker, Georg August Schweinfurth, David Livingstone, and others praised Africans' agriculture and cattle raising; because Heinrich Barth described the weaving of cotton in the Sudan in the eleventh century, Monbutto smiths making high-quality steel chains, and the Fan people making spearheads and knives to "the wonder of European travelers"; and because Franz Boas, one of the United States' leading anthropologists, credited the Negro with inventing the smelting of iron and credited Africans with using vehicles with wheels from time immemorial. Harrison observed that an Indian was seated in "the Congress of the United States from which the Negro is debarred because he is an 'inferior' race!" He concluded that "the white Anglo-Saxon lacks both logic and humor."[97]

In "America's Backward Race," in the same September issue, Harrison described a backward race as one that, if "surrounded by civilization and culture, falls behind other races in physical, moral and intellectual efficiency." An "extreme example" would be a people living under favorable conditions, such as "the 'poor whites' of the southern states," which still "degenerates physically, socially and mentally." He then cited an August 10 *New York Times* summary of a U.S. Bureau of Education report by Dr. Harold W. Foght that maintained that these "poor whites" were homogeneous: "English-speaking and of Anglo-Saxon and Huguenot origin" and "of good blood." "But," added Harrison wryly, "the goodness of their blood—contrary to those theories of race which have been so brilliantly expounded by the Herren [Heinrich von] Treitschke, [Friedrich] Nietschke and [Friedrich A. J.] von Bernhardi, the British imperialists and the *New York Times*" was really not so apparent. After the *Times* commented on their illiteracy, it added, "it is well to emphasize, on the other hand, that the average mill family should not be considered inferior to other people." Harrison again commented: "Emphasizing what 'should not be' has long been a peculiar form of logic possessed exclusively by the *Times*. In this instance it occurred to the editorial 'mind' that it had based the inferiority of the Negro on the same identical fact!" He then added: "Chickens of argument will now and then come home to the editorial roosts, and one must be prepared to shoo them away 'on the other hand.'"[98]

Harrison emphasized that "Negroes who have lived in the south, have long been aware of the ignorance and illiteracy of the great majority of our white southern people" and were glad that the U.S. Bureau of Education, via Dr. Foght and the *Times*, was bringing those facts "to the attention of the world at large." This helped "to furnish an explanation of some of the things that are done to us in the south." In addition, while newspapers were speaking about ignorant and illiterate foreigners, it was "Massachusetts, New York, Pennsylvania, and the other states with large numbers of European immigrants that "lead the nation in wealth, culture and intelligence." In fact, those sections where "the undiluted Anglo-Saxon languishes in his native wilds" were the "most backward in brains, brawn and business." Harrison added that "these hill-billies, red-necks and crackers constitute the 'white man's burden' in America" and that "their illiteracy, as revealed in the official records of the late war, is appalling." Their murder rate ran "22 times as high as that of the British Isles," in West Virginia's mountains "they shoot down one another in church," and in Georgia and Tennessee "they roast women and rip out their unborn children," "use charred fingers as souvenirs," and "play foot-ball with severed human heads."[99]

The South, wrote Harrison, presented "a great opportunity for the use of those Christian missionaries whom we are wasting on China, India, and Africa." Noting that "he who would keep another in a ditch must stay in the ditch to hold him there," Harrison explained that the "main business of the south, since slavery, has been that of keeping the Negro 'in his place.'" He concluded that the situation in the South "calls for federal aid in education," though he realized that "such aid would necessarily include the Negroes." However, perhaps "the south would rather rot than accept any benefit in which the Negro shared." The question thus became "whether the nation could afford to let the white south drag it down?"—and that, he emphasized, was a question for the nation to answer.[100]

In the September 1919 *New Negro* Harrison began his "In the Melting Pot" column under the pseudonym "The Taster." In it he satirically discussed one "of the most surprising traits of the American Negro": the "ease with which he becomes grateful." One could "load him with shackles, crush him with insults; then give him a kind word, and all his sufferings are forgotten" as "the one faint favor pervades his soul." This gratefulness brought to mind a "celebrated witticism" of Oscar Wilde: "The virtues of the poor are conceded, and are much to be regretted." Harrison used this lead-in to discuss the *New York World*, which, though claiming to be Republican, acted as Democratic as any New York paper by "damning the Negro race by skillful manipulation of head-lines."[101]

The Taster explained that he had preserved the press's record "in his clipping-collection running back for twenty years." He noted that the *New York World* in its November 15, 1910, issue "played-up" in a three-column news article with lurid "illustrations" the case of ten-year-old Marie Smith, whose dead body was found in the Dead Lake woods in Asbury Park, New Jersey. Thomas Williams, "the big Negro accused of the outrage," was the person "slated for mob-violence at that time," and the *New York World* "assisted in fine style." "But," the Taster added, "when the real culprit was found a few days later to be a white German degenerate, the *World* set it down in three inches of space on the inside." This incident resulted in "editorial denunciation even from the *Amsterdam News.*" Now, however, wrote Harrison sarcastically, the *New York World* was "backing us up for not being 'too proud to fight' in Washington and Chicago. And, naturally, we feel grateful."[102]

In "In the Melting Pot" for October, the Taster commented satirically on how the editorials of the *New York Times* were being "used to foment 'Bolshevism' among Negroes" and described encountering "a prominent Negro radical" who had hanging over his desk "a frame on which were pasted certain editorials from the big dailies." The June 30 *New York Times* editorial "Enemies of Democracy" was underlined and written on by the friend, who replaced "class" with "race," "Russia" with "America," and so on. This led Harrison (as the Taster) to conclude that, rather than "Negro agitators," it was the *New York Times* that was "one of the sources of Bolshevist agitation among Negroes."[103]

In the same column Harrison described how a recent rereading of Herodotus, the "Father of History," brought to mind "a favorite ambition of his earlier years": the "issuing of a series of reprints dealing with the history of Negro lands and lands in which Negroes are interested, from the works of those great writers of the past whose works are no longer 'protected by copyright'" for "a price to suit . . . the average man, women or child—say at 25 and 50 cents." He suggested that "a good beginning could be made with the second book of Herodotus," which offered "invaluable and interesting facts about Egyptian history, as known to the Greeks." Herodotus pointed out "that many of the Egyptians were black and all of them were dark; that the Greeks derived their art and science and religion from them; that the black Ethiopians gave civilization to Egypt and often reigned and ruled over them." Harrison concluded, "in face of the lies of Anglo-Saxon scholars, and the cheap assumption of our near-scholars that Herodotus (in English) is hard to read, such a reprint would be a blessing to our Negro youth."[104]

Finally, in the October "In the Melting Pot" Harrison quoted the white Southerner, H. L. Mencken, who noted that "the southern white is falling behind the procession." Citing a recent issue of the *Maryland Historical Magazine*, which made this "distressingly obvious," he added, "we have never seen such a pitiable product even in the backwoods of the black belt."[105]

In the September 1919 *New Negro* Harrison dedicated two pages to "Poems for the People" and included "The Village Lynch-Smith (with Apologies to Longfellow)," a poem by Andrea Razafkeriefo; "Sixty Years After," a poem by James Russell Lowell; and "To a Negro Belle," a poem by Adolf Wolff. "Raz," Harrison's friend and one of the great poets of the "New Negro" era, had a number of his early poems published by Harrison and later gained fame as lyricist for Eubie Blake, Fats Waller, and others. Lowell, an opponent of slavery, was one of the United States' leading nineteenth-century poets and essayists. Harrison described Wolff, his friend from the Modern School, as "a white man and a brilliant Belgian of the New School" who had "done remarkable work as poet, painter, and sculptor."[106]

The September issue also included Harrison's "Sonnet to a Sick Friend." It is not known for whom, if anyone, this was written.

> If one should learn that all his early hope
> Were doomed to wither and fade away
> Ere it had blossomed in the light of day,
> He would be anguished—would he not?—and grope
> For some strong hands to lead him up the slope
> Of Tribulation's mount; and fondly pray
> The gods to grant him but one kindly ray
> Of sweet celestial comfort. Such a hope
> I cherished for your sake, and if to-night
> Some dim foreboding brings my soul unrest—
> I am too weak to trust the Larger Light
> And put the temper of my faith to test;
> For things that nearest to our hearts do lie
> Gather an added dearness when they die.[107]

In "Poems for the People" in the October *New Negro* Harrison included "Prayer of the Lowly" by Raz and his own "The Black Man's Burden (a Reply to Rudyard Kipling)," which had first appeared in the *Colored American Review* of December 1915 as a response to Rudyard Kipling's 1899 poem "The White Man's Burden: The United States and the Philippine Islands."[108]

————

In addition to his "Poems for the People" Harrison also ran an "Our Little Library" column in which he furnished lists of books "For General Education" and also for the study of "Negro History and Culture." They were "intended" as "a firm foundation on the understanding that in knowledge as in other matters first things should come first." He suggested "the formation of Study Clubs," which could "meet every week to take up, one by one, the study of the works." The books he recommended in the September 1919 *New Negro* "For General Education" were *Man's Place in Nature*, by Thomas Henry Huxley; *The Childhood of the World*, by Edward Clodd; *Modern Science and Modern Thought*, by Samuel Laing; *A History of Modern Science*, by Arabella Buckley; *Education*, by Herbert Spencer; *Anthropology*, by Edward B. Tylor; *Mutual Aid*, by Prince Peter Kropotkin; *Elementary Principles of Economics*, by Richard T. Ely and (George Ray) Wicker; *Readings in European History*, by James Harvey Robinson; *A Short History of the English People*, by John R. Green; *Civilization in England*, by Henry T. Buckle; *Modern Europe*, by Christopher Fyffe; *(History of) The Conflict Between Religion and Science*, by John William Draper; and *Workers in American History*, by James Oneal.[109]

The books he recommended on "Negro History and Culture" included *African Life and Customs*, by Edward Wilmot Blyden; *White Capital and Coloured Labor*, by Sir Sidney Olivier; *Negro Culture in West Africa*, by George W. Ellis; *Europe in Africa in the Nineteenth Century*, by Elizabeth Wormeley Latimer; *Ethiopia Unbound: Studies in Race Emancipation*, by Joseph Ephraim Casely Hayford (Acca Agrimun); *From "Superman" to Man*, by J. A. Rogers; *The Aftermath of Slavery*, by Dr. William A. Sinclair; *The Haytian Revolution*, by T. G. Stewart; *West African Studies*, by Mary H. Kingsley; *A Tropical Dependency*, by Lady Florence Lugard; and his own *The Negro and the Nation*. Harrison also promised that "a review and summary" of one of these books would appear each month "for the benefit of our readers." This same "Our Little Library" article was reprinted in the October *New Negro*.[110]

In September Harrison began his "Books of the Month" column, with a section on books by those "Outside" the "Darker Races" and another section by those "Inside." In the first category he included *Russia in 1919*, by Arthur Ransome, which he described as "the most informative and authoritative account of what happened and is happening in Russia that exists in English." Harrison also included *Ireland's Fight for Freedom*, by George Creel; *Theodore Roosevelt: A Tribute*, by William Hard-Mosher; *Hurrah for Sin!*, by Charles W. Wood; *What Happened to Europe*, by Frank A. Vanderline; and the *Decrees and Constitution of Soviet Russia*, by *The Nation* (which he described as "absolutely necessary to every one who thinks or talks about Russia").[111]

Books from "Inside" the "Darker Races" included *Young India*, by Lajpat Rai (described as "a temperate statement of the horrors of British rule in India, by an exiled leader"); *From Superman to Man*, by J. A. Rogers ("the greatest book of information on the Negro's history, status and capabilities in English," "written by a Negro and absolutely reliable"); and *Complete History of the Colored Soldiers in the World War*, by Sgt. J. A. Jamieson and Comrades of the Fighting Fifteenth. In the "Outside" the color line section of "Books of the Month" for October Harrison listed *The Listener's Guide to Music*, by Percy A. Scholes; and *The Happiness of Nations*, by James MacKaye. For those from "Inside" the color line he listed *Local Governments in Ancient India*, by Radhakamud Mookerji; and *The Children of the Sun*, by George Wells Parker.[112]

In the "Our Book Review" section of the September *New Negro* Harrison published, under the pseudonym "Ignacio Sanchez," his review of Rogers's *From "Superman" to Man*, entitled "The Negro in History and Civilization." Harrison described Rogers's book as "the greatest little book on the Negro that we remember to have read."[113] Years later Rogers would write to Harrison from Paris that "it was due to your [Harrison's] stimulation that I made the effort to get out F.[rom] S.[uperman] to M.[an]" and "I shall never be able to thank [you]," especially "for the publicity given 'F.S. to M.' in *When Africa Awakes*" (where, in 1920, Harrison reprinted his laudatory 1919 *New Negro* review). Interestingly, long after his death, Harrison's comments continued to adorn the dust jacket of subsequent reprints of *From "Superman" to Man* —a fact that points to the respect and friendship (Rogers lived at times with Harrison and his family) between these two outstanding, autodidactic intellectuals.[114]

In the *New Negro* review Sanchez explained that though the book made "no great parade of being 'scientific,'" it was "one of the most scientific that has been produced by a Negro writer," if "science consists fundamentally of facts, of information and of principles derived from those facts." It "sweeps the circle of all social sciences," and "history, sociology, anthropology, psychology, economics and politics—even theology" are used to "yield a store of information . . . [in] a presentation so plain and clear that the simplest can read and understand it, and yet so fortified by proofs from the greatest standard authorities of the past and present that there is no joint in its armor in which the keenest spear of a white scientist may enter." In Rogers's book one learned "not that newspaper science which keeps even 'educated' Americans so complacently ignorant, but the science of the scientists themselves" and what it has "to tell of the relative capacity and standing of the black and white races." For the facts of history and ethnology Rogers went to historians and ethnologists; for the facts of anthropology he went to anthropologists. The result was "information which stands the searching tests of any inquirer." Rogers explained that "his race . . . founded great civilizations" while "the white race was wallowing in barbarism." He added that "cannibalism has been a practice among white populations," "white races have been slaves," and "here in America the slavery of white men was a fact as late as the 19th century" (and, "according to Professor Cigrand,

Grover Cleveland's grandfather, Richard Falley, was an Irish slave in Connecticut").[115]

Sanchez added that Rogers "also deals with the facts of the present position of the Negro in America and the West Indies" and "questions of religion, education, politics and political parties, war work, lynching, miscegenation on both sides, the beauty of Negro women and race prejudice," and "on every one of these topics it gives a maximum of information." The information "flows forth during the course of a series of discussions between an educated Negro Pullman porter and a Southern white statesman on a train running between Chicago and San Francisco," and "the superior urbanity of the Negro, coupled with his wider information and higher intelligence, eventually wins over the Caucasian to admit that the whole mental attitude of himself and his race in regard to the Negro was wrong and based on nothing better than prejudice." To Harrison "this conversational device" gave "the author an opportunity to present all the conflicting views on both sides of the Color Line," and the result was "a wealth of information which makes this book a necessity on the bookshelf of everyone, Negro or Caucasian, who has some use for knowledge on the subject of the Negro."[116]

In October 1919 Harrison printed a laudatory letter in the *New Negro* in which Rogers explained how he received the publication and "started in to examine it coldly, critically, aye, even with that tinge of hostility" with which he "usually regard[ed] new publications." Then, however,

> I found myself simply bubbling over with enthusiasm. The *New Negro* has, by its initial appearance easily attained the eminence of being the leading literary Negro journal. It has filled what I have long been yearning for, that which I have suggested to many friends who told me of their ambition to start a magazine—that is a Negro journal that would be international in thought. The *New Negro* is a first-class literary journal ranking with the best in America.
>
> I am of the firmest conviction that if merit and quality counts for anything, *The New Negro* is already assured of an audience, not only of the masses, but of the cultured and most intellectual thought of the day.[117]

Support for the *New Negro* also came from Cyril V. Briggs's *Crusader*, which considered it "worth while," with "intelligent articles and [a] fearless attitude on the Negro question."[118]

Despite such praise, the *New Negro* ceased publication with the October issue. No reason is offered in Harrison's papers or diary, and no reference to the whys of its closing have been found. Finances were a frequent problem for Harrison and probably were a factor in this case. Other possible reasons concern the deportation provisions of the Alien Act approved by Congress on October 16, 1918. The act, an amendment to the Immigration Act of 1917, decreed that any "alien who, at any time after entering the United States, is found to have been at the time of entry or to have become thereafter" an advocate of anarchy, syndicalism, or violent revolution, "shall upon warrant of the secretary of labor, to be taken into custody and deported." During the Red Scare of 1919–1920 the act was invoked, and BI agents launched nationwide raids against left-wing organizations with large alien memberships. From November 1919 to January 1920, approximately five thousand arrest warrants were issued and 556 upheld. Some 591 aliens were ultimately deported under the 1918 amendment. Though the climate was clearly repressive, it does not appear that any of the alien West Indians, whether "white" or Black, were ever arrested or charged under the amended act.[119]

———

While in Harlem, on Tuesday, September 30, Harrison noted in his diary how he had "a great surprise" that evening. His daughters "Frances and Alice united to tell a lie." As he reproved one of them "for doing the 'shimmy,'" what he described as "a vulgar ventral dance," the girls "insisted to my teeth that they had both seen me do it many times at Miss [Julie] Petersen's." To Harrison this was "a thing impossible physically, because I *can't* dance it—apart from the fact that I detest it." It was also "a revelation" to him, however, "as to the possibilities of my daughters."[120]

As the *New Negro* was ceasing publication Harrison recorded in his diary of Wednesday, October 1, that he had completed reading *The Life of John L. Waller*, the former U.S. minister to Madagascar, a book from which he "got something substantial." Presumably aware that Waller was the grandfather of his brilliant friend "Raz," he added, "perhaps the biologic germ of a life's richest possession and foundation of its richest treasure."[121]

Also on October 1, the Harlem assemblyman John C. Hawkins, in an attempt to help Harrison's financial situation, wrote a letter for Harrison to the superintendent of buildings of the Board of Education, New York City. It explained that Hawkins had "known for ten years Mr. Hubert Harrison, Editor of the *New Negro* and Adjunct Professor of History at the Baptist Seminary and College of Lynchburg, Va.; and can testify of my certain knowledge that he is competent to manage a Community Lecture Forum in any Public School building with credit to the community." Hawkins then took "the liberty of seconding his request for the use of the lecture room in P.S. 89 for the above purpose."[122]

A month later, on November 1, Harrison handwrote what was intended to be an introduction to a book, which was followed by some pages on "The Attitude

Figure 3.4. Alice Genevieve Harrison. Alice Genevieve Harrison (May 22, 1911–September 10, 1987), the second-born daughter of Hubert Harrison and his wife, Lin, attended Public School 119 and Public School 136 Junior High School in Harlem, went on to a profession as a state tax worker, and died in Arizona. She outlived two of her sisters, Frances Marion Harrison (October 21, 1909–December 18, 1932) and Ilva Henrietta Harrison (August 25, 1914–August 7, 1933), both of whom died of (the often poverty-related) tuberculosis. She also outlived her younger brother, William (September 17, 1920–February 22, 1984), who was an attorney and who was, along with his sister Aida M. Harrison Richardson (July 4, 1912–June 28, 2001), instrumental in preserving the Hubert H. Harrison Papers. *Source:* Hubert H. Harrison Papers, Box 15, Folder 12, Rare Book and Manuscript Library, Columbia University Library. See https://dlc.library.columbia.edu/catalog /cul:6djh9w0xgm.

of the American Press Toward the American Negro." On the first page of the "Introduction," Harrison began:

> An introduction to a book is seldom necessary; but it may sometimes be serviceable to the prospective reader who would like to know beforehand the scope of the author's purpose and the spirit in which he has approached the task that he set himself. Especially is this so when the book itself partakes of the nature of a polemic. . . . When the overwhelming majority of one's fellows hold to a particular view of a subject, however ill supported by facts, the very setting forth of the facts which controvert that view constitute a polemic substance.[123]

He then went on and developed some of the thoughts he had articulated in the *New Negro* and described with historic sweep "the world in which this book is written":

> The White Man's World of the 20th century in which people of Negro blood are held down to an inferior status. Their ancestral lands are the prizes of international finance policies and war, and in these they are governed on the basis of a theory which excludes their consent as a necessary factor. Here in the United States, the chief land of their dispersion in the Western World, they are prevented from worshipping in the same churches, living in the same residences, and striving for the same goals in civic, political and military life as their fellows of the white race. In short, they are held to be inferior in the present; and this belief grows out of the knowledge that in this land they have been slaves—inferiors—in the past.[124]

Harrison made clear that it was not his intention to argue the point, but "the intelligent reader" could "readily see how easy it is from this data to draw the conclusion that the Negro must have been an inferior in that historic past beyond the vision of the average white person and beyond the range of interests of even the educated white." He added that "the slightest consideration of historical cases (for example, a comparison of [William] Mitford's *History of Greece* with that of [George] Grote)" would "suffice to show that what men believe to be they often wish to be, and so wishing and believing, when they come to write or speak," they "reduce it to a demonstration and set the question at rest." He noted "that scholars, scientists and writers of books are human in spite of their claims and share the same defects of human nature with the exceptional people," and he observed that "the very helplessness of the Negro in the republic of letters in this White Man's World is a standing temptation to the intellectual vice referred to above." This suggested why "there may be grounds for suspecting that the pious wishes and beliefs of many scholars and scientists of the white race are doing duty as authentic information concerning the Negro's past position and achievements."[125]

In his "Introduction" Harrison considered taking up "these wishes and beliefs in detail, to prove them to be only wishes and beliefs, to invalidate their claim to be considered as facts," but felt "it would be a wearisome task, and a thankless [one]." He did, however, discuss "sensationalism" in the press, which he defined "to mean not merely the pampering of diseased imaginations, but also the pandering to a disordered social conscience." He offered that "whenever justice and truth . . . are sacrificed by any section of the press upon the altar of popular approval," it was "a loss to true democracy and a triumph of sensationalism." He explained that "the direct victims of sensationalism" in the press were "many," including "those whose vocations erect a wall of ignorance between themselves and the public," "those who follow Truth," and "those whom society has injured and, therefore, in its own defense, must hate." He emphasized that sensationalism was "essentially anti-social."[126]

Harrison also described how "those who are allied to unpopular causes—socialists, suffragettes, vivisectionists and pacifists—can tell the same story of facts suppressed, distorted, falsified" by "the public press" in America. He commented on "'how natural it seems!'" and how "kicking the man who is down has become a national habit." He then emphasized:

Of all those who suffer from this misuse of the press in America the Negro is easily first. For his is the most unpopular race—and this means much in America. Therefore, for as much as the treatment accorded to him is illustrative and typical of that accorded to other unpopular groups, an examination of that treatment may serve to set forth at the same time the relation of the underdog to public opinion in American life. And because the conditions which determine such treatment here are at work wherever subject races are dominated by ruling races, an exposure of that treatment and a temperate but vigorous remonstrance addressed to the public conscience of enlightened people everywhere are worthy of grave and serious consideration.[127]

In "The Attitude of the American Press Toward the Negro" Harrison elaborated on what he had written in these introduction notes. He saw his task to be "to demonstrate to the impartial world that the word of the American press can not safely be taken in the case of the American Negro; to discredit and set aside the dicta of interested prejudice, and so, clear the way for a fair, unbiased estimate of ten million human beings." He thought "it would be strange, indeed, if that race-prejudice which is so pronounced in the great majority of white Americans should play no part in the printed portion of their lives." Moving outside the United States to amplify his point, he described how "those who have met Americans in London and Paris are impressed by the vigorous, assertive, racial antipathy which they exhibit on those occasions when they come in contact with their darker compatriots." He added, "surely a prejudice which survives the more democratic atmosphere of these two cities must be strong enough at home to color the reports of the press." He also pointed out "one must be a victim of injustice and oppression to know fully what injustice and oppression mean; and it needs a Negro in the twentieth century to put with the pitiless logic of experience the case of the Negro before the impartial world."[128]

In a short while he would be afforded the opportunity to do just that. As 1919 moved into 1920, Harrison, the "Father of Harlem Radicalism," the founder of the first organization and first newspaper of the militant "New Negro Movement," and the editor of the *New Negro*, "an organ of the international consciousness of the darker races—especially of the Negro race," would soon begin work as the principal editor of the *Negro World*, the newspaper of Marcus Garvey's Universal Negro Improvement Association. He would reshape that paper into a superbly edited, mass-based, race-conscious paper that would sweep the globe and be eagerly read by Black people around the world.

Editor of the *Negro World*

CHAPTER

4

Reshaping the *Negro World* and Comments
on Garvey (December 1919–May 1920)

By early December 1919, the New Negro was no longer publishing, Harrison was
living at home in Harlem with his family, and he was now working with the
Pioneer Development Corporation as chairman of the Organizing Committee,
director of publicity, and head of the Speakers' Bureau. The PDC had a temporary office at 178 West 135th Street; its chairman was Samuel A. Duncan, from
St. Kitts, a Harrison acquaintance from the Lyceum days a decade earlier. The
corporation advocated "A Colored Bank for the Colored People of New York"
and aimed to "Promote and Protect the Business, Commercial and Financial
Interests of the Colored Race." Among those prominently involved with the PDC
were Duncan, a rival of Garvey and a former president (in February 1918) of a
competing UNIA; William Sherrill, who would later become, in Garvey's
absence, the interim UNIA president; and Walter J. Conway, an attorney and
friend of Harrison for over a decade who had served as an original founding
director and first vice president of the UNIA.[1]

Garvey's Universal Negro Improvement Association and African Communities (Imperial) League was a struggling organization in June 1919. According to its founder and leader, Marcus Garvey, it "did not have one nickel."[2] By
the end of the year, however, the UNIA and its Black Star Steamship Line were
undergoing tremendous growth spurts, Garvey was beginning to take on mythical proportions, and the UNIA was on the verge of seeing its newspaper, the
Negro World, develop into an extraordinarily powerful propaganda tool, with
Hubert Harrison serving as its unofficial managing editor for most of 1920.

In 1920 Harrison significantly reshaped the *Negro World* and turned it into
the nation's foremost radical, race-conscious paper. The publication, under his
editorship, also swept the globe and became the world's leading international

Figure 4.1. Hubert Harrison (c. 1919). This photograph of Hubert Harrison is from a photo reel of three photos. *Source:* Hubert H. Harrison Papers, Box 15, Folder 14, Rare Book and Manuscript Library, Columbia University Library. See https://dlc.library.columbia.edu/catalog/cul:zpc866t338.

organ of Black thought. The historian Tony Martin considered "the most effective of Garvey's propaganda devices" to be "his newspapers" and the "most important" of these papers and "possibly his single greatest propaganda device" to be "the *Negro World*."[3] As the paper spread its race-conscious message, the UNIA grew into the largest and (claimed Garvey) the "richest Negro organization in the United States."[4]

Garvey's rise and Harrison's transformation of the *Negro World* were made possible by a combination of events. This conjuncture included a heightened race consciousness growing out of the system of racial oppression in the United

States and "the dogma of the color line" internationally; "capitalist imperialism"; the war and the bloody summer of 1919; the work of activists like Harrison, Garvey, and others; heightened class struggle and related social upheaval during and after the war; new employment and migration opportunities; an April 1919–January 1920 postwar economic boom and wave of financial speculation; a new appreciation of Garvey among race radicals triggered by Harrison's important October 1919 "Two Negro Radicalisms" article; and the startling growth of the Garvey mystique in the wake of a disgruntled stockholder's October 14, 1919, assassination attempt on his life. To the *Negro World*'s editor William H. Ferris, Garvey "was a man of the hour who appeared at the psychological moment." Ferris was correct regarding the psychological moment, but it was not only a psychological moment—it was also a social moment, a period of ripening social conditions. Garvey, with his intense drive, developing mass appeal, and functioning organization and newspaper, was well situated to take advantage of the subjective and objective conditions of late 1919 and early 1920.[5]

In the summer of 1914, Marcus Garvey, a twenty-seven-year-old Jamaican printer, established two separate organizations in his homeland: a fraternal-benevolent organization, the Universal Negro Improvement and Conservation Association; and an "imperial" organization, the African Communities League. These organizations reflected two major influences on his life—Booker T. Washington and British imperialism—about which Harrison was strongly critical. Regarding Washington, one of Garvey's aim was to establish an industrial farm and institute "on the same plan" as Washington's Tuskegee Normal and Industrial School. To pursue this effort he declared that the UNIA was "non-political" and urged his followers "to eschew politics as a means of social improvement." Regarding the influence of British imperialism, Garvey's second aim was to develop the African Communities League—an African-dominated empire modeled after the British Empire. With the ACL he sought "to strengthen the imperialism of independent African States" while simultaneously establishing agencies to protect Africans and "Negroes" in other countries of the world, and the organization specifically sought to "assist in civilizing the backward tribes of Africa." ("Civilizing the backward tribes of Africa," in particular, was a concept that Harrison did not agree with.) In his plans, Garvey envisioned a particularly important role for West Indians, whom he considered to be "the instruments of uniting a scattered race" that would "found an Empire on which the sun shall shine as ceaselessly as it shines on the empire of the North." Four years after their founding, the separate UNIA and ACL organizations would merge, but Garvey's new unified organization was created in the United States, not Jamaica.[6]

Harrison's work over the years had been very political, and it stood in distinction to both the "civilizing" and the imperial aspects of the Garvey program. Regarding Garvey's desire to "assist in civilizing the backward tribes of Africa," the historian Winston James accurately points out that one of "the most distinctive features of Harrison's political thought" was that he had both "confidence in and humility before the peoples and cultures of Africa." Having studied the continent's history and culture, Harrison evidenced "none of the arrogant New World 'civilizationism' that one finds, for instance, in Garvey's pronouncements; none of the 'civilizing the backward tribes of Africa,' as Garvey and the UNIA" promised. To Harrison, "Africa was primarily a teacher; not a primitive unschooled child in need of 'civilization' and instruction."[7]

Regarding "capitalist imperialism" and its "color line," in "'Democracy' in America," an October 8, 1921, *Negro World* article, Harrison began by explaining:

> All over the world today the subject peoples of all colors are rising to the call of democracy to formulate their grievances and plan their own enfranchisement from the chains of slavery—social, political and economic. . . .
>
> Of all these peoples the darker races are the ones who have suffered most. In addition to the economic evils under which the others suffer they must endure those which flow from the degrading dogma of the color line, that dogma which has been set up by the Anglo-Saxon peoples and adopted in varying degrees by other white peoples who have followed their footsteps in the path of capitalist imperialism; that dogma which declares that the lands and labors of colored races everywhere shall be the legitimate prey of white peoples and that the Negro, the Hindu, the Chinese and Japanese must endure insult and contumely in a world that was made for all.[8]

Earlier, in a May 28, 1921 *Negro World* article, "Wanted—A Colored International," Harrison outlined a plan of action that included an "anti-imperialistic" call for "a congress" to struggle against "the capitalist imperialism which mercilessly exploits the darker races":

> Our first duty is to come together in mind as well as in mass; to take counsel from each other and to gather strength from contact; to organize and plan effective resistance to race prejudice wherever it may raise its head; . . . We must organize, plan and act, and the time for the action is now. A call should be issued for a congress of the darker races, which should be frankly anti-imperialistic and should serve as an international center of co-operation from which strength may be drawn for the several sections of the world of color. Such a congress should be worldwide in scope; it should . . . be made up of

those who realize that capitalist imperialism which mercilessly exploits the darker races for its own financial purposes is the enemy which we must combine to fight with arms as varied as those by which it is fighting to destroy our manhood, independence and self-respect. Against the pseudo-internationalism of the short-sighted savants who are posturing on the stage of capitalist culture it should oppose the stark internationalism of clear vision which sees that capitalism means conflict of races and nations, and that war and oppression of the weak spring from the same economic motive—which is at the very root of capitalist culture.[9]

While in Jamaica between 1914 and 1916, Garvey's UNIA made little headway, and Garvey concluded that Jamaicans "were not sufficiently racially conscious to appreciate a racial movement because they lived under a common system of sociological hypocrisy that deprived them of that very racial consciousness." The "difficulty about the West Indies," he later maintained, was "that the Negroes there haven't the racial consciousness possessed by the Negroes of the United States nor those of Africa." In contrast, after spending time in the United States, Garvey grew to believe that

the American Negroes are the best organized and the most conscious of all the Negroes in the world. They have become so because of their peculiar position. They live in very close contact with organized racial prejudice, and this very prejudice forces them to a race consciousness that they would not have had otherwise.

Prompted by his Jamaican experience (which also included a reported "great [financial] scandal" that he was involved in) and his developing views, Garvey made up his mind to travel to the U.S. where "the Negro was forced to a consciousness of his racial responsibility."[10]

Garvey's comment brings to mind Harrison's experience, as well that of many other early twentieth-century Afro-Caribbean immigrants, who found that organized white supremacy was more pronounced in the United States than in the Anglo-Caribbean. When Harrison arrived in the United States in 1900, he encountered a vicious white supremacy that was quite unlike anything he knew previously. The key was that "the color line" was drawn differently in the United States than in St. Croix, where roughly 80 percent of the population was Black, 5 percent European, and 15 percent "colored" (of mixed African and European ancestry) and where the greatly outnumbered European ruling elite had, for social-control reasons, implemented a policy of promoting a significant sector of the African-descended population. During slavery, "free coloreds" served in the militia, the principal instrument of social control, and in 1834 "free coloreds" were extended an "Edict of Full Equality." In contrast, in the United States, slave patrols were basically "lily white"; "Negroes," as codified in the *Dred Scott* decision of 1856–1857, "had no rights that a white was bound to respect"; and the general policy was one of severe racial proscriptions for African Americans.[11]

The contrasting promotion-versus-proscription policies led to markedly different social practices. In St. Croix there was no history of lynch terror and no formal segregation; class promotion among people of African descent was fostered, and white supremacy was not as virulent or as organized as in the United States. Harrison and other early twentieth-century Afro-Caribbean immigrants coming from countries with similar tripartite social structures often commented on the difference between the United States and their homelands. When Harrison, at age twenty, first started writing letters in the *New York Times*, he was prompted by the racial oppression he encountered in the United States. He expressed "shock" at the horror of, and support for, lynching in America and described himself as "a Negro who feels the injustice and veiled oppression under which his race struggles [in the United States]." His friend Claude McKay, who was from Jamaica (like Garvey), explained that when he came to the United States it marked "the first time" he "had ever come face to face with such manifest, implacable hatred of my race," and though he had heard of prejudice in America he "never dreamed of it being so intensely bitter."[12]

When Garvey arrived in the United States on March 23, 1916, it was to learn more about the Booker T. Washington–founded Tuskegee Institute in Alabama (though Washington had recently died in November 1915) and to garner support for his similar organization in Jamaica. He planned a five-month tour of the South. Instead, over the next few years, according to the historian Robert A. Hill, Garvey "became converted in America to the primacy and efficacy of political goals." The transformation took some time and was greatly influenced by the nature of racial oppression in the United States and by Harrison, the Liberty League, and *The Voice*. Garvey learned, as he later explained in a passage that suggests both his own political development and the influence of Harrison, editor of *The Voice* and *New Negro*, that the "new spirit of the new Negro does not seek industrial opportunity"; rather, it "seeks a political voice, and the world is amazed, the world is astounded that the Negro should desire a political voice, because after the voice comes a political place, and nobody thought the Negro would have asked for a place in the political sun of the world."[13]

Based on his experience in the United States and on the new mood that was emerging in the era of violent "race riots" and racial oppression, Garvey developed over the next few years a "radically transformed vision of political independence." Harrison was the leading architect of that new race-conscious, politically independent political voice seeking a mass-based new orientation. Garvey, according to Hill, became, "the foremost beneficiary" of the "mood that emerged full-scale among blacks after 1918."[14] Many of the key leaders of the Garvey movement came from Harrison's Liberty League, and Harrison's influence on the movement was clear.[15]

After almost a year of addressing and being influenced by many of the individuals and activists that were in and around Harrison's Liberty League and *Voice*, Garvey incorporated the UNIA under the laws of New York on July 2, 1918. Then, on July 29, 1918, the African Communities League was incorporated as a business corporation, and on August 3, 1918, Garvey published the first edition of his paper, the *Negro World*. The paper started modestly, with free distribution. In that same year of 1918 Garvey also started several business ventures, including a restaurant. In June 1919, Garvey and four others incorporated the Black Star Line.[16]

Before the extraordinary growth of the UNIA in late 1919, Garvey underwent a summer of internal and external difficulties of the sort that would continue to beset both him and his organizations. Each of his principal enterprises—the UNIA, the BSL, the *Negro World*, a restaurant, and a factory corporation—faced difficulties. Troubles in the UNIA and BSL soon led to complaints, charges, leadership changes, and legal actions.

According to a Bureau of Investigation report, Garvey had reportedly found in New York "that to get a good following . . . among his race, it was necessary to be a Soap-box orator" (à la Harrison), so he "took up his stand on Lenox Avenue." In addition, when his "resources were running low," he "posed as a Catholic, got some classy letter-heads printed, with cable address, etc., and started to send out hundreds of begging letters to Catholic priests, Bishops, and even to the then Arch-Bishop . . . appealing to them for money to help him on the imaginary Jamaica school proposition, turning their moneys to his own account." He also sold over $2,000 in bonds for a restaurant and over $1,000 in bonds for a grocery store. By June 1919 the "restaurant and newspaper were bordering on bankruptcy," yet Garvey held Sunday and Thursday meetings and continued "to borrow from his members," who were described as "fanatics." "Debts were piling up, bills were pouring in, collectors were busy," and so far as was known, between June and October, Garvey had "seven convictions for non-payment of wages." Around the same time, he announced his steamship line (the BSL) and, after he started mass meetings, collected $400 on the first Sunday.[17]

With such a questionable and shaky beginning, complaints and attacks began in earnest in June 1919. Three members of the UNIA whom Garvey had appointed as an audit committee claimed Garvey was "mismanaging the funds of the two organizations [UNIA and BSL] and collecting money from the members under false pretenses." According to records, the UNIA had only 334 members (paying $.35 a month) and $264.50 on May 1; Garvey then sold $4,000 in promissory notes, which he called Black Star Line bonds (the BSL was incorporated in June), to members. The auditors said the money was used to pay expenses for his mismanaged and nearly bankrupt restaurant at 56 West 135th Street. While they supported the idea of the steamship line, they objected to Garvey's "unlawful and autocratic methods"—he was the only officer and chairman of both the UNIA and BSL, and neither organization held directors' meetings.[18]

The auditors were not Garvey's only critics. In June, William Bridges (a Florida-born former waiter who had joined the SP's People's Educational Forum in 1917 and started the newspaper *Challenge* in 1918–1919) began to attack Garvey openly from street corners. Garvey dubbed him a race traitor; Garvey's supporters chased Bridges off his Lenox Avenue soapbox.[19]

The district attorney's office also went after Garvey. On June 18 Assistant DA Edwin Patrick Kilroe, acting on the complaints of the audit committee, "instructed" Garvey "to refrain from collecting any more funds" for the BSL.[20] Garvey promised to refrain from such collections and reportedly claimed that "white" men were against him. After the DA's office had detectives block his next collection, Garvey traveled to Virginia. When he returned, according to a BI report, it was "with the same lame excuse, that the stock certificate was lost with the names and record of the people who bought stocks." Critical articles in the *World* and the *Harlem Home News* followed, and these prompted legal action from Garvey, who sought $100,000 from the *World* for libel and $25,000 from the *Harlem Home News* for "maliciously publishing articles they knew to be manufactured and untrue." This response—of taking court action—is one that the litigious Garvey would repeatedly use against his critics. It is also one that would be used against him.[21]

Shortly after the audit committee's report, Edgar M. Grey, the general secretary of the UNIA and secretary of the New York local, advertising and business manager of the *Negro World*, and director and assistant secretary of the BSL, severed connections with Garvey. Garvey responded by expelling Grey on July 2 and announced his intent to prosecute him. Grey, a former Liberty League officer, then gave a July 18 statement to the authorities on Garvey's use of BSL funds for the restaurant and on Garvey's loss of $1,200 worth of BSL stocks while on tour in Virginia.[22]

In July, Richard E. Warner, the executive secretary of the UNIA and secretary of the BSL, resigned, after only four weeks of work, charging that Garvey was "bent on misappropriating the funds collected by the Black Star Line."[23] Also in July 1919 the former Liberty Leaguer W. A. Domingo resigned as editor of the *Negro World*, a position he had held since the paper's inception. Domingo was brought up on Garvey-initiated internal charges for writing editorials not in keeping with the UNIA program. Domingo described Garvey's methods as "medieval, obscure, and dishonest" and claimed that the BSL was "bordering on a huge swindle."[24] Domingo would be subjected to physical attack for his comments. He explained that in 1919 he raised his voice "in protest against the execrable exaggerations, stupidities, blundering bombast and abominable assininities of our black Barnum [Garvey]" and that he and his fellow socialist Thomas Potter subsequently were "assaulted, kicked, and placed under arrest by Garveyites in the spring of 1920."[25] Over the next few years physical attacks against other Garvey critics would intensify, to the point of murder, and it would take extreme courage to criticize Garvey among his followers publicly.

On July 28, 1919, Garvey was brought before Assistant DA Kilroe for a sixth time.[26] He was then formally indicted on criminal libel charges based on a Kilroe complaint on August 4. He was indicted a second time, on August 28, on three charges of libel against Kilroe, Warner, and Grey, and he posted $3,000 bail and was released. These cases would be amalgamated, and Garvey would ultimately be forced to issue a retraction and to place a public apology on the front page of the *Negro World*.[27]

With fundraising difficult in New York, Garvey traveled to Chicago, where he encountered more difficulties, in the form of a lawsuit and an arrest. Robert Abbott, the editor of the *Chicago Defender*, filed a $100,000 malicious libel damage suit against him on September 29, 1919. Garvey countered with an October 1 suit for $200,000 damages against Abbott. Ultimately, a trial jury would award Abbott damages of $5,000.[28] On September 30, 1919, Garvey was arrested for violating the Illinois Blue Sky law, which regulated the sale and disposition of securities. Though he plead guilty to selling BSL stock in Illinois without license or authority and paid a fine and court costs,[29] his problems continued.[30]

An ominous development was BI surveillance of Garvey during the summer of 1919. This was prompted by an anonymous letter, which cited various "unlawful activities on the part of Marcus Garvey (alleged to be a citizen of Great Britain)." The letter was probably sent by Edgar Grey and was called to the BI's attention by way of an August 8 letter from the State Department's L. Lanier Winslow (assistant to the Office of the Counselor and "expert" on Black affairs) to the Bureau's Frank Burke (assistant to Bureau Director William J. Flynn and overseer of the BI's day-to-day operations).[31] On August 15 the Bureau's Washington office instructed the New York office to "immediately forward" a "complete summary [of] all of the information in your files upon the activities of this subject [Garvey] and prepare . . . at the earliest moment a case for deportation."[32] Within a week, the BI agent Mortimer J. Davis reported that although the *Negro World* had, in the past, "shown its sympathy with Socialism [he was probably referring to the period of Domingo's editorship] and particularly with Bolshevism, Garvey has been clever enough to see the error of his tactics in entering the field upon a partisan political standpoint."[33]

On October 11, 1919, J. Edgar Hoover of the Bureau's Washington office wrote a memorandum on Garvey that said he was attempting to establish the BSL and that he was "active among the radical elements in New York City in agitating the negro movement." Hoover had no information that Garvey had "violated any federal law whereby he could be proceeded against on the grounds of being an undesirable alien, from the point of view of deportation," but he did suggest "that there might be some proceeding against him for fraud in connection with his BSL propaganda."[34]

Overall, the period between June and October 1919 was a particularly difficult one for Garvey. Internally, there were heated disputes with many leaders of the organizations, and, according to a BI report, in that period alone there were reported to be seventy-eight cases against him, including the district attorney's libel charge and three other libel cases that came from grand juries and involved the *Chicago Defender*, Grey, and Warren.[35] Nevertheless, Garvey persisted with his financial programs and organizational efforts.

––––––––

Despite his difficulties, in the fall of 1919 Garvey had a functioning organization and newspaper, both of which had been developed thanks to crucial assistance from former members of Harrison's Liberty League. He also had a remarkable source of income from the sale of BSL stock. This was a markedly different situation than Harrison's, who no longer had a functioning organization (the Liberty League was inactive), whose publication the *New Negro* would cease publishing in October, and who had no regular source of income.

Though he did not have his own paper or organization, the influence of Harrison on Garvey's work was unmistakable. This was clearly seen in the *Negro World*'s "Race First!" editorial of July 26, 1919. The editorial, written by the former Liberty Leaguer W. A. Domingo, emphasized that "perhaps no phrase has done more to consolidate the sentiment of the Negroes of the world than that summed up in the two words: 'Negroes First.' . . . [which was] coined by the well-known lecturer and scholar, Hubert Harrison."[36]

In 1920 Harrison offered some background to his pioneering use of "Race First." He explained "it was the direct product of the outdoor and indoor lecturers [Harrison in particular] who flourished in Harlem between 1914 and 1916." It also appeared prominently in the "Declaration of Principles" of his Liberty League ("We must be loyal to our race first in everything") and in his talk of "Africa First," with "Africa" being understood in the racial, not geographic, sense. In the July 4, 1917, issue of *The Voice* two editorials proclaimed "Africa First" and "Negroes First," and the August 7, 1917, issue of *The Voice* took to task the *Amsterdam News* and the *New York News* for criticizing those who preach "Race First."[37]

Harrison had made clear that he developed "race first" in response to the "white first" of socialists and the labor movement in the United States. It also appears related to Woodrow Wilson's "America First," which he challenged, and to the Sinn Fein's "Ourselves First," which he supported. The slogan, however, was prompted primarily by the struggle against white supremacy domestically and internationally.[38]

J. A. Rogers explained that since "white" American socialists "habitually thought 'White First,'" Harrison's slogan "became 'Race First'—in opposition to his earlier socialistic one of 'Class First.'" Though Harrison still considered himself a socialist at this time—he simply refused to put "either Socialism or . . . [the Socialist] party above the call of his race." As the war progressed, if Blacks functioned "in terms of [the wartime slogan] 'America First,' or 'Class First,' they would be neglecting their own interests—at least until the time that the Whites—socialist-minded and otherwise—underwent a real change of heart." Hence, explained Rogers, Harrison argued that "in self-defense, Negroes must think 'Negro First.'"[39]

Domingo's July 26, 1919, *Negro World* editorial on "Race First!" was soon followed by several other important developments. In September, Garvey announced that the BSL was buying its first boat. (The thirty-two-year-old steamship, *Yarmouth*, needed extensive repairs, yet it was to be bought for $165,000, to be paid in ten monthly installments, which never materialized.)[40] Garvey used this announcement to push BSL sales and to make the purchase of BSL stock almost a measure of race loyalty. In an editorial letter from around September 25 he declared that "Any Negro after the 31st of October not a stockholder in the Black Star Line Steamship Corporation will be worse than a traitor . . . [and their behavior] no less than a crime."[41]

It was in this setting, and in an intense racial climate marked by growing mass interest in Garvey and the BSL, that Harrison, who had not previously defended Garvey, came to his public defense. His powerful October 1919 polemic in the *New Negro* on "Two Negro Radicalisms" defended Garvey, who had "attracted tens of thousands of Negroes," against the "socialist" radicals (such as A. Philip Randolph and Chandler Owen).[42]

Why did Harrison make the decision to write such an editorial? Certainly the conjuncture of events in 1919 set the stage. In the absence of any other indicators, however, Harrison's own words offer the best explanation of what finally prompted his public support: "Where "Negro' radicals of the type known to white radicals can scarce get a handful of people, Garvey fills the largest halls" because he holds "up to the Negro masses those things which bloom in their hearts—racialism, race-consciousness, racial solidarity—things taught first in 1917 by THE VOICE and the Liberty League. That is the secret of his success so far."[43]

During October 1919 Garvey's supporters grew both in numbers and determination. At a UNIA meeting on October 12 in Virginia, J. S. Taylor, president of the Newport News UNIA branch, contributed $10,000 from his division to the BSL. Garvey followed the announcement of this monumental gift with an announcement of plans for a giant mass meeting at Madison Square Garden on October 30 to celebrate the launching of the BSL's SS *Frederick Douglass*, the unofficial new name of the *Yarmouth*, the ship they were in the process of attempting to purchase.[44]

On the heels of Garvey's announcement, on Tuesday morning, October 14, George W. Tyler,[45] a disgruntled thirty-eight-year-old investor of $50 in the UNIA's Harlem restaurant, attempted to kill Garvey at his office. Garvey was wounded on the left side of his forehead and in his right leg by Tyler, who had repeatedly requested that his money be returned but was told that it had been used to promote the Black Star Line. After the shooting, the *Negro World* announced that though Garvey was still in Harlem Hospital, he planned to address the October 30 meeting. The "attack on his life" was treated as an "assassination" attempt emanating from his "critics," and Garvey began to take on mythical proportions as his popularity skyrocketed. Though his recent effort at selling BSL stock in the Midwest had been "less than successful," sale of the stock now soared, and in October 1919 over 11,000 shares were sold.[46]

On October 19, the Sunday after the attempt on Garvey's life (according to a U.S. MI report received from British MI), Hubert Harrison reportedly spoke at an afternoon talk on the Black Star Line at Rush Memorial Church. The historian Robert A. Hill identifies the speaker listed as "Robert [*Hubert*] Har[r]ison" as Hubert Harrison. The speaker reportedly said: "That nations and people never rose to power without ships; that by means of ships they could carry passengers and men to other countries, that they could be passed th[ro] ugh as working men; that they could get their literature through; that the promotion of the Black Star Line was not for its present value but for its future value." Later that evening, at the Lafayette Hotel, Harrison reportedly maintained, according to MI, that "the negroes should centralize like the Irish and other nations in one place . . . their fatherland . . . [and] Africa was their fatherland. . . . [That] if they kept together they could create a power in Africa, centralizing their forces with those of Egypt, Abyssinia, Liberia and other countries."[47]

While Harrison was reportedly speaking on October 19 at Lafayette Hall (on Seventh Avenue and 131st Street), a mass meeting was held at Liberty Hall (on 138th Street, near Lenox Avenue). The *Negro World* claimed that "Ten Thousand Negroes" tried to attend and that "nearly three thousand were jammed into Liberty Hall." Garvey made his first post-shooting appearance and told the crowd that the six- or seven-month-old restaurant promissory notes would be redeemable in January 1920 and that the BSL planned to launch its first ship on October 31. He claimed "Tyler fell into the hands of enemies of the U.N.I.A[.] because I had caused some politicians to lose their jobs [and] . . . they doped him and sent him to me." In response to articles in the *New York World* and *New York News* claiming Tyler shot Garvey "because he had borrowed $25" from Tyler, Garvey responded: "That is a lie. I have never borrowed a dollar from any man in my life."[48]

After Garvey's talk at Liberty Hall, he again traveled to Virginia. The *Negro World* covered his October 25 Newport News talk, where he reportedly said that "the New Negro, backed by the Universal Negro Improvement Association," had "given up the idea of white leadership" and was "determined to restore Africa to the world."[49] In an editorial letter from Newport News that appeared in the *Negro World* of November 1, Garvey stated that "the New Negro manhood movement [a phrase used by Harrison since 1916] is not confined to the North alone, it has found its way far down South and there are millions of black folks here who mean to have all that is coming to them or they are going to die in the attempt of getting same."[50]

Back in New York at Madison Square Garden on October 30, Garvey headed a large meeting of six thousand "to celebrate the purchase of the first vessel of the Black Star Line." It was reported that many in attendance "wore the colors of the new colored flag—red, green and black." (The colors of the flag of Harrison's Liberty League in 1917 were black, brown, and yellow.) In his talk Garvey, without basis, claimed the UNIA had "grown into an organization of over two million active members."[51]

Garvey was taking full advantage of the postwar economic boom, which was affecting most of the industrialized world. During the period of conversion from war production there was increased demand for goods and investment opportunities.[52] The large crowds Garvey was attracting were buying stocks, and records show that from July 1919 to August 1920 BSL sales reached 96,285 shares.[53]

Many of those buying stocks were from what Judith Stein refers to as "the enlarged black working class." She emphasizes that the "idea of accumulating wealth through stocks and bonds had been widely publicized during the war." This "world of paper wealth" had first been entered through Liberty bonds, the purchase of which had often been encouraged by Black leaders. Both war workers and returning soldiers had some savings, which were "readily targeted by capital-starved marginal businessmen and promoters, both legitimate and fraudulent."[54]

The desire to invest was so pronounced that the *New York Age* in January 1920 warned its readers that "in this era of get-rich-quick enterprises, which promise the gullible investor all sorts of interest on a small investment, it behooves the capitalist to look well before he leaps." A year and a half later, *Age* editors described "the craze for buying stocks" as "almost epidemic in Harlem." People who had money in savings banks or Liberty bonds were often using that money to invest in questionable enterprises promising loans of 10 or 20 percent.[55] As Stein points out, people who had recently responded to patriotic appeals for money now responded to Garvey's appeal, which offered both the promise of racial advance and prompt financial return on a five-dollar investment.[56]

During November 1919, as Garvey's popularity continued to rise, an interesting harbinger of future developments appeared: a UNIA leaflet, which drew directly on Harrison's previous work. That leaflet urged people to join the UNIA & ACL and used Harrison's old slogan (derived from the British poet George Linnaeus Banks) from his column in the 1915 *New York News* and from *The Voice*'s masthead of October 31, 1917:

> For the cause that lacks assistance
> For the wrongs that need resistance.
> For the future in the distance.
> And the good that we can do.[57]

In the first week of December 1919 Garvey approached Harrison on West 136th Street, between Lenox and Fifth Avenues, and, "after a hearty handshake," told him that he had been looking for him "for several weeks and had concluded" that he "had gone out of town." Harrison explained that, although Dr. R. C. Woods, president of the Baptist Seminary and College of Lynchburg, Virginia, had "engaged" him "to come down there and organize and set going a Department of Negro History," he "had finally decided to remain in New York and was at that time acting as Director of Publicity and head of the Speakers' Bureau for Sam Duncan's project of a Negro Bank (The Pioneer Development

Corporation)." Garvey then asked Harrison to accept "the presidency or principalship of the new college which he had projected as one of the main institutions of the U.N.I.A." Harrison told him that he "would consider it seriously" and give his answer.[58]

A week later Harrison went to Garvey's office "to give him my reply," and, as Harrison recounted, the "office was at the time a curious shambles" in which "the work of the U.N.I.A., of the Black Star Line and of the newspaper, were all jumbled together in one room—although much of the financial work of the B.S.L. and also that of the U.N.I.A. was done on the floor above." Given this arrangement, there was "no privacy for the discussion of business in the office," so he and Garvey went out onto the landing, where Garvey told him that he "wanted to associate" Harrison "with Ferris ('Professor' and 'Rev.' Wm. H. Ferris, 'author of 'The African Abroad') in the editing of the paper [the *Negro World*] at that time and later to assume the leadership of the school or college when it was organized."[59]

Harrison "accepted provisionally, and asked for more time to make my acceptance binding and to formulate the conditions under which I would work." Then, "on the 24th of December, the day before his [Garvey's] wedding [to Amy Ashwood],"[60] Harrison made his acceptance final. He would "work for $30 a week as Associate Editor (not *Assistant* Editor)," and he stipulated that he "was not to be expected to lecture at Liberty Hall" as any part of his duties, although he was "willing to help out in an emergency." At that time Ferris was earning $25 per week. Harrison actually wrote a letter detailing the "terms of acceptance" and specifying that he was "not to lecture for [the] U.N.I.A."[61]

When it became known that Harrison "was to be connected with the *Negro World* many of the rank and file and the officials of the movement were enthusiastic in their congratulations." Chief support came from "the bright young secretary E. D. Smith-Green," who was convalescing from a "pistol shot wound in his leg inflicted by a murderous footpad who, for the purpose of robbery, had waylaid him in the dark hallway of his home."[62]

One aspect of Harrison's hiring that merits attention is the fact that though he was arguably Harlem's finest journalist, he was very dark-skinned. He was never able to secure permanent work with the *Amsterdam News*, the *New York News*, the *New York Age*, or *Opportunity*. He believed that attitudes about his skin color were a factor in this. Several years later he wrote that he was "'too dark' to get employment at any but one Negro paper or periodical in New York."[63]

In January and February 1920, while he was still planning on heading the UNIA's proposed college, Harrison worked up some notes entitled "Plans for a Negro College." Though not fully developed, they offer an instructive look at his maturing views on the importance of "racial internationalism" on the education needed by the race. He began by focusing on "the nature of our needs" and defined three broad areas. First was "the problem of rejection," which necessitated building "on a different basis and for other ends than whites." He believed that it would be necessary "to eschew some things considered necessary in their program" but added that "we must take stock of that program that we may know how to eschew intelligently." Second, he identified "some present defects of Negro education," including the "general ignorance of [the] masses," a "placid acceptance of standards of excellence inferior to those of whites on the part of our educated classes," and "our race's education motivated by cultural-standards and cultural necessities of whites." Third, Harrison emphasized that "our racial aims must furnish our academic program and methods." To do this it was necessary that "racial history [serve as] the root of racial self-respect." He stressed that "racial internationalism, world commerce and political interests will dictate" that "Hausa and Arabic [should be learned] instead of Latin and Greek; Spanish and French instead of Hebrew; physics and chemistry instead of philosophy and metaphysics; and business and handicrafts instead of literature."[64]

In early 1920 Harrison found time for several social activities of note. On Monday, January 25, he attended what he described in his diary as "the most interesting dinner of the [Freethought-influenced and interracial] Sunrise Club that I have ever attended." After the meal the diners were treated to "a demonstration of spiritualistic phenomena" by Joseph F. Rinn, ex-president of the Brooklyn Philosophical Society, who "worked wonders" on an improvised stage of kitchen tables. Rinn "gave illustrations of thought-transference" in the room and in Brooklyn. After his assortment of feats was completed, Rinn "exposed the whole show, declared that everything he had done had been fraudulent, demonstrated the nature and method of some of the 'stunts', and showed that Sir Oliver Lodge, Mayer [Frederic W. H. Myers], [James H.] Hyslop and other psychical researchers are and have been the easiest kind of 'easy marks.'" He stressed "that the ordinary person, whether a scientist or not could not be independently relied on for a correct interpretation of the evidence of his senses." Rinn spoke from his experience of thirty years as a member of the Society for Psychical Research, during which he was "associated with Prof. Hyslop and others" and had "exposed Eusapia Palladino, Diss de Barr and many other mediums." He publicly "offered to deposit $5,000 with any newspaper that no spiritualistic medium could furnish a single genuine message from the dead or present a single contravention of natural laws under prescribed scientific conditions of observation."[65]

In February, Harrison stepped outside the no-lecture clause in his contract with Garvey and delivered lectures for the UNIA at Liberty Hall on "Lincoln and Liberty: Fact Versus Fiction" on February 10 and on conditions in Liberia on February 17. His notes for the Lincoln talks indicate that his focus was on "our present political plight" and that he emphasized that "the burden of gratitude alone keeps us from using our political power safely in our own behalf." He therefore saw our "duty" to be that of investigating "the grounds of our 'gratitude.'" To do this he detailed how records of the past had been falsified "in the interest of [the] present," and, in so doing, he challenged some of the major "historical myths of America."[66]

The first myth that he challenged was that concerning the "purity of 'The Fathers,'" and he did this by citing the work of the historian John Bach McMaster on New England's "White Slavery," George Washington, and Abraham Lincoln. He focused on Lincoln in particular and emphasized that he was the country's "greatest president," despite the fact that the "current notion of him as a god" was "not supported by the facts"—at least not "those relating to us." Harrison argued that a "Morally Reconstructed" Civil War would properly emphasize the efforts of abolitionists such as the editor Elijah Lovejoy, who was murdered by a mob at Alton, Illinois, in 1837; the *Liberator* editor William Lloyd Garrison; the legendary warrior John Brown, who was executed by hanging; and the orator, activist, and social reformer Wendell Phillips, who was also mobbed.[67]

Harrison saw "the real causes of the Civil War" as related to the "economics of slavery," the "necessity of its extension," and the "conflict of interests (capitalists [vs.] free laborers)." He discussed "attempts at compromise ending with [that proposed by John J.] Crittenden" and analyzed "why the south would not abide the verdict of the voters." In the course of his discourse he analyzed "Lincoln's relation to slavery" and argued that Lincoln "was not an abolitionist," "had no special love for Negroes," "opposed citizenship for Negroes," "favored making slavery perpetual in 1861," "denied officially that the war was fought to free the slaves," and "refused to pay Negro soldiers the same wages that he paid white soldiers." Harrison aimed to "prove" that the Emancipation Proclamation "did not abolish slavery and was not intended to" and that it "was issued not for the slave's sake but as an act to cripple the enemies of the South." He also sought to show that "the war was fought for economic and not for moral reasons," that "the Rep[ublican]. party opposed the abolitionist doctrines" and "offered to 'sell out' the Negro in 1861," and that "as late as 1864" the Republicans "refused to pass an amendment to the Constitution abolishing slavery."[68]

To prove his charges Harrison detailed Lincoln's "hypocrisy" and quoted his words from the August 27, 1858, Freeport, Illinois, debate with Stephen A. Douglas, where Lincoln supported the fugitive slave law ("I think, under the Constitution of the United States, the people of the Southern States are entitled to a congressional fugitive-slave law") and opposed abolition of the domestic slave trade ("As to the question of the abolition of the slave-trade between the different States, I can truly answer, as I have, that I am pledged to nothing about it"). Harrison also cited Lincoln's August 14, 1862, answer to a Colored deputation in which he indicated support for colonization; Lincoln's letter to Governor Michael Hahn of Louisiana March 13, 1864, on extending the franchise to "some colored people"; James G. Blaine's autobiography; Lincoln's first inaugural address of March 4, 1861, which discussed the proposed "13th" Amendment (prohibiting federal intervention in slavery, to which Lincoln had "no objection to its being made express and irrevocable"); the oft-related requests of the British workers Conway, Stallo, and Taft; Horace Greeley's open letter to Lincoln entitled "The Prayer of Twenty Millions" in the *Tribune* of August 20, 1862; and Lincoln's response of August 22, 1862, in which he explained his "paramount object in this struggle is to save the Union, and is not either to save or destroy slavery." Harrison argued that these examples "effectively" dispose "of any claim to our gratitude on the high moral ground of altruism and benevolence." He stressed that Lincoln was against arming Negroes in 1862, and he cited the story of the 54th and 55th Massachusetts Infantry, which included Lewis Douglass (Frederick Douglass's son), Col. Thomas Wentworth Higginson's *Part of a Man's Life*, the Story of Capt. André Calliou's First Louisiana Volunteers (an all-Black unit that fought with the federal forces), and the letter to C. D. Robinson, Washington, DC, of August 17, 1864, indicating that the North could not win the war without the Black soldiers. Harrison concluded by noting that his proofs were all documentary and that "most damaging" were "Lincoln's own words."[69]

———

Along with his busy work and social schedule, and probably related to it, Hubert had problems at home. On Sunday, February 15, he wrote in his diary of a brief marital spat. After getting out of bed at noon and washing his face in preparation for a bath he said to his wife "courteously and without offense Lin have you got . . . this." She was apparently absorbed in a conversation with herself, and after fifteen seconds he "asked louder." She then screamed, "Don't raise your voice at me! Don't raise your voice at me." Hubert responded, "I will raise my voice at you if you won't . . . and if you don't like it you can lump it." "Lump it said she, 'I'll lump it with a garbage? bag? of shit.'" Hubert noted in his "Diary" that she said this "in the presence of the baby [five-year-old Ilva]—the others having gone to church." He then told Lin that he and she "couldn't get along in that [way] . . . and with that spirit." He added, "If . . . I had done anything myself or failed in my duty in any way you could say that it was my fault; but you can't now."[70]

One other incident of note from this period concerns a "curious dream" about himself and his family that Hubert chose to record in his diary. He wrote that on the leap-year night of Sunday, February 29:

For the first time in my life, I dreamt that I was dead and went around as a disembodied spirit. I had always thought that this was psychologically impossible. How I had died was not known to me in the dream and at first, I didn't know that I was dead until people and birds had passed thru me and I couldn't make myself heard or seen by others. Then, as I thought of my children left fatherless and unprovided for, I burst out weeping and just at the same instant I heard (but did not see) one of my children bewailing the loss or absence of her father. Then I suddenly found myself awake. A curious dream.[71]

In fewer than eight years Harrison would in fact be dead and his children "fatherless and unprovided for."

Shortly after his "curious dream," on St. Patrick's Day, Wednesday, March 17, 1920, Harrison began to "attempt to set down" in his diary the "early history of my connection with the Garvey movement [The Universal Negro Improvement Association and African Communities League, and its products: The Black Star Line Corporation, The Negro Factories' Corporation and the Negro World]." He feared that if he "should delay it longer the fine edge of certain impressions might be worn down and certain minor details might vanish from my memory." He would leave "the account of my own labors in the field of New Negro sentiment" for "later shaping," noting "the materials for that narrative may be found partly in the pages of *The Voice*, the weekly newspaper which I issued between July 4th 1917 and March 1919—especially in the first number." In his diary he intended to "confine myself to my connection with the later and larger movement." (Harrison would offer a powerful and extraordinary sample of his "labors in the field of New Negro sentiment" in August 1920, in publishing *When Africa Awakes: The "Inside Story" of the Stirrings and Strivings of the New Negro in the Western World*.)[72]

The reshaping of the *Negro World* was undoubtedly Harrison's most important work in early 1920, and his March 17 diary entry offers unique, inside testimony at what he accomplished. Given Harrison's brilliance and the *Negro World*'s importance in the history of Black journalism, the diary entry is a key artifact. He begins by describing how his actual connection with the *Negro World* began on January 2, 1920, although he had no involvement in the Saturday, January 3 issue, which hit newsstands on Tuesday, December 30. Garvey was honeymooning in Canada with his first wife, Amy Ashwood, at that time, and they did not return until January 8. The first issue Harrison edited was that of January 10.[73] (He would serve as the effective managing editor from January 1920 to sometime in September to November. He was listed as "Associate Editor" on the masthead from March 6, 1920, until December 25, 1920, and as "Contributing Editor" from January 1, 1921, to c. September 9, 1922.)[74]

In his diary Harrison detailed the *"New Methods"* and *"Changes"* he, as effective managing editor, brought to the *Negro World*. He specifically mentioned:

"improv[in]g gen'[era]l appearance; heads & sub-heads & 'banks'";
taking "letters off [the] front page";
changing the "quality of editorials" into "Editorials that were not Literary
    essays";
issuing a "Call for NEWS";
offering a "Description of "[News]"";
establishing a ""Questions"" "[+ Answers]" section;
"Herding 'poetry' to 1 section" and establishing a "Poetry for the People"
    section;
establishing a "West Indian News Notes" section;
developing "Book-Reviews";
establishing a "To Our Readers & Friends" from January 17, 1920 et seq.;
writing "The Crab-Barrel" series (which began on April 3, 1920);
writing "Negro Culture & Negro College";
introducing "[an] Office File";
introducing "Letter Files";
and being "given final authority on copy and make-up."[75]

In existing copies of the *Negro World* from the period (up to late August 1920), when he was serving as effective managing editor, Harrison's impact (in terms of editorials, news, "Book Reviews," "West Indian News Notes," "Poetry for the People," "Correspondence," and the "Magazine Section") is readily discernible.[76]

Harrison's March 17, 1920, diary description of how he worked various changes is revealing:

My first business was to improve the appearance and general makeup of the paper. A reference to the files will show how much has been achieved in two months and a half. The "heads" of news articles and special articles often ran to six and eight lines, with "banks" of eight and ten lines that sprawlingly attempted to tell all about what was contained in the articles. Letters went galloping all over its ten pages and opinion-items, which should have been sparingly used and confined to the supplementary sections, appeared on the front page all in the wasteful glory of "heads", "subheads" and "banks" eight lines long. It seemed that every ass in the universe who was of the Negro race was writing "poetry", and everyone spewed his hog-wosh [*sic*] in the pages of the *Negro World*. The general idea seemed to be that if each line began with a capital letter, if grammar's neck was wrung and rhymes like "boat" and "joke" were occasionally interspersed, "poetry" was achieved.

I had to stop all this. I began by herding the poetry on page one under the standing future-head, "Poetry For the People". I made that page the Magazine Page and tethered there the literary effusions in which Mr. Ferris and his friends were prolific. Then I set to work cutting down the "heads" and "banks" and guiding a large portion of the letters into the harmless harbor of the waste-basket.[77]

Harrison next worked on two other "defects." First, as he described, "the editorials were almost endless," and "many of them consumed nearly four columns (set as two double-columns)." While these "might have been all right as literary essays," a "newspaper (especially one designated for the masses black or white) cannot afford to let its editorials run to literary essays." Newspaper editorials needed "terseness, point, pungency and force." Harrison "did not criticize"; rather, he "turned out samples instead, and, by dint of putting my initials at the end of my editorials during the first few weeks, I soon forced on my associate a change of form; for readers began to note the difference."[78]

He also focused on "the matter of clippings." As he explained, when he took over "most of our news came from that source—mainly from the white newspapers." Unfortunately, "Mr. Ferris, although a Harvard and Yale M.A.[,] hasn't the slightest idea of newspaper work" and "seemed to read certain papers by chance and if he found in them something which pleased him he would snip it out and put it in even if it were six months or a year old, never changing a word or a heading." Ferris's "desk was as untidy as his person, strewn with the accumulated rubbish of months," which "he could never arrange into any semblance of order and in it he could consequently find nothing when it was wanted." Harrison judged him "a brilliant 'scholar' within a certain narrow rut or range" whose "mind is innocent of order, plan, or arrangement." He added that "anyone who has read his two volumes, 'The African Abroad,' that gigantic rubbish heap of ill-digested and structureless learning, will be able to verify the judgment from his mental products, wherein sermons, lectures, valuable historical data and whole pages of names are jumbled together pell-mell like the scraps in the wallet of one of [Scottish poet Robert] Burns's Jolly Beggars." To overcome this situation, Harrison began to "shape up the clippings to snip off, insert and re-write many portions of them." As he described, "this wasn't by any means an easy task, and we had many an unvoiced conflict of opinion." On several occasions Ferris asked Harrison "in his innocence and wrath, 'Who is the editor, you or I?'" Harrison added, "That was before he knew better." At that time Harrison "was getting $30 a week: whereas he was getting $25," although by March Ferris was raised to $30.[79]

Harrison explained how he "gradually . . . got the strings of management in a letter to the printers," which he "dictated to a stenographer and had Mr. Garvey sign," making him "the sole and final authority on matters relating to the admission of 'copy' and to the 'make-up' of the paper." He emphasized that he "had to do this for the salvation of the paper," but such ultimate authority also entailed "a burdensome increase of work and responsibility." This now meant that he "had to read again and re-shape every item of 'copy' that came from his [Ferris's] hand to mine—except his editorials and 'Literary Mirror' articles."[80]

Harrison also went after "the lucubrations of officials of the movement." Two officials were "especially" described as "veritable thorns" in his side. One was the Rev. Mr. H. M. Mickens, who had taken the place of "Prof." B. C. Buck "as Secretary-General of the U.N.I.A."; the other was "the Rev. Mr. Gilliard," a Baptist divinity student. According to Harrison, "both of these men work in the offices and, seemingly, when time hangs heavy on their hands they turn to the production of pronounciamentos for public consumption." To such efforts he became "the mute with the bowstrings."[81]

Ferris's "irresponsibility" added to Harrison's workload. By mid-March 1920 Ferris was chancellor of the Convention Fund for the planned month-long August Convention, and he shirked his work as associate editor. Harrison cited as an example Saturday, March 13, when he received from Garvey's office "about 60 letters for the editors—an unusually heavy budget." Harrison took "a proper pride in seeing that every letter that is sent to my desk gets read and attended to on the same day." But this was an "unusually large" batch, and he "divided up with Ferris by asking him to take a portion of them." Ferris took twenty-four, and Harrison "impressed on him the necessity of attending to them on that same day because some of them might contain timely matter of consequence." Nevertheless, at six o'clock, as Harrison "was getting ready to clean up and go home the letters were still there and Ferris was nowhere in sight." Harrison "was exasperated and sent the bundle to him by one of the messengers to Liberty Hall where he was to preside that night."[82]

On Sunday evening, when Harrison went to work alone at his desk, the letters were back "on his desk unattended to." He "had to go thru them, and it was well" that he did. One of the letters was from Schiller Nicholas, a Haitian who had written a "manuscript on American Rule In Hayti." Earlier, Harrison had read, corrected, and turned that manuscript in to the printers. In his letter Nicholas had "requested that his name, for his own protection, should not appear as author of the article." Harrison was able to delete it on Monday, but if he "had not gone through Ferris' share of the mail it would have appeared," to Nicholas's "injury, since Ferris did not touch those letters until" Wednesday—even though the paper was set up on Monday and came out on Tuesday.[83]

To Harrison, "crass and cowardly stupidity [were] even worse dangers than laziness." On this matter he cited the case of Captain Joshua Cockburn's speech at Liberty Hall during the first week of January 1920. Captain Cockburn had commanded the *Yarmouth*, the first ship of the BSL, on her maiden voyage "under the Black, Red and Green." Harrison felt there was "some underhanded business done to make the trip a failure and to prevent the ship from reaching port." In one instance, "the Captain retired about midnight leaving explicit instructions, a man at the wheel, and the ship on a certain course." Then, "at four o'clock he awoke to find the fixes banked, the ship on a reef, wireless messages already sent out saying that the ship was sinking, life-belts distributed to passengers and crew and the boats being swung out from the davits—and all this done without any attempt being made to wake or call him." He then "had to threaten to shoot before he could get things again under control," and "with the help of an officer who was not an engineer he got steam up and backed his ship off the reef." On this trip there was a "white" chief engineer and a "white" first mate, and "the treachery was generally supposed to have been the work of the engineer mainly."[84]

Captain Cockburn had explained "all this" in a "speech at Liberty Hall the night after the ship docked on her return; although he told much of it indirectly and with an evident desire to suppress the more sensational aspects of the story." But, "as he told it the stenographers set it down." Such a "Liberty Hall news story" was "generally set on the front page of the paper." On the night Cockburn spoke, however, Garvey was in Canada on his honeymoon, having left on December 26. Harrison attended the talk "and took copious notes of the Captain's speech." He was, as he described, "thunderstruck on Monday to find that Ferris had brought down the speech as reported by the stenographers and, after reading it, had given it to the printers to set, with all the unsavory details which, when read, would have destroyed the confidence of the public and stockholders and split the project of the Black Star Line wide open." Harrison "immediately, upon seeing the 'proofs', ordered the story 'killed' and re-wrote an account of the meeting and the speech from which these details were elided." According to Harrison, "This was one of the things which helped to induce Mr. Garvey to give" him "control of 'copy' for the printers."[85]

The Harrison-initiated "Poetry for the People" section was a major contribution. Tony Martin dedicates a lengthy chapter in his book *Literary Garveyism* to this section of the paper and points out that by 1920 "the *Negro World* was already well on its way to becoming the focal point of a mass preoccupation with the arts, especially poetry, unequalled by any of the better known publications of the Harlem Renaissance."[86] Martin adds that "Poetry was a regular feature of the *Negro World*" and that the "greatest number of poems appeared in 1920 and 1921, most of them part of the 'Poetry for the People' section of the newspaper," which "began in 1920 as part of the 'Magazine Page' of the *Negro World*."[87]

The Letters to the Editor section under Harrison was increasingly receptive to differences of opinion. This undoubtedly reflected Harrison's own willingness to air different positions on issues. Martin, after commenting on one such difference of opinion between Harrison and a 1920 letter writer, emphasizes that there was a "willingness of the *Negro World* to engage in real debate."[88]

In those first few months of 1920 Harrison also "inaugurated" in the *Negro World* what he described on March 4, 1922, as "the first (and up to now the only) regular book-review section known to Negro newspaperdom." Martin describes how "the *Negro World* prided itself on being the first Afro-American popular publication to carry a regular book review section," and he correctly describes Harrison as "the pioneer in this field." He also points out that "Harrison's reviews were only part of his wider interest in literary criticism," noting that he later also "lectured regularly at the 135th Street library in Harlem on such literary figures as Edgar Allan Poe, [Thomas Babington] Macaulay, Victor Hugo, 'Lincoln as a Master of English,' Lewis Carroll and James Russell Lowell."[89] Within two years after Harrison initiated book reviews in the *Negro World* his practice had caught on enough for him to write: "I foresee that in the near future there will be many book reviewers . . . among us. Indeed, they are already treading on my heels in this paper."[90]

In 1922 Harrison explained in more detail how his book reviews had a "twofold aim: [1] to bring to the knowledge of the Negro reading public those books which were necessary" to "know what the white world was thinking and planning and doing in regard to the colored world; and [2] to bring the white publisher and his wares to a market which needed those wares." Sometimes, the books reviewed were "written by Negro authors with whose works Negro readers were thus made acquainted." In rendering this "common service" Harrison judged that "to a certain extent" he had "succeeded." In light of this success, one "would have thought," he added, "that the white publishers would be eager to avail themselves of the novel opportunity thus offered to get some more pennies for their pumpkins." "But," he observed, this "was not to be."[91]

Overall, particularly under Harrison's editorship, the *Negro World* evidenced a remarkable combination of political and literary coverage. Martin found "the large number of *Negro World* editorials devoted to literary subjects" to be "particularly striking" and observed that "The *Negro World* was the most highly political of newspapers. Yet it was simultaneously the most literary of newspapers." He was "hard put" to identify any similar "primarily political oriented newspaper which devoted so much space, even on its editorial pages, to literary concerns."[92]

The *Negro World*, reshaped by Harrison, was a real key to the phenomenal organizational growth of the UNIA in 1920. It was a superbly edited newspaper with mass appeal. Harrison was the consummate race-conscious journalist[93] and, in addition, as the BI special agent "WW" (William A. Bailey) wrote after attending a UNIA meeting at Liberty Hall, Harrison was considered a man "who knew every principle of Socialism."[94] According to Martin, he was "Harlem's best known and most respected intellectual," and the "*Negro World* weekly had a purely literary and artistic influence on masses of people" while "provid[ing] an artistic outlet for hundreds of New Negroes."[95] Martin emphasized that "No other publication of this time," neither the Urban League's soon-to-be-started *Opportunity*, nor the NAACP's *Crisis*, nor anything else, "came close to the *Negro World* for the sheer magnitude of its literary output," which "peaked" during the period beginning in 1920 (under Harrison's editorship).[96]

As Harrison assumed the editorship, his friends and supporters came more fully into the *Negro World*/UNIA orbit. The venerable journalist John E. Bruce ("Grit"), a former Garvey critic, became a regular columnist and later a contributing editor.[97] The poet Claude McKay described how he was encouraged by his friend Harrison to write articles for the paper.[98] By April 11, Harrison's friends Bruce, Arthur Schomburg, and Bob Douglas (coach of the Harlem Renaissance Five Basketball Team) would speak at Liberty Hall.[99] Joel A. Rogers, Hodge Kirnon, and Andy Razaf, three other Harrison friends, wrote for the *Negro World*. Harrison also encouraged the poet Lucian B. Watkins to submit his poems.[100]

Other writers similarly came forward under Harrison's editorship as the UNIA reached a high point of its radicalism. In Harrison's words, "no movement among American Negroes since slavery was abolished" had "ever attained the gigantic proportions" of the UNIA. It was Harrison who added the radical tone to the movement through the *Negro World*. With his brand of "news" for the race, his editorials, and the new features, the paper came to be viewed as a publication of the masses. On May 1 the *Negro World* went from six to ten pages an issue, and in June it reached a circulation of fifty thousand, sweeping the globe with its race-conscious message.[101] Though Garvey didn't say it, the growth was in large part thanks to Harrison's skillful editing and powerful writing.

In evaluating Harrison's role it is important to recognize the type of paper the *Negro World* became. Martin writes that it "published a truly massive amount of poems, stories and criticism weekly." Its editors—Harrison, Ferris, Bruce, Eric Walrond, Ted and Ulysses Poston, Fortune, and Garvey—"were the intellectual equals of any anywhere." Its "regular contributors," including Duse

Mohamad Ali, Schomburg, Carter G. Woodson, Rogers, and Lucian B. Watkins, "were every bit as impressive as the editors."[102]

The *Negro World*, under Harrison's editorship, seemed to solve the problem of financing that had beset so many previous publications, including *The Voice*. The old dispute in the Liberty League had included discussion over "white" or Black financing of *The Voice*. Harrison had opted for Black financing, but that was a difficult proposition considering the general impoverishment and low national literacy level of the Black masses at the time. Other radicals, such as Owen, Randolph, and Domingo, as well as Du Bois, opted for major "white" support for their efforts. Garvey, like Harrison, opted for Black support, but Garvey had additional (non-newspaper) means of financial support. Whereas it was difficult to finance a newspaper, Garvey found it not so difficult to entice support for his financial projects. He seemed to solve the problem of *Negro World*'s finances at first, at least in part, through financial projects such as the Black Star Line, Liberian Construction Fund, and other lesser efforts, which in total brought in hundreds of thousands of dollars. According to Harrison, however, during the period of his editorship, the paper not only paid for itself, but "the papers' money was being used to pay for Black Star Line work and things of that sort."[103]

The Harrison-reshaped *Negro World* was extremely well received. In July 1920 William H. Ferris wrote, "Nowhere in the history of Negro journalism has any paper attained a circulation which the Negro World has in 21 months." In particular, he described how in the past eleven months its circulation had jumped almost threefold from 17,000 to 50,000.[104] Similarly, a letter to the editor of the *Negro World* from J. S. Patterson of Vancouver, British Columbia, published in the June 26, 1920, issue said simply that "After reading your valuable paper for the past four or five months I must confess that in all the years that I have been reading news print I have never read a paper half as interesting as your paper." That four-to-five-month period coincided with Harrison's beginning months as principal editor.[105]

———

While Harrison was busy reshaping the *Negro World* and preparing for the Negro College, Garvey informed him on February 16, 1920, that he had selected him "to go to Liberia as chairman of a Commission" that would have "a delicate diplomatic mission connected with the world-wide work of the U.N.I.A." Liberia was central to all of Garvey's plans related to Africa, and the trip was a major Garvey concern. As soon as Garvey asked him to participate, Harrison, who was still not a U.S. citizen, "advised him [Garvey] . . . against spreading the news of his intent until he had completed all his arrangements." Nevertheless, around March 10 it was announced at Liberty Hall, and this caused Harrison to

comment in his diary that Garvey "blabs it." Though the details were not specified, Harrison observed "some people know of it in a vague and general way."[106]

By early March, the "special UNIA delegation," on Harrison's suggestion,
included the elder statesman and journalist John E. Bruce. Harrison mentioned
the trip to Bruce on March 6, and Bruce immediately "expressed a wish to go
as a member of the Commission." Harrison told him he thought he "could manage it," since Garvey "had not yet decided who the others should be." He advised
Bruce to write to Garvey, after which he would, "as head" of the commission,
pursue the matter. Harrison then waited for Bruce's letter until the following
Wednesday. Then, not having heard from Bruce, he mentioned the request to
Garvey "and described his [Bruce's] relations by correspondence and otherwise with the leading men of Liberia and other parts of West Africa." Garvey
"accepted the suggestion" and told Harrison to write Bruce to that effect. Ten
minutes later Harrison received Bruce's letter.[107]

After getting him approved, Harrison tried "to get Bruce up to dinner." He
apparently had not been adequately addressing issues at home, however, and
he noted in his diary that Lin's "termagant temper has put obstacles in the way."
On Saturday, March 13, after inviting Bruce "to dinner and a conference,"
Hubert "was forced by Madame's recalcitrance to phone him and cancel the
engagement." They finally met on March 16, but "the dinner had to be given at
Miss Julie Petersen's (670 Lenox Ave)." Julie Petersen was an extremely close
female friend of Hubert with whom his wife believed, perhaps accurately, that
he was having an affair. Julie Petersen took Harrison and Bruce in "at moment's
notice," and Hubert was "very grateful to her." But since four other young women
lived with Miss Petersen, and since Harrison was to preside at the author and
political activist Henry F. Downing's lecture on Liberia at Liberty Hall, he and
Bruce "had neither privacy nor time enough to get down to an interchange of
ideas." Hubert had already shown him notes, which he had drawn up for Garvey's perusal, "outlining the duties of the Commissioners, the principles which
should guide their conduct, the results for which they were to work, and presenting a schedule of expenses involved."[108]

Before their meeting on March 16 there "came a slight hitch." When Harrison phoned Bruce on the night of March 13 Bruce "began to express doubts
as to whether he could go." He said he had received a letter from the Sudanese-
Egyptian historian, journalist, editor, and publisher Duse Mohammed (Duse
Mohamed Ali), who was coming to America and was to be his guest. When
pressed for details, Bruce "could not give [Harrison] anything precise as to
Mohammed's trip," and Harrison "couldn't help thinking that since Bruce was
sharing Arthur Schomburg's house and Schomburg was as well known to
Mohammed as Bruce, that there was 'a nigger in the woodpile' somewhere."
When Harrison saw Bruce at Miss Petersen's, he "made it clear that 'expenses'

would be borne by the Association." "As a consequence," Bruce "ceased to waver," and on March 18 he sent Harrison "a letter asking, among other things, whether he would be paid for the time spent on the mission, since he was getting leave of absence 'without pay.'"[109]

To Harrison the whole series of events was evidence of "one of the besetting sins of the American Negro—especially the male: they lack straightforwardness; that spiritual quality whose cruder form is known as courage." In his diary he wrote, "Why couldn't Bruce have spoken up like a man and said that he was financially unable to stand the strain of going unless his expenses were paid?" He noted, that in contrast, he "didn't keep Garvey guessing as to *my* financial status: I set it forth." Nevertheless, he commented, "all's well that ends well, so far."[110]

Bruce wrote a March 5 letter of introduction for Harrison and the delegation to Charles D. B. King, the president of Liberia. He described Harrison as "a warm personal friend," the "duly accredited Chairman of a deputation visiting Liberia," and a representative of "the Universal Negro Improvement Association and African Communities League, and its subsidiary branches—the Black Star Line and Negro Factories Corporations." He explained that Harrison was coming to Africa at Garvey's direction:

> to confer with its leading public business men and prominent private citizens, for the purpose of strengthening the bonds of amity between the two English speaking branches of the Negro race, for closer business union, a stronger and more diversified commercial relations and a better understanding of the relations which ought . . . to exist between us, [since] though widely separated by distance[, we] have a common destiny.

Bruce emphasized that the delegates were "gentlemen of culture and refinement, character and ability" representing "3.000.000, of our race on this side of the Atlantic, the West Indies, Central and South America," who "sent them to the Mother Country to study the condition of its people and in cooperation with its men of light and leading to open wider the door of opportunity in Africa, commercially, industrially and intellectually for the sons of Africa throughout the world."[111]

Under the same date Bruce also wrote to Supreme Court Judge J. J. Dossen, of Monrovia. This letter was to introduce Harrison (whom Bruce claimed was replacing him as head of the delegation) and the other delegates. Harrison was described as "a brilliant, able, scholarly young gentleman" and "a warm personal friend" and the other delegates as "men of integrity and character and imbued with desire to render to Africa, such service as will make for its greater uplift, nationally, commercially, industrially and educationally."[112]

On April 15 Francis Wilcum Ellegor, who was ordained a priest in the Protestant Episcopal Church in Monrovia in 1910 and had taught at Liberia College before immigrating to the United States in 1916, wrote to Gabriel M. Johnson, the mayor of Monrovia and head of the UNIA division in that city. Using UNIA stationery, Ellegor, soon to become the UNIA's commissioner general, described "Dr." Harrison as an "['interesting'] friend" and possessor of "a fund of information on American and world affairs" who was coming to Liberia "with an open mind." He considered him "worthy of the confidence of the best minds of Liberia." The same day Ellegor also wrote a more general letter of introduction, which said that Harrison was traveling to Liberia "in the interest of the largest Negro Corporation in the World, the UNIA and ACL and its associate bodies the BSL and the NFC." Ellegor stressed that Harrison was "a journalist and public man of repute of long standing" and expressed "every confidence in his ability, not only to serve as chairman of the commission but the Negro race as a whole as one of its most able and intrepid exponents."[113]

As plans for the proposed Liberian trip continued, Harrison put out a call for improved relations with Africa and Africans in a talk before a reported six thousand people at a BSL meeting in the Manhattan Casino on May 1, 1920. He apologized for speaking on the BSL, since he had planned to speak on "The Call to Africa" but had to change his topic because of the "call of the audience." He said he stood before them "as a way-side representative of the African spirit to point out that the biggest thing in the entire organization is that response to the call of Africa." He discussed what the "call" meant to him and very significantly injected in his comments the concept of "Africans of the dispersion":

> For a very long time it ["The Call to Africa"] has meant a great deal. It has meant to me that we who are Africans of the dispersion, just like the Jews who were carried away into captivity and were asked to sing the songs of their country. "How can we sing the Lord's songs in a strange land?" they replied. And when we are told what Africa was, when we are told what Africa is today, it does not strike quite the responsive chord that it should.[114]

He then added that he had "been told that a certain lady was talking about me the other day, and was told by a friend of mine that I had gone away—well, diplomatically speaking, let me say downtown." The woman reportedly said, "Why, how can he go there?" "How can he eat raw meat and human flesh with those people down there?" And this, he pointed out, "was from a Negro lady!" She apparently "thought her own people were eaters of human flesh and that they could not do anything else." He used this point "to show how necessary it is that we get in proper touch with Africa and Africans—our own Africans." This statement was met with cheers. He suggested that the way to do this was

"By way of the convention": a "great convention of the Negroes of the world" meeting in Liberty Hall, "a hall owned by Negroes." Such a convention would "be different from anything that they have ever had," since "Negro delegates, Negro commissioners, [and] Negro representatives" would "put the problem of Negroes all over the world" to the fore and work to "bring the race together."[115]

Harrison contrasted such an assembly with the First Universal Races Congress at the University of London in 1911 organized by Gustav Spiller and others, where "White men drew black men, drew red men and yellow men together." Even "our own Professor Du Bois happened to be there," though "he never learned what for." Harrison explained that the purpose of the earlier convention was "because the white men of the world wanted to get colored men in council to study them, to learn what ached them, so that they could take proper steps by yielding so much to avoid a catastrophe, or by using the strong hand where they were sure the strong hand would go—to rivet the fetters of their own racial [domination?], and our great professor could not see it." In contrast, he stressed: "This will be our convention. It is a thing worthy of the soberest, the gravest, the deepest thought on our part." Thought, however, would not "solve any human problems"—to do that, "You have to dig down in your own jeans and throw up 'plunks' to make it go. We have got to raise $2,000,000 and more for that convention, and for the college to educate the New Negro free from the money to establish the headquarters of the Negroes of the world. We have got to make sure that our connections with our mother country—our motherland—will b[e] firm, stable and secure." Harrison closed by telling a cheering crowd that he was there "to get money" from them, to get them "to make the . . . sacrifice."[116]

By May 1920, difficulties with the proposed Liberian trip had fully surfaced. On May 24 Harrison wrote in his diary that "it does not now appear that the 'Commission' to Liberia will be allowed to materialize." He had "been knocking at the door of the State Department for the past two months, but no passports" were "forthcoming." He cited as the "reason" an issue of the *Negro World* in which was published "an insane collection of bombastic rantings as to what the 'Commission' would do in Liberia, delivered in Liberty Hall by pin-headed preachers and other ignorant howlers." All of this was done before Rev. Eason (the person chosen to fill the spot of Bruce, who, on his doctor's advice, had to give up his spot) and Harrison had obtained their passports. When Hudson C. Pryce, "the new (third) editor [of the *Negro World*] was correcting the proofs at the printers' and came across this senseless slobber he called up Mr. Garvey on the phone and pointed out to him that if the stuff went in his 'delegates' would hardly be able to get their passports." Garvey reportedly "replied that he had heard it all spoken and had read it in type and that, in his opinion, it was 'good propaganda' and should go in. So it went in."[117]

Harrison's suspicion was, in fact, correct. On May 7, 1920, Frank Burke, assistant director and chief of the BI wrote to Charles Brelsford Welsh, acting chief of the Passport Division of the Department of State, regarding Harrison and Eason, who, "for the past month, have been making every possible effort to leave this country for the purpose of making necessary arrangement with the Liberian Government in Africa, to establish headquarters of the 'UNIVERSAL NEGRO IMPROVEMENT ASSOCIATION.'" He added that they were "being sent to Africa, for this purpose by Marcus Garvey," who was considered "the cause of the greater portion of the negro agitation in this country." Burke emphasized that it was "the opinion of the Bureau that it would be simply furthering the operations of this organization [the UNIA] should these passports be granted," and he "requested" that they "be declined." He asked that "this information" be treated as "strictly confidential," since it "was obtained from a very confidential source."[118]

In the interim, as Harrison was "credibly informed," Sam Duncan, "who has two old scores to pay off and who is a mean dirty s.o.b. had written secretly to the State Dept. and set them on the trail just as he had previously done to the governors of the various British West Indian islands, resulting in the outlawing of the Negro World in those islands." Harrison was sure "there will be no passports for us," and he felt this was "mainly due to Marcus Garvey's prime defect, bombastic blabbing." Garvey, he felt, "talks too much and too foolishly."[119]

Harrison's observation that Garvey's "prime defect" was "bombastic blabbing" served as a lead-in for him to write "a general estimate of Mr. Garvey's character and abilities" in his diary of May 24, 1920. He began by recounting some of his history with Garvey. He described how, when the Liberty League was organized, "Garvey used to attend our meetings," and "at the same time he began to organize a branch of the Jamaica Improvement Association, which finally blossomed out into the U.N.I.A. and A.C.L." "Everything that I did he copied . . . yet I was generous enough to introduce him to my audiences in New York at the Bethel meeting on the night of May 12th [June 12], 1917 and also at my lecture-forum in Lafayette Hall, as also in Brooklyn later." Sometimes Harrison even closed his meetings in Lafayette Hall "earlier than usual" and asked his audience "to go down to give him a crowd." Yet "when Garvey had gone up in the world and the U.N.I.A. was 'going strong' never a reciprocal courtesy was forthcoming from him." Harrison, knowing full well that his work, "which had failed[,] had laid the foundation for his [Garvey's] success," refrained from burdening Garvey's movement with his presence. Edgar Grey claimed "that he again and again asked Garvey to call me in and utilize my abilities in counsel

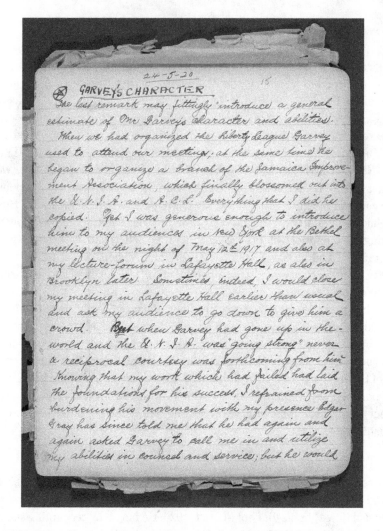

Figure 4.2. Hubert Harrison, "Garvey's Character," diary entry, May 24, 1920, first page. On May 24, 1920, Hubert Harrison offered a three-plus-page assessment of Marcus "Garvey's Character." In offering his "general estimate of Mr. Garvey's character and abilities" he began by recounting some of his history with Garvey. He described how, when the Liberty League was organized, "Garvey used to attend our meetings." "At the same time he began to organize a branch of the Jamaica Improvement Association, which finally blossomed out into the U.N.I.A. and A.C.L." "Everything that I did he copied," "yet I was generous enough to introduce him to my audiences in New York at the Bethel meeting on the night of May 12th [June 12], 1917 and also at my lecture-forum in Lafayette Hall, as also in Brooklyn later." Sometimes Harrison even closed his meetings in Lafayette Hall "earlier than usual" and asked his audience "to go down to give him a crowd." But "when Garvey had gone up in the world and the U.N.I.A. was going strong," "never a reciprocal courtesy was forthcoming from him." Harrison adds, "The first big defect, then, in Mr. Garvey's make-up is a defect in the size of his soul. He is spiritually as well as intellectually a little man. That is why he doesn't want around him men who are of larger girth either way. Or if he gets them he does not utilize them in any way which would aid, amplify, or modify his chaotic plans and notions. If he can use them as his hired bravos, then so far so good." *Source:* Hubert H. Harrison Papers, Box 9, Folder 1, Rare Book and Manuscript Library, Columbia University Library. See https://dlc.library.columbia.edu/catalog/cul:mpg4f4qt3x.

and service; but he would always refuse with the groundless excuse that 'Harrison has his own propaganda', and that he was 'dangerous." In his diary Harrison countered that "at that time I had no propaganda of any sort except 'Race First!" and that "[I] was devoting my time to purely educational lectures outdoors and indoors."[120]

Reviewing all this Harrison concluded: "The first big defect, then, in Mr. Garvey's make-up is a defect in the size of his soul. He is spiritually as well as intellectually a little man. That is why he doesn't want around him men who are of larger girth either way. Or if he gets them he does not utilize them in any way which would aid, amplify, or modify his chaotic plans and notions. If he can use them as his hired bravos, then so far, so good."[121] Elaborating further on this, Harrison, in his personal copy of Jerome Dowd's *The Negro Races*, underlined Dowd's comments on how in "primitive" societies the "king" is "the most gaudily dressed" and how "his subjects or inferiors seek in all possible ways to flatter him and magnify his greatness. They fawn at his feet and lavish upon him thousands of complimentary phrases and thousands of little attentions, with the hope of receiving some crumbs from his royal table, or of escaping some exaction." Harrison compared the first to "Garvey's imperial costume [of] Aug. 1920" and the second to "The Garvey retinue of sycophants."[122]

In his May 24 diary entry Harrison noted that "today, most Negroes in and out of the U.N.I.A. who are interested in its work assume that the men of abilities like Smith-Green, Ferris and myself who are with Mr. Garvey, are, somehow, permitted to lend the aid of their knowledge and abilities to the work in hand. But it isn't so at all." Ferris was "a mere pseudo-intellectual flunky with no more personality than a painted stick." Harrison was "only the editor of the Negro World" and was "in no way connected with either the U.N.I.A. the B.S.L. or the N.F.C. except as a dues-paying member of the first." Smith-Green, secretary of the BSL, "had to chafe against being over-reached, brow-beaten and superseded in his own department, and right now, Garvey is trying to make a scape-goat of him by a blanket-insinuation of malversation to cover up the snarled results of his own autocratic interference."[123]

Since January 1 there had "been but one meeting of the Board of Directors," that of last Monday, May 17, and Garvey, according to "Smith-Green, Johnson, [traffic and passenger agent] Cyril Henry, and others," had "paid money on ships, published the news of the new acquisitions and *then* called the board to inform them that *he had done* this." Garvey's "ignorance of ships and shipping matters" had "resulted in his paying out tens of thousands of dollars unnecessarily and he has been victimized again and again by the white men from whom ships and ships' accessories were bought." According to Harrison, "In the midst of all this he lies to the people magniloquently, bragging about impossible things while not owning the ships outright." The *Yarmouth* was "lying at her pier" at

Figure 4.3. Marcus Garvey at Liberty Hall c. 1922. In this photo a sitting Marcus Garvey is wearing what Hubert Harrison elsewhere described as his "imperial costume." Elaborating further on this, Harrison, in his personal copy of Jerome Dowd, *The Negro Races*, underlined Dowd's comments on how in "primitive" societies the "king" is "the most gaudily dressed" and how "his subjects or inferiors seek in all possible ways to flatter him and magnify his greatness. They fawn at his feet and lavish upon him thousands of complimentary phrases and thousands of little attentions, with the hope of receiving some crumbs from his royal table, or of escaping some exaction." Harrison compared the first to "Garvey's imperial costume [of] Aug. 1920," and he compared the second to "the Garvey retinue of sycophants." *Source:* James Van Der Zee, photographer, © Donna Mussenden Van Der Zee.

a cost, Harrison was told, "of $150 a day while her black captain has been relieved of his command—although still in the company's service—and a white captain has been assigned to command her."[124]

Harrison's May 24, 1920, commentary on Garvey was revealing, and it accurately suggested many future problem areas for Garvey, the UNIA, and the BSL—particularly in terms of his character traits and approach to business. Harrison would have much more to say later. His comments make clear that his differences with Garvey were not petty and personal—they concerned matters of profound importance. For the moment, however, Harrison was still preoccupied with developing the *Negro World* as the world's premier "Negro" race-conscious publication.

5

Debate with *The Emancipator*
(March–April 1920)

In his diary discussion of the "New Methods" and "Changes" that he brought to the Negro World Harrison mentioned "writing 'The Crab-Barrel' series which began on April 3, 1920." That series was part of a larger debate with the socialist-leaning editors of a new weekly, *The Emancipator.* In that debate Harrison maintained he defended "not Mr. Garvey personally, but the principles of the New Negro Manhood Movement, a portion of which had been incorporated by him and his followers of the U.N.I.A. and A.C.L."[1]

The debate was at times personal and seemed, at least temporarily, to silence criticism from some major Garvey opponents. It may also have had a role in the rightward political shift of Chandler Owen, who, over the next few years, and after physical threats against him from Garvey and disillusionment with the socialist-led garment workers' unions for not granting membership to his brother, would abandon socialism and move toward the Republicans (from whence, according to Harrison, he came). In addition, the debate offers comments of interest from the activists Randolph, Owen, Domingo, and Harrison.[2]

The short-lived *Emancipator*, "A Paper with Principle and Purpose," first appeared with an issue dated March 13 and last appeared in an issue dated April 24, 1920. It was published by the New Negro Publishing Co., Inc., headed by its president, Thomas A. E. Potter, a seventeen-year Socialist Party member, along with Domingo, who served as treasurer, and Frank R. Crosswaith, who served as secretary. *The Emancipator's* articles came from Black radicals in or near the Socialist Party, including its editor and former Liberty Leaguer Domingo and from the activists Owen, Randolph, Cyril Briggs, Richard B.

Moore, Anselmo Jackson, and Crosswaith. Of that group Owen and Randolph were U.S.-born; Domingo was from Jamaica, Moore from Barbados, Briggs born in Nevis and educated in St. Kitts, and Jackson and Crosswaith from the Virgin Islands. In the editorial, "Our Reason for Being," the editors explained that the paper was the outgrowth of a merger of two monthlies, *The Crusader* (of Briggs) and *The Messenger* (of Randolph and Owen), and that it would work for industrial unionism, cooperation, social democracy, and a more complete emancipation than that achieved fifty-five years earlier.[3]

In fact, much of the paper's reason for being was to challenge the Garvey movement, and that campaign began in full force with an investigation of Garvey and the BSL in its March 27 issue. As that issue was likely out several days before its publication date, it appears that Garvey's response was swift and familiar. On March 25, Gerald Rosenheim, attorney for the BSL, filed a suit for $200,000 in damages in the New York County Supreme Court against the New Negro Publishing Co. and for another $200,000 against "William" A. Domingo.[4]

The Emancipator's editors, it should be noted, were not of one mind, particularly on the subject of "Class First" versus "Race First." Harrison considered Owen and Randolph to be "Class First" socialists.[5] Cyril Briggs, who edited *The Crusader*, expressed strong sympathies for the "Race First" position. In the March 1920 *Crusader* he published an editorial entitled "Race First!" which cited examples of how "whites" put race first and expressed the hope that those examples were "sufficient to convince the asses who would have the Negro give loyalty first to any country, while white men who derive the greatest benefits and protection from those countries give their first loyalty, not to the country, but to their race." *The Crusader* would offer a similar "race first" appeal again in June,[6] after a Harrison article entitled "An Open Letter to the Socialist Party of New York City" that appeared in the May 8, 1920, *Negro World* mentioned Briggs by name. Briggs then advised ABB members and other "Negroes" to "Adopt the policy of race first, without, however, ignoring useful alliances with other groups" and to "help propagate the 'race first idea.'" He had earlier emphasized his allegiance to the doctrine of "NEGRO FIRST, LAST, AND ALL THE TIME!" Robert A. Hill observes that "Briggs found no difficulty" preaching race first while simultaneously considering himself a "Bolshevist!!!"[7]

Before the appearance of *The Emancipator*, Briggs had started a campaign against Garvey. On March 8, 1920, on *Crusader* stationery, he wrote to the registrar of British shipping in Nova Scotia seeking information on the ownership of the *Yarmouth*. The response said the *Yarmouth* was owned by the North American Shipping Corporation (not by the Black Star Line). The date stamped on the letter by the Canadian authorities was March 15; the letter was promptly reprinted in *The Emancipator* of March 27.[8]

The Emancipator's first issue of March 13 contained a cautionary article entitled "An Era of 'Wild-Cat' Business Promotions," which described how "the Negro race" was "passing through a period of feverish, wild-cat business promotions," largely the result of the war and the "new get-together spirit permeating the race." Wartime jobs in shipyards, ammunition plants, and other lucrative, though dangerous, occupations had provided "opportunities to accumulate, what were to them small fortunes," and this new wealth was widely distributed. In addition, "increased racial consciousness, intensified by oppression and fostered by increasing propaganda, created in the masses a desire for more tangible evidence of solidarity and progress." In this setting, conditions were favorable for launching all kinds of business enterprises, and "stock companies ranging from a modest capitalization of $5000 to hundreds of thousands of dollars were organized." These mushrooming businesses met with varied success—a few did well, but the majority, directed by "dreamers who would substitute emotion for knowledge and foolhardiness for prudence," were "doomed to failure" and would "injure the race."[9]

The second (March 20) issue of *The Emancipator* included discussion of the DOJ report on radicalism among "Negroes," an editorial on "Labor Unions and the Negro" that supported organized labor, and another editorial entitled "Bubbles," which discussed "Negro" get-rich-quick schemes that turned out to be "bubbles." In an obvious reference to Garvey, the "Bubbles" editorial stated that "in this age of . . . widespread education and great world changes, there is no place for the blower of bubbles, and the Negro race should profit from past experience and avoid a South Sea Bubble or another Chief Sam Movement." (Chief Alfred Sam's career in the United States in 1913–1914, complete with African repatriation schemes and stock sales, in some ways foreshadowed Garvey's.)[10]

The second issue also featured a piece on "Our News Policy," an apparent reference to the "West Indian News Notes" section of the *Negro World* started by Harrison. The piece explained that *The Emancipator* did not aim to insult West Indians by keeping them off the first page or by placing them in a separate section. It emphasized that it would not boost any individual and would contain no nationalistic propaganda. In addition, the March 20 issue also included Frank Crosswaith's "Declare Yourself"; a letter dubbed "The Weekly Message of the Satanic Majesty, Potentate," by "Mephistophense, Potentate"; and a letter from William Bridges, editor of *The Challenge*, to Domingo, which advised not only to oppose the "white" aristocrat but also "The Black one," who was "equally a menace to the continued progress of our Race."[11] The March 27 issue contained a satirical poem, "The Potentate Flounders in the Deep of Diplomacy: Empire Building in Harlem," by "Incog."[12]

Most importantly, the March 27 *Emancipator* carried the first installment of Anselmo Jackson's "An Analysis of the Black Star Line." Jackson described how Garvey arrived in New York from Jamaica, "circularized the Negro Section of Harlem to the effect that 'Professor' Garvey, 'The World-Famed Orator' would make his first public appearance in New York City at St. Mark's Hall, 55 West 138th Street," and at a talk (on May 9, 1916) "completely lost his nerve," "was obviously self-conscious," and suffered an "attack of stage fright" so serious that "he fell off the stage, much to the amazement of the audience."[13]

Jackson explained that Garvey then left New York to tour the country, "seeking funds for a proposed Tuskegee Institute in Jamaica." When he returned,

> outdoors and indoors, Hubert Harrison was preaching an advanced type of radicalism with a view to impressing race consciousness and effecting racial solidarity among Negroes. . . . The . . . atmosphere was charged with Harrison's propaganda; . . . .
>
> Garvey publicly eulogized Harrison, joined the Liberty League and took a keen interest in its affairs. . . . Harrison was the forerunner of Garvey and contributed largely to the success of the latter by preparing the minds of Negroes through his lectures, thereby molding and developing a new temper among Negroes which undoubtedly made the task of the Jamaican much easier than it otherwise would have been.

To Jackson, however, "Harrison blundered fatally," and his "errors were so evident" and "costly" that "interest in the Liberty League waned and Harrison's deserters soon became enthusiastic admirers of Garvey" and "joined the New York branch of the Universal Negro Improvement Association and African Communities League which Garvey, in the meantime had formed." Jackson concluded: "The success of Garvey was built on the ruins of Harrison's failure."[14]

———

It was around the time of the Jackson article, and in the wake of *The Emancipator*'s previous criticism of the "West Indian News Notes" column, that Harrison's "Race First Versus Class First" appeared in the *Negro World* of March 27. In that pointed article he argued that the Socialist Party had "secretly subsidized, both a magazine [presumably the *Messenger*] and a newspaper [presumably *The Emancipator*] to attempt to cut into the splendid solidarity which Negroes are achieving in response to the call of racial necessity." He warned of a betrayal of race interest into "alien hands" by the "'radical' young Negroes" along the line of the betrayal of the "old crowd."[15]

Harrison began, "In the old days white people derived their knowledge of what Negroes were doing from those Negroes who were nearest to them, largely their own selected exponents of Negro activity or of their white point of view."

Now, as they became "vaguely, but disquietingly, aware that Negroes are awake," they still retained their "traditional method of interpreting the mass by the Negro nearest to themselves in affiliation or contact." For that reason, the Socialist Party persisted "in thinking that the unrest . . . in the Negro masses" was "due to their propaganda which its paid adherents support" and that it would "function largely along the lines of Socialist political thought."[16]

The "essence" of this betrayal, argued Harrison, was "in making the racial requirements play second fiddle to the requirements dictated as best for it by other groups with other interests to serve." He then cited some examples from past SP history. He explained that "when the Socialist Party of America was respectable," and never drew lines of racial separation in the North, it still "permitted those lines to be drawn in the South." It thus offered "no word of official condemnation for the Socialists of Tennessee who prevented Theresa Malkiel in 1912 from lecturing to Negroes on Socialism either in the same hall with them or in meetings of their own." That same year key party leaders "wanted the votes of the white South" and "were willing to betray by silence the principles of inter-racial solidarity which they espoused on paper." This was done when the SP's national office "refused to route [presidential candidate] Eugene V. Debs in the South because the Grand Old Man let it be known that he would not remain silent on the race question while in the South."[17]

Now, since the party had "shrunk considerably in popular support and sentiment," they were "willing to take up our cause." While Harrison was willing to "thank honest white people everywhere who take up our cause," he wanted them to know

that we have already taken it up ourselves. While they were refusing to diagnose our case we diagnosed it ourselves, and, now that we have prescribed the remedy—Race Solidarity—they came to us with their prescription—Class Solidarity. It is too late, gentlemen! This racial alignment is all our own product, and we have no desire to turn it over to you at this late day, when we are beginning to reap its benefits. And if you are simple enough to believe that those among us who serve your interests ahead of ours have any monopoly of intellect or information along the lines of modern learning, then you are the greater gulls indeed.

Harrison made clear that he was not opposed to socialism, just to practices of the Socialist Party of America. "We can respect the Socialists of Scandinavia, France, Germany or England on their record," but "your record so far does not entitle you to the respect of those who can see all around a subject." He stressed: "We say Race First, because you have all along insisted on Race First and class after when you didn't need our help."[18]

Harrison then posed a challenge. He reproduced a quote (without identifying its source) that had been adopted at a recent National Convention of the Socialist Party by one of its national committees and asked the socialists "to explain it." He suggested that if they were "unable to do so," they should set their "lackeys to work" so that they "may be able to do it in terms of their own 'radical scientific' surface slush." The unidentified quote was from the "Majority Report on Immigration" of the 1912 Socialist Party National Convention. Its signers were Ernest Untermann and J. Stit Wilson representing the West and Joshua Wanhope (editor of the *Call*) and Robert Hunter representing the East. The quote that Harrison reprinted read:

Race feeling is not so much a result of social as of biological evolution. It does not change essentially with changes of economic systems. It is deeper than any class feeling and will outlast the capitalist system. It persists even after race prejudice has been outgrown. It exists not because the capitalists nurse it for economic reasons, but the capitalists rather have an opportunity to nurse it for economic reasons because it exists [as] a product of biology. It is bound to play a role in the economics of the future society. If it should not assert itself in open warfare under a Socialist form of society, it will nevertheless lead to a rivalry of races for expansion over the globe as a result of the play of natural and sexual selection. We may temper this race feeling by education, but we can never hope to extinguish it altogether. Class-consciousness must be learned, but race consciousness is inborn and cannot be wholly unlearned. A few individuals may indulge in the luxury of ignoring race and posing as utterly raceless humanitarians, but whole races never.

Where races struggle for the means of life, racial animosities cannot be avoided. When working people struggle for jobs, self-preservation enforces its decrees. Economic and political considerations lead to racial fights and to legislation restricting the invasion of the white man's domain by other races.[19]

While in the SP, Harrison had argued that racism-is-innate arguments (such as the statement "race consciousness is inborn and cannot be wholly unlearned") were at the core of all racist arguments, and he opposed them. With that background, he thought it important "that the New Negro should know this" quoted SP position, since it justified giving Socialists a taste of their "own medicine." Harrison noted that he was "also a Socialist," but he refused, "in this crisis of the world's history to put either Socialism or your party above the call of his race." He did this "on the very grounds" that the party gave (and had not repudiated) "in the document quoted" and because he was "not a fool."[20]

———

The Emancipator of April 3 contained a host of articles focusing on Garvey. These included: (1) *"Emancipator* Dares Leader to Publish Sworn Statement," which emphasized that in its first two issues *The Emancipator* had gone easy on Garvey; (2) "Garvey Sues *Emancipator*"; and (3) "$500 Reward," which offered that amount to anyone who could prove that on March 15, 1920, the SS *Yarmouth* was owned by Garvey or the BSL and not by the North American Steamship Corporation. In addition, in part 2 of his exposé on the BSL, Anselmo Jackson explained that Garvey's movement had attracted not only people of "unimpeachable integrity" but also "professional politicians and all kinds of unprincipled opportunists in quest of easy berths and financially advantageous positions." This latter category "unintentionally" gave Garvey "a pretext for becoming despotic" because "his arbitrary attitude" could be "excused as being absolutely essential to protect the association from members with selfish and sinister purposes."[21]

Harrison was targeted in an article with no byline entitled *"Emancipator* Dares Leader to Publish Sworn Statements." The article stated that *The Emancipator* editor "is not an ungrateful renegade" and that "35 pieces of green paper a week cannot buy his soul as they apparently have bought the soul of others who privately refer to the very black people whose sweat and labor buys the food they eat, the Derby they wear and the present good condition of their sight, as 'a choice collection of contemptible hogs.'" The thirty-five pieces of green paper referred to a salary of $35 per week that *The Emancipator* apparently believed Harrison was receiving from the *Negro World*, the derby to the fact that by 1919 Harrison had started to wear that style hat, and the sight to the fact that he had started to wear glasses.[22]

Another article with no byline in the April 3 *Emancipator*, entitled "Before and After," also targeted Harrison (and quoted from his October 1919 *New Negro* article "Two Negro Radicalisms"). *The Emancipator* commented that Harrison "used to sell the magazine [*New Negro*] from stepladders on street corners in Harlem" but was "now employed by Mr. Garvey as editor of the *Negro World*." It added that the *Negro World*, in its last issue (March 27, 1920), contained "an editorial signed H.H." (the editorial was probably entitled "The Negro's Own Radicalism"), which (as noted in chapter 3) quoted from Harrison's 1919 "Two Negro Radicalisms" article. *The Emancipator*, then, perhaps in an effort to sow some dissension between Harrison and Garvey, quoted the following Harrison passage, which was in the original 1919 *New Negro* article (but would be elided in the August 1920 publication of "The Negro's Own Radicalism" in *When Africa Awakes*):

One of the most taking enterprises at present is the Black Star Line, a steamship enterprise being floated by Mr. Marcus Garvey of New York. Garvey's project (whatever may be its ultimate fate) has attracted tens of thousands of Negroes. Where Negro "radicals" of the type known to white radicals can scarce get a handful of people, Garvey fills the largest halls and the Negro people rain money on him. This is not to be explained by the argument of "superior brains" for this man's education and intelligence are markedly inferior to those of the brilliant "radicals" whose "internationalism" is drawn from other than radical sources. But this man holds up to the Negro masses those things which bloom in their hearts—racialism, race-consciousness, racial solidarity—things taught first in 1917 by *The Voice* and The Liberty League. That is the secret to his success, so far.[23]

The April 3 *Emancipator* editorial entitled "Opinion of [Chandler] Owen & [A. Philip] Randolph Editors of the *Messenger*" explained that *The Emancipator* had recently been presenting facts concerning different business enterprises in New York "calmly and dispassionately," and "the reply by some of those enterprises was a suit for $200,000, tearing up signs of the publication announcing the exposure, destroying the papers themselves . . . and making personal attacks upon Socialism—the political philosophy of *The Emancipator*." The $200,000 suit was a reference to the March 25, 1920, suit brought by the BSL against the New Negro Publishing Co., owner of *The Emancipator*. In regard to the legal suits, *The Emancipator* replied, "let them come," so that they could "present the facts in court where demagogy and emotion will be curbed." It suggested that "offended parties sue for two million or two billion dollars instead of a piker's $200,000!" since the chances are about as good for one as the other, and it would "not stop for a moment a thing in the New Negro's program." Regarding the tearing up of signs and paper, it deemed it "a very suspicious course of action," since one "cannot answer argument by tearing up the paper through which you are exposed" but rather by "logic and facts." As far as the attacks on socialism, "no answer" was "necessary because of the weakness and superficiality of the arguments presented."[24]

Owen and Randolph then addressed the "editor [Harrison] of the *Negro World*, who signs his name 'H.H.'" and whose article in the previous week's issue "was too shoddy in logic, too fragile in facts, and too forceless in presentation to be entitled to a decorous answer." They suggested that "'H.H.' will have to do better before we can give him any serious consideration," since, "as the old adage goes, He looked like a Man, but was nothing but a dog." They concluded, "Who is 'H.H.' anyhow? Does H.H. stand for Ha, ha? And does this mean that the 'ha, ha' editor who signs his name thus is a joke?"[25]

In "Race First Versus Class First," the April 3 *Emancipator* argued that "the paramount question confronting the Negro race is whether race or class should be first." *The Emancipator* editors argued "Race first" was "justifiable biologically" as a "defensive" measure but was not justifiable "economically." The question was so important that "supporters of race first" (a reference to Harrison) had to "buttress their argument" with "liberal quotations from their own writings." They then wrote, in a thinly veiled barb at Harrison and his personal life:

> To answer so momentous a question by an offhand "yes" or "no" is to put one's self in the position of the man who is asked to answer yes or no as to whether he had stopped mistreating his family and imposing upon the generosity of white radicals. Such a question would be more difficult than if some individuals who are today condemning the Socialist Party were asked to explain scientifically the nature of the magnetism that inheres in 35 pieces of green paper.

The *Emancipator* editors explained that they recognized "the value and limitation of the race first doctrine," since "in a condition of conflict, whether racial or otherwise, the weakest group only weakens itself by racial disunity." They argued: "Race first is forced upon oppressed peoples as a weapon of defense." Since the prejudice exerted against a group made "no discrimination between the members of the group," and since the "Negro landlord" was "as much discriminated against in public places as is the Negro tenant," it was important "in fighting that discrimination" that "all Negroes must unite, must 'close ranks.'"[26]

To *The Emancipator* the real question was what constituted "the best strategy" to provide "the solution of the Negro problem." Though "all Negroes" were agreed "that Africa should be free, that racial discrimination should cease, [and] that their race should be economically free," there were "honest differences of opinion" as to how this could best be achieved. The editors felt that "race first" as a doctrine had "validity only where it is possible of success," that it needed "strength to make it effective," and that those people without weapons had to "fight according to the rules laid down by fully armed men" and "should not challenge them." "Race first" reached "its limit" when it touched "upon individual interests." Thus, while "the Negro landlord and tenant" could "unite as to the necessity of fighting discrimination in places of public accommodation," it was also true that the "black tenant" would "unite with white tenants to fight their landlord" and that "black landlords" would "support white landlords who go to Albany to see that rents are not reduced." At these points, "the race interests of Negroes and Caucasians" became "confused" and class interests appeared. Since class interests related "to the sustenance of life," they could not "be ignored!"[27]

Then, in a final dig at Harrison, who was not mentioned by name, the editors wrote, "If some whose economic necessities logically place them in a certain class sacrifice their class loyalty" for that "of race," then "they deserve to be condemned, but in condemning them we must not turn a mental somersault and advocate the very things of which they are guilty!"[28]

The Emancipator concluded, "Race first is, therefore, justifiable for defensive purposes only, while class first is essential to the rendering of race first unnecessary." If "economic and political considerations" led "to racial fights and to legislation restricting the invasion of the white man's domain by other races, then the only sensible thing for a weak people . . . to do" was "to fight as a race to save themselves from extinction while assisting groups inside the ranks of their oppressors which are striving to abolish the same 'economic and political considerations.'" This "sound strategy of military warfare," of "dividing of the 'enemy' while maintaining your own ranks intact," was used by "the Jews in Russia" and "should" be used by "the Negro masses of the world." But, added the editors, "in the present crisis in world history," when "plans for a League of Nations to enslave the darker races" were being discussed, it was "crass folly" for any one "to do anything" that would "break down class lines among the whites by sending out challenges on behalf of the black race."[29]

On April 3, Harrison's "Just Crabs" appeared in the *Negro World*. He later described it as "a delightful inspiration in the course of defending, not Mr. Garvey personally, but the principles of the New Negro Manhood Movement, a portion of which had been incorporated by him and his followers of the U.N.I.A. and A.C.L." The piece was "the opening gun of the defense, of which some other salvos were given in the serial satire of The Crab Barrel," and it "gave rise to related editorials." "Just Crabs" was an apparent barb directed at the *Emancipator* group of "Negro" socialists, whom it referred to as "The Subsidized Sixth," in seeming allusions to W. E. B. Du Bois's "Talented Tenth" concept, to the socialist editors of *The Emancipator*, and to their financial backing from the Socialist Party and other sources. Harrison described the series of prose and poetry as the "Crab and Just So" stories, likely alluding to both Booker T. Washington's homespun "Crab" stories and Rudyard Kipling's *Just So Stories for Little Children* (1902).[30]

Harrison's "Just Crabs" told of "a Greedy Person" who "went rummaging along the lagoon with a basket and a stick in quest of Crabs, which he needed for the Home Market." The crabs were "Land Crabs," which were "more luscious than Sea Crabs, being more primitive and more full of meat." The "greedy person" did this several times and dumped all the crabs into a huge barrel with no cover, but he "was not at all worried about his Crabs" because he knew "Crab Nature." Just "as soon as any one Crab began to climb up on the side of the barrel to work his way toward the top the other Crabs would reach up, grab him by the legs, and down he would come, kerplunk! 'If we can't get up, you shan't get up, either. We'll pull you down.'" The crabs added, "you should wait until the barrel bursts" because "there are Kind Friends on the Outside who will burst the barrel if we only wait, and then, when the Great Day dawns, we will all be Emancipated and there'll be no need for Climbing."[31]

Harrison explained how in "the Beginning," the "Greedy Person could always get as many Crabs as he needed for the Home Market, because they all depended on him for their food." While this happened, "all the creatures stood around and laughed," and "this was funny in the Beginning of Things" because "all the creatures said that the Reason for this kink in Crab Nature was that when the Creator was giving out heads he didn't have enough to go around, so the poor Crabs didn't get any." The "Greedy Person thanked the lucky stars that Crabs had been made in that Peculiar way, since it made it unnecessary to put a cover on his barrel or to waste his precious time a-watching of them."[32]

This was "the first" of Harrison's "Just-So Stories—with," he noted, "no apologies to Rudyard Kipling or any one else," since "at this time the Crabs are at work in Harlem, and there is a tremendous clashing of the claws as the 'Pull 'Em Down' program goes forward." That old program didn't seem to get any-one anywhere, and a "new day" had "dawned for the Negroes of Harlem," a "day of business accomplishment" in which people were "going into business, saving their money and collectively putting it into enterprises" that would "mean roofs over their heads and an economic future for themselves and their little ones."[33]

"But," added Harrison, "the Subsidized Sixth" were sure that this was "all wrong and that we have no right to move an inch until the Socialist millennium dawns, when we will all get 'out of the barrel' together." It had apparently not "occurred to them that making an imperfect heaven now does not unfit any one for enjoying the perfect paradise which they promise us—if it ever comes." It was true, however, "that 'the power over a man's subsistence is the power over his will'—and over his 'scientific radicalism,' too." Harrison remembered having stated this as "'Show me whose bread you eat, and I'll tell you whose songs you'll sing.'" He emphasized: "This applies to radicals overnight as well as to ordinary folk." These last comments were presumably directed at Randolph and Owen. Harrison added, "'White Men's Niggers' is a phrase that need not be restricted to old-line politicians and editors."[34]

Then, in a pointed reference to *The Emancipator*'s absence of bylines in key articles, Harrison commented that though "criticism pungent and insistent is due to every man in public life and to every movement which bids for public support," it was "the cowardly insinuator who from the safe shelter of name-less charges launches his poisoned arrows at other people's reputation." He deemed such a person to be "a contemptible character to have on any side of any movement" and added that "generally" such a person is "a liar who fears that he will be called to account for his lies if he should venture to name his foes." He argued that no person "with the truth to tell indulges in this pastime." He urged: "Let us, by all means, have lean, hard-hitting criticism," and, in "the name of common sense and common decency, quit being Just Crabs."[35]

On April 3 Harrison's *Negro World* editorial, "The Lion and the Lamb," signed "H.H.," began by stating that "We have always understood that the *Messenger*," which called itself "the only Negro magazine of scientific radicalism in the world," was "engaged in a fight to the finish with the N.A.A.C.P. and all that it stands for." This understanding was based, in part, on words expressed by the *Messenger*, for example, when it observed that "A man will not oppose his bene-factor" and that "The old crowd of Negro leaders has been and is subsidized by the old crowd of white Americans—a group which viciously opposes every demand made by organized labor for an opportunity to live a better life." It was also based on their words that "there is no organization of national prominence which ostensibly is working in the interest of the Negro which is not dominated by the old crowd of white people"—because "they receive their funds—their revenue—from it."[36]

Harrison added that to the editors of the *Messenger* it was "a matter of com-mon knowledge that Du Bois does not determine the policy of the National Association for the Advancement of Colored People; nor does [Eugene] Kinckle Jones or George E. Haynes control the National Urban League." These organizations were "not responsible to Negroes because Negroes do not maintain them." *The Crisis*, in fact, had "reached its crisis" and "no lon-ger" represented "the opinion of the millions of Negroes of the United States who are insisting upon justice without compensation or apology"—it did "not voice their sentiments any more than the *Tuskegee Student*." *The Messenger* had also claimed that *The Crisis*'s editor, Du Bois, "lacks" "intelligence" and "courage" and was "undoubtedly controlled by the capitalist board of the National Association for the Advancement of Colored People." Thus, to them, the "problem of the *Crisis*" was "the problem of intelligence, courage and control"—it was "the crisis of the *Crisis*." They reasoned that "the sooner its influence wanes among Negroes, the sooner they will have begun to pass their crisis."[37]

Given that background, and since *The Messenger* emphasized that "the chief problem of the American Negro today is the ridding himself of misleadership of all kinds, and especially the so-called organs of public opinion," Harrison found it "bewildering" to read that it now proposed "a radical convention" for Washington, DC, in May 1920, in which it would "co-operate or work hand in glove with the N.A.A.C.P." He rhetorically asked: has "the nature of the orga-nization [the NAACP] changed so much in the meantime, or has the *Messenger* changed?" Harrison sarcastically hoped "that the six Socialists who are staging this grand transformation scene will not swallow the dear N.A.A.C.P.," and he hoped "that 'the capitalist board of the N.A.A.C.P.,' which 'will not permit the editor of the *Crisis* [Du Bois] to lead Negroes in their own interests,' will not swallow our Bolshevist Bonapartes." Either event would be "a calamity of large dimensions." He warned, "'Beware of the Greeks, especially when they bring gifts.'" Harrison also wondered what the NAACP would say "to this offer of the olive branch" so "adroitly tendered." He admitted he was tickled "to see the lion and the lamb making friendly passes at each other," though he couldn't "help wondering (since we do understand the Socialist philosophy) whether there isn't an economic advantage basis, past, present, or expected [to] this latest moral transformation."[38]

———

In the April 3 "Poetry for the People" section of the *Negro World* Harrison began some verses, which continued on April 10 and 17. His preface explained that as far as he knew "the poetic literature of the Negro has not been enriched by satire—except by those who wrote in Arabic, a language with which we of the Western world are not sufficiently acquainted." This fact seemed odd considering "the many striking opportunities which their situation affords for the use of the intellectual instrument." He then offered a screed from "one who is not a poet."[39]

The "subject of the satire" was "a group of persons within the confines of the Negro race, whose activities seem[ed] . . . to merit some form of castigation." Harrison endeavored "to restrict" his "blows" to "those features of these persons" that had "some bearing on their public sins." He explained that "the device of separate items, incidents and parts has been deliberately resorted to, partly because of the exigencies of publication in a weekly newspaper and partly because it allows a greater amount of variation in the verse-forms." He did not "indulge more freely in classical allusions and the ampler forms of verse, which he would have preferred." The reason, he explained, was that "the satire is written mainly for the man in the street, and must therefore be swift in movement, and terse and direct in manner" because "if it gets to him, and hits the bullseye of his understanding, its aim will have been achieved."[40]

After explaining that "The Crab Barrel" series was "Dedicated to the Little Tin Gods of the Fool's Paradise," Harrison offered a lengthy poem with the following opening lines:

> When envy from the realm of Night
> Came forth with her attendant Spite,
> Armed mischief marshalled her array,

> And formed her red ranks for the fray
> Against Achievement's fearless son
> Whose strong arm had already won
> Success from the hand of Fate,
> A Shining target for their hate.
> Envy looked, dubious, on the scene,
> Scanning the space that lay between
> Th' opposing forces. Far and nigh
> She glanced; then kindled her wild eye
> With baleful fire.

The poem had numerous barbs (including ones directed at Owen, Domingo, and Randolph), which he thought would be picked up on by those they were aimed at as well as by others.[41]

———

The Emancipator of April 10, again apparently trying to sow dissent between Garvey and Harrison and to challenge Harrison, featured the article "'H.H.' Challenged." That piece, "in the interest of the workers of the Negro race," challenged "the editor of the *Negro World* who signs his articles with the initials H.H." to enlighten his readers as to "his true and sincere opinion" of "(1) Mr. Marcus Garvey (his character, intellect, knowledge, integrity and other qualifications for leadership) (2) the Black Star Line (as an investment proposition) and (3) the feasibility of the program of the U.N.I.A. and A.C.L. as outlined by Mr. Garvey in his weekly 'messages' and similar outpourings." The article asked "H.H." to "base his opinion upon his knowledge of economics, history, commerce and geography, entirely eliminating the factor of emotion." It added that the "failure to render such an opinion" would be "regarded as proof of the doctrine quoted by H.H. that 'he who pays the piper (editor) calls the tune' (editorial) and that H.H. is an intellectual harlot." Interestingly, this article and these questions may have been based on Harrison's discussion(s) with one or more members or contacts of the *Emancipator* staff, since they address serious concerns he had noted previously in his diary assessment of Garvey on March 17–18, 1920 (and concerns he would also subsequently address on "Garvey's Character" in his diary of on May 24, 1920).[42]

Another article in that April 10 issue of *The Emancipator*, by Cyril Briggs, commented that "the President of the Black Star Line [Garvey] and his satellites" had "seen fit to meet facts with vituperation and abuse." Such a course was dictated "by the advantage which Truth ever holds over Error an advantage none the less overwhelming because of the frantic efforts of prostituted literati [a probable reference to Harrison] to defend their newly won and so-soon endangered meal ticket."[43]

––––––––––

In the *Negro World* of April 10 appeared a piece signed "H.H." that was a direct, and at times very personal, attack on Chandler Owen entitled "'Just Suppose' a Riddle for 'Scientific Radical' Liars, with Apologies to C. OW" (Chandler Owen). The article began: "Just suppose that by long and judicious lying you had kidded yourself and other fools into the belief that you were the only Pebble on the Beach; that you were the only person in the race who knew anything of sociology, economics and history, and that on the strength of that you had blown yourself up a nice, new baby's bladder of conceit." Then, "if Another Fellow had come along [Harrison] who by thirty years of reading and study had amassed much more knowledge than you—and everybody knew it—you would be careful never to mention his name in your sheet, wouldn't you?"[44]

Further, if he was "in possession of facts which would show up some of your lies, wouldn't you just hate him?" He added:

Just suppose you had met him last summer in Norfolk and had bragged to him of how all the big white labor unions and Socialist locals had bought up big slices of your magazine stock, and you had mentioned the names of people in Washington and elsewhere (which same can be produced on demand) as having each taken five hundred dollars' worth of stock and had said that Richard R. Wright, Jr., editor of the *Christian Recorder*, had given you $500 "because he thought so highly of your work," and that you were getting out an edition of one hundred thousand copies?" Then, "If you were unable to produce even paper proof to show that labor unions and S.P. locals had invested in your stock (which in itself is no disgrace), and the Other People said that you lied "heap much," and it warnt so, nohow, and Richard R. Wright had printed only ten thousand copies, and the man who helped you "tote" the two bundles containing one thousand copies to the station was now working as one of the associate editors [Harrison] of the *Negro World*, and that the other 9,000 copies were still in the office of Richard R. Wright, Jr. in Philadelphia, and you never called for them, and never paid for them, and he had already filed a suit in New York City last week to get you to "loosen up," and the Other Fellow knew all this and more.[45]

Harrison went on: "Just suppose you had kidded people into the belief that you were a graduate of Columbia University—although you 'couldn't make it' and hadn't a diploma to show, and you had kidded Miss [Mary White] Ovington and other white Socialists into believing that you were such a graduate." Just suppose "the Other Fellow [Harrison], as well as Edgar Grey and others, knew the facts in the case, even to the Jarmelowsky [*sic*, a possible reference to the Jarmulowsky financial scandal], that wasn't quite in good odor," and that "you had been bluffing about your deep knowledge of 'sociology,' whereas your knowledge of Lester Ward wasn't critical enough to enable you to see how he was on even the question of lynching and its causes."[46]

In contrast, wrote Harrison, "J. A. Rogers (who doesn't brag so much) saw and exposed your idol's [Lester Ward's] lack of logic and ignorance of the facts bearing on that point, although Rogers, like Herbert Spencer, had never been to college." Just suppose "if you were asked a critical question regarding the works of such standard writers on sociology as Fustel de Coulanges, [Georges] Vacher de Lapourge, [Herbert] Spencer, [Ludwig] Gumplowitcz and Letomeau, or such widely known anthropologists as [Friedrich] Ratzel, [Lewis H.] Morgan, [James G.] Frazer, [John] Lubbock, [Edward] Tylor, Taylor and [Georg] Schweinfurth, or the critical economists like [Eugen von] Bohm-Rawerk and Cliff-Leslie, you wouldn't know beans about them." Even more:

If the Other Fellow expressed his ability to prove these things to your teeth on any public platform, and (for very shame) you couldn't describe him as one of "the old crowd Negroes," Wouldn't [*sic*] you conclude that his editorials were "too shoddy in logic, too fragile in facts, and too forceless in presentation" to be entitled to a decorous answer, and wouldn't you stick your cute little cranium in the sand when you saw his initials and lyingly pretend that you don't know what they stood for, so that you wouldn't have to meet his arguments (which he ventures to think that you can't)?[47]

Harrison next discussed the Moens case:

Just suppose that in your career of bluff and swagger you had, for the sake of peddling a putrid sensation, declared that you had just spoken five minutes with a Dutch scientist [Herman Benelot Moens] and were sure that he "knew nothing of sociology or anthropology" (of which you suppose yourself the king) . . . [though] "scientists like [Dr. R. W.] Schufeldt and Jacques Loeb had put their signatures, along with those of other scientists, to the statement that they had examined this man's work and found it scientific to the core, and, to cap the climax, if Professor Franz Boas, the greatest anthropologist in America, who has given more years to the subject than you gave minutes, had written a long letter asserting that this man was a scientist and that everything which he did was necessary in anthropological researches, and that, consequently, you were a bombastic, empty-headed ass, and the Other Fellow had got hold of it and published it in a Chicago publication [the *Chicago Enterprise*] for everybody to see—wouldn't it rock your mighty intellect?[48]

On a more personal note, Harrison asked: "Just suppose you had found a haven of refuge in the S.P. [Socialist Party] ranks and were picking up less than 35 bones a week—which isn't the Other Fellow's pay, by the way—and which you have every moral right to do. But just suppose you were 'making a front' on the ground of your honesty and sincerity." On the political front Harrison, with a quick review of some recent personal history of Owen, rhetorically asked what

if the Other Fellow [Harrison] knew how you [Owen] went down to Charley Murphy of Tammany Hall every week from June to August 1917, to get him to put you on his payroll, how he blocked your game finally by sending you back to the local organization of which F[erdinand]. Q. Morton was the head, and knew, further, how you got on [Board of Education President] Thomas Churchill's preliminary payroll when you picked him to get the Mayoralty nomination, and then when he failed to get it the jig was up with you, and, since you found the Republican and Democratic doors closed to your itching palms, you rang the Socialist bell and they let you in.

Further, "if the Other Fellow knew these things because you were so fond of bragging on your prospects that you 'spilled the beans' to him every day that you went down, and he could refer enquiries to [Virgin Island–born political activist] Harold Simmelkjaer and others, wouldn't it hit you right in the bread basket and bust open your base of supplies? And wouldn't this 'economic consideration' make you gnash your teeth when you fore gather with your equals in 'the Crab Barrel.'"[49]

Finally, asked Harrison, "Just suppose you had posed as a 'radical' hero, and told the bunch that when you were drafted you had stood as a Conscientious Objector and by your knowledge of the law and your manliness you had secured a non-combatant's job," and "if the man who has kept your records were also employed on the editorial staff of the *Negro World* and knew that you were given such a job only because you had been classified as 'physically unfit'—wouldn't it make you sick?"[50]

Harrison then closed with: "The writer of the above despises anonymous journalism and has put his case in the form only to show the defenders and champions of that sort of thing how it can hurt." He was, however, "willing to waive any slight moral advantage which could be claimed on the ground that the article bears his initials." Nevertheless, he asserted that the statements he made "in the form of 'just suppose'" were "all true," and he stood "ready to make them over again in a form sufficiently direct to satisfy any Sexless twins [a probable reference to Owen and A. Philip Randolph] in the barrel of Crabs."[51]

Harrison's multifaceted challenge, plus his apparent reference to the sexual preference, nonpreference, or indifference of Owen and Randolph in "Just Suppose" and in the soon-to-be-published April 17 "Crab-Barrel" piece in the *Negro World,* may have been important factors in ending *The Emancipator.* They may also have been comments related to Owen's turn away from the radical movement.[52]

In the same April 10 issue of the *Negro World* Harrison offered part 2 of "The Crab Barrel" poem.[53] Then in the April 17 issue he offered part 3, which yet again seemed to offer pointed attacks on Owen and Randolph and said, in part, that "Shamus Glendowen":

> This learned liar has a pal
> Who stuck to him as close's his gal.
> The secret bond between these two
> Was queer indeed, but no one knew
> The essence of the tie that bound
> The arms of Pythias around
> The neck of Damon; none could clear
> The mystery of this mated pair
> (For many another case *hoc tailis*
> See *Psycopathia Sexualis.*)
> This other quaint prevaricator
> Had a somewhat peculiar nature.
> When he essayed to speak the sound
> Came rumbling up from underground
> And sticking twix his throat and jaw
> Transformed itself to words of awe
> Like "boorjwahzee" and "working-clorss"
> (The later word he rhymed with horse.[)][54]

Harrison added in a "Note" that "if the Crab-Barrelites were as learned as they think they are they would find something in the . . . [full verse] (apart from a bad rhyme or two) which they could throw at my head." "The Crab Barrel" was to "be discontinued" until Harrison got back from his "trip home" (to Liberia, then in the planning stages, though it never happened), at which time he would "be ready to resume, unless the Crabs have quieted themselves in the meanwhile," in which case he would "spare the rod."[55]

On April 17 *The Emancipator* ran the fourth part of Anselmo R. Jackson's "An Analysis of the Black Star Line." Jackson described how Garvey's followers' faith in Garvey and the BSL was "somewhat similar to one's faith in religious doctrines," in that it was "acquired and maintained by unreasoning belief rather than by enlightened examination of facts and subsequent logical deductions." These followers "believe that to be loyal to Garvey is to be loyal to their race," though "what they call race loyalty, other Negroes [would] call folly, fanaticism and race frenzy." Jackson considered it "surprisingly strange that in spite of the blatancy of Garvey's critics and the movement's calamity-howlers . . . only one of these dared to challenge him to a public debate." This was a reference to the street-corner affair involving William Bridges, which was described as either an example of "commendable courage or extraordinary foolhardiness." Other critics, "knowing the temper of the followers" of the UNIA and realizing that there were "no limits to which they would not go for Garvey," were "more judicious as to when, where and how they express their criticisms." In addition, there also was "that element," presumably including Harrison, which was "deterred from expressing its antagonism by the economic urge" and had "been unusually cautious, probably fearing that their attacks on Garvey and Black Star Line would be more personally costly than beneficial."[56]

The April 17 *Emancipator* also included "Discard Ambition and Ignorance," which appeared either to sow dissension between Garvey and Harrison or to promote Harrison within the ranks of the UNIA. It suggested that at "the much advertised [forthcoming August] convention of the U.N.I.A," one man in particular, "Mr. Hubert H. Harrison, (not his Mr. Hyde, H. H.)," should be "a candidate not for such an archaic anachronism as potentate, (for that is evidently a bad joke) but for the highest office within the gift of members of the Association." *The Emancipator* considered Harrison to be "fitted by his knowledge of history, international affairs, politics, economics and things pertaining to the Negro race to head the association which has such ambitious international plans," and it regretted "that the meagre mental attainments of the principal aspirant for the office [Garvey]" prevented their support of his candidacy. In addition, it advised Harrison against going on the proposed Liberian Commission, warning, "If Mr. Harrison leaves the United States it will remove him from the field."[57]

In the editorial "Character Assassination Must Stop!" in the same issue, *The Emancipator* again went after Harrison. It argued that it had "become the fashion nowadays for certain self-seeking individuals, posing as leaders of the race, to arrogate to themselves the position of guardians of public pocket and morals, censors of all kinds of racial enterprises." Then, if a new movement or company formed, "those leaders, themselves resenting any kind of criticism," would feel "called upon to exercise their officious and self-assumed tasks of arming the public." While "as Socialists" *The Emancipator*'s editors had "no interest in business enterprises as such" and did not endorse any particular business, they did "regard it as a public duty and a racial obligation to examine all business enterprises" and "warn" readers "against palpable frauds and swindling schemes" that would "impoverish investors while enriching their wily promoters." Similarly, "with respect to racial movements," they considered it their "duty to subject them to the X-ray of public scrutiny." Thus, "when a leader, demonstrably lacking in the essentials of leadership,—tact, democratic spirit and a due regard for realities—condemns other movements we immediately become suspicious and feel impelled to censor the censor."[58]

The Emancipator then described how "cunningly worded warnings" had "multiplied" and many a legitimate enterprise, conceived in sound capitalist morals, has been irreparably injured because some leader with a scheme to promote was jealous that the enterprise might interest some of the lambs he had marked out for shearing." Similarly, "many an honest man" (perhaps a reference to Owen) had "found his name and reputation besmirched by a cunningly worded warning, containing sufficient suggestiveness of moral turpitude as to damage the man's character, yet not direct enough as to permit a suit for libel." *The Emancipator* argued that it was "time that a halt is called to this cowardly campaign of character assassination," which was "in many cases but a mask for the furtherance of selfish schemes for plundering the public pocket." It protested, "because colored Socialists and radicals have had their sincerity impugned by these same leaders who, being impelled by cupidity, cannot conceive of others being actuated by motives of principle." It argued further that "if any 'leader' who controls a newspaper is honest in his attacks upon individuals, then he would be willing, out of ordinary decency, to open his columns to the attacked parties for defense." The time was "past for these veiled and unproven attacks," and if one made assertions, one "should be compelled by an intelligent public to furnish conclusive proof," since "character assassination" was "too insidious and vicious for an enlightened people to encourage." The public "should demand reasons, specific proof of charges," and "no longer must self-advertising and self-adulating mountebanks be permitted to divert attention from themselves and their public activities by making unproven and cowardly attacks upon others . . . no longer must these cowardly human hyenas put into practice the theory that the best defense is sometimes a vigorous campaign of offense." The "human hyenas" alliteration appears clearly aimed at Harrison.[59]

In the April 17 *Emancipator*'s "Opinion of Randolph & Owen Editors of the *Messenger*: Supposing—with Apologies to the Ha Ha Editor," Randolph and Owen directly responded to Harrison. In arguing against ad hominem attacks, they explained that "facts are indifferent to their author" and that "you cannot overthrow the theory of evolution by saying that you saw Darwin shooting craps." To them, one should not answer an argument "by trying to throw up a smoke screen" behind which to hide. Randolph and Owen then made an effort "to sum up a little." They suggested that "a certain gentleman whose initials are R.R.W. [R. R. Wright] printed a magazine for editors [Owen and Randolph] who have a recognized literary reputation," and "even though the proofs were read by one of the present editors of *The Negro World* and (not withstanding that editor has two or three degrees and as many more diplomas from well known universities)," the magazine had "about two hundred and fifty misspelled words and few or no pages in consecutive order." Then, "supposing all of this (keeping in mind the recognized literary reputation of radical scientific editors)," they asked if it wouldn't "be most natural to reject such work?" Then they added, "it must be remembered that these are not ha ha editors who stood in Madison Square Garden and sold Guy Empey's *Over the Top* and endorsed it as scientific history of the war and high calibre English literature."[60]

The article went on: "Supposing also that a 'ha ha' editor [Harrison] had intimated that a certain radical scientist [Owen] alleged to have been a conscientious objector, was not a conscientious objector" but that the "ha ha editor, not being a scientist himself, had relied upon hearsay evidence of a Negro stool pigeon [Grey?], who while just as competent as H.H. was nevertheless, just as unreliable and as lacking in veracity." Further, while Randolph and Owen would not attempt to answer "each irrelevant and immaterial argument raised by an easily proved licentious, lecherous and libidinous prevaricator like H.H.," they suggested that readers "take this typical instance of his untruthfulness as a means of setting his entire irreputation and honesty forever at rest." On their investigation they found "a radical scientist editor, alleged to have been a conscientious objector [Owen] to be a real, recognized, conscientious objector." They then offered, "Supposing we pursue a different policy from a Black Star philosopher and have no fear of turning on light." They pointed out that "this conscientious objector bore the number 4170485 in the army" and was "drafted on September 2, 1918," was given "a certificate of a conscientious objector, number 68" on September 9, 1918, signed by Roscoe F. Rupp, 2nd Lieutenant Infantry, Assistant Camp Personnel Adjutant, Camp Upton, New York. On the back of the certificate was an executive order, signed by Woodrow Wilson, March 20, 1918. Further, on December 19, 1918, in Special Order no. 309, Headquarters Eastern Department, Governor's Island, New York, Major General J. Franklin Bell "issued an order for the discharge of a radical scientist editor, whose name on the order is in italics and following the name, in parenthesis, the words 'conscientious objector.'" That order was countersigned by W. A. Simpson, Colonel, Retired, Adjutant, and on the thirty-first day of December 1918, "a discharge was granted this radical scientist with a special statement upon that discharge, in parenthesis, 'this is a conscientious objector.'" Also, "question 11, referring to physical condition, says very distinctly—'good'—and the entire record of the radical scientist in the army shows the only physical defect at any time was sore throat and swollen tonsils." "Supposing these facts are well-established upon documentary evidence—would it not prove that H.H. is either a ha ha editor or an unmitigated fabricator?"[61]

"With respect to [Lester] Ward and other scientists," they couldn't "permit H.H. to take the floor to make a motion on scientific authority," because "supposing that you know anything about science, you must know that life began in the sea," and "you would not call a land crab more primitive than the sea crab," or "to illustrate from your own species, the shark—the land variety is later than the sea variety . . . and also more cunning." They concluded (with allusions to two BSL ships) that he "must be a 'shady-side' scientist" whose "knowledge of science is pretty shady-shady! And not much truth emanates from 'yar-mouth!'"[62]

In light of the foregoing, "the three big gun editors have had a conference, in which there was some disagreement, namely, C.O. [Chandler Owen] maintains that H.H. means Ha Ha and that the editor is a joke. A.P.R. [A. Philip Randolph] holds that H.H. may also mean hat-in-hand and that the Ha Ha editor is a sycophant and a lacky; while W.A.D. [W. A. Domingo] contends that the two are not mutually exclusive and that H.H. may stand for both at the same time." The "Big 3" then "voted unanimously to sustain the argument of W.A.D.," who held that he "looked like a lion but was nothing but a dog."[63]

The April 24 issue of *The Emancipator* included "Now for the Dirty Work," by Cyril Briggs, which explained that the paper "interfered with the orderly carrying out of certain schemes in Harlem" and had "pricked" one "iridescent bubble . . . before the hour set by his infinitessimalness." The referred to plan was "to remove headquarters from America—[to Liberia] . . . —beyond the reach of irate stock-holders and American District Attorneys who might be interested in investigation and punishment." With the plan exposed, Briggs predicted that "the crash impends and the way of escape is blocked." There still remained, however, "that double-edged weapon of their own creation: fanaticism!" which, in "desperation," they (Garvey and those who had most closely been working on behalf of him and his various efforts) sought to direct "from themselves" by "openly and secretly advocating the assassination of those who are directing upon their questionable transactions the X-ray of Truth."[64]

While Briggs's claim that *The Emancipator* had fulfilled its role by blocking Garvey's planned relocation to Africa (before angry stockholders and legal authorities could deal with him) offers one explanation for the paper's termination, it is not at all clear that it was the only reason. Among other possible factors were Harrison's pointed criticisms and the possibility of physical harm: there would be a threat on Owen by Garvey, Domingo would later report a threat on his life by followers of Garvey, and Randolph would later reportedly receive a human hand in the mail.[65]

In the May 1, 1920, issue of the *Negro World* Harrison offered "Patronize Your Own" to argue his position and to offer another response to Chandler Owen. The editorial was not identified as his when printed, though he did claim it later in the year when it was republished in August 1920 in his *When Africa Awakes*. The omission may have been more the typographer's fault than Harrison's, since on a number of occasions he complained of typographical errors and regularly used his initials for identification. "Patronize Your Own" explained that "the doctrine of 'Race First'" was "the direct product of the out-door and indoor lecturers" that "flourished in Harlem between 1914 and 1916," and although it was "utilized largely by the Negro businessmen of Harlem," it had "never received any large general support from them." The editorial added that "not all who were radical shared this sentiment" and cited Harrison's December 1918 Palace Casino debate with Owen, where the "radical" Owen "fiercely maintained that the doctrine of race first was an indefensible doctrine," while Harrison maintained "that it was the source of salvation for the race." It added, "Both these gentlemen have run true to form ever since."[66]

The editorial also noted that there had now "grown up in Harlem Negro businesses, groceries, ice cream parlors, etc., in which the application of prices, courtesy and selling efficiency are maintained." In a direct challenge to the "class first" Socialists, it wished "more power" to this "New Negro business man" and expressed the opinion that if such a method of applying the principle of "Patronize Your Own" continued to increase in popularity in Harlem and elsewhere there was sure to be "a full and flowing tide of Negro business enterprises gladly and loyally supported by the mass of Negro purchasers to their mutual benefit."[67]

In the *Negro World* of May 8 the relentless Harrison wrote several pieces, including "An Open Letter to the Socialist Party of New York City" and "Is An Answer Impossible," which referred to his challenge to the editors of the *Emancipator* issued in the March 27 *Negro World*. He also wrote "Scientific Radical Liars" and probably wrote the letter to the editor from "Hagar" entitled "Negroes Should Be Taught Pride of Race" as well as the response to Hagar. Each of these pieces was fuel in the struggle against the Black socialists who had been in and around the *Emancipator*.[68]

In "Is an Answer Impossible?" Harrison reminded readers that the *Negro World* of March 27 published an "official statement of the Socialist Party of America, which proves conclusively that *with them* it is Race First and not Class First, as certain of their subsidized bellwethers insist—when preaching to us." He then reprinted the passage previously cited in the March 27 issue, which read in part:

> Race feeling is not so much a result of social as of biological evolution. It does not change essentially with changes of economic systems. It is deeper than any class feeling and will outlast the capitalist system. It persists even after race prejudice has been outgrown. . . . . Class-consciousness must be learned, but race consciousness is inborn and cannot be wholly unlearned. *A few individuals may indulge in the luxury of ignoring race and posing as utterly raceless humanitarians, but whole races never.*[69]

He had asked the Socialists to explain the passage, and in the six weeks since, "not one of those brilliant bellwethers" knew "the Socialist records well enough to be able to find the source of the above quotation." The "present interest in the matter" was because "the controversy on this and other matters" had been "waged freely" since that date, and "neither 'the big three [Owen, Randolph, and Domingo],' the little three, nor any other of the Negro Socialist scribes has been able to answer this shot from their own side." Instead "they have filled the air with poison gas, while dodging this big crack in their case." Harrison asked: "What's the matter, gentlemen? Are your brains asleep? Or do you realize that you can't answer? Speak up—but speak to the point." Although he again didn't explain it in his article, the document Harrison referred to came from the majority position on immigration at the 1912 SP Convention, and the "Negro Socialists" in 1920 apparently never did identify it.[70]

On May 8 in the *Negro World* Harrison also offered the very important "Open Letter to the Socialist Party of New York City." In that article, which was initialed "H.H.," he explained that during the 1917 election "white leaders of the Republican party were warned that the Negroes" of New York City "were in a mood unfavorable to the success of their party at the polls and that this mood was likely to last until they changed their party's attitude toward the Negro masses." They rejected the warning "because the Negroes whom they had selected to interpret Negro sentiment for them still confidently assured them that there had been no change of sentiment on the part of the Negro people," and these "white politicians did not think it necessary to come and find out for themselves." In effect, "they were lied to by those whose bread and butter depended on such lying," and in the mayoralty campaign, "when it was too late[,] they discovered their mistake." Then at a "memorable" Palace Casino meeting of October 29, 1917, both John Purroy Mitchel, the Republican Party candidate, and Theodore Roosevelt, its idol, "were almost hissed off the stage, while the Mitchel outdoor speakers found it impossible to speak on the street corners of Harlem." The Republicans "went down to defeat and Judge [John] Hyland was elected."[71]

Harrison reminded his readers of this history to call attention to the danger of similar mistakes being made by Socialists who had "selected Negro spokesmen [Randolph, Owen, et al.] on whose word [they] choose to rely for information as to the tone and temper of Negro political sentiment." This was "the same faulty method of the white Republican politicians." Thus, when Socialists relied on the word of their own "selected exponents of Negro thought and feeling," they received a "pitiful vote" in the last election. Harrison then recounted how, during the war, "the Negro in America was taught that while white people spoke of patriotism, religion, democracy and other sounding themes, they remained loyal to one concept above all others, and that was the concept of race." While "in the throes of war, and on the battlefields of France it was 'race first' with them" ("them" being "white" people), it was "out of this relation [that] was born the new Negro ideal of 'race first' for us." Because of such experience, "whether Negroes be Catholics or Protestants, capitalists or wage workers, Republicans or Democrats, native or foreign-born," they now began life "anew on this basis." They were "responding to this sentiment which has been bred by the attitude of white men here and everywhere else where white rules black." Neither Attorney A. Mitchell Palmer nor Postmaster General Albert S. Burleson would admit this because "the Anglo-Saxon white man is a notorious hypocrite." They "preferred to prate of Bolshevism—your 'radicalism'—rather than tell the truth of racialism, our 'radicalism,' because this was an easier explanation, more in keeping with official stupidity." Harrison wryly added, "we had supposed that you [Socialists] were intelligent enough to find this out," but, "evidently, you were not."[72]

Harrison commented that the Socialist Party's "official Negro exponents," concerned with their own "bread and butter," had "seized on this widely-published official explanation to make you believe that the changed attitude of the Negro masses was due to the propaganda which you were paying them (at their published request) to preach." This, however, was "a lie." If Socialists would do some reading and "get a hundred different Negro newspapers and magazines, outside of those which you have subsidized, and study their editorial and other pronouncements," they would "see that this is so." Coming "nearer home," Harrison explained how "the propaganda of Socialism has been preached in times past in Harlem by different people without awakening hostility of any sort." Now, however, it elicited "a hostility which is outspoken." The reason was not that "socialist propaganda was neglected by you between 1912 and 1917" but that "Negro Harlem [is] reborn, with business enterprises and cultural arrangements" that "have been established without any help from you or those who eat your bread." He advised the Socialists to "consult your own memories and the columns of the *Call*" (the SP newspaper). "All these things" were "the recent products of the principle of 'race first,'" and "among them the biggest" was "the Universal Negro Improvement Association, with its associate bodies, the Black Star Line and the Negro Factories Corporation." "No movement among American Negroes since slavery was abolished [had] ever attained the gigantic proportions of this." The UNIA attracted the "love and loyalty of millions" as well "as the cold cash of tens of thousands." Nevertheless, the SP's "Negro hirelings have seen fit to use the organs which you give them to spread Socialist propaganda for the purpose of attacking all these things, and the Black Star Line in particular." These "Negro" Socialists "meet with such outspoken opposition that they have been driven to seek an underhanded alliance with the police (as your Negro Socialist organ avows in its latest issue)" and with such "a glorious alliance for purposes of Negro propaganda," it is clear that "someone has been fooling you." Harrison then named some names (in a sentence that did not appear when the article was republished later in the year in August in *When Africa Awakes*): "On their own avowal your chief militant representatives among us are Messrs. Chandler Owen, A. P. Randolph, W. A. Domingo and Cyril V. Briggs."[73]

Just like "the white Republicans," Socialists "assumed that those whom chance or change brought" their way had "somehow, achieved a monopoly of the intellect and virtue of the Negro race." He again described how on March 27 the *Negro World* had quoted an official Socialist document (the 1912 convention position on immigration) "showing that the white men of your party officially put 'race first' rather than 'class first,' which latter phrase is your henchmen's sole contribution to 'sociology'—for us." He emphasized that the quoted passage "cuts the very heart out of their case," yet "those whom you have selected to represent you are so green and sappy in their Socialism that, although six weeks have elapsed since this was hurled at their thick heads, not one of them has yet been able to trace its source, this quotation from one of your own official documents."[74]

Meanwhile, "you yourselves are such 'easy marks' that you believe them, on their own assertion, to be the ablest among the Negroes of America," and it is difficult "to decide which of the two groups is the bigger joke—you or they." "You have constantly insisted that 'there is no race problem, only an economic problem,'" but you will soon "find out otherwise." And "some day you will, perhaps, have learned enough to cease being 'suckers' for perpetual candidates [a reference to Randolph and Owen] who dickered with the Democrats up to within a month of 'flopping' to your party only because they 'couldn't make it' elsewhere; some day, perhaps you will know enough to put Socialism's cause in the hands of those who will refrain from using your party's organ for purposes of personal pique, spite and venom."[75]

When that day comes, Harrison predicted, "Socialism will have a chance to be heard by Negroes on its merits." He noted that "even now, if you should send anyone up here (black or white) to put the cause of Karl Marx, freed from admixture of rancor and hatred of the Negro's own defensive racial propaganda, you may find that it will have as good a chance of gaining adherents as any other political creed." But, "until you change your tactics or make your exponents change theirs your case among us will be hopeless indeed." The historian Winston James has concluded that Harrison, "an intellectual steeped in the work of Marx, willingly acknowledging its analytical power in understanding the perplexing world in which he lived. He shared in the vision of classical socialism" and was "in essence, a black socialist, waiting for a better day that he feared would never come."[76]

———————

Harrison had vigorously challenged Owen, Randolph, and Domingo in print. Through June and July he would continue with other articles, which he later claimed were "defending, not Mr. Garvey personally, but the principles of the New Negro Manhood Movement, a portion of which had been incorporated by him and his followers of the U.N.I.A. and A.C.L." While putting forth this defense, Harrison would also address the question of leadership with some pointed editorials that focused on the NAACP. As he defended the principles of the New Negro Movement, however, Harrison's criticisms of Garvey were also growing. By the August 1920 convention he would be taking steps to move away from being the unofficial principal editor of the *Negro World*—steps that further distanced him from Garvey.

6

Early *Negro World* Writings
(January–July 1920)

After Harrison assumed the managing editor position at the Negro World in early January 1920, he transformed the paper not only through his editing efforts but also with his own editorials and articles. Throughout the period leading up to the August 1920 UNIA Convention, he sought to help develop a radical, race-conscious, internationalist perspective among the Black masses and to point the way forward with a militant, New Negro–led direction in the struggle for equality. The themes he treated and subjects he covered—the leadership question, international and domestic issues, education, poetry, and book and theater reviews—were extremely wide-ranging. His writings over the course of this short, seventh-month period were remarkable and offer an important look at the seminal, radical, race-conscious, internationalist message that he offered to readers.

———

A subject that Harrison considered of prime importance was the question of leadership. He was convinced that amid "all the tangles of . . . awakening race consciousness" there were "perhaps none more knotty" than those relating to leadership, and he paid special attention to leadership issues in his early 1920 writings. One of his first *Negro World* articles concerned a February 1920 *Crisis* editorial by Du Bois and how Du Bois's "white friends" had been "fervidly ignoring the occurrence and the consequent collapse of his leadership" since July 1918.[1]

In "When the Blind Lead" Harrison explained how Du Bois (in February 1920) offered a "brief editorial on 'Leadership,' with the touching reminder that 'Many a good cause has been killed by suspected leadership.'" Harrison commented on how "these words bring back to us Negroes those dark days of 1918," when Du Bois "was offering certain unique formulas of leadership" that "didn't 'take." He was referring to Du Bois's July 1918 "Close Ranks" editorial and his urging "Negroes" to "forget our special grievances" (lynching, segregation, and disfranchisement) during World War I. To Harrison, Du Bois's "'Close Ranks' editorial and the subsequent slump in the stock of his leadership" illustrated "that, while it's as easy as eggs for a leader to fall off the fence, it is devilishly difficult to boost him up again." Harrison added that while in September 1918 those following Du Bois's lead could say "The *Crisis* says *first* your Country, *then* your Rights!" today "Negro people everywhere" were responding to the sentiment "it's Race, not Country, first." "The gist" of Du Bois's "Leadership" editorial was "the moral downfall of another great leader."[2]

Harrison then quoted from Du Bois's February 1920 "Leadership" editorial: "Woodrow Wilson, in following a great ideal of World Unity, forgot all his pledges to the German people, forgot all his large words to Russia, did not hesitate to betray [Samuel] Gompers and his unions, *and never at any single moment meant to include in his democracy twelve millions of his fellow Americans, whom he categorically promised 'more than mere grudging justice,' and then allowed 350 of them to be lynched during his Presidency.*" Du Bois also went on to explain, as noted by Harrison, that "out of the World War, with the Allies triumphant, have come Britain's brutal domination of the seas, her conquest of Persia, Arabia and Egypt, and her tremendous tyranny imposed on two-thirds of Africa."[3]

After citing these remarks by Du Bois, Harrison commented that as "early as 1917" he and others saw these things as "the necessary consequences of the Allies' success," yet Du Bois in the *Crisis* "was telling his race: 'You are not fighting simply for Europe; you are fighting for the world.'" Harrison pointedly asked, "Was Dr. Du Bois so blind that he couldn't see then? And if he was, is he any less blind today?" Harrison explained that in 1918, while lynchings were still going on, Du Bois "was solemnly advising us to 'forget our grievances.'" Anyone who insisted "on putting such grievances as lynchings, disfranchisement and segregation in the foreground was described by the *Crisis'* editor as seeking 'to turn his country's tragic predicament to his own personal gain.'" At that time Du Bois "either believed or pretended to believe every one of the empty words that flowed from Woodrow Wilson's lips, and on the basis of this belief he was willing to act as a brilliant bellwether to the rest of the flock," but the flock "refused to follow the lost leader." Harrison then pointedly explained:

"If the blind lead the blind they will both fall into the ditch." But in this case those being led were not quite so blind as those who wanted to lead them by way of captaincies in the army [a reference to Du Bois seeking a captaincy in Military Intelligence in 1918] which was why some captaincies were not

forthcoming. The test of vision in a leader is the ability to foresee the immediate future, the necessary consequences of a course of conduct and the
dependable sentiments of those whom he assumes to lead. In all these things
Dr. Du Bois has failed; and neither his ungrateful attack on Emmett Scott
nor his belated discovery of Wilsonian hypocrisy will, we fear, enable him to
climb back into the saddle of race leadership. This is a pity, because he has
rendered good service in his day. But that day is past. The magazine which
he edits still remains as a splendid example of Negro journalism. But the personal primacy of its editor has departed, never to return. Other times, other
men; other men, other manners.

Even the Negro people are now insisting that their leaders shall in thought
and moral stamina keep ahead of, and not behind, them.[4]

This change in "the [Negro] people's spiritual appetite" was "commended to . . .
all those good white friends who are out selecting Negro 'leaders.'" It was "a
fact" that, if carefully considered, would "save them thousands of dollars." Harrison closed by stating: "The Negro leaders of the future will be expected not
only to begin straight, take a moral vacation, and then go straight again. They
will be expected to go straight all the time; to stand by us in war as well as in
peace; not to blow hot and cold" but "to stand four-square to *all* the winds that
blow."[5]

"When the Blind Lead" was soon followed in the April 17 *Negro World* by a
reprint of Harrison's January 1919 *Voice* article "An Open Letter to the Young
Men of My Race."[6] Seven weeks later, in a June 5 *Negro World* column on
"The U.N.I.A. and Politics," Harrison published a letter from Granville H. Martin, along with Harrison's response as editor. Martin had a history of activism
and was a butler when he and Maude and William Monroe Trotter led a 1903
protest of a Booker T. Washington talk (known as the Boston Riot). In his May 9
letter Martin expressed regret over "the apparent misunderstanding" between
"Garvey and the Socialist Party, particularly the Negro end of that party." In
particular, he "deeply regret[ted]" that "Garvey advises renunciation of politics
in toto" and "hoped that some of the friends who lived in the good graces of
Mr. Garvey would dissuade him from this disastrous course." Martin reminded
readers that Booker T. Washington "preached a vote-less doctrine to the
Race" and had "never been pardoned for it." He added that "the ballot, well-
directed," was "the stay chain of the defense of any oppressed people" and that
it was misleading to "arraign the whole Socialist Party" for what appears to be
"misrepresentations on the part of two or three constituents." Martin suggested that "every ounce of the Negro's strength should be brought to bear
upon the common enemy—politically, commercially, morally and industrially," and if it was necessary to "fight party politics," he asked, why not fight

against "the two big sinners, the Republican and Democratic parties, whose crimes against us are known throughout the world?"[7]

"Associate Editor" Harrison responded to Martin, whom he thought misunderstood Garvey's position. This appears to have been a diplomatic approach, both because Harrison repeatedly attempted to push Garvey (who was known to have eschewed political involvement) to take more political action and because Harrison also wanted to encourage the building of a Black economic base. Harrison explained that "no Negro of prominence would tell Negroes to forego the use of the ballot," since the "vote as a protector of property, lives, and liberties is certainly of great value; and if properly used by the Negroes in the North it would be of still greater value." In addition, "policemen and politicians" did "respond to the pressure of a voting population where they would not respond to the mere voices of a voteless people." "But," according to Harrison, "Garvey, like some others of us, realizes that at this time it is worth while for Negroes to spend most of their energies to the main thing first. And that main thing is the creation and maintenance of the economic basis of our own survival."[8]

"Personally," Harrison hoped that the time would come "when this mass of awakened Negroes, motivated by racial necessity," would "take with them into politics the same 'Race First' spirit and principle which now makes the U.N.I.A. and the Black Star Line known and noted all over the Negro world." When "that same spirit" had "organized itself politically all over the nation" one could "confidently expect to see black Negro legislators in the United States Congress protecting our interests there and crippling the Southern cracker at the central source of crackerism in the United States."[9]

Harrison thought that there was "no 'misunderstanding between Mr. Garvey and the Socialist Party.'" It had its "field of activities" and "we have ours," and "just as the Socialist party officially declares that it exercises no control or veto power over the religious beliefs of its individual member[,] so the U.N.I.A. does not dictate to any member what his economic or political beliefs shall be." "But," he added, with *The Emancipator* debate fresh in mind, "we are justified in defending ourselves from the attacks of other people, even if those other people attack us from behind the shelter of Socialist propaganda." Under such circumstances there might even be "occasion to counter-attack in our own behalf." Nevertheless, if the SP felt "that any injury" was "done to its propaganda on this score" it could "easily put a stop to it by forcing these cowards to come out from behind its shelter and do their own personal spitework on their own personal grounds and by insisting that only Socialist propaganda shall be spread by force of the funds which it furnishes." Finally, "as to the existence of the Socialist Party in the South," Harrison urged Martin "to consult the Party's own record," in which he "would find a procedure [segregation] both interesting and instructive." He closed, as had Martin, "for Race solidarity."[10]

In an "H.H."-initialed June 19 *Negro World* article, "A Negro for President," Harrison further extended some of the political themes he discussed in his response to Martin. He described how "for many years the Negro has been the football of American politics . . . kicked from pillar to post"; "begging, hat in hand, from a Republican convention, to a Democratic one"; and "always . . . begging, pleading, demanding or threatening." "The Negro" was dependent "on the good will, sense of justice or gratitude of the other fellow," and this meant the race's fate was never "within the control of the Negro." But "a change for the better" was "approaching." For four years Harrison had been "propounding in indoor and outdoor lectures" the thesis that "the Negro people of America would never amount to anything much politically until they should see fit to imitate the Irish of Britain and to organize themselves into a political party of their own whose leaders, on the basis of this large collective vote, could 'hold up' Republican, Democrats, Socialists or any other political group of American whites." Now, he explained, "as in many other cases [a likely reference to both the socialists Randolph and Owen, on one hand, and to Garvey, on the other], we have lived to see time ripen the fruits of our own thought for some one else to pluck." He then pointed to the fact that William Bridges, editor of the *Challenge*, was making a campaign along these lines by "advocating the nomination of a Negro for the Presidency of the United States." Harrison didn't have "the slightest doubt" that the idea would "meet with a great deal of ridicule and contempt," but he nevertheless prophesied "that, whether in the hands of Mr. Bridges or another," it would "come to be ultimately accepted as one of the finest contributions to Negro statesmanship."[11]

Harrison did not think "that the votes of Negroes can elect a Negro" or that "white people will be forthcoming to assist them in such a project." The "only way" this would be done "would be by virtue of the voters not knowing that the particular candidate was of Negro ancestry"—which, he wryly added, "we believe, has already happened within the memory of living men." But "the essential intent of this new plan" was "to furnish a focussing-point around which the ballots of the Negro voters may be concentrated for the realization of racial demands for justice and equality of opportunity and treatment." Such a plan "would be carrying 'Race First' with a vengeance into the arena of politics" and "would take the Negro voter out of the ranks of the Republican, Democratic and Socialist parties and would enable their leaders to trade the votes of their followers, openly and above-board, for those things for which masses of men largely exchange their votes."[12]

Harrison predicted that Bridges would "find that the idea of a Negro candidate for President presupposes the creation of a purely Negro party and upon the prerequisite" he would be "compelled to concentrate." While "the political wise-acres of the Negro race" would argue "the idea is impossible because it antagonizes the white politicians of the various parties," they would be closing their eyes "to the fact that politics implies antagonism and a conflict of interest." They would also "fail to see that the only things which count with politicians are votes" and that "just as one white man will cheerfully cut another white man's throat to get the dollars which a black man has, so will one white politician or party cut another one's throat politically to get the votes which black men may cast at the polls." While "these considerations" would "finally carry the day," he stressed, in one of his more pointed statements of the period, that there should be "no mistake":

> The Negro will never be accepted by the white American democracy except in so far as he can by the use of force, financial, political or other, win, seize or maintain in the teeth of the opposition that position which he finds necessary to his own security and salvation. And we Negroes may as well make up our own minds now that we can't depend upon the good-will of white men in anything or at any point where our interests and theirs conflict. Disguise it as we may, in business, politics, education or other departments of life, we as Negroes are compelled to fight for what we want to win from the white world.[13]

Harrison next approached the "color" question. It was, he argued, "easy enough for those colored men whose psychology is shaped by their white inheritance to argue the ethics of compromise and inter-racial co-operation." "But," he countered, "we whose brains are still unbastardized, must face the frank realities of this situation" and "marshal our forces to withstand and make head against the constant racial pressure." He added that "it is this philosophy which must furnish the motive for such a new and radical departure as is implied in the joint idea of a Negro party in American politics and a Negro candidate for the Presidency of these United States."[14]

The same June 19 *Negro World* offered two other pieces dealing with the NAACP (which had long been a subject of Harrison criticism) and the question of leadership. In "The Crisis Asleep" Harrison described how the previous summer the London-based *African Telegraph* reported at length on a lawsuit in which its editor was the defendant against a Captain Joseph Frederick John Fitzpatrick, who had been charged with being responsible for brutal floggings perpetrated on Black women in northern Nigeria. Several hundred copies of the magazine reached people in upper Manhattan in August or September 1919, and "the trial and the principle involved were of transcendent importance to Negroes everywhere as illustrations of the methods of white overlordship." These matters were repeatedly discussed in West African journals, in the *Negro World*, and in the *New Negro*, yet it was only in the June 1920 issue (in a piece entitled "English Rule in Africa") that the editor of the *Crisis* mentioned the *African Telegraph* account of "'a law-suit in Nigeria in which one Captain Fitz-patrick brought action against John Eldred Taylor, a West African journalist,' etc. etc." To Harrison it seemed as if the *Crisis* and its editor (Du Bois), who was not mentioned by name, were "fast asleep since last June, and even now must be only imperfectly awake," since "the law-suit didn't occur in Nigeria, but in London, the largest city of the white world."[15]

In a similar vein, about three months earlier the *Negro World*, in both a "West Indian News Notes" article and its "Special Articles" section, carried accounts of "the case of the silver [Black] as opposed to the 'gold' ["white"] employees, conditions, strikes and sufferings in the Panama Canal Zone." Then, in the cur-rent *Crisis*, there was an interesting account of these workers "suffering all the horrors of peonage," but it was regrettable "that the *Crisis* should just now have heard of the case." Because of its inadequate coverage of these two matters of international interest, which may "have [ultimately] been inserted as 'fillers,'" Harrison pointedly asked "whether the *Crisis* and its editor are awake or asleep."[16]

In "Shillady Resigns" in the June 19 *Negro World*, Harrison discussed some implications brought forth by the recent resignation of John R. Shillady, the "white" ex–executive secretary of the NAACP. In August 1919, Shillady had been beaten into unconsciousness by a group of "white" men led by a county judge when he unsuccessfully attempted to meet with the governor and attor-ney general of Texas in Austin. In his letter of resignation Shillady stated that he was "less confident than heretofore of the speedy success of the association's full program and of the probability of overcoming within a reasonable period the forces opposed to Negro equality by the means and methods which are within the association's power to employ."[17]

To Harrison, "in this one sentence Mr. Shillady, the worker on the inside," put "in suave and serenely diplomatic phrase the truth which people on the out-side have long perceived, namely, that the N.A.A.C.P. makes a joke of itself when it affects to think that lynching and the other evils which beset the Negro in the South can be abolished by simple publicity." Harrison then put forth that

the great weakness of the National Association for the Advancement of Col-ored People has been and is that, whereas it aims to secure certain results by affecting the minds of white people and making them friendly to it, it has no control over these minds and has absolutely no answers to the question, "What steps do you propose to take if these minds at which you are aiming remain unaffected? What do you propose to do to secure life and liberty for the Negro if the white Southerner persists, as he has persisted for sixty years, in refus-ing to grant guarantees of life and liberty?"[18]

While the NAACP had done "some good and worth-while work as an organization of protest," Harrison emphasized that the times now called "for something more effective than protests addressed to the other fellow's consciousness." What was needed was "more of the mobilizing of the Negro's political power, pocketbook power and intellectual power (which are absolutely within the Negro's own control) to do for the Negro the things which the Negro needs to have done without depending upon or waiting for the co-operative action of white people." Any such "co-operative action," if it did come, would be "a boon that no Negro, intelligent or unintelligent," should affect to despise. On the other hand, "no Negro of clear vision, whether . . . a leader or not," could "afford to predicate the progress of the Negro upon such co-operative action, because it may not come." Thus, while Mr. Shillady may have seen these things, it was "high time that all Negroes see things whether their white professional friends see them or not."[19]

Some years later the poet Claude McKay offered some personal recollections regarding Harrison's attitude toward the NAACP. One involved himself, Mary White Ovington, and Harrison. Ovington, the prominent socialist and NAACP leader, told McKay of a meeting she had with Booker T. Washington and how Washington was indifferent to her until he found she came from a family of higher-ups. At that point he became obsequious. McKay repeated the story to Harrison, who "exploded in his large sugary black African way, which sounded like the rustling of dry bamboo leaves agitated by the wind." McKay knew that Harrison had criticized Washington's policies "in powerful volcanic English, and subsequently, by some mysterious grapevine chicanery, he had lost his government job." According to McKay, Harrison "finally came to the conclusion that out of the purgatory of their own social confusion, Negroes would sooner or later have to develop their own leaders, independent of white control." McKay's second example concerned Harrison's "personal resentment against the N.A.A.C.P.," which he nicknamed the "National Association for the Advancement of Certain People." McKay described Harrison's humor as "ebony hard," and he recalled how Harrison found it "exciting to think that the N.A.A.C.P. was the progeny of black snobbery and white pride, and had developed into a great organization, with Du Bois like a wasp in Booker Washington's hide until the day of his death."[20]

In another *Negro World* matter related to the NAACP, Harrison was drawn into a mild controversy over Du Bois and the NAACP's principal annual award, the Spingarn Medal. The medal had been instituted by Joel E. Spingarn, chairman of the board of directors of the NAACP, and it was awarded "for the highest or noblest achievement by a living American Negro during the preceding year or years." In February 1919, in Paris, Du Bois had convened a Pan-African Congress, which he referred to as the "first." In 1920 the NAACP awarded him the Spingarn Medal for the "founding and calling together of the first Pan-African Congress." In the *Negro World* of June 19, 1920, William H. Ferris wrote a response to a letter to the editor from Henry F. Downing, which had accurately pointed out that the first Pan-African Congress had been in 1901 in London and that he had been chairman of its executive committee. Ferris, as editor of the *Negro World*, replied that the correction was "substantial and detailed enough to merit a reply from the editor of *The Crisis*." If the facts stated by Downing and supported by contemporary clippings were accurate, then the awarding of the Spingarn Medal to Dr. Du Bois on the ground of his organizing the first Pan-African Congress, according to Ferris, was "a discredible fraud, and the assertion upon which it rests is a falsehood, pure and simple."[21]

On June 26, a June 17 letter from Arthur Schomburg to Harrison was printed in the *Negro World*. Schomburg said he had read Downing's letter on the first Pan-African meeting, and there was "no doubt whatever that it originated in London" and that "soon thereafter Mr. H[enry]. Sylvester Williams came to this country to interest us over here in the movement." Louis A. Joppe chaired a meeting in New York, and Schomburg mailed meeting notices to the press. He enclosed a clipping from the *New York Times*, which showed "that to Brooklyn goes some of the credit." Schomburg offered that "the trouble with many of us is that we . . . jump at conclusions" and "are ready to swallow general statements without checking up the details." "Why should you be harping over the Spingarn Medal?" he asked; they can give it to whomever they please. Schomburg added, "Of all the recipients of the medal Mr. Du Bois, in my opinion, has the best claim to wear it. In the field of letters, polite letters, I am sure he would grace any academy with dignity and authority. He is as good as anybody in America in economics, and when it comes to painting sky poetry you got to hand it to the learned professor." Harrison then affixed an addendum indicating that "the Spingarn Medal editorial was written by Professor Wm. H. Ferris and not by Mr. Harrison" and that "Schomburg's [enclosed] clipping proves his point, but, unfortunately, bears no date."[22]

———

In the July 3 issue of the *Negro World* Harrison discussed two important aspects of the leadership question. First he looked at "the problem of 'outside interference'"—of whether "the leading of our group in any sense [should] be the product of our group's consciousness or of a consciousness originating from outside that group." Second, he examined a part of the leadership problem "seldom touched upon by Negro Americans who characteristically avoid any public presentation of a thing about which they will talk interminably in private; namely, the claim advanced, explicitly and implicitly, by Negroids of mixed blood to be considered the natural leaders of Negro activities on the ground of some alleged 'superiority' inherent in their white blood."[23]

The discussion of outside interference opened with a reprint article that described a Sunday June 20, 1920, incident in Chicago in which Grover Cleveland Redding led a procession of members of the Star Order of Ethiopia in front of a South Chicago café and burned an American flag. A Black police officer who attempted to stop the destruction of a second American flag was shot and wounded, a "white" sailor who intervened was killed, and a restaurant employee was also killed when "Abyssinians" fired into the café.[24] As of June 23 the police planned to arrest Redding, a self-styled "prince of Abyssinia," considered a ringleader in the incident. He was to be formally charged with murder, accessory to murder, and rioting.[25] "Dr." R. D. Jonas, a Southside agitator, had been released with no evidence found of his direct connection with the shooting.[26] The incident related to the "Back to Abyssinia Movement" headed by Jonas, a "white" minister who had served as the secretary of the League of Darker Peoples (whose founders included the hair-products millionaire Madame C. J. Walker and *Messenger* editors Chandler Owen and A. Philip Randolph).[27] Jonas was reportedly "able to show he had no part in the riot" and said he was "gathering information for the government" and "had connection with the British Secret Service." Redding denied participating in the parade, denied that he was Redding, and claimed he was "George Brown" of St. Louis and "had just come to the city." Ultimately, Jonas's role as an undercover agent was widely exposed, and Redding was convicted of murder and hanged on June 24, 1921.[28]

Harrison's scathing July 3 *Negro World* editorial, "Our White Friends," began by discussing how "in the good old days" the "black man's highest value in the white man's eye" was as "an object of benevolence" for "those tender outpourings of charity which were so dear to the self-satisfied Caucasian." At that time "whites" who fraternized with Blacks "could do so as their guides, philosophers and friends without incurring any hostility on the part of black folk." That practice had continued, and there were "many white men who will befriend the Negro, who will give their dollars to his comfort and welfare, so long as the idea of what constitutes the comfort and welfare comes entirely from the white man's mind." Two examples he cited were Joel Spingarn and E. D. Morel.[29]

The racial climate had changed, however, and "the white man who mixes with the black brother" was now "having a hard time of it." Now, when "whites" insist on mixing, "the colored brother will persist in attributing ulterior motives." The cause of this difference could be found by those who refuse to wear "the parochial blinkers of Anglo-Saxon civilization" (a concept similar to what was later referred to as "the Blindspot in the eyes of America" and the "white blindspot"), by those who see "that the relations of the white and the black race" had "changed" and were "changing all over the world." The change was attributable to "the growing race consciousness" found in the "second half of the world." It was "because they have developed consciousness, intelligence, understanding," and "have learned that the white brother is perfectly willing to love them—'in their place.'" That place was one "in which they are not to develop brains and initiative, but must furnish the brawn and muscle whereby the white man's brain and initiative can take eternally the products of their brawn and muscle."[30]

Harrison was not surprised that "the black man balk[ed] at the white man's 'mixing in,'" since there were "spies everywhere" and "the *agent provocateur*" was "abroad in the land." He cited an article from the Chicago "Associated Press (white)" that held that Dr. Jonas, who had "always insisted in sticking his nose into the Negro people's affairs as their guide, philosopher and friend," was "forced to confess" that he was "a government agent." Jonas reportedly said that he was "connected with the British secret service," but, added Harrison wryly, "since the second year of the European war, it has been rather difficult for us poor devils to tell where the American government ended and the British government began, especially in these matters." Nevertheless, with Dr. Jonas's confession it appeared that "all the silly Negroes who listened approvingly to the senseless allegations made by Messrs. Jonas, [George] Gabriel and others of a standing army of 4,000,000 in Abyssinia and of Japan-Abyssinian diplomatic relations and intentions" were "very foolish."[31]

Harrison then commented on "how natural it was that Jonas, the white leader, should have gone scot free, while Redding and his other Negro dupes are held!" and "how natural" that "Jonas should be the one to positively identify Redding as the slayer of the Negro policeman!" Once again, "that section of the Negro race that will not follow except where a white man leads" would "have to pay that stern penalty." He pointedly concluded:

> Under present circumstances we, the Negroes of the Western world, do pledge our allegiance to leaders of our own race, selected by our own group and supported financially and otherwise exclusively by us. Their leadership may be wise or otherwise; they may make mistakes here and there; nevertheless, such sins as they may commit will be our sins, and all the glory that they may achieve will be our glory. We prefer it so. It may be worth the while of the white men who desire to be "Our Professional Friends" to take note of this preference.[32]

In the same July 3 issue of the *Negro World* Harrison wrote "A Tender Point," which discussed the "alleged superiority of white blood." It described how "whenever a leader of the Irish has to be selected by the Irish" it was "an

Irishman who is selected," and "no Irishman would be inclined to dispute the fact that other men, even Englishmen like John Stuart Mill and the late Keir Hardie, could feel the woes of Ireland as profoundly as any Irishman." Simply put, the Irish "prefer to live up to the principle of 'Safety First.'"[33]

He then broached a subject "not often discussed in the Negro press" because "black, brown and parti-colored—fear to offend each other." The subject was "the biological breed of persons who should be selected by Negroes as leaders of their race." He emphasized that one couldn't be "too tender" in these matters "of prejudice" that stood "in the way of desirable results." Harrison recounted how for two centuries in America the "descendants of the black Negroes of Africa" were "told by white men that we cannot and will not amount to anything except in so far as we accept the bar sinister of their mixing with us." In addition, when white people would "select a leader for Negroes," they would "always" select "one who had in his veins the blood of the selectors." During "the good old days when slavery was in flower, it was those whom Denmark Vesey of Charleston described as 'house niggers' who got the master's cast-off clothes, the better scraps of food and culture which fell from the white man's table, who were looked upon as the Talented Tenth of the Negro race." At that time "the opportunities of self-improvement" that "lay within the hand of the white race" were "accorded exclusively to this class of people who were the left-hand progeny of the white masters."[34]

Out of this practice, explained Harrison, "grew a certain attitude on their part toward the rest of the Negro people." In cities like Washington, Boston, Charleston, New York, and Chicago, "proponents of the lily-white idea" were "prone to erect around their sacred personalities a high wall of caste, based on the grounds of color," and "black Negroes" had "heretofore worshipped at the altars erected on these walls." This was evidenced "in the Baptist, Methodist and Episcopal churches" and at various conventions and fraternal organizations where "Black people themselves seem to hold the degrading view that a man who is but half a Negro is twice as worthy of their respect and support as one who is entirely black." Based on this, "women, undeniably black and undeniably beautiful" were "shunned and ostracized at public functions by men who should be presumed to know better." Similarly, "fervid jeremiads of 'colored' men who, when addressing the whites on behalf of some privilege which they wished to share with them, would be in words as black as the ace of spades" but were "professional lily-whites" when it came to "mixing with 'their kind.'" It had to be pointed out to them "that there is no color prejudice in America—except among 'colored' people."[35]

In this matter of color prejudice, Harrison observed that "white people, even in America" were "inclined to be more liberal than colored people." Thus, "if a white man" had "no race prejudice" it didn't matter "how black is the Negro friend that he takes to his home and bosom." In recent years this had even been extended to "white people who pick leaders for Negroes," who gave "formal and official expression to this principle." Accordingly, when Tuskegee Normal and Industrial Institute trustees had to elect "a head of Tuskegee and a putative leader of the Negroes of America to succeed the late Dr. [Booker T.] Washington" in 1915, they argued "that it was now necessary to select as leader for the Negro people a man who could not be mistaken by any one for anything other than a Negro." For this reason, "Mr. Emmett Scott was passed over and Dr. Robert R. Moton was selected." By citing this example Harrison was "not approving . . . the results of this selection, but merely holding up to Negroes the principle by which it was governed."[36]

The point Harrison sought to make was that "so long as we ourselves acquiesce in the selection of leaders on the ground of their unlikeness to our racial type, just so long will we be met by the invincible argument that white blood is necessary to make a Negro worth while." He recognized, however, that "every Negro" with "respect for himself and for his race," when "contemplating such examples as Toussaint Louverture [L'Ouverture], Phillis Wheatley, Paul Laurence Dunbar and Samuel Ringgold Ward," felt a "thrill of pride" that differed "in quality and intensity" from the feeling experienced "when contemplating other examples of great Negroes who are not entirely black." Part of the reason was because it was "impossible in such cases for the white men to argue that they owed their greatness or their prominence to the blood of the white race which was mingled in their veins." Thus, the "thrill of pride" was "legitimate"—it offered "a hope nobler than the hope of amalgamation whereby, in order to become men, we must lose our racial identity." Harrison urged "sober and serious reflection" on this matter.[37]

Two other Harrison editorials published circa July 1920 concerned the national political parties. "When the Tail Wags the Dog" discussed the growing "new manhood" dedicated to "the proposition that, if all Americans are equal in the matter of baring their breasts to foreign bayonet, then all Americans must, by their own efforts, be made equal in balloting for President and other officers of the government." It was that principle that was "compelling the Republican party in certain localities to consider the necessity of nominating Negroes on its local electoral tickets," despite the fact that "the old attitude of that party on the political rights of Negroes" was unchanged.[38]

At the Republican Party's June 8–12, 1920, Chicago convention, which nominated Warren G. Harding for president and Calvin Coolidge for vice president, "Negro delegates were lined up to do their duty by the party," but there was an "odd feature of the entire affair"—"*Whereas the Negro people in the South are not free to cast their votes, it was precisely from these voteless areas that the national Republican leaders selected the political spokesman for the voting Negroes of the North.*" Thus, men who could not vote in the coming election and men who "like Roscoe Simmons, never cast a vote in their lives," were "the accredited representatives in whose hands lay the destiny of a million Negro voters." Unfortunately, "the average Negro Republican" was "too stupid to see and too meek to mind." Harrison saw this as "Fate's retribution for the black man in the North who has never cared enough to fight (the Republican party) for the political freedom of his brother in the South, but left him to rot under poll-tax laws and grandfather clauses." It was, he emphasized, "the Northern white Democrats," who let "their Southern brethren run riot through the Constitution," who now had to "pay the penalty of being led into the ditch by the most ignorant, stupid and vicious portion of the party." Similarly, it was "the Northern Negro Republican," who let "his Southern brother remain a political ragamuffin," who now had to "stomach the insult of this same ragamuffin dictating the destiny of the freer Negroes of the North." In both these cases, Harrison tersely pointed out, "the tail doth wag the dog because of 'the solid South.'"[39]

In a July 1920 editorial on "The Grand Old Party" Harrison called attention to the fact that "most Negro Americans (and white ones, too)" considered it "fashionable to maintain the most fervid faith and deepest ignorance about points in their national history of which they should be informed." In an effort at overcoming such ignorance he discussed the Republican Party, which he considered to be "the most corrupt influence among Negro Americans."[40]

Particularly since the 1906 Brownsville, Texas, incident, Harrison had increasingly become disillusioned with the Republicans. On the day after the 1906 election, President Theodore Roosevelt, a Republican, on insufficient evidence and without courts-martial, dishonorably discharged from the army and debarred from future government employment all 167 men of three companies of Black troops of the Twenty-Fifth Regiment stationed near Brownsville. From that point on Harrison would continually urge African American voters to break from the Republican Party (the party to which Booker T. Washington and the "Tuskegee Machine" were so fully aligned). He first turned to the Socialists, as did W. E. B. Du Bois, but by 1914 he had left the Socialists. (Du Bois left earlier, in 1912, to support the Democratic Party's Woodrow Wilson.) Beginning in 1916, Harrison had repeatedly called upon African Americans to maintain their political independence, put "race interests" first in evaluating candidates, organize politically, seek a political voice, and run "Negro" candidates for office (even during his short-lived return to the Socialist Party in 1918). Overall, this quest to develop a new and independent Black political voice had distinguished the leadership of Harrison (who had named his paper *The Voice*) from the leadership of Washington and Du Bois.[41]

His work in this area also influenced Garvey. According to the historian Robert A. Hill, Garvey had eschewed political involvement in the early days of his UNIA, and in 1915 he renounced participation in Jamaican politics and reportedly asked his followers "to eschew politics as a means of social improvements." In the United States, however, Garvey was influenced by the new era of racial consciousness that Harrison was so instrumental in developing with his newspaper *The Voice*, his organization the Liberty League (which Garvey joined), his monthly *New Negro*, and his editorials (such as "The Grand Old Party") in the *Negro World*. It was in America, writes Hill, that Garvey became converted "to the primacy and efficacy of political goals." Garvey explained in 1921 that the "new spirit of the new Negro" now "seeks a political voice, and the world is amazed, the world is astounded that the Negro should desire a political voice, because after the political voice comes a political place, and nobody thought the Negro would have asked for a place in the political sun of the world."[42]

In "The Grand Old Party" Harrison argued that historical facts were "open and notorious" but that there were "'intellectual' Negroes" who were "striving secretly" to "perpetuate the bonds of serfdom which bind the Negro Americans to the Republican party." In light of this, Harrison appealed "to the historical record" in order to show that "if the Negro owes any debt to the Republican party it is a debt of execration and of punishment rather than one of gratitude."[43]

Harrison called special attention to some little-known but extremely important antebellum history from the period between Abraham Lincoln's November 1860 election and his first inaugural address, on March 4, 1861. He described how the Republican Party in Congress, under the leadership of Massachusetts's Charles Francis Adams, organized a joint committee of thirteen Senators and thirty-three Representatives "to make overture to the seceding Southerners." This resulted in "a proposed thirteenth amendment, which, if the Southerners had not been so obstinate, would have bridged the chasm" and made "the slavery of the black man in America eternal and inescapable." Among other things, it would have "provided that no amendment to the Constitution, or any other proposition affecting slavery" could ever be legally presented in Congress "unless its mover had secured the previous consent of *every Senator and Representative from the slave-holding States*." This proposal "put teeth into the Fugitive Slave Law" and "absolutely gave the Negro over into the keeping of his oppressors."[44]

This proposed legislation took various forms, including the resolutions proposed to the Senate and House by John J. Crittenden on December 18, 1860, and the proposed amendment of Thomas Corwin, which was approved by the House on February 28, 1861, and by the Senate on March 2, 1861. Harrison wrote that Lincoln, in his inaugural address, "gave his explicit approval to the

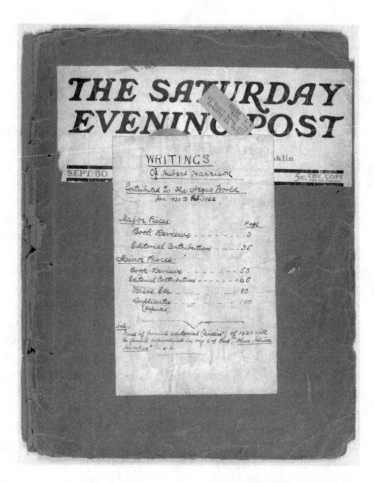

Figure 6.1. "Writings of Hubert Harrison Contributed to the *Negro World*," scrapbook of Hubert Harrison, January 1920 to February 1922, cover. Around 1910 Hubert Harrison began to organize and paste his writings, clippings, and similar materials in scrapbooks (using publications such as the *Saturday Evening Post* as a base). These scrapbooks served as files for him. Some forty-three Harrison scrapbooks have been located, including this one: "'Writings of Hubert Harrison Contributed to the Negro World Jan 1920 to Feb 1922': Major Pieces—Book Reviews, Editorial Contributions, Minor Pieces, Book Reviews, Editorial, Contributions, Verses, Etc., Duplicates (unpasted)." *Source:* Hubert H. Harrison Papers, Box 13, Folder 7, Rare Book and Manuscript Library, Columbia University Library.

substance of the Crittenden resolutions which the joint committee referred to above had collectively taken over." Since this initial Thirteenth Amendment was adopted by six of eight northern states, including Pennsylvania and Illinois, this clearly demonstrated "that the Republican party at the very beginning of its contact with the Negro was willing to sell the Negro, bound hand and foot, for the substance of its own political control." It was also clear that "if Fort Sumter had not been fired upon [on April 12, 1861] it would have become by State action the law of the land." Citing the historical record, Harrison concluded that "the Republican party's only interest in the Negro is to get his vote for nothing; and so long as Negro Republican leaders remain the contemptible grafters and political procurers that they are at present, so long will it get Negro votes for nothing."[45]

In the "Grand Old Party" Harrison also discussed how, after the Republican Party obtained control, "thousands of square miles of the people's property were given away to Wall Street magnates." He detailed how in 1876 "the overwhelmingly Republican Congress" shamelessly "made a deal" to "pacify the white 'crackers' of the South," how "the Negro was given over into the hands of the triumphant Ku-Klux," and how "soldiers who protected their access to the ballot box in the worst southern states were withdrawn," while the "crackers" agreed "as the price of this favor to withdraw their opposition to the election of [the Republican Rutherford B.] Hayes." He also described how Reconstruction was "settled against the Negro by the aid and abetting of the Republican party" and how since then "lynching, disfranchisement and segregation have grown" under mostly Republican control of the government. He then drove home his point that "the new Negro in America will never amount to anything politically until he enfranchises himself from the Grand Old Party which has made a political joke of him."[46]

Harrison repeatedly sought to encourage Black enfranchisement by movement away from the Republican Party, and his emphasis on that point increased significantly over the course of the 1920s. It would gain additional strength with the March 1921 publication of his four-part series "Lincoln and Liberty—Fact Versus Fiction" in the *Negro World*.[47]

———

In his 1920 *Negro World* writings on domestic issues Harrison evinced both a class and a race consciousness. In "Curbing the Gouging Landlords" in the April 17 issue he described bench decisions under new tenant legislation that afforded "some measure of protections from greedy, gouging landlords" who would use the courts in efforts at dispossession. Harlem, in particular, was "infested" with bad landlords, and "the Negro landlord [was] just as oppressive, and very often more so than the white landlord." If "these bullying, get-rich-quick" landlords weren't curbed, Harrison predicted, "a serious situation" would arise "out of sheer desperation on the part of oppressed tenants." In a large majority of cases Harlem landlords had increased rents "indiscriminately," sometimes "way over the 25 per cent limit." Existing judicial interpretation actually maintained that the 25 percent provision in the new legislation did not "allow" such increases. Harrison stressed this fact "as a warning to those landlords in Harlem who not infrequently evict white tenants and immediately boost the rents of vacated apartments as high as 75 per cent. to Negro tenants." He also advised that before taking an apartment, "Negroes should take steps to ascertain, as far as possible, the rent paid by the former occupant."[48]

In the May 29 *Negro World* Harrison's "A 'Cheap' Administration" recounted that during the war the U.S. government insisted "we should pay for the nurses and hospital supplies, the candy, tobacco and books which were as necessary as bullets to our brothers who fought in the trenches." It somehow "didn't seem just right that great governments should run their wars on a 'pan-handling' basis," especially since "they got our brothers to do the work of war at one-fifth to one-tenth of what they were paid by businessmen in the piping times of peace." Having seen "the various shifts and tricks" whereby governments were "evading the payment of a bonus to their returned soldiers," Harrison offered "a word in criticism" of the "government's policy of treating its civil and military employees as if they were as 'cheap as common dirt.'"[49]

Harrison, a former postal clerk, then cited the case of postal employees, who were "as faithful and efficient a body of men and women as ever did work for the government." In the current era of "sky-high prices," they received less than a hundred dollars a month from the government. The ordinary postal clerk had to memorize by heart a general separation scheme, a city scheme, and various state schemes, many of which contained thousands of names, and they had to route mail without error to these places. Any mistakes would appear on an individual's record as demerits and were used to block raises. In addition, most postal clerks had to do "laborious porter's work 'juggling' and shaking out sacks of mail from which escape[d] clouds of international dust" and that "in many cases" resulted in "consumption." Though performing such services and incurring the health risks, and despite a rise in the cost of living, postal pay "remained stationary down to 1907," when there had been "a slight increase." During the war there was a second slight increase—a bonus of 150 dollars. But, as of May 1920, postal clerks and carriers received "an average salary of 1,400 dollars a year." In comparison, a porter in a drug store often received $1,560 a year. In arguing for a raise Harrison, who began his postal work in 1907, recalled how the Postal Commission of the Fifty-Ninth Congress in that year declared "'upon the postal service more than upon anything else does the general economic, as well as the social and political development of the country depend.'" Nevertheless, these same Congressmen who "load[ed] the mail with millions of [franked] copies of speeches which they never delivered" held up the Joint Postal Commission report designed to relieve the situation, and clerks and carriers "were driven from the service in droves" and "forced to seek other employment." Conditions in the Post Office were "as rotten as that of the teachers," and Harrison suggested that Postmaster Albert Sidney Burleson "would do well to take a day off from censoring the press and bend his blooming intellect to the mighty task of getting a square deal for the postal employees." He admonished that "Uncle Sam can't afford to be the 'cheapest' employer of labor in his own land."[50]

In response to this editorial Harrison received a letter from five "Negro" postal clerks from Manhattan, offering their "heartiest thanks" for his "able, lucid, and bold 'write-up.'" They fully appreciated the good it would do and stressed that "Negro readers though only porters, chauffeurs, etc.—if interested—can have equal influence with their employers as the interests of any other race group." They also added that the *Negro World* was "not only read locally" but "all over these United States." Among the five signatories was Julius A. Thomas, Harrison's friend from the Liberty League.[51]

The June 26 *Negro World* included Harrison's "Lynching: Its Cause and Cure," which began by quoting John R. Shillady's resignation from the NAACP (published in the June 1920 *Crisis*) and declared it obvious "that the N.A.A.C.P. is not likely to affect the lynchings in this land." Cited as proof were the previous week's comments by Minnesota's governor Joseph A. A. Burnquist, the president of the St. Paul NAACP branch. Burnquist described a Duluth, Minnesota, lynching as "one of the most cynically brutal that has occurred North or South in the last ten years" and offered all assistance possible in apprehending the culprits.[52]

Burnquist's description of the brutality was accurate. On Tuesday night, June 15, between 11:15 and 11:45 p.m., a mob of five thousand lynched three African American men, Isaac McGhie, Elmer Jackson, and Nate Green. The victims, who were in town with a circus, were hanged from a telephone pole at First Street and Second Avenue East in downtown Duluth. They had been arrested and were taken from the police by the mob along with three other Black men. In their seizure, the mob used no firearms; the thirty police on duty did not fire a shot and offered little resistance. The mob then held a mock "trial" and found three of the six guilty of sexual assault on a local seventeen-year-old "white" woman. Hundreds in the mob cried "lynch them" and "burn them" as the victims were dragged through the streets. According to the Minneapolis *Morning Tribune*, a "peculiar feature of the lynching was the great number of aged men, young girls, and young matrons who looked on as the three negroes

Figure 6.2. The Duluth, Minnesota, lynchings, June 15, 1920. On Tuesday night, June 15, 1920, a mob of five thousand lynched three African American men, Isaac McGhie, Elmer Jackson, and Nate Green, in downtown Duluth. The victims, who were in town with a circus, were hanged from a telephone pole and were among six men taken from over thirty police on duty by a mob that used no firearms. The mob then held a mock "trial" and found three of the six guilty of sexual assault on a local seventeen-year-old "white" woman. Hundreds in the mob cried "lynch them" and "burn them" as the victims were dragged through the streets. According to the Minneapolis *Morning Tribune* a "peculiar feature of the lynching was the great number of aged men, young girls, and young matrons who looked on as the three negroes were strung up." In this photo two of the victims are still hanging; the third is on the ground.

Hubert Harrison wrote, "white men lynch Negroes . . . because Negroes' lives are cheap." The "cure," he suggested, "follows from the nature of the cause," and if "Negroes determine that their lives shall no longer be cheap," then we will see "the cracker" thinking twice "before he joins [such] a mob." *Source:* Public domain.

were strung up." "No word of regret was uttered by them," though "they cheered and laughed at the crude wit from immature boys' mouths." On June 16 several Duluth city officials said they were "not certain of the guilt" of the six and that "at least one innocent man fell victim to the mob."[53]

Harrison pointed out that "in most of the other cases of lynching" it was "assumed that all the officials were in collusion with the forces of violence, or were at any rate in acquiescence." The Minnesota case was different, however, since the governor was a high officer of the association. Nevertheless, Harrison prophesied "no more will be done in the case of the Minnesota lynching than in the case of lynchings further south."[54] This assessment led him "to a front face consideration of the problem of lynching," of why "white men lynch black men in America." He concluded, as he would repeatedly conclude, "white men lynch black men or any other men because those men's lives are unprotected either by the authorities of the commonwealth or by the victims themselves." In short, "white men lynch Negroes . . . because Negroes' lives are cheap."[55]

"The cure," he suggested, "follows from the nature of the cause." If "Negroes determine that their lives shall no longer be cheap; but that they will exact for them as high a price as any other element in the community under similar circumstances would exact," and if they see to it that their lives are protected and defended, "if not by the State, then certainly by themselves," then we will see "the cracker" thinking twice "before he joins a mob in whose gruesome holiday sport he himself is likely to furnish one of the casualties." If "Negroes help to make murder costly," Harrison counseled, they "will aid the officers of the city, State and nation in instilling respect for law and order into the minds of the worst and lowest element of our American cities." Since laws in every state declared killing in defense of one's own life to be "proper, legal and justifiable," he urged that "Negroes determine to defend themselves from the horrible outrage of lynching." If this were done, "they should have the support of every official and every citizen who really believes in law and order and is determined to make the law of the land stand as a living reality among the people that made it."[56]

In all the publications that he edited, Harrison stressed international matters. This was particularly true of the *Negro World*. Though many issues of the paper from the period of his editorship have not been located, those that are available contain articles revealing a decidedly anti-imperialist perspective and particular concern with Africa, Africans of the diaspora, and the peoples of Asia, the Caribbean, the Mideast, and Latin America. The fact that these articles reached such a broad domestic and international audience amplifies their significance.

In the May 15, 1920, issue Harrison put forth one of his more important articles on "The New International." It began by pointing out how "in the eyes of our overlords internationalism is a thing of varying value." Thus, "when Mr. [J. Pierpont] Morgan wants to float a French or British loan in the United States," or "when Messrs. [Woodrow] Wilson, [Georges] Clemenceau, [David] Lloyd George and [Vittorio] Orlando want to stabilize their joint credit and commerce," or "when areas like the Belgian Congo are to be handed over to certain rulers without the consent of their inhabitants," "then the paeans of praise go up to the god of 'internationalism' in the temple of civilization." In contrast, "when any portion of the world's disinherited (whether white or black) seeks to join hands with other groups in the same condition, then the lords of misrule denounce the idea of internationalism as anarchy, sedition, Bolshevism and disruptive propaganda."[57]

The "difference" was because the international linking up of peoples was "a source of strength to those who are linked up." The overlords sought "to strengthen themselves" and to "keep their subject masses from strengthening themselves in the same way." But, as "the great world-majority, made up of black, brown and yellow peoples" stretched out their hands to one another and developed what the Columbia University professor Franklin H. Giddings called "a 'consciousness of kind,'" they also sought "to establish their own centers of diffusion for their own internationalism." This reality gave "nightmares to Downing street [in London], the Quai d'Orsay [in Paris] and other centers of white capitalist internationalism."[58]

As the "white" statesmen equated "civilization" with "their own overlordship, with their right and power to dictate to the darker millions," they "aroused [the] sentiment of the world's darker majority," who desired "to be as free as England, America or France" and did not want to be "'wards of the nations' of Europe any longer." The problem for "white" statesmen of the future would be how "to square democracy with the subjection of this dark majority." A continuation of suppression might "be fraught with consequences disastrous to white overlordship," and "the tendency toward an international of the darker races" could not be set back. Harrison attributed this new situation to "increasing enlightenment, the spread of technical science, and the recently acquired knowledge of the weak points of white 'civilization' gained by the darker peoples during the recent World War." He predicted that "the darker peoples" would "strive increasingly for their share of sunlight, and if this is what white 'civilization' opposes," it would "have a hard time of it."[59]

To Harrison "the object of the capitalist international" was "to unify and standardize the exploitation of black, brown and yellow peoples in such a way that the danger to the exploiting groups of cutting each other's throats over the spoils may be reduced to a minimum." This desire led to "various agreements, mandates and spheres of influence" and to the League of Nations, which was "not a league of the white masses, but of their gold-braided governors." When "faced by such a tendency," the "darker peoples of the world" began "to realize that their first duty is to themselves." In this way, he concluded, the "similarity of suffering" was "producing in them a similarity of sentiment."[60]

The Harrison article "Bolshevism in Barbados" was probably written in early 1920, after the October 1919 suppression of the *Negro World* in the West Indies.[61]

It described how the *Barbados Standard*, worried "about the signs of awakening . . . yells to all" that "there is 'Bolshevism among Negroes.'" The paper even saw "evidences of a Bolshevist R-r-r-revolution in Trinidad, and, presumptively, all over the British West Indies." In reality, explained Harrison, "they point at the thing for which they alone are responsible and shriek for salvation." Harrison suggested "the white Englishman learn that justice exists not only for white Englishmen, but for all men" and that he "get off the black man's back." If this were done, there would be "very little need for wasting tons of print paper and thousands of pounds in a crusade against the specter of Bolshevism."[62]

In another brief article, "Help Wanted for Hayti," Harrison described how, while the United States was at war, "our President declared, over and over again, that we were calling upon the flower of our manhood to go to France and make itself into manure in order that the world might be made safe for democracy." The "deluded people of the earth" now realized that "Ireland, India and Egypt" were "living proofs that the world has been lied to." Those who said "the world would be made safe for democracy have lied to us." In truth, people worldwide were "finding out that when an American President, a British Premier or a French 'tiger' speaks of 'the world,' he does not include the black and brown and yellow millions, who make up the vast majority of the earth's population." Haiti was a case in point: "British India and Ireland, Turkish Armenia or Russian Poland" had never witnessed "such ruthless savagery as has been let loose in Hayti in a private war for which President Wilson has never had the consent of Congress." Harrison charged that the "white daily newspapers" spoke "complacently about the repulse of 'bandits'" in order "to put the blinkers of a catchword over the eyes of the spirit."[63]

In fact, Haiti was the "American Ireland"—its people were "being shot, sabered and bombed, while resisting an illegal invasion of their homes." Harrison urged "America white and black" to insist on a congressional investigation:

> When Ireland feels the pressure of the English heel, the Irish in America make their voices heard and help to line up American public opinion on their side. When [Ignacy] Paderewski's government massacres Jews in Poland, the Jews of America raise money, organize committees, put the U.S. Government on the job—and get results. But when Negroes are massacred—not in Africa, but in Hayti, under American control—what do we American Negroes do? So far, nothing. But that inaction will not last. Negroes must write their Congressmen and Senators concerning the atrocity perpetrated at Port au Prince last week [on January 15, 1920, in "la débâcle" of Port-au-Prince]. They should organize committees to go before Congress and put the pitiful facts, demanding investigation, redress and punishment.

He concluded by arguing that "as long as such things can be done without effective protest or redress, black people every where will refuse to believe that the democracy advertised by lying white politicians can be anything but a ghastly joke."[64]

The Harrison article "The Cracker in the Caribbean" discussed "the bloody rape of the republics of Hayti and Santo Domingo." This aggression was "perpetrated by the bayonets of American sailors and marines, with the silent and shameful acquiescence of 12,000,000 American Negroes too cowardly to lift a voice in effective protest or too ignorant of political affairs to know what is taking place." Harrison bemoaned the fact that "we strike heroic attitudes and talk grandiloquently of Ethiopia stretching forth her hands" while "we Africans of the dispersion" let "the land of [Toussaint] L'O[u]verture lie like a fallen flower beneath the feet of swine."[65]

The brutal military occupation had to be challenged. The situation as described in *The Nation* and elsewhere was "a tale of shuddering horror in comparison with which the Putumayo [of the Amazon] pales into insignificance and the Congo atrocities of Belgium are tame." The two West Indian republics had been "murderously assaulted" and their citizens "shot down by armed ruffians, bombed by aeroplanes, hunted into concentration camps and there starved to death." In their homelands their "civil liberties" were "taken away," their governments "blackjacked and their property stolen." All of this was made possible "by the 'cracker' statesmanship of 'the South,' without one word of protest from that defunct department, the Congress of the United States!"[66]

The U.S. Congress had "shamelessly ignored" the fact that the Constitution gave it the exclusive power to declare war. To further "the God-given 'cracker' mandate to 'keep the nigger in his place,'" a "mere Secretary of the Navy," Josephus Daniels, had "assumed over the head of Congress the right to conquer and annex two nations and to establish on their shores the 'cracker-democracy' of his native [North] Carolina slave-runs." To Harrison it was "high time that the Negro people of the United States call the hand of Josephus Daniels" by appealing to Congress "to resume its political functions, investigate this high-handed outrage and impeach the Secretary of the Navy of high crimes and misdemeanors against the peace and good name of the United States." This would not violate any law and would be an effort "to put an end to a flagrant violation of the Constitution itself on the part of a high officer." He emphasized: "That is our right and our duty."[67]

Harrison explained that Irishmen "sell the bonds of an Irish loan to free Ireland from the tyranny of [U.S. ally] Britain" on the steps of New York's City Hall, while "we black people are not manly enough to get up even a petition on behalf of our brothers in Hayti." He then put forth a call for a "monster petition" to Congress: "Out upon such crawling cowardice! Rouse, ye slaves, and show the spirit of liberty is not quite dead among you! You who elected 'delegates' to a Peace Conference to which you had neither passport nor invitation, on behalf of bleeding Africa, get together and present a monster petition to the American Congress, over which you have some control."[68] An extremely instructive lesson was then drawn from the past: In the eighteenth century "George the Third [of Great Britain] engaged in a contest with the colonies" because he "could not defeat the Pitts, Burkes and Foxes at home." "Had he succeeded," however, "in setting his foot on their necks he would have returned home with increased prestige and power to bend the free spirits of England to his will." William Pitt (the Elder), Charles James Fox, and Edmund Burke knew this, which is why "they took the side of their distant cousins against the British kings." Harrison noted "the British liberals of today thank their memories for it." He emphasized: "If the 'crackers' of the South can fasten their yoke on the necks of our brothers overseas, then God help us Negroes in America in the years to come!"[69]

In the July 3 *Negro World* Harrison cited a June 16 letter from "L. F. Bowler," originally printed in the *New York Evening Sun* of June 18. Bowler wrote how "Africa offers a great field for medical research and discovery." Harrison used Bowler's letter as a point of departure for his own July 3 editorial, "Getting Excited and Nervous," which discussed how Africa had "Bulala Gwai, to put its enemies to sleep or to death" and advised, "Africa is going to teach the teachers who imagine that they know it all a great many wonderful things in the coming years, because she is now awakening."[70]

In a July 17 *Negro World* editorial Harrison discussed a popular advertisement in magazines, on streets, and on billboards that was "a masterly illustration of the principle of repetition." Its "flaring sign" said "U-need-a Biscuit." Uneeda Biscuit was the name of a popular National Biscuit Company soda cracker. Even if ignored at first, the advertisement reached one's "inner consciousness" by its "constant insistence" and prompted people to "decide that perhaps after all we do need a biscuit." He called this story "to the attention of the white people of this country who guide the ship of state either in the halls of Congress or through the columns of the white newspapers" who were "seemingly at a loss to account for the new spirit which has come over the Negro people in the Western world." While some claimed it was "Bolshevism— whatever that may be," others said it was "the product of alien agitators," and yet others contended that it sprang "from a desire to mingle" blood "with that of white people." Such answers were all inadequate, but "the Anglo-Saxon" was "such a professional liar that with the plain truth before his eyes" he would "still profess to be seeing something else."[71]

Harrison offered an explanation for this new spirit. He began by asking if any reader who lived through the years 1914–1919 could remember "what

'Democracy' was." "It was," he wrote, "the U-need-a Biscuit advertised by Messrs. Woodrow Wilson, Lloyd George, Georges Clemenceau and thousands of perspiring publicists, preachers and thinkers, who were on one side of a conflict then raging in Europe." One could not "get men to go out and get killed by telling them plainly that you are sending them to get the other fellow's land, trade and wealth, and you are too cowardly or too intelligent to go yourself and risk getting shot over the acquisition." Instead, "you whoop it up with any catchword which will serve as sufficient bait for the silly fools whom you keep silly in order that you may always use them in this way." "'Democracy' was such a catch-word," and the leaders Harrison listed "advertised it for all it was worth—to them." But, explained Harrison, "just as we prophesied in 1915, there was an unavoidable flare-back": "When you advertise U-need-a Biscuit incessantly people will want it; and when you advertise democracy incessantly the people to whom you trumpet forth its deliciousness are likely to believe you, take you at your word, and, later on, demand that you make good and furnish them with the article for which you yourself have created the appetite." Thus, while "Negroes, Egyptians and Hindoos, under the pressure of democracy's commercial drummers, have developed a democratic complex," which was "apt to trouble the firms for whom these drummers drummed," they had not received any of the advertised goods—nor was there "the slightest intention" of passing any to them.[72]

Harrison advised "white" men that "when you read of the Mullah, of Said Zagloul [Saad Zaghlul] Pasha and Marcus Garvey or Casely Hayford; when you hear of Egyptian and Indian nationalist uprisings, of Black Star Lines and West Indian 'seditions'—kindly remember (because *we* know) that these fruits spring from the seeds of your own sowing." You "have said to us 'U need a biscuit,' and, after long listening to you, we have replied, 'We do!'" Harrison pointedly added, "Perhaps next time—if there is a next time—you will think twice before you furnish to 'inferior' peoples such a stick as 'democracy.'" The work had been "too well done," and now "the Negro of the Western world" could "truthfully say to the white man and the Anglo-Saxon in particular, 'You made me what I am today, I hope you're satisfied.'"[73]

This editorial drew praise from Leonard Braithwaite of New York, who, in a letter to the editor, wrote that he had "so much pleasure in reading" it that he was prompted to acclaim his approval. It accurately described "the correct cause of the new spirit that has overshadowed the Negro peoples of the western world as well as the people of all the world." Braithwaite added that he had "been reading the *Negro World* for some time," and while the editorials were often "masterfully written," special attention was due this one for revealing both "the character of the writer—a close observer of humanity" and "the ills that affect us."[74]

Another Harrison editorial, "When Might Makes Right," probably written in early 1920, discussed a letter to the editor that raised the question "of the relation between mental competence and property rights." It provocatively asked, "'Does inability to govern destroy title to ownership?'" It seemed that "the white race" assumed so "in every case in which the national property of darker and weaker races" was concerned but denied it in cases involving "their own national property rights." Thus, "disturbances" occurring in the southern states were "never considered sufficient to justify the destruction of their sovereignty," while "such disturbances occurring in Hayti or Mexico" were considered "a sufficient reason for invasion and conquest by white Americans." England, France, and Italy acted similarly, and disturbances "in Alexandria, Delhi, Ashanti or the Cameroons" sufficed "to fix upon those territories and cities the badge of inferiority and incompetence to rule themselves."[75]

In all such cases it was declared "that the white race" was "called by this fortunate combination of circumstances to do the ruling for them." In contrast, "similar disturbances occurring in Wales, Essen or Marseilles would never be considered as sufficient to justify the dictatorship of foreign powers in the interest of 'law and order.'" Thus, it was "'might makes right,'" though "white statesmen" would "often deny this" while "using 'force without stint'" to "establish 'rights' which they claim over territories, peoples, commerce and the high seas."[76]

Such "characteristic hypocrisy" kept them from "telling the truth as plainly" as "Friedrich A. J. Von Bernhardi did in his [bellicose, 1911] book, *Germany and the Next War.*" The "'sociological' reason for this hypocrisy" was that they needed "to preach 'goodness,' 'right' and 'justice' to those over whom they rule in order that their ruling may be made easy by the consequent good behavior of the ruled." In fact, however, they themselves had to "practice ruthlessness, injustice and the rule of the strong hand to make their governance go," and it was this fact that caused "intelligent Negroes, Filipinos, Chinese and Egyptians to spurn with contempt the claims which Caucasian diplomats, statesmen, writers and missionaries make on behalf of their moral superiority." While "they lie; they know that they lie, and . . . they're beginning to know that we know it also." Such "knowledge on our part," emphasized Harrison, was "a loss of prestige for them" and would inform "our actions in the future."[77]

———

In "Education and the Race," which appeared in his August 1920 book *When Africa Awakes: The "Inside Story" of the Stirrings and Strivings of the New Negro in the Western World*, Harrison cited the example of Russia as instructive for African Americans. He opened by explaining how "in the dark days of Russia, when the iron heel of Czarist despotism was heaviest on the necks of the people, those who wished to rule decreed that the people should remain ignorant." At that time "Leo Tolstoi and the other intelligentsia began to carry knowledge to the masses." Though "most of this work was underground at first," it "took," and "thousands of educated persons gave themselves to this work—without pay." Their "only hope of reward" was "in the future effectiveness of an instructed mass movement." Then, "as knowledge spread, enthusiasm was backed by brains," and "the Russian revolution began to be sure of itself."[78]

Meanwhile, "the workingmen of the cities studied the thing that they were 'up against'" and "gauged their own weakness and strength as well as their opponents." With this developing consciousness, "the despotism of the Czar could not provoke them to a mass movement before they were ready and had the means." Then, "when at last they moved, they swept not only the Czar's regime but the whole exploiting system upon which it stood into utter oblivion." The importance of this example "to the Negro of the Western world," wrote Harrison, was still to be determined. If these experiences were to "have value for the New Negro Manhood Movement," it should seek to support "the new fervor of faith in itself" with "knowledge." Harrison stressed, "we Negroes who have shown our *manhood* must back it by our *mind*." Since the "world, at present," was "a white man's world—even in Africa," the task was to "either *accept* his domination and our inferiority" or "contend against it." The struggle must be waged "to win," and whether undertaken "with ballots, bullets or business," victory would not come "unless we know at least as much as the white man knows. For, after all, knowledge *is* power."[79]

But, added Harrison, the kind of knowledge that "enables white men to rule black men's lands" was not "knowledge of Hebrew and Greek, philosophy or literature." Rather, it was "knowledge of explosives and deadly compounds: that is chemistry," "knowledge which can build ships, bridges, railroads and factories: that is engineering," and "knowledge which harnesses the visible and invisible forces of the earth and air and water": "that is science, modern science." These were "what the New Negro must enlist upon his side." "Let us," Harrison urged, "like the Japanese, become a race of knowledge-getters, preserving our racial soul, but digesting into it all that we can glean or grasp," so that we are competent to control our destiny. To begin to develop such competence Harrison advised: "Those who have knowledge must come down from their Sinais and give it to the common people. Theirs is the great duty to simplify and make clear, to light the lamps of knowledge that the eyes of their race may see; that the feet of their people may not stumble."[80] This, Harrison emphasized, was "the task of the Talented Tenth." The "masses" also had a task, and to the "masses" Harrison's instructive message was:

Read! Get the reading habit; spend your spare time not so much in training the feet to dance, as in training the head to think. And, at the very outset, draw the line between books of opinion and books of information. Saturate your minds with the latter and you will be forming your own opinions, which will be worth ten times more to you than the opinions of the greatest minds on earth. Go to school whenever you can. If you can't go in the day, go at night. But remember always that the best college is that on your bookshelf: the best education is that on the inside of your own head. For in this work-a-day world people ask first, not "Where were you educated?" but "What do you know?" and next, "What can you do with it?" And if we of the Negro race can master modern knowledge—the kind that counts—we will be able to win for ourselves the priceless gifts of freedom and power, and we will be able to hold them against the world.[81]

The *Negro World* of May 8 published an April 17 letter entitled "Negroes Should Be Taught Pride of Race," signed "Hagar." In the Bible, Hagar is the wife of Abraham and mother of Ishmael who, along with her son, was cast out of Abraham's family by Sarah. "Aunt Hagar" and "Aunt Hagar's chillum" were slang terms in the African American community for African Americans. (*Hagar* was also the title of, and protagonist in, a feminist novel by Mary Johnson published in 1913.) The author of the *Negro World* letter was very possibly Harrison: the style of writing was similar to his, the subject touched on the education work Garvey had approached him about, Harrison had four daughters currently in school, he at times used meaning-laden pseudonyms, and "Hagar" is formed from a melding of HArrison and GARvey.[82]

Hagar stated that "Negroes all over the world" were "beginning to feel the imperative need of a determined race consciousness and to realize that such consciousness can be solidly built only upon the foundation of knowledge." Unfortunately, this was "no easy matter for a Negro man or woman" whose time was often "occupied with the problem of making a living." Hagar knew "of no institution to which Negro children may be sent to learn the facts about themselves" and urged "that a school for Negro children, with sessions that do not interfere with their attendance at the public or parochial school, that taught those facts about the Negro's status during the several civilizations," was "a vital necessity" and "would instill a pride of race in our coming generation." Hagar added that there was "no more fertile field for this work of education than here in Harlem" and that such work could be supplemented "by courses of lectures for adults and the organization of Negro culture clubs." In addition, "text books could be edited to meet the particular demands of such an institution and systems of instruction by correspondence would make it possible to reach people living in remote districts." Hagar thought the UNIA was "the logical body to undertake this work" and asked "to have the editor's opinion of her idea" as well as the opinions of "other readers, especially mothers." The editor, very possibly Harrison, responded that "the U.N.I.A. has had this idea under consideration for some time" and that "plans to put it in operation have been held in abeyance pending the convention in August."[83]

Harrison's "The Racial Roots of Culture" appeared in the July 31 *Negro World*. It was a slightly shortened form of "Negro Culture and the Negro College," which had appeared in the *New Negro* of September 1919. The article again outlined Harrison's views on the type of university education needed by "Negroes" and called for attention to the "stored-up knowledge and experience of the past and present generations of Negroes in their ancestral lands."[84]

One of Harrison's special accomplishments at the *Negro World* was to aid and encourage Black poets in publishing their works. Claude McKay, Lucian Watkins, and Walter Everett Hawkins were three such poets. Harrison also encouraged efforts from his friend Andy Razaf and from *Negro World* readers when he established the "Poetry for the People" section in the paper.

In late 1919 McKay had discussed a personal "dilemma" with Harrison. He was undecided as to whether to go to Spain for a year or two as the guest of a pair of patrons referred to as Mr. and Mrs. "Gray."[85] McKay described Mr. Gray as having "parentage [that] was international—a mixture of Italian, German, and other Nordic strains. He was born in the Orient." Harrison advised that it would be foolish to hesitate over the Grays' offer. He thought that McKay was "too conscientious" and pointed out how "in civilized life it was not necessary for one to like one's hosts." Harrison suggested that he, McKay, and Mr. "Gray" talk the plan over. When they did, Harrison also discussed the Pan-African movement and, according to McKay, claimed he had "had a similar idea . . . but Garvey, being more spectacular, had run away with it." He also told Gray that it was gracious of him to take McKay to Europe, and, according to McKay, he (falsely) told him that he had lived in Denmark and Japan and that the experience aided his later work. Harrison didn't discuss McKay's "real feelings about taking the trip." Harrison also received a personal donation of fifty dollars from Gray "to help in the work of black enlightenment." When McKay told Harrison that he had refused the trip, Harrison called him "an impossible poet."[86]

"Gray" soon offered McKay the alternative of a brief vacation abroad, and McKay chose to go to England, where he stayed for a year and a half. While McKay was abroad, Harrison asked him to submit articles to the *Negro World* from England. McKay complied with a series of articles "about the colored soldiers and their club" (the "Coloured Men's Y.M.C.A.," located on the corner of

Drury Lane and York Street, in London), which Harrison featured in the *Negro World*.[87]

One of the first letters Harrison received as editor of the *Negro World* was dated December 17, 1919 (before Harrison was editor), sent from McKay, in England, to Marcus Garvey, the *Negro World*'s editor. McKay explained that he was sending some news matters and an editorial from the London *Daily Herald* of December 15, which "might interest you." He thought it "splendid" to "have a representative organ of British Labor denouncing so strongly imperial abomination and endorsing the self-determination of Britain's subject peoples."[88]

McKay emphasized what he had said before in the *Negro World*: "Radical Negroes should be more interested in the white radical movements" because "they are supporting our cause, at least in principle." To McKay they were "the great destructive forces [within], while the subject races are fighting without." He made clear he was not saying to "accept them unreservedly and put our cause into their hands," since "they are fighting their own battle & so are we," but, he stressed, "at present we meet on common ground against the common enemy." Since there was "a great wall to batter down," he recommended, "while we are working on one side we should hail those who are working on the other." He reassured his readers that "we need have no fear if, as a race, we have ability to safeguard our own peculiar rights."[89]

McKay considered it "amusing, but very pathetic, to see Negroes under British rule wasting valuable money sending deputations and petitions to the officials of the Imperial capitalists in Downing Street." Said officials only viewed them as "poor black devils" a "little lower down in the scale of human life than their poor white devils." It would be "better," he thought, "for us to let the thinking white workers of the British Isles know of the real conditions obtaining among England's subject races."[90]

Another poet aided by Harrison was Lucian B. Watkins, a former sergeant during World War I and known as the "soldier-poet." Harrison, describing himself as "Associate Editor" of the "Negro World," first wrote to Watkins on January 2, 1920, expressing his "very high appreciation of the poetic genius and craftsmanship of the 'Sonnet on the New Negro', dedicated to the Honorable Marcus Garvey, in the Negro World of December 6." He was "preserving [it] in his private collection of poetic gleanings" and encouraged the Virginia-born Watkins to submit his poetry to the *Negro World*. On April 3, 1920, Harrison again wrote to Watkins, who had just come out of the hospital for treatment of war wounds (he would die on February 1, 1921), and sent him some copies of the *Negro World*. Watkins responded on April 8 and informed Harrison that he had read a letter from Robert Kerlin in the *Negro World* and, though he had never met him, had received four letters from him seeking permission to use two poems in his forthcoming book *The Voice of the Negro: 1919*. Watkins granted permission, and Kerlin also inquired about Watkins's book of poems, the manuscript of which was held by the Cornhill Company of Boston. When Watkins wrote to Harrison he included correspondence from Walter E. Reid, Cornhill's owner, apologizing for a long delay in rendering a decision in regard to his manuscript poems and offering to publish an edition of not fewer than one thousand copies if Watkins would put up $380.[91]

Trying to assist Watkins, Harrison wrote to Cornhill on April 9 on behalf of the *Negro World*. He inquired as to the status of "the manuscript of a book of poems" by Watkins, whom he described as "our staff poet." He explained that the *Negro World* wanted "to be certain of our facts, and to be sure that you have been given an opportunity to explain your side of the matter before we put into print the account of the facts which we have gleaned from Mr. Watkins," who had indicated Cornhill "held his manuscripts for nearly a year" and "neither published nor returned them to him" despite repeated correspondence. Harrison added that "on the face we should be justified in giving the story to the readers of the *Negro World*" but "preferred" to write to the publisher first.[92]

That same day Harrison wrote to Watkins to tell him that after receiving his previous letter he had immediately written to the Cornhill people. Watkins had apparently been back at the hospital, and Harrison added his sincere hope "that, having cheated the undertaker," he would "proceed to climb the height of health."[93] Also on April 9, Reid wrote to Watkins that Cornhill had received his letter of March 24 as well as correspondence from Kerlin indicating his desire to publish the poems. Reid now indicated that it was "possible" that they "could bring it out during the late spring or early summer."[94]

On April 13 Watkins wrote to Harrison "heartily" thanking him for his April 9 letter and the copy of his letter to Cornhill. He said he considered him a "live wire" who possessed "the rare intellectual quality known as initiative—and that gets things done." He also confided that there was "one phase of the matter" that he thought had "tended to keep my book out of print, and that is the poems are all written in classical English with no so-called Negro dialect among them." He felt that "the white race in America" was "slow to recognize anything creditably artistis [*sic*] in the Negro." Watkins also sent, under separate cover, a booklet entitled "Origin of the White Race" and "The End of the White Race's Rule Over the Black Man in 1921" along with two clippings, all of which he thought Harrison would find interesting.[95]

Cornhill responded to Harrison on April 15 that they had received his letter of April 9 regarding Watkins's manuscript. They thought "there must be a slight mistake regarding the facts." They had written Watkins many times, and though they had "refrained from advising him definitely regarding its publication," they were "hoping that conditions in the publishing world would improve sufficiently to warrant our offering Mr. Watkins an acceptable contract for their publication." They also mentioned that on April 9 they wrote Watkins "at length regarding the book, and requesting his opinion."[96]

Yet another poet whose work Harrison appreciated and supported was Walter Everette Hawkins. On May 20 Harrison received a copy of Hawkins's *Chords and Discords* from his poet friend Andrea Razafkeriefko. Then, in a June 5 review in the *Negro World*, Harrison described this "first fruit of a new poet" as a volume with "few of the defects of youth [and] with many of the brilliant qualities." He quoted from various poems and explained that Hawkins had his "'discords' as well as his 'chords.'" One of the former described "the 'sport of burning human flesh'—a sport peculiar to the land which recently marshalled its hosts of young men 'to make the world safe for democracy.'" He described the poem "A Festival in Christendom" as "a piece of mordant irony in verse, addressed to the American conscience on the evil of lynching," which effectively "sears and tears, leaving the raw blisters behind." Harrison noted, however, that Hawkins was "mainly a singer of glad things," utilizing "voices of a rustic upbringing" with humor "of the sod" and pathos "of the soul rather than of the sod." His "radical breadth of view and his higher reaches of thought" were "the product of his contact with men in the crowded centers of civilization," and though the collection had "a few crudities of technique," it also had "genius" and "the true Parnassian ring." Harrison predicted that Hawkins would "continue to climb the steps of Poesy," and, "when he shall have trimmed his wings to the pressure of the upper air we may look to him to realize the promise of perfection which these poems contain."[97]

These examples indicate that Harrison was an important discoverer and encourager of poets. He also helped bring the work of his friends, including the poet Razaf and the bibliophile Schomburg, into the UNIA/*Negro World* orbit. Tony Martin emphasizes that Harrison was "very much a part of the wider Harlem literary community" and that his "role as a discoverer and nurturer of Black talent was as important as it has been unacknowledged." In addition to those "he exposed through his pioneering book review columns, he was among the first to actively promote McKay, J. A. Rogers, the South African Solomon Plaatje and, indeed, Marcus Garvey himself."[98]

————————

In early 1920 Harrison developed the "Our Book Review" section as another regular feature of the *Negro World*. It was, he wrote, "the first" and "only" "regular book-review section known to Negro newspaperdom," and it sought "to bring to the knowledge of the Negro reading public those books which were necessary" to "know what the white world was thinking and planning and doing in regard to the colored world." It also sought "to bring the white publisher and his wares to a market which needed those wares."[99]

In a 1922 article he offered insightful advice on his approach to book review-ing (advice cited favorably some eighty-seven years later by Scott McLemee, the "Intellectual Affairs" columnist for *Inside Higher Ed*). Harrison wrote:

> In the first place, remember that in a book review you are writing for a public who want to know whether it is worth their while to read the book about which you are writing. They are primarily interested more in what the author set himself to do and how he does it than in your own private loves and hates. Not that these are without value, but they are strictly secondary. In the next place, respect yourself and your office so much that you will not complacently pass and praise drivel and rubbish. Grant that you don't know everything; you still must steer true to the lights of your knowledge. Give honest service; only so will your opinion come to have weight with your readers. Remember, too, that you can not well review a work on African history, for instance, if that is the only work on the subject that you have read. Therefore, read widely and be well informed. Get the widest basis of knowledge for your judgment; then back your judgment to the limit. Here endeth the First Encyclical.[100]

Harrison implemented his views and skills in three reviews he published in the April 17, 1920, *Negro World*. He described Upton Sinclair's *Press-Titution* as "one of the series of wonderful little books" sold by the Appeal to Reason at Girard, Kansas, for 25 cents. Only 188 pages, it was a portion of Sinclair's larger work, *The Brass Check: A Study of American Journalism*. Harrison explained that "the brass check" was "a symbol of commercialized self-selling," and "the bril-liant author" showed why the term "'prostitutes of the press'" was "a correct description of American newspaperdom." Sinclair exposed "the methods of the Associated Press in suppressing news, distorting news and poisoning the sources of information in the interest of Big Business." Harrison advised that "every one who reads the big newspapers and thinks that he gets the truth from them should read this little book," which was "written in a simple, direct and incisive manner" and could "hold the interest of 'the man in the street.'"[101]

In the same April 17 issue Harrison also reviewed *The Negro Year Book, 1918–1919*, edited by Monroe N. Work, the director of records and research at the Tuskegee Institute in Alabama, the school formerly headed by Booker T. Washington. He considered Work's publication "the most serviceable" of "all the books produced in Negro America." It was "truly 'an annual encyclopedia of the Negro'" and covered "every department of Negro activity, from banking to radicalism"; dealt "with Racial Co-operation, Education, Religion, the War, Riots, Lynching, Politics, Literature, Science and History, Abyssinia, Haiti, Libe-ria, Sports, Population, Office Holding and Music"; and contained "many lists of books on various aspects of race relations here and abroad." *The Negro Year*

Book also had a convenient index, and despite "a few minor defects—mainly of omission," and "many typographical errors due to inefficient proofreading," the book remained "an indispensable necessity, with no rival in its field."[102]

———

Finally, in the April 17 *Negro World*, Harrison offered an important review of W. E. B. Du Bois's *Darkwater*. He began by offering additional comments on the subject of book reviewing and explained that "an unwritten law" had "existed for a long time to the effect that the critical estimates which fix the status of a book by a Negro author shall be written by white men." "Praise or blame—the elementary criticism which expresses only the reviewer's feelings in reference to the book—has generally been the sole function of the Negro critic"—and "the results have not been good." First of all, "white critics (except in music) have been too prone to judge the product of a Negro author as Dr. [Samuel] Johnson judged the dancing dog [which he paraphrased]: 'It isn't at all like dancing; but then one shouldn't expect more from a dog.'" For that reason, "many Negro poets of fifth grade merit" were "able to marshal encomiums by the bushel from friendly white critics who ought to know better." In addition, there was "a danger of disparagement arising solely from racial prejudice and the Caucasian refusal to take Negro literary products seriously." In both cases the work failed "to secure consideration solely on its merits."[103]

Harrison judged it "high time that competent appraisal of Negro books should come from 'our side of the street.'" For that to happen, "the Negro reading public" had to be "taught what to expect," specifically

> that criticism is neither "knocking" nor "boosting"; but an attempt, in the first place, to furnish a correct and adequate idea of the scope and literary method of the book under review, of the author's success in realizing his objects, and of the spirit in which he does his work. In the second place, the critic should be expected to bring his own understanding of the subject matter of the book to bear upon the problem of enlightening the readers' understanding, that at the end the reader may decide whether the work is worth his particular while.[104]

Du Bois's *Darkwater*, according to Harrison, was "free thinking and plain speaking." At the outset the publisher made an assumption about the author's status ("Even more than the late Booker Washington, Mr. Du Bois is now chief spokesman of the two hundred million men and women of African blood") that Harrison considered "outrageously untrue." Harrison judged that "once upon a time Dr. Du Bois held a sort of spiritual primacy among The Talented Tenth, not at all comparable to that of Booker Washington in scope, but vital and compelling for all that." The power of Du Bois's leadership, however, "instead of increasing since Mr. Washington's death, has decreased" and was "now openly flouted by the most active and outspoken members of The Talented Tenth in Negro America," while "outside of the twelve or fifteen millions 'of African blood' in the United States, the mass of that race in South and West Africa, Egypt and the Philippines know, unfortunately, very little of Dr. Du Bois."[105]

Harrison felt that *The Souls of Black Folk* was "a greater book than *Darkwater* in many ways." First, "its high standard of craftsmanship" was maintained throughout; there were "no fag-ends, as in the chapter 'Of Beauty and Death' in the present volume, where the rhetoric bogs down, the author loses the thread of his purpose and goes spilling off into space, spinning a series of incongruous purple patches." "Artistically," that chapter was "an awful thing," and Harrison assumed the author was "artist enough to be ashamed of it." In addition, *The Souls of Black Folk* "was more artistically 'gotten' up—to use the grammar of its author," while *Darkwater* was "cheaply bound and cheaply printed on paper which is almost down to the level of the Seaside Library [of inexpensive publications]." Thus, "neither in mechanical nor mental quality" did the book of 1920 "come up to the level of that of 1903."[106]

Despite "some defects," *Darkwater,* "with the exception of chapters six, seven, eight and nine," was "a book well worth reading." It was a collection of papers written between 1908 and 1920 "strung loosely on the string of race." Harrison wished that it included the earlier essay on "The Talented Tenth" and the address on the aims and ideals of modern education, delivered in 1908 to the colored schoolchildren of Washington, DC. Each paper was a separate chapter, "followed by a rhetorical sprig of symbolism in prose or verse in which the tone-color of the preceding piece" was "made manifest to the reader." Harrison considered the "best" of the "tone-poems in prose and verse" to be "the Credo; A Litany at Atlanta; the Riddle of the Sphinx, and Jesus Christ in Texas." In these "the lyrical quality of the author's prose" reached "high levels." The "elegance" did not "slop over into turgid declamation and rhetorical claptrap," a "common fault of the author's recent prose as shown in *The Crisis.*" In the first part of the book, the work was "genuine" and its rhetoric rang "true"; nevertheless, "the sustained artistic swing of *The Souls of Black Folk*, which placed that work (as a matter of form and style) on the level of Edgar Saltus' *Imperial Purple*" was "not attained in *Darkwater.*"[107]

Du Bois's book largely dealt "with the broad international aspects of the problem of the color line and its reactions on statecraft welt-politik, international peace and international trade, industry, education and the brotherhood of man." Each chapter was devoted to one of these topics. It also had "a charming autobiographical paper, 'The Shadow of Years,'" which had appeared in the *Crisis* three years earlier. In this Du Bois offered a "study of soul by itself," and the growth of his mind "under the bewildering shadow cast by the color line" was "tragically set forth." This, "despite its fine disguise," was to Harrison "the smoldering resentment of the mulatto who finds the beckoning white doors of the world barred on his approach." Harrison sensed "that, if they had remained open, the gifted spirit would have entered and made his home within them" and offered "no one has the right to quarrel with the author on that doubtful score."[108]

The chapter on "The Souls of White Folk" was "a fine piece, not so much of analysis, as of exposition," and Du Bois puts "his best into it," though it "seems to have failed to bite with acid brutality into the essential iron of the white man's soul." The "basic elements of that soul are Hypocrisy, Greed and Cruelty," and though Du Bois "brings this out," he "doesn't burn it in." His "indictment" is presented as "an appeal to shocked sensibilities and a moral sense which exists, for the white man, only in print; whereas it might have been made in other terms which come nearer to his self-love." Nevertheless it was "unanswerable in its logic." "In 'The Hands of Ethiopia,' as in 'The Souls of White Folk,'" was evidenced "the stern note of that threat which (disguise it as our journals will), the colored races are making, of an ultimate appeal in terms of color and race to the white man's only God—the God of Armed Force." "But," emphasized Harrison, Du Bois "never reaches the height of that newer thought—an international alliance of Black, Brown and Yellow against the arrogance of White."[109]

"In 'Work and Wealth' and 'The Servant in the House' the problems of work and its reward, and the tragedy of that reward, are grippingly set forth in relation to the Negro in America and in the civilized world." The book ends "with a fantastic short story, 'The Comet' which, like 'The Coming of John' in 'The Souls of Black Folk,'" suggests "Du Bois could be a compelling writer of this shorter form of fiction." Harrison concluded:

> Dr. Du Bois, in the looseness of phrase current in our time in America, is called a scholar—on what grounds we are not informed. But Dr. Du Bois is not a scholar; his claim to consideration rests upon a different basis, but one no less high. And when the Negro culture of the next century shall assay the products of its own it will seem remarkable that this supreme wizard of words, this splendid literary artist, should have left his own demesne to claim the crown of scholarship. Surely, there is honest credit enough in being what he is, our foremost man of culture. And this *Darkwater*, despite its lapses from artistic grace, helps to rivet his claim to that consideration. It is a book which will well repay reading.[110]

———

On July 3 and again on July 17 Harrison ran a short article entitled "Our Little Library." He explained that the editors of the *Negro World* had often been asked to furnish lists of "books for general education and also for the study of Negro history and culture." A list of twenty-five books was provided "as a collective answer to these enquiries." It was intended "as a firm foundation," and the editors suggested formation of weekly study clubs to take up a reading of these works one by one. Readers could write for advice and assistance. The list for "General Education" included: (1) *Man's Place in Nature*, Thomas Henry Huxley, with *Six Lectures to Workingmen*; (2) *The Childhood of the World*, Edward Clodd; (3) *Modern Science and Modern Thought*, Samuel Laing; (4) *A History of Modern Science*, Arabella Buckley; (5) *Education*, Herbert Spencer; (6) *Anthropology*, Edward B. Tylor; (7) *Mutual Aid*, Prince Peter Kropotkin; (8) *Elementary Principles of Economics*, Richard T. Ely and (George Ray) Wicker; (9) *Readings in European History*, James Harvey Robinson; (10) *A Short History of the English People*, John R. Green; (11) *Civilization in England*, Henry Thomas Buckle; (12) *Modern Europe* (one vol. edition) (Charles Alan) Fyffe; (13) *The Conflict Between Religion and Science*, John William Draper; and (14) *Workers in American History*, James Oneal. Harrison's list "For Negro History and Culture" included: (15) *African Life and Customs*, Edward Wilmot Blyden; (16) *White Capital and Coloured Labor*, Sir Sidney (Sydney) Olivier; (17) *Negro Culture in West Africa*, George W. Ellis; (18) *Europe in Africa in the Nineteenth Century*, Elizabeth Wormeley Latimer; (19) *Ethiopia Unbound*, Casely Hayford (Acca Agrimun); (20) *From Superman to Man*, J. A. Rogers; (21) *As Nature Leads*, J. A. Rogers (this replaced *The Aftermath of Slavery* by Dr. Wm. A. Sinclair in the first list); (22) *The Haytian Revolution*, T. G. Stewart; (23) *West African Studies*, Mary H. Kingsley; and (24) *A Tropical Dependency*, Lady Florence Lugard. Harrison's *The Negro and the Nation* (25) was missing from the first published lists and appeared along with William H. Ferris's *The African Abroad* (26) in the August 21 issue.[111]

In the July 3 *Negro World* Harrison reviewed J. A. Rogers's second book, *As Nature Leads*, noting that it followed "the now famous" *From "Superman" to Man* (1917). Like its predecessor, it was "a masterpiece of sociological handling." Four weeks later Harrison reprinted his review of *From "Superman" to Man*, which had originally appeared in the *New Negro* of October 1919.[112]

In his July 3 review of *As Nature Leads* Harrison detailed Rogers's discussion of "some of the reasons why Negro and Caucasian are mixing in spite of opposition." He presented "facts of Negro psychology as shown by the ideas and preferences of the black people in their native environment in Africa," where they "used to exhibit aversion and repugnance and even terror at the sight of a white person." This was cited "as proof that the responsibility for blood mingling" did "not rest with them." In comparing "the attitude of the transplanted Negro with that of his brother at home," Rogers reached "some radical conclusions" on why "dark men and women prefer to mate with white men and women and vice versa." Rogers utilized "the best authorities white and black," and the book was "a treasure house of illustrative material." He also suggested "the best books to read on religion, psychology, sex, history, politics, aesthetics and philosophy as they relate to the Negro question" and answered "interesting questions" with "a wealth of information and a breadth of view unsurpassed by any other author black or white."[113]

Harrison emphasized that *As Nature Leads* did "more than merely digest the information coming from others"; it also made "competent contributions to the sociology of the race question." Rogers "very gently but firmly [tore] to pieces some of the theses of Lester F. Ward," and, as far as Harrison knew, "no one ha[d] hitherto discovered the part played by 'inferior' races in the total process of social evolution." Rogers also stated "his own law of descansion [descension]" quite modestly and found reason for "the daring dresses which white women wear so wantonly." Harrison concluded that "all in all," Rogers's first two books "constitute the greatest contribution yet made by any Negro writer to the race question."[114]

In the July 10 *Negro World* Harrison reviewed *In Spite of the Handicap*, an autobiography by the poet, journalist, and minister James D. Corrothers (1869–1917), DD. He considered it "not a great book" and the author not "a great man," though he was "moved to think that there are human qualities more desirable than greatness," which "exist in overflowing measure in this life." His autobiography was "a story from which one rises with expanded soul, with greater courage and a richer sense of the meaning of manhood." Basically, said Harrison, it was "the simple story of one who began life almost in the dirt and lived to climb a more than normal distance up the ladder of achievement." His sole fault seemed to be "to think too thankfully of kind white friends." His "philosophy of life" had undoubtedly "grown out of his experiences, and these cannot be altered."[115]

Harrison considered *In Spite of the Handicap* "in the same class" as Booker T. Washington's *Up from Slavery*. It was the "record of a Negro who has shared the common life of the common Negro people and by achieving intellect, culture and fame, has put heart into the common mass by letting them see what each and every one of them is capable of." The book was "a work of inspiration" that would "inspire others of the same race to aspire and achieve." Harrison sat up until four o'clock to finish the book "for the pure pleasure and profit which I got from it," and as he got up from reading it he wrote "not as a review, but as a spontaneous tribute to the stalwart soul whose strivings, hardships and successes are therein recorded." He felt "sure that both pleasure and profit await other Negroes—especially those under 30" who read the book.[116]

In the July 24 *Negro World* Harrison reviewed *The Menace of Immorality in Church and State* by John Roach Straton, "pastor of Calvary Baptist Church at

123 W. 57th St., New York City." Straton had prepared a collection of messages of wrath and judgment, which Harrison recommended to *Negro World* readers because he felt "that a cross-section of white civilization done by a white minister ought to be a stimulating bit of spiritual food." He entitled his article "The Seamy Side of White Christian Civilization: As Seen by a White Medicine Man" and explained that "medicine-men, wizards, shamans and witch doctors" were "substantially the same all over," whether called by such names, "which are generally used only for the colored members of the tribe," or by "the more dignified ones of reverends, canons, bishops, etc. generally restricted to the white ones."[117]

In discussing Straton's criticisms Harrison offered the opinion that while he was "a good man," it was nevertheless true that "when a good man becomes a priest he tends to nag, and "nagging develops a murderous impulse in the victims." Because of this one could "readily understand why prophets and martyrs have been slain by angry mobs, and the preacher who really trains his guns on particular and popular vices, especially in Christian civilization, is assuredly fitting himself for the dignity of martyrdom." It was "for that very reason," according to Straton, that "most Christian preachers choose to inveigh against sin in general ['because no one ever commits sin in general' is added in HH's handwriting] while the particular sins of their particular congregation are permitted to go uncriticized." To Harrison, "this fashionable pastor of a fashionable church in the nastiest city of the western world" did not refrain from "laying bare the rottenness of its rotten spots." According to Harrison, Straton "takes a dive into the sexual cesspool of New York and comes up with an awful stench." He considers the "greatest danger point" to be "the relationship between the sexes, under the conditions of our congested, overwrought modern life." Noting that "every great civilization of the past has decayed precisely at this point," he sees the "danger signals" for "our age." Straton says, "The very life of the ([white]) [Harrison inserted the brackets] race is at stake in these tremendous issues, and instead of rebelling against rebuke or justifying ourselves in pride and haughtiness, we need to bow in the very dust of repentance, and turn back in humility to God and His truth." Elsewhere Straton writes that "we are now witnessing the widest wave of immorality in the history of the human race," and according to the testimony he provides, "the whites, tested by their own moral standards, have fallen far below the level of the heathen[the pluralizing *s* is crossed out] to whom they send missionaries."[118]

Harrison added, when Straton says that this "whole social evil" is "part of that heritage of sin" that belongs to all humanity, he "illustrates the blindness of the average white man who talks about humanity as if his race were IT." Further, notes Harrison, "it is only of the white race that what he says of prostitution" is true, namely, that it is "organized and exploited in a large business way" as never before, it capitalizes for gain the passions of men as never before, and that it is now "an organized business; a nation-wide trust as it were." Straton himself "points out that according to [August] Forel, whom he calls 'a great authority,' prostitution never became established among primitive peoples." Harrison then offers, if "educated white men were not so distressingly ignorant of comparative racial facts, they would know that this is the converging testimony of all the anthropology and sociology." He stresses that "the sex sociologists like Dr. [William W.] Sanger (*The History of Prostitution*), Havelock Ellis (*Studies in the Psychology of Sex*) and Iwan Bloch (*The Sexual Life of Our Time*) are particularly explicit about this," while "the general anthropologists like [Edward B.] Tylor, [Friedrich] Ratzel and Perschel are not a whit less clear."[119]

In Straton's book, "the white woman . . . comes in for a thundering broadside of denunciation," especially those of the higher classes. He writes, "The greatest evil in modern styles is . . . the present tendency towards undress is so obviously for the purpose of directing attention to the sex area," and "this area is tremendously over-emphasized in our modern life." Harrison comments that "the good doctor has made no attempt to study the connection between types of clothes and types of civilization," and "such social explanations as those given by Thorstein Veblen (*Theory of the Leisure Class*) escape him all together." He feels that Straton is also not "any more open to the crushing force of that explanation by [J. A.] Rogers (*As Nature Leads*), who contends that it is the waning sex power of the white women's men-folk that prompts them to over-emphasize the idea of sex in their way of dressing in order that stimulation might be lifted to the level of efficiency." Straton, however, goes on to vent his wrath against "the fact that many of our modern women have lowered their standards of life."[120]

In another sermon, entitled "Dogs Versus Babies," Straton offers that "the declining birth rate among the well-to-do classes of America should give us pause" and notes that "on all our 'fashionable' streets dogs are taking the place of babies." "There are not only dog nurses to-day, but there are dog doctors and dog hospitals and dog dressmakers, and even dog cemeteries—expensive, elaborate ones, with tombstones, caretakers, and all such things!" He sees "the substitution of the dog for the baby" as "just about complete in certain social circles of New York." Elsewhere, Straton "thunders at the gambling craze, the money madness and ragtime religion." The "net result," according to Harrison, is "to burn into our very souls a realization of the fact that the religious and moral system which a lying white world insists on exporting to Africa is certainly not the system by which it governs its life at home." Though "we have all known for years that it did not govern its life by its advertised system *abroad*," he adds, "now we have the assurance that those who are liars and hypocrites abroad are first liars and hypocrites at home." Harrison concludes that "a copy of a daily Christian newspaper published in London or New York should be sent" to "every Christian missionary in Africa," but "failing that, we might send a copy of Dr. Straton's book."[121]

Harrison next reviewed *The Influence of Animism on Islam*, by Samuel M. Zwemer, FRGS (Fellow of the Royal Geographical Society), in the *Negro World* of July 31. His review, "Myth, Magic and Religion: A Study of Pagan Influences in the Religion of Islam," described Zwemer's work as "a learned book in which [William] Robertson Smith and El Shibli, Al Bukhari and [D. U.] Brinton, [C.] Meinhof, [Earnest Alfred] Wallis Budge and Sir. J[ames]. G. Frazier elbow each other across the printed pages." It was "not a treatment of religion which would commend itself to the average believer"; nor would it strengthen such a person's faith. Rather, it was "essentially . . . written for men of learning" and discussed the "tendency which exists in all great religions . . . to partake of the nature of the common dirt of superstition on which most religions are grounded." Zwemer studied "the religion of Mohammed not as it was promulgated in its original purity, but as it finds itself to-day, compelled to adopt and assimilate the various local superstitions and magical practices which have developed within the area over which it holds ostensible sway."[122]

According to Harrison, however, Zwemer "pointedly ignores the fact that what is true of Islam in this respect is just as true of Christianity." As examples from New York he cites "people who go to church on Sunday [and] refuse to put the number 13 on their doors, but compromise on 12A"; people who "go to fortune-tellers for divination and witch-craft" and "pursue 'familiar' spirits by way of the Ouija board and the spiritualistic seance"; how "fine ladies and gentlemen walk all around a black cat rather than let it cross their path"; and how "folk who expect to go to heaven depend for luck upon the left hindleg of a grave-yard rabbit." To Harrison, Zwemer was "in good company, for most of the white men who write on these subjects like [W. T.] Elmore, [D. U.] Brinton, [J. J.] DeGroot, and [W. W.] Skeat can see a certain significance and value in the religious practices of 'inferior' folk while remaining as blind as bats to exactly similar things in the religious practices of their own 'superior' people."[123]

Harrison then describes how Zwemer, as he "follows the crescent into Africa, Asia and Europe studies the way in which it adopts its ritual to that lower religion which is the actual belief of the various populations that come under its sway." Zwemer suggests that "demons, stone-worship, magic, the prayer-bead or rosary, and other animistic elements in prayer and practice run riot over the Muslim world," and his illustrations "make good his contentions." The part of the book "which should be of particular interest to the new Negro," adds Harrison, "is that which shows the kinship between native Negro West African practices and similar practices among Muslim and Jews"—how "what the obeahmar does in the delta of Niger is shown to be spiritually akin to what the muezzin does in Cairo, the Rabbi in Kishinev and the Roman Catholic priest under the dome of St. Peter's."[124]

In some respects, "as regards scholarship and breadth of view," Harrison considers Zwemer's work "deserving of high praise." He also judges it "a great advance in the respect shown by white men for the culture-products of men who are not white." For those "interested in a scholarly treatment of religion and superstition," Harrison thought "this work will be found to be a genuine service."[125]

———

In August 1920 Harrison would complete his second book, *When Africa Awakes: The "Inside Story" of the Stirrings and Strivings of the New Negro in the Western World*. In a section on "Our International Consciousness" he explained that "as early as 1915," he offered in indoor and outdoor lectures an "explanation of the racial significance of the whole process of the war," which preceded "the sweeping tide of racial consciousness which found expression subsequently in those Negro newspapers and magazines . . . called radical." Harrison stressed this "point of priority" because in 1920 *The Rising Tide of Color Against White World-Supremacy*, a "remarkable book" by Theodore Lothrop Stoddard, became "an instant success."[126]

The Harvard-educated Stoddard was the grandson of the wealthy abolitionist Lewis Tappan and, according to the historian I. A. Newby, was one of "the nation's most influential race theorists" and the writer who assumed "the most important role in popularizing historical racism." Stoddard's book was published in April, and Harrison reviewed it in the May 29, 1920, *Negro World*.[127]

Harrison began by recounting how ten years earlier, B. L. Putnam Weale, in *The Conflict of Color*, "tried to open the eyes of the white men of the world to the fact that they were acting as their own grave diggers." Around that time, the Associated Press's president Melville E. Stone "reinforced the same grisly truth" in a talk on "Race Prejudice in the Far East" before the Quill Club of New York City. Five years later T. Shirby Hodge (a pseudonym for Roger Sherman Tracy) wrote *The White Man's Burden: A Satirical Forecast*, which ended "with these pregnant words: 'The white man's burden is—himself.'" While Hodge's publishers, Gorham Press, "practically suppressed his book," Harrison felt it "should have been in the library of every intelligent Negro." At that time "the white world was indisposed . . . to listen to its voices of warning." Now, however, "the physical, economic and racial ravages of the World War have so changed the white world's mind that within four weeks of its appearance *The Rising Tide of Color*, . . . struck the bull's-eye of attention" and became "the most widely talked-of book of the year." "White men of power" discussed "its facts and its conclusions with bated breath and considerable disquietude."[128]

It was "a book written by a white man which causes white men to shiver" because it shows "the writing on the wall" and "proves that the white race in its mad struggle for dominion over others has been exhausting its vital resources and is exhausting them further." It also "proves to the hilt" Harrison's 1917 thesis advanced in "The White World War and the Colored Races" that "whereas the white race was on top by virtue of its guns, ships, money, intellect and massed man-power, in the World War it was busy burning up, depleting and destroying these very resources on which its primacy depended." Further, "even though the white capitalists knew all this their mad greed was still their master," and that "great race is still so low spiritually that it sells even its racial integrity for dollars and cents." While "Stoddard's book may disturb its sense of security," it "cannot keep white 'civilization' from its mad dance of death."[129]

Harrison noted that "at the very outset" Stoddard's book suffered "from the unwelcome assistance of Dr. Madison Grant, 'chairman of the New York Zoological Society and trustee of the American Museum of Natural History.'" Grant (who in 1916 had authored *The Passing of the Great Race*) offered "a large stock of many ethnological ideas," but without that "freightage the book would be much better." To Harrison, "the difference in value and accuracy" between "Stoddard's text and the pseudo-scientific introduction of Dr. Grant would furnish material for philosophic satire."[130]

Stoddard's thesis, according to Harrison, "starts from the proposition that of the seventeen hundred million people on our earth today the great majority is made up of black, brown, red and yellow people," but "the white race, being in the minority, still dominates over the lands of black, brown, red and (in the case of China) has assumed a right of dictatorship and disposal even in the yellow man's lands." Further, "in the course of this dictatorship and domination the white race has erected the barrier of the color line to keep the other races in their place." But "this barrier is cracking and giving way at many points and the flood of racial self-assertion, hitherto damned up, threatens to overflow the outer and inner dikes and sweep away the domination of the whites." Stoddard approaches this theme "with a curiously graduated respect for other races," and this respect "is always in direct proportion to the present power and discernible potentialities of the races discussed." Thus, to

the yellow man of Japan and China he shows the greatest deference. . . . The browns (of India, Persia, Afghanistan, Egypt and the Mohammedan world in general) are, of course, inferior, but must be respected for their militancy. . . . The reds (the original American stock which is the backbone of the population of Mexico, Central and South America) are a source of contamination for white blood and an infernal nuisance, capable of uniting with Japan and China in an onslaught on the land areas reserved for white exploitation in the western world; while the blacks, at the foot of the ladder, have never amounted to anything, don't amount to anything now, and can never seriously menace the superiority of the whites.[131]

This gradation was "full of meaning, especially to those fervid theorists who affect to believe [that] religion, morality, loyalty and good citizenship constitute a good claim to the white man's respect," since "it is Japan's actual military might and China's impending military might which have put them in Grade A, while the brown man's show of resistance in Egypt, India, and elsewhere under Islam, and his general physical unrest and active discontent have secured for him a classification in Grade B." While "the American in Mexico and South America keeps his window open toward the east," the "black man still seems, in our author's eyes, to be the same loyal, gentle, stupid beast of burden that the white man's history has known—except in those parts of Africa in which he has accepted the Mohammedan religion and thus become a past of the potential terror of the Moslem world." In this Harrison thought Stoddard was "mistaken," but, he reasoned, "it is neither arguments nor logic that will determine these matters, but deeds and accomplishments."[132]

However the "racial aspect may be apportioned," it was clear that "Stoddard holds that his race is doomed." Harrison quotes Stoddard: "'If the present drift be not changed we whites are ultimately doomed. Unless we set our house in order the doom will sooner or later overtake us all.'" Harrison stakes his money "on 'the doom,'" because "the white race's disease is an ingrowing one whose development inheres in their very nature," and "they are so singularly constituted that they would rather tear themselves to pieces parading as the lords of creation than see any other people achieve an equal favor of fortune." Harrison noted that Stoddard "presents many chastening truths and wide vistas of international politics which are enlightening when carefully studied." He hoped his review indicated "the high value and suggestiveness of the work" even though "all the way through the author, though clear and enlightened, remains an unreconstructed Anglo-Saxon, desirous of opening the eyes of his race to the dangers which beset them through their racial injustice and arrogance; but sternly, resolutely, intent that they shall not share their overlordship with any other of the sons of the earth." The book was "written in a clear and commendable style" with "few defects of temper" and "a shrewd mastery of his materials." Harrison considered it "well worth" its $3 price and urged it "should be widely read by intelligent men of color from Tokio to Tallahassee."[133]

Harrison followed his May 29 review of Stoddard's book with a June 12, 1920, *Negro World* piece on *The Rising Tide of Color*. He began by explaining that

William Randolph Hearst, "the ablest white publicist in America," had "broken loose, and, in a recent editorial in the New York *American* has absolutely endorsed every word of the warning recently issued by Lothrop Stoddard" in his book. In justice to Hearst, Harrison "pointed out (as we ourselves did in 1916) that we saw this handwriting on the wall long ago." Since Hearst was "not particularly famous as a friend of the darker races," Harrison nevertheless gave him "credit for having seen what was involved in the war between the white nations of Europe and America."[134]

Harrison then recounted that "as far back as 1915," he himself "was engaged in pointing out to white people that the racial aspect of the war in Europe was easily the most important, despite the fact that no American paper, not even Mr. Hearst's, would present that side of the matter for the consideration of its readers." Now, however, they were "beginning to wake up—as people generally do when disaster is upon them—frantically with much screaming and flapping of arms." The "doom approaching," however, was "but the ripened result of deeds that have been done" and was "therefore absolutely inescapable." The "White race" had "lied and strutted its way to greatness and prominence over the corpses of other peoples"; "capitalized, christianized, and made respectable, 'scientific,' and 'natural,' the fact of its dominion"; and "read back into history the race relations of today, striving to make the point that previous to its advent on the stage of human history, there was no civilization or culture worthy of the name." Now, it "admonishes us that if it were to pass off the stage as the controlling factor in the World's destiny, there would be no civilization or culture remaining." "Naturally," Harrison continued, "we take exception to both these views, because, for the past, we know better and, for the future, we think better of the many peoples who make up the cycle of civilization."[135]

Nevertheless, to Harrison these conditions were "not the gravest at present." Rather, "the fact of most tremendous import is that the white race in trying to settle its own quarrels has called in black, brown and yellow to do its fighting for it, with the result that black, brown and yellow will learn thereby how to fight for themselves, even against those whom they were called in to assist." The "consequences of conquest" made it "thumbs down for the white race in the world's arena," and it would not be able to "escape from its dilemma," in which its peoples would "be the dealers of their own death blow." To him "the analogies between the present situation of the white race and the situation of the Roman Empire in the fourth century of the Christian era" were "too many and too striking to be easily ignored."[136]

On June 17, 1920, Stoddard wrote to Harrison, asking him to send "one or two copies of your extremely interesting review of my book, *The Rising Tide of Color*," from the May 29 *Negro World*. This letter initiated a fascinating correspondence, which the two men carried on over the next few years. A week later

THE WHITE WAR AND THE COLORED RACES.

By Hubert Harrison.

[See slip.]

The 19th Christian Century saw the international expansion of capitalism -
the economic system of the white peoples of Western Europe and America - and its
establishment by force and fraud over the lands of the colored races, black and
brown and yellow. The opening years of the 20th Century present us with the sorry spectacle of these same white nations cutting each other's throats to determine
which of them shall enjoy the property which has been so acquired. For this is
the real sum and substance of the original "war aims" of the belligerents; although
in conformity with Christian cunning, this is the one which is never frankly vowed.
Instead, we are fed with the information that they are fighting for "Kultur", and
"on behalf of small nationalities". Let us look carefully at this camouflage.

In the first place, we in America need not leave our own land to seek
reasons for suspecting the sincerity of democratic professions. While we are
waging war to establish democracy three-thousand miles away, millions of Negroes
are disfranchised in our own land by the "cracker" democracy of the Southern states
which is more intent upon making slaves of their black countrymen than upon freeing
the French and Belgians from the similar brutalities of the German Junkers. The
horrible holocaust of East St. Louis was possible only in three modern states - Russia of the Romanoffs, Turkey, and the United States - and it ill becomes any one of
them to point a critical finger at the others.

But East St. Louis was simply the climax of a long series of butcheries
perpetrated on defenseless Negroes which has made the murder rate of Christian America higher than that of heathen Africa and of every other civilized land. And, although our government can order the execution of thirteen Negro soldiers for resenting wholesale insults to the uniform of the United States and defending their lives
from civilian aggressors, not one of the murderers of black men, women and children
has been executed or even ferreted out. Nor has our war Congress seen fit as yet
to make lynching a federal crime. What wonder that the Negro masses are insisting
that before they can be expected to enthuse over the vague formula of making the
world "safe for democracy" they must receive some assurance that their corner of the
world - the South - shall first be made "safe for democracy"! Who knows but that
perhaps the situation and treatment of the American Negro by our own government and
people may have kept the Central Powers from believing that we meant to fight for
democracy in Europe, and caused them to persist in a course which has driven us into this war in which we must spend billions of treasure and rivers of blood.

It should seem, then, that "democracy", like "Kultur", is more valuable as
a battle-cry than as a real belief to be practiced by those who profess it. And
the plea of "small nationalities" is estopped by three facts: Ireland, Greece, and
Egypt, whose Khedive, Abbas Hilmi, was tumbled off his throne for failing to enthuse
over the claims of "civilization"

But this is merely disproof. The average American citizen needs some positive proof of the assertion that this war is being waged to determine who shall dictate the destinies of the darker races and enjoy the usufruct of their labor and
their lands. For the average American citizen is blandly ignorant of the major
facts of history and has to be told. For his benefit I present the following statement from Sir Harry Johnston, in the Sphere of London. Sir Harry Johnston is the
foremost English authority on Africa and is in a position to know something of imperial aims.

"Rightly governed, I venture to predict that Africa will, if we are victorious, repay us and our allies the cost of our struggle with Germany and Austria.
The war, deny it who may, was really fought over African questions. The Germans
wished, as the chief gain of victory, to wrest rich Morocco from French control, to
take the French Congo from France, and the Portugese Congo from Portugal, to secure

---

Figure 6.3. Hubert H. Harrison, "The White War and the Colored Races," c. 1917–1918, page 1 (of 4). Hubert Harrison's "The White War and the Colored Races" was a powerful statement based on his indoor and outdoor talks of 1915 and 1916. He wrote it c. 1917–1918 ("when the Great War still raged"), for "a certain well known radical magazine," which found it "to be 'too radical' for publication at that time." Harrison was possibly referring to the *International Socialist Review*, which ceased publishing in February 1918, or, more likely, to *The Messenger*, edited by A. Philip Randolph and Chandler Owen. Harrison's article of this title was published in October 1919 in the *New Negro*, in February 1920 in the *Negro World*, and in August 1920 in *When Africa Awakes: The "Inside Story" of the Stirrings and Strivings of the New Negro in the Western World.* "The White Man's War," with a "radical indictment," though included in the original publication plan, similarly did not make it into the publication of the March 1925, Alain Locke–edited, *Survey Graphic* "Harlem: Mecca of the New Negro" issue, which was later expanded into the 1925 Locke-edited anthology *The New Negro: An Interpretation.* Harrison began "The White War and the Colored Races" with a description of "the international expansion of capitalism—the economic system of the white peoples of Western Europe and America— and its establishment by force and fraud over the lands of the colored races, black and brown and yellow." He pays special attention to how "people were fed with the 'camouflage'" that "they are fighting for 'Kultur' and 'on behalf of small nationalities.'" In looking more carefully at such camouflage Harrison would focus on what he referred to (in a subheading in his 1920 reprint of this article) as "The Sham of 'Democracy.'" *Source:* Hubert H. Harrison Papers, Box 6, Folder 61, Rare Book and Manuscript Library, Columbia University Library. See https://dlc.library.columbia.edu/catalog/cul:t76hdr7vcf.

Harrison sent Stoddard two copies of the review and added his "regret" that he "had not the time to make my review more ample and to extend my criticism to many minor but salient aspects of the book." He would have liked to "seize upon the deeper under-lying essentials and strive to make those clear to my own people." He extended his "congratulations upon the matter and manner" of the book and added, "within its fold, it stands unrivalled at present as a piece of international journalism." He added, "since I am a Negro, my sympathies are not at all with you: that which you fear, I naturally hope for." "But" he did "not suppose that the necessities of crowd-conflict and of sociological purpose constrain any of us to be surly and mulish in regards to other individuals whose position in the conflict of races has been as much a matter of pre-determination as his own." He trusted that "Across the Color Line" they could "still respect one another individually and praise good work when we see it."[137]

Harrison also enclosed a copy of his article on "The White War and the Colored Races," written in 1918 and reprinted in the *Negro World* in February 1920. The substance of the article "had been previously delivered in Wall St. and Washington Heights, Madison Square and other places, in-doors and out to white audiences during 1915 and 1916," and he thought it would help Stoddard "to realize that some black men, unknown and unnoticed by the white world in America, have been thinking their thoughts on this subject without waiting for the 'lead.'" Harrison told Stoddard that he planned "to bring out soon a small book of editorials, near-editorials and articles similar to the enclosed, dealing exclusively with the reaction of the Negro in America and in the world at large to the great war and its sociological results." This would be his *When Africa Awakes*, which would come out in two months, in August 1920.[138]

On July 14 Harrison wrote again to Stoddard extending a "tardy thanks" for a copy of Stoddard's *The French Revolution in San Domingo*, which Scribner's had sent him on Stoddard's request. He had "not yet had the time to go through it, inasmuch as editorial duties crowd on me and a batch of books for review has accumulated on my back." When he did get to it he would "most likely write a book review that may be more substantial than my review of *The Rising Tide of Color*." Harrison wrote, however, "not merely to thank" Stoddard but to seek his assistance on "one or two difficulties" he was having in bringing out his own book. He asked Stoddard "as a casual human favor" to tell him whether it was "likely" that his publisher, Charles Scribner's Sons, "could be induced to handle such a book, i.e. to publish it for me." Harrison stressed "the elements of 'timeliness.'" He had first intended to have the book brought out "in the same size as Arthur Henderson's *The Aims of Labor*," which Huebsch printed in paper and sold for 50 cents. From his "eight years experience in the selling of books at out-door and in-door lectures," Harrison "judged that I could sell a minimum of 300 copies of such a book weekly." If, however, he "could get the Scribners to publish the book in a style like that of Frederick Starr's *Liberia* which would sell for $1.00 or $1.25," he felt he "might be able to surmount the difficulties which trouble me now." He would agree "to sell 3000 copies of an edition of 5000" and would enter a contract to that effect. He realized "it might be well to show you the 'manuscript' of the book which would enable you to form your own opinion of its value and might also be an inducement to you to use your kindly offices in the matter." He also asked that if Stoddard found "any part of this service to be burdensome" that he "feel at perfect liberty to refuse it." He hoped to hear from him soon.[139]

After a weekend in the Catskills, Stoddard responded to Harrison's "good letter" on July 20. He was "very pleased" that Harrison would review the San Domingo book and awaited the review "with interest." He was also "exceedingly sorry to hear of the difficulties" Harrison "encountered in publishing" his book. Based on what he had seen of his work he expected the book to be "distinctly interesting," and he offered to read the manuscript "and to be of any assistance possible if (as I am morally certain will be the case) I consider it a publishable proposition by any house with which I have contacts." He would have time to do the reading around August 20 and asked Harrison to send the manuscript around then.[140]

On August 4 Stoddard again wrote to Harrison and told him that several days earlier he had read Harrison's review of his book to Dr. Ernest H. Gruening, managing editor of *The Nation*, who was "much interested, and said that if you would call him some time he would be glad to see you." Stoddard advised Harrison "to do this" because he felt Gruening could give "valuable advice about publishing your book." Stoddard also asked for a copy of Harrison's *Negro World*, which covered the current (August 1920) convention, since he was "naturally interested in it" but it was "being wretchedly reported in the daily press." Harrison sent Stoddard the requested copies of the *Negro World*, and on August 21 Stoddard wrote back, thanking him for providing a "much fuller and completer account" of the convention than the metropolitan press. He assumed Harrison had been "too much engrossed with the Convention to have called up Dr. Gruening at *The Nation*" but "strongly advise[d]" him to do so when he had "breathing-space." Gruening was "genuinely interested" in Harrison's "mentality," as evidenced by the Stoddard review and correspondence, and Stoddard knew Gruening "would be of assistance" regarding "advice and possibly in more direct ways, regarding publication" of the material.[141]

On August 21 Harrison wrote to Stoddard that he had "been down to see Dr. Gruening according to your suggestion" and "found him an amiable liberal with views of his own, some of them very ideological." After speaking with him Harrison began "to understand the reason for the aloof Olympian cynicism of the *Freeman*'s radicalism." Gruening thought that Stoddard's book was "faultily conceived in that it panders too much to 'wrong' conceptions of racial superiority etc." Harrison said he "tried to get him to see that inasmuch as you were describing a world in which these things are most powerful forces, it would have been absurd on your part to shirk the task of stating them and their workings as they actually exist." Harrison perceived Gruening's devotion "to be exclusively to an ideological 'rightness' in which somehow I cannot bring myself to believe in more than in the christian's God." Gruening also "had some very definite opinions about the primacy of Prof. Du Bois" that Harrison thought would "be severely shocked by one or two of the items in my book." He "regretted that white people from outside will persist in making their selections as to Negro leaders and leadership solely on the basis of such persons as happen to stand nearest to them, in point of view and to presume upon the existence of an adequate representative character inherent in their selection." However, he thought "that on the whole" he liked Gruening but judged "that we will need to 'factuate' him out of a few of his pet ideological liberalisms." He hadn't discussed publishing his book with Dr. Gruening because he had made alternative plans, and the book would be out "by the middle of next week." It was being published at his "own expense," and he planned to send Stoddard a copy as soon as it appeared. He asked "whether it would still be possible—after a book has been circulated in paper covers at 50c to the extent of 5,000 or 10,000 copies in three months—to persuade a respectable publisher to bring it out." He would discuss that question with him shortly.[142]

In sending the issues of *Negro World* Harrison "sincerely hope[d]" that Stoddard would "not judge the quality" of his "intellect by the material and method of this movement as expressed in the *Negro World*." His "function in the paper," he explained, was "that of one brought in to give a little 'tone.'" He judged "that in that character, my work is nearing the end of the fifth act" and that "the materials for Falstaffian farces are being ground out at a pretty rapid rate," since "our Tartuffe has developed a strong streak of Megalomania."[143]

Stoddard responded to Harrison on August 25. He was glad Harrison's book was out and looked forward to reading it and, if desired, to offering his opinion "as to the possibilities of publishing it through regular trade channels." Stoddard was also pleased that Harrison "had such a satisfactory interview with Dr. Gruening." After Harrison sent him *When Africa Awakes*, Stoddard wrote back on September 18, thanked him, and apologized for not acknowledging sooner his receipt of the book. His "excuse" was that the book arrived the day he had moved from New York back to his native town, Brookline, Massachusetts. He "only had time to glance at the book" but thought "it looks well worth reading." He was pleased to see the "complimentary reference" to his book and the inclusion of Harrison's "most excellent review."[144]

On September 30, 1920, Harrison wrote to Stoddard and asked him to give him his impression of the book as promised, reminding him that he "had promised" to let him know "whether, upon perusal, you think that the chances are good for subsequent publication through the regular trade channels." Stoddard responded on November 1 that he had read the book "with a great deal of interest . . . not only because of the generalizations which it contains, but also because it is a chronological record of the Negro movement since the beginning of the war and because it throws light on the internal frictions of Negro thought." It was "just those last two elements" which made the book interesting to him as "a specialist on world-affairs" but that would, in his opinion, "render the book unlikely to succeed with the general public" and therefore make it "unacceptable to the publisher." He noted that "its chronological character involves a good deal of repetition—which the average reader does not like," and he felt that "the discussion of Negro internal politics would not interest many non-Negro readers." He suggested that "if I were you I should group my broad, general material and present it in the form of a series of essays or chapters." That would "make a publishable book, since the present volume contains much which, if presented as I suggest, should, in my opinion, interest a fairly wide circle of non-Negro readers." He suggested "Huebsch, Harcourt, Brace & Howe, or T. Y. Crowell" as "the most likely publishers to approach."[145]

"Unfortunately," he had "no personal acquaintance with any of these houses," though he thought Gruening might. If Harrison made the changes Stoddard suggested, then he advised him to see Gruening. He closed by explaining that he was "exceedingly sorry" that he couldn't tell Harrison that he considered the "present volume publishable in the regular channels" but that he was offering the "honest opinion" as requested. Stoddard added, however, "so far as I am concerned, your book as it stands interests me more than if it were written as I suggest." But, he quickly added, "the general public has not got my specialist's taste."[146]

On November 13 Harrison wrote back to Stoddard and was "glad to know" that he had read the book and liked it. He also appreciated the comments regarding "the necessity of casting the contained matter in another way to make it available for publication by the regular trade channels." But, wrote Harrison, in a revealing response, "I fear that I am too lazy to go over the thing again. Having done it once, I am through." While he considered Stoddard "old in the business of publishing," he was "young yet in that line," and "after having read my own stuff six or eight times, I am so thoroughly sick at looking at one of the pages that I almost hope I will never see it again except as marketable commodity." He stood "to make about $2,000 on the edition now printed," and he thought "that is good enough."[147]

Harrison was now turning his hand to some other things, to "plotting and charting the previously-covered ground of my studies in African history and culture—a fairly big job in itself." He was also "thinking seriously of perpetrating a book which I had planned about five years ago and of which two or three chapters were written; viz. 'Negro and the Negro Stage.'" "Apart from Negro matters," he also had beside him as he wrote "the manuscript of a book on 'Sex and Society' covering the subject in a more popular manner than was done by Prof. [William I.] Thomas of Chicago some years ago; and the ragged skeleton and finished first chapter of 'The Idols of the Tribe' a study of the sociological foundations of modern civilized thinking: common, scientific, and philosophical." He expressed a desire to "get away to Egypt or the West Indies for a year of leisure in which I could work up some of my multifarious thoughts." Unfortunately, he couldn't, and he therefore chose "to go a step at a time" and added that "in the near future, you may expect to hear more of 'Sex and Society' or 'Negro Society and the Stage.'" There is no indication these manuscripts were ever published as books.[148]

Harrison added that the other night he had read about twenty pages of Stoddard's *French Revolution in San Domingo* and "liked it very much as a scholarly piece of work." He considered it "very well documented" but thought that it "neglected to till one section of the field: that is, the valuable biographical studies made by black Haytian scholars within the last forty years." He suggested "it should be easy to get a full list of these by writing to some of the prominent Negroes of Port-au-Prince." He added, "inasmuch as I happen to be the Honorary President of the Club Dessalines in this city, I could, if you wish, get such a list and send it on to you."[149]

In July 1920 Harrison also began "a regular weekly [news] summary of the leading and significant happenings in the various West Indian islands" entitled "West Indian News Notes by Hubert H. Harrison." The size of the section varied from week to week based on "the amount of news" obtainable "from the newspapers, handbills, proclamations and letters" sent to the paper. Harrison, as editor, was "responsible for the final form of the news items," except when he expressly quoted other papers. Examples of the content include: July 3—articles on Jamaica, Barbados, St. Thomas, Trinidad, Demerara, St. Vincent, and Dominica; July 17—after readers were urged to "send all available papers of recent dates, as well as letters and other documents," there were pieces on Grenada, Barbados, St. Lucia, Panama, and Dominica; August 21—articles on Barbados, St. Vincent, and England and her colonies; August 28—articles on Barbados, Trinidad, and Jamaica; and February 26, 1921—articles on British Honduras, Barbados, and Liberia.[150]

With his "West Indian News Notes" column started, his book-review section and "Poetry for the People" along with his major and minor editorials attracting wide attention, and his masterful editing of the *Negro World* all being major factors in the newspaper's extraordinary domestic and international growth, the stage was set for major new developments. These would include the August 1920 UNIA Convention, publication and distribution of his *When Africa Awakes*, and his participation in an all-"Negro" Liberty Party effort.

7

The 1920 UNIA Convention and Influence on Garvey (August–November 1920)

The month-long UNIA convention—"The First International Convention of the Negro Peoples of the World"—began with a giant mass meeting at Madison Square Garden (at Twenty-Sixth Street and Madison Avenue in Manhattan), on Monday, August 2, 1920. Marcus Garvey publicized the convention as "a turning point in the history of black-white relations," and his "vision of racial greatness," according to the historian Robert A. Hill, "fired the popular imagination of blacks." The BSL, whose first ship had sailed ten months earlier, was a symbol of the emotional and political climate, and in the thirteen months leading to the convention that its stock was available some 96,285 shares (worth almost a half-million dollars) were purchased.[1]

"From the standpoint of members," wrote Harrison in his diary, the opening ceremony was "a splendid success." He estimated 15,000 attended, and "the Garden was packed from top to bottom." It was a golden opportunity. "But, instead of putting forth a constructive radical program," Garvey "sank into silly rhodomentades [rodomontades] about ordering the white nations to 'get out of here' (Africa)." Harrison considered Garvey "a joke" as a speaker, said he "looked like a dog," and contrasted him with James Hood Eason, the AME Zion minister from Philadelphia, who "proved himself a splendid orator." (Eason, who would increasingly be considered a serious Garvey rival, would be assassinated by UNIA activists in New Orleans in January 1923—just before the start of Garvey's mail-fraud trial.) Harrison noted that when Garvey appealed for money, the people "walked out on him" by "the thousands."[2]

The first week of the convention at Liberty Hall included numerous delegates' reports on conditions in their sections. According to Harrison, "most of the delegates were from the West Indies," though "many of them were simply residents of New York whom he [Garvey] called in to pose as delegates *sent* from the West Indies and Africa."[3] Examples he cited included Bishop Alexander McGuire, who represented Antigua, and "Prince" Madarikan Deniyi of Lagos, Nigeria, who had been studying in the United States for more than six years. (Both became critics of Garvey.) Harrison's "credentials" stated that he was "the delegate of the Negro-Foreign-Born Citizens' Political Alliance," and Garvey insisted on recognizing him when he rose to speak as "the gentleman from the Virgin Islands." The Virgin Islands sent no delegates, although Virgin Islanders, like others, brought a banner to Liberty Hall and marched behind it in the parade of Tuesday, August 2.[4]

Harrison's outdoor talks continued during the convention and received favorable comment. Willard T. Holmes wrote a letter to the editor on "Radical Negro Orators" that appeared in the August 5 *Globe*. He explained that his business took him "through the Negro section of Harlem" and that "out of curiosity" he "stopped to listen to one or two colored speakers who nightly address huge audiences of their fellows on various topics." It was, he said, "a revelation to me." Holmes described himself as "a loyal American who loves his country," and he was "worried" because "the average complacent American" doesn't "realize how radical our black fellow-citizens are becoming." He commented on "three principal speakers," who "represent three wings" and whose "every argument (and they are forceful speakers) is socialistic." Harrison marked a copy of the newspaper clipping, which described "One speaker" (Harrison—as identified by HH) as "a man of much learning, [who] gives talks on Africa and Negro sociology which seek to prove that African culture is superior to European culture because it [African culture] is communistic." The other speakers discussed by Holmes were William Bridges and W. A. Domingo.[5]

An important subtext to the UNIA convention concerned Garvey's legal difficulties. Jamaica-born Herbert S. Boulin, president of the Berry & Ross Toy and Doll Manufacturing Co. (makers of "Negro dolls"), who was also undercover Special Agent P-138 of the BI, reported that a main topic on August 8 at the convention was Garvey's trial and how to defend him. Boulin, who would become friends with Garvey and whose doll company would be bought by the UNIA, claimed in his August 9 "Report" to have "heard many" speakers "threatening to kill R[ichard]. E. WARREN [Warner] and EDGAR M. GREY, colored, the District Attorney's two star witnesses" against Garvey.[6]

The witnesses were to testify in District Attorney Edwin P. Kilroe's year-old charges against Garvey, which stemmed from an article in the August 2, 1919, *Negro World*. On August 11, 1920, in open court, Garvey publicly and openly retracted all statements he had made "orally or in print" concerning Kilroe,

Grey, and Warner. He also stipulated that in the next issue of the *Negro World* he would publish a retraction (which appeared in the August 21 issue).[7] Grey was not mentioned in the retraction and, according to Harrison's diary, received $700 on the day that Garvey agreed to print the retractions.[8]

The *New York Age* highlighted another subtext of the convention: the sale of BSL stock. The August 14 issue described the "adroit manner" in which the convention leaders "played to the galleries." "No detail" was "omitted in the matter of high sounding titles for the officers, elaborate robes of office and the artificial aids of bands of music and impassioned orators, to arouse the sentiments of racial pride and enthusiasm among their followers." The *Age* maintained, however, that "the real motive actuating the entire movement is to be found in the insistent demand for the common herd to buy stock in the various enterprises promoted by the leaders." It added, "Whether these enterprises are legitimate or not, from the standpoint of ordinary business, we have no means of telling, but the persistent appeal for subscriptions gives the whole meeting the appearance of a gigantic stock jobbing scheme, put forth under the guise of racial improvement."[9]

The second week's work sessions, according to Harrison, were "devoted to the formulation of a Bill of Rights, afterwards called a Declaration of Rights." He commented, "One would have thought that the best brains would have been brought together in a committee to elaborate such a document. But this would not have suited Garvey's book. He is afraid of brains." Instead, Garvey "put forth the silly proposal that each delegate should present resolutions from the floor, all resolutions to be worked up later by the Convention into the Declaration of Rights." Meanwhile, Garvey "had prepared his own D[eclaration of]. R[ights]. and presented it from the chair (as a delegate)." As a consequence, "the other delegates' resolutions were brought forward as amendments and extensions of this document," and whenever anything was brought up that Garvey didn't approve, "he ruled it 'out of order.'"[10]

Agent Boulin, in his report of August 14, wrote that Harrison, "a Socialist and pronounced Negro agitator of the rabid type, joined the convention as a delegate" on August 12. He explained that Harrison had been "keeping street meetings for years" and was "holding a series of meetings at 138th St. and Lenox Ave. [down the block from the convention after it moved from Madison Square Garden] every night." As the convention started framing the Declaration of the Bill of Rights on August 12, Harrison reportedly "insisted that the majority of the bills were not strong and outspoken enough; that the white man must be denounced in the strongest of language in the Bill of Rights." Then, "on his suggestion, a number of them were sent back to the framers," and Harrison offered his help "to put the necessary 'kick' in them." On August 13 the "Declaration of Rights of the Negro Peoples of the World," with 122 signers, was completed. Boulin correctly noted in his report, however, that "Garvey still rules with an iron hand."[11]

The convention's third week, according to Harrison in his diary, included "aimless talks and the 'election' of a 'Provisional President of Africa.'—himself [Garvey]; a leader of the American Negroes (Dr. James Hood Eason) to dwell in a 'Black House' to be built in Washington, D.C., to hob-nob with 'the other ambassadors' and draw, I think, $10,000 a year (The P[rovisional]. P[resident]. of A[frica]. is to draw $25,000)."[12] In addition, "two 'leaders' of the West Indian Negroes were also 'elected' and a leader for the Negroes of the world (400,000,000 according to him [Garvey])."[13]

Agent Boulin reported that "Garvey insisted that a native born African should not be elected as President of Africa, as in his opinion, such a man would be under very grave suspicion by England, France and other European countries who own territory there." This ruling, "that native born Africans were not eligible to the office of president of that country," led to "the una[lterable] resentment of an African delegate," who "insisted that they as Africans can better understand the nature of African chiefs, kings etc. who would resent an outsider." Again, "Garvey ruled him out of order, told him to shut up, sit down and be quiet, thereby carrying out his own ruling." According to Boulin, "Garvey exercises perfect control over the so called delegates who vote just as he wants them to, and those who differ are clapped down and called traitors of the race by the audience, hence a delegate is utterly afraid to vote against Garvey's will."[14]

One incident of ominous intrigue occurred during the third week of the convention. On Tuesday, August 18, Harrison, as noted in his diary, was told by Rev. Eason, the chaplain-general of the UNIA, that Henrietta Vinton Davis was the person "intriguing against" him with Garvey in an effort to have him "dismissed from the editorship of the paper." Eason recounted that when William Ferris, the chancellor of the convention, "refused to sign the silly document which they call a Declaration of Rights," Garvey "turned to Miss Davis who was seated by his side on the platform and said: 'Now, you see? If I had taken your advice and removed Harrison from the paper I wouldn't have had anybody left.'" Eason did not tell Harrison this "in confidence," but according to Harrison "didn't care to whom" it was repeated. Harrison was subsequently told by Hodge Kirnon "that Fred Toote told him that when Miss Davis and Mr. Watkiss [Harry R. Watkis, who worked in the BSL office] were in Philadelphia they both asked him point-blank to use his interest with Mr. Garvey to have me [Harrison] removed from the paper—on the ground that I was 'an enemy of the movement.'" Toote, president of the Philadelphia chapter of the UNIA, said that when he asked them for specific acts and instances "they couldn't produce any, but insisted on the general blanket-assertion."[15]

During the fourth week of the convention Harrison delivered a Wednesday night, August 25, talk at Liberty Hall on "What Shall We Do to Be Saved?"[16] He once again left a strong impression. The *Negro World* of September 4, in reviewing the convention, called Harrison "a Walking Encyclopedia." The Rev. Dr. John Dawson Gordon of Los Angeles and Harrison both spoke, and each man held "his audience by different means: the one by the wonderful personality and magnetism he possesses, coupled with his original, inimitable style of expression; the other by the weightiness of his words and the valuable information he invariably imparts in all his addresses." Harrison "not only interests his hearers, but also never fails to gain their approval of what he says," and this was "the result of long, careful study on his part of innumerable practical subjects." The *Negro World* then added:

Mr. Harrison is the most scholarly and learned member of the convention no one will deny; for that matter, there is scarcely a man in all the race whose learning is so profound, whose knowledge of economics, religion, sociology, science, art, politics, literature is such as seems inexhaustible. So all-comprehensive are his vast stores of knowledge in general that he is sometimes alluded to as a walking encyclopedia; so that, like Lord McCauley [Thomas Babington Macaulay], who in this respect he resembles, his great storehouse of information is ever ready to serve his purposes, whether by way of clarifying a subject upon which he is speaking, or whether simply to embellish it from a literary or rhetorical point of view. But, best of all, this man of remarkable erudition is daily endeavoring to use his learning and knowledge in helping to solve the problems of his race, a very commendable example to others possessing talents and training of a very high order.[17]

During the convention's fourth week, as Harrison recorded in his diary, "the high officers of the U.N.I.A." were elected, "including a Potentate," Gabriel M. Johnson of Liberia, "the only delegate elected in Africa," at a salary of $12,000 a year. Also elected were High Commissioner General Wilcum F. Ellegor; International Organizer Henrietta Vinton Davis, at $6,000 a year; Chaplain General Bishop Alexander McGuire; a minister of legions, at $3,000; a surgeon general "and other such high-sounding magnificos"—yet, pointed out Harrison, all this while "the Chancellor's report showed that the organization has about $2,000."[18] Harrison then commented on the election procedures, which he considered

the most shameless thing that I have seen. Garvey shamelessly electioneered for the candidates whose names he had "suggested" to the Convention while condemning canvassing and electioneering for others. He sent people like Watkiss—also [Henry V.] Plummer & [Arden A.] Bryan—from his office who were not delegates and they voted for his candidates. He even sent his mistress Miss Amy Jacques, but Arnold [J.] Ford, the Sergeant-at-Arms took the question up with him point-blank and he had to rule against her voting (This was done conversationally tete-a-tete, and not in public business). Several of his candidates were defeated on Thurs 26th and he ruled, therefore, that no one was elected who didn't have "a two-thirds majority". Then it was pointed out that "The Rev. Dr.["] [John Dawson] Gordon, his personal flunkey and not three weeks in the Association, was not elected either, not having received a 2/3 majority. This he fiercely debated but finally was forced to yield.[19]

According to Harrison, in a new election held the next day, "there was a tie on Gordon's office." Though "Garvey had already voted," he "insisted that it was his right to cast another vote 'as President General of the U.N.I.A.,'" and "he did so and thus elected his henchman." This act, however, "revealed Garvey to the delegates and lined up much sentiment against him." Harrison "had been nominated for the office of Speaker In Convention, the last but one in the list," and on the first ballot his vote "was 39, Toote's 30 and Garvey's designees (a Rev. [B. F.] Smith of Philadelphia) 17." The next morning, Friday, August 27, before the new elections, Harrison withdrew his name, "and while doing so asked all those who voted for me to cast their votes for Toote." Harrison noted that then "Toote, on the balloting, (I stayed away from the hall) got 69 votes and was elected." Harrison wrote in his diary that delegates asked why he withdrew, and he commented, "Time will tell them: I won't."[20]

Harrison also discussed additional aspects of the convention in his diary. He noted, as he had previously predicted to the UNIA leader F. Wilcum Ellegor, that "Garvey insisted on presiding." Harrison was especially critical of Garvey's chairing of the meetings and claimed that he "made the welkin ring [made loud noise] with his insane and bombastic rhodomontades [boastful talks]." He then offered details:

In plain English, he [Garvey] has made an ass of himself and has made the movement a matter of ridicule. He has had not the shadow of a program and when he was kept away from the meeting everything was up in the air. He has plastered the air with lies. Imprimis, his circulars advertising the Madison Square Garden meeting asserted that 25,000 (Twenty-Five Thousand) delegates were present from all parts of the world whereas the official balloting for the officers showed that Mr. Ellegor, who was the sole nominee for the office of Commissioner-General, and presumably received the votes of all the delegates, received 103 (one hundred and three) the highest number cast for any office. Garvey himself, sole nominee also, received 92 votes for President-General. Yet, despite such facts, he is again declaring in circulars out today that there will be 20,000 delegates in the parade on Tuesday [August 31].[21]

Harrison went on and again described Garvey as "an ass" who, "although he has been presiding for 3 years" didn't "know enough to put the simple formula: 'You have heard the motion; are you ready for the question?'" Instead, Garvey "always" got it "snarled up" as 'Yo'ave heard de motion: are yo' ready?'" In this way, delegates "evolved a document" that Garvey said "would make the white world tremble when given to the white papers." To the contrary, however, Harrison observed that "the papers have only laughed and jeered at his arrant imbecilities, altho' they began (the New York ones) with studious fairness— except the *Globe*." Harrison noted that Garvey hadn't given his Declaration to the *Negro World* so Negroes could read it but had read it in the presence of white reporters in attendance only at the evening sessions. Harrison also added an ominous prediction: "The man has a perfect mania for flamboyant publicity. And this, I think, will wind a rope around his neck later."[22]

On Monday, August 30, Harrison "met Mr. Jackson" (possibly James A. Jackson), a "colored newspaper man." Jackson was "seeking data for an article on Garvey and his movement for a white newspaper" (possibly the *Herald* or the *Sun*). They were scheduled to meet again, since Harrison wrote in his diary on Sunday, September 5, "I disappointed Mr. Jackson, being away at Rye Beach [seaside resort] with the children."[23]

The UNIA's third parade was held on Tuesday, August 31, but Harrison "did not march." In his diary he explained, "Once may be a duty; but when it becomes a habit, I abstain." He then observed that Garvey had "declared Aug. 31st an international holiday for all the Negro peoples of the world; but the hypocrite kept the people employed at 54–56 W. 135th St. [offices of the UNIA, *Negro World*, and the Black Star Line] hard at work." Then on the morning of August 31 Garvey "gave the honors (The African Cross and D.S.O.E. [Distinguished Service Order of Ethiopia]) to the fortunate (I stayed away)" and that night had "'a grand reception' and dance at 107th St, the New Star Casino." Harrison closed: "Thus ends the most colossal joke in Negrodom, engineered and staged by its chief mountebank."[24]

After the UNIA convention ended Harrison went, on Friday, September 3, to 217 West 139th Street to call on Mrs. Adelaide Casely-Hayford, the African activist, educator, and feminist originally from Freetown, Sierra Leone. Mrs. Casely-Hayford had been married to the Gold Coast (now Ghana) nationalist and distinguished barrister J. E. Casely-Hayford from 1903 until their separation in 1914. She and Hubert had "a most enjoyable chat"; he "found her to be one of the most thoroughly cultivated Negro women whom I have ever met." She had been head, for a time, of the ladies' division of the UNIA in Sierra Leone but, according to Harrison's diary, "gave it up—for cause." He, in turn, "gave her many inside details of the Garvey fiasco."[25]

On Sunday, September 5, at 3 p.m., Harrison was to meet the Barbados-born Clifford Stanley Bourne, whom he described in his diary as "an intelligent delegate to the Convention . . . in revolt." Bourne had previously earned a reputation as protector of West Indian immigrants in Puerto Barrios, Guatemala. Harrison waited till 3:25 p.m., but Bourne "failed to put in his appearance."[26]

Hubert also spent Labor Day, Monday, September 6, with his daughters Frances, Alice, and Aida at Rye Beach; Ilva stayed home "with Mama." The foursome "had a delightful time." Frances and Alice went swimming and played on the sands; Aida and her dad "loafed on the beach" and went to see the sights. They encountered Miss (Julie) Petersen and Mrs. Jackson (the mother of Peter Jackson Jr.), and when they came back, after more swimming by Frances and Alice, a fine drizzle started. They then all went to the amusement park, "where Mrs. Jackson, Miss Petersen and her girls had secured a good place." Hubert left the girls in charge of the women, with two dollars to be spent on them, and went swimming for nearly two hours, making it out to a big launch. While he swam the children "explored nearly all the pleasure places," and he then took them to some more, including "the scenic railway (shooting the shoots) which they seemed to like" but which "was too much" for him. They all sailed in a tub and rode on the merry-go-round, the children played on the swings, and Hubert "used the rifle" and found that the fact that he was now wearing glasses hadn't "spoiled" his aim. At six they "*began* to go home," but "the Irish ignoramus who drove the truck (for Toussaint Welcome) fooled around so getting gasoline and passengers that he didn't make an actual start before 7:10." Then "he lost his way and had to ask it several times." Traveling at "a snail's pace . . . he finally got us back to Harlem at 10 p.m.— although it had taken us (on one of Toussaint's regular autos) only an hour and ten minutes up."[27]

When they returned, "Mrs. Harrison," who was in the last stages of a pregnancy, "promised to lick the children for eating food that Miss Petersen had given them." She "had warned them not to do this" on the ground that Miss Petersen was Hubert's "concubine," and, "since she hated the mother, would not hesitate to poison the children!" Hubert commented in his diary: "*Some* wife!" Eleven days later, on Friday, September 17, at 3 p.m., Hubert and Lin's fifth and last child, a son, William, was born.[28]

In his diary entry of August 31, 1920, Harrison somewhat cryptically wrote that "Time will tell" why he withdrew from the "Speaker in Convention" race.[29] The timing and content of that remark suggests that it may have been in part related to the August 1920 "Confidential Report" from Elie Garcia, resident secretary in Liberia, on conditions there and on the UNIA's prospects for investment in that African country. According to Harrison, he obtained a copy of this report from Garcia, "when Garcia came back in 1920 from Africa in August or July." Garcia showed it to him to get his reaction before it was given to Garvey. While he had it, and before Garvey saw it, he made a copy. Harrison undoubtedly sensed its importance—the document both suggested that efforts in Liberia would be enormously difficult and that Garvey might be guilty of political conspiracy against the government of Liberia.[30]

The background of this report goes back to April, when Harrison was unable to head the UNIA delegation to Liberia. Elie Garcia,[31] a Haitian-born BSL stock salesperson in Philadelphia, took his place. Garcia left New York on April 17, 1920, reached Liverpool on the April 27, and arrived at Freetown, Sierra Leone (about 225 direct miles from Monrovia, Liberia), on May 22 to evaluate investment prospects. The report written by Garcia, as UNIA resident secretary in Liberia, to Garvey had two parts and was completed in August. Part 1 was started on June 27, and "Part 2: Notes" offered virtually no hope for the UNIA effort regarding Liberian development. Garcia also detailed hostility emanating from the UNIA potentate and the mayor of Monrovia, Gabriel Johnson.[32]

So the UNIA would know with whom it was dealing, Garcia felt compelled "to make some statements very unfavorable to the Liberians." He began by explaining that "Liberia, although a very rich country in natural resources, is the poorest place on the face of the earth and the people are actually facing 'starvation.'" He attributed this to many facts, including "the strong repulsion of the Liberians for any kind of work"; that there "is no cultivated land in the Republic and rice which is the national food is imported from England and other places and sold at a fabulous price, although it can be produced in enormous quantities there"; and that "Class distinction" is "also a great hindrance to the developments of Liberia," where there are "two classes of people, the Americo-Liberians, also called 'Sons of the Soil,' and the natives." He described the "first class, although the educated one," to be "*the most despicable element in Liberia*," who, because of their education, "are conceited and believe that the only honorable way for them to make a living is by having a 'Government job.'" He noted that most of them were "educated in England or other European places" and "are used to a life which the salaries paid by the Government do not suffice to maintain. Therefore, dishonesty is prevalent. To any man who can write and read, there is but one goal: a government office, *where he can graft*." For this reason, "they are absolutely hostile to 'immigration['] of American or West Indian Negroes," and "this fact is of great importance . . . *words must be given to any one going to Liberia in the interest of the U.N.I.A. to deny firmly any intention on our part to enter into politics in Liberia.*"[33]

Garcia suggested that the UNIA "policy for the present must be to limit our program to commercial, industrial and agricultural developments," and because of "the attitude of the Americo-Liberians toward enlightening the native tribes," this *"intention of the U.N.I.A.* must be kept quiet for a while." He pointed out that "the Americo-Liberians are using the natives as slaves and human chattels." They "buy men or women to serve them and the least little insignificant Americo-Liberian has half a dozen boys at his service" and does not "even carry his own umbrella in the street." Garcia also considered it deplorable that the highest Liberian official lives in a state of polygamy and added that there "is not a mile of road in all of Liberia and in Monrovia, which is the capital, not a street worthy of the name." For such reasons, contrary to his instructions, Garcia did not work "for immediate concession of land" because he found out "it was [*not*] in the power of the Government to grant such concessions without the approval of the Senate."[34]

The historian Tony Martin judges Garcia "an astute observer" and emphasizes that his report "contained within it all the major elements in the relationship which would develop over the next few years between the UNIA and Liberia." He adds that its later discovery by the Liberian government helped assure the failure of Garvey's plans for Liberia.[35]

Garcia's report, which Garvey did not release at that time, was yet another matter that distanced Harrison from Garvey. While the report may have been the final straw as far as Harrison's consideration of the "Speaker In Convention" position and even as regards his continuing as managing editor of the *Negro World*, it was not the only problem Harrison had with Garvey. Harrison had probably already developed a full-blown critique of Garvey, and he was developing plans of his own to build an all-Black Liberty Party.[36]

By the end of the 1920 UNIA convention, it was clear that Harrison was breaking from Garvey. Sometime in 1921 or later he jotted down notes on his appraisal of Garvey, which suggest some of the likely reasons for his ceasing to serve as managing editor of the *Negro World* in late 1920. His list read:[37]

I Observe Things

1. Insincere Boastings[38]
2. Cowardly Evasions on Lynching / Nyassaland[39]
3. Lies (20,000 delegates)[40] ([Elie] Garcia's Report)

Daily Trips

("90 days from now . . .")

4,000,000 members vs. 73,000 off. rep. 4/8/21[41]

(Retraction: [Assistant District Attorney, Edwin P.] Kilroe, [Richard E.] Warner & [Edgar] Grey Collects $700 on day when we had agreed to publish retraction)[42]

4. Changed Policy from Negro Self-Help to Invasion of Africa

"Kink-no-more ads"[43]

(My Speech of Aug. 25th—"Lion & Dead Mule")

5. I Observe His Character

    A. Delusions of Grandeur[44]

    B. Delusions of Persecution[45]

    C. Insane Hoggishness: [Samuel George Kpakpa-]Quartey Case told by Mrs. Young[46]

    D. Jealousy of Successful Subordinates[47]

    E. Active Ingratitude: Mrs. [Ashwood] Garvey, [Edward D.] Smith-Green, Grey.

    F. Greed for Domination[48]: Voting Twice in Convention:

      Rescinding Votes.[49]

    G. Ignorance: "Denizens" of Africa.[50]

    * "Yo've heard de question, are yo' ready?"

      Nyassaland as independent [Nyasaland was a British protectorate in Africa]

      Africa as *a country* & *all Negroes*[51]

      17-1-20 Editorial: The Black Star of Achievement[52]

Previously, around the time of the Paris Peace Conference, Harrison had suggested a major difference with Garvey. Harrison criticized those, including Garvey, who were "seeking to get money from the unsuspecting masses of our people 'for the purpose of sending delegates.'" He considered such efforts "sublimely silly" and "a useless waste of the money of poor people who can ill afford it" and emphasized that "lynching, disfranchisement and segregation are evils HERE; and the place in which we must fight them is HERE." He added that instead of elaborating plans on how to liberate Africa, African Americans should "LEARN WHAT THEY HAVE TO TEACH US."[53]

Harrison would later, far more emphatically, emphasize that he sought "the harnessing up of Negro energies in the United States for the promotion of their own economic, political and spiritual self-help and advancement" and not to found "a Negro state . . . in Africa, as Marcus Garvey would have done." He added "that African Negroes," not "American Negroes," were capable of leading the struggle in Africa.[54]

Toward the end of the year, on Friday, December 10, Harrison learned from Cyril Crichlow, of Crichlow and [Isaac Newton] Braithwaite, Shorthand Reporters, "that Garvey had paid them *one hundred dollars a day* to report the convention proceedings." Harrison commented in his diary, "Good Lord! Think of the way in which this insane ass, Garvey wasted thirty one hundred dollars of the people's money!"[55]

Also on the night of December 10, 1920, Harrison had a conference with Hudson Pryce, one of the editors of the *Negro World*, at his house, and they "agreed to collaborate on a book of about two hundred pages, a history of the Rise and Fall of Garvey—to be ready for immediate publication when the crash comes." Harrison began "to lay out the work and assemble the documents" that night, but Pryce "developed into an Old Guard," as Harrison noted in his March 3, 1921, diary entry.[56] Harrison would later restart work on a similar book. His collaborator in that effort would not be Pryce but Garvey's first wife, Any Ashwood Garvey.[57]

———

During the UNIA convention Harrison mixed articles and editorials in with the *Negro World*'s general coverage of the convention. In the August 7 issue his "A Difference of Opinion" responded to "Progress" by John E. Bruce in the same issue. He quoted Bruce: "The American Negro of today, had slavery not existed, would probably now be a gibbering ignoramus. And what is true of the benefits and civilizing and Christianizing influences of slavery in the case of the Negro is true of every race that has ever been enslaved and that was not quite ready for civilization at the time of its enslavement."[58]

Harrison took exception "to that conception of the Negroes' place in the world of men." He presumed that "among us Negroes, as among other people, men may differ in a friendly fashion without disrespect to each other's person and views," and he did not think that all *Negro World* writers "should have the same opinion upon every subject." "Such unanimity," he posited, "could only be expected in a graveyard and not on a live newspaper." After those prefatory remarks he then publicly dissented from his friend, "worthy colleague and father in journalism," because he considered "the point of view expressed" to be "quite false" and "subversive of Negro pride and self respect." Harrison reasoned, "If the Negro in America and the West Indies today would have been a 'gibbering ignoramus' without the 'benefits and civilizing and Christianizing influences of slavery,' then wherever the Negro exists today without having passed through these beneficial influences he should be a gibbering ignoramus." To counter this position he cited the "notorious fact that the Negroes of West Africa, in Nigeria and the Gold Coast who have not passed through this white Christian slavery are among the most intelligent, self-respecting and able in the entire Negro race." He rated the *Lagos Weekly Record*, the *Gold Coast Independent*, and "other Gold Coast and Nigerian papers and magazines" as "above the best publications of their sort that we have produced in the Western World." Finally, he pointed to the West African leaders Casely-Hayford and John Mensah Sarbah, whom he listed "at the very tiptop of Negro intellect, enterprise and achievement."[59]

Harrison also extended his remarks to consider the notion "that the white man's destruction of the Negro's family life, of Negro honesty, of Negro respect for women and Negro sobriety were designed by Almighty God as a means of lifting the race." This, he argued, was "a dangerous modern form of the older notion that Negroes were nothing, are nothing and will be nothing except in so far as white people make them something." Harrison signed his reply as "Editor of the *Negro World*" and emphasized that "The U.N.I.A. and A.C.L., the Black Star Line and, indeed, the New Negro Manhood Movement, of which they are portions," were "based upon the directly opposite principle [from Bruce's]." He also asked to hear from Bruce on this matter, since "some of the points advanced in the same article [were] well worthy of respectful consideration."[60]

On August 7 [Dave?] Louis Thompson wrote to "*My* Dear *Harry*" (Harrison) to thank him "for disavowing the statement of Mr. John E. Bruce in your splendid letter in the current issue." Thompson was "distinctly opposed to Mr. Bruce's conclusion" but aware of his own "inability to properly and convincingly refute his statement." He was therefore "more than glad" to see this done "by one who is admittedly known to be more than capable to do so." Thompson added that he appreciated Harrison's letter for three reasons—first, "because the *great* you is agreed with *little* me"; second, because "no one of my acquaintance could so convincingly, fairly, and scholarly combat Bruce-Grit deductions, as Mr. Hubert H. Harrison"; and third, because with Bruce's "wide and deserved renown as one of our most brilliant scholars and journalists" his "assertion would at once be taken verbatim as correct by the unthinking—those who are in the habit of allowing others to do their thinking for them—as conclusive as axiomatic." Thompson closed, "With much pride in 'Our Harry.'"[61] That same day, L. M. Meade of New York City also wrote and thanked Harrison for his "brilliant and effective reply" to Bruce's article."[62] The August 21 *Negro World* then included Bruce's reply to Harrison. It thanked "Dear H. H." for his "courteous and friendly criticism" of the paragraph, which was "written in an ironical vein, and intended to be so understood." Bruce attempted to clarify what he said and closed, "I plead 'not guilty' to the charge."[63]

In the August 14 issue of *Negro World*, in the middle of the UNIA convention, Harrison published his powerful "A New International," which had appeared in the May 15, 1920, issue as "The New International" (see chapter 6) and described how "continued [white] suppression" would propel "the tendency toward an international of the darker races." He also offered a succinct and powerful new editorial on "The U.N.I.A." This editorial explained that racial self-help and self-sufficiency were at the core of much of the message of both the New Negro and the UNIA:

> The Universal Negro Improvement Association in the scope of its appeal embraces and expresses the spiritual standpoint of the new Negro. The essence of the appeal is the call to racial self-help and self-sufficiency. Begging, leading, arguing and threatening are all methods addressed to the other man's mind. The Universal Negro Improvement Association eschews these ancient and futile methods of propaganda. The new Negro does not control the decisions of the other man's mind anymore than did the old. But he does control his own body and brain, manhood and pocketbook, and out of these materials can erect the splendid fabric of his future. To mass our manhood, our might and our money is the special object of this organization.
>
> Here is a call to both the splendid idealism and the practical effort of the young Negro to manhood. To have done with wishing and waiting; to replace a wishbone by a backbone, to finance our own future and to make for ourselves in the world of business, politics and culture that place which we deserve, without waiting upon the good will of those who have been responsible for being down—such are the ideals, aspirations and aims with which the Universal Negro Improvement Association makes its appeal to the young men of the race.[64]

Harrison's August 21 editorial, "Our Political Power," also written during the convention, emphasized the need for self-help and true political independence. It called attention to the fact that "the Negro in America is lynched, disfranchised, jim-crowed and discriminated against," but it also pointed out "that the Negro in America has a few opportunities, rights and privileges which he does not enjoy in the West Indies." In the "Northern States," in particular, "the Negro" had "only himself to blame" for not utilizing "these powers and privileges in his own behalf." In New York City "any Negro" could send a child to the public schools for "an education identically the same in every respect" with that provided "to the most favored Anglo-Saxon." Similarly, both Hunter College and City College furnished collegiate instruction, including BA and MA degrees, "absolutely free." He asked, "How many of us avail ourselves of these educational rights and privileges?"[65]

Harrison then cited an example to stress his point. There was a trade school on 138th Street ("in the Negro neighborhood") attended on any afternoon "by hundreds of white boys from the Bronx and downtown" who sought instruction "to begin life above the level of a railroad porter or waiter." One "seldom" saw "a black boy among them," although "in the days to come," he predicted that "black men who are now black boys will be insisting that all the fault for their low economic condition is due to the white people." He then added: "No one who knows us will accuse us of any excessive friendliness for white people, but we must point out that it is the Negro's duty to avail himself of every means to power which is now furnished in New York and America at large, if he would eventually and successfully maintain a position of independence in the world uncontrolled by the whims and prejudices of whites."[66]

It was, he offered, "in politics particularly that we Negroes fail in this respect," especially since "agitation and propaganda which have been outlawed in Hayti, the Virgin Islands and the British West Indies can still be carried on in the Northern states of the union." Since conditions in those territories could "be affected for better or for worse by the action of the American Government, it becomes our duty here in the North to exercise some effective influence on the machinery of that government." He emphasized:

> If Negroes in the North had intelligently organized their votes they would be able to now call the hand of the Secretary of the Navy [Josephus Daniels], who has been waging brutal war against the liberties and property of our brothers in black in Hayti and Santo Domingo and has given to the Virgin Islands the awful anomaly of Danish laws in American territory, and sexual and physical outrage perpetrated by the marines.[67]

What could be done to utilize "our privileged position" in the North "on behalf of our brothers not so far away?" Harrison's answer: "We have done nothing, although we could do much," and "because we have virtually made ourselves impotent, we can expect nothing." Steps could be taken, however: "Every Negro in the North who hasn't the vote" should "acquire it" and "use it," and, if done wisely, they could "secure the ballot for their voteless brethren in the South by withholding their votes from the Republican party or any other party and by using their votes in the city, State and nation to compel the enforcement of the 13th, 14th and 15th amendments to the American Constitution." In addition, "they could also secure the appointment of Negro governors for the Virgin Islands" or at least "bring effective pressure to bear against the horrifying brutalities which black people are now compelled to endure from the 'cracker' in the Caribbean." As "the machinery of government" was already provided, the task was "to lay our hands to guide, direct and control some of its application."

Failing to do this, "the blame will be laid squarely by future generations, not upon the criminality of the white but upon the stupidity and cowardice of the black." Harrison urged "that we make . . . a record which our posterity will respect."[68]

The author, editor, and Montserrat-born Harlem activist Hodge Kirnon was greatly impressed by such writings, and the August 21 *Negro World* reprinted his "Contemporary Comment: As to 'HH'" from the monthly magazine that he edited, *The Promoter.* Perhaps aware of Harrison's possible impending departure from the editorship of the *Negro World*, it suggested that Harrison again edit his own paper. Kirnon described Harrison as a "radical forerunner writer and speaker," as "the first Negro who boldly preached racialism and all forms of radicalism in New York," and as "the first Negro whose radicalism was comprehensive enough to include racialism, science, politics, sociology and education in a thorough going, scientific manner." Noting that East St. Louis (the site of the 1917 "pogrom" previously discussed by Harrison) "demonstrated to every Negro that the lackey cringing and conservative spirit was not a help to him, but a decided hindrance," he pointed out that "this event more than anything else" is what "gave rise" to *The Voice*, the "radical, fearless and outspoken [weekly], published and edited by Harrison." It was, he added, "this paper that really crystallized the radicalism of the Negro in New York and its environs." Kirnon then stressed that "what the race now needs is a weekly paper to fill the place of the *Voice*, a paper containing news of general interest and editorials touching upon radical, social, educational and labor questions connected directly or indirectly with the race."[69]

In the August 21, 1920, *Negro World*, published during the UNIA convention, Harrison also printed a review of William Z. Foster's *The Great Steel Strike and Its Lessons.* Foster, a former socialist and syndicalist, was one of the outstanding radical labor organizers in the country and would become a leading member of the Workers Party and later of the Communist Party USA. The steel strike of 1919 was one of the great labor battles of the decade. The review, particularly with its comments on the role of "white" workers, was one of Harrison's more important pieces.[70]

Harrison noted that Foster's book had received "so many well merited encomiums from periodicals and newspapers of national scope" that he didn't think it necessary to dwell upon its "general excellence." It stood "almost unrivalled" as "a first-hand study of the actual machinery of industrial control in one great department of the nation's economical life." Any reader would "realize that the great trusts which are empowered to organize, arm and equip a military and police of their own, control in addition the political machinery of government, national and state, and utilize this machinery to beat down the opposition of the workers, organized and unorganized." Harrison's main concern was with "the relation of the Negro worker to the white workers and to this militant machinery of brutal repression." He noted that the facts in Foster's eleventh chapter "produce the impression that the Negro worker at present is largely hostile to organized labor," and he then quoted Foster: "The indifference, verging often into open hostility with which Negroes largely regard Labor's activities, manifested itself strongly in the steel campaign. Those employed in the industry were extremely resistant to the trade-union program; those on the outside allowed themselves to be used freely as strike-breakers." Harrison also noted that Foster had pointed out that "in the Homestead steel works out of 14,000 employees, 1700 were Negroes." He then again quoted Foster:

> During the organized campaign, of all these men, only eight joined the union. And of these, but one struck. . . . The degree of this abstention may be gauged when it is recalled that of the white unskilled workers in the same plants, at least 75 per cent. joined the union and 90 per cent. struck. . . . Similar tendencies were shown in Chicago, Youngstown, Buffalo, Pueblo, Sparrows' Point, and other districts. In the entire steel industry, the Negroes beyond compare, gave the movement less co-operation than any other element, skilled or unskilled, foreign or native. . . . Those on the outside of the industry seemed equally unsympathetic. National committee secretaries' reports indicate that the Steel Trust recruited and shipped from 30,000 to 40,000 Negroes into the mills as strike-breakers. Many of these were picked up in the northern cities, but the most of them came from the South. They were used in all the large districts and were a big factor in breaking the strike. . . . Most of them seemed to take keen delight in stealing the white men's jobs and crushing the strike.[71]

Harrison considered this to be "a terrible indictment of the Negroes' failure to respond to the call of labor." He emphasized, however, "for this, labor [presumably, in part, because of statements about 'white men's jobs'] itself is to blame, as Mr. Foster very cheerfully admits further on," when he insists that "the unions will have to meet the issue honestly and broad-mindedly. They must open their ranks to Negroes, make an earnest effort to organize them and then give them a square deal when they do join. Nothing short of this will accomplish the desired result." To Harrison, however, Negroes were "at a loss to understand why Mr. Foster should expect that 'the best Negro leaders must join heartily in destroying the pernicious anti-union attitude so deeply rooted among their people.'" In contrast, Harrison stressed:

> It is up to the white unions and the American Federation of Labor and the great railroad brotherhoods themselves and not up to the Negro leaders to change this deep seated aversion which American Negroes have for white

American labor. It is conceded on all sides that the white organized labor movement has been and still is pronouncedly anti-Negro. And as long as that remains true, just so long will self-respecting Negro leaders abstain from urging the laboring masses of their race to join forces with the stupid and short-sighted labor oligarchy which refuses to join forces with them."[72]

"But, apart from this matter," Harrison found *The Great Steel Strike and Its Lessons* to be "a book for intelligent, work-a-day Negroes to read." They needed to see the photographs of Pennsylvania Cossacks "in brutal action on the streets of Homestead, Gary and other cities"; to look at the pictures of Mrs. Fannie Sellins, the union organizer, "disfigured and shot to death by steel trust gunmen in West Natrona, Pa."; and to see "the forces of respectability marshalled in favor of disorder and violence against white workers whose only crime is the demand that enough of the profits of their labor be deflected into their pockets to enable them to live with the ordinary decency of a common horse or cow." Harrison predicted that "when the Negro sees this he will know how to estimate properly the lying statements made in newspapers and on pulpits concerning the criminality of the laboring man."[73]

––––––––––

While the UNIA convention was underway and his dissatisfaction with Garvey was intensifying, Harrison completed his second book, *When Africa Awakes: The "Inside Story" of the Stirrings and Strivings of the New Negro in the Western World*. Harrison had planned this book for some time. Previously, in August 1917, in the midst of the heightened activity around the founding of the Liberty League and *The Voice*, he had completed his first book, *The Negro and the Nation*, which was published in New York by the Cosmo-Advocate Publishing Company, headed by Orlando M. Thompson, Barbados born and a future vice president of the BSL. In his preface to that work Harrison indicated that he planned, in the near future, to write a book "on the New Negro" that would "set forth the aims and ideals of the new Manhood Movement among American Negroes which has grown out of the international crusade 'for democracy—for the right to have A VOICE in their own government'—as President Wilson so sincerely put it."[74]

As suggested by its subtitle, Harrison's second book offered firsthand testimony to social, political, literary, educational, and internationalist aspects of the World War I–era New Negro movement and to Harrison's role in its growth. The book consisted of nine chapters, some with introductions, comprising fifty-one articles, an opening "Introductory," and a concluding "Epilogue" (his 1915 poem "The Black Man's Burden [a Reply to Rudyard Kipling]"). It contained articles from *The Voice*, the *New Negro*, and the 1920 *Negro World*. Harrison believed, as he explained in his August 1920 "Introductory," that these articles "were the foundation for the mighty structures of racial propaganda" that had arisen. Reviews included in the "A Few Books" chapter had been published in the Harrison-inaugurated book-review section of the *Negro World*, which he later described as "the first" such "regular book-review section known to Negro newspaperdom"—another extraordinary but much-ignored Harrison achievement.[75]

The "Introductory," completed on August 15, 1920, stressed familiar themes and described the setting in which the book appeared. Harrison detailed how the Great War of 1914–1918 "liberated many ideas undreamt of by those who rushed humanity into that bath of blood" and how the "flamboyant advertising" of "democracy" had "returned to plague the inventors" as the "subject millions" clamored "for their share of it." The "racial" aspect of this demand was the most acute, and in the United States this was reflected "in the mental attitude of the Negro people," who had "developed new ideas of their own place in the category of races" and "evolved new conceptions of their powers and destiny." These ideas "quickened their race-consciousness" and led to "new demands" in "politics," "education," "culture," and "commerce and industry," which were made "on themselves, on their leaders and on the white people in whose midst they live."[76]

Harrison felt that the publication of *When Africa Awakes* could meet a "dual Need." On one hand, "white people of America should know what these demands are and should understand the spirit in which they are being urged," rather than have them "misrepresented and lied about." Any "fulminations about the spread of 'Bolshevism' among Negroes by 'agitators'" didn't help toward understanding this "new phenomenon." On the other hand, "the Negro people" would also "profit by a clarified presentation of their own side of the case."[77]

The book's listed publisher was the "Porro Press, 513 Lenox Ave., New York City," though no information on the publisher was provided, and the name was not explained. One possible derivation of the name was suggested in a July 3, 1920, Harrison *Negro World* editorial that described the "Poro" society of Africa as one that "never allowed a white man or woman to enter the 'bush'" where mysteries were taught and never let them "understand the process by which things are done in Africa." A second possible derivation was from the cosmetologist Annie M. Pope Turnbo-Malone, who developed a "Poro method" emphasizing economic self-sufficiency, a "Poro system" of beauty products, a Poro College in St. Louis, and a monthly newspaper, the *Poro Purpose*.[78]

In his *"Inside Story" of the Stirrings and Strivings of the New Negro in the Western World* Harrison selected pieces that could be considered as "expositions of the new point of view evolved during the Great War and coming into prominence since the peace was signed." This perspective had "not been fully presented—by the Negro," though "white men, like Messrs. [Carl] Sandburg and [Herbert J.] Seligmann," sought "to interpret it to the white world." He judged that his writings would "stand the test" as "literature" and he was "willing to assume the risks." He felt he owed it "to my people to preserve this cross-section of their new-found soul," since it was his "privilege to assist in shaping some of the forms of the new consciousness."[79]

In his "Introductory," Harrison explained that in 1916, when he gave up his work as a lecturer and teacher among "white" people to work exclusively "among my own people," he "first began to hammer out some of the ideas" in the book. Then, in the summer of 1917, "with the financial aid of many poor but willing hearts" he brought out *The Voice*, "the first Negro journal of the new dispensation, and, for some time, the only one." Though it "failed in March, 1919," it made "an indelible impression." He then edited the *New Negro* "for a short time" before assuming "the joint editorship" of the *Negro World*. Harrison clarified "that the AFRICA of the title" (of *When Africa Awakes*) was "to be taken in its racial rather than its geographical sense," and he called attention to the account of the launching of the Liberty League presented in the first chapter "because *that meeting at historic Bethel [Church] on June 12, 1917, and the labor of tongue and pen out of which that meeting emerged were the foundation for the mighty structures of racial propaganda which have been raised since then*." This, he added, was a fact "not generally known" because he had "not hankered after newspaper publicity."[80]

In publishing the book, Harrison laid claim to the principal role in developing the New Negro movement, of which the Garvey movement was the most visible manifestation. Such a pronouncement may have been made because he thought, particularly with Garvey's difficulties, that he might contend for leadership of such a movement. It may also have been a factor in Harrison's difficulties at the *Negro World*.

The front page of the August 28 issue of the *Negro World* contained a short piece entitled "Personal Letters," which indicated that Harrison's book was out and suggested that his mail was being opened. The article stated that money for the *Negro World* should be sent care of the paper and "not to individuals" and explained that because some correspondents had failed to do this it had "been found necessary to maintain in the office of *The Negro World* a system of dealing with correspondence whereby each letter has to be opened and examined before being distributed to the person to whom it is addressed." In light of these new procedures, Harrison urged those who wished to write him "personally or confidentially" to address their letters to him care of the Porro Press, 513 Lenox Avenue, New York, and also to "Please send there all queries relative to my recently published book."[81]

Despite such difficulties Harrison did use the *Negro World* issue of August 28 to mention his "recently published book." He also mentioned, in a September 11 letter to Thomas Wallace Swann, of Philadelphia, that *When Africa Awakes*, with ten chapters (he probably was counting the "Introductory") and 146 pages, was out. He was "sure" Swann would like it and planned to bring a copy with him to Philadelphia.[82]

In his letter to Swann, Harrison also noted that in the September 11 issue of the *Negro World* Hodge Kirnon had reviewed the book. In that review Kirnon recommended *When Africa Awakes* yet felt justified in saying "that the author is still far from being at his best." He quoted approvingly from the "Introductory" and said that Harrison "not only caught the glimpse and heard the rumbling of the rising wave of the spirit of the New Negro, but he assisted in molding and directing these ideals into their most effective channels." Kirnon added that "the infant spirit of the New Negro was nursed, cradled and championed by Mr. Harrison, and throughout the pages of his book we remain conscious of his entire consistency."[83]

Kirnon acknowledged that one might "find room for disagreement or even strong criticism with much that he [Harrison] says and the manner in which he says it," but he was nevertheless "perfectly cognizant of the fact that there is not the slightest discordant note in the spirit which actuated his writings." Harrison had "the insight and prophetic vision of a seer," and he sounded "the strong and strident note of his awakened race with all the indignation and fury of a vexed spirit—a note to which time adds only luster and testifies to its wisdom and correctness of its interpretation." Thus, judged Kirnon, "in the ardent championship of the rights of the new Negro, one might feel that Mr. Harrison occasionally struck his opponents below the belt, but then one is forced to conclude that if such a method was resorted to, it was necessar[il]y efficacious to arouse their sense of proper manhood."[84]

Overall, Kirnon felt that Harrison's "bold and aggressive statements" made "thrilling and interesting reading" and that the book was "full of interest" and "instructive" in helping "to understand both the author and the varying fortunes and principles of the new Negro movement." Though most of the writings had appeared previously, Kirnon found that "to re-read them in proper arrangement" rendered them "more instructive and fascinating," and he recommended the book to readers "really desirous of acquainting themselves with the new Negro movement." He concluded by comparing Harrison's work with that of Max Stirner and Friedrich Wilhelm Nietzsche, with its "wonderful and strange admixture of tone, vigor, [and] the appeal to manhood and an empirical pragmatism," which so "contrasted with the supine feeble and boot-licking attitude of the old Negro crowd."[85]

The *Negro World* mentions and the letter to Swann take on added importance in light of the fact that when Harrison finally made application to the U.S. Copyright Office on December 29, 1920, he enclosed two copies of *When Africa Awakes* and added that his "ignorance" compelled him to ask that he be informed "of any other proper procedures." He claimed that when he wrote the "Introductory" on August 15 he "expected prompt printing," but the book had only recently been published, and he was sending "these copies before putting it on sale."[86]

John E. Bruce was also favorably impressed by *When Africa Awakes*, and, on January 12, 1921, he sent Harrison a press notice that appeared in the January 8 Kansas City, Missouri, *Call*. Bruce hoped the piece "pleased" him and might bring "some orders." He also appended a note commending Harrison on his "illuminating" *Negro World* article "An Economic Suggestion to the UNIA." Bruce told Harrison that the article was "forceful" and "yous's a 'smart nigra.'"[87]

The referred-to press notice said "Hubert 'Heavy Hitter' Harrison[']s" new book was "written in his best style" and was "as interesting and illuminating as, all the products of his facile pen usually are." Bruce commented that "Harrison has the incis[iv]eness and directness of statement which is characteristic of the silvery emanations of Tho[ma]s. Carlyle, that crabbed old Scotchman, who called things by their proper names, and hit hard whenever he saw them." He described the book as "the best thing that has ever come from the fountain pen of this brainy and courageous young Negro author" and predicted that it was "going to have a big sale because Harrison has said what the average Negro of intellect has been thinking for the past thirty years or more." Bruce concluded that any who read the book would "know that Africa the wide world over is awake."[88]

In another "Bruce Grit" column of that period, Bruce described Harrison as "a polished orator" of the "tantalizing sort" who possessed "an acid tongue a tenacious memory and a fund of general information on many subjects." Although "Nature made him a controversialist," it also "gave him a voice which is pleasing and a style that is persuasive." The column ended by describing Harrison as "our oratorical mesmerist"—a speaker who could "force a smile out of a wooden Indian and compel him by the witchery of his eloquence to subscribe for Black Star Line stock in any amount."[89]

On February 13, 1921, Chester A. Scott, president of the Milwaukee UNIA division, wrote to Harrison to thank him "for the excellent Christmas present" of his "wonderful book *When Africa Awakes*." He had "read and re-read the contents" and enjoyed it very much. The chapter on politics was a particular "wealth of information," and he "enjoyed every word of it." Scott thought every member of his UNIA division should have "a liberal knowledge of the affairs of Africa and themselves," and he requested "special terms on . . . 50 or 100 lots" of the "wonderful book." He thanked Harrison for "many past favors" and asked "what our friend[?] Mr. [William] Bridges is doing" and how "the ambitious young man" was "getting along."[90]

Scott was not the only UNIA member impressed with Harrison's book. It was well enough received throughout the organization that within a year it was listed as training material for UNIA and ACL cadets (aged thirteen to sixteen years) in the UNIA's "Rules and Regulations for Juveniles" in the *Constitution and Book of Laws* revised and amended in August 1921.[91] The book also circulated widely among the common people. In Harlem, according to the historian David Levering Lewis, it was read and sold "in barbershops"—a clear indication that it was reaching some of the masses Harrison sought.[92]

By the end of the 1920 UNIA convention Harrison was clearly dissatisfied with Garvey. While critical, however, he continued his lecturing, writing, and book promoting, and he also became a principal organizer, along with William Bridges, of a new, all-Black political party—the Liberty Party. The new organization had a short life—it existed from about August to November 1920—yet in that time it actively sought to put into practice the militant political independence that Harrison had been advocating. It broke from the established political parties, sought to develop a plan to run its own candidates for political office, and argued for militant self-defense in the face of white supremacist attacks. It was a major departure from Garvey's relatively apolitical approach, and with the Liberty Party Harrison hoped to reach people involved in the Garvey movement and the broader New Negro movement as well as the Black masses. Bridges, from Florida, had attacked Garvey and the BSL in outdoor speeches and edited the short-lived magazine *Challenge*. He later drew criticism in a *Negro World* article, which said he made "a specialty of 'knocking'" people who rose "into prominence in Harlem."[93]

The Liberty Party was mentioned in the *Negro World* of August 28, as the UNIA convention came to a close. The paper noted that Harlem would have the distinction of holding the first and last national conventions of the year: the Socialists had met in June at Finnish Hall, at 2056 Fifth Avenue, and the several-months-old Liberty Party was scheduled to meet on September 15. The Liberty Party planned to nominate candidates for various offices, including for the twenty-first congressional district of New York and president of the United States. (Harrison was not a citizen and would not be nominated for any office.) Bridges was quoted as saying: "We were disgusted with the Republican Party and so we are organizing our own party."[94]

Bridges explained that the Liberty Party aimed "to keep Miss Margaret Smith [a Republican] from returning to the Assembly" in Harlem's nineteenth

State Assembly district. She had reportedly voted to oust the Socialist assemblymen elected the previous year because "the colored men in her district were radical." Since she said she wanted to get rid of the radicals in the nineteenth district, the Liberty Party now sought "to get rid of Miss Smith." The party would also run a candidate in the twenty-first State Assembly district to oppose J. C. Hawkins, the city's "only colored assemblyman," because they claimed not to know what he had done in Albany for two years and didn't want "a man who sits and is satisfied to answer 'yes' or 'no.'" They wanted "a real live wire" who would "let himself be heard and not be bossed by the machine," and they would "fight . . . all the Republicans who are doing nothing but follow[ing] the rule of the machine." As for the party's candidates, Bridges predicted that Harrison would "probably get the permanent chairmanship of the [Liberty Party] convention," and leading candidates for the presidential nomination were James Weldon Johnson, Dr. James Hood Eason (who would "receive the backing of the Garvey element"), W. E. B. Du Bois, and Professor S. W. Scarborough, of Wilberforce University. Bridges denied rumors that he would be the party's candidate for president. The *Negro World* judged that the failure of the leading parties "to nominate a colored man for Congress in the 21st district" had "added greatly to the impetus of the new party," and it looked as if it would "carry off several offices in Harlem."[95]

By September, with the UNIA convention completed, Harrison and Bridges were regularly stumping for the Liberty Party. The Bureau of Investigation agent Tucker, in his report of September 4, noted that Bridges was holding open-air meetings in Harlem and Philadelphia for the party and calling for "a Negro for President." The party reportedly planned to run "a full ticket of Negroes" in November and urged people "not to vote for any member of the white political parties"—to vote "the negro ticket only." Tucker added that Harrison was one "of the moving spirits in the party."[96]

In his report for September 9, Agent P-138 (Boulin) wrote that "the radical Negro Socialists have been keeping their nightly campaign on the Harlem street corners" and that those "making very great hay are the Negro Liberty Party" headed by Bridges and Harrison. They reportedly held meetings "telling the Negroes not to vote for any white men this year." Boulin noted, "Harrison has been in everything—every Negro movement—every party and a street speaker for over eight years."[97]

In two very similar reports of September 25, BI agents Tucker and Boulin noted that the Liberty Party was fostered by the "radical agitator[s]" Harrison and Bridges, who were "holding nightly meetings in the Negro district of Harlem" advocating that "the Negroes" this year "vote only for Negroes." Tucker described Harrison as "a very intelligent man" who "in the course of his speeches advises his hearers to learn chemistry so that they will be able to make gunpowder, gas, etc. in the event of their being attacked by the Whites either here or in the South." He added that this "advice" was "clothed in such language that while his meaning is unmistakable, it would be a difficult matter to prove that he was inciting his audience to violence or suggesting it."[98]

A confidential report of September 30 by the BI in New York reported that Herman Marie Bernolet Moens had recently been in the office of Garvey and had "a long conversation" with Harrison. Moens had shaved off his beard, making him difficult to recognize. The report also claimed that Harrison had reportedly "recently joined some secret society" and that Moen's visit had "some connection with the fact." (Since there is no indication of Harrison joining any secret society at this time, this may simply be an ill-informed reference to Harrison's article on the Poro society of Africa.)[99]

In his report for October 5 Boulin wrote that Harrison was continuing his lectures in Harlem "with a large following" and that his "radical" speeches posed "as educational lectures so as to cover up his tracks."[100] Four days later Boulin reported that Harrison and Bridges were promoting the Liberty Party on street corners and saying "they will be the first to nominate a negro president of the U.S.A." They were also reportedly "filling their pockets with nickels and dimes from the collections," yet Boulin claimed to be "at a loss to know what they are about or what these fellows are after." With only two days left before the close of voter registration he noted that "the negro radicals" were "exceptionally busy in the neighborhood."[101] Also on October 9 both Agent Tucker and the Department of Justice's Radical Division in its "General Intelligence Bulletin" pointed out that Harrison and Bridges were continuing their "radical" Liberty Party activities and that Harrison "advises his audience to use force in putting down any movement against them."[102]

The Liberty Party convention led by Harrison and Bridges and attended by about 150 people was held at Public School 89 on October 10. Boulin reported that after "a lot of anti-white and anti-Democratic and Republican talk" the convention nominated "nine negroes" for president, "none of whom were present at this meeting." Most of the nominees, with the possible exception of James W. Hood Eason, were probably not interested. The results showed Rev. Eason, 32 votes; Du Bois, 22; ex-assemblyman E. A. Johnson, 15; James Weldon Johnson, of the NAACP, 5; James Wormely Jones (an undercover BI agent), 5; Kelly Miller, of Howard, 2; William Pickens, of the NAACP, 2; and William Monroe Trotter, an illegible amount. Bridges declared Eason the party's candidate.[103]

A *Negro World* article of November 6 revealed more about both the October 10 convention meeting and internal problems in the Liberty Party. The article, intended for the issue of October 30 and probably written by Harrison, was entitled "Negro Party Brands Bridges as a Faker: Accused of Secretly Working for the Democratic Party." The article claimed, regarding the October 10 nominating meeting, that Bridges had failed to notify the nominees of their candidacies for president and vice president. Bridges had also failed to discuss his stay in Milwaukee "during the four weeks when his presence was needed to enable the party to function in the primaries" and misled members into believing that they would be able to vote for their candidates by writing their names on the ballot. In addition, the article charged Bridges with using "the name of the Liberty Party without warrant or authority, to 'indorse' Republicans, Democrats and Socialists" with whom he was "on friendly terms." Mention of "Milwaukee" referred to the fact that Bridges had visited Wisconsin in September to seek support from the SP and the IWW and had met with the Socialist congressman Victor Berger, who, he claimed, "assured the party of moral and financial aid." Bridges subsequently returned to New York and called for Black support of the SP and the IWW. Regarding the voting procedures, one could only vote for presidential electors, by whom the president and vice president would afterward be elected. Since the Liberty Party had no presidential electors, it would be impossible for its adherents to vote for president and vice president "without invalidating their ballots."[104]

The clear purpose of the *Negro World* article was to attack Bridges. It went on to claim that "another of Harlem's ikons was knocked from its pedestal" on Thursday, October 28, at PS 89 (at the southwest corner of Lenox Avenue, between 134th and 135th Streets), when the Liberty Party held its first public meeting since nominating Eason for president on October 10. Party members reportedly "presented an indictment of the crooked courses of their former organizer, William Bridges," who was scheduled to appear at a mass meeting on Thursday, November 4, "to show cause why he should not be expelled from the party." Harrison, the party's state chairman, and others asserted that Bridges "had been honey-fugling the members and had said many things that were very far from the truth," including that he "had organized branches in Philadelphia, Milwaukee and Boston"; that "the party had indorsed certain Republican and Socialist candidates"; that "he had financed its recent convention"; and "that one of the members had been guilty of 'a serious misappropriation of funds.'" These statements were reportedly "shown to be false and uttered with intent to deceive the members." It was also disclosed that Bridges "was a secret official of the Democratic party" and a "Tammany Hall district captain in the thirtieth election district of the twenty-first Assembly district." According to the *Negro World*, when members saw how they were "duped" they immediately voted that Bridges show cause in a mass meeting as to why he should not be expelled. They also reportedly urged the party "to take legal proceedings to recover from [treasurer] Bridges" the books and funds of the organization. Legal action was also sought to obtain "a gold ring which was entrusted to him [Bridges] to be raffled off to raise funds for the party's campaign."[105]

On November 6 Bridges wrote a letter to the editor of the *Negro World*, which appeared in the issue of November 13. Judging by the contents of Bridges's letter, and given that there was no editor's response, it seems likely that Harrison was no longer the managing editor of the paper. Bridges said: "In the last issue of the *Negro World* there is an article written by Hubert H. Harrison attacking me in a manner that is not justified by the real facts." Bridges then offered his version of events. He did acknowledge being a Tammany captain, saying it would put him "in a position at all times to enter any poll in the five counties of New York to see that no canvasser throws out a vote cast for Liberty Party candidates." Bridges also called Harrison's charge—"that the party urged legal means as a method of getting its books, funds and a gold ring"—"the hugest joke in all of his silly rantings." He said that there were "at present in use by the Liberty Party three books," one "owned by Joseph Gordon, Recording Secretary; the other two by the National Negro and Realty Holding Co., of which I am the President," and that "the funds we had [six dollars] were turned over to Harrison in payment of a loan he had made. That leaves a ring. Let him get it."[106]

As to Harrison's charge that "he [Bridges] should have reminded you that during the month of September," at both "138th and 139th Streets and Lenox Avenues," he "severely criticized Mrs. Henrietta Vinton Davis and the U.N.I.A." and that "I [Harrison] mounted the same platform behind him and pointed out the importance of every Negro supporting that organization," Bridges responded, "There has been no bitterer opponent of Marcus Garvey in all New York than this same Hubert H. Harrison." "He says that I have knocked every man that ventures to rise into prominence. It is difficult to believe that he would say this, he who is known everywhere as the knocker of everybody and everything." Bridges listed from Harrison's book *When Africa Awakes* a few of those who had "come under his ceaseless trip-hammer," including "Kelly Miller, Emmett Scott, [W. E. B.] Du Bois, [Robert Russa] Moton[,] . . . Henrietta Vinton Davis, Chas. W. Anderson, Geo. Harris, Fenton Johnson, Jas. W. Anderson, and all the ministers now associated with the U.N.I.A." (Interestingly, Henrietta Vinton Davis, Chas. W. Anderson, Fenton Johnson, and Jas. W. Anderson were not mentioned in Harrison's book.)[107]

———

On November 9 Harrison wrote to the Philadelphia activist Thomas Wallace Swann that at its last meeting the Liberty Party was "quite dissatisfied with the methods and tactics of Mr. Bridges" and had "elected me to the position of State Chairman of the party in New York, pending the Convention at which time those assembled will vote for a National Chairman." Harrison trusted that Swann would make "it clear to the friends that the fiasco of the last Olympia Theatre meeting is not to be laid at my door." He proposed "to come to

Philadelphia as soon as possible to speak." He hoped Swann could "get a certain theatre free of charge" as he had promised, and, if he couldn't, Harrison "would be glad" if he, "in company with the live wire young men who have been drawn to the movement in Philadelphia," would be able to "arrange some kind of public meeting." Harrison would speak "on the subject of The New Negro in Politics" and asked that Swann write back as to the prospects at his earliest convenience. He also mentioned that *When Africa Awakes* was available, he was "sure" Swann would like it, and he would bring a copy with him. Finally, he asked that "the young men (whose names I have forgotten)" write him "on their own account" care of the Porro Press.[108]

The Liberty Party reportedly held occasional street meetings into the next year, but according to Hill "no record of it has been found after August 1921." For Harrison, however, the Liberty Party effort appears to have ended in November 1920.[109]

————

As Harrison moved out of his role as managing editor of the *Negro World*, he once again looked to use lectures as a principal means of supporting himself and his family. In the last week of October, probably after having submitted his article on Bridges to the *Negro World*, he traveled to Virginia to deliver a "series of six lessons on topics of import for the betterment and progress of the race." The Petersburg *Evening Progress* reported that "a large enthusiastic and appreciative audience greeted Dr. Hubert H. Harrison" on October 25, when "the *Negro World* editor" delivered his first lecture at the Metropolitan Baptist Church in that city. The meeting was chaired by Edward H. Evans, a correspondent to out-of-town race papers and president of the local division of the BSL. Harrison offered a few complimentary words on the city, its inhabitants, and "the cordial relations existing," and then "critically, elaborately and masterfully" discussed the "New Negro." Comparing those who accomplished their emancipation and those who were given many privileges, he "eloquently portrayed the different races, their rise and fall and their achievements in words that burned and inspired." The paper claimed with "great force," "material facts," and "citations from sacred and profane history" he pointed the way "to heights that must be reached" and "sustained his reputation as a polished and finished orator."[110]

Harrison delivered his second lecture, on "Politics and the Southern Negro," at the Harrison Street Baptist Church in Petersburg on October 26. The *Progress* reported that Evans again presided, and "quite a large gathering of enthusiastic people turned out." Harrison was "in splendid form and voice" and was generously applauded as he offered "many sane, practical and useful suggestions." His third and fourth talks of the series were scheduled for October 27 and 28, on "Education and the Race" and "The Old Negro and the New Bondage."[111]

According to the *Progress*, "Dr." Harrison's talk on October 29 on "The Purposes and Principles of the Universal Improvement Association and the Black Star Line," originally scheduled for the Oak Street AME Zion Church, was changed to an 8 p.m. mass meeting at Metropolitan Baptist Church. An overflow audience was anticipated. Evans informed the author of the "Colored Dots" column in the *Progress* that all information concerning the BSL was under supervision of the division and that Harrison's lecture was to "climax in a mass meeting" for the purpose of organizing a branch of the UNIA and BSL. Harrison was then scheduled to speak at the First Ebenezer Baptist Church, on Halifax Street, before what was expected to be another large audience.[112]

After his Virginia tour, Harrison returned to New York to lecture and to continue work as associate editor of the *Negro World*. He developed a handout card to promote free lectures he offered at a restarted Harlem People's Forum, on Sundays at 8 p.m. at Lafayette Hall. The card included laudatory quotes about him from the *Truth Seeker*; the *New York Times*; Professor Henry Carr, of City College; Dr. George Frazier Miller, of St. Augustine's Church, Brooklyn; and Kendrick P. Shedd, of Rochester University and the Socialist Sunday Schools. The handout explained that the Harlem People's Forum had been established in 1916, "under the leadership" of Harrison, at a time "when it was dangerous to think." His proposed talks for the period of November 21 through December 12 included "The Black Man in History," "How Old Is Your Lodge? A Lecture on Masons, Odd Fellows, Elks and Other Fraternals," "How Things Happen to Happen," and "Is Spiritualism Worth While?"[113]

While his Harlem People's Forum was underway, Harrison also made arrangements to lecture in Philadelphia. On November 22, he wrote to Joseph St. Prix of the Philadelphia branch of the UNIA and sent him copy for a leaflet announcing his upcoming talk, which was to be used to help build the Liberty League, which he was apparently trying to resurrect in the wake of the Liberty Party's demise. Harrison thought two thousand flyers would be appropriate for an expected audience of two to three hundred. He left blank the site and asked to see the proof before it was printed. He also indicated that he would bring one hundred copies of *When Africa Awakes* and requested that St. Prix handle the sales for a 10 percent commission on the list price of fifty cents per book.[114]

Harrison preferred an afternoon meeting but suggested St. Prix make the decision based on his understanding of local concerns. He also asked if they could get as a chairperson, with the chair's name listed on the leaflet: either Thomas Wallace Swann; the AME minister, community activist, and former

Niagara Movement member Dr. Richard R. Wright Jr.; or the pastor of Union Baptist, Philadelphia's largest Black church, Rev. William G. Parks. Harrison, who so often lived at the edge of poverty, claimed he only had a dollar left and asked if St. Prix and friends could handle the printing and hall rental until he could send money within a day or two or until he came to town. In closing, Harrison suggested that St. Prix, or the man who had written a certain letter in a libel case, chair a committee of three or four to handle monies and arrange future meetings. Harrison's return address was again care of the Porro Press, 513 Lenox Avenue.[115]

This effort resulted in a leaflet announcing "Dr." Hubert H. Harrison's free Sunday November 28 talk at 2 p.m. on "Heaven, Earth and Hell, or A Race in Search of Its Soul" at the Women's Christian Alliance Hall, 610 South Sixteenth Street, in Philadelphia. Harrison was billed as a contributing editor of the *Negro World*; president of the Liberty League; and author of *The Negro and the Nation*, "The Black Man's Burden," and *When Africa Awakes*. The quote from the September 4 *Negro World* calling Harrison "the most scholarly and learned member of the [UNIA] Convention" and that there was "scarcely a man in all the race whose knowledge of economics, religion, sociology, politics and literature is so nearly inexhaustible" was attributed to Marcus Garvey. Also quoted was the *New York Times* of September 11 [14], 1912, describing Harrison as "an eloquent and forceful Negro Speaker who broke all records in an address at the Stock Exchange Building Yesterday." Finally, the Rev. Dr. George Frazier Miller of St. Augustine's Church, Brooklyn, was quoted describing Harrison, "with his Exquisite English," as "the marvel and idol of New York."[116]

On November 29 St. Prix sent Harrison a list of expenditures from the November 28 talk, including "telephone $.25, hall $6.25, leaflets $3.50, and postage $.16." Some $10.16 had been paid; $5.51 was still outstanding. St. Prix indicated that while Harrison spoke, the UNIA's "Mr. Gains" (probably E. L. Gaines, the UNIA's "Right Honorable Minister of Legions") came to town and said "British gold is being circulated to prostrate the jealous of the U.N.I.A. by a certain N.Y. gentleman." He left Harrison to draw his own conclusions and indicated that he and others were planning "more elaborate advertising" for Harrison's next lecture.[117]

On December 1 Harrison wrote to St. Prix on *Negro World* stationery but used the return address of the Porro Press, 513 Lenox Avenue. He asked St. Prix to go ahead with the "more elaborate advertising" but indicated he was "still 'broke' as I have been for two weeks," since "the people [*Negro World*] who employ me haven't paid me yet." He added, "Now that the Big Chief [Marcus Garvey] is in town we are hoping to see some cash this week." He asked that if St. Prix ran into any further financial difficulties he "show this letter to my friend [Henry] Dolphin and ask him to advance you some money in my name."

Harrison indicated he was pleased with the November 28 turnout and expected an overflow for Sunday, December 5. If he got paid, he thought he might come on Saturday, stay over, and give himself "a chance to meet some people who will 'join the chorus.'" Harrison added that Mr. Gain[e]s seemed "to be a great, big joke. He must have 'British gold' on the brain. Don't mind the old f—t, but go right ahead. Our motto is 'Not Busting, But Building,' and we can afford to stick to that. If we do good work and neither attack anyone or notice any attacks made on us, the Liberty League will attract hosts of friends in the City of Brotherly Love."[118]

Harrison suggested that St. Prix use the previous week's circular as a basis, change the lecture title to "What the New Negro Wants," and ask Swann to help with newspaper publicity. He was also having books sent to him from Petersburg, Virginia, care of St. Prix, and if enough were sold at the meeting he would use the money, minus his travel expenses, to pay the bills for the first two lectures. The Philadelphia forum lecture could be canceled in order to gain time to go around together and "meet some more friends." If St. Prix thought Sunday night in Philadelphia would be better, Harrison was prepared to make up a card announcing his lectures for December 19, December 25, and January 2 and then change his New York lecture from Sunday night to the afternoon. Harrison also sought St. Prix's "candid opinion" of his plan to teach educational classes in Philadelphia two evenings per week, and he wanted the Sunday audience's opinion about the idea of organizing either "a Local Committee or a branch of the Liberty League." Finally, wrote Harrison: "Speaking as one human being to another, I am deeply impressed by the spirit of comradeship and helpfulness which you and the others have shown and are showing, and whatever may develop from our joint efforts in Phila., I will never forget that I owe it to you."[119]

On December 6 Harrison wrote to "Dear Friend St. Prix" that he was "very sorry" that he (St. Prix) hadn't come to hear his talk on Sunday: "It would have done your heart good. We had a full house and an appreciative one." Unfortunately, because they "had to hurry to get out" Harrison didn't sell as many books as he otherwise would. Nevertheless, he felt the talks were "catching on," and he ventured "to prophesy that if we can get out some cards and can afford to hire a theatre or larger hall after two or three weeks more we will attract more than a thousand people." He added that he "had the pleasure of meeting Mrs. St. Prix on Sunday at the hall" and judged "that she and Mr. [Anderson?], your very able lieutenant, have given you a cheering account of the meeting."[120]

Harrison indicated that he had canceled his New York lecture for Sunday night, December 12, in order to stop over in Philadelphia "and use Monday to hitch up the people who can and should help us in the work." He included "'copy' for the circular and also a news account for the editor of *The American*." He asked that it be given to Mr. Parks or Mr. Swann "in time for this week's issue." He also asked St. Prix to try to "make arrangements that no other meeting will be held *down-stairs*" and looked forward to "a very interesting discussion 'from the floor' after the answering of questions." Harrison advised that "[floor discussion] is one of the very best sources of popular enthusiasm for any movement. The electric contagion spreads in that way. One spark starts another and the gathering is ablaze with it, and the result is earnest conviction of the value of the work, which can then be effectually shaped and directed by those who are leading it." Harrison closed by again reminding St. Prix of the educational classes and expressed "the liveliest feeling of gratitude for the good work already done."[121]

The circular Harrison prepared announced his free talk on "The 'Back to Africa' Movement" at the Women's Christian Alliance Hall, on Sunday, December 12. It described Harrison as a "Doctor of Civil Science" and a man "Who has traveled in AFRICA." Bishop Coffin of Philadelphia was quoted as describing the previous week's lecture as "the most wonderful and able address that I have ever heard." The leaflet also quoted from J. A. Rogers in *From "Superman" to Man* that "Hubert Harrison is the most modern and effective thinker of our race, ranking with many of the best among the whites" and from the December issue of the *World's Work* ("the great white magazine") that "Hubert Harrison, is a man of great Learning and World Wide Education." Those who didn't want to miss "Eloquence, Learning and Sound Sense" were urged not to avail themselves of this opportunity. Harrison followed this Philadelphia lecture with one more, on December 19, on "The Black Man in History, or Africa's Contribution to White Civilization."[122]

Harrison left his position as unofficial managing editor of the *Negro World* shortly after the UNIA convention, probably toward the end of October 1920, and Garvey again took over. In Harrison's opinion, Garvey's "instinct for self-worship" then "prompted him to appropriate the entire front page of the *Negro World* each week with his stupid declamations addressed to his 'fellowmen of the Negro Race.' It reduced the circulation of the paper from 50,000 to 3,000 copies." There were, of course, other significant factors in the decline of the *Negro World* and the UNIA, as noted by the historians Ernest Allen Jr. and Robert A. Hill. These included internal financial difficulties aggravated by a postwar recession and general economic downswing, government attacks and court actions, political opposition from other Black leaders, internal infighting, and politically conservative shifts in Garvey's general philosophy. The loss of Harrison as principal editor of the *Negro World* seems to have clearly rendered the UNIA far less prepared to handle such difficulties. Harrison's departure coincides with the period that Ernest Allen Jr. suggests was the beginning of the UNIA's gradual retreat "from an ideological position championing black

Figure 7.1. Hubert Harrison (1920). This photo is found in the original 1920 edition of *When Africa Awakes: The "Inside Story" of the Stirrings and Strivings of the New Negro in the Western World.* *Source:* Hubert H. Harrison Papers, Box 19, Folder 6, Rare Book and Manuscript Library, Columbia University Library. See https://dlc.library.columbia.edu/catalog/cul:18931zct54.

America social equality, to one in which any struggle for equal rights in the United States was deemed futile."[123]

Garvey's paper had spread amid a period of heightened racial consciousness and under Harrison's editorship. Its large circulation addressed the problem of financing. The old dispute in the Liberty League had included discussion of "white" or Black financing of *The Voice*. Harrison had opted for Black financing, a principled but difficult proposition considering the general impoverishment and low national literacy level of the Black masses at the time. It was a

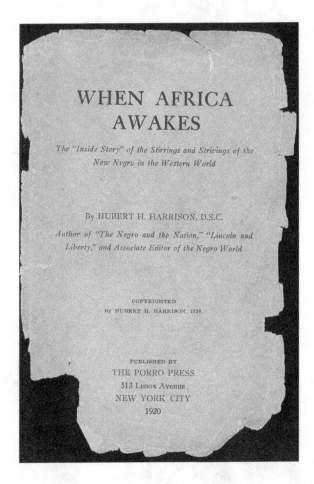

Figure 7.2. Hubert H. Harrison, *When Africa Awakes: The "Inside Story" of the Stirrings and Strivings of the New Negro in the Western World*, title page from the original 1920 edition. This title page appeared in the original 1920 publication and also appeared in the 2015 edition, with new introduction and notes by Jeffrey B. Perry, published by Diasporic Africa Press. The book contains fifty-three of Harrison's writings between 1915 and 1920 that establish his pioneering theoretical, educational, and organizational role in the founding of the militant New Negro Movement. *Source:* Hubert H. Harrison Papers, Box 19, Folder 6, Rare Book and Manuscript Library, Columbia University Library. See https://dlc.library.columbia.edu/catalog/cul:18931zct54.

different policy than the "white"-financed efforts of Booker T. Washington.[124] It was also a different policy than that of W. E. B. Du Bois and of Eugene Kinckle Jones and George E. Haynes of the National Urban League. Other radicals, such as Chandler Owen, A. Philip Randolph, and W. A. Domingo, had also opted for "white" support. Garvey, like Harrison, opted for Black support and urged a strong racial appeal. Garvey took an approach different from Harrison's, however. Whereas it was difficult to get the Negro masses to finance a newspaper, Garvey found it less difficult to entice support for his financial schemes. He solved the problem of finances (at least for a while) through the BSL, the Liberian Construction Fund, and lesser efforts, through which hundreds of thousands of dollars came into his hands.[125]

In "The Lion and the Lamb," in the *Negro World* of April 3, 1920, Harrison had quoted extensively from past *Messenger* articles that were critical of the NAACP and the National Urban League for accepting "white" financial support. He quoted, for example: "A man will not oppose his benefactor. The old crowd of Negro leaders has been and is subsidized by the old crowd of white Americans" and

> there is no organization of national prominence which ostensibly is working in the interest of the Negro which is not dominated by the old crowd of white people. And they are controlled by the white people because they receive their funds—their revenue—from it [*sic*]. It is, of course, a matter of common knowledge that Du Bois does not determine the policy of the National Association for the Advancement of Colored People; nor does [Eugene] Kinckle Jones or George E. Haynes control the National Urban League. The organizations are not responsible to Negroes because Negroes do not maintain them.

Harrison then mentioned efforts by the "six Socialists" of the *Messenger* who were calling for a convention in Washington, DC, in May to "work hand in glove with the N.A.A.C.P." Harrison publicly questioned "whether there isn't an economic advantage basis, past, present or expected, [to] this latest moral transformation."[126]

In "Just Crabs" in the *Negro World* (c. April 1920), Harrison had charged that socialist money was the key to the "scientific radicalism" of Owen and Randolph. He added that Owen and Randolph became "radicals overnight" after they were given socialist money. To Harrison those who put their propaganda efforts on such a paying basis were "'White Men's Niggers'" every bit as much as the "old-line politicians and editors." In notes from c. 1927 regarding "The Red Record of Radicalism," Harrison would refer to Owen and Randolph as "The Gold Dust Twins."[127]

———

The matter of Harrison's radical influence on the *Negro World* and UNIA merits discussion. The socialist/communist-leaning radicals of the era who worked on *The Emancipator*—including Domingo, Briggs, Moore, Randolph, Owen,

Anselmo Jackson, and Frank Crosswaith—left no doubt that they thought Harrison was the real leading radical figure around the UNIA. *The Emancipator* advised Harrison against going to Liberia as a UNIA representative and argued that he would best serve by becoming the head of the UNIA instead of Garvey. It added that Harrison was the person suited for the UNIA's "highest office" by virtue of "his knowledge of history, international affairs, politics, economics, and things pertaining to the Negro race," and it regretted that Garvey's "meagre mental attainments" prohibited him "from favoring his [Harrison's] obvious candidacy."[128] Harrison, however, was opposed to taking any executive position and claimed he never joined the UNIA, although membership dues were withheld from his pay. When he was the leading vote getter for "Speaker In Convention," he withdrew his candidacy.[129]

Contemporaries recognized Harrison's influence on Garvey. The *New York Age* claimed that Harrison's paper, *The Voice*, in its "spreading of propaganda on the universal brotherhood of the Negroes," was "a forerunner of the Marcus Garvey idea." The *Pittsburgh Courier* said that Harrison's "Liberty League [was] an idea which Marcus Garvey later made famous as the U.N.I.A." Hodge Kirnon maintained that "an interest in Africa and matters of culture relating to Africa and the Africans . . . were being shaped and brought to a near maturity by Harrison before Mr. Garvey came upon the scene." Years later, the historian John Henrik Clarke echoed this analysis and wrote that Harrison "had a profound influence on the thinking of Marcus Garvey during the formative years of his movement in America."[130]

Harrison offered important insights regarding his influence on Garvey. In "Two Negro Radicalisms" Harrison took the Black socialists, particularly A. Philip Randolph and Chandler Owen, to task as he explained the essence of Garvey's appeal:

> Where Negro "radicals" of the type known to white radicals can scarce get a handful of people, Garvey fills the largest halls and the Negro people rain money on him. This is not to be explained by the arguments of "superior brains," for this man's education and intelligence are markedly inferior to those of the brilliant "radicals" whose "internationalism" is drawn from other than radical sources. But this man holds up to the Negro masses those things which bloom in their hearts—racialism, race-consciousness, racial solidarity—things taught first in 1917 by The Voice and The Liberty League. That is the secret of his success so far.[131]

Some of the most revealing comments about Harrison's influence on Garvey would appear in a 1923 article Harrison wrote for the Associated Negro Press.

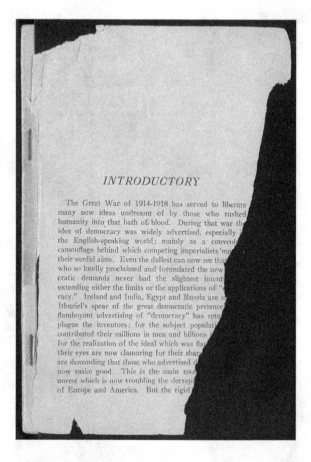

Figure 7.3. Hubert Harrison, "Introductory" (page 5). This is the first page from the "Introductory" of the original 1920 edition of Hubert Harrison's *When Africa Awakes: The "Inside Story" of the Stirrings and Strivings of the New Negro in the Western World.* Here Harrison explains how "the Great War of 1914–1918 has served to liberate many ideas undreamt of by those who rushed humanity into that bath of blood" and that during the war "the idea of democracy was widely advertised, especially in the English-speaking world; mainly as a convenient camouflage behind which competing imperialists masked their sordid aims." It was now clear "that those who so loudly proclaimed and formulated the new democratic demands never had the slightest intention of extending the limits or the applications of 'democracy.'" The "flamboyant advertising of 'democracy' has returned to plague the inventors; for the subject populations who contributed their millions in men and billions in treasure for the realization of the ideal which was flaunted before their eyes are now clamoring for their share of it. They are demanding that those who advertised democracy shall make good. This is the main root of that great unrest which is now troubling the decrepit statesmanship of Europe and America." *Source:* Hubert H. Harrison Papers, Box 19, Folder 6, Rare Book and Manuscript Library, Columbia University Library. See https://dlc.library .columbia.edu/catalog/cul:18931zct54.

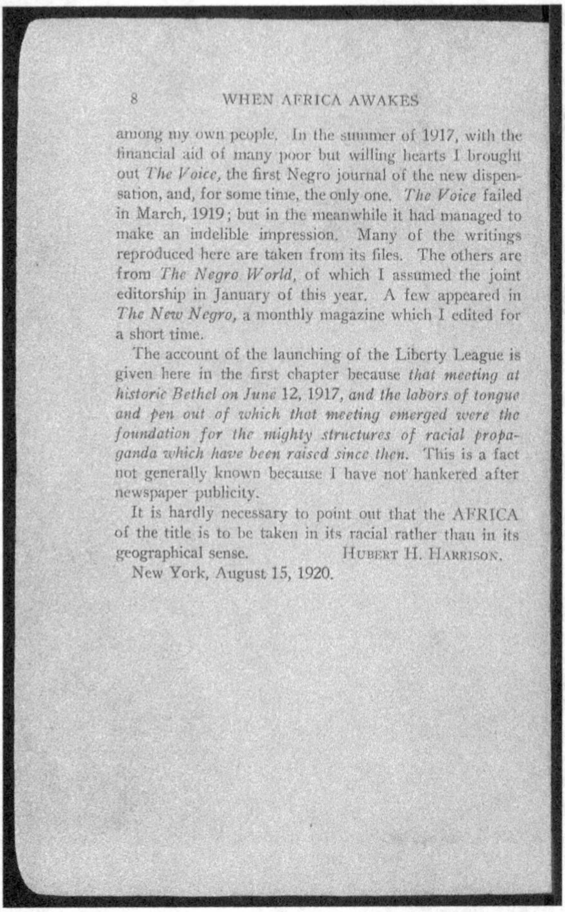

8 WHEN AFRICA AWAKES

among my own people. In the summer of 1917, with the financial aid of many poor but willing hearts I brought out *The Voice*, the first Negro journal of the new dispensation, and, for some time, the only one. *The Voice* failed in March, 1919; but in the meanwhile it had managed to make an indelible impression. Many of the writings reproduced here are taken from its files. The others are from *The Negro World*, of which I assumed the joint editorship in January of this year. A few appeared in *The New Negro*, a monthly magazine which I edited for a short time.

The account of the launching of the Liberty League is given here in the first chapter because *that meeting at historic Bethel on June* 12, 1917, *and the labors of tongue and pen out of which that meeting emerged were the foundation for the mighty structures of racial propaganda which have been raised since then.* This is a fact not generally known because I have not hankered after newspaper publicity.

It is hardly necessary to point out that the AFRICA of the title is to be taken in its racial rather than in its geographical sense. HUBERT H. HARRISON.

New York, August 15, 1920.

Figure 7.4. Hubert Harrison, "Introductory" (page 8). This is the final page from the "Introductory" of the original 1920 edition of Hubert Harrison's *When Africa Awakes: The "Inside Story" of the Stirrings and Strivings of the New Negro in the Western World*. Here Harrison writes that in the summer of 1917 "I brought out *The Voice*, the first Negro journal of the new dispensation, and, for some time, the only one. *The Voice* failed in March, 1919; but in the meanwhile it had managed to make an indelible impression. Many of the writings here reproduced are taken from its files. The others are from *The Negro World*, of which I assumed the joint editorship in January of this year. A few appeared in *The New Negro*, a monthly magazine which I edited for a short time." He then adds that the "account of the launching of the Liberty League is given here in the first chapter because *that meeting at historic Bethel on June 12, 1917, and the labors of tongue and pen out of which that meeting emerged were the foundation for the mighty structures of racial propaganda which have been raised since then*. This is a fact not generally known because I have not hankered after newspaper publicity." He closed by pointing out "that the AFRICA of the title is to be taken in its racial rather than its geographical sense." *Source:* Hubert H. Harrison Papers, Box 19, Folder 6, Rare Book and Manuscript Library, Columbia University Library. See https://dlc.library.columbia.edu/catalog/cul:18931zct54.

The original program of the Universal Negro Improvement Association was a good one, and it is still good. That program was based on the belief that Negroes should finance the foundations of their future and not go begging to the white race either for help, leadership or a program. But this was not a novel contribution by Garvey. It had been the program of the Liberty League of which Garvey was a member in 1917 in New York. From that league Garvey appropriated every feature that was worth while in his movement. His notion of a racial flag was one, and the flag of the Liberty League lies beside me as I write: black, brown, and yellow, symbolic of the three colors of the people of the Negro race in America. Red, black, and green were more discordant and bizarre and appealed to Garvey's cruder esthetic sense. Outdoor and indoor lectures, a newspaper, protests in terms of democracy—all these were adopted from the Liberty League. Garvey added an intensive propaganda more shrewdly adopted to the cruder psychology of the less intelligent masses, the sensationalism, self-glorification, and African liberation— although he knew next to nothing of Africa. But since Africa was far away and wild statements about its "400 millions" could not be disproved in New York that feature of it was a money-getter always. Then came the Black Star Line—an idea which Garvey took bodily from [Charles] Seifert, one of the original members of the Liberty League.[132]

The evidence is ample that Harrison—the "Father of Harlem Radicalism," the nurturer of the New Negro, the founder of the militant New Negro Movement, and the proponent of a mass-based race consciousness and racial solidarity—was the major influence on Garvey's radical political transformation. The key was the political development and consolidation of organized, independent, race-conscious efforts.[133]

Garvey had failed to make headway with his UNIA in Jamaica, and that had pushed him to visit the United States in 1916. Garvey's assessment was that Jamaicans, in 1916, "were not sufficiently racially conscious to appreciate a racial movement because they lived under a common system of sociological hypocrisy that deprived them of that very racial consciousness." In contrast, he believed "that the American Negro would respond to his call to racial action because in the United States, 'the Negro was forced to a consciousness of his racial responsibility.'"[134]

The political growth of what has come to be known as the Garvey movement/ UNIA was but one facet of the New Negro Movement of which Harrison was the recognized early leader. By late 1919, as his appeal started to grow, Garvey was delivering lectures on two of Harrison's favorite subjects: "Negro Manhood" and the "New Negro." According to Hodge Kirnon, this was the "infant" that Harrison had "nurtured." Frank R. Crosswaith, the Virgin Island–born

Brotherhood of Sleeping Car Porters Special organizer and a leading Black socialist of the 1920s, wrote simply that "the story of the New Negro's fascinating fight for a man's place in our time, is the story of Hubert Harrison."[135]

The most important political aspect of this militant New Negro Movement was the development of race consciousness combined with racial solidarity—a race consciousness of which Harrison was a pioneer and the leading and the most consistent proponent. It was this racial appeal that was the key drawing power of the movement, not dreams of African empire or get-rich-quick schemes. This point was well made by William H. Ferris, who emphasized that the majority of those drawn to the movement were attracted by the racial appeal. The UNIA leader William Sherrill agreed that the development of race consciousness was the real success of the Garvey movement. This concern for developing race consciousness in a political direction was what J. A. Rogers described as Harrison's "saner and more effective program" to lead the masses forward. It was central to the core program and the key ideas that fueled the radical political development of the UNIA.[136]

———————

The historian Robert A. Hill, in his seminal fourteen-volume documentation of Garvey and the UNIA, states, "Garvey originally came to America to learn more about Tuskegee and to enlist support for his own Jamaican version." Then, "he became converted in America to the primacy and efficacy of political goals." This was a marked change from his "earlier static view of political abstinence" in which, similar to Booker T. Washington, he urged that his followers "eschew politics as a means of social improvement."[137]

Hill then argues that while he was in America "the Irish cause provided the major ideological mainspring for Garvey's radical political transformation." To support this thesis Hill discusses the desire for a political voice, the slogans Garvey employed, the naming of his meeting hall Liberty Hall ("after the center of the Irish Transport Workers' Union in Dublin, which served as a center for militant nationalist politics in Ireland and the site from which was launched the Easter Rebellion in 1916"), and the use of a tricolor flag. On each count, however, it appears that Harrison, more than the Irish, was the major influence.[138]

First, there is the matter of the new radicalism of Garvey. Hill quotes Garvey in 1921, in the high period of his radicalism, that the "new spirit of the new Negro does not seek industrial opportunity; it seeks a political voice, and the world is amazed, the world is astounded that the Negro should desire a political voice, because after the voice comes a political place . . . and we are going to fight and die for that place."[139]

This desire for a political "Voice," however, is nothing other than the plan that Harrison had articulated in 1916 and implemented in 1917 in his newspaper *The Voice* and in the preface to his book *The Negro and the Nation*. As Harrison (quoting Woodrow Wilson) explained in an early *Voice* editorial, the essence of democracy is "the right of those who submit to authority to have a voice in their own government." This quote ran across the top of the front page of *The Voice*—for all to see. Further, the call for a political voice was a continuing push by Harrison in his work with the *Negro World*. In June 1921, in response to a letter to the editor of the *Negro World* bemoaning "that Mr. Garvey advises renunciation of politics in toto," it was Harrison who would explain that what was needed was for "this mass of awakened Negroes" to "take with them into politics the same 'Race First' spirit and principle which now makes the U.N.I.A. and the Black Star Line known and noted all over the Negro world."[140]

Hill adds: "In place of [Booker T.] Washington's outdated accommodationism Garvey claimed to offer 'a correct interpretation of the new spirit of the new Negro,' which presented 'a new problem—a problem that must be solved not only by the industrial leader but by the political leader.'" This "radically transformed vision of political independence" made Garvey, according to Hill, "the foremost beneficiary of the nationalist mood that emerged full-scale among blacks after 1918."[141]

Again, the New Negro, the call for political independence, and the new spirit were all efforts in which Harrison took the lead. It was Harrison who was the principal architect of the New Negro Movement. It was Harrison who advocated race consciousness and led the way with appeals to "Race First" and "Africa First," and it was Harrison, *The Voice*, and the Liberty League that championed the way toward political independence in the struggle for equality.[142]

Hill adds, "Even the slogan made famous by Garvey, 'Africa for the Africans at home and abroad,' echoed the oft-repeated Irish slogan 'the Irish race at home and abroad.'" Elsewhere, however, he points out that "Hubert Harrison was also instrumental in popularizing the slogan ['Africa for the Africans'] before Garvey arrived, but the 'Africa for the Africans' theme did not originate with him."[143] To the historians Tony Martin and Edmund D. Cronon the key slogans of the Garvey movement were, respectively, "Race First" and "Up You Might Race." "Race First" and "Negroes First" were, it should be noted, all used and pioneered by Harrison and the Liberty League.[144]

Hill seeks to buttress his claim about the primacy of the Irish influence by emphasizing that Garvey's "familiarity with the ideas and rhetoric of Irish nationalism dated from before the war." He cites Garvey's association, c. 1910, with the National Club of Jamaica. He points out that the founder of the club, S. A. G. Cox, "absorbed the influence of the Sinn Fein movement [and] . . . Cox chose the name *Our Own*, a rough translation of the Irish nationalists' *Sinn Fein*." This statement seems to contradict one in an earlier work where Hill wrote that Garvey's "experiences in England and Europe . . . did not produce in him anything that could be described as truly radical." Hill also notes that "literally, *sinn fein* means 'ourselves alone' or 'we ourselves.'"[145]

Again, it is important to realize that even this slogan was adopted and discussed by Harrison in 1917, well before Garvey's radical phase. Harrison explained that the Negro must use a similar slogan and that any man "who aspires to lead the Negro race" must understand it and put "squarely before his face the idea of 'Race First.'"[146]

In addition, Hill argues that "the name chosen for the UNIA meeting place reflected an appreciation for Liberty Hall, Dublin, the symbolic seat of the Irish revolution on the site where the Irish Citizen Army had launched the Easter Rising on 23 April 1916."[147] It is, however, far more likely that Garvey's Liberty Hall, which was named in 1919, was directly related to Harrison's Liberty League; his repeated calls for "Liberty" on the mastheads of *The Voice* and the *New Negro*; his establishing of "Liberty Corner" (which he made famous) at 134th Street and Lenox Avenue; and the Liberty Congress, which he chaired in 1918. (Harrison would also serve as chair for the Liberty Party in 1920.) Further, J. Dominick Simmons stated unequivocally that Harrison named Garvey's first Liberty Hall at 138th Street, and Harrison's son, William, in his notebook, similarly indicated that Harrison named the Garveyites' Liberty Hall.[148]

Finally, Hill quotes Charles Mowbray White to the effect that, in the interview of August 18, 1920, Garvey designated the symbolic meaning of the UNIA's tricolor as: "The Red shows their sympathy with the 'Reds' of the world, and the Green their sympathy for the Irish in their fight for freedom, and the Black— The Negro."[149]

Harrison, however, stated that the tricolor notion came from the Liberty League, that the colors were originally "black, brown, and yellow, symbolic of the three colors of the Negro race in America," and of "our [Blacks'] dual relationship to our own and other people [of color]." Harrison added that Garvey's change to red, black, and green was because they "were more discordant and bizarre." Such a non-Irish-related origin of Garvey's tricolor was confirmed by Garvey himself, on November 12, 1918. On that date, well before the Charles Mowbray White interview that Hill cites, Garvey explained that the tricolor represented "the black race between blood and nature to win its rights." He did not mention the Irish.[150]

The stage was set for the tricolor as well as for the UNIA's later growth and radicalism by the work of Harrison. Anselmo Jackson, writing in March 1920, said that "the success of Garvey" was "built on the ruins of Harrison's failure." Considering Garvey's success at that time (March 1920), however, it seems clear that Harrison's important, pioneering, and groundbreaking work had not been a "failure."[151]

8

Post-Convention Meditations, Writings, and Reviews
(September–December 1920)

In late 1920 Harrison and his family, particularly after the September 17 birth of his fifth child, William, continued to face economic problems. Hubert also continued to write for both the *Negro World* and in preparation for the lectures he would deliver. Though he left the managing editor position of the *Negro World*, he submitted articles, editorials, and book and theater reviews as a contributing editor, and these writings were probably a main source of his income in that period. They offer testimony to the breadth, depth, and insightful historical and political analysis that characterized his work over the remaining seven years of his life.[1]

During this period Harrison wrote some wonderful meditative pieces in the *Negro World*. In the September 20 issue "The Black Man's Burden" was published under the general heading of "Meditations of Mustapha as translated by Hubert H. Harrison." (Mustapha is one of the names of Muhammad and means chosen, selected, preferred, etc.) "Mustapha" (Harrison) began:

Down the dim dusk of the ages the man from Africa appears as the burden bearer of Western civilization. Long ago, while yet the world was wrapped in ignorance and slavery, he laid in ancient Ethiopia the sure foundations of Egyptian culture, as Egypt's own sons have confessed; and later, by the lotus-laden waters of old Nile he mingled his blood and brain in the mightiest edifice of social craftsmanship and work that the world had seen for six thousand years. There, as the Father of History has told us, did white Greece come to learn letters and law, religion and art, science and philosophy; to light her torch of culture at the resplendent blaze built by the black and brown children of the land of Khem and from this torch to kindle the fire of civilization upon the altars of barbarian Rome, whence sottish Saxon and brute German, wild Celt and wandering Goth have taken tribute of light and heat to warm themselves and enlighten the world of the present.

In ancient Rhodesia rose the mighty walls of Monomotapa as the awed Portuguese named it, where the majestic towers of the Great Zimbabwe astound the eyes of a white man's world, which thinks that only white men can build. The exhausting working of its great gold mines from which hundreds of millions had been taken furnished food for speculation to world-wanderers from the banks of the Tagus and the Thames. And today the science of archaeology plays pander to the prejudices of Anglo-Saxon savants who would claim the credit of these mighty ruins for the thieving race of which they are part.[2]

The Great Zimbabwe ruins in southeastern Zimbabwe are on a site estimated to have first been settled between 500 and 900 CE and then developed into a monumental stone-walled settlement of seven hundred hectares and some 18,000 Shona people between 1270 and 1450. After Europeans encountered the site Cecil Rhodes and others argued it was a long-lost Phoenician city and that Africans were too lazy and barbarous to have built such structures. Harrison's comments, breaking from the "prejudices" of "Anglo-Saxon savants," were consistent with some of the leading thinking of his day, since, in the period between 1906 and 1929, leading British archaeologists confirmed the veracity of the African oral tradition and the African origins of the Great Zimbabwe ruins.

Mustapha went on:

From the days before Christ walked in Galilee the black men within the lordly-sweep of the Niger were building city-states in Benin and Yoruba, in Sokoto, Kanem and Timbuktu. And these, expanded by conquest, commerce and culture, developed into the two-fold empire of the Mellestine Songhay and Ghana, which from the sixth to the sixteenth century, over a territory as vast as two-thirds of the present United States, maintained agriculture and the industrial art, commerce and science, while semi-savage Europe was burning witches, eating food with its fingers, and touching for the King's evil. This great Negro empire ran its course, as others have done before and since, and was finally subverted as Rome was, by the barbarians of [HH inserts western] Europe, cruder in culture but stronger in brute force; who finally by the slave-trade destroyed what was left of the ruins of its social and political order as Major Felix DuBois, Dr. [Heinrich] Barth and Lady Lugard [Flora Shaw] testify.[3]

According to the historian Basil Davidson, Heinrich Barth's "great work" (in five volumes) *Travels and Discoveries in North and Central Africa, etc.*, published in 1857–1858, was "the first scholarly and comprehensive understanding of this vast region that any European had ever secured," but for many years afterward it was appreciated by only a handful of specialists. Harrison's calling attention to such work was another pioneering effort on his part.[4]

Mustapha went on to explain that European attacks on its social and political order had "raped and ruined Africa," which "has been the captive of proud Europe," and "the black man has been indeed, 'despised and rejected of men.'" While the missionary counseled "faith in Christ," it was true that "slaughter and syphilis, gin and consumption, imported by the whites, ravish[ed] still further the vital resources of a hitherto helpless people." He saw these all as "portions of the black man's burden," as were "lynching and disfranchisement, mocking . . . and a Jim Crow Jesus made by the white man in his own image and in horrid mockery of the . . . [people] in Africa." But, he advised, times were changing, and "the burden bearer" was lifting up his eyes "to behold in the East the dawning of a better day."[5]

The October 16 *Negro World* carried Harrison's thought-filled "Meditation: Heroes and Hero-Worship, and the Heroic in Human History." He wrote, "At sundry times and in diverse manners man has made God in his own image," and "from the beginning until now most men have worshipped something set above themselves in honor and dignity and power." In its varied forms "its substance was the same: It was the best that man could see in himself. This he abstracted and offered homage to." Thus, "his god (or good) has nearly always served as a dynamic ideal to lift man further from the mud and nearer to the stars." Understood in this way, "the doctrine of the incarnation, shared by many religions," was "a tribute to the deepest truth and the most ancient spiritual fact" that "the divinity that dreams within us often awakes to reality in the life of some other person in whom we perceive a greater measure of the same effulgence." Harrison then quoted "old [Thomas] Carlyle": "Know that there is in man a quite indestructible reverence for whatsoever holds of Heaven, or even plausibly counterfeits such holding. Show the dullest clodpole, show the haughtiest featherhead, that a soul higher than himself is actually here: were his knees stiffened into brass, he must down and worship."[6]

Harrison explained that "hero worship is a tribute which humanity pays to its better nature"; "it changes with the stress of times and circumstance, and the Hero bears always the imprint of the age that brought him forth." Thus "Buddha, Mohammed and [Oliver] Cromwell; [Julius] Caesar, St. Francis [of Assisi] and Charles Darwin are all the embodiments of social tendencies peculiar to particular ages." Each hero "in his own way and for his own time led the world to a fuller realization of its latent powers and hidden

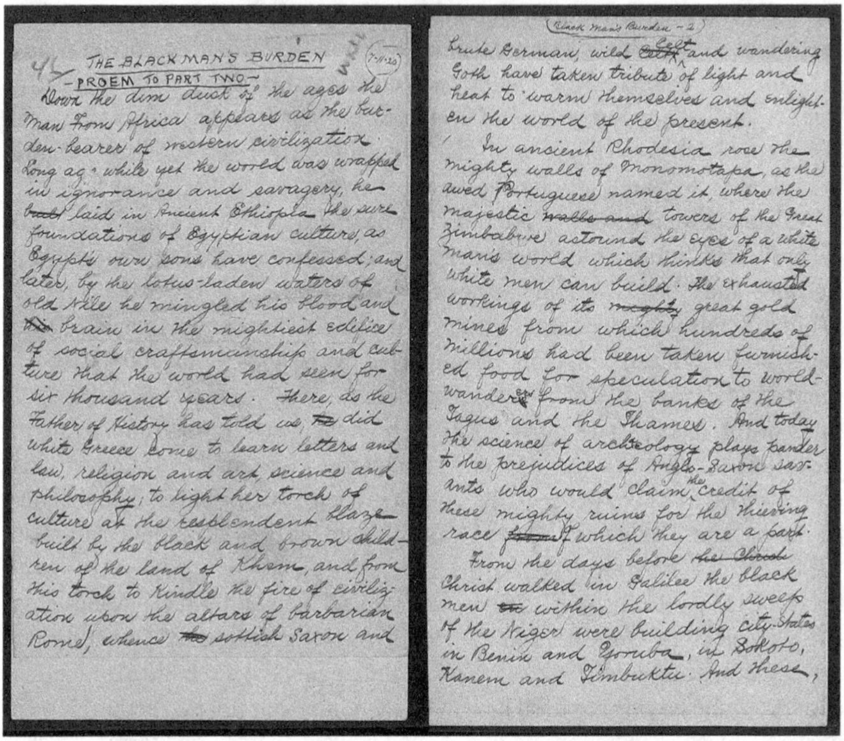
THE BLACK MAN'S BURDEN (7-11-20)
-PROEM TO PART TWO-
Down the dim dusk of the ages the man from Africa appears as the burden-bearer of western civilization. Long ago while yet the world was wrapped in ignorance and savagery, he ~~built~~ laid in Ancient Ethiopia the sure foundations of Egyptian culture, as Egypt's own sons have confessed; and later, by the lotus-laden waters of old Nile he mingled his blood and ~~his~~ brain in the mightiest edifice of social craftsmanship and culture that the world had seen for six thousand years. There, as the Father of History has told us, ~~to~~ did white Greece come to learn letters and law, religion and art, science and philosophy; to light her torch of culture at the resplendent blaze built by the black and brown children of the land of Khem, and from this torch to kindle the fire of civilization upon the altars of barbarian Rome, whence ~~the~~ sottish Saxon and

(Black Man's Burden – 2)
brute German, wild ~~Celt~~ Gaul and wandering Goth have taken tribute of light and heat to warm themselves and enlighten the world of the present.
In ancient Rhodesia rose the mighty walls of Monomotapa, as the awed Portuguese named it, where the majestic ~~walls and~~ towers of the Great Zimbabwe astound the eyes of a white man's world which thinks that only white men can build. The exhausted workings of its ~~mighty~~ great gold mines from which hundreds of millions had been taken furnished food for speculation to world-wanderers from the banks of the Tagus and the Thames. And today the science of archeology plays pander to the prejudices of Anglo-Saxon savants who would claim the credit of these mighty ruins for the thieving race ~~from~~ of which they are a part.
From the days before ~~the Christ~~ Christ walked in Galilee the black men ~~were~~ within the lordly sweep of the Niger were building city-states in Benin and Yoruba, in Sokoto, Kanem and Timbuktu. And these,

Figure 8.1. "The Black Man's Burden—Proem to Part Two," November 7, 1920, first two pages. In this piece, as in his September 20, 1920, *Negro World* article "The Black Man's Burden," Hubert Harrison discusses (in wonderful prose) wide-ranging aspects of African history. He writes: "Down the dim dusk of the ages the man from Africa appears as the burden bearer of Western civilization. Long ago, while yet the world was wrapped in ignorance and slavery, he laid in Ancient Ethiopia the sure foundations of Egyptian culture, as Egypt's own sons have confessed; and later, by the lotus-laden waters of old Nile he mingled his blood and brain in the mightiest edifice of social craftsmanship and culture that the world had seen for six thousand years. There, as the Father of History has told us, did white Greece come to learn letters and law, religion and art, science and philosophy; to light her torch of culture at the resplendent blaze built by the black and brown children of the land of Khem. . . . In ancient Rhodesia rose the mighty walls of Monomotapa as the awed Portuguese named it, where the majestic towers of the Great Zimbabwe astound the eyes of a white man's world, which thinks that only white men can build. The exhausting working of its great gold mines from which hundreds of millions had been taken furnished food for speculation to world-wanderers from the banks of the Tagus and the Thames. And today the science of archaeology plays pander to the prejudices of Anglo-Saxon savants who would claim the credit of these mighty ruins for the thieving race of which they are a part." *Source:* Hubert H. Harrison Papers, Box 4, Folder 15, Rare Book and Manuscript Library, Columbia University Library. See https://dlc.library.columbia.edu/catalog/cul:p2ngf1vk45.

inclinations," and "their own humanity looked up to them for guidance, shaping and control."[7]

"But," he added, "such leadership carries its own stern necessities of duty and responsibility," and as John Milton said, "he who would write an epic poem must be himself a true epic poem." To Harrison, "He who would be a Hero must be a true heroic soul, rising like a mountain-peak"; the "Hero must rise to heights of spiritual grandeur in which he will have perhaps no cheering companionship"; "he must follow the bent of his own nature and not the course mapped out for him by the multitude"; and "so only can he dwell with God above the clouds 'in private duty and in public thinking.'" This was "one reason why Heroes are so very rare," because "it is the virtue of the crowd to be crowd-minded, and the hounds of slander and the curs of foul abuse often follow yelping at the heels of him who dares to venture on the Better way." To Harrison, it was "humanity's eternal tragedy that its Heroes who were worshipped after death were most often in life the very"

> souls that stood alone
> While the men they agonized
> for hurled the co[n]tumelios stone.

In ending, Harrison emphasized "that imminent tragedy deters no high heroic soul."[8]

Six and a half years later, Harrison would write more on the topic, offering that "the worship of its great men is one root of self-respect of a group, a nation, a race; it is high time that Negroes should become familiar with the heroic deeds and splendid achievements of their brothers in blood."[9]

Around October 23, 1920, Harrison handwrote "The Meditations of Mustapha: A Soul in Search of Itself," which was to be delivered at the Radical Forum and was also to be used for the *Negro World*. It opened with a passage from Tennyson's *In Memoriam*:

> Perplexed in faith but pure in deeds,
> At last he beat his music out.
> There lies more faith in honest doubt,
> Believe me, than in half the creeds

Harrison went on to describe how "kind Christian friends" were "wont to assume that all those who fail to share their faith disbelieve also in goodness" and how "they firmly believe that all those outside the shelter of their fold are bound to a sad and sordid materialism of the flesh." Harrison, however, found "examples of great and good men in all times, from Socrates to [Herbert] Spencer and from

Hadrian to [Thomas] Huxley," who "might plead for a more neighborly estimate." He understood that "it would be pushing the point too far to insinuate
that a good pagan may be better than a good Christian," "but surely," he contended, "it is safe to say that he is no worse." He suggested, "if we could see
into one another's souls we might find that we could respect each other."[10]

Then, "to help in forwarding the dawning of the larger day one of these
souls," Harrison, who had "wandered" in search of himself because it was his
"destiny," proceeded to set forth "something of his find" on "the meaning and
the mystery of this life." He then offered his personal creed:

> I believe in Man my brother, his duties and his rights. I believe in the sacra-
> ment of sacrifice in giving myself in varying degrees to those who are about
> me; first to my friends, secondly to my race, next to my country, and lastly to
> humanity. I believe that man should not live by bread alone. If to eat and sleep
> and dress, to run the gamut of selfish success and to play at precedence with
> a next-door neighbor were all that there was to live and labor for I would as
> life be dead. For if these were the ends of life wherein would man be higher
> than the brutes?
>
> . . . to be tolerant of all men's honest opinions while holding by my own; to
> follow after the truth as it is given me to see the truth; to prove all things
> where proof is possible and to suspend judgement where there is no proof; to
> continually diminish by knowledge the number of my prejudices and to give
> even the devil a hearing before condemning him; to live my own life in my
> own way, with pleasure to myself if possible and if not, with satisfaction at
> least; to try my best to make this world a little better for my being in it, and to
> pay back to Nature something of what was expended in putting me here;
> to keep my face toward the light and my feet in the way of that Nobler Life—
> these are my principles which if I fail to keep I hope the charitable forgive-
> ness of mankind, since no man was ever as good as his creed.[11]

He next offered his thoughts on the subject of mortality:

> To subsist in the grave—or elsewhere—until the day of resurrection, or to
> live on forever and from everlasting unto everlasting, is something for which
> I have had no relish even as a child. To live for a few hundred years beyond
> my mortal term might indeed engage my thoughts and win me to seeming
> assent. But, however the poet may sing, the heart of man, undriven by the
> dogmas of his creed, longs for some *final* resting place and finds it not in
> the grave which opes again. To lay down once [and] for all the burden not of
> life but of *existence*; to make an end of being; to be done with life, its sorrows
> and elations, its golden tints and deeper shadows; to be done with pain and

pleasure, good and evil, contentment and care; to quaff the cup of Lethe [to lose all memories] and decline into an endless oblivion—this is, to me, a blessed boon and privilege greater than all the blessings of an immortal life.[12]

Harrison followed "A Soul in Search of Itself" with more of "The Meditations of Mustapha." His next piece, entitled "Peace on Earth," appeared around October 30 and opened by quoting from Du Bois's "unconventional credo" of October 1904. Du Bois said he believed in "the Prince of Peace," "that war is murder," "that armies and navies are at the bottom the tinsel and braggadocio of oppression and wrong," and "that the wicked conquest of weaker and darker nations by nations whiter and stronger but foreshadows the death of their strength."[13]

Harrison used this starting point to argue that it was "necessary to preach peace today when the great nations of the earth lay claim to their proud pre-eminence by virtue of their greater proficiency in the art of war; when three-fifths of the resources of a mighty nation are expended upon wars, past and present, and to come, and the mighty burden of taxation presses with ever-increasing force upon the faces of the poor." Throughout the world, people seemed "to live in an eager expectation of war," and "the feverish activity displayed in the manufacture of novel instruments of slaughter" suggested "that the savagery of civilization" was a "more potent force" at present than the "boasted brotherhood of man." To Harrison, "the efficient motive of war" was "simply human hate" and "every social instrument that ministers to hate" made "for the perpetuation of war." He placed "double shame upon those who preach the gospel of the Prince of Peace and yet can sit in silence while such atrocities are committed in His name."[14]

The Christian creed, he explained, had once proudly boasted "that it had brought to man a new and nobler sense of the sacred dignity of human life," but now "it is in Christendom that human life is held to be as cheap as common dirt." Since "the Christian nations" were "pre-eminently the warlike nations," he asked, who could deny "that the gospel of the meek and lowly Nazarene has been betrayed?" He then reasoned, if we "look for peace among the nations, we must seek it in those which are heathen," for "they are the ones that rest in peace—until the influence of Christian Europe and America compels them to be warlike in their own defense." A prime example was five hundred million Chinese in "a nation devoted to the ideal of peace for more than a thousand years," who were being "driven to arm themselves with Krupp guns to resist the aggression of the followers of the Prince of Peace."[15]

In public schools in the United States and elsewhere, boys and girls were "taught the detestable doctrine that organized murder is commendable" and, "in the name of patriotism," were "given to understand that the possession of superior brute force entitles them to oppress, insult and tyrannize over those who are weaker than themselves." Women, "gentle and refined," now "look[ed] on the soldier's uniform with pride and affection." Harrison, perhaps foreshadowing events of the 1930s and 1940s, forecast that "all the signs of the times" pointed "to a preparation for a more perfect holocaust."[16]

The "plea for peace" by "better minds," Harrison observed, was made "not on the ground that "they who take the sword shall perish by the sword" but "upon the broader and more certain ground that the doctrine of social hate upon which war is based is demonstrably a relic of certain savage, anti-social instincts of primitive man." While in the early days of small tribes it might be "natural that each group should hold every other group as its enemy," that was no longer the case. The "very process of civilization consists in a growing sense of the inter-dependence of human beings, in an extension of the bonds of human sympathy—in short, in a process of social integration," and it was therefore necessary "to insist that the worship of war is a rank reversion to the savagery of a barbarous age." Therefore, argued Harrison, "those of us who believe that war is murder and dissent from the current opinion in that respect should make our dissent known—should make it uncompromising and clear."

He predicted that some day "the worship of war, of the organized butchery of human beings by other human beings, will be rightly regarded as a hateful, hideous and horrible thing which men had to overcome in the lower stages of his progress from savagery to civilization." In the meantime, each person could "do something to advance the day when war will become odious." One could "lift a voice in protest against the sanguinary sentiments" that were "ascendant" and "speak a brave word now and then in favor of the Gospel of Peace which the Gospel of the Golden Dollar has elbowed out."[17]

On November 10, shortly after Harrison's "Peace on Earth" cited his "Credo," Du Bois wrote to him that the *"Crisis* would like to exchange with *Negro World"* and asked if he could arrange it. Harrison responded on November 18 that the *Crisis* had been put on the exchange list with the *Negro World*, and he trusted the exchange would be "mutually satisfactory."[18]

———

In the November 13 *Negro World* Harrison wrote on the Ku Klux Klan, which had been revived in 1915 and by 1920 was a nationwide phenomenon. His article described how in 1865 in Pulaski, Tennessee, it "first reared its grisly head as an instrument whereby Negroes could be terrorized back into working for nothing." This "economic purpose" had "always been at the root of the social subjection of the Negro in the South," and as the KKK reorganized anew Harrison argued that "the same desire for economic subjection" was at work. Thus it was "the Negro in the cotton fields whom the present day Ku Klux would terrorize," and the reason was "to keep him away from all the instruments of social power and protection like shot guns, juries and ballot boxes."[19]

With his biting satire Harrison argued that the "Ku Klux idea is, we think, a very good one": "it works," and "we should like to see the Negroes of the South adopt the idea themselves" and stand behind it "with the necessary manhood." He reasoned that "if white men can publicly organize and publicly parade for illegal purposes, including murder and arson, the Negroes ought to be able to organize for the legal purpose of self-defense, even if it involves murder and arson." He recommended this course because it was "obvious that not until they teach the Southern 'cracker' a lesson will he cease to treat them like dumb driven cattle."[20]

Harrison wryly noted how it was "notorious that, South of Virginia, the only Negro whose lives are secure are those whom the cracker knows as 'bad Negroes.'" The "decent, respectable, law-abiding, white-folk-fearing colored man" was "the one most likely to be slapped in the face by a white school boy or kicked by a 'cracker' and subject in various ways to humiliation and insult, while white men who love their lives keep away from the Negro who will cut, shoot and kill upon sufficient provocation." The "moral and meaning" were "as clear as day, and if the Negro people of the South" would consider them, they might be able "to solve the problem of lynching without waiting for the Federal Government to act." "As soon as Negroes . . . demand a respectable toll of killed and crippled for each life that goes out, then only those who have the courage of big game hunters will venture to go gunning for them." It was, he added, "well known that the 'crackers' who have that kind of courage don't amount to more than one in ten thousand."[21]

Harrison also mentioned that a humorist was "buzzing" the northern press, suggesting that the Ku Klux had proposed to organize and parade in New York. New York, however, was "home of the 'Phantom Fifteenth,'" the National Guard units called up during the war as the 369th Infantry Regiment and known as the Harlem Hellfighters. Before they went to France, they had "chased the 'crackers' in Tennessee and a few other places and gave such a good account of themselves that the crackers at the head of the War Department had to bring them out of the South." Since "New York Negroes" were "law-abiding" and "not particularly notorious as white-men-fearing," Harrison predicted "we Negroes in New York would most particularly welcome the advent of the Ku Klux to New York, and especially a parade of them through the Harlem streets." He did "not say more," for he was sure "that every 'cracker' as well as every one of our white friends in New York" would "understand what we mean."[22]

———

An extremely important Harrison article, "The Line-Up on the Color Line," appeared in the December 4 *Negro World*. It recounted how in 1909 the "National Negro Committee," the forerunner to the NAACP, met in New York at the United Charities Building and heard speeches from "the great defenders of our race." One striking speech was by Mrs. Celia Parker Woolley (a Unitarian minister, author, and founder of the interracial, Chicago-based Frederick Douglass Woman's Club). Mrs. Woolley pointed out that whereas the "white" press, the publicists and writers of books, and politicians were talking about the race hatred of the Caucasian, "it was a most sinister fact that, there had grown up and was growing up, on the part of black folk in America, a corresponding and countervailing race hatred." Harrison felt this fact "was important to bring out," and it did appear in the *Evening Post* at that time.[23]

"But," he added, when the National Negro Committee printed the proceedings of that conference, "those words of Mrs. Celia Parker Wool[l]ey were elided from the records." To Harrison this suggested "that some white people seem to think a certain public attitude towards white people to be fit and proper, and a certain other attitude—an attitude which white people would maintain if they were in the same situation—as unbecoming to black people." Previously, "the white man" discussed race problems and attempted to solve them from the point of view of "'What would be done with the Negro?' without asking what the Negro himself thinks of it." Under this conception the problem was "to be settled by the words, the mandates, the principles, the judgments and the opinions coming from one side only." The cases "of the Egyptian, of the South African, and the West African, the Hindu and the China Men" were similar to the "case of the Negro in America."[24]

Harrison viewed this as "the dominant race . . . walking rough-shod over the hearts, the sentiments, the feelings, the rights, the riches of the black, brown, and the yellow peoples of the world." The white race thought "that the only question for them to decide was: 'What shall we do with them?'" Now, however, "the big, sinister fact of international politics," recognized dimly in the writings of T. Lothrop Stoddard and B. L. Putnam Weale (Bertram Lennox Simpson), "is the demand on the part of black, brown and yellow people, that their voices shall be heard in any solution affecting their welfare and their future." This "world conflict of color" entailed "a very definite danger to the present supremacy of the white races."[25]

The necessary response, advised Harrison, was in "keeping in touch with the thought and the movements of the colored races." The "young Turk movement; the young Egypt movement; the Swadesh movement; the All-India Congress movement, and the radical movement led by the second Chinese president, Sun Yat Sen, in China," all were evidence "that these people intend and desire to take their destinies out of the hands of the white lords of misrule."

These movements did not maintain that they were competent "to meet in arms and to overthrow the white nations of the world now," though Japan did say so. Rather, China, under Japanese tutelage, was "beginning to grumble," and India was "a sort of seething, raging, but suppressed volcano, with a cover on which the Englishman sits," though the Hindus believed "that some day the wooden cover will burn through and something will get scorched." That was why the Maharajah of Baroda, "the most enlightened Indian prince in all India today," a few years ago turned his back and walked away from the British king at the Durbar. Another Hindu, "a quietist," whom the British rajah had recommended for the Nobel Prize in Literature, "a man decorated with medals and titles of knighthood—Rabindranath Tagore—tore off the decorations and sent them back to the British king, saying that 'the blood you are spilling in India will be upon my hands if I accept any decoration from you.'" For such reasons, men in India who were "fighting for Swadesha and Swaraj" and for "home rule" were sent by the British to the Andaman Islands and "exiled for twenty years and more."[26]

Harrison then discussed the Belgians, who were doing in their dominions the same as the British in theirs. In the African Congo, "in about three decades, the Belgians reduced the population of that most prolific area from 20,000,000 to 8,000,000." One could read of this in Sir Arthur Conan Doyle's *The Crime of the Congo* or in the writings of Edmund D. Morel, who made himself an English authority on that question, based on "the reports of the consul general, the great, glorious, lamented and martyred Sir Roger Casement," which included "photographs of hands chopped off, legs and feet chopped off by bunches, bundles, barrels full, when the Belgian king could not get those Congo people to make rubber enough for him." The International Association for the Exploitation of the Congo had received its grant "under the most sweeping and assuring statements about the goodness of their hearts and the sincerity of their minds." They said they "wanted to save Africa, Christianize and civilize it," but "the first thing that King Leopold did was to pass a law saying that all the land belonged to the State; a poor Kongolese had no right even to go out and gather firewood because the land was the State's." The United States, which was so long in recognizing independence in Hayti "and so quick to jump in now to destroy the reality of Haytian independence," and "so long in recognizing the independence of Liberia, her own foster child," was nevertheless "the first to recognize the independence of the Congo Free State."[27]

Next, Harrison discussed Nigeria. In that country, "when black meets white—in black's ancestral land—black must go down on his knees and wait until white goes by in a palanquin, and if he does not he will go to jail or will be beaten with many stripes." In "the civilized section of Southern Nigeria" the white English Christian minister who goes there "proceeds to settle down and organize a Negro church." The country had now developed "Negro graveyards and all the separatist things that we have got here, including the Jim Crow car."[28]

Finally, in his brief "summary of the series of grievances which black men, brown men and yellow men have against white there is the question of sex." Harrison wondered "how the white men with millions of Urasians whom they have produced in India and whom they despise after having created them" and "millions of mulattoes and interbloods that they have created in the United States, the West Indies and elsewhere . . . can look themselves in the face and talk about the sexual criminality of the black man." These "white" men "have gone all over the world using up the womanhood of the other races—dividing up with them—lightening them up," and "now when the other races stand up and say, 'If you have divided with us we are going to divide with you,'" their answer "is the lynching bee." That answer, however, would not stand, commented Harrison, because "we breed faster than they do," "we double our population in forty years, when they take eighty years to double theirs." In fact, "we breed so fast that the white doctors in their hospitals from the South to Harlem are driven to perform operations upon colored women—unbeknown to them—to be sure that they will not be breeders of men."[29]

"But," predicted Harrison, "we will survive, although some of us who study too hard and drink too hard and do some other things too hard may go crazy once in a while." He noted, however, that "we do not go crazy one-tenth as fast as they do" and cited statistics from England, France, the United States, and Canada. That meant, he argued, "that their physiological organization . . . breaks down under the weight of the burdens they have . . . shouldered for themselves." Harrison concluded "The Line-Up on the Color Line" by commenting on the tasks at hand:

In the face of these facts the first great international duty of the black man in America is to get in international touch with his fellows of the downtrodden section of the human populations of the globe and establish business, industrial and commercial relations with them. We need to join hands across the sea. We need to know what they are doing in India; we need to know what they are doing in China; we need to know what they are doing in Africa, and we need to let them know what we are doing over here. We must link up with the other colored races of the world, beginning with our own, and after we have linked up the various sections of the black race the black race will see that it is in its interest and advantage to link up with the yellow and the brown races. We must establish friendly relations with each other because the white man is at present more powerful than we are, and we must do this to help us in deciding what our section shall do to avail itself of the power of the white man to be used against the white man. The conflict of color is the call to the black race, the brown race, the yellow race today. It is a bid for their self-emancipation.

In the *Negro World* article was added, though Harrison crossed it out in his scrapbook as not being his, the concluding phrase: "and the U.N.I.A. is the instrument which the Negroes must use in that conflict for his own liberation."[30]

———————

In early September 1920 Harrison published a series of insightful book reviews that were probably prepared during the period of the UNIA convention. Four such Harrison reviews appeared in the "Our Book Review" section of the September 4 *Negro World*; three of them focused on topics related to the "Negro" in America.

In "The Soul of a Sycophant" he unsparingly discussed Robert Russa Moton's autobiography, *Finding a Way Out*. Moton was the education administrator chosen to succeed Booker T. Washington as principal of Tuskegee Institute. His autobiography had been sitting on Harrison's table for four weeks. He "hesitated after reading it to write about it in the hope that something might happen to prevent . . . doing so." It was, he explained, not his "policy to write about worthless books," and he preferred "to expound and illustrate those principles of appreciation by books which will make people who read them better or wiser." Unfortunately, Moton's autobiography did "neither of these two things," and its only virtue was "the virtue of self-revealment," for it showed "'The Soul of a Sycophant,' of a natural born boot-licker."[31]

Harrison acknowledged that Moton had a difficult life and had "come up from the dirt," which was "a great achievement for any man, whether we like him or not." "Unfortunately, however, the dirt has not come up from him," and though it was "one thing to get the Negro out of slavery," it was "a far more formidable task" to "get slavery out of the Negro." Harrison noted that Moton had served the interests of "good white friends" and that his autobiography was "a faithful record of faithful services rendered to himself and to these friends." No one reading the book "would ever imagine that there were such things as lynching, disfranchisement and jim-crowism in these United States," since in his autobiography "everything is happy and the goose hangs high." Harrison found that "Moton paints the degradation of his own soul with an engaging naivete." He said "he condemned an Indian fellow-student at Hampton for refusing to shake hands with the murderer of his father," who was a "white" American army officer. To Harrison, however, this was a "manly Indian" and a "very natural show of spirit" that did not "dishonor his father's memory." Harrison felt that "Negro America must thank its lucky stars" that though Moton had succeeded Booker

Washington as principal of Tuskegee, he hadn't "succeeded to that primacy of leadership and influence which was Booker Washington's." He added: "An enfranchised people cannot stomach a slavish soul as their representative, and Dr. Moton's soul as exhibited in this book is super-abundantly slavish."[32]

Harrison's second review in the September 4 *Negro World*, "The New Negro as Seen by a White Man," discussed NAACP Director of Publicity Herbert J. Seligmann's *The Negro Faces America*. He considered this book "quite different" from Moton's because Seligmann wrote "as a man to men": he "dissects the weak points of American democracy," "analyzes the current race prejudice," and "with a warning finger points to its potent possibilities of social and political disaster." Seligmann recognized "a new spirit in the Negro of today" and illustrated that spirit "by the facts of the race 'riots' in Washington, Chicago and elsewhere," which were "pitched battles in which the Negroes organized to fight back with vigor and with venom in defense of their hearth and homes." To Harrison "this was the striking contribution of that new Negro which had waded through blood on the European battlefields or gone through hell at home while giving until it hurt to a Red Cross which barred his sisters from effective membership and Liberty Loans which offered no liberty to him." Seligmann didn't share the opinion of the *New York Times* writers "who blame this new spirit upon Bolshevism, a product from outside." Rather, he realized "that American injustice, brutality and arrogance plus the new situations initiated by the great war are responsible for that disturbing phenomenon, the new Negro."[33]

After that opening, Harrison then described how Seligmann successfully "pulverize[d] some of the asinine assumptions" that passed "as scientific bases of race prejudice in America" in his chapter on "Anthropology and Myth"; how he argued that "Science has not meant the extinction of God, but it has sounded the doom of tribal and racial gods"; and how science held forth "the promise of a brighter dawn" in which races would "be valued not by any sense of superior or inferior, quantitatively, but as different colors in civilization, qualitatively, different." Though Seligmann discussed "the Negro" as "the football and the scapegoat of cheap politicians, white and black," his presentation lacked "historical treatment" and a discussion of "the economic conditions under which the relations between white and black were historically developed in America." Nevertheless, Harrison felt he did "good work with the current materials" and "helps the Negro people, as well as the whites, to realize that race prejudice cannot be independently interpreted up in the air of psychology, philosophy, and the eternal verities' of [Thomas] Carlyle, but must seek its sufficient explanation upon the firm ground of economic fact." In sum, Harrison considered the book to be "written primarily for white people," and as such it was "of the very highest value as a present-day interpretation of what's what." "Even to Negroes," however, its value was "immense." It was "lucidly written, full of facts and citations from authoritative sources," and "bound to prove 'a very present help in time of trouble.'"[34]

Harrison's third book review of September 4 was on Robert Kerlin's *The Voice of the Negro: 1919*. He explained that it contained "a cross-section of the Negro's intellectual life" in "selections made from over 300 Negro publications during the four months immediately succeeding the Washington race riots." In this book, as in *When Africa Awakes*, Harrison noted, "the Negro is permitted to speak for himself," and this made "most disagreeable reading for those white gentlemen of idiotic intellect who adorn the Attorney General's office and pretend that 'foreign propaganda' is responsible for Negro unrest." Anyone seeking "to learn what the Negro newspapers themselves have been saying on the subject of human rights for their race in America" could "turn to this book." Harrison regretted, however, that Kerlin didn't seem to know of the *Negro World*, since no citations from its pages were included. This was one of its few weaknesses. Overall, Harrison found it "a valuable and informing assemblage of what the university scholars describe as primary documentation."[35]

————

In the September 4, 1920, *Negro World* Harrison's fourth review, entitled "The Superscientist," discussed *The Place of Science in Modern Civilization and Other Essays*, by Thorstein Veblen. He commented that it was "some time since Professor Thorstein Veblen (Danish in name as in thoroughness of thought) burst upon our jaded world with a new and thought-compelling vocabulary of his own." As with Thomas Carlyle and Herbert Spencer, "this unique vocabulary was itself an index to a new and unique method of looking at things"—and, "like a blistering blaze of truth" it "provoked thought" and "shocked our jaded sensibilities." Above all, it offered "the irony of superior perception" and "it was neither wit, humor nor cynicism; yet it partook of the nature of all three." Harrison commented that when he encountered across such phases as "the pecuniary canons of taste," "exploit and industry," "Vicarious consumption," "conspicuous consumption," "requirements of conspicuous waste," or "requirements of pecuniary decency" he felt "the vigor of an alert and critical intelligence that had worked out not merely words for itself but standards of judgment and interpretation which challenged serious attention and respect."[36]

Though the field of economic and institutional science had been tilled by the late Nathaniel S. Shaler "with an equipment vastly inferior in scientific scope and power to that of our brilliant Danish-American," Harrison now took the "opportunity" to "introduce Negro America" to Veblen. He recognized that *The Place of Science* was "one of the hardest" of Veblen's "notoriously hard to read" books and was hard to review. Nevertheless, he thought it "high time" Veblen's work "should be recommended to the intellectual leaders of Negro America for their instruction and enjoyment." This was because "for years it has been noto-rious among us that our leaders of thought, whether selected by us or by oth-ers," have been "playing at a child's game of imitation scholarship," but "the increasing number of educated Negro laymen are demanding more." Harrison explained that fourteen of Veblen's eighteen essays were "concerned mostly with criticism of the claims and conduct of the higher intellectual science." He felt the limitations of the *Negro World* constrained him to pass over those four-teen "scholastic achievements," though he recommended the title essay and "The Evolution of the Scientific Point of View." In those essays and in "The Blond Race and Aryan Culture," Veblen didn't merely show "the drift and intent of scientific spirit," but "as a critic of that spirit who shares its general mental attitude," he revealed himself as "a super-scientist," and to Harrison this was "his value to us who have suffered so much from pseudo-science masquerad-ing as science." Harrison recommended "our young and enthusiastic Socialists to a careful study" of "The Nature of Capital" and "The Socialist Economics of Karl Marx," from which they might "learn a great deal." Despite the book's value, Harrison did "not expect that very many 'educated' Negroes" would want to read it—and this was a "pity."[37]

That was not true, however, of *The Theory of the Leisure Class*, which Harri-son considered "a work which should be on the bookshelf of every cultivated liberal and radical, white or black." Veblen called the book "an economic study of institutions," and it was "that, and more." It discussed "such institutions as leisure class, political government, manners, press, the higher learning and religion"—all with brilliant interpretations "from the standpoint of the highest and deepest modern standards of evaluation." The critical comments on "Reli-gious Mummery" were "highly diverting and instructive." In *The Theory of the Leisure Class* he analyzed "'the shaven face of the priest,' 'his livery of a very expensive character,' 'his wasteful expenditure,' and the other ear-marks of devout ceremonial." Veblen's discussion of "women's dress, particularly the cor-set," introduces and illustrates "a theory of economic values and their function in a class of society which contains the key to a new world of thought." No study of sociology and economics would be complete without this work.[38] Besides these two books Harrison also recommended Veblen's *The Instinct of Workman-ship*, *The Theory of Business Enterprise*, and *The Higher Learning in America*. He felt "sure" that whoever became acquainted with any of Veblen's books "through our recommendation" would "live to thank us for it."[39]

———

In early December 1920 Harrison, as was his custom, prepared a handwritten copy of his forthcoming *Negro World* article, "Books About Africa," which appeared in his "With the Contributing Editor" column of December 11. He began by discussing the "present wave of interest in Africa and things African" that was "sweeping over the race consciousness of Negroes in the western world," and he noted that this provided "a splendid opportunity to those who are leading them to diffuse reliable information on the subject among the masses of our people."[40]

Taking up that task, he first challenged the "stupid notion" that "white writers never publish the facts and conclusions about Africa which would minister to our racial pride." To the contrary, he argued, "if anyone should take the trouble to ask any black scholar who is well acquainted with African history and social science he would find that nine-tenths of the worth-while books which he would cite on these subjects were written by white men." He speculated that the current impression of "whites" being ignorant was attributable to the fact that, "since the intellectual pursuit of white men on the whole are limited by their racial interests most of them (even the intelligent and the well-informed ones, like Mr. Lothrop Stoddard) have never interested themselves in that direction and, consequently, know next to nothing of Africa except in the popular sense of its being a 'dark' continent whose only worthwhile affairs are sufficiently comprehended in the missionary and commercial exploits of white intruders." "But" this was "just as true of the vast majority of Negroes . . . even the intelligent and well-informed ones," and "until Negro editors, lawyers, ministers and teachers know the facts, at least, about Africa and Africans," there was no reason to "expect white editors, lawyers, ministers and teachers to know them." Harrison pointed out that "while some white men, especially in America, have written some awful things about us from the profundity of their ignorance," others, "with wide knowledge, like Sir. Richard F. Burton and Sir Harry Johnston," had also "scored heavily against us." Nevertheless, those who weren't "too lazy" could "easily get books on Africa, written by white men of the highest ability, and full of the bread of life for our intellects." He then proceeded to call attention "to a few of the best" (books on Africa), restricting himself to books on his "own book shelves," most of which could "be easily obtained at the public library or the ordinary book store in any large city."[41]

First, Harrison discussed Dr. Frederick Starr's *Liberia*, a small book "packed [with] every bit of information on that little republic that is worth while." It discussed "climate, economic resources, political history, her people, tribal and 'civilized,' her present problems diplomatic and social," and "explained with the knowledge of a master, the method of a scientist and the sympathy of a friend." He recommended it highly.[42]

He next discussed the late George W. Ellis's *Negro Culture in West Africa*, which he described as an "authoritative and readable study of the Vai people of Liberia" written by "a Negro American." The Vai have "their own domestic industries and arts, successful social institutions and a system of writing—the

Vis syllabic system—invented by themselves." Ellis had worked for the U.S. government in Liberia, wrote about them "ably" and "charmingly," and interpreted "the inner life of the people" while he unfolded "the significance of their institutions." Harrison emphasized that anyone who reads the book "will not only know the Vais; he will also understand them."[43]

Harrison considered *In the Shadow of the Bush* by P. Amaury Talbot to be "a magnificent volume in size and substance." It dealt with the life and customs of the Ekoi people of northwestern Nigeria where Talbot served as district commissioner. The volume offered "a cross-section of native African life" and, "in a splendid panorama," discussed "African religion, science, law, philosophy and culture; the position of women, secret societies, active clubs for men, women and children; their method of telling news by drum-tap code, their secret hieroglyphic language called Naibidi, agriculture and industrial arts." Talbot's work stood "supreme" as "a competent and clear picture of the West Coast native and his ways," and it dwarfed "into insignificance" the "ponderous and pretentious volumes of Sir Harry Johnston on the native West African in another West Coast country." Both the Ellis and Talbot books were "handsomely illustrated from photographs" and contained "many African tales translated by the authors from the folk-lore of the natives." *A Transformed Colony*, by T. J. Alldridge, the former resident commissioner in Sierra Leone, discussed the British colony north of Liberia. Harrison noted his description of the "soapstone images called Nomolis carved by the hands of black sculptors thousands of years ago" on Sherbo Island as well as his description of the land and the natives, "Mohammedan and pagan and their mode of life." Harrison also found that his "word-pictures of freedom and its Christianized free descendants of former slaves" left an indelible mark.[44]

Harrison considered the missionary Rev. Dan Crawford's *Thinking Black* "a masterpiece." Crawford spent twenty-two years in the Shire highlands of south-central Africa, "where he saw black so steadily that he learned to think black." Harrison observed, "He is one of the few, white men who have managed to penetrate under the skin of the African Negro and understand the roots of his soul." The "well illustrated" book had a "literary charm" and "beauty" of language as well as "supremely solid values."[45]

Sir Arthur Conan Doyle's *Crime of the Congo* offered "innumerable facts" and a good summary of recent developments in the Congo. It detailed the "bloody, gruesome, nauseous tale" that "had to be told." Harrison added that "any black person" who wanted "to preserve a lurking love for white Christian, 'civilized' people . . . should not read either this book or Morel's *The Black Man's Burden*."[46]

Harrison next turned "from the present to the past" to consider four books by four "distinguished" travelers who had "helped to make Africa and the Africans better known to us all—black and white alike." He noted that two authors were "British," the Scots Mungo Park and David Livingstone, and two were German, Heinrich Barth and George August Schweinfurth. Mungo Park's *Travels in the Interior Districts of Africa* described African life "as few Europeans have seen it," as he traveled "without the backing of his government." Despite "much rough treatment, (including slavery), which he suffered in some places, he preserved his balance" and wrote "naught in malice." His "penetrating and philosophic eye saw much good in the African's nature and disposition," and to read his book was "to take a trip into Africa as it was at the end of the Eighteenth Century, to rub elbows with Arab slave raiders, Joloffs and Mandingos; to feel the burning heart of the desert and the fever of the fans." The narrative of "adventure and discovery" constantly held the reader's interest.[47]

In the December 18 *Negro World* Harrison offered "On 'Civilizing' Africa." In his opening remarks he commented, "When white people today talk of civilizing Africa and assert that the Africans are uncivilized they awaken in the minds of well-informed Africans a doubt as to whether white people know what is meant by the term." This doubt arose because "various 'civilizations'" had existed, and still existed, in Africa, independent "of that particular brand which white people" brought there "in exchange for the untold millions of dollars which they take from there."[48]

If "civilization" meant a stable, self-supporting society that maintains a system of government and laws, industry, and commerce, then "the Hausas and Mandingoes, the people of the Ashanti and Dahomey, and the Yorubas of the Gold Coast had and have all these" and were "civilized." So also were "the Zulus and Bechuanas, the Swazis and Mashonas of South Africa, as well as the Raganda people of Uganda." Further, according to Staudinger, Schweinfurth, Barth, and Boas, "smithwork and the smelting or iron were original with some of the West African peoples," and "the weaving of cotton was known in the Sudan as early as the eleventh century, and is known there today."[49]

Most recently, Jerome Dowd, whom Harrison described as "a southern savant," had written that "some of the most important medical discoveries of modern times were first made in Africa." He cited "the fact that flies and mosquitoes are the purveyors of disease," which was known by "the medical men of Yoruba," who didn't always rely on magic, spirits, and deities but also had a considerable knowledge of "scientific principles" and examined patients, located the seat of disease, and prescribed certain diets and medicines. In addition, "long before [Edward] Jenner [the British pioneer of the smallpox vaccine, 1749–1823] lived black African doctors were inoculating as a preventive against smallpox," and white South Africans very often took "cures prescribed by Negro physicians for the African fever." Many of these physicians possessed "an intelligent knowledge of the pathology of the disease," and thus Europeans who went to Africa should not say "that there is no civilization already there."[50]

While the "missionary-minded" often maintained "that the Africans have no knowledge of God," in fact, "one of the most learned Egyptologists, Dr. Wallis Budge, curator of Egyptian antiques in the British Museum," challenged that assumption. In his *Osiris and the Egyptian Resurrection* he summarized testimony from "dozens of scientists and travellers from all countries of Africa," and showed "that not only do Africans believe in Gods" but that they do so "under many names and forms from the Bobowissi of the Ashanti, the Mawa of Dahomey, the Olorun of the Yoruba, down to the Umhulunkulu of the Zulus." Bishop Henry Calloway similarly "established this fact for the Bantus of South Africa" and Dr. Duff MacDonald "for the Bantus of the Shire Region." There was one other point on this that Harrison mentioned: "the Africans' religion works." In "Northern Nigeria, among the Vais of Liberia and in Congoland whenever the holy symbol of their religion (i.e. fetish) is left to protect goods," it is respected, and the goods are not touched because "these people really *believe* their religion." Thus, on this religious test, "there is *seen* to be civilization in Africa."[51]

Harrison suggested that the "real civilization meant by most whites who talk of civilizing Africa is the system which produces profits by taking the land from under the feet of the workers, producing a propertyless, landless proletarian class which must either work (for wages) or starve." Such a class didn't "exist anywhere among black Africans except where white peoples have robbed them of their lands by force direct, as in Rhodesia and the Cape." In these cases "the 'civilizing' of Africa" meant the "establishment of the European system, of 'concessions' for rubber, railroads, factories and mines, whereby the labor of the native population and the new tastes developed in their minds yield enormous revenues to the white people who rule these lands."[52]

For the December 11, 1920, *Negro World* Harrison wrote a review of the year-old *The Black Man's Burden* by E. D. Morel. In discussing the American edition of the English book he noted that Morel had already earned recognition "as an authority of the very first rank" on African history and social science, and his published works included "many valuable contributions, such as *The Affairs of West Africa, King Leopold's Rule in Africa, The Congo Slave State, Trading Monopolies in West Africa, Nigeria, Its People and Its Problems, Red Rubber, Africa and the Prince of Europe*, and a host of lesser writings, besides a staggering quantity of contributions to periodicals and much controversial literature." As a writer he was "worthy of serious attention," and *The Black Man's Burden* especially deserved "the serious attention of intelligent Negroes."[53]

Harrison described how Morel's book was a "summary of the history of the white Christians' attempt to take to the African peoples his own peculiar brand of civilization and culture," and it made for "particularly nasty reading." If "any servile Negro" wanted "to preserve his traditional love and respect for the white race he had better not read this book," advised Harrison, because it showed "that the best and highest of that race—its king and queens, its statesmen, generals, editors and industrial magnates—are, in plain English, professional liars, slimy hypocrites, and blood-thirsty thieves." England, France, Italy, Germany, Portugal, and Belgium were all guilty "in their game of African expansion," and "lying, cunning, brute force and slavery" were still "the main methods of controlling the destinies of the unhappy people of the African continent." To Harrison, "no story of marauding buccaneers" rivaled "in brutal blood-lust" the "history of these six Christian nations in their dealings with the black Africans." The recorded deeds of "Captain Kidd, John Watling, Edward Teach ('Blackbeard'), and the pirates of the Spanish Main paled into insignificance beside the deliberate and atrocious butcheries engineered and carried out by Dr. [Leander] Jameson in Rhodesia, [Lothar] von Trotha in Damaraland [the north-central region of present-day Namibia], [King] Leopold [II] in the Congo, and bearers of 'the white man's burden' everywhere in Africa."[54]

Nevertheless, wrote Harrison, as long as "fools on our side" speak of "the 'reconciliation of the races' and persist in preaching 'love' to the lamb rather than to the lion, books like this one of Mr. Morel will serve a useful purpose among us." This wasn't Morel's purpose, however, for he sought "'to lay down the fundamental principles of a human and practical policy for the government of Africa by white men,'" and his emotions were "limited to the philanthropic round." Thus, as long as Africans could furnish fit subjects for Morel's sympathies he would remain their "champion and defender," but he would not "rise above that philanthropic role and consider the black race as humanly the equal of his, or as an independent shaper of its own destiny." Morel held that the "actual government of tropical Africa in the proper sense of the term, by the whiteman," was "only beginning," and he saw "the real problem" as how "to insure that a material relationship, which is inevitable, shall not preclude just, humane, and enlightened government of tropical African peoples by European States." Harrison sarcastically responded to this as a member of a "struggling, handicapped race" and pointed out that "the rule of white men and brutality to us are inseparable." Even "if the separation of the two were possible," he added, "we should still prefer (as they would in our place) our own rule over ourselves to their rule over us."[55]

Morel began with an account of the slave trade led by the Portuguese and Spaniards, who bore "unctuous phrases of religion on their lips." These "were quickly followed by the English, Dutch, Danish, French and others." The English, especially after the Treaty of Utrecht (1713), became "most notorious both for the extent of their traffic and its savage brutality." During the sixteenth century "Queen Elizabeth was the silent partner of the infamous John Hawkins, whom she sent out on the good ship Jesus to burn peaceful towns and villages on the Guinea coast and seize the inhabitants as slaves." Then, in the seventeenth century, "Queen Anne added to her private income in the same way," and, in the Treaty of Utrecht, "England forced the Spaniards to give her the monopoly of supplying slaves to the Spanish colonies, and the wealth which flowed from this source was used to pay the expense of the war with Spain which had just ended." Thus, as early as 1713, "white Christians of England had already adopted the pernicious principle which Sir Harry Johnson announced in 1914 and the Colonial Office is now living up to: That the costs of white Christian warfare must be paid by black 'heathen' Africa." Both the elder (1708–1778) and the younger (1759–1806) William Pitt "proceeded on this principle, as a result of which the English government persisted in forcing the slave trade upon the American colonies—a fact not generally known by 'educated' and loyal British Negroes." Then "the nineteenth century brought this traffic to an end."[56]

But in the nineteenth century "the other form of slavery was established: the slavery of entire peoples and lands to the armed buccaneers of imperial expansion." Harrison describes how Morel provides an "account of this new horror, with its horde of suave and subtle missionaries in front, its traders and concessionaires in the middle, and its legions of licentious soldiery behind," in seven significant episodes, including

> the British acquisition of Rhodesia, the German conquest of the Hereros [of South West Africa], France's seizure of Morocco, Italy's grab at Tripoli, Belgium's Congo horror and France's similar hell in the French Congo, and the Portuguese slave raid on Angola and the Cocoa Islands [Coco Islands, in the northeast of the Bay of Bengal] where one-tenth of the male population is worked, beaten and starved to death every year.

To Harrison, all these crimes were equally horrible, and if the English-speaking public still thought of "Belgium's Congo as the supreme atrocity," it should be remembered "that England, by its cable monopoly, controlled the news of the world and Belgium did not. The English (and Americans) could, therefore, 'play up' the Congo atrocities to a gasping world while the Belgians couldn't 'play up' theirs." As Morel points out, Harrison added, "each one of the imperialist groups can be perfectly trusted to tell the full and complete truth about the other," and thus "by collating these several national truths we can get the entire international story."[57]

Harrison discussed in more detail Morel's account of the British robbery of Rhodesia because it directly challenged "the lying account of native conditions in that country given in 1895 by Mr. E. F. Knight in his book *Rhodesia of Today*," which was still found in the local public library. Morel detailed the seizure and occupation and described how "the son of the missionary, [John] Moffat," acted "the congenial role of decoy or 'come-on' to poor old Lobengula [Khumalo]," the "misguided monarch" who "trusted too much to 'the word of God' as interpreted by Christian Englishmen." Since then, the native inhabitants were permitted, by the "grace of the English," to live on reservations in "the bleakest and least productive" corner of the country, "while the good white people have instituted a collective slavery which compels the former owners of the soil to labor for next to nothing in the mines and on the farms of their masters," and "any white settler may take up land occupied by natives who are then compelled to pay him $5 a year for the privilege of living on that land and $5 more to the Chartered Company." Such "money must be earned by working for the invaders," who brought into existence in that part of Africa "one of the chief blessings of Christian capitalist civilization; a propertyless, landless, proletarian class." Harrison emphasized that "in this spoilation of Mashona and Matabele people it was the official and responsible arm of collective English Christianity which was unable to protect the duped king from his own landsharks; but as soon as they had attacked him it sent its soldiers to slay him and his people and seize their lands."[58] Harrison then described "the collective character of white Christians" from this "small slice of the imperialistic record." He wrote that they were "crooked and contemptible liars, cold-blooded bandits and canting, psalm-singing hypocrites."[59]

Finally, Harrison mentioned one of Morel's "pet horrors"—the "danger (to Europe) of armed Africans enrolled in the military service of white nations"—and he pointed out that "we, on the contrary, desire [it because] . . . we can't forget that Rome came to an end in that way, and we are hoping that the white man's blind and greedy imperialism will meet the same fate by the very products of its own rapacity." He warned that "'Whatsoever a man soweth, that also shall he reap,'" and, just "as Belgium between 1914 and 1918 reaped in disaster and destruction some fruits of her sowing in Africa," so also might England and others "reap her whirlwind of destruction in the days to come." After his lengthy review, Harrison recommended Morel's book to "everyone who can afford a copy," since "it will furnish the facts on which we rest our case against the white man's domination of our own motherland."[60]

Toward the end of 1920 Harrison also wrote several theater reviews, which provide wonderful glimpses of actors and plays of that period. He began with an October 30 *Negro World* review of *Canary Cottage*, the previous week's musical comedy at the Lafayette Theatre in Harlem. It was his first effort at dramatic criticism in over two years. He described Quality Amusement's presentation of Shelton Brooks and his associate players as a "marvel of melody and stagecraft" of "such commanding excellence that it sheerly lifted me out of my seat."[61]

Harrison had seen musical comedy at the Lafayette since it was first built in 1915, and he was familiar with the *Darktown Follies*, the *Smart Set* and the *Smarter Set, Darkydom*, and *Broadway Rastus*. He had also critically observed the Lafayette's presentations of Broadway musical comedies since the days of "Madame Sherry." But "not one of these 'shows'" had "ever come within hailing distance of 'Canary Cottage,'" which "outshines them all in cleverness" and "has something to which none of them except the recent 'Bamboula' ever made any pretense, namely, melodic consistency." The musical had a real plot, "cleverness," and it "convulsed" the audience with "the increasing humor of its situations and dialogue." Its chorus was "in a class by itself" in "form, dancing dress and efficient team-work."[62]

While *Broadway Rastus* had risen "to the level of theatrical dignity only in the able acting of one person, Emmett Anthony," and "'Bamboula' lacked able actors," *Canary Cottage* was qualitatively different. It was built by Oliver Morosco "as firmly and consistently as a drama," and it made "considerable demands on the dramatic abilities of the cast." The result was that "every part was acted as it should be," and though there were "few gleams of great genius," there was "good acting everywhere," and this was "unusual in a musical comedy in Harlem." The show's "only observable defect" seemed to be in "the enunciation" of most speaking parts, since "words were often unintelligible in the first balcony." In his publicly printed article Harrison wrote that "this could have been due to the defective acoustics of the Lafayette Theatre," but in his manuscript copy he added, "It wasn't though—H.H."[63]

The musical numbers were "excellently rendered" by the chorus and orchestra, and Shelton Brooks at the piano in the second act offered "highly diverting . . . harmonic 'stunts.'" In a handwritten insert Harrison added that the printer left out that "the numbers sung by Mr. Powers and Misses Brooks and Edith Purnell were exceptionally good" and that Miss Purnell as Pauline Hugg attained the distinction of being "the most beautiful young woman seen on the Lafayette's stage in many a day." He added, "Miss Purnell, by the way, is brown instead of 'white.'"[64]

Harrison described the chorus as "clothed and costumed" in "perfect" detail, noting that this was a rarity for the Harlem stage. The females of *Canary Cottage* knew "what dancing is," and they danced "not as if the stage manager was holding a whip over them" but "as if they enjoyed it." "Altogether," he judged "this musical comedy" to be "the best yet"—it "pleases without dirt and tickles without the usual contemptible 'niggerisms' which so many of our actors insistently obtrude even into a Broadway show." He thought that "if the name of the piece could be changed to one with more meaning it should have a long and pleasant run at the various theatres on the Q[uality]. A[musement]. C[orporation?]. circuit."[65]

Harrison wrote "Last Week at Lafayette" for the November 13 *Negro World* and reviewed *Fair and Warmer*, a "rather thin" Broadway comedy by Avery Hapgood, performed by a cast including Charlie Olden, Ida Anderson, and Susie Sutton. The amusing story was of "a happy-go-lucky combination of young and inexperienced married folk." Ida Anderson, as Blanche Wheeler, "tried (with but a fair measure of success) to transcend the limits of her personality," while Charles Olden, as Billy Bartlett, a male ingénue, "showed that he still needed to study the difference between comedy acting and shenanigans." Harrison described Edward Brown, as Jack Wheeler, as "the most competent actor in the cast." After mentioning the work of Alice Gorgas, A. de Comathiere, Henry Jones, and James Norman he concluded that the show offered "good second-class acting of a good, clean second-class play, and it deserved the full houses which it received."[66]

In the same November 13 issue Harrison reviewed the return of the popular hit, "The Darktown Follies," to the Lafayette. This rendition by the Lafayette Players, assisted by a few "old performers who made the Follies famous," featured "the best-known female impersonator," Evon Robinson, "in a wealth of smiles," and the return of Dink Stewart, "a conscientious and hard-working actor, who has been in the shade for some time." The show had "brilliancy in spots, with just a bit too much of the old 'niggersims' from which the Quality Amusement people departed long ago." To Harrison, "the crap-shooting game in the second act served no useful purpose either of art or amusement." Anthony Tribble, as Mandy Lee, "gave a very effective rendering to a comic female part"; Dink Stewart "was his old superb self"; E. B. Fraction, as Mose Lewis, a prominent lawyer, "lived up to the best Lafayette traditions"; Edward Thompson and Leon Diggs were "worthy of extra-special mention"; "[E]Lida Webb had her talents hidden under a bushel"; May Crowder and Jennie Day did "excellent work in the chorus"; and Lottie Harris couldn't sing too well but could "act a song to perfection" and created "an atmosphere for 'Rock Me in the Cradle of Love' that carries it over the top." Catherine Reeve, as little Susie Lee, brought back "memories of the late Hattie Akers in the original Smart Set," and her work showed "wonderful promise."[67]

Harrison observed that the Lafayette audience had made "such wonderful progress in artistic perception that they laugh (as they should) at the magnificent monkey-shine suits worn by the swell dudes at the dinner party" and "even snicker knowingly at the dance, of Evon Robinson in Act 2" and to "the song and dance of Mattie Wilkes in 'A Good Time While I Can.'" Overall he viewed "The Darktown Follies" as "a fairly good show of its kind"—the kind that "is being superseded by others."[68]

Harrison also wrote a review of "The Darktown Follies" for the November 19 *New York Dispatch*. He commented that the play "proved such an overwhelming success last week that its run has been extended another week." Dink Stewart, Andrew Tribble, Evon Robinson, Will Cook, and Catherine Reeve continued "to shine," and "the work of all the performers" showed "a decided improvement this week," suggesting "that long runs mean better acting." The show was scheduled to move to Philadelphia, Pittsburgh, Chicago, Cincinnati, St. Louis, and Indianapolis, and Harrison predicted that "by the time it gets to the end of its tour there will be very little difference between the excellence of the Broadway performers and the present company's."[69]

The action of the musical production developed around the misadventures of Jim Jackson Lee, who mortgaged his property in Leesburgh, Virginia, left his wife, and went to Washington, DC, where he became engaged to Miss Lucinda Langtree, "a belle of the smart set—'high' as to color and social standing." Jim assumed "the high-sounding cognomen of 'James J. Booker,' under the influence of that dapper young man of the world, Bill Simmons," who helps him in many situations, including time in jail, out of which he emerges "a sadder and a wiser man." From "this thread of romantic comedy" was "hung a choice collection of humorous incidents and tuneful melodies," which provided a medium "for the talents of some really good male and female artists of ability." Dink Stewart, as Jim Jackson Lee, was the star, and his acting combined "intelligence, artistic ability, and the result of hard work." Andrew Tribble played the feminine role of Jim Jackson Lee's wife, Mandy Lee, and Harrison felt it "would be difficult to praise him too highly," since he did "good, clean, high-class comedy with the stamp of genius on it." Miss Catherine Reeve was the "Juvenile" star, Susie Lee, and her work was "worthy of especial commendation." Miss Evon Robinson, in the Follies from its inception, maintained "her original radiance," and he praised "her wealth of good looks, smiles and dancing manner as Madame Langtree." Edward Thompson, who gave up a newspaper career, played Bill Simmons (alias "Molasses Candy"), "a representative of the Colored Men's Business League," and stood out "as an actor of class and distinction with an original manner of interpreting his role." Miss Elida Webb, Madame's eldest daughter, had a minor role, but she was "already well-known as a conscientious and capable worker in connection with the chorus," and her work as chorus director manifested "in the increased efficiency of the present chorus." Harrison's "old friend, Will A. Cooke," appeared as Jasper Green, a rich colored plantation owner of Leesburgh, and as a humorist he held his own "in the midst of younger players." Cooke was also "stage-manager—and the result was a credit to him and to director Jesse Ship, as things ran as smooth as clock-work."[70]

The play had many fine situations. When Mandy Lee made her entrance in pursuit of her husband, the audience was "galvanized at once into attention and enjoyment." This effect was repeated in scenes between the two in every act.

In addition, "the colloquy between her and the cabdriver and redcap" was "a masterpiece of comedy." As in his earlier review, Harrison found the "one weak part of the play," without "artistic excuse," to be "the news' boys crap-game," which he hoped would "be eliminated." The song "Rock Me in the Cradle of Love" was an old tune, but it became "new when sung—and acted—by Miss Lottie Harris, whom he referred to as "our own Theda Bara." The audience was "shaken into an electric brain-storm," and her dancing partner, Molasses Candy, had "to hold himself down." "This song received more encores than anything else in the play except Dink Stewart's powerful 'Blues' song at the end of the first scene of Act 3." Harrison also gave "special mention" to Miss Evon Robinson's symbolic dance-song "That's the Kind of Man I Want." The chorus of "The Darktown Follies" sang as well as danced; the orchestra, led by Miss Marie Lucas, was "as usual almost flawless"; and "the genial Mr. Snow" presided at the trap drum in place of Miss Alice Calloway and made "a very favorable impression." In sum, "taking it altogether," Harrison considered "'The Darktown Follies' under the present management" to be "well worth seeing."[71]

————

In his December 1, 1920, correspondence with Joseph St. Prix of Philadelphia, Harrison indicated that he had been "broke" for two weeks. He was the principal source of income for his family of seven, and his financial situation was indeed precarious. Around 1920 he had obtained and cosigned for a loan of two hundred dollars from the Globe Credit Union, 621 Broadway. "Hubert and Irene Harrison of 570 Lenox Ave, Timothy Walsh of 68 Broad St. N.Y, Cyril Wallace of 653 Lenox Avenue, and Edward Benners [Benner] of 109 West 141 Street" were responsible for the debt.[72] Then, on November 15, 1920, the Unique Operating Company of 167 West 145th Street, which handled real estate investments and managed properties, sent a "Mr. Herbert H. Harrison" a bill for the balance on his contract for stock.[73] On February 16, 1921, agent JFK of Berley & Co. Inc. Real Estate Sales & Management, on Broadway at Madison Square, left a final notice of rent due for Harrison, who was not in.[74]

To meet his financial responsibilities Harrison again attempted to develop his book-selling efforts and billed himself in printed literature as "Book-Seller to the Reading Public of Harlem." He offered the "Lowest Prices on New and Old Books on the Negro, History, Sociology, Economics, Literature, Religion, Psychology, Fiction, Poetry; Text Books of Travel and Dictionaries," along with home delivery and free special searches that utilized his "thirty years acquaintance with books." The literature indicated he could be contacted at 513 Lenox Avenue or through the New York Age Press. In this period Harrison may also have done some private tutoring and dabbled at short-story writing; he also continued to rely on monies received for his *Negro World* columns.[75]

9

Early 1921 *Negro World* Writings and Reviews
(January–April 1921)

In early 1921, while doing some bookselling and tutoring, Harrison continued work as associate editor of the *Negro World* and used his "Contributing Editor" column to provide articles, editorials, and book reviews. He opened the year on January 1 with "On Praise: From the Arabic of Abulfeda, Prince of Humah (in Syria), 1328. Done into modern English by Hubert H. Harrison." In this insightful, Harrison-authored piece, he suggests why his intellectual bent, personality characteristics, and reaction to praise may have placed limits on his becoming a Garvey-like mass leader. He began:

> If there is one thing I hate next to lying and hypocrisy in human beings it is praise coming from human beings. Through most of life it has been a hard medicine to swallow. The first dose bewilders, the next annoys, the third irritates and the added installments make me feel murderous. And yet I believe I am quite human. I do enjoy the kindly appreciation of my elders and the critical appreciation of my equals. But this spiritual pawing over one's soul by the soiled hands of every chance comer is a thing abhorrent to me.
>
> Why will people obtrude their praise on one? Why should they be so silly? . . . I really think that if most of them could know how it nauseates they might be induced to withhold their sentimental slobberings over the thing that they like to enjoy.
>
> I understand, of course, that most people are different. Well, I am what I am and I don't want to be different. I therefore have no apologies to offer on the point. I hate the praise of people because I look upon nine-tenths of it as sniffling insincerity, and therefore an insult to my intelligence. And then, too, I despise it when it takes the form of crowd approbation because I appraise it

at its true value and recognize it as merely a momentary mood and fashion of their shallow souls.[1]

The following week Harrison reprinted in the January 8 *Negro World* an important letter that took the Socialist Party to task on the issue of white supremacy. He identified the piece as one that he had written in 1914 or 1915 "in reply to a Southern 'Comrade'" (and sent to the *New Review*). In the introduction to the letter Harrison explained that it was written in response to a "'Comrade' (Ida Raymond) whose ideas of the Ku Klux Klan and its relation to the Negro people seemed to have gotten mixed up." He thought the "implications will be clear to the discerning" and pointed out that the socialist periodical to which it was sent "didn't see fit to print it."[2]

Harrison wrote that "Mrs. Raymond opposes Miss [Mary White] Ovington's advocacy of having the white and black people meet on equal terms 'at this present time.' I should like to know whether she would be in favor of it at any future time." He felt that Mrs. Raymond had "imbibed the Southern attitude from her Southern environment, and it vitiates even her notions of history." For example, he noted she asserted that "the South had a taste of what the Negroes would do if they were to be allowed [the] full political rights accorded them by the Constitution," and "the Ku Klux Klan had to take matters in their own hands and save their women, their homes, and their country from the terrible outrages that were perpetrated by the Negroes." Harrison, citing Walter L. Fleming's *Documentary History of Reconstruction*, countered that "the constitutional right to vote was given to Negroes in 1868, while the Ku Klux Klan began its terrorism in the winter of 1865, long before the vote was given to Negroes in the South." He explained that Congress "was induced to give the vote to the Negro to enable him to protect himself" from "the Ku Klux Klan, the Society of the Pale Faces, and the Knights of the White Camelias."[3]

What most interested Harrison was "not the misstatements of well-known facts in her letter, but the attitude of Southern Socialists which it so naively reveals." He described how the experience of the Socialist Party speaker Theresa Malkiel in Tennessee ("where she was prevented by certain people from addressing a meeting of Negroes on the subject of Socialism") and the letter of a "Southern Socialist" (Raymond) to the *Call* "have shown us that Southern Socialists are 'Southerners' first and 'Socialists' after. And the Socialist party, in the laudable ambition of increasing its membership and vote among all classes of the population is apt to keep in the rear whatever implications of its doctrine may offend and scare off the desired elements." He added: "So long as the tattered remains of the Granger and Populist movements rally to your standards in the South, we shall have to keep from saying that Socialism stands for the full civic and political equality of all workers."[4]

Harrison contrasted the Socialist Party with the Industrial Workers of the World, which had no difficulty "affirming the full import of its revolutionary doctrine at all times and all places—even in the South." He detailed how it "oppose[d] race prejudice, with success," in Louisiana," where it "organized 14,000 black timber workers, together with 18,000 white timber workers, with 'mixed' locals," and he wondered "whether any Socialist, Southern or other" could "blame" one for supporting the I.W.W."[5]

In the same January 8, 1921, issue of the *Negro World* Harrison's "Education and the U.N.I.A." maintained that "one of the most hopeful things in the U.N.I.A." was "its stand on education," which "realize[d] that head, heart and hand must combine to do effectively the work of racial regeneration." Noting that "heart and hand" had already "done their share," he found "encouraging" signs of the head linking up with them and cited "recent official declarations in regard to Liberia," where "schools, colleges and universities" were to be established in addition to industrial and political enterprises. While "the Negro Baptists and Methodists, and even the white Episcopalians" had done "some good work in this direction" over the last thirty years, Liberia College, because of "lack of funds," had "fallen" from its former "high standard of usefulness" and needed "the invigorating influence of financial support."[6]

Harrison urged that "if the U.N.I.A. could give effectual aid it would earn the undying gratitude of all Liberians," and, if it went further and "establish[ed] other colleges equal to those of Europe and America," it would "keep in Africa the young Krus, Yorubas and Gold Coast men" who were "forced to go to England and America in search of that higher education for which they hunger and thirst." "On this side" he thought "the membership of the U.N.I.A. should hail the new declaration with enthusiasm, because education is valuable on either side," and "we need it to clarify our vision, to make us sure of ourselves, and to aid us in the conquest of a hostile world from whose hard hands we must wring whatever gains we may make." He encouraged, "Let the good work go on!"[7]

In "'Subject' vs. 'Citizen,'" his January 22 *Negro World* editorial, Harrison responded to a correspondent from the West Indies who asked him "to write an article on 'the full political meaning of the terms, subject and citizen.'" The theme was "timely and important," so he gladly took on the task. He explained that a "subject" was "a person who owes allegiance to a government, its laws and officials without having, as a right, the power to make or remake that government or these laws." In contrast, citizens could elect their officials when their governments "derive[d] their powers from the consent of the governed."[8]

Through the "twentieth century . . . [the] white voter in England often describe[d] himself as 'a loyal subject of the king'"; it was just "one of those political fictions (like the Congo Free State and independent Egypt of ten years ago)." At "the beginning of the nineteenth century hardly one-tenth of the white people of England had the right to vote," but, during the last eighty years, between the reigns of Charles I and Queen Victoria, "the British people trimmed their king down to a political nonentity" and "wrested" the right to vote "from their masters." Since, "in theory at least," the "people" now had "the power to change their masters and their laws to suit their needs," they had secured "the essence of citizenship." Based on this analysis Harrison concluded "the Negro people in the Northern States are citizens, while they are subjects in the Southern States, the West Indies and the British possessions."[9]

Harrison's "The New Conscience" in his April 2, 1921, *Negro World* column described how until the beginning of the war, "the private right to hold, dispose of, and to fix a valuation upon one's possessions was held to be sacred, and as a rule, inalienable." Then, the "grave necessities of the war compelled governments to revise this world-old notion" and adhere to the dictates of a "new conscience." The "growth of population made specialization necessary," and the change from independent units (as when families produced their necessities for food, shelter, and clothing) to the "present state of absolute in[ter]dependence, should logically have been followed by a changed attitude towards the individual's responsibility" to others. But the "failure to make this change . . . made profiteering, with its grinding, crushing, insatiable greed possible," and it became "the prolific, hydra-headed begetter of wars" at "great cost in human lives." Harrison emphasized, "The way—the only way—to end war is to take the profit out of it," and that could not be done "until we recognize our true relation toward one another."[10]

He also explained that since "we have become specialists," this necessitated a "system of apportionment [that] involves a mutual dependence upon, an obligation towards, one another." Bringing this to a local level, he described how the masses and the government were "awakening to the clarion call of the new conscience," as evidenced by the "Tenant's Protective Association" (TPA). The TPA, growing out of the housing situation, waged "a fight for human rights against conscienceless human sharks." Harrison stressed that tenants' rights, like other rights, would "not be secured by asking for them, but by demanding them, and putting back of that demand the power to enforce it."[11]

In early 1921, after ending his managing editor duties at the *Negro World*, Harrison wrote numerous book reviews, describing himself as being "the only professional Negro book reviewer in captivity."[12] In the *Negro World* of January 29 he reviewed *Two Colored Women with the American Expeditionary Forces*, by Addie W. Hunton and Kathryn M. Johnson, who had served fifteen months as YWCA welfare workers at a supply base in France and then at a recreation center. Harrison began by noting that Hunton and Johnson offered "no revelations" on the "persistent prejudice of which he [the Negro soldier] was a victim," and they seemed to "carefully" select from what was in print. He also noted that they did not discuss "the vile way in which officials made wealth a standard of acceptance for women who wanted to serve the country overseas" by informing applicants "that 'only women able to pay their way' into social activities, etc., would be accepted." These officials also didn't mention "the 'rape propaganda' by which white American—men and women—sought to poison the minds of the French against their dusky compatriots." It was, he wrote, the "lives led by the colored lads" that "showed the French the cruel falsity" of that propaganda and "the stark rottenness of the heart of white Christian America."[13]

Noting how at some places where Black soldiers were billeted they were ordered "to carry on the necessary trade relations without opening their mouths to speak," Harrison compared this to the "silent trade" of African history. He pointed out that America unconsciously "hark[ed] back to one of the most ancient practices of West Africa" described by Herodotus, early Portuguese and French travelers, and Mary Henrietta Kinglsey. The difference was that the ancient "'silent trade' was a voluntary testimonial to the superior honesty of the African: whereas in Europe's war time it was enforced as a fitting illustration of the white man's desire to humiliate the descendants of 'the blameless Ethiopians.'"[14]

Harrison recounted other affronts including: how at either Bordeaux or Brest "the white officers had a gigantic dice, three feet high, made of concrete, set up at the entrance to the Negro troop's quarters," where "gambling was encouraged, and [Army chief of staff] General [Hugh L.] Scott contributed to their morale a special house of ill-fame"; how "Mr. Kitter [Jerome Faber Kidder], the white Y.M.C.A. secretary sent them ['Negro troops'] exclusively to white *fillies de joie*, who were suffering from unmentionable diseases"; and how, "when the colored Y worker, who noted these facts, sent the information by letters to Emmett J. Scott, Dr. Du Bois and others, the letters were opened and read and the Y. Worker was ordered home as *persona non grata*, although no charges had been preferred." Harrison also described how at Chambray, France, the "'propaganda of preparation' reached its highest levels" when the people of that town were "told by white officers of the United States Army and of the Y.M.C.A. that the Negroes were rapists and that they should be treated like dogs, as they were treated in 'democratic' America." The "superiority of the Negro troops and 'Y' workers to the white compatriots was so apparent," however, that they soon won all hearts." Significantly, "not a single case of rape, housebreaking or murder, occurred while they were there, and when they marched out the entire population lined the sidewalks and pelted them with roses."[15]

"These facts" were not given in the book under review but formed a part of the story, which these two women "so splendidly told." Nevertheless, their narrative was "packed with facts and fine feeling" as they told the story of the soldier's sufferings and "nobly" omitted their own. "Theirs was the mothers' task; to minister to the physical and spiritual needs of the Negro section of the American Expeditionary Forces, to cheer and enliven men who had to fight not only Germans in France but American race prejudice of the rankest kind." Hunton and Johnson skirted "the darker edges of their duty with tact and fine discernment," though they did provide "innumerable illustrations of soul-shocking injustice and degradation." They also "sketch[ed] the history of the Negro soldiers in France—manly, patient, efficient and heroic," as "combat troops," "S.O.S. units," and "in the terrible task to which they alone of all Americans were assigned—that of digging up the American corpses that had been dead for months and burying them again at Romagne." Such "heroism" ranked "with any in the records of the ages," and though Harrison could not "share the authors' hope that such heroism on the part of the Negro" would "enhance his value as a man and a brother in the eyes of the whites," we "would not have had him do otherwise," because "such training of the spirit and the flesh" was "good" for "those who triumphantly endure[d] it." Harrison warned that "the Negroes of America in the dark days yet to come may need the greatest reserve of character to be . . . utilized on their own behalf." Overall, Harrison judged that Hunton and Johnson "splendidly succeeded" in "writing a human history" of the "American Negro soldiers in France," which former soldiers of the 92nd Division would read "with pleasure and appreciation." The story would "thrill the hearts of all Negroes." As for the "two colored women with the American Expeditionary Forces," he considered them to be "high exemplars of what is best in Negro womanhood."[16]

In his February 12, 1921, *Negro World* column Harrison reviewed *The Soul of John Brown*, by the English writer Stephen Graham (who would later be active with the Workers' [Communist] Party). He explained that Graham had served in the English army during the war, a war in which the "white men of Europe were cutting each other's throats by the million to determine which should gobble up the lands and labors of Africa in the name of white Christianity." After the war Graham came to America "to see what white Christianity has done for the African." Harrison commented that Graham wrote with his "tongue in his cheek" and with "luscious contempt" for "both the white and black American"—and was not "a friend of either." He sneered openly "at the insincerity of the white American's democratic pretensions."[17]

In setting out on a trip through the South, "following the trail of General [William Tecumseh] Sherman in his famous march to the sea," Graham sought to explain to "the white sections of the English-speaking world" exactly "where the Southern Negroes stand today." He tried "to combine the merits and methods of two famous works of the middle of the last century," Frederick Law Olmstead's *A Journey Through the Seaboard Slave States* and Fanny Kemble's *Journal of Residence on a Georgia Plantation*, but in Harrison's estimation he "fell far short of the intimate knowledge of the one and the profound comprehension of the other." It was, however, "unfair to expect either of these qualities in a strolling Englishman who had only a few months to spend on his quest for the truth in such a tangled matter as that of our American race-relations." Graham's result was "midway between that of a superficial impressionist, and . . . a serious seeker after truth." Harrison thought similar work had recently been "done much better by Messrs. White and [Herbert J.] Seligmann," particularly in the latter's *The Negro Faces America*. Nevertheless, "on the whole," Harrison judged his effort to be "meritorious."[18]

Harrison considered Graham's "errors of observation" to be "diverting" but "not deadly." Examples of "laughable errors" included that "Du Bois 'is the greatest force among the Negroes today,'" that "Booker T. Washington was 'more sooty' than he [Du Bois]," that James Weldon Johnson was "also 'a darker man,'" that *The Crisis* was "a newspaper," that there were "only about a hundred Negro newspapers in the United States," that Madame Walker sold "a nostrum called 'Anti-Kink,'" and that there were "Negro marines in the United States Navy." Sometimes, however, "this gift of inaccuracy" led "to serious results," as when "he cheerfully chatters of the cowardice of the American Negro troops in France."[19]

Harrison felt he would be false to his trust as a book reviewer if he "failed to call attention to the good side" of Graham's work. Graham saw "in America's attitude toward her Negro population not only a real danger . . . in the event of invasion" but "a menace to the white race as well," and he occasionally exhorted "a heedless nation to return to the elementary decencies of justice and fair dealing." Harrison quoted Graham's warning: "'If ill treatment of the Negroes should at last force the twelve millions of them to make cause with a revolutionary mob,'" then "'polite America might be overwhelmed and the larger portion of the world be lost.'" He meant "the Anglo-Saxon world . . . as most Anglo-Saxons do when they speak of 'civilization' and 'the world,'" but his warning was "no less solemn and portentous." Graham had "no doubt that almost any insurrection of Negroes could ultimately be put down by force and that it would be very bad for the Negroes and for their cause," but he wondered "what might happen" if "it synchronize[d] with revolutionary disturbances among the whites themselves, or with a foreign war." Harrison felt that such thought, "though seldom expressed often comes to the minds of white men who, judging by what they themselves would do, easily impute the same intention to Negroes." Whether the imputation was well or ill-founded, it was "certainly dishonest and unfair to impute such intentions to Dr. Du Bois," as Graham did. To Harrison, Du Bois "obviously lacks the toughness of fiber needed for such intentions, which would imply too stark a rejection of the 'sweet reasonableness' of literary and parliamentary discussion and the other modes of approach to ultimate 'reconciliation' with the white man's world of which his genius is so fine a flower."[20]

Graham saw "the sinister problem of lynching from many different angles" and noted "its roots in the simple brutish desire to keep the Negro down—to the level where his work, wealth and women can be most safely and successfully appropriated." He also saw "the importance of 'race' in the study of its reactions," and he observed that "if the white race which inhabits the south were French or Russian or Polish or Greek there would be no lynchings.'" However, it was "the Anglo-Saxon and the Irish-American section of the population who determines the way of politics . . . in the South.'"[21]

Very importantly, Graham explained "the Negro masses' apathy to Socialism and Bolshevism" as related to the fact that the "white proletariat of the South" were considered "the worst enemies of the Negro"—the "Negro is afraid of Bolshevism or Socialism because he knows that the common white people, 'those who have nothing and are nothing,' are the last people likely to give him justice." Graham quoted approvingly the words of a prominent Negro who said that "'as long as Socialism is followed by the lower classes of whites, we can see that there is more danger coming from Socialism to the Negro than from anything else, because below the Mason and Dixon li[n]e the people who lynch Negroes are the low down whites.'" This, Harrison noted, was "the very reaction" he "foretold in 1912 to the bourgeois opportunists of the Socialist Party," and it "should carry concern, if not conviction, even to the editors of *The Messenger*." Graham also contended "the theory of sex-perversion" applied "to the white mobs who dance with ghoulish glee around a roasting Negro." This "popular form of sadism was noted by a German scholar about fifteen years ago" but still needed "pungent presentation," added Harrison.[22]

Harrison felt "the Negro reader" would at times "find helpful criticisms of his race's demerits," as when Graham commented "in caustic vein on certain tendencies of the educated Negro." He cited "'a marked disposition to quarrel'" and concluded that "loyalty to one another was not one of their characteristics." To Graham, "sin" was "written" in most "mulattoes'" bodies and was "sharpest in the mulattoes and near-whites," since the "moral character of the black Negroes is simpler than that of the pallid ones." Harrison also commented on Graham's statements on "mulattoes" and on "our 'odor'" and wished he "had space to correct" Graham's "absolutely erroneous impression as to the services rendered in white civilization by the Ku Klux." He recommended that the author read Albert Bushnell Hart, James G. Blaine, and William Archibald Dunning and "take the trouble to find out the dates and recorded facts."[23]

———

In the February 19 *Negro World* Harrison reviewed *Africa: Slave or Free?* by the Rev. John H. Harris, a former missionary in Africa and the secretary of the Aborigines' Protection Society (APS) of London. The APS, Harrison explained, "formerly functioned in the British Empire in a role similar to that of the Anti-Slavery Society before the American Civil War" but in the last two decades had been "'liberalized' by the ethical mandates of refined imperialism." Now one could no longer "tell exactly what it stands for." Its members, however, still produced "some of the best literature . . . on Africa and African questions," and Harris's book, which openly spoke of the "dirty" work of the white soldier and missionary, was "the best written book on Africa . . . in recent years" and "indispensable" for "the New Negro" at "home or abroad."[24]

Harris brought a "breadth of view and a soundness of judgment . . . lacking in the works of most missionaries." His book dealt "understandingly and comprehensively with every important feature of Africa and the life of the African, from labor to religion." Its scope was "encyclopedic," yet it could be read "rapidly." It moved "in a clear and steady stream of narrative and interpretation" and was "the spontaneous overflow of an able mind and a generous spirit which has lived in close contact with the theme on which it writes." Harris's book offered a "survey of the Sudanic and Bantu portions of the continent, of its peoples and of the problems which are presented by the reactions of white Christian culture on the native institutions economic, political and cultural." It was "a reliable handbook" that Harrison recommended to those Baptist ministers and to "every other body of Negroes" expecting "to do missionary work in Africa."[25]

Harris's first chapter on "Africa and Her People" was "a labor of love which chains one to the rest of the book." He discussed "the land and labor systems of old Africa" and "the changes wrought in these by the white man's overlordship," and he wrote on "polygamy and government and missionary education, on alcohol, slavery, [and] religion." Harrison stressed that the "supreme issue of life to the African is his land," and while "franchise, cattle, industry, labor and polygamy all involve their respective difficulties . . . land overtops each." It was the issue on which the African would "stake all in battle, no matter what the forces arrayed against him." To Harrison, this suggested that "British control of the continent" was "based upon ruthless brute force," as in South Africa (as Harris showed), where "white people have 'retained' 200,000,000 acres for one million whites and 'restricted' the 4,000,000 Negroes to 40,000,000 acres of the most arid lands." In this fact lay "the promise of future upheavals." Harris claimed that influences were at work "with the object of taking from the native the land which he occupies today in order that labor may be provided for white capitalist enterprises." He noted that this was "true of every British dependency in Negro Africa except Basutoland and the Gold Coast" and added that after such a "revelation of British intent toward the African" it was clear "that the only hope for him lies in the downfall of the British Empire." Harris, "being British," never considered "the possibility of such a revolutionary outcome," but, noted Harrison, "such revolutionary conclusions continuously shape themselves in the minds of thinking Africans."[26]

In considering labor, "'the most precious asset in Africa,'" what "the white race had done" was "criminal folly," wrote Harris. It was probable that the population of the African continent was "only half what it was a century ago," and this was "largely" attributable to "contact with the white races." Harris cited "'specific causes' for the population decline," including "the earlier slave trade, modern slavery and modern labor systems; the destruction of the communes and tribal systems; punitive expeditions; imported sexual diseases; rum, gin and consumption.'" But his "message of hope—for the black people of Africa," wrote Harrison, was that it was "possible to change the spirit of the white man, especially the Anglo-Saxon." He added that this "optimism," like that of E. D. Morel, was "maintained in the face of awful facts." Nevertheless, it was not "blind optimism"; it was built "upon intelligible factors in the present situation" and appealed to white people "in terms of racial self-interest."[27]

On the subject of religion, Harrison commented that "after 300 years of Christian contact with Africa" there were "less than 3,000,000 in a population of 120,000,000 who even profess Christianity," and this included "1,000,000 white people of South Africa." The "spread of Islam" during the previous decade gave "grave concern to the various missionary conferences," but Harrison attributed its success to the fact that "it practices toward the black African more of the square dealing of Jesus Christ than race-prejudiced Christianity ever has practiced." Harrison added:

The African Negro, who is not quite the fool that some of his friends think, knows, as they know, that it is only when Christianity comes into this continent that gin comes with its blight and degradation; that it is only where Christianity goes that prostitution finds an entrance, with its dirty diseases that destroy life or make it a living curse; he knows that when Christianity reaches him he loses the land on which he lives and must become a landless legal bond servant to the white Christians of all sorts; he knows that, whereas all true believers are equal under Islam not only "in the sight of God" but in the sight of the magistrate, and in every right, Christianity, as organized and made effective in all her institutions, from the church to the jail, insists that only white men are men and that Negroes especially must be treated like dogs, whether kindly or cruelly. The African Negro knows this; the missionary and his friends know it; and the African knows that they know it. Is it any wonder, then, that when the missionary and his fellow Christians speak to the African at home of "the stability of the Christian Church" and her intention "to establish herself *permanently* as the *consistent* guide in the evolution of the higher African civilization," the African answers in the words of one whom the Christian Church crucifies anew each day by its deeds: "Thou hypocrite! first cast out the beam from thine own eye, and then shalt thou see clearly to cast out the mote from thy brother's."[28]

Harrison could not quite understand "the ground on which white Christians offer Christianity to the black African," though he did understand "why white capitalists insist on taking capitalism to him." He wondered how "the white missionary" could "justify his religion," since charity begins at home, and at home there were "white women in Europe (including the queens) . . . snatch[ing] each other's husbands as a pastime in the upper classes" and "a large jail population in every Christian country." In addition, there were "atheists . . . agnostics and rationalists . . . by the millions," and missionaries had failed to teach "love of Christ" to "legislators like Lloyd George and the 'sinister liars' like Lord [Edward] Grey who plunged millions of British Christians into a bath of blood [by encouraging support of France over Germany]." They also had done nothing "to reach the suffering children of Russia and . . . the black Christians excluded from white churches." The "truth" was "that the work of the white missionary" was "dirty work," like that of the "white soldier," whose job was "to carry destruction wherever he may be sent . . . regardless of the innocence of the 'enemy' or the guilt of his own government." Similarly, "the white missionary's function is to spread that form of religion which will soft-soap the soil of black Africa so that the business of robbing and ruling it shall be less costly and less dangerous." Harrison then offered insightful words on hegemony in the modern European state:

In the modern European state every institution is used by the dominant class to some end which contributes to the general social purpose of that class. It is not necessary that any personal part of such institution should understand the purpose of his calling. Quite possibly he may realize his own intents and aims; indeed it is better for his masters that he should not see them as his master's. Then he can be quite "sincere," earnest and spiritually-minded.[29]

The fact nevertheless remained that "the white missionary's function" was "necessary," and this was "conceded by 'liberals' like Sir Sydney Olivier, Sir Harry Johnston, the Liverpool Chamber of Commerce, and a certain wing of the Aborigines' Protection Society." For that purpose such "infidels" as "Johnston, Olivier and [B. L.] Putnam-Weale [pseud. for Bertram Lennox Simpson] joined hands with the fervid believers of the National Liberal Club to missionarize the African into contentment and submission while the robbing and the ruling go forward." Putnam-Weale in *The Conflict of Color* stated "the naked truth nakedly" and explained "why 'infidels' like himself and Sir Harry Johnston" were "so keen on backing the Cross against the Crescent."[30]

Similarly, Rev. Cornelius Howard Patton, secretary of the American Board of Foreign Missions, in his missionary handbook, *The Lure of Africa*, after studying the political work of the missionaries in Uganda and Rhodesia, said that the missionaries could "be trusted to preach to the Negro the ethics of submission and subservience," and the British government, knowing this, was "eager to put the work of education into the hands of white missionaries." As they said, "'one missionary is worth more to us than a battalion of soldiers.'" To Harris, it was not the African who needs religion so much as the European. He considered the African "deeply religious" and acknowledged that in certain respects African worship of religion "appears to go deeper and is not less pure than the general religious atmosphere of so-called civilized races."[31]

Harrison also discussed "the easy insouciance" with which Harris indicated "his acceptance of a certain view of African capacity" that was "both false and injurious." He referred to "the great Zimbabwe ruins of Rhodesia and to the question of the racial character of the people who left these mighty ruins of temples, fortresses and abandoned gold mines." Harris claimed that they "were not the work of the indigenous African, but that of some immigrant race bent not upon colonization, but the exploitation of the resources of the valley." Though he claimed there was "abundant evidence in support of this theory," he never indicated "any." Harrison noted that "the mines, ruined temples and residences, with the products of human workmanship found in them," testified "to the past experience of a people in a relatively high state of culture." The question was: "To what race did this people belong?" "Anglo-Saxon opinion" maintained that "they must have been Asiatics" because "no native African race could have been capable . . . of producing them," but no proof was offered for this opinion. Since "no one" alleged "that any such building as the Zimbabwes" was "found anywhere in Asia," the presumption that it was Asiatic was "pure prejudice." Further, "Egypt, which is African," had "erected stone structures and other works as mighty as these." The "mighty pyramids and temples" of sixty centuries were reason to "reject with cold contempt the prejudiced conjectures of an upstart race."[32]

————————

Harrison commented on the poet Claude McKay in the March 12, 1921, *Negro World*. He opened by discussing the recent death of the poet Lucian B. Watkins and observed that Watkins's passing "served to remind us that our Negro poets never get properly noticed by us until they have been taken up either by death or by the white people." This was "most unfortunate" and would hopefully end. There was, however, "another great black poet," recently returned after a year in London where "his poetic gifts . . . received fitting acknowledgements from the British people."[33]

Claude McKay, while in England, had brought out his "small volume of high grade verse entitled *Spring in New Hampshire and Other Poems*." (McKay had sent Harrison an author-inscribed copy.) The book received much commendation, including in the *Cambridge Magazine*, yet Harrison asked pointedly, "which of our Negro literatii [*sic*] knows anything about McKay?" His talents were "so well known among the whites that upon his return from England he was promptly offered a position as associate editor of the *Liberator*, one of the most prominent of America's magazines." This was "the first time that a Negro has held such a position in America," though Harrison had been on the staff of the same magazine in 1911, when it was edited by Piet Vlag and known as *The Masses*. Harrison projected that "if McKay had waited until one of our 'race' publications had given such recognition to his genius he would have starved to death first"—and this despite the fact that "his famous poem of Negro manhood, entitled 'If We Must Die,'" had "been quoted in Congress" and "recited by many of our readers and elocutionists."[34]

On May 21 Harrison reviewed *Spring in New Hampshire*. Jamaica, he said, had "given us three Negroes who, along different lines, have risen into permanent prominence: Marcus Garvey, president of the Black Star Line and head of the most widely discussed movement in modern Negrodom; Joel A. Rogers, author of two books which stand without a peer in the output of Negro writing (*From "Superman" to Man* and *As Nature Leads*); and Claude McKay, whose proud title to distinction consists of two simple words: The Poet."[35]

Harrison related how "McKay began to write poetry before he left Jamaica, where he published three volumes of verse," but his "interest in his own fame" was "so slim that he did not take the trouble to preserve any copies of these earlier volumes." After coming to America, McKay worked at various jobs, depending on his hands to earn a living. While at one of these "he was 'discovered' by *Pearson's Magazine* and Max Eastman's *Liberator*," where he served as associate editor. He came "to the fore by sheer virtue of the spiritual quality of

Figure 9.1. Claude McKay, c. 1920. Jamaica-born Claude McKay (September 15, 1889–May 22, 1948) arrived in the United States in 1912. When he came to the United States it marked "the first time" he "had ever come face to face with such manifest, implacable hatred of my race," and though he had heard of prejudice in America he "never dreamed of it being so intensely bitter." This was a reaction similar to Harrison's after he arrived in the United States from St. Croix. McKay described how he was encouraged by his friend Harrison to write articles for the *Negro World*. Harrison favorably reviewed works by McKay and by 1922 described him as "the greatest living poet of Negro blood in America today." Interestingly, when the Third Communist International commissioned McKay to write its first book-length treatment on "The Negro Race" (1923), they provided McKay, in Moscow, with a copy of *The Negro and the Nation* by his close friend Harrison. *Source:* Public domain.

poetic ability which no hardships could suppress," and he made his way "without any aid from Negro editors or publications . . . because white people who noted his gifts were eager to give him a chance while Negro editors, as usual, were either too blind or too mean-spirited to proclaim them to the world." His "manly, stirring poem, 'If We Must Die,' first appeared in a white publication [the July 1919 *Liberator*] from which it was elevated to the dignity of a place in the *Congressional Record*," and it "was then that the Negro reading public discovered him for themselves without any aid from their top-lofty mentors," who were "always 'ready to bring forward young writers'—after they have been proclaimed by white critics."[36]

Spring in New Hampshire revealed McKay "as a poet with a fine and delicate technique and a curiously cultivated restraint." It was "free from jingling and splurging and from the flaring fan-tolds of the free-verse comedians" who held "the centre of the stage in the garish masquerade entitled 'The New Poetry.'" The "genuine breath of the tropics" was "felt in most of these poems," yet the "fine artistic feeling of the poet controls and tempers it to fine effects." Harrison excerpted from "North and South," which created an "appropriate tone-color (or 'atmosphere')" in which the "golden touch of genius" appeared. In "Exhortation" (to Ethiopia) McKay's "thinking" stood out: "He means something," and he didn't "let the rhyme rule the thought nor the ink guide the pen." Harrison considered "The Lynching," "On Broadway," "Harlem Shadows," and "The Harlem Dancer" as "note worthy presentations of familiar themes" and "A Memory of June" as the "most arresting poem in this volume." Overall, McKay's work was "high in aim, in thought, in technique," and his "genuine poetry" merited "a place in the affections of our folk."[37]

Over the years Harrison would try to help McKay in other ways. When McKay was invited to meetings in Harlem and "had to sit on a platform and pretend to enjoy being introduced and praised" and "had to respond pleasantly," Harrison suggested that he "owed it" to his race "to stand up and repeat his poems."[38] Later, when McKay was in Europe, he received "monies from many friends," including Eric Walrond, Harold Jackman, Mrs. A. Philip Randolph, Grace Campbell, and the often impoverished Harrison.[39]

———

According to J. A. Rogers, Harrison's health "was excellent though at times he suffered from vertigo while speaking and had to steady himself. Small wonder, for he spent the night in reading, even after his strenuous three-hour lectures. He could retire at daybreak, sleep for two or three hours, and start the day all over again." Probably related to this schedule, on Thursday, March 17, 1921, in the period between the two McKay pieces, Dr. Leon Fitz Nearon diagnosed Harrison as having "nervous exhaustion" and ordered that he give up reading for some time.[40]

Harrison may have followed the advice for a week or two but was soon back reading and writing—his review of *The Story of a Style*, the "psycho-analytic study of Woodrow Wilson" by William Bayard Hale, appeared in the April 9, 1921, *Negro World*. His preliminary note stated that although "a book review should be a review of a book, not a review of a person," in this case, where a person was the subject of the book, he would "draw upon a wider knowledge of that subject." Further, since the book was "decidedly 'personal,'" he had an excuse for the "strong personal tone" of his review.[41]

To begin, Harrison recounted that "in 1915 after two years of the Wilson administration" he had "prophesied that Woodrow Wilson would go out of office the most thoroughly discredited President since Andrew Johnson." He based this on "what had been said and done by Mr. Wilson in two years . . . as President of the United States," on "some slight acquaintance with the facts of his career as a professor at Princeton and later as president of the university," and "on his *History of the American People* and *The State*." It was evident to Harrison that "Wilson was a sayer of great things whose deeds bore no consistent relation to his words." Wilson was reelected president in November 1916 on "a campaign whose slogan was, 'He Kept Us Out of War!'" Yet, observed Harrison, on Good Friday, 1917, he asked a joint session of both houses of Congress "to put America into the world war on the side of England." Though Wilson had previously declared it "to be a capitalist's war, a war for commerce and colonial possessions, he and his Attorney-General sent Eugene V. Debs to Atlanta Penitentiary for putting the same interpretation on the facts about a year later" and, till the end, refused to pardon him. During the war Wilson "rode on the highest wave of international popularity that had ever lifted any man into the heart of humanity," and his subsequent "fall from that tremendous pinnacle was such a fall as has come to but few individuals." Wilson "had posed before all the world as a champion of democracy." He prated of "the rights of small nationalities," of "self-determination," of "the right of all who submit to authority to have a voice in their own government"—yet it was, as Harrison observed,

this greatest of hypocrites who suppressed freedom of speech and of the press in these United States, let loose upon Hayti and Santo Domingo the awful horrors of unlicensed butchery, and sold out the hopes of all the world for peace and democracy at the Congress of Versailles in a foul compact with cunning crooks like Lloyd George and cynically blind beasts like Clemenceau.

To Harrison, "the outstanding quality of Mr. Wilson's career" was "the divergence of what is in his heart from that which is on his lips," and "the real tragedy of his fall" was "in the fact that humanity has found him out!"[42]

In his book Hale utilized what Harrison described as "a dark application of the Freudian method," and though the book was "a psycho-analytic study" it wasn't "restricted to sex-repressions." Hale's book had "scientific rigor," yet in spite of "its thoroughgoing thesis," it was "so simple an application of the principles of Freud that even 'the common run of people' [quoting Wilson]" could "read and understand" it. Hale was a student of Thorstein Veblen, and his phrases were "deftly drawn upon."[43]

According to Harrison, Hale saw Wilson as a man of words whose "real self" was revealed "in his language." In analyzing "a characteristic passage" from Wilson's first magazine article in 1879 he found 108 words, of which only one was "a pure verb"; thirty were adjectives. Wilson was described as "windy" and as one who "trims and dodges the vital issues of reality which are generally to be found in action." In a special chapter on "Aristocratic Affectations," Hale followed "every trick of expression" whereby Wilson showed himself to be "a fawning servile on aristocracy and what he conceive[d] to be the virtues of aristocracy." His "worship of Britain and the British aristocracy" was shown "in its strongest light." Wilson had previously been called "the greatest living Englishman born in America," and this was shown "in many ways, not the least costly of which was the way in which he made American interests subservient to British interests during the war"—as the journalist William Randolph Hearst "so frequently pointed out." The United States entered the war "because, without our participation, Britain would have been well licked by Germany," as Admiral (William Sowden) Sims made clear. Then, when the peace was concluded, "Wilson left all the gains of victory, in treaties, territory, guns and merchant ships—to England." He "kept American commerce out of Russia, while he waged a costly but ineffective war against the hard-pressed nation," and, at the same time, the British Government, which had "opened our commercial mail with impunity and stole our commercial secrets" with Wilson's "servile acquiescence," lined up its businessmen "to snap up the Russian trade from which we are still excluded to the great loss of both people." Harrison added that Hale helped readers see Wilson's role was "as a conscious or unconscious lackey of Britain."[44]

As an undergraduate at the College of New Jersey (now Princeton University), Wilson published "an argument for the reconstruction of the American Congress and Cabinet to Conform to the English Parliamentary Plan" in the *International Review*. Later, in *George Washington*, "with aristocratic 'affectations,'" he tried to show "that Washington 'longed to be quit of the narrow life of the colonies and to stretch himself for a little upon the broad, English stage at home.'" Hale thought "Washington would hardly have called England 'home'" and added that "the whole spirit and tone of Mr. Wilson's legendary story of Washington is so completely that of devotion to caste, that no scant quotations can convey a sense of the author's profound reverence for rank and the virtues of those who have it, his glowing gratitude to them, and his happiness in being permitted to write of them." Hale added Wilson "is never so eloquent as when talking of kings, and he never misses a chance to mention them, however remote the connection." This was "the pronounced worship of a servile soul for the top-dog, which, in this case, is Britain." Hale discussed Wilson's pet phrases, including his predilection for "process," "counsel," "processes of counsel," "voices," and "fountains," and saw them as "simply a disease of the intellect." He considered Wilson to be "of inferior mental power" based on his writings. In discussing "Wilson's pathetic futility during the war," Hale suggested that "amidst the tortures" he could "only alliterate and generalize." Further, it was only in a country "where four-fifths of the college graduates are ignoramuses and the reading masses too stupid to know how to vote in their own interests" that a "belief in Mr. Wilson's 'ability'" could originate. His "ignorance" was "deplorable," as evidenced by the fact that he did not know that Sarajevo was the Bosnian capital and was, consequently, in Austrian territory in 1914, and he did not know that the Bremen-to-Baghdad railroad did not pass within a hundred miles of Poland, didn't touch Romania, and didn't pass through Persia.[45]

Harrison closed by observing that, to Hale, such ignorance was bad, but "deliberate falsifying" was "much worse." He cited Wilson's September 4, 1920, talk in Columbus, Ohio, on his tour "to reconcile the American people to the Paris Treaty and the League of Nations," where he said: "I have been bred and am proud to have been bred, of the old Revolutionary stock which set this government up." Hale noted that only Wilson's father had been born in America, and that was in 1822, well after the American Revolution. He did what he could "to atone for not having been present in 1776, by supporting the leaders of the Confederacy in 1861" and by "preaching eloquent sermons in advocacy of slavery and secession." Other than "this participation in 'Revolutionary' affairs," however, "the stock from which Woodrow Wilson was bred . . . had slight 'Revolutionary' opportunities," since his mother was born in England and reached Canada in 1833. All four of his grandparents were British, and all eight of his great-grandparents had lived and died in Britain.[46]

———

On April 7 José Clarana wrote a letter to "Contributing Editor Harrison" that was published in the April 16, 1921, *Negro World*.[47] Clarana thought Harrison should have given his "own original criticism" of Wilson, "rather than to fall back on that of William Bayard Hale." He sarcastically added, even if "it was only 'in 1915, after two years of the Wilson regime,' that you became sufficiently aware of the utter incapacity of Woodrow Wilson . . . to prophesy his downfall, you surely have had time to formulate your own opinion . . . without relying on the judgment of Hale," which in 1921 was "dictated by unjustifiable vindictiveness as in 1911 it was by unwarranted admiration." Clarana noted that Hale had at first praised Wilson, in *The World's Work* and elsewhere, and "did more than any other newspaper writer to foist [him] upon the Baltimore Convention [of the Democratic Party] and the electorate of 1912." It was "upon Hale's advice" that Wilson

> took possession of Haiti and Nicaragua; but refused to recognize as Presi- dent of Mexico a "one-eyed Indian subsisting on brandy [Victoriano Huerta]," caused the exile of said "one-eyed Indian" from his native land and hastened his death as a prisoner of the United States; became, in effect, the super- dictator of Mexico until the white man of his and Hale's choice [Venustiano Carranza] to replace the "one-eyed Indian" refused to comply with the instruc- tions of the alien usurpers and was eventually overthrown by their influence, which he died in resisting.

Clarana added that this was "the same Wilson, who, a toy in the hands of Hale and others like him, was too proud to pick up the gauntlet thrown in his face by the Germans in the sinking of the *Lusitania* and too cowardly to say the word or words which might have brought the war to a close in 1915 instead of 1918."[48]

To Clarana, the material for Hale's current book was also the material that "furnished the articles in which Hale sought to make the unregenerated son of a Confederate preacher and advocate of slavery, President of the United States and controller of the destinies of twelve million slaves or descendants of slaves, black men not all, but brown men, yellow men" and others who "have no Eng- lish blood." While "Wilson has happily been consigned to a merciful oblivion," "the story of his career should be instructive and corrective." Clarana then pointedly added:

> The defects of Wilson, so clearly exhibited by Hale in 1921 and so care- fully dissimulated by Hale in 1911, are the defects of the men who would promote the advancement of the colored people of the United States or the improvement of black people everywhere. The impartial observer finds in these chieftains the same baseless conceit, the same boundless self- assurance, an ignorance often vastly more crass by comparison with that of Wilson with regard to matters in which action cannot be beneficent and lead- ership cannot be efficient in the absence of knowledge. And yet these men persist in the way of Wilson, refusing good counsel, rejecting all enlighten- ment, for fear that their own glory might otherwise be diminished. With them, as with Wilson, their accomplishment must therefore be restricted to the domain of words and their reward must be the oblivion, if not the execra- tion of those who place their trust in them.

Clarana closed with the hope that "some day . . . the black man may enjoy every- where the opportunity to improve himself in contact with his fellow men, whether or not he enjoys the protection of a Nigritian Empire" and "that civilization will soon be so far advanced in the United States that the so-called Anglo-Saxon would poison himself rather than roast, drown, or bury alive his brother of more obscure lineage."[49]

Harrison wrote his reply to Clarana's letter for the same April 16 issue but, "through no fault" of his, "it was not printed at the same time." He believed "that the appearance of the answer along with the letter would have shorn the latter of any appearance of evil," and on April 23 he offered it, "better late than never." He also offered an addendum because Mr. Clarana and "many other persons have quite a wrong notion about my relation to *The Negro World* in particular and the U.N.I.A. in general." They presumed that his "relations to both" were "necessarily like those of other men like Dr. [Rev. George Alexander] McGuire, Dr. [Rev. John Dawson] Gordon, Dr. [Rev. James David] Brooks or Mr. [Orlando M.] Thompson," so Harrison felt it "necessary to point out that soon after the convention closed" in 1920 he "ceased to be the editor of *The Negro World*—as had been prophesied before," and he now turned in "a book review and other items each week for . . . the sum of $15," just as he would "for doing similar work for any other publication." It "should not be expected," therefore, that he would "have that passion for magnificent titles which Mr. Clarana seems to sarcastically ascribe" to him and others. Harrison explained: "I have never cared for such titles, and Mr. Clarana may rest assured that I never shall." Even though he was now an instructor in embryology at the College of Chiropractic, he saw to it that the students call him "'Mr. Harrison' and not 'Professor or 'Doctor.'" Parenthetically, he remarked, it was "left to white people to utilize my services in this way, although black people have had these services offered to them collectively and individually for the longest while."[50]

The April 30 *Negro World* carried Harrison's more detailed response to Clarana, which was supposed to have appeared on both April 16 and April 23, as well as his explanatory paragraph, which also appeared on April 23. Harrison noted that Clarana seemed "to assume that a book review is necessarily an original contribution to the subject," but "it isn't." Hale's work "was well done," and Harrison said he hadn't commented on Hale's previous connection with Wilson "because I knew nothing beyond the fact that he had written a biography of the former President." Clarana's letter provided additional information, which Harrison had not yet had an opportunity to check and for which sources were not cited. He doubted "that, apart from Colonel [Edward M.] House, Woodrow Wilson's international policies were dictated by any single person outside of Woodrow Wilson," and he wanted to see "strong evidence on this point." While he knew "that the imperialist tendencies of American capitalism impel the capitalists of this country to seek for investment outlets in the territories of their weaker neighbors in the West Indies, Central and South America," he thought this tendency expressed itself "without any reference to the personal views of the President in the White House." Harrison found Clarana's "insistence that we should guard against the same faults in our own [Negro] leaders which we condemn in white leaders" to be "evidently justified." He emphasized that "the same lack of knowledge" and "the same swaggering pretentiousness" were "just as dangerous, from the standpoint of effective action, on the one side as on the other." He concluded: "Many Negro organizations (such as the Friends of Negro Freedom) could profit from what Mr. Clarana says."[51]

———

On March 17, 1921, Harrison went to the 135th Street Public Library, where he heard Mrs. Adelaide Casely Hayford and her niece Miss Kathleen Easmon, both of Freetown, Sierra Leone, lecture on "Woman in West Africa." A Mr. Sinango, of Portuguese East Africa, introduced them, played on the marimba, and sang several songs, in one of which he was assisted by Sol Plaatje, of Cape Colony, South Africa, who was in the audience. Plaatje, a founder of the South African National Congress in 1912, had participated in two delegations to England protesting the treatment of Black people in South Africa. A little over a month after the library event, Harrison offered a small biographical piece on Plaatje (1876–1932) in the April 23 *Negro World*.[52]

In that piece on Plaatje Harrison declared it "a great pity" that his *Native Life in South Africa* was "not better known to the Negro-reading public on this side." The "able book," published in London in 1916, argued against South Africa's Native Land Act of 1913, which forced Black sharecroppers into landless laborers and prohibited the purchase of land by Blacks in "white" areas, thus placing about 90 percent of the land off limits. Around 1918 Plaatje had sent Du Bois several hundred copies, but, said Harrison, "no honest effort has been made so far to get the book advertised and sold and the copies sent have been largely left to gather age and dust." Harrison "promise[d] to introduce the book" in his column "in a few weeks" and meanwhile called readers' attention "to a pamphlet and another book by this Sechuana author."[53]

The eleven-page pamphlet, *The Mote and the Beam*, was "an epic on sex-relationship between black and white in British South Africa." To Harrison its "chief value" to "Negro Americans" was "to demonstrate to them that their provincial notion of the unique character of race prejudice in this country" was "entirely wrong." "Every feature of outrage and hypocrisy, of cruelty and legalized social injustice" in the United States was duplicated in the Union of South Africa. Plaatje noted "that the gist of the complaints made by white men to black men's love for white women" was "really the fact that white women have begun to exercise on their own account that same privilege of sexual mixing and mingling which has been for so many years an exclusive privilege of white men in their relations with black women." This, he noted, was similar to what he had observed and to J. A. Rogers's assessment in *As Nature Leads*—that "all history is full of the attraction exercised by the men and the women from outside on the women and men inside of the group." Harrison felt "the women of the white race" were "no exceptions to these natural laws—although it suits the book of the white Anglo-Saxon to pretend that they are." Overall, he considered *The Mote and the Beam* "a nifty little pamphlet," though overpriced "at 25 cents for a pamphlet of eleven pages, however good."[54]

In reviewing *Sechuana Proverbs* Harrison discussed correct forms of African tribal names and explained that the "Sechuana" of Plaatje's title was the plural form of the more familiar "Bechuana." The book was a collection of 732 "short, pithy proverbs in which the wisdom of one section of Bantu people of South Africa" was "preserved for posterity." Each page was "divided into three parallel sections, in the first of which the original Sechuana proverbs appear, while the second is made up of the literal translations of these proverbs; [and] the third contains their European equivalents." The proverbs, "largely codifications of the experience of a cattle-raising people who live habitually in the open," clearly "demonstrate that wisdom is not the exclusive possession of any single human group" and "certainly not the exclusive possession of the white people." In the preface and introduction Plaatje described "some of the troubles that beset a writer in a language whose orthography has been tampered with by the white missionaries without their being able to reach definite decisions as to its principles of pronunciation and literal representation." The illustrations were "beautifully reproduced," and the book and pamphlet were available from George Young at 135 West 135th Street.[55]

As he promised, Harrison reviewed Plaatje's *Native Life in South Africa*, published by *The Crisis*, in his column of August 13, 1921. He mentioned that "press opinions" stated that it described "the treatment of the loyal natives under the South African flag," that "Plaatje's articles on native affairs" were "marked by the robust common sense and moderation so characteristic of Mr. Booker Washington," that Plaatje "realized the great debt which the natives owe to the [white] men who brought civilization to South Africa," and that Plaatje was "no agitator or fire-brand, no stirrer-up of bad feelings between black and white," but one who "accepts the position which the natives occupy today in the body politic as the natural result of their lack of education and civilization." Harrison dryly concluded: "The 332 pages of this interesting book seem to bear out the promise of its introduction."[56]

———

In the *Negro World* of April 30, 1921, Harrison reviewed *The American Empire*, by Scott Nearing.[57] He had put "the finishing touches" to that review on April 6 and planned to submit it to "*The Liberator,* nee *Masses,*" whose costumed ball at Tammany Hall he attended on Friday night, April 1. Harrison noted in his diary that at that affair, "I found dozens of my white friends whom I haven't seen for four or five years, and made some new ones: Dr. Newman, Mrs. Cox and Miss [Augusta ?] Woskoff." In the review Harrison began by offering his powerful overview of imperialism:

> The most dangerous phase of developed capitalism is that of imperialism— when, having subjugated its workers and exploited its natural resources at home, it turns with grim determination toward "undeveloped" races and areas to renew the same process there. This is the phase in which militarism and navalism develop with dizzying speed with their accumulating burden of taxation for "preparedness" against the day when the capitalist class of the nation must use the final argument of force against its foreign competitor for markets. These markets change their character under the impact of international trade and are no longer simply markets for the absorption of finished products, but become fields for the investment of accumulated surplus profits, in which process they are transformed into original sources for the production of profits by the opening up of mines, railroads and other large scale capitalist enterprises. It becomes necessary to take over the government of the selected areas in order that the profits may be effectually guaranteed; and "spheres of interest," "protectorates" and "mandates" are set up.
>
> Thus the lands of "backward" peoples are brought within the central influence of the capitalist economic system and the subjection of black, bro[w]n and other colored workers to the rigors of "the white man's burden" comes as a consequence of the successful exploitation of white workers at home, and binds them both in an international of opposition to the continuance of the capitalist regime.[58]

Harrison commented that Americans who could see this process in other nations were largely "unable to see the same process implicit and explicit in the career of their own country." Nearing's book, however, attempted "to open their eyes." It made clear "some of the political implications of our 'manifest destiny' in extending the mantle of our own imperialism over Hawai[i], Cuba, Hayti, Porto Rico and the Philippines"; it demonstrated "the trend of the same commercial purpose toward our weaker neighbors to the south"; and it showed "what the mass of workers are 'up against.'"[59]

Nearing cleverly combined "the aims of the historian, the economist and the propagandist," though, "as a historian of the imperial process in American affairs," his work was "of uneven merit," since it took "claims advanced on behalf of the high motives of the early fathers at their full face value." Though contradictory material was "well set forth and properly documented by original scholars like Gustavus Myers (*History of the Great American Fortunes, History of the U.S. Supreme Court*, and *History of Tammany Hall*), [John Bach] McMaster (*History of the People of the United States*) and [Sydney G.] Fisher (*The True American Revolution*)," Nearing appeared "to be unacquainted with the work that has been done in that field," and he still seemed to share "the illusions of 'the Golden Age.'" He was also evidently unacquainted with "the system of 'indentured servants' which was the name given to the chattel-slavery of whitemen and women in America which for more than two centuries, was substantially on all-fours with the chattel slavery of blackmen and women." This was "all the more strange" because James Oneal's book *The Workers in American History* was "the best authority at second hand on this significant phase of our early industrial life" and was sold at the Socialist Party's Rand School bookstore. Nevertheless, "in regard to some of the later phases and incidents of American history" Harrison considered Nearing's grip "sure" and his presentation of the facts "illuminating." That was "especially true of his treatment of Negro slavery and the slave-trade, the acquisition of Texas, the Spanish-American War, and the suppression of Hawaiian and Philippine independence."[60]

Harrison judged Nearing "well-fitted for the task of opening the eyes of our economic illiterates to the nature and meaning of the economic processes that are going on all around us." His "implicit indictment of the crumbling system of capitalist exploitation at home and abroad" was "put with a fine reasonableness and good temper" that stood to "gain him many readers from among that inert mass . . . impervious to ordinary Socialist propaganda." It was "for those 'outsiders' that such works are primarily written," and Nearing, "in making his program implicit rather than explicit," showed "that he sets a proper valuation upon missionary success." "On the whole," Harrison found the book "a worthy contribution to the literature of radical economic thought," its "grip on the mechanics of imperialism" to be "firm," and its "exposition . . . always clear and sound."[61]

From March 5 through March 26, 1921, in four "With the Contributing Editor" columns in the *Negro World*, Harrison offered "Lincoln and Liberty—Fact Versus Fiction." It was a subject he had been discussing since 1911, and in these columns he put forth his important historical analysis, which reached "Negro" peoples worldwide. Harrison repeatedly sought to encourage Black movement out of the Republican Party, and that movement increased significantly during the decade of the 1920s. The fact that much of the information in this series was not known by the general public suggests what a remarkable contribution this was by Harrison and the *Negro World*. Chapter 1, "Historical Fictions," maintained that the current "political plight of the Negro people of America" was that, "with a certain amount of political power available for use in their own interests, they use that power, year after year to add to the value of the Republican party's control of the country and the government—a control which has not so far redounded to the political advantage of the Negro people." While the Fourteenth and Fifteenth Amendments expressly stated that Congress shall have power to enforce them by appropriate legislation, that had not been the case. Harrison explained that these amendments aimed to put "all people in the United States of the male sex upon an equal footing as regards the qualification for voting," and "the punishment" for any state that discriminated "against black people or other people on petty, unfair grounds" was supposed to be that their representation in Congress would be "reduced in proportion to the number of males of voting age whom they exclude from the ballot."[62]

In fact, however, "from 1878 the vote of four-fifths of the Negro people ha[d] been taken away from them by the Democratic white men of the South," and, from then till Woodrow Wilson's time, with the exception of Grover Cleveland's administration, the U.S. government was "in the hands of white Republicans" who "stood by with a continuing consent." In this period "the Negro was being robbed of the ballot," the "only protection" that could "keep off" the "lynchers of the South, from his body, and prejudice from his property." While one might expect "that the Negro would use his political power to set these things right," he had not; he had "gone into the booth to vote with the belief that he owed a debt of gratitude to Abraham Lincoln and the Republican party, and that his first duty was not to himself but to those white persons to whom the debt of gratitude was owed." Thus, explained Harrison, "our women, our children, our property, our education, have all been unprotected and unprovided for," with "our continuing consent," and this "burden of gratitude alone keeps us from using our political power solely in our own behalf." He reasoned, therefore, "our consequent duty" was "to investigate the grounds of our gratitude." In discussing the "falsifying [of] the records of the past," a "lucrative and popular occupation" in the United States, Harrison acknowledged "the statesmanlike proposition" that "in order to rule men you must fool them." He pointed out that while "they certainly fool us, black and white, the common people," they also "falsify the records of the past in the interest of the present" by painting "for us a picture of glorious-minded men who came out, clad in the rich robes of idealism to do battle for the principles of right, justice and equality." Harrison found "this assumption in many of the state papers of America," including "the opening sentences of Lincoln's Gettysburg address," where we are told that our fathers at Plymouth Rock and Jamestown "were high-minded men, not at all like the present politicians with their selfish aims and objects, their strivings for political advantage, to the exclusion of the interests of the community." But, this was "not so," and it led to a class of books from writers who "think it necessary to append to them the adjective 'true.'" Thus, *The True George Washington* by Paul Leicester Ford; *The True History of the American Revolution* by Sydney George Fisher; "the 'true' this, that and the other." Such efforts were necessary because "the things that we generally get as history—are lies," and the person "who studies, goes back to the original documents, realizes the enormity of the lies."[63]

In America, Harrison explained, "we have cultivated" the "worship of certain historical myths." As an example he quoted from memory *With the Fathers*, by John Bach McMaster, "the greatest historian of America." In discussing "gerrymandering," which "the ignorant voter believes to be a product of Tammany Hall," he noted that it "was started by Colonel Ellbridge Gerry [1744–1814] in Massachusetts," and McMaster wrote "when it comes to vote stealing, bribery and political chicanery the fathers were always our equals and often our superiors." In a similar vein, Harrison claimed he could present "some evidence in regard to white slavery among the puritans of Massachusetts, and some information about George Washington," but here he would focus on Abraham Lincoln. "Personally," Harrison considered Lincoln "the greatest President that the United States had up to his time." But, he pointed out, "the current opinion of Abraham Lincoln as a god is not supported by the facts."[64]

Harrison began by discussing the causes of the Civil War, which had "been morally re-constructed" so that "the average white person" now believed that "the North went to war with the Southerners in order to free the Negroes"— and "the average Negro himself believes that!" The reason was because "the schoolbooks . . . your political fairy stories," say so. These "memories," however, did "not square with the facts, which revealed: "[Elijah Parish] Lovejoy was lynched. John Brown was executed. Wendell Phillips was ostracized. [William Lloyd] Garrison was mobbed and dragged through the streets of Boston with a rope around his neck. These were the champions—the white champions—of the Negro's freedom; and the Republican Party and the general white sentiment of the day, repudiated and execrated and tabooed them. Their motives were not the prevailing ones in that period."

To Harrison, "the real causes of the Civil War" concerned "the economics of slavery" and the "two, types of civilization established in our country." The "type that became dominant in New England" tried "to arrange itself on the basis of a free white working-class," though in fact "it never did at any time have a quite free white working class." In fact, "in 1630 . . . the first Fugitive Slave Law was passed in this country . . . in the legislature of Massachusetts" regarding "white men, white women, white children," who "were at that time sold like cattle!" When "they ran away the *posse comitatus* was supposed to go out and hunt them down with dogs and guns and ropes and bring them back to their tasks." From New England to New York was "established (under the impulse given by Thomas Slater of Rhode Island who established the first factory and Alexander Hamilton who laid the financial foundation under government arrangements) the factory capitalist system of the North."[65]

The type of civilization that "became dominant in the South . . . sent to Africa to get black people . . . as workers." The "Southerner then developed agricultural domestic slavery," a very "wasteful" system, "as conceded by every economist who investigated it." It lacked "rotation of crops in the growing of cotton, tobacco and cane," and "the soil was worn out." Because of this it was in "the interests of the slave-holders to continue expanding the area of the territory which was given over to their form of wealth-getting," and "this necessity expressed itself in changes in the structure of our government." Periodically "the government itself [would] reach out under pressure of this necessity to acquire land," as when "it bought Louisiana from Napoleon" and when the nation, "controlled by the Southerners as presidents, as heads of the army, navy, Supreme Court and the legislature, insisted upon raids in the territory of Mexico." The raids on Mexico "were intended to provoke war . . . in the interests of the Southern extension of slave territory" and led to the annexation of Texas.[66]

Then, "when the capitalists of the North began to develop their factory systems and to take their goods to Europe to Asia to Africa, their method of making a dollar turn over resulted in a quicker turnover than the slaves method did." These northern capitalists found "it was easier to make a dollar yield another dollar when that dollar was invested in a worker whom you did not have to support when he was sick; whose wife and children you did not have to support if they were not working for you." Meanwhile, "the capitalist in the South, having bought the black slave, had to pay for his board and lodging" and "that of his wife and children" during "those periods when the black slave was sick and was not producing any surplus value for the capitalist." In the North, "the capitalists paid only for the actual working time of the white free laborer," and "their method of fructifying the dollar yielded larger results than the other method."[67]

Under this, as "any capitalists competition, that form will win out which secures the most profit; and the Northern system . . . secured the maximum of profits as compared with the Southern system." The "goods which the factory capitalists of the North turned out could be sold cheaper than the goods turned out by the slaveholding capitalists of the South," and "these two forms competed for political power in Washington and for profits in the markets of the world."

The "competition was expressed also in the changes in the government," as "the Northern capitalists began to say: 'Why should we let the nation go to work and tax our capital up North to get taxes to spend on the Crackers of the South? Why should we let the Southerners control the Supreme Court, the Army and the Navy?'" Then, "in their own protection, the capitalists of the North had to work to attempt to seize control of the government within the political structure; and that was the contest which culminated in the electoral campaign of 1860 when Abraham Lincoln was elected to office and the South seceded." At that time, "Lincoln and the Republican party, scared at what they had evoked, offered to drop all discussion of slavery, to give the South everything it wanted, including the perpetuation of slavery on American soil." They were prepared to make it "a thing that should exist forever, whose disturbance by agitators or by legislators should be forever illegal." The South seceded because they knew that "Government functions in the interest of the class that controls it," and they "realized that with the powers of government in the hands of the white capitalists of the North, promises could be made a thousand a day:—but when it came to square dealing, the government would function against the interests of the slaveholders. They knew on whose side government was." Thus, "because Abraham Lincoln was elected and the powers of government were put in the hands of the people of the North, they insisted for the sake of the perpetuation of their kind of property that they must have a government of their own in which their kind of property was paramount and, consequently, one in which their interests would always be advanced."[68]

Harrison maintained "that the war was fought for economic and not for moral reasons," and in his second and third "Lincoln and Liberty" articles he sought

> to show that Lincoln was not an Abolitionist; that he had no special love for Negroes; that he opposed the abolition of the Domestic Slave Trade and favored the Fugitive Slave Law; that he opposed citizenship for Negroes; that he favored making slavery perpetual in 1861; that he denied officially that the war was fought to free the slaves; that he refused to pay Negro soldiers the same wage that he paid the white soldiers; that without these Negro soldiers the North could not have won the war; that the Emancipation Proclamation was issued, not for the slave's sake, but solely as an act to cripple the army of the South; and finally, that it did not abolish slavery and was not intended to.

By demonstrating this he aimed to "prove that: the Republican party opposed the Abolitionist doctrine; that they offered to sell out the Negro in 1861, and the only reason why the sale was not consummated was that the buyer picked up his basket and went home." He would further "prove that as late as 1864 the Republican party, in control of the Government, refused to pass an amendment to the Constitution abolishing slavery."[69]

For "proof" Harrison quoted from Lincoln's opening speech in his second joint debate with Stephen A. Douglas, August 27, 1858, at Freeport, Illinois, where he said "the people of the Southern States are entitled to a congressional fugitive-slave law." Lincoln added that he would not, with his "present views," be "in favor of endeavoring to abolish slavery in the District of Columbia unless it would be upon these conditions: First, that the abolition should be gradual; second, that it should be on a vote of the majority of qualified voters in the District; and third, that compensation should be made to unwilling owners." He also would not be in favor of Congress seeking "to abolish the slave trade among the different states."[70]

Harrison also quoted from Lincoln's first inaugural address, where he discussed the "apprehension . . . among the people of the Southern States" that a Republican administration would endanger "their property and their peace and personal security." Lincoln saw no "reasonable cause for such apprehension" and reiterated his position that "I have no purpose, directly or indirectly, to interfere with this institution of slavery in the states where it exists." In that same speech he quoted from the Republican Party's platform, which aimed to maintain inviolate "the rights of the states, and especially the right of each state to order and control its own domestic institutions according to its own judgment exclusively." The platform also denounced "the lawless invasion by armed force of the soil of any state or territory, no matter under what pretext." Harrison emphasized that he did "not mean to insinuate" that "Abraham Lincoln was a hypocrite." His own view was simply that he was "a politician [and] a statesman." He cited Lincoln's opening speech at Charleston, Illinois, on September 18, 1858, where he proclaimed "I am not, nor ever have been, in favor of the bringing about in any way the social and political equality of the white and black races" and "I am not, nor have ever been, in favor of making voters or jurors of Negroes, nor of qualifying them to hold office." Later, in a direct rejoinder to Stephen A. Douglas, he stated "that I am not in favor of Negro citizenship." He also added that he would uphold the *Dred Scott* decision and oppose any state's effort "to make a Negro a citizen under the Constitution of the United States" in violation of that decision.[71]

Harrison added to this "proof" by showing that Lincoln "favored making slavery perpetual in 1861." Citing James G. Blaine's *Twenty Years of Congress*, Harrison demonstrated "that the first thirteenth Amendment was proposed to entrench slavery so securely that it should be safe from attack by the Supreme

Court of the United States," and it was supported by "the Republican party and Abraham Lincoln." In early 1861, "the Southern representatives in Congress began to drop out as their states seceded," and then "the northern politicians . . . compromised" and "offered to sell out the cause of the Negro." At that time, "white men of the North did not, on the whole, care much about Negroes," and "those who did were called Abolitionists, and . . . had no party." There had been "a break between Frederick Douglass and William Lloyd Garrison, between the Radical and Abolitionist groups, as to whether they should support the Free Soil or any other party, by which they could get a percentage of their demands realized and enacted into law."[72]

In his third article Harrison explained that "early in 1861, while the Northern legislators were kow-towing to the Southern sentiment, a committee composed of thirteen members of the Senate and thirty-one members of the House was created to bring in resolutions on the basis of the Crittenden compromise, which had been previously offered to Congress." The committee record, according to Blaine, "cannot be reviewed with pride or satisfaction by any citizen of a State that was loyal to the Union." Charles Francis Adams proposed that the U.S. Constitution "be so amended that no subsequent amendment thereto 'having for its object any interference with slavery' shall originate with any State that does not recognize that relation, within its own limits, or shall be valid without the assent of every one of the States composing the Union." Blaine commented that "no Southern man during the long agitation of the slavery question extending from 1820 to 1860 had ever submitted so extreme a proposition as that of Mr. Adams . . . for the protection of slavery." Nevertheless, the proposition was opposed by only three members of the committee—Mason W. Tappan of New Hampshire, Cadwallader C. Washburn of Wisconsin, and William Kellogg of Illinois.[73]

The proposed amendment, Blaine explained, "provided for a perpetual existence" of slavery by "declaring that no future amendment . . . shall ever be passed" that shall affect any of the proposed proslavery amendments, that "the provision in the original Constitution which guarantees the count of three-fifths of the slaves in the basis of representation shall never be changed," that "no amendment shall ever be made which alters or impairs the original provision of the recovery of fugitives," and that "no amendment shall be made that shall ever permit Congress to interfere in any way with slavery in the States where it may be permitted." After several days of angry debate, a large majority adopted the resolutions on February 27, 1861. Then, "when the constitutional amendment was reached Mr. [Thomas] Corwin substituted for that which was originally drafted by Adams an amendment declaring that 'no amendment shall be made to the Constitution which will authorize or give to Congress the power to abolish or interfere within any State with the domestic institutions thereof, including that of persons held to labor or service by the law of said State.'" This was adopted by a vote of 133 to 63 and numbered the Thirteenth Amendment. It "would have made slavery perpetual in the United States so far as any influence or power of the national government could affect it," and it "received the votes of a large number of Republicans who were then and afterwards prominent in the councils of the party," including "Mr. [John] Sherman of Ohio, Mr. [Schuyler] Colfax, Mr. C[harles]. F[rancis]. Adams, Mr. [Jacob] Howard of Michigan, Mr. Winton of Minnesota and Messrs. Moorhead and McPherson of Pennsylvania." In his first inaugural address Lincoln said, in reference to the proposed amendment, "I have no objection to its being made express and irrevocable."[74]

"During the first year and a half of the war," according to Harrison, "the white working men of England and Europe made repeated requests to Lincoln to declare that the freedom of the Negro slaves was one of the objects of the war." In particular, "Karl Marx and the working men of Great Britain . . . urged him to do this" and pointed out "that the Tories of England were making capital of the fact that they could get England into the war on the side of the Confederacy." The English workers said: "If you would now declare that this is a war to free the slaves, we will smoke them out and in the name of human altruism we will compel the Government of Britain to keep its hands off." Lincoln, however, "would not say that the war was a war to free the slaves, but insisted instead in saying again and again that the war was not a war to free slaves."[75]

Horace Greeley, in particular, "was impatient" with such "ignoble Morality—the morality of the slick politician," and he wrote an open letter to the president that stated his view. In response, Lincoln wrote:

> I would save the union. I would save it the shortest way under the Constitution. The sooner the national authority can be restored, the nearer the union will be "the union as it was." If there be those who would not save the union unless they could at the same time save slavery, I do not agree with them. If there be those who would not save the union unless they could at the same time destroy slavery, I do not agree with them. *My paramount object in this struggle is to save the union and is not either to save or destroy slavery. If I can save the union without freeing any slave, I would do it. If I can save it by freeing all the slaves, I would do it, and if I could save it by freeing some and leaving others alone—I would also do that.*

"That is exactly what he did," commented Harrison. This was Lincoln's "statesmanship," and it merited "approval for statesmanship." But the statement also "effectively disposes of any claim to the Negroes' gratitude on the grounds of high moral altruism and benevolence."[76]

Harrison's fourth "Lincoln and Liberty" article, "A Crooked Deal for the Black Patriot," argued that Lincoln was not a friend of freedom and noted that he "refused to pay Negro soldiers the same wages that he paid to white soldiers." Harrison referred to Colonel Thomas Wentworth Higginson's autobiographical *Price of a Man's Life*, which discussed the 54th and 55th Massachusetts infantry regiments of "free blackmen," who "took up guns to go out and save the Union" in "the hope that one of the consequences of the conflict, would be the emancipation of the slaves." When Jefferson Davis and the South "saw that Negroes were fighting against them, they issued proclamations saying that if they captured any Negroes they would treat them, not as soldiers captured in war, but as 'niggers'; they would lash them; [and] they would sell them further South into slavery to hoe corn and tend cotton." Lincoln "knew this," the proclamations were reproduced in the North, and it was "clear that the black soldier in fighting, ran a risk that the white soldier did not run."[77]

In the face of these developments, Lincoln and his government "went back on their pledged word and offered to the Negro soldiers half the wage which they had promised in the proclamations issued to call soldiers into the Union ranks." These Black men "were good enough to stop bullets—they were men there—but when it came to the recompense they were only 'niggers' in the opinion of Lincoln and his Republican government." When Frederick Douglass, who had a son in the 54th Massachusetts, and a delegation of Black men went to Lincoln to protest this—the president said he "could not afford to antagonize the sentiment of the white people of the country," and therefore these soldiers would be given half-pay. The 54th and 55th Massachusetts, "like the other colored troops that came in afterwards," were "men enough to refuse it" and went without pay for a year and a half. They borrowed money from officers and, according to Higginson, said, "We will not take the half pay; we will fight, and if need be, die; but if we are offered half pay and we are only to get that, we will let it stand in history to the eternal disgrace of the nation that is using us as men and treating us as slaves." Finally, after the year and a half, representatives from Massachusetts, Rhode Island, and Connecticut got the government to vote them the same pay as other soldiers.[78]

A "sidelight" on this story that Harrison added concerned Captain André Callioux, of Louisiana, who "represented a type of mulatto produced in Louisiana that certainly deserves the high praise of Negroes and the friends of the Negroes in that conflict between slavery and anti-slavery." These "colored men—half white and half Negro" owned slaves and plantations and were "cultured," having "gone to France to get the finest education available in France, which was finer than that available in any college or university in the United States at the time." As the war developed "Calliaux [*sic*] let his money go and put his race first." He "organized a regiment of men—Negro men—to fight for freedom" and included "such slaves as he freed before the emancipation proclamation." He offered these men "to Abraham Lincoln's government," which "took white men that he had trained, drilled and equipped at his own expense—his and others." They also "took the regiment's from them, put white men at the head and gave them mere captains' and lieutenants' commissions— because Captain Calliaux began as a lieutenant." That was "the recompense" offered "for sacrifice under Abraham Lincoln's government."[79]

Harrison also attempted to show "that without these Negro soldiers the North could not have licked the South." Lincoln said so in an August 17, 1864, letter to Charles D. Robinson of Washington, which stated:

> Drive back to the support of the rebellion the physical force which the colored people now give and promise us, and neither the present nor any coming administration could save the Union. Take from us and give to the enemy the one hundred and thirty, forty and [or] fifty thousand colored persons now serving us as soldiers, seamen and laborers, and we cannot longer maintain the contest. The party who could elect a President on a war and slavery restoration platform would, of necessity, lose the colored force; and the colored force being lost, would be as powerless to save the Union as to do any other impossible thing.[80]

To Harrison this was "as precise and as explicit" as possible. If the South had agreed to rejoin the union, Lincoln would not have issued the Emancipation Proclamation, he argued. Lincoln's September 22, 1862, proclamation maintained that on January 1, 1863, "all persons held as slaves within any State or designated part of a State the people whereof shall then be in rebellion against the United States, shall be then, thence forward and forever free." Lincoln explained the action was taken "*as a fit and necessary war measure for suppressing said rebellion.*" Harrison stressed that Lincoln did this "in order to bring Negroes into the ranks of the army" and to let slaves who were working on southern plantations know that they were free and could run away without the risk of being sent back. The measure provided "that the slaves shall be declared free, only in those States that are in rebellion." It explicitly excepted the forty-eight counties of Virginia which became West Virginia; the Virginia counties of Berkeley, Accomack, Northampton, Elizabeth, York, Princess Anne, and Norfolk; Arkansas; Texas; and thirteen Louisiana parishes. The exceptions were "because the northern troops were in control in these sections and it was not needed 'as a fit and necessary war measure.'" Lincoln "was not declaring a freedom measure—he was declaring a war measure; he was tearing the tools of war out of the hands of his enemy." According to Harrison, Lincoln spoke accurately when he said "that if he could only win the war by freeing some of the slaves and leaving the others bound to servitude he would do that." Harrison rested his "eye opening" case.[81]

In his presentation Harrison made no claim to "profound scholarship." He did think it a "shame" that the facts were "right there on the surface," though largely unknown. With information of this sort "left to 'bookish' people," it tended "to affect the practical political life of our people, and the way in which they cast their votes." The result was that "we have lived in lies; lulled ourselves in the luxury of lies told us by white people and black politicians who were feeding out of their hands." To counter this situation, his publication of his series on Lincoln in the *Negro World* was a major effort at getting this information out to a wide audience. Harrison concluded that though Lincoln had "a great character," it was "not what we have been told." He "was not a friend of freedom" and "not an altruist," and it was "high time that we Negroes of today who boast of our education and culture should be aware of this simple historical fact." It was "time that we Negroes should do our own historical work instead of taking our food pelican-wise from the white people's pouch." After this was done, Harrison predicted, "we will have rectifications to make." He added, "while we patter about race emancipation we still be brain-bound to the white man's mental products and his mental interpretation of our people to the world in which they live," and this was "after all, a more hopeless slavery than physical bondage could ever be."[82]

In the *Negro World* of April 9 Addie Sisco of Chicago wrote requesting a copy of the four chapters on "Lincoln and Liberty," from the paper or in "pamphlet form." Sisco thanked Harrison "so much for giving that contribution to the world" and added, "we have been asleep, but we are waking." Harrison responded that "the four articles . . . on 'Lincoln and Liberty: Fact versus Fiction,' will be printed as a pamphlet during the late spring and distributed at nominal cost." He added that the talks "were originally delivered as a lecture at Liberty Hall in February, 1920," and were "an indication of some of the kind of work that could be done at Liberty Hall if the propaganda work permitted."[83]

In the *Negro World* of February 12, 1921, Harrison described how the Lafayette Theatre management was "trying the experiment of converting it into a high-class moving picture house." The previous week they had shown the actress Pola Negri in *Passion*, "a study of love in the high-life of pre-revolutionary-France." In the movie "the celebrated courtesan, DuBarry, who began life in the gutter was shown in the successive steps by which she rose to be the chief manager of the great King Louis whom she brought to degradation and finally to death, and got her own head cut off by the public executioner during the Reign of Terror." Harrison judged it "a splendid picture" and added that "many first-run dramas and comedies" were scheduled.[84]

In the *Negro World* of March 12 Harrison wrote "Are Negro Actors White," which included a reprint of an article by Cyril V. Briggs from the March 1919 *Crusader* and a poem, "Two Whites at the Show," by Andrea Razaf. Harrison began by discussing comments on Black actors offered by Stephen Graham in *The Soul of John Brown*. These actors "would blush for shame," said Harrison, "for while the white critic praises them sparingly for their histrionic gifts he pokes insulting fun at them for their persistence in 'making up' as if they were white people playing to white audiences." His "ridicule" was "well merited," and Harrison asked his readers to "consider what the practice implies": "If Negroes were people then it would be proper that Negro audiences should get accustomed to seeing Negroes as drawing room guests, doctors, detectives, governors, financiers, etc. in the glow of the footlights," but, "if folks can't be considered as people unless they are unlike Negroes, then, of course, our actors should never look like Negroes."[85]

Harrison believed that "one of the fine features of Charles Gilpin's acting while at the Lafayette (where 'we' couldn't recognize that he was our greatest actor until white people told us so) was that he was never ashamed in 'making up' for his parts to let the audience see the race to which he belonged." This, however, was exactly "what the Lafayette Players are never permitted to do, except in the mockery of 'musical comedy.'" Harrison did not "intend this as any disparagement of their work or their abilities," for he "firmly believe[d] that they are as fine a body of actors as America can show—when the short time given to them to prepare a play is taken into consideration." He did, however, think "that this matter of their identity on the stage could be cleared up to the great satisfaction of the community which furnishes for them, not white, but Negro play-goers."[86]

It had been "a mooted question for some time whether black girls like Blanche Deas and Fannie Tarkington, both of whom appeared successfully among the whites on Broadway, could gain admission to the chromatically select circles of the Lafayette." Harrison "believe[d] that culture and ability are not limited by color," and he asked, "How can we consistently demand that white people shall act up to this altruistic principle in our case when we hypocritically and with much cowardly lying refuse to act up to it in our own case?" He "sincerely hope[d] that the new management of the Lafayette" would "see their way clear to find a place for talent regardless of its color" and noted that "[Clarence] Muse and Miss [Cleo] Desmond are there," but they were "top-notchers and were the very soul of the original nucleus out of which the stock company grew." He also wished the company "the long lease of life which it deserved" and hoped that it "take to heart these words of an earnest and consistent friend."[87]

"By way of proof" that his "complaint" came from others and had been heard before, Harrison offered an article and poem from the March 1919 *Crusader.* He assured his readers that his own paragraph "was written and in the hands of the editor of the *Negro World* ten days before we stumbled on Mr. Briggs' articles." He added that it was "more than coincidence that Mr. Briggs should have put the case of the black girl's chance as an actress right after the argument as to make up" and noted that he was "quite black," while Mr. Briggs was "a very light Mulatto." Both, however, "as self-respecting Negroes," took "the same stand on this matter." Raz's poem, "Two Whites at the Show," which followed the Briggs piece, ended:

> But what a funny race!
> If I were doing such great work
> I'd never hide my face![88]

By March 1921 Harrison was having difficulty receiving his mail at the *Negro World*, and in the March 26 issue he asked all who wanted to get in touch with him "for business or other personal purposes" to write him care of Porro Press, 513 Lenox Avenue, in the back of the drugstore. He disclaimed responsibility for letters "left or sent anywhere else." Two weeks later he explained that "a brown stiff-paper portfolio containing manuscript papers, including an unfinished article entitled 'Are We All White?' an unfinished article on 'The Ku Klux and History,' and other writings intended for *The Negro World* and of no use to anyone but the writer" had been lost. He thought the material "was probably left at the Baptist Ministers' Conference at the Metropolitan Baptist Church on Monday, March 21," but allowed that it "may have been left elsewhere." He offered a "suitable reward" if the material was returned. The historian Hill points out that James Wormley Jones, BI confidential informant "800," had been responsible for registering all incoming mail at UNIA headquarters. There is no indication that Harrison was aware of this.[89]

On Wednesday, April 13, Harrison wrote in his diary that he had just received a letter from D. Hamilton Jackson, his old schoolmate from St. Croix and now a prominent labor leader and editor on the island. Jackson wrote "in reply to a casual note" and asked Harrison "to go out to the West Indies and lecture on the racial phases of the labor problem, as an introduction to the people of St. Croix." He asked Harrison to consider "associating . . . permanently with him and his work there." Two days later they had a meeting at Jackson's West 144th Street apartment, where Jackson told Harrison he wanted him "to go out to Santa Cruz during the coming winter for a three-months trial as a lecturer and field secretary of his labor union movement." At that meeting Harrison left Jackson his "outline notes of the Liberty League," which, while Marcus Garvey was outside the United States, had been "resurrected."[90]

Right before meeting with Jackson, on Thursday, April 14, Harrison began "two parallel series of lectures" on "Negro history" and "African culture" at St. Savior's Church, 73 Schenectady Avenue, Brooklyn, where Rev. Bridgeman of the UNIA was pastor. The Thursday afternoon African history series ran through May 12 and included lectures on "African Life and Customs," "The African Family System," "How Africans Worship God," "The Secret Societies of Negroland," and "African Systems of Government." The Sunday series from April 17 through May 22 included talks on "The Black Man in History," "Egypt and Ethiopia," "The Cradle of Civilization," "One Thousand Years of West African History," "The War of Races in Africa (Early Colonization and the Slave Trade)," and "The Partition of Africa." The talks would include questions and discussions, and book lists would be available.[91]

Harrison's difficulty receiving mail at the *Negro World* office as well as his efforts to again resurrect the Liberty League and his increased public speaking suggest that deeper issues were affecting his relationship with Garvey and the UNIA. These issues would soon manifest themselves in a developing crisis within the Garvey movement and in increased attention being paid to Harrison by Black radicals, Garveyites, and the Bureau of Investigation.

10

The Liberty League, Tulsa, and Mid-1921 Writings
(May–September 1921)

Despite the dissatisfaction of Harrison and others, the organizational momentum of the Garvey movement was growing by the middle of 1921. Garvey and his followers began a new round of promotional tours selling BSL stock, reorganizing weak UNIA divisions, and starting new ones. While *Negro World* circulation had dropped in early 1921, by the middle of the year it was estimated at 75,000. The paper reportedly was self-supporting and contributed some $1,000 monthly to the UNIA. Its editor, William Ferris, estimated that by July 1921 the Garvey movement was employing nearly two hundred people in New York and another two hundred around the world. At the August 1921 UNIA convention it was claimed that the number of divisions had increased from ninety-five to 418 in one year and that there were 422 branches awaiting charters. The historian Robert A. Hill writes, "the UNIA was the major political force among blacks in the postwar world."[1]

There was, however, a developing crisis in the movement. Though BSL stock sales amounted to $55,147 in the eleven months between the close of the 1920 convention and the start of the August 1921 convention, the postwar economic slump was continuing, and Black unemployment was rising. To counter the increasingly difficult economic times, Garvey introduced new financial schemes. In October 1920 he started a Liberian Construction Loan that sought $2 million to finance a loan to Liberia to replace Liberian Liberty bonds. On December 1, 1920, he issued a circular seeking $250,000 by mid-January 1921 for another ship to bring workers and materials to Liberia. The Liberian Construction Loan and the BSL virtually merged as a promotional package, and the loan-campaign monies were used in a desperate attempt to stave off the financial crisis of the BSL. In search of additional funds, Garvey left on a promotional tour of the West Indies and Central America in late February 1921. During Garvey's almost five months abroad, Harrison regularly held mass meetings in Harlem, urged action against white supremacist violence, sold *When Africa Awakes,* and "made little effort to hide his differences with Garvey." His lectures were "well attended, especially by Garveyites, who flocked to him during Garvey's absence." By June 1921 he was again publicly promoting the Liberty League.[2]

During Garvey's tour, J. Edgar Hoover of the BI moved against him. Hoover believed that Garvey was partially subsidized by the British government, and he sought help from the U.S. State Department, which could deny Garvey a visa and block his reentry to the United States. The State Department at first worked with Hoover on this plan but then abandoned it and allowed Garvey's reentry. Hoover retaliated by not helping the State Department block the admission of Gabriel M. Johnson (a UNIA potentate from Liberia), in July 1921. Johnson attended the UNIA's August 1921 convention.[3]

Garvey was aware, before embarking on his February 1921 trip, that he might have difficulty returning. He badly needed a "major fund-raising tour in previously untapped regions." His trip, however, according to Hill, "marked a major turning point in the history of the UNIA." The individuals he left in charge of the UNIA and BSL argued, the movement faltered, and Garvey faced increased legal difficulties. Nevertheless, great crowds greeted him abroad, he sold much BSL stock, and he raised large sums from admission fees at his talks. The proposed five-week tour lasted months, and when he returned in the middle of July Garvey was much more aware of the U.S. government's opposition to him and his movement. A serious crisis also arose when the U.S. Shipping Board did not produce the promised ship, the so-called *Phyllis Wheatley,* which was to be used for travel to Africa (and which delegates to the 1921 convention were expecting to see).[4]

In Garvey's absence, leading Garveyites including UNIA Secretary-General James D. Brooks, John Dawson Gordon, and Bishop Gorge A. McGuire paid increased attention to Harrison. On April 7 Harrison wrote in his diary:

> *Hodic prim-participium cum* Rev. Dr. J[ames]. D. Brooks, Secretary General of the U.N.I.A. *Magna cum laude! Il ef avaient trois de l'espece opposant a centrum et triginbatr via ad num centum et duo.* Both Dr. Brooks and Dr. [Rev. John Dawson] Gordon [the assistant president general of the UNIA] are evincing an outspoken liking for me which seems to indicate that, in their minds, Garvey's star is setting. [Bishop George A.] McGuire

[the chaplain general of the UNIA] too is making approaches. I shall watch and wait.

The Antigua-born and St. Thomas–educated McGuire was at that time seeking to build his independent Black church into the official religious body of the UNIA but was receiving strong opposition from Garvey. Six days later, Harrison wrote in his diary: "Habui alterum participium cum Brooks last night and *Dominam* [Boss] Mitchell, W. 132nd Street. He pays for these."[5]

One of the first steps taken by the BI as Garvey was preparing to depart was a February 14 "Memorandum" prepared by M. K. Bunde for Parker Hitt, the assistant chief of staff. Though focusing on Garvey, it suggested much about the Harrison-Garvey relationship and why there would be increased attention on Harrison by both radicals and by the BI. Bunde wrote:

> The radical Negro leaders, while giving their support to the various projects of Marcus Garvey, deplore the fact that he is too reactionary. They claim that he could do a lot of good for the radical cause if he would follow the advice of some of the bright and clever men like H. Harrison, for instance. . . . The trouble with Garvey, they said, is that he does not want anyone around him who exhibits brain power enough to become a danger by over-shadowing him, so when he was elected Provisional President of Africa, he succeeded in having elected as leaders of the various factions, such as the West Indies, America, etc., men who would do his bidding without question and who were sufficiently impressed with his—Garvey's—greatness, so that they would not be dangerous as rivals for office or leadership. Garvey, according to these leaders, is now surrounded by a group of intellectual nincompoops.[6]

Around the same time, a section of the "Program of the United Communist Party" on the "Negro Question," reprinted in the *Toiler* of February 12, 1921, hinted at why someone like Harrison would attract interest from the communists. The program described "the negro population of the United States" as "the most exploited people in America"—an "outlaw race"—and emphasized that "the only possible solution of the negro problem" was "the abolition of wage slavery, through the overthrow of the capitalist State and the erection of the Communist society." In order "to break down the barrier of race prejudice that separates and keeps apart the white and the negro workers, and to bind them into a union of revolutionary forces for the overthrow of their common enemy," the UCP aimed to "find the revolutionary and potential revolutionary elements among the negroes and select those most likely to develop into revolutionary propagandists" for training in "revolutionary work."[7]

Two and a half months later, BI Special Agent Joseph G. Tucker described in a "Special Report" a May 1 "Negro Forum" at 131st Street and Seventh Avenue, where Max Feigenbaum, the associate editor of the SP's *Call*, spoke on "May Day and what it means to the Negro." Feigenbaum declared that "the only country today which is free is Russia and that the Negroes should not join in [the] 'Back to Africa' movement, but should remain in this country, join hands with the white 'wage slave brothers' and overthrow the capitalists." Feigenbaum was followed by Harrison, Domingo, and Grace Campbell, who all reportedly "pointed out to the audience the advantages of Communism."[8]

As the radicals began to pay more interest to Harrison, one person who was deeply impressed by him was Claude McKay. McKay described Harrison in his autobiography as "very black" and "compact of figure," with a "head [that] resembled an African replica of Socrates." As an orator he described him as one who spoke "precisely and clearly, with fine intelligence and masses of facts." McKay emphasized that "for a time he [Harrison] was the black hope of the Socialists."[9]

In early May 1921 McKay was working as an assistant editor of *The Liberator*, a communist-influenced monthly, on Fourteenth Street. When Harrison stopped by the office "to offer his congratulations," McKay introduced him to Robert Minor,[10] the former cartoonist for the *Masses* and now working for the *Daily Worker* and the *Liberator*. Minor would become a member of the Central Executive Committee of the Communist Party of America in 1921, would specialize on the "Negro Question," and "was interested in the activities of the advanced Negro radicals." According to McKay, Harrison "suggested a little meeting that would include the rest of the black Reds." The meeting took place at the *Liberator* office,

> and besides Harrison there were Grace Campbell, one of the pioneer Negro members of the Socialist Party; Richard Moore and W. A. Domingo, who edited *The Emancipator*; Cyril Briggs, the founder of the African Blood Brotherhood and editor of the monthly magazine, *The Crusader*; Mr. [Joseph P.] Fanning, who owned the only Negro cigar store in Harlem; and one Otto Huiswood [who was active with the Communists and] who hailed from Curacao the birthplace of [the late Socialist Labor Party leader] Daniel Deleon [De Leon].

The "real object of the meeting," according to McKay, "was to discuss the possibility of making the Garvey Back-to-Africa Movement . . . more class-conscious." A second meeting was also held.[11]

The BI accumulated information on that second meeting. Special Agent "P- 138," Jamaica-born Herbert Simeon Boulin, in a report for July 10 on "Negro

Activities," wrote that Edgar M. Grey, secretary of the Liberty League, "and assistant street corner lecturer of Harrison," reportedly told him "in confidence" that Briggs's ABB was "purely a COMMUNIST organization" and that its periodical, *The Crusader,* was "subsidized by the COMMUNIST PARTY." Grey also discussed the second May meeting with the communists and said that "about a month and a half ago [in late May]" Rose Pastor Stokes, an advocate for an aboveground and legal CP, "had invited several radical negroes to a supper at her house in Ann Street at Greenwich Village, for a conference on how to spread the communist [message]." Among those present were Domingo, McKay, Briggs, Grey, and Harrison. Grey said that "Stokes put up to HARRISON a proposition by which she, who represents the COMMUNIST PARTY, would finance him so that he could use the LIBERTY LEAGUE as a branch of spreading communism among negroes by agitation with white people—which HARRISON refused." Stokes reportedly "told them that there was plenty of Russian gold here and they will spend it in any negro movement as to further their cause." She also "offered aid to Briggs and his magazine *THE CRUSADER,*" which Briggs's ABB reportedly accepted. Grey added that McKay was "a communist and attached to the *LIBERATOR*" and lived at the magazine's office building. He has just arrived from England and was "supported by the Communists." Grey stated that "HARRISON and himself refused to join MRS. ROSE PASTOR STOKES, in her proposition" because Harrison "prefers to make the Liberty League a purely negro organization, fighting for the negro cause." According to Hill, Harrison's rejection of Stokes's overture showed he would not be the communists' "stalking horse against Garvey." Hill adds that Briggs, on the other hand, joined the communist Workers Party around this time. An MI report claimed that Grey reportedly said that Harrison refused money from the CP and wanted an all-Negro organization, while the ABB took money from the communists.[12]

———

Around the time of his rejection of the communist offer, Harrison wrote his call for a "Colored International," which appeared in the May 28, 1921, *Negro World.* It reflected the fact that he was increasingly distancing himself from Garvey by his more class-conscious and anti-imperialist views, that he was posing an alternative approach for "Negroes" to that being put forth by U.S. communists and the Communist International at that time, and that he was trying in Garvey's absence to resurrect the Liberty League. Harrison's powerful *Negro World* article was an articulate response to communists' efforts to woo him and other African Americans and one of his most significant political statements.[13]

The article explained, "All over the world . . . subject peoples of all colors are rising to the call of democracy, to formulate their grievances and plan their own enfranchisement from the chains of slavery, social, political and economic." People "from Ireland and Armenia . . . Russia and Finland . . . India, Egypt and West Africa" were "looking for their relief from the thralldom of centuries of oppression." Among those peoples, "the darker races" were "the ones who have suffered most," as they faced both "the economic evils under which the others suffer" and "those which flow from the degrading dogma of the color line." That dogma, which was "set up by the Anglo-Saxon peoples and adopted in varying degrees by other white peoples who have followed their footsteps in the path of capitalistic imperialism," declared "that the lands and labors of colored races everywhere shall be the legitimate prey of white peoples and that the Negro, the Hindu, the Chinese and Japanese must endure insult and contumely in a world that was made for all."[14]

In America, explained Harrison, "we who are of African ancestry and Negro blood have drunk this cup of gall and wormwood to the bitter dregs." Though "our labor built the greatness of this land," we "are shut out from places of public accommodation: from the church, the ballot and the laws' protection," and we are "Jim-Crowed, disfranchised and lynched without redress from law or public sentiment, which vigorously exercises its humanity on behalf of the Irish, Armenians and Germans thousands of miles away, but can find no time to concern itself with the barbarism and savagery perpetrated on black fellow citizens in its very midst." This "cynical indifference" extended "to the leaders of the Christian Church, the high-priests of democracy and the . . . exponents of the aims of labor," as "the Negro" was "left out of the plans being put forward by these groups for the reorganization and reconstruction of American affairs on the basis of 'democracy.'" Because of this, Harrison added:

We Negroes have no faith in American democracy, and can have none so long as lynching, economic and social serfdom lie in the dark alleys of its mental reservations. When a president of this country can become famous abroad for his preachments on "The New Freedom" while pregnant Negro women are roasted by white savages in his section of the South with not one word of protest coming from his lips; when a church which calls itself Christian can grow hysterically "alarmed" over the souls of savages in Central Africa, while it sees everyday the bodies of its black fellow Christians brutalized and their souls blasted and smirks in gleeful acquiescence; when the "aims of labor" on its march to justice exclude all reference to the masses of black workers whom conservative labor leaders would condemn in America to the shards and sweepings of economic existence—when such things represent what happens every day in a "sweet land of liberty" where "democracy" is the great watchword, then we Negroes must be excused for feeling neither love nor respect for the rotten hypocrisy which masquerades as democracy in America.

When we look upon the Negro republics of Hayti and Santo Domingo where American marines murder and rape at their pleasure while the financial vultures of Wall Street scream with joy over the bloody execution which brings the wealth of these countries under their control; when we see the Virgin Islanders in the deadly coils of American capitalism gasping for a breath of liberty, and Mexico menaced by the same monster, we begin to realize that we must organize our forces to save ourselves from further degradation and ultimate extinction.[15]

Harrison's profound statement, written almost a decade earlier in the *New York Call*, still rang true: "Politically, the Negro is the touchstone of the modern democratic idea."[16]

Harrison then reviewed previous attempts at redress and the lessons learned. When we "appealed to the common Christian sentiment of the white people for justice," he wrote, we were "told that with the white people of this country race is more powerful than religion." When we "appealed to the common patriotism which should bind us together in a common loyalty to the practice rather than the preachments of democracy," we were "in every case . . . rebuffed and spurned." Our "protest and publicity addressed to the humane sentiments of white America have availed us nothing." Harrison concluded: "We are too weak to wage war against these evil conditions with force, yet we cannot afford to wait for help to come to us from those who are our oppressors. We must, therefore, learn a lesson from those others who suffer elsewhere from evils similar to ours. Whether it be Sinn Fein or Swadesha, their experiences should be serviceable for us."[17]

He then outlined a plan of action:

Our first duty is to come together in mind as well as in mass; to take counsel from each other and to gather strength from contact; to organize and plan effective resistance to race prejudice wherever it may raise its head; to attract the attention of all possible friends whose circumstances may have put them in the same plight and whose program may involve the same way of escape. We must organize, plan and act, and the time for the action is now. A call should be issued for a congress of the darker races, which should be frankly anti-imperialistic and should serve as an international center of co-operation from which strength may be drawn for the several sections of the world of color. Such a congress should be worldwide in scope; it should include representatives and spokesmen of the oppressed peoples of India, Egypt, China, West and South Africa, and the West Indies, Hawaii, the Philippines, Afghanistan, Algeria and Morocco. It should be made up of those who realize that capitalist imperialism which mercilessly exploits the darker races for its own financial purposes is the enemy which we must combine to fight with arms as varied as those by which it is fighting to destroy our manhood, independence and self-respect. Against the pseudo-internationalism of the short-sighted savants who are posturing on the stage of capitalist culture it should oppose the stark internationalism of clear vision which sees that capitalism means conflict of races and nations, and the war and oppression of the weak spring from the same economic motive—which is at the very root of capitalist culture.[18]

Harrison envisioned the coming together of "the darker races" in an "anti-imperialist" congress to challenge "capitalist imperialism." He then explained the economic basis of that capitalist imperialism:

It is the same economic motive that has been back of every modern war since the merchant and trading classes secured control of the powers of the modern state from the battle of Plassy [Plassey, June 23, 1757] to the present world war. This is the natural and inevitable effect of the capitalist system. For that system is based upon the wage relationship between those who own and those who operate the gigantic forces of land and machinery. Under this system no capitalist employs a worker for two dollars a day unless the worker creates more than two dollars worth of wealth for him. Only out of this surplus can profits come. If ten million workers should thus create one hundred million dollars worth of wealth each day and get twenty or fifty millions in wages it is obvious that they can expend only what they have received, and that, therefore, every nation whose industrial system is organized on a capitalist basis must produce a mass of surplus products over and above, not the need, but the purchasing power of the nation's producers. Before these products can return to their owners as profits they must be sold somewhere. Hence the need for foreign markets, for fields of exploitation and "spheres of influence" in "undeveloped" countries whose virgin resources are exploited in their turn after the capitalist fashion. But since every industrial nation is seeking the same outlet for its products clashes are inevitable, and in these clashes beaks and claws—must come into play. Hence beaks and claws must be provided beforehand against the day of conflict, and hence the exploitation of white men in Europe and America becomes the reason for the exploitation of black and brown and yellow men in Africa and Asia. Just as long as black men are exploited by white men in Africa, so long must white men cut each other's throats over that exploitation.[19]

Under such oppression, added Harrison, "the subject races and the subject classes are tied to each other like Kilkenny cats in a condominium of conflict which they cannot escape until the system which so binds them both is smashed beyond possibility of 'reconstruction.'" Therefore, "it becomes the duty of the darker races to fight against the continuance of this system from without and within," and "the international of the darker races must avail itself of whatever help it can get from those groups within the white race which are seeking to destroy the capitalist international of race prejudice and exploitation which is known as bourgeois 'democracy' at home and colonial imperialism abroad." With such internationalism "we meet our oppressors upon their own ground." Thus:

When Mr. [J. P.] Morgan wants to float a French or British loan in the United States; when Messrs. [Woodrow] Wilson, [Georges] Clemenceau, [David] Lloyd George and [Vittorio Emanuele] Orlando want to stabilize their joint credit and commerce or to wage war on Germany or Russia; when areas like the Belgian Congo are to be handed over to certain capitalist cliques without the consent of their inhabitants—then the paeans of praise go to the god of "internationalism" in the temple of "civilization." [But,] when any portion of the world's disinherited (whether white or black) seeks to join hands with any other group in the same condition, then the lords of misrule denounce the idea of internationalism as anarchy, sedition, Bolshevism and "disruptive propaganda," because the international linking up of peoples is a source of strength to those who are linked up.

"Naturally," the "overlords want to strengthen themselves," and "quite as naturally, they wish to keep their various victims from strengthening themselves in the same way."[20]

Today, however, explained Harrison, "the great world majority, made up of black, brown and yellow peoples, are stretching out their hands to each other and developing a 'consciousness of kind.'" "They are seeking to establish their own centers of diffusion of their own internationalism, and this fact is giving nightmares to Downing Street [in London], the Quai d'Orsay [in Paris] and the other centers of white capitalist internationalism." The "object of the capitalist international is to unify and standardize the exploitation of black, brown and yellow peoples in such a way that the danger to the exploiting groups of cutting each other's throats over the spoils may be reduced to a minimum," and this leads to "the various agreements, mandates and spheres of influence" and "the League of Nations, which is notoriously not a league of the white masses, but of their gold-brained governors." The "darker peoples of the world have begun to realize that their first duty is to themselves" as "a similarity of suffering is producing in them a similarity of sentiment, and the temper of that sentiment is not to be mistaken."[21]

Of particular importance in Harrison's article (in addition to his call to develop international colored unity) was his call to develop racial solidarity among "Negroes" and his emphasis (as it was earlier when he was with the SP) on the need for "white" labor and leftist forces (in this case communist and socialist) to focus on "breaking down the exclusion walls of white workingmen" (that is, to "breaking down the . . . racial solidarity of the ranks of white labor"). As Harrison explained:

We in America, in attempting to win life, liberty and happiness for ourselves, must utilize this sentiment to strengthen our position. Our enforced participation in the first World War brought us into contact with the wider world of color, and we have learned from that contact much that has enlightened us. We have learned that American race prejudice was not willing to stay at home, but insisted on pursuing us as far as France, where it sought to establish itself in the hearts of a European people to whom it was previously unknown. We have learned that capitalist America was quite willing to co-operate with Bolshevik Russia when it thought that its own ends could be served by so doing. We have learned that jim-crow cars exist in Nigeria, India and Egypt, and that lynching, disfranchisement and segregation are current practices in the French Congo and in South and East Africa. And, having learned these things, we have done our own thinking, and reached our own decision to avail ourselves of the international forces and factors which will aid us to work out for ourselves a fairer destiny than the doom which threatens us if we submit supinely to the forces of racial aggression.

We should, therefore, take the lead in linking up with those agencies and groups which tend to disrupt the white man's world as at present constituted, because it is from its present constitution that we chiefly suffer to pull chestnuts from the fire for either radical or conservative groups. Until we can co-operate with them on our own terms we choose not to co-operate at all, but to pursue our own way of salvation. We will not allow either communists or Quakers to break down our developing racial solidarity, and we shall denounce every attempt to stampede us into their camps on their terms until they shall have first succeeded in breaking down the opposing racial solidarity of the ranks of white labor in the lands in which we live. Sauce for the black goose ought to be sauce for the white gander, and the temporary revolutionists of today should show their sincerity by first breaking down the exclusion walls of white workingmen before they ask us to demolish our own defensive structures of racial self-protection. The latter arose as a consequence of the former and the cause should be removed before the consequence can fairly be expected to disappear.

But those who will meet us on our own ground will find that we recognize a common enemy in the present world order and are willing to advance to attack it in our joint behalf.[22]

———

In early June 1921, after his call for "A Colored International" was published, Harrison discussed the purpose of the Liberty League of Negro-Americans, which he was attempting to resurrect, with a reporter for the SP newspaper *The Call*. He said it aimed to carry on "educational and propaganda work among Negroes" and to "exercise political pressure wherever possible to carry into effect certain practical measures which would abate lynching," and it "was not afraid openly to take the position that lynching would never be stopped or effectively checked until it became a costly business to the white people who undertook it." Overall, the Liberty League's "political program" was "based on the idea of 'Race First'"—and it reportedly sought "to waken the Negro to the realization that he must make his rights absolutely the only issue when he takes part in American political life."[23]

The Liberty League, according to Harrison, was also "strongly behind the program of the advanced labor movement in this country" and was "using every effort to line up all colored workers in the union composed of colored workers only," which would "co-operate in every possible way with the white unions when we are allowed that right." The League's labor policy was "adopted not because we consider it the best, but because it is the most helpful." Though Harrison "would prefer to see workers of all colors and creeds working for emancipation in one union," he judged that "the white workers of America on the whole do not yet realize the need for lining the colored worker alongside of him and treating him as his social equal." As "long as that condition exists," he concluded, "the colored man must fight for his economic betterment independently of the white trade union movement."[24]

Harrison further explained that the League was "endeavoring to teach the Negro the facts of the social system in which he lives" and to "evoke in him a respect for his own history." It would "teach African ethnology along the lines suggested by Dr. Franz Boas and others" and would emphasize that the Negro "was not altogether a creature rescued from savagery by the white slave dealer" but that "the Negro race in Africa" had "at different times in its history reached a high stage of civilization." "Civilization," Harrison clarified, was "not a specialty of the white race"; "Negroes [had] made their contribution," as was "tentatively realized by some of the more liberal scientists."[25]

———

While Harrison attempted to resurrect the Liberty League, the organization was thrust into national attention after white supremacist attacks on the Black community of Tulsa, Oklahoma. On May 31 and June 1 Tulsa was torn by what the *New York Times* described as "one of the most disastrous race wars ever visited upon an American city." The fighting started after a Black man was arrested on a questionable charge of assaulting a "white" woman (by allegedly grabbing her arm in an elevator). A crowd of "white" men then gathered and talked of lynching, and a responding crowd of African Americans assembled. Early reports indicated eighty-five or more deaths, and "the Negro quarter" in North Tulsa, comprising over "thirty densely populated blocks, was wiped out by fire." Six thousand "Negroes" were put "under heavy guard in hastily established detention camps," and on June 1 "500 whites began the invasion of the negro quarter." Private airplanes circled the city and dropped deadly bombs on the Black community, in what has been described as the first-ever air attack on U.S. soil. Some forty city blocks were looted and leveled, twenty-three churches and one thousand homes and businesses ruined, and Black men were forced to march, en masse, with hands up, through town. The state militia was activated, and Police Chief Charles W. Daley estimated 175 deaths.[26]

Liberty League President Harrison called a 4 p.m. meeting for Sunday, June 5, at the Public Library on 135th Street in Harlem to "protest against the Tulsa massacre and to elect a committee to go to Oklahoma to get the facts at first hand." On behalf of the League he sent a telegram to Oklahoma's governor, James B. Robertson, warning that unless the authorities took dramatic measures against those responsible "this condition will give an immense impetus to the movement among the Negroes for arming themselves against white aggression." Harrison added, "Unless the state authorities repudiate and punish such lawlessness, Negroes will develop as militant a spirit as the Irish in Ireland." Other scheduled speakers at the rally were Rev. Dr. Williams the elder; Irena Moorman Blackstone, president of the Women's National Business Association; Arthur E. King, publicist; and Edgar M. Grey, secretary of the Liberty League, who was to preside.[27]

In mid-1921 BI monitoring of Garvey, Harrison, and other Black radicals intensified. Special Agent Tucker prepared a report on the June 5 Harlem meeting, in which he quoted Harrison as saying:

It is not only those negroes [in Tulsa] but those everywhere in the country of whom we are thinking. I am not making predictions, but I should not be surprised if we saw three splendid riots by next September. There may not be any in New York, but I advise you to be ready to defend yourselves. I notice that the State Government has removed none of the restrictions upon owning firearms, and one form of life insurance for your wives and children might be the possession of some of these handy implements and it is absolutely necessary for your protection to join the Liberty League which is carrying on a wide campaign for the interest of our race.

To Tucker, these comments demonstrated that while Harrison "does not openly advise his followers to purchase firearms," he "does so by innuendo and has a reputation of being a very dangerous agitator." Tucker added that it was said Harrison was born in the Virgin Islands, had been in the United States for about fifteen years (it had been about twenty-one years), and that it was "not at present known whether he is a citizen."[28]

The MID's General Staff, Negative Intelligence Branch, in Washington, in a "Confidential Weekly Situation Survey," also discussed the June 5 meeting to collect money "to aid the negroes of Oklahoma." The report stated that Harrison "urged the negroes of New York to arm themselves," "denied the negroes of Tulsa were in any way responsible for the rioting and chaos," and charged "that the police and troops took sides with the rioters until restrained by the authorities." After quoting Harrison's other remarks, the MID report pointed out that the meeting was called to elect a committee to investigate conditions in Tulsa and that at the close Harrison asked that he and Liberty League secretary Grey be allowed to go. Harrison reportedly maintained that the names of those chosen to go would not be revealed until after their return, so that "some white man's darkey in the back" didn't "write them down" for someone who "would be waiting for them, [when they] got out to Tulsa."[29]

In its coverage of the June 5 meeting, the *New York Evening Journal* said Harrison had predicted three "splendid race riots by next September" and advised "his colored friends to arm themselves and get ready for anti-negro riots." Harrison reportedly claimed that in Tulsa "a group of fifty colored men merely went to patrol the jail when rumors of intended violence to a colored prisoner reached their ears." The *Journal* suggested the possibility that this "patrol of fifty armed colored men started the riots" and added that it was "absolutely certain that the colored men were bound to come out second best when the rioting began." The *World* issued a similar report and added that Oklahoma Adjutant General Charles Barrett, who led the National Guard in suppression of the riot, claimed the lawless "patrol" should have been at once disarmed and dispersed because its presence aggravated, if it did not cause, the ensuing horrors. The *World* termed Harrison's advice "bad policy."[30]

On June 6 Harrison wrote a letter to the editor of the *New York Times*. It was not published there, but it was reprinted in the *Negro World* of June 18. He claimed that a *Times* reporter in that day's paper had "done me and the organization which I represent a grave injury," and he offered "a few brief corrections." First, he criticized "the somewhat sensational caption 'Urges Negroes Here to Arm Themselves.'" He then explained that the meeting was called by the Liberty League of Negro Americans, "an organization with branches extending in flourishing fashion as far west as St. Louis, Mo., and not by the Liberal League," as the *Times* reported. He noted that it was "not true that the speakers were all colored" and pointed out that a "white woman who indorsed every step of our program in a brief but able speech is, perhaps, the most famous high school teacher in the state of New York." He withheld "her name now only because she might be bothered by the dangerous impression created by the carelessness (or worse) of your reporter." He clarified that "no funds were solicited," since, as he told the audience, "we were not yet sure as to whether funds were needed, or would be welcomed by the Tulsa authorities from outside sources." Harrison did "prophecy that we would have at least three great race riots in America before September," but he "didn't describe them as 'splendid,'" since "as a man of African extraction" he was "unable to see anything 'splendid' in race riots."

Harrison also stated that he did "not make any special appeals to Negroes to arm themselves—in New York," and to substantiate this he quoted from the League's telegram to the governor of Oklahoma: "If this sort of thing can be done with impunity in a southern state, then it will become necessary for Negroes all over the South to arm for self-defense." Since "no sane man" would "argue that they must and should die like defenseless sheep," Harrison reasoned, as did "one of the (white) speakers," that "a Negro who shoots down lawless murderers in defense of his home is contributing to the creation of a wholesome respect for law and order and orderly legal processes." Harrison insisted that this "right of self-defense is conceded by all laws, Southern as well as Northern, and . . . my people are defending themselves now, as a last resort." He thought it a "pity," however, that this was "necessary" in "a land where, in theory, all are entitled to the equal protection of the law" but "only white men get it—in the South."[31]

On June 6, Harrison sarcastically wrote to thank the editor of the *New York World* for their article of that day and for "the giving of good advice," which the paper was "always ready and willing to render us ['Negroes']." In regards to the paper's "ill-informed editorial" Harrison "was somewhat surprised to see that the writer based himself so solidly upon the news item printed in the *Times* the day before," since "The *Times*' account was a false and prejudiced one, designed to do as much damage as was possible to the cause of the

Liberty League." He felt the *World* had "no excuse for writing an editorial based on anything less reliable than its own report," and he added that the *Times* "was one of the papers which had not been invited to send a reporter to the meeting," while the *World* "had been invited and sent none." Harrison also explained that the people at that meeting would "testify" that "no lawlessness . . . was advocated by any speaker," though "we do insist . . . on calling the attention of Negroes to the fact that, ultimately, the reasons why Negroes or Irishmen are the victims of violence is because they are defenseless." The League would continue to insist "that one way for Negroes to put down lawless violence" was "by resisting it to the full with the lawful violence of self-defense." If the *World* editor and "other so-called white friends of the Negro" were opposed to this, then, reasoned Harrison: "You simply stand in the position of one who would look on and see a friend get his throat cut out without offering him a gun or a knife to prevent that throat cutting: but as soon as he grabs a gun or takes a knife to save his throat, you will always be found ready and willing to run up and offer against his self-defense the protest which you never offered against the original aggression." Harrison closed: "For such frightful friendship . . . the Negro of America today does not care two pins."[32]

––––––––

On Tuesday, June 7, according to BI Special Agent Boulin, Harrison, the "promoter and president of the 'Liberty League,'" held a street meeting at 135th Street and Lenox Avenue before about six hundred people, where he lectured and sold his book *When Africa Awakes*. He reportedly spoke on "the negroes part in helping to stop lynchings," saying that since "the law allows a man to use his gun or any other weapon to defend himself . . . that the same is true when white murderers, called lynchers, attack black men." Harrison also asked for brave men to come forward and form the Liberty League, saying "he did not want cowards who would be *found hiding under a bed if they were in East St. Louis, or Tulsa when a race riot started*." He wanted "men who are not afraid to die; men with red blood; strong young men as he needs their services and the race needs them also." According to Boulin, "Only about four came forward and gave their names"; nevertheless, this was the first time Harrison had asked for members since reviving the defunct Liberty League several days earlier. Boulin thought that the St. Louis branch of the League was going strong but that the New York branch had stopped functioning a few years earlier and Harrison was now attempting to revive it. (No record of any St. Louis branch has been located.) Harrison was League president; Grey, the secretary; and Arthur Reid, the treasurer. At the meeting's end, Harrison announced a meeting on "What Happened in Hayti" for the following Sunday in the 135th Street Public Library basement. A former Haytian minister to the United States and a delegate to

Washington from a commission protesting U.S. occupation of the island would also speak.[33]

In his report, Boulin provided a background portrait of the Liberty League president. He said Harrison was "well read, was a rabid Socialist speaker and one of the star lecturers for the Socialist Party a few years ago. He broke with the Party, came up in the negro section and organize[d] the 'Liberty league of Negro America' in 1917 and a radical weekly paper called 'The Voice.'" Garvey "gave Harrison a job as Associate Editor of the 'Negro World,'" but afterwards he "was reduced to the position as contributing editor." Now, "with Garvey absent and the recent race riot in Tulsa," he was trying "to revive his defunct Liberty League." The "Garvey followers especially distrust Harrison [centering their criticism on] . . . his attacks on their leader, but despite this they flock to hear him as the type of anti-white lecturer . . . [that appeals] to them, especially when he tells negroes to prepare to . . . [be] attacked and don't be cowards." Boulin added that Harrison "lives on his wit and has a wonderful method of telling . . . [his audience] to learn the use of T.N.T., guns, fires, etc., so as to kill whites if attacked, but he has practiced a way of clothing his dangerous . . . [advice] in such subtle words and phrases that his audience understands him . . . at the same time he seeks to evade the clutches of the law."[34]

Boulin's next report detailed community reaction to Harrison. On June 8 he visited "the rendezvous [Martin Luther Campbell's tailor shop] of the negro radicals at 127 West 135th Street" in order to get their opinion of Harrison and the Liberty League. Campbell told him "he endorsed every word and action of Harrison in advising Negroes to arm themselves to prepare for race riot, and said that was the best advice ever given to the Negroes." Carpenter, another radical, "also endorsed Harrison's action."[35]

Boulin then reported on June 11 that on the night of June 9 Harrison and League Secretary Grey held a Liberty League street meeting on a Lenox Avenue corner before "a big crowd." Harrison condemned the editorials in the *World* and *Evening Journal* for blaming him for "telling negroes to arm and be prepared." He reportedly said that he would "always tell negroes to get guns, T.N.T., kerosene, etc., and fight back against the white people in self-defense [since] that was the only way to stop lynching and race riots." He mentioned that he had written a letter to the *World* and emphasized that "negroes were not fools anymore" and that "they had enough sense to be prepared." He reasoned, "if the natives of the Congo Free State in Africa were armed, Belgium would not dare to have killed them off as she did," emphasizing that "no strong nation would easily invade a weaker one if the weak nation was well armed and prepared." Since the United States was guilty of spending "ninety-four per cent of the country's revenue for war—army and navy preparation," he further reasoned that he "was simply telling the negroes" the "same lesson that he learned from the U.S.A." (which had gone "three thousand miles to fight a war of defense"): "train and be prepared." When he ended his talk he was "*loudly applauded*," took up a collection, and sold some items.[36]

On June 11 Special Agent Tucker reported on Harrison's June 5 talk and also raised the issue of Harrison's citizenship status.[37]

The newspaper coverage of Tulsa especially interested J. Edgar Hoover. On June 13 he wrote a memorandum to George F. Ruch in which he attached two clippings forwarded by "informant 800" (James Wormley Jones, who had infiltrated both the UNIA and the ABB). The material referred "to the activities of 'Herbert' Harrison, President of the Liberal [*sic*] league of negro Americans," who was reported to be "an alien, having emigrated from the West Indies." Citing "the statement attributed to Mr. Harrison," Hoover requested "a thorough investigation be made of the subject, with a view to effecting his deportation, if in fact he made statements inciting to riot."[38]

Agent P-138 (Boulin) continued his monitoring of Harrison, discussed a speech during the week of June 12, and noted that Harrison had become "so very active a few weeks ago in the re-organization of his 'Liberty League' of negro America." Boulin added that Harrison had "not [been] attracting very much attention for the past few days" and that, in addition, "the radicals" were holding "their regular street meeting[s], attracting moderate crowds," with "no sign of foreign interference."[39] In a follow-up June 24 report Boulin wrote that Harrison had spoken that afternoon at the Socialist Forum on Seventh Avenue on "The Negro and the World's [Race?] Problem."[40]

———

Harrison wrote on armed self-defense under the heading "Frightful Friendship vs. Self-Defense" in his June 18 *Negro World* column. He warned of the dangers that come from "friends" who, when "a race riot loses its American character of being a one-sided massacre of frightened and defenseless sheep and casualties," appear "on both sides." He also described how "the Associated Press and the other news-gathering agencies . . . magnify the Negro's losses and minimize the whites as a fixed policy, whose object is to convince Negroes that fighting back in self-defense is useless and dangerous—to them." Then, if anyone speaks in favor of "the new policy which American Negroes have been pursuing since 1917," these "good white friends insist that is 'bad advice'—for Negroes." They do this despite the fact that "it is the very policy in pursuit of which the United States Government is this year [1921] is spending ninety-four percent of its revenues on wars past, present and future." While papers like the *Times*, *World*, and *Journal* "denounce self-defense for Negroes on the editorial page," they "carry on the front page, in bold headlines, Secretary [of the Navy,

Edwin] Denby's address, in which he upholds and expounds the national policy, 'In times of peace prepare for war.'" Harrison added that "every reader of these same newspapers knows that, in the South, the Negro who is arrested, is absolutely at the mercy of any lawless mob," that "the officers of the law always fail to protect his life," and that "any colored community in the South may be invaded at any time by armed mobs eager and able to kill, burn and loot, at their own sweet will unchecked by the legal authorities whose power always breaks down when such communities require their protection."[41]

Harrison accordingly asked: "What can be the objection to Negroes, in such cases, arming in defense of their own lives and the majesty of that law which the mob has outraged?" It couldn't be "legality, because every statute book— even in the South—concedes that self-defense is legal and proper." The "real reason" was "that every one of these fake friends thinks it is a lesser evil that law-abiding Negroes should be killed by lawless whites, than that lawless whites should be killed, even in self-defense, by law-abiding Negroes, because this is, after all, 'a white man's country.'" He promptly added, with biting sarcasm, "Naturally, we Negroes are . . . unable to concede this point of precedence," and he advised that "such white newspapers are wasting their time and space advising us to let ourselves be killed. It would be much better if they develop the same amount of time and space to the 'cracker' in the South, and the enforcement of law and order among them."[42]

Harrison's remarks were a result of "white newspaper comments" on the June 5 meeting. He discussed the speech he had delivered that day and said that he had told "the inside facts of the Tulsa race riots, which the white newspapers had suppressed"; "insisted (as I have done since 1916) that . . . Negroes in America (like Irishmen in Ireland) were the victims of violence because they had been defenseless"; stressed that "lynching and pogroms were indulged in because they cost the aggressors nothing"; and argued that if "the prospective victims should put up a stout and costly defense the violence would be indulged in only by those who were willing to pay the price, and would be very much reduced even at that." He noted that such statements seemed "to rile" the *World*, *Times*, and *Journal*.[43]

He then described how the *"Times* lied" about the meeting "like a southern gentleman," the *World* "took the *Times'* report as gospel truth" and offered "a rather confused and illogical editorial," and the *Journal*, "whose owner [William Randolph Hearst] controls the photoplay, 'The Birth of a Nation,'" offered "to protect the dear Negroes from 'bad advice.'" Harrison emphasized "that the *World* deliberately lies when it says that any of the speakers advocated lawlessness in the East, West, North or South," and he appended the editorials from the *World* and the *Journal* with his answers to the *World* and *Times* so that readers might "compare Caucasian and Negro reasoning and decide, for themselves, which is worth their while."[44]

The timing of all this was important. As Harrison was arguing for armed self-defense, the House of Representatives Committee on the Judiciary was about to begin hearings on the constitutionality of a federal antilynching law. The hearings, which began on June 18, 1921, would be heated but again fail to lead to any antilynching legislation.[45]

The investigations of Harrison continued. On June 22 Cyril V. Briggs, editor of *The Crusader*, was interviewed by a representative of MI, and a report was written on June 23 by Parker Hitt, assistant chief of staff for MI, to the director of the MID. Briggs reportedly said: "The Liberty League was started some five years ago" by Harrison and was "to be an organization for the civil rights of the Negro, but soon disclosed its radical character." According to Briggs, "It never had more than a few hundred members," and Garvey had taken it over. Briggs also reportedly said that Harrison had "stopped his attacks on Garvey" and was "at present busy trying to revive the Liberty League," having held "a few meetings for that purpose." Since he hadn't "been able to obtain any members," Briggs considered the League "defunct." The report also indicated that Harrison still called himself "President of this League," and Edgar Grey, who dominates Harrison, was the secretary. The report added, "One of the chief reasons why Harrison, who is really a very intelligent and highly educated man and scholar, has failed in nearly all his undertakings is said to be his abnormal sexualism, in spite of the fact that he is the father of several children." Hitt's report concluded that "the Liberty League can be discountenanced as an organization. There are hardly any members and they have no influence with the colored people." The Briggs interview was certainly questionable and self-serving. There is no truth in the assertion that Garvey had taken over the Liberty League or that Grey dominated Harrison. Similarly, Briggs's claim that his African Blood Brotherhood was "a flourishing organization" with "about 23,000 members, scattered all over the world," including "five posts in New York City, with a membership of 1000," appears to be tremendously exaggerated—indications are that the ABB may have been a largely paper organization that received communist financial support to help put out its monthly publication *The Crusader.*[46]

On June 26 T. M. Reddy, acting division superintendent for the BI in New York, sent his June 25 report to Hoover, which described how *"Negro World* editor Harrison" was "active in several street meetings during the past week in the Harlem district and has taken advantage of every opportunity to stir up race hatred and urge all negroes 'to be prepared for the next race riot.'"[47] The response, probably written by Hoover, came from the Washington bureau "chief" Baley, on July 1. Reddy's attention was directed to Harrison's recent speeches and the related press coverage. Baley added, "According to our information, Harrison is an alien and in view of these recent speeches, it is desired that you make a complete and thorough investigation of this individual, looking toward deportation proceedings." It was noted, with no evidence provided, that Harrison had previously taken people's money while agitating for the Liberty League.[48]

One week later, on July 8, Bureau Special Agent W. R. Palmera, pursuant to instructions from Agent Tucker and based on "confidential information," prepared a report on Harrison, who he said was born in the Virgin Islands and had resided in the United States for fifteen (it was twenty-one) years. Palmera interviewed Charles Miller, the acting chief naturalization examiner in New York, to determine Harrison's "U.S. citizenship status" and "was advised that the purchase of the Virgin Islands from the Danish Government by the United States government did not automatically make the inhabitants of the islands United States citizen." Miller said he would "make [a] thorough investigation" of Harrison "to ascertain whether he is a immigrant [?] or a full citizen of the United States." Palmera added that his office would also "continue to investigate" Harrison, who, according to *Trow's Directory*, had lived at 231 West 134th Street from 1911 to 1918.[49] On July 10 Miller wrote to Palmera that the investigation of "whether a petition for his [Harrison's] naturalization was pending in either of the Naturalization Courts in New York County resulted in finding no record whatsoever."[50]

As Palmera was doing his investigation, Agent Boulin prepared a report on "NEGRO ACTIVITIES," for the period ending July 6. He indicated that Harrison continued to hold his Liberty League street meetings "every evening, advising the Negroes to be prepared for possible race riot." Harrison "again appealed for funds to continue his work," and Palmera reported that he heard that Harrison "does not work" (he was reportedly still being paid by Garvey at this time) and has no visible means of support "apart from the collection which he gets from the poor people."[51]

On July 13, 1921, as Harrison continued his Liberty League speaking, Garvey returned from the Caribbean. Garvey's return, which was not desired by the BI, was facilitated by the U.S. State Department. On the same day as Garvey's return, Boulin issued a report on "Negro Activities" that discussed the communist offer to Harrison. Baley (very possibly via Hoover), took quick action. On July 14 he wrote to Frank O'Connell of the New York City office and referred to the Bureau's July 1 correspondence, "requesting a thorough investigation" of Harrison "for the purpose of instigating deportation proceedings, if the evidence secured warrants such action." Baley pointed out that no reports had yet been received and asked O'Connell to "kindly forward some without delay." The BI, which had tried to keep Garvey out of the country, also wanted Harrison deported.[52]

On July 14 Palmera filed his report on Harrison for the period of July 10. Pursuant to instructions, he had interviewed Clerk Schmaltz, the recorder and superintendent of elections for Manhattan, in order to ascertain whether Harrison had registered to vote in the district covering 231 West 134th Street between 1915 and 1918, when he lived there. Palmera was told "no such name appears in the records for the years 1915, 1916, 1917, and 1918."[53]

Boulin, in his Bureau report for July 15, wrote that he "had another talk" with Grey that day "relative to the [African] Blood Brotherhood and the Harrison organization." Boulin said that Grey and Harrison told him "so far as they are concerned they had no inclination to throw in their lot with either the Socialists or Communists, the BLOOD BROTHERHOOD or any other organization for the benefit and control of white men. They refuse to be catspaws, as their cause is 'the Negro first.'"[54]

Charles J. Scully, the acting division superintendent, wrote to the BI chief (Baley), with an attention to Hoover, in reply to Baley's (probably Hoover's) letter of July 14. He called attention to the July 8 and 14 reports of Palmera and added that "further inquiry is being made regarding Harrison's citizenship status and his present activities, and you will be advised immediately upon the completion of this investigation."[55]

Boulin in his report of July 20 wrote that Harrison had held a Liberty League street meeting at 139th Street and Lenox Avenue and asked the audience "to pledge themselves not to fight for the U.S. again and go to war with Japan" but instead to oppose "lynchings and disfranchisement." He predicted a great war between the United States and Japan within two years and said they would be called upon to fight. He also reportedly "advised members of the Liberty League and all negroes" to refrain "until lynchings were stopped."[56] In his report for the period ending July 22, Boulin again noted "HARRISON kept his regular street meetings" and was "planning [something] . . . big."[57]

In his next report, on July 25, Boulin detailed an interview with Grey, secretary of the Liberty League, whom he described as a "very close personal friend" of Harrison and an "involuntary informant." Grey, who, with Harrison, was still holding regular street meetings each night, told Boulin that Harrison was "a native of the DANISH WEST INDIES and not a citizen of the United States" and that he had "never taken out his papers but had given the impression to the general public that he was a citizen." Boulin added that "so far as is known he [Harrison] has never voted, but spent his time as an agitator and living on his wits." Boulin also "learned" that natives of the former Danish islands "are not citizens of the U.S.," and orders were sent to the Elections Bureau not to allow them to register to vote. On July 28 Boulin again reported that Harrison held "his regular street meeting" that night and was "planning" a "big unemployment parade."[58]

Around July 25 BI Chief Baley (probably via Hoover) again wrote to Frank O'Donnell of the New York office. He was concerned about the recent reports on Harrison and suggested that O'Donnell "have a few of his speeches covered" as part of their investigation "in order that the Bureau may secure the required [materials] . . . to have instituted deportation proceedings."[59]

While the government investigations continued, deeper problems arose within the Garvey movement. Cyril A. Crichlow, the resident secretary of the UNIA at Monrovia, Liberia, wrote a June 12 letter of resignation to Garvey. He made it "effective at once," for reasons he would set forth in a "Special Personal Report to Your Excellency [Garvey] dated June 24, 1921" (and in a "Supplement" of July 4, 1921).[60] This report was just the tip of the iceberg; by the time the second convention was to begin in August, there were, according to Hill, "ominous signs of crisis within the movement." Officials expressed many doubts about the finances of the BSL and Garvey's fundraising regarding Liberia. The $70,000 in annual UNIA salaries approved at the 1920 convention could not be paid. By late August 1921, the *Yarmouth* was out of service, the (yacht) *Kanawha* was disabled in Cuban waters, and the (the Hudson River excursion boat) *Shadyside* was losing money. The BSL was at the brink of bankruptcy, and, in addition, a steep overall decline in the shipping business made its future prospects particularly gloomy.[61]

L. B. Weeks, the acting chief of staff for MI, on Governors Island in New York, reported on September 3 that various Harlem leaders opposed to Garvey were predicting his demise within two weeks. Crichlow's books were said to have been confiscated by DA William A. Hayward, and prominent officers were leaving the UNIA, including Chaplain General George A. McGuire, Dr. F. Wilcom Ellegor, Richard H. Tobitt, and Assistant-President-General Dr. J. D. Gordon.[62]

Amid these difficulties, Garvey held the second UNIA convention determined to expose and remove UNIA and BSL officials he blamed for the troubles. At the convention, his leadership came under direct challenge by Cyril Briggs's ABB. Briggs, a member of the Workers Party, outwardly offered unity to Garvey while also developing more pronounced criticisms of him. At the convention the ABB raised serious questions about the BSL and published convention bulletins highlighting controversies. Its members were then expelled from the convention by Garvey. During the convention Garvey also attacked other

Black leaders he perceived as his opponents, often labeling them advocates of "social equality" between the races (which he contrasted with his newly advocated philosophy of "racial purity"). In particular, Garvey focused on Du Bois, whose Second Pan-African Congress was beginning in London and who had investigated Garvey and the BSL and offered critical comments in the December 1920 and January 1921 *Crisis*.[63]

As the UNIA convention progressed, Harrison continued to hold his nightly street meetings and, according to a "General Intelligence Bulletin" of the DOJ, on August 6 he again advised his audience "to prepare for another race riot which may take place at any moment."[64] Agent Boulin in his report for August 8 cited a special meeting at 138th Street and Lenox Avenue that evening, where Harrison "spoke to a large crowd that almost blocked the sidewalk" and again "called for members to join the LIBERTY LEAGUE" and prepare "to meet the next race riot."[65]

On Friday August 15 Harrison wrote in his diary that "Garvey's second convention is here" and that it was "going to pieces in his hand." At the same time, according to Boulin, Harrison continued his nightly Liberty League meetings and appeals.[66] In his report for the period ending August 21, Boulin noted that Harrison, assisted by Grey, now cited recent race friction in Massachusetts and Ku Klux Klan activities in New Jersey at their nightly meeting, in which they "urge[d] the negroes to be prepared for trouble." Boulin added that "as a rule, every time there is a race riot or a near riot H. Harrison capitalizes" and that "Hubert Harrison is a most dangerous and disturbing faction [*sic*] among the thousands of idle Negroes who walk the streets of Harlem, listening to his militant talk."[67]

Boulin next reported that on August 23 he had visited a Liberty League meeting held by Harrison and Grey on Lenox Avenue, at which there was "quite a large crowd of negroes assembled to hear them until 11:45 p.m." Grey also spoke with Boulin and reportedly told him that they were "expecting to start a magazine soon and that this magazine will be the mouthpiece of the Liberty League."[68]

In his report for the period ending August 30, Boulin, possibly based on self-promoting conversations with Grey, reported that Grey was secretary and Harrison president of the Liberty League and that "Harrison and Gray are like twin[e?] and lifelong friends and will die for each other" (there is no basis for this statement); that Harrison felt that Garvey should make him a high officer in the UNIA (there is no basis for this); and that "Gray joined the African Blood Brotherhood just to get even with DOMINGO and the other socialists group who were against Harrison because he refused to join them in the terms offered by STOKES, when they were all invited down to her home . . . months ago."[69]

On August 27 the acting division superintendent of the BI in New York, Edward J. Brennan, sent a "Special Report on Radical Activities in Greater New

York District" to William J. Burns, the Bureau director in Washington. Brennan reiterated that Harrison was "nightly holding street corner meetings throughout the negro district in Harlem," dwelling "particularly on the so-called race friction in Massachusetts and New Jersey and on the Ku Klux Klan." He emphasized that Harrison was "intelligent and well educated and takes advantage of any opportunity to spread radical propaganda."[70] That same day, the *Negro World* mentioned that Harrison was teaching "a free class in Negro history" Monday nights at 149 West 136th Street "under the auspices of the Liberty League."[71]

———

Edgar Grey, whom Harrison reportedly never liked nor trusted as much as the government thought he did, was apparently quite willing to help the government in its investigation of Garvey. The BI was looking into alleged Garvey violations of the White Slave Act and into "information regarding the payment of a sum of money for Garvey to . . . [obtain a] visa which would enable him to return" to the United States. Frank B. Faulhaber, a BI special agent in New York, in a report for the period ending August 29, indicated that he interviewed Grey, who was "anxious to assist the government in this matter" and "furnished the hearsay evidence in his possession concerning the allegation that Garvey paid someone $2000 to be allowed to re-enter the United States." According to Faulhaber, Grey said he had first met Garvey in 1917 and that it was "common gossip in the community" that Garvey's "Vice-Attorney General, whose name is [William Clarence] MATTHEWS, (a Harvard Graduate and practicing attorney)" approached "HENRY LINCOLN JOHNSON, Negro National Political [figure] . . . at Washington, D.C., asking that he use his good office for the purpose of convincing the State Department that should Mr. Garvey not be allowed to return to the United States that negro citizens who had invested moneys in various of his organizations would sustain losses." It was also "rumored" that Johnson "called on Secretary of State, [Charles Evans] Hughes, and so informed him; whereupon Mr. Garvey was made to promise in a written statement that he would not . . . [make] inflammatory statements in his speeches against the American Government or the white people of this country, upon penalty of being deported."[72]

Confidential Informant 800 (Jones) wrote to George F. Ruch on September 4 that on Friday morning, September 2, he had met the attorney Matthews and Cleveland Jacques on the street and that Mathews had said "that a man by the name of Anderson in the New York office of the Dept of Justice had sent for him and had asked him what about the $4000 (four thousand dollars) that Garvey had paid to get back in the country." Jones added, "I think this fellow [Edgar] Grey is working both ends from the middle and is double crossing everybody he comes in contact with. . . . Grey is such a liar that I don't believe anything he says."[73]

In his September 3 report L. B. Weeks of MI in New York reported that Harrison was still being paid by Garvey even though "he does not send anything in for the paper" and "is still conducting meetings nightly and attacking the great leader, Garvey, without using his name." Weeks added, "It is stated that Garvey is afraid to dismiss him."[74]

In late August the UNIA convention wound to a close. The ABB's third weekly *Bulletin*, "Negro Congress at a Standstill—Many Delegates Dissatisfied with Failure to Produce Results," was distributed on August 25. Garvey called them traitors and Bolshevists, and a resolution was put forward and passed calling for their expulsion.[75] After the 1921 UNIA convention the ABB's criticism of Garvey intensified.[76]

————

During the spring and summer of 1921 Harrison produced a flow of writings, primarily in the *Negro World* but in other periodicals as well. He did this amid the growing crisis in the Garvey movement and as he tried to resurrect the Liberty League. He also engaged in some correspondence with leading literary lights of the day, including Eugene O'Neill, H. L. Mencken, and Theodore Lothrop Stoddard.

In the May 7 *Negro World* Harrison wrote on "The Harlem Hospital," an important topic in the community in which he lived. With the devastating impact of the 1918 influenza pandemic undoubtedly in his mind, he began by pointing out that the "public hospital" in the "modern city" was "a piece of social insurance against disease and its consequences." As such, it was "no more a public charity" than "public schools and libraries," which provided "social insurance against ignorance and its social consequences." If administrators of such institutions, paid by public funds, failed "in the performance of the public duties," then they should "receive severe castigation from that public whose taxes furnish the funds which they waste."[77]

From these general remarks Harrison moved to particulars of Harlem Hospital's administration, which "for quite a long time" had been "a stench in the nostrils of the Negro people of Harlem" and "should have been changed." His first example concerned a seriously sick woman who had to wait over two hours for an ambulance before having a young intern in the ambulance, on the basis of a mere cough, "hastily" diagnose "tuberculosis." At the hospital the woman "was stripped" and "let to lie naked . . . for four hours" as a doctor "insultingly inquired why she had waited till after midnight to come in." After several days of starvation, she called her husband to go home. Subsequently, doctors from Mt. Sinai Hospital, "after due examination," declared they were "unable to find any evidence of tuberculosis." The woman continued in good health four years later, with no sign of the "dread disease," which the "ignorant undergraduate pronounced so infallibly." In a second case, a woman "lay in the hospital for three days with a temperature of 104 and a pulse of 150 constant, presenting a clear case of pneumonia." Another "ignorant doctor" diagnosed "tuberculosis" and, "if she had not been taken by her relatives to a competent colored physician," she would have died. In a third case, "a Negro child was sent from public school to the Harlem Hospital for medical attention" at the two o'clock clinic. By 2:05 the medical student in charge of the child had not appeared, and the child went home unattended. Harrison concluded that as long as such "carelessness, ignorance and cruelty continue the Negro population of upper New York City can have no confidence in the management of what should be a well-ordered public institution." He urged "the city fathers" to "conduct a thorough examination into the treatment of patients and the general management of the Harlem Hospital."[78]

Related to these community concerns, in August 1921 Harrison prepared some informal notes on community-related "Liberty League demands." They included:

1. 5,000 in Bank for Food Relief During Winter.
2. Municipal Works, street cleaning . . .
3. Negro judicial district & court house
4. Negro principal for New School
5. Two Negro Assemblymen[79]

In the May 7 *Negro World* Harrison wrote "The Racial Roots of Education," which discussed social inheritance. He began by defining education "as that process by which the ripened generation brings to bear upon the rising generation the accumulated knowledge and experience of the past and present generations to fit it for the business of life." That definition applied "to human beings everywhere and on every level of culture" and implied that "the educational machinery and its effectiveness" would be "determined directly by the level of general intelligence in any society" and that "educational methods" would "vary in societies according to their social structure, their mode of social functioning and, above all . . . the purpose." It also implied a belief in a process of social inheritance. Harrison explained:

As we inherit our houses and lands, our arts and institutions from our ancestors, so also do we inherit our bodies and minds, our aptitudes and inclinations from thme [*sic*]. Modify them how we may, they still remain our original inheritance. Thus the social structure and purposes which determine our educational ideals and methods are in their turn determined by our social inheritance; thus the marrow of tradition is in the very bones of our being, and through the eyes of the individual soul looks out the social ancestry—the race.[80]

Harrison argued that "race may mean whatever you choose it to mean, as long as your meaning is clear and definite" and that "no argument maintaining the superiority or inferiority of any race can be erected on this foundation": he would "merely argue for the difference." He admitted, for "argument's sake, the converting power of certain educational processes" but still contended "that the things which you have to convert differ in racial instances." "Tradition, history, literature, art and science relate us to our past," and if you "change any one of these factors" then "you change the racial result."[81]

These views were probably included in a talk Harrison delivered for the People's Educational Forum at Lafayette Hall on Sunday, May 8. They also elicited a rejoinder. The *New York Dispatch* reported that two weeks later Richard B. Moore lectured on "Racial Imperatives."[82]

In the *Negro World* of May 14 Harrison wrote "Stupidity and the NAACP," in which he pointedly asked: "Do the letters N.A.A.C.P. also mean the Nincompoops' Association for the Advertisement of Certain Plays?" His comments were prompted by the white supremacist film *The Birth of a Nation*, which had "dropped down to the level of a third-class attraction, in a fair way to be forgotten," when "the pig-headed enthusiasts of the N.A.A.C.P." decided to "picket the theatre in uniform and placards and thus elevate it to the level of a first-class sensation and money-maker for its promoters." To Harrison, this was sheer "stupidity" by a "collection of amiable idiots" who thought they could "stop a play by picketing." If they "really believe[d] that 'publicity' of this sort" would "turn white theatregoers away from an evening's enjoyment," they were "the simplest fools that ever wandered through Wonderland." Harrison knew a white friend who went to see the play after being "prompted" by "seeing the demonstration advertised in the daily papers," and he wondered: "How many thousands of white people will do the same thing for the same reason?"[83]

In analyzing the situation, Harrison observed that the NAACP's "strong point" is "publicity"—and they think they "will end lynching," "put down Jim Crow," and "abolish disfranchisement by 'publicity.'" Yet, in this "first chance which their particular brand of 'publicity' had to function freely it made an ass of itself." The film's producers "would be willing to pay a thousand dollars into the 'Campaign Fund' of the Nincompoops' Association for the very generous 'publicity' which they so freely and foolishly give to that play." Harrison concluded that the NAACP "needs brains very badly," but if they can't get them, it is "hightime for a more intelligent group to take the field," since "it certainly couldn't do anything to look more like a doddering idiot than the N.A.A.C.P. had done."[84]

A Harrison diary entry on the NAACP from this period is revealing. Six weeks before publishing this column, on Monday night, April 11, he was approached by a young man, whose name he didn't know, "on behalf of the N.A.A.C.P." He was asked "in their official name to take part as a street speaker in their great drive for ten thousand members in New York City." Harrison wrote in his diary: "I gave him hell."[85]

———

In the July 16 *Negro World* appeared "What's in a Name: An Open Letter from a White Man to the People Who Have No Home [Name]." The article was listed as being by "Edwin T. Duke per Hubert Harrison." When published, the last word in the subtitle of the article was changed from "Name" to "Home." This was apparently done against the intent of, and without the permission of, the author. Harrison corrected his copy of the article in his scrapbook, as was his practice with both typographical and content errors. The letter began with a Garvey-like greeting: "Fellowmen of the Negro Race!" It said that the author had read "Take the Negro Out of the Negro Problem," an article written under the name John Crosby Gordon in the *New York News* of June 23, and thought the readers "might relish a little good advice coming from a white fellowman." He began by asking: "What is really the little matter outstanding between your people and mine? Isn't it the fact that we insist on giving you less justice, security, protection and pay than we ourselves get?" If this was true, "Duke" continued, "haven't you got sense enough to see that it is a question of things—status, relationships, acts—and not a question of names?" Duke explained that the writer of a recent *New York News* article "insists that 'When the [word] Negro disappears from the popular mind [the white people of] the United States will see that this is a united nation." To this, Duke replied, "Do you think that any of us who hate and hurt you now will love and help you because you change your racial designation? . . . Call yourself or be called Negro, colored people, Afro-Americans, Race men or Africannibals," and "you will still have the same hard fight to make."[86]

On August 6 the *Negro World* ran "As to the Name Negro," a letter from Harrison, identified by his "H.H.H.," which referred "to the article by the white man two weeks previous about the race which has no name." Harrison began by taking up "the matter of Señor Jaime Gil," who, writing under the name of John Crosby Gordon in the June 23 *New York News*, insisted: "We should 'take the "Negro" out of the Negro problem.'" Harrison pointed out that "ten years ago Señor Gil's own name was Mr. James Clark" but that he had "seen fit to change it." Harrison speculated that "the facility of changing personal names may have

Figure 10.1. Frances Marion Harrison, c. 1921. Frances Marion Harrison (October 21, 1909–December 18, 1932), eldest daughter of Hubert Harrison and Irene "Lin" Horton Harrison. Frances did well in Junior High School at PS 90 and then attended Wadleigh High School (215 West 114th Street, the first public high school for girls in New York City). In 1926 Frances worked at the Lafayette Theatre, and in November of that year she left for Pittsburgh with a role in the Irvin C. Miller show *Desires of 1927.* Frances died of tuberculosis in 1932, five years after her father's death. *Source:* Hubert H. Harrison Papers, Box 15, Folder 13, Rare Book and Manuscript Library, Columbia University Library. See https://dlc.library.columbia.edu/catalog/cul:n8pk0p2q4k.

misled him into thinking that changing a racial name is equally easy, irresponsible, and whimsical." On July 16 the matter had been "dealt with under the form of a letter from a white man to 'the race that has no name.' (The printers made it 'the race that has no home.')" Because that answer "was brief and ignored all but the gist of his article," Señor Gil assumed it was inadequate. The *Negro World* therefore took the liberty of reprinting the "definitive answer, written by a former editor [probably W. A. Domingo] of *The Negro World,* in June 1919." This would close their side of the case, and if Señor Gil was not satisfied, "millions of Negroes . . . undoubtedly will be."[87]

Harrison wrote "An Apology" in the August 13 *Negro World*. "Like most other men I dislike to seem in the wrong," adding, "I dislike even more to do wrong to another." Therefore, as "a duty of contrition" he pointed out that the previous week "I was guilty of 'fouling' my opponent John Crosby Gordon." The matter "of his name or names was not a proper part of my reply to him and was really a violation of the ethics of the controversy." Harrison "tender[ed] him this public apology," which he hoped would be accepted "in the spirit in which it is offered." Harrison, however, "still remained unconvinced of the value of his arguments on the merits of the case in controversy."[88]

Harrison's "The Negro and the Census" in the August 27 *Negro World* cited a recent *New York Age* reprint of a letter from Professor Kelly Miller, of Howard University, to the director of the census that focused on "the fact that the white men of America habitually tell lies about the Negro people." Harrison remarked that "figures don't lie; but it is a notorious fact that liars do figure— especially in the census office," where the practice went back as far as 1850. In Harriet Beecher Stowe's "greatest book," *The Key to Uncle Tom's Cabin*, one could see "detailed proof of this falsifying." More recently, the American Statistic Association had brought the matter before the U.S. Senate, but "despite the revelations of deliberate lying, these errors were not corrected and the controversy [was] forgotten." Harrison saw the "present [census] Director's aversion to correcting the errors" as "part and parcel of a definite purpose historically established."[89]

Harrison argued that "of all the available instruments of control in the hands of the white overlords the lie is the most effective for subverting the spirit of the subject races and classes," and "in the case of the English-speaking Negroes," it had been used "with deadly effect." The census showed "that the people classed as Negroes have increased and are increasing far beyond the comfortable expectations of the whites." Using the 1850 census, *DeBow's Review* had "prophesied that the Negro in America would have died out by 1922, but, in this, like "so much American 'science' the wish was father to the thought." In fact, "if it had not been for the great tide of white immigrants into America from 1800 to 1921, this country would now have had a population largely Negroid." Harrison had heard it said "that the breeding powers of the Negro are so great that he can double his own population in half the time required by the whites." The "whites who are in authority" were "worried at this power of expansion, especially in the face of the shrinkage in the birth-rate of the American whites." Though "lynching, race riots, degradation and slums" had "failed to decrease their numbers," now "white physicians . . . [were] recommending operations which leave Negro women incapable of child-bearing."

But, as the number of Negro physicians increased, that move was defeated, and "whites" had to "fall back upon their great god [god crossed out] Lie, to help them to a spurious appearance of triumph. Hence the census figures." In response, Harrison urged, "we Negroes must let it be known that the great U.S. census is a lying document so far, at least, as the Negro population is concerned, and that it stands discredited."[90]

In the September 3 *Negro World* Harrison wrote a tribute to his friend, Arthur A. Schomburg, grand secretary of the Prince Hall body of Ancient Free and Accepted Masons of New York and secretary of the Negro Society for Historical Research. The society was established "to collect and preserve the memorials of Negro achievement" and "to diffuse among the descendants of the Africans . . . some knowledge of their nobler past." To Harrison, it was as "a book collector" that Schomburg "deserve[d] to be best known and remembered by the people of his race." He had traveled extensively in pursuit of books, and his efforts were well known "to English, French, German, Dutch, Danish and Spanish booksellers." His "collection of books dealing with the Negro" was "the greatest in the United States" and a "compact, systematic and well-ordered engine of research."[91]

Though Harrison prided himself "on knowing something of Negro history and literature," he "unhesitatingly declare[d] that Schomburg's knowledge on these points" was "at least eight or ten times as extensive." Schomburg, however, was "emphatically not a bookish recluse, but a well-rounded personality, a man of the world . . . 'a regular feller.'" His native language was Spanish (he was born in Puerto Rico and his mother, Mary Joseph, was from St. Croix), and he spoke English "with something of a Spanish intonation." He was "unrivalled" for "sheer erudition on Negro history and literature."[92]

Harrison encouraged him to "write a book on Negro history." Schomburg, however, was "like the late Lord Acton" (John Emerich Edward Dalberg Acton), the planner of "the great Cambridge Modern History" and "great English scholar [who] had more learning than any of his ponderous German compeers; yet he was always too busy pursuing knowledge to turn out a single volume worthy of his great powers" and left, as far as Harrison knew, only "two volumes of historical essays." Schomburg had similarly "only" provided "a few occasional papers": an "ably edited edition" of Phillis Wheatley's poems and a "splendid pamphlet" entitled *Racial Integrity: A Plea for the Establishment of a Chair of Negro History in Our Schools and Colleges*. That last piece furnished "knowledge and inspiration" and packed "more precise information about the great Negroes of the past than can be found in many a large and learned tome." Schomburg ranged "from Aesop to Crispus Attucks" and discussed "Negroes of Europe, Africa, America and the West Indies" as well as "savants, philosophers, divines, poets, warriors and educators." Harrison concluded, "If Schomburg would but write as he reads when the sun of the New Negro shall be shining in the zenith of its glory to come, his name would be hailed with acclaim as that of the first great historiographer of the Africans of the dispersion."[93]

———

In the September 10 *Negro World* Harrison wrote "Hands Across the Sea," about imperialism and Haiti. It was one of his most forceful critiques of imperialism and a moving plea to action on behalf of the Haitian people. He began by defining the general nature of the problem and drew his first two paragraphs from his "Imperialist America" review of Scott Nearing's *The American Empire* in the April 30 *Negro World*. Those paragraphs discussed how "the most dangerous phase of capitalism" was "imperialism," how "the lands of 'backward' peoples are brought within the central influence of the capitalist economic system and the subjection of black, bro[w]n and other colored workers to the rigors of 'the white man's burden' comes as a consequence of the successful exploitation of white workers at home," and how this "binds them both in an international of opposition to the continuance of the capitalist regime." He then added, "Most Americans who are able to see this process more or less clearly in the case of other nations are unable to see the same process implicit and explicit in the career of their own."[94]

After this general description Harrison discussed "the present plight of the Haytian people," which clearly resulted from "the aims of our own American imperialists." He wrote how, in Haiti, "a people of African descent" had "their government suppressed and their liberties destroyed by the Navy Department of the United States without even the slightest formality of a declaration of war by the United States Congress as required by the Constitution." U.S. "'cracker' marines" installed a puppet president, Monsieur (Phillipe Sudre) D'Artiguenave, "to carry out their will" as "the legislative bodies of the erstwhile republic" were "either suppressed or degraded," as "unoffending black citizens" were "wantonly butchered in cold blood," and as "thousands" were "forced into slavery to labor on the military roads without pay." This was "American imperialism in its stark, repulsive nakedness."[95]

The fight that would soon be waged in Congress for the restoration of Haitian rights was, however, "receiving no help from the millions of Negroes," though it was "high time that it should." The opportunity was present—if the "Negro American . . . would use our votes here in an intelligent, purposeful way we could at least make our voices heard and heeded in Washington on behalf of our brothers in black who are suffering seven hundred miles away." There could be "gigantic propaganda meetings in such places as [Boston's] Faneuil Hall, Madison Square Garden and the Negro churches" and agitation

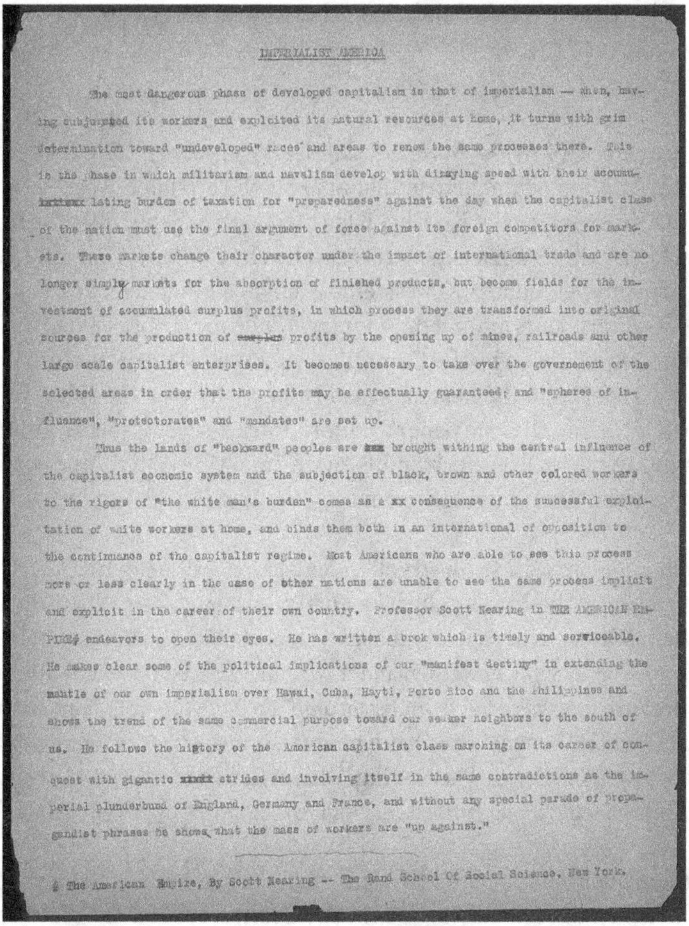

IMPERIALIST AMERICA

The most dangerous phase of developed capitalism is that of imperialism — when, having subjugated its workers and exploited its natural resources at home, it turns with grim determination toward "undeveloped" races and areas to renew the same processes there. This is the phase in which militarism and navalism develop with dizzying speed with their accumulating burden of taxation for "preparedness" against the day when the capitalist class of the nation must use the final argument of force against its foreign competitors for markets. These markets change their character under the impact of international trade and are no longer simply markets for the absorption of finished products, but become fields for the investment of accumulated surplus profits, in which process they are transformed into original sources for the production of profits by the opening up of mines, railroads and other large scale capitalist enterprises. It becomes necessary to take over the governement of the selected areas in order that the profits may be effectually guaranteed; and "spheres of influence", "protectorates" and "mandates" are set up.

Thus the lands of "backward" peoples are brought withing the central influence of the capitalist economic system and the subjection of black, brown and other colored workers to the rigors of "the white man's burden" comes as a consequence of the successful exploitation of white workers at home, and binds them both in an international of opposition to the continuance of the capitalist regime. Most Americans who are able to see this process more or less clearly in the case of other nations are unable to see the same process implicit and explicit in the career of their own country. Professor Scott Nearing in THE AMERICAN EMPIRE¥ endeavors to open their eyes. He has written a book which is timely and serviceable. He makes clear some of the political implications of our "manifest destiny" in extending the mantle of our own imperialism over Hawai, Cuba, Hayti, Porto Rico and the Philippines and shows the trend of the same commercial purpose toward our weaker neighbors to the south of us. He follows the history of the American capitalist class marching on its career of conquest with gigantic strides and involving itself in the same contradictions as the imperial plunderbund of England, Germany and France, and without any special parade of propagandist phrases he shows what the mass of workers are "up against."

¥ The American Empire, By Scott Nearing -- The Rand School Of Social Science, New York.

Figure 10.2. Hubert Harrison, "Imperialist America: Review of *The American Empire* by Scott Nearing," April 30, 1921, page 1. Hubert Harrison begins by explaining that "the most dangerous phase of developed capitalism is that of imperialism." He then elaborates on that point in his review of Nearing's work, which he describes as "a worthy contribution to the literature of radical economic thought." *Source:* Hubert H. Harrison Papers, Box 5, Folder 3, Rare Book and Manuscript Library, Columbia University Library. See https://dlc.library.columbia.edu/catalog/cul:msbcc2fsm2.

"for the withdrawal of the forces of the American occupation, as the Irish did on behalf of Ireland," in our newspapers. A "gigantic petition with a million signatures" could be carried to Congress, and "even a 'silent protest parade' would become us better than this slavish apathy and servile acquiescence in which we are now sunk." Harrison emphasized that "French, British and Belgian imperialism is a limb of the same tree of white domination on which our home-made branch grows" and that "the Negro American is now on trial before the eyes of the world."[96]

———

In his September 24 *Negro World* column Harrison wrote "The Ku Klux Klan in the Past," an important article that applauded the "good work" of the *New York World* "in exposing the Ku Klux Klan of today." In September the *New York World* had run a three-week exposé, researched by Rowland Thomas. It focused on Klan violence, estimated Klan strength at half a million, and was carried by eighteen leading papers around the country. While the report was partly responsible for an investigation by the Committee on Rules of the House of Representatives, the report and the hearings also helped publicize the Klan. Harrison, in his article, feared that the paper's editorial writers were "just as ill-informed concerning the facts of American history as most educated Americans are." Harrison quoted disapprovingly from the *New York World*:

> Nobody familiar with reconstruction legislation will deny that there was justification for the Klan's political activities, although its methods in innumerable cases were brutal, criminal and indefensible. Its practices of intimidation were uniformly cowardly, and it was tolerated by decent Southerners only because they were living under an autocratic government imposed upon them by Federal bayonets and were ready to use any weapon on which they could lay their hands. . . . The Ku Klux Klan of Reconstruction days even at its worst represented an organized resistance to political oppression only.[97]

To Harrison such "justification by concession of that band of bloody midnight assassins which terrorized Negroes in the South from 1865 to 1870" revealed "an abysmal ignorance of the proven facts of that period" and caused "educated black men to wonder whether educated American whites ever read any sourcebooks of information on American history." Harrison didn't contend such a view was "dishonest"; he "merely insist[ed] that it isn't true." The facts of Reconstruction were recorded in the report of the Congressional Committee of Investigation, which it appeared the editors had not read. To overcome such ignorance Harrison recommended the second volume of James G. Blaine's *Twenty Years of Congress*, William Garrott Brown's *The Lower South in the Civil War*, Alexander Johnson's article in *Labor's Cyclopedia of American History*, Carl Schurz's *Report*, Edwin Lawrence Godkind's series in *The Nation* in 1865 and 1866, and the third volume of Albert Bushnell Hart's *American History Told by Contemporaries*. He felt these volumes would show "that the Ku Klux Klan was organized in 1865 (the date *is* very important), during the interregnum between the dastardly murder of Abraham Lincoln and the convening of Congress which took place in December of that year."[98]

In that period "the people of the South were given an absolutely free hand to deal with the Negro and their other domestic problems as they should see fit." Those "(who had been defeated) proceeded to pass laws reducing the Negroes to a new condition of serfdom more galling and hopeless than slavery had been." In Alabama and elsewhere "it was decreed that any [former] slave who did not possess $250 cash, should be declared a vagrant, taken into custody and sentenced to hard labor on the public works for six months." This was described by Blaine as "the meanest piece of legislation on the statute books of any civilized State." On such labor Mobile, Alabama, and other southern cities were rebuilt. In addition, "Negro children were ordered 'bound out' to their former masters to work without pay until they were twenty-one." It was also "made a crime for three Negroes to converse together; they were ordered not to practice the trades of carpenter, wheelright [sic], blacksmith, etc., unless they could first pay to the state several hundred dollars." Harrison stressed: "All these things were done during the summer, fall and winter of 1865," and "it was during that period that the Ku Klux Klan was organized." The date was "approximately fixed by the testimony of Gen. Nathaniel B. Forrest, who became its head upon the first general reorganization of the Klan." Harrison cited the testimony of Brown in his book *The Lower South in American History* and the book *Ku Klux Klan: Its Origin, Growth, and Disbandment*, by John C. Lester and Daniel Love Wilson, two Klansmen.[99]

With "the date of its organization thus fixed," Harrison considered it "an evident absurdity to argue," as had the *New York World* "and so many others," that "the Klan was organized to put down 'black supremacy,' or to keep the Negroes from the ballot box." The "southern Negro was not given the ballot box until 1866 [HH changed it to 1868]!" and "it was the attitude of the South toward the Negro as illustrated by the Ku Klux killings and whippings, and the legislation above described (the celebrated Black Code), which forced Congress to give the ballot to the Negro in order that he might be able to protect himself from the unreconstructed slavists." When Congress met in December 1865, it "considered the Black Code and the other facts of the situation" and "found that, if the fruits of victory were not to go to the losers in the conflict, it had to take some drastic steps." First it passed "the Thirteenth Amendment to the United States Constitution, forever abolishing slavery; since Lincoln's proclamation was only a war measure and did not free all the slaves." Congress "made the acceptance of this amendment a condition precedent to re-entry into the union and submitted it as such to the conquered Confederacy." The "South would not accept it," and Harrison quoted Congressman James A. Garfield from memory that "The last one of the sinful ten" had "flung back into our teeth with scorn the magnanimous offer to a generous nation." This was the clearest "indication of the rebels' intentions toward the Negro." Congress "thereupon divided the South into military districts, each of which was under the command of a major-general of the United States Army, and proceeded to elaborate and enact the Fourteenth and Fifteenth Amendments, and to govern the rebellious States under martial law until they should accept the three war amendments." Meanwhile, the government strove to implement civil reconstruction, and when "in 1868, the South was reconstructed, the Negroes, as the largest body of people . . . loyal to the United States, aided by white ex-soldiers from the North and a handful of white Southerners, played, of necessity, a large part in that process." Less than two years after "the Negro got the ballot, the Ku Klux was disbanded."[100]

These were "the essential facts of history" relating to the Ku Klux of the past. They were confirmed in the Sunday, September 11 *World*, when the former Klansman Colonel N. F. Thompson said that he "became a member of the Klan in 1866, as did nearly every Confederate soldier." Nevertheless, "white Americans of education, as ignorant of their country's history as [Klan leader] 'Colonel' [William J.] Simmons and Tom Dixon [author of *The Clansman*, the basis of the film *Birth of a Nation*]," kept repeating "that the earlier Klan was really organized 'to save white civilization from the domination of ignorance.'" To Harrison, was it not "high time that white Americans cease being so grossly ignorant of the facts of their history?"[101]

Harrison was also particularly critical of the fact that "our Negro 'scholars' and near-scholars, professors, educators and journalists" had "never set forth these facts, but have accepted instead the historical glosses of white people from James Ford Rhodes to *The World's* writers and readers." He concluded that these scholars were themselves "grossly ignorant" and had "never done any independent study of the original sources of American history as it affects their race." While they prated "about 'alien education,'" they were "either too lazy or too monkeyfied to sift facts" themselves. He emphasized: "The Negro race needs real scholars and real students now as it never did before, and they must come from this generation of Negroes."[102]

He also called attention to the fact that "if the revived Ku Klux had not gone out and meddled with Catholics, Jews and other foreigners no great newspaper would ever have organized its forces to hunt them down." He considered it "the duty of our editors and publicists" to point out that "if white Americans ignore" disfranchisement and other injustices "because they only affect Negroes, the time must come, sooner or later, when these things will also be set in motion against whites." On "that basis"—of "their self-interest"—Harrison believed "whites" could be enlisted "to investigate and squelch those other things." He stressed: "Intelligent statesmanship for the weak consists in making allies of the strong who stand within the same danger."[103]

———————

Harrison's main reviews in the period from May to August 1921 were in the *Negro World*. He did, however, review Dr. Algernon Sidney Crapsy's *The Ways of the Gods* in the May 4 Indianapolis *Freeman*. This review criticized the author's "excited, belated rationalism" and "rambling nature," which made "a hash of anthropology theology and history." Harrison thought Crapsy's claims that "Moses led a labour-strike in Egypt" and "early Christianity was a labour-movement" were made "with a serene unconsciousness of mythical elements in the records" and that his view of "the evolution of Greek and Roman religion" was "equally bizarre."[104]

In the May 14 *Negro World* Harrison reviewed *The Real South Africa* by Ambrose Pratt, an Australian journalist who had visited South Africa with Australia's prime minister, Andrew Fisher, in 1910. Harrison considered Pratt's book, which was "packed full of facts" and "well documented," to be "one of the most informing and courageous books" on the subject. It told "a story which the whites of South Africa would rather not see in print." Pratt made South Africa appear not as "an earthly paradise for the white race" but as "an imposing edifice, gorgeously gilt on the outside but reeking with the stenches of decay on the inside." He provided "the sinister spectacle of a race in the process of collapsing under the weight of 'the white man's burden' which it was driven by greed and pride to assume in the course of capitalistic expansion and imperial conquest." Pratt described "a 'superior' race, with laziness, crime, disease and arrogance eating its very vitals out." He also depicted "the white man, with all his parade of 'civilization,' wilting under the fierce sun of Africa, while the dominated black increases in numbers, strength, solidarity and the sense of power—in spite of oppression, subjection and outrage." Pratt reasoned that in light of "the wind that he has sown and the whirlwind which he must reap the South African white is in an unenviable position."[105]

South Africa, between the Zambesi and the Cape of Good Hope, was an enormous stretch of 1,250,000 square miles thinly populated by Bantus, Bush Men, and Hottentots. Over four centuries "Boers and British, Dutch, German, French and Portuguese" had "endeavored to subjugate and exploit various portions of this immense area," and, ultimately, the British, "who beat the world in swiping everything which has not been nailed down—and most things that are," finally "succeeded in ousting from political control all the other Europeans." They "consolidated the sub-continent under the title of the Union of South Africa, in which Boers and Britons subsist upon the underpaid labor of millions of aborigines." The "significance of this experiment" was that it was "the first attempt made by a white European population in historic times to establish themselves as denizens of the Black Continent." Previously, "overlordship, not settlement," had been "the only practicable form of exploiting African resources," and "white men . . . confined their control over Africans in Africa to the administration of government and the control of trade and commerce."[106]

In establishing the South African Union, explained Harrison, "the European believed that he had found a section of the continent suitable for his habitation where he could live and rear his children, duplicate his peculiar form of civilization, and add another permanent extension to the white areas of the world." These "whites," however, were "'corrupted and enervated by their long and uninterrupted dependence on the blacks,'" and the "total white population" scarcely exceeded "1,200,000 souls." To Harrison, the "natives" were "so physically vigorous and mentally virile," their numbers so vast, "their rate of natural increase . . . so great and rapid," and "their desire to exceed the bounds of the white man's caste prejudice . . . so keen," that it was "obvious that their aspirations must be restricted and repressed as a condition precedent to the preservation of white supremacy." This "recognition of white dependence and black strength" gave rise to the "policy of brutal repression," which paralleled "in almost every respect that of the 'crackers' of the southern United States": "Lynching, segregation disfranchisement and educational starvation" were "rampant there as here." In addition, as "the South African 'cracker,' like . . . [the American] variety, declines in physical and mental vigor, becomes increasingly lazy, vicious, degenerate and washed-out"; his "children grow up illiterate and shiftless and his women fail to breed as they should." For Harrison, it seemed "as if fate had decreed as a law of inexorable retribution that wherever the white race enslaves and oppresses the black the white shall sink and the black shall rise." He then quoted Pratt:

> South Africa is a black man's country. . . . The white man's rule depends on keeping the blacks ignorant and mentally benighted. . . . The native is doing all the rough and unskilled work in South Africa. The whites are merely overseers. . . . The practice is injurious and short-sighted to the last degree. . . . [It] undermines and diminishes the white man's industrial efficiency and it trains the native to supplant him. But it is the iron custom of South Africa, and nobody dares to break it.[107]

Harrison cited Pratt's depiction of how the native miner received two and a half shillings a day and the white miner twenty-two and a half and how, "in the ordinary industrial occupations the 'superior' white laborer plays the part of a racial aristocrat." The black worker was forced to "carry his tools," and "every white bricklayer must be attended by natives, who hand him the bricks which he lays." A line was "drawn between 'white man's work' and 'Kaffir's work' and no white man must soil his hands with the latter, or white supremacy is done for." Pratt warned "white men of the working classes that they should shun South Africa as they would the plague" because there was "no work there for them, as a result of this very attitude." In addition, "profitable industry" could not "be made to support an excess number of overseers," whose salaries were "a charge against the profits of production." Harrison reasoned that "capitalists will not knowingly forgo their profits for racial reasons—and the work of production must go forward." Thus, since "the white laborer" couldn't survive "on anything like the same wage," Harrison predicted that the "result in South Africa must eventually be that the white working class will be squeezed out in the contest, and instead of South Africa['s] becoming a white workers paradise it will be, for weal or woe, the heaven of black workers."[108]

Pratt added that the "attitude of the white man has greatly affected his efficiency as a laborer" and that "the standard of efficiency of white unskilled labor in South Africa has fallen very much lower than in countries where there is no colored labor." He cited a Royal Commission that found that 85 percent of the mechanics in Kimberly were "colored," the wagon-building industry was almost completely in the hands of the "Negro," 30 percent of those in the printing trade were "Negroes," and "that black competition" was "acute in the trades of carpentering, plastering, saddlery, painting, tailoring and bricklaying." Even if the prejudice were broken down tomorrow, "there would be little or no unskilled work for the white man to do, since the black man does it better and much cheaper." The commission found "an immense amount of white indigency prevailing in all parts of South Africa," including special settlements subsidized by the Union government, at Goedodorp, Donkey Camp, and Vrededorp. Harrison underscored that "the crime[s] which the white people have perpetrated on the Negroes of South Africa recoil upon . . . [them]."[109]

In conclusion, Harrison praised Pratt for telling his story well and for showing that Negroes were "climbing steadily and making great gains in education and enlightenment in spite of their severe handicaps." He also praised the book "to all thinking Negroes," and he thanked his friend George Young for making the book available at his Harlem bookstore.[110]

———

In the July 16 *Negro World* Harrison reviewed Herbert Spencer's *First Principles* and offered a guide to its reading. He described how "in these days of our awakening" many were "asking for guidance in reading" and were beginning to realize that "the educated person is the well-informed person" and "apt to be the well-read person." Harrison emphasized "well-read rather than much-read," because the two things were "not necessarily the same." On this he quoted the "great English thinker" Thomas Hobbes: "'If I had read as much as some people I should have been as great a fool.'" Harrison emphasized that it required "a very strong intellect to read extensively and retain ones own mental independence" and cited Edward Gibbon, Thomas Babington Macaulay, Herbert Spencer, Lord Acton, Sir J. G. Frazer, Joseph McCabe, and J. M. Robertson as "splendid examples in English of thinkers who read widely and yet retained their vigor and originality."[111]

Harrison then offered a historical review: In the early sixteenth century Francis Bacon wrote *The Advancement of Learning* and the *Novum Organon*, "the first works since the Greek [Harrison changed it to 'Islamic'] science in which a European writer had massed all the available information about the universe into a systematic survey." Bacon's effort "laid down the law that the basic business of an educated man was to know the world in which he lived in every important aspect." Since then the same thing was "done several times by different writers in France, England, Germany and America." Harrison cited (Paul-Henri Thiry) d'Holbach, in 1770, with his *System of Nature*; Alexander von Humboldt's *The Cosmos*; Auguste Comte's *Course of Positive Philosophy*; Ludwig Buchner's *Force and Matter*; Ernst Haeckel's *The Riddle of the Universe*; Herbert Spencer's *First Principles*; and John Fiske's *Outlines of Positive Philosophy*. Each of these works was "practically a 'system of nature,'" and all were "foundation works" that "anyone who is genuinely in search of an education should read." Harrison particularly favored "the last three," which were "products of the era of evolution." He noted that Fiske's was "the easiest to read" but was "only an American simplified version of Spencer's," which was "the greatest of them all."[112]

Spencer's *First Principles* was a compendium of his nine-volume *Synthetic Philosophy*, which Harrison considered "the ablest attempt yet made by the mind of man to understand, describe and explain" creation. It discussed "religion" under the title of "The Unknowable" and "facts and the problems connected with space, time, matter, motion, force, mind and society" under "The Knowable." Spencer drew on "every department of human knowledge," including "physics, chemistry, law, grammar, literature, biology, psychology, sociology, engineering, geology, [and] art," and he detailed "the marvelous way in which the universe and everything in it . . . show order and harmony." To Harrison, "to master this one book is to have a fuller, deeper and more genuine education than you could get in twenty years dabbling in 'theology,' 'philosophy,' 'literature' and some other forms of time-wasting theoretics and mystical moonshine." One learns from it "how things happen to happen," and one's mind is "better able to think for itself and to master and understand the thoughts of other men."

Harrison adds, Spencer "makes a man think and think clearly" and asks: "Isn't that the object of our higher education?"[113]

––––––––––

In the *Negro World* of July 23 Harrison's "Germany, England, and the African" reviewed *Colonies and Calumnies: A Reply to Sir Hugh Clifford's "German Colonies,"* by Dietrich Reimer and Hans Georg von Doering (the former acting governor of Togoland), and *France's Black Militarism: Sidelights on the French Colonial System*, by "Ajax." Harrison began by quoting William S. Gilbert, the English humorous poet, librettist, and co-collaborator in comic operas with Arthur Sullivan, on the "colossal conceit of the British," who thought that "everything that England does is right, from slaughtering Chinese [in order] that the British merchants of Singapore and the Straits Settlements might rivet the opium traffic on the Chinese people, to swiping the lands and cattle of Lolangula's helpless Mashonas and Matabeles in South Africa." England did these things "in a spirit of the highest unselfishness," in order to bring "the superior blessings of the white man's burden," and the "English conscience" then justified this "with due parade of 'logic' and 'eternal truth.'" Gilbert's words reminded Harrison of the following "caustic and correct summary" of "English character," which was put into the mouth of Napoleon by the Irish-born George Bernard Shaw in *Man of Destiny*:

> The English are a race apart. No Englishman is too low to have scruples; no Englishman is high enough to be free from their tyranny. When he wants a thing, he never tells himself that he wants it. He waits patiently until there comes into his mind, no one knows how, a burning conviction that it is his moral and religious duty to conquer those who have got the thing he wants. Then he becomes irresistible. Like the aristocrat, he does what pleases him and grabs what he wants: like the shopkeeper, he pursues his purpose with the industry and steadfastness that come from strong religious conviction and deep sense of moral responsibility. He is never at a loss for an effective moral attitude. As the great champion of freedom and national independence, he conquers and annexes half the world, and calls it colonization. When he wants a new market for his adulterated Manchester goods, he sends a missionary to teach the natives the gospel of peace. The natives kill the missionary: he flies to arms in defense of Christianity; fights for it; conquers for it; and takes the market as a reward from Heaven. In defense of his island shores, he puts a chaplain on board his ship; nails a flag with a cross on it to his top-gallant mast; and sails to the ends of the earth, sinking, burning and destroying all who dispute the empire of the seas with him. He boasts that a slave is free the moment his foot touches British soil, and he

sells the children of his poor at six years of age to work under the lash in his factories for sixteen hours a day. He makes two revolutions, and then declares war on our one in the name of law and order. There is nothing so bad or so good that you will not find Englishmen doing it; but you will never find an Englishman in the wrong. He does everything on principle. He fights you on patriotic principles; he robs you on business principles; he enslaves you on imperial principles; he bullies you on manly principles; he supports his kin on loyal principles and cuts off his king's head on republican principles. His watchword is always duty; and he never forgets that the nation which lets its duty get on the opposite side to its interest is lost.[114]

With such conceit, reasoned Harrison, "it was natural, when England went to war with Germany for the commerce and colonial possessions which Germany had that she should put Germany in the wrong" while she spoke of "'democracy,' 'freedom of the seas' and 'the rights of small nationalities.'" These matters, however, had "nothing to do with England's war aims," as both the *London Times* and Sir Edward Grey admitted "as early as November, 1914." After the war ended and England "coolly annexed Germany's possessions," she sought to "keep up the shabby pretense of 'moral justification' by endeavoring to show that Germany had governed her colonies in ways that were not quite proper." That was "the thesis" of Clifford's *German Colonies: A Plea for the Native Races*, written while he was the governor of the Gold Coast Colony. Harrison described *Colonies and Calumnies* as "a temperate and convincing reply to the English governor's charges" and noted that "the burden of the Englishman's strictures" was "laid on the German administration of Togoland." Herr von Doering pointed out "that the very title of the Englishman's book" reflected "that material expediency veiled under a moral pretext by means of which England has always carried on her raids for plunder as divine crusades for liberty, humanity and all those other blessings."[115]

Harrison agreed with both the German governor and the Irish philosopher "that England, being a thief, will also lie," but he insisted that this was "equally true of France, Germany, Belgium, the United States and all other bearers of 'the white man's burden.'" England occupied Nigeria and the Gold Coast "by trampling on her pledged word"; she occupied Mashonaland and Matableleland "by sheer outrage, violence and highway robbery"; and her occupation of Egypt was "on moral principles, the shame of the centuries." Nevertheless, Clifford, with "canting hypocrisy," dared to say that British colonial occupation in Africa "was 'impelled by no other necessity save the dictates of conscience, a sense of moral responsibility and obligation, and above all by a characteristic love of fair play.'"[116]

Regarding "corporal punishment" Clifford alleged "that in the German colony every official enjoys the privilege of flogging," while von Doering denied this and presented "solid proof to the contrary," explaining that "authority to inflict punishment" is "given only to the judge of the native courts, their representatives and certain sub officials." The Germans reportedly regulated corporal punishment by "rigid laws to guard against abuses," while in the neighboring British colony of Nigeria "the whipping privilege had grown to the proportions of a scandal." Captain Macdonald's libel case against J. Eldridge Taylor in London in the summer of 1919 revealed "that British officials could summon black women to their compounds with immoral intent and, upon the women refusing to agree to these most immoral demands, the officials could and did have them arrested as trespassers or thieves and have them tried, condemned, stripped naked in the public square and flogged until the blood ran down their bodies." In addition, a practice existed in large sections of Nigeria "whereby when a white man goes by in his litter every black person whom he meets must 'kow-tow' by going down on one knee until the august personage goes by." The overall "damning fact" remained, wrote Harrison, "that in the African colonies of Germany, England, France and Belgium the white man thinks that it is his 'superior' right to beat the Blackman— and woman." He warned: "Black people all over the world will work for the overthrow of the alien rule of white over black in Africa because we perceive that such methods of repression are part and parcel of it."[117]

Herr von Doering cited testimony to prove that in such matters the German colony was superior to the British, and Clifford, in turn, trotted out "that grand old British bogey of 'sexual immorality.'" Von Doering countered "that whereas Englishmen who begot half-breed children, of native concubines left them to tender mercies of nature, the German colonial laws 'imposed upon the white father the duty of depositing a certain sum for the child.'" Further, "proof of the greater laxity of British morals" was found in the "larger number of unfathered mulattoes both in the Gold Coast Colony and in Nigeria than in Togoland" and in "the prostitution of Black women for white purposes," which didn't exist in Togoland yet was "a flourishing institution" in the two adjoining British colonies. Von Doering also cited the case of Attorney General Willoughby Osborne, who took his wife and "a black concubine" back to England, where a clash between the two women led to a public scandal. In regard to the land and labor questions, von Doering argued that Togoland was "far superior to the British West African colonies," and his book, "written in a temperate spirit," offered "detailed proof of every specific point."[118]

Quite different "in form and temper" was the pamphlet by the anonymous Ajax, who wrote "like an unreconstructed German Junker of the worst

Prussian proclivities." While "imperialistic France" had "many sins to answer for," and its "recruiting of her African armies" approached "the compulsory standards of slavery" (and was "a suppressed chapter of modern capitalist brutality"), Harrison felt the charges brought by Ajax needed "solid proof" and offered "very little." The pamphlet was "a disgrace to German methods of 'thoroughness' in writing." Nevertheless, the few facts it contained would be "of some value" to those who shared "the illusion that French colonialism differs in its imperialist aspects from that of other European nations which have stolen African lands." The lesson in all this, said Harrison, was "when the spokesmen of the white plunderbunds tell uncomplimentary truths about each other we Africans of the dispersion can catch a glimpse of the greater truth whose minatory finger points to the approaching downfall of the white autocracy which holds the darker world in subjection."[119]

On July 22 "L.M.M." wrote "to thank" Harrison "for his very timely and interesting article on 'England, Germany and the Africans'" and added that "upon subjects of timely, vital and educational interest Mr. Harrison always speaks and writes to the mental illumination and benefit of our people." "L.M.M." considered it a pleasure to read "such able and well written articles in a Negro paper" because they did "credit not only to the writer, but also to the paper and the race." "L.M.M." hoped to see Harrison's "powerful and penetrating mind working more closely and intimately within the U.N.I.A. the greatest of all Negro movements."[120]

———

In the August 13 *Negro World* Harrison reviewed *The Aftermath of Slavery* by William A. Sinclair. He opened with a translated quote (one of his favorites) from Vergil's Eneas (Aeneas), from the *Aeneid*:

> Through this stern mesh of circumstance,
> Of grim misfortune and mischance
> We hold our steady onward way
> Toward Latium and the light of day.

Harrison explained that he had "always felt that the whole heartening speech of Eneas might be fittingly applied to our race's situation, especially in America. For we, too, 'have suffered weightier woes,' and have the stern task of steering between Scylla and Charybdis." He used this introduction to discuss how Dr. Sinclair's book charted "the currents of the raging sea of racial prejudice" and differed "from many of our Negro books that have risen to fame in at least one important respect"—it was "not a collection of more or less occasional papers which have been brought together for collective publication," as were

The Souls of Black Folk, Darkwater, and *Out of the House of Bondage.* Rather, it was "planned and written" as a book, eight of its ten chapters were "distinctly historical," and it served "as a modest history of American race prejudice from the end of the Civil War to Roosevelt's second administration."[121]

Harrison, noting the "striking fact" that many "Negro" historians in America, "from George [Washington] Williams to Dr. Sinclair, have been clergymen," suggested that this had led to "too much of sermonizing" in "many of our historical narratives." In Sinclair's case, however, the "sermonizings" were "often serviceable," although often "weighted down with old-fashioned loyalties to old-fashioned faiths" like "the Republican party." Sinclair seemed unaware "that the party's existence developed out of a definite economic and political need of the rising industrialism of the North," and he didn't "see its necessary relation to the great and large aggregations of capital whose guardian and wet nurse" it remained. His "loyalty to the Republican party" led Sinclair "to gloss over the fact that the Negroes have lost the vote in the South because the party while in continued control of the national means of law enforcement refused to enforce a single one of the constitutional amendments which were enacted to protect the Negroes' lives, liberties and political rights."[122]

In spite of this, Harrison evaluated *The Aftermath of Slavery* as "a valuable storehouse of historical information" that "furnishes food for thought." It used authoritative sources to provide the facts of Reconstruction and made clear that the Southerner's charge "that the Northerners forced Negro suffrage upon them" was "a gratuitous insult." He discussed how in 1865–1866 the South "set its hand to the cowardly task of reducing the recently enfranchised Negroes to a slavery more hopeless and degrading than that from which the war had liberated them, and that in each instance 'the slavery which was abolished by the organic law of a nation was now to be revised by the enactment of a State.'" Sinclair demonstrated how "the poverty of the Negroes was made a crime and they were everywhere seized, taken to court and put upon the chain gang to labor for Southern society without pay"; how "children were 'apprenticed' to their former masters"; how "laborers were prevented from keeping livestock and from working at trades, except when doing so as some white man's chattels"; and how "the master or his agent might assail the ear with profaneness aimed at the Negro man and outrage every sense of decency in foul language addressed to the Negro women." But, if one of those "goaded to resistance . . . should answer back with impudence . . . he did so at the cost of . . . one dollar for every outburst, which 'fine' he had to work out." This was "the condition of the freeman when Congress intervened," yet "Southern liars and Northern hypocrites" still deplored "the 'mistake' made by granting the suffrage to the Southern Negro."[123]

Sinclair, according to Harrison, traced the history of Southern opposition to reconstruction and "the war against Negro suffrage which was finally won by the South, when in 1877, the Republican party surrendered the Negro to the tender mercies of the 'crackers.'" He also described the "awful horrors of lynchings and the convict camps," the "hell of modern peonage and the present plantation system," the "political plight of the Negro," and the "determination of the Southern whites to hold the race in eternal bondage and hopeless degradation." Harrison concluded by pointing to passages in Sinclair that, he said, show why "Negroes can feel no obligation of respect toward a government which by its silence acquiesces in disloyalty coming from those who treat its Constitution as 'a scrap of paper'" and why "the New Negro hates the 'crackers' with an undying hatred."[124]

In the *Negro World* of August 27 Harrison's "Why Books?" explained that "no movement for emancipation" could hope to succeed "in our time" unless it is based "upon knowledge and competent thinking." It was also "rather unfortunate," he added, "that the people who stand most in need of these things should be the ones least aware of it." This fact made it "necessary that those among us who have some knowledge should direct the people of our race to the books— the sources of that knowledge without which no competent thinking can be done." He then quoted his "poetic friend 'Razz'" (Andy Razaf):

> Read, Read, Read!
> Make this your family creed
> Or else, though you have eyes to see
> You will be blind indeed.[125]

Harrison described the "great opportunity for our people in the reading line" at the 135th Street branch of the New York Public Library, which had "'stocked up' during the last three or four months with about 500 books on the Negro and Africa." The books he reviewed in the *Negro World* were available there, as were other "outstanding books" such as W. Hannibal Thomas's "remarkable" *The American Negro* ("in which a Negro writer puts his race under the microscope and takes a good 'close-up' of its foibles and failings"). Also available were works by Booker T. Washington, W. E. B. Du Bois, "poetry, fiction, history, travel, sociology," as well as books about Africa, including "geographies, travels, descriptions, compilations, missionary and scientific studies and treatises." In particular, the branch had the "three big volumes of [Heinrich] Barth [probably volumes 1–3 of his five-volume *Travels and Discourses in North and Central Africa*] and the two of Georg August Schweinfurth," including *The Heart of Africa*. There was also Major Felix Dubois's ("not Dr. Du Bois") *Timbuctoo the Mysterious* and Maspero's *Art in Egypt*, with "over 300 pages, full of photographs of the art products of Ancient Egypt," wherein one could "look and decide . . . whether the ancient Egyptians were Negroes or not"; David Livingstone's *Travels and Researches* [*in South Africa*]; the Scottish explorer Mungo Park's *Travels* [*in the Interior Districts of Africa*]; and modern studies by E. D. Morel, Mary Kingsley, John H. Harris, and George W. Ellis. Since this "wealth of information" could be had by anyone in Harlem without spending one cent, there was "no excuse for any Negro who can read to be ignorant of the past history of his race in Africa or of the actual fact of their present existence." In addition, Harrison mentioned he taught a free class in "Negro history" on Monday nights at 149 West 146th Street, under the auspices of the Liberty League.[126]

———

During 1921 Harrison began a correspondence with Eugene O'Neill, America's leading playwright and future winner of the Nobel Prize for Literature. In the process, revealing comments on O'Neill's brilliant play *The Emperor Jones* were offered.[127] The play had opened on November 1, 1920, at the Provincetown Playhouse on MacDougal Street in Greenwich Village. It was then scheduled for a two-week run at the Princess Theatre on Broadway; that turned into six months and 204 performances, beginning January 29, 1921. The Broadway show starred the former Lafayette player Charles Gilpin in the title role and was a tremendous success. Subsequently *The Emperor Jones* went on a two-year road tour in the United States, after which it played in Paris in 1923 and then opened in London at the Ambassador's Theatre in the West End in September 1925. It closed in five weeks, after receiving mixed reviews. In London the work of Paul Robeson as Jones drew raves, though O'Neill was criticized for mounting "a brutal attack on the nerves." It was said that he "shocks and surprises but he does not charm, he does not amuse."[128]

Harrison reviewed the Broadway/Gilpin show in the *Negro World* of June 4. The paper had previously published on March 26 a letter from William Bridges, which argued that *The Emperor Jones* slandered Negroes. O'Neill viewed matters differently and subsequently explained that he wrote *The Emperor Jones* to provide a precedent to facilitate playwrights creating plays "for the Negro as a serious actor," to counter the existing practice whereby major Black roles were played by white actors in blackface, with the exception of musical comedy and vaudeville. While much of the Black press agreed with Bridges's criticism, Harrison, like O'Neill, saw things differently.[129]

In the *Negro World* Harrison argued that he saw the "joint product of the genius of Eugene O'Neill and Charles Gilpin" on the last day of its run at the Princess Theatre. Since he had "plotted Mr. Gilpin's curve as early as 1917 in *The Voice*" and since he knew "that his abilities as an actor placed him in

Class A," Harrison felt "the pull of the white critics' praise was not so strong" on him as on many others in "the colored fraternity." After seeing the play, he commented: "I would not have missed it for a trip to France." He was "at a loss to understand," however, how the play could ever become a Broadway success, since "its character, quality and excellence" were far above Broadway's level. As written, the play was "a work of genius, too delicate in its technique to be lightly classed in any of the usual groups." Though the publishers, Boni and Liveright, described it as "a study of the psychology of fear and race superstition," Harrison judged it as "pre-eminently a psychological study."[130]

Harrison then described how the play "presents the spiritual changes that take place in the soul of Brutus Jones when fear strips from him one by one his success, bravado, self-sufficiency, grit and the accumulated stock of restraints and supports with which 'civilization' had supplied him." Through telescoping back, O'Neill strips "the soul of 'the emperor' down to its bare essentials"; the fact that it is mostly a one-man monologue was why the play did "not follow the conventional European order of acts and scenes." Because of this, "the external setting of the drama" was "really of no importance whatsoever," and "instead of being set in 'an island in the West Indies as yet not self-determined by white marines' it could just as readily be set in Africa or South Carolina." "The 'action' is within the man, not without," and the play "doesn't purport to give history," making "the question of historic accuracy or even probability . . . quite beside the point."[131]

In the first of the play's eight scenes Brutus Jones appears "as a successful faker lording it over a group of his people in the style of emperor." According to Harrison, this former "Alabama field hand who had done time as a convict" and killed several people had "landed among a mass of Negroes in a primitive state of intellect," and through "the superior cunning, chicanery and cool nerve supplied by civilization" he "managed to rise 'from stowaway to emperor in two years.'" Jones appealed "to the supernatural and the far away" and managed "to fool and cow the people while he suck[ed] up every dollar in sight." He then justified "his methods to the cringing cockney" who served "as foil to 'his majesty'":

Dere's little stealin' like you does and dere's big stealin' like I does. For de little stealin' dey gets you in jail soon or late. For de big stealin' dey makes you emperor and puts you in de hall of fame when you croaks. . . .

SMITHERS: And I bet you got yer pile o' money in some safe place.

JONES: I sho' has! And it's in a foreign bank, where no pusson don't ever git it out but me, no matter what come. You didn't s'pose I was holdin' down dis

Emperor job for de glory in it, did you? Sho'! De fuss and glory part of it, dat's only to turn de heads o'de low-flung bush niggers dat's here. Dey wants de big circus show for deir mony. I gives it to 'm, an' I gits de money. De long green; dat's me every time.[132]

In the play, "the people 'get wise' in time to their Emperor's graft, and under the leadership of Lem set out to 'get' him." They first "desert the 'palace' and take to the woods, whence the coughing boom of the tom-tom warns Jones of the beginning of the end of his imperial job." They then "begin to make power-ful 'medicine' to offset the might of the Emperor's charm—a silver bullet." Jones meanwhile makes "the necessary preparations for absconding (i.e. his 'get away') and sets out for the edge of the forest through which he must pass." When he reaches there, "tired and hungry," he finds that the food, which he had hidden there for such an emergency, had been removed. He now "must face the awful ordeal of crossing the dark forest at night worn, weary and hungry." With courage and determination he attempts to do this, "but fate is against him," and "the forest is full of specters which haunt him." "As the visions of his past life appear," Jones "fires the shots from his pistol, including the silver bullet, which was his 'charm.'"[133]

In the selection of the six episodes in scenes 2 through 7, Harrison felt "the skill" of the playwright. The "first shot drives off 'the little formless fears,' which indicate the origin of the other specters," the "second shuts out the spectre of Jeff, the man whom he had killed in a game of craps," and the "third dissipates the horrors of the convict-camp of his earlier days in which he had killed a prison guard who haunts him." These were from "his own personal existence which 'telescopes' back," "but," writes Harrison, "the soul of the individual is a bud on the stem of ancestry; the base of the individual's mind is bedded in the roots of his race, which is moulded of that race's experience." Thus, in succeeding scenes "the specters are the past horrors of racial experi-ence, which rise from the roots of Jones's subconscious mind," and "he finds himself put up for sale as a slave on a special auction block, then on a ghostly slaveship in the dreaded 'middle passage,' and, finally, he is about to be offered by a Congo-witch-doctor as a human sacrifice to a phantom crocodile-god on the banks of the Congo." From "each agony he frees himself by a shot from his pistol," until "in the seventh scene his last shot is spent." As this goes on "the beat of the tom-tom grows at each shot louder, nearer, more rapid and menac-ing, and the man's soul is stripped by his increasing terror down to its primi-tive essentials." Then, "in the grip of this terror, instead of getting through the forest, he loses his way, turns in a circle and comes back to the point at which he first entered it." At that spot, "led by Lem, a chief whom he had injured and who waits there with a sublime confidence that the power of his 'charm' will bring the Emperor back, he is shot by the soldiers of his own Negro army." Harrison suggestively offered that if the tale had any moral, it might be: "That the good Lord watches over the poor and ignorant to protect them even from clever sharpies of their own tribe."[134]

That was "the play as written." As produced, Harrison considered it "a marvel of stage-setting and stage-effects" whose "great success" was attributable to the "effective handling" of the stage director. Though originally scheduled for two weeks at the Princess Theatre, "the genius of Charles Gilpin in the title-role made it a six months' sensation." Gilpin's "creative acting" showed "comprehension, power, mastery," and "in the character of an inflated mountebank with a ballast of a shrewd common sense and a cargo of cool confidence," he played "up to" but "never overplay[ed], the part." Even as his naked soul was "stripped by terror of all its trappings, we see the terror, yet cannot blink the courage which carries Brutus Jones through to the awful end of his ordeal." Gilpin acted "with taste and discrimination" and held "reserves of dramatic vigor well in hand" until he needed them. Then, "in the third, fourth, fifth and six scenes, he 'turns them loose' and rises to crescendos of effective intensity," and "in this, as in other things, it can be truly said that no white actor on Broadway during recent years has surpassed this Negro actor." Harrison "questioned whether any has equalled him." Gilpin's "genius" was "a credit to the dramatic powers of the race to which the great Ira Aldridge belonged."[135]

Harrison criticized those "among our own writers" for whom "a previous study of the technique of the drama is not considered a necessary prerequisite to the uttering of opinions on things dramatic," including those who, "unable to form any qualified judgments of their own, simply re-echo the encomiums of the white writers without understanding the whys and wherefores" and those who "with commendable racial pride, but unfortunate misunderstanding, object that the play 'does not elevate the Negro.'" He thought it "necessary to explain" that "the drama is intended to mirror life, either in realistic outward terms, or, as in this case, in the imaginative terms of inner experience." Thus, "Mr. O'Neill, in portraying the soul of an ignorant and superstitious person of any race could not be so silly as to put in that person's mouth the language of a different sort of person." O'Neill "did the best he could—and he did it very well," and "Gilpin, in acting the play, had to act what was in the play"; he "couldn't act anything else." Harrison added, "when the forms of expression now current among our illiterates should have died out, then, and not till then, will [it] be unseemly in a play of contemporary character to reproduce these terms." He concluded: "To those who have an understanding of the drama and its laws, 'The Emperor

Jones,' as written by O'Neill and acted by Gilpin, will be known for what it is: a great play acted by a great actor and in a noble manner."[136]

––––––––––

On June 9, O'Neill wrote to Harrison from Provincetown, Massachusetts, and said that he was "indeed grateful" to Harrison for sending his review. He added: "I have read it with the greatest interest and consider it one of the very few intelligent criticisms of the piece that have come to my notice. You know what you are writing about. I wish I could say the same for many others who have praised it unwisely for what it is not." O'Neill also said that he would be "only too glad to give all the publicity I can to your article," though there was little chance at the time, since "the season ended and the play closed." When it reopened in the fall he would do more. He hoped "in the time between now and the end of the play's career to write another Negro play," which he had in mind—in which case his association "with Mr. Gilpin, always a pleasant one from the very start, may be continued and his [Gilpin's] 'Where do I go from here?' may find a solution to his liking." O'Neill considered Gilpin "a wonderful actor" who "should not go playless," and he asked Harrison: "Don't you think the writers among your race should be encouraged—and urged—to try and write plays for him? Something very fine for the Negro in general might evolve from such an attempt." In addition, O'Neill offered this thoughtful comment:

> I am glad to see you remonstrate with those of your people who find fault with the play because it does not "elevate." Such folk do not realize that the only propaganda that ever strikes home is the truth about the human soul, black or white. Intentional uplift plays never amount to a damn—especially as uplift. To portray a human being, that is all that counts.
>
> And, by the way, the same criticism of "Jones" which you protest against is a very common one made by a similar class of white people about my other plays—they don't "elevate" them. So you see!

O'Neill then assured Harrison "that in any theatre with which I have any connection, all the usual courtesies to a dramatic critic will be extended to you."[137]

Harrison's review of O'Neill's play also led to a critical letter to the editor by Mrs. William A. Corbi, of Cambridge, Massachusetts, in the *Negro World* of July 30, 1921. According to the historian Tony Martin, Mrs. Corbi articulated "the correct Garveyite aesthetic as against one of the *Negro World*'s own editors." Corbi wrote: "O'Neill's so-called wonderful play, described as a study of the psychology of fear and race superstition, which Mr. Harrison so readily commends to negroes as a work of genius, cannot and will not be accepted by race-loving Negroes as a work of genius." Surely, she added, "'Something is rotten in Denmark,' when Hubert Harrison lauds 'Emperor Jones.' That is the trouble with our educated and intelligent men. They are using their brains to keep down their own race." Corbi went on: "Anything that causes the white man to believe that the Negroes are superstitious, immoral and illiterate . . . can make a hit on Broadway. . . . One does not need 'an understanding of drama and its laws,' to quote Mr. Harrison, to realize that 'Emperor Jones' is of no racial value to the Negroes of the World." The play "does not elevate the Negro, and such plays never will." She felt such men as Harrison "who encourage white playwrights by lauding them to the skies, are of no racial value to the Negroes." "Remember always the man who allows a man to make a fool of him will always be a fool." Corbi concluded: "The time has come when Negroes will not accept such plays as great."[138]

There is one other interesting aspect of Harrison's review in the *Negro World*, one that perhaps sheds light on some of the criticism in terms of the "Garvey aesthetic." The story of *The Emperor Jones* can be interpreted as an inversion of the career of Marcus Garvey, as was later suggested by Charles S. Johnson, Robert Morse Lovett, and James Weldon Johnson. Garvey came from a West Indian island to a modern, large country; Brutus Jones left a modern, large country for a West Indian island. Each, with considerable pomp, attracted a large passionate following, which contributed generously, and each leader's life followed a tragic course. To Harrison, the parallels and similarities were evident from the beginning. In his review, although he knew it not to be the case, he wrote that "the play was written about eight or ten years ago." Later, when O'Neill informed him that "I wrote the play last summer, not eight or ten years ago," Harrison wrote on his copy of the letter, "as I knew very well." Harrison's phrase "about eight or ten years ago" suggests he saw the parallels with Garvey and put the incorrect date in the article so that he could make his point while being able to skirt charges that he was attacking Garvey.[139]

In 1923, when Garvey was convicted of mail fraud, Harrison directly suggested parallels between Jones and Garvey in an Associated Negro Press article:

> The Garvey Case will go down in history as a splendid illustration of the race's gullibility. After all, it is not so much Garvey's fault, but his people's. A leader who would have made no promises that he couldn't keep, no statement that wasn't true, who always accounted for every penny and who made less "whoo-pin' and hollerin'" would not have appealed to them. He gave them what they wanted. And at this point I am reminded of "The Emperor Jones"—a fine picture of the psychology of the whole Garvey movement.
>
> "Smithers—And I bet you got yer pile o' money in some safe place.

Jones—I sho' has! . . . Dey wants de big circus show for deir money. I gives it to 'em, an' I gits de money. De long green; dat's me every time."

Harrison concluded his 1923 article with: "And now, at the end of the spectacular career of *our* Emperor Jones, Judge Mack sticks up a sign marked 'Five Years in Prison for Fraud.'"[140]

———

During 1921 Harrison also corresponded with one of the country's leading journalists, H. L. Mencken; one of its leading authors, T. Lothrop Stoddard; the editor Frederick R. Moore; and J. P. Williams, of Gold Coast, West Africa. Shortly after Harrison's review of *The Emperor Jones* appeared in the *Negro World* he sent a copy to H. L. Mencken. Mencken responded on July 10 that the review "seems very good stuff to me, though I am densely ignorant of the theatre." Unfortunately, Mencken couldn't use it for his magazine, the *Smart Set*, since his coeditor, George Jean Nathan, "exhausts also the space we can give to the drama." He did, however, ask Harrison to "write something else for us" and said he would "be delighted to see a frank and merciless treatise on the Caucasian, and particularly upon the Nordic Blond, from the standpoint of an observant Negro." Mencken added:

As I told you in our conversation at the Liveright soiree, it seems to me that the Negroes are too mild and conciliating; what is needed is a strong and challenging assertion of the Negro ego. I tried to induce Dr. Du Bois to do such an article, but it seems to me that he was rather ineffective. Why don't you attempt it? The normal Americano is a puerile and transparent fellow. He seems ridiculous, even to me. What must he look like to you?[141]

On July 19 Mencken again wrote to Harrison, saying, "Your plan sounds very interesting. Let me see the article by all means." He said the "ideal length would be about 4,000 words." He thought there was "little chance that we will disagree," and he hoped Harrison didn't "waste any effort on politeness." Then, on January 11, 1922, Mencken again wrote, saying, "This, unluckily, is not for us." He asked, "What has become of the article you promised to write last summer?"[142]

In 1921 Harrison was not having great success selling his literary wares, and around May he wrote to Fred R. Moore, editor of *The Age*, indicating that two weeks earlier he had sent him a letter "bearing upon" a Du Bois editorial in the May 6 *Age*. The article had not been printed, and though return postage had been included, "neither the stamp nor the manuscript has been returned." Harrison would "not languish over that" but suggested that *The Age* "may have a permanent reduction to show if it persists in its present policy of publishing . . . falsehoods."[143]

On May 20, 1921, T. Lothrop Stoddard, who had apparently last corresponded with Harrison the previous November, wrote and asked if he would, at his leisure, provide "a few bibliographical hints as to the Ethiopian or Pan-African Movement, in its broader aspects." Stoddard was "tentatively looking into the material available to see whether or not there may be a book in it." He said he had found "quite a good bit of material on the South African phase, and of course the Garvey phase in this country," and noted that the Harvard Library possessed a file of the *Negro World* "for the past year or more" and a file of *The Crisis* "for a couple of years back." But there were "many aspects of the movement, such as the historical beginnings, the Pan-African Congress at Paris (the first, I believe), and the West Indian phase," on which Stoddard said he could "find very little." He added that *The Rising Tide* continued "to rise as fast as ever" and that sales to date were somewhere around 14,000.[144]

On June 19 Harrison responded to Stoddard with a letter not sent until July 1. He apologized for his tardiness in replying to the May 20 letter and explained that he was "kept exceedingly busy these days by the work necessary to rebuild the Liberty League." He then offered "what help—bibliographic or other" that he could, explaining that "a good deal depends on what *you* understand by the Pan African Movement," since the phrase was "used to cover many different things." Harrison then put forth his understanding of the Pan African Movement:

> The Pan African Movement as I have come to understand it, is the conscious expression by Africans of their desire to rule their own ancestral lands free from the domination of foreigners however exalted and benevolent. But this isn't all. As a cultural movement it connotes a desire to preserve the soul of the African by laying respect for his own institutions as the basis for any access of knowledge that may come to him through the more highly developed technologic process of the European which are at the same time spiritually disintegrating—not only to a people to whom they are new—but in their real essence, as determined by their persistent effects as revealed in the history of European civilization. For you must know that we Africans do not see in "progress" that be-all and end—which you Europeans do. We think that stability is more important to society than this restless, wearisome striving after the wind which *always* leaves 9/10 of your people short of such specific satisfactions as food, clothing and shelter while mocking them with a mirage of civilization including an increasing neurasthenia and the loss of their *Soul*. Let me put a biologic analogy. The female element in life conserves and protects. The restless masculine element fertilizes it is true, but it also

destroys. It is the symbol of aggression, conquest, conflict and destruction by all of which it works changes. And the cycle of changes comes finally round to the point from which it started. The "efficient reason" for this may be found in the dialectic formula of Hegel. But the main point is that the female principle is the more important. (I teach embryology myself and in that branch of science we learn that the male is only the female—at a further stage of evolution.) It is like capital and labor. Before capital came into existence labor was; I have seen labor functioning without capital, but never capital without labor. Before maleness came femaleness; before "progress" there was stability—which presupposes organization. So did Old Egypt last for fully five thousand years. China and India also have had age-long civilizations. Europe has never had them. And if you ask why, the answer will be found in that book *The White Man's Burden*, by T. Shirby Hodge [Roger Sherman Tracy], which the Gorham Press suppressed after they had published it. It is also an answer which goes well with the thesis of your book *The Rising Tide of Color*. We older races prefer stability to progress: that is the wisdom of old stocks.[145]

Stoddard wrote back to Harrison on July 15 and thanked him for his "most helpful and enlightening letter." He expressed deep appreciation for the "kindness" in writing "so fully, not merely on the bibliographical, but also on the philosophical side." He noted that "for us intellectuals, our most precious possession is our *time*," and he knew "what a considerable expenditure of time" the writing of Harrison's "carefully formulated letter must have entailed." Most of the books that Harrison mentioned Stoddard was "already through," and some of them he had "succeeded in buying" for his own library. He was not, however, familiar "with Duse Mohammed's organ, and neither the Harvard Library nor the Boston Public Library seem to possess it." He would follow Harrison's advice and write to John E. Bruce about it, and he would also write Casely Hayford. Stoddard assumed, based on what Harrison said, "practically nothing has been published about Pan-Africanism or 'Ethiopian' stirrings in the West Indies or Latin America."[146]

On May 8, 1921, J. P. Williams wrote Harrison from Gold Coast, West Africa. He indicated that for "a very long time" he had "been admiring" Harrison's articles in the *Negro World* and wanted to correspond with him, "but the opportunity seems not to have presented itself with you." When he started to receive the paper irregularly he forwarded a year's subscription by mail. He had previously written "inquiring as to the progress of the Building scheme of Liberia," thinking that he "might have been of service," but he "had not received any reply." Since he was "an aspirant from a Racial viewpoint," he was "most anxious in collecting all the Negro literature that may be available," and, as a West Indian from Trinidad, he was called "an American and sought after by every lettered man within my District for information about the U.N.I.A. and the Black Star Line." He was also a member of the Lagos Branch of the UNIA, and people in the Gold Coast were anxious about the arrival of the boats from Accra and "read Negro Books and adorn their walls with Negro Pictures." He hoped Harrison would give him "the necessary assistance in fostering a long lost Brotherhood" and stressed both that "the idea of the African at Home is far more complex" than most thought and that there was "a latent intelligence in the man which would be a new education to Europe." In closing, Williams mentioned that he intended to start a correspondence club and hoped Harrison would be interested.[147]

On November 6, Williams again wrote to Harrison thanking him for his "kind letter" of August 30, which arrived on October 3, along with some books for him and for Casely Hayford (which he promptly sent to "Sihondi"). Williams described Harrison's "most valuable book" *When Africa Awakes* as "a treasure." He then explained that in his effort to start the Correspondence Club International "the question of Finance is out of the programme," and it was "a hard struggle on my own to bring to the knowledge of the African reader a necessity to correspond with persons abroad on matters of all kinds and that it will form a sort of education." He asked Harrison to do him "the favour of collecting most of the Negro Works for me." If he was sent a price list he would remit the necessary amount. He also was interested in wholesale prices and possibly becoming an agent for booksellers. Williams included a form for the Adonis Correspondence Club, for which he sought twenty members, in the hope that this club could "'find its fruition' in an international monthly magazine beginning with 24 pages." He added that he looked forward to the Liberty League magazine that Harrison planned and was "of [the] opinion that such a paper would sell like hot cakes in this country" because "the African at home is eager to know everything and would sometimes spend much to achieve such a knowledge." His hope was that Africa was indeed "awakening," and he wanted to hear from Harrison.[148]

Perhaps in part inspired by this letter, Harrison would continue writing the types of pieces that J. P. Williams so admired in the *Negro World* through the early portion of 1922.

11

Negro World Writings and Reviews
(September 1921–April 1922)

From the end of 1921 into early 1922 Harrison wrote a number of important articles, editorials, and reviews as associate editor at the *Negro World*. He focused on such themes as "democracy," imperialism, racism, high rents, electoral politics, the Washington Conference, and disarmament. His book reviews were wide ranging and included pieces on Africa, Islam, and works by Black authors. These reviews sparked correspondence with the authors T. Lothrop Stoddard and J. A. Rogers, and though they have largely been inaccessible, they (like most of Harrison's writings) have much to offer. During this period the forces arrayed against Garvey grew stronger, and Harrison, while still writing for the *Negro World*, maintained a noticeable distance from him.

On October 1, 1921, Harrison took up the issue of democracy in a discussion of the surplus laborers created by "white [capitalist] civilization." His letter to the editor of the *Negro World* discussed a recent visit he had made to the New York Public Library at Forty-Second Street. His attention had been "arrested" by "a vast multitude" of "dirty, unshaven, hungry and homeless" men ("all but four" of whom "were white"), who assembled in the adjacent Bryant Park. As he watched, other men lined them up and then proceeded to give a few pennies or a meal ticket to each man. Those receiving "first consideration" were men who "had been mobilized . . . to 'make the world safe for—' something" and could show army discharges. As they presented their identification papers Harrison "couldn't help thinking that the white race was exposing . . . one of its cankering sores," which was "eating into its vitals and under which it must soon succumb." He tersely commented:

Here was a mass of muscle and mind produced by the forces of white civilization, and for these it could find no use either in work or war. War was over and work was over, too. And this sort of thing recurs at shorter and shorter periods—in the white man's world of blessing which he is anxious to impose upon people of other colors. A civilization which regularly grinds out such horrors deserves to die.[1]

Developing this theme further, Harrison wrote "'Democracy' in America" in his *Negro World* column of October 8. His powerful first three paragraphs reproduced the opening four paragraphs from "Wanted—A Colored International" in the May 28, 1921, *Negro World*. They put forth his critique of "capitalist imperialism," moved from the international to the domestic situation, and reiterated that "we Negroes have no faith in American democracy and can have none so long as lynching, economic and social serfdom lie in the dark alleys of its mental reservations."[2]

"Democracy in America" was a theme Harrison would often discuss. He would allude to pronouncements of Woodrow Wilson and to the "rotten hypocrisy which masquerades as democracy in America." To Harrison, Wilson, who in 1917 had proclaimed that the United States had declared war against Germany to make the world "safe for democracy," was probably "the most prominent proponent of democracy." While such words stirred strivings for democracy throughout the world, Harrison repeatedly stressed that the call for "democracy" was "a convenient camouflage behind which competing imperialists masked their sordid aims," those who proclaimed the new democratic demands never had any intention of extending them, and "the cant of democracy" was intended as "dust in the eyes of the white voters" and "bait for the clever statesmen." He consistently argued that the flamboyantly advertised "democracy" would return "to plague the inventors" and that those who "took democracy at its face value," which was "equality," would "demand that the promise be made good." The failure to extend true democracy was becoming "the main root of that great unrest" that was developing throughout the world.[3]

After his opening three paragraphs, Harrison broached the subject of Christianity. He cited the author Mary Kingsley, who said "she did not believe that Christianity could be a solution of the African's problem 'because, while it may be possible to convert Africans *en masse* to Christianity, it is not possible to so convert Europeans.'" Harrison thought this to be "substantially true." The African viewed Christianity "with unfriendly eyes," though making "a distinction between the religion of Jesus Christ and Christianity." He thought the former "would be a good thing not only for Africa, but also for Europe," while the latter did "not benefit Europe and America" and was "a curse to Africa." In Christian Europe and America there was "hatred and race prejudice, greed, obscenity, drunkenness and organized bloodshed and banditry," which caused Harrison to wonder how Christian ministers "turn[ed] their backs upon iniquity at home" yet had "such a fine eye for it in Africa." He concluded that there was work to do in all Christian lands.[4]

Harrison then examined Christianity from the perspective of the "African Negro." He discussed how "missionaries can be trusted to preach to the Negro the ethics of submission and subservience" and how the British government is aware that this is "putting the education of the black African more and more into the hands of the white Christian missionary," a positive development, in its opinion, because "one missionary is worth more than a battalion of soldiers." He again emphasized that under capitalist conditions "the work of the white missionary, like that of the white soldier is dirty work" and that "the African . . . knew this." That knowledge, explained Harrison, was why, "after five hundred years of Christian contact with Africa, only four million of its two hundred million inhabitants," including "a million and a half white Afrikaners in South Africa," were "nominally Christians."[5]

In his November 26, 1921, *Negro World* column on "The Negro and the Health and Tenement House Departments," Harrison focused on an important domestic issue—the infant mortality rate. He cited a Department of Health publication that showed that the infant mortality rate "among the Negroes of the Columbus Hill area" (the area around Broadway and Columbus Avenue and Sixty-Fifth and Sixty-Sixth Streets in Manhattan, near where Harrison had lived two decades earlier) had been reduced from 314 per thousand children to 164 between 1915 and 1920. He considered this "a creditable showing," though both rates were "twice as high . . . as that for whites." The disparity was, in part, because "the majority of the houses inhabited by Negroes in the Sixties" were "less wholesome and healthy than those inhabited by whites of the same class." The disparity also existed because both the Health Department and the Tenement House Department were "not so solicitous regarding violations of their respective codes when the complaining residents are colored as when they are white."[6]

Harrison had made this charge earlier. In 1919 he "cited specific instances" when speaking at the Palace Casino, when the Rent-Payers' League met in the presence of Commissioner of Health Dr. Royal S. Copeland. He cited 570 Lenox Avenue (between 138th and 139th Streets), where he lived and "where at that time there had been for over a year no dumb-waiter service and the agents of the building had instructed the tenants, in plain violation of the code, to dump their garbage down the shaft." "The same condition" had remained for two years without even a violation placed against the house, though he had complained four times over the past three weeks to the Tenement House Department and spoken with the commissioner. Only when he went down to Mayor John F. Hylan's Committee on Rent Profiteering was he able to get an inspector to visit. There were children in this building, and the absence of heat and other things for nearly two weeks was "injuring their health." Harrison hadn't "observed any inclination on the part of either of these departments to act," and he concluded that these and similar conditions "wherever colored people live in New York" adequately explained "the difference in infant mortality statistics." If such conditions weren't remedied, he warned, "we colored people will have to get up a gigantic petition to the Mayor of New York." He also insisted that the various health agencies, "including the Harlem Hospital, must stop treating us as if we were beggars . . . and begin to bestir themselves when we are the victims of covetous child-slayers, as they do when white people are." Harrison considered New York to be "a fine and splendid" city with "Police, Fire and other departments . . . unusually efficient." Residents, while proud of its municipal grandeur, did not like "to find that any department voluntarily defaults on its efficiency record when it reaches the color line." As first steps toward a proactive response, he urged "Negro mothers" to write to the *Weekly Bulletin* and to the Department of Health for "valuable pamphlets" such as *The Work of the Department of Health's Dental Clinic for School Children* and for the June and July bulletins on "Open-Air Classes in the Public Schools" and "Preventing Preventable Diseases in New York City."[7]

Several months later, on March 4, 1922, Harrison's "The Negro and High Rents" in the *Negro World* noted that the New York Charity Organization Society's annual report had demonstrated that "high rents are responsible for more destitution in this city than any other single factor." Since the average monthly rent paid by white families in 1921 was $17.36 and "the average monthly rent paid by Negroes in Harlem" was "about fifty dollars," it was clear that "to keep their heads above water the average Negro family has to struggle more fiercely [often needing to take in lodgers] than the average white family." Nevertheless, it was "a noteworthy social fact that the average Negro home is neater and cleaner than the home of the average white worker who is in the same social class." The society's figures also showed "that the number of West Indian families who were assisted was exactly equal to that of the Negro Americans." Harrison concluded by complementing the Urban League under James H. Hubert for "doing splendid work in relieving distress among scores of West Indian unfortunates."[8]

———

In "The Theory and Practice of International Relations Among Negro-Americans" in the October 22, 1921, *Negro World*, Harrison offered a brief statement on the "theory of international relations, racially speaking," of "the Negro" in the United States. He noted how "over twelve hundred million" of the "more than seventeen hundred million people" of the world were "colored—black, brown, and yellow" and that "about half of the white remainder" held "more than half of the colored majority" in "permanent political subjection" and "control[led] in various ways most of the others." The theory by which this was justified was known variously as "the Color Line, the White Man's Burden and Racial Superiority." It was "against the theory and the situation which it expressed" that "colored peoples" were "contending everywhere." A "similarity of suffering" was "producing a similarity of sentiment," which was "finding expression in deeds, in spoken words and in print, in the newspapers and magazines published by colored people in Turkestan, China, Japan, India, Egypt, West Africa, Persia, the West Indies and elsewhere." The colored world was "internationally on the move," and its different sections could "profit by each other's experience and catch inspiration and understanding from one another." It was, therefore, "absolutely necessary" that "any one part . . . should know what is happening in all the other parts and keep in touch with . . . international developments occurring in the international world of color." Harrison then asked "the American reader of color" to try to answer, without using a book, ten imposing questions on "the big and significant occurrences and features of the international world of color." His questions were:

1. What is the difference between the programs and following of said [Said] Zaghlul [Zafhloul] Pasha and Adly Yeghen Pasha? Which one is supported by the British—and why?

2. Where, when and why did the National Congress of British West Africa meet and who were its leaders?

3. Who is General [Reginald Edward Harry] Dyer? What are the Rowlatt Acts, and why have they driven the conservative Indian nationalists into the arms of the radicals?

4. How many republics are there in China at present? Who is Sun Yat Sen? Are the policemen in Hongkong Chinese—or what are they? (This is really important and not at all trivial).

5. General [Henri Joseph Eugene] Gouraud had 200,000 French troops in Syria and the Arab hinterland, and the British 100,000. Against what colored general did they fight and why? Gouraud held up the people of Damascus and made them pay ten million francs ransom. Why?

6. What is the name of the white Englishman who was in 1917 "the soul of the Arabian revolution?" Why has he since denounced the British secret treaties? What are these treaties?

7. If the Moors overthrow the Spaniards whom would they have to defeat next in order to free Morocco from European control?

8. What new Latin-American republic was created within the past two weeks? Where is it situated?

9. What island off Hongkong and Canton is owned by Japan? What lands on the continent of Asia?

10. What countries in West Africa have jim-crow cars? Which in South Africa has segregation laws ten times worse than those of the United States?[9]

Harrison stated that inability to answer correctly two-thirds of this questionnaire was "absolute proof of ignorance on racial international affairs," and he predicted that "more than nine-tenths of our 'leaders' and 'intellectuals' would fail to answer correctly—unless they first looked up the questions in a book." Since there were "thousands of white men who could ['not' was inserted by the printer, but Harrison did not want it here] answer them offhand," he concluded that "here in America white men know more about the international world of color than colored men do." To Harrison that was "our damning disgrace." Since "the difference between our THEORY and our PRACTICE" was so "glaring," he asked the readers to suggest "the answer."[10]

In the November 5 *Negro World* Harrison commented that there had been only one response to the questionnaire, and he hadn't seen it until it appeared in print. In response to the one written reply, he explained that Judge (Sir Sidney A. T.) Rowlatt "was not a peer; he was a puisne [that is, a superior court] judge" and that the acts bearing his name "were not political, but punitive." They "penalized any expression of opinion, even in a private letter, that carried any criticism of the British regime" and "deprived the accused of the right of trial by jury, the right to be faced by his accuser or to know who he was, and the right to have his case judged on good evidence or even on the original bill of indictment." Harrison recognized that his questions were "not fair as a test for 'the masses,'" though they were "a test for the 'intellectuals' who should be able to teach the masses these things"—but, he emphasized, "one must first learn in order to teach." He also offered that anyone who felt like "being unmannerly" to him could do so "safely" in the *Negro World*, since he didn't "answer personal slurs in it," except "on a point of public importance to racial concerns," as when he "carried on the 'Crab-Barrel' controversy" (in 1920).[11]

Harrison's November 19 *Negro World* article was on "The Washington Conference," the meeting on naval disarmament held from November 12, 1921, to February 6, 1922. That international meeting was attended by delegations from the United States, Great Britain, Italy, France, and Japan as well as by representatives from China, Belgium, Portugal, and the Netherlands, who came together to discuss Far Eastern questions. The conference grew out of the post–World War I, post–Paris Peace Conference naval race between the United

States, Great Britain, and Japan, which intensified after the United States stationed a large fleet in the Pacific.[12]

President Harding called for the conference as an alternative to U.S. participation in the League of Nations and as a way to relieve the burdens of military and naval establishments. The U.S. Congress had previously passed legislation for a naval buildup in response to the increasing buildup of Britain and Japan and possible renewal of the Anglo-Japanese alliance. Then, on November 12, 1921, as the conference opened, Secretary of State Charles Evans Hughes and President Harding announced a proposed plan for the United States to scrap thirty ships (845,000 tons), Britain nineteen ships (583,375 tons), and Japan seventeen ships (448,928 tons). The conference ultimately agreed on a ratio of naval tonnage for the major powers in which Britain conceded superiority to the United States, a call for an end to the Anglo-Japanese alliance, and recognition of colonial possessions in the Far East as well as Japan's role as an international power.[13]

Harrison considered the Washington Conference to be "of supreme importance" and analyzed it from "the point of view of the Colored International." He emphasized that a consideration of the "Disarmament Conference properly begins with Japan," and he considered it "significant" that in recent pronouncements made by experts on international tensions "Japan has been set up as the main target in the discussion." A prime example involved Stoddard's *The New World of Islam*, which had caused "much disquietude" and led to an effort "to dispel this" by a long article by General Charles-Marie-Emmanuel Mangin, of the Superior War Council of France, in the October 23 *New York Times*. Mangin attempted "to argue away the impression left by Stoddard's book, viz., that the darker peoples of Near, Middle and Far East are preparing to challenge the supremacy of the whites in Asia and North Africa." His answer followed "step by step the plan of Stoddard's book" yet never mentioned it. Mangin also "dragged Japan into it" by stating that "a small amount of wisdom will be sufficient to enable her [Japan] to assure herself and to demonstrate to the eyes of the world that she repudiates the idea of entering into rivalry with the European powers in Asia or of nursing a latent and dangerous hostility against the United States in the Pacific."[14]

Harrison cited additional evidence on the centrality of Japan to the conference. He mentioned *Le Matin* of October 7, in which its foreign editor Jules Sauerwein emphasized, "'Popular excitation and race hatred are increasing every day between America and Japan.'" There was also the November 5 *Evening Post*, in which a correspondent stated that "official Washington is trying to get a line on the leading Asiatic statesmen," and the words of Motosada Zumoto, editor of the *Herald* of Asia and former secretary to Marquis Ito, who, at a press congress in Honolulu, "told the white men there assembled what all Japanese felt, but no Japanese diplomat cared to express in public": "If the West persistently refuses to listen to the voice of reason and justice and aggravates the antagonism of culture by injecting race prejudice, it is not inconceivable that the result may possibly be war between the races incomparably more calamitous than the last great war and wider in extent." Zumoto added, "The question of cultural antagonism cannot be settled by official conventions. . . . Japan and America are the respective vanguards of two civilizations, expressing temperaments and modes of thought so different that when they come into contact the shock is bound to be unpleasant and disconcerting." Finally, General Sir Ian Hamilton, a veteran of some forty years of military campaigns, told the members of the London Press Club that "the Japanese know that if battleships should cross the Pacific to attack them they would never get back, because of lack of adequate naval bases. If we had trouble with the Japanese they would be able to take Hong Kong and the Philippines and it would be a long time before they could be ousted."[15]

Harrison said the Washington Conference was a "Peace Congress" only because Wilson's "Peace Congress and its resultant fake League of Nations were flat failures." Something had to be done: since there were now "twice as many soldiers . . . under arms as there were in 1914, and the burden of taxation presse[d] heavily on the purses of white nations"; since millions were "out of work and starving"; and since "shells and bombs" were going "up (and down) in tests," some at costs that "would feed a village for a year." The "overlordship" of these countries entailed "the maintenance of 'white supremacy,'" and given that some of the darker peoples had arms it was "obvious" that "the white powers must first disarm them before they themselves can disarm." Japan was the most powerful of these darker nations, and "she alone" had "'entered into rivalry with the European powers in Asia'": therefore, Japan was "their main concern" at the second Peace Congress—it had to be disarmed.[16]

Japan, Harrison stressed, was "only an index." There were hundreds of millions in Asia and Africa who were "restive under white control," and if Japan took up arms "against any white nation at this time it would be 'all Hell let loose'—and they know it." Thus, "the main business of the bearers of 'the white man's burden'" was "to trick Japan into a position where she can be prevented from fighting—except at a great disadvantage." Yet, "with all this talk of disarmament, the white nations do not intend to forego 'white supremacy,' the power of the white nations of Europe and America to interfere in the affairs of Africa and Asia." While they "must bar the Asiatic . . . from the Western world," it was clear that "no white nation" would "agree to let itself be barred from the Orient." Therefore, argued Harrison, the Washington Conference was "a patent fraud." He supported this with a statement made by the Dutch trade union head

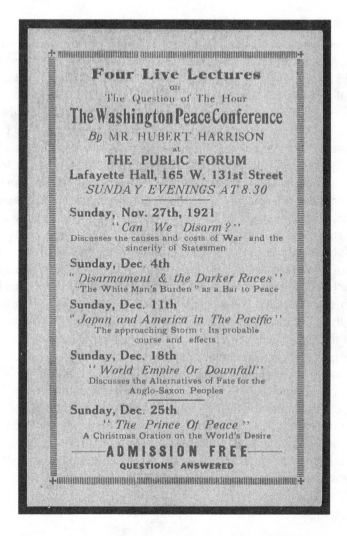

Figure 11.1. "Four Live Lectures on the Question of the Hour; The Washington Peace Conference, by Mr. Hubert Harrison, 27 November–25 December 1921." Hubert Harrison's free lectures on "The Washington Peace Conference" for "The Public Forum" at Lafayette Hall, 165 West 131st Street, are listed on this broadside. In his December 4 talk on "Disarmament and the Darker Races" Harrison discussed "imperialism" and attempts by the "white race" at "lowering the price of racial control" by moving "from stark force to moral camouflage: from soldier to savant," by means of "'alien education,' 'Christianity,' and 'friendliness.'" In this context, he declared the Washington Conference "a fake—yet a reality" whose "objects" were "to trap Japan," "to lower costs of control," and "to extend Anglo-Saxon over-lordship & fix its foundations." He saw potential causes of future disturbances in "exploitable areas" such as China and "centers of future disturbance" such as the "U.S. vs. Japan." Harrison concluded by emphasizing that "The Dialectic of Racial Rule" was that "White 'civilization' [was] likely to destroy itself." *Source:* Hubert H. Harrison Papers, Box 16, Folder 17, Rare Book and Manuscript Library, Columbia University Library. See https://dlc.library.columbia.edu/catalog/cul:8gtht76k0s.

Ido Fimmen at The Hague one month earlier: "I do not believe for an instant that the gentlemen are serious in their talk of disarmament. The most important delegates are military chiefs from the recent war—[French Marshall Ferdinand] Foch, [Douglas] Haig [Great Britain], [David] Beatty [Great Britain], [Armando] Diaz, [Italy] etc."[17]

Harrison also cited another reason for restraint. Since "no nation wars except in self-defense," its "safety must depend upon its military might." But if such a nation could not know "how many nations may attack it at once," it could not be expected "to voluntarily decrease its powers of resistance," and, accordingly, he expected "the usual . . . lying, the secret treaties and reservations and all the paraphernalia of 'diplomacy.'" "'Civilization' as determined by the white race," wrote Harrison, "sees itself on the toboggan slide, knows where it is going, but can not stop nor deflect its course." The Washington Conference was "simply one of its last heroic gestures," and the "only man of them all who seems to know what's what will be in the press gallery—Herbert George Wells." If one wanted to know "just how hopeless is the case for white civilization—Japan or no Japan," Harrison recommended Wells's recent book *The Salvaging of Civilization*.[18]

Shortly after his article on "The Washington Conference" appeared Harrison was scheduled to deliver a series of "Lectures on the Question of the Hour: The Washington Peace Conference" for the Public Forum at Lafayette Hall, 165 West 131st Street, on Sunday evenings. His topics included "Can We Disarm?" (on "the causes and costs of war and the sincerity of Statesmen) on November 27, "Disarmament and the Darker Races" (and "'The White Man's Burden' as a Bar to Peace") on December 4, "Japan and America in the Pacific" (and "The Approaching Storm: Its Probable Course and Effects") on December 11, "World Empire or Downfall" ("the Alternatives . . . for the Anglo-Saxon People") on December 18, and "The Price of Peace" ("A Christmas Oration on the World's Desire") on December 25.[19]

––––––––––

Notes from his December 4 talk on "Disarmament and the Darker Races" indicate that Harrison opened by describing "imperialism." Under the subtopic "Metaphysics of Imperialism" he discussed how "the white man's burden" maintained that other races were unfit for self-government and how democracy and self-government were "in conflict with Race-Superiority." In discussing the "realities of rulership" he described exploitation in terms of area, numbers, health control, and physical force and emphasized that the maintenance of "White Civilization" required "armaments" and that the "white powers could not disarm—if they wished." After discussing these "outer conflicts" Harrison moved to the "inner conflicts . . . within the white race" and described attempts at "lowering the price of racial control" by moving "from stark force to moral camouflage: from soldier to savant"—as by means of "'alien education,' 'Christianity,' and 'friendliness.'" In this context, he declared the Washington Conference "a fake—yet a reality," whose "objects" were "to trap Japan," "to lower costs of control," and "to extend Anglo-Saxon over-lordship & fix its foundations." Potential causes of future disturbances existed in "exploitable areas," particularly "China, Asia Minor, [and] Siberia," and "centers of future disturbance" included "England vs. France," the "U.S. vs. Japan," and the "U.S. vs. England." The "'safe' nations" were "those who will be fought for." Harrison concluded by emphasizing that "the Dialectic of Racial Rule" was that "White 'civilization' [was] likely to destroy itself."[20]

Harrison handwrote his December 4 talk on "Disarmament and the Darker Races." Then, later in the month, he wrote a three-page piece, with the same title, under the pseudonym "Hira Lal Ganesha." Finally, in the *Negro World* of December 31, he published the article in modified form. The core message of all three pieces was similar.[21]

In the talk Harrison explained that the world's population was over seventeen hundred millions, of which over twelve hundred millions were people of color. The "white populations of Great Britain, the United States, France, Italy, Belgium, Holland, Spain and Portugal" did not exceed two hundred and eighty-three millions, yet their representatives met to settle the future of "the world" and ignored "the reactions of the twelve hundred million colored people." There was, accordingly, an explosive possibility "for future trouble" because "the voice of an overwhelming *majority*—linked unwillingly in a state of unstable subordination to a permanent ruling minority" was suppressed.[22]

After these comments Harrison described how "the white race" was "undoubtedly the superior" at present. It was "superior" because it had "invented and amassed more powerful means for the subjugation of Nature and of man than any other race"; it was "the top-dog by virtue of its soldiers, guns, ships, money, resources and brains." Yet, in Europe, between 1914 and 1918, "the white race" consumed and destroyed "these very soldiers, ships, money, resources and brains" upon which its superiority was based. It was naturally weaker "after such a war" and "less able to maintain its will as against the will of other races." The war not only "decrease[d] the numbers of the white race"; it also "lower[ed] for a time its moral and intellectual quality." This was so because "war, as waged by the white race, destroys first the strongest and bravest, the best stocks, the young men who were to father the next generation." Since the "next generation must . . . be fathered by the weaker stocks of the white race," it would, "in physical stamina and in brain power . . . be less equal to the task of maintaining their 'superior' position in the conflict of the races than their fathers were." It was these "lands, labours, and resources of the backward and weaker peoples" that constituted the "stakes of war and diplomacy" for "Europe and America."

A glance at the map showed the "danger points" in places "like Persia, China[,] Asia Minor and Africa where white nations have staked out competing claims to the ownership, control and 'development' of the land of colored peoples." Since Britain, Belgium, and France had "absorbed most of Africa," Asia now remained "a fruitful source of future troubles." Overall, however, based on "the subsequent apportionment of the spoil," the "last [general war] between white nations" was fought "mainly for slices of Africa," and it now looked "as if the next would be fought over slices of Asia." Japan, "the only colored nation which was ceded the status of a Great Power exists in Asia, and [the] only alliance formally entered into with any [colored] nation was made with this one—and made [by the] mightiest white Powers." Before concluding Harrison added, "the real reason" for the "Anglo-Japanese alliance was and is . . . India," which he declared to be "the key-stone of Britain's imperial structure."[23]

In "Disarmament and the Darker Races" Harrison again emphasized the "explosive possibilities" that "lurk in every . . . suppressed minority" and how they were more explosive when the suppressed "is an overwhelming majority linked unwillingly in a state of unstable subordination to a permanent ruling minority." Out of this unstable domestic subordination sprang "the permanent need of the police machinery of the State, with its consequent burden to the taxpayers," while internationally, "colonial and imperial control" provided "the greater portion of the need for armaments." Thus, at the disarmament conference in Washington, "the French delegates demurred to the demand for reductions in the size of the French Navy," and Stephen Luzanne stated "the main ground of their objection"—it had extensive coasts and was "the second greatest colonial empire."[24]

"Just as the 'inferior' blacks of four Southern States dominate the domestic policies of those States, so do the 'inferior' Asiatic groups dominate the international policies of white Europe and America." In America, Harrison explained, "our white political experts have managed to dodge the real inner reason for England's Asiatic alliance with Japan . . . India, which [he emphasized again] is the key-stone of the British imperial system." The "mere existence of a colored great power in Asia" was "a tremendous stimulant to Asiatic self-assertion," and given that "this colored power" had "defeated successively two white powers and driven them from Asia's eastern front," it was no wonder "what trouble it could stir up in India," with its 150,000,000 people, "if it should, in a spirit of unfriendliness assume the role of liberator or leader."[25]

Harrison then quoted Stephen Bosnal in the *Times' Current History* magazine that "China is a market which . . . we cannot afford to lose." Bosnal, a "white publicist," painted "a beautiful ethical picture" of the United States "as the champion of China against Japanese aggression," but he "deliberately" hid "the racial implication of his thesis." Though he claimed that the United States' pledge to support China against outside aggression went back to the treaty of 1858, in fact, explained Harrison, the United States never protested when "large slices of China" were "taken by England, Germany, France and Russia." Then, in 1894, "when the rising empire of Japan defeated the empire of China, the Japanese attempted to do what England did after she had defeated Germany—to take some of the territory of the conquered." That was when "Russia presented a note to the powers" maintaining "that any taking of territory by Japan would be opposed by the armed forces of Russia, England, Germany and France." Japan realized "she could not fight these four powers," but then those powers "proceeded to take what they had denied Japan": "England took Wei Hai Wei, Germany took Shantung, Russia took Port Arthur, and France also took her slice," and this "showed the Japanese that strong armies and navies were the only things respected by the righteous powers." Japan then proceeded to develop them, and with them "she ousted Russia in 1905, and Germany in 1915." Since the United States "did not assume any ethical role" when "the white powers were stripping China," it seemed clear to men of color, wrote Harrison, that "she does so now only because Japan, as a colored nation, has assumed in China a prerogative exclusively appropriated hitherto by the dominant and superior whites."[26]

Harrison hoped that "those who act as spokesmen for the enlightened sections of the white world could be candid enough to admit openly" that the "fundamental dictum of their present political philosophy" was "to have their own stock eternally on top." The "philosophy of the White Man's Burden" could "be justified on pragmatic grounds" in formulations by "white statesmen and publicists," but "yellow, brown and black men all over the world" were "laughing . . . at the thought that the white men can hold firmly by that philosophy and still talk of disarmament." As long as there was the "will-to-be-free" held by "these darker millions" and the "will-to-power of the white people of Europe and America, just so long must these white people stay armed." Harrison then predicted that "when the next great war breaks out the nations involved will be divided into two groups—those fighting and those being fought for." With the "tremendously increased destructiveness of chemical warfare the amount and range of the destruction wrought will be far greater than that of the first great war," and it seemed "a safe guess that the greater the technical development of the nations in the first group the greater will be the destruction which they will wreak upon each other." He suggested, "perhaps civilization (as they know it) will be wiped out" and "the nations which will escape destruction will be those that are being fought for." Thus, "the doctrine of domination will end . . . and 'they that take the sword shall perish by the sword.'"[27]

In late 1921 Harrison also wrote a number of book and theater reviews. In the October 15 *Negro World* he discussed Angelina Weld Grimké's *Rachel*, a three-act play that became a successful stage drama. Since "the art of playwriting" was "not so common among us Negro-Americans," he did not think a "serious attempt" should be overlooked. Since he knew "absolutely nothing" of Grimké, this might make for "impartiality."[28]

Based on her craftsmanship Harrison guessed that Grimké was "a young writer" (she was twenty-six when the play was written), while the theme indicated she was "a grave and serious" dramatist who looked at the "world of color problems" with "somewhat unusual eyes." With an "economy of means" she worked out "a tragedy in the conflict of character within one human breast," an achievement Harrison did not remember having seen before. Rachel, "a Negro girl, sweet, sincere and high-minded," loved children, "especially colored children." She had a big heart and a "passion for motherhood." Nevertheless, she refused to marry the man she loved because she "would not bring into the world Negro children foredoomed by fate to run the gauntlet of American race prejudice." This, observed Harrison, was "the deadliest indictment of American race prejudice that could be framed," and "it took the fertile genius of a woman to frame it."[29]

Harrison considered the play's "values" to be "ideal rather than real." He compared it to "the Chinese gentlemen who, when insulted by a neighbor, retaliate[s] by committing suicide upon the neighbor's doorstep." Harrison hoped that Miss Grimké would "see the point," for it was "obvious that your neighbor can at any time blot you out as a problem of his existence if you are given to this . . . form of reaction." He thought the play exhibited "splendid promise" but not "great achievement." It contained "glimpses of tremendous powers struggling to get themselves exposed," but the "dialogue was mostly 'defective,'" and Grimké's "control of the mechanics of stagecraft" was "not yet up to standard." Overall, Harrison felt if she would "devote herself a little more to the concrete study of characterization and learn to limit and differentiate her characters by the form as well as the substance of their language," he felt that Grimké would "achieve not only a fine play—as 'Rachel' is—but a great play."[30]

In the *Negro World* of November 12 Harrison reviewed three 1921 books: *The Wings of Oppression*, by Leslie Pinckney Hill; *Night Drums*, by Achmed Abdullah (born Alexander Nicholayevitch Romanoff); and *An African Adventure*, by Isaac F. Marcosson. He described *The Wings of Oppression* as "a small and unpretentious collection of verse by a Negro schoolmaster" whose themes reflect "the preferences of the intellectual." Hill's treatment was "simple and sincere" and spoke "directly to the heart of the ordinary man." The poems "My Race" and "The Black Man's Bit" were "well worth the reading" and would "bring throbs of pride to the darker reader whose deeper interests they so well express." Hill's "range" was "not restricted to such themes," however, and other verses would "appeal to men and women everywhere."[31]

Night Drums was "romantic fiction," a "novel of Africa" in which a son of Africa in the days of "wireless telegraphy, aeroplanes and high-powered guns" was supposed to plan "a mighty uprising in the Motherland" amid a great gathering of the clans. As Nubians, Tuaregs, Fantis, and other "tribes of Africa north of the equator" rallied to M'yanna M'bi-likini, he welded them "into a mighty force." They defeated the French and almost drove "the whites out of Africa," until the leader was "destroyed by a knife in the hand of the woman whom he loved and to whom he had trusted his life." The story's two heroes were "a white American officer of the French Foreign Legion and El Mokrani, a Senussi mokaddem, an Arab whom the author causes to insist that he is white." Overall, Harrison considered *Night Drums* to be "a stirring tale" that would keep one from sleep until finished.[32]

Achmed Abdullah, born to a Russian father and Afghan mother, had traveled in many lands and lived in New York. He pursued "the Western white man's way of prosperity—giving them what their 'taste' demands," and he made "a rattling good yarn in the process." Though the author was a Senussi, Harrison judged that he had not traveled in Sudanic and central Africa, since he didn't know what a "jigger" (a parasitic insect) was. Abdullah's novel was recommended to *Negro World* readers.[33]

In reviewing *An African Adventure*, Harrison noted that this was Marcosson's eighth book and that he had previously "sprang into literary notice" with an *Adventure in Interviewing*, which recorded his tour from Capetown to the Congo but was not "worth-while." Harrison couldn't "recall any one who has travelled so far and seen so little" and thought Marcosson typified "the average cocksure American reporter who, with an all too inadequate education, bluffs his way through the world." Marcosson's "'interview' and account of" General Jan Christian Smuts, the leading architect of many of South Africa's "whites only" policies, was "very well done," but his travel accounts of South and Central Africa were "a dismal failure." His "ignorance of African history" was "colossal," and he was "always the willing dupe of those who feted and dined him." The Congo was a good example: Marcosson always referred to Congo atrocities as "German propaganda." In this he besmirched the late Sir Roger Casement, who was killed by the British in a "wartime attempt to free his native Ireland." Marcosson didn't know that Casement's charges were supported "by dozens of actual photographs of collections of human hands and legs chopped from the Congo natives by Leopold's savage Belgian soldiers because they didn't bring in enough rubber—to which the king had no claim." Marcosson similarly didn't "know of the existence of the official British blue books on the subject"; of *"The Crime of the Congo,* by Sir Arthur Conan Doyle; of "the

Belgian Commission's Report"; of the admissions made "even in the official 'whitewash,' of the proofs presented in the Belgian Parliament by Emile Vandervelde and Lorande"; and of the testimony of the Swedish clergyman Mr. Sjoblom and that of Joseph Clarke, "an American missionary who lived in King Leopold's private domain." Harrison didn't expect more "from a literary Johnnie" who took to Africa such works as Miguel de Cervantes's *Don Quixote*, Michel de Montaigne, William Henry Prescott, Thomas Carlyle, and Charles Dickens but "no book on African history and African affairs." It was "natural, therefore, to find no mention of the real labor problem in South Africa, nor the tens of thousands of white paupers in the Union." Harrison found only the first and last chapters on "Smuts" and "America in the Congo" to be "worth reading."[34]

In the *Negro World* of December 10 Harrison reviewed Octavus Roy Cohen's new book, *Highly Colored*. He began by observing that the "highly specialized life, which the Negro lives in his highly specialized American world," had "produced many interesting social types . . . tempting to the true fictionalist." He "regretted," however, that "Negro writers since [Paul Laurence] Dunbar and [Charles Waddell] Chesnutt" had "not seen fit to limn the larger number of these types for posterity." Unfortunately,

> just as the callow representatives of "culture" turned in top-lofty disdain from the hymns of the colored Baptists and Methodists of the plantation South until white men like [Antonín Leopold] Dvorak and [Henry Edward] Krehbiel pointed out to white and black that these were the only genuine music produced in America, so, the dress-coated devotees of a hand-me-down elegance have refused to deal with the rich mine of human material to be found in the daily lives lived by nine-tenths of our people.[35]

Harrison used this introduction to comment, "When a young Negro college graduate puts pen to paper to portray imaginatively the life of the American Negro he either produces a propaganda pamphlet in the guise of 'a story,' or he writes almost exclusively of the upper-class Negro types and pushes the lives below that level into the background of obscurity." While he didn't "condemn this tendency," since it was "quite natural" and "the way in which all literatures begin," he did think it important "to insist that we need not stop." The time had come to say "let's go!" to "Negro writers of fiction." The "white man" was "already exploiting the field which should be theirs" and "not always to our liking."[36]

How Cohen's book would be received by African Americans would "depend upon their sense of humor." Though "we boast" of "the Negro's 'unfailing humor,'" observed Harrison, "we are still touchy about our tribe and tend to get huffy when the type that is amusing happens to be 'colored.'" There was "the humor of malice and the humor of sympathy as well as the humor of sheer pleasure without any ulterior purpose," and Cohen's humor was "of the latter sort." Harrison went on to predict that the "supreme dandy and man-about town, Mr. Florian Slappey, Lawyer Evans Chew and that close-fisted man of money, Mr. Semore Mashby, will live in the memory as outstanding types together with the stalwart society known as 'The Sons and Daughters of I Will Arise.'" They were "drawn to the scale of humor, and on that scale they bulk large—even for Birmingham, Alabama." Cohen stuck to Birmingham, "although the types" he drew "would be just as representative of Norfolk or any other large Southern city." Harrison felt that "no normal human" would read "these delightful stories without bubbling over with enjoyment." He added that as a "book-hardened" reviewer he didn't "read a book over as a rule" but planned to read this one again. All but one of the short stories were "shaped to perfection," and the dialect was "lovingly chiseled to a high and fine finish." His "one regret" was that the book had only one illustration. *Highly Colored* was noteworthy, he added, because there were "no criminal or contemptible types" represented, "'just folks.'"[37]

Harrison reviewed Frederick Palmer's *The Folly of Nations* in the *Negro World* of January 21, 1922. He described how "all the world" was praying "for deliverance from the aims of patriotism," and Palmer, a veteran war correspondent who in early 1914 wrote "a great polemic against war" (*The Last Shot*), now offered "proof that men grow old." While his impressions of war "from his wide experience in Turkey, Greece, the Philippines and Manchuria" were "valuable as first-hand records," and while he knew "the dirt and cruelty, the whoop-las and the lies, the cynical indifference of statesmen drunk with power to the miseries they invoke," he saw them through "a haze of pathetic optimism and futile sentimentality." The "deep underlying causes" seemed "to escape him altogether." Palmer's argument was "so weak," explained Harrison, because he was "blind" to "Imperialism, which puts the war-making powers of the modern state in the hands of those who own the earth and its products, and sends its millions of men to die abroad for markets when they lack meat at home." He was "a humanitarian" who saw that war was "all wrong and wasteful," but he dodged his "duty of diagnosing the cause of war" and therefore failed "to exert any appreciable influence on the recovery of a sick world." Harrison closed his review, paraphrasing Claudius, king of Denmark, in Shakespeare's *Hamlet*: "diseases desperate in their nature grown require desperate remedies."[38]

On February 18, 1922, Harrison reviewed Hendrik Van Loon's overnight bestseller *The Story of Mankind*, which was "a history of civilization in which the African's contribution received generous acknowledgement." Van Loon "wrote for young people" with a "mild and gentle humor" while remaining a "champion of the wider world, as against the narrowing claims of countries, creeds and dogmas." Harrison then provided background to one of the strong points of Van Loon's *Story*—it was "entirely free" from the "vicious view of history" that "generally begins with Greece; because there was no white group anywhere which played any commendable part on the stage of civilization prior to twenty-four hundred years ago." Van Loon, however, points out that "the valley of the Nile had developed a high stage of civilization thousands of years before the people of the West had dreamed of the possibilities of a fork, or a wheel or a horse." The Egyptians "taught us many things," he wrote. They "were excellent farmers," "knew all about irrigation," "built temples which were afterwards copied by the Greeks . . . which served as the earliest models" for current churches, and "invented a calendar" that has survived with "few changes until today." Van Loon went on to explain "how our letters, which lie at the roots of civilization, have been developed out of the ancient Egyptian hieroglyphs." In "the same spirit" he "sweeps over Asia Minor, bringing before the reader the spectral sciences figures of Sumerians, Akkadians and the other elements of the great Semitic melting." Then "the Greeks enter the tale and from that point the story follows the usual course," though "it never sinks to the usual level."[39]

An additional Harrison review, "A Good Word for the Stage," in the *Negro World* of March 4, explained how the actors of the "Shuffle Along" company were again "going out of their way to give a benefit performance" to raise $3,000 for the Manassas Industrial School. He observed that "no class of people in the public eye has so many sneers thrown at its morals as . . . actors," especially from ministers. Nevertheless, "these hard-working people have exemplified in their helpfulness to each other in distress and to others who stood in need of their help, that sympathy and charity which are the backbone of real religion." The Shuffle Along company "pointed out the path of social service." Harrison hoped that those who attended the benefit performance on Sunday, March 5, would "learn the lesson which those actors have been giving to a selfish world!" He emphasized that ministers, in particular, could "learn a lesson in practical Christianity from these followers of Thespis."[40]

––––––––

Harrison published his "major critique of white supremacism in the publishing industry" in his "On a Certain Condescension in White Publishers" in the March 4 and March 11, 1922, issues of the *Negro World*. His "With the Contributing Editor" column described how in 1920 he had "inaugurated" in the *Negro World* "the first (and up to now the only) regular book-review section known to Negro newspaperdom." Since that time, *The Crisis* "has been attempting to follow my footsteps in the trail—with such success as was achievable by youth and inexperience." This comment, according to the historian Tony Martin, was probably a "scornful allusion" to Jessie Redmon Fauset, who "had for long been one of Harlem's respected intellectuals." Fauset was the literary editor (but not regular book reviewer) for *The Crisis* from 1919 to 1926. When he began the book reviews, Harrison continued, "it was with a "two-fold aim": "to bring to the knowledge of the Negro reading public those books which were necessary if he would know what the white world was thinking and planning and doing in regard to the colored world; and to bring the white publisher and his wares to a market which needed those wares." He "aimed to render a common service," and to "a certain extent" he felt he "succeeded," though "white" publishers were generally not "eager to avail themselves of the novel opportunity thus offered to get some more pennies for their pumpkins."[41]

With "humorous amazement" Harrison recalled how, after writing to Boni and Liveright for a review copy of a book dealing with "the anthropology of colored peoples," he received their reply of "supercilious magnificence." They wanted him "to supply them with back numbers of the journal" and seemed to wonder, "What could Negroes know of anthropology . . . ?" It reminded him of when John Mensa Sarbah wrote to the anthropologist Elsie Clews Parsons for an exchange copy of her book *The Family*. She replied "to his courteous request that the book was not of a sort to interest him and that, perhaps, he had been misled." Her response "created laughter from Lagos to Sierra Leone." Sarbah was the illustrious author of *Fanti Customary Laws* and "knew just about five times as much of social anthropology as Mrs. Parsons." Harrison also "laughed at the top-lofty airs of Boni and Liveright at that time."[42]

Harrison had recently, on February 18, 1922, reviewed Van Loon's *The Story of Mankind*, published by Boni and Liveright, yet in their reply they were "only an index." He similarly could not get the New York representatives of Macmillan and Company "to take the Negro reading public seriously." Over three months before he had written seeking a review copy of *A Social History of the American Negro*, by Benjamin Brawley, and had "not even deigned to reply." If it were a "question of the intrinsic quality of the literary criticism," then Harrison could cite Eugene O'Neill, the author of *The Emperor Jones*, who described his review as "one of the two or three best that had come from any source." Harrison added that he felt he had done "workman-like work in book-reviewing'. . . [William Bayard] Hale's *Story of a Style*, [Edmund D.] Morel's *The Black Man's Burden*, [John H.] Harris *Africa Slave or Free*, and [Ambrose] Pratt's *Real South Africa*."[43]

Harrison concluded "On a Certain Condescension in White Publishers" in the March 11, 1922, *Negro World*. He explained that the publishers of Lothrop Stoddard's two books, *The Rising Tide of Color* and *The New World of Islam*, had commended the thoroughness of his literary criticism of those books and that he and Stoddard had "entered into friendly and faithful correspondence." He had also reviewed books by Huebsch, Scribner, Doran, and Dutton to *Negro World* readers "to their mutual profit." Even the Macmillans had *The Soul of John Brown*, by Stephen Graham, and *The Influence of Animism on Islam*, by Dr. Samuel M. Zwemer, reviewed. Nevertheless, he found "the force of an ancient attitude is strong" and publishing houses seemingly unaware of "the fact that many of the 12,000,000 Negroes in this country do buy and read not only books on the Negro but other literary and scientific works."[44]

"As the only 'certified' Negro book-reviewer in captivity," Harrison felt "the onus of this backward view which white publishers take of the market which the Negro reading public furnishes for their wares." He considered it uncomplimentary, "short-sighted and unsound" and expressed his belief "that the Negro reading public will buy books—when they know of their existence." In particular he cited "the amazing stream of letters and money orders" flowing to J. A. Rogers at 513 Lenox Avenue. Rogers's "continued success" was "proof of the great intellectual awakening which has been brought about by the forces of the last decade." To his "Negro" readers Harrison predicted "that in the near future there will be many book reviewers," which, he explained, "is the name for literary critics in their working clothes." They were already treading on his heels in the *Negro World*. He stated that his own book reviewing began in the *New York Times* in 1906, and he offered advice to those who would follow in his wake.[45]

———

On August 1, 1921, T. Lothrop Stoddard continued his correspondence with Harrison, informing him that he had requested that Scribner's send him a copy of the forthcoming *The New World of Islam* as well as "two 'highlight' articles" on the book from *Scribner's Magazine*. Harrison responded by sending Stoddard his review of the *New World of Islam* from the *Negro World* issue dated October 29, 1921. On October 27 Stoddard wrote back thanking him for the "interesting review"; he indicated that he was looking forward "to reading the next part" (which appeared the following week). Stoddard also requested that Harrison send "a couple of extra copies of both" articles and asked if Harrison saw "the favorable mention" of the *Rising Tide of Color* in President Harding's October 26 "Birmingham address."[46]

Part 1 of Harrison's review in the October 29 *Negro World* opened by discussing how Stoddard had provided "a respectable and well-documented study" in *The French Revolution in San Domingo*; had "plotted the descending curve of the white race's contacts with the colored race in Asia, Africa and America" in *The Rising Tide of Color Against White World-Supremacy*; and was currently engaged in "preparatory work for a study of the Pan-African movement in Africa." Harrison then explained that in *The New World of Islam* Stoddard offered "an intensive and detailed study of the various ferments at work in the Near and Middle East," where "the brown Mohammedan millions" were "lining up for the final struggle against the domination of the white men of the Western world." Harrison commended the fact that Stoddard showed "an increasing measure of respect for the ideas and institutions of men of color" and noted that this kept pace with "his increasing knowledge of their activities and purposes."[47]

In his book Stoddard provided "a bird's eye view" of the series of movements that, wrote Harrison, "started with Mohammed ibn Abd-al-Wahhab in the first half of the eighteenth century," rose to "grave and disquieting proportions under Seyid Mohammed ben Senussi and Djemal-el-Din Sherif and Sir Syed Ahmed Khan in the early part of the nineteenth century," and under a "variety of forms" reached a "dangerous and revolutionary head" under leaders like the Emir Feisal, Mohammed Farid Bey, Yahya Siddik, Ahmed el Sherif and Sir Sed Ahmed Khan "in this revolutionary [twentieth] century." The "geographic and racial scope of these movements" was extensive: "Abd-el-Wahab was born and bred in the heart of the Arabian desert, and Feisal in Mecca; ben Senussi and his grandson, el Sherif, in Algeria; Djemal-el-Din, in Persia; Siddik and Farid Bey, in Egypt, and Sir Syed Ahmed Khan in India." The "'far flung battle line' stretched clear across Northern Africa from West to East" and ran "through Asia Minor, the Arab peninsula, Persia, Afghanistan, Turkestan and India, and . . . right through into China." To treat such a movement "through one hundred degrees of latitude and two centuries of time" required "a competent historian," and Stoddard was "quite competent."[48]

Harrison showed the way in which Stoddard turned to history to explain "the full meaning of the Islamic ferment." He described how in the seventh century "there erupted out of the backyard of Africa a race of fighting brown men with a new religion, a genius for democracy and civilizing gifts of a high order." Then, "in less than a hundred years they had spread that religion over half the earth":

> Shattering great empires, over-throwing long established religions, remoulding the souls of races and building up a whole new world—the world of Islam . . . . Intermarrying freely and professing a common belief; conquerors and conquered rapidly fused, and from this fusion arose a new civilization—the Saracenic civilization in which the ancient cultures of Greece, Rome and Persia were revitalized by Arab vigor . . . Arab genius and the Islamic spirit. . . . Studded with splendid cities, gracious mosques and quiet universities where the wisdom of the ancient world was preserved and appreciated; the Moslem East offered a striking contrast to the Christian West . . . then sunk in the night of the Dark Ages.[49]

Harrison next described how "the glory of Islam was dimmed when the seat of government was shifted to Baghdad" and "its democracy dampened under the influence of Persian despotism." According to Stoddard, "the fierce, free-born Arabs of the desert would tolerate no master, and their innate democracy had been sanctioned by the prophet who had explicitly declared that all believers were brothers." "Persian primacy," however, was "the beginning of the downfall of imperial Islam," and "when the Turanian Turks fell upon the luxurious Iranians," the latter "crumbled before a more vigorous people whose barbarian brutality" remained "the continuing cloud in the Mohammedan sky." The "Turk was a barbarian then and, despite his commendable transformation," remained "substantially a barbarian" and "almost as brutish as the British in Ireland," added Harrison (perhaps with the recent Armenian genocide in mind).[50]

Meanwhile, the Western nations of Europe had acquired "gunpowder and a thirst for wealth," and "these white barbarians, like the yellow ones on the Eastern front, had one great advantage in common with all other barbarians—constant fighting had made them harder fighters than the more civilized people who fought less frequently." Through the Crusades, they were "brought into contact with the higher civilization and culture of the Saracenic world," they had "their own period of renascence," and "their expanding powers were set to serve an awakening greed for gold." "Commerce and discovery were the two handmaidens of the new desire," and, "fronting on the sea," they "evolved into maritime powers at the time when the Mohammedan lands had lost their central unity and the powers of further propagation." Then "the sceptre of sovereignty" was "seized by the newer nations of the Christian world." It was "hardly six hundred years since the Turks were thundering at the gates of Vienna, and not quite twelve hundred since Moslems were arrayed against all Europe on the battlefields of Spain and Southern France, and Moslem armies were encamped before Lyons and Besancon." Nevertheless, in a few centuries, "the white man has risen to the heights of rulership from which he looks down with flattering self-complacency on all the rest of the world."[51]

Islam's "earlier world-domination . . . was in many respects superior in moral and spiritual values to that of the white man," since "it was not eaten by the corroding canker of race prejudice." To the contrary, "in political and civic matters character counted for much; color and race for nothing at all." Harrison quoted Stoddard: "'All true believers were brothers.' Black and brown and yellow were not, as in the Christian system, brothers in theology only, but they were genuinely so in practice before the magistrates and in all the relations of daily life." Harrison then added that Shaikh Mushir Hosain Kidwai, "a dark son of India," explained in his book *Pan Islam* that

it is the Christian white, "dis-colored" European people who are fanatically prejudiced against the "colored" and Asiatic races . . . . It is they who constantly disturb the amity and fraternity that should exist and which did exist under the true Islamic civilization. The black men of Abyssinia, the white of Spain, the yellow of China and the brown of Asiatic countries loved one another like brothers and treated each other on terms of perfect equality—and so they do even today if they are Mohammedans .... Christianity has also (on this account) failed altogether in bringing peace (on earth). It is the Christian people who have shed the greatest quantity of human blood in the past and who are still bent on their bloody pursuits.[52]

Harrison stressed that "those who profess Mohammedanism practice what they preach" and that "the sons of the Prophet [Muhammad]" were "nearer to 'the kingdom of Heaven' than those who parade the principle of the Judean carpenter [Jesus], yet never put them into practice." "Islam's superiority" was clearly "demonstrated" in education:

Christianity as an ecclesiastical system controlled Europe's educational systems and institutions, no thinker dared to think a new thought. The inquisition and the lesser tribunals sat cross-legged at the birth of every scientific idea to insure that it would be stillborn. The facts of science upon which Christian civilization now besets its claim to intellectual supremacy had to fight for their lives in the teeth of that Christian bigotry and ignorance that made the Dark Ages dark. And if that bigotry and ignorance had prevailed the telephone, wireless, steamship and traction plow would still exist only in the womb of the future. On the conceded facts of history the Christian system was in its own domain incompatible with knowledge and free inquiry.[53]

"On the other hand," Harrison added, "the Mohammedan system from its very beginning strove to promote knowledge and free inquiry," as detailed by Western scholars such as John William Draper in *The History of the Conflict Between Religion and Science*. Stoddard emphasized that "Mohammed reverenced knowledge," and he cited Mohammed's own words in the Koran:

"Seek Knowledge even if it be on the borders of China."
"Seek Knowledge from the cradle to the grave."
"One work of Knowledge is of more value than the reciting of a hundred prayers."
"God has created nothing better than reason."
"The ink of sages is more precious than the blood of martyrs."
"In truth, a man may have prayed, fasted, given alms, made pilgrimage, and all other good works; nevertheless he shall be rewarded only in the measure that he has used his common-sense."[54]

Harrison observed that this "was the religion which linked together and still links the souls of hundreds of millions of black, brown and yellow peoples from the Senegal to the shores of the Yellow Sea," and it was "this multitudinous mass" that was "on the move, struggling upward to their 'place in the sun,' under the impact of white arrogance, greed and race-prejudice" supported by "the forces of religion, business, imperialism and war." Stoddard's book included "the purely Hindu movement of Mr. [Mohandas] Gandhi, the people of Turkestan (who are not brown in any sense of the word)[,] the black populations of portions of India and Africa," and even references "the Moslem part of the population of Yellow China." In India "the brunt of the struggle for liberation has been borne mainly by the non-Moslem Hindus whose leader, M. K. Gandhi, stands out among men of all colors today as the greatest, most unselfish and powerful leader of the modern world." Since Stoddard wrote on "unrest in the Islamic world," he did not focus on this and other movements, and Harrison saw "justification for this in terms of Weltpolitik," since "the Moslem movement" was "the chief disquieting feature of the Eastern problem today." He also added that the "Japanese aspiration" was "dangerous" for "what it may evoke out of this ferment."[55]

To Harrison, the Islamic world was "awakening" from its "somnolence," as evidenced by "the conversion of new millions to the religious tenets of Mohammedanism." He cited the "marvelous progress in the interior of Africa" and quoted the French Protestant missionary D. A. Forget, who wrote that "While Christians dream of the conquest of Africa, the Mohammedans accomplish it." In West Africa European missionaries had lost many of their converts to Islam, while across the continent "the ancient Abyssinian Church, so long an outpost against Islam," was threatened "by the rising Moslem tide." Tribes were converting to Islam; the Russian Tartars, "despite the persistent efforts of the Orthodox Russian Church to convert them to Christianity, reverted to Islam"; and "Chinese in Yunan province and its hinterland" and in Chinese Turkestan had "come under the Crescent." It was "the same story" in "India, the Dutch East Indies and the Philippines." In the second part of the article Harrison promised to discuss "the source of this new strength" and the "machinery by which it expresses itself."[56]

On November 5 the *Negro World* republished Harrison's "The Brown Man Leads the Way," with corrections made on "14 glaring typographical errors" that had appeared in the first printing. In his accompanying column Harrison also clarified that the October 22 questionnaire was "for intellectuals." Then, in the concluding part of his article, he described how

the new and awakened Islam had its roots in the consciousness of humiliation with which the leaders of the people faced the fact of subjection to white

Christian Europe. This subjection was not only political: there was also the cultural superiority of the European peoples. Theirs were the new advances on the older knowledge, the inventions and improvements by which they had harnessed up the mighty forces of earth and air and sky and converted them into servants of their "will to power" over other human beings. The leaders of the brown man's world foresaw that truth[,] which has been stated in *When Africa Awakes*, namely that "never until the black man's knowledge of nitrates, machinery, textiles, engineering, etc. shall at least equal that of the white will the black man be able to measure arms successfully with him." They made up their minds that the brown man must go to school—even if he had to learn from the white.

But they also perceived that a part of the difficulty lay inside their world and that its removal must precede the removal of that part which lay outside of it. Selfishness, greed, fanaticism, and ignorance—these must be grappled with. The first great necessity, therefore, was one of Regeneration.[57]

As they addressed themselves to this task of regeneration they first addressed the "'messianic hope of Mahdism' and its bloody but abortive uprisings," which "accomplished nothing whether in the Egyptian Sudan or under the powerful Makechabendlya in Turkestan and China." The movement was "a mere straw fire; flaring up lively here and there, then dying down, leaving the disillusioned masses more discouraged and apathetic than before." The lesson learned from "the wildest outbursts of local fanaticism against the methodological might of Europe convinced thinking Moslems that long preparation and complete coordination of effort were necessary if Islam was to have any chance of throwing off the European yoke."[58]

These Moslems "also realized that they must study Western methods and adopt much of the Western technic of power." This new realization expressed itself "through the new type of religious fraternities like the Sednussiya [Senussi] in Algeria, the Ikhwna in Arabia and the Saiafi [Saifai] movement in India" and "through the propaganda of a new group of thinkers like Djemal-ed-Din, Mustapha Kemal, Kheir-ed-Din and Ahmed bey Agayeff." These "new fraternities" devoted themselves "to elevating the morals of the people, giving them education and enlightenment, uplifting their souls and welding them together in a discipline inner and outer."[59]

Stoddard described these organizations with sympathetic comprehension but made "no mention of the Bahai Movement—a most significant off-shoot of the Mohammedan reformation." For, "even though the Bab and his successor, Baba'ollah suffered martyrdom at the hands of Moslem tyrants, they and their more famous successor Abbas Effendi (better known as Abduh Baha)" were still "Moslem reformers." The "increasing number of the truly spiritual" who followed Bahai teachings in the Western lands were—to Harrison—"a living proof of the spiritual superiority of rejuvenated Islam over obsolescent Christianity."[60]

Thinkers and scholars "in all the Islamic countries" had striven "to evoke a group response to their native cultural needs." Sometimes, explained Harrison, "the appeal was put in terms of religion" and sometimes in terms of what he described as "that shifting reality called race," but "always it was in terms of themselves." It bore fruit "in the present Pan-Islamic movement and in the various movements of Islamic nationalism in Egypt, Turkey, Persia, Turkestan and elsewhere." The "result of this" was "a very real 'International' of Islamic peoples (mainly brown, but also black and yellow)," which kept England and France "in a perpetual fit of the jumps at the thought of what might happen should Japan, the foremost colored nation and the only colored Power, assume the leadership of this group or cast in her lot with it." All of this "gave point to the thesis" Harrison had expounded in his *Negro World* column of October 22 on "The Theory and the Practice of International Relations Among Negro-Americans," which he considered to be "a necessary part of our preparation for ultimate 'redemption.'"[61]

In reviewing Stoddard's description of how the recent war had intensified the unrest in the Islamic world, Harrison quoted:

> When the Sultan Abdul Hamid—who was also the Caliph of Islam—issued the call for a Jehad or Holy War it was not the flat failure which allied reports led the West to believe at the time. As a matter of fact, there was trouble in practically every Mohammedan land under Allied control. Egypt broke into a tumult smothered only by overwhelming British reinforcements; Tripoli burst into a flame of insurrection that drove the Italians headlong to the coast; Persia was prevented from joining Turkey only by prompt Russo-British intervention; while the Indian northwest frontier was the scene of fighting that required the presence of a quarter of a million Anglo-Indian troops. The British government has officially admitted that during 1915 the Allies' Asiatic and African possessions stood within a hand's breadth of a cataclysmic insurrection.[62]

In light of this, and in a direct slap at the wartime leadership of Du Bois and the others at the June 1918 Editors' Conference, Harrison stressed "how silly and shortsighted was the advice given by our educated but ignorant editor-leaders when they asked their befuddled followers to work, fight and pray for Allied success." It was "obvious that if the Allies had lost before America went in the colored peoples now under British subjection in Africa and Asia would have won their freedom at the same time." The war also "made for a tightening of the strings of Islam's resolution to be free," and "the democratic pretense of the Allies furnished a ferment" which remained at work. As Stoddard described, "during the war years" Allied statesmen repeatedly proclaimed "that the war was being fought to establish a new world order based on such principles as the rights of small nations and the liberty of all peoples." These pronouncements were "treasured and memorized throughout the East," and when "the East saw a peace settlement based "upon the imperialistic secret treaties, it was fired with a moral indignation and sense of outraged justice never known before." "A tide of impassioned determination began rising which . . . set the entire East in tumultuous ferment, and which seems merely the premonitory ground swell of a greater storm." "The great war . . . shattered European prestige in the East" and "opened the eyes of Orientals to the weaknesses of the West." Stoddard predicted that Asia and Africa would "make use of that knowledge."[63]

Harrison next examined Stoddard's rather "comprehensive analyses" of the "effects of Western contacts on the structure and institutions of the Mohammedan world." Stoddard's chapters offered "a liberal education to the Negro-American" on "the international world of color," their "broad sweep" was not "superficial," and their errors were "few and venial." He sometimes minimized "European moral turpitude," as when he ignored "the deliberate 'fakery' of the [Alfred] Milner commission to Egypt." While Lord Milner may have been sincere, "those who sent him to delude the Egyptians with false hopes while they settled with India and Russia" were aware "that they were using his sincerity as they had previously used that of [Lieutenant] Colonel [Thomas Edward] Lawrence [Lawrence of Arabia] with the Arabs." Harrison added that the likely "qualified 'independence' for Egypt" would not be thanks "to any original sincerity of the English Government" but rather to the "popular strength" of those who "really wanted independence unqualified." In sum, Harrison judged Stoddard's book to be "a masterly epic of the facts of international Islam" and "a welcome handbook."[64]

———

On November 5 Stoddard wrote to Harrison that he had "read with interest the second part of the review" and considered it "an excellent resume, though I regret (as you yourself deplore) that the character of your audience precluded you from analyzing the book as I know you could have done it." He also thanked him for sending a clipping from the *Evening Post*, which he was returning, since his clipping bureau had sent him a copy, and for the offer to lend him an article by General Charles-Marie-Emmanuel Mangin from the *New York Times* (which he had already clipped). Stoddard felt sure that Mangin had read his *Rising Tide*, as "the arrangement of the argument" was "a very close parallel."[65]

On the subject of Harrison's "prospects of doing book-reviewing and other literary work for standard magazines," Stoddard hoped to see him do it and offered to do what he could "as opportunity offers." He emphasized that this was not "a mere polite gesture." He really meant it, and his reasons were because Harrison had given his work "an excellent presentation" among African Americans, because he had provided "valuable advice regarding Pan-African material," and because his work interested Stoddard and he wanted to see it "given a good show." He also thought "it would be a good thing for the white public to have the movements and tendencies of the negro world intelligently and accurately presented," as he felt Harrison "could do." It was Stoddard's "belief that the greater part of the trouble in the world" was "due to ignorance—especially ignorance of the other man's point of view." Thus, if "the intelligent men on both sides of a controversy" could "set forth the facts and the philosophy of their side and get the other side to listen," then both sides could "find out where they are"; "look at things as they are, free from either prejudice or sentimentality"; "see where concessions can be made"; and "fight the issue out intelligently and cleanly." Stoddard wanted Harrison to "get an entree to the white public," but this would "not be easy," and he didn't "at present see any very good opening." Stoddard also asked if Harrison had "kept up with Dr. [Ernest] Gruening and the rest of the *Nation* crowd" and advised him to do so, "if feasible." He offered to "speak to the editor [Glenn Frank] of *The Century*" the next time he was in New York. Those two were the only places he felt he could help; he didn't know other editorial offices that would be interested and where his word would have any weight. He promised to keep Harrison "in mind and say a good word" if anything turned up and trusted that Harrison would "be able to effect some opening ere long."[66]

On December 16 Stoddard again wrote to Harrison thanking him for his willingness to loan material on Pan-Africanism. Since he wasn't planning to write that book until next year, he would avail himself of the kind offer later. Meanwhile, he offered to write to Glenn Frank, at *The Century*, telling him of Harrison's "projected article on the Negro Church." Harrison could then follow up with a phone call and make an appointment.[67] Several months later, on April 28, 1922, Stoddard wrote to Harrison that his new book, *The Revolt Against Civilization: The Menace of the Under-Man*, would be out in a fortnight and that he had instructed Scribner's to send him a copy. He described the book as "an analysis of the biological basis of revolutionary social unrest, Bolshevism, etc." This was what "side-tracked" him from the "projected Pan-African volume," and he now expected that it would "be some time" before he could tackle that.[68]

J. A. Rogers was a Jamaica-born Pullman porter who would become one of the most significant lay historian/journalists of the twentieth century, but in the early 1920s his career was progressing slowly. Harrison had the highest praise for his work and was one of his biggest supporters. At times Rogers would live with Harrison's family, and they became close friends.[69] Rogers greatly appreciated Harrison's support, and around 1921 he wrote Harrison, "it was due to your stimulation that I made the effort to get out F. S. to M. [*From 'Superman' to Man*]." He added with a friendly playfulness that Harrison was therefore obligated to help him "sell it." With the money from this edition he hoped "to get out a classic one next time." Rogers admitted, "I am a poor salesman," as he had sent the last twenty-five copies he had. He planned to get the money for twenty and pay the printer, and he asked Harrison to "be sure to send" the money "in the time promised." He repeated that he was "much indebted" and would "never be able to thank" Harrison enough "for the publicity given 'F.S. to M.' in *When Africa Awakes*," where Harrison reprinted his laudatory review.[70] Harrison's comments continued to adorn the dust jacket of reprints of *From "Superman" to Man* long after both men's deaths—a statement seemingly reflective not only of Harrison's appreciation of the book and of Rogers's appreciation of the comment but also of the friendship and respect between these two outstanding lay intellectuals.[71]

In the January 7, 1922, issue of the *Negro World* Harrison again discussed Rogers's *From "Superman" to Man* in an article entitled "White People Versus Negroes: Being the Story of a Great Book." He described how he had first picked up the book in August 1917 "in a Negro book shop" (possibly that of George Young). He sat down to read it and didn't get up until he "had read it through." Then he paid for it and took it home, realizing that he had found "a genuine treasure." He could learn nothing of the author who had published it at his own expense. Then, while in Washington in 1919, he came across a second edition of the book, published by "The Goodspeed Press." He immediately wrote them, got Rogers's address, and wrote to him to tell him "how highly" he thought of the book. Since then he reviewed it in the *Negro World* and elsewhere and insisted that it was "the greatest book ever written in English on the Negro by a Negro." He was "glad to know that increasing thousands of black and white readers" had the same "high opinion" he expressed.[72]

Harrison observed that since 1917

this book has made its way to success without one word of encouragement or praise from any of the more prominent Negro writers or editors except Mr. [William H.] Ferris and myself, although free copies had been sent to Dr. Du Bois, Kelly Miller, Benjamin Brawley, Monroe Trotter, Prof. [William Sanders] Scarborough, [William Stanley Beaumont] Braithwaite, and many others, including the National Association for the Advancement of Colored People.

He added, "Almost the only colored people who helped to spread its fame were the lesser known and humble classes, who still pilgrimage to 513 Lenox avenue in quest of it." Unfortunately, "the best known Negroes have failed to notice it."[73]

Interestingly, some "whites" had proved supportive. A "colored" woman who did day work at the University of Chicago showed a copy to Professor (Zonia) Baber, a southern white woman, who read it and wrote Rogers saying she considered it "'the finest bit of literature she had read on the subject.'" She made it required reading for her classes, placed it in the university library, bought fourteen copies to send to leading scientific libraries and "white" educators at universities including Minnesota and Michigan, and gave a reception at her home to her all "white" students, at which she invited Rogers to speak. Similarly, the Catholic Board for Mission Work Among Colored People sent a "white" priest to Chicago to look up the author. Unable to find him (Rogers "was away from home working as a Pullman porter"), they sent him a letter expressing their "interest and pleasure" in the book and adding that "there are more objections against the colored race answered satisfactorily and convincingly in this book than in any book we have read upon the question." They intended to use it "as a textbook" and ordered twenty-five copies. The Catholic College in Greensburg, Pennsylvania (probably Seton Hill Junior College), similarly ordered ten copies for use in a sociology class and asked Rogers "to write for them a catechism on the race question for use in their schools," which could be printed in their magazine, which had a circulation of sixty thousand. They also sent Rogers a Christmas present of $200 "as a recognition of genius" and as encouragement.[74]

Rogers had mailed a letter and a copy of the book "to every leading Negro college in the country," including Atlanta, Fiske, Wilberforce, Howard, Tuskegee, and Shaw; to Du Bois, Joel A. Spingarn, Kelly Miller, William Stanley Braithwaite, President Scarborough, Isaac Fisher of Tuskegee, Benjamin Brawley of Morehouse, Charles Banks of Mound Bayou (Mississippi), Dr. Bentley (Chicago's head of the NAACP), the New York NAACP, and many others. Miller and Fisher "acknowledged receipt but made no comments." Brawley said "that the book was 'rather interesting,' but that the author [had] made a great error in putting philosophy in the form of fiction, and hoped that if he ever wrote again he wouldn't commit the same grave error against the transcendental technics of the exalted act of saying nothing." Harrison countered that the book was "no more a work of fiction than is [Thomas] Carlyle's *Sartor Resartus*, or the *Dialogues of Plato*. The truth is that Brawley, as usual, was too stupid too form any critical opinion worth a tinker's damn—as Brander Matthews, of Columbia, gently hinted a short while ago." All the rest didn't answer. They were "too ill-bred and unmannerly to vouchsafe him a reply." Interestingly, James Vardaman, of

Mississippi, sent a courteous note of acknowledgment even though he was attacked in the book. The leading Negro publications, such as the *Chicago Defender, Boston Guardian, Crisis,* and *Christian Recorder,* "all got copies but took no notice of it." The *Indianapolis Freemen* did write an article on it, and "the writer sent Rogers a bill for that!" Around 1920 the *Chicago Defender* "carried a notice of the book, and charged him $28." The *Journal of Negro History* and *Crisis* also received copies of Rogers's second book, *As Nature Leads,* but, added Harrison, they had "taken no notice so far."[75]

In contrast, "Negroes to whom the book was not sent recognized it for themselves" and sought Rogers out "with helpful greetings and generous praise." This support came from people like the Rev. George Frazier Miller, Arthur Schomburg, William. H. Ferris, John E. Bruce, and Harrison. None of these men knew him personally at the time except Ferris. Harrison not only reviewed the book in the *New Negro* and the *Negro World;* he also wrote in 1919 what Rogers described as a "warm letter of congratulation." In addition he suggested that Rogers send a copy of the book to *The Crisis,* while satirically advising, "'don't let them know that you are colored or they'll never publish you.' They are somewhat color-blind on genius.'" Harrison maintained that his belief had been confirmed previously, since "the book had been sent two years before, and no notice had been taken of it." Harrison contrasted this treatment with that by "two colored school teachers of Washington—Mrs. N. T. Myers and Mrs. R. G. Moore" (who "sold hundreds of copies refusing any remuneration") and that by Nathaniel Guy, who "sent a copy at his own expense to every judge and truant officer in the District of Columbia." With such bottom-up support the book was now in its third edition.[76]

Harrison ventured two explanations for the "conduct of the colored big-wigs" in relation to this "masterpiece of literature." First, "the Negroes whom Christian slavery reduced to the social level of brutes still have today some of the traits of the slave." One of these traits of "our 'big Negroes'" was that they "don't help to push any other Negro into notice" if they have themselves won notice, because "notice for them detracts from your notice." Thus, Harrison found that "big Negroes prefer to advance ignoramuses since their own superiority will be thereby enhanced. To advance a 'comer' might abate their own brilliance." He commented, "God help us as a race, so long as this contemptible trait shall flourish among us!"[77]

Harrison felt his second explanation would be shocking to many. "The truth is," he wrote, "that many of our 'brightest' minds have not yet developed any intellect of their own. They can give you the most brilliant expositions of [George Bernard] Shaw, [Paul Laurence] Dunbar or [the painter John Cheri] Marin— provided he has been previously explained for them. But when they are asked to explain a new writer whom no one from whom they draw their opinions has yet seen or sampled, they are 'stuck.'" He knew young men, for example, Willis J. King and "Mr. Sunday," who could develop their own explanation, but they were "not prominent yet. No one knows them." But "Du Bois and Owen, Brawley and Randolph, [James Weldon] Johnson and Kelly Miller can't do it" because it required "a quality of independent judgment that is certain of itself and sure of its ground."[78]

Harrison explained that "'education' (which can be poured into a person)" is "no substitute for intellect, which is one's own." The men he just named were "men of 'education.'" In contrast Ernest Just, Alain Leroy Locke, Willis J. King, and Hodge Kirnon were cited by Harrison as "men of intellect" who can "think for themselves in the face of a brand-new fact." The others couldn't, but it was "these others that our black world mistakes for men of light and leading." In a similar vein, "When Claude McKay erupted into notice these colored pseudo-intellectuals couldn't tell from reading his poems that he was worth noticing." Now, however, after "their superiors have spoken," they "take Claude out to lunch and lionize him 'most much.'" Harrison predicted that "as with McKay so with Rogers," and when "these copy cats shall have learned from their teachers how great is *From* [']*Superman*['] *to Man*, they will slobber over him and give space to his book." Harrison then rhetorically asked, "Who shall put brains in our brainy men?"[79]

On February 4, 1922, in his *Negro World* column, Harrison included an open letter from Rogers to Arthur Brisbane, which he claimed "tears off the mask of pretended knowledge and fairness behind which the great Hearst editor has been hiding his ugly race prejudice." Brisbane was the editor of the *New York American* and the close personal friend and business partner of the paper's owner, William Randolph Hearst. Rogers had been reading his editorials "continuously for fifteen years" and thought he had "a pretty accurate gauge" of his intellectual power. In the letter Rogers wrote, "Here in Harlem is a full-blooded Negro, Hubert Harrison, who, with all your great breadth of learning and white man's chance, could out match you." He emphasized that he spoke without "so-called 'race pride'" and emphasized that "in all my arguments I consciously strive for fair play and exactness of thought, recognizing no differences whatever between man and man, race and race, in my writings."[80]

Brisbane had recently endorsed President Warren G. Harding's "doctrine of 'eternal inescapable differences,'" articulated before a segregated crowd, in his famous Birmingham, Alabama, speech of August 26, 1921. Rogers pointed out, however, that "most of the leading anthropologists of the world—men such as [Felix] Von Luschan, [Franz] Boas, [Jean] Finot, [Sir Henry Hamilton (Harry)] Johnston, [Gustave] Spiller, [Ludwig Lejzer] Zamenhof [the inventor of Esperanto]—met in a Universal Races Congress in London" in 1911 and that the "consensus of opinion of the most learned body was that all varieties of mankind, commonly called races, 'are essentially equal in intellect, enterprise, morality and physique.' Existing differences, the body agreed, were caused by environment, and hence subject to change by environment." This view was "diametrically opposed" to Harding's, and the 1911 Congress's report published by Gustave Spiller was easily available. Rogers was "firmly convinced that if President Harding had spoken more as a reasoning human being and less as a politician he would not have given utterance to such nonsense" as "Eternal inescapable differences!" Rogers emphasized: "There are no 'eternal differences' between 'races' of mankind. It is a matter of most elementary knowledge that the so-called races of the human race have been blending and disappearing one into the other from time immemorial to the present to form new varieties." There were "no fixed differences, except perhaps that of sex," and even "certain of these functions intrude on the other," resulting in "an intermediate sex or even sexes." Rogers noted that he was "self-taught since the age of ten" and had acquired his information "in the teeth of the great obstacles that the race you boast so much of has thrown in his way, evidently in the hope of proving your theory of 'eternal inescapable difference.'"[81]

Rogers again wrote to Harrison, and the letter was published in the *Negro World* of February 11, 1922. He thanked him for publishing his open letter to Brisbane but regretted "that the meaning was so much distorted in the printing—words spelt wrongly, paragraphs out of place, etc." and "uninformed" spelled as "uniformed." He added that Brisbane replied and said the opinion Rogers quoted was not his own "but that of Huxley and other scientists of acknowledged reputations." Rogers responded: "To the best of my knowledge Huxley did not say that, and would not." Brisbane also said he did "not think the question involved a very important one," and Rogers added, "Evidently not, or I am sure that he would be more careful in his statements about race." Rogers had been an eyewitness to the Chicago race riot, in which he claimed "some eleven hundred persons lost their lives." That "riot had been brewing for a long time in the newspapers, indeed was started by them, as riots usually are." In that race battle "hundreds of white persons were killed and injured, nearly all of the lower class," and Rogers pointedly asked, "Had Mr. Brisbane or any of his relatives and friends been caught in the mob, would he have thought the race situation of so little importance, or better yet had attacking whites joined hands with the blacks after the riot and went after the real culprits?"[82]

In the same column Harrison wrote "to assure Mr. Rogers and the readers of this section that the statement which Mr. Brisbane blandly ascribes to [Thomas] Huxley must have been received from that eminent biologist since his death. For no such statement is to be found in anything that he wrote while alive." He added that "if the statement is in any of Huxley's writings just let Mr. Brisbane cite the volume and the chapter or page" and similarly be more precise with the other scientists: "Who are they? And in which of their writings do these statements appear?" Harrison noted that "Huxley once carried on a controversy with professor [Sir Richard] Owen [an anti-Darwinian from the British Museum] over the question of the existence of the hippocampus major in the brains of apes—a fact now open and admitted by all who know—and he closed his remarks by saying that it was a question of veracity (not of opinion) between them and that he refused to see it otherwise." Similarly, Harrison insisted, "Mr. Brisbane was simply not telling the truth, that he was caught in the act, and that he now acts as if he were ashamed to admit it." "Of course," he added, "the readers of *The American* don't know the difference and don't care so long as their silly racial arrogance is sufficiently pampered and patted."[83]

In his "With the Contributing Editor" column of February 4, 1922, Harrison announced that his "West Indian News Notes" was to be resumed. He wrote that in a recent meeting, Garvey expressed that he "would like to see a resumption of that section of the N.W. which we created in 1920—the 'West Indian News Notes.'" Harrison promised to start the section again but said it would not be possible "to make them as elaborate as 1920," since he was now "only a Contributing Editor, not the Editor." He would do the best he could "under the circumstances" and hoped readers would enjoy his "summaries and comments." In the *Negro World* of March 25, in his "West Indian News Notes" column, Harrison discussed developments relating to Dominica, Jamaica, Demerara, Trinidad, and a West Indian Federation.[84]

He would also try to continue reviewing "books on the Negro which are consistently appearing, in order that Negro readers may keep in touch with the extensive literature of information and interpretation on that subject." Since the 135th Street Public Library was now encouraging the reading of such books, he wanted to continue "community help in that direction." Unfortunately, the "News Notes" would "inevitably curtail the time and space" devoted to the book reviews. Harrison was also starting "a brief oral review and discussion of new books on the Negro" on Sundays at Lafayette Hall in Harlem; over the next four weeks he planned to discuss William H. Ferris's *The African Abroad*, Rene Maran's *Batouala*, Carter G. Woodson's *The History of the Negro Church*, and Benjamin G. Brawley's *Social History of the American Negro*.[85]

Despite his announced efforts to keep writing for the *Negro World*, by April 1, 1922, Harrison's name was missing from the *Negro World* publication box. It would never appear again.[86]

Around December 1921 Harrison wrote "The Black Tide Turns in Politics," under the pseudonym "Frances Dearborn." Frances was the name of his first-born child. Dearborn (Harrison) began: "It is a singular fact that the white people of America know more about the white people of England and Ireland than they do about the twelve million black people in their midst. And nowhere is this shown more strikingly than in the domain of politics." This was the area "where superstitions are rife," particularly "the great superstition" that "the Negro is a born Republican" whose "political philosophy is presumed to be summed up in the aphorism [associated with Frederick Douglass] that 'The Republican Party is the ship and all else is the open sea.'"

There "was a period when the superficial observer" might have felt "justified in holding by the myth of the Negro's simon-pure Republicanism," but that period was "now at an end." Nevertheless, "those white people who shape the ideas of the nation on this and other matters" were "strangely ignorant of that fact," and "editors, lecturers, authors and politicians" seemed "equally unaware of this transformation of the Negro's political sentiments." Harrison explained:

> Here in America the white world and the black world move side by side; but they seldom intermingle. Those white people, like the politicians, who have business in the black world generally do their business in the following fashion. They select one Negro as their exponent of Negro activities who is also the exponent of their own white point of view. They then multiply him indefinitely to serve as a working concept of "The Negro", taking his word religiously and excluding from their consideration any other whose word is not in tune with that of their selected bell-wether. This has been the traditional method of getting at the Negro's mind employed by politicians and patriots, professional Southerners and Vesey Street Liberals. [20 Vesey Street was at various times the home to the Oswald Garrison Villard–owned *New York Evening Post*, *Crisis*, and *Nation*.] It is small wonder, then, that their easy complacence comes a cropper in the face of revolutionary facts.[87]

This was particularly true "in the domain of politics," and a prime example concerned the New York municipal campaign of 1917, when Colonel Theodore Roosevelt and Mayor John Purroy Mitchel "were hissed off the platform at the Palace Casino by an audience of more than three thousand Negroes." In that case "the editor of the *New York Age*," Fred R. Moore, was "the selected index," and "most of the Negro ministers had received for their support sums ranging from two to six hundred dollars, and the high-priests of pure government from whom the money came were assured that the votes were safely stowed away in some one's vest pocket ready for delivery." "The real truth," however, "was that the Negro masses were seething with hostility." "Republican leaders only learned this when it was too late," and "during the rest of the campaign their speakers were hardly able to show their faces at street-meetings in Harlem, the Negro section." Nevertheless, these Republican leaders "learned nothing from the lesson; but lapsed again into their traditional dependence on a selected exponent."[88]

Another example occurred during the last week of the 1921 election campaign, when two large mass meetings were held "in Liberty Hall the home of Marcus Garvey's adherents." In both cases the hall was hired by politicians, the Democrats on Thursday and the Republicans on Friday, and "both were cases of political thimble-rigging":

> The hall holds six thousand people and is filled nearly every night in the week by Garvey's crowd—who have no votes, being for the most part aliens. It was this same crowd, plus about 400 voters, who filled the house on both nights. But this, although known to the canny colored local leaders, was not even suspected by the white politicians who naturally gave great credit to the local party-riggers for turning out such a multitude of "voters" to listen to them. But although the Garvey people hadn't votes they had plenty of the local feeling in regard to politics. So they applauded the Democrats with enthusiasm Thursday night and Garvey himself spoke in their behalf. But when Major [Henry H.] Curran and his Republican team-mates attempted to speak for their ticket the next night they were heckled, hissed, jeered and booed. The reserves were called out and the meeting broke up in disorder. The audience was expressing the deep detestation in which the Republican Party is held in Negro Harlem. But of this detestation which was enough to reach even the remote non-voters the official Republican Party hadn't an inkling.[89]

The afternoon before that meeting at the headquarters of one of the Republican candidates "a colored campaign worker had asked 'how could they expect to carry Harlem without spending money for Republican workers to canvass the district?'Oh,' said one of the chiefs, airily, 'they always vote the Republican ticket!'" This same chief, the day after the meeting, called "with the tears streaming down his face" and asked "the same colored worker appealingly, 'what can we do? Tell us, what can we do?'" What had happened was that "only one out of nine local Negro newspapers pumped for the Republicans during the campaign." Fred Moore, the editor of that paper, the *New York Age*, had been "'the selected index' and the bursar of party funds for years." The other papers "were either quiescent like the *Amsterdam News*, insurgent like the *Despatch*, or Democratic like the *Pictorial News*." Then, "for the first time in all the long history of American politics more than 65 per cent of the Negro vote was cast for the Democratic Party."[90]

Despite these developments, Harrison explained, "the American white continues to know less of the Negro in his midst than of any other people except
the Russian." Thus, *The Nation*, "in its post-election issue blandly informed us
that 'the colored vote is now more than ever attached to the Republican Party.'"
All this certainly suggested "that if white people want to get accurate interpretations of what's what in the colored world they must go to properly equipped
Negroes who are not in leading-strings to them." Given "the present disturbed
state of race-relations in America the thinking portion of the white public needs
the truth about the Negro situation as it never did before." The facts, which challenged the correctness of *The Nation*'s assertion, were "very much wider than
has been indicated," and "in many states like Maryland and Virginia the
Negroes, with the hope of defeating the Republicans, put independent tickets
in the field." This had also "been done once before in the last Presidential campaign," claimed Harrison. In Virginia in 1920 "they put up a complete state ticket
and voted exclusively for men and women of their race with the result that the
'Lily-White' Republicans who were squeezing the Negroes out of the party went
down in ignominious defeat," and "as one Negro newspaper expressed it . . . 'The
Republican Party can not close its eyes to the fact that a measure of resentment
entered into the results.'"[91]

The causes of the "tremendous change in the political sentiment of the
Negroes" were then detailed by Harrison. These included the fact that they
were "beginning to read American history" and finding out things "not consistent" with the claims utilized to keep them in "political tutelage." He cited Lincoln's reply to Horace Greeley; James G. Blaine's *Twenty Years of Congress*,
with its account of how "the joint committee of Congress secured the passage
of an amendment to the U.S. Constitution making slavery perpetual, as a sop
to the seceding Southerners"; "Lincoln's explicit concurrence in that move as
stated in his First Inaugural"; and the increase of "'Jim-Crow,' lynching and disfranchisement" while "the Republican Party was in control of both Houses of
Congress, the Army, Navy and Supreme Court." This last matter was all the
more important because both "the 14th and 15th amendments to the Constitution" maintain "that 'Congress shall have power to enforce this article by appropriate legislation,'" yet these powers were not utilized. Harrison continued citing reasons why African Americans were awakening. He included "the
disputed count of the Hayes-Tilden electoral contest in 1877" and how "a deal
was put through by which the Republicans sold them out and left them politically naked to the tender mercies of the Southern Whites"; how "in every sec-
tional party-crisis they have been sacrificed as an offering on the altar of
friendship"; how Theodore Roosevelt "paid the South for the Booker Washington [October 16, 1901] lunch with the discharge of the Brownsville Battalion . . . after the [1906 election] votes were in"; how William Howard Taft then

"offered them up as a wedding present when he laid down the famous dictum that no Negro should ever be appointed to office anywhere if white men any-where objected"; how a "few appointments" were "the only return which the Republican Party made for the Negro vote in the 'doubtful' states"; how Repub-lican "Lily-White-ism" increased "from [William] McKinley to [chairman of the Republican National Committee from 1918–1921] Will Hayes [Hays]" under the theory "that the Southern Negro is a liability rather than an asset" and "should be politely thrown overboard"; and how Republican President Harding had re-expounded "the principle laid down by Taft" and in his Birmingham address asked African Americans "to leave the party." For such reasons, Har-rison explained, they were now "taking him at his word and leaving it."[92]

To Harrison, President Harding's invitation came "just a trifle late," since "Negroes have been leaving the party for some time." "Twenty years ago those Negroes who joined the Democratic Party were regarded by their fellows much as white Americans regarded pacifists and pro-Germans in War time—and they were treated accordingly," but "now the pendulum has swung to the other side." The "Negro voter" was "developing political common-sense," "seeking to work out for himself his own political emancipation," and "striving to win political consideration for his vote." In the past, "both parties in an overwhelmingly Jew-ish district would put Jews on the local ticket to insure the Jewish vote," but they would put "no Negro at all" in a "Negro neighborhood." Now, however, "Negroes [we]re demanding this right of 'Elective representation.'" In New York City "the one party" to fight against this was 'The Grand Old [Republi-can] Party,'" but the change had gone "so far that in the 21st Aldermanic Dis-trict the Aldermanic candidates of all three parties were Negroes." African Americans were now "forcing the politicians to give them something for something."[93]

The "ultimate aims of this new spirit" were to "not rest satisfied until Negroes return to Congress as national legislators," which, Harrison predicted, would likely "first be done in the North." They would likely "capitalize [on] the neigh-borhood segregation . . . forced on them . . . in Chicago and New York, and thus reap some of 'the advantages of their disadvantages.'" They certainly intended to make "use of their balance of power in the doubtful States to trade with the enemy" as had been done in Ireland by "the Irish Parliamentary *bloc* under [Charles Stewart] Parnell and [Justin] McCarthy." Harrison "confidently look[ed] for a *rapprochement* between Negro voters and the Democrats of Vir-ginia and the other Southern States" where they still had the ballot, since this would enable them "to block the 'Lily-White' Republicans." Since they could "defeat the Republicans (as they did in Virginia last fall) they might as well do it for something as do it for nothing." Harrison predicted that "from now on, the two major parties will have to compete for the Negro vote"—and this would be a sure "sign of healthy political life."[94]

————

On December 20, 1921, Harrison began work on a notebook of "Aphorisms and Reflections" and a "Common Place Book." The idea for the latter was derived from *The Memoirs of the Life of Edward Gibbon*, where Gibbon spoke of "A Common-Place Book into which he digested his reading 'according to the precept and model of Mr. [John] Locke.'" Harrison quoted Gibbon's explanation from his *Memoirs*: "After glancing my eye over the design and orders of a new book, I suspended the perusal till I had finished the task of self-examination, till I had resolved in a solitary walk, all that I knew or believed, or had thought on the subject of the whole work, or of some particular chapter: I was then qualified to discern how much the author added to my original stock." Harrison noted that this was a practice he did not "strenuously recommend."[95]

The actual aphorisms, which Harrison included, as well as a "words" section started at age thirty-eight, are revealing. Among his thought-provoking aphorisms are the following:

> Not to do the right thing, but to tell the right lie: that is the essence or morality as I have observed it in the *actions* of my fellow-men.
>
> It was a wise American who had travelled all over the world who said that "Human beings love to be humbugged". Patriotism, spiritualism and the 2nd debate newspapers are cases in point. Wherefore, *to rule men you must fool them*. Spend your life in serving them unselfishly, and they will let you die of starvation. But fool them to the top of their bent and they will pour their wealth into your pockets and enshrine you in their administration. Jesus, John Brown and Father Damien [Joseph De Veuster, who served on the leper colony Molokai I] died poor and despised; while Billy Sunday, Marcus Garvey and Woodrow Wilson lived in luxury and ease.[96]

Harrison's mention of Garvey fooling the people and living in "luxury and ease" was an indicator of the new problems Garvey would face in 1922.

12

The Period of Garvey's Arrest
(October 1921–March 1922)

The period from the end of the second UNIA convention (August 1–31, 1921) through March 1922 was one of political decline and mounting economic and legal difficulties for Marcus Garvey and the UNIA. Membership morale deteriorated and internal dissent grew as Garvey faced court battles, which culminated in his arrest for mail fraud. After September 1921 there was little money for officer salaries (which were cut 40 to 50 percent by January), *Negro World* circulation and UNIA membership decreased noticeably, and the crisis in the movement was visible. Political attacks intensified, government investigators put together their case, and internal revolts broke out in a number of cities, including Philadelphia, Chicago, and Los Angeles. The BSL was in deep financial and legal trouble, and by early 1922 some $144,000 raised for the Liberian Construction Loan had been spent.[1]

The Garvey situation affected Harrison in several ways over these months. As contributing editor to the financially troubled *Negro World*, a significant source of income was threatened, and the well-being of his family of seven was in jeopardy. To supplement his income he sought additional work as a lecturer, writer, and teacher. A short-lived career as an instructor at a chiropractic school lasted from April to the latter part of 1921, but when it ended, Harrison's financial difficulties worsened. Though he stumped two months for the Democratic Party, by December he was in court over nonpayment of rent, and the maintenance of his family's apartment was threatened. Through all this his disenchantment with Garvey grew, as did his eagerness to utilize his skills and energies in a politically positive way. He sought to get out his ideas, and he and others worked to challenge Garvey while he continued to write columns for the *Negro World* and search for other meaningful employment. In addition, toward the end of this period, Harrison appears to have engaged in a short-lived extramarital affair.[2] Occupying much of this period in Harrison's life was Garvey's early 1922 arrest for mail fraud. These events involved Cyril V. Briggs, legal officials, the Bureau of Investigation, postal inspectors, and other activists.

————

By October 1921 Garvey had come under increased pressure from the federal government. This was shortly after a September 1 letter by Madarikan Deniyi, from Lagos, Nigeria, which claimed that Garvey's African Redemption Fund was a "fraudulent" scheme for scamming "poor and needy Negroes" for the purpose of paying the salaries of Garvey and other officers.[3] Garvey attempted to placate government officials by adopting a more conservative political direction. As a counter to the Du Bois–led, Second Pan-African Congress (of August–September 1921 in Brussels and Paris) Garvey raised the banner of "racial purity" and criticized that body as the creation of "an admixture of white and colored people."[4] In October Garvey praised the controversial October 26, 1921, Birmingham, Alabama, speech of President Warren G. Harding before a segregated crowd, which opposed "race amalgamation."[5] In the summer of 1922, building off such views and political direction, Garvey would meet with Edward Young Clarke, the acting imperial wizard and principal recruiter for the white supremacist and antiradical Ku Klux Klan.[6]

In the political climate of Garvey's growing conservatism and political difficulties, Cyril Valentine Briggs and the ABB, apparently influenced by the Communist Party,[7] which Briggs had joined,[8] moved into action against Garvey on both the political and legal fronts and unsuccessfully tried to influence the 1921 UNIA convention.[9] Garvey at this time would refer to the very light-skinned Briggs as a "little boy" and a "white man"—actions clearly intended to arouse Briggs's ire.[10] Briggs then attacked Garvey publicly in *The Crusader*, took him to court, wrote to the Department of Commerce in Washington about him, and approached postal and federal investigators with evidence that contributed to Garvey's indictment for mail fraud in relation to what proved to be a phantom ship, the SS *Phyllis Wheatley* (named after Phillis Wheatley). The mail-fraud case against Garvey was finalized in late 1921, and on January 12, 1922, the government presented its case and had Garvey arrested. Since the BSL was a corporation and not Garvey's alone, this action was superseded by a February 15 indictment citing twelve counts of mail fraud and coindicting BSL officials Elie Garcia, George Tobias, and Orlando Thompson.[11]

The October 1921 *Crusader* fired an important salvo against Garvey. In one article Briggs charged that Garvey had recently "put $12,500 'in escrow,' and now it's disappeared."[12] A second article implied that Garvey was "contemplating a trip to Europe" as a possible "alibi" regarding financial improprieties. A

Figure 12.1. Madarikan Deniyi, May 28, 1920. Madarikan Deniyi (1892–1959), from Lagos, Nigeria, came to the United States in 1914, attended the 1920 UNIA convention, and in 1921 publicly criticized Marcus Garvey, claiming that Garvey's African Redemption Fund was a "fraudulent" scheme for defrauding "poor and needy Negroes" for the purpose of paying the salaries of Garvey and other officers. *Source:* Hubert H. Harrison Papers, Box 15, Folder 5, Rare Book and Manuscript Library, Columbia University Library. See https://dlc.library.columbia.edu/catalog/cul:r2280gb77n.

third article claimed the UNIA financial report from the August convention gave evidence of "a state of affairs in the finances of the Association as to challenge the efficiency of its executives," cause "serious thought to its intelligent followers," and "check the truculent enthusiasm of its most fanatical adherents." It concluded: "This is no time for Mr. Garvey to go to Europe or Africa. He is needed here to assume the responsibilities of his many offices."[13]

The most pointed article in the October *Crusader* was "Figures Never Lie, but Liars Do Figure," by W. A. Domingo, the former Liberty League officer and *Negro World* editor. Domingo claimed that the financial report of the UNIA from the August 13, 1921, *Negro World* indicated "death taxes" proved that "the actual membership, far from being the millions of Mr. Garvey's fettle fancy, is less than 20,000!" Domingo also criticized the handling of the "convention funds." Regarding the Liberian Construction Loan, Domingo found the loan had raised $144,450.58 but that only $4,000 had reached Africa.[14]

As the October *Crusader* circulated, the October 15 *Negro World* contained a special "Notice" explaining that "a copy of the records of all Divisions, Branches, Chapters and members of the Universal Negro Improvement Association has been stolen from the Secretary-General's office by some one who was employed by the organization." While the membership and mailing lists had possibly been taken by Bishop George Alexander McGuire, one additional document that Garvey may have believed had been stolen was the secret report on Liberia prepared by the UNIA commissioner to Liberia, Elie Garcia. The report was the same document that Harrison had been given earlier. Briggs planned to publish that year-old report in *The Crusader*, when it was "stolen from him" by Cyril Crichlow, who allegedly gave it to Captain James Wormley Jones (Agent "800"), a confidential informant of the BI, who was in charge of registering all incoming mail at UNIA headquarters and had infiltrated the ABB. Jones then allegedly passed Garcia's report to "diplomatic quarters" before it was returned to Garvey.[15]

On October 18, 1921, Jones reported that on his advice Briggs had gone to the DA to sue Garvey for calling him a "white man" in the *Negro World*. The case was scheduled for October 20, and, according to Briggs, on that day Garvey played the role of informer. He presented to Justice Renaud of New York's Twelfth District's Magistrate Court an August 15, 1921, letter written by Briggs on ABB stationery, which he claimed invited him to help overthrow the white government.[16]

DA Edward Swann took up Briggs's complaint and on October 26 charged Garvey with libel regarding pieces in the October 8, 15, and 22 *Negro World*. The pieces were headlined: "White Man Negro for Convenience a White Man in New York by the Name of Cyril Briggs Has Started the 'African Blood Brotherhood.'" Swann's statement noted that Briggs was "a person of color" who had received threatening phone calls during the week of October 10 and was derided by a group of ten or twelve men at 136th Street and Lenox Avenue during the week of October 17.[17] Briggs's charge of criminal libel was soon sustained by Renaud, and a hearing was scheduled for October 31.[18]

On the same day that Swann took action against Garvey, Jones sent a report on Garvey's trial to George F. Ruch, the special agent of the BI in Washington, who was a friend of and worked closely with J. Edgar Hoover, then principal assistant to BI Director William J. Burns. Jones noted that Garvey had a previous conviction for a similar libel offense against former DA Kilroe over a year before, "for which he apologized, through the columns of his paper and the court suspended sentence." Jones added that Briggs had "started action against Garvey for using the mails to defraud," since circulars "Garvey sent out" had "the name Phyl[l]is Wheatley on the ship."[19]

Briggs's campaign saw some success. There were minor defections from the UNIA to the ABB in October,[20] and then Crichlow, Rev. John Dawson Gordon (former assistant president general of the UNIA), and Bishop McGuire (former chaplain general and member of the UNIA Executive Council) all joined the ABB.[21] According to Jones, the circulation of the *Negro World* decreased from 35,000 to 26,000 in the four weeks ending November 5, and this was "due to Briggs' action."[22]

The November *Crusader* continued the attack and blasted on its front page "Extra! 'S. S. Phyllis Wheatley' a Garvey Myth," which was the title of an article inside. It also included an editorial, "Garvey Turns Informer," written by Briggs under the pseudonym "C. Valentine," which described Garvey's October 20 attempt "to turn State Witness for the white oppressors of the Negro Race" by presenting Briggs's letter, which Garvey claimed was an invitation to him "to join Briggs in the overthrow of white governments, as a means of liberating Africa from those said governments." Valentine added that this "latest Judas-act of Marcus Garvey's" was "the climax in a long list of traitorous acts enumerated at length in the October *Crusader* and unrefuted by Garvey." Valentine concluded that "Garvey's attempt to 'inform' on one of his boldest leaders in the Liberation Struggle should convince even the most rabid Garveyite of the insincerity of the man," if such a follower were "*not too pro-Garvey to be really pro-Negro.*"[23]

The Briggs-Garvey matter drew increased attention from the BI. On November 5 Agent Ruch wrote to Hoover that informant "800" (Jones) had reported that Briggs was "making every effort possible to have the Post Office Inspectors take action against Garvey for the publication in the 'Negro World' of an advertisement showing a picture of the 'Phyllis Wheatley' which, according to the statements of Garvey, had been purchased by the Black Star Line." Ruch pointed out that "this was an ordinary steamboat with the name 'Phyllis Wheatley' placed on same and used for a 'cut' for the advertisement and used for the purpose of securing further purchases for Black Star Line stock."[24] Also on November 5, Agent W. W. Grimes wrote a memo to Hoover that stated, "I understand that Crichlow will talk."[25]

BI Director Burns then wrote a November 9 letter to Agent Mortimer J. Davis, in New York, explaining that Briggs was endeavoring to get the Post Office to take action against Garvey and the BSL for using the mails to defraud shareholders. His letter led Davis to interview Briggs on November 15, and, according to Davis, Briggs "appeared very willing to give his assistance in this matter." Briggs indicated that he based his charge on a BSL circular that contained a photo of a large freighter with the name *Phyllis Wheatley* on the bow. The circular was to solicit stock subscriptions, and, while it was not stated that the *Phyllis Wheatley* was owned by the BSL, the "entire effect" was to "lead one falsely to that impression." Briggs mentioned that he had written to the Department of Commerce's Bureau of Navigation on October 29 and asked whether the *Phyllis Wheatley* actually existed. He showed Davis the reply, which said that the Bureau of Navigation was "unable to find in its record or maritime reports the steamships 'Antonio Maceo' and 'Phyllis Wheatley.'" Briggs reprinted that letter in the November *Crusader* along with an editorial saying that the BSL did not own the *Phyllis Wheatley*. Briggs also said he was "positive" that the circular "had been widely circulated through the mails." Briggs then promised to obtain the name and address of at least one person who had received the circular, believed the BSL owned the *Phyllis Wheatley*, and purchased BSL stock.[26]

Bishop McGuire was present with Briggs during the interview and reportedly told Davis that he had "come to the conclusion that he [Garvey] was a swindler." He explained that he had left the UNIA, lost $300 in stock enterprises, and was now working with Briggs. Both Briggs and McGuire claimed, and Davis verified in the *Negro World*, that the BSL was advertising passenger and freight sailings from New York on the steamship *Phyllis Wheatley*. Briggs also asserted that many families had lost their savings and belongings and again said he would provide names. According to Jones, Garvey was furious with Briggs for what he had wrought, and "he raved like a mad man," saying "that if Briggs wasn't careful something would happen to him some night that would stop his mouth."[27]

Garvey responded, as he had so often in the past, through lawyers and the courts. On November 11 Wilford Smith, an attorney, represented him before Justice Renaud and requested Garvey be allowed to make a retraction in the Briggs case. Briggs agreed, and the case was adjourned until November 29. Five days later, Garvey sued Briggs for criminal libel over the October *Crusader*.[28]

Then, on November 16, William C. Matthews, "a colored attorney of Boston and New York" who said he was working "in the interests of Marcus Garvey," called on Hoover. Matthews reportedly showed Hoover a letter that Garvey had received from Briggs, inviting him to join the ABB and implying that the ABB had caused the Tulsa riot. Hoover added, in a memo to Ruch, that Matthews stated that "he would send us any information which might come to Garvey or himself relating to Briggs' pernicious activities, which he considered to be a menace to this country."[29]

On November 25 Garvey had Briggs held in a $500 bond for Special Sessions Court. Jones, still acting as a confidential informant, reported that he was supposed to be a witness for Garvey and say that he inferred that Briggs meant Garvey when he said "that he [Briggs] had not been driven out of London for rape on a young girl and that he [Briggs] did not live with a woman that was not his wife." The inference, according to Jones, "was that Garvey did do them." Garvey also reportedly told Jones "that when Briggs had him in court the Judge had been influenced against him but that there was a different Judge on the bench and he had seen that the Judge had been influenced against Briggs." To Jones this suggested "Garvey had 'fixed' things."[30]

When they spoke, Garvey also reportedly told Jones that he was "going to keep after Briggs until he breaks him." His plan was to enter three suits against Briggs in special sessions the following week, and he thought that might stop him. Based on this information Jones suggested to Ruch that his office take steps to "see that this doesn't happen," since Briggs was "the biggest thorn in Garvey's side." Jones also recommended that the mail-fraud case "be called as soon as possible so there will be no let up in Briggs' propaganda, as Garvey seems to keep just enough within the law to keep out of prison."[31]

Agent Jones met with Crichlow and then wrote to Ruch on November 26. He stated that the next *Crusader* would begin Crichlow's report and predicted the articles would "certainly do Garvey no good as they expose Garvey and his African plan." Jones also mentioned that Crichlow had told him that "Garvey had sent for his attorney to see if they couldn't come to some agreement" regarding Crichlow's suit. Crichlow offered to settle for $1,000, the salary he said Garvey had promised to pay him for his work in Liberia.[32]

As a result of Garvey's settlement with Briggs, the December 3, 1921, *Negro World* ran a correction explaining that in three issues it had published a news release that "Cyril Briggs, a white man, was passing for a Negro in New York." Garvey, the paper's managing editor, had been summoned to court for those publications, and the *Negro World* now announced that "Briggs' mother, who attended the hearing, is a colored woman." It added, "Mr. Briggs is not a white man in race, but a Negro." Though the retraction was made "gladly,"[33] it did not deter Garvey's litigious ways. The same day that it appeared, the *New York News* headlined "Garvey Arrests Brooks, Charging Theft of Black Star Line Funds, and Cyril Briggs for Criminal Libel."[34]

By early December 1921 the Bureau of Investigation was ready to put together its case against Garvey. On December 7 Director Burns wrote to Rush D. Simmons, chief inspector of the Post Office Department, that they had "for many months . . . been investigating MARCUS GARVEY, an alien Negro who, for more than two years has been living lavishly off the meagre savings of poor Negroes throughout the United States." The investigation disclosed "violations of several federal statutes, not the least in importance being the violation of Postal laws." Burns requested the immediate assignment of "a competent post office inspector, who can go over the information procured by us and work with our agents here in the pre[pa]ration of the case against Garvey, which will include the postal angles."[35]

Special Agent Davis called Briggs on December 8, 1921, "to obtain from him any information in his possession with regard to the alleged misrepresentation by the Black Star Line in its sale of stock." Though Briggs had promised to obtain the names of persons who could be used as witnesses against Garvey and had located several, "none of them would care to make any statements against Garvey." Davis judged this to be attributable to "fear of consequences or embarrassment among their friends." Briggs, however, "promised to continue his efforts" and keep Davis "informed."[36]

The deeply involved agent Jones submitted his December 14 report to Ruch in the form of a brief that made the case of "using the mails to defraud" against Garvey. Jones asserted that "the best evidence" was in the *Negro World*, since the paper had passed through the mails each week with second-class privilege. He explained that in issues from January and February 1921 "you will find advertis[e]ments for the sailing of the ship Yarmouth on March 27, 1921[,] for Liberia for which money was accepted for passage: this ship has never sailed and books kept by Mason t[raffic] manager[,] and [Orlando] Thompson, secretary of the Black Star Line, will [show] that only a part of the money has been returned to pa[ssengers]." He added, "you will find pictures of ships that were suppos[ed to have] been purchased by the Black Star Line and all of those speeches have been published in the Negro World and subsequently sent through [the] mails. The books of the corporation will show that the stock [sold] through advertising has not been used as stated." In his sample brief Jones next discussed the Negro Factories Corporation, which was running an advertisement that read, "When you invest $5.00 (five dollars) or $200.00 (two hundred dollars) in the shares of the stock it means that at the end of the financial year you will gather so much money by the way of dividends." This advertisement had run for almost a year, but "no dividends have ever been paid." In that time, "about $25[,]00[0] (twenty five thousand dollars) worth of stock has been sold." Jones also reviewed the "Convention Fund" advertised in the June, July, and August 1920 issues of the *Negro World*. The advertisements stated that every contributor would have his or her name entered in a book to be published after the convention, which they all would receive. Through this method, claimed Jones, Garvey received nearly $20,000; the book was never published. The plea for funds also claimed that the funds would be used to defray the expenses of the delegates, but nothing over $500 was used for this purpose. Jones suggested that BSL Treasurer George Tobias "should be a willing witness" and could testify "to these facts." Regarding the Liberian Construction Loan, Jones wrote that its bonds "had been advertised in the *Negro World*" in advertisements that claimed the money would be used "to build factories, schools, and etc. in Liberia." The UNIA books showed, and Tobias could testify, wrote Jones, "that almost $150,000 had been collected and only $10,000 used for the purpose for which it was subscribed." The rest had "been used for propaganda."[37]

Jones closed his sample brief with mention of several other violations. The December 3 and 10, 1921, *Negro World*s contained advertisements saying that 200,000 copies of the Christmas issue would be circulated, yet only 50,000 copies were printed and only 25,000 sold. There were also circulars sent through the mails to solicit funds for various causes, and H. V. Plummer, "Agent of Publicity and Propaganda," could testify on this. The State Insurance Law was violated, Jones maintained, by use of the "Death Fund of the U.N.I.A. for any purpose he [Garvey] sees fit." Similarly, the Corporation Law was violated when the funds of one corporation were transferred to the credit of another without a Board of Directors meeting. Based on such examples, Jones suggested that Garcia, the auditor; Tobias, the treasurer; and Gabriel E. Stewart, the chancellor, be secured as witnesses.[38]

Jones met with Crichlow on December 16 and then wrote to Ruch that Garvey was very worried over articles in the last *Crusader*. He mentioned that he had read Garcia's report to Garvey made upon his return from Africa and that Crichlow claimed that he had obtained the report from Harrison, who saw it before Garvey did. Garcia had shown it to Harrison because Harrison was supposed to have gone on the trip, and Garcia wanted to see what Harrison thought of it. While in Harrison's possession, Harrison made a copy of it. Crichlow then obtained it and now planned to publish it "in full" in the next *Crusader*. Briggs was allegedly "paying Crichlow a good price for this" because he knew it would be "a blow to Garvey to publish it." Jones "tried very hard to get a copy of this report but Crichlow would not let it out of his possession." After reading the report Jones was convinced there was "enough evidence to convict G[arvey] of a criminal political conspiracy against the government of Liberia." He added that, if he were "an open agent," he "could buy this report from Crichlow." As a secret agent, however, "such an offer" would "arouse his suspicion." When "the proper time" came he was sure [Crichlow would] "be only to[o] glad to tell all that he knows if he thinks th[at it would] clear him." In light of these developments Jones recommended that they "wait" until Garcia's report was published.[39]

Jones also mentioned other developments. Two former Garveyites, Bishop McGuire and John Dawson Gordon, were scheduled to speak at an ABB meeting and would make good witnesses against Garvey. There were circulars sent through the mails that promised to pay dividends at the end of the year and Garvey's news release "to the colored press warning of libel charges if they printed any of Briggs's stories." Regarding finances, Garvey had only turned in $155 from his last trip to Washington, Baltimore, and Wilmington, although he had collected $1,000 in ticket sales alone. "This," commented Jones, was "the way" Garvey gets his money. Finally, the Christmas issue of the *Negro World* contained "Garvey's latest scheme," which asked members to give a dollar toward printing "four million" copies of the paper each week in 1922.[40]

On December 19 Jones sent another report to Ruch and included circulars and a Garvey news release announcing that "the fight is on." The Garvey critics McGuire, Gordon, and Crichlow "had to leave a church meeting by the back door in order to avoid Garvey's supporters." Jones thought that such occurrences seemed to give Garvey more confidence and a tighter hold on the masses. Some of his most ardent supporters were the largest stockholders; they "know he has spent the money foolishly, but . . . still trust him." Garvey, aware of Briggs's next publication, was reportedly planning to try to have Briggs and Crichlow jailed before it was printed.[41]

On December 21 Special Agent Davis reported from New York that Post Office Inspector "Wilkinson" (*sic*, probably Oliver B. Williamson) had gone to the Bureau Office in the afternoon to be interviewed by Davis and the agent in charge, Edward J. Brennan. The postal inspector stated he had evidence indicating a prima facie case against Garvey and other BSL officials for using the mails to defraud. He sought BI assistance in the form of an agent, an accountant, and any additional information. Brennan promptly assigned Davis to work with him.[42]

Inspector Williamson said that he had interviewed Garvey on December 20. He had no doubt that a violation had been committed and that there would be no trouble securing a warrant for Garvey's arrest and a subpoena *duces tecum* requiring (under penalty) that the corporation's papers be presented. Williamson thought it best to wait until after the holidays, but Brennan saw no reason to delay and requested that Davis accompany Williamson to the U.S. Attorney's office to procure the necessary warrants and subpoenas, for service the next day. Williamson then placed the matter before Assistant U.S. Attorney Maurice Joyce, who suggested that it would be better to secure a grand jury indictment in preference to a commissioner's warrant, which might force the government to a hearing before Williamson was ready. The case would be presented to the grand jury in January.[43]

————

Jones, the confidential informant, spoke with Harrison on December 24. He reported to Ruch that Harrison had told him that "there was something going to happen to Garvey in a very short time and that he would know a few days before it happened and if Garvey wasn't such a fool he would go to him and tell him about it and tell him how to make a get away and where to go." Jones told Ruch that he didn't know "if Harrison was trying to pump me," but he didn't think so, since he knew "that Harrison doesn't like Garvey." The fact that Harrison knew so much, however, led Jones to suggest to Ruch "there must be a 'leak' somewhere."[44]

On January 7, 1922, Jones wrote to Ruch to tell him that Edgar Grey and Elie Garcia were working against Garvey. Grey "had been to Washington about Garvey and before the month was up Garvey would be in jail." Jones was also "told that Garcia was seen leaving the office one night last week after midnight with a bundle of papers under his arm." Garvey was reportedly "expecting something to happen," and Jones recommended "Garvey ought to be watched" because "men better known than Garvey have gotten away from the country." Jones also noted that "local authorities" were also "checking up on Garvey," and he knew that Harrison had "been to see one of the District Attorneys by name of [James C.?] Thomas."[45]

In his January 7 correspondence Jones provided background on Garcia's report. He mentioned "when Garcia got back from Liberia he let Hubert Harrison see it and while in his possession he made a copy," then "Crichlow got a copy from Harrison." Jones added:

When Garvey is taken to court be sure and have Harrison as a witness as he has kept on file all of Garvey's speeches and has made notes on those parts of his speeches that could be used against Garvey in court. Harrison has written articles for the paper [*Negro World*] in fact does so at the present time but he has never had any use for Garvey. He said to me the other day that he hoped he would get a chance to go to court and testify against Garvey when they got him, as he had been keeping data on Garvey ever since he started his organization.[46]

By early January 1922 the government was ready to proceed. On Monday, January 9, BI Agent Davis met with Postal Inspector Williamson and Assistant U.S. Attorney Maurice Joyce to prepare the case against Garvey. Williamson drew up the complaint and prepared subpoenas. Davis collected data regarding the BSL's purchase of the steamships *Yarmouth*, *Kanawha*, and *Shadyside*.[47]

On January 12, 1922, Williamson, in a sworn complaint, charged that on and before May 24, 1921, Marcus Garvey "did unlawfully, willfully and knowingly devise and intend to devise a scheme and artifice to defraud." The particulars:

That the defendant would by means of false and fraudulent representations, pretenses and promises induce, solicit and procure divers persons . . . referred to as the victims, to pay and transmit to him, the said defendant, money and property for the purchase of stock in the Black Star Line, Inc., and for the purpose of inducing said victims to part with their money and property in the purchase of said stock and said memberships so intended to be sold and offered for sale.[48]

As indicated by the complaint, Garvey was at first indicted alone. Then, when the government officials realized that the BSL was a corporation, not a private firm, the first indictment was withdrawn and two new ones instituted. The new indictments named Garvey as president, Orlando Thompson as vice president, Elie Garcia as secretary, and George Tobias as treasurer, though Garvey continued to be the real target. The other three would eventually be acquitted;[49] Garvey would ultimately be convicted on one count.[50]

Garvey was arrested on the day of Williamson's initial complaint (January 12). He was arraigned before U.S. Commissioner S. M. Hitchcock and released on $2,500 bail for a January 19 hearing. Meanwhile, the accountants worked on the books of two of the corporations and other accumulated material. Williamson, discussing the case in a letter six days after the arrest, offered what he thought was the essence of the matter: "Garvey, through his several schemes has filched from the public as much as $1,000,000." The New York papers covered the case in detail. The *New York Tribune* reported that postal inspectors charged that Garvey had used the mails to defraud in selling BSL stock, advertising and selling steamship passages to Africa without having made arrangements to carry out his contracts, and promoting a "ghost ship." It noted that the arrest "was brought about through private investigations conducted by members of the accused man's own race who have been engaged in the case for many weeks."[51]

———

The *New York World* of January 13, 1922, in "Garvey, Financier and 'Sir President' of Africa Is Held," published coverage that appears to have been influenced by, perhaps even largely written by, Harrison. The article described Garvey's arrest as "a climax to a bizarre career" that lifted him "from obscurity to mellifluous titles, hero worship and wealth." It claimed that four months of intense investigation, "prompted by antagonistic members of his race," led to his arrest on charges of making "fraudulent representations" to enlist membership in his organizations, "of advertising and selling passage to Africa on a mythical vessel," and of using the mails to defraud in disposing of stock in the Black Star

Line. The article also mentioned how the "provisional President" organized the "'Distinguished Service Order of Ethiopia'" to "obtain his Knighthood," how he wore "a vivid gown of green and red," how as he was arraigned he wore a fur-covered overcoat and carried an ornamental cane on his arm, and how, when he sought to telephone his home, he remarked petulantly: "I can never remember my private telephone number!"[52]

In reviewing general financial operations the *New York World* article cited the BSL's capitalization at $10,000,000, the alleged four million UNIA members each paying 35 cents a month in dues (10 cents of which went to the home office and the rest to the local branch), and the special levy of $1 placed on each member at the last convention. It also stated that the BSL was composed of two unlisted vessels, the *"Shady Side"* (an excursion boat for the Hudson, damaged by ice the previous winter) and the *"Kanawha"* (a pleasure yacht, in Cuba in the custody of the American consul, whose captain and crew had sued for back wages). The SS *Phyllis Wheatley* was described as a mythical ship used to sell passage and, when *The Crusader* had written to the Department of Commerce to learn if it was listed, "no record of it was found." This was said to have prompted *The Crusader*'s "bitter attack" on Garvey.[53]

In a follow-up January 14 article in the *New York World* Garvey was described as a "Negro 'Napoleon'" who blamed his arrest on "plotters of my own race— villains who are envious of me because I have done more than they have done for the colored people, because they know I am honest." Garvey reportedly assured the interviewer for the paper that "this is a big cause I am leading, the establishment of an African republic for the Negro race." He then disposed of the charges of irregularity by saying, "I am clean of heart. Dollars and cents are insignificant. This isn't a money making proposition. We have lost money because of the plots against us. But the chief thing is, we have helped the cause, stimulated morale. That's the big thing."[54]

The interviewer, identified as "Spewak," read to the "Provisional President of the Republic of Africa" figures on the Liberian Construction Fund that purported to show that $144,450 had been collected, $44,461 spent in salaries and traveling expenses, $34,440 in Black Star Line stock, and $46,555 "for the good will of the *Negro World*, his publication." These figures also showed only $4,000 sent to Liberia and $4,461 paid for a sawmill. A balance of $8,530 was left. "Absolutely false," said Garvey. "What I would like to know," Garvey continued, "is why the public should worry about me when the stockholders are completely satisfied. They know what is going on. They can't be fooled." When the interviewer asked Garvey about the charge that he had sold passage on a mythical ship, Garvey said he was away at the time, but "the ship was to have been bought yesterday." It had been named, however, before its purchase. "I can't control all

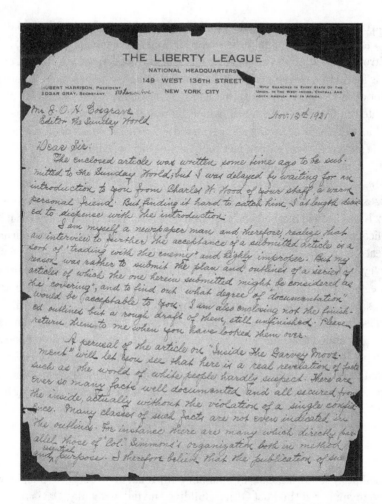

Figure 12.2. Hubert Harrison to J. O. H. Cosgrave, editor of the *New York World*, November 13, 1921, page 1 (of 2 pages). In this letter to J. O. H. Cosgrave, editor of the *New York World*, Harrison offers to provide articles on "Inside the Garvey Movement" with "well documented" facts. It makes reference to "many" facts, "which directly parallel those of Col. [William Joseph] Simmons'" organization (the Ku Klux Klan). Harrison's materials may have strongly influenced the articles on Garvey in *The World* of January 13 and 14, 1922, as well as an important article by Herbert J. Seligmann on Garvey in *The World* of December 4, 1921. In the summer of 1922, in a very controversial move, Garvey would meet with Edward Young Clarke, the acting imperial wizard and principal recruiter for the white supremacist and antiradical Ku Klux Klan. *Source:* Hubert H. Harrison Papers, Box 2, Folder 16, Rare Book and Manuscript Library, Columbia University Library. See https://dlc.library.columbia.edu/catalog/cul:w3r2280j02.

departments," he emphasized. "I have much work to do." Asked to explain his plans for the African republic, he snapped, "Did Napoleon make known . . . ?"[55]

Strong indication of Harrison's involvement in the *New York World*'s coverage is found in a November 13, 1921, letter that he wrote to J. O. H. Cosgrave, editor of the *Sunday World*. In that letter Harrison enclosed an article entitled "Inside the Garvey Movement," which he indicated was written "some time ago," as well as notes for a series of related articles. He described the enclosed article as "a real revelation of fact such as the world of white people hardly suspect." It included "'many facts well documented and all secured from the inside . . . without the violation of a single confidence." He noted that many classes of facts "directly parallel those of 'Col.' Simmons's organization [the Ku Klux Klan] both in method and essential purpose." Harrison believed that "the publication of such a series [the outlined articles] would be a minor journalistic feat—also a 'beat' on some other papers which have gullibly swallowed what Garvey had to say of himself, instead of investigating." Harrison expressly requested that if the *Sunday World* accepted either the submitted article or the series, "my name shall not appear in any connection with them." He did this because he did not want to lose his paying job as contributing editor at the *Negro World*. He added that "morally" he felt "free" to do what he was doing because "I am not in cahoots with Mr. Garvey and his crazy ideas—and have never pretended to be. This fact is well known both inside and outside the movement." Harrison's materials may have strongly influenced the articles on Garvey in the *New York World* of January 13 and 14, 1922, as well as an important article by Herbert J. Seligmann on Garvey in the *New York World* of December 4, 1921.[56]

Immediately following Garvey's January 12, 1922, arrest several people were asked to appear at the Post Office Building the following day. Davis reported that Garcia, Thompson, Jones, Tobias, and Fred A. Toote appeared and "signified their willingness" to make voluntary statements. On January 14 James D. Brooks voluntarily gave a statement. He returned again on January 16 with Harrison and said that Harrison wanted to make a statement. Then, while Inspector Williamson went to Pittsburgh, Assistant U.S. Attorney Joyce urged that Davis make an investigation of the BSL ship purchases.[57]

Captain Jones (confidential informant 800) stated in his January 13 testimony that he had begun work for Garvey in March 1920 and that the bills of the *Negro World* had been paid by the BSL checks. At first, the printing bill ran between $2,100 and $2,300 a week, while the paper was turning in from $500 to $700 a week, a deficit of about $1,500 a week. It was Garvey's idea that whether newsdealers paid or not wasn't as important as it was "to get the sheet before the public." Then, "some weeks," said Jones, "that deficit would be made up from funds from the U.N.I.A. or from any other fund available." At that time the BSL was selling $5,000 to $10,000 a week in stock and had money available.[58]

Also discussed was the alleged purchase of the *Negro World*. In order to cover up $46,000 of the death fund, the UNIA was supposed to have bought the *Negro World* for $46,000. In fact, said Jones, not a cent was transferred. He had been circulation manager of the *Negro World* since March 1921, and in July 1921 the paper's ownership passed from the UNIA to the general association, known as the parent body or ACL. The sale price was $46,000, an amount that the ACL never had in its treasury. Jones claimed to have "personal knowledge that when bills are to be paid, no distinction is made between the funds of the A.C.L., the Black Star Line, Inc., or the parent body." Later, as the *Negro World* developed a surplus, the other corporations helped consume that. The printer Rogowski, for example, was variously paid by funds from the ACL, the UNIA, and the BSL. Jones added that until around July 1921, the principal source of income was through the sale of stock in the BSL; recently it was from sale of the Liberian construction bonds. As the BSL began to dwindle, Garvey started the Liberian Construction Loan and issued bonds for construction purposes in Liberia; he sold about $144,000 worth and spent only about $5,000 related to Liberia. Regarding the SS *Phyllis Wheatley*, Garvey had held a March 1921 conference with thirteen presidents of large UNIA divisions where he reportedly told them if he could raise $25,000 he could purchase a boat to be named the *Phyllis Wheatley*. The money was raised, and in *Negro World* issues the BSL advertised the sailing of the *Phyllis Wheatley* for a certain date around April 25. Through these advertisements and others, they sold fares to Liberia, perhaps $22,000.[59]

Elie Garcia, BSL secretary and UNIA auditor, in his statement of January 13, when asked by Inspector Williamson "How did you get the name 'Phyllis Wheatley'[?]" marked on a photograph of the "*Orion*," responded, "I do not know. Mr. [Orlando] Thompson handled all that." He added, "Without consulting the books I would say that some $8,000 was collected for the passage on the 'Phyllis Wheatley' and that of it something like $4,000 was returned."[60] Orlando M. Thompson, the BSL's vice president, in his January 13 statement was asked by Inspector Williamson: "Who was responsible for the circular [with the name *Phyllis Wheatley* marked on a photograph of the *Orion*]?" Thompson responded, "I was connected with it. Mr. [Elie] Garcia and I got it out."[61] In his statement of January 13, James D. Brooks, former secretary general of the UNIA and former seller of BSL stock, said, "We began collecting money in January [1921] to purchase the *Phyllis Wheatley*, and that is where Garvey enters, before we began collecting, before Garvey left the country" (in February 1921).[62]

On January 14 Cyril V. Briggs and his attorney visited Post Office inspector Williamson. When agent Davis went to meet with Williamson on the afternoon of the 14th he found him speaking with Briggs and his legal adviser, Murray Bernays, of the law firm of Hale, Shorr. Bernays had recently defended communist leaders Edward Lindgren, Israel Amter, and Abram Jakira and was known to be personally and legally active in communist circles. Briggs's efforts were likely supported by the communist Workers Party, which he had joined.[63]

Harrison waited until the authorities arrested Garvey before he provided them a statement and brought material to them. How voluntary his testimony was is not clear. The historian Theodore Kornweibel Jr. suggests that though Harrison, like other officials in the Garvey movement, gave a "voluntary" statement, he was in fact "compelled" to testify. While there is no indication at all that Harrison had a fear of prosecution for possible involvement in wrongdoing, as did Thompson, Garcia, and others, his testimony may have been partially related to his vulnerable status as an "alien" and his desire to obtain U.S. citizenship. Politically, however, Harrison's belief that Garvey was engaged in a big swindle and was robbing poor people of their monies and needed to be stopped was likely the major factor. On January 17, the informant Jones reported to George F. Ruch in Washington, DC, that "Hubert Harrison was down to the District Attorney's Office yesterday and I know that he told them all that he knew. I saw him on his way down there and he had a large bundle of records that he has kept on Garvey for the past two years."[64]

Harrison's testimony was provided to Post Office Inspector Williamson on Monday, January 16, 1922, at the Post Office Building in New York. The stenographic minutes were taken by Mortimer J. Davis. Harrison stated that he was currently "associate editor of the *Negro World*—one of the contributing editors," a position he had held since November 1920, antecedent to which he was "editor of the *Negro World*."[65]

He explained that the first owners of the *Negro World* were the "same people who are the owners of it now, that is, the U.N.I.A. and A.C.L." When asked, "Where did Garvey get the money to buy the paper?" Harrison replied, "What do you mean?" Williamson asked, "Didn't he pay the paper some money?" Harrison responded, "I guess you are referring to that statement [about the alleged $46,455.20 spent in purchasing 'the good will' of the *Negro World*].... That is bunk. No such transaction ever occurred." When asked "Did Garvey ever use any Black Star Line funds to make payments to that paper?" Harrison responded, "Prior to my going there in January, 1920, I do not know. Between January 1920 and November 1921, when I gave up the editorship, I can but say I do not believe so. I saw no signs of it, and on the contrary, the paper's money was being used to pay for Black Star Line work and things of that sort. They owed the paper money."[66]

Williamson asked, "Did Garvey and his agents, in selling Black Star Line stock, hold out the hope of colonizing Africa or some part of it?" Harrison answered, "Always," and added, "that was one of the main inducements and the Black Star Line was to run the ships." When Williamson asked Harrison if he had "ever seen a report made by [Elie] Garcia to Garvey as to the feasibility of this plan," Harrison replied: "I have seen the report made by Garcia to Garvey when Garcia came back in 1920 from Africa in August or July. I do not know that the report could be fairly described as a report on the feasibility of his invasion of Africa, but in the course of the report he [g]ave information which indicated that they had no base to work from or on."[67]

Harrison indicated that though the seat of the Garvey government was to be in Liberia, Garcia's report indicated that Garvey owned nothing in Liberia, that "the Liberians themselves" opposed any colonization scheme, and that Garcia "advised that if they [the UNIA] wanted to exert any influence in Liberia they must soft-pedal and rather persuasively permeate the situation rather than buck it." Harrison then added that "the gab" about gaining control of the Liberian government was "abundantly furnished at Liberty Hall." In addition, there was "a certain issue of the *Negro World* in 1920 about March or April . . . [in which] they opened up at Liberty Hall and told all that they intended to do in Africa and what they were going to say to the Chiefs, and Garvey was chump enough to put it in the paper."[68]

Williamson asked if "the Garcia report discouraged the colonization project," and Harrison answered, "Yes," adding that in trying to sell stock in the Black Star Line,

[Garvey] ar[g]ued that the race needed ships and needed to be in commerce. He told them that they had to free themselves from the domination of the whites and if they could do that by owning ships; that at the same time Africa was to be redeemed and that part of the work of redeeming Africa would be done by the Black Star Line by building it into a great big thing, and he assured them that there was wealth in Africa, that the wealth was waiting for our people, and that all our people needed to do was to go over there and get it.[69]

Regarding getting in there, Harrison answered that "he [Garvey] explained that all he had to do was to drive the British out."[70]

When asked what representations Garvey made "as to the ownership or c[on]trol or operation of any ships," Harrison replied that "[Garvey] said—more than said—that they owned the S/S Yarmouth, to be rechristened the 'Frederick Douglas[s]'; that they owned the 'Kanawha,' which they called the Maceo;

that they owned the Shadyside, and I have read the circular showing that they owned—had taken over the S/S Phyllis Wheatley."[71] Harrison confirmed that he heard Garvey make those statements in speeches. Regarding the *Phyllis Wheatley*, Harrison stated:

> About February, 1921[,] I heard Garvey, in Liberty Hall, make these statements as to the Phyllis Wheatley: That he had been examining the ship; that the ship suited him and the company and that the sole reason why he did not take her over then was that it was a Sunday on which he was looking her over. Furthermore, that at the time of his looking her over the Black Star Line stood so strong in six banks that they could have bought the Phyllis Wheatley any time, and in the same speech he made the statement that if they wanted to raise a million dollars any time they could do it in less than a month.[72]

Garvey was "selling stock at the time." Harrison next answered a question about "the printed representations as to the ownership or [c]on[t]rol of the Phyllis Wheatley" that he had seen. He said that "insofar as they were a reproduction of this speech. He further [than] that, coming down to 1921 I think, read the statements [ma]de in Liberty [H]all. Subsequent to this, I heard, in [F]eb. 1921, to the effect that they had the Phyllis Wheatley."[73]

According to Agent Davis's report for January 18, Harrison that day brought "Cyril Crichlow" to the BI office "to have him make a statement of his knowledge of Garvey's affairs." Davis "deferred taking such statement" until Inspector Williamson, who was out of town, returned to New York. Crichlow advised him that he was "willing to testify" to conditions in Africa, speeches delivered by Garvey in the United States, and the purpose of Garvey's 1921 trip to the West Indies. Davis noted that "Crichlow was for a long period Official Reporter of the U.N.I.A." and "travelled throughout the United States with Marcus Garvey, reporting stenographically his various speeches, many of which subsequently appeared in the *Negro World* verbatim." During 1920 "Crichlow was selected by the U.N.I.A. to head a delegation of its members, which made a trip to Liberia," and his "findings" were "embodied in several letters, photostats of which are in possession of this office." He was reportedly "willing to testify as to the African situation," and, in general, he "found that neither Garvey [n]or the U.N.I.A. had any standing in Liberia; that the Liberian Government was antagonistic to Garvey's proposed colonization scheme," and "that climatic and economic conditions were such that this scheme would be impracticable." Crichlow "notified Garvey in writing and in person of these facts," and it was "well known that not only did Garvey sup[p]ress Crichlow's report, but, in addition, continued to publicly misrepresent the facts after receiving it." In addition, Crichlow was "suing Garvey for $1300 back pay . . . from the African trip."[74]

Crichlow added that Garvey told him in 1921 "that things looked very bad financially for the Black Star Line" and that "a crash was imminent." Garvey allegedly said that "he intended leaving the country so that should anything happen he could claim ignorance because of his absence." Davis thought this was "probably true" because he had "received information from several sources duri[n]g the week that Garvey's defense in this case, so far as it refers to the phantom 'Phyllis Wheatley' will be that all transactions regarding it took place during his absence from the country."[75]

Special Agent Davis also reported on January 21, 1922, that "Harrison today submitted voluntarily memoranda," which Davis then copied for Williamson. The Harrison "memoranda"[76] read as follows:

Mrs.—[Nancy or T.?] PARRIS, 117–119 West 142 St., one flight up, front, east side. Bought passage for Africa (for herself and family). Sold land in Yonkers and in St. Croix, V.I. Also sold household furniture in preparation for trip. Constant attendant at Liberty Hall. Sick of Garvey's lies and crookedness, but has pathetic regard for "welfare of movement" for which reason she is slightly inclined to rally around him until they on the inside can deal with him themselves. Rich in witness stand possibilities. I could coach you somewhat on line of questioning her.[77]

Capt. Joshua Cockburn, 201 W. 128 St. Very valuable person, from whom could be had the addresses of Edward Smith Green, former secretary of Black Star Line, and Mr. Johnson, former passenger and Traffic Agent. All three "have it in" for Garvey. Perhaps they would be more valuable for Dept. of Justice than for restricted limits of P.O. case. Their names might be passed on.

Capt. [James W.] Jones [Harrison apparently didn't realize he was an agent, undercover informant "800"], of Negro World. *If privately examined*, could give name and address of man to whom passage to Africa on the phantom "Phyllis Wheatley" was sold as late as Dec. 6th, 1921[,] for $250. At any rate, he talked in office with many to whom such passage was sold in summer of 1921. He too, could be benevolently "forced."

Cyril A. Crichlow, 92 Ege Ave. Jersey City. Eager to testify. Went to Liberia for Garvey in 1921. Can expose the whole swindle and prove that Garvey has no U.N.I.A. lands or concessions in Liberia and never had.[78]

In re Negro World of Jan. 21, 1922. Garvey seeks to shift responsibility by pretending that he was not here when certain things were planned. But the series of "book your passage" ads (now in the hands of Mr. [Samuel] Spewa[c]k of *New York World*) began as early as Jan. 1921 when Garvey was here, and ran uninterruptedly to Dec. 17th of same year.

If you look up Negro World for April and October 1921 you will find statements of ownership of paper (African Communities League). This was sworn to, and proves that there has been no transfer of ownership as alleged by Garvey, and Garcia, in print, to explain speculations and wastage of funds of Liberian Construction Loan (about $46,000) as payment for the Negro World.[79]

Harrison bought a bond of this loan which was advertised for months as a "Liberian Loan." In speeches printed in the Negro World, Garvey first convey[ed] the impression that it was a loan *to* Liberia. Harrison paid in weekly installments of a dollar each, missing many weeks, and taking about 20 weeks to pay. So that during all that time he was under the impression first created by Garvey. Then, when he had paid, he received the bond and noted that Liberia's name never occurred once on it, and the word "Africa" only once, near the end. It had been transformed into a loan to "The Parent Body of the U.N.I.A." All the office employees were *forced* to buy bonds, even the poor typists on $12 and $15 a week. The money was simply taken from their pay envelope without any precedent explanation. So it was in Harrison's case.[80]

Re African Construction Loan "Bonds": Garcia's report made to Garvey on his return from Liberia in 1920 before first [UNIA] convention shows that Garvey knew that U.N.I.A. had no lands or concessions of any sort when he launched this swindle. Harrison was head of a delegation to go to Liberia and could be "forced" to show in his testimony that Garvey had no plans whatever for getting concessions up to time set for sailing.[81]

In the New York World of Sat., Jan. 14, 1922, Garvey said to Spewa[c]k that the figures showing that only about $6,000 out of $144,000 went to Liberia, were the lying work of an enemy. One of the Negro World issues for August [1921] shows that these were Garvey's own official figures given by [UNIA & ACL High] Chancellor [G. E.] Stewart and "explained" in a 2[nd] column by Garcia as Auditor Genl. The printing was forced by Noah D. Thompson, delegate from Los Angeles.[82]

The "memoranda" merit some additional comment. Nancy Paris emigrated to the United States from the Virgin Islands. She, her husband, Thomas Paris, and their daughter, Eudora, were early members of the UNIA and active in the synagogue of Rabbi Arnold Ford, a Harrison friend who had been active with the UNIA as musical director of Liberty Hall. Harrison's diary lists a sister named Emma who had three children, including Carmelita Maria Parris, born in June 1893 at Mt. Pleasant (Colguhoon), St. Croix, and it is quite possible that Thomas Paris and Nancy Paris were related to Harrison.[83]

Captain Joshua Cockburn had commanded the *Yarmouth*, the first ship of the BSL, on her maiden voyage. He delivered a speech at Liberty Hall the night after the ship docked in early January 1920, which, according to Harrison, referred to the "underhanded business done to make the trip a failure and to prevent the ship from reaching port." By the end of July 1920 he was no longer involved with Garvey and by late 1921 was prepared to speak along with Briggs, McGuire, Gordon, and Crichlow at an ABB meeting at Rush Memorial Church to expose Garvey and the BSL. At that December 18, 1921, meeting Cockburn, like others, was shouted down, and ultimately off the platform, by cries of "Traitor! Traitor!" from Garvey's followers. He would later testify at Garvey's mail-fraud trial in 1923 and was reportedly threatened with physical harm both before and after his testimony.[84]

Edward Smith-Green was the former secretary of the BSL who had been shot on December 10, 1919. In January 1920 he accompanied the SS *Yarmouth* on its second voyage to Cuba, but shortly after his return, he resigned from his positions with the BSL and the UNIA. Smith-Green broke from Garvey in late June or early July 1920, and Garvey subsequently put out a warning against him and blamed some of the BSL losses on him. The reference to being "more valuable" for Justice than postal inspectors may have referred to either the loss of funds on the maiden voyage or possible information on Mann Act violations by Marcus Garvey with Amy Jacques before they were married.[85]

Cyril Crichlow, the UNIA stenographer, was a member of the high executive council of the UNIA and former resident secretary in Liberia in 1921. He had access to all of the UNIA's records, data, and reports. After breaking with Garvey and joining the ABB, Crichlow sued Garvey for lost wages and an unrepaid loan and prepared various reports on the situation in Liberia. In general, as Agent Davis writes, Crichlow "found that neither Garvey [n]or the U.N.I.A. had any standing in Liberia; that the Liberian Government was antagonistic to Garvey's proposed colonization scheme," and "that climatic and economic conditions were such that this scheme would be impracticable." At the December 18, 1921, ABB meeting to criticize Garvey he was shouted off the platform. For these reasons Harrison reasonably thought that Crichlow could "expose the whole swindle and prove that Garvey has no U.N.I.A. lands or concessions in Liberia and never had."[86]

On January 26, 1922, the grand jury investigating Garvey returned a true bill. The Justice Department was charging Garvey with mail fraud—the charge that would eventually put him behind bars and lead to his deportation.[87]

Harrison's "memoranda" were not the last material that he gave the Justice Department regarding the case against Garvey for mail fraud. On October 3, 1922, one week after becoming a citizen of the United States (a day he referred to as "One of the Redletter days of my life"), Harrison gave to Special Agent

Davis of the BI, "for use of U.S. Dept. of Justice," an important series of documents. These materials included:

1) Delegates to 1920 U.N.I.A. Convention
2) Bond #3244 of Parent Body UNIA Loan 7/26/21
3) Garvey's Leaflets and Circulars
4) Anti Garvey Leaflets & Circulars
5) "The Phantom Phyllis Wheatley"
6) Black Star Line Ads.
7) Course of Events Clippings
8) "African Construction Fund"
9) "Miscellaneous indications"
10) "Threatenings and Slaughter"
11) Convention fund
12) Official Record bundle
13) Constitution and By Laws of UNIA.[88]

Though Harrison had both political and personal objections to Garvey, and though his citizenship status had hung over his head for a long time, the providing of these additional materials after he obtained citizenship supports the position that the reasons he gave testimony and provided documents regarding Garvey were primarily political. Harrison, as he would make clear in July 1923, considered Garvey guilty of "swindling members of his race by means of the . . . the 'Black Star Line' whose fleet of ships to sail the seven seas existed mainly on paper and in the mind of Marcus Garvey." He explained: "The S.S. Yarmouth which, . . . was 'soon to be rechristened['] the 'Frederick Douglass' was never rechristened, but went back to its original owners because it was not quite paid for; the 'Shadyside' was a bluff, and the S.S. Phyllis Wheatley, a phantom ship which was never bought nor seen, but on which Garvey by false and misleading advertisements had collected thousands of dollars paid in as passage-money to Africa and as stock sales."[89] The BSL was, he maintained, "designed as a money-getter for Garvey," and this was shown "by the fact that he 'collected' money for it for many months without any legal safeguards until [Edwin P.] Kilroe, an assistant district attorney of New York got after him and he was forced to incorporate in due legal form." Garvey, however, "never accounted for the monies which he 'collected' before the incorporation." The "broken-down ships which he got were intended to seduce credulous Negroes who saw them into putting more of their money into Garvey's hands, and not as a bona-fide business procedure." According to Harrison, Garvey "would let a cargo of perishable freight for New York rot while he paraded the Yarmouth in Philadelphia to catch more suckers. Then, instead of going to New York to unload it he would take the ship to Boston, declaring that it was 'good propaganda.'"

Harrison recognized that

as a propagandist Garvey was without a peer; but, unfortunately most of his propaganda consisted of selling himself. He was the most valuable asset of the entire chain of enterprises—not one of which succeeded. That didn't phase him, however. He knew the value of appearances and, while a sane man would have finished paying for one ship before proclaiming a second, third and fourth, he flung himself from the unpaid "Yarmouth," to the rotten "Shadyside" which sunk at her moorings; then to the "Kanawha" whose machinery was a mess; finally to the phantom "Phyllis Wheatley." This flying Dutchman was advertised as sailing for Africa in January 1921. As she failed to materialize her sailing date was successively (and successfully) put off to February, March, April, May, etc. Pictures of her were faked in the office of the B.S.L. and printed in the Negro Worlds, each picture showing a different type of ship. But always he said he had her in possession . . .

In the meanwhile he sold passage to Africa . . . on the ship which he knew didn't exist.[90]

Harrison felt that Garvey developed "propaganda more shrewdly adopted to the cruder psychology of the less intelligent masses, the sensationalism, self-glorification, and African liberation—although he knew next to nothing of Africa. But since Africa was far away and wild statements about its '400 millions' could not be disproved in New York that feature of it was a money-getter always."[91]

On a personal/political level, Harrison thought that:

Garvey has a great talent for lying. In 1920 when he attacked his first wife in Liberty Hall he said that if she had ever bought any houses he was absolutely ignorant of the transaction. But, on the stand, when shown a check of the B.S.L. for $5,000 made out to her and drawn and paid by him to a real estate agent for the purchase of a house for her, he "explained" that that was for a lien on the property. A check as a lien is a new thing in real estate deals. . . .

For months before every convention he would run a "Convention Fund" in the Negro World, which frequently ran to tens of thousands of dollars. Yet no visiting delegate ever got even a glass of lemonade that delegates didn't pay for. What he did with the Convention funds is as much a mystery today as the Liberian Loan fund, the fund for "Certificates of Race Loyalty," the "African Redemption Fund," the money collected in 1918 to send delegates to the Peace Congress and the other bally-hoo devices by which money was extracted from his dupes while he prated of "dying for his race.[92]

Harrison's presentation of materials indicated that he was "sick of Garvey's lies and crookedness" and saw his financial schemes as a "swindle."[93] He realized that many poor and working people had lost and were losing significant sums of money. He was disappointed that Garvey failed to "[put] forth a constructive radical program." Personally he considered Garvey to have "a defect in the size of his soul" and viewed him "spiritually as well as intellectually [as] a little man" complete with "delusions of grandeur" and "persecution," "insane hoggishness," "jealousy of successful subordinates," "ingratitude," "greed for domination," "ignorance," and "bombastic blabbing." As a speaker he thought he was "a joke" with "silly rhodomentades [*sic*]," "insincere boastings," "bombastic blabbing," "cowardly evasions on lynching," "lies," and a changing policy.[94]

Harrison also believed, as he had for some time, in the possibility of the federal government helping to ameliorate conditions when other methods failed. This had been the case when the federal government took steps to end slavery and when Reconstruction governments intervened against recalcitrant Southern state governments and the rise of the KKK after the Civil War. This was also implicit in repeated appeals by Harrison and others for federal antilynching and civil rights legislation.

Another reason that Harrison presented evidence against Garvey may be related to the fact that Garvey himself, since 1919, had repeatedly and seemingly excessively used the courts and state against his critics and opponents. In August 1922, after he was indicted and while he awaited trial, Garvey would file nine more libel suits, for a total of $750,000, in the Supreme Court of New York against his critics and opponents for publishing or making slanderous statements concerning him.[95]

On January 22, 1922, Agent Jones wrote to BI Special Agent George F. Ruch that Harrison had given Davis "some valuable information and is now securing the names and addresses of some of the discontented stockholders; work that would not do for me as it is best that I not be seen mixing with any discontented stockholders." Harrison was also planning to "write a series of articles for the *New York World* under the name of 'Spewak' disclosing the inner workings of the association." He said he would send these articles as soon as they appeared; this was confirmed by Davis.[96]

Jones advised that "when the indictments are returned" Garvey should "be rearrested and the maximum bond [should] be required in each separate count." Such action was "necessary to show Garvey's members that Garvey is not greater than the Government, as they believe him to be." He also thought that "if Garvey is put in jail and he can't raise the bond," it would "kill Garvey's defiant spirit as well as that of his members."[97]

On February 21, Orlando Thompson provided a statement to special agents Davis and James E. Amos, in which he explained that "some time in January, 1921, an advertisement came out in the Negro World advising of regular sailings to Africa, but it didn't state the name of the boat." Thompson added that Garvey wasn't in the United States "when the first advertisement specifically mentioning the Phyllis Wheatley appeared in the Negro World," though he was in the United States "when that [earlier] advertisement [about regular sailings to Africa on the un-named boat] appeared." Though Thompson had asked Garvey to cancel the listing of sailing dates to Africa (since the BSL had no boat that could make it there), Garvey refused to cancel the advertisement. He did, however, take out the sailing dates, though the sailings remained without a specified time.[98]

In his report of March 8, Agent Davis indicated that Thompson, under advisement of his attorney, stated his willingness to give a second statement at which he turned over "all letters, telegrams, and memoranda regarding his official acts" with the BSL to Inspector Williamson. Davis noted that Garvey was using the *Negro World* and public speeches to place the blame "for the phantom 'Phyllis Wheatley'" on Thompson's shoulders, since "negotiations for it, and the publication of the circulars in [q]uestion occurred during the time Garvey was in the West Indies." Garvey also claimed "that Thompson has made away with $25,000," which was believed to be "th[e] amount now held by the Shipping Board as deposit on the S/S 'Orion,'" a fact "well known to Garvey but which he is apparently misrepresenting for his own purposes." Davis believed this situation "led to Thompson's attitude" and that his offer to help the Government was "a matter of self-protection."[99]

In the same report Davis indicated that Cyril Crichlow, who had gone to Africa for the UNIA and was the official stenographer for the organization, came to his office. Crichlow had brought suit against the UNIA for $1,300 in salary upon his return to the United States, won a judgment for $750, and reportedly said that nothing would prevent him from testifying. Davis cautioned, however, that on March 7 he was "confidentially informed that the association had handed Crichlow $550 in settlement of his judgment, on the promise that he would not testify against them at the trial." The promise was allegedly "extracted from Crichlow" by "Bishop Gainse [Rev. E. L. Gaines?]." On the same day Davis also "learned confidentially that Elie Garcia, being in charge of the Black Star Line during the absence of . . . Marcus Garvey, ordered, on Feb. 20th, that the sale of stock be stopped." Davis also heard from "Thomas Merril[e]es" that while the sale of stock of the BSL had continued since the indictment, the monies received were deposited into the BSL account by way of the Black Star Steamship Co., Inc., a New Jersey corporation. This was done to avoid an attachment that had been obtained against the bank account of the BSL for unpaid bills.[100]

Gwendolyn Campbell, in charge of the stenographic force in Garvey's office, told Agent Davis that the Board of Directors gave Garvey permission to draw money for his expenses without giving itemized statements. Thus, when he went out of town, he merely submitted a slip stating how much was spent and how much collected, without itemization. Campbell also said she saw Crichlow's unfavorable report on UNIA aims and objectives in Liberia and personally gave it to Garvey and saw him read it. She explained all the various funds collected were interchangeable and that officers, particularly Garvey, "drew promiscuously on each and every fund available regardless of whether or not the use of the money had any direct connection with same." Regarding Garvey's trip to Jamaica, Campbell said she thought Garvey took $1,000 for expenses, and Amy Jacques indicated they sold about $12,000 worth of stock. They only turned in a few hundred dollars to the BSL and dismissed the rest as undetailed expenses.[101]

Around April 1922 Du Bois offered a more private assessment of Garvey in a letter to D. J. Steyne-Parve, consul general for the Netherlands in New York. Du Bois thought "this organization [UNIA] is ineffective, foolish and even dangerous," although it had "started out with some good ideas" including "the establishment of commercial intercourse between colored people of the eastern and western hemispheres." Its "business methods," however, "were from the beginning faulty if not fraudulent." He added that "recent disclosures" indicated "grave inefficiency together with wild and silly plans and propaganda."[102]

In April 1922 Garvey received an ominous and "severe rebuke" from Justice Jacob Panken in New York's Seventh District Court, at 125th Street and St. Nicholas Avenue, when Garvey was a defendant before him in three actions. An unidentified newspaper article explained that Panken's comments came after "it was brought out that the $600,000 invested in the Black Star Line by thousands of small investors among the colored people was practically wiped out." On the stand, Garvey reportedly said that the BSL had spent $600,000, including the *Yarmouth*'s cost of $145,000 and $300,000 on its first trip; $65,000 for the purchase of the *Maceo* and $75,000 on its first voyage; and money for the old ferryboat the *Shadyside*, the amount of which was not mentioned. He also admitted that the mythical ship *Phyllis Wheatley* was never seen, though it was advertised. Garvey reportedly denied knowing anything about the *Phyllis Wheatley*'s advertisements, which were being looked into by the federal government.[103]

When the trial ended, Justice Panken told Garvey:

> It seems to me that you have been preying upon the gullibility of your own people, having kept no proper accounts of the money received for investment, being an organization of high finance in which the officers received outrageously high salaries and were permitted to have exorbitant expense accounts for pleasure-jaunts throughout the country. I adv[ise] these "dupes" who have contributed [to] these organizations to go into c[ourt] and ask for the appointment of a [re]ceiver. You should have taken [the] $600,000 and built a hospital [for] colored people in this city inste[ad of] purchasing a few old boats. Th[ere is] a form of paranoia which manif[ests it]self in believing oneself to be a [great] man.[104]

Later, in his chambers, Panken added:

> These various mo[vements] that have been fostered by [Garvey?] have taken millions of dollar[s out of] the pockets of the colored pe[ople] F[or?] the Universal Negro Improvement Association he claims [has] a member[ship of] 4,500,000 who have been paying [dues.] He says nothing is left of the [Black] Star Line. . . . [All] the officers cared about was ha[ving a] salary they would receive [and having] enormous expense accounts.[105]

In the May 20, 1922, *Jamaica Times*, E. Ethelred Brown, who knew Garvey since their Jamaica days and who would later found the Hubert Harrison Memorial Church, wrote "Garveyism, a Dispassionate, Unprejudiced Appraisement." He quoted Justice Panken's rebuke to Garvey and emphasized that his objective was "to call the attention of Jamaicans to the fact apparently unknown to them that in the words of Garvey himself 'the $600,000 invested are all gone and the Co[r]p[o]ration has suspended operations.'" Brown also felt that Judge Panken's criticism of the outrageous salaries was "justified especially, in the case of high officers of the U.N.I.A.," whose salaries voted at the last convention "were simply ridiculous." Panken's criticism was also justified regarding the "Liberia Construction Loan Fund," which started after the 1920 convention and collected $144,450 "for the especial purpose of carrying out reconstruction work in Liberia [and] only the sum of $8,464 was used for that purpose, if the sawmill did eventually reach Liberia." BSL shares claimed $34,400, and "a highly questionable and unexplained transaction entered up a[s] a purchase of the goodwill of the 'Negro World' swallowed up $46,000." Since the *Negro World* "owns no printing plant" Brown asked, "Why should money contributed to reconstruct Liberia be spent on a New York weekly?"[106]

In August 1923, Brown would describe how "the Black Star Line was criminally mismanaged." The "business proposition" had been turned "into a propaganda agency, resulting in a waste of time and consequently heavy loss of money" as "speculation went mad in the purchase of old rotten boats." He compared Garvey to Charles Ponzi and Horatio Bottomley. "Ponzi [the great swindler of 1920] had his day of popularity, but his end came; and his victims knew him [then] for what he was and wasted on him neither pity, nor sympathy. Horatio Bottomley for years played his part as the champion of the rights of England's poor." Bottomley "became bold & bolder in success, but he walked the slippery path once too often, and now lies in an English prison at the eventide of life dishonoured and disgraced. The English people were stunned at the revelations of his dishonesty. They were shocked at the fall of their idol—the fearless uncompromising Editor of 'John Bull.'" Garvey, however, though "a prisoner in the Tombs [at the time of Brown's 1923 article], is still the idol of his people, and enjoys today even in greater measure than in the days of his freedom, the loyal affection and undim[in]ished devotion." He was "their martyred saint, their crucified Saviour." "The victims of his waste [remain] his loyal friends! the dupes of his ill considered schemes are his passionate defenders!" Brown asked, "How could one explain . . . this unique, this unparall[el]ed, this Garveyistic devotion?"[107]

Additional comments on Ponzi merit attention. In August 1923 Garvey was described as the "Black Ponzi" by Charles S. Johnson. Charles Ponzi was an Italian-born swindler in Boston who in 1919 and 1920 promised investors he would "double their money in 90 days." He told them his Securities Exchange Company, a kind of pyramid scheme, took advantage of favorable exchange rates in purchasing International Postal Union coupons. At first Ponzi paid his investors, but his overall operation was found by federal authorities to be bankrupt, with liabilities totaling some $3 million over assets. The state of Massachusetts indicted him for larceny. He was sentenced to seven years and freed on bail; he then attempted to recoup his losses with a Florida land scheme for which he was convicted for fraud. He then jumped bail, was captured in New Orleans, and extradited to Massachusetts. In 1934 he was released from jail and deported to Italy. He died a pauper in Rio de Janeiro in 1949. Since his efforts, a scheme that pays off original investors with money from succeeding investors has often been referred to as a "Ponzi scheme."[108] Robert A. Hill notes, "Garvey was frequently compared to Charles Ponzi."[109]

———

Garvey, after his arrest and while awaiting trial, took one of the most controversial steps of his career when he secretly interviewed Edward Young Clarke, acting imperial wizard and principal recruiter for the KKK. Garvey later said that in the two-hour conference Clarke "outlined the aims and objects of the Klan," "denied any hostility toward the Negro as a race," expressed "sympathy for aims and objects" of the UNIA, maintained that America should "be a white man's country," and argued "that the Negro should have a country of his own in Africa." He also "denied that his organization, since its re-organization, ever officially attacked the negro." According to Garvey, Clark was "invited to speak at [the] forthcoming [UNIA] convention to further assure the race of the stand of the Klan." Garvey also committed to publishing the interview in the *Negro World*.[110]

In the wake of the meeting with the Klan, Garvey's supporters became more volatile. When he attributed his prosecution to Black opponents and European governments he temporarily strengthened his leadership, but the secret meeting backfired noticeably. Although Garvey argued that the KKK and UNIA had similar goals—they opposed racial "miscegenation," favored racial "purity," and opposed the NAACP—as the organization approached its 1922 convention there was major dissent within the UNIA. The "leader of American Negroes," the Rev. James W. H. Eason, a prominent, U.S.-born minister, planned to oppose Garvey, and the overall split in the organization heightened tensions between U.S.-born and West Indian–born delegates.[111]

A. Philip Randolph and Chandler Owen, operating outside the UNIA sphere of influence, took anti-Garvey protests to the streets with a new "Garvey Must Go" campaign supported by the Friends of Negro Freedom. They had first organized the FNF in the spring of 1920, with Robert W. Bagnall as chair of the executive committee and Grace Campbell as vice chair; they held their first national convention on May 25, 1920, in Washington, DC. By 1922 the "Garvey Must Go" campaign, which also prominently involved William Pickens of the NAACP, worked "with a view to driving out of the country the influence of Marcus Garvey and his worthless schemes through which negroes are losing their hard-earned dollars."[112]

By August 1922 their outdoor rallies against Garvey were drawing large crowds. At one activity, on August 6, two thousand Harlem residents reportedly heard several speakers at a "Garvey Must Go" meeting at Seventh Avenue and 131st Street, sponsored by the FNF and presided over by Randolph, editor of

The Messenger. William Pickens, field organizer for the NAACP, spoke on "What to Do When Negro Leaders League with Negro Lynchers." He said he had received many threats from friends of Garvey who said they would not only interrupt the meeting but also "do away" with him. Pickens stated that Garvey, with his endorsements of the KKK, appeared to be organizing a Black Ku Klux Klan. He thought that Garvey's scheme was "nothing new," noting that under Abraham Lincoln some people wanted to send the "Negroes" back to Africa. Garvey's sympathizers interrupted the speakers so often that police patrols were stationed throughout the audience to preserve order. The anti-Garvey campaign continued throughout the month, and on August 20 Bagnall, director of branches for the NAACP, spoke on "The Madness of Marcus Garvey."[113]

On August 13 a meeting was held in Harlem by the FNF at which Randolph charged that Garvey was "a Crook or Liar." Randolph reviewed Garvey's claim of a UNIA membership of 4.5 million in light of forty-cent dues and pointed out that that would bring $21,600,000 a year. Since Garvey was being sued in court because the UNIA couldn't pay employee's wages, he concluded: "Either Garvey is stealing the money, or there is no 4,500,000 membership." Similarly, Garvey claimed 150,000 delegates to the 1922 convention, but a count by competent observers had revealed only four hundred. In response to Garvey's plans for empire building, Randolph countered, "People now are fighting for the erection of democracies, not of empires. The Negroes don't want to be the victims of black despotism any more than white despotism." Also at the meeting, Pickens charged that Garvey had advised "Negroes desirous of winning leadership" to "form an association of their own similar to the Ku Klux Klan." The meeting was repeatedly interrupted by Garvey's followers.[114]

The communist Workers Party was also more publicly attempting to develop work in Harlem. On August 5, 1922, *The Toiler* announced that the city convention of the Workers Party had nominated Grace Campbell for the Twenty-First Congressional District and Otto Huiswoud for the Twenty-Second Assembly District. It also announced that the Harlem West Side Branch of the Workers' Party of America was now organized and meeting twice monthly at 147 West 136th Street. Provisional officers of the branch included Otto Huiswoud, organizer; Cyril Briggs, recording and financial secretary; Comrade Pierre, delegate to the City Central Committee; and Comrade Silverman, literature agent. Richard B. Moore, Grace Campbell, and Claude McKay were elected to the Propaganda and Educational Committee; Comrade Hirsch was elected the friends of Soviet Russia agent. Jack Jampolsky of the Organization Committee reported that nearly one hundred dollars had been raised toward a headquarters fund.[115]

In preparation for its December 25, 1922, convention, the Workers Party issued its proposed "Program." It differed from its previous January 14, 1922, program of the Workers Party of America in two key ways—it omitted mention of Black people as victims of rape and changed the demand for social equality to one for educational equality. It added more about discrimination and race riots in northern industrial cities and explained, "the Workers Party will support the Negroes in their struggle for liberation and will help them in their fight for economic, political, and educational equality." The *New York Times* of December 26, 1922, emphasized, "The proposal of some delegates to add to the resolution the words 'and for social equality' was turned down by an overwhelming majority."[116]

On August 23, 1922, Garvey, who had criticized the efforts of his opponents to have him prosecuted, retaliated by filing nine libel suits, for a total of $750,000, in the Supreme Court of New York. He accused his critics and opponents of publishing or making slanderous statements concerning him. The defendants named and the amounts involved were the *New York Times*, $200,000; *New York Call*, $100,000; *Amsterdam News*, $50,000; *New York News*, $50,000; Robert W. Bagnall, $100,000; Chandler Owen, $100,000 and $50,000 respectively; William Pickens, $50,000; and A. Philip Randolph, $50,000. Garvey took offense at such statements as those that his organization was "robbing ignorant negroes" and "seeking an alliance with the Ku Klux Klan."[117]

While a large number of his followers remained vehemently loyal, sentiment against Garvey was mounting. According to BI Special Agent James E. Amos, in his report for the period of August 30 to September 6, 1922, the Rev. J. D. Gordon, James Brooks, and James Eason had now indicated that they were quite willing to testify against Garvey.[118]

After terminating his managing editor duties with the *Negro World* the financial and personal pressures on Harrison intensified. In November 1921 he had papers served on him by the Manco Realty Co. for nonpayment of rent. He was desperate for a job, and as he searched for work as a writer, lecturer, and instructor, making a living became extremely difficult.[119]

His job search had taken an unusual course earlier in the year. In March 1921 Dr. J. Freeman Otto, chief executive of the Cosmopolitan College [School] of Chiropractic at 240 West 138th Street, had "urged" him to join the faculty of the school. Otto's offer was conveyed to him by Mrs. Gertrude Miller Faide, and, after "slight demur," Harrison "consented." On Wednesday, April 6, he taught his first class as an instructor in embryology to a group of "highly enthusiastic" students. In his diary he noted he was "the only Negro on the Faculty and the only member of it who is not a doctor." From May 14 through June 18 he delivered a series of six evening lectures on "Sex and Sex Problems" in the college building. His talks on "The Nature and Origin of Sex," "The Origins of

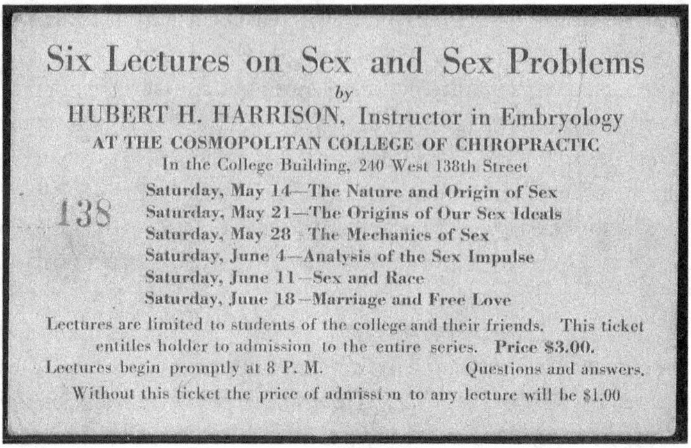

Six Lectures on Sex and Sex Problems
by
HUBERT H. HARRISON, Instructor in Embryology
AT THE COSMOPOLITAN COLLEGE OF CHIROPRACTIC
In the College Building, 240 West 138th Street

Saturday, May 14—The Nature and Origin of Sex
Saturday, May 21—The Origins of Our Sex Ideals
Saturday, May 28—The Mechanics of Sex
Saturday, June 4—Analysis of the Sex Impulse
Saturday, June 11—Sex and Race
Saturday, June 18—Marriage and Free Love

Lectures are limited to students of the college and their friends. This ticket
entitles holder to admission to the entire series. Price $3.00.
Lectures begin promptly at 8 P. M.   Questions and answers.
Without this ticket the price of admission to any lecture will be $1.00

Figure 12.3. Hubert H. Harrison, instructor in embryology, "Six Lectures on Sex and Sex Problems," May 14–June 18, 1921, at Cosmopolitan College of Chiropractic, 1921. In his search for work in 1921 Hubert Harrison was aided by Mrs. Gertrude Miller Faide and Dr. J. Freeman Otto, chief executive of the Cosmopolitan College [School] of Chiropractic at 240 West 138th Street, in Harlem. Otto "urged" him to join the faculty of the school as an instructor in embryology. In his diary Harrison noted that he was "the only Negro on the Faculty and the only member of it who is not a doctor." A list of his "Six Lectures on Sex and Sex Problems," May 14–June 18, 1921, is printed on this broadside. *Source:* Hubert H. Harrison Papers, Box 16, Folder 39, Rare Book and Manuscript Library, Columbia University Library. See https://dlc.library.columbia.edu/catalog /cul:zkh18933m2.

Our Sex Ideals," "The Mechanics of Sex," "Analysis of the Sex Impulse," "Sex and Race," and "Marriage and Free Love" included a question-and-answer period, were limited to students of the college and their friends, and cost $1 per session or $3 for the series.[120]

In the month following his lecture series Harrison took part in efforts to secure a public bath in the 134th Street neighborhood in which he lived. On July 26 he wrote to Blanche Wylie Welzmiller, deputy commissioner of the Bureau of Information and Conservation of the Department of Public Markets, and asked her to support community residents' efforts to secure a public bath. On August 4 she responded and said the matter was a subject for the Board of Estimate and that the board passed a resolution and would "proceed under the Resolution to secure the property for the bath," which she thought would be on Lenox Avenue and 134th Street.[121]

Conditions at home were not good for Harrison in the summer of 1921. Matters came to a head on Wednesday, August 13, when Hubert rented a room (apartment 11) from a Mrs. Rogers at 59 West 140th Street. He wrote in his diary that he did this "in order to free [himself] from wifely nagging, cursing and swearing, dirt and deviltry" and "to do some work." Despite moving out he still tried to see his children regularly, and a little over a month later, on Saturday, September 17, when his son Billy celebrated his first birthday, he wrote in his diary that Billy already "steps around (when some one holds his hands), and even seems eager to dance." Billy could utter "a few words, more or less clearly," "deliver a fair-sized oration—in his own language," and "hold a serious conversation—with himself." Hubert felt that Billy gave "promise of being a bright child," though he still didn't have "a tooth in his head." A month later, on Thursday, October 17, Hubert "went down to the family's residence for supper," and "'Little Billee' was yelling . . . to 'Come here; come here!'" These were "the first intelligible words from him—except his 'No!' when he doesn't like an action or a thing." As an infant, Hubert recollected, his oldest daughter "Frances used to double it" and "say 'No, No!'"[122]

With his economic situation worsening, Harrison, as president of the Liberty League, wrote a letter to the Mayor John F. Hylan, a Democrat. His letter was published on September 12 in an unidentifiable paper; it clearly appears to have been calculated to help him secure employment. Harrison answered a recent "open letter" by the Black Republican alderman (from the Twenty-Sixth Aldermanic District) George W. Harris, publisher of the *New York News*. Writing "on behalf of thousands of law-abiding and respectable people of Harlem" who were "outrageously slandered" by what Harris's open letter said about conditions in their community, Harrison responded. He pointed out that Harris was "the only Republican Alderman in Harlem who managed to escape last year's Democratic landslide when over 70% of the Negro votes went to Tammany Hall," and with the 1921 elections fast approaching it was "natural that Mr. Harris should begin now to scare up an 'issue.'" "But," added Harrison—that was "no reason . . . why he should seek to give the district a black eye before he bids it goodbye." "As the father of a family," Harrison claimed "to be even more deeply concerned in the moral conditions of the district than Alderman Harris." "As a practical student of sociology who has combed the district for facts during the past fifteen years," he wanted to assure the mayor "that Harlem is in no such awful plight as Mr. Harris intimates." Harrison claimed "the official record of criminal statistics for the past ten years and the blotter of West 135th Street Police Station" would bear him out. While Harlem was "not heaven," it was "as human as any other section of New York," complete with "our criminals as the other sections have" and with Volstead Act violations.[123]

Harrison added that anyone who says that "there are at least 100 delicatessens, grocery stores, furniture stores, and whatnots selling the most poisonous and maddening brands of liquor," as Harris claimed, was "indulging in gross and deliberate falsification for an ulterior purpose." If Alderman Harris knew of "at least 100" such places, it was "his duty as a citizen . . . to point them out to the police." That he was unable to do so raised questions about "his character as a citizen, his courage as a reformer, or his reputation as a teller of truth." Regarding the "poisonous and maddening brands of liquor," Harrison asked Harris "whether the whiskey served at the West Harlem Republican Club of which he [Harris] is well-known head was bought in one of the local liquor shops to which he refers." Was he conniving to violate the law at his own place, "while playing the reformer as to similar violations on other people's premises?" On the matter of Harris's "charges that 'the morals of both the uniformed and detective forces seems to have broken down,'" Harrison claimed that Harris "sacrifices the good repute of a hardworking body of men on the altar of his own self-interest." Harrison recognized that "violations of the law occur in Harlem—and violations of the law occur elsewhere," and "some policeman in Harlem ought to be off the force—and the same is true elsewhere," "but, by and large, both the conduct of the force and the general moral conditions in this city have grown steadily better, and I challenge Alderman Harris or any other person to deny this with the criminal statistics before him." Harrison concluded wryly that in the coming campaign "Mr. Harris may have to face those statistics" and "explain to the voters of Harlem why he has been the only Harlem Alderman to besmirch the civic standing and moral character of the Negro people of West Harlem." Of course, if "the work in the Aldermanic Chamber" had "been too much for Mr. Harris's nerves," then the voting public would "see to it that he gets the rest which he so sorely needs."[124]

The September letter to Hylan appears to have kicked off an intense eight-week period leading up to the November election in which Harrison worked for the Democratic Party. Over the last four weeks of the 1921 election season, by his own account, he "delivered thirty speeches, fourteen in automobiles, seven on the auto truck, and nine on the Liberty League Platform," for the Democratic party. He also wrote two leaflets at the request of Ferdinand Q. Morton, the United Colored Democracy head. Harrison emphasized in a letter to Morton "every item of this work was of high efficiency."[125]

A little over a month after his open letter and while he was actively campaigning for the Democrats, Harrison received an October 14 letter from Ernest R. Crandall, director of lectures for the NYC Board of Education, asking him to fill out some forms to be considered as a lecturer for a winter course in January and February 1922.[126] Harrison quickly sought letters of recommendation from Morton, head of the UCD; Van Wyck Brooks, editor of the *Freeman*; State Assemblyman John C. Hawkins; Father Thomas M. O'Keefe, of St. Benedict the Moor Roman Catholic Church, at 342 West Fifty-Third Street; and

Father C. J. Plunkett, of St. Mark the Evangelist Roman Catholic Church, at 65 West 138th Street. On October 20, Brooks wrote to Harrison and apparently included a recommendation.[127] On October 24, Hawkins, the Republican assemblyman from the state's Twenty-First Assembly District, wrote to Crandall that he had known Harrison "favorably for a period of ten or more years," was "deeply interested in his ability as a lecturer and teacher," that he possessed "an unusual capability of expressing himself intelligently on any topic of the day," and that his services as lecturer for the board "would be of great value to the community as a whole." Hawkins took the significant step of stating "the Board would do well to secure his services for any place in the city." O'Keefe and Plunkett also wrote recommendations, but the key one from Morton was not provided, though Harrison did not find this out until May 1922.[128]

Harrison also unsuccessfully sought work with the *Amsterdam News*. On October 20, John E. Robinson, the paper's managing editor, wrote to him in an apparent response and explained that the paper was not in a position to pay for news items but that it would perhaps pay for a personal column in the future.[129]

By November 19 Harrison's financial situation was reaching the desperate stage. On that date he had papers served on him for nonpayment of rent. He wrote to Morton "in a final attempt to find whether goodwill is one of your attributes" and reminded him that he had seen at first hand the "work I did during the last *four weeks* of the campaign when I was under your jurisdiction and control." Harrison cited in detail his speeches in automobiles, on the auto truck, and on the Liberty League Platform, as well as his leaflet writing. Nevertheless:

On the last Saturday of the campaign Chappelle on your authorization gave me 20 dollars—half of which I still have. Of course you wouldn't pretend that that was paying me; and payment of some sort is urgently needed. And I don't feel that I am asking for charity either—Do you? Remember that during those last four weeks—as during the four preceding—I had to give up my night work in order to do yours. Now I find myself with a family of seven on my hands, none of them earning anything; and papers served by the Manco Realty Co. for non-payment of rent. On Tuesday I must appear in the 7th District Court. Can you guess the result if I am unable to pay? If I had obtained a job of course, things would be different. But somehow I can't indulge the costly illusion of getting one through you. But it does seem to me that if you cared at all you could make some arrangement with me (in recognition, if not in payment of my services to the party), whereby I could keep the roof over our heads until some literary work now at the editors desk gets paid for. If you care to see me send a message to 570 Lenox Ave., Apt 9.[130]

On November 25 Van Wyck Brooks wrote to Harrison that an article he had sent was "excellent" and "interesting in many ways" but that the subject was "too political and also too local in its appeal for the *Freeman*." He hoped that Harrison would send other material, including those referenced in his (Harrison's) headings: "Methods of Penetration—II," "Social Contacts," and "White Ignorance of Slave's Thought-World."[131]

On December 7 Harrison wrote to Martin J. Healy, the Democratic Party leader, alderman from the nineteenth district, and head of the Cayuga Club. The Cayuga Club, located in Harlem, was, according to the Tammany politician J. Raymond Jones, one of those "racially discriminatory white clubs" where African Americans were not wanted. Harrison asked Healy to use his "influence" on his behalf "in a certain matter." He reminded him "during the campaign this fall" he did work "as a Tammany Hall speaker and organizer of political sentiment in Negro neighborhoods." Harrison included a copy of the letter he had written to Ferdinand Q. Morton "in which some of those services are set forth, but not all." He noted "over 65 per cent of the Negro votes" went "to our party" and thought he might "fairly claim most of the credit for the increased enrollment." He added that "Mr. John William Smith will testify that at the first meeting of his campaign committee 7–8 weeks before election time and before registration I made the proposition that we should make a drive for enrollment in the party as that alone could insure party power and prestige." Then "night after night it was I and I alone of the speakers who presented this point of view." Harrison didn't "care to ask for a reward for work done" but stressed:

> I am a very poor man. If I had some work to do in keeping with my abilities, some definite source of income, then I could and would be able to work for Tammany Hall next year—and at every election without thought of recompense. That is why I am striving to get assigned as lecturer under the Board of Education this coming season. I have done this work before . . . and thousands of white people who have listened to me . . . will testify that I can do credit to the Board. So will Father O'Keefe of St. Benedict's Church, Father Plunkett of St. Mark's, Van Wyck Brooks of The Freeman.[132]

He added that his lecture application was in the hands of Dr. Crandall, as were his testimonials. He sent Healy "additional ones and some clippings including one from the *Globe* that shows the impression I made on 'One Southerner'" (John T. Carroll). Harrison asked if Healy would "peruse these proofs" and then take one with him to see Dr. Crandall and find out if he could get Harrison "first an early assignment then assurances that if my work is as good as its [*sic*] cracked up to be that I can get enough regular assignments to keep the wolf away from the door." Harrison explained to Healy that he had "submitted Negro themes to Dr. Crandall," but he knew that he could "substitute for any of the Board's lecturers on Literature—Modern or Classical, History—American, European or Classical, Current Events, Political Science, or General Anthropology." He originally "kept from suggesting such themes" in his application because he "feared that no white man would believe off-hand that any Negro could have correct knowledge of these things" unless he was heard "many times before." Harrison hoped that Healy could get Crandall "to consider widening the range of subjects," and he asked him, "Please do the best" he could, "remembering that I have a family of seven and work is urgently needed."[133]

Around November or December 1921 it appears that Harrison wrote to Max Eastman, editor of *The Liberator,* describing his great financial difficulty. Eastman responded and asked that Harrison "forgive" his "habit of procrastination." He had only read Harrison's letter that day and told him that he felt sorry at his "helplessness," but *The Liberator* was "down to the last expedient—borrowing money." Eastman's own salary had "ceased 4 weeks ago," and he, too, was "borrowing money to get along." He suggested that Harrison "write to Charlie [Chaplin]" in Hollywood, "reminding him who you are" but not mentioning that Eastman had made the suggestion. Eastman closed with "sincere esteem and regret" that he could not help more.[134]

Harrison had met Chaplin with Eastman at the *Liberator* office on October 20, 1921, at a meeting at which Claude McKay was probably present. Some years later McKay recounted how "Chaplin had met Hubert Harrison at my office and admired his black Socratic head and its precise encyclopedic knowledge." Harrison noted in his diary that Chaplin had "expressed a wish to see me again," and on the evening of Tuesday, October 25, Harrison went "down to the house of Eugene Boisservain" to meet Chaplin, whom he described as "the most popular person in the world." Others at the party that evening were Eastman and his sister Crystal, Dudley Field Malone, McKay, and five others. They had "a reasonably good time with drinks of all sorts sparingly indulged in." Harrison found Chaplin to be "a fine gentlemanly and intelligent going man—not at all 'freakish', as one might think from his pictures" (*The Idle Class* was, at that time, on the screen).[135]

Harrison was able to secure a speaking engagement at the 135th Street Public Library around December, but it may not have paid any money. It was part of a course on "modern racial problems and solutions" at the library that was offered free to those with "involvement in the Negro race." On Thursday, December 1, Duse Mohammed Ali was scheduled to deliver the first lecture on "Some Impressions of Africa." He was to be followed in subsequent weeks by Dr. George N. Haynes; Dean Kelly Miller, of Howard University; Dr. J. E. Woodland; James Weldon Johnson; and Harrison.[136]

On January 13, 1922, Harrison received a letter from Glenn Frank, the editor of *Century Magazine*, who indicated he was interested in his folder of manuscripts and syllabi. He hoped in the future to have Harrison do something for *The Century*. Frank was currently running a review of *Birthright* and couldn't "give space to the implications of the racial question." He claimed that he didn't want to "play one string too much"—he expected that Harrison would "understand" this and hoped that he would let him "know when a good idea strikes."[137]

In December 1921 Harrison also engaged in a *Negro World* debate over chiropractic. His December 10 article "Chiropractic—Good and Bad" spoke favorably of chiropractic and by its indirect comments may have smoothed the way for some remuneration from one school (the Metropolitan School of Chiropractic), while paying back another (the Cosmopolitan School of Chiropractic) with bad publicity. He began by describing chiropractic as an important and popular form "of drugless and preventive therapy" based on "the principle that the central nervous system" was "the machine" by which Nature sent "her stream of healthful influences through the body." While he was aware of quackery in the medical field, made possible by the general public's "wide-spread ignorance of the body and the laws of its operations," Harrison claimed that chiropractic was fast spreading and could effect marvelous cures, "even of blindness," as he personally knew.[138]

Because he evaluated chiropractic so highly, Harrison called for the establishment of "a school of chiropractic in Harlem" where "Negro students can go to learn this noble art." He advocated this "even though the downtown school" (Cosmopolitan) had a branch here (at 240 West 138th Street), because the branch appears to have been established to keep local residents "from thrusting their black, brown and yellow faces into its white classrooms [downtown]" and to pursue "their prime purpose": "to coin money from the Negro neighborhood." "But," he now added, "if we find such a school pretending to give instruction which is a farce . . . then we should proclaim to the public that such quack-institutions are a menace to public health and a disgrace both to the art of teaching and to Chiropractic." Harrison warned the public to insist on seeing chiropractic certification and to look for the name of "one of the downtown schools, like the Metropolitan College of Chiropractic, or the American School of Naturopathy." Regarding individual chiropractors he recommended insistence "on seeing a duly-inscribed certificate of D.C. (Doctor of Chiropractic)" and urged "for public and professional reasons: KEEP KIROPRACTIC KLEAN!"[139]

On December 10 Dr. Otto of Cosmopolitan wrote a letter to the editor of the *Negro World*, William H. Ferris, which was printed in the December 31 issue.

Though Cosmopolitan was not mentioned by name in Harrison's article, it was the only chiropractic school in Harlem. Otto was critical of Harrison's article and explained that "some months ago" Harrison had been recommended to him as "a man of exceptional teaching ability" and was hired by the college to lecture on embryology. While on the faculty Harrison was a "booster," but, "after he had been relieved of his position," he became "a 'knocker.'"[140]

In a December 13 letter to Harrison, T. Benedict Furniss, the registrar of Metropolitan College of Chiropractic, applauded Harrison's "splendid article," which had mentioned his school. He noted that Harrison had "some intimate friends" in Metropolitan's student body and asked him to "stop by" so they could arrange a talk for him. After they spoke Furniss wrote that "the officers of the College" had empowered him "to negotiate some suitable arrangement" that would "be mutually helpful." He offered Harrison the "opportunity to study Chiropractic" while they "work[ed] out some plan" that would enable Harrison "to help us."[141]

On December 17 eight students of Cosmopolitan wrote a letter to Garvey that appeared in the *Negro World* of December 24. They stated that they were members of the UNIA, stockholders in the BSL, and at "the only Chiropractic College in Harlem." They wished to protest Harrison's December 10 article. They felt that as "students" they were "better able to judge" than Harrison, who had merely delivered a series of twelve lectures in embryology to the freshman class. They then issued a "challenge" to any chiropractic institution to prove in open competition by any means they choose that they are as well trained as are the students of Cosmopolitan.[142]

Harrison's response to the students, entitled "Safety First," appeared alongside their letter in the *Negro World* of December 24. He found the students' letter "a trifle amusing," since "no one was named" in his article. "But," he noted, their protests "MUST mean me." He added if they were "so keen on the U.N.I.A.," why didn't they "use their influence to insure that the U.N.I.A.'s paper gets paid for the advertisements which it carried?"[143]

Harrison then called the students' "bluff" and suggested that three of them meet him in the office of the *Negro World* on Wednesday, December 14, at 2 p.m. Harrison would "bring three colored undergraduate students from downtown schools of Chiropractic" and "two compend[ium]s of anatomy and physiology," from which he would select twenty questions to be answered by all six. If the "time and place" did not "suit," then the Cosmopolitan students could select their "own time and place; but it must be in Harlem and before December 31." He would arrange to have Professor Ferris judge and to have the results published in the *Negro World*. The students were urged to "put up or shut up."[144]

Harrison added that one of the students at Cosmopolitan, a Mr. Smith, had "just jumped his bail in the unsavory case of the 15-year-old McAllister girl" and was "'practising' although he was not graduated and hasn't the necessary knowledge." Harrison felt "that to let such students practice" was "a grave public danger—especially to women." Perhaps "that student would have also signed the empty boast" of the students if "he hadn't been compelled to fly from justice." Harrison hoped that they would respond to his challenge and emphasized that he "took up this matter only in the people's interest" to make it "impossible for green and ignorant students who have not yet graduated to fool with the public's health." His aim, he said, was to "KEEP IT [chiropractic] CLEAN!"[145]

A week later, in the *Negro World* of December 31, Harrison wrote "Finale," in which he explained "the date given for the test of chiropractic knowledge in last week's issue must have seemed strange to many readers," since "in reality a later date had already been fixed in another portion of the article which had been shifted to the editorial page by Mr. Pryce, but was removed by Mr. Ferris to make way for something else after 'page proofs' had been made." Harrison claimed, however, that he "had personally appraised [*sic*]" the students "of the changed date" and "sent a registered letter to the head of his school," which he refrained from naming "because it still has an advertising bill with this paper unpaid for six months, and it isn't customary among manly editors to give free advertising on the top of such bills." Harrison claimed that "the students backed down on their boasts." He "waited at the office in vain, and finally called up the head of the college." A "group of colored students from downtown colleges" were at the phone when the college head called and "refused to send his students to the very test which he pretended to ask for." Harrison suggested the "readers draw their own conclusions."[146]

In the *Negro World* of January 21, 1922, Harrison wrote "Put Up or Shut Up," which explained that in the *Negro World* of December 24, six chiropractic students challenged "ANY student of ANY Chiropractic institution in the world to prove in open competition by any means they choose that they are not[?] as well trained as are the students of [our] college." Harrison "called their bluff" and although four weeks had gone by, "they have seemingly crawled into a hole." Though they had "received three separate and distinct invitations to come over and make good their boast, they have chosen to 'shut up' rather than 'put up.'" How "the people of Harlem" would "judge them after this grand fiasco" he couldn't say, but, "in the meanwhile the student of the college who had to jump his $1,000 bail in the unsavory scandal of the McAllister case" was still missing. Harrison added that, as a consequence, the New York State Chiropractic Association had issued "a ruling that it will not recognize any college or 'school' that permits its students to practice before they have been graduated." The NYSCA also decided "to withhold recognition from any college (or 'school') that doesn't put its students through a full three years' course of training before peddling a degree." Harrison concluded by suggesting that "all those who need the valuable services of a chiropractor insist on seeing his doctor's diploma" and to "remember that you are safe in the hands of a graduate of the downtown chiropractic college."[147]

On March 1, 1922, Metropolitan College's president, Louis S. Siegfried, wrote to Harrison, mentioning reports that came to him "thick and fast, of the splendid showing" Harrison had made in a Saturday evening, February 25, debate on Lincoln. He asked that they meet at five o'clock the next day to discuss "some plans" he had "in mind." Three days later, Metropolitan's registrar, Furniss, asked Harrison to "please come in and discuss this with us as soon as you can."[148] Then in the March 11 *Negro World* appeared Furniss's "In Defense of Chiropractic," which was addressed to the "Contributing Editor *The Negro World*." Furniss, also of Metropolitan, said that for twenty-six years "the science of chiropractic" had "been put to the acid test," and it was "here to stay."[149]

Around the beginning of February 1922 it appears that Harrison became involved in a passionate and literary romance with a woman named Elsie, a romance that produced emotional and revealing correspondence. Indications are that Elsie took the first portion of their correspondence for copying and Hubert had the last portion, and it is those later letters that remain in his papers. Hubert retained letters for the month and a half from early February through mid-late March. Harrison was married with five children, and, despite this and other affairs and occasional separations, he stayed with his wife and family. This correspondence was left with his wife and family posthumously and likely added to bitterness his wife, Lin, harbored after his death.[150]

Elsie is not fully identified in the correspondence, and little is known of her. It appears that she, like Hubert, was married. In addition, she was apparently "white," and at times they spoke of the racial as well as sexual aspects of their relationship. Attempts have been made to identify her; women such as Evelyn Scott and Beatrice Wood have been considered, along with an otherwise unidentified Elizabeth Dearborn, but no firm conclusion has been reached. In one letter she makes reference to having written a short piece, entitled "Realization," in *Snappy Stories* a few years earlier, but that article has not been located. There is a possibility that the correspondence was largely the creation of Harrison's fertile imagination, foreshadowing the "Love Letters of Sappho and Phaon" he would write a few years later.[151]

Based on available correspondence in Harrison's papers, "Elsie" wrote to Hubert around February 1, 1922, of the love "that consumes me when I give thee headway with you."[152] She wrote to him again, often in similar fashion, including on February 3, 4, 6, 7, 9, 10, 20, 24, and 26 and March 8, 9 or 10, 17, and 20. Harrison wrote her on February 8, saying, "you made me deliriously drunk last night and this morning. . . . You are never out of my mind for a single minute . . . I love you so," and he wrote to her again on February 13.[153]

Around February 1922, probably during this affair with Elsie, Harrison handwrote a poem, "Drifting," which read:

> Out of the tide of life's unending sea
> Love's current bears our bark, with you and me
> Lolling in languorous ecstasy beside
> The flower strewn banks down whose marge we glide
> But whether you and I adrift may go
> We do not know
> Let it suffice that we know where we are
> Here in each others arms: the world afar
> Floats out beyond the blue horizon's rim
> And melts away the twilight dim
> What can it matter, Sweet? Love's sky is clear—
> We do not care.[154]

In March 1922, after Harrison's involvement with Elsie had subsided, he again focused on other pressing matters, such as getting work, supporting his family, and obtaining U.S. citizenship.

"Free-lance Educator"

13

Lecturer, Book Reviewer, and Citizenship
(March 1922–June 1923)

On Saturday, March 4, 1922, "Dr. Hubert H. Harrison" delivered a talk on "The Brother in Black" for the New York City Board of Education Lecture Bureau's public lecture series at the Cooper Institute's Great Hall. It was a significant speaking event; the site had been a venue for many famous radicals, reformers, writers, and important political figures, including Frederick Douglass, Susan B. Anthony, Victoria Woodhull, Samuel Gompers, Harriet Beecher Stowe, Thomas Huxley, Ulysses S. Grant, William Howard Taft, Grover Cleveland, Theodore Roosevelt, and Woodrow Wilson. According to his diary, the audience gave him "a rising vote of thanks—which was unusual."[1]

Two days after the talk, one of those in attendance, M. F. Ruiz, wrote to Harrison to congratulate him on his "masterly . . . exposé." Ruiz asked for the title of a book Harrison recommended on "white prejudices of old." He also sought "to learn more fully about a thesis," with which he agreed, namely, that "the difference between the white and Negro—as men—is only a question of pigment, [which is based on] climatic or functional, distribution of local influences," and that, "mentally," there were "two distinct trainings to which the two races have been submitted" and, "socially," there were "impositions that the artificial forms of society have created." Ruiz commended Harrison for his "clear tendency to eradicate the mystical education on religious fanaticisms, which seem to be the prevalent form of 'uplifting'" from "whites." He added, "men of your mentality can foresee the pit into which a newly educated mass (educated to the present social artifices) can fall."[2]

On March 9 Harrison, who was looking for permanent work with the Board of Ed, replied to Ruiz and suggested that he write to Dr. Crandall, director of lectures and visual instruction of the Board's Extension Division Lecture

Bureau, about his appreciation of the lecture. Ruiz wrote to Crandall on March 12, and on March 16 Crandall responded that he was glad to hear that Ruiz had "greatly enjoyed" Harrison at Cooper Union. Ruiz then wrote Harrison on March 18, enclosing a copy of the Crandall correspondence.[3]

After writing to Ruiz, Harrison wrote to Crandall on March 17 to say that he understood Crandall had planned to assign him "to 'fixed post' duty at the 135th St. center next fall as a 'Trend of The Times' lecturer." Since that center would be closed, Harrison made an alternative offer. He had been "Associate Editor of a fairly large newspaper [the *Negro World*] for nearly three years," and the "biggest part" of his work was to review books. His work had "been considered highly meritorious" by Van Wyck Brooks, editor of *The Freeman*; Lothrop Stoddard had provided him "letters of high commendation"; and Eugene O'Neill considered his review of *The Emperor Jones* to be "one of the two or three ablest critiques of that work." He thought he had "some special competence in the interpretation of books and the drift and current of ideas," and he requested the chance to "do regular work in a composite series of lectures in which 'Great Writers Of the 19th century' would alternate with 'Books of the Hour.'" Such a plan would offer "valuable instruction to any intelligent audience." After making this proposal Harrison submitted a list of works to be discussed, including Thomas Carlyle's *Sartor Resartus*, Tennyson's poems, James Russell Lowell's political and patriotic poems, Jack London's writings, Charles Dickens's best works, Edgar Allan Poe's poetry, Rudyard Kipling's prose and poetry, and Mark Twain's writings. Crandall didn't accept Harrison's proposal at that time, but in 1924, after Harrison had demonstrated the caliber of his work, Crandall engaged him to deliver these lectures.[4]

Ruiz's March 19 letter to Crandall congratulated him on the selection of "Dr." Harrison for Cooper Union and emphasized that he was "one of the most brilliant speakers you have had this year." He demonstrated "a vast amount of knowledge" and was "candid and sincere" in delivering his lectures in an "impartial and straight forward" way. Ruiz admired Crandall's "openmindedness and courage" in "selecting a Negro to lecture." Since "Race prejudices" were of so "deep a root in our society," he thought it "high time" that men of Crandall's "mental caliber" were "directing the educational efforts made to carry our Americanism to the mind of the public at large." Ruiz next wrote to Harrison on March 21 and told him he hoped his letter to Crandall would "have the desired effect." He found it "hard to believe" that he could influence the board's opinions, particularly since its recent attention seemed "directed towards [the] spread of flimsy literary lectures" that were "more often the performances of mediocre artists and empty perorators than real cultural efforts."[5]

Crandall wrote to Harrison on March 27 and said he had tried to find one of the young stenography students who had recorded his Cooper Institute talk.

Crandall applauded Harrison's "well thought out" talk, with its "strong appeal for justice for 'The Brother in Black.'" He also liked the way he "answered questions" and put to rout "prejudiced critics." Since Harrison asked for suggestions, Crandall offered he would not "put quite so much weight on the Colored Soldiers winning the Civil War when speaking to a white crowd." He ended with the hope that he would hear Harrison again in the future.[6]

––––––––

Around April 1922 Harrison prepared another lecture, "Bridging the Gulf of Color," which he sent to Crandall in support of his desire to be hired on a regular basis. His opening message was that "one of the most regrettable features of the great American race-problem" was "the wide gulf existing between the mind of the Negro and the mind of the Caucasian." Since the gulf appeared almost "permanent," he thought that "any improvement" would be "the joint product of the better minds of both groups." He therefore sought to "throw a bridge across this gulf" to allow "tides of mental traffic" to "flow over it in both directions."[7]

Such a bridge would "tend to improve and stabilize the relations between the two races and reduce to a minimum the friction of new and necessary adjustments." The lack of such a bridge was "felt on both sides." "White" investigators were "often amazed at the great differences in quality between the standards of their own race's output and those of the Negro's." Students at Howard University were "taking elementary lessons in civics and calling them courses in sociology," "Negro sociologists and economists [were] restricting their 'science' to the compilation of tables of statistics in proof of Negro progress," and "Negro 'scholars' [were] still expressing the intellectual viewpoints of the eighteenth century." When these students "read Negro newspapers," they found "school-boy errors in English in every paragraph and bushels of 'poetry.'" To Harrison, the cause and meaning of the gulf was clear:

> Christian America created the Color Line; and all the great currents of culture and ideas which have been making for self-criticism, from the eighteenth century to our own time have found that great gap impassable. Behind the Color Line one has to think perpetually of the Color Line, and most of those who grow up behind it can think of nothing else. Even when one essays to think of other things that thinking is tinged with the shades of the environment. Add to this the fact that in South Carolina, which is a typical Southern state, each Negro child gets in Lawrence county 97 cents worth of education a year; in Bamberg, 89; in Saluda, 68; and in Calhoun, 58 cents worth—and the differences in quality of output between the higher levels of both races will be easy to understand. Unless the stream of modern

ideas can flow unhindered through such a mass it will continue to be a back-water in which cultural crudities take root; and when able intellects arise among Negroes, like Alain Leroy Locke, the scholar, William Browne [William Henry Brown], the mathematician, and Ernest Just, the biologist, their superiority, unperceived by their own race, escapes the assessing observation of the whites; and so, lack[ing] of proper recognition, fails to exert its full force as standard and example.[8]

Harrison then stressed an important point in his analysis—with such a gulf, "the white race also suffers." During "the good old days white people derived their knowledge of what Negroes were doing from those Negroes who were nearest them; generally, their own selected exponents of Negro activity or of their own white point of view." The "classic illustration of this mode of 'Knowing the Negro'" was "the Republican Party," and it was "now paying the penalty of losing the Negro vote in New York, New Jersey, Maryland and other states." Other "equally good examples" were the "Episcopal and Methodist churches, the Urban League[,] the white heads of the N.A.A.C.P.," and "the United States government." Harrison felt "the white world" was "vaguely but disquietingly aware that Negroes are awake, different, and perplexingly uncertain," yet it retained "its traditional method of interpreting the mass of Negroes by the one nearest to itself." It was "amusing to well-informed Negroes to observe the gullibility of white news-gatherers in the presence of hysterical developments on the other side of the Color Line." Harrison considered "their Brocken specter" to be "but the magnified and distorted shadow of their own ignorance and fears." But, that was not all, for

[it is] easy for those who have learnt wisdom in the school of slavery to play up to the racial egotism of the Caucasian. Subserviency is often the goats-horn on which the fox climbs out of the well. And the Negroes who know this are not all on the lower levels. Booker Washington was a case in point. Undoubtedly he was a great man. But he was also astute. It was his astuteness which pointed out the way to greatness; by fawning and flattering the whites he got their assistance and so was able to serve his race successfully.[9]

As a classic example Harrison cited "the case of Bert Williams, the actor." He explained:

It is hardly reasonable to expect, when we take a people as inferiors, as the butt of our jokes, that we should allow representatives of that people to become the recipients of our serious admiration and applause unmodified by a due sense of our own superiority. The comedian ministers to our own enjoyment in the capacity of an inferior—as: mountebank. Wherefore we will accept Negro comedians, but hardly Negro actors in the legitimate drama. For Bert Williams the way to personal success lay in flattering the white people's sense of superiority by always playing the clown. Had he done otherwise the tens of thousands of dollars which finally found their way to his pocket would have remained in the pockets of the whites. When [Bob] Cole and [J. Rosamond] Johnson at the Fifth Avenue Theater in the fall of 1910 appeared before white audiences in unobtrusive evening dress with an act of "high class" singing, piano playing and clever dialogue their audiences fell off suddenly. It didn't pay. Then they made a quick change back to the standard of "A Trip to Coontown"—fair part: Success.[10]

While "this was done on the level of honesty," Harrison pointed out, "below that level the thing is done by millions every day." "If white people could overhear the opinion of their sapience expressed by their colored servants and henchmen in the privacy of their homes," he thought, "they might soon realize that 'inferiors' may dupe and despise their 'superiors'—and 'work' them for 'a good thing.'" In such an "atmosphere of deception and ignorance mistrust maintains herself," and, in so doing, "the seeds of race-hatred and race-riots spring up in her footsteps to embitter the permanent relations between the two races."[11]

Harrison argued that "we of today must straighten the racial tangles which our fathers have bequeathed to us," and a first step would be to develop "some way in which Black men can speak to white men across this gulf before either or both can hope to bridge it. Correct information must somehow come across from the black man's world." For this to happen,

white men must be willing to let unfettered black people interpret to them the facts and situations of the black world. Whether it be Ray Stannard Baker, Carl Sandburg, Mr. [Herbert J.] Seligmann or Professor [Robert] Kerlin, no white man can understand and interpret the Negroes to white people as well as black men who live behind the Veil. Provided of course, that the black men are as well-equipped as the whites. And white America would do well to realize that, here and there, there are black men in our country as well-equipped mentally as any of the white men mentioned. But these men have not in their past been free to function as interpreters of their world. Before a black man could get a hearing he had to be somebody's man, whether that somebody was a Vesey Street Liberal, or Northern millionaire or a powerful politician; and as somebody's man he could only tell somebody's truth—not the truth which is now necessary to a better understanding. If American newspapers and magazines want this truth they should assign Negroes to the task of interpreting for their reader the trend of events among Negroes and the drift of the current of Negro thought and feeling. But these Negroes must be free. That is the only guarantee which the whites can have that these blacks are *not lying to them* for their own advantage.[12]

In the meantime, however, "white America" had to "be willing to make a genuine gesture of friendship to the Negro people, not as a mawkish condescension but as a human investment for safety sake." Harrison stressed that "when Southern white men burn to death a gravid Negro woman [such as Mary Turner] and trample to a pulp her unborn babe . . . thousands of Negro mothers pledge their children to purposes as far from playful as was that of Hannibal's youthful oath" and that "Negroes who fought in France for a democracy denied them on their return to Florida . . . [harbor] . . . deep and dark resolutions in the event of war with a nation that isn't white." Harrison suggested the implications if "revolutionary disturbances among them should synchronize with revolutionary disturbance among the whites themselves, or with a foreign war." He thought such matters "worth serious thought and earnest efforts toward some bridging of the gulf." He concluded:

> At present such social contact as exists between both people is furtive and surreptitious except on the lower levels as in the dives of northern cities and the plantations of the south where white men who have "an instinctive aversion against compromising the purity of their race" manufacture the millions of mulattoes who testify against them. On the higher levels the social approach is a thing of diffidence. One may sometimes find Negroes and whites commingling on temporary terms of social and intellectual equality at the Sunrise Club in New York and in a few radical organizations in some of the Northern cities, notably in Boston and Chicago. And as late as six years ago there met every Sunday at Lenox Casino in New York a lecture forum made up of hundreds of cultivated whites who had selected as the leader and teacher a man of undiluted Negro blood [Harrison]. Here and there one finds black doctors who have white patients, black lawyers with white clients and black teachers with white pupils. But, on the whole, the amount of social contact is not extreme enough to guarantee any adequate exchange of correct information. And correct information however it may come is still the first desideratum. For whatever theory of racial relations may be the correct one, it is only by the fruits of knowledge that the correctness of such theory can be tested. And until white and black know each other better there can be no bridging of the gulf that divides them.[13]

On April 22 Crandall wrote to Harrison that his article "Bridging the Gulf" was "startlingly illuminating" and his "conclusion inescapable." He found it "curious" that Harrison "assume[d] throughout that the black man does understand the white man." Crandall noted "some minor defects," suggested that Harrison wrote "too well not to write better," and asked him to visit so he could find out about a talk Harrison had "with Dr. Finley" (possibly Dr. John H. Finley, since 1921 editor of the *New York Times*).[14]

H. E. Miller, superintendent of the Newark (New Jersey) Works of Westinghouse Electric & Manufacturing Company, Radiophone Broadcasting Division, wrote to Harrison on May 23 that they had his letter of May 4 about the Cooper Union lecture on "The Brother in Black." Miller advised Harrison they needed "a word for word copy" of the speech he expected to deliver before they could assign it a broadcast date. Miller explained it was "necessary . . . to cover every word that goes into the air in order that the proper material may be sent out and that nothing offensive to the prejudices of the public be given."[15]

In May 1922 Harrison also received a letter from Crandall dated November 14, 1921, which said that he had "not yet received [a] recommendation from Ferdinand Q. Morton," the head of the United Colored Democracy. No reason was indicated for the delay, but the letter suggested the political nature of Board of Education appointments.[16]

Throughout 1922 Harrison faced constant financial pressure. On May 8 he was summoned to the Municipal Court for the Borough of Manhattan, First District, to answer charges that he and defendants Timothy Walsh, John W. Connor, and Barbados-born Eustace Oxley had borrowed $150 from Globe Credit Union on February 27 and repaid only $9. He was badly in need of income, and besides seeking employment with the Board of Ed he continually sought work as a writer, book reviewer, and lecturer.[17]

Early in the year he wrote to Funk & Wagnall's *Literary Digest* and received a March 16 response from George A. Dame, advertising manager, which said they were sending him *Woodrow Wilson as I Know Him*, by his private secretary, Joseph P. Tumulty, and asked that he send a clip of anything he wrote on it. On June 14 Margaret Williamson, literary editor of the *Christian Science Monitor*, wrote that the editor had passed Harrison's letter to her on the very day when the "Literary Page" carried reviews of both *Birthright* and *White and Black*. She was interested in what Harrison indicated of his experience and said she would gladly ask him to write a review if the opportunity arose. A June 17 Harrison letter to Rand McNally & Company led to a June 23 response indicating that the titles he was interested in, presumably to review, were discontinued. A July 20 letter from Monroe N. Work indicated that it would not be till the "last part of the summer or the early fall" before the new edition of the *Negro Year Book* would be available. At that time he would be pleased to mail three copies "for reviewing purposes," as Harrison requested. Late in the year, on November 2, Harrison had "a long and enjoyable" forty-five-minute talk with Robert Littell, editor of the *New Republic*, and he left with E. H. Culbertson's *Goat Alley*, which Littell assigned him to review. Littell also asked him "for a sketch of the interior of the Negro's mind—how he *really* regards the white man," and Harrison replied, "the truth in such matters is—something awful."[18]

Lecturing offered more immediate cash, but to do outdoor lecturing Harrison had to avoid harassment from the police. He sought to use his contacts with Democratic Party politicians to do this, and on April 5 Martin J. Healy, the Democratic alderman from the Nineteenth District, wrote a letter of introduction for him to Police Commissioner Richard E. Enright. Healy described him as "one of our most effective campaigners & *staunch advocate of the present city administration*," adding that Harrison desired "a courtesy" and it would bring "great pleasure if you will grant same."[19] On April 13 Enright signed a certificate addressed "To the members of the Police Force," which asked that they "Permit Hubert Harrison, President of the Labor League, 513 Lenox Ave., New York City, to speak at certain different places where it will not unnecessarily interfer[e] with street or pedestrian traffic."[20]

Two weeks later, on his thirty-ninth birthday, Harrison reviewed Hubert Anthony Shands's novel of Texas life, *White and Black*, in the *New York World*. The daily described Liberty League president Harrison as "a Negro author and editor, winner of the 1905 Board of Education medal for oratory, teacher, globetrotter, porter, elevator man, postal clerk, lecturer and soldier" and holder of "a degree in science from the University of Copenhagen" who was "seeking to complete his education in medicine." There was no basis for the Copenhagen and medicine references.[21]

Harrison described the novel as "a story that stands out strikingly from the ordinary run of 'best sellers.'" It was "not a 'problem' novel," nor was it burdened with "the mawkish sentimentality of the officious 'uplifter,'" and though it was the work of "a Southern writer," it said "nothing about the Southern claim to solve the race problem by its own peculiar methods." Shand's work would not "please the Ku Klux Klan" or "give solace to the Vesey Street radicals [of *The Nation* and the NAACP]," but, to "the vast majority of common-sense Americans," it would "bring knowledge and understanding."[22]

White and Black, wrote Harrison, was "a stark realistic study of racial relations in a country district of Southeastern Texas." It contained "tenant-farming and share-farming, the religion and morality of Negroes and poor whites, [and] all the shades of character possible in such an environment." It dug down "to the essential tragedies"—the "miscegenation which is so widespread and so generally winked at, the hollowness of religious professions, the Ku Klux menace, lynching, and the shiftlessness of black laborers." All these subjects were "burnt into the reader's memory in an unforgettable way." The story's "hero," Will Robertson, was "not a dressed-up copy-book hero, but one of nature's noblemen; a white farmer who scorns to defraud or oppress his black tenants, and is too much of a practical Christian to condone inter-racial concubinage even in the case of his own son." Robertson was "a type of that better South . . . germinating amid the husks of the old." He and a "few others like him" banded together "to withstand lynching and the Ku Klux," and while opposing one of those raids Robertson is shot to death. On that "note of tragedy" the story came "to an abrupt but by no means inconclusive end."[23]

Harrison considered it "remarkable" that *White and Black* and *Birthright*, which he also reviewed, should simultaneously come "out of the heart of the South," both "with the same objective realism," painting "two pictures of conditions out of which the authors keep their own emotions and conclusions." Such works suggested that "an intellectual renaissance" was "afoot south of Mason and Dixon's line." Though novels of this sort were "all too scarce," Harrison thought they would "do much to substitute light for heat in the dark place of our American race problem."[24]

––––––––

Shortly after penning these words Harrison had cause to take to task Thomas S. Stribling, the author of *Birthright*, for a letter on "Dumb St. Croix" he wrote in the May 6 *New York Evening Post*. Harrison responded with a May 7 letter to the editor published in the May 15 issue under the pseudonym "A St. Croix Creole." The pseudonym was probably used because the letter called attention to the noncitizenship status of Cruzans in the United States, and Harrison was not yet a U.S. citizen. The *Post* stated that the "writer was born in St. Croix"; had "taught in its largest rural school, the one at Friedensfeld"; and was "at present a lecturer for the Board of Education . . . as well as a regular contributor (under other names) to some of the better known periodicals." The letter began by commenting on "the fictional quality of Mr. Stribling's picture of St. Croix." It explained that "D. Hamilton Jackson (a former classmate of the writer)" was a lawyer, trained in the United States, whose "father was the most prominent teacher, white or black, in the three islands, and presided over the Danish school in Christiansted." When Jackson began "to regenerate the Negro laborers they were dispirited and hopeless on a daily wage of 20 cents." Jackson "licked them into such cooperative shape that they now own eight of the 'estates' on which they formerly worked for hire; they have a newspaper, a warehouse, and a bank." They obtained these "only by banding together," and "it was the success of this cooperative labor movement which, more than anything else, disposed the Danes to sell the islands, in order that resident whites could control their black labor problem in approved American fashion."[25]

When Stribling said that Jackson had taught "his people to hate whites," he substituted "fiction for fact." To the contrary, Jackson was "now in trouble with his own group because he refuses to exploit race hatred in their behalf." Harrison added that "Virgin Islanders occupy a most anomalous position" and that "in consequence of the dodging tactics of the State Department the 20,000 of them living in New York City are neither citizens nor aliens" and "cannot vote" or "get naturalized because they have no 'allegiance' to forswear." Their status was "a standing disgrace to democracy and ought to be speedily changed," he urged, but as of yet there had been "no discussion of the facts before the American people."[26]

———

Harrison's review of Claude McKay's *Harlem Shadows*, appeared in the May 21 *New York World*. He was laudatory and thought that McKay revealed himself "as a Negro poet of parts, with a fine and delicate technique and a curiously cultivated restraint." The work was "equally free from jingling and splurge and from the flaring fantods of the 'free vers' school." In "most" of the poems the "genuine breath of the Tropics" was felt, yet it seldom blew "tornado blasts," since the "fine artistic feeling of the poet" controlled and tempered it "to fine effects." The book's title was "slightly misleading," however, since "only a few" of the poems were "concerned with Negro Harlem." The "majority of the themes" were "simply such as any good poet, irrespective of race, would select." This fact might "keep them from standing out in public appreciation," wrote Harrison, since "it was the distinctive treatment of Negro themes which attracted the American reading public to the poetic powers of Paul Laurence Dunbar," and since, "in the treatment of such themes the Negro poet, because of his more intimate contact with his people, can easily outshine the white."[27]

Harrison felt that McKay's handling of "Negro themes" was "characterized by a quiet dignity that charms if it does not thrill." In "If We Must Die" McKay offered "a revolutionary portent": "a protest of impressive dignity" with "a hint of the dangerous possibilities to which lynching and race riots may give rise." The fact that McKay was born and bred in Jamaica helped explain "the constant recurrence of tropical landscape themes in his verse." He was, however, "also a cosmopolitan" who had "lived in the larger world," and "this broad contact with life in Europe and America" was "reflected in his taste, temperament and ideas." To those who wanted to know "how the Negro can react to world culture as a man," Harrison offered, "this little volume should prove a human document of the highest value."[28]

In the introduction Max Eastman set forth "with a sweet reasonableness McKay's claims to consideration on his merits." Eastman also supplied "necessary biographic material for a proper estimate of his genius." Harrison concluded: "Taking everything into consideration, there can be no doubt that in range, technique and mastery of the medium of verse Claude McKay is the greatest living poet of Negro blood in America today."[29]

After his review of *Harlem Shadows* Harrison published a July 23 *New York World* review of *The History of the Negro Church*, by Carter G. Woodson. He felt it "unfortunate that this book of a Negro scholar should succumb, as it does, to the passion of the propagandist." While Woodson maintained that the church had "surrendered to the capitalistic system and developed into an agency seeking to assuage the pains of those suffering from the very economic evils which the institution has not the courage to attack," he overlooked "obvious points of scholarship," which his work needed. In particular, wrote Harrison, "every scholarly historian should know that when the Negro slaves were brought to the Western world they had been uprooted from a culture of their own in which were embedded their own religious habits and institutions. These constituted the new religious foundations upon which Christianity was set, and these foundations determine even in our own day the form which the religious consciousness of the Negro takes." Dr. Woodson, however, made "no attempt . . . even to sketch these African foundations of his theme, consequently no one will learn from his work how differently Negroes worship God, or anything of their emotionalism, or of their age-long divorce of practical ethics from religious preachments under Christian teaching and example." Though Woodson did tell "the story of the Christian Church in America so far as . . . recoverable from the records and proceedings of the various church bodies," Harrison found his "range of documents . . . narrow" and thought that "he nowhere rises to more than mediocre respectability." While the story he tells "is itself highly interesting," his telling "serves to lower that interest to the point of dullness." Overall, Harrison felt the book abounded in "slovenly English" and, "as a piece of historical scholarship," was "distinctly disappointing and far inferior to the author's other works."[30]

A month later in the August 20 *New York World* Harrison reviewed *Batouala*, by the Martinique native René Maran, which was set in the French colony of Ubangui-Shari (later the Central African Republic), in French Equatorial Africa. In July, Ernest Hemingway, then reporting for the *Toronto Star*, declared it a great novel and in September *The Crisis* would claim "the whole world [was] reading it."[31]

Harrison opened by explaining that the book "created an unusual furore in French literary and administrative circles" and had won the Prix Goncourt (the most prestigious in French literature) the previous winter. "Despite its stark and sombre realism," it was "of atmosphere and flavors": "precisely the things . . . most difficult to transfer from one language to another." Though some of "the fine Gallic flavor" had evaporated from the English version, "enough of the basic quality of the book survive[d] to justify its claims to special consideration."[32]

Batouala, he explained, was not exactly a novel "but rather a series of sketches of the inner and outer life of the degraded natives of the section of the French Congo which lies between three different culture-areas; the Egyptian Soudan, Soudanic and Bantu Africa." The people depicted, "a branch of the cannibal group known as the Nyam-Nyam" who had been described by Georg Schweinfurth, were "no more representative of the average African cultures, surrounding them than the Basques of the Cantabrian Mountains are representative of the average culture of England, France or Germany." The "tax gatherers of French imperialism" superimposed "an additional degradation" on these people; according to Maran, they had "the vices of Europe . . . deliberately imported among them."[33]

Though "not a polemic," *Batouala* was "timely," since the "Negro question" had been made "a present reality" by "the Americans and by the newspaper campaign from the other side of the Rhine." Interestingly, Maran offered no "defense of the Negro," and his "objective, artistic conscience" made him "paint the Negro before him as he really is in that particular section of Central Africa—a stark and brutal savage without a single glimmer of uplifting hope." Even that picture "could have been worse in its brutal savagery" if it contained a "direct description" of the "orgies of ceremonial cannibalism"—something "which French rule has suppressed, although, like the ga'nza, it crops up from time to time in those sections which are not effectively supervised."[34]

Overall, Harrison found the story "as sordidly primitive as the natural surroundings," which Maran described "with a power and poignancy." Maran had a "seeing eye," "understanding mind," and drew with a "steady and true" hand. Harrison considered him "a great artist" who, if he stuck "to this field of French Colonial Africa," would "enjoy a primacy all his own." As for "the genuine atmosphere of the French section of Congoland," one would assuredly find it "in this book, which is, as its author describes it, '*un veritable roman Negre.*'"[35]

Maran read Harrison's review and wrote from his home in Fort Achambault, French Equatorial Africa (present-day Chad), saying he had received little financial profit from *Batouala*. He asked that Harrison make known his financial situation in the hope that readers could offer some financial assistance. In yet another effort to help a struggling Black artist, Harrison had this information publicized in the April 5, 1923, *Chicago Defender.*[36]

A few weeks after his review of *Batouala*, Harrison reviewed *Early Civilization: An Introduction to Anthropology,* by A. A. Goldenweiser, in the *Negro World.*[37]

———

In June 1922 Harrison made efforts to finalize his naturalization as a U.S. citizen. He had first filed a Declaration of Intention to become a U.S. citizen in the Supreme Court of the County of New York on June 22, 1915. At that time he described himself as a thirty-two-year-old lecturer whose color was Black, complexion dark, 5 feet 7 inches tall, and 170 pounds. He said he was born in Santa Cruz, Danish West Indies, on April 27, 1883, and had come to the United States aboard the *Roraima* on September 21, 1900. He also declared his intent to renounce his allegiance to King Christian X of Denmark. The declaration was to become valid in seven years.[38]

Seven years to the day later, on June 22, 1922, Harrison filed his Petition for Naturalization in the presence of two witnesses and friends, the musician Melville A. Charlton, of 405 Lenox Avenue, and the author Joel A. Rogers, of 570 Lenox Avenue. On that petition Harrison claimed he was a writer, inadvertently incorrectly dated the births of his first four children, and "renounced absolutely and forever all allegiance and fidelity to any foreign power . . . particularly to Christian X, King of Denmark." After receiving his petition, the Naturalization Office in New York instructed him to write to the War Department. The next day he wrote "requesting information from the records for naturalization purposes in the case of Hubert Henry Harrison, a resident of 231 West 134th St., New York City, at the time of registration."[39]

On July 1 Robert C. Davis, acting adjutant general of the War Department, responded to Harrison at 570 Lenox Avenue and informed him that "the draft records on file" showed his addresses as "2441 7th Ave., c.o. Tippet and at 231 West 134th St." His order was no. 4743, his serial no. 2795, and he had registered at Local Board no. 144 in New York on September 12, 1918. On page 1 of his questionnaire he claimed classification under the Selective Service Law as "Classes 4-D (necessary sole managing, controlling, or directing head of necessary industrial enterprise); 3-L (necessary assistant or associate manager of necessary industrial enterprise); and 4-A (man whose wife or children are mainly dependent on his labor for support)." Under series VII, Citizenship, to the question "If you are not a citizen of the United States and have not declared your intention of becoming a citizen, do you claim exemption for service in the Army of the United States on the ground," he made no answer. To the question "If you are not a citizen of the United States and have not declared your intention to become a citizen, are you willing to return to your native country and enter its military service," he made no answer. To the question "Do you wish to be relieved from liability to military service by withdrawing your intention to become a citizen of the United States," he made no answer. The final classification of the draft board in this case was "Class 1-A (Single man without dependent relatives) but apparently never called for service." Davis suggested "this official communication be submitted with any application for citizenship made to the Commissioner of Naturalization, Department of Labor, Washington, D.C., or to any representative in the States of the Bureau of Naturalization."[40]

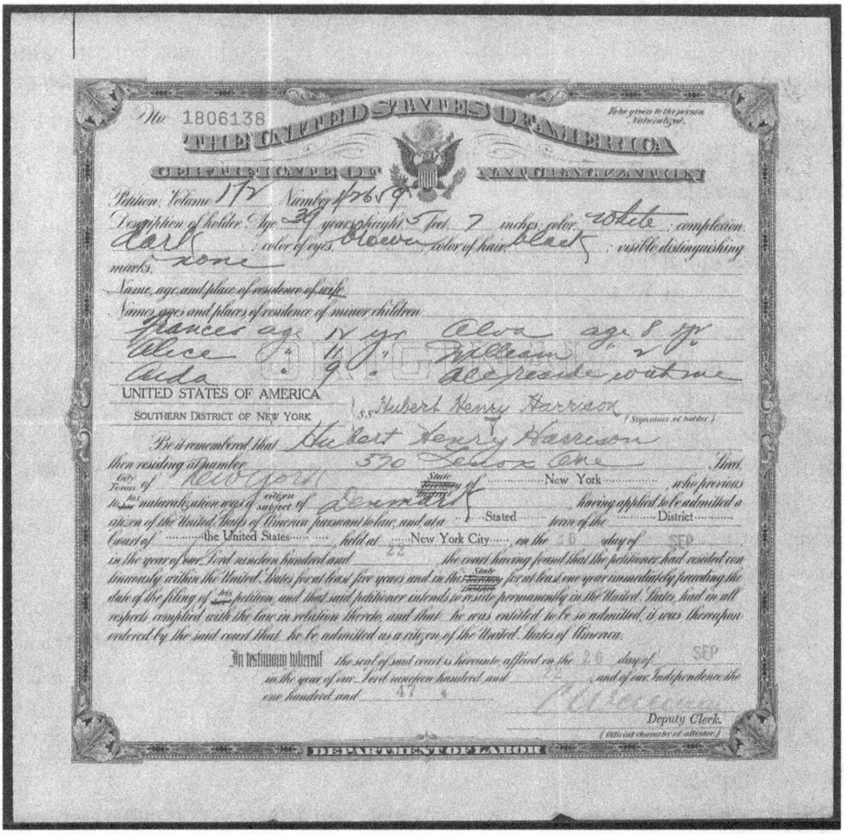
No 1806138
To be given to the person Naturalized.
THE UNITED STATES OF AMERICA
CERTIFICATE OF NATURALIZATION
Petition Volume 172 Number 47659
Description of holder. Age 39 years; height 5 feet 7 inches; color white; complexion dark; color of eyes brown; color of hair black; visible distinguishing marks none
Name, age and place of residence of wife
Names, ages and places of residence of minor children
Frances age 12 yr Alva age 8 yr
Alice " 11 " William " 2 "
Aida " 9 " All reside with me
UNITED STATES OF AMERICA
SOUTHERN DISTRICT OF NEW YORK } ss. Hubert Henry Harrison (Signature of holder)
Be it remembered that Hubert Henry Harrison then residing at number 570 Lenox Ave Street, City of New York State of New York who previous to his naturalization was a citizen subject of Denmark having applied to be admitted a citizen of the United States of America pursuant to law, and at a Stated term of the District Court of the United States held at New York City on the 26 day of SEP in the year of our Lord nineteen hundred and 22 the court having found that the petitioner had resided continuously within the United States for at least five years and in this State for at least one year immediately preceding the date of the filing of his petition, and that said petitioner intends to reside permanently in the United States, had in all respects complied with the law in relation thereto, and that he was entitled to be so admitted, it was thereupon ordered by the said court that he be admitted as a citizen of the United States of America.
In testimony whereof the seal of said court is hereunto affixed on the 26 day of SEP in the year of our Lord nineteen hundred and 22, and of our Independence the one hundred and 47.
Deputy Clerk.
(Official character of attester)
DEPARTMENT OF LABOR

Figure 13.1. Hubert Harrison's Certificate of Naturalization, September 26, 1922. Hubert Harrison was described as "color white" on his September 26, 1922, Certificate of Naturalization. A friend, the historian J. A. Rogers, sarcastically attributed the listing to "the ethnological omniscience of the [U.S.] State Department," which assumed "Danes are white." Of interest is the fact that Bureau of Investigation Special Agent W. R. Palmera, pursuant to instructions from Agent Joseph G. Tucker and based on "confidential information," had prepared a report on Harrison, who he said was born in the Virgin Islands and had resided in the United States for fifteen (it was in fact twenty-two) years. Palmera interviewed Charles Miller, the acting chief naturalization examiner in New York, to determine Harrison's "U.S. citizenship status" and "was advised that the purchase of the Virgin Islands from the Danish Government by the United States government did not automatically make the inhabitants of the islands United States citizen." This may be the reason why on Harrison's Certificate of Naturalization he "renounced absolutely and forever all allegiance and fidelity to any foreign power . . . particularly to Christian X, King of Denmark." In his diary Harrison described the day he became a U.S. citizen as "One of the Redletter days of my life." *Source:* Hubert H. Harrison Papers, Box 14, Folder 4, Rare Book and Manuscript Library, Columbia University Library. See https://dlc.library.columbia.edu/catalog/cul:zpc866t337.

Harrison wrote to the Naturalization Examiner at 151 Nassau Street, New York City, on July 5 that "in accordance with your instruction I wrote the War Department on June 23rd and have just received their answer," which he enclosed. He asked Naturalization to "please note the departmental discrepancy between what I said (4A man, wife & children) and their final classification (1A Single man, etc.). But that's their fault, not mine." He asked them also to "please note too that at the time of registration I didn't know whether I was citizen, half-citizen or alien, due to my not being quite clear as to certain meanings of the treaty by which St. Croix was acquired by the U.S.A. in 1916–1917." He closed stating he would be "pleased and proud when my final papers are issued and I become in the fullest sense Hubert H. Harrison American Citizen." He added a PS: "When the children's births were given by me on June 22nd I did not remember the exact dates of birth. Very few fathers do. The actual dates, as per my wife, are as follows: Frances Marion Harrison October 21, 1909[;] Alice Genevieve [Harrison] May 22nd 1911[;] Aida May [Harrison] July 4th 1912[;] Ilva Henrietta Harrison August 25th 1914[;] William Adolphous [Harrison] [September 17, 1920]." He also explained that the addresses in the record were his residence and his place of business (as editor of a newspaper).[41]

On July 26 the commissioner of Naturalization wrote that Harrison had "filed in this office a letter addressed to him by the Adjutant General of the War Department, under date of July 1, 1922, in which he is advised that the records of the Department show that he . . . claimed exemption on three different grounds, among which a claim appears in Class 4A (man whose wife and children are mainly dependent on his labor for support)." The War Department's letter explained that "the alien was placed in 'Class 1-A', (single man without dependent relatives) but apparently never called for service." The commissioner added that "in view of this anomalous situation and the further fact that the alien was married and had four children at the time he filed his questionnaire," he "respectfully asked that the Bureau obtain a further report from the War department and forward it" to him.[42]

The same day, in a "Brief Slip," Chief Naturalization Examiner Sturges recommended that at Harrison's final hearing the examiner should "invite the Court's attention to the attached letter from the petitioner dated July 5th, in which he furnishes the correct dates of birth of his children and indicates that the dates of birth furnished in the petition are not corrected."[43]

Chief Naturalization Examiner "AM" prepared a memorandum on July 27, which explained that Harrison called at the office that day and was "very carefully interrogated." He was described as "clearly a man of unusual education and culture," who had "maintained himself for a number of years past by writing book reviews and other articles for magazines, periodicals and newspapers."

Harrison informed AM that "he receives assignments and in fact executed some of them recently for *The New York Tribune, The World and The Times*" and "lectures on the public streets on Spencer, Huxley, anthropology and allied science, and supports these lectures by selling books written by Huxley and other authors." "He was also for a period, the Editor of the *Voice*, a weekly negro newspaper," and, "for a period of about two years up to very recently he was the President and very actively connected with the Labor League, an organization which was formed for the educational uplift of the negro." Harrison also provided AM the certificate addressed "To the members of the Police Force" signed by Police Commissioner Enright on April 13, which asked that he be permitted "to speak at certain different places." AM added that Harrison said "he was summoned to court on two or three occasions prior to 1914 for obstructing traffic, by reasons of crowds which gathered while he was delivering street lectures, and that he was discharged on each occasion," and that "in 1913 or 1914, he was set upon and assaulted by a white boy about 19 years of age . . . with an iron bar; that he succeeded in gaining possession of the bar and struck the boy in his own defense; that a charge of assault was then brought against him which was tried in the Magistrate Court on 57th Street, and that he was discharged by Magistrate Campbell." Harrison added that he was "never arrested at any other time or for any other offense."[44]

The chief naturalization examiner wrote to the police commissioner of New York on July 28, asking to be advised of any police records on Harrison, who, as "an applicant for naturalization," had presented Police Commissioner Enright's "certificate addressed to all members of the Police Force, dated April 13, 1922," which was enclosed. It was explained that the information was being requested for official government use and an early response was desired.[45]

On August 8 Robert C. Davis, of the Adjutant General's Office of the War Department, wrote to the commissioner of naturalization, U.S. Department of Labor, in Washington and referred to the commissioner's August 1 letter, in which was enclosed a copy of chief examiner at New York's letter requesting a further report on Harrison. Davis stated "at the time of filling out his questionnaire, September 28, 1918, [Harrison] claimed classification in Class 3-L, Class 4-A and Class 4-D. On page 16 of questionnaire, Local Board stated: 'Class 1, claim not established.' The reason for this classification is not apparent."[46]

The acting chief naturalization examiner wrote to the commissioner of naturalization on August 21 and asked that the duplicate petition for naturalization be forwarded to that office so that it could be presented at the final hearing. It was added, "It appears that the dates of birth of one or more of the alien's children are not correctly stated in the petition."[47]

On September 12 Harrison, as president of the Liberty League, wrote his open letter to Mayor John F. Hylan criticizing George W. Harris, the only

Republican alderman in Harlem who "managed to escape last year's Democratic landslide."[48]

Exactly two weeks later, on September 26, 1922, Harrison's Certificate of Naturalization #1806138, Vol. 172, Number 42659 was signed. He was listed as thirty-nine years old, five feet seven inches tall, "color—white," "complexion dark," eyes brown, hair black, with five children—Frances, twelve; Alice, eleven; Aida, nine; Alva, eight; William, two. He stated that all children resided with him at 570 Lenox Ave. The name, age, and place of residence of his wife was left blank. He stated he was a subject of Denmark before becoming naturalized on September 26, 1922. The day he was naturalized he also received correspondence, including the citizenship oath, and a U.S. flag, from the New York Chapter Colonial Dames of 541 Madison Avenue. He wrote in his diary, "On this day I became a full-fledged citizen of the United States in Judge Hough's court. One of the Redletter days of my life." Interestingly, Harrison was described as "color—white" on this document, a fact noted later by his friend, the historian J. A. Rogers, who sarcastically attributed the listing to "the ethnological omniscience of the [U.S.] State Department," which assumed "Danes are white."[49]

On October 3, one week after becoming a naturalized citizen, in a possible quid pro quo, Harrison provided a collection of materials to Mortimer J. Davis, a special agent of the Bureau of Investigation, "for use of U.S. Dept. of Justice" in the case being built against Marcus Garvey. Davis gave Harrison a written receipt of the items he provided. The following day, on October 4, the commissioner of naturalization wrote to Harrison: "The duplicate petition which accompanied your letter is returned herewith. At the final hearing on this petition the Court declined to direct amendment of the petition in any respect, holding that the exact dates of birth of the children under the circumstances as they appear was not material." Then on Thursday, October 5, 1922, Harrison wrote in his diary, "Received my naturalization papers by registered mail." His naturalization papers came two days after he turned over material to the postal inspector.[50]

Nine days after he received his citizenship papers, on Saturday, October 14, Harrison lectured to the Single Tax Party at their office at 201 West Thirteenth Street, at Seventh Avenue, on "The Real Negro Problem." The lecture consisted mainly of the first chapter of a book he was planning, *Caliban Considers*, which he read with collateral remarks. In his diary he described the discussion as "vigorous and ample."[51]

After the talk Harrison was taken by the party treasurer Morris Van Veen and some of the older Single Taxers to a Fourteenth Street coffeehouse for coffee, pie, and "enjoyable chat." Van Veen offered him the party's nomination for state senator, which Harrison declined, as he explained in his diary, "since I am a regular member of the Democratic party and a member (the only Negro member) of the Speaker's Committee of Tammany Hall." Van Veen then promised to put him in touch with an influential friend who could get him "a connection with one of the large lecture bureaus." Van Veen also gave him a check for ten dollars, not as pay (the lecture was free), but for "the circulars to be printed" for his lecture forum. Joe Miller, one of Van Veen's friends, asked Harrison to submit his book to Appleton's when finished. One of his friends was a reader there, and Miller pledged his assistance. Miss Charlotte Sebetter, the chairperson, presented Harrison with an abridgement of Patrick Edward Dove's *The Theory of Human Progression*—which was made by Julia A. Kellogg "*at the age of eight.*" Another old Single Taxer gave him a fine lithograph of Henry George.[52]

On November 1 Harrison had "a conference" with Van Veen at a restaurant by the subway at the northwestern corner of 135th Street and Lenox Avenue, and it was agreed Harrison would introduce him on November 2 on Seventh Avenue and 136th Street and "help him in other ways to get the propaganda of the Single Tax before Negroes." Van Veen assured Harrison that he, in turn, would "start the ball a-rolling" to get, as Harrison described it, "something for me to do this winter."[53] A month later, on December 2, Harrison was scheduled to speak for the Single Tax Forum on West Thirteenth Street on "The Single Taxers' Opportunity." He was described in a promotional flyer as "one of the ablest men of his race; an Author, Publicist and Orator of the most convincing character and logic" and whose "ability to tell an absorbing and interesting story is unquestioned."[54]

While Harrison had a few involvements with the Single Taxers, he was far more active with the Democratic Party during this period. Six days after Van Veen's offer, Harrison attended an October 20 Democratic meeting at William "Kid" Banks's club on West 133rd Street. "Chicken" Banks had reputed underworld ties and was, according to the Tammany politician J. Raymond Jones, the representative to the "white Tammany" leader from the Harlem United Colored Democracy Club. His "club," as Jones was told in 1921, was the "[Tammany Democrat] club for coloreds" in the same Nineteenth Assembly District as Martin Healy's "Cayuga Club," which was for "whites." At the October 20 meeting, many candidates spoke, including Judges O'Brien and Collins, James Male, the assemblyman from the Nineteenth, and Ferdinand Q. Morton. Harrison noted in his diary that at the meeting he had two drinks with William S. [H.?] Simmons.[55]

Harrison also did "some work" for Tammany under Morton's "control," though, as of the beginning of November, he was "not speaking as often" as the previous year for the Democrats and had "only done three or four talks during two weeks." On November 1, he went to the Harlem Democratic Party head-quarters at 2295 Seventh Avenue and asked Morton, who headed the UCD, to let him "accept" a "form of the offer which he made me two weeks" earlier, "which was that he would pay me $100 for the two weeks of the campaign." Harrison "had asked him to make it $50—and a job later," but he now felt, as he wrote in his diary—"I can't trust Morton to bestir himself on my behalf," and if he could "get some help in the form of work elsewhere" he "might as well put that other $50" in his "own pocket." Morton told him that "the matter would be arranged," but according to Harrison, "it wasn't."[56]

On November 11, Henri W. Shields, whose law offices were at 135 West 135th Street, wrote to Harrison, thanking him for his "very kind words of interest" and "for the many nice things you said on my behalf and the wonderful things you did for me during the campaign." Shields (who had just become New York's first "Negro" to win a seat in the state legislature when he was elected from Harlem's Twenty-First Assembly District) added, "It shall always be a source of pleasure to me to know that I had your good will and confidence; and it shall always be my aim to deserve your continued good will and confidence." In December, Dr. Royal S. Copeland wrote similarly to Harrison to express his "appreciation for the splendid work you did for me during the election campaign."[57]

During the election period of October 1922 the first issue of *Loyal Citizen Sovereignty*, edited by James F. Morton Jr., appeared. Harrison knew Morton from his previous Freethought and Modern School work. The first page of the debut issue explained that *Loyal Citizen Sovereignty* was "an American magazine published for Americans" and was not "an exponent of jingoism nor a fatuous adulator of all things as they actually, exist in this country." The paper held that "every land and every race" had "much to teach the world" and "much to learn from sister nations" and that "love of one's own country" did "not imply disparagement of any other, nor even an assumption of genuine superiority." The "development of the spirit of loyalty to American principles" did not stem from the belief "that our own ways are best" but rather rested "on the plain fact that our special duty is here." On the second page the editors wrote: "Race and religious prejudice will have no place in these columns." They welcomed "loyal men and women of all racial origins, of every class and of every phase of religious conviction" and emphasized that "'America for Americanism' is our single motto: and our appeal is to all who believe in the American spirit."[58]

Harrison was listed as an editorial contributor beginning with the November issue. On October 30 he wrote a letter to the editor in which he offered his "sincere congratulations on the first issue" of the "very promising publication." He observed, "it does two things that seldom go together in civic and political publications": "stirs the blood and keys up the intellect." There was "need at present for just such a publication which, in the midst of much howling jingo-ism on the one hand and shortsighted radicalism on the other," would "try to hold the scales level for the great bulk of intelligent Americans who love Amer-ica and yet find in it things which they should like to see bettered." "One of the greatest dangers to American political advancement today," Harrison offered, was "the widespread indifference in the matter of assuming the obligation of citizenship to perform the political duties that pertain to that status." Referring to an article in the October issue, he wrote that "the real reason for the control of cities and states by corrupt machines" was that "the upholders of such machines will register, enroll and vote," but "the good citizens who outnumber them ten to one will not." Then they "grumble at the horrible results or fold their arms with the smug complacent assertion that 'politics is a dirty game anyhow.'" Harrison offered to "help the movement and the paper in any way" and was "glad to note the broad, liberal basis of this new publication." He, like many, had "become 'sick and tired' of movements that have no other principles but that of being anti-this or anti-that." "Americanism, as the Loyal Citizen Sov-ereignty interpret[ed] it," was "breezily, helpfully constructive—building and invigorating, rather than dividing and destroying." He hoped the publication lived long and served "as an inspiration to the millions of citizens to whom patri-otism and national betterment" were "an adventure of the spirit and an ideal worthy, not only of glorified lip-service, but of daily work and constant striving."[59]

Morton replied that Harrison's letter was "from one who is excessively criti-cal, and is therefore the more gratifying." He added that Harrison was "a remark-able man, of high culture, well educated and extraordinarily well-read," who, as "one of the lecturers of the New York Board of Education," was "admired by audiences everywhere."[60]

On November 17 J. Winfield Scott, the manager of *Loyal Citizen Sovereignty*, wrote to Harrison on stationery of "The Loyal-Sovereign Citizen Carry-On Cor-poration," of 35 Hawthorne Street, West Somerville, Massachusetts, of which he was also manager. He had just read the proofs of Harrison's comments and wrote that "all here are greatly pleased with your endorsement of the great work we believe we are inaugurating and we are some what elated at the possibility of your scholarly support." He thought that Harrison could help, particularly with "the urgency of adequately broadcasting love and loyalty as the antidotes for the prevalent anti-Americanism of creedal and racial hatred and alienism." Harrison's "keen vision, scholarship and ability peculiarly fit" him "for a pow-erful part" in what Scott believed to be "the greatest movement since 1776." He told Harrison, undoubtedly unaware of his "Lincoln vs. Liberty" talks, that he (Harrison) could "become the Abraham Lincoln in this Emancipation Move-ment." Scott was pleased that Harrison was apparently "willing to lead in a large way educationally and financially." Morton had written Scott that Harrison's "logic and eloquence sweep audiences off their feet," and he thought "those skills can move many to loyal, constructive action—to contribute the $50,000 we need as an extension fund." He asked that Harrison, at his convenience, confer with Morton "respecting the wisest co-operation course of joint action." He also noted that they had "already taken the liberty" to add Harrison's name to the list of editorial contributors and hoped to hear from him soon.[61]

Scott's letter may have played a part in Harrison distancing himself from the publication. In the December 1922 issue Morton was listed as editor and Scott as manager; Harrison was still an editorial contributor, along with Scott and Edwin C. Walker, of the Sunrise Club. In the January 1923 issue Harrison was no longer a contributor.[62]

Throughout the summer of 1922 Hubert continued to have difficulties at home with his wife, Lin, and he moved to 118 West 130th Street on August 18, where he agreed to pay his landlady, Mrs. Reynolds, eight dollars per week. In his diary he stated that he moved "to escape from hell at home and to get some literary work done." He cared deeply for his children and noted some of their achievements in his diary. In September his daughters returned to school, where all seemed "to be doing well in their classes." Frances, who had graduated from PS 90, the Riverside Junior High School, on July 14, was in the second-year class at Wadleigh High School (215 West 114th Street, the first public high school for girls in New York City); Alice was in 6B at PS 89 (Lenox Avenue, between 134th and 135th Streets); Aida had "almost caught up with her" and was "in 6a at the age of ten"; and "Little Ilva" was in the fourth grade. Hubert added that "at her own request" he was "helping Aida with her lessons every afternoon after school." On Sunday, September 17, his son Billy "completed his second year of life" and, according to Hubert, had "done well," being "a jolly, lively, strong little fellow, fond of laughter and jollity and a very promising specimen of humanity."[63]

On Sunday, September 19, Harrison attended the opening of the first Negro lodge of Moose in New York City, at St. Marks' Hall. Officers were elected at the meeting that day, and "Director General Ridley himself" nominated Harrison ("the first to be nominated") as "Past Dictator." Harrison was one of eleven or twelve elected to office.[64]

Earlier in the month, at a September 10 Liberty Hall meeting, Garvey had announced the appearance of the first issue of the *Daily Negro Times* and reported on the UNIA delegation's efforts to secure a mandate over parts of Africa.[65] The *Daily Negro Times* was a short-lived publication that ran from approximately September 25 to October 26, 1922. It listed a talented staff that included Garvey, executive editor; T. Thomas Fortune, editor; Ulysses S. Poston, managing editor; Joel A. Rogers, sub–news editor; John E. Bruce and Robert L. Poston, editorial writers; and Romeo L. Daugherty, sports editor. Rogers claimed that Garvey had bought a secondhand newspaper press and acquired a United Press ticker, which made the paper "probably the first Negro newspaper in America with a ticker that gave the news of the world." It ceased publication after twenty-six issues; the cost of printing had far exceeded daily receipts.[66]

The first issue of the *Daily Negro Times* featured a "Book Reviews by Hubert Harrison" column, which reviewed Arthur Sommers Roche's novel *The Day of Faith*. Though Harrison didn't consider it a great novel, it was "the kind of book which to the semi-literate" was "bound to seem great." He objected to the fact that it pretended "to offer a story pregnant with deep social significance while palming off instead a mass of mushy sentimentality." The protagonist, Bland Hendricks, "a lawyer of philanthropic views," adopted as his principle "the idea embodied in the slogan: 'My neighbor is perfect.'" This failed when he attempted to apply it to the case of a burglar caught red-handed in his house, whom he let go, and who later that same night committed a second burglary in which Marley Maynard, "an eminent and respectable citizen," was killed. Though Maynard was his lifelong friend, Hendricks retained "an able New York lawyer" to save the criminal's life, "in furtherance of his faith in the perfection of all men." His fellow citizens were so outraged that they tarred and feathered him, rode him on a rail, and inflicted other physical injuries, from which he died. Maynard's daughter suffered a mental shock, which led to temporary insanity and treatment in a sanitarium, after which she confronted another shock—that of suddenly meeting the escaped convict who caused her father's death. Her "first rational act" was "to help him on his way to freedom," after which she traveled to New York "with a changed heart to establish the Bland Hendricks Foundation to perpetuate the principles which had had such splendid results." Beyond the general principle, however, "she had no plan," and she erected a building at which all who entered "must repeat the words, 'My neighbor is perfect.'" The new foundation attracted many people, rich and poor, including John Anstell, "the son and heir of Michael Anstell, a billionaire magnate." The billionaire father soon became a supporter of the cause. The "Great Idea" was spread worldwide, and a "Day of Faith" was established by Congress for general affirmation that "My Neighbor is Perfect." On the Day of Faith "everyone is transfigured"; jail populations are released; "policemen, soldiers and detectives knock off"; and "under cover of the New Religion," the billionaire and his son grab "all the property in Europe, Asia, Africa and America that wasn't under lock and key." A public mob then kills young Anstell. The book featured "thick gobs, of drooling propagandist preachments" and was of "bad taste and bad workmanship."[67]

Harrison's social activities in the latter part of 1922, particularly with other women, continued as they had for years. One woman he became involved with was Jessie Morris, a thirty-five-year-old Englishwoman. They met during the summer at the Civic Club on West Twelfth Street, where he was her guest for diner. After dinner they went to her studio and were joined by Eva Wyeth, an old friend from the Sunrise Club. By September 6 he and Morris "were to have a party of about 8 persons—white and Negro" at her apartment at 43 Washington Square South. When Harrison came up from the subway at Fourteenth Street into a great downpour of rain and phoned her, she informed him that she had called off the party but asked whether he "minded joining her tete-a-tete." Harrison "took a taxi and went to the house." They "had a very interesting talk on the more intimate phases of the race-problem in America," and Morris indicated she had "recently suffered from some of Dr. Du Bois's bad manners, and she was willing to look at some of the uglier aspects of the question—from our side." Then, added Harrison, "after some heart-searching and confessions we came, by her leading, to the sexual aspects of it," and he "told her all the *intimes* of the matter." She "intimated that, personally, Negro men made a strong appeal to her," but Harrison "for-bore to press the point." He then "gave her a list of ten good books on the realities of the race-problem and left with a promise to make one of a party of three (with herself and Mrs. Wyeth) in the near future."[68]

About a month later, on Thursday, October 5, Morris called him on the phone while he was out. When he returned he called back, and they had what he described as "a long and delightful chat of about 40 minutes," in which she "was rather playful and inviting," called him by his "first name" several times, and "urged" him "again and again" to attend the Sunrise Club the following Monday "as her guest." He accepted. On October 18 he spoke again with her, and she gave him "a kiss (by phone)." He also "received a letter from her with a forget-me-not in it, mailed from Sharon, Connecticut, on October 15. On October 30 Harrison went to the Sunrise Club dinner with Morris and Mrs. Eva Wyeth. James F. Morton spoke on "What Is Love?" and Harrison enjoyed the dinner, speeches, and atmosphere. When Harrison rose to speak he was "greeted with tremendous applause." He then "played [a] trick on the chairman," who rose to tell him that his time of five minutes was up but that he would let him finish his sentence. Harrison "so expanded [the] sentence" that it was evident he "could speak a whole speech in it," but he "didn't torture dear old [Edwin C.] Walker long." Walker had founded the Sunrise Club in 1889 and served as its secretary until 1931.[69]

Friday, September 29, Harrison wrote in his diary of another relationship. He had been "visited by 'Pmjwfuvsofs'" (Olive Tu(n)er?), who "came to consult" and copy his "book-list study-course." She was "the same young lady who some years ago shot and killed a West Indian man who was trying at the time to shoot

her, after having pestered her with his affections which, it seems, were unso-
licited and unreciprocated. She was exonerated in court." Harrison added, "I
have always had a high regard for her as a young woman of unusual mental ability." Their talk that day confirmed his "first impressions," and their "mutual
interest had a happy culmination + which she enjoyed immensely."[70]

The next day Harrison made a politically foreboding diary entry: "The war
clouds that have been lowering over the Dardanelles have begun to release light-
ning." It looked "as if there will be war in a week between Mustapha Kemal
Pasha's Turks and Great Britain." For over two weeks Harrison had "been keeping in touch with developments in the Near East thru the reports in the *N.Y.
Times*," and he "filed away much valuable material among the clippings in vol. 2
of [his scrapbook] 'Weltpolotik,'" a volume he subsequently lost. Harrison, who
maintained three other "Weltpolotik" scrapbooks, noted that it seemed "to be
a common apprehension among those who understand that the losing of the
levin at this moment may be the beginning of the end of Britain's Empire, the
explosion of the Indian powder-magazine and a real world-war in which all
Islam—from the Barbary Coast to Turkestan—may draw the sword of Race and
Religion."[71]

"Naturally," wrote Harrison, "I want to see the British Empire smashed;
yet if I were Kemal I should rest content with having forced her to back down
when France and Italy (sick at her double-dealings) refused to act as collusive
cats-paws." He realized that "Kemal who is the man on the ground should know
his business better than I do, and there are hints and indications in the news
reports that England has been doing things provocative while pretending to be
passive," such as "using her control of the Sea of Marmora and the straits to
aid the Greeks in getting an army into Thrace by ferrying them across the
'neutral' waters." Kemal had "forced a cessation of this about four days ago,"
and his army currently had surrounded the British "general [Charles] Harrington's [Harington's] forces at Chanak!" To Harrison it looked as if there
would be "a duplicate of the siege of Alesia again, both at Chanak and Constantinople." Despite the presence of "British dreadnoughts in the Dardanelles," he expected "to see many of them sunk by the Turkish land-batteries"
if war was declared, "because land-batteries with the kind of Skoda guns that
battered [the Belgian cities] Liege & Namur to pieces in 1914" were "bound to
be destructive of warships" lacking "freedom of maneouvre" and "cooped up
in a narrow strait."[72]

The "really important part of the conflict" would be the "repercussions in
Asia," which he would watch "with much interest." He wryly observed, "How
odd it is that England should be talking of keeping the Turk out of Europe while
she herself is in danger of being kicked out of Asia!" Finally, Harrison indicated
he was not at all surprised by the fact that "our government" was "sending a

destroyer flotilla to the scene of impending hostilities" and that William Randolph Hearst was "beginning to explain the racial significance of what Lothrop Stoddard described as the impending doom."[73]

On Tuesday night, October 3, Harrison spoke on "Religion and Race" at the Bridge St. Church in Brooklyn, before the Zion Ministers' Union. Rev. W. C. Brown, "the church's pastor and a great friend" whom he knew from "Washington in 1919 when he was pastor of the John Wesley Memorial Church" had invited him.[74]

In the fall and early winter of 1922 Harrison also became involved in the issues of access to books in libraries and noncensorship. In 1922 John S. Sumner, secretary for the Society for the Prevention of Vice, led a campaign of censorship against the *Satyricon* of Petronius, the first novel in Latin. The satirical masterpiece was available in France, England, and Germany, but access was being delayed in New York.[75]

On September 14, Ernestine Rose, the popular and skilled librarian who had succeeded Gertrude Cohen at the 135th Street Public Library in June 1920 and did much to help staff that branch with Blacks and to develop a collection and programs that served the Harlem community, wrote to Harrison, probably in response to his request that the library purchase the *Satyricon* of Petronius and other books. She said there was a delay about entering the book "officially" in their catalogue "because of the possibility of censorship." She added, "The placing of the English translation in our branch collection has been delayed by the discussion of its treatment by the library system as a whole." Rose also noted that "a number of such copies are being purchased" and that "within a day or two, also, cards for *Batouala* as well as for Mr. Rogers' book will be filed in our catalogue.[76]

Harrison, as president of the Liberty League, wrote an October 16 letter to the editor of the *New York Times* entitled "Satyricon of Petronius." It appeared in the October 22 issue and asked: "Isn't the contention of the New York Vice Society in the matter of Petronius getting to be more than a little absurd? There isn't the slightest danger of any intelligent person confounding the *Satyricon* of Petronius with the work of John Barclay, unless that person is entirely ignorant of Latin literature in general and Petronius in particular." Barclay, a Scottish satirical poet, had written *Euphormionis Lusinini Satyricon*, a politico-satirical romance directed against the Jesuits and the medical profession in the early seventeenth century. Harrison explained that he had his own copy of Petronius's *Satyricon*, published by Robert Garnier, with the Latin text and a French translation by Heguin de Guerle, with critical commentaries by J. N. M. de Guerle, for more than fourteen years, "yet it has never occurred to me that it was a nasty book." He felt "able to glean from its pages a much better understand[ing] of how people actually lived in Imperial Rome than could be had from the pages of [Theodor] Mommsen, [William] Ihne or even [Victor] Duruy." He added, "the *Satyricon* is a classic in both senses of the word; and as a classic it should be better known." Harrison also explained that some years earlier Professor Harry Thurston Peck, of Columbia University, published a translation of a portion of it under the title of *Trimalchio's Feats* (*Coena Trimalchionis*) and that this translation "was remarkable for the fidelity with which the linguistic flavor of the Latin original was reproduced in English." "Every bit of Latin slang was represented by an equivalent piece of English argot," and it was undoubtedly "one of the finest bits of American classical scholarship that had appeared in our period." Nevertheless, the New York Public Library "put it on their disingenuous Index Expurgatorious." Harrison stressed that he didn't "want to poison the morals of youth," though "the sensational newspapers" and the "comic supplements" would. He thought "grown-ups" also had "some rights in this matter," since they paid for the literature that was bought. Though "Shakespeare, Balzac, Rabelais, Vergil and Juvenal were grown-ups, writing for grown-ups," the censors seemed "to take it for granted that [August J. Evans's] *St. Elmo*, *Eric*, and Jasper's Old Shad should set the standards for all literature."[77]

Some two months later, on December 13, Floyd Calvin, editor of the "Educational Supplement" of *The Messenger*, wrote to Harrison that they were "planning publication of an educational supplement for May 1923 composed of book reviews by 62 of the most prominent and able Negro writers in America." They asked if he would review *Noncensorship*, a symposium by noted authors on the question of censorship. Calvin explained, "We think you are the most deserving man of this particular task." If Harrison accepted, they would send the book promptly and would want his manuscript by February 15, for a projected *Messenger* run of 25,000 copies, which would include mailings "to every Negro College and High School in America."[78]

In October 1922, after providing his documents on Garvey to the Justice Department, gaining his citizenship, and nurturing his friendships with the Democrats and with Single Taxer James F. Morton Jr., Harrison was hired to deliver a regular series of Saturday evening lectures for the New York City Board of Ed Lecture Bureau. The series on "Literary Lights of Yesterday and Today" at the 135th Street Public Library was "the first instance of any Negro attaining to that height." The board occasionally had Black lecturers, "but not a series." Harrison's lectures sought to expose minds to "those beacon lights of experience that genius has shed upon the pages of imperishable literature." Printed handouts for the series falsely claimed that "Dr." Harrison had obtaining his degree from the University of Copenhagen and had "since encircled the globe, visiting Europe, Asia, Africa and the Islands of the Pacific." His schedule was: "The Novels and Stories of [Charles] Dickens" (October 28), "[Henry Wadsworth] Longfellow—The Poet of the Hearthside" (November 4), "[Rudyard] Kipling in Prose and Verse" (November 1), "Our Own Mark Twain" (November 18), "The Poetry of [Alfred, Lord] Tennyson" (November 25), "Edgar Allan Poe, Poet and Prose Writer" (December 9), and "Thirty Years of H. G. Wells" (December 16).[79]

At the end of October Harrison approached Dr. Crandall "about an additional course somewhere else in Harlem." Crandall was willing, and Harrison proposed lectures in elementary science. He then could have been "knocked" over "with a feather" when Crandall suggested instead that he "should lecture on 'The Trend of the Times.'" That topic was assigned only to "the Board's seven or eight ablest lecturers, including professors from Columbia, City College and New York University." Harrison accepted, and in December 1922 or January 1923 he began the series at Public School 89 on Lenox Avenue and 135th Street. Before he started those lectures, Crandall also responded, on November 6, to a Harrison letter of October 26 seeking a continuation of his current services. Crandall told him that his "lectures have created much enthusiasm wherever they have been heard" and that "one of our local superintendents recommended that your lecture on 'The Brother in Black' ought to be heard in every lecture centre." He not only wanted "to continue the present series"; he would also gladly consider extending it.[80]

––––––––

Around November 1922 Harrison wrote "At the Back of the Black Man's Mind," the idea of which resulted from his "casual conversation with the editor of the *New Republic*," Robert Littell. Though he couldn't remember where his "initial impulse" came from, Harrison knew that when he left the office he was "committed to this project of rushing in where angels feared to tread." He also remembered "pleading in deprecation that the people of my putative race (I am black) would tear the scalp from my quivering cranium if they should see this thing in print." As he recollected, he was "assured that the white race (among whom I have many thousands of friends) would protect me in such an event." But, when he "intimated" that it was his intention "to be no less disrespectful to certain subliminal certitudes of white people than to those of Negroes, the editor threw up his hands" and commended him "to the care of that kindly Providence which always looks after little children, drunken men and fools."[81]

In the article, Harrison set about to reveal "the secrets of the prison house." He explained: "An opportunity to tell the truth is a privilege so rarely proffered to a black writer that I gladly dare even the damnations of the professional colored men for the sake of the luxury." That "professional colored man always maintains 'the indivulged pretence' as against any white friend or foe," he added.

Always "his soul is on parade . . . dressed up for inspection, like the belle at a ball who maintains a simulated unconsciousness of the 'killing' effect of her silks." Harrison stressed that "the individual Negro when under inspection maintains a pose through which very few of his white friends can pierce." This was not a "bar to an adequate comprehension of the 'race problem', which concerns the relation between white people on the one hand, and black and colored people on the other and which need take no note of the essential nature of the souls of either." That was "why some white *simpaticos* who understand the Negro problem assume that they understand the Negro," but "they don't."[82]

"Before getting to the back of the black man's mind," Harrison first explained "what that mind is." He first had to overcome the obstacle "of the kind-headed people who imagine that race is not a ['social and' is crossed out] psychic reality just because there is no point at which one can say: 'here is the true dividing line, on the one side of which you have one thing for certain and on the other something different.'" He admitted that "social psychology" was "misused [?] by those other extremists who talk about 'the Teutonic mentality', 'the race-mind of the Anglo-Saxon' and the 'Aryan consciousness,'" but he left them "to [Jean] Finot and [John] Oakesmith and [Alexander A.] Goldenweiser." He then explained:

In the first place, then, the "mind" of the American Negro of today is largely embryonic; a great psychic smear, as of something rubbed out or rubbed off with nothing to replace it except the other fellow's mental furniture to which the rooms are not yet quite adjusted. For instance: it always happens that the gods that men make are made in their images: the gods of yellow men are always yellow; of brown men, brown; of white men, white; and of black men (in Africa), black. The only racial group of whom this is not true is the Westernized Negro of the United States and the West Indies. It has always made me laugh to hear them singing: "Wash me and I shall be whiter than snow." But it is a bit tragic when that same subversion of an ethnic ideal works itself out in the forms of "Kongolene Knocks Kinks", "Bleach Your Black Skin" and those ghastly advertisements of a similar sort with which Negro newspapers are replete—in America. Let the *reason* be what it may, the *fact* remains that the Westernized Negro (of whatever nationality) is what the white man has made him—a psychic hybrid—and his struggle for self-expression must take place in a house spiritually divided against itself.[83]

He then described the influence of environment:

Our environment develops in us characters to suit. The environment which the white man provided for the black was that of slavery and subjection.

After three hundred and fifty years the slavery was removed: the subjection remained. If social environments shape psychic characters then it is non-sense to suppose that there has been no slave-inheritance for the Western Negro. Ask yourself why was John Brown overpowered? Because the Virginia slaves did not rise as he expected. And why didn't they rise? Because the whips of slavery had beaten the heart out of them. Again, what is the greatest *moral* claim of American Negroes? That, even after Lincoln had issued a proclamation declaring them free and specifically calling on them to rise and do something; when their masters were at the front fighting to keep them in slavery—the slaves of the South never struck *one* violent blow in their own behalf. That is the *boast!* Would the Irish, Greek, English or any other white group *boast* about such a thing? They have never done so. *The Slave Inheritance, then, is a substratum of Negro consciousness.*[84]

To Harrison it was "obvious, that those who are robbed of rights and power turn to guile and deceit," and "the Negro is no exception"—"it is here that his strength lies." For so long "he had to pretend and pose and express everything but his real thoughts and feelings" that "it has now become a second nature to him." The "particular individual may have studied at Oxford, Yale or Gottingen [in Germany]; he may be a 'scientific radical'; a suave symbol of pseudo-culture, or a New York legislator—if he is of the stock that Lincoln freed, it is ten to one that he will always pretend and never own up to the freightage of original evil which he now knows is in his cargo."[85]

Another product "of the slave-psychology" concerned the fact that "there is no color prejudice in America—except among colored people." Though Harrison himself wrote "for the *New York World*, the *Tribune*, and the *Nation* . . . the editors of those journals, like the editor of the *New Republic*, require assurances only on the two points immediately germane. Does he know? Can he write? They care nothing about my color." If "they had race-prejudice they would then refuse my writings altogether because of my being a Negro. They wouldn't care whether I was a light one or a dark one." In contrast, he was "'too dark' to get employment at any but one Negro paper or periodical in New York" (a probable reference to the *Negro World*). While some Negroes kept "the white newspapers warm with their protests against what they call, with unconscious humor, the color-prejudice of the whites, and in their published writings are "as black as the proverbial ace of spades," one would nevertheless find that "they have their own 'light' churches as in Washington, 'light' graveyards as in Charleston and 'light' social sets as in New York." This "contempt for the Negro's characteristic color is fully shared by the black people themselves," yet "one will find no reference to this dominant obsession in the writings or speeches of those who 'represent' the race," as "it is considered very bad form to see the grinning head of the skeleton in the closet." Yet "another slave-product" was "the inferiority complex—that consciousness of unimportance which needs the aid of garish uniforms, swords, strutting and 'big-talk' for its temporary suppression."[86]

All was not bad, however, for there were "the twin gifts of lying and of laughter; of pretence and poetry wherein," according to Harrison, "consists our real claim to consideration." Alongside "developing civilization" there "developed some means of escape from the pressure of present reality," and "the Negro . . . has what the cold and critical western white calls 'a vivid imagination.'" Harrison maintained that "when the western Negro shall have developed self-reliance and a soul of his own," this "will count for much," but even now, he is able "to 'put it all over' the white man." This is possible because the "white man—especially the Anglo-Saxon—is keen on the assertion of his own superiority," and "the Negro has learnt how to play up to this racial egotism of the white, by flattering [from] which he often gets some of the durable satisfactions of life." Among Harrison's "striking illustrations" was how "the exclusive exponent of Negro activities[']" relationship to the "uplifting agencies, rich philanthropists, big politicians or professional 'friends of the Negro'" was maintained, and how, as "spot-light artist," it was not in his interest "to reveal to them the existence of any other personality in the background or any disturbing element in the order of things which they have complacently schematized by multiplying him ten million times to represent 'the Negro.'" But these "colored savants and henchmen in the privacy of their own homes" reveal that they "may dupe and despise their 'superiors' and 'work them for a good thing.'" But, since the whites "never venture to 'check-up' on their bell-weathers" they "consequently remain blind—and workable."[87]

Politics furnished "many amusing illustrations," such as the previous year's election rally at Liberty Hall (see "The Black Tide Turns in Politics," in chapter 11), at which the Republican Party "had been successfully duped by their dark 'inferiors' whose cleverness they had held in collective contempt." He added, "Let it not be supposed for a moment that the Republicans are alone in this matter. There are others—although *they* have not yet discovered themselves."[88]

Even Uncle Sam was "not exempt from this exploitation from below." He, in the person of the Republicans, "maintains in Washington a 'kitchen cabinet' of three colored appointees who act as almoners for the distribution of such crumbs of patronage as may be left over for Negro uses." These men are "generally selected from those sections of the south in which the Negro is not permitted to cast his vote; to the end that they may be doubly dutiful, subservient—and despised." Then in a direct reference to the Garvey situation he sketched how

> when a well-known black Boanerges [the vigorous orator Garvey] wished to return to this Land of Easy Pickings, and the white man's government held him at arm's length away from its shores, it was these three that (unbeknown to Uncle Sam) heard the tempting tinkle coming from the royal mountebank's coffers, hurried to get some golden grease on their hands and wrought so connivingly at the office of State that orders were issued to let him in. And to this day those same men have been able to baffle all the special agents of a certain department [Justice] and to keep their private provider from coming to trial.

To Harrison this showed that "on the whole, the white man can hold the black man to be a fool only at the risk of becoming himself the fool of this fool," and "in America today the black man finds the white man [just] such an 'easy mark.'"[89]

"Dr." Harrison began his "Trend of the Times" lectures on the fourth floor of Public School 89 in late December 1922 or early January 1923. His Sunday talks covered "Politics, History, Science, [and] International Affairs." The series was described in a handout as "a continuous course in current events, supplemented by the discussion of social and economic problems and followed by an open forum." The efforts of the new governor, Alfred E. Smith, the new state legislature, the new U.S. Senate, and the virtually new Congress were watched "to compare post-election performances with pre-election promises." England's "new deal," Italy's "bloodless revolution," the Near East, and Russia were discussed, as well as other "trends, currents, tendencies and movements of national and world significance." This work, which the Board of Education ordinarily entrusted "only to its ten or twelve ablest men," was quite an honor, "the first time that any Negro has been so honored by any Municipality in America." The *Harlem Home News* reported that Harrison was the only Negro lecturer on the Board of Ed's general staff of five hundred.[90]

While doing the "Trend of the Times" talks, from January 6 through February 24 Harrison also delivered Saturday night lectures on "Literary Lights of Yesterday and Today," sponsored by the Independent Lecture Committee of the New York Public Library on 135th Street. That committee consisted of Minnie G. (Mrs. William) Pickens, Mrs. Sadie M. Petersen, Miss Jessie Morris, Miss Doris Browne, Miss Madeline H. C. Wales, Dr. W. M. Hawenstein,

Edgar M. Grey, Melville Charlton, Eustace Dryden, Charles Johnson, Wilfred A. Domingo, and Charles Gilpin. Promotional material explained: "To Insure that Harlem shall get the very best in Free Education the Lecture Department of the Board of Education has secured the services of The Ablest Lecturer of the Negro Race Dr. Hubert Harrison." Harrison was identified as the author of *The Negro and the Nation*, *When Africa Awakes*, and *Natural Health* and as a writer of literary criticism for the *New York World*, *Tribune*, *New Republic*, and *Nation*. The schedule included "A Night With Negro Poets" (January 6), "The Novels and Poems of Walter Scott" (January 13), "[Ralph Waldo] Emerson's Essays" (January 20), "McCauley [Thomas Babington Macaulay] the Essayist and Historian" (January 27), "Victor Hugo's 'Les Miserables'" (February 3), "[Abraham] Lincoln as Master of English" (February 10), "Charles Reade's 'The Cloister and the Hearth'" (February 17); and "Bret Harte's 'Out of the Wild West'" (February 24?).[91]

Harrison was now taking on a new public education persona. The *Harlem Home News* reported incorrectly that he had "a D. Sc. from Copenhagen, Denmark," and Dr. Crandall was quoted as saying that "he has encircled the globe, visiting Europe, Asia, Africa and the islands of the Pacific" and listed his books and newspapers and magazines that had published his works.[92]

Besides his weekly talks at the library and at PS 89 Harrison was also scheduled to speak to children at the school, under the auspices of the Literary Forum. On Thursday evening, February 1, he lectured on Lewis Carroll's *Alice in Wonderland*, and on Saturday evening, February 3, on Victor Hugo's *Les Miserables*. The North Harlem Community Forum planned to celebrate Carroll's birthday at its February 15 meeting with "Dr." Harrison, who had "long been a devoted admirer of Lewis Carroll and his book," as the featured speaker. Parents were urged to bring their children and also to visit the exhibit on Carroll and *Alice in Wonderland* in the children's room.[93]

Around February 5, 1923, William Pickens, field secretary of the NAACP, wrote an evaluation of the Board of Ed's 135th Street Library lecture program and the Sunday afternoon forum at PS 89, which he sent to Crandall. Pickens stated: "None of these have a fair attendance, altho the Hubert Harrison forums have grown nearly one hundred percent in attendance and interest over the last year's record." He noted, "Harrison undoubtedly gives the most thought-provoking talks on history, literature, international politics and current topics, of all the forums and lectures being given in the city in any forum." Nevertheless, "only a relatively small number attend, and some of the most faithful attendants are white students and scholars." "In a generation," he added, "those whites and blacks who attend these forums now, will be found far ahead of others in their knowledge of politics, social evolution and literature."[94]

Pickens elaborated on and publicized his laudatory appraisal of Harrison in the February 7 *Amsterdam News* under the title "Hubert Harrison Philosopher of Harlem." After he and his wife, Minnie, visited some Harrison lectures, Pickens wrote:

> It is not possible that Socrates could have outdone Hubert Harrison in making the most commonplace subject interesting. Here is a plain black man who can speak more easily, effectively and interestingly on a greater variety of subjects than any other man we have ever met, even in any of the great universities. . . . He is a "walking cyclopedia" of current human facts, and more especially of history and literature. And it makes no difference whether he is talking about *Alice in Wonderland* or the most extensive work of H. G. Wells; about the lightest shadows of Edgar Allan Poe or the heaviest depths of Kant; about music, or art, or science, or political history—he is equally interesting.
>
> We know how hard it is to believe this, and we confess that we could never have believed it ourself, by report. But continual visits to the lectures which Harrison has been giving this winter in the New York Public Library, and elsewhere, under the auspices of the public school system, have convinced us. That is all. We had heard Harrison talk on the street corners before . . . go and sit down comfortably, anywhere under the dome of heaven, and hear Hubert Harrison TALK, evenly, easily, readily, wittily, but not too wittily, about ANYTHING under the sun, and if you have brains you will concede him the palm as an educational lecturer.[95]

The first few times Mrs. Pickens induced her husband to go to a Harrison lecture they were both interested and acknowledged Harrison's excellence but didn't believe he could repeat the feat. William Pickens explained, "We had no idea the man could keep up the same informing and interesting talk on a great variety of subjects, twice or more every week, for all winter!" He added:

> The unfortunate thing is, that a man like Hubert Harrison cannot yet find his proper place among us. He ought to be a lecturer in some great American university. Not one out of a hundred of those lecturing in the universities have half his real information, and not one out of a thousand can convey it so interestingly. And we poor American people, white and black, have been so used to the white ideal, that it is next to impossible for us to believe that of any black man—until we become convinced. And most of us will never become

convinced, but we will not even allow ourselves enough preliminary faith in the proposition to "Come and see!"

This difficulty in finding work comparable with his ability was, to Pickens, largely explained by racial discrimination:

> There is hardly a place for such a black man in America. If Mr. Harrison were white (and we say it boldly), he might be one of the most prominent lecturers and professors of Columbia University, under the shadow of which he is passing his days. Many white university people can be found sitting among the colored people at the Public Library on West 135th Street, or in some public school auditorium in Harlem, patiently listening to Harrison and writing rapidly in their note books—gathering material for their classes at the institution. And the strange human thing is, THAT THESE SAME WHITE DEVOTEES WOULD OBJECT AND PERHAPS WOULD EVEN REFUSE TO ATTEND COLUMBIA UNIVERSITY, IF HARRISON WAS TO BE THEIR LECTURER AND LEADER THERE. On such poor stuff is human nature made. And yet these same students, if they bravely confessed, would acknowledge that they can listen interestedly to Harrison lecturing at ten o'clock at night on a subject in which their university professors could hardly interest them at ten o'clock in the morning.[96]

Parallels came immediately to Pickens's mind. "People used to go and sit on the hard rocks by the river to hear the Nazarene, or trudge through the woods to the wilderness to listen to the Baptist, who would not have accepted either Jesus or John as heads or leaders in their synagogues." Similarly, "Fellows were charmed by Socrates on the corners of the small streets and in the market places, who would have felt too 'proud' to enroll in a school or university course headed up by that bare-foot pot-gutted old gentleman." Pickens attributed this to "human nature," and in Harrison's case there were the added factors of "race prejudice and color mania." While "Charles Gilpin might have gone on in cheap vaudeville and back street shows for the rest of his life—but for an accident"—so too might Harrison "go on for the rest of his life—with his full mind and most instructive deliverance, in the less prominent corners of public education—for accidents do not work so readily in his class of performance."[97]

On February 19 Dr. Crandall wrote to Pickens and thanked him for his February 5 letter, which included a copy of the "note" sent to Harlem newspapers. Crandall was pleased to find that Harrison's work was "so well appreciated."[98]

———

In the December 10 *New York World* Harrison wrote "Potentate and Poet," a review of *Penitent*, by Edna Worthley Underwood. He thought the book offered the "promise of great things to come," though its author was "not yet habituated to the mode of the historical novel." The "broad sweep of her imagination" created "an arresting atmosphere." Mrs. Underwood depicted Russia under the Romanovs, and the "two chief characters" were Czar Alexander I and "that wonderful poet of Negro blood who laid the foundations of Russian literature—Alexis Sergevitch Poushkin." Unfortunately, "the connection between these two (in the story)" was "a matter of forced construction," which sprawled "out of the author's control." Nevertheless, the characters in the book were "well drawn," and there was "no doubt" that Underwood had "the gift of portraiture," though Harrison felt that she didn't "know how to group" the characters "and relate them to each other so as to get the grand and convincing effect." "In short," she was "deficient in what painters call the knack of composition." The two main characters were the poet, "the typical aristocrat, idle, irresponsible, petulant"; and the potentate, "like an American business man . . . devoted to his tasks, earnest, easygoing and steadfast to the end." Despite "some historical myth and invented" history Harrison found *The Penitent* "worth reading."[99]

Following the Underwood review, in the December 11 issue of the *New York Tribune* Harrison reviewed *Nigger*, by Clement Wood. He described it as "hardly a novel in the accepted sense, but a series of dissolving views in which the author gives imperfect silhouettes of the Southern Negro on the march from slavery to the present day." Wood selected "two slave families in the dismal swamps of Alabama" and followed "their joint careers in a sketchy fashion for three generations" during which they were "mocked by the mirage of freedom."[100]

Wood tried to tell his story in the "objective manner" that T. S. Stribling's *Birthright* and Hubert Anthony Shands's *White and Black* offered "serious treatment of Negro life," but he seemed "to lack the necessary equipment." While he could "put atmospheres in his scenes," he "fails utterly to make his human characters convincing." Nevertheless, his "intent" was "an honest one," and one realizes "that the harsh lot of the Southern negro has not changed very much in the last sixty years." Whether "as an agricultural peon or an urban industrial worker he is still faced with the stern alternatives of terror or abject submission." "In spite of these handicaps," however, "he is consciously striving to realize the newer ideals of freedom."[101]

While writing the Underwood and Wood reviews Harrison was trying hard to quit smoking. On November 1 he began a "skirmish with Nick [O'Teen]." Then, after twenty-three days of his "abstention from tobacco," he described feeling "like being racked to pieces." He had "got tobacco down," however, "and, hurt as it may," he knew that he could "keep him down." He predicted that "when 3 months shall have gone by I shall know then that I am quite free from the shackles of the drug nicotine." He "abstained for 93 days" before starting smoking again.[102]

On Monday, January 1, 1923, Harrison delivered a 3 p.m. address at "The Annual Celebration of the Emancipation Proclamation" held under the auspices of the Brown Knights of Honor of Fleet Street AME Zion Church, in Brooklyn. Other speakers included the Rev. W. C. Brown and A. L. Comither, secretary of the Carlton branch of the YMCA, in Brooklyn. Harrison's notes indicate that he spoke about the Declaration of Independence and the Emancipation Proclamation while emphasizing that it was the Thirteenth Amendment that granted freedom. He described the Emancipation Proclamation as a "war measure" by which Lincoln hoped for "a slave revolt," and he stressed that it was preceded by Lincoln's (August 22, 1862) letter to Horace Greeley. Harrison focused on the emotion of Lincoln's emancipation idea and noted that "we were freed in the course of the struggle of a nation which had neglected Justice & Truth & Right." He added that "today" people face the task of completing "The Unfinished Emancipation."[103]

Harrison's positive review of *The Negro in Our History*, by Carter G. Woodson, appeared in the January 7, 1923, *New York Tribune*. "Here at last," he wrote, was "a history of the American Negro in succinct and readable form, suitable as a text book for high school or college and for the general reader who wishes to acquaint himself with the ways in which the presence of the Negro population has influenced the march of great events in the United States." While the book didn't have "the range and sweep" of Benjamin Brawley's *Social History of the American Negro*, he felt "its compressed materials" and "fine illustrations" made it "a more handy work of reference." Harrison described Dr. Woodson (whose *Journal of Negro History* was "the only learned periodical published by American Negroes") as a man who had "assumed the role of professional historian of the Negro." Woodson brought to that task "considerable erudition and remarkable industry," and Harrison referred to previous Woodson works he had reviewed, including *The Education of the Negro Prior to 1861*, *A Century of Negro Migration*, and *The History of the Negro Church*. In those earlier volumes Harrison considered Woodson's style to be "cramped and slovenly," but the "subject matter" of this volume was "so compelling" that it enabled one "to overlook this prime defect." Woodson's book demonstrated "the various form of American slavery," from "the first soul-grinding phase which changed to a mild patriarchal form as the South became saturated, changing again to intensified exploitation as [Samuel] Crompton's [spinning] 'mule' and [Eli] Whitney's cotton-gin made cotton king and dictated the extension of slavery with its consequent political conflict which gradually estranged the two great sections of the country from each other and led to the Civil War." Woodson also graphically treated "freedom, reconstruction, and the rise of the freedmen" and presented "a wealth of material" that would "open the eyes of many American readers whose knowledge of the history of their darker fellow citizens rests mainly on a mass of myths."[104]

The review of Woodson's book would be followed in 1923 by other important Harrison reviews, articles, and talks. The year would also see Harrison continuing to face financial difficulties and searching for work. In addition, it would be the year that Garvey was sentenced to five years in prison for using the mail to defraud.

14

The KKK, Garvey's Conviction, Speaking, Virgin Islands, and Reviews (1923)

In the early 1920s the revived Ku Klux Klan became extremely active in the U.S. North and Midwest, as well as in its original home in the South. This reality came to national attention after a three-week *New York World* exposé (September 6 to 26, 1921), based on research by Rowland Thomas, was reprinted in eighteen leading papers across the nation. In the September 19 installment the *World* provided a chronology of 152 separate aggressions committed by the new Klan. The following month the U.S. House of Representatives held a series of hearings on Klan atrocities and heard extensive testimony by William Joseph Simmons, who had founded the new organization in 1915. The *World* exposé claimed that Klan membership approached one million and that two hundred new local chapters had recently been established.[1]

The Klan spread from Pennsylvania and upstate New York, and the Leif Erickson Klan no. 1 of Paterson was established as "the first major unit" in New Jersey (a state whose Klan membership would grow to sixty thousand). On July 4, 1922, the Klan formally announced its arrival by burning a cross on Garret Mountain, overlooking Paterson. It was to this new Klan target, within twenty miles of New York City, that Harrison traveled on Sunday, January 7, 1923, to speak on "The Menace of the Ku Klux Klan," at Salzberg Hall, 211 Market Street, under the auspices of the Paterson Philosophical Society. A large and vocal audience, which included Klan members, a police sergeant, and patrolman, was waiting. The police were assigned to cover the meeting because Harrison, while in New York, had received a threatening letter (reportedly from the New York Klan) warning that he would be kidnapped if he tried to speak.[2]

Harrison was undaunted, and he opened his talk by commenting on how regrettable it was that people didn't know more of their own history. This lack of knowledge made Americans "the dupes of all kinds of boobs that come along with pretentious versions of the past with which to kid us." Returning to themes he often discussed, Harrison challenged several historical myths: "Lincoln did not free the slaves," and the "emancipation proclamation was nothing more than a war measure." He emphasized that it was Congress that freed the slaves ("with enactment of the thirteenth amendment") and granted full citizenship rights ("with passage of the fourteenth amendment"). In similar fashion Harrison discussed the origins of the first KKK. He detailed its founding in Giles County, Tennessee, under the leadership of Major General Nathaniel Bedford Forrest in 1865 and in its reorganized form in 1866. Based on these dates, he asked: How could the claim be made that the Klan grew in opposition to "Negro political domination," especially since it was not until 1868 "that the Negro got the vote?" He then described the horrible treatment "Negroes" received from former Confederate soldiers who resented the outcome of the war and the fact "that the Negro was no longer their slave." These Confederate Klansmen "did not care for the American form of government"; they "wanted to establish a sort of empire, in which the white man should be ruler over the negro." In pursuit of that aim, "the Klan was responsible for many negro massacres and outrages, and on one occasion slew 260 white men and women of the North who had come to the Southland to assist the negro." The Klan continued "its ravages against the negroes in order to keep them in slavery," and it was this "band of midnight assassins, with the nightgowns," which was finally "put down in 1874, by an army." Today "in the South," continued Harrison, "they consider that the negro is meant for the ditch, and in order to hold him there, ['whites'] have gone down in the ditch with him." For that reason, "the South is the most illiterate and backward section of the nation." When the Klan revived in 1915–1916, it first directed its efforts "against the negro and then, as it grew, against the Jew." After gaining greater strength it "attacked Roman Catholics and later still all foreigners," all the while "peddling 'bunk' and 'essential hate.'"[3]

Harrison's point was that the KKK was directly opposed to "true Americanism" because it fostered the spirit of antipathy to fellow Americans. He warned his audience to beware of associating with Klansmen and stressed that "our highest duty is to be American citizens, whether white or black, Southerner or Northerner, Jew or Gentile, Protestant or Catholic." In his concluding remarks Harrison scathingly denounced the type of men who had started the Klan, declaring them to be Southern tobacco-chewing "crackers" of a low type of intellect. They would claim "We must keep our race pure" yet would "make use" of Black women. In addition, there were also many senators and congressmen of similar low morality and who had fathered Black families. Harrison then urged his listeners: "Do your duty. Put down racial and religious prejudices, and the menace will collapse."[4]

When the chairperson announced that Harrison (who had been heckled by about a dozen men not recognized as residents of Paterson and believed to be Klansmen) would answer questions, the audience became excited, and several people, including apparent Klansmen, responded. The crowd, however, was on Harrison's side and cheered as he answered the hecklers effectively. Then a tall young man who would not reveal his name (but who was later identified as Arthur Bell) stood up and introduced himself as a Klansman. The chair invited him to the platform, where he charged that Harrison had confused the old KKK with the new, which was "not anti-negro" but merely "a one hundred per cent Protestant white man's organization." Bell claimed that he had "many friends who are Jews, Catholics, negroes and foreigners" and that "the klan helps all who are needy, regardless of race, color or creed." Unashamed of his affiliation, he maintained that the "bed-sheet" robes were not worn to scare people and were never seen outside of the lodge room, except when Klan members went to church to make a donation or attend a funeral or when they held an official parade with permission from the proper authorities. After these comments both Bell and Harrison answered questions as the heckling continued. The *Paterson Morning Times* judged that though the Klansman received some applause, "he was far eclipsed in argumentative powers by the lecturer, whose contentions appeared to evince a more thorough knowledge of the subject." As a final gesture, before finishing for the night, Harrison issued a challenge to "any member of the Ku Klux Klan who may desire to meet me in any hall of this city to public debate on the proposition [that] The Ku Klux Klan is a menace to American liberty." Harrison said he would take the affirmative, and the challenge was greeted with tumultuous applause. Bell responded that he was not a KKK lecturer but that he would secure one for the debate, possibly a Dr. Maloney, of New York State.[5]

Three days after Harrison's Paterson talk the Paterson Philosophical Society met to discuss Harrison's lecture and the views of Bell and the KKK. It scheduled a debate between Harrison and any member of the Klan for Sunday, January 14, with free admission and freedom to ask any question from the floor. The PPS then drafted a statement to the *Paterson Evening News* expressing its dissatisfaction with Bell's "public statement" and informing the public that proceeds from the debate would "be turned over to local hospitals in equal amounts to Jew, Catholic and Protestant." If the Klan did not appear, the PPS and Harrison would discuss "Whom will we go to war with or against?" A handout explained that "since England and France were teamed up for trouble and wanted oil and empire," and "since both wanted them at the expense of Turkey, which was backed up by 260,000,000 black and brown Mohammedians from Algiers to India," the question really raised was "'Shall the U.S.A. get into the game and under what diplomatic guise?'"[6]

In early 1923 Harrison made a number of efforts at earning additional money to supplement his Board of Ed salary. On February 8 he wrote to Arthur E. Bestor, president of the Chautauqua Institution, seeking lecturing work. Chautauqua, in southwestern New York State, was a utopian community founded in 1874 that featured speakers and correspondence courses, provided educational opportunities for women, and was an important cultural institution of the late nineteenth and early twentieth century. Bestor responded that Harrison perhaps misapprehended the institution, which was "A System of Popular Education" and did not sponsor a lecture bureau (though in the early twentieth century there were thirty other local chautauquas that did). He suggested that Harrison "try the assemblies called chautauquas" and included some names and addresses.[7]

On February 23 Harrison wrote to Clifford Smyth, editor of the *International Book Review*, seeking an assignment to do book reviews:

> I am colored—in fact black. And it has become such a common thing in our corner of the world to measure ability chromatically, that I am not quite to be blamed for thinking of my looks as a literary obstacle. However, and in spite of it, I happen to be the only professional Negro book-reviewer in captivity, and I have been plying the tools of the trade since 1917. At present I review books dealing with the Negro here and in Africa for the *New York World, Tribune* and *Evening Post*. But that doesn't give my "extreme range." I have just turned in a (triple) review of Davis' *Near East*, Sykes' *Persia* and Seneville's *Balkan Peninsula*—all histories—to Mr. [John] Macy of *The Nation*, and am now getting ready to review Reinach's *History of Christianity* for the same discriminating critic.

He closed by asking, "Can I do any book-reviewing for you?" There is no indication that he received a response or was ever offered any work.[8]

Harrison wrote to Margaret Normil, of the Redpath Lyceum Bureau, on April 7 requesting lecture dates. She responded that they were "so situated that, for at least another year," they wouldn't need lecturers, though they would keep his work in mind. Nineteen months later the answer was the same. Marguerite R. Brown, of Redpath, wrote thanking him "for again writing us" but regretted that it was "still not possible" to consider him. Also on April 7 Harrison wrote to Robert E. Ely, trustee of the League for Political Education, at New

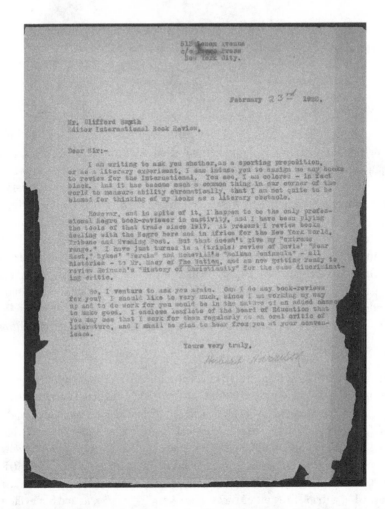

Figure 14.1. Hubert Harrison to Clifford Smyth, editor of the *International Book Review*, February 23, 1923. In this letter to Smyth, Harrison describes himself as "the only professional Negro book-reviewer in captivity," who has "been plying the tools of that trade since 1917." He adds that because he is "colored—in fact black" he can't help "thinking of my looks as a literary obstacle." Nevertheless, he sought to be assigned to review any books for the *International*. There is no indication that he received a response or was ever offered any work by Smyth or by the *International Book Review*. *Source:* Hubert H. Harrison Papers, Box 2, Folder 4, Rare Book and Manuscript Library, Columbia University Library. See https://dlc.library.columbia.edu/catalog/cul:z8w9ghx53d.

York's Town Hall. In his April 18 response Ely "hope[d] it is unnecessary to say that we do not discriminate on ground of race or color, [though] we are obliged to choose our lecturers with great care." He didn't "hold out much chance" of offering Harrison "an engagement" but assured him that the matter would receive "careful attention." Again, there is no indication Harrison was ever called upon by the League for Political Education.[9]

––––––––––

Sometime in the period between 1922 and March 1923, while writing and lecturing but having difficulty obtaining additional work and money, Harrison wrote personal notes entitled "The Control of Negro Sentiment" and "What I Think I Can Do." These notes focused on the current sociopolitical situation and on what role he thought he could play in reshaping public consciousness. They noted from the start that most "specific organs" of pulpit and press were, under the "present method of press control," simply a "reflection of news matter & favorable editorial opinion of [the] white press." Harrison paid particular attention to the Associated Negro Press (ANP), the Crusader News Agency (CNA), and the NAACP press releases. He considered the ANP of Claude Barnett as "Easy to influence, directly & indirectly" and the CNA of Cyril Briggs as a "Bolshevistic agency: [with] no visible means of support." The NAACP was in the midst of "a tremendous slump falling off in number of branches [by] more than 100 in a year, [including a] falling off in circulation of [the] *Crisis* [by] 40% & [a] great falling off in pop[ular]. support due to [the] failure of [the] Dyer Bill & aristocratic aloofness of N.A.A.C.P.'s social contact methods." Harrison described the "Garvey Propaganda" as "Dying: alive only in last strongholds" and barely mentioned the Urban League's *Opportunity* magazine. He thought that it was possible "to establish [a] benevolent liaison of publicity now along lines of spiritual assistance [that] would take ground from under [the] feet of present inefficient controllers of publicity." Harrison also thought he could represent "a point of view agreed on among Negroes" in public speeches, public writings, and in a newspaper, which he planned to edit soon, and he hoped to represent that point of view among "whites" in lectures for the Board of Ed, in articles "prepared for the corporation & released to newspapers," and by "direct influence on writings" (both his own ["in newspapers & magazines e.g. Book Reviews"], and those "issued by others").[10]

In his Board of Ed work Harrison was achieving considerable "success" as a lecturer, and in early March he was selected to speak at New York's City Hall. When the Board of Ed secured the Aldermanic Chamber as a lecture forum it selected him "as the first resident lecturer on its staff to lecture there." All previous speakers had been "national notabilities not on its staff"—and "white." In assigning Harrison, Dr. Crandall reportedly "passed over two professors from Columbia, one from New York university and two from New York city college," all Board of Ed staff members. Harrison's lecture, delivered on Saturday, March 10 at 1:30 p.m., was entitled "The Brother in Black." The hall was "packed," and there was "a generous sprinkling of Negroes from up-town." The lecture took "half-an-hour longer than usual," although "the entire audience remained to hear the questions asked and answers." This audience, similar to his audience at Cooper Union, gave "a rising vote of thanks—which was unusual." After the speech was delivered it was sent to the Edison Company at Newark for broadcasting from station WJZ, in compliance with a special request from the Edison Company.[11]

One who heard Harrison lecture in this period was M. F. Ruiz, a resident of Manhattan. Ruiz, who had corresponded with Harrison in 1922, wrote a March 19, 1923, letter to Harrison complimenting him on his lecture on "Pan-Americanism" and on his "sound ideas" and asking whether he would continue as a Board of Ed lecturer. Ruiz considered U.S. "overlordship over the South American entities" to be "irksome and ethically wrong," and he suggested that the contemporary Pan-American movement was "the result of the iniciation [sic] made by James G. Blaine in the grouping of the Pan-American Republics and the Pan America Conferences." Ruiz also wrote to Crandall on March 21 and suggested Harrison be used at "other centres." Crandall responded, saying that the Board of Ed used Harrison "in white centres" and would "do so increasingly."[12]

In March and April Harrison delivered a Board of Ed "Literary Lights of Yesterday and Today" lecture series, on Saturday evenings at 8:15 p.m. at the New York Public Library, 103 West 135th Street. The lectures included "Thomas Moore, the Poet of Irish Patriotism" (March 3), "Rider Haggard's African Romances (March 10), "Carlyle as a Spiritual Teacher" (March 17), "The Patriotic Poems of James Russell Lowell" (April 7), "The Mightiest Master of Musical Prose" (April 14), "The Romantic Writings of Sir Arthur Conan Doyle" (April 21), and "The Literature of the Victorian Age" (April 28). The April 28 lecture marked the completion of his first full lecture year (October–April) at the 135th Street Public Library.[13]

In late May Harrison received a letter from Crandall notifying him of his reappointment for two courses during the coming lecture season and offering him the option of changing the literary series. Harrison responded with the suggestion that his lecture series "be interspersed with two other series: on 'The History of Civilization' and 'The Outlines of Science.'" He apparently got his wish. His diary indicates that the lectures on "Literary Lights of Yesterday and Today" were interspersed with the "History" series until the middle of December and then with "Outlines."[14]

After the Board of Ed's spring term ended on April 19 Harrison planned to travel to Chicago in late June to lecture outdoors until the end of October. He contacted the Charles H. Kerr Publishing Company in Chicago, and the Proletarian Party considered using him "in the colored districts." In his diary he expressed the hope this would be his "last year of lecturing on the streets in summer." His plans met with difficulty, however, and he did not go to Chicago until 1924. Badly in need of income, he was forced to remain "on the streets" in New York.[15]

Dr. Crandall wrote to him on June 4 and enclosed wording he planned to use with Harrison's picture in a forthcoming Board of Ed lecture reel. In a written blurb Crandall described Harrison as a lecturer who spoke before "mixed audiences of whites and Blacks in Harlem" and sought "to bring about a more sympathetic understanding of his people." The blurb also mentioned that Harrison talked all over the city on "The Brother in Black."[16]

———————

In the summer of 1923 Harrison also delivered another radio talk. On Thursday, June 21, he lectured from handwritten notes on "The Negro and the Nation" for the Lecture Bureau of the Department of Education. In his diary he noted that this "unique" talk was broadcast on "the most powerful radio" station in the eastern United States, the American Telephone and Telegraph Co.'s WEAF.[17]

The important "The Negro and the Nation" manuscript opened with a discussion of how "Americans are a composite people" and have been such "from the beginning," when "Swede and Spaniard, Dutch and English, German, French and Irish" helped make the country. The current "melting-pot" included people "of many races: Nordic, Slav, Latin, Celt, Jew, Negro and Red Indians," who had "fought at various times to keep this country free and to make it great and united." Such efforts involved "mutual forbearance," understanding, and "the practice of the great democratic principle of 'live and let live.'" There was more, however, for the "different stocks" brought "custom and tradition from other climes" as well as "different habits of thought and feeling," all of which "had been built up into the spiritual fabric of their lives." In this way, explained Harrison:

> An American character, physically and spiritually one, is emerging from this complex of cultural forces; while at the same time each contributes its special gifts toward the building of that national character. The Irish, the Jew, the Italian have enriched America by being what they are and have themselves gained (from the normal interplay of forces which have been at work on them and around them). Thus the fingers of Fate have been shaping us on the iron anvil of necessity into the outline of a great experiment in democracy that will yet make these United States the herald of the Dawn that is to be.[18]

It was from this point of view that Harrison chose to discuss "The Negro and the Nation." He specifically did not want to treat "the Negro Problem" in "the traditional manner" of "sentiments and feelings" that might "stand in the way of that wider appeal." He preferred, instead, to examine "the relations between black and white in America" as if they were "neighbors who realize that they must live together and are willing to take counsel together in a neighborhood spirit as to the ways in which they may get the greatest value out of their relationship."[19]

In his manuscript he then started at "the beginning," explaining how, having preceded both "the Pilgrim Fathers" (by "more than a year") and the legislation of the first Virginia Assembly, the "American Negro antedates American democracy." In fact, he pointed out, "the Negro" was here "under the Spanish *conquistadores*" ("long before any of the people of Anglo-Saxon stock") and "is very near to being the oldest American in our melting pot." "Unfortunately," however, having "come here as a bond-servant, as the man farthest down," "the Negro" had "to do the nation's dirtiest work and get for it no more than food and blows." This, Harrison emphasized, was not "unfortunate for the black man alone"; "it was even more unfortunate for the white men who took part in that social evil and its tragic consequences. Because the white Americans, of 1791 acquiesced in the slavery of black Americans, white Americans in 1861 had to slay each other by hundreds of thousands. This was the moral retribution for 'following a multitude to do evil'—and our account is not yet closed."[20]

Harrison next focused on the important part the Negro played in the Civil War. He called particular attention (as he had done previously in the March 26, 1921, *Negro World*) to Lincoln's August 17, 1864, letter to Charles D. Robinson, of Washington, DC, in which Lincoln offered: "Take from us and give to the enemy the hundred and [thirty, forty, or fifty] eighty thousand colored persons now serving us as soldiers, seamen and laborers, and we cannot longer maintain the contest." If Lincoln's words in this letter "were true," Harrison observed, "then America would seem to owe a tremendous debt of gratitude to the Negro." In addition, there was the "Negro's long record of loyalty and patriotism"—as manifest in "the battlefields of the Revolutionary War, the War of 1812, the Civil War, the Spanish American and that other war in which he went 3000 miles to help 'make the world safe for Democracy.'" In that last war "the Fighting Fifteenth" [of New York] and the 8th Illinois, were decorated with the Croix de Guerre.[21]

This "co-operation with his white fellow-citizens" was not "restricted to the work of War," however. Similar efforts were extended in "our only bona-fide American music," "our world-beating cotton," "industrial activity," "ownership of homes," and "scores of banks and life-insurance companies." "Negroes" were "represented in education, religion, art, science and the professions" and had created "group-organizations" such as "churches and church schools, law-and-order leagues, fraternal-bodies and that greatest of Negro civic bodies, the National Federation of Colored Women's Clubs." These achievements came "in the face of repressions, restrictions and handicaps" including "Jim-Crow cars," "educational starvation," disfranchisement, and lynching, which were "imposed on no other race in America."[22]

All of this, wrote Harrison, pointed to "an eternal obligation resting on the white man of America to help and not hinder the black man in his efforts to make the best of himself." This was "not an obligation of charity but one of self-protection." Since "the white man brought the Negro here against his will," "all the Negro's problems" were, "therefore, of the white man's making." "Not until the white man has spent his last surplus dollar and exhausted the last faculty of his brain in the effort to lift up his weaker brother" could he "stand in the presence of infinite justice and complain of the ignorance of the black."[23]

While there were good signs of "the new spirit of neighbors" (even in Dixie), it was in the North that work must be done immediately. On one hand, it was "the duty of the white man of the north to set his face like flint against any attempt to make him give ground against invading prejudice" and to "holdup the hands of that better element in the south" so as to nourish its "nascent conscience." On the other hand, the North offered "the Negro better opportunities of civic advancement than the south"—including "all available facilities for education, opportunities for civic advancement, respect for his manhood and citizenship and safeguards for decency." Northern philanthropy even reached into the South "to help the Negroes there, as the Jeannes, Stokes and Carnegie funds have shown" and as the Roman Catholic Church was showing, by sending teachers "to build industrial schools and colleges." Even "individual Catholics like Sister Drexel of Philadelphia and Monsignor Burke of New York" were "spending themselves heroically in the service of the Brother in Black."[24]

Typical among Northern cities in terms of opportunities offered was New York. The "same high grade of education" was available, "not in segregated buildings but in the same class-rooms where early contact breeds civic goodwill and inter-racial tolerance and appreciation." The city's "two great free colleges," City and Hunter, were open to all, and their graduates could teach in the city's public schools. The city's dental and medical clinics were "available to Negro children as to others," and "the free milk stations" maintained by the municipal authorities aided "the lives of black babies as well as white ones." Politically, "the rights of civic participation; the ballot and elective representation" were "enjoyed by the Negro in New York" (who had elected three assemblymen and one alderman and who had a civil service commissioner and an assistant to the Corporation counsel). There were "over 40 Negro policemen and two detective sergeants, scores of school-teachers, and hundreds of Negro employees in the Municipal Civil Service," and Dr. Earnest L. Crandall, of the Department of Ed, had placed the speaker on his staff of lecturers. In New York, said Harrison, "the average Negro gets justice in the courts, freedom from mob-violence, freedom to work out his own salvation and the opportunity to rise in the world to the measure of his own abilities."[25]

Harrison emphasized that this "New York doctrine is the democratic doctrine" and that it is "not grudging justice but helpful co-operation." Because of it, "the Negro American may always have more to give whenever America calls." This led to Harrison's main thesis—a thesis that contrasted with what was propounded by Marcus Garvey:

> The Negro is an integral part of the American nation: not a mere incident or problem. The strands of his soul are woven into the fabric of our national existence and no mere demagogue can untwist them. The destiny of the American Negro lies in the future of America and no one need think that he will mortgage that future for the sake of a barbaric dream of African Empire with Dukes of Uganda and Ladies of the Nile. The present Negro population of Africa is quite able to work out its own salvation on the spot. And while the racial heart of the American Negro will always beat in response to the call of the blood, he recognizes that he is part and parcel of the American civilization. It is here that he has been the burden-bearer; having borne the burden and heat of the day he intends to receive the wages due him here for that work.[26]

Harrison also lectured outside of his Board of Ed schedule. One of his favorite venues was the Sunrise Club, a dining society with yearly dues of $1 that met each three weeks and two weeks, alternately. The club sought "to blend alert thought and sociability" and to bring together "men and women of all vocations, parties, creeds, nations and races." While its dinners sometimes featured debates and symposiums, its typical format included an opening presentation of thirty to fifty minutes, followed by several seven-minute speeches, and then closing remarks by the opening speaker. Wide ranges of opinion were welcomed, and members could bring guests. The club's secretary and driving force since its 1883 inception was Edwin C. Walker, of 211 West 138th Street.[27]

On Monday evening, March 19, "Dr." Harrison was the principal speaker before four hundred people at a Sunrise Club dinner at the Cafe Boulevard on Forty-First Street, near Broadway, in Manhattan. His talk was on "The Ku Klux Klan Past and Present." On April 3 he took "Gertie" (his friend from the Cosmopolitan Chiropractic School, Dr. Gertrude Miller-Faide) to a Sunrise Club dinner at the Hotel Continental. Hubert had seen Gertie on March 21, visited her at the house of a friend of hers, and "had a most enjoyable time . . . there from 11:30 to 4:30." In his diary he added, "Gertie *ist eine Wunder-Madchen!* [Gertie is a Wonder-Girl!] Her wonderful art completes her resemblance to Bee [an otherwise unidentified old and intimate friend] and caps the climax indeed."[28]

The April 3 Sunrise talk that Hubert and Gertie attended was by Mrs. Winifred Sackville Stoner, who spoke on "The Pilgrim's Script," which, as he noted in his diary, "might mean anything at all." She argued "we should join the League of Nations and help Europe to get upon its feet again" and "that all this sad world needs is just to sing the official songs of the 'joy-izers' and smile its griefs away." She set "her ideas in the key of rapt adoration of all the aristocratic virtues" and "adored Mussolini, the sadistic degenerate who heads the Fascist movement in Italy." Stoner "abhorred all Bolsheviks," a term she "used indiscriminately for all people who are poor and oppressed, all democrats and liberals, and all persons who couldn't qualify as stark reactionaries." In his diary Harrison noted that among those in attendance were the attorney Adolph Feldbloom, who sat at his table and described himself as "'the comic relief'" (though he "made some able and serious contributions to the discussion"); James F. Morton Jr.; Miss Ida Vera Simonton, an artist and recent traveler into the interior of Africa; Miss Elizabeth Ballou, of the *Brooklyn Daily Eagle* staff; and Mrs. Winifred Harper Cooley, "the able and witty chieftainess of the Moron Club." At the close of the affair Miss Simonton extended an invitation to Harrison and Dr. Faide to come to her studio on Friday evening.[29]

Vera Simonton's studio was at 24 East Fortieth Street, and Hubert was asked to bring "some colored people of your own intelligence and up-to-dateness" to a Friday evening get-together. She was to speak on her book *Personal Adventures in Savage Africa,* and she thought they might "learn something about the dark continent not contained in books or admitted by the white powers which rule it." Simonton mentioned that Dr. Moens, whom she hadn't seen in over a month (he had been knocked down by an automobile and was laid up for two weeks with an injured leg), had been by that afternoon for tea and "asked about" Harrison. She said he didn't look well and was "naturally, low spirited because of his unjust and unnecessary detention in this country."[30]

———

On April 14, 1923, less than two weeks before his fortieth birthday, Hubert wrote a poem entitled *"Post Multos Annos,"* which was probably intended for his wife, Lin:

> Take me on trust. I may not seem to be
> As good, as sugar-sweet as long ago
> When you and I did first begin to know

That love put apple-blossoms on the tree
Of Life whose fragrance was for you and me
A thing of joy forever; but I know,
Spite of shortcomings that torment you so,
That I still love you and that this must be
My fate forever. You and I are bound
Each to the other like daylight to the sun.
My soul and yours will always circle round
Each other's course where Love's race is run;
And not hell's depths nor heaven's heights can part
Soul's love from soul or my heart from your heart.[31]

A few weeks later, on April 30 at one-thirty in the morning, he began a book "at the end of my fortieth year, not intending it as a diary (which I also keep) but a book in which I can scribble from time to time *thoughts and ideas* as they occur to me." What he would call it would "be determined later," although he had already rejected "'Common Place Book'" because it was "not intended exclusively as a record of common-place thoughts and ideas." Rather, he described it "as an outlet for my less specially mental overflows: partly as a stylistic hippocampus or exercise-ground and partly as a series of dissolving views of life and things." Because at some future time he might "think it worth publishing (though not in its unpruned form)," he wrote only on one side of each sheet. "For the purposes of subjective record" he planned to date each entry, and, at the very outset, he appended two pages from a short collection of "Aphorisms and Reflections," which he had begun in December 1921. Whenever he ran "across another writer's expression of an idea or opinion" that he thought "worthy of a place in my own thoughts," he would "transfer it to my book."[32]

Samples of his entries for April 30, 1923, are of interest. He described "Saphead" as "a piece of current American slang the vulgar employ as an epithet to describe one whose mental machinery is perpetually out of gear. To save time they often shorten it by a syllable." After commenting, "God must have loved, fools because he made so many of them," he wryly noted "that it must have been a cynical wag who first described man as *Homo Sapiens*. Had he abbreviated the adjective by two syllables he would have achieved a perfect description of the animal."[33]

Harrison also discussed the "popular belief that 'murder will out'" (murder will become public and cannot remain undetected). It was, he thought, "psychologically akin to the beliefs of the superstitious people who erect an entire philosophy of faith on a dozen instances in which a dream fore-runs a reality with which it agrees, while purposely dropping out of the account the ten thousand instances in which it doesn't agree with the reality which it fore-runs."

Thus, "When murder doesn't out nobody keeps the account, but when it does everybody records it in the ledger which has a credit but no debit side." He quoted Sir Thomas Browne (1605–1682), an English physician and author of *Religio Medici* (which included confessions of a skeptic): "'Who knows whether the best of men be known or whether there are not more . . . dead to fame than ever stood recorded in the known account of Time?'"[34]

In May Harrison entered some insightful comments. Sparked by W. E. H. Lecky's "Biographical Introduction" to volume 1 of Thomas Carlyle's *French Revolution*, he wrote: "Character is more important than intellect, but genuine intellect is closely allied to character, for it shows itself chiefly in true insight into the facts of life." While reading Carlyle on the French Revolution and looking through Jules Michilet on May 31, he wrote "WITHOUT A GREAT ENTHUSIASM NO GREAT WORK WAS EVER DONE." He then again quoted Lecky: "The pride in good and thorough work is one of the best elements of character." Finally, he quoted from John Milton's 1637 poem *Lycidas* that

> Fame is the spur which the pure spirit doth raise
> (The last infirmity of noble mind)
> To scorn delight and win laborious days.[35]

On July 2, 1923, Harrison added additional "Notes and Aphorisms." He commented that "Johnson's old Boswell and I seem to have agreed on one point." In his introduction to the "Life of S[amuel]. J[ohnson]" his biographer James Boswell speaks of "the greatest man of any age, Julius Caesar." Harrison also cited John Fiske's *The Discovery of America*: "With everyone of them [the Spanish historians of Las Casas's time (1477–1566)] the nine digits seem to have gone on a glorious spree." He added, "The same was true of Marcus Garvey."[36]

Harrison's reference to Garvey came shortly after Garvey's June 19 conviction and June 21, 1923, sentencing for mail fraud. For most of the past year—after Garvey's June 1922 meeting with Edward M. Clarke, imperial wizard of the KKK, in Atlanta, and while he awaited trial, the criticisms against Garvey had grown, and intimidation and violence against his opponents had intensified. Such criticisms and intimidation are additional, important elements of the background to the critique of Garvey that Harrison had developed and would write about publicly. The bullying and violence against Garvey critics was evident as far back as the fall of 1919, when Domingo protested "the execrable exaggerations, stupidities, blundering bombast and abominable assininities [*sic*] of our black Barnum [Garvey]," and both he and the socialist Thomas Potter came under attack, which culminated in the spring of 1920, when they were "assaulted, kicked, and placed under arrest by Garveyites." Later that year, on August 22, a few hundred Garveyites invaded a tent revival meeting at West 138th Street chaired by the Reverend Adam Clayton Powell Sr. in response to a sermon critical of Garvey by Reverend Charles S. Morris, of Norfolk, Virginia.[37]

On September 5, 1922, A. Philip Randolph, another Garvey critic, received a package containing a human hand cut off below the wrist. The package was marked "From a friend, New Orleans," and contained a letter allegedly signed by the KKK and ordering Randolph to join the UNIA. Police at the 139th Street station indicated they suspected the package had been sent by a Garvey supporter. New Orleans, the origin of the package, is where the Rev. James W. Hood Eason, perhaps Garvey's foremost rival in the UNIA, would be assassinated four months later by Garveyites.[38]

W. E. B. Du Bois later reported that after criticizing Garvey he had received letters of unbelievable filth and was threatened with death by men who said they followed Garvey. The historian and journalist J. A. Rogers, in the context of noting strong similarities between Garveyism and fascism and Nazism, called attention to the movement's violent streak. Rogers also mentioned the calls to fierce nationalism and "racial purity," fascination with uniforms, appeals to crowd psychology, general anticommunism, impassioned oratory, and pageantry.[39]

The evening after the Randolph incident, the Rev. Gabriel E. Stewart, the former high chancellor of the UNIA, called on BI special employee Andrew M. Battle and said that he had written to Garvey in April regarding "the reckless manner in which Garvey was expending the organization's money." He also said that he believed "Garvey was mixed up in the matter of the human hand being sent to Philip Randolph through the mail." Finally, Stewart said that Garvey had been very foolish in his August 6 convention speech to remark that Chandler Owen and others who disagreed with him should "get themselves another job," since he could not be responsible for anything that might happen to them "because they might come up with a hand off or a leg or a broken head."[40]

In the wake of the Randolph incident, others gave testimony against Garvey. On September 6, 1922, Rev. J. D. Gordon, of Brooklyn, said he had provided all the papers he had in connection with the Garvey mail-fraud case, and though he did not want to take the witness stand, he did promise "to testify at any time the Government wanted him to," since he had concluded that Garvey was "a menace to the negro race." J. D. Brooks, of Newark, the former UNIA general secretary, had been arrested at Garvey's urging for allegedly stealing $400,000. After being found not guilty, he said he intended to sue Garvey for $100,000 for false arrest and defamation of character and added that he had traveled the country selling stock for the mythical *Phyllis Wheatley* and was ready and willing to testify at any time for the government against Garvey. James W. Hood Eason, the former "leader of American Negroes in the U.N.I.A.," wanted to testify on moneys he sent to Garvey by mail for Garvey's fraudulent stock sales. According to one Agent Amos, Eason and "hundreds of others" were willing to testify for the government.[41]

The opposition to Garvey continued to grow, and on September 11, 1922, the Friends of Negro Freedom, a Randolph- and Owen-led anti-Garvey group, held a meeting in Harlem at which Randolph, Eason, and J. Austin Norris spoke. Norris strongly criticized Garvey's June 25, 1922, meeting in Atlanta with Edward Young Clarke, the acting imperial wizard of the KKK.[42] Eason, who had been expelled from the UNIA for ninety-nine years and one day, went public with his criticisms, and the *New York Age* of October 14 quoted him as saying that he could have still been in the UNIA if he had kept his "mouth shut" and not told "the truth to the members of the association as to what has become of the nearly a million dollars collected from the members, with absolutely nothing to show for it on hand." Eason had reportedly gone to New Orleans in 1921 "and put the Garvey movement in good shape" and now claimed that Garvey owed him $5,000.[43] Walter White, assistant secretary of the NAACP, reportedly told Amos that Garvey was "doing more to hurt the negro than anyone has ever done" and that if he avoided jail it would be "the worst calamity the negroes have ever experienced."[44]

On October 27, 1922, the accountant Thomas P. Merrilees completed his "Summary Report of the Books and Records of the Black Star Line and UNIA" for the Department of Justice. It was to be used in the upcoming case against Garvey, and it called especial attention to "Unearned passage money" for the SS *Phyllis Wheatley*, noting that since "this boat was advertised to sail for West Africa on a given date in April, 1921, the collection of these monies was a palpable fraud." Another key point, which was included but not emphasized, was that the BSL accounts hid major deficits, which to Merrilees looked "very much like woeful misrepresentation, which is another way of saying fraud."[45]

Cyril Briggs's Crusader News Agency kept after Garvey. Its October 30, 1922, article "Black Star Line Has No Ships" described the furor created in New York by the publication of Garvey's testimony in the Bronx Supreme Court, where, on August 19, he admitted that the BSL had no ships and only had an interest in two boats—one, the *Kanawha*, which was abandoned in Cuba as a wreck, and the other, the *Shadyside*, a wreck "somewhere in New York Harbor." The Crusader News Agency also pointed with some pride to the fact that developing federal case against Garvey had grown out of the original *Crusader Magazine* exposure of advertising and selling passage on a "ghost steam ship," the "Phyl[l]is Wheatley." These matters had subsequently been developed into the charge "that Garvey used the mails to misrepresent and defraud."[46]

As the attacks continued, Garvey took more determined action. On November 9, 1922, he sent Esau Ramus, a former officer of the Philadelphia UNIA, to the New Orleans Division, with a letter of introduction. The St. Kitts–born Ramus, also known as John Jeffries and Prince, later said he was sent there to found a UNIA police division.[47]

As the opening of the Garvey case approached, one of the principal witnesses against Garvey, the Rev. James W. Hood Eason, was assassinated on January 1, 1923, in New Orleans. The *Times-Picayune* of January 2 reported that Eason, who was scheduled to have left for New York that morning to testify against Garvey, was "shot twice from behind by unidentified assailants as he was leaving church last night." Though shot in the head and back, he was able to describe the attack and reportedly claimed, "I am positive . . . that my assailants were acting on instructions to put me out of the way and prevent my appearing as a witness against Garvey at the trial. I have already been threatened several times."[48]

On January 5, 1923, two loyal Garvey followers, William Shakespeare and Constantine Fred Dyer, were arrested for the murder and charged with manslaughter. They would be indicted in New Orleans on January 30, convicted on March 22, and sentenced to eighteen to twenty years in the Louisiana State Penitentiary on April 2. Their appeal was turned down on April 2, but the Supreme Court of Louisiana remanded the case to Judge Frank T. Echezabal, of New Orleans, for retrial.[49]

In a January 6, 1923, report, BI agent Mortimer Davis wrote that several weeks earlier Eason had provided a statement on his connection with Garvey and that "he was looked upon as one of the Government's leading witnesses in the case." Agent Amos reported that Garvey learned of the Eason assassination within minutes by means of a telegram, and Davis claimed that Garvey reportedly said "upon hearing of it," "'that's the way they treat them in the West!'"[50]

Anti-Garvey sentiment intensified after the assassination. The *New York News* explained that the attack was the second on "star witness" Eason since he had severed relations with Garvey and concluded that the UNIA "must be routed out of the life of the people of this community and this country," since it was "more dangerous to the people of color than the Ku Klux Klan."[51] The *Negro World* editor Robert L. Poston reportedly told BI special employee Andrew M. Battle that Garvey had Eason killed. D. T. Tobias, former manager of the Forum at 131st Street and Seventh Avenue, said Garvey had Eason "knocked off" and had very foolishly stated around August 13 that he would not be responsible for any UNIA opponent who might "lose an eye, an arm, a leg, or head."[52] Battle reported on January 16 that several nights earlier Garvey bragged at Liberty Hall about Eason's death.[53]

As the start of Garvey's trial was delayed, eight prominent African Americans sent a letter of complaint to Attorney General Harry M. Daugherty, asking to have him deported. The signers included Harry H. Pace, president of the Pace Phonograph Corporation; Robert S. Abbott, editor and publisher of the *Chicago Defender*; John E. Nail, president of Nail & Parker, Inc., Real Estate; Dr. Julia P. Coleman, president of the Hair-Vim Chemical Co., Inc.; William Pickens, field secretary of the NAACP; Chandler Owen, coeditor of *The Messenger* and co–executive secretary of the Friends of Negro Freedom; Robert W. Bagnall, director of branches of the NAACP; and George W. Harris, member of the Board of Aldermen of New York City and editor of the *New York News*. Randolph, who had received the human hand in the mail, did not sign.[54]

The letter said they desired action because they wanted to counter the "erroneous conception held by many" that "Negroes try to cloak and hide their criminals." The "truth" was that "the great majority of Negroes" knew "that such criminals will cause increased discrimination against themselves." Their letter read in part:

> There are in our midst certain Negro criminals and potential murderers, both foreign and American born, who are actuated by intense hatred against the white race. . . . They have become so fanatical that they have threatened and attempted the death of their opponents, actually assassinating in one instance.
>
> The movement known as the Universal Negro Improvement Association has done much to stimulate the violent temper of this dangerous element. Its president and moving spirit is one Marcus Garvey, an unscrupulous demagogue who has ceaselessly and assiduously sought to spread among Negroes distrust and hatred of all white people. . . .
>
> The *Negro World* . . . sedulously and continually seeks to arouse ill-feeling between the races. Evidence has also been presented of an apparent alliance of Garvey with the Ku Klux Klan. . . .
>
> The U.N.I.A. is composed chiefly of the most primitive and ignorant element of West Indian and American Negroes. The so-called respectable element of the movement are . . . usually in search of "easy money." In short, this organization is composed in the main of Negro sharks and ignorant Negro fanatics.
>
> The organization and its fundamental laws encourage violence. In its constitution there is an article prohibiting office holding by a convicted

criminal, EXCEPT SUCH CRIME IS COMMITTED IN THE INTEREST OF THE U.N.I.A. Marcus Garvey is intolerant of free speech when it is exercised in criticism of him and his movement, his followers seeking to prevent such threats and violence.[55]

As "proof" the letter cited Charles S. Morris being threatened with bodily harm; attempts at bodily harm against W. Ashbie Hawkins by members of the Baltimore UNIA; attacks on Cyril Briggs and an anti-Garvey meeting at Rush Memorial Church by Garveyites; recent violence by members of the Philadelphia UNIA against Norris and Eason; physical attacks in Los Angeles against Noah D. Thompson, of the *Los Angeles Daily Express*, who reported adversely on the Garvey movement; a veritable riot in Cleveland when Dr. Leroy Bundy, Garvey's chief assistant, was asked for an accounting of funds; the attempted assault by Garveyites on Owen in Pittsburgh on October 23; attempts by Garveyites to intimidate Pickens in Toronto; and August death threats and meeting disruptions against members of the Friends of Negro Freedom.[56]

The letter added that Garvey's UNIA constitution, article 5, section 3, "condones and invites to crime" and cited yet other instances, including the UNIA official William Sherrill in Baltimore, on August 18, 1922, stating that "BLACK FOLK AS WELL AS WHITE WHO TAMPER WITH THE U.N.I.A. ARE GOING TO DIE"; an assault and razor slashing of S. T. Saxon, by Garveyites, in Cincinnati in October; and the January 1 assassination of Eason, whose dying words were quoted. The letter also quoted from Judge Jacob Panken in his remarks accusing Garvey of "preying upon the gullibility" of the people. The signers advocated "that the Attorney General use his full influence completely to disband and extirpate this vicious movement" and "that he vigorously and speedily push the Government's case against Marcus Garvey for using the mails to defraud," "in the interest of justice" and "as a matter of practical expediency."[57]

———

In a January 23, 1923, report, agents Davis and Amos described Eason's death as "the culmination of many threats which have been made against Government witnesses in this case." They cited the experiences of Mrs. Dorothy Lawson (a dressmaker who said she had invested her entire savings of $100 in BSL stock and then tried to retrieve it) and Captain Joshua Cockburn. Lawson was subpoenaed in the Garvey case and then had a revolver drawn and death threats made on her and her husband if they did not cease their attacks on Garvey. The convicted assailant was a member of Garvey's "secret service." On January 20 she was again molested by two men, one of whom she had seen outside Liberty

Hall. Captain Joshua Cockburn similarly reported that threats were made against him.[58]

Special Agent Battle, in his report of January 26, wrote that he had interviewed J. B. Yearwood, who said that he actually saw the letter given to Ramus by Garvey when he was sent to New Orleans; that it was absolutely true that Ramus was the third party in Eason's killing; that a telegram had actually come to Garvey after the shooting; and that Garvey had paid $60, which was listed as bond money in the UNIA books. Sydney DeBourg said that the telegram was sent by Ramus from New Orleans.[59] J. Edgar Hoover in a January 27 memo indicated that "Ramus, made a mysterious trip to New Orleans" and that Eason "was murdered by three Garvey men, two of whom he identified before he died. Ramus got away, but the others are now held."[60] BI agent Harry D. Gulley, in charge of the New Orleans office, reported that E. Strain said "she was present at the home of Cornelius Dyer on January 3rd, 1923 when Esau Ramus entered the rooming house . . . and in her presence stated that he had killed Eason."[61]

Agent Mortimer Davis, in his report of February 1, 1923, wrote that on January 25 Garvey, along with his attorney William C. Matthews, went to the office of U.S. Attorney Maxwell S. Mattuck and held an informal conference that also included him and Inspector Oliver Williamson. Garvey maintained that "a group of willful men has caused the Government to bring this unfounded charge against him." He reportedly admitted mailing the circular with the picture of the SS *Phyllis Wheatley*. The following day Mattuck presented the matter to the grand jury, with Inspector Williamson as his witness. The indictment contained eight counts and named as defendants Garvey, Elie Garcia, Orlando M. Thompson, and George Tobias.[62]

On February 14 Davis reported that the attorney (and close friend of Eason) J. Austin Norris, of Philadelphia, advised him that Esau Ramus's correct name was John Jeffries and that he was hiding in Detroit, as indicated by a letter he sent to his wife, Mary Prince, in Philadelphia. Norris brought a sample of Ramus's handwriting to show that he had written an anonymous letter to the *Chicago Defender*, published on February 3, purportedly from Eason's murderer. A man named Dixon, who was assisting agents, also confidentially reported that Elie Garcia had told him that before Ramus left New York for New Orleans in the fall he was given $100 by Garvey, who, as a matter of course, sent him to Garcia to receive the money order. Garcia also reportedly said that five days after Eason's shooting Ramus again came to the office, and Garvey gave him another money order for $60, which Garcia transacted.[63] Six days after Davis's report, Ramus was apprehended in Detroit by the Detroit office of the BI. He was arrested for Eason's murder.[64]

The BI came to believe that Ramus, the low-level UNIA official sent to the New Orleans division by Garvey, was the real murderer. Garvey publicly denied any involvement in the matter, but publicity around the murder negatively affected the image of both Garvey and the UNIA.[65]

Battle, in his report of April 27, wrote that he had interviewed Mrs. T. Parris, 117 West 142nd Street, New York, who said she was one of the first to buy stock in the BSL. She also gave $45 to help raise money to buy the *Phyllis Wheatley* and had given additional money to buy oil and linen for it; she was currently packing her furniture and planning to go to Africa. She said she would willingly tell everything she knew about Garvey. She had signed a petition in 1922 finding no fault with Garvey, who, at that time, she did not believe was crooked. She said she was now convinced of his guilt and that nearly everyone who had signed that petition was now against Garvey.[66]

Jeffries (Ramus), who had been moved to New York on another matter, was interviewed by Davis and Amos on May 7, 1923, at the Tombs, New York City's prison. He said that while in Philadelphia in 1922 he received a letter from Garvey stating that Eason was to speak there and that "his meeting must be broken up or he must not return to New York alive." Jeffries and members of the African Legion succeeded in breaking up the meeting, but Eason was not harmed. Subsequently Jeffries was informed that New York police were looking for him, so he came to New York and saw Garvey, who advised him to proceed to New Orleans and change his name. Garvey gave him $100 from the treasury of the UNIA for the trip, and in New Orleans he received a letter signed by Garvey informing him that Eason was to speak there on a certain date and instructing him that "Eason has turned State's evidence against him [Garvey] and must not be allowed to return to New York alive." Jeffries said he showed this letter to Shakespeare and Dyer as well as to other members of the African Legion. On May 7, Jeffries told Amos and Davis that Dyer was the gunman, accompanied and assisted by Shakespeare. Jeffries added that he destroyed Garvey's letter, as instructed in the letter itself. Mary Prince (formerly of New York but now whereabouts unknown) could prove all of this and might have possession of the letter and other papers.[67]

Agent Davis, in his report of May 10, wrote that in his report of April 27 he had noted that Esau Ramus, alias James Jeffries, had pleaded guilty to first degree assault, was very anxious to talk, and was the subject of a writ of habeas corpus in the Southern District of New York. Jeffries subsequently appeared in the office of Assistant U.S. Attorney Mattuck on the writ and told Mattuck and agents Amos and Davis that he was willing and anxious to testify against Garvey but wanted a promise of a suspended sentence. Mattuck advised him that no promise could be made, but he would speak to Judge Talley in Part I, General Sessions, where Jeffries was to be sentenced, to the effect that he had assisted the government. Jeffries agreed to have his sentence postponed until the BSL case was heard. On May 3, on request of Mattuck, he obtained a postponement.[68]

———

On May 18, 1923, the government, having consolidated indictments in Garvey's trial for mail fraud, was ready to proceed.[69] The trial opened before Judge Julian William Mack on May 21. As previously discussed (see chapter 12), at first Garvey had been indicted alone, but the government withdrew the original indictment and, to avoid dismissal on a technicality, submitted two new ones after realizing that the BSL was a corporation, not a private firm. The new indictment named as president, Garvey; vice president, Orlando Thompson; secretary, Elie Garcia; and treasurer, George Tobias. Garvey was clearly the target; the others were eventually acquitted. There had been a number of anonymous threats against various government witnesses, and agents Amos and Davis and Special Employee Battle, upon a request by Mattuck, cooperated with the U.S. marshals in tracking down these threats and affording protection to subpoenaed persons. Among the incidents was a May 23 threat on the life of Capt. Joshua Cockburn, made in the federal building after he testified for the government against Garvey. Richard E. Warner, who testified on May 21, reported that his wife had told him that on the night of May 22 two Garveyites were hanging around his house, saying they were there to "get" Warner. Agent Davis was told by Hugh Mulzac, who testified under government subpoena from Baltimore, that he and government witness John Sydney de Bourg had been threatened. Mulzac without hesitation pointed out Linous Charles, whom the deputy marshal placed under arrest. When Judge Mack returned to court, he excused the jury and heard the charges against Charles, found him guilty of criminal contempt, and sentenced him to six months, which was reduced to two months. Mulzac and de Bourg stated that they had been threatened that if they testified against Garvey, he would "get them" if it took the rest of his life. Mack Davis also reported there were "many rumors that Garvey sympathizers have been carrying weapons while attending the trial."[70]

The key government witness turned out to be Benny Dancy, a cleaner at Pennsylvania Station in New York. He stated that he had heard Garvey speak, read the *Negro World*, and had purchased fifty-three BSL shares. Subsequently he received letters from the UNIA and Negro Factories Corp. as well as solicitations and circulars for investments in ships from the BSL. He identified one particular envelope, marked "Black Star Line," as one that was mailed to him at his Brooklyn home. The prosecution charged that the BSL had mailed circulars advertising the sale of shares in a ship it did not own. Their proof centered on a circular identical to one they said was sent to Benny Dancy, which contained a doctored photograph of a ship with the name *Phyllis Wheatley* super-imposed over the original name, *Orion*—a ship the BSL did not own.[71]

On June 15 Garvey made the final appeal in his case, on June 16 Shakespeare and Dyer lost the appeal to their case (after a new trial in 1924 they would be found innocent and freed), and on June 19 Garvey was found guilty by jury of using the mails to defraud by advertising the sale of shares in a ship that was not owned by the BSL. Garvey's conviction was covered under the third count of the first indictment, which held that on or about December 13, 1920, "for the purpose of executing said scheme," Garvey placed in a post office in New York's Southern District "a certain letter or circular enclosed in a postpaid envelope addressed to 'Benny Dancy, 34 W. 131 St., N.Y.C.'" The principal evidence was an empty BSL envelope addressed to Dancy, which had allegedly contained the circular and was postmarked at College Station on December 21, 1920. All the other defendants were acquitted. Garvey was sentenced to five years in Atlanta Penitentiary and had to pay a $1,000 fine and the costs of the suit.[72] Efforts at a pardon in the 1980s did not succeed, nor have subsequent efforts.[73]

———

On June 21, 1923, the day that Garvey was sentenced after being found guilty on Monday, June 19, Harrison wrote in his diary that "today Marcus Garvey was sentenced by Mr. Justice Mack to 5 years in a Federal prison for using the mails to defraud his 'fellow-men of the Negro race.'"[74] Then, using a July 1 date-line, he wrote a major piece on Garvey entitled "Marcus Garvey at the Bar of United States Justice" for the Associated Negro Press. This piece, with a different title, also appeared in the *Kansas City Call* of July 5, 1923. Nahum Daniel Brascher, editor-in-chief of the Associated Negro Press, wrote to Harrison on July 3 thanking him "for [the] excellent story on Marcus Garvey" and included a copy of its release.[75]

Harrison's article explained that on Monday night in the Federal Court in New York

> the curtain went down on the last act of the drama staged by Marcus Garvey, self-styled "Provisional President of Africa" and head of the "Distinguished Service Order of Ethiopia", president of the "Black Star Line", the Negro Factories Corporation and President-General of the Universal Negro Improvement Association and African Communities League, Managing Editor of the *Negro World*, the *Negro Times*, and the *Black Man*, etc., etc.

The assistant U.S. district attorney for the second district of New York, Maxwell Mattuck, "had conducted the government's side of the case with commendable zeal and skill." Harrison noted that "it was somewhat of a surprise to the score of people who were present in the court-room at half-past ten that all the other defendants who were represented by colored lawyers were acquitted while Garvey who had discharged his colored lawyer and retained two white ones 'for advice' while he conducted his own case in the full glow of dramatic publicity, was convicted." Harrison observed, however, that "it might have been expected," since "all through his public career, Garvey had loved the limelight. He loved to be the center of everything. He has always wanted to be the 'whole cheese,' and the jury took him at his own estimate."[76]

Harrison described Garvey's trial as eminently fair:

No sane person who sat in the courtroom can deny that he got a fair trial. In fact, the judge strained both his temper and the court's rules of procedure to give him more leeway than had ever been granted to any lawyer. In his charge to the jury he was scrupulously fair and even fore-bore to press portions of the case which told against the defendant. When touching on the question of the credibility of Garvey, he drew the jury's attention to the fact that a bishop had testified that Garvey's reputation for veracity in the West Indies was "doubtful," he refrained from pointing out that it was Garvey himself who had subpoenaed the bishop as a character witness. But the Judge's fairness did not weigh with Garvey, who when he was ordered to be taken to the tombs [prison], broke out into an undignified tirade of foul abuse and low language describing both Judge and district attorney as "damned dirty Jews" and threatened that he would make them suffer for his conviction.[77]

"Naturally," wrote Harrison, "bail was denied," Garvey's motion for appeal was set aside, and "the ruler of over '400 million Negroes' was remanded to the Tombs prison to await his sentence to a term of years in a Federal penitentiary, having been convicted on the charge of swindling members of his race by means of the marine bucket-shop known as the 'Black Star Line' whose fleet of ships to sail the seven seas existed mainly on paper and in the mind of Marcus Garvey." Harrison harshly described how "the S.S. Yarmouth," which, according to William H. Ferris, "was 'soon to be rechristened['] the 'Frederick Douglass' was never rechristened, but went back to its original owners because it was not quite paid for; the 'Shadyside' was a bluff, and the S.S. Phyllis Wheatley, [was] a phantom ship which was never bought nor seen, but on which Garvey by false and misleading advertisements had collected thousands of dollars paid in as passage-money to Africa and as stock sales."[78]

Harrison was aware of the depth of feeling of Garvey's followers and the inherent danger in their worshipful devotion.

[To] that type of West-Indian peasant from the hoe-handle and cow tail brigade to whom Garvey is a god, and whose intolerant fanaticism may still compromise the thousands of intelligent and respectable West Indians in the United States; these people still believe that Garvey never did a crooked thing in his life. To them the receipts of the poor people for passage money, the advertisements in the *Negro World* of sailings of the Phyllis Wheatley, put off month by month from January to November 1921, the printed lies telling of 20,000 delegates to a convention in which anyone who could count would find only a hundred; to them these facts don't exist and they go about threatening to shoot even the lawyer whom Garvey discharged, as if [Cornelius W.] McDougall [McDougald] fired himself to injure Garvey, and making dangerous statements which, if the authorities choose to notice them, will cause the closing of Liberty Hall and the suppression of Garvey's African legion as dangers to domestic tranquility.

Harrison added: "The District Attorney of New York already has his eye on them."[79]

Garvey's program, however, had merit. Harrison's discussion of the "original program of the Universal Negro Improvement Association" (see chapter 7) was "based on the belief that Negroes should finance the foundations of their future and not go begging to the white race either for help, leadership or a program," and Harrison maintained that this "had been the program of the Liberty League" from which "Garvey appropriated every feature that was worth while in his movement."[80]

Harrison emphasized (see chapter 7) that "the B.S.L. was designed as a money-getter for Garvey."[81] Garvey "sold passage to Africa (receipts for such passage money were presented during the trial) on the ship which he knew didn't exist, and this was one of the things that got him in trouble." Harrison felt that

the fact that the jury convicted him on one count only doesn't mean that they found him guiltless on the others. They knew that a conviction on five counts would have made him liable to five years on each count and they had no desire to press him too hard. His trial was one of the fairest in the annals of New York. The Judge allowed him every latitude. Yet when the jury found him guilty he proceeded to accuse both the court and the public prosecutor of collusion with other dirty Jews—just as he had accused Kilroe, Grey, and Warner in 1919 and 1920. Yet on the 21st of August, 1920, he published a retraction in the *Negro World* in which he admitted that he had lied about them.[82]

To Harrison, as previously noted, Garvey had "a great talent for lying."[83]

In reviewing Garvey's history in the United States Harrison commented, "When Garvey came to America," he "was so poor that some of us had to give him food and clothes. He wouldn't work, not he. He had discovered a method of living without working." Now, "today, he is well-fed, well-groomed, and well-off. In his flat for which he pays a rent of $150 a month, there are splendid couches swinging by chains from the ceiling. Yet this paranoiac has the nerve to talk about his 'sacrifices for the race,' although he refrains from telling what those sacrifices consist of."[84]

Harrison elaborated further:

Garvey is a worshiper of Garvey. On the "Yarmouth" he had two life-sized oil-paintings of himself. His office and his apartments contain dozens of such paintings. It was his instinct for self-worship that prompted him to appropriate the entire front page of the *Negro World* each week with his stupid declamations addressed to his "fellowmen of the Negro Race." It reduced the circulation of the paper from 50,000 to 3,000 copies; but Garvey didn't care. Instead of putting news in his paper he gave the readers his speeches. He quarreled with every person he ever worked with unless they were willing boot-lickers and glorifiers of himself. His insane egotism and jealousy were boundless. In 1920 he paid $100 *a day* for 31 days to [Cyril] Crichlow and [Isaac Newton] Braithwaite, stenographers, to report all the twaddle talked at the first convention. He promised to bring out the reports of that pow-wow in volumes that would startle the world. But although he started a fund for that purpose and said in his paper that the book was in the press, it never did come out.[85]

To Harrison the Garvey Case would "go down in history as a splendid illustration of the race's gullibility." It was "not so much Garvey's fault, but his people's," for "a leader who would have made no promises that he couldn't keep, no statement that wasn't true, who always accounted for every penny and who made less whoopin' and hollerin'" would "not have appealed to them." Garvey "gave them what they wanted." Harrison then quoted from *The Emperor Jones*, which he considered "a fine picture of the psychology of the whole Garvey movement":

Smithers—And I bet you got yer pile o' money in some safe place.
    Jones—I sho' has! And it's in a foreign bank where no pusson don't ever git it out but me, no matter what come. You din't s'pose I was holdin' down dis Emperor job for de glory in it, did you? Sho'! De fuss and glory part of it, dat's only to turn de heads o' de low-flung bush niggers dat's here. Dey wants de big circus show for deir money. I gives it to 'em, an' I gits de money. De long green; dat's me every time.[86]

Thus "at the end of the spectacular career of *our* Emperor Jones," Judge Mack put up "a sign marked 'Five Years in Prison for Fraud.'" Harrison, however, did not think this would be the end, and he

> look[ed] forward confidently to some winter morning two or three years from now when Convict No. [ ] will point his finger majestically at a white warden and bellow, "Ho, there valet! Take a message to the Provisional Field Marshall of my African Legions and tell him to order out the Tenth and Eleventh Army Corps, for I have it in mind to hold a high field dry and general review. Quick, begone!" Then they will take that convict with the light of developed insanity in his eyes and put him in a room where he can't hurt his head when he hits it against the walls—because those walls will be padded. This may seem a bold prediction today. But wait three years and see.[87]

Under the heading of "Religion and Education" Harrison reviewed two works by Upton Sinclair in the May 2, 1923, *Amsterdam News*. He described Sinclair as "the greatest propagandist of our day"—one who sometimes "writes briefs in behalf of the workingman," sometimes "tweaks the nose of the capitalist class and exposes the corruption of the press," and sometimes "turns the thunders of Mount Sinai against the faithless servants of the Christ." In "every instance" Sinclair was a "doughty and swashbuckling journalist," and "everything" that he wrote was "journalism."[88]

In *They Call Me Carpenter: A Tale of the Second Coming* Sinclair pictures "what a world of Christian Pharisees would do to Jesus if he ventured back into it" and associated "with common working people and the riff-raff of the earth." In this story he is "hunted by the American Legion, rejected by the Church, and despised by the rich and respectable," until, "in sheer despair," he "goes back to the sad but safer task of being a silent symbol in the stained glass window of a rich man's church." He then is loved "so long as he remains in the Bible or the gorgeous decorations of a Christless creed." Harrison judged this "a sad story" that "glitters cheaply with rhetorical tinsel" while its "obvious propaganda murders its art." Nevertheless, its "punch" was "like the left hind leg of a Georgia mule!" and it would "grip" anyone "interested in religion."[89]

The Goose Step: A Study of American Education revealed the extent to which "famous colleges like Harvard, Columbia and Yale are controlled by the millionaire masters of everything else." Harrison thought Sinclair's thesis was "sound enough," but "some of his specific aspirations" wouldn't "hold water." He did demonstrate that "in most of the large colleges and some of the smaller ones students are not allowed to learn nor professors to teach anything except

Figure 14.2. "When You Want a Book Place Your Order with Hubert H. Harrison," n.d.

Hubert Harrison was an extraordinary bibliophile with wide-ranging interests, and he was able to make some money through the sale of books. As indicated in this broadside the types of books he offered, in addition to searches for rare books, included "Books on the Negro, History, Sociology, Economics, Literature, Religion, Psychology, Fiction, Poetry; Text Books of Travel and Dictionaries." Among the pallbearers at Harrison's funeral in December 1927 were such outstanding bibliophiles as Richard B. Moore, Arthur Schomburg, and George Young. *Source:* Hubert H. Harrison Papers, Box 16, Folder 46, Rare Book and Manuscript Library, Columbia University Library. See https://dlc.library.columbia.edu/catalog/cul:mw6m905s2n.

what the lawyers, bankers and businessmen on their boards of trustees think safe and sweet for them." As such, the book was recommended to both "leaders" and "those who are lead."[90]

Harrison's scheduled May 10 lecture before the North Harlem Community Forum on "Books and How to Read Them" prompted a letter from Robert Reiss, of the *Harlem Home News*. Reiss requested a copy of the lecture for use in the paper's book section and asked Harrison to please "keep in touch" regarding "other literary activities of your section of the city."[91]

On May 26 Harrison was a specially invited guest of the Mayor's Committee on Celebration of the Twenty-Fifth Anniversary of the Greater City of New York at its Silver Jubilee Parade of the Municipal Departments. He was also a guest at the June 16 dinner for the same Mayor's Committee at the New York State Conference of Mayors at the Waldorf-Astoria. Also, on May 29, "D. Sc." Harrison was a guest of honor of Sigma Tau Sigma.[92]

The summer of 1923 approached in what Harrison described in his diary as "a most distracting" manner. May had been "unusually cold." It was "so cold" at the end of May that he "was forced to take off" his "mohair summer suit" and get back into his "cutaway-coat-suit," which he wore as his "ordinaire on the advice of Casper Holstein."[93]

June 14, 1923, was the date of one of Harrison's more memorable literary social events. That evening he attended at the Hotel Brevoort a testimonial dinner honoring the book publisher Horace B. Liveright for his role in the successful fight against the so-called Clean Books Bill, which Harrison correctly pointed out was "a piece of legislation designed to terrorize publishers and writers of books." "Dr." Harrison sat at the guest table along with the toastmaster, Park Commissioner Franklin D. Gallatin; the state senator and future mayor of New York, James J. Walker; the writers Fannie Hurst and Anita Loos; the journalist Elmer Davis; Frederick W. Hume; Walter Guest Kellogg; Dr. Charles L. Fleisher; the cartoonist Ryan Walker and his wife; and a host of literary personages including Heywood Broun, the critic and *New York World* columnist; Burton Rascoe, the literary editor of the *New York Tribune*; Mr. and Mrs. Horace Liveright; Mr. and Mrs. Ludwig Lewisohn; Mr. and Mrs. Carl Van Vechten; Theodore Dreiser; Henry L. Mencken; B. W. Huebsch, the publisher; Konrad Bercovici; and the author/editor Charles Hanson Towne. Speakers included Gallatin, Walker, Broun, Rascoe, and Harrison.[94]

Rascoe, in his column in the *Tribune* the following day, described how at the dinner Mencken had asked him for an introduction to "Dr. Hubert Harrison." Within a short while "Dr. Harrison was the center of the most serious discussion of the evening" as "Dreiser, Broun, Towne and Fleisher came and talked with him." Mencken, chewing on his cigar and hitching his trousers, told Harrison "that the trouble with negroes in the South is that 'they are always trying to prove that they are as good as whites.'" He said this was "bad tactics" and "won't get them anywhere." "What they have to do is set about proving not that they are as good as the whites but better." Mencken didn't feel there would be "any difficulty establishing their case," since "the Southern whites in the mass are an awful mess of idiots." He added, however, "another trouble with the nigger is that their defenders, propagandists and apologists are too indignant." As an example he cited "this fellow, Du Bois," who "hurts the nigger's case every time because he is always getting sore." Mencken then argued: "To be indignant is a confession of inferiority; it is to be licked from the start: the superior man retains his advantage by never losing his temper. The cultured niggers ought to be having some fun at the expense of the illiterate and imbecile whites instead of setting up walls like Du Bois."[95]

In his column Rascoe also wrote that Dreiser "tried vainly to convince Dr. Harrison that the Ethiopian Art Players were the finest actors ever seen on Broadway and that their version of 'Salome' had every other white production" beat badly (and he claimed to have "seen them all"). According to Rascoe, Harrison regretted to say that he didn't know much about Broadway productions, "but if what you say is true, that the negro players are better than the whites," it was "distressing evidence as to the low state to which the American theater has fallen" because "the negro players' 'Salome' was rotten." When Dreiser countered that "the negro's voice is superior to the white man's. . . . It is more musical and more resonant," Harrison was again "sorry to disagree." He offered, "On the contrary, the negro's voice is a nasal monotone. His speech is slovenly. He garbles and mushes his words, without a proper regard for their texture, their sound or meaning. The negro is too lazy to pronounce his words correctly. What the whites mistake for charming idiosyncrasy is simply a vice—mental shiftlessness, a refusal to take the trouble to give syllabic stress and nuance to words." After listening to such conversations, Rascoe "took a cab home," having "enjoyed myself as thoroughly as at any party."[96]

Late on the evening of the dinner-table discussion on Black actors, in an elaboration of his earlier comments, Harrison handwrote eight pages on "The Negro Actor on Broadway: A Critical Interpretation by a Negro Critic." He explained that the Ethiopian Art Theatre, which was "a company of actors and not a play-house," had "come and gone" and had "furnished in the interim a seven day sensation for sophisticated Broadway." He had seen both their plays, *The Chip Woman's Fortune* and Oscar Wilde's *Salome*, and critical opinion was divided only on *Salome*. It was generally agreed that in *The Chip Woman's Fortune* the "Negro actors achieved as notable a success" as had Charles Gilpin in *The Emperor Jones*. Given this general consensus he thought a "brief estimate of the relative merits of both plays by a writer of the race to which the players belong" was "in order."[97]

Harrison began his analysis by reasoning that "on general human and artistic grounds, a company of Negro actors on Broadway" was "simply a company of actors, and the racial identity of the performers would seem to have no value in the esthetic estimate of their work, provided that they were at home in the English language and the conventions of the American stage." But, this was "reasoning *in vacuo*," and the fact was "that a company of Negro actors on Broadway" was "an unusual phenomenon." This "special fact" had to be explained "on special grounds" that "take into consideration the expectations of the world of white critics, playgoers and the public at large in the light of their previous contact, with Negro actors in the legitimate drama." Since a play was "a projection of life and life's forces onto the stage," as were "the opinions, judgments and the other reactions of human minds in regard to the play and the players," it was clear that "these Negro actors and their acting" were "new things which must *justify* themselves." Therefore, the first question to be addressed was: "What was the contribution, the new and unique thing, which these players contributed to 'Broadway'?"[98]

The Chip Woman's Fortune was "a Negro play, conceived by a Negro playwright [Willis Richardson], presenting a characteristic Negro situation, with a distinct racial atmosphere and background," and in this sense it was "something which Broadway as such did not have." For that reason it ranked "higher than . . . 'Salome,'" which was "distinctively a hot-house product" dealing with "hot-house passions, situations and characters" in a "strongly decadent" atmosphere. Harrison felt it wasn't necessary "to argue that Negro actors are either temperamental or artistically unable to present such an exotic as capably as white actors" because "even if they had done it better their achievement would still not be as valuable a contribution to Broadway as 'The Chip Woman's Fortune.'" To him, it was "obvious that any group of workers can do more and better work on their own ground with materials native to their experience than they can on alien ground with alien materials."[99]

After discussing "the argument on general critical grounds," he moved to specifics. Since *The Chip Woman's Fortune* was "surprisingly thin" (it concerned "an incident in the daily life of a Negro worker's family which was living beyond its means"), it was "the acting, and the acting only, that gave this thin and feeble theme life, depth and poignancy." Among the performers, Harrison was most impressed by the work of Miss Evelyn Preer, who "revealed herself as an actress of power, originality and imagination." The "mere reading of her lines was a revelation of the range and reach" of her "art," which was unlike any seen "since the palmy days of [the famed Helena] Modjeska and Eleanor Duse." Her performance was "a study in tonality and nuances" and "one of the memorable achievements of the American stage." In her physical presentation, she "lifted Broadway's art of two-dimensional acting into the body, breadth and depth of three dimensions." She "embodied all that there was of the whimsical, the humorous, the sordid, pathetic and tragic in the character and its surroundings and circumstances," and "what she did, as art," would "never escape from the memory of those who have seen it." Sydney Kirkpatrick, "the impecunious husband," was "adequate—but no more"; Laura Bowman's rendition of the old chip woman was "excellent." In sum Harrison evaluated *The Chip Woman's Fortune* as "great as art and high in interpretive quality." It "made Broadway realize the novel possibilities that lie in Negro life apart from its mountebank moments" and "suggested that no white actors anywhere can equal Negro actors in the interpretation of Negro life." If Broadway took "these two lessons to heart," it would be "splendidly benefitted."[100]

Salome was a difficult interpretation, and Harrison commended the Ethiopian Art Theatre for its effort. When he saw the play "it suffered from poor and imperfect lighting," and Kirkpatrick's work as Herod "was markedly uneven" and "a cardinal error" in understanding of the play. Regarding the female leads he felt that Miss Bowman offered a very effective rendering of Herodias but that Miss Preer's Salome was "not as good as her rendering of the Negro wife in 'The Chip Woman's Fortune.'"[101]

Overall, Harrison judged the presentation of *Salome* as "good rather than great," and he maintained, as he said to Theodore Dreiser, "that there are at least ten white companies on Broadway that could do it as well." "But not one of them," in his opinion, "could even come near to the flawless perfection of 'The Chip Woman's Fortune.'" It was in "this dramatic gem, rather than in the more ambitious *piece de resistance*, [that] the Negro actors of the Ethiopian Art Theatre justified to the full their temporary presence on Broadway." Harrison concluded that "if white producers want to be fair to the histrionic gifts of the American Negro; if they wish to give Broadway a genuine opportunity to judge of the dramatic richness of Negro life and the possibilities of the enrichment of the resources of the American stage from that source," they would "turn to pieces like 'The Chip Woman's Fortune' and Ridgely Torrence's 'Granny Maumee' and 'The Rider of Dreams,'" for in such plays they would find "the basis and justification for a real Negro theater."[102]

A little over a month after the Liveright dinner Harrison reviewed Ernest Howard Culbertson's *Goat Alley* in the July 18 *New Republic* under the heading "Caliban in the Slums." Culbertson, a "white" playwright, had produced a play with a Black cast, and Harrison began by observing that when Rudyard Kipling "let loose on English readers a shoal of stories about Indian life which were clever, pungent and delightful, every literary critic who had never been to India went into ecstasies over 'the convincing realism' of their local color." "No one," however, "asked the Indian anything." He didn't complete "that apologoue," but he used it to move into his comments on Culbertson's "drama of Negro life," which "failed on the stage."[103]

Though reviewers such as H. L. Mencken, George Jean Nathan, and Ludwig Lewisohn swore that *Goat Alley* was "true to life and even true to art," Harrison "courteously but explicitly" chose to "deny" this. The first act was "too long, loose and erratic," and the dialogue grasped "blindly for the trail of the theme." The play was "top-heavy," and the dialect "pure blind guess-work," although it might look "correct" to those who studied "Negro English in the pages of [the humorist of Southern life] Octavus Roy Cohen."[104]

Harrison was aware that the critic had to "leave to the creative artist free-dom of choice in the selection of his materials," but he nevertheless felt that the "unrelieved moral, physical, and spiritual squalor of the picture of Negro life in Washington" painted by Culbertson did not correspond to reality any more than did the dialect. While there was a "sincerity of his striving" regard-ing characters such as Sam and Lucy Bell Dorsey, played by Evelyn Ellis, whose love was "sweet and pure and passionate" before "bursting pathetically into flower on a reeking dung-hill," and while "every one of the types presented undoubtedly exist[ed]," *Goat Alley* didn't work as "either as art or life." Harri-son concluded that "inaccurate observation and incompetent transcription" stood "in the way of its acceptance as a great, good, or even worth-while play."[105]

———

Shortly after his *Goat Alley* review, Harrison and Paul Jones, a professional lec-turer, were the first two public speakers arrested under New York City's new May 23, 1923, ordinance requiring that an American flag no smaller than thirty-six inches by forty-eight inches be displayed "at every meeting, parade, etc. held by local organizations." On Friday, July 27, Officer Herbert Kennedy charged them with violating section 24, chapter 23, of the city ordinances for displaying emblems only sixteen inches long and ten inches wide as they spoke at Columbus Circle. While both men admitted knowing of the law, neither real-ized that a special flag size had been designated. Jones, of 396 Broadway, who spoke on "No More War," appeared in the West Side Court before Magistrate Hatting, faced a possible $100 fine, and was permitted to choose between pay-ing a fine of $5 or spending two days in jail. Harrison, who had served on vari-ous committees established by Mayor Hylan, was arrested an hour later while lecturing on "Man's Place in Nature." He pleaded guilty, paid a $5 fine, and, as he left the court, reportedly said that he was "going around the corner to buy a bigger flag immediately."[106]

Less than a week later, on August 2, President Warren G. Harding died sud-denly while on a speaking tour in San Francisco. Harrison wrote in his diary that he "deeply sympathize[d] with Mrs. Harding" and sent what he considered to be an "undistinguished letter of condolence." He later "received a treasured acknowledgement letter." Three days before Harding's death he had sent a let-ter "of sympathy" to the president, who he thought "had turned the corner on the high-road to health." Harrison judged that Harding "was not a great presi-dent"; he had "no great abilities," though he did have "a kindly heart and wished well to all men."[107]

On the night that Harding died, Harrison also had a little incident at home. His daughter Ilva (age eight) told him that his daughter Aida (age eleven) "had told her to '*baiser son cul et sugere ex ea sanguinem.*'" He asked her if she had told her mother, and she said, "'Yes; but she didn't do anything to her.'" He asked if she said anything, and the answer was "No." When he asked Lin "whether she had not given either punishment or admonition she indifferently replied in the negative." He wrote in his diary, "Such is the TRAINING which my wife gives to her children."[108]

Two months later, on October 10, Harrison wrote to Dr. Jacob Ross about Ilva and "some elementary principles of sanitation." Ilva was a pupil in an open art class taught by a Mrs. Quinn, and previously the children's milk glasses had been washed and allowed to drain in an icebox, but on the ninth, a Mrs. Hirsch "issued an order to the effect that the child who is assigned to the task of washing up on any particular day should bring *her* towel from home and wipe all the glasses with it." Harrison cited "the city's efforts to do away with common drinking, common towels, and other similar things in public places" and protested "strongly" against it "as dangerous and unsanitary." He was concerned with the bacterial cleanliness of such towels and insisted "that no such towel be used in any glass from which my daughter is to drink milk." He did not, however, limit the scope of his objection to his own daughter's health, and "as a tax payer," he took the position "that the health of all the children is equally involved." He wrote first to Ross "as a matter of departmental propriety," but he "reserve[d] the right to take the matter as far as may be necessary to secure the recall of the unsanitary order."[109]

On Monday, December 3, Hubert wrote in his diary that he now knew "something of the bitterness of being a father." On Saturday he had received a card saying that his eldest daughter Frances (age thirteen) "had not been to school *for 9 days*." When he showed it to her she told him "that it must be a mistake of the school authorities." He told her that he was going to Wadleigh High School "to find out the truth of the matter and that if the card told the truth she'd catch it." When he got home on the evening of the third, he learned from Lin that the truant officer had been there to say that Frances hadn't been to school on Monday, either. She also hadn't returned home, so he went to the police station to inform Sergeant McLoughlin and seek his help. Aida said that she had seen Frances at the Roosevelt Movie Theatre; Hubert waited there for an hour and a half but couldn't find her. In his diary he wrote: "I couldn't eat at the house; *her mother's singing* and the situation were too much for me. Good God!" Frances wound up staying away for four days and three nights because of some trouble at school.[110]

———

While attending to his domestic situation, lecturing for the Board of Ed, and writing occasional reviews, Harrison managed to finish an exceptional nineteen-page article, "The Virgin Islands: A Colonial Problem," on October 31, 1923,

for *The Nation*. It offered important historical analysis and little-known historical anecdotes. *The Nation* had editorially separated from the *New York Evening
Post* earlier in the year, and its editor Ernest Gruening and its literary editor
Mary Marcy had previously corresponded with Harrison. The completed article was to be one in a series of articles entitled "These United States," which
were to appear on alternate weeks. Though *The Nation* ultimately did such a
series (and it was later republished as *These "Colored" United States* and included
a piece on St. Croix by Ashley Totten), Harrison's article was never published
in *The Nation* (or in *These "Colored" United States*). This important piece was
not published until 2001 in *A Hubert Harrison Reader*.[111]

Harrison began by emphasizing that it "is hardly possible" to tell the story
of the Virgin Islands without mentioning that the Virgin Islands' "population is
93 per cent Negro." The islands of St. Croix, St. Thomas, and St. John are "part
of our far-flung colonial empire and represent one portion of 'the white man's
burden,'" which, he sarcastically added, "our republic has been driven by 'manifest destiny' to assume." This "assumption of sovereignty over darker peoples" carried an "obligation to know something of them" and "unfortunately,
most Americans—from our statesmen up," believed they could "dispense with
this obligation." Such an attitude resulted in "singular anomalies," one of which
was that the U.S. Navy, an arm of war, though "never intended as a co-ordinate
branch of our own government," was "the Executive, Legislative and Judicial
departments" of the islands. Since the opening of the twentieth century the
United States had used this Navy "to hold Hayti, Santo Domingo and Nicaragua in thrall" under the assumption that "these people are all foreigners who
had to be either subjugated or intimidated." Their lands, however, were not part
of the United States, whereas "the Virgin Islands were peaceably purchased
from Denmark"—yet they too were "administered entirely by the officials of
the Navy Department instead of the Bureau of Insular Affairs, the Department
of State or the Department of the Interior." Another anomaly that Harrison cited
concerned the fact that the United States inclined toward "a government by law."
It was a "primary principle" of the Founding Fathers "that the executive,
legislative and judicial functions should never be united in any one person" and
"that no person . . . should at the same time make the law, interpret the law and
apply the law" (because that would be "autocracy as opposed to democracy").
Yet, exactly that power was "conceded" by Congress "not only to every naval
Jack-in-office who may be temporarily promoted to the governorship of the Virgin Islands but even to official underlings, like Mr. George Washington Williams, a gentleman from the South, who is at the same time district attorney,
magistrate, police commissioner and quite a few other things."[112]

In reviewing the history of U.S. acquisition of the islands, Harrison stressed
that the "'foundation reasons' for U.S. interest" was "'their geographic position

and consequent strategic importance.'" These were reasons that might "in time bring the entire West Indian group under our control." Harrison recounted how, during the "roaring days of [Henry] Morgan, [Edward] Teach ['Blackbeard'] and the other pirates and buccaneers the strategic and commercial importance of St. Thomas had exalted the port of that island into a position of unrivalled supremacy over all the other West Indian islands." Some 2,500 ships annually called there through the middle of the nineteenth century. The harbor at St. John could handle an entire fleet, and the island was at one time dotted with scores of plantations producing sugar, rum, and molasses. St. Croix, or "Santa Cruz," "the largest, most important and most beautiful of the three" islands, was acquired by Denmark much later than the other two, though it soon surpassed them in the production of sugar and rum. For over two centuries Santa Cruz rum was "the most famous of West Indian spirits," and in 1810 the island alone exported forty-six million pounds of sugar. The production of cotton was "attempted several times," and in the last decade of the eighteenth century the annual crop was around 157,000 bales.[113]

For "the tourist in search of romance" there were "the grim walls of Blue-beard's Castle" overlooking Charlotte Amalie. The Salt River plantation "stands at the north of a lagoon in which tradition says Columbus landed on St. Ursu-la's day when he named the group of islands in honor of her and her eleven thousand virgins." In "the little town of Bass End or Christiansted," Alexander Hamilton "labored as a clerk and first exhibited those remarkable mental pow-ers that took him through Columbia College in New York" and made him "the active genius of the American Constitution." Also, "on this same island slavery was abolished by the slaves themselves after a bloody uprising in 1848." Long before that, however, "the fierce love of freedom characteristic of the Danish blacks had blown a spark over on the mainland where in 1822 one of them by the name of Denmark Vesey had organized a slave revolt in Charleston, South Carolina which all but succeeded."[114]

Harrison described the "black people of the Virgin Islands" as "almost entirely of African extraction," since "the few Carib Indians who were found there in the 16th century . . . died off very quickly upon contact with the first white men." He then discussed how

the social characteristics of the Negro populations of the Virgin Islands are only to be adequately understood and appreciated by reference to similar characteristics to be found in the West African Negroes from among whom the slaves for the Danish Islands were mainly drawn—the locale extending from the Upper Gold Coast to the south-eastern limits of Nigeria. Their cus-toms are rooted in the African communal system; and the planters of the Dan-ish islands left these inherited customs generally undisturbed.

Up until twenty years earlier the Africa-based "communal extensions of individual economics" had enabled agricultural laborers to survive under Danish rule, but now "under the rigid American economic system a dollar and a half a day (which he doesn't get) would be insufficient to give him one-half the well being which he formerly enjoyed."[115]

There were "certain well-defined economic limits to the prosperity of the islands," including "the thinness of the soil on a volcanic foundation" and the "frequent disappointing fluctuations in the rainfall," but these were countered by "actual and potential resources." The island was rich in sugarcane, bay trees, cotton, mahogany, dogwood, mangineel ("a sort of vegetable carbonic acid"), cashews, pigs, and oxen. Despite "the present deplorable economic depression" he thought there was still "an opening for any ambitious American whose capital does not exceed five thousand dollars."[116]

Reviewing the history of U.S. interest in the islands, Harrison explained that American efforts to possess this "key to the Caribbean" went back to 1867, when Danish colonial officials held a plebiscite that supported a transfer, which could have been effected for fifteen million dollars. Ratification by the U.S. Senate was "blocked by the spitefulness of Charles Sumner who used his position as chairman of the Senate Committee on Foreign Relations to pay off his personal scores against the administrations of [Andrew] Johnson and [Ulysses S.] Grant." Over the next half-century acquisition remained "on the margin of our political field of vision." It "required" the European war to rush Congress into doing what, "as a necessity of our new imperialism, should have been done at leisure long ago." The "final reasons for the acquisition were, like our first, almost entirely strategic" and "implied an intention on the part of the Wilson Administration to get us into the war as an opponent of Germany as early as 1916."[117]

In the period after the United States first expressed interest in the islands, the West Indian sugar industry, under fierce competition from German and American sugar, "had shrunk disastrously," and "black West Indian laborers had begun to pour into the cities of our North Atlantic states in numbers that steadily increased as the years rolled by." In the British West Indies "conditions were intensified by the fact that the younger sons of the English upper classes descended like a swarm of hungry locusts on the already impoverished colonies." Though not generally known, the governor of Jamaica received a salary that "was, down to 15 years ago, as large as that of the governor of the richest state in our Union" and then, when the term in office ended, could go "home to England to receive for the rest of his natural life a pension drawn from the revenues of that poverty-stricken place." Similar provisions existed in other British islands, while the "pinch of poverty was felt, in consequence, by the masses of the West Indian people." Thus, the "main source of the pressure was economic rather than bureaucratic," and in the Virgin Islands there developed a response: "a definite labor movement with clear-cut radical aims," headed by Harrison's boyhood friend, D. Hamilton Jackson. Those in power sought to control this labor movement, and Harrison emphasized:

> It was the rise and potency of this labor-movement as expressed mainly in the St. Croix Labor Union which determined the planter-element in the islands to revive and support the movement for the transfer of the Virgin Islands to the United States. In the days before the union the regular wage of an agricultural worker was twenty cents a day. By organizing the workers the union was soon able to pull up wages to fifty cents, seventy-five, and finally a dollar a day. Nor was this all. These black Danish workers began to give evidence of a social vision far in advance of that which was being exhibited by white workers in the United States. They organized a bank of their own, secured a printing-press, published a newspaper and brought up seven of the estates on which they had formerly been employed. It became evident that they meant to try conclusions with the capitalists of their own ground. Against such organized economic co-operation the planters could not hope to compete successfully. They realized that transfer to the United States, in which racial subordination was most effectively organized and entrenched in the politico-economic structure of the actual government, would redress the balance and restore their effective control over wages and working conditions.[118]

The planter's "propaganda for the sale happened to coincide with the urgent strategic needs of the United States and the financial embarrassments of the Danish Colonial office." Their voice was "heard more effectively in Copenhagen than that of the laborers," and the press in Denmark popularized the cause. Under such "convergent pressures the sale was consummated on March 31, 1917," and, "having perfected all his preliminary arrangements, the president who had 'kept us out of war' went before Congress and ordered us in."[119]

In late 1923 David Lloyd George, the British prime minister, commented on the German situation and "justified his demand for a dictatorship in Germany with the remark that both England and America had had 'a practical dictatorship' during the war." During the U.S. "dictatorship most of the functions of Congress were taken over by the Executive," and it was during that period that the United States took over the Virgin Islands. It was "perfectly natural" that the administration then set up "followed the fashion of autocracy rather than that of democracy." The "present government of the Virgin Islands is that of a naval autocracy responsible not to the Congress of the United States but, in a dim and remote way, to the President alone":

The naval commandant and the governor are one and the same person; the lieutenant-commander of the Signal Corps is the Government Secretary, the Captain of the Marine Corps is head of the Legal Department, the aide to the Naval Chief of Staff is the head of the Department of Public Works, and the head of the naval hospital Director of Health for the islands. These are but a few of the official identities which exist to prove that the government of the Virgin Islands is a naval government. The point is of vital importance and the naval officials, realizing this, have been busy explaining it away. During his two-day visit to the islands in April last [Naval] Secretary [Edwin] Denby in the first two sentences of his address delivered in St. Thomas declared, "I am only a visitor here. The administration of these islands is a civil administration which the Navy furnishes with men to carry on." Then he immediately explained that "I have no authority here *outside of a strictly military authority*"—which, of course, gave the whole show away.[120]

The islanders continued "to protest against the hitherto unheard of theory of political serfdom which puts the government of an American colony into the hands of the Navy Department." While this approach might be used for "*a conquered territory*, prior to the setting-up of civil government," Virgin Islanders

fail to find any precedent in the history and laws of the United States, or those of any other English-speaking country, for the present arrangement which turns over the civil rights of a free people whose territory has been peacefully acquired by treaty and purchase to the by no means tender mercies of that same Navy Department which has already achieved such an unsavory reputation in Haiti; and insist that the dignity, self-respect and good faith of the United States are involved until such time as the government of the Virgin Islands shall be put under the appropriate department of the United States government.[121]

Their "objections to the naval regime" went "deeper than the question of political form" because it is "a notorious fact, known in every seaport of the world," that the behavior of U.S. seamen "when on shore is more unruly than that of the seamen of any other great nation." This is "especially" so "when they have to deal with colored inhabitants." Their behavior in Kingston, Jamaica, was "responsible for the drastic order" of Governor Sir Alexander Swettenham after Jamaica's earthquake, which sent the American marines back to their ships and rejected their "aid" in policing Kingston. In explanation of the unauthorized landing the American admiral declared, "You know, niggers will loot." The "wrathful Swettenham" retorted, "Sir, we have no 'niggers' in Jamaica—only black and white citizens. Take your men off at once."[122]

These things were "not known in America," where there is "a national preference for knowing only the good things about ourselves." They were "well known, however, all over the Caribbean and also in South and Central America." Harrison added, "Whatever may be said of the American army, it has less race-prejudice than the navy—in which 'Southernism' runs riot." Under such circumstances, "control of a Negro community by the Navy Department" was "nothing short of a social and civic calamity." Under Danish control "there were 'superior' and 'inferior' people on the islands; but in no instance were they made so by the color of their skin"; the "doctrine of chromatic inferiors and superiors has been violently thrust upon the islanders by the personnel of the naval administration." In an official report for 1920–1921, Governor Sumner Kittelle attempted to create "a Negro class." Other Americans, like the Rev. Mr. White-head and Thomas Stribling, went further and sought "to make it appear that the darker people are laborers and the lighter ones middle class." Harrison pointed out, "If the lines of social and economic cleavage had at anytime followed those of chromatics some knowledge of this fact might well have vouchsafed by divine providence to one who, like myself, grew up in the islands. But I know of no such thing."[123]

With such thinking it was "easy" for "naval Americans to believe that *all* white people are fore-ordained to enjoy the prerogatives of rulership while *all* black or mixed-blood people are pre-ordained to obey their orders and serve them to the end of time." This was "a rational and defensible doctrine, like that of a war to end war," but it was "better suited to sailors and soldiers than to those who administer governments: in that sphere it provokes friction and causes no end of trouble." This had been the case from its first application in the former Danish Islands, where "in the very first week of the American occupation marines and sailors began to assault citizens and shoot up the town." One case offered "a bird's-eye view of what marine brutality means to the Virgin Islanders." Harrison quoted from a St. Thomas newspaper of April 10, 1921, when, on the eve of the fourth anniversary of U.S. occupation of the island, "a gang of marines went on a rampage for several days, shooting at defenseless citizens indiscriminately." According to reports, "the casualties amount[ed] to nearly a score of severely injured civilians and several who received minor injuries and a number of houses damaged by rifle fire."[124]

None of the marauders had yet been punished, though they "would have been punished had this taken place in the United States—as the Negro soldiers now in Leavenworth prison [over the August 1917 Houston, Texas, incident] can testify." "But," he sarcastically added, "the brutality which is consequent upon helplessness has not been restricted to shooting." "Rape, a serious crime hitherto unknown to the islands, began to appear with distressing frequency"; "the offenders" in "every case" were "white." The "number of illegitimate children" was "astonishing," and "Colored girls" were "insulted with impunity" as "marines, in many instances" invaded "the sanctity of respectable private homes." Some "social consequences" were referred to in the official report of ex-governor Kittelle, which declared that "venereal diseases are [now] very prevalent" and that "statistics for several years back show that this increase . . . appeared first in the figures for 1917, co-incident with the arrival of the Americans."

"Concretely," Harrison emphasized, "this is what a naval autocracy must of necessity mean; and this is only one of the reasons why Virgin Islanders want Congress to abolish the naval rule under which they are suffering. They want *responsible* government—responsible to themselves, if possible, and if not, then responsible at least to the United States Congress." The Congressional Council of the Virgin Islands recently stated that they felt "civic bewilderment and political uncertainty as to our status" because it was unclear whether Virgin Islanders were "American citizens or American subjects." Until Congress decides, "we remain mere subjects, suffering from the same civic disabilities as the subjects of Europe's Kings and Asia's Emperors—a status not at all creditable to the democratic integrity of the *republic* which rules our destinies."[125]

"Under the present regime criticism of naval autocracy is tantamount to . . . crime.'" The U.S. Navy "frowns upon that crime," and it had already led to two deportations, the Reverend Reginald G. Barrow and Thomas Morenga-Bonaparte, and in the latter case "a Negro editor [Rothschild Francis in the *Emancipator*] had ventured to reprint a mildly critical quotation from the report of that Congressional Commission which went out to whitewash the Navy in 1921."[126]

In the meanwhile, out of a population of 26,000, only 424 could vote; neither the Fifteenth nor the Nineteenth Amendment applied, although "the 18th [Prohibition] is in all its rigor and at the cost of tremendous economic suffering." The "voting arrangement" followed old Danish law that placed a property limitation on the suffrage, a limitation that "was lifted in Denmark itself many years ago but remained in force in the colony." Thus "the bulk of the people were denied the right of adult suffrage because American officials, paid from the taxes of the American people," administered "the laws of the foreign country (Denmark)—a situation without parallel on earth today." Nevertheless, "the welcome which the inhabitants gave the Americans when they took over the islands was genuine and sincere enough." "Not knowing any better, they expected friendship and co-operation. They had had no previous acquaintance with the psychology of race-prejudice and the harsh superciliousness of the Navy officials has done much to disillusion them."[127]

To such "disillusionment" the "horrors of quasi starvation have now been added." During the previous three years there had "been practically no rain."

Crops failed, work fell off, and wages "declined below the subsistence level." Agricultural laborers getting only two days of work a week at thirty cents a day faced prices for staples as high as in the United States. The "distressing poverty and semi-starvation" was "a scandal all over the West Indies," and the U.S. Virgins were now "pointed to as an earnest of what may be expected under American rule." This was not "unjust," since, despite "hard luck" and "uncontrollable natural conditions," a "fairly large part of it is due to callous indifference on the part of the American overlords." A glaring example was the fact that rum manufacture was prohibited even though "much of the economic welfare" of the Virgin Islanders depended on it, "while the prosperous Philippine Islands are exempted from the operation of the Prohibition Amendment."[128]

If this were not enough, the Navy Department "imposed a number of troublesome port-regulations," which "had the effect of driving away four-fifths of the shipping that brought work and wages to the islands." Tariff restrictions on American imports and insular sports were "another preventable root of the present depression." The U.S. Navy, instead of purchasing available supplies in the islands, chose to import "most from the United States and the rest (including fresh vegetables and fruits) from the British islands." Governor Kittelle's report said "fruits and vegetables are imported in large quantities from Tortola and other British islands and from Porto Rico where conditions of growth are not markedly more favorable." The "land from which the overwhelming majority of the people must get their living is overburdened with new taxes." Thus, while "the land-tax in prosperous Porto Rico is $2.50 an acre it is set at $8.27 cents an acre in the impoverished Virgin Islands." The "direct consequence of such preventable conditions is barely hinted at in the ex-governors report when he says that 'deaths of children under one year comprise 25 per cent of all deaths in the Virgin Islands.'"[129]

To Harrison, the official record of American rule as administered by the Navy Department, which was reprinted in 1923 in "*Lightbournes's* [*Lightbourn's*] *Annual of* [*Annual for*] *the Virgin Islands*," provided "the accumulated evidence of a vast disaster that has come upon the islanders 'co-incident with the arrival of the Americans,' to use the ex-governor's phraseology." The "official figures" showed "social conditions of today are worse than those of 1915," and everywhere it was said that "bad as the Danes were painted they never sponsored so much social misery as the . . . Navy Department," whose "policy" seemingly was "to depopulate the Virgin Islands" and confront the inhabitants "with starvation if they stay." Thus, working people who could raise passage money were "leaving the islands in droves."[130]

A little over a month after Harrison completed this article, on December 6, Gruening wrote back that the article "isn't quite what we want. It is much too long and has altogether too much about the military occupation." Gruening said he would get in touch with Harrison to tell him what they had in mind and sent his phone number. Meanwhile, they held his article at *The Nation*'s office. On January 19, 1924, Gruening again wrote to tell Harrison that Adolph A. Berle had told him that when the United States took over the Virgin Islands, the population was 42,000, and it was now under 20,000. "Under the present policy the population of the Virgin Islands might cease to exist," and it seemed to Gruening that "this might be the lead" of the article, "with a comparison of the conditions under the Danes and the conditions now but written colorfully and with atmosphere and background—the article should not exceed 3500 words." Harrison apparently never delivered what Gruening wanted, and *The Nation* wound up using a two-part series by Ashley L. Totten, "The Truth Neglected in the Virgin Islands," which appeared in the July and August 1926 issues.[131] Interestingly, in 1934, the United States would set up its first official colonial office for the Virgin Islands—the Interior Division of Territories and Island Possessions—under Director Ernest Gruening (who would serve in that capacity to 1939).[132]

Toward the end of 1923 Harrison worked at book reviews, which he submitted to *The Nation*, the *New York World*, and other publications. In the September 5 *Nation* he reviewed *The Partition and Colonization of Africa*, by Charles Lucas, which he described as "a valuable compendium of useful information on the subject of the European penetration of Africa." It sketched "the history of racial contacts from classical times to the present period of mandates" and briefly discussed the problems that have arisen. With "admirable compression," Lucas discussed the "slave trade and its attendant horrors, and the mitigation of these by the efforts of good men in England and elsewhere"; the "abolition of the traffic in slaves and the rise of the colonial exploitation of African peoples in their homelands which immediately took its place"; the "international scramble for choice sections of African territory"; the "wars, diplomatic and military, which the nations of Europe waged with each other in consequence"; and the "horrors of the Congo, and the various campaigns in Africa from the times of Henry the Navigator to those of General Smuts." Harrison noted, however, that the story was told "exclusively from one side—the side of the European who administers Africa for the African's good." The "broad humanitarianism of [E. D.] Morel, [Samuel P.?] Oliver, and De Brazza [Pierre Savorgnan de Brazza]" was missing, as was "the warm Christian kindness of [John H.] Harris and [Rev. Cornelius Howard] Patton." "Within its limits," though, the book was "a correct and competent piece of work, easy to read and easy to remember."[133]

Harrison next reviewed *A Short History of Christianity*, by Salomon Reinach, in the October 3 *Nation*. The book provided "a history of the Christian *church*" and "the organized form of its worship and the dogmas of its creed." As "a brief history of these" Harrison found it "interesting, serviceable, and at times significant."[134]

In the October 23 *New York World* Harrison reviewed *Dark Days and Black Knights*, by the humorist Octavus Roy Cohen. Cohen had "carved for himself a little corner in our contemporary literature," and Harrison appreciated his work and wanted to contest the position of those who were offended by it. He began by arguing that Cohen's niche was in part made possible by "the inferiority-complex," which seemed "to keep Negro writers of fiction from utilizing the inexhaustible veins of humor and comic value which run under their racial sod." Though this rich humor was "known far and near," it was not evident "in the works of the representative Negro writer" of the day. Instead, when a young Black writer sought to portray "the life and soul of his people" imaginatively, it was either as "a propaganda pamphlet in the guise of a 'story'" or a piece that depicted a "race" that "consisted exclusively of lawyers, doctors, savants and millionaires." The "rich human values that lie in the lives of the rank and file" were thus "surrendered to the pens of white writers"—and when they concentrated "on the humorous aspects of the material 'the talented tenth'" got "touchy."[135]

A better understanding of humor was needed, and Harrison made two important points. First, he noted the recent remarks by H. L. Mencken to the effect that those "with a sense of adequacy" can "find humor in a situation of conflict," while those "with a sense of inferiority" quickly go "'up in the air.'" The English, Irish, and American had "all been served up" in "literary dishes highly spiced with humor, and no one was injured"; now, commented Harrison, "it was "the Negro's turn." His second point concerned the fact that there was "the humor of malice and the humor of sympathy, as well as the humor of sheer pleasure without any ulterior purpose." Harrison thought Cohen's humor was of the last sort.[136]

In *Dark Days and Black Knights* Cohen provided "a gallery of outstanding Negro types" around which he developed "comic situations of amazing fidelity to fact." Florian Slappey was a "supreme dandy" and "man-about-town," and a host of other characters, including the lawyer Evans Chew, Rev. Plato Tubb, Sis Callie, Flukers, Gussie Muck, Eli Gouch (a "close-fisted man of money"), Semore Mashby, and the "stalwart society" known as "The Sons and Daughters of I Will Arise," all had "their counterparts in [contemporary] Negro life" in any large city. They were, "of course," drawn "to the scale of humor," and on that scale "they bulk[ed] large—even for Birmingham," where the scene was laid. Harrison felt that "to one . . . on the inside of Negro life" it was "obvious" that Cohen was "not so much creating characters as transcribing them from life." He had "a thoroughness of comprehension which no other white man ever had" of "the inner motives and springs of character to be found in the Negro society of a large Southern city." Though he purposely distorted, it did not "disguise the intimate accuracy of his knowledge." His humor was not especially pointed, and he had "no conventional lay figure like those of the 'good old darky' and 'Massa John's man,'" who was "helpless apart from the kickings and crusts of some bogus 'Kunnel,' 'Jedge' or 'Gen'ral.'" Cohen's "colored people" were "individualized and self-sufficing," and "the rich and rollicking humor" grew "out of their changing relations to each other and to organic social situations." As such it was "not inconsistent with patches of the pathetic, ironic insight and the flavor of romance." This was "the broad essential difference between Cohen and a whole raft of writers like [Hugh] Wiley and 'Judge' [Thomas] Dixon who have used the Negro as humorous material." They produced "'slapstick comedy' while Cohen produces humor." Harrison concluded that, like "Mark Twain, Rabelais and Anatole France," Cohen had shown that an "intellect above the average, a deep knowledge of humanity and the sympathy of perfect comprehension are necessary for the finest flavors of the humorist."[137]

Shortly after the Cohen review Harrison received a personal copy of William Pickens's autobiography, *Bursting Bonds*, inscribed by the author and thanking him for "an hour's entertainment Nov. 4, 1923" (a probable reference to Harrison's Board of Education lecture on Henry Wadsworth Longfellow at the 135th Street Public Library on that date). Harrison enjoyed *Bursting Bonds* "immensely" and prepared a review for the Associated Negro Press entitled "What a Profound Literary Scholar Thinks of Pickens' Book." He had planned to read only a few pages, but the book kept him in all night. What attracted him was "that quality" found in Julius Caesar's pages, missing in Cicero's, and encountered again in Plutarch: "swift and simple directness, with no backward glance at the audience." This was also found in Booker Washington's *Up from Slavery*—a 1901 book unencumbered by "the artificial ingenuity of the chap 'who loves to hear himself talk'" (which, he adds, is often the case "when the tale is bigger than the man"). In Pickens's case, "the man is bigger than the tale," and the tale got told. Harrison noted that the book's last five chapters were strategically and "richly furnished with the commentary on life which was candidly kept out of the first nine." Overall it was "a well done piece of work, though only a sketch." As a "fitting summary" he quoted Vergil's *Aeneid*:

> Per varios casus, per tot discrimina rerum,
> Tendimus in Latium.
> [Through various misfortunes, through so many dangerous
> things, we strive (forward) into Latium][138]

Harrison's critical review of *The Book of American Negro Poetry*, selected and edited by James Weldon Johnson, appeared in the December 16 *National Star* of New York. Noting that "very few Americans" were "acquainted with the quantity and quality of poetry which has been produced by their colored compatriots," Harrison "regretted" that Johnson's volume did not "tend to increase either their understanding or appreciation." The bulk of its poems were "below the standards of mediocrity," and "the best Negro poems" were "omitted." Unfortunately, readers were asked to form an "opinion on the total body of Negro poetry from what is very near to the worst."[139]

As an example of his point Harrison cited the selections from Paul Laurence Dunbar. Johnson "was a friend of the poet," but, writes Harrison, "if he had entered into a conspiracy to suppress the record of which Dunbar's claims to consideration rest, he could hardly have done worse by him." He compared Johnson's treatment of Dunbar to an anthologist of Tennyson failing to include "anything from 'In Memoriam,' the songs in 'The Princess,' 'St. Agnes' Eve,' 'Ulysses,' 'The Lotus Eaters,' 'The Two Voices,' 'The Dreams of Fair Women,' or 'The Idylls of the King.'" While some poems might be omitted, "to omit all of them from any list of eight would savor of incompetence—or something worse." "Lovers of poetry" would surely "fail to understand the unknown principle of selection" by which Johnson similarly omitted Dunbar's "Ode to Ethiopia," "When Malindy Sings," "Love's Apotheosis," and "When Sleep Comes Down" and substituted poems "uniformly below Dunbar's highest standards of excellence" (exemplified in the *Lyrics of Lowly Life* and *Lyrics of the Hearthside*). A second example concerned Theodore Henry Shackleford's "Lissauer, a 'Hymn of Hate.'" It was "a perfect expression of perfect hate" and "out and out" his "ablest" poem, but Johnson "in emasculating Shackleford dodged this one and represented this young master by one of the silliest pieces of his earliest days that could be found." Similarly, Lucian B. Watkins, whom Harrison felt "wrote some things as beautiful as McKay at his best," was "treated in the same dishonest fashion." Harrison attributed these omissions to a "literary dishonesty" that was "seen all through Mr. Johnson's book." He thought "someone should protest emphatically against this contemptible attempt of Mr. Johnson to glorify his own mediocre verses by stripping off the gold from the genius of others that they may not outshine his own drab productions."[140]

In sum, Harrison considered the book to be "a hopeless fizzle" that served to enforce what he had said in the *Negro World* several months earlier, "that Negro writers like Mr. Johnson lack the power of critical judgment." To emphasize his point he added: "No person with a modicum of that power could imagine that there was any poetry in the 'Litany of Atlanta,' by Dr. Du Bois; in D. Webster Davis' 'Weh Down Souf'; Mr. Johnson's 'Sence You Went Away' and

'O Southland'; the first two poems by John Wesley Holloway, or the absolute trash of William Stanley Braithwaite." Harrison added that "to call these things poetry is to drive young and aspiring bards like Walter Everett Hawkins and [Andrea] Razafkeriefo to write simple trash in sheer despair. Every time we dishonestly praise trash we, as a race, keep back our artists from doing as good work as white artists are doing. And for this contemptible trick of Mr. Johnson's there is very little excuse."[141]

Regarding the verses of W. S. Braithwaite, Harrison refused to consider them "poetry." In eleven of the twelve offerings that Johnson printed there was "not a single gleam of either genius or efficiency in versifying," and only one was "above the capacity of a 12-year-old school-boy." It was obvious that Johnson was "paying his debt to a mutual admiration society and not doing honest work as a guide to public taste." Unfortunately, Braithwaite's "Song of a Syrian Lace Seller," which was "better" than any of the twelve, was omitted.

Johnson's collection also "lack[ed] proportion": Dunbar got only eight pages, while Johnson allocated "20 for himself, of which only two poems" were "worth while." His "idea of poetry" was "so bizarre" that he printed "five pages of Asiatic prose ('The Litany of Atlanta') by his associate, Dr. Du Bois, in this queer hodge-podge as poetry." In contrast, "three of the ablest young poets" of the day—Theodore Henry Shackleford, Lucian B. Watkins, and George Reginald Margetson, were "emasculated in this selection," as "their early endeavors, full of imperfections, from which their latter work is free," were chosen "as representative" of their work.[142]

Around 1923 Harrison drafted some notes on George Louis Beer's new book *African Questions at the Paris Peace Conference*, which he described as "a one-sided presentation of African colonial problems" justified by the fact that it dealt "only with those African questions that came up before the Paris Peace Conference." In its pages, "the peonage and pass-systems of British South Africa, the devastating-act of 1916; the physical and economic massacre of the Mashonas and Matebeles under British Colonial Rule, the historic holocaust of the Belgian Congo; the forced strangulation of native West African economic rights in palm oil profits by recent act of Parliament—all these are absent from the picture." France, Britain, and Belgium "had the whip-hand at the Conference," and "their tons of dirty clothes were shoved decently out of sight, while Germany's were pinned on the line of publicity." Though he did not blame Beer, Harrison considered these necessary background "items," since, without them, Beer "was able to cite as specific German 'horrors' methods of colonial procedure which the other European countries had practiced far longer than Germany and on a much larger scale." Beer "was an expert 'on documents only,'" but because he "had never been to Africa," he couldn't "become an expert on Africa without that pre-requisite." Further, "none of the

200 million Africans wrote any of the governmental documents" he used, so "their point of view never entered into the raw materials of his ideas and conclusions."[143]

———

On November 12 the journalist Floyd Calvin wrote a letter to Harrison from which Harrison extracted portions, including a brief biographical sketch. Calvin commented that "we are often very slow in according exceptional recognition to our own" and then discussed the September 1 Golden Jubilee of the "white radical" weekly the *Truth Seeker,* which listed Harrison along with Mark Twain, Thomas Huxley, Ernst Haeckel, Moncure Conway, Lester Ward, and Luther Burbank. In contrast, not many "Negro papers" had mentioned Harrison "in regards to the cause of education and uplift."[144]

Calvin went on, explaining that for the past two years Harrison had served as a lecturer for the Board of Education on "Trend of Times," lecturing at the 135th Street Library and at PS 89 on Lenox Avenue and 134th Street. His lectures outdrew other "Trend" lecturers, who were professors at NYU, Columbia, and City College. While "all New York magazine publishers" knew this, "not one ha[d] ever mentioned it." Harrison was the "only Negro in [the] country to have a regular staff lectureship" with a Board of Education, and as a "Trend" lecturer he "receive[d] 50% more than other staff lecturers." The letter also mentioned Harrison's book *Natural Health* and that "Sex and Society" was to be published by Boni and Liveright in the fall. At present he was preparing articles for the *New York Times, Current History,* and the *American Mercury.*[145]

Around the time of his Board of Ed lectures, Harrison prepared two handwritten pages of lecture notes on "The League of Nations and the Present European Crisis" for a Board of Education lecture at PS 89 on November 18. He began by discussing the background to the League of Nations and how the "War to end War" had not ended wars. He considered the League "a League of Victors," in which the "inner circle dominates" and from which Germany, Austria, and Russia were omitted. He also critically evaluated its work in the context of "Britain's wars in Mesopotamia," "Poland's aggression on Russia," "England in Egypt," "Italy's raid on Greece and successful defiance of League," and "France in the Ruhr" ("in violation of the treaty"). In analyzing "the present crisis" Harrison insightfully observed that while "France tries to eat her cake and have it too," Germany's "economic destruction" crippled all Europe, and these problems affected "England—and other countries," since the mark was "no longer money," and one could get "ten million for one cent!"[146]

In this situation the German government, "weakened by [the] allies' acts, [was] powerless to pay or rule," and the consequences were seen in the growth of "Hitler & Bavarian monarchists" and the "People's Party." Harrison emphasized that "Hitler's—an Austrian" and that the "German Nat'l socialist Party is strictly *anti-socialist*, anti-semite and *anti-rational* & anti-Republican." He added that "the moderate socialist ministry in their effort to down soviet-ism (soldiers & workers' councils) in Munich, call[ed] in [Gustave] Noske's guards from Prussia" and that the "reaction supported by Bav. People's Party & [Gustav Ritter] von Kahr, [meant that a] monarchist, becomes dictator." When the "strongly financed" Adolf Hitler was "charged with receiving money from [the] French," he failed "to deny it convincingly" and continued to receive arms and drill extensively.[147]

Regarding French imperialism, Harrison noted that it was "as old as Napo-leon III"; that its "African Empire ([was] largest of all)"; that it was in "Asia, East & West (Gouraud in Mesopotamia)"; and that "France arms Poland et al." In terms of "America and the Crisis" Harrison discussed how the "economic food dependence of Europe" was on the United States. The key question was "Should U.S. collect the loans?" On the probable future Harrison discussed "England's grapple with France," "her probable alliance: [an] Anglo-Saxon entent[e]," and the fact that "European dominance [was] in peril," as evidenced by "poverty—starvation, disease, revolution, collapse of capitalism" all of which suggested "a dark future."[148]

Also on November 18, Harrison wrote some notes on Lew Leslie's *The Plan-tation Review*, starring Florence Mills, Cora Green, Eddie Rector, and Hamtree Harrington, which "deserve[d] its unique popularity as the society's noblest fad." The "select assemblage of dusky artists combine[d] the efficiency of clock-work with the flash of genius and the fire of personality" and carried "the stamp of perfection and the mark of genius" from start to finish. Florence Mills's "vivacity, charm, dash and sparkling personality," along with "her well-known genius for hard work," kept her "in the fore-front of Broadway's entertainers and artists." She sang, danced, and acted "in winning and wonderful ways."[149]

Harrison went to see John Barrymore in *Hamlet* at the Manhattan Opera House on West Thirty-Fourth Street on Monday, November 26. He considered Barrymore's acting "a marvelously good piece of interpretation," though the company that acted with him "was beneath contempt."[150]

On Saturday night, December 1, Harrison gave a lecture, "On the Essence of Government," before the Single Tax Forum at the Hotel McAlpin at Broad-way, Sixth Avenue, and Thirty-Third Street. He attended with Mrs. Elizabeth Davis and Miss Madelyn Wales, an artist who had "a queer obsession" that kept her "from trusting herself to an elevator." He knew three of the Wales sisters, "and two of the three are 'queer', Madelyn and Catherine, neither of whom cares for men, *as men*. Madelyn and Mrs. Davis act like Husband and Wife, and she (M.) really has what amounts to *horror hominis*." While Catherine had "formed no such noticeable attachment," she also had "an aversion to men," though James Bell seemed "to be bringing her to the verge of a conversion." Both women shared "a horror for babies and an excessive love for cats," as did Mrs. Davis. The three Wales girls were "beautiful brown creatures," and Catherine had "the most wonderful gray-green eyes." Anna, the youngest, seemed "quite normal." In his diary Harrison soon added a PS: "I learnt since from Anna that she too is fond of cats and afraid of young children."[151]

Charles S. Johnson of the National Urban League's *Opportunity* magazine wrote to Harrison on December 8 that he would "like nothing better than the opportunity to meet" and "talk over the matter of those chapters of your proposed book." He had to go to Buffalo but hoped to discuss the matter after he returned around December 20. On December 26 he wrote Harrison "a note of apology." He had been delayed in Buffalo and now had to go to Washington. He planned to contact him when he returned.[152]

On December 20, 1923, the *Chicago Defender*'s editor Phil A. Jones wrote to Harrison to say he was sorry he hadn't seen him again before leaving New York. He would be back in January and hoped they could discuss the matters in Harrison's letter of December 18. He asked Harrison to send his articles from the *World* and other publications and thanked him "for the publicity given the Chicago Defender in The Cat's Meow," adding that they were "reproducing the same in our issue of December 22nd." He hoped that "early in the New Year we can make arrangements to have you join the staff of 'The World's Greatest Weekly.'" Jones wrote again on January 4, 1924, and thanked Harrison "for forwarding me clippings from publications that have printed your literary efforts." He was returning all manuscripts by registered mail and during 1924 hoped "to increase circulation to 50,000" and would "seek efficient writers" like Harrison. When he again came to New York he would "bring a contract" and asked that meanwhile Harrison send "any news articles" he thought "would interest" *Defender* readers.[153]

As 1923 moved into 1924 Harrison would continue his constant search for work. In early 1924 he would lecture for the Board of Education, he would then write a very important series of articles for the *Boston Chronicle*, and he would have one of his articles that was proposed for publication go unpublished in the Alain Leroy Locke–edited *Survey Graphic* on "The New Negro."

15

Boston Chronicle, Board of Ed, and the New Negro
(January–June 1924)

In early 1924, in his continuing search for work, Harrison (under the pen name "Master Alcofribas") wrote a short-lived column entitled "The Fish-Kettle" in the weekly *The Tattler*. The pen name was likely derived from "Alcofribas Nasier," the anagrammatic pseudonym used by François Rabelais, the sixteenth-century French satirist of contemporary events, whose work Harrison appreciated. The use of "Alcofribas," the jocular and racy yet serious voice used by Rabelais, perhaps suggests Harrison's aim for the series, which he offered from January 20 through February 3, 1924, and which focused on aspects of Harlem life. The first article in the January 20 issue, entitled "The Demi-Men," mentioned that he knew "three of them on one sheet (paper, not linen) and they can hate—in little spiteful ways." (This was a probable reference to *The Messenger* magazine.) This article was soon followed by "Flappers and Bachelors" in the January 27 issue.[1]

In the February 3 *Tattler* "Master Alcofribas" wrote "Over at Joe's," a restaurant that was "the best in black Harlem." During the day it was an ordinary place where quiet brown waitresses would serve you, but in the evening the intellectuals gathered "from the four corners of the *Colorado Mundo* [colored world] to smoke, eat, drink coffee and discuss the race problem, religion, art, science, scholarship and sex." If you met one of them and asked where you could meet for a chat, you would be told, "over at Joe's, after eleven."[2]

On a typical night in the northeast corner of the old dining room where Bert Williams, Charlie Anderson, Babe Townsend, Charlie Gilpin, and other notables gathered in the days before the Volstead Act, the "little brown chap in the president's chair is a famous singer, head of a post of the American Legion"; the "handsome fellow on his left with the wonderful eyes and shapely mustache is a world-wanderer from the West Indies, who has lived in England, Scotland, Wales, Germany and Scandinavia [McKay?]"; the "dark man on his right, the scholar of his group, writes for the white newspapers and magazines and lectures for the Board of Education [Harrison]." There also was the "man with the prominent nose" who "combines poetry and business and is well known among white song writers, publishers and theatrical producers down town [Razaf]. And so on." At the table behind them are "two girlfriends, the sprightly one is [the popular singer and comedienne who had starred in *Shuffle Along* in 1921] Gertrude Saunders, a capable queen of the footlights," while the "third table is held by the Junior Section of the Intelligentsia, 'Bridgie,' Stout, [the musician Elmer] Snowden and the rest of 'the gang.'" "The feast of reason and flow of soul," anecdotes, arguments, jests, wit, humor, raillery—all these are on tap "over at Joe's" between 11 p.m. and 2 a.m., where they might be discussing Nan Bigby Stephens's drama "'Roseanne,' the League of Nations or the latest book by [H. L.] Mencken."[3]

There, wrote Master Alcofribas, amid much tobacco mist, is proof "that Harlem has brains of its own." *The Tattler* circulates along with the cigarettes, "and even the Bible gets a hearing." "Writers, thinkers, artists, musicians, actors, business men; each of them able to stand on his own feet mentally— they are Harlem's present pledge of future greatness, this 'gang' that meets 'over at Joe's.' In this crucible is being melted that ore of Africa which will contribute to the golden glory later on." The following week's column was to discuss "Fakers and Fakerines," but no subsequent "Master Alcofribas" column has been located; instead Harrison began writing a series of more serious articles for the weekly *Boston Chronicle*.[4]

Before his first "Master Alcofribas" column, Wendell K. Thomas, assistant director of lectures for the NYC Board of Ed, wrote to Harrison on January 16, 1924, on behalf of the Committee on Entertainment of the Public Lecture Association. Thomas asked Harrison to replace a scheduled speaker, Dr. Hillis, who was ill, at a luncheon on Saturday, January 19, at the Park Avenue Hotel. They wanted him to speak for ten minutes on almost any subject, and Thomas suggested he might also want to give the other lecturers a little idea of the work that he does in Harlem under the auspices of the Board of Ed.[5]

The day after the luncheon Harrison spoke on "The Rent and Housing Situation" for the Board of Ed. Based on his notes, his focus was on the causes of high rents. The "general cause," he argued, was "the pressure of city populations" given the "scarcity of land in and near cities." The "special cause" was the war-related "increase in prices," including the "high cost of living" and "*the cost of high-living*" that "(helped to increase rents in Harlem [from] 1916–19)."

The "war profiteers set the pace" with "rent-profiteering during the war" in New York, Washington, and Chicago. While the state had tried to keep rents under control with the New York rent laws during Democratic governor Al Smith's first administration, "their usefulness [was] checked by the cowardice and stupidity of many tenants." Though there was a demand to make these laws permanent and to allow tax exemption on buildings for a period, Harrison thought "more radical and constructive measures seem necessary." He suggested "Municipal Housing," "Taxing land out of use," "building loans from [the] mun[icipal]-treasury," and "municipal land purchase."[6]

On February 17 and again on November 30, 1924, Harrison prepared handwritten notes for a lecture on "What Should Be the Immigration Policy of the U.S.A.?" In May 1924 the United States would pass restrictive immigration legislation (the Johnson-Reed Act) based on the U.S. ethnic composition of 1920. This policy would favor peoples from northwestern Europe, limit southwestern Europeans, virtually exclude Asians, and severely limit other peoples of color. Harrison argued against the proposed immigration policy and for a more absolute restriction policy, not because he was anti-immigrant but because he was concerned with the bettering of conditions of all laborers, both those currently in the United States and those in the countries of the immigrants' origins. He thought cutting off immigration would work in that direction.[7]

He began by discussing "immigration and the time-element" and how it was "necessary in filling the country; [but] not necessary today." In discussing the history of immigration in the United States he quoted from an article by Secretary of Labor James J. Davis in the *New York Times* of February 17. Harrison emphasized that he was not asserting that immigrants bring "crime and ignorance" or that northern and western European immigrants "are better than those" of the south and west. He considered the army tests, which were used to make such arguments pure "rot." He also did not assert "that immigrants and descendants divide their allegiance" (which, he noted, did not happen in the last war, despite the "lies of propagandists"); nor did he assert "that they take our money and send it back home" (because, in fact, "they leave their labor here in fair exchange").[8]

In discussing "our dangers from continued immigration" he included the drag on "labor—wages—standards of living" and "un-assimilation" (noting that out of 14 million foreign-born under half were naturalized). He argued that "we don't owe them more than we owe ourselves," and on this subject he cited the issue of "political asylum" offered to "refugees from Russia [in] 1904" and in 1924. He noted that "a policy of restriction (absolute)" "until the melting-pot melts," would "oppose quota-ed restrictions as troublesome & unfair (cf. *Asiatics*)" and would "better assimilation & distribution of laborers already here" (such as "THE NEGRO"). He also pointed out "the good to Europe (& elsewhere) If they have nowhere to escape they'll stay and fight and secure better conditions."[9]

From March through April 1924 "Dr." Harrison lectured on Saturday evenings for the Board of Ed's free public lecture series "Shining Lights of Literature" at 103 West 135th Street. A handout card for these talks said they were geared toward those "craving for the inner life," "the joys of poesy and romance," and "the higher and serener philosophy of living as reflected in history and in the pages of the masters of literature." His scheduled subjects included: "The Negro in American Literature" (March 1); "John Keats and the Romantic Movement in English Poetry" (March 8); "[James Fenimore] Cooper's Leather Stocking Tales" (March 15); "[Henry] Wadsworth [Longfellow] and the Poetry of Nature" (March 22); "Mrs. Minnie M. Mundy, 'Folk Songs of the American Negro,' Illustrated by songs by Miss Minnie Brown" (March 29); "The Historical Novels of Mary Johnston" (April 5); "Moby Dick: The Unique Masterpiece of Herman Melville" (April 12); "The Poetry of Bliss Carman" (April 19); and "Summing Up Shaw; A Critical Estimate of G. Bernard Shaw" (April 26).[10]

Around March Harrison also hand wrote notes for a lecture on "The Record of the 68th Congress and Problems of the 69th." His notes began by looking at "the problem of law-making," of establishing rules to govern human relations, which increase in number and complexity, though not at "an annual, biennial or quadrennial necessary rate." Under such conditions an annual, biennial, or quadrennial legislature must, therefore, "either make laws in excess of the real relations" or "mark the time," and both options result in a "lack of rhythm in [the] legislative process." The 68th Congress had some 18,000 legislative proposals—13,000 bills and resolutions in the House of Representatives and 4,800 in the Senate—and under such pressure, Congress met the difficulty "by hearkening to pressing popular demands." Its "congressional program" was, therefore, "dependent upon democracy's demands." Harrison's notes focused on some of the outstanding legislation of the 68th Congress, including the "economy and tax reduction"; the "resumption of oil lands" and "conservation of other natural resources"; "the farmer, the laborer and the ex-serviceman"; "Congress, child-labor and the supreme court"; "the Department of Justice"; "living up to the Washington Treaty of limited Naval Disarmament"; "the helping hand to Europe—the Dawes Plan, the World Court, 'bills receivable'"; and a "few heroic failures: the Ku Klux bills, child labor, the lynching filibuster, postal salaries, Muscle Shoals," and "immigration: European and Asiatic." Under the heading "problems facing the 69th Congress" he mentioned "the problem of the 'lame duck'" (noting how England meets the problem), the

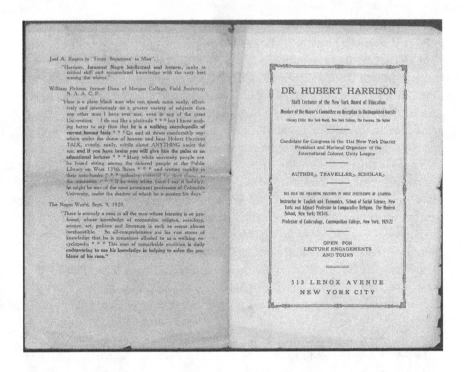

Figure 15.1. "Dr. Hubert Harrison, Staff Lecturer for the New York City Board of Education . . . Open for Lecture Engagements and Tours," promotional brochure, c. 1924–1926, pages 1 and 4. In this promotional brochure a number of Harrison's roles and achievements are listed, and laudatory comments are provided by Joel A. Rogers, William Pickens, and the Negro World. *Source:* Hubert H. Harrison Papers, Box 16, Folder 23, Rare Book and Manuscript Library, Columbia University Library. See https://dlc.library.columbia.edu/catalog/cul:qv9s4mw885.

"child labor" amendment (and the "significance of southern states' attitude"), "the European debt situation," "postal salaries again," "the problem of the Virgin Islands . . . and of the Philippines" (including the recent naturalization case and the courts vs. State Department). Harrison's notes also listed "Congress and the citizen," including "pessimism voiced by the *Times*."[11]

On March 30 Harrison prepared handwritten notes for a lecture on "The West Indian in the United States." His notes listed "two periods of West Indian immigration": "down to 1905" and "since 1905" and emphasized that the "character (social & intellectual) of the earlier immigrants" was that of "the adventurous middle class" including "students, doctors, lawyers." As examples of people who came at that time he included "York Russell, Dr. Tunnell, Rev. [Everard W.] Daniel [of St. Philip's Protestant Church, 134th Street and Seventh Avenue], Arthur Schomburg, [and] Bert Williams." Among "descendants of

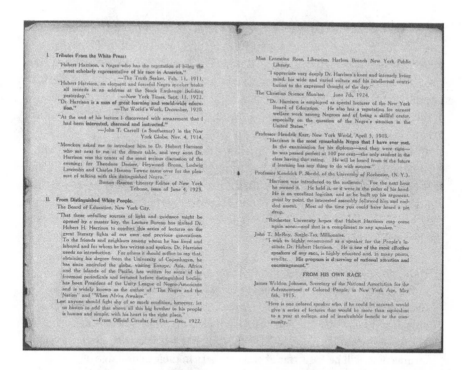

Figure 15.2. "Dr. Hubert Harrison, Staff Lecturer for the New York City Board of Education . . . Open for Lecture Engagements and Tours," promotional brochure, c. 1924–1926, pages 2 and 3. Laudatory comments on Harrison are provided by a variety of publications and notable figures. *Source:* Hubert H. Harrison Papers, Box 16, Folder 22, Rare Book and Manuscript Library, Columbia University Library. See https://dlc.library.columbia.edu/catalog/cul:qv9s4mw885.

West Indians" from this period were Du Bois, Charles W. Anderson, and [postal foreman, Elks officer, and Republican Party activist] George Wibecan. The "character of the later immigrants" he depicted as "the peasantry packs up," and he tied this migration to the "downfall of [the] sugar industry." In discussing *"Adjustments"* he mentioned "W. I. separatism (how bro't about)," "backbone," "lack of humor & flexibility," and "West Indian myths." Finally he noted "recent troubles" and the "necessity of a new rapproachment."[12]

During the early spring of 1924 a group called the Permanent Committee of the Public Lecture Forum wrote to Ernest Crandall that the Board of Ed's lectures had been "an educational blessing thanks to the Board and Drs. Crandall and Harrison." The committee suggested the transfer of the "Trend" and "Literary" lectures to the new PS 139 (at 120 West 140th Street, between Lenox and Seventh Avenues) auditorium, which would open in the fall and allow five hundred or more to attend. The seats at PS 89 (on Lenox Avenue between

134th and 135th Streets) were for small children and limited the audience. If the "Trend" lectures were changed from Sunday afternoon to Thursday evenings, it would allow many more to attend. The committee also asked that Harrison be allowed to speak more on such topics as "The Negro in American Literature," "West Indians in America," "Egyptian Civilization," and "Beauties of the Bible," since his lectures were "well attended, especially by our culture group."[13]

In an undated letter probably from this period, William Pickens of the NAACP wrote that Harrison could be seen working for the New York Board of Ed and at the New York Public Library's 135th Street branch and that he also held a Sunday afternoon forum in PS 89. None of these had "a fair attendance," although they had "grown nearly one hundred percent in attendance and interest over the last year's record." Pickens added:

> Harrison undoubtedly gives the most thought-provoking talks on history, literature, international politics and current topics, of all the forums and lectures being given in the city in any forum. Yet only a relatively small number attend, and some of the most faithful attendants are white students and scholars. In a generation more [of] those whites and blacks who attend these forums now, will be found far ahead of others in their knowledge of politics, social evolution and literature.—Any community of 500 colored people could have a good forum.[14]

Crandall wrote to Harrison on May 20 that he was "gratified to hear that you contemplate sending your daughters to Catholic School." He added that "you have been so near being a good Catholic I have hoped your foot would slip and you would become one." Crandall was "not familiar with St. Francis in Baltimore" (which was founded in 1828 as the St. Francis School for Colored Girls) but hoped Harrison was successful in getting his daughters in there. He offered a letter "as testimonial that you are a high-minded, clean-minded Christian gentleman and your home training would make your children a credit to any institution." While Hubert's wife, Lin, was a Christian, why Crandall believed that Hubert, a free thinker, was a "Christian" was not indicated.[15]

On October 6 Wendell K. Thomas responded to a previous Harrison letter of October 3 and indicated that his lecture subject (which has not been located) was satisfactory. He added that he had notified radio station WEAF (New York's first commercially licensed radio station, owned by AT&T Western Electric and started on March 2, 1922) that Harrison would speak on that subject, but the date was changed from October 28 to November 25 at 10:50 a.m. Harrison would be expected to begin speaking at 11:00 a.m.; he would be given fifteen minutes.[16]

Harrison prepared handwritten lecture notes on the "History and Forecast of the Disarmament Movement" for a Board of Ed lecture at the Public Library on November 16, 1924. The notes discussed "the war and its results." In "human costs" the "9 big wars from 1790 to 1913" resulted in 4,449,000 killed in battle, and the "war of 1914–1918 resulted in 13,000,000 killed in battle as well as 20,000,000 wounded, 6,000,000 dead from disease, and over 20 million civilian deaths." In terms of "money costs," "property losses" were $37,000,000,000; government spending by the Allies, Germany, and Austria was $186,000,000,000, and the "continuing expenses [of the] U.S. by way of example of what is true of all powers" were astronomical. This was based on an analysis by Dr. Edward B. Ross, U.S. Bureau of Standards. Harrison also mentioned the "expected horrors of the future," including "airplanes, submarines," and "luisite gas (2 drops on skin will kill)."[17]

Harrison then moved to an analysis of "the problem" and a discussion of "what complete disarmament means," as opposed to "what reduction of armament means." The latter was "the current acceptable meaning of 'Disarmament.'" He commented on the "difficulties of discrimination," including "national defence vs. disarmament," "offensive vs. defensive armaments" ("e.g. bow-guns or stern-guns for merchant ships during war"), and "maintenance of peace and national security." Regarding "Post-War Endeavors" Harrison noted that "the war failed to end war" and that armies were now "bigger" (he cited "Europe 1913—3,750,000" and Europe "1922—4,355,000," and this "despite reduction of 700,000 = G. Aus. Bulg").[18]

In discussing the Washington Conference he noted that the *New York Times* had pointed out the "general subject of the relation of Asia to Europe & America, whether for peace or war, was indeed the main occasion and material of the Wash[ington]. Conf[erence]." The conference, called by U.S. President Harding and held in Washington, DC, lasted from November 12, 1921, to February 6, 1922. Among the invited attendees were the United States, Japan, China, Britain, France, Italy, Belgium, Portugal, and the Netherlands. It was to focus on interests in the Pacific Ocean and East Asia; Russia was specifically not invited. Harrison, in his notes, emphasized that the Washington Conference was "only a *Naval* disarmament" conference "and only for *capital* ships to which alone the 5–5–3 ratio" was applicable based on "existing naval strengths." He also listed "some remoter reactions," such as Japan returning Shantung to China on October 12, 1922, and Britain's labor ministry giving up its "Singapore project—*for the present*." Particularly "significant" was that Britain "was defeated on two horns of Pacifistic policy Singapore and Soviet Russia." Under "recent developments" Harrison added Congress's vote "for more disarmament"; "the premiers balk"; "[Charles Evans] Hughes[,] [James Ramsay] MacDonald[,] [Édouard Marie] Herriot"; "the Treaty of Mutual Assistance"; and "the American Plan" (the "Shotwell Treaty"). Harrison did not "forecast" "any real hope."[19]

––––––––

One significant development in 1924 concerned the weekly *Boston Chronicle* (which had started in 1915), for which Harrison would apparently write twenty-one articles over six months. On December 21, 1923, Alfred C. Haughton, managing editor for the *Chronicle*, wrote to Harrison, seeking to have him contribute one or two articles per month. Harrison responded promptly, and on January 4, 1924, Haughton wrote back indicating that the *Chronicle* could pay ten dollars per month "for weekly article on current subjects." The subjects were to be nonpolitical, and Haughton included copies of the paper and a check. He indicated that in six months they might be able to pay more and that he was also interested in obtaining Harrison's services as a lecturer. Harrison responded favorably, and on January 22 Haughton wrote that the *Chronicle* would pay forty dollars for a Harrison lecture on "Lincoln etc." He thought the activity would "attract the best white and black citizens of the city," and by next year he hoped to have Harrison speak before the large "white" forum, which annually engaged William Pickens.[20]

A *Chronicle* editorial of January 26, 1924, proudly announced that the paper had "secured the services of Dr. Hubert H. Harrison, a lecturer of the New York Board of Education, graduate of the University of Copenhagen [not true], author, soldier [not true], and literary critic of several large magazines." Harrison was to write "The Trend of the Times" column on the editorial page each week. The editorial added that Harrison had lectured on a wide variety of subjects including "[Rudyard] Kipling, [Henry Wadsworth] Longfellow, [Alfred, Lord] Tennyson, . . . The Earliest Civilizations, . . . Greece, . . . the Bible, the Brother in Black, and Irish Affairs" and that on the latter he had received "a special letter of commendation from James Larkin, the famous Irish leader." The *Chronicle* also mentioned that during the war Harrison had "rendered distinguished aid to the National War Savings Committee of greater New York in their drives." Finally, it directed readers to a "Pickens Says" (where Harrison was referred to as "The Philosopher of Harlem") and to Harrison's upcoming lecture on Lincoln on February 12.[21]

"Dr." Harrison, "president" of the International Colored Unity League, appears to have offered his first 1924 column on "Our International Consciousness" for the January 12 issue of the *Chronicle*. He had apparently written for the paper before, and he explained that to "get back to work in the columns of the *Boston Chronicle*" was an opportunity he would "gladly grasp" in the hope that he might "assist in the work of stimulating the thought of its readers." It was "not vitally necessary that they should agree" with his "particular views"; he wanted more to "prod them into thinking" and did not care "whether they think as I do or otherwise." His series of columns from January through June provided readers with brief and generally high-quality Harrison essays.[22]

In discussing "Our International Consciousness," one of his more important articles, Harrison explained that

> before the World War broke loose one of the classic slogans of "the old Negro" in these United States was: "This is the only country we know anything about." And it was said boastfully, as if our colossal ignorance of the vast world were something to be proud of. At that time our "leaders" and "thinkers" didn't even know that there were "Jim Crow" cars in Nigeria, a pass-system in South Africa or parks in Shanghai [especially People's Park], with such signs as "Chinese and dogs not allowed." The solutions which they advanced for the Negro problem were tinged with the insular notion that it stood in peculiar isolation from all the other political, economic and racial problems of the world. The Swadesha movement in India, the West African National Congress movement, the Egyptian Nationalist movement and the Senussi movement in North Africa were as unknown to them as the geometry of the fourth dimension. So ignorant were our Negro intelligentsia that one of them [Jessie Fauset,[23] literary editor of *The Crisis*] openly confessed in the "Crisis" that, until she met Africans at the "second Pan-African Congress", she did not know that the Bantus were not at all of one "tribe"! And yet such innocents had set themselves up as guides to the masses of Negroes in this twentieth-century world![24]

He went on:

> Then we entered into the World War. Our men went "over there" and discovered that there were white men in the world to whom a dark face was not an invitation to be mean and nasty. . . . The Negroes from Mississippi and Massachusetts contacted with other colored people from Senegal, Cochin-China, Cape Colony, India and Egypt, and learned something of their differences in "language, institutions and laws" and the essential similarity of their sufferings and sentiments in the shadow of that Color Line which runs from Boston to Benares and from Tulsa to Tientsin. In this new Crusade, and in the earlier one, the multiplication of contacts was the mother of culture. The very cause for which they believed that they were fighting evoked questions and speculations which reached out far beyond the parochial limits to which their "leaders" had accustomed them; and the first, faint stirrings of an international consciousness began to make themselves felt.[25]

It was now true, he explained, that "we read of inter-racial complications in Morocco and Syria"; that "we learn that the people of India under Mohandas Gandhi are on the march toward national self-expression"; that "China is bent on being mistress in her own house"; and that "Japan, for her own protection, has assumed all the military and imperial trappings of the land grabbing Christian communities of Western Europe and America." And "what does it all *mean* to us Negroes in America?" Harrison answered:

> Unfortunately, our "leaders" know so little of international affairs that they can only tell us what they read in the white newspapers. . . . Not a single one of our newspapers and magazines can *interpret* for us the meaning of the significant events now unfolding themselves before our eyes. . . . And in the meanwhile, the various currents of "the rising tide of color against white world supremacy" are everywhere also establishing contacts with each other; so that publicists of color in West Africa, North Africa, Egypt, Afghanistan, India and China relate the international aspects of their local problems so that their common implications are equally clear to all of them while to us the only thing that is clear is our need for clarity.[26]

To "meet this need" Harrison proposed "to present from time to time in this column some brief interpretations of what's [happening] in the larger world of international affairs" so that "some needful light might be shed on the trend of the times as it affects colored people here and elsewhere." In the intervals he would focus on "domestic problems and the internal questions of our racial strivings here in America."[27]

———

In the January 19 *Chronicle* Harrison followed with "The World We Live In," which began by discussing the fact that "Most of us never think how new is this world in which we live, or how strange the world of our great grandfathers would seem to us." He described the world "our ancestors lived in" and how "their world has been transformed . . . in the last hundred and fifty years." He argued that "the magician responsible for this change" was "Science," which was "nothing more than organized observation, experiment, [and] commonsense." Divisions of science "had 'transformed the world' in less than two centuries," and it was "a singular fact that those peoples who have most of it are able to impose their will on those who have less or none at all." He then briefly discussed "some of the social effects" of science:

> It brings people nearer to each other, increasing social knowledge and social sympathy, so that when an earthquake occurs in Japan the pocket-book of

the world flies open. On the other hand, as soon as diamonds are discovered in South Africa or other things in Hayti we civilized people can rush there to stake out our claims and back them up with our regiments and battleships. . . . Isolation is over for us. What with our International News reels and Pathe Weekly films, books and newspapers, it is easier for us to keep well-informed about what people look like and what they do in Siam, China, the Virgin Islands, Germany or Russia. Lies find it harder to maintain themselves in any mind that's not too lazy to look around and inquire. But, at the same time, if India, Egypt, West Africa and Hayti can not be successfully lied to about "democracy," they have a harder job shaking off its yoke, so long as "democracy" has the equipment of science and they have not. So, in the wider world, the social effects shade off into the political. With more knowledge of what's what all people are less content with inequalities: they realize them more keenly. The more they know, the more they want. So, the demand for democracy (the real thing) becomes a constant factor in political life whether external or internal. At the same time, they feel the urgent need to treat the main things on which their social needs depend for satisfaction in ways that will better serve the common interest. . . .

But that brings us to economic matters; to things that have to do with wealth, work and wages, buying and selling, trade and commerce and industry.[28]

Harrison said that he "merely wanted to hint . . . that science and scientific things are . . . matters that concern you and me and the other 1700 million humans down to the very roots of our everyday lives." Both the "Fiji Island cannibal" and "the Wall Street millionaire" were "equally affected by this thing that has transformed the world: the one works it and wins while the other knows nothing of it and *therefore* stays on the losing side." Harrison asked his readers, "On which side are you?[29]

Harrison's *Chronicle* column of January 26 was entitled "'English as She Is Spoke.'" He began by describing how for "Negroes," "our ordinary speech, as well as our ordinary writing, is a thing set apart, bearing the badge of an inferior product, as if we were in a mental class by ourselves." He asked, "What is the basic reason of all this?"[30] He observed that "the Polish Jew can use five different languages: Hebrew and Yiddish, Polish, German and Russian," while in contrast, "The American Negro has but the one language to learn," yet "most of us speak and write ours as if it were, for us, the hardest thing in the world." Harrison believed firmly that "our manner of speaking is an absolute indication of the manner of our thinking," that "the man who slurs his words always slurs his thoughts," and "he who runs his words together does the same thing with his ideas."[31]

Harrison pointed out that "the question of our speech is closely connected with the larger question of our mental capacity" and that "the white man . . . naturally concludes that when you speak like 'inferior cattle' you are 'inferior cattle.'" He then offered some advice to his readers:

You may know only three thousand words; but if you can use them properly, then you must go back to the little grammar, the spelling book and the dictionary. . . . You will find that as you master your language you will be mastering your ideas. And, until you master them your mental life will be a muddle.

Reading a few good books will be a great help. . . . Commit a few paragraphs of each to memory, and they will serve as standards by which to test your own everyday speech.[32]

"Science and Race Prejudice" was the subject of Harrison's February 2 *Chronicle* column. It began with a discussion of how Birmingham, Alabama, police injected scopolamine ("the drug which rumor says will make even a policeman tell the truth") into "a number of helpless Negroes," who, according to the police, then confessed to a series of murders. "Oddly," added Harrison, no one had "thought of injecting scopolomine [*sic*] into the policemen"—the "logical next step." This led him to ask: "What is the value of science in American hands?" He responded that the answer "depends on circumstances," since the "physical sciences like engineering, chemistry and hydraulics cannot be 'worked' to produce results according to the prejudices of the scientist," while "the social and psychological sciences can."[33]

In sociology and psychology "exponents like Macdougall [William McDougall], [Franklin H.] Giddings, [Madison] Grant and those who construe the army intelligence tests, seem to think that the rest of us are fools." Clearly, "when we know a man to be a Catholic, a Russian Grand Duke, a Ku Kluxer or a Californian Senator we expect that the bias of his religion, class or nationality will enter into the results of his mental processes and prejudice his views on birth-control, Bolshevism, patriotism and Chinese immigration," and "we make allowances accordingly." Similarly, "a scientist is . . . a human being—subject as such to the pressure of his environment, educational, social, racial and others," though "men like Macdougal and the Birmingham police seem to think that when they put on the cloak of 'science' the thing under the cloak becomes at once insulated from the human currents of prejudice and error." To Harrison this was "sheer nonsense," since "in reality they assume the cloak in order to 'put over' their prejudices with greater authority and effect."[34]

Harrison predicted that the "poor Negroes in Alabama will find that the results of the scopolamine tests "depend upon the hands that apply them and the purposes for which they are applied." Extending this point, he argued that "from the Bible to the census, from philosophy to the civil service examinations: when race prejudice applies the test and fixes the standards, the results will always be in favor of race prejudice." That was "one great reason" why he had been "urging Negroes for the past ten years to produce their own scholars and scientists to the end that they may be able to keep the hands of prejudice from juggling with the weights."[35]

If this were not done, "unscholarly 'social psychologists'" like Professor McDougall would "continue to dress propaganda in the garb of science and always 'prove' Negroes to be 'unfit,'" while "scholarly ethnologists" would "keep Christian Negroes believing that no worthwhile contributions to culture and civilization have ever come or can ever come from any Negroid or dark-skinned group." He concluded that "as a group we Negroes have not produced many scientists" and that "Professor [George Washington] Carver and Professor Ernest Just" were "the only two" whom he could "recall off-hand in the present generation." Instead, "our crop runs mostly to ministers, lawyers and literateurs; and we make up for the deficiency by classifying our mere writers as scholars, sociologists and philosophers." But, he predicted, "the generation now in school will . . . give us, not what we want, but what we need—men who can challenge white scientists and scholars on their own ground and make them toe the mark."[36]

In the February 9 *Boston Chronicle* column on "The Newspaper and Social Service" Harrison opened with broad comments describing how "the main social service which a newspaper can render to its readers is the gathering and publishing of news." But he promptly clarified that "in journalism, as in art, the first necessity is that of selection." The selection process "expresses the intent of the selector," and thus "news selection is generally an index to the Policy of a newspaper," which in turn "always mirrors its makers' intents." While providing a "record of events" might be "the main social service of the newspaper," it was "not the only, nor even the highest social service." There was also "social value" in a newspaper that explained "what is being thought in the world" and "what the editors themselves think is valuable as light and guidance to their readers." Thus "institutions and how they work; ideas and how they affect us": "all these come within the scope of the up-to-date newspaper."[37]

"In the light of these principles" Harrison moved to "consider the policies of some Negro newspapers." He wrote from New York where there were "some of the ablest minds and some of the shoddiest papers in Negro-America." He noted, "Some of our weeklies limit their news to what they clip from the columns of the white papers." Since "the white papers feature[d] the Negro only in his lower, or police court, aspects . . . a Negro paper with such a policy" would "never be an aid in Negro uplift." "Besides," he added, "'where there is no Vision the people perish.'"[38]

Harrison also discussed some other practices critically. He described the elevating of paid advertising matter "to the news columns as news" and how, when readers realize what this implies, "they lose respect for the news-columns of such papers, and cease to patronize them." He added that though "Negroes possess a good deal of deep humor and genuine wit," it was too often the case that "'personal' digs" and "taste for the scandal" took the place "of an intelligent interest in the world around them" and that "enlivening and instructive controversy," such as provided when Timothy Thomas Fortune edited *The Age* (in the period from 1885 to 1907), was "considered too 'high-brow.'"[39]

In such a situation Harrison knew that "changes of policy are effected mainly by the *readers* who, by turning their backs on such papers, can make their circulation drop," and they can apply pressure "by refusing to advertise in them." In these ways "the 'followers' lead the 'leaders' and educate those who should educate them."[40]

———

While writing his weekly columns for the *Boston Chronicle*, Harrison went on a lecture tour of the Boston area in February 1924. In New Bedford on February 11, he spoke on Abraham Lincoln before a group of small businessmen, who paid him $25. He spoke on the "Ku Klux and the Negro" and on "Frederick Douglass" in Cambridge on February 12 and 13 and in Haverhill on February 14. His big talk, however, on "Lincoln & Liberty," was at Ford Hall in Boston on February 12, and the *Boston Chronicle* reported that a twenty-five-person committee on arrangements "representing influential Boston organizations and clubs" was established. A mixed audience of five hundred attended the talk, in which "Dr." Harrison honored Lincoln, discussed his expediency, and "pointed the way to a sane historical consideration of the true worth of 'the greatest of white Americans.'"[41]

In his opening remarks Harrison introduced himself as "a native of the outer America, living near the center of government, for safety's sake." He said he considered Frederick Douglass the "greatest single figure in American history," and he "won over" his audience with his "somewhat novel interpretation of the character of Lincoln." His delivery was said to be "forceful" yet familiar, with "an eloquence that drove home the gist of his assertions" in a style likened to that of William Pickens. He demonstrated "wide reading" and "acquaintance with the historical facts of the period" while omitting "the stock of jests which characterize the lectures of Dean Pickens." His remarks were "punctuated with frequent outbursts of applause."[42]

The *Chronicle* reported that his announced intent was "to unshackle the mind of the American Negro from the sense of debt of gratitude . . . [to] Abraham Lincoln, and . . . the government and administration which he served." Harrison argued that "the Negro owes a debt of gratitude that he stands ever ready to acknowledge" to "abolitionists of the stamp of Wendell Phillips, of William Lloyd Garrison, and of [Elijah Paris] Lovejoy," "but," he added, "the Negro student today is resenting vigorously the insinuation that to the men whose government of the nation through the trying Civil War period was motivated by purely political instincts, the Negro is under many obligations." He explained:

> For his work in steering the Union through a political crisis, Lincoln merits the praise which history has given him in full measure. Abraham Lincoln proved himself a statesman, when the country needed a statesman of the highest order. It is therefore only natural that the country which benefited from his political foresight should bestowe upon him a degree of posthumous admiration equivalent almost to hero-worship.
>
> But to say that the Negro, became a beneficiary of Lincoln's policies only because emancipation proved expedient is asking too much.

"As a Negro," Harrison did not "blame Lincoln because he declined to follow the advice of the idealist abolitionists, and sacrifice the politically expedient to the morally sublime." He had followed "the course politically most expedient" and merited credit for this. Lincoln "sought the nation's good above the interests of any factors within it" and "should be regarded as a great statesman who followed expediency to a wise end" and not as "a sort of archangel ministering to the ills of down-trodden groups regardless of the political exigencies of the moment." Harrison also described the work of the 54th and 55th Massachusetts regiments and the Louisiana volunteer outfits, "whose work in the field Lincoln acknowledged was a vital factor in the ultimate success of the war."[43]

On Wednesday evening, February 13, Harrison spoke before another large gathering in the First Church, Cambridge, on "Frederick Douglass." At his February 14 talk on "Lincoln and Liberty" sponsored by the Congregational, Universalist, and Unitarian churches at the North Congregational Church in Haverhill, he declared that

> the civil war was a war not to abolish slavery but to save the union. Although Abraham Lincoln set the negro free in the south during the Civil war, the war was for the safety of the union: such action was the demand of the vast majority who saw what the enlistment of the negro in the Confederate army would mean and to prevent England from siding with the Confederacy by showing

that the war was for the freedom of the negro slave. Slavery was only abolished in this country with the adoption of the 13th amendment to the constitution of the United States long after Lincoln had died, but it was Lincoln's action that led to the adoption of this amendment, and we hail him as the hero of the negro.[44]

The church was filled into the vestry. Harrison explained that he didn't "propose to launch forth a traditional and conventional eulogy of America's great commoner, Abraham Lincoln." Lincoln "did not come from poor stock," he said. His ancestors "were sturdy folk of good American stock," and he "was not a sociological miracle" but "a self-made man." He "was a politician at the time when politicians could be great . . . when a politician could fix upon one strong issue," when politicians "would not trim their sails to every breeze." Lincoln "was not an abolitionist"; the abolitionist "was a crazy radical who was so crazy that he did not care a thing for common political consideration." The abolitionist "realized that slavery was politically improper" and "economically rotten"; that "nothing would come from successive compromises"; that a "new party, the Republican party" needed to be organized. Lincoln's opponents "called him all sorts of names and filthy stories of his ancestry and origin were circulated," and, after he won the presidency, the southern states that opposed his political platform "seceded and organized a southern confederacy." Lincoln "sought to do the expedient thing," which was "to save the union." He "was not thinking entirely of the Negro but considered the interests of the majority." Even when the war broke out, "he still kept from saying that it was to abolish slavery." He said it was "a war not to abolish slavery but to save the union," and he "stuck to this until southern generals began to enlist the black men."[45]

At this time, when "England was the recognized 'Mistress of the Seas,'" the "cotton from the south was being held back from England by the blockade of the southern ports by the federal warships, and the English people were thrown out of work and were reduced to starvation." They were "coming to recognize the southern cause," and "the working class of England at this time was under harsh government and was looking for more freedom itself." Lincoln "came to see the feeling of the English people in regard to the war" as the English government "threatened to take sides with the Confederacy." Then, "to quiet this feeling," he saw "that the only move would be to capture the ethical support of the English people by declaring the war [was] for the freedom of the negro." This "satisfied" the English, who "pulled their belts tighter, saying that it was a war for freedom."[46]

When Lincoln said that "negroes were free," they "immediately enlisted in the union armies" and at the height of the war 180,000 Black men fought in the union ranks. Lincoln said "it was the black fighters that won the war for the union," and his "declaring the negro free during the Civil war" did lead to adoption of the Thirteenth Amendment, which ordered "the abolishment of slavery forever in this country." Harrison explained that "we negroes come together with the white people to worship Lincoln as one because we owe him a special debt," but, he reminded his readers, "the negro . . . did his share in the war" and "died on the field of the battle and suffered for the cause." Harrison concluded: "This nation of ours owes the negro a debt of gratitude, and, although we should worship Lincoln as the greatest American that ever held public office in this country, we should also show our respect to the negroes that died for the union."[47]

Harrison apparently wrote to William Pickens about his Massachusetts lectures, and on February 20 Pickens responded while on a train between Pittsburgh and Columbus, Ohio. He had just read "thoroughly" a letter Harrison's "little daughter" had brought the night before and was "elated" to know that the Ford Hall talk went "just as I told them things would" and that Haverhill had worked out also. "Once they get acquainted with you, I have no doubt about the demand for you," he added. Pickens said he was working on a "unique new book" (possibly *American Aesop: Negro and Other Humor*) and would be away for some weeks. He hoped to see Harrison on his return, acknowledged what he said "about beginning work for the [Chicago] *Defender*," and noted Harrison's plan to review his book.[48]

While Pickens didn't mention which daughter brought the letter, it may have been Harrison's youngest, nine-year-old Ilva. Hubert wrote a poem to her from Boston on February 15 and included a copy of it in his copy of *Gems from Tennyson*. He wrote:

> All precious things discovered late,
> To those that seek them issue forth
> and then added—
> How'er it be,
> it seems to me
> Tis only noble to be good.
> Kind hearts are more than coronets,
> And simple faith than Norman blood.[49]

The February 16 *Chronicle* carried Harrison's "Lincoln and Douglass," which was probably the basis of his Cambridge talk and which noted that February contained "two anniversaries of men who were unique and outstanding in the life of the American people. One . . . white, the other colored." It was based on his talks and writings on the subject for over a decade. He described how an "ancestor of the white man [Lincoln] came to Massachusetts in 1637 and settled in New Hingham," where he became "the first ironmaster in America." From him there descended "a stream of sturdy pioneers, landowners and adventurers who fared forth under favorable conditions to conquer the fading frontiers." They went from New England, "through New Jersey, Pennsylvania, Virginia and Kentucky, where the line finally flowered in Abraham Lincoln, the 16th President of the United States." In contrast, "the ancestor of the colored man [Douglass] was unknown—in fact, he came into the world not a man, but a thing, to whom wandering, adventure and ambition were alike forbidden."[50]

While Lincoln "lifted himself from the level of a landowner's son, through law and politics to the presidency of a people made up of his equals only," Douglass "lifted himself from the level of a piece of property . . . through Journalism and oratory to a position of conceded equality with the best men of a race which held itself superior to his." Thus, concluded Harrison, "if the length of the journey is the measure of the travelling powers, then it must be allowed that the colored man travelled farther than the white." Add to this "that the black man had no ancestry" and "that no man's hand held this white man down while all men's hands held the other down," and we "must face the startling conclusion that Frederick Douglass, the Negro, was greater than Abraham Lincoln, the Caucasian."[51]

Harrison emphasized that "Lincoln was great in every sense of the word, the greatest soul that ever occupied the presidential seat," and that it was "natural" that "every white church and household should celebrate his anniversary." "Douglass was even greater," however. "But how many Negro churches and households are celebrating his life and deeds in memorial service this month?" he asked. While "Lincoln looms like a god" to white Americans, to "how many Negro Americans" did "Douglass loom like a god?" Harrison concluded that "we Negroes are a singular folk," and since "the worship of its great men is one root of the self-respect of a group, a nation, a race," it was "high time that Negroes should become familiar with the heroic deeds and splendid achievements of their brothers in blood."[52]

––––––––––

Harrison's next two *Chronicle* articles focused on self-education. In his February 23 *Chronicle* column Harrison wrote on "Education out of School," which began:

To the Negro America offers Jim Crow, segregation, disfranchisement and the lynching-bee. But at the same time she also offers him free schools and colleges, free public libraries and the second-hand bookshops where he can "sit with Shakespeare," walk with Shaw, commune with poets, philosophers, scientists, historians, novelists, and draw "sweetness and light" from the noblest souls of the past and present. What a blessing it would be if, while we fight against the evil in America's left hand, we should utilize the powers which she holds in her right to make our fight more effective![53]

He reasoned that "it is the wisdom of the weak that enables them to overthrow the strength of the strong." Thus, "when the European Jews found themselves proscribed and trampled on, without rights or protection in the Middle Ages they began to specialize in two things: mind-power and money-power—and the first was parent of the second." They soon "became the most intelligent people in all Europe, and although they number less than the Negroes in America and are hated more cordially both there and here, they have become by their intelligence more powerful than any people in Europe in proportion to their numbers."[54]

The situation was different in the United States. "With education open to us, in the North, as freely as to others, we fail to avail ourselves of the golden opportunity." Though "some of our boys go to college," that "is not necessarily education." The final day in college is called "Commencement Day" because "it is only after college that the youth *commences* to learn." One's "college course (if well conducted)" can provide "the key to the door of the Temple of Learning." But, "too often," our youth stand "twirling the key in . . . hand for others to admire" and never open the door, while others, who forge keys for themselves, go in and enjoy "all her treasures."[55]

Examples abounded. Herbert Spencer "knew more than any other European of the nineteenth century, yet he had never been in college." Henry Thomas Buckle, Abraham Lincoln, Toussaint Louverture, and Frederick Douglass "were all educated men, but none of them had ever been to college or high school." They made their mark through "determined study," which was "still open to every American, black as well as white." In college one is taught "how to gather knowledge" but not "how to use knowledge"—"that no one can teach you, either in college or out of it." He concluded:

Knowledge is power. While we chatter about "segregation" we segregate ourselves from that community of culture and knowledge that is as wide open to us as the winds of heaven and limitless as the eternal sea. In this respect the West Africans are far ahead of us. Let us pray for the will to follow in the footsteps of John Mensah Sarbah, [J. E.] Casely Hayford, [Ernest] S. Beoku Betts, Kobyna [Kobina] Sekyi and our other black brothers whom we ignorantly aspire to lead.[56]

Harrison's March 1, 1924, *Chronicle* column, "A Few Books," responded to a reader who asked for a list of "indispensable books to be read and studied by those who are anxious to educate themselves at home." It was a request that constantly cropped up, and Harrison gladly answered it, though the list he provided was stripped down to "bare essentials" and omitted "literature." Nevertheless, he "confidently assert[ed] that anyone who masters these ten will possess a better, broader and more modern education than the average graduate of Yale or Harvard." The ten books were: (1) *The Childhood of the World*, by Edward Clodd; (2) *Man's Place in Nature (with Six Lectures to Working Men)*, by Thomas H. Huxley; (3) *The Descent of Man*, by Charles Darwin; (4) *Anthropology*, by Edward B. Tylor; (5) *Modern Science and Modern Thought*, by Samuel Laing; (6) *The Evolution of Civilization*, by Joseph McCabe; (7) (*Ancient Times: A History of*) *The Early World*, by James H. Breasted; (8) *Modern Europe* (the one-volume edition) by (Christopher) Fyffe (Fyfe); (9) *The Evolution of States*, by John M. Robertson; and (10) *First Principles*, by Herbert Spencer. [57]

Harrison explained that some of the books could be obtained at secondhand bookshops and that numbers 1, 2, 3, 5, and 6 were available from the Truth Seeker Publishing Co., 61 Vesey Street, New York. These five books suggested how important freethought writings still were to his worldview. In addition, and since one "should know of his own group, as well as something of the wider world to be educated," he added "a list of ten books indispensable to an educated Negro": (1) *African Life and Customs*, by Edward Wilmot Blyden; (2) *White Capital and Coloured Labor*, by Sir Sidney (Sydney) Olivier; (3) *Negro Culture in West Africa*, by George W. Ellis; (4) *The Black Man's Burden*, by E. D. Morel; (5) *From "Superman" to Man*, by J. A. Rogers; (6) *The Aftermath of Slavery*, by William A. Sinclair; (7) *The Haytian Revolution*, by T. G. Steward; (8) *West African Studies*, by Mary H. Kingsley; (9) *The Negro Year Book* (published annually) by Monroe N. Work; and (10) *The Negro in Our History*, by Carter G. Woodson.[58]

For his "literature" list Harrison included: (1) *The Bible*; (2) Shakespeare; (3) *Don Quixote*, by Miguel de Cervantes; (4) *The Arabian Nights*; (5) *Penguin Island*, by Anatole France; (6) ten of (Sir Walter) Scott's novels; (7) six of (Charles) Dickens's novels; (8) four of (H. G.) Wells's novels; (9) five of (Alexandre) Dumas's (*pere*) novels; (10) *Quo Vadis*; (11) (François) Rabelais; (12) (Alfred, Lord) Tennyson's poems; and a host of others. He added, "There would be not less than a hundred 'indispensables' in such a list, which should run back to Virgil, Horace, Sophocles, Aeschylus, Homer, and Anacreon." But, he added, "such a list can easily be obtained," and with the two other lists one would "have laid the secure foundations of knowledge"—foundations "all too sadly neglected in our day."[59]

―――――――

Harrison's important article on "Race Consciousness" appeared in the March 15 *Boston Chronicle*. It offered his mature, well-thought-out views on the subject and had a more temporal and conditional tone than was suggested by his reflexive and absolutist "race first" of seven years earlier. His pithy essay began:

> The general facts of the outside world reflect themselves not only in ideas but in our feelings. The facts that make up a general social condition are reflected in social states of mind. Thus the feeling of racial superiority which the white races so generally exhibit is produced by the external fact of their domination in most parts of the world. That same fact, by the way, produces in the minds of the masses of black, brown and yellow peoples in Africa, Asia and elsewhere what is called in psychology a protective reaction; and that is their race-consciousness. So that race-consciousness is like loyalty, neither an evil nor a good. The good or evil of it depends upon the uses to which it is put.[60]

The recent war had "chiseled the channels of race-consciousness deeper among American Negroes than any previous external circumstances." "American army officers treated their Negro fellow soldiers worse than they did the German enemy," and "we learnt that the Other People held race to be higher than patriotism." Similarly, in peace, the message imparted was "that race is stronger than religion"—hence "the existence of Negro churches." While "this need not mean that we have to hate white people," it did mean "that in sheer self-defense, we too must put race very high on our list of necessities." Only because this had been done "all along" was there "'Negro progress' to boast about as proof of our equal human possibilities." In conclusion, he emphasized:

> Negro churches, Negro newspapers, Negro life-insurance-companies, banks, fraternities, colleges and political appointees—all mean Negro race-consciousness.
>
> So even if self-seekers have vilely exploited the thing that is no reason why we should condemn it as an evil. What is an evil is the ignorance and gullibility of those who let themselves be exploited. So long as the outer situation remains what it is we must evoke race-consciousness to furnish a background for our aspiration, readers for our writers, a clientele for our artists and professional people, and ideals for our future. For so long as a black boy may not aspire to be Governor of Massachusetts or President of the United States, like the son of an immigrant German or Russian, so long will we need race-consciousness.[61]

In the March 22 *Boston Chronicle* Harrison's "The Feet of the Young Men" aimed to inspire young Black males to a new level of leadership. He began with a discussion of how the older generation attempts "to hold on and dispute control with the young ones" and how this was a "part of the social tragedy" affecting "our race." He knew "men who on behalf of higher education stormed the sage of Tuskegee's citadel a quarter of a century ago; yet, now that another generation has risen round them equipped with the same 'higher education,' they do all they can to hold back these militant youngsters from reaching the limelight of publicity." Despite such resistance, he predicted, "'Youth will be served'" because "the feet of the young men tend to be level with the heads of the old." Harrison then charted the course ahead:

> Whenever we speak of Regeneration it is the young men whom we have in mind. It is to them that the race must look for the removal of its inner and outer disabilities. Those petty meannesses that hold us, and that help us to hold others, back; that smug satisfaction that keeps us contented with lower standards of social and intellectual efficiency; that complex of inferiority which prompts us to "the flight from Fact" and makes us waste so much energy in trying to shun our real selves—all these are products of a genera- tion that is dying and is already mentally dead. Whether in their day they called themselves radicals or subservients is nothing to the point. . . . Having done what little they could for progress, their control of the line of march is now a bar to further progress. They must make way for Youth—gladly or sadly, but they must make way.

In closing he emphasized, "The feet of the young men are giving the new marching-time, and those who can't keep step with them must fall out because they cumber the ground." There were new lines forming "for the new attack on the twin citadels of Self[ishness] and Stupidity."[62]

In "The Negro-American Speaks" in the March 29 *Chronicle* Harrison offered a vision for the future and an implicit response to those like the Garveyites who might advocate a "Back to Africa" movement. He began with comments on how "the American Negro" was "called to live as strange a life as the Christian paci- fist who works in a munitions factory in war-time to support a large family." Like that pacifist, "he is driven to effect the best compromise that he can." To Har- rison, "the American Negro" was "an American; and generally a deeper, truer American than nine-tenths of the whites." This fact was "so well . . . known" that when Woodrow Wilson's life was in danger "he put a guard around the White House made up *of Negro soldiers!*" When U.S. armies were being mobilized, "every white person who sought admission to the camp [Upton, on Long Island] was stopped by the sentry, questioned and searched," while "the only Negroes who were stopped and questioned were those who at first sight seemed white." The "meaning" of all this, Harrison added, was that "while the Negro is no happier than the Jew, he, like the Jew, is here to stay and make the best of it.

His problem is an American problem and he will settle it here in America upon American lines."[63]

Harrison then commented on the type of leadership that was needed, consistent with the "here in America" perspective he articulated:

What the Negro needs in this new day is a Negro-American Messiah, a prince of promise who will gild his people's soul with the gleams of a glorious future—in America, who will show them how they can rise to heights hitherto undreamed of—in America, and help them to change proscription into power and salvation. It was Jesus who said "The kingdom of heaven is within you", while [James Russell] Lowell's Sir Launfal had to be taught that one need not mount and ride away to find the Holy Grail. If we flee from lions in our back yard be sure we shall not face them in their own jungles. Strength, courage and persistence will work wonders at home as well as elsewhere. We who have helped to build America with our blood and tears and sweat, who have eaten her bread and salt, and have looked the white man in the eye and lived and grown numerous and intelligent, we propose to reap the fruits of our labor and partake of the harvest which we have helped to produce.

And that is why twelve millions of us are still calling for a leader who will have some living message for us in terms of what we are—Americans![64]

In "Opening the Doors," which appeared in the April 5 *Chronicle*, Harrison recounted how on the previous Saturday (March 29) he had had the "good fortune to stand upon the same platform where Abraham Lincoln stood sixty-four years ago—in historic Cooper Institute—representing the Board of Education of the first city in the world" in order to "lecture to an intelligent educated audience of four thousand white people on 'America's Interest in the Reparations Problem.'" The occasion "brought a thrill," for "never before in the history of race-contact in this country has any black man been sent by white men to white men to instruct them on any subject that was independent of the Race Question." As Harrison "looked upon the vast sea of whites—Irish, Jews, Germans, Russians and Anglo-Saxons" and the "slight sprinkling of . . . 'fellow-men of the Negro Race' who had come down from Harlem," he "realized to the full that America (in the North, at least) does hold out to the Negro some opportunities unsurpassed anywhere else."[65]

The "generous and enthusiastic" applause at the close of the lecture brought to mind "the fine words of Herbert Spencer when he said that 'in the Republic of Letters there is no such thing as Race.'" Harrison added, "No one found my hair in need of Zura-Kink-out or my complexion too dark. They listened with respect to my interpretations of America's financial relations with Europe, and the few who differed from me in the ensuing discussion differed respectfully."

He mentioned this because it had "a solid significance for our people," suggesting as it did, "that when the Negro enters fully into the intellectual life of the white American the customary barriers based on the assumption of his inferiority tend to break down. For there, as in the financial world, every man's dollar is worth one hundred cents—if it is genuine."[66]

Harrison emphasized that "Knowledge . . . is power" and, as he had in his February 23 *Chronicle* column, that "when the Jew was oppressed on all sides in medieval Europe he steadily and stealthily developed two powers: mind-power and money-power." The "former showed him the value of the latter," and "the Jews have been for many centuries the most intellectual people in Europe." Today, "while they are less in numbers than the Negroes of the United States, they wield an international power which is both respected and feared." Harrison then drove home his point:

> The American Negro is more favorably situated than the Jew was seven centuries ago. Despite the poor schools provided for Negroes in the South the whole enginery of crackerdom can not prevent the poorest Negro boy in Mississippi from learning to read. Frederick Douglass, Booker Washington, Isaiah Montgomery, William Pickens and many others have proved this again and again. The wisdom of the weak is still more than a match for the strength of the strong. It is still possible for Negroes to make themselves the most intellectual element in America. Don't say "it can't be done", my brothers. It can. Try it and see. Only by brains and by the product of brains can we pull ourselves up. Without it we shall remain as we are. With it we can remove mountains. There is in knowledge the power to open doors, political, social and economic. Let us use this key while yet we may to unlock the golden doors of promise.[67]

On April 19 Harrison's "Population, Immigration, and the Negro" appeared in the *Chronicle*. It stated "when the Negro was declared free in 1863 there were four million of them," while "the white race numbered at that time twenty-seven million and a half." The latest "imperfect census concede[d] the known existence of twelve million Negroes," indicating a tripling in sixty years—without the aid of immigration ("since foreign-born Negroes numbered less than sixty thousand"). Between 1790 and 1890 some 17,363,977 immigrants entered the United States, yet the 1890 census "showed that the foreign-born and those of foreign parentage amounted to thirty million, approximately forty-eight per cent of the total population which was then fifty three million and a quarter." Then, "between 1907 and 1914 the tide of white immigration flowed in an annual wave of more than a million and a quarter," and these numbers showed that "if it had not been for the white immigration during the last hundred years the Negroes in America would today outnumber the whites!" and "this fact would have made a tremendous difference in the present status of the American Negro." It also suggested "despite all the racial pessimists on our side and the dogmatists of doom on the other, that the black race under similar and equal conditions can out-breed and out-live the white." He then added, "Clear as this fact is—I have yet to learn that any of our intellectuals have discovered it."[68]

Harrison realized that "conditions are not equal." In 1910 "there was one Negro physician for every 3320 Negroes while every 517 whites had a physician," and since then the ratio had "not much improved." Similarly, in "the most unhealthy portions of the cities" one would "find the bulk of the Negroes" with rents higher and wages lower than their white counterparts. They would also be the first to "go without parks, schools, play grounds, and libraries." Yet this situation was not hopeless—progress had been made despite handicaps, and the facts, as Harrison read them, showed "inferior status, but superior stamina."[69]

Harrison's "'Superior'—to Whom" in the *Chronicle* of May 3 began by summarizing J. A. Rogers in *As Nature Leads*, which showed "that the white man in America really desires the presence of the Negro as a setting for the white man's egotism." He similarly cited the story of the little Southern girl who was asked why she objected to the removal of the Negroes and replied, "Cause then Ah wouldn' have nobody to be better than." Harrison then wryly offered that "the great majority of us who prate of 'democracy', 'liberty', 'equality', black as well as white, when put to the test, want to have something 'to be better than.'" This went to "very laughable lengths," such as the "white Anglo-Saxons" who find themselves "top-dog on the heap" and thereupon "proceed to write social science and re-write history to prove" that "top-ness (superiority) is Anglo-Saxon-ness (racial) and that's that." Then, however, "along come some other Nordics . . . ahead of us with poison-gas and submarine." The Anglo-Saxons then "call upon non-Nordics to help save—civilization." Another example concerned the taking of "the lands, lives and labor of black, brown and yellow" because "they may be inferior." Now, however, "Lothrop Stoddard and the prestidigitators of the Army intelligence tests assure us" that "more than ninety per cent" of the "'superior' whites in America" are "hopelessly and inescapably 'inferior!'" To Harrison these were "the absurdities of that modern form of an ancient disease—Egotism—which we miscall 'superiority!'"[70]

On May 10 Harrison wrote the important and insightful "The Right Way to Unity" in the *Chronicle*. He explained that during the last decade there had been "a commendable striving on the part of prominent Negroes to attain unity for the masses." Unfortunately, however, many were not clear as to just what they meant. "Some seemed to mean unity of thought and ideas; others unity of purpose; and yet others meant unity of action." It was "self-evident," however, that not all were "humanly possible, or even quite desirable." Harrison reasoned there was "one place in which one may reasonably expect unanimity of thought and ideas . . . —the grave-yard." Similarly, "unity of organization," while not impossible," was difficult to achieve. The largest "Negro" organization in the world was the Baptist Church, with over four million members, yet it couldn't "get all the Negroes of America with-in one fold after more than a hundred years."[71]

In contrast, "unity of purpose and aim is well within our possibilities," and though it had "received recently the attention of some of our best minds" the goal was not nearer. Harrison believed that "the fault" was "entirely with the uniters," who had "generally gone at the problem from the wrong end." They had "begun at the top when they should have begun at the bottom." The "attempt to unite the 'intellectuals' at the top" was "not the same thing as uniting the Negro masses." Too often, "the 'intellectuals'" assumed an "air of superior beings" and "expect that the others will run to seek them out." Since these intellectuals were "unable to reduce the number of lynchings" over thirty years while "the ordinary uneducated Negroes did this just by picking up their feet and coming away from the South in large numbers," it was "apparent that these Negro masses sometimes have more effective brains in their feet than the 'intellectuals' have in their heads." Accordingly, Harrison suggested that

> the way to unity lies through the hearts of the multitude. First set those hearts on fire with a common zeal for a common object, equally desired and equally attained by all in common, and the fire of that common feeling will flame in every lodge, every church, every city and state in the nation. From the nature of the case unselfishness, humility, courage, and helpfulness must be the fuel that will go to the kindling of such a flame. But light the fire at the bottom of the pile. . . . Then "your young men shall see visions"—and your young women too. And, in the meanwhile, "where there is no vision the people perish."[72]

Harrison's position was clearly distinct from Du Bois's (from as far back as 1903), that the "Talented Tenth" were the "educated and gifted" group whose members "must be made leaders of thought and missionaries of culture among their people" in order to lead African Americans forward. Harrison, in contrast, emphasized education and self-development of the masses, the so-called common people. He also increasingly equated the Talented Tenth concept with the concept of "Colored" (or "Mulatto") as opposed to "Negro" leadership of the "Negro race." His opposition to such a leadership was because he did not think that such a Talented Tenth was in any way preordained to lead the "Negro race," nor did he think that it had provided the leadership needed by African Americans. Harrison rejected the "white" domination that unchallenged acceptance of such leadership implied. As he explained, for two centuries African Americans "have been told by white Americans that we cannot and will not amount to anything except in so far as we first accept the bar sinister of their mixing with us." Thus, "always when white people had to select a leader for Negroes they would select some one who had in his veins the blood of the selector." Under slavery, according to Harrison, "it was those whom Denmark Vesey of Charleston described as 'house niggers' who got the master's cut-off clothes, the better scraps of food and culture which fell from the white man's table, who were looked upon as the Talented Tenth of the Negro race." Historically, "the opportunities of self-improvement, in so far as they lay within the hand of the white race, were accorded exclusively to this class of people who were the left-handed progeny of the white masters."[73]

What was particularly important in Harrison's strategic approach was his conception of and approach to race unity. He sought "unity of action," focusing on "uniting the Negro masses," who were "the key to racial solidarity." Interestingly, Du Bois would reach a somewhat similar conclusion in 1940 in his autobiography *Dusk of Dawn*. At that time Du Bois explained that Booker T. Washington had proposed "a flight of class from mass in wealth with the idea of escaping the masses or ruling the masses through power placed by white capitalists." Du Bois added that he, in turn, had opted for "flight of class from mass through the development of a Talented Tenth; but the power of this aristocracy of talent was to lie in its knowledge and talent and not in its wealth." The problem with this, as Du Bois later realized, was that it, too, "left controls to wealth"—a problem he admitted that he had not foreseen. By 1940 Du Bois concluded that "the mass and class must unite for the world's salvation." In this can be seen the position—the racial unity of the mass with the leadership class, with focus on the unity of purpose of the masses—that Harrison had arrived at as early as 1916 and that is reflected in his 1924 article.[74]

Harrison's politically important May 17 *Chronicle* article gave evidence of his deep-rooted love of and confidence in the "common people." He opened with a quote from Lincoln that "God must have loved the common people because he made so many of them." The idea implied, he wrote, was "that since they make up the great majority of human kind they deserve more devotion than the aristocrats." He noted that "the Carpenter of Nazareth stuck to the 'publicans and sinners' and people who were not respectable or in 'good society', avoiding the Pharisees and Sadduces, the Scribes, the Sanhedrin and the high priests." Harrison said he often thought of this when he heard "great masses of my fellow-men referred to as 'rats.'" Since "in the great Washington and

Chicago race-riots it was the 'rats' who upheld the honor of the race and fought to maintain its safety from murderous assaults," he felt that they were owed "a vast debt of gratitude, even though they belong to the lowest levels of those whom we call the Common People."[75]

He then "plead for those" who are "despised and rejected of men," since they were "the real tests" for "our theories of brotherhood and racial solidarity":

> By and large, the Common People are the real race. They may not have much to give, but, such as it is, they give it without stint: loyalty, respect, friendliness and help in the hour of need. Sometimes their ignorance is played upon and their loyalty and devotion outraged; but when you do the right thing by them they always do the right thing by you. They are a perpetual reservoir of healthy enthusiasm and their rough but genuine appreciation is like a tonic to the soul that is sick of the shams and insincerities of those who call themselves "cultured". They are the dependable back-bone of every good cause and making of many. Out of the bosom of the Common people rise the sources of our literature and art, and the real, living virile society is the genuine life they live. Divorced from that, art is finical and literature flabby and what is called "society" becomes only the drumming [insincerities of drones in the hive or the foolish fluttering of those who call themselves butterflies]. It is better to have their good opinion when you are dead than the blessing of the Brahmins while you live. For while the one is real and abiding, the other is like "a tale told by an idiot, full of sound and fury and signifying—nothing."[76]

Two weeks later Harrison's "Seeking a Way Out" in the *Chronicle* of May 31, 1924, further pointed the way forward and also briefly introduced readers to his new organization, the International Colored Unity League. In his article Harrison explained "a race-problem" had to be "worked out or fought out by forces more complex than those of mere logic and argument." In light of this "the Negro problem in America" was "not insoluble," for "no human social problem ever was," and while it was "primarily of the white man's making," the "colored man must do most of the work" because he was the one "mainly concerned in it."

How would this be done? Harrison asked his "Negro" readers. "First, by organizing," which involved "cohesion, solidarity . . . [and] *LOVE*: love of race, love for one another, a blood-is-thicker-than-water policy, racial support and self-support, racial respect and self-respect." "Every lynching-bee and Jim Crow car" taught "that we must stand by each other: one for all and all for one, in matters of money, mind, politics and religion," in order "to survive and succeed."

Organizing was "work," and "that work is always where we are. In Boston or Bridgetown, Jamaica or Georgia, the old advice was still valuable: "Cast down your buckets *where you are!*" That was why, explained Harrison, that "the new nation-wide organization, of 'race-loving men and women,' The International Colored Unity League," had sprung up. Harrison added that he would be in Boston in June to "expound to Negroes and whites" on its program which, in part, was

> to stop Negroes from hating one another and Negro leaders from attacking each other; to mobilize all that energy against lynching, disfranchisement and Jim Crow; to use the ballot of the Northern Negro to secure such enforcement of the Constitution as will put the ballot into the hands of the Southern Negro, by which means-to-power he will be able to safeguard his own life, property and the future of his children; to encourage our people to buy, to own and to use property in town and country, building up by cooperative action such economic structures as will enable them to stand on their own legs and keep the dollars of the race; to co-operate with the Negro church, lodge, and other organizations that are already doing good work, and to help them to do better.[77]

Harrison's June 7 column in the *Chronicle*, "On Reading Negro Books," argued that "the young Negro writer" had an especially "hard row to hoe." If one wrote a book "which tells the truth about Negroes," then "white publishers [generally] want something else." If one secures a publisher, then "our people don't buy enough copies to afford . . . a living from the royalties." Part of this was "due to the old notion," which many retained, "that Negro books are necessarily of inferior quality." This, however, was "not true," and "Negro writers like Alain Leroy Locke and Charles Johnson of *Opportunity*, J. A. Rogers, William A. Sinclair, W. E. B. Du Bois and Kelly Miller" wrote "quite as well as white people—some of them better." Nevertheless, "Negroes bought more copies of the *Outline of History* (which attenuates the race's contributions to culture) than of *The Aftermath of Slavery*." Harrison added, only with "Racial Self-Consciousness and Solidarity will the Negro author's really big chance come. The Negro author and the Negro artist must both await the Negro Renaissance when the soul of the race is on fire with the purpose of proving its mettle, achieving for itself the things by which it will be judged in the future, and eager to listen to." Harrison here draws from Paul Laurence Dunbar's "Ode to Ethiopia":

> Bards who from thy roots shall spring
> And proudly tune their lyres to sing
> Of Ethiopia's glory.[78]

In the meantime, Harrison suggested that "each of us" make it "a point of pride to buy a Negro book—and read it." Many contained "genuine inspiration" and some "genuine greatness." He concluded by explaining to readers that

> neither in literature and history nor in the social sciences can we depend on writers of the white race to do justice to ours. I have always urged that we should raise up our own historians, scholars, sociologists, anthropologists—and even Egyptologists. But what is the use of their writing if we will not read? They also [require] appreciation and support; and we should give these to them. For by so doing we will keep alive the sparks of genius and kindle them into a blaze which will light our footsteps up the heights.
>
> What they can give us cannot be given [by] any other group of writers—to us. To get from them we must give to them and the more we give them the more they can and will give us. Suppose YOU begin![79]

Harrison's "In Case of War—What?" in the *Boston Chronicle* of June 14 called attention to the fact that three years earlier, in his lecture course at the public library in New York, he had said that "before five years had passed one of three wars would have come: between England and France, between England and the United States, between the United States and Japan." At that time, "hypocrisy's howl was raised for peace, universal and lasting peace," but he thought he "knew better and took occasion to say so." While "it seemed very presumptuous then," it no longer seemed to be the case. He insightfully commented that the "trouble between the United States and Japan" was one that, "given a knowledge of the currents and channels of the imperialist stream," was "bound to come." He didn't "want it," but he thought that its "imminence" would "play a part in the closing days of the political campaign." Harrison went further: "what is to be has already been decided upon." The war between the United States and Japan actually came seventeen years later.[80]

In addressing the question "How will the Negro be affected by a war between Japan and the United States?" Harrison quickly interjected that "one aspect of the problem is, of necessity, barred from discussion. Intelligent readers will know what it is without any word from me." He then considered other aspects, including the fact that "during the last war the government was just getting ready to open the officers training camps to Negroes when some of our stupid old women in trousers piped up for a Jim Crow training camp" and "got it." Harrison advised putting a price on patriotism this time, adding some remarks that included implicit and very pointed criticism of Du Bois for his stand during and after World War I:

Let us decide now, clearly and unequivocally, that we are going to fight for America. We are hers and she is ours. But we insist on having a Negro general or two, Negro colonels for every Negro regiment, Negro artillery regiments added to the standing army, Negro nurses and a square deal for Negro patriotism. We want no cultured cowards to go peep at battlefields after victory is won and tell us that "in the name of the Great Jehovah they come back fighting"—when the war is over. We want them to shoot off their mouths while the boys are shooting off their guns—not afterwards. If our "brave" leaders had done their duty as men while our boys were fighting to make the world "safe for democracy," these boys would have found America safer when they got back. But if they try any more of that "Close Ranks" cowardice on us in another war we will run them out of this race for keeps.

We are going to be patriotic this time, enthusiastically so; but the price of our patriotism, now and forever will be "Political EQUALITY, Social JUSTICE, and Civic OPPORTUNITY". That is the Slogan of the International Colored Unity League.[81]

———

Harrison's June 14 *Chronicle* article, entitled "The Roots of Power," put out a call for economic cooperation. It was an important plank in the program of his ICUL, and the *Chronicle* column both disseminated these ideas and set the stage for his planned speaking tour in New England. In his efforts to encourage economic cooperation Harrison wanted to get beyond a preoccupation with blaming "whites" and to elaborate a constructive program that "Negroes" could begin to implement.[82]

Harrison felt that it was "high time to undertake the removal of some of the things that stand in the way of our progress." He started with "our spendings" and noted that "in the city districts where so many of us live in the North" there was "a streak of daily emigration pouring out every morning" and "a thin stream of daily white immigration flowing in." Then, "on Saturday nights the returning colored flood sweeps back into its home areas with its wages; but most of it floats out with the thin white tide." "None of that cash" was "available for the building of economic structures in the home district which would spur the ambition of Negro boys and girls or increase the power of its inhabitants over newspapers and public opinion." Meanwhile, the grumblings continued "when the bank that collects our savings lends them out to white men to fertilize white politicians," when "their colored lackeys gerrymander our districts so that we can not get the control of Negro district by Negro voters," and when we "'sing the blues' over the way in which we are treated by the police, the boards of health and street cleaning, and the wielders of power." Harrison saw all of this as related to "our own neglect of economic co-operation." He emphasized that "the American Negro, like the European Jew in the middle ages, is shut out of a great many things. But he isn't shut out of making money—and hanging on to it. And now, as then, money is power. But power, to be effective, must be concentrated; and that concentration must be in our own hands."[83]

On June 28 Harrison's "How to End Lynching" appeared in his *Chronicle* column. He wrote that "lynching is the greatest of our outdoor sports for just one reason: it is the safest." A "decrease in the safety of it" would "inevitably decrease its attractiveness and popularity." He reasoned that since "Negroes have the greatest stake in the reduction of lynching, any steps toward its decrease must therefore be initiated by us." Similarly, since "most lynchings occur in the South," it is "to the Southern Negro that we must look for direction against lynching." Those in the North could "only help indirectly." He then explained how lynching could be abolished:

> First by direct action: That is, action on the job—at the places where lynching occur; at the times when they are attempted. The Southern Negro has already decreased lynchings by more than 50 percent by the action involved in migration from the places where most lynchings occurred. By migration from those places he has utilized a power absolutely within his own control. By affecting the production of wealth he has struck a body blow at the most powerful interests in the South and has compelled them to exert their influence against lynching. And he has done this without a single petition or appeal to the kindness, the Christianity, or the democracy of the white folk.[84]

Such "appeals," commented Harrison, "were always the product of certain groups of Northern Negroes," and it was "clear" that lynching could not "be stopped from a distance." This apparent reference to the NAACP continued as Harrison argued that it could "never be stopped by wasting money on 'publicity' whether that 'publicity' takes the form of fervid appeals to a moral sense which exists only on paper, of indignant protests, or bombastic ravings." Neither could lynching "be stopped by national legislation." He indicated his dissatisfaction with developments since World War I when he asked, since the "14th and 15th [amendments] cannot be enforced," what chance had "any mere Congressional enactment?" Harrison explained that in the 1890s, when the Ku Klux Klan "rampaged in West Virginia," "the Federal Government sent soldiers and put them out of business." The concern was "the revenue from whiskey [and] the Government found that it had an interest in law-enforcement then." If "Northern Negroes were really sincere in the desire to give genuine though indirect help to our Southern brothers in putting down lynching," he reasoned, "we would so use our votes in [Virginia, crossed out] Ohio, Indiana, Pennsylvania and New York, as to make the administration find an interest in enforcing the 14th and 15th amendments." He added:

> We don't need a single new law: only the enactment of what we already have. For with the two amendments enforced either the South will become so weak politically that it will be unable to oppose liberal legislation from the North; or the Southern Negro, having won the ballot, with Southern governors, judges, sheriffs and militia responsive to their votes, will be able to solve for themselves the problems of lynchings, Jim Crow, Education and all other problems that some of us in the North make a living by pretending to solve for them. In any case our one best bet is to concentrate on the enforcement of the 14th and 15th Amendments.[85]

While Harrison was writing his series of articles for the *Boston Chronicle*, there was another development of note. On March 13, 1924, Charles S. Johnson of the National Urban League's *Opportunity* magazine wrote to Harrison, informing him that a "group of younger Negro writers," including the short-story writer Eric Walrond; the novelist and literary editor of the *Crisis* Jessie Fauset; the poets Countée Cullen, Langston Hughes, and Gwendolyn Bennett; the critic and educator Alain Locke; and a few others had planned "a rather informal '6:30' Dinner Meeting" on March 21 at the Civic Club. The idea originated with a suggestion to ask a few interested persons to meet with the Writer's Guild on the appearance of Jessie Fauset's novel (*There is Confusion*); which was being published by Boni & Liveright. The idea had grown to the point of making this a "coming-out party" for the entire younger school of Negro writers, and about forty people had been asked to join the group, including people he doubtless knew—Carl Van Doren, of *Century Magazine*; the playwright Ridgeley Torrence; the *World* columnist (and future founder of the American Newspaper Guild) Heywood Broun; Du Bois of *The Crisis*; Oswald Garrison Villard, of *The Nation*; the publishers John Farrar and Horace Liveright; among others, some of whom already said they would come.[86]

Jeffrey C. Stewart describes how Johnson had written to Locke on March 4 about the planned event and in a follow-up letter explained that he wanted him to play a role as emcee and as leader in coming up "with an interpretation acceptable to young writers, old race leaders, and tentative White literary allies so that they could find common language to talk about the prospects for a vital Negro literature." Stewart explains that Locke, at first, "demurred," not feeling that he wanted to take part in an event that honored Fauset's new novel and represented it "as exemplary of the new literature." But after the focus of the meeting was adjusted to Locke's liking he agreed to take part in its planning, emceeing, and leading.[87]

While there is no indication that Harrison attended the March 21 event, Paul Kellogg, the editor of *Survey Graphic* (a New York City–based magazine launched in 1921 that focused on sociological and political research and analysis of national and international issues) did attend. At the meeting Kellogg approached Johnson and Locke about doing a special issue of *Survey Graphic* on the younger writers movement among "Negroes." Kellogg planned a meeting with Johnson and Locke for Saturday, April 19, in New York, at the *Survey Graphic* offices, at 112 East Nineteenth Street. (Though Johnson could not attend, Kellogg and Locke would meet.) Kellogg also asked Locke to prepare an outline for the special issue. Locke returned to Washington, DC, and prepared and mailed his outline to Kellogg.[88] He then sent Kellogg a "revised makeup prospectus of the Harlem issue" on April 16; Kellogg received it two days later.[89]

On April 30 Kellogg wrote to "GS" (probably the *Survey Graphic* staff member Gertrude Springer) in preparation for a May 1 *Survey Graphic* staff meeting:

> Following our conference of Saturday [April 26], Mr. Locke has drafted this syllabus for the Harlem issue. Can you glance it through so we can discuss it at staff meeting tomorrow?
>
> Note that unless we are prepared to swing a larger number . . . some of these features must go. . . .
>
> We have already, of course, cut out certain phases of the situation entirely in drawing into a skein the various strands of suggestions made at our first conference. It may be that you will have some topic to suggest, therefore, which you consider more important that these set down. Authors as well as titles are merely suggested.
>
> The plan would be to get invitations right out, however, and most of the article in hand in June for fall publication.[90]

In what appears to be Locke's outline for the *Survey Graphic Harlem Issue*, section 3, "Black and White: Studies in Rough Contact and Reactions," four articles were proposed, one each by Melville J. Herskovitz, Walter White, Kelly Miller, and Hubert Harrison. In that syllabus, Harrison's article, "The White Man's War," was projected at 2,200 words and two pages in length and was described as follows: "The effect of the war upon the Negro, and the analysis of the disillusionment of the treatment inconsistent with the principles of democracy and self-determination, reaction among the generation that took part in it toward the church, the state, and capitalism. The points of radical indictment and the forces of agitation and protest,—the attitude of radical organizations toward the Negro, and of the Negro to radical social programs."[91]

On May 10 Kellogg wrote to Locke:

At our [staff] meeting the general scheme of the issue met with enthusiasm: and we are all for section I entire, Section II with one query; but various questions were raised with regard to Section III which covers that phase of the number with which our staff is best acquainted, and . . . as outlined is disproportionately long. It seemed that here the cuts should be made which would bring the number within the compass of an 80-page issue including editorials and advertisements. . . .

With respect to section III, go ahead with Walter White, Kelly Miller and Charles S. Johnson. . . . Let's let the rest of Section III swing until we get together.[92]

The Harrison article was to be omitted based on a recommendation from the Kellogg-led staff; there is no indication that Locke in any way opposed this suggestion. The historian Barbara Foley writes: "It is surely no coincidence, however, that it was Harrison's piece that fell under the axe, even though it had been accorded one of the shortest word limits of all the pieces under consideration. Perhaps Harrison's 'radical indictment/ of 'capitalism' . . . was too much for Kellogg and his colleagues." Foley adds, "There is also no evidence that Locke contested this decision." Foley was referring to the failure to include Harrison's article in the *Survey Graphic* issue of March 1925 entitled "Harlem: Mecca of the New Negro." Harrison's article also did not appear in the Locke-edited *New Negro* anthology published in book form less than a year later. The 1926 book republished the contents of the March 1925 *Survey Graphic* in expanded form as the *New Negro* anthology, and it is a work that has long been used by students of the "Harlem Renaissance."[93]

If a Harrison article was submitted to Locke or to *Survey Graphic*, given the brief description and size allotment of 2,200 words in the "Memo," it is very possible that it was drawn from Harrison's 2,400-word article "The White War and the Colored Races." According to Harrison that article was written in 1918 (he elsewhere says 1917) for "a certain well known radical magazine," which found it "to be 'too radical' for publication at that time." Harrison was very possibly referring to *The Messenger* (edited by A. Philip Randolph and Chandler Owen), which ironically got considerable coverage in the "white" press for its "radical" antiwar stand. Harrison then published it in the *New Negro* in October 1919 and in the *Negro World* in February 1920. Harrison also published it in his *When Africa Awakes: The "Inside Story" of the Stirrings and Strivings of the New Negro in the Western World* (August 1920), where he explained that he did so "partly because the underlying explanation which it offers of the root-cause of the war has not yet received treatment (even among socialist radicals) and partly because recent events in China, India, Africa and the United States have proved the accuracy of its forecasts." Harrison's thesis—that "the war in Europe is the result of the desire of the white governments of Europe to exploit for their own benefit the lands and labor of the darker races, and, as the war continues, it must decrease the white man's stock of ability to do this success-fully against the wishes of the inhabitants of those lands" and that this "will result in their freedom from thralldom and the extension of political, social and industrial democracy to the twelve hundred million black and brown and yel-low peoples of the world"—certainly offered a "radical" analysis of events.[94]

Besides being a "radical" indictment, perhaps too radical for Kellogg, Locke, et al., it also appears that Harrison's submission—if published in *Survey Graphic* and Locke's "New Negro" journal and book—would seemingly (especially if his earlier articles were referenced) raise serious questions regarding Locke's "pri-macy" in the historiography of the "New Negro."

In mid-1924, however, Harrison's desire to point the way forward politically, while making some type of living for himself and his family, continued.

IV

The Struggle for International Colored Unity

16

ICUL, Midwest Tour, Board of Ed, NYPL, and 1925 (March 1924–December 1925)

On a beautiful spring day, Sunday, March 23, 1924, Harrison, in the midst of writing the *Boston Chronicle* series, exited the Douglas Theatre and took a long walk up and down the streets of Harlem with Edgar Grey. During that walk they discussed "for the first time" his "plans for a new drive for a nationwide Negro organization and movement to be launched this Spring." The "central idea" was to be "a Negro State in the American Union." Grey "was tremendously enthused with the idea" and "pledged . . . support . . . with all his power." They "went into many details of principles, propaganda, methods of appeal, etc." In apparent reference to feeling betrayed by Grey before, Harrison commented in his diary that he hadn't "forgotten, and while seeking a way out for my race I keep my eyes wide open and trust no man fully." He later added, "When the plans were put before a gathering at the Library Edgar Grey was the only one who tried to raise objections. Consequently, we have eliminated him."[1]

According to Harrison, the International Colored Unity League advocated "the setting aside of a section of the United States to be occupied exclusively by Negroes who will thus have an outlet for their 'racial egoism.'" The ICUL's purpose was "the harnessing up of Negro energies in the United States for the promotion of their own economic, political and spiritual self-help and advancement," and its "ultimate aim" was "to found a Negro state, not in Africa, as Marcus Garvey would have done, but in the United States," in "one or more of the sparsely-settled states of the American Union, where, under American institutions the American Negro can work out his independent political destiny in an American way." The word "international" in the organization's title emphasized "all Negroes in America, no matter what part of the world they originally came from, were eligible for membership in the new organization."

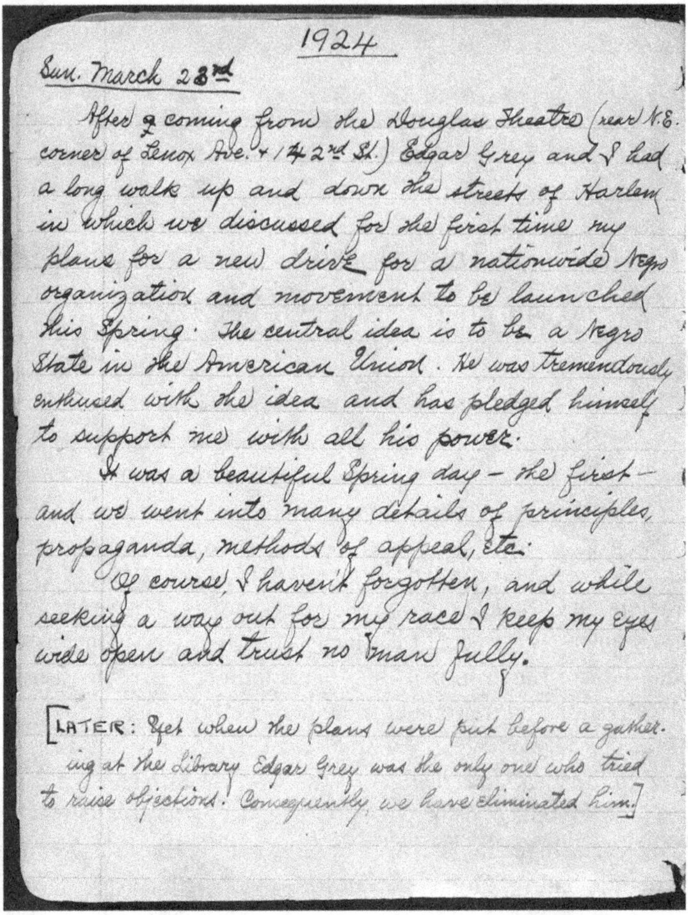

Figure 16.1. Hubert Harrison, diary entry, March 23, 1924. In this diary entry Harrison describes discussing with Edgar Grey his plans "for a nationwide Negro organization and movement" to be launched in the spring of 1924 behind the "central idea" of "a Negro State in the American Union." While Harrison and Grey discussed "many details of principles, propaganda, methods of appeal, etc.," Harrison went on in his diary entry to say: "While seeking a way out for my race I keep my eyes wide open and trust no man fully." He later added, "When the plans were put forth before a gathering of the Library Edgar Grey was the only one who tried to raise objections." *Source:* Hubert H. Harrison Papers, Box 9, Folder 2, Rare Book and Manuscript Library, Columbia University Library. See https://dlc.library.columbia.edu/catalog/cul:tmpg4f4sfs.

He was "opposed to any scheme to take the race out of the United States" but thought that a state "where colored people would have an outlet for their 'racial egoism' would work for the betterment of his people." The "ultimate aim of the league" was "to found a State in the country, and not in Africa, where colored people would not be 'denied a man's chance and a square deal.'" Harrison claimed that the idea of establishing "a Negro State in Africa" is "not practicable," and "African Negroes do not need any help and if they do it could not come from American Negroes."[2]

Interestingly, Harrison's agitation for a separate "Negro State" in the United States preceded by four years the Communist Party's call for self-determination for a Negro homeland in the South—a call that the historian Theodore Draper has argued was "Made in Moscow."[3] It should be noted that Harrison's writings were appreciated by the international communist movement. When the Third Communist International commissioned Claude McKay to write its first book-length treatment on "The Negro Race" (1923), they provided McKay, in Moscow, with a copy of *The Negro and the Nation* by his close friend Harrison.[4]

One month after Harrison's announced 1924 speaking tour for a "Negro State" or states in the United States the Fourth Plenum (enlarged executive committee) of the Third Communist International, on July 12–13, 1924, discussed self-determination and a separate government for "Negroes" in the United States. The discussion resulted in mixed views and reportedly received "no help from the American comrades."[5]

In regard to his views on a separate state or states for "Negroes" in the United States, Harrison had a book in his collection, *The Color Question in the Two Americas* (1922), written by a Cuban friend, Dr. Bernardo Ruiz Suarez. Suarez's book carried a history of the Independent Colored Party in Cuba, called for an independent Black party in the United States, spoke of "a black nation within a white nation" in the United States, and opposed Garvey's "Back to Africa" plans.[6] Also of interest is the fact that in early 1921 Harrison essentially treated the situation of "Negroes" in the South as one of oppressed subjects.[7]

Harrison's detailed program for the ICUL was divided into three parts: "political, economic, and social." The general political aim was "to unite the power of the Negro demanding proper representation in Congress, and in state and municipal governing bodies" and to "utilize the balance of voting power held by Negroes in doubtful states, such as Ohio and Illinois, irrespective of previous party affiliations." The political program called for "the return of Race legislators to congress, first from the North and finally from the South," since under present social conditions, "the most fair minded white man in congress . . . can only speak about our group; he cannot speak for him." Concretely, the ICUL proposed to unite the political power of the Negro in the Negro's own hands; to pledge all Congressional candidates in time not only to demand the enforcement of the 14th and 15th Amendments, but to filibuster in Congress and tie-up the legislative process until Congress itself respects the Constitution by enforcing it; to utilize the balance of power possessed by Negroes in certain states by getting not only Negroes, but black men, into Congress thus demonstrating the political equality of the black race under the folds of Old Glory.[8]

Economically the ICUL sought to "have the united Negro race become self-sustaining by raising all elementary food staples" and "to help the race everywhere to finance the foundation of its own future." Specifically it urged plans

to encourage the Race populations of large cities like Chicago and New York to buy large farms on a cooperative basis near to the cities, to raise their own beef, pork, potatoes, chickens, eggs, milk and vegetables; to transport these products on their own motor trucks, retail them in their own city stores and butcher shops and thus cut out the foreign middle men who in every Race neighborhood keep up the high cost of living by charging for these things higher prices than those paid by white people whose wages are higher than those which our group gets.

Similarly, by buying and building "co-operative apartments in the cities and suburbs . . . the vast sums which now pass out of the Race's control in the form of rent may remain within the Race" and "the race's pockets in the form of profits and employment to architects, engineers, experts, artists, mechanics and laborers." By such means the ICUL aimed "to give the Race man's dollar the same magic as the white man's dollar, and use it as a means toward the future well-being, security and financial independence of the Race."[9]

The ICUL's social program included "the foundation of scholarships for colored youth in the best northern schools, and the abrogation of restrictive laws and injustices against Negroes in the United States." Harrison emphasized that "our group must seek the solution of his problem in terms of the American culture and consciousness to which he has so greatly contributed," and he argued for a Race homeland in America as an ultimate objective. In "a Race state, or states," the "Race American" could demonstrate that it is "as competent as any other racial element in America to produce governors, United States, senators, legislators, judges and public officials under the protection of Old Glory and under modern civilized conditions." By setting apart one or more of the sparsely settled states of the American Union, "the American Negro" could, "under American institutions," work out an "independent political destiny in an American way." Harrison expressed a desire to "visit Idaho, Wyoming and Montana as well, with a view to selecting territory suitable for ultimately housing the future Negro commonwealth." He emphasized, "Negroes were not to be forced to live in these states, but that he would try and convince them his plan was sound and advantageous." These "Negro states would serve," he said, "as a 'conduit to drain off Negroes from other parts of the country where they are denied a man's chance and a square deal.'" The "idea of a Negro state in Africa was deplored," and Harrison again declared that African Negroes "did not need any help, and if they did, it could not come from American Negroes."[10]

Harrison believed that with this program it would be "possible to unite the Race without the sorry spectacle of Race leaders wasting their energies in internal squabbles." The ICUL emphasized cooperation and deplored the "envy, malice and uncharitableness" that "kept Negro 'leaders' eternally bickering and fighting with each other." He explained, "If half the energy and fighting power now devoted by Negro leaders to tearing down each other were concentrated against such products of race-prejudice as lynching, disfranchisement or Jim Crow, we who are supposed to be 'led' would have something to show. What we need is less fighting among ourselves and more fighting against the common enemy." "Mutual help, not mutual hate, is what we most need," and "the sort of unity which helps us most will not come from the 'intellectuals' for the Race, many of whom keep too far away from the masses. It must come from the masses themselves in a rush of racial enthusiasms and good-will, in a common purpose and a common aim." To set "a good example" the ICUL, in its writing and speeches, would "refrain from criticism of any Negro organizations or movements" and, in its proposed magazine, *The Voice*, would "do its utmost to present to Negroes the better side of Negro strivings and achievements."[11]

Harrison also evidenced a new attitude toward church leaders. He saw "the Race churches and the Race ministers, school teachers and journalists" as "a mighty instrument for racial betterment" and felt that "any such program as that of the Unity league must put itself under their protection and enlist their support." He emphasized that "what we need . . . is leading, rather than leaders, and the ministers, teachers and newspapermen are already giving us a good deal of that. If we can link it up and make it conscious of itself the league will be rendering a true patriotic service to the nation and the Race."[12]

Also of note was the ICUL's emphasis on the "Negro's" role in the United States. "America," according to Harrison, "needs the Negro, and the Negro needs America." "Either the Negro belongs or he doesn't," he reasoned, "and if he belongs here he must make his plans for the future consistent with his duty to the country. Only so can we hope for success in forcing the country to do its duty by him." The New York branch of the ICUL had already "shown its understanding of its patriotic relations by lending its platform, indoors and outdoors, to the task of helping to fill the ranks of the Fifteenth Regiment of

Infantry, which was the first National Guard regiment to be mustered into service by the United States during the last war."[13]

———

By early June the ICUL was already organized in Harlem; Orange, New Jersey; and Montclair, New Jersey. In the second week of June Harrison and his friend J. A. Rogers embarked on a speaking tour, which sought to "spread the principles" of the ICUL and urge "the harnessing-up of Negro energies" in the United States "for the promotion of their own economic, political and spiritual self-help and advancement" while establishing local organizations. Though Harrison wanted to bring his theories to the floor of the House of Representatives and was listed variously as a Single Tax or Socialist Party candidate for Congress in the Twenty-First District of New York, he had "decided that the political awakening and enlightening of the masses of his people all over the country" was "of more importance than the number of votes cast for him in Harlem."[14]

Harrison and Rogers spoke on Thursday night, June 12, before an open forum of the League of Women for Community Service, an organization of Black women with offices at 558 Massachusetts Avenue, in Boston. The group had been founded in 1918 as a soldier's comfort unit; it focused on local problems and consistently opposed lynching. He outlined the program of the ICUL while Rogers spoke on "the new censorship" and described the "American effort to suppress certain books by negro authors." Harrison was to be in Boston organizing and raising funds for a week or ten days or more. After Boston he was scheduled to go to Philadelphia, Virginia, Washington, and then proceed westward through Ohio, Indiana, Michigan, Illinois, Wisconsin, Missouri, and Kansas. He expected to spend two weeks in Chicago, either in late July or early August, "to extend the work and carry on a crusade for the League's program," after which he planned "to return to New York" to "carry on his campaign for congress."[15]

The June 7 *Chicago Defender* quoted Harrison, who noted that "the chief feature" of the ICUL program was "already disturbing some of the smaller political fry," since it proposed "the consolidation of our vote, irrespective of previous and present political affiliations," and was dedicated "to the task of securing the ballot for the Race masses in the South by using it solidly against any party which opposes the enforcement of the Fourteenth and Fifteenth amendments to the United States Constitution." This attitude was recently manifested "in the attitude of the Race voters of Indiana and Missouri," and in Virginia "Negro" voters who "put up an entire independent ticket and thereby caused the election to go Democratic, despite the best efforts of [the Republican Party politician and former six-time U.S. Congressman] C. Bascom Slemp, who had closed the door of the Republican convention in their faces." Harrison believed "that if the Southerners of our group can get the vote back into their hands, they will be able to solve their own problems of lynching, Jim Crow and limited education, since sheriffs, school boards and legislators will be responsible to Race voters as well as to whites."[16]

During this campaign the Bureau of Investigation continued monitoring Harrison, and Agent Joseph G. Tucker, in his report for the period ending July 5, described the purpose of the ICUL. Harrison apparently encountered some difficulty from the police in promoting his program. Tucker, in his report for July 26, wrote that Harrison had recently been arrested in the Negro section of Harlem while addressing a large crowd on the 'Uplift of the Colored Race.'" He reportedly "refused to obey the order of a policeman to move." In his report for August 9 Tucker repeated information from his two previous reports on Harrison and the ICUL, added that Harrison planned "to make a trip to Kansas, Missouri, Illinois, Virginia and Ohio in the interest of his project," and quoted from several other ICUL positions.[17]

———————

On March 15, 1924, Eugene O'Neill, responding to a letter he "was immensely pleased to get," wrote to Harrison from the Hotel Lafayette, on University Place in Manhattan, asking him to call him the next morning, Sunday, at eleven or twelve, so he could "answer this seemingly unpardonable delay" in responding and so that he might "have the pleasure of meeting" him. Later in the year, on October 12, O'Neill wrote again, "I owe you an apology for my forgetfulness—but you'll surely get that book [*The Emperor Jones*] sometime!" He didn't have a copy with him, but he would be in New York in about ten days and would get one from the publisher "Cross my heart." Harrison wrote on his copy of the letter: "When this came I was in Indianapolis."[18]

O'Neill wrote again to Harrison on January 10, 1925, and told him he hadn't received his letter till after Christmas and that "[Fitzgerald]—promised to send me a copy of *Jones* to autograph and to send back to you." She hadn't sent O'Neill the book, and he suggested that Harrison contact her. O'Neill had no copies of his books with him, and though he was "a lot too late for Christmas," he said he would send a copy as soon as he got it from her. He also extended "All best wishes . . . and much gratitude for giving me an opportunity to read again your splendid appreciation of *Jones*—(which I will release[?] in book[?])." Harrison, who had lost his previous copy, did obtain a new copy of *The Emperor Jones*, probably later that year.[19]

In March 1924, Harrison, as a member of Mayor John F. Hylan's "Mayor's Committee on Celebration of the Twenty-Fifth Anniversary of the Greater City of New York," received an invitation to attend the premiere of the New York

Silver Jubilee Motion Picture at Carnegie Hall on Monday evening, March 31. In the spring of 1924 Harrison was also on the list of the "Mayor's Committee on Reception to Distinguished Guests." As a member of that committee he was invited to attend the May 20 presentation by His Excellency Baron De Cartier De Marchienna, the Belgian ambassador to the United States, of a monument at Battery Park to commemorate the tercentenary of the settlement of New York by the Walloons.[20]

In early 1924 Harrison became a founder and executive committee member of the Virgin Islands Committee. The VIC was headquartered at 70 Fifth Avenue in New York and led by its chairman, Rothschild (Polly) Francis, editor of the *Emancipator*, which was published by the Working People's Committee of St. Thomas. The VIC legal counsel was Adolph Berle, who also was legal counsel for the ACLU and the Virgin Islands Congressional Council (VICC). The aim of the VIC was to secure measures that would promote the economic and political reconstruction of the Virgin Islands. Other executive committee members included Lewis S. Gannett, editor of the *Nation*; A. Elizabeth Hendrickson, of the Virgin Islands Civil Rights Association; James Weldon Johnson, of the NAACP; Arthur Warner, of the *Nation*; Horace Williams, of the Working People's Committee of the Virgin Islands; Casper Holstein, of the VICC; John Connolly, a Rochester businessman; and A. Philip Randolph, of the *Messenger*. The committee's major activities included mass meetings, and at one such meeting, in the Grace Congregational Church on West 139th Street, Francis lectured on "What's Wrong in the Virgin Islands of the United States?" Attendees passed a resolution calling on the U.S. Congress to grant a democratic form of government to the islands, remove trade and commerce restrictions, and grant full citizenship to Virgin Islanders residing in the United States. Shortly after the meeting a memorandum was submitted to Congress in support of pending legislation calling for a permanent civil government in the Virgin Islands.[21]

Harrison was a featured speaker before three thousand people at a Virgin Island Congressional Council meeting at the Renaissance Casino on his forty-first birthday, April 27. The rally was described as "one of the most largely attended meetings of a political nature that New York has ever seen." Other speakers included Charles W. Mitchell, secretary of the federal commission sent by President Coolidge to investigate conditions in the Virgin Islands; the Rev. Reginald G. Barrow, a Barbadian attending Northwestern University, who had been deported from the Virgin Islands over a year before "because he dared defend a slander against his wife"; and Louis F. Jeppe, a leading figure in the islands' affairs for twenty-five years. Roger N. Baldwin, director of the ACLU (from 1920 to 1950), was unable to attend but sent a message, and Casper

Holstein, president of the two-year-old VICC, helped arrange for Rev. Barrow to see his wife for the first time in over a year.[22]

Francis described Harrison in the *Emancipator* as "the most illustrious Virgin Islander since Dr. [Edward Wilmot] Blyden." In his speech, Harrison reportedly "asserted that the white race everywhere had determined a policy of denying to black, brown and yellow peoples equal government with them." He also indicated his disagreement with a statement made by Dr. Charles E. Mitchell that "the American white race could be relied on to mete out justice to weaker peoples." Harrison maintained that "the reasons the United States purchased the [Virgin] islands was protective and military," and he emphasized that the "Hope of the Virgin Islanders must be placed not upon the Republican and Democratic parties, but upon the Congress of the United States." His speech "brought the audience to its feet."[23]

Two weeks after the VICC meeting, on Sunday, May 11, Harrison was one of several hundred to attend the first mass meeting of the newly formed West Indian Reform Association at the Renaissance Casino. The meeting was to protest against recently passed legislation in the Leeward Islands that prevented laborers from leaving those islands to better their conditions elsewhere. Mrs. (York?) Russell came over from Montclair, accompanied by her son, and sat with Harrison in the front row. The meeting was "a great success," and $307 was collected. Afterward, the younger Russell went home, and Edgar Grey, Mrs. Russell, and Harrison went to a local eatery, Eddie's, "but didn't dine as the service was slow." Then they went to Loew's Victoria Theatre on Seventh Avenue and 124th Street and saw what Harrison described as "some good moving pictures." After Grey left, Mrs. Russell and Harrison were, as he described it, *"manibus junctus in theatro* [holding hands in the theater]"; they then went back up to Seventh Avenue, "dined at Eddie's, lingered a long time, were joined by James Bell, and finally took the Subway" to begin the long trip back to Montclair. After getting "lost in the Fulton St. Subway Station (*quo primo osculation est*) [which was the first kiss]," Harrison "escorted her home (*ubi semel osc.*) [where one more kiss]," and didn't get back to New York until after 4 a.m. on what he described as "a memorable *day*."[24]

Such activity seemed to have its repercussions at home: Hubert recorded one instance in his diary of Thursday, May 22. He returned home after 6 a.m. and, according to his diary entry, from 8 a.m. till at least 12:45 p.m. his wife, Lin, "raved, quarreled, [and] cursed." After over four hours she was "still going strong . . . talking indecencies to the children in a flat coarse West Indian brogue." She dramatized her "story into different 'acts'" in which she sometimes took off a favorite hated character among Harrison's friends "and sometimes just barging and Billingsgating along." In the meantime, Hubert counted thirty-four times that three-year-old Billy screamed for her. Her face, however, had "a rapt and far-away expression," and she didn't answer him once. Hubert, who apparently chose to count screams rather than to help his son, wrote, "When this child grows up with a peevish, quarrelsome disposition she [Lin] will lay it to the will of God, or its own innate depravity."[25]

Such spats with Lin did not seem to slow Hubert's social life. On Monday, May 26, he spoke before two to three hundred diners at the Sunrise Club on "The Tempest in the Theologic Teapot, or the Warfare Between Modernists and 'Fundamentalists' as Seen from the Side-lines." There were "over 37 Negroes" in attendance, and, according to the Sunrise Club secretary, Edwin C. Walker, this was "the most that the club has ever had at a function." Walker attributed the high turnout to Harrison's "personal popularity" and "the subject." Harrison's guests at the speaker's table were Miss Ruth Bradley and the "Princess Kathryn de Rigo."[26]

The following day Rigo wrote to him: "The honor that was bestowed on you last evening by a gathering of the most interesting people in our city was only a small compliment to what you deserve." She added, "you spoke a few words last night that will live forever[,] words that make people *think* deeply and [are] doing more good on earth than all the books that were ever written." She told him that she planned "to erect a lasting monument" in his honor.[27]

Harrison had also been deeply impressing others, and on Saturday night, May 31, the "Dr." was given his first testimonial dinner at Craig's Restaurant, 102 West 130th Street. The "moving spirits" were Mrs. Elizabeth H. Davis and Miss Madelyn St. Clair Wales. Edwin C. Walker chaired; about forty-one attended, including "a majority of the literary and artistic lights of Harlem" and "10 or 12 white peoples." Harrison considered it "a genuine success as a testimonial," and the journalist J. A. Jackson observed that "seldom has a Negro man of letters been honored by so many important literary folks."[28]

Harrison had many friends, and a close friend of his, Richard B. Moore, later commented that he was "generally amiable and never pompous," "bore a reserved but pleasant mien," and always carried himself "with conscious dignity."[29] J. A. Rogers, another close friend, remarked years later, "In his personal contacts Harrison was kindly and good-natured, and both among the common people and the broad-minded intellectual whites he had many friends." Rogers added, "He was happiest and at his best on a 'soap-box' surrounded by admiring listeners and a heckler or two to match in a combat of wits."[30]

At the testimonial Dr. Crandall of the Board of Ed "delivered a splendid eulogium," which Harrison deemed "worthy of the great and good soul that he is." Crandall called Harrison "one of the most intellectually honest men, and one of the ablest speakers I have ever met." He added, "The Board of Education of New York City is indeed fortunate to have a man of such profound and universal learning on its staff." Crandall explained that "attendance at the Harlem lecture centre at the 135th Street Library" had "dwindled almost to nothing," before Harrison and then "I wanted to build it up again and selected Dr. Harrison, not because he was colored, and the majority of the audience is colored, but because he was the best man white or colored, that I could find." Attendance "had increased many times since Dr. Harrison had been speaking there," and "some white centre would have been only too glad to have him as testified by the manner in which he is received whenever he speaks at other centres."[31]

Vocal music at the testimonial was rendered by the tenor Carl Boxlull and baritone William Service Bell, who sang William Ernest Henley's "Invictus" in "a marvelously fine voice" and was "received with tumultuous applause." Harrison's "dear old friend," Melville Charlton, presided at the piano; another "dear old" friend, the public school teacher Percy Green, "said a world of good things." Hubert described his words, delivered at 12:45 a.m., as "some what lame, because of the excessive emotion evoked by the expressed goodwill of my neighbors and friends."[32]

Among those unable to attend but there "in spirit" was Assemblyman Henri Shields, from the Twenty-First Assembly District, who wrote of his "very high personal regard for Dr. Harrison" and told Mrs. Davis that "Dr. Harrison has contributed much to the community; he has given of his broad experiences without stint and of his knowledge in an ungrudging way." It would "be difficult to place a price" upon this work, which couldn't be measured "from a pecuniary view point." Shields knew that Harrison's "services have been appreciated" and felt he was "entitled to know that his friends feel that way."[33]

Scheduled speakers unable to attend included Ernestine Rose of the 135th Public Library and the poet Countée Cullen. On May 29 Miss Rose wrote to Mrs. Davis that she would be out of town and deeply regretted not being able to attend the testimonial. She held "a warm personal regard" for the honoree, who was one of her "oldest friends in Harlem," and she "appreciate[d] very deeply" his "keen and intensely living mind, his wide and varied culture, and his intellectual contribution to the expressed thought of the day." The same day Rose also wrote "a personal word" in which she told Harrison she was "heartily glad" that the "token of appreciation" was being offered and assured him of her "own appreciation, and very deep personal esteem" for him and his work.[34] The afternoon after the testimonial Hubert spent "with Otutwuugnn" and wrote in his diary, "we enjoyed ourselves immensely!"[35]

Harrison was still having difficulty making ends meet, and in June he contacted several entertainers, perhaps over the possibilities of publicity work or arranging of personal appearances. On June 18 he wrote to the musical team of Eubie Blake and Noble Sissle, and on June 23 the pianist and composer Blake, per H. Brill, responded that he had received the "splendid letter" and hoped to meet him in New York in August.[36] A week later, on June 30, the actor Charles S.

Gilpin wrote a letter "To Whom it may concern" in which he delegated "authority . . . to Mr. Hubert H. Harrison to make any and all arrangements for my personal appearance in connection with dramatic societies, or literary organizations." He added, "Any dates set, contracts signed, and other details settled by
Mr. Harrison in my behalf will be honored by me."[37]

In the July 16 *Nation* Harrison reviewed *The Irresistible Movement of Democracy*, by John Simpson Penman. Penman described democracy "as a series of
social movements" whose "immediate political aim" was "the establishment of
'a form of government based upon the popular will as expressed in universal
suffrage'" and that, in England, France, and America, "noticeably diverge[d]
from the established order after the middle of the eighteenth century." Because
the "democratic spirit" challenged "property, social privilege, religion, art, and
literature," it was in constant conflict with "conservatism." To Harrison "the crucial test for democracy's supporters" came "with revolution," which he
described as "the crisis in a series of social changes when it becomes evident
that the social forces have outgrown the fixed forms or institutions of society."
Then, "under the impact of these developing forces," existing institutions
"decompose and make way for new structures," which "are subject in turn to
the ever-recurrent cycle of social forces." Penman's book offered a political history of the three national revolutions in which the modern democratic forces
were first liberated and later institutionalized in new forms. It made "no new
contribution to democratic theory," which, according to Harrison, had "lost its
attraction for thinking people." Nevertheless Harrison considered the book of
value and felt that in it "history lives and has meaning." Penman concluded with
the warning that "Democracy stands at the crisis of its history" and that "the
future of society hangs in the balance between a movement toward socialism
and a development of the principles of democracy." Harrison felt Penman's book
would "help the thoughtful citizen to make his choice."[38]

On August 11, 1924, G. Victor Cools, national manager of the Negro Bureau of
the (Robert M.) La Follette–for–President Committee, wrote to Harrison asking him to come to Chicago. La Follette, a Wisconsin senator from 1905 to 1925,
widely known for his opposition both to U.S. entry into World War I and the
KKK, was running for president on a third party, the Conference for Progressive Political Action (Progressive Party) ticket. He would garner almost five
million of the thirty million votes cast and win the state of Wisconsin. Cools
said to Harrison that William Pickens had recommended him as a willing
speaker for La Follette's national campaign. He added that La Follette appealed
"to the oppressed masses, to the rational Negro—the New Negro" and that he
was "the only candidate to oppose the KKK." Harrison, aware of La Follette's

political program, in need of money, and eager to publicize the ICUL, agreed to go to Chicago. Within six weeks, however, after many hassles over payment, he would be livid at Cools and describe him as "a damned little ass."[39]

The KKK, with two million members, moved deeply into national politics at the national party conventions of 1924, most particularly at the Democratic convention, where a plank was proposed condemning secret societies in general and a minority plank named the Klan in particular. Two major Democratic presidential contenders, Al Smith and Oscar Underwood, condemned the Klan and supported the minority plank. William Gibbs McAdoo, the leading contender, opposed the minority plank and supported instead a plank calling for enforcement of existing laws. Bitterness over the Klan issue carried into the selection of the Democratic nominee. Forces for McAdoo, Smith, and Underwood were unable to agree, and, after a nine-day debate, the compromise candidate, John W. Davis, was nominated. The acrimony engendered by the Klan fight cost McAdoo the nomination and probably cost the Democrats the presidential election.[40]

Before leaving for the Midwest, Harrison "saw Emma" in Newark on Thursday, August 14. Then, on August 17 he said good-bye to his family and took a twenty-seven-hour trip to Chicago on the Erie Railroad for a fare of $30 and an additional $5.80 for Pullman accommodation. He arrived at seven p.m. the next day and stayed at the Hotel Vincennes (on Thirtieth Street and Vincennes Avenue), which he described as "an up-to-date Negro Hotel" that shamed "our indolence and backwardness in New York," where there was "no such structure for the accommodation of the travelling Negro public." As far as he knew, there was "only one Negro hotel—the Whitelaw in Washington"—that compared to the Vincennes.[41]

When he emerged from the station on a State Street car, he went to 9 East State Street, to the home of Mr. W. H. Tibbs, who took him in his automobile to see Louis Anderson, alderman for the Second Ward, for whom he had a letter of introduction. After failing to find Anderson, Harrison and Tibbs went to the colored YMCA to look for Rev. Reginald G. Barrow, who had spoken at the VICC meeting in April and edited *The Herald* with D. Hamilton Jackson in St. Croix. At the desk Harrison saw Ida Wells Barnett; they chatted for a while, after which she invited him to dinner the next evening. Then Tibbs drove him back to the Vincennes.[42]

On Wednesday, August 20, Harrison received "a cordial reception" at Mrs. Barnett's, where he also met her two daughters, one of whom attended the University of Chicago, and her husband, Ferdinand Lee Barnett, "a kindly man, and chatty." Back at the Vincennes he met Claude Barnett, of the Associated Negro Press, and his partner, Nahum D. Brascher; "many other of Chicago's elite"; and "many famous strangers who had come for the sessions of the National Business League." These included Walter L. Cohen, of Louisiana; Henry Lincoln "Link" Johnson (a prominent Republican); a Mr. Best, of Georgia; Lucille Greene Randolph (the wife of A. Philip Randolph), of New York; Lester Walton, of the *New York World*; and "others too numerous to mention."[43]

Harrison stayed at the Vincennes for three days. But as his "money had dwindled to the vanishing point," he left and was "'put up' for two days" by Dr. Monroe Alpheus Majors (a former editor of the *Chicago Conservator*) at 4450 Prairie Avenue (Harrison wrote Indiana Avenue). While in Chicago he saw Mattie Edwards, an old friend from New York who was now Mrs. Cleaves and a practitioner of Christian Science. She gave him $5, since their "former relations admitted of such an intimacy" (they "had often shared each other's financial burdens"), and he used the money to get a room at Mrs. Davis's, at 4310 Vincennes Avenue. Harrison "had sent a telegram to Emma asking for some money" on Wednesday, but he later learned it was not delivered until Sunday, August 24. That day he had breakfast by invitation at Mrs. Myers', at 4435 Indiana Avenue, where he met Mr. Garnet Wilkinson, the superintendent of colored schools in Washington, DC; Mr. Woodlee, a lawyer who also worked as a postal clerk, and his wife; Charles Summer Duke, a civil engineer who had served on the Zoning Commission; and two ladies whose names he couldn't recall. After breakfast Wilkinson, Duke, Woodlee, and Harrison went for a sightseeing spin in Woodlee's car, with his chauffeur driving. Harrison learned about Chicago and saw Jackson Park, the lakefront, and Washington Park, where he saw Tibbs at "the famous 'Bug' Club (white)."[44]

Harrison was asked to speak at "Bug House Square," at the back of the Newberry Library near Walton and Clark Streets, and his audience of five hundred "seemed pleased" as he addressed "this unique 'gathering on the grass' on 'Culture and Politics.'" He "made many acquaintances" and saw some "old acquaintances from New York," including Dr. Ben Reitman, "former anarchist and hobo-leader, now a respected city physician"; and Pat Quinlan, the IWW activist involved in the Lawrence, Massachusetts, and Paterson, New Jersey, strikes. Harrison returned to Tibbs's place and then came back to the "Bug" Club, where he spoke at 8 p.m. on "Lincoln and Liberty: Fact Versus Fiction" and answered questions. On August 26, at Reitman's request, he spoke on "Science and Civilization" and on August 28 he spoke again on "Where Did Man Come From?" At the square the custom was to take up a collection; on Tuesday night $5.43 was collected, and on Thursday, $8.50.[45]

By early September Harrison had "been kept cooling [his] heals [*sic*] for three weeks" in Chicago. Then, Cools and the LaFollette Campaign Committee people, whom he referred to as that "bunch of soul-less brutal exploiters," asked him "to go out to various cities in the Middle West *without even an advance for transportation.*" They said they would pay him "a hundred dollars *at the end of each week.*" Harrison was broke and "in a trap any how," so he "managed to borrow money to get to Milwaukee (had to borrow to get back to Chicago)" and returned on September 16. He still did not receive any money, and "Cools coolly demanded" that Harrison "go to Indianapolis forthwith." Harrison "finally managed to get an advance of 25 dollars" and paid for his food and other incidentals, though he had not yet paid for his room. He filed his "required expense-account before leaving," although he saw "no sense to it," since he would have to pay his own expenses out of the hundred dollars.[46]

Harrison did write a favorable article on Chicago distributed by the Associated Negro Press that appeared (while he was in Indianapolis) in the September 19 *Black Dispatch* (Oklahoma City), owned by Roscoe Dunjee. Entitled "City of Success," it opened with his observation that the "Windy City" had enough to justify any amount of "blowing" by its citizens, yet they "blew" less than the citizens of many smaller cities. He suspected that it was because "they take it out in the doing of deeds . . . rather than in vain brag and empty bluster." This "common trait of Chicagoans" was "shared by the Negroes as well as by the whites," so he would "do some of the necessary 'blowing' for them."[47]

He then pointed out that "in nearly every civic respect," Chicago was ahead of New York. He mentioned his "love at first sight" traveling up State Street and along Thirty-Fifth and seeing the "long lines of Negro business houses." As a "Negro visitor from the East" he was "amazed" by "the Restaurants, drugstores, beauty-parlors, furniture shops, furnishing stores, trust companies, banks, State and National, taxi-cab companies, each with its fleet of cars and all owned and operated by Negroes." Although Chicago's Negro population was much lower than that of New York, it had "31 drugstores, 123 groceries, 87 restaurants, and 42 bona fide real estate dealers." In addition, Chicago boasted "the largest Negro weekly newspaper in America [the *Defender*], two Aldermen and an Assemblyman." Harrison predicted that in two years it would have "the first Negro in Congress to come from a Northern state." (In November 1928, Alderman Oscar DePriest, of Chicago's Second Ward, was elected to Congress.) It also had "the one and only Associated Negro Press," which served "more than a hundred Negro newspapers every week," as well as "the largest Negro business north of Washington, D.C.," and "the largest Baptist church in the whole United States." Chicago was "easily the most beautiful" large city he had seen; "not even Washington" could "boast a street as lovely as the Grand Boulevard." The city had spent millions of dollars to beautify and enlarge and "in the midst of all this loveliness" lived "tens of thousands of Negroes" in houses "far more beautiful than any which adorn Harlem's Seventh Avenue or Washington's great North-west section." There were "hardly any bee-hive apartment houses"; the population spread out rather than piled up, and even the architecture was "distinct and individual": it didn't "imitate that of the Old World" but rather combined "utility and strength with beauty and charm and loveliness."[48]

Harrison was impressed with the "spirit of enterprise, of healthy striving and accomplishment," that was "everywhere apparent among Chicago's Negroes," who "support one another." He cited the *Chicago Defender* "with an output of more than a quarter of a million every week and correspondents in every city large and small." Its owner, Robert S. Abbott, was perceived as an example of "bull-dog tenacity and successful achievement" whose life story merited being written. There were

> scores of similar cases, like Anthony Overton of the Douglass National Bank, Dr. Lacey Kirk Williams of Olivet Baptist Church which boasts a congregation of more than ten thousand, "Toney" Langston, alias "Tony the Great" who draws a larger salary than any other Negro newspaper man, Jesse Binga of the Binga State Bank, Frank L. Gillespie, founder and president of the Liberty Life Insurance Company and Louis H. Anderson, Alderman for the second ward.[49]

Despite "the riots of 1919" and "occasional prejudice here and there" Harrison viewed race relations in the city as "much more harmonious and satisfactory than in any other large Northern city, not excepting Boston." Charles S. Duke, "a young civil engineer, represented the colored people effectively and looked upon the interests of colored property owners" on the recent zoning commission. Even the political situation showed "a healthy division of the Negro vote," which was "well represented in official positions of honor and public trust." In sum, Harrison described "the Negroes of Chicago" as "a shining example of what the American Negro can attain to in the land of his birth."[50]

Harrison traveled from Chicago to Indianapolis, and while sitting in his room at Mrs. Henderson's at 514 Blackford Street, in Indianapolis, on Wednesday, September 24, 1924, he wrote in his diary that he was "afraid even to think of the condition of [his] family in New York." They had received nothing from him since he left on August 17, except for a $2 birthday present for Billy around September 20. As he finished his second week's work for the LaFollette Committee he commented that they had not sent his "*first* week's pay yet," though they were aware of his "desperate family and personal needs." "God damn their heartless souls!"[51] A week later, while still in Indianapolis, Harrison wrote his letter to "Miss Dearborn" (see chapter 12).

After leaving Chicago Harrison spoke on Friday, October 10, at Crawfordsville, Indiana, on Monday, October 13, in Indianapolis outside a church, and on

Tuesday, October 14, in Princeton, at the courthouse. He addressed the Vincennes Democratic Colored Men's Club's Wednesday night meeting at the county courthouse on October 15; the *Vincennes Sun* said that it "turned out to be one of the best attended and most enthusiastic [talks] of any held in this county in this campaign." In Vincennes Joseph W. Kimmell, the Democratic candidate for judge, introduced "Dr." Harrison, who urged "the colored voters" of Knox County "to break away from the political slavery they have been under for the past fifty years, and vote the Democratic ticket."[52]

On October 16 Harrison spoke at the Indianapolis Democratic headquarters "(Colored)." Later that night he wrote in his diary that he had sent "a decoy telegram to Roscoe Simmons in Chicago to find out whether our Mr. Henry Fleming, the ex-Republican gambler is 'straight' or is still in the pay of the G.O.P. with secret connections." Harrison was "clean disgusted" with the way Fleming was "double crossing the Dem. Party." The following evening, at 8 p.m., he spoke, along with the Hon. W. A. Kersey, of Indianapolis, on the "Constitutional Rights of the Negro." In his diary he wrote that the talk before a "crowded courthouse" was a "Great success."[53]

"Dr." Harrison next addressed "a colored democratic mass meeting" at Evans Hall, Evansville, before one thousand people, on October 21. He was a replacement speaker for William H. Lewis, of Boston, the former assistant attorney general of the United States, who had taken ill Monday night at Terre Haute. According to the *Evansville Courier* Harrison "supported his enviable reputation for logical, historical scintillating oratory, and was enthusiastically received." He "denounced actions of the present republican national administration during its tenure of office and exploded the myth of the 'Silent' [Cal] Coolidge by declaring that [the] official had nothing to say." "Dr." Harrison was introduced by the chairperson James McFarland, who said that Harrison was "the democratic nominee for representative in congress in New York City and regular staff lecturer and official organizer for the International Colored Unity league." In his talk Harrison focused on national campaign issues including the Teapot Dome, Wyoming, oil scandal, and he specifically mentioned the roles of Secretary of the Interior Albert B. Fall, Pan-American Petroleum president Edward Doheny, Mammoth Oil president Harry Sinclair, Secretary of the Navy Edwin Denby, and others. He then criticized Secretary of the Treasury Andrew Mellon, who headed the aluminum trust, pointing out that Mellon's interests stood to make $69,000,000 a year through inflated aluminum prices. Harrison described the soldiers' bonus as a "last minute vote-getting measure" on the part of Congress: "Congress pushed it up; Cal Coolidge pushed it down; then congress put it over," and this was done "to show congress wasn't behind the president." He added, "The republicans have not one bit of party leadership. It's no wonder the head of the party can't talk." The

Evansville meeting was chaired by Sumner George, a local attorney, and other speakers included a Dr. Norrell; A. J. Smitherman, editor of the *New World* of Springfield, Massachusetts; and W. E. Henderson, an Indianapolis attorney and president of the Independent Voters' League of Marion County. A campaign handout entitled "Advice to Colored Voters!" listed the 1924 Indianapolis Democratic and Republican candidates. The handout noted that virtually all the Republican candidates were Klansmen while most Democrats were anti-Klan. Henderson added that "the colored people . . . have not left the republican party; the republican party has left us."[54]

On October 31 the political campaign in Marion featured Democratic and Republican meetings. "Dr." Harrison "delivered a fine address" for the Democratic national and state tickets before three hundred people at Beshore Hall, on South Washington Street. Harrison stated: "my people go to the polls carrying Lincoln on their backs and the republican party on their necks. I am a democrat, and have never voted the republican ticket." He then examined the contention that "The republicans say the negro owes them a debt of gratitude" and countered, "The republican party has never enforced the amendment which gives the right to voting to our people over the whole United States"; it had "promised to enforce the constitution of the United States which protects the negro, but has never done it." He added, "Only when the colored people go into the democratic party" would the Republicans "wake up and do something." Harrison made clear: "I have never said that the democratic party loves the negro. No party should. The negro should love himself." The Democratic Party was "willing to extend the right hand to colored people," and its slogan was "'equal rights to all and special privileges to none.'" It was "a party against privilege," "fighting for the common people," and had "always stood for the individual." In closing Harrison reportedly urged the colored people to vote early and to vote for John W. Davis and Carlton B. McCulloch for governor.[55]

Harrison next spoke before a large crowd at the circuit courtroom on Saturday, November 1. The meeting was little advertised, yet the courtroom was standing room only. According to the *Leader Tribune* Harrison said that "The republican party" was "now singing in this campaign, 'We Ain't a Goin' to Steal No More,'" while the democratic party on election day is going to sing, 'We Know You Ain't Goin' to Steal No More.'" He went on:

> There was a time when the republican party was great, but it is now bankrupt in honesty, in intelligence and in leadership. The republicans say there is no issue in this campaign. If there is no issue, why this campaign? There is not one issue that the republican party can stand on this year. . . . When the votes are counted, if they are counted, the people of this country will register a repudiation of the republican party throughout the state and nation.[56]

He urged "Negroes" to "vote the straight democratic ticket, both state and nation." He asserted that "Negroes" are "waking up" and that the "young negro in Indiana, as well as New York, is doing his own thinking. Abraham Lincoln is dead and I am not going to vote for a dead man." As his talk ended, many urged Harrison to speak again in the city.[57]

The work of Harrison and others could not stem the Republican tide. In the 1924 Indiana gubernatorial race both the Klan and Republicans claimed victory. Nationally, the Republican Coolidge won with a popular vote of 15,725,016 to Davis's 8,383,586 and La Follette's 4,822,856.[58]

———

While he was in the Midwest Harrison continued to seek lecture work. On September 5, Mildred Chatfield Smith, executive secretary of the Open Forum Speakers Bureau of Boston, wrote back to him that they currently had a large number of available speakers on race relations. She wasn't sure what opportunities would arise, but she would add his name to the list for the coming season if he filled out and returned their form. Ms. Smith later sent a form letter to Harrison indicating that "the forum season just closed has been the busiest the Bureau has ever had" and invited him to cooperate with them with "a dozen Sundays or only one or two," since they needed him and his message.[59]

On September 15 Walter White, assistant secretary of the NAACP, wrote to Harrison: "You have no idea how happy your letter of September 9th made me." Harrison's had written in praise of White's first novel, *The Fire in the Flint*, which he had received for review from the publisher Alfred A. Knopf. White added, "I tried to do an honest piece of work and to know that you with all of your experience feel that I have 'hit the bull's eye' is encouraging indeed. I do hope that you will do the review for *The Christian Science Monitor*."[60]

Harrison was back in New York for the 1924 elections, and around November 2, he received a copy of a campaign leaflet from the Democratic congressman (from 1923–1929), Royal H. Weller, whose district covered part of Manhattan and the Bronx. The leaflet asked, "Colored Voters: Can You Forget?" and then criticized the Republican candidate Emanuel Hertz, who in 1923 "urged the defeat of Henri W. Shields[,] your Alderman, because he was a colored man." Weller, who claimed to have secured a yearly appropriation of one million dollars for Howard University and to have "worked for the erection of a monument in France to the COLORED soldiers," urged people to vote for him and "Keep Hertz out of office."[61]

After the election, on December 18, 1924, Walter Yust, editor of the *Literary Review* of the *New York Evening Post*, wrote to Harrison thanking him for what he had sent. Harrison had apparently sent the names of two books he might review as well as his review of *The Emperor Jones*. Yust, who would later become

editor in chief of the *Encyclopedia Britannica*, described the review as "illuminating" and O'Neill's letter as "characteristic." He added that he hoped to talk
to Harrison again but regretted that the two books he suggested in his letter
had already been reviewed. He asked Harrison to send another list.[62]

The year 1925 proved to be one of the most difficult of Harrison's life. He was
beset by ill health, had very limited income, and did little writing. He did continue his philandering, however, right from the beginning of the year. On New
Year's Eve, an old friend from Boston, "V," arrived in New York and left a note
for him at a neighborhood drugstore. He didn't get it till late on New Year's afternoon while on his way "to join ifs tjtufs nbsz [her sister Mary]." He called for
"V" on the second and "spent much of each day" with her until January 10, when
he put her in a cab at his corner of 139th Street. She returned to Boston. During those eight days they "dined twice at Eddie's." He described her in his diary
as "full of charm and baby-ways, jealous as the devil, requires constant sooth-
ing, and as full of the will-to-love as the sky is full of stars."[63]

One of Harrison's job-search efforts involved an offer to write articles and
coordinate New York distribution for *Reflexus* magazine. On February 10, R.
Irving Johnson, general manager of the Popular Magazine Corporation of Chicago, sent Harrison a detailed distribution plan and said his next letter would
include Harrison's contract. He also enclosed a general agency contract under
which Harrison's special agents would work. Johnson mailed under separate
cover "a sufficient quantity of literature and material" for the next two to three
weeks. In his postscript he asked about the progress of "our special article."
The contract for the appointment of city supervisors was sent on February 21, and Harrison, in order to be in charge of newsstand distribution in
New York, was to sign it and return it. Three days later Johnson sent a signed
two-page contract for Harrison to sign by March 1. In an accompanying letter he added that he had mailed final instructions and supervisors' contracts
and requested that Harrison rush his manuscript on "Civilization's Black
Beginnings," which they "hoped to feature next month."[64]

On March 5 Johnson wrote that he had received Harrison's contract and
"very interesting letter." He was glad that Harrison had "already been over the
field" but was "not a bit surprised that the new dealers are unwilling to put our
[out?] their money before they see the magazine." He said that Harrison's efforts
"paved the way for the immediate sale of the magazine once it appears on the
streets," agreed that "a sample copy will tell more than an ocean of words," and
planned to mail Harrison copies to be used as he thought best. Harrison's manuscript had also been received "in excellent condition," could be "readily handled without being typewritten," and "received very favorable comment" from

Figure 16.2. "Mass Meeting of Colored Citizens of Floyd County, ... New Albany, Indiana, October 17, 1924 [featuring Huber[t] Harrison], Sponsored by the Independent Voters League of Floyd County." In 1924 Hubert Harrison, consistent with a "chief feature" of the International Colored Unity League program, traveled to Indiana, seeking to consolidate the "Negro" vote in an effort at helping secure "the ballot for the Race masses in the South by using it solidly against any party which opposes the enforcement of the Fourteenth and Fifteenth amendments to the United States Constitution." This attitude was recently manifested "in the attitude of the Race voters of Indiana," where the Ku Klux Klan was growing rapidly. Harrison believed "that if the Southerners of our group can get the vote back into their hands, they will be able to solve their own problems of lynching, Jim Crow and limited education, since sheriffs, school boards and legislators will be responsible to Race voters as well as to white." *Source:* Hubert H. Harrison Collection, Box 16, Folder 29, Rare Book and Manuscript Library, Columbia University Library. See https://dlc.library.columbia.edu/catalog/cul:4f4qrfj8d7.

their editor. He thanked Harrison for his promptness but would not be able to send a proof for correction before deadline. If Harrison would trust them he felt sure there would not be any mistake in typography. Johnson also wanted Harrison to "prepare other articles of a similar nature for subsequent issues of *Reflexus*." If that was agreeable he would mail a check to Harrison upon date of publication. Though he only expected an article of two thousand words it was "thoroughly acceptable in its present form," and he would be paid at "1c per word." Harrison's "Poro article" would not run until August, so he would have time to prepare it. The magazine would solve the problem of a proper illustration and cooperate with Harrison in every way possible. Johnson wished for Harrison's continued success and "improved health with which to carry on."[65]

Shortly thereafter, on April 29, 1925, the *Amsterdam News* reported that there were shortages of $125,000 at the *Chicago Defender*. Though there were no arrests, Phil. A. Jones, general manager; Roscoe Conkling Simmons, of the Republican Lincoln League and a columnist related to Booker T. Washington; J. Delos Baker, a bookkeeper; and Alfred Anderson, chief editorial writer, were implicated. The publisher, Robert S. Abbott, had probably sensed something wrong when Jones and Bell came out with the elaborate *Reflexus*. It was its first and only issue and probably cost $10,000.[66]

On March 18 C. Spencer, of the Douglass Society of the City College of New York, an organization that aimed "to disseminate [information on] good qualities of the Negro Race," wrote to Harrison that they were "looking forward" to his speaking on "Civilization's Black Beginnings." He suggested a time of Thursday at 1 p.m. Harrison would "be the drawing card," and they needed time to advertise. He asked for an available manuscript for their bulletin board and raised the issue of possible participation in a symposium on the race problem. In addition, Harrison spoke on "Civilization's Black Beginnings" at Columbia University, under the auspices of the Douglass Society and the Young Men's Christian Association.[67]

Harrison also sought to write for the *New York Sun* and on February 14, the *Sun*'s editor, Allan Nevins, wrote thanking him for his note of February 11 and explaining that "the two volumes" that Harrison sought to review would be "worth, in combination, a thousand words." He was sorry that the paper had not received a copy of Du Bois's *The Gift of Black Folk* and was writing the publishers that day for a copy to send to Harrison. In a postscript he asked Harrison to "Please keep under the 1000 words rather than above," adding, "750 might be better."[68]

———

Around February 14 Harrison reviewed, probably in the *New York Sun*, *The Everlasting Stain*, by Kelly Miller, and *The Negro in South Carolina During the*

Reconstruction, by Alrutheus Ambush Taylor. He explained that "the negro in America is finding his voice; and year after year it can be heard clearer and more emphatic as he invades field after field of discussion, where he insists on elbowing out of the way the hitherto accredited spokesmen on his behalf that he may speak for himself." He added, "The results are often interesting." These two books "by negro writers" illustrated at the same time "two different types of negro mentality and two widely differing phases in the development of the negro intellect."[69]

Professor Miller represented "the earlier phase of scholastic development among negroes when some superficial acquaintance with 'letters' and a flair for cryptic phrases did duty behind the color line for the culture demanded by modern life." His book was "a loose collection of occasional papers on the negroes problem, with no organic connection between them." Harrison found no "definite point of view" but did detect "a certain evangelical pietism" and "placid self-contradictions," which were "so pathetically naive" that the author's brother professor, who penned the introduction, was driven to remark that 'one might almost regard Kelly Miller as a belated rationalist of the eighteenth century, or a Jesuit strayed from the cloister into the arena.'" To Harrison, however, "no Jesuit—not even St. Ignatius himself—was ever so innocent of learning as is Prof. Miller." *The Everlasting Stain* was "a horrible example of the futility of the old type of negro education against which Booker T. Washington thundered thirty years ago. It doesn't illuminate the racial discussion with a single idea or a solitary item of knowledge."[70]

Harrison found that to read Taylor's book, in contrast to Miller's, was "to enter an entirely different world," one in which "the discipline of historical studies tends to promote sharp, clear outlines in one's mental perspectives." Taylor offered "a clear picture . . . of a period of our national history over which there have often hovered the fogs of illusion and conventional mythology." "Popular historians from [Henry William] Elson and [John W.] Burgess to [Hendrik Willem] Van Loon have either played . . . with the facts of reconstruction or been serenely ignorant of them." Too often "the negro's part in the process has been [described as] that of shuttlecock," and educated Americans seemed "content to repeat *ad nauseam* the stale falsehoods . . . disproved by the works of even Southern historians like [Walter L.] Fleming and Garner." Taylor's book, however, was "not in the controversial spirit." It "set down aught in malice" and "proceeded in the spirit and according to the methods of that 'new history' for which [James Harvey] Robinson of Columbia has been so long contending." Through "painstaking study" of original sources such as "legislative records, contemporary daily newspapers, census reports, budgets, diaries, correspondence, books of travel, church and school publications," Taylor was able to let the reader "see, as with his own eyes, the stirring scenes that filled the time between the accession of Andrew Johnson to the Presidency and that of [Benjamin] Hayes, and the part which the negro played in those scenes in the State of South Carolina."[71]

The Negro in South Carolina During the Reconstruction contained fourteen chapters. The first seven discussed how the Negroes lived, what they wore and ate, how they acquired land, and how they took to religion, church building, and school attendance. Despite the fact that Reconstruction was generally conceived as a political process of adjustment, it was only in the eighth chapter that Taylor entered upon the political aspects of Reconstruction. The chapters on "The Constitutional Convention of 1868" and "Reconstructionists and Their Measures" were well documented and recorded "the demonstrated capacity of Southern negroes in the administration of public affairs." This was "an astounding revelation to those who have steeped themselves in such current mythology" as that which "Prof. [John Moffatt] Mecklin repeats in his book on the Ku Klux [*The Ku Klux Klan: A Study of the American Mind*]."

Taylor's "entire book" was "replete with garnered and sifted knowledge" that illuminated. The merit of the historian, however, concerned "his judgments no less than his narrative," and Taylor did "not shine in respect to the former faculty." To Harrison, "the form of subvention under which the study was undertaken" helped "explain this defect." Though Taylor's "mastery of his period" was "gratifying," the "toils of his syntax" were "very often pathetic." Nevertheless, his work was "a substantial achievement of the modern negro intellect in terms of the historical scholarship of its own time."[72]

———

On February 21, Ernest R. Crandall of the Board of Ed sent Harrison a schedule of "Trend of Times" lectures for the first eight weeks of the spring course. He wrote again on March 7 and informed him that since all announcements had been made, if he wanted to do "Trend" for half an hour and then a short lecture on a literary topic, he should submit an outline of the lecture "in plenty of time," so, "if necessary," he could request "a different topic."[73]

One of Harrison's lectures in this period, probably for the "Trend" series, was on "The United States Air Service." His March 14 handwritten notes began by discussing "the importance of aeronautics in national security" as the "eyes for the Army and Navy" and as "a means of offence and defence." He explained how "the war taught" new skills like "bombing and gassing from planes" and how America's "aerial development [was] not as marked as that of some other nations"—particularly because, "since the war," U.S. airships were "built in Germany & Italy." This was so despite the fact that "our inventors had the primacy in aeronautic experimentation" from "the Wright bros. & Roy Knabenshue."

Interest in aeronautics was "re-awakened" by the topic of "Round-the-World by Aeroplane (with assistance of the Navy)" and by the military and commercial significance of the *Shenandoah* and *Los Angeles*. Harrison also discussed recent congressional inquiries including "the Navy's point of view," "General [William] Mitchell's [pro-air power] point of view," and the "prospects [from Congress]," particularly "from [Edward V.] Rickenbacker's group."[74]

Around 1925 Harrison crossed out parts in his copy of a newspaper article entitled "Miscegenation and the Rhinelander Case." The case, which drew considerable national attention, was a divorce matter between the millionaire Leonard Kip Rhinelander, a Huguenot descendant and member of one of "New York's 400" elite families, and his "Negro" wife, Alice Jones Rhinelander. The article, which was probably written by Harrison and may have been the basis for a "Trend" lecture, begins by describing miscegenation as an "ancient monument to man's humanity," which, "like Janus, [has] two faces": "A White Man's Privilege" and "A Way of Escape." The "furtive and underhanded" "White Man's Privilege," he said, "has the silent and sinister sanction of white society" and "is a thing which the much-feared 'social equality' would inevitably decrease"—since "if white men were made to realize that they would have to marry where they mate, the chances are that all but the few who honorably love would leave Negro women alone."[75]

"The other face of miscegenation"—"A Way of Escape"—was "lit with hope" for "some Negroes who are already part white and are tired of struggle" and had "no pride of race to back them, since they are not truly (that is, biologically) of either race." Thus, "every year more and more" were "'passing for white' among the Caucasians," and as they "cross over the line" they "make the American white man what he is—a race whose mixture of black blood is largely unknown and unsuspected." While "no fair-minded person can very well blame them for it," the consequence of this was "that in America, while we can tell who is a Negro, we never can tell who isn't." Nature, however, had "her own way of redressing the balances and fooling those" who desired "to see an early breeding-out of the Negro stock"—it was that "most mulatto women bear children who are darker than themselves." The "'yellow fever' which causes black men and maidens to put an extra premium on the light woman and man as prospective partners is the very thing which is trimming lightness down to brownness (a decided gain in beauty) in this race of ours." Another side issue was that there was "an ever-increasing number of white women who in Negro Harlem, Washington and elsewhere are 'passing for colored' because as poor white women, they could only secure car conductors as husbands; while, as white-Negroes, the pick of black lawyers, doctors, ministers and big business men will compete for the chance to become their meal-tickets for life." All of this was "a tremendous counter-weight" to "the force of that social impulse among 'society' Negroes which prompts them to lend the white man a hand in promoting the whitening process."[76]

———

On February 3, 1925, the U.S. Circuit Court of Appeals for the Second Circuit issued an opinion that affirmed the original judgment finding Marcus Garvey guilty of a single count of using the mails to defraud in violation of Section 214

Figure 16.3. Amy Ashwood Garvey, 1920s. Jamaica-born Amy Ashwood Garvey (January 10, 1897–May 3, 1969), described by her biographer Tony Martin as a "Pan-Africanist, Feminist," was the first wife of Marcus Garvey. She had an affair with Hubert Harrison and worked with him on "The Rise and Fall of Marcus Garvey" in 1925. Harrison was called as a witness during her 1926 divorce trial with Marcus Garvey, and correspondence between Amy Ashwood Garvey and Hubert Harrison was presented. *Source:* Public domain.

of the U.S. Criminal Code. After the conviction was sustained, Assistant U.S. Attorney Maxwell Mattuck demanded his immediate arrest. On February 5 Special Agent Amos boarded a train at 125th Street and, along with deputy U.S. marshals Walter B. Carr and James Hyer, took Garvey into custody as he was voluntarily returning from Detroit to surrender. He was placed in the Manhattan House of Detention (the Tombs); arraigned before Judge Hand, who denied a stay and bail and ordered Garvey removed to the Atlanta Federal penitentiary; and then, on February 7, handcuffed to federal marshals and placed on a train to begin his five-year prison sentence in Atlanta.[77]

On February 7, as Amy Jacques and Marcus Garvey traveled by train to Atlanta, Amy Ashwood Garvey went to the apartment of her former husband at 133 West 129th Street in New York and, with the help of friends, sought to remove furniture she claimed Marcus had bought her during their marriage. A scuffle ensued with neighbors and UNIA members; police were called. Amy Ashwood, accompanied by a police officer, took an inventory of items, which included $5,000 worth of items purchased from the Harlem Furniture Co. on credit in March 1920, the month they separated, and a player piano. On February 9 she obtained a restraining order in municipal court that prohibited Amy Jacques Garvey from taking any property until the court ruled.[78]

Seventeen days later, on February 24, 1925, Amy Ashwood Garvey wrote to Harrison that she had not replied to his "missive ere this, as I wanted." In her letter, which Harrison later described as "wonderful" and "fascinating," Amy added:

> You are a wonderful man and I could die in your arms. You are so fascinating and tender I am going to remain in America for one year, if I may, and I know it is going to be a blissful, happy, mental communion of souls—maybe I have it, just perfect—the combining of one nature with tender impression, the meeting of their lips and then—then the climax. Oh, the ecstasy of it is truly an art.
>
> Dear, as soon as I can, I am going to fix up a love nest. I am short of funds right now and must wait some developments, but if I can get a loan of $300 for say, ninety days, we would soon begin to live. I know what you want dear, a nice environment. Your ten fingers and brain are worth millions. Between us, we could move the colored world. All we need is a start; if hard work and pluck has anything to do with success, we are going to succeed, I know [where you] stand financially, I don't think I have ever cared about that. I love you for yourself.
>
> Your love,
> ADE.[79]

As Hubert became more involved with Amy Ashwood there were, once again, repercussions at home in the form of tensions with his wife, Lin. On Sunday morning, March 1, as he lay in bed, Hubert heard his sixteen-year-old daughter Frances in the kitchen singing "a vulgar version" of the recent song "The West Indian Blues," by J. Edgar Dowell, Spencer Williams, and Clarence Williams:

> In days of old when knights were bold
> And toilets not invented,
> They left their load in the middle of the road
> And went away contented!

When he went into the kitchen to talk to Frances, he "found that her mother was there" and "had been there all the time," yet "she 'never said a murmurin' word.'" Hubert judged that "by the deliberate consent of their mother" the children "vary in this direction." He "frequently heard 'Lin' 'singing' in their presence the vulgar and often suggestive songs of the street" and considered it "Small wonder that they know so many of them!"[80]

The next day, on Monday, March 2, Hubert wrote in his diary that he had "been working for over a week with Mrs. Amy Ashwood Garvey, the first wife of Marcus Garvey." Their project was "a biography of her husband to be entitled 'The Rise and Fall of Marcus Garvey—By Amy A. Garvey.'" Harrison explained that she would write out the story and he would "cast it into literary form and re-write it, eliciting by questions such additional information as the structure of the biography may demand." He added: "She and I get along like a house afire. A very ambitious woman is this little Jamaican, very ambitious." That first week in March they planned to shift their workshop from the house at 227 West 126th Street to 486 St. Nicholas Avenue, apt. 6 (the corner of West 134th Street), which was the apartment of a friend of hers named Bishop. Harrison added that Mrs. Garvey promised "to acquire a flat—this one or another—and wants me in that event to come and live there."[81]

He then entered in his diary more intimate details about Amy Ashwood Garvey:

She is by the way, a very, very passionate woman. She tells me that one reason for the failure of her marriage to Marcus was the fact that the fellow couldn't—satisfactorily. It seems that on the night when they got together—which she avers was the fourth night after the wedding (though this was by no means the *first*) he—her twelve times! And yet, so coarse, crude and clumsy was this "Provisional President of Africa" that she never had even a single orgasm, either then or at any subsequent time with him. Her first orgasm, she insists, came while asleep in London about 3 or 4 years ago. She was dreaming—so she says—*about me*! Well, one needn't dream these things at present![82]

Later that week, on Thursday, March 5, Harrison wrote in his diary that

Mrs. Garvey and I have been writing at her book for nearly two weeks now, and are just in the middle of the second chapter. Our friendship develops wonderfully too. Usually, a Negro woman when she is very passionate has no room in her soul for any "higher" things. But this little West Indian is a well-spring of ambition and inspiration. No wonder Garvey called her his "Star of Destiny"! She veritably was; and when he "dished" her he had the same result that Napoleon had when he "dished" his Josephine. I wish it were possible for me to get her as my helpnest. I think I should rise to giddy heights of achievement!

In the meanwhile I am learning a great deal of this magnificent and mendacious mountebank, Garvey. He was, evidently, the dirtiest robber that ever rose to prominence. Well, his wife makes up for much, and, in any case, I am getting a glorious revenge! With this woman to spur me on, (as she is doing already) and with such gifts as I have, I could become the most famous Negro in America. 'Tis well worth thinking on—and acting on, too. Bah![83]

Only two weeks after his diary entry on Amy Ashwood Garvey, on Thursday, March 19, 1925, Hubert "looked up 'Diva Augusta [Savage],'" the wonderfully talented Florida-born sculptor. He "spent almost the entire day at her house, up to midnight," adding, "Her kisses were delicious! And today we established ourselves upon a sounder footing. *Gloria in sedibus*—!" The following Wednesday, March 25, Hubert again went to Augusta's house. This time, however, he "got in before she did and waited in for her until about 4 in the afternoon when she came." While he was there a Mr. Paul came to look for her, with a letter in his hand, and left. Then came Arnold Reiss, "the white artist in tow of Mr. Gaillard, a young Negro artist" (who he thought lived on Cornelia Street in Greenwich Village). They didn't stay either, so Hubert "'Kept house' alone until Augusta came in. . . . [when they] spent some very pleasant hours together." He observed "Augusta seems quite a little cynic—especially in matters of Eros." Nevertheless, he had "the exquisite pleasure of kissing away the tears from her eyes." He then wrote, "She has not only intelligence, but genius; and as a sculptor she has, to my mind, already made her mark."[84]

Toward the end of March into April Harrison looked to pick up his lecture schedule. On March 30 "Dr." Harrison spoke at the Sunrise Club's eleventh dinner of its thirty-second season, at Cafe Boulevard, Forty-First Street, near Broadway. The topic was "'High-Brows,' 'Low Brows,' and Bell-Wethers—The Psychography of the Social Crazy-Horse."[85]

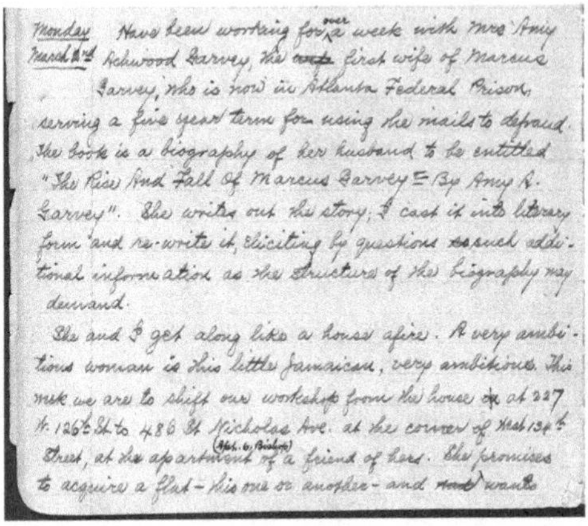

Monday March 2nd Have been working for over a week with Mrs. Amy Ashwood Garvey, the first wife of Marcus Garvey, who is now in Atlanta Federal Prison, serving a five year term for using the mails to defraud. The book is a biography of her husband to be entitled "The Rise And Fall Of Marcus Garvey" By Amy A. Garvey". She writes out the story; I cast it into literary form and re-write it, eliciting by questions such additional information as the structure of the biography may demand.

She and I get along like a house afire. A very ambitious woman is this little Jamaican, very ambitious. This week we are to shift our workshop from the house at 227 W. 126th St to 486 St Nicholas Ave. at the corner of West 134th Street, at the apartment (Mrs. L. Bishop) of a friend of hers. She promises to acquire a flat—this one or another—and wants

Figure 16.4. Hubert Harrison, diary entry, March 2, 1925, page 1. In his diary of March 2, 1925, Harrison wrote of having "been working for over a week with Mrs. Amy Ashwood Garvey, the first wife of Marcus Garvey," on her book "to be entitled 'The Rise and Fall of Marcus Garvey,' by Amy Ashwood Garvey." He explained that she "writes out the story, I cast it into literary form and rewrite it." Harrison added, "She and I get a long like a house afire." *Source:* Hubert H. Harrison Papers, Box 9, Folder 2, Rare Book and Manuscript Library, Columbia University Library. See https://dlc.library.columbia.edu/catalog/cul:tmpg4f4sfs.

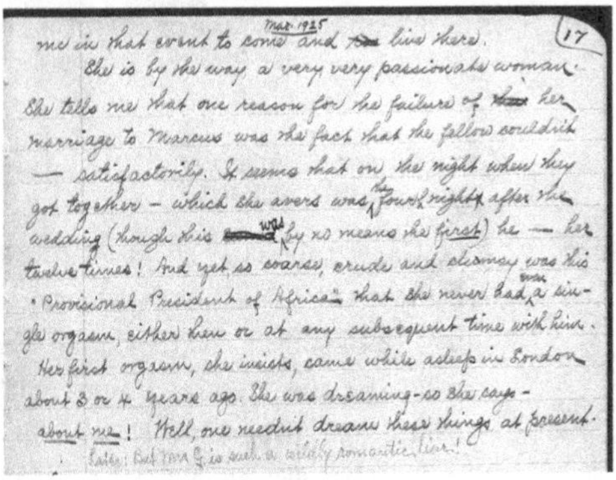

Mar. 1925 17

me in that event to come and live there.

She is by the way a very very passionate woman. She tells me that one reason for the failure of her marriage to Marcus was the fact that the fellow couldn't — satisfactorily. It seems that on the night when they got together — which she avers was the fourth night after the wedding (though this was by no means the first) he — her twelve times! And yet so coarse, crude and clumsy was this "Provisional President of Africa" that she never had a single orgasm, either then or at any subsequent time with him. Her first orgasm, she insists, came while asleep in London about 3 or 4 years ago. She was dreaming—so she says—about me! Well, one needn't dream these things at present.

Later: But Mrs G is such a wildly romantic liar!

Figure 16.5. Hubert Harrison, diary entry, March 2, 1925, continued on page 2. In this continuation of his March 2, 1925, diary entry Hubert Harrison describes Amy Ashwood Garvey as "a very, very passionate woman" who told him that "one reason for the failure of her marriage to Marcus was the fact that the fellow couldn't—satisfactorily" and that "she never had a single orgasm" with him. She added, "Her first orgasm . . . came while in London about 3 or 4 years ago" while "dreaming" about Harrison. Later, Harrison added to this entry: "But Mrs. G is such a wildly romantic liar!" *Source:* Hubert H. Harrison Papers, Box 9, Folder 2, Rare Book and Manuscript Library, Columbia University Library. See https://dlc.library.columbia.edu/catalog/cul:tmpg4f4sfs.

On April 14, F. D. Bluford, acting president of North Carolina A&T, wrote to Harrison asking his terms for one lecture and the dates when he would be traveling south. He said that C. P. Johnson had suggested him for a lecture at the school and added that he would "be coming south sometime in the near future." The *Chicago Defender* also reported that "Dr." Harrison planned to go south on a lecture tour at the end of May 1925.[86]

On December 16, 1924, a meeting was held in the 135th Street New York Public Library to discuss establishing a major reference collection in Black history and culture on the library's third floor. The bibliophile Arthur Schomburg chaired, and other prominent community members involved from the beginning included Harrison, James Weldon Johnson, and Johnson's brother-in-law,

Figure 16.6. Augusta Savage. Florida-born Augusta Fells Savage (February 29, 1892–March 27, 1962) was a brilliant sculptor. After spending time with Hubert Harrison in New York in 1925 he wrote in his diary: "She has not only intelligence, but genius; and as a sculptor she has, to my mind, already made her mark." In the early part of 1926 Harrison became involved in efforts to enable her to study at the Academy of Fine Arts in Rome, where she had been accepted (she had been accepted previously to study at Fontainebleau in France but could not afford to attend). After Harrison's passing, Augusta Savage made a death mask of him that was to be the basis for a life-sized bust. *Source:* Schomburg Center for Research in Black Culture, Photographs and Prints Division, New York Public Library Digital Collections.

John Nail, a wealthy real estate investor and entrepreneur. Ernestine Rose, the librarian, and her assistant, Catherine Allen Latimer, the library's first Black librarian, had already started separating material for this purpose and wanted a community-led group to assist in formulating a plan for the collection.[87]

Ms. Rose subsequently sent a more formal product of this preliminary work to Harrison—it was a plan for establishing a Department of Negro History, Literature, and Art in the 135th Street branch in order "to make easily available for permanent public use a large and representative body of material expressive of Negro culture in the past and present." She suggested "a Society or Foundation: to secure permanency and active public support" and to support and control such a collection of materials. She also proposed that "the collection be housed at the 135th Street Branch of the N.Y. Public Library until such time as it has attained sufficient size and financial support as to require and deserve an independent building" and that it "be administered by a properly equipped colored person, under the supervision of the N.Y. Public Library." She asked Harrison to participate in a meeting to discuss the formation of a Negroid Department in the library on Tuesday, March 11, 1925, at 8:30. Her postscript said she was "particularly anxious" to have him attend and "to lend counsel in this matter of vital significance.[88]

The organization that was formed had Schomburg as president; Rose, first vice president; Johnson, second vice president; Harrison, secretary; and Nail, treasurer. The group decided to seek to preserve resources in this field, and their first formal decision was "to withdraw from circulation books relating to the Negro which were difficult to replace." The community quickly responded with loans and gifts from the private libraries and collections of Harrison, George Young, Schomburg, the late John E. Bruce, Louise Lattimer, and Dr. Charles D. Martin.[89]

The Department of Negro Literature and History of the West 135th Street Public Library formally opened with a literary and musical program and an exhibition of paintings by W. E. Braxton on Thursday evening, May 7. Schomburg presided, Miss Rose discussed the aims of the library in establishing the new department, and other speakers included Harrison, Dr. Alain Leroy Locke, and Franklin F. Hopper, chief of the circulation department of the NYPL (from 1919 to 1941).[90]

By 1925 the branch libraries of the NYPL were doing much to further adult education. Branches served as bureaus of information, maintained ties with educational agents in their neighborhoods, and readily supplied books and reading lists. Evening classes in the schools would visit the libraries so students could be instructed in library use and receive encouragement to become borrowers. At the 135th Street branch there were weekly lecture courses given by the Board of Ed, and Harrison was the principal speaker. According to the

report of the director of the NYPL, Harrison "uses the Library freely and rec-
ommends to his hearers the books which he himself finds most useful there."[91]

Notes in Harrison's papers entitled "Some Reasons Why Such a Collection
Is Necessary" suggest the possible subject matter of one of his talks. He begins
by pointing to an article in an April issue of the *New York Times* that stated that
the Prince of Wales had depicted West Africa as a series of trading stations. He
thought it might surprise *Times* readers to know of Sir. E. Lewis; Henry Carr,
Esq.; Edward Wilmot Blyden; John Mensah Sarbah; and Joseph Ephraim Casely
Hayford, and of millionaires such as Obassa [Orisadipe Obasa]. Harrison also
thought it important to know that "W. Africa turns in to [the] coffers of Britain
more wealth than all India."[92]

Another example was the article by Carl Shoup in the Sunday *New York World*
of March 5, 1925, in which he tells of Plato's comments on Atlantis but doesn't
mention a word "of the fact that the story is not Plato's but was given [to] him
by Egyptian priests whom Plato, Herodotus, Heliodorus, Aeschylus, & Diode-
rus describe as black people." Harrison notes that Lewis Spence's recent book
on Atlantis was not in any branch of the public library, nor was Dr. Albert
Churchward's book on Matt Henson and the North Pole. Harrison also mentions the "Ignorance of those who come 'to study us,'" describes a "flock of
fledgling philosophers & one-evening experts in sociology," and cites *Survey
Graphic* and statistics from Konrad Bercovici, Winthrop D. Lane, and Kelly
Miller that have "Harlem's 200,000—Now 300,000." Harrison emphasizes that
a crucial reason for such a collection is "to build [the] shattered self-respect of
[the] Negro."[93]

As background to the idea of building self-respect, Harrison prepared additional pages of notes on "One Decade of Harlem's Mental Growth." He mentioned the 135th Street branch of the New York Public Library and the fact that
only two Blacks attended its 1908 Crampton Lectures on Biology and Evolution. Then in 1915 Miss Gertrude Cohen, the librarian, requested that he develop
a series of lectures on sociology, literature, and theology, after which he "gave
up the white forum: [to] organize [the] Harlem People's Forum," where he developed "Lectures on Negro Liter[ature]. & History and World-Aspects of Race."
Harrison added that "'Twas here that the Race-Cons[ciousness]. dev[eloped]
out of which came ev[entually]. Garvey Mov[emen]t." Harrison developed "outdoor lectures on Negro affairs" and sold books including James G. Blaine's
autobiography, Joel A. Rogers, Kelly Miller, his own books, and books from
George Young's bookshop. He also discussed how "the germ" of this racial consciousness was nurtured in St. Benedict's Catholic Lyceum, how "*Cultural
Inertia*" had to be overcome, and how "the Callow Colored Socialists [a probable reference to Owen and possibly to Randolph]: ignorant alike of History and
Literature asserted there was no such thing as Negro History or Negro

lit[erature: one of their editors [a probable reference to Owen] even denied that there was such a thing as *Negro music*." He cited "Jaime C. Gil: [that] 'there is no Negro literature'" and stressed the important role in developing race consciousness played by the Negro Historical Society, the Schomburg Collection, and West Indians.[94]

On December 24, 1925, in Room 112 of the 135th Street branch, an exhibit illustrative of Black Harlem was displayed. The exhibit ran until March 15, 1926, and included historical and geographical influences and material on "the Negro in early New York," literary Harlem, "the Negro's contributions in poetry, the drama, and music, as well as his folklore, in song and story," business and professional life, and the library's place in Harlem life (with a particular stress on the Department of Negro Literature and History). Much of the source material was lent by the book collector Arthur A. Schomburg, the book dealer George T. Young, Harrison, and Dr. Charles D. Martin, pastor of the Moravian Church. In connection with the exhibit "a selected bibliography on the Negro" was compiled by the 135th Street branch and published in the December "Branch Library Book Notes."[95]

———

Other matters also attracted Harrison's attention in late 1925. On August 11, Melvin J. Chisum, field secretary of the National Negro Press Association, had written to Harrison that he wanted "to make the acquaintance of the brilliant Dr. Harrison" and asked him to "break bread" with him at noon on August 12 at the Broadway Central Hotel, where he was staying. He said the meeting would be "a very great honor and a distinct pleasure on an itinerant member of the Fourth Estate." Harrison added an addendum at the bottom of Chisum's letter: "Of all the hypocritical frauds that I have ever met among Negroes this smooth fellow is the worst." Harrison initialed this and dated it July 11, 1926.[96]

U(lysses). S. Poston, chairman of the Harlem Branch of the John F. Hylan 5-Cent Fare Club (named for the effort to preserve the subway fare at five cents), wrote an August 27, 1925, letter of introduction that described New York Board of Ed staff lecturer Harrison as "a man who has been instrumental in shaping the political thought of Harlem" and "a journalist of wide experience." He added that in pursuance of "the publicity policy of campaign work of having some of the influential men of the community to write for publication news releases as they effect our group politically, I am recommending Dr. Harrison as being one eminently qualified to serve us in this capacity." Poston added that "an article from him released in the daily press would go a long ways in enhancing the cause of Mayor Hylan among the colored voters." He hoped that it would be found "convenient to use Dr. Harrison in this capacity."[97]

On September 21, 1925, A. L. Schwartz, acting secretary of the Bronx Fellowship Club, wrote to Harrison that he was authorized to offer $25 per lecture for two lectures on the first and third Wednesdays in October. Harrison would then have an option for continuing the series at $20 per lecture. Schwartz suggested Harrison speak on "The Problems before the Next Congress."[98]

Then, on October 27, 1925, Harrison wrote to Arthur Hillard about an upcoming election campaign activity. He explained: "The Unity League is an organization of Negro men and women of different political creeds who find a common bond of union in the present and future welfare of their race." He added that "the core and center of the League's influence is between 550–600" and that they had authorized him to contact "Mr. Caulkin [the Tammany politician Charles W. Culkin] and pledge him the support of the organization at the polls in November and to urge him to address us on the evening of Sunday Nov[ember]. 1st when Miss Annie Mat[t]hews, Mr. Holahan, and Dr. Williams, his team-mates on the Democratic ticket are also to speak." This was not to be an ordinary political meeting, since they were "not a political organization." They would have their own program, which would be shortened, and Harrison would serve as chair. He enclosed a folder on who he was and added that for four years he had been "a member of the speakers committee of Tammany hall," the "only Negro on the staff of the Board of Education," and a "member of Mayor's Committee on Reception of Distinguished Guests." He could "be vouched for by Miss Bessie Bea[? . . .], Dr. Crandall, [and] Martin J. Healy leader of the Cayuga Democratic Club." Offering "to be of some service . . . in Harlem," he closed, "Yours for a Tammany triumph, Hubert H. Harrison, pres[ident]., Colored Unity League." The endorsement from Healy was noteworthy, since Healy's political club in the Nineteenth Assembly District of Harlem did not welcome Blacks.[99]

Also around 1926 Harrison prepared notes for *"An American History for Public Schools"* and for "The Art of the Short Story." His table of contents for the history included an "Index," "Major Plans and Ideas," "Materials, Sources, Etc.," "Emendations," and "Particular Facts to Be Mentioned."[100] His notes to himself included: "Tell the story of the Cincinnati and Thos. Mooney" and "Imitation of Indian Democracy." Under "Major Plans and Ideas," he wrote that "the book must present a *novel* feature so as to attract attention, comment and favor." He would "Let New York City bulk large in it," since "this will appeal to the local patriotism." He would therefore "use N.Y.C., as often as possible, as index and illustration of events and institutions in the history of the nation." He suggested that he "insert photographs of historic persons and places and in N.Y. e.g. [Theodore] Roosevelt, [Elihu] Root, [Charles Francis] Murphy; the Jumel Mansion, [and] Fraunces Tavern[.]"

In his notes on "The Art of the Short Story" he emphasized that "a short story . . . must lead up to something. It should have for its structure a plot, a bit of life, an incident such as you would find in a brief newspaper paragraph." Then, "as nearly as possible it must deal with a single person, in a single action, at a single place, in a single time." "In general a short story should not exceed 10,000 words," though "from 3,000 to 5,000 is the most usual length." Harrison felt that it was "this isolation, this magnifying of one character or incident, that constitutes the chief difference between the novel and the short story." To him "the true method for the making of a plot" was "the development of what may be called a plot-germ" from which the author can "take two or three characters strongly individualized morally and mentally, place them in a strong situation and let them develop." "Every plot" should be "founded upon fact which may be utilized in its original form, or so skillfully disguised or ingeniously distorted that it will seem like a product of the imagination." He advised to try "to get a new light on the plot that you purpose to use; to view it from an unexpected side; to handle it in an unusual manner—in short, try to be original." The plot "should allow of expression in a single short, fairly simple sentence," and "if it can not be so compressed there is something radically wrong with it," he added.[101]

On the subject of "*TITLES*" Harrison felt that "fragments of proverbs and poems are always attractive, as well as Biblical phrases and colloquial expressions; but the magic title is the one that excites and baffles curiosity." He thought that a title "should grow out of the phase of the plot, rather than the basic theme, else it will be too abstract & general."

In discussing "The Use of Facts" Harrison offered: "Be content to write of what you personally and intimately know, and not attempt to treat of matters of which you have only a vague and superficial knowledge, or of which you are totally ignorant." He added, "Nature can take liberties with fact that Art dare not—a truth that has passed into a proverb."

Regarding "Characters," Harrison wrote, "Despite the apparent paradox—a character must be exaggerated to appear natural." Thus, "the character which seems most real is usually a composite of the most striking characteristics of several real persons."

Discussing "Narrative" he thought that "First person narrative is better adapted to adventure, than analysis and better to the expression of humor than to the realization of tragedy."

In discussing "The Beginning" Harrison wrote that "the background of a story should always be the last thing to be chosen; But it is the first thing to consider when one comes to the actual writing-out. . . . Simple portraits need less background."

He emphasized that "unless a scene influences the action of the story, or is necessary for the understanding of what is to come it has no place in the

narrative, no matter how great may be its beauties or how artistic your description of them."

He advised to "be specific in minor details: it is a great aid to vividness" and
to "suggest the scene, as you do the character, by the few specific features which
distinguish it from other familiar scenes—then permit the reader's imagination to fill in the details."

On "Materials, Sources, Etc." he writes "select a few good sources: Hugh
Macatamney's *Cradle Days of New York* and a few more on New York City." "For
the nation: [Horace] Greeley, [James G.] Blaine, [Senator Thomas Hart] Ben-
ton, *Appleton's Cyclopedia*, Macpherson's Manuals of Politics, etc." "Read, compare, collate and digest the school histories of [John Bach] McMaster, [Albert
Bushnell] Hart and Perry and Price, also the *History of the U.S.* by Henry W.
Elson, Blaine, vols." He added, "Make plentiful use of citations from patriotic
poems and sprinkle them liberally through the book."

On "Emendations" he advises to "eliminate bibliographies: Teachers should
know the better books. Pupils should not have their attention dissipated. They
cannot read them anyhow and will not until they get to high-school—and perhaps not even then." On "Particular Facts" he mentions "1. Thomas Slater of
R.I. His visit to England; forbidden to take any drawings of the new machinery
out of the country, he memorizes its every part, constructs it when he gets back.
Ref. Carrol D. Wright—*Ind[ustria]l Hist. of U.S.*, Levasseur+"; "2. Black Sam
Fraunces' Tavern—Consult Schomburg.;" "3. Ethan Allen "In the name of the
great Jehovah etc[.]"[102]

Harrison apparently taught privately from November 1925 through January 1926 and then from January through March 1926. In his papers he had
student lists for each class; among the names listed were Mrs. William Pickens and John I. Lewis.[103]

In 1926 Harrison would see his work for the New York City Board of Education terminated. Once again, he would have to turn to freelance lecturing and
writing to make a living while carrying on his educational and political work.

17

NYC Talks, Workers School, and *Modern Quarterly* (January–September 1926)

Harrison started the year 1926 delivering lectures in Harlem. He spoke on Sunday, January 3, at the 135th Street "Y" on "The Rising Tide of Color" and considered it "very well received, by a full house." In addition to this talk, his "Trend of the Times" lectures at the 135th Street Library were regularly held on Saturday nights at 8:15 p.m.[1]

Handwritten notes for his Saturday, January 23 talk—"Is the Housing Problem Still with Us?"—show that he treated the housing problem as considerably more than a matter of "high rents." Since there would still be a housing problem even "if rooms were $1 a month," he reasoned that the real question was that "of furnishing adequate housing to our people." In analyzing "the relation of population to facilities" he discussed the "Natural—and illimitable" factors such as "air," the "Social—and producible" factors such as "schools," and the "Natural—and restricted" factors such as "land." Nationwide, the housing problem was evidenced in the fact that rent levels had increased 62.5 percent from 1917 to 1925—51 percent in the East, 64 percent in the South, 66 percent in the Midwest, and 69 percent on the Pacific Coast. The "economic roots" of the increase were related to "the city-ward flow of population," a trend that was "greatest" in countries "highest in economic development." Harrison saw this in general terms as the "pressure of a distributable population upon land (an undistributable resource)." The situation in New York had been "acute since 1917—co-incident with a great increase in economic activities caused by war and an influx of industrial population," and some "two-thirds of the population [was] in peril," according to the *Literary Digest*.[2]

Harrison's notes addressed politicians' efforts to deal with the situation, including those of Democratic governor Al Smith of New York (through emergency rent laws, tax relief, and loans) and Sam Koenig, chairman of the New York County Republican Committee. His notes also discussed the story of 570 Lenox Avenue since 1917, the Tenement House Department, the Municipal Term Court, the landlords' magistrates, and the helpful magistrates in the Seventh District. Also discussed was the need for "extending the emergency rent laws" against the "political power of landlords" in spite of the recent "collapse of the tenants associations."[3]

Around January 19 Harrison apparently started work on "The Love-Letters of Sappho and Phaon: A Peep Into the Privacy of a [Modern—crossed out] Royal Romance as transcribed by Elbert Harborn [Harrison]. New York: Boni and Liveright 1926." It was subtitled "Love passages between H.R.H. and an American girl Un verifiable Roman." The "Note (for preface)" read:

> The prince maintained his incognito to the very last, and it was not until two years had gone by that the lady was aware that her royal lover was not the journalist and author which her host represented himself to be. . . . The lady is now . . . residing in Europe but has authorized the publication of the letters because, as she thinks, ["]they may give joy to other lovers present and prospective." It is hardly necessary to say that all the names given on the title page are fictitious. Every precaution has been taken to insure that the real names of the real writers shall remain an eternal secret.[4]

This introduction was used to introduce the "love letters comprising this little volume," which the author said were "genuine" and "were written, sent and received by the two persons who actually called each other by the love names 'Sappho' and 'Phaon.'" (In Greek mythology Sappho [c. 620–c. 565 BC] was a poetess born on Lesbos, the island of lesbians, and Phaon was an aged boatsman given youth by Aphrodite.) The "actual names of the writers" would "remain for the present, a secret," though it was said that the man was "a titled European well known to many millions of people" and the "amatory history that is here recorded occurred some years ago while he was residing in America, incognito."[5]

February 1926 was marked by a series of activities around the Virgin Islands. On February 10 the *Amsterdam News* reported that members of the Virgin Islands Colonial Council were speaking before the House Committee on Insular Affairs on the report of Rufus S. Tucker, special investigator for the Treasury Department, on "Economic Conditions in the Virgin Islands." Tucker's report indicated that the population of the islands was 26,000, 7.4 percent white, 74.9 percent Negro, and 17.5 percent mixed; that exports of sugar had fallen from 30 million to 12 million; and that cotton production and value were also down. The House would soon pass a Senate bill that conferred citizenship upon the inhabitants of the Virgin Islands and extended the naturalization laws to these insular possessions. At that time there were 3,500 Virgin Islanders in New York City.[6]

On Friday afternoon, March 5, Hubert's eleven-year-old daughter Ilva "came home elated" after "she had just won her first debate—against boys, too"—at the 135th Street Library. She was a member of a team of four girls who beat four boys when they took the negative in a debate on whether the American whites had dealt justly with the American Indians. Hubert "gave her a dime a hug and a kiss."[7]

In the early part of 1926 Harrison also became very involved in efforts to enable the sculptress Augusta Savage to travel to Europe to study. The Florida-born Savage was Harrison's intimate friend and one of the most talented artists of the era. She had been accepted previously to study at Fontainebleau in France but was unable to attend. Now she was accepted to study at the Academy of Fine Arts in Rome. On March 13 the nationally prominent defense attorney Clarence Darrow wrote to Harrison that he was "interested in [the] letter you wrote re Savage." Though Darrow was "unfamiliar with her work," he offered that "if she has [the] right stuff in her" he "might get some friends interested in a small way." He asked Harrison to write him "about how much money needs to be raised," and he would "investigate further."[8]

Darrow possibly contacted Walter White, assistant secretary of the NAACP, because White wrote to Savage on March 15, "One of the persons to whom Mr. Hubert Harrison wrote so splendid a letter about you and your work and your ambition to go to Europe, has written me asking for more detailed information regarding your exact plans." That person indicated "that not only will he be willing to contribute something but will get some of his friends to do so." White asked Savage to write about her plans and to give "some idea as to just what amount of money you need and what amounts are already assured you, together with any other pertinent data which will enable me to advise the inquirer," which, he indicated, he would "be glad to do so."[9]

A March 18 letter from 1230 Druid Hill [Avenue], Baltimore, Maryland, to Savage read: "Pardon delay, so busy and not well." The writer had heard that morning "from Mr. Harrison." Admitting the possibility of being wrong, the writer nevertheless explained that

> my experience teaches that people will respond more freely to an appeal which is sent out from some recognized organ like the N.A.A.C.P. or some newspaper with a good reputation, or Y.W.C.A. as headquarters to receive and account for subscriptions sent to a fund, rather than direct to the individual, because where the individual is not known to the subscriber, there is always the thought "Suppose the necessary amount is not raised what then becomes of my subscription?"

The writer wrote a friend from the Associated Press, "asking his advice," and suggested that Harrison "sign about four of the letters he wrote for you and enclose at least six of his circulars with them to me at his earliest convenience." The writer also wanted "to enclose them in the appeals" to be "sent out, together with a photo of your work, if you please," and also suggested that they "let Dr. Harrison send out the appeal in his own name and ask the N.A.A.C.P. or some other KNOWN organization or some creditable newspaper be your headquarters for receiving the funds," suggesting that this "should make much faster headway." Finally, as a place to receive the funds, the letter writer suggested *Opportunity*, *The Crisis*, and the *New York Age* "might serve."[10]

———

On February 6, 1926, Edgar Grey, now associate editor of the *New York News*, wrote to Harrison that he had heard that Harrison was planning to be the editor of "a new newspaper-magazine." Grey suggested that because of Harrison's past "work in this field among us" the "coming paper merits some notice from us, quite apart from the ordinary duty of professional courtesy." He asked for whatever information was available on the periodical.[11]

Harrison was indeed attempting to start a new publication, and it was to be the organ of the ICUL, which was being revived. ICUL stationery from the period indicates that the organization was calling for "Political Equality, Social Justice and Civic Opportunity"; its officers included "Dr." Harrison, president; Hodge Kirnon, vice president; John I. Lewis, secretary; J. Dominick Simmons, treasurer; and an executive committee of Reuben Berry, Casper Holstein, Rabbi Arnold Josiah Ford, William H. Price, William J. Gordon, and Mme. Marie Barrier Houston.[12]

The *New York Times* reported on a February 22 afternoon event (at St. Luke's Hall, 125 West 130th Street) at which Harrison, who was identified as the chairman of the IICUL, proposed the publication of a Harlem-based magazine, the *Voice of the Negro*.[13]

———

On March 11 "Dr." Harrison spoke on "Science and Race Prejudice" before the Social Problems Club of NYU, uptown at noon. The *NYU Daily News* described him as a literary critic and contributor affiliated with the *New York World*, *Herald-Tribune*, *Freeman*, and *Nation*, who "matriculated and received his Ph.D. at the University of Copenhagen" and "spent the following years travelling around the world . . . [visiting] Europe, Asia, Africa, and islands in the Pacific Ocean," making "an intensive study of the Negro problem in various countries." In his talk Harrison discussed how "people nowadays believe things without really finding out if they are true," often taking "science's word for it." On the subject of races, he stated "none are pure," and "the Anglo-Saxon race which is considered pure" is, in fact, "made up of Angles, Saxons, Jutes, Picts, and Danes." He added that personally he didn't "blame people for having race prejudice," though he was "wholly against groups trying to rationalize" it. In conclusion he reportedly said "race prejudice to be nothing more than caste and an inferiority complex."[14]

The *Amsterdam News* commented that Harrison had totally surprised his audience by not mentioning "the Negro problem" in his lecture. By handling his subject in this "objective manner of the scientist," he said that he felt he could bring "to the bar of psychology and sociology all the proponents of race prejudice." The students were pleased and invited him back to lecture the following week. He accepted, spoke on "Locarno, Imperialism and the League of Nations," and reportedly "made an even greater impression than the first [talk]." Harrison commented to the *Amsterdam News* that the "unique" aspect of his NYU lectures was that "a black scholar, without even touching on the Negro problem, discusses with the authority of modern scholarship problems of science and international affairs, and is warmly welcomed and sought after by white university students, the intellectual cream of the white race."[15]

An NYU student leader, Daniel Ecker, described "many pleasant, inspiring and helpful reactions" to Harrison's talk, which induced the university students to do some original thinking. Ecker said Harrison's lectures seemed "to carry just that element the boys are looking for" and added that if it were possible to secure an adjunct professorship in the "Science of Things in General" he would do everything possible to help Harrison obtain it. Harrison was invited back. He at first declined but, after the students persisted, agreed to speak.[16] Harrison's April 8 noontime talk was entitled "Is the Politician Necessary?" and in it he put forth the position "the politician is a parasite in our government today."[17]

The downtown section of NYU heard that the students at the Heights campus "thoroughly enjoyed" Harrison's lecture, and Fred L. Kriete, the temporary chair of NYU's Washington Square YMCA, wrote on March 30 asking him to speak downtown. Harrison agreed, and his lecture, like all his NYU lectures, was free to outsiders. In announcing the talk the *NYU Daily News* stated that "Dr." Harrison was "now doing research work at Columbia University."[18] In his Washington Square "Y"–sponsored talk of April 13 on "Science and Race Prejudice" Harrison was quoted as saying that "human beings of to-day do not think with their minds, as is commonly supposed"; rather, "they think with their dominant prepossessions of age old prejudices and habits." He added that though science largely dominates present-day thought, that didn't mean that nature didn't count or that miracles couldn't happen. He advised his listeners to "note that these dominant prepossessions exist" and to "make allowances accordingly." As he moved to the subject of "race prejudice" he explained, "This race prejudice does not spring from any illogical thinking." The "white race is on top at present and its will goes. But it is rapidly sliding into a devolutionary pace."[19]

In the midst of his NYU lectures "Dr." Harrison also was scheduled to deliver several other outside lectures. On Sunday, March 21, at 8:15 p.m. at Lafayette Hall, he was to speak on "Negro Traitors I Have Known" in a presentation that would focus on two questions: "Who is a Traitor?" and "Can One Betray His Race as Well as His Country?" He planned to provide "Startling Revelations (with Facts, Dates, and Names) of Prominent Racial Renegades and False prophets who pose as 'leaders' while selling out the Race's Cause." Later in the month, on March 29, Harrison offered his "Is the White Race Doomed?" lecture before the "extremely critical thinkers" of the Sunrise Club, which provoked "spirited discussion."[20]

On Sunday afternoon, April 18, the Harlem Educational Forum, at 200 West 135th Street, reopened with "Dr." Harrison again lecturing on "Is the White Race Doomed?" The HEF, according to its printed material, had played an "important . . . role in awakening and stimulating the intellectual renaissance in Harlem, the Mecca of the New Negro" between 1918 and 1923. It was led by a committee headed by Grace B. Campbell, who was "ably supported by many of her former co-workers and by the progressive thinkers of the community," including Richard B. Moore (secretary), Walter T. Brandon, Hodge Kirnon, Dr. Louis Miller, Thomas J. Dillon, Mrs. Ruth Whaley, August V. Bernier, Miss H. A. Dumont, Arthur Wharton, Peter R. Codrington, Otto E. Huiswood, and "Dr." Hubert H. Harrison. "Every effort" was "being made to reestablish an institution" that would "disseminate light, truth and knowledge," and "the support of the public" was "warmly invited." The committee believed "in the necessity of full, free and vigorous discussion as the only means of discovering the truth," and its "guiding principles" were "Know the Truth and the Truth shall make you free" (New Testament), "All great Truths begin as blasphemies" (G. B. Shaw), and "If there is anything which cannot bear free discussion, let it crack" (Wendell Phillips). The motto of the HEF was "Lay on Macbeth, and damned be he who first cries, Hold, enough!" "Virile thinkers of both races" were invited to "the intellectual arena to do battle for ideas and ideals" under the HEF's slogan of "Admission free, thought free, speech free—eventually, mankind free."[21]

Harrison's April 18 talk was to be "a thorough and illuminating summary" of the "world [racial] problem," in which he planned to describe the exact status of the races while offering "a revealing analysis of the process by which the white race has achieved ascendance." He would also describe how that process had "set in motion the forces which now threaten and will inevitably destroy white supremacy." An announcement for the activity declared, "The imperialist rulers are their own grave diggers."[22]

The month following his HEF talk, Harrison was given a second testimonial dinner at Craig's Restaurant. The Saturday evening, May 22, event marked the end of his fourth year as a staff lecturer at the Board of Ed, and Percy F. Greene, his longtime friend and chair of the lecture course at the 135th Street Public Library, was in charge of arrangements. Short talks were given by Greene, Wendell Thomas (of the Board of Ed), Domingo, Moore, Campbell, Rogers, and others who "praised" "Dr." Harrison for his "breadth of learning," "intellectual honesty," and "splendid work . . . in the educational field."[23]

Ernestine Rose, branch librarian for the 135th Street Public Library, was ill and unable to attend, but Eliza Buckner Marquess, an assistant librarian, wrote to Cyril Wallace, chair of the Entertainment Committee of the ICUL, extending apologies for Ms. Rose, who would be replaced by Miss Sonya Krutchkoff, representing the staff (who all keenly appreciated Dr. Harrison's community work). Marquess added that Dr. Harrison had been "one of our most helpful friends and critics," and "the entire staff" joined in extending "best wishes . . . for the success of the dinner and for the continued work of Dr. Harrison in the community." She added that the library was "fortunate enough" to have had Dr. Harrison lecture "in its auditorium for several years and many members of the staff, as well as of our reading public, have profited by the lectures."[24]

During the first few months of 1926, Harrison started working with the American Negro Labor Congress. The ANLC had been formed in Chicago in October 1925 under the auspices of the Workers (Communist) Party. It was the party's major effort at organizing "Negro" workers and farmers, and, according to its constitution, it sought "to bring the Negro working people into the trade unions and the general labor movement with white people"; "to remove all bars and discrimination against Negroes and other races in the trade unions"; and "to aid the general liberation of the darker races and the working people throughout all countries." The ANLC sought "the abolition of all discrimination, persecution and exploitation of the Negro race and working people generally." The W(C)P maintained that such labor organizing was being ignored by the NAACP, which favored siding with the capitalists. Lovett Fort-Whiteman was ANLC general secretary-treasurer and national organizer, and H. V. Phillips was business manager. Fort-Whiteman also edited the ANLC's official organ, the *Negro Champion*, along with managing editor Irving Dunjee and contributing editors W. C. Francis and William Scarville, of Pittsburgh; A. Warreno, of Philadelphia; C. W. Fulp, of Primrose, Pennsylvania; Joseph A. Gordon, of Galveston, Texas; John H. Owens of Ripley, California; Richard B. Moore, of New York; J. Gotham Lunion, of West Africa; and Clements Kadalie, of South Africa.[25]

Around April 1 Fort-Whiteman wrote to Harrison that he was back in Chicago and had spoken with Lydia Gibson, the wife of the Workers Party of America national leader Robert Minor, the day before. She informed him that she had sent the sculptress Augusta Savage a contribution and some names of persons who would be friendly to her. Fort-Whiteman had Harrison's letter and appeals for Savage in hand and was planning to "send one to the lady in the University in Texas [Fort-Whiteman's mother]" and distribute the rest among persons who he felt would contribute. He also suggested that Harrison send Robert Minor a copy of "your book 'Africa Awakening' [*sic*], it is quite worthwhile." The following day Fort-Whiteman wrote to Harrison that he had just seen Robert Abbott, editor and publisher of the *Chicago Defender,* and had provided him a copy of Harrison's letter of appeals and showed him Miss Savage's work from a portfolio she had provided. Abbott seemed "quite pleased and instructed Dewy Jones to publish the appeal, perhaps in next issue of the *Defender.*" He described Jones as "a good friend" and said he had "asked him to write up a nice story" and give Ms. Savage's address.[26]

In his April 1 letter Fort-Whiteman also asked that Harrison inform him when he would "be free from Bd. of Ed. in order that we can line up a tour for you." He was "glad to know that the committee of the ANLC of New York" was "functioning" and that Harrison was "one of its officers." Under separate cover he planned to send Harrison the ANLC constitution and program in order that he might "familiarize" himself with it. Fort-Whiteman would also "look over 2 articles" Harrison sent regarding their publication and would send Harrison and William Pickens copies of Bukharin's *Historical Materialism.* He asked Harrison to keep him informed of affairs in New York and added a postscript: "Int. Conf of Colonial and Semi-Colonial Peoples in Brussels has taken on large proportions, will keep you informed." The conference would ultimately be held in 1927, and Richard B. Moore would attend as the ANLC representative.[27]

On April 2 the *New York Times* reported that Solomon Abramovitch Lozovsky, general secretary of the international communist movement's Red Trades Union International (RILU, or Profintern) in Moscow, had urged "members of that organization to insist on the inclusion of negro workers in all foreign trade unions, especially in the United States." Lozovsky took the position that "if American trade unions refuse to admit negroes we must not be afraid to create parallel negro trade unions to compete with them." This was a new position for international and U.S. communists, though it was a position that Harrison had long maintained. Such a change in communist tactics undoubtedly drew Harrison closer to the ANLC and the Workers Party.[28]

In June the ANLC's *Negro Champion* featured two articles on Harrison. One claimed that "a number of outstanding figures in present day American life" were joining the ANLC and that "Standing in the front rank" was "Dr. Hubert

Harrison of New York City, staff lecturer of the New York board of education, member of the mayor's committee on reception to distinguished guest[s], traveler and scholar of note." It added that "Harrison has been known for many years as a serious, fearless and energetic student of Negro life and its problems," and it was therefore "accepted as natural that he finally takes his place in the ranks of the A.N.L.C." in order to serve "in an organized struggle on the part of the Negro workers to win their economic emancipation; which in turn means his social and spiritual emancipation." The article called attention to the fact that Harrison had served as literary critic for the *New York World, New York Tribune, Freeman,* and *Nation*; was organizer of the ICUL; and was to "begin a speaking tour of the eastern locals of the A.N.L.C. in the near future." The *Negro Champion* also reprinted the *Amsterdam News* article "Negro Scholar Receives Remarkable Tribute at N.Y. University." That article reported that Harrison had been engaged at the Workers School in New York to give twelve lectures on the American race problem and to provide for the students a selected reading list that included seven books by Negro authors.[29]

The Workers School, at 106–108 East Fourteenth Street, described itself as "the first serious attempt of the Workers Party to set up a permanent educational institution in the New York district." It was originally organized as a private undertaking, and, according to the school's leader, Rebecca Grecht, it "became an instrument for Communist training and the spreading of Communist ideology when it was brought under the direct control and supervision first of the District Executive Committee and later of the National Executive Committee of the Workers Party." The school was "a Communist educational institution" following the spirit of the "Thesis on Agitation and Propaganda" of the Fifth Congress of the Communist International, which called upon all communist parties "to intensify their educational efforts so as to make their organizations real parties of Lenin, and extend Communist influence amongst the masses." The Workers School aimed "to spread the teachings of Marx and Lenin so as to develop a Bolshevist ideology" and "to train comrades to take active leadership both in the various units of the party and in the shops and trade unions." Students at its evening classes included party members and potential party activists.[30]

In the October "Announcement of Courses" for the 1926–1927 session, Workers School director Bertram D. Wolfe stated that its curriculum was "based on the assumption that Marx, Engels and Lenin in their works and deeds, have given the proletariat a science of understanding, organization and action which directs it along its march towards power and emancipation." The "Announcement," in its section on "Special Problems of the American Working Class," listed "Course No. 30" as "Problems of Race," which was to be given by Harrison on Friday evenings from 8:00 to 9:30 p.m. It was to provide "a comprehensive presentation of the relations between the white and colored races" and would "cover every outstanding and significant aspect of the Negro problem—internal and external, historic, economic, cultural, including the tabooed topic of sex and the bugaboo of 'Social equality.'" "The Negro question in relation to Imperialism, recent changes in Negro racial movements, [and] the effect of the changing South upon the Negro" would be discussed. Registration was from October 11 to 25, most courses were scheduled to begin the first week in November, and school enrollment reached about seven hundred.[31]

In addition to working with the Communists, Harrison also provided services to the Urban League during the summer of 1926. On May 8, James H. Hubert, the New York Urban League's executive secretary, wrote asking him to "Stop by and see me next week I want to talk with you about the proposition which you and I discussed." The referred to proposition likely concerned employment, for within six weeks the Urban League would announce that it had hired Harrison.[32]

Harrison's signing on with both the Workers' Party and the Urban League was undoubtedly related to the fact that his work with the Board of Ed was being terminated. On June 11, Ernest Crandall wrote to him canceling his lecture dates for the Board of Ed at the 135th Street Library. Crandall said the action was "necessary due to lack of funds," because the Board was "forced to close all centres which show an average attendance of less than 100," and because the 135th Street Library lectures, in particular, showed small attendance.[33]

The loss of the Board of Ed job affected Harrison and his family severely. J. A. Rogers wrote some years later that "in his last years" Harrison "suffered acutely from poverty. His clothes became shabby and his shoes heavily patched, quite in contrast to the appearance of many other Negro leaders, less sincere and less capable than he. All that he owned at the time of his [1927] death were his favorite books." Rogers added, "In the pursuit of an ideal surely no more can be demanded of one than to sacrifice literally everything, as Harrison did."[34]

A week after Crandall's letter the *Chicago Defender* reported that the Urban League had announced that for its special $50,000 fundraising campaign it had "secured Dr. Hubert H. Harrison, veteran staff lecturer of the New York board of education, as a promoter of publicity in Harlem." The *Defender* noted that "Dr." Harrison, despite the weather being abnormally cold, had "been speaking indoors and outdoors, in churches, forums and lyceums" and was "creating much favorable sentiment for the urban league on the part of the general public."[35]

The following month the July 1926 issue of the Urban League's *Opportunity* contained a Harrison review of *Lulu Belle*, the new Broadway success at the David Belasco Theatre. Harrison considered the play "sufficiently noteworthy" because it was "a slice of Negro life, given without malice and without sentimentality." But, he added, "its chief and abiding significance" was that Mr. Belasco had "done something for American drama which most of the critics—especially those 'on our side of the street'—have managed somehow to miss." Specifically, the play "presented for the first time, a new type of realism, devoid of the conventional stereotypes which have so long done duty as veritable pictures of 'Negro life' on the American stage." Previously "the American play-goer" had "esthetic perceptions restricted to the narrow choice between the comic stereotype of the black buffoon, the pathetic lay-figure of Uncle Tom or his more modern equivalent, and that man of straw, the 'problem' Negro who serves occasionally as an awful example of the social horrors of miscegenation." In virtually every case "it was the white impersonating the Negro and imitating black humanity abominably as a rule." There had been exceptions—including Ridgeley Torrence's three plays, *The Emperor Jones*, and *The Chip Woman's Fortune*—but they were rare.[36]

The Belasco production of *Lulu Belle*, however, broke new ground, according to Harrison. Even though its two chief characters were "white," "the dominant atmosphere of the play" was "furnished by the overwhelming mass of Negro actors on the stage, many of whom [were] . . . visibly whiter than the two chief characters themselves." The mixed theater company was "so inextricably blent that, except for the French viconte and his slumming party, one would take the entire cast to be colored." By "this double device" Belasco hamstrung in advance "any possible protest on the basis of race-prejudice," beguiled Broadway "into seeing double," and made it "easier for the next step—an all-Negro cast in a serious presentation of some other and more significant slice of Negro life." Harrison felt that "if this one achievement" was "clearly grasped by Negroes" they would realize "that they owe a vote of thanks to the veteran actor-manager-producer who for half a century has striven to make the stage a realistic mirror of life."[37]

Unfortunately, added Harrison, "on our side" the early responses came "from those who had not seen it and who were burdened, moreover, with the somewhat naive notion that the first duty of the stage is to present exclusively rich, noble, and educated types of black humanity." They held this belief, he commented, "despite the fact that in their own theatres, over which they wield the whip of patronage, they invariably prefer the debased types of racial representation." The matter, however, "was soon righted—after the critics had been brought face-to-face with 'Lulu Belle'"—and seats had to be purchased many weeks in advance as "the value and significance" of the play came home.[38]

Harrison explained that in *Lulu Belle* a devotee of "the higher life," who "graduated from the cabaret college of the University of Hard Knocks into a post-graduate paradise of her own in the Rue Marigny, Paris . . . meets and maims the soul of an erstwhile respectable young Negro" on her way up. He is "from the purer atmosphere of 'up-state,'" and she runs him "through the wringer of her sordid, savage, passions," after which he comes out "a limp slave, forgetful of friends and family and of elementary self-respect." He is then "cast off by the modern Messalina [an ancient Roman symbol of vanity and immorality] who has set her heart on a French nobleman who takes her from Harlem to the city on the Seine and establishes her in his palatial residence." In France she is followed by her former lover after he serves time in a New York prison for felonious assault and, "after a fruitless attempt on his part to have her return with him to America and live in a cottage, he finally throttles the life out of her with his bare hands."[39]

The scenes are in "San Juan Hill," Harlem, and Paris, and the show attempts "to reproduce as nearly as possible the actual appearance of the localities." The social background was "well worked with a number of actual types; the washer-woman at their windows, the casual stroller, the street dandy, the prize-fighter, the hanger-on, 'the big butter-and-egg man,' the respectable colored citizen and the cabaret 'jazz hound.'" Amid these characters Miss Lenore Ulric, in the title role, dominates the scene "from her first entrance on the stage to the moment of her spectacular 'finish.'" The "magic of her personality, as well as of her acting," put "a garish gleam over the sordid situations" and marked her "as a great actress, in spite of the limitations of the piece."[40]

Overall, there was "no great acting in 'Lulu Belle,'" but there was "great impersonating." Harrison explained: "Great acting is of the depths, and 'Lulu Belle' is a slice of the surface." The play did have "the hard glitter of the surface," but it lacked "the rich color of the depths." While the dialogue was "the most brilliant and nimble" that Harrison had "heard for some time"; "no attempt" was made "to catch, or even hint at, any valid emotional experience beneath the surface appearances." In the second and third acts the playwright shirked "the sub-surface values in the situation presented" and failed "to achieve poignancy and pathos." Then, in the last act, when the action was "chopped off at the very moment of the murder," the descending curtain denied the audience "any assessment of the tragedy in terms of reflective or explanatory consequences." The second act was the only place where the playwright made "the grade." Miss Ulric's "conception of the character" was "vivid, arresting and amazingly adequate," and the "details of stage-craft . . . well attended to—even the peculiar voice of the Harlem cabaret singer." It was also "gratifying to note that John Harrington as 'Butch Cooper,' the Negro prize-fighter, had changed from the 'darky' type of the rehearsals to a genuine colored person in the presented play—much to the improvement of his characterization and the enjoyment of his audience; while Henry Hull as 'George Randall' almost attained to the dignity of a pathetic figure."[41]

In sum, Harrison judged the play "impressive and satisfying as genuine drama," while its "sociologic complications" gave it "an added value and significance which put it in a class by itself." It had "a few dramatic errors" in detail, which would "be well to iron out," but, overall, "the ensemble effect of 'Lulu Belle'" was "one of vivid reality," and the result was "'something attempted, something done'" that redounded "to the credit of the American stage."[42]

Shortly after Harrison's favorable *Opportunity* review of *Lulu Belle*, with its laudatory comments on Belasco, he received an interesting letter from the Urban League's James Hubert. Harrison had apparently written a fundraising letter, possibly for Augusta Savage, and Mr. Hubert informed him of a response from David Belasco with a $25 contribution. This was to be forwarded to Mr. Wendell, the treasurer.[43]

On July 28, eleven days after Mr. Hubert informed him of Belasco's $25 contribution, Harrison's favorable review of Belasco's *Lulu Belle* appeared in the *Amsterdam News*. The paper stated that a few months earlier Harrison had written the review for the *Amsterdam News*, "but circumstances arose [probably his employment by the Urban League] which induced him to place his opinion on the David Belasco show in *Opportunity Magazine*." The *Amsterdam News* considered the article to be "so brilliantly written" that they "were very glad of his decision to let this promising publication of the Urban League use it, knowing that our readers would welcome it no matter how late." Much had been written about the play, which was a Broadway success at the Belasco Theatre, and the paper felt it "timely to reproduce the article and direct the attention of our readers to the fact that it is the most comprehensive thing yet written on the show by white or colored critics." In his brief introductory Harrison added, "To write about a book or play and to say something worth-while and significant long after the corps of critics have completed their labors is at once a difficult and thankless task." Nevertheless, since *Lulu Belle* was still drawing record crowds on Broadway, he thought "the attempt may prove interesting."[44]

The *Amsterdam News* also informed readers that Harrison's "remarkable grasp of . . . things affecting the race" gave it

> pardonable pride in pointing out that it is more than likely that he will from
> time to time contribute to these columns on subjects which will be food for
> thought for readers of the amusement pages and those in the theatrical world
> who have hypnotized themselves into believing they are great producers
> because of their ability to assemble a jazz band, a gathering of half-naked

(more than half, to be exact) young women and vulgar and suggestive jokes to hold the kind of audience which feeds the vulgar output of the times.

The addition of such "a learned mind" would "prove" that the paper was "leaving no stone unturned in giving to its large number of readers the very best to be secured along all lines to which an up-to-date publication of this kind must adhere in turning out a bigger, better and brighter newspaper." It was thus, "with a great deal of pleasure, a heroic pose and a dramatic flourish" that they presented Harrison's review.[45]

————————

In *Opportunity* Harrison followed his July review with an August one on the book *Digging for Lost African Gods*, by Byron Khun de Prorok. Harrison noted that archaeologists and explorers worldwide were "digging up a bewildering mass of 'new' materials, the conscious and unconscious records of the ways and works of other people who have preceded us upon this planet," and the "net result" of their findings was making it necessary "to revise our notions of the origins of mankind, civilization and society." As "new vistas" were opened, "many old familiar landmarks—like the Aryan migration" and "the priority and self-origination of classic Greek culture" had "faded away." Scholars like Albert Churchward were "pushing back the period of man's origin nearer to a million years," the "mighty Frederick Soddy asks if it hasn't all happened before," and the Doheny expedition of 1924 in Northern Arizona "revealed human art in America as contemporaneous with the dinosaur." "Dogmatism" was "out of date" and it was "all very bewildering" to those who took "easy refuge in fixed notions."[46]

In developing this new understanding "the French savants" played "a worthy part," and in North and West Africa "Maurice Delafosse, Stephen G[e]sell and Reygasse loom[ed] large in the fields of archaeology and cultural anthropology." Harrison suggested adding the name of "Count de Prorok," whose book was "intended as a 'popular' presentation of that work rather than a formal and scholarly discussion." Most of Prorok's excavating "was done amid the ruins of Carthage, that ancient metropolis founded by Tyrian merchant-mariners more than twenty-eight centuries ago," and "a large proportion" of current "cultural arrangements" were "available" and "familiar to the African people of Carthage," including "Seven-story houses, central heating systems, elevators, theatre programs, sports, cheer-leaders, marble, checkers, eye-glasses, bills of exchange, bankers and a banking system, and cross-word puzzles." Even "the great game of advertising seems to have been well developed there" by the makers of lamps, who wrote, "Please buy our lamps, the cheapest in Carthage—only one cent!"[47]

But, "just as [Heinrich] Schliemann at Mykenae [in ancient Greece] found more than one civilization embedded in the earth, so in North Africa, the Count tells us that 'the sifted earth of Carthage contains the relics of a dozen different civilizations, each definitely marked, and capable of identification.'" All North Africa was now "an archaeological park," and "in this great work of historical recovery America plays a large part and 'the wealthy people of the United States do take very much to heart the advancement of science in all its departments,' as the Count de Prorok says." They furnish most of the funds, and "a goodly number of the working staff of the expeditions—to say nothing of invaluable publicity which has kept three continents awake to the vast significance of the work and familiar with some of its outstanding results." Harrison felt the last chapters on "The Civilizations of the Sahara," "The Ancient Tombs of the Sahara," and "Prehistoric Man in Africa" would "prove especially stimulating to young Negro-Americans." In sum, he found the book "well illustrated with photographs and a map" and thought it would "serve a useful purpose as an introduction to the methods and results of African exploration and archaeology in the scientific phase."[48]

In the October 1926 *Opportunity* Harrison reviewed *The Negro in American Life*, by Willis J. King. The book was issued by the Methodist Book Concern, and he described its "tone and temper" as "a far cry from" the Reverend Charles Carrol's *The Negro a Beast*, published in 1904 by the St. Louis Bible House. During the last ten years "many of the more important religious bodies" had been "atoning for the previous apathy of organized Christianity in the matter of race-relations by publishing safe, dependable and informative books on the various aspects of race-contacts here and elsewhere." He cited Dr. Cornelius Howard Patton's *Lure of Africa*, Mrs. Lily (Hardy) Hammond's *In the Vanguard of a Race*, and Dr. George Edmund Haynes's *The Trend of the Races*, which were "designed to set the Negro at home and abroad in a better light and to soften the asperities of race-prejudice by cleansing douches of common-sense, dependable information and helpful discussion." King's book and Mrs. Sophia Lyon Fahs's *Race Relations* were "especially designed for study classes." King's book described itself as "an elective course for young people on Christian race relationships," but an "impartial, almost impersonal, tone" pervaded it, and "the Christian part" was separated "from the rest of the volume" and "restricted" to the "interesting and instructive" twelfth chapter.[49]

The chapters on "The Negro Among the Races of Mankind" and "The Theory of Racial Inferiority" provided "a serviceable summary of modern anthropologic knowledge for the too busy man-in-the-street." The chapter on "The Negro Prior to His Coming to America" opened with the challenging sentence that "if one would fully understand the American Negro one must know his African background." It was "not only white men like [T. Lothrop] Stoddard,

Simpson and Gregory" who were "ignorant of that background and its cultural implications, but even Negro writers like Dr. Du Bois and Woodson, whose *History of the Negro Church* collapses at the outset for lack of this underpinning." Even Mr. King, "while conversant with the more accessible white writers on Africa like Miss [Mary] Kingsley, Mungo Park, [Thomas] Naylor and Lady [Flora Luisa] Lugard," was "unfortunately unacquainted with the sometimes more authoritative works of African Negroes like [John Mensah] Sarbah, [J. E. Casely] Hayford, [Edward Wilmot] Blyden, [D. D. T.] Jabavu, [Solomon Tshekisho] Plaatje and [Ernest Samuel Beoku] Betts."[50]

In his last nine chapters King details "the story of the Negroes' participation in the building of this country, his handicaps and achievements in industry, politics, education and home-building," and he summarizes "the social and spiritual contributions which he has made and is making to the sum-total of American life." King "deftly" dodges controversy by "stating dispassionately both sides of most questions," and by so doing, he puts "the facts in the record without evoking dissent," an "ideal" method "for a volume designed as a text-book." King's "discussions of slavery, Reconstruction (1865–1878), race riots, intermarriage, social equality, the recent migrations and inter-racial cooperation penetrate to the roots of these matters; they are clear, concise and informative, and they really elucidate." Harrison thought the book "will commend itself to all those who need a brief, yet comprehensive summary of the origin, evolution and present status of the Negro problem in the United States."[51]

The October 13 *Amsterdam News*, which announced that Harrison had been engaged by the Workers School, also mentioned that he would give a series of lectures on international politics at NYU's University Heights campus. He was scheduled to speak on "China's Challenge to the Powers" and "The Significance of Germany's [September 8, 1926] Entrance Into the League of Nations." The newspaper emphasized that it was "the first time . . . a Negro has been secured to lecture at the university on a subject other than the 'Negro Problem.'"[52]

According to the *NYU Daily News* Harrison's October 13 noontime talk on "China's Challenge to the Powers" at NYU's South Hall, sponsored by the "Y," was the first of his four scheduled lectures on "High Lights of International Politics." Forty students attended the "enlightening, authentic and imposing" talk. Harrison reportedly stressed the sociological differences of progression and stability as evidenced by the Occident and the Orient and detailed how the West had imposed by force its "advances" on China, resulting in depredations and exploitations of that country. He explained that from the sixteenth century to the present Europe had interfered in China; that greedy interests of Great

Britain had nurtured a lucrative opium trade, which China fought against; and that the Opium War of 1839, which resulted in much pillaging and bloodshed in China, was precipitated by the avarice of the British opium traders who had been unable to force Hong Kong to import opium. Harrison traced the wholesale exploitation of China by the imperialist powers of the West and by Japan, detailing how they gradually assumed control of many important ports and established their unwelcome civilizations while often extending their interests into neighboring Chinese territories. The Boxer Uprising of 1900 was seen as the culmination of a series of petty revolts of the Chinese in opposition to brutal and inhuman treatment in sections of the country under foreign control. A particular example was how the British in Hong Kong had excluded Chinese citizens from their own parks and posted placards bearing the insulting words "Chinese and Dogs Not Allowed."[53]

Harrison also discussed contemporary conditions and how China's diplomatic policy was changing from arbitration to secret preparation along militaristic lines. He sounded an ominous note of warning, declaring that China could mobilize an army of forty million men, which, with proper training, would develop into the finest disciplined human weapon of destruction in history. China, having torn herself free from the injustice of former treaties, would abrogate them one by one, as was shown in its recent decision to ignore French and Belgian treaties. Harrison emphasized the lurking danger that would face Europe if the Western powers attempted to quell China's spirit of rebellion. The *Amsterdam News* said that given time limitations, "Dr." Harrison "was not able to deal intensively with his subject," but he "made a remarkable interpretation of the unchanging East, which was one of his salient points." He emphasized how China had slept peacefully "until she was awakened by the thunders of guns," and he enumerated the "broken promises" from the 1921 Arms Conference at Washington. After the lecture representatives from student councils at Columbia and the College of the City of New York invited him to address their student bodies.[54]

Every Thursday night at 8:15 p.m., from July 8 to September 9, 1926, "Dr." Harrison delivered a lecture in a special ten-week seminar course on the "World Problems of Race," for $3, at the Institute for Social Study's (ISS) office, in room 213 at 200 West 135th Street. The institute was established "to meet the need of this [Harlem] community for an independent agency of education devoted to a thorough study of the vital, social problems which affect the lives and welfare of the great masses of the people." It sought "to discover and to diffuse knowledge of the true nature of these challenging social situations, of the causes of social evil and oppression arising therefrom, and the means whereby complete

Figure 17.1. Hubert H. Harrison, teaching his class in "World Problems of Race," September 9, 1926. Hubert Harrison and his class at the Thursday night, September 9, 1926, final session of his course on "World Problems of Race," at 200 West 135th Street. In attendance are numerous outstanding Harlem activists including Richard B. Moore (far left, with book in hand) and W. A. Domingo (sitting front row center, with several items on his lap). Williana Jones Burroughs (?) is sitting in the front row behind Harrison and Hermie Huiswoud (?) is in the back row above Harrison. *Source:* Hubert H. Harrison Papers, Box 15, Folder 3, Rare Book and Manuscript Library, Columbia University Library. See https://dlc.library.columbia.edu/catalog/cul:47d7wm399p.

social emancipation may be achieved." The ISS's method was to conduct "study classes and lectures at a price within the reach of all, wherein the facts and findings of the social sciences" could be presented "in clear, simple terms" that could "be readily grasped by the masses and properly applied for the improvement of their condition."[55] The ISS's eleven-member executive council included Willis N. Huggins,[56] chairman; Mrs. Williana Burroughs, secretary; Dr. E. Elliot Rawlins, treasurer; Richard B. Moore, director; and Miss Louise Jackson, Miss Mabel Byrd, F. Eugene Corbie, Peter D. Codrington, N. E. White, Grace P. Campbell, and "Dr." Harrison.[57]

The epilogue ("Caliban Considers") on the brochure for Harrison's course said it would provide "an unusual opportunity to acquire a full and thorough knowledge of the fundamental facts about the great and challenging problem of race." It added that Harrison was "widely known for his breadth of knowledge and profundity of thought" and described him as "the outstanding pioneer of the intellectual renaissance which has made Harlem, 'the Mecca of the New Negro.'" He was, it claimed, "particularly appreciated for his remarkable skill in rendering difficult matters clear, vivid, and simple, and for his animated, forceful and stimulating mode of presentation." His years of study "devoted to mastering the social sciences: Biology, Politics, Sociology" were being made available "for the benefit of students of this course" to help "provide the equipment necessary for intelligent participation in the work of Inter-racial Conferences and Committees" and to "furnish the mental back-ground for that rare but needful quality wherein is hope for the future, namely, *intelligent and courageous race-statesmanship*." The brochure advertised "education for freedom" and included quotations including: "Knowledge ... the direct pathway from slavery to freedom" (Frederick Douglass); "There should be thrown open to the public in every large crowd of population the means of studying the great sciences of the day" (Wendell Phillips); "There can be no equality and no justice, not to speak of equity, so long as society is composed of members—a few of whom only possess the social heritage of truth and ideas—while the great mass are shut out from all the light that human achievement has shed upon the world" (Lester F. Ward); and "Give light and the people will find their own way" (Dante).[58]

The syllabus for the "World Problems of Race" course focused, in the first week, on the "Rise of the Modern Idea of Race," contrasted ancient and modern views, discussed race theories and definitions, including "Race as 'Breed' and as 'Quality,'" treated the influence of prejudice upon race theories, and considered the "measurement" of intelligence. The second week discussed "The Expansion and Dominance of Europeans," emphasized that Europe had been behind Asia five hundred years earlier and had received its awakening impulse from the darker races and described the causes and methods of Europe's ascendancy, including the racial aspects of European imperialism and the economic and political factors of European dominance. The third week, "The Black Man's Burden: Africa," treated African culture, ancient and modern; the invasion and partition of Africa, including the slave trade and slavery on African soil; typical areas and situations; and the awakening Africa. The fourth week, on "Race Problems in America," began with "materialistic roots and typical facts" and discussed the emergence of the "New Negro," international aspirations, and "The West Indies, Haiti, and Latin-America." The fifth session, on "India and the British Empire," explained how India, "The Heel of Achilles," was acquired and governed and how it felt about it. The sixth week covered "China and the Powers" and examined China's long peace, followed by intrusion and partition, its enforced awakening, recent revolt, and the future. The seventh week discussed "Japan: The Frankenstein of European Imperialism," analyzed its transformation, its method of "learning the lesson," and its "dual challenge to white supremacy." The eighth session, on "The Revolt of Islam," discussed Islam's splendid past, the "religion of racial-co-operation," the Mohammedan world, its militant

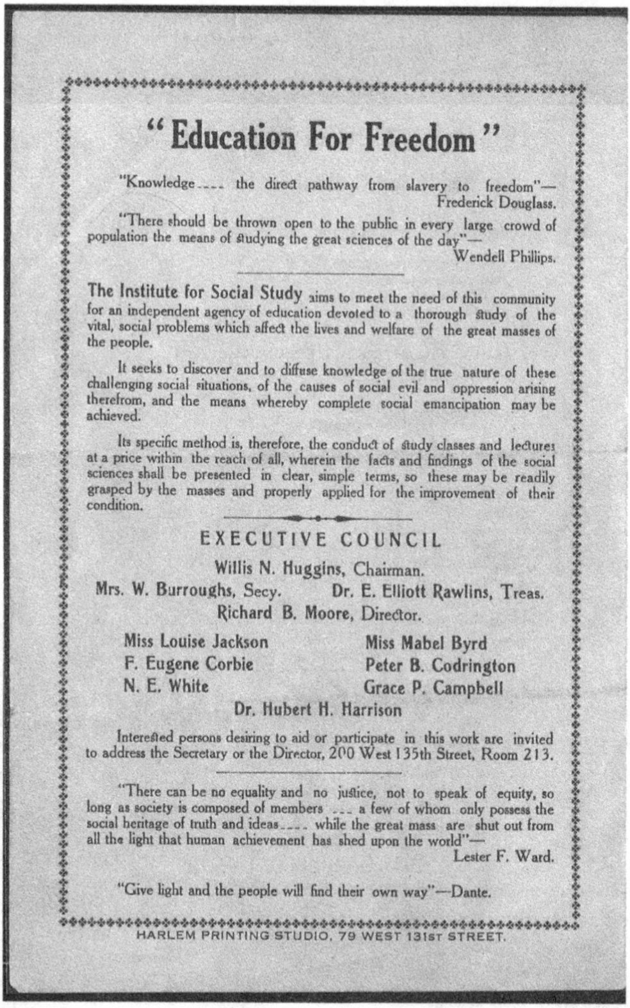

" Education For Freedom "

"Knowledge ____ the direct pathway from slavery to freedom"—
Frederick Douglass.

"There should be thrown open to the public in every large crowd of population the means of studying the great sciences of the day"—
Wendell Phillips.

The Institute for Social Study aims to meet the need of this community for an independent agency of education devoted to a thorough study of the vital, social problems which affect the lives and welfare of the great masses of the people.

It seeks to discover and to diffuse knowledge of the true nature of these challenging social situations, of the causes of social evil and oppression arising therefrom, and the means whereby complete social emancipation may be achieved.

Its specific method is, therefore, the conduct of study classes and lectures at a price within the reach of all, wherein the facts and findings of the social sciences shall be presented in clear, simple terms, so these may be readily grasped by the masses and properly applied for the improvement of their condition.

EXECUTIVE COUNCIL

Willis N. Huggins, Chairman.

Mrs. W. Burroughs, Secy.   Dr. E. Elliott Rawlins, Treas.

Richard B. Moore, Director.

Miss Louise Jackson   Miss Mabel Byrd
F. Eugene Corbie   Peter B. Codrington
N. E. White   Grace P. Campbell

Dr. Hubert H. Harrison

Interested persons desiring to aid or participate in this work are invited to address the Secretary or the Director, 200 West 135th Street, Room 213.

"There can be no equality and no justice, not to speak of equity, so long as society is composed of members ____ a few of whom only possess the social heritage of truth and ideas____ while the great mass are shut out from all the light that human achievement has shed upon the world"—
Lester F. Ward.

"Give light and the people will find their own way"—Dante.

HARLEM PRINTING STUDIO, 79 WEST 131st STREET.

Figure 17.2. "World Problems of Race: Syllabus, Dr. Hubert H. Harrison, Instructor," brochure, July 8–September 9, 1926, page 1. Between July 8 and September 9, 1926, Hubert Harrison offered an extraordinary "Special Seminar Course" on "World Problems of Race," hosted by the Institute for Social Study and held at 200 West 135th Street, Room 213, in Harlem. The ISS's eleven-member executive council included Willis N. Huggins, chairman; Mrs. Williana Burroughs, secretary; Dr. E. Elliot Rawlins, treasurer; Richard B. Moore, director; and Miss Louise Jackson, Miss Mabel Byrd, F. Eugene Corbie, Peter D. Codrington, N. E. White, Grace P. Campbell, and "Dr." Harrison. The list of important Harlem activists associated with the ISS, the subject matter of the course, and the wide range of topics discussed mark this as a seminal effort in the history of Harlem radicalism. *Source:* Hubert H. Harrison Papers, Box 16, Folder 46, and Box 13, Folders 5–6, Rare Book and Manuscript Library, Columbia University Library. See https://dlc.library.columbia.edu /catalog/cul:m905qftw32.

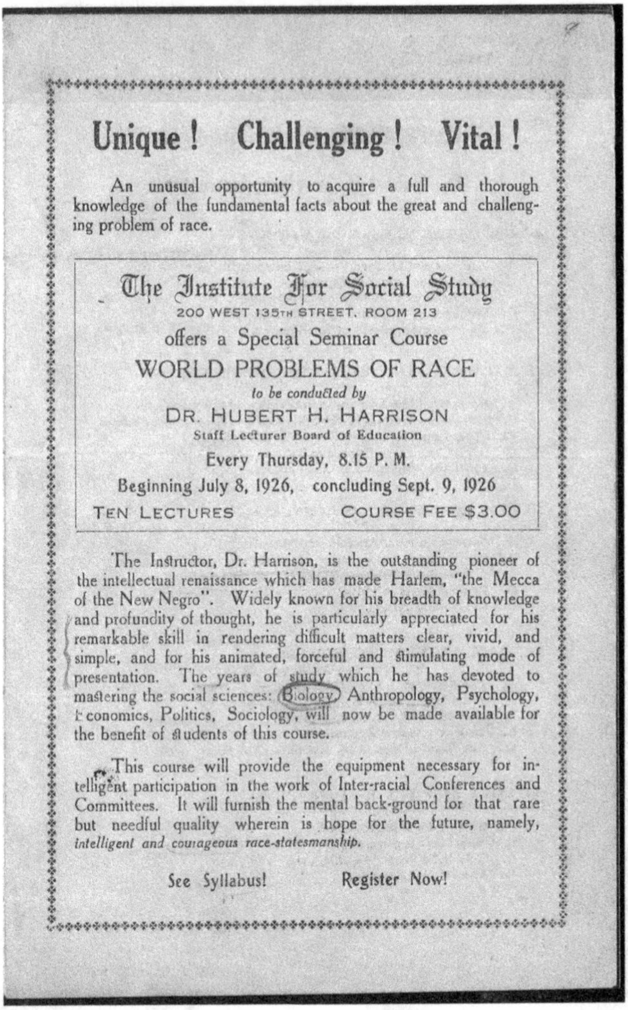

Unique! Challenging! Vital!

An unusual opportunity to acquire a full and thorough knowledge of the fundamental facts about the great and challenging problem of race.

The Institute For Social Study
200 WEST 135TH STREET, ROOM 213
offers a Special Seminar Course
WORLD PROBLEMS OF RACE
to be conducted by
DR. HUBERT H. HARRISON
Staff Lecturer Board of Education
Every Thursday, 8.15 P. M.
Beginning July 8, 1926, concluding Sept. 9, 1926
TEN LECTURES COURSE FEE $3.00

The Instructor, Dr. Harrison, is the outstanding pioneer of the intellectual renaissance which has made Harlem, "the Mecca of the New Negro". Widely known for his breadth of knowledge and profundity of thought, he is particularly appreciated for his remarkable skill in rendering difficult matters clear, vivid, and simple, and for his animated, forceful and stimulating mode of presentation. The years of study which he has devoted to mastering the social sciences: Biology, Anthropology, Psychology, Economics, Politics, Sociology, will now be made available for the benefit of students of this course.

This course will provide the equipment necessary for intelligent participation in the work of Inter-racial Conferences and Committees. It will furnish the mental back-ground for that rare but needful quality wherein is hope for the future, namely, *intelligent and courageous race-statesmanship.*

See Syllabus! Register Now!

Figure 17.3. "World Problems of Race: Syllabus, Dr. Hubert H. Harrison, Instructor," brochure, July 8–September 9, 1926, page 2. This second page of the 1926 Institute for Social Study's "World Problems of Race: Syllabus" describes Hubert Harrison as "the outstanding pioneer of the intellectual renaissance which has made Harlem, 'the Mecca of the New Negro'. Widely known for his breadth of knowledge and profundity of thought, he is particularly appreciated for his remarkable skill in rendering difficult matters clear, vivid, and simple, and for his animated, forceful and stimulating mode of presentation." *Source:* Hubert H. Harrison Papers, Box 16, Folder 46, and Box 13, Folders 5–6, Rare Book and Manuscript Library, Columbia University Library.

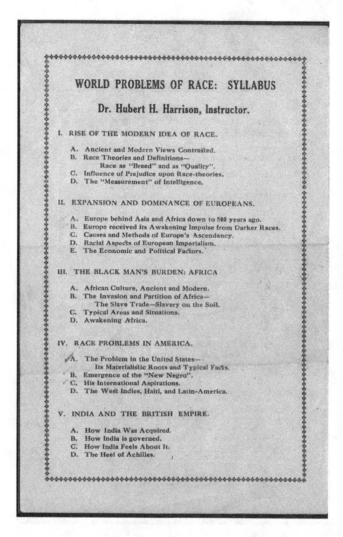

WORLD PROBLEMS OF RACE: SYLLABUS

Dr. Hubert H. Harrison, Instructor.

I. RISE OF THE MODERN IDEA OF RACE.

    A. Ancient and Modern Views Contrasted.
    B. Race Theories and Definitions—
        Race as "Breed" and as "Quality".
    C. Influence of Prejudice upon Race-theories.
    D. The "Measurement" of Intelligence.

II. EXPANSION AND DOMINANCE OF EUROPEANS.

    A. Europe behind Asia and Africa down to 500 years ago.
    B. Europe received its Awakening Impulse from Darker Races.
    C. Causes and Methods of Europe's Ascendancy.
    D. Racial Aspects of European Imperialism.
    E. The Economic and Political Factors.

III. THE BLACK MAN'S BURDEN: AFRICA

    A. African Culture, Ancient and Modern.
    B. The Invasion and Partition of Africa—
        The Slave Trade—Slavery on the Soil.
    C. Typical Areas and Situations.
    D. Awakening Africa.

IV. RACE PROBLEMS IN AMERICA.

    A. The Problem in the United States—
        Its Materialistic Roots and Typical Facts.
    B. Emergence of the "New Negro".
    C. His International Aspirations.
    D. The West Indies, Haiti, and Latin-America.

V. INDIA AND THE BRITISH EMPIRE.

    A. How India Was Acquired.
    B. How India is governed.
    C. How India Feels About It.
    D. The Heel of Achilles.

Figure 17.4. "World Problems of Race: Syllabus, Dr. Hubert H. Harrison, Instructor," brochure, July 8–September 9, 1926, page 3. This third page of the 1926 Institute for Social Study's "World Problems of Race: Syllabus" lists the first five topics in Hubert Harrison's course as "Rise of the Modern Idea of Race," "Expansion and Dominance of Europeans," The Black Man's Burden: Africa," "Race Problems in America" (including discussion of the "Emergence of the 'New Negro'"), and "India and the British Empire." *Source:* Hubert H. Harrison Papers; Box 16, Folder 46, and Box 13, Folders 5–6, Rare Book and Manuscript Library, Columbia University Library. See https://dlc.library.columbia.edu/catalog/cul:m905qftw32.

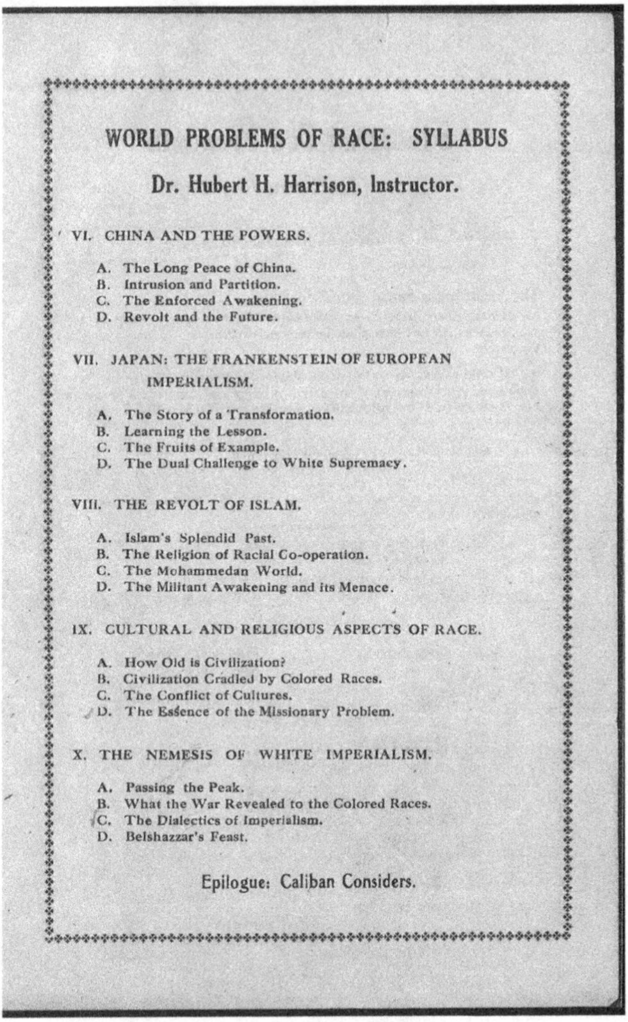

WORLD PROBLEMS OF RACE: SYLLABUS

Dr. Hubert H. Harrison, Instructor.

VI. CHINA AND THE POWERS.

    A. The Long Peace of China.
    B. Intrusion and Partition.
    C. The Enforced Awakening.
    D. Revolt and the Future.

VII. JAPAN: THE FRANKENSTEIN OF EUROPEAN
       IMPERIALISM.

    A. The Story of a Transformation.
    B. Learning the Lesson.
    C. The Fruits of Example.
    D. The Dual Challenge to White Supremacy.

VIII. THE REVOLT OF ISLAM.

    A. Islam's Splendid Past.
    B. The Religion of Racial Co-operation.
    C. The Mohammedan World.
    D. The Militant Awakening and its Menace.

IX. CULTURAL AND RELIGIOUS ASPECTS OF RACE.

    A. How Old is Civilization?
    B. Civilization Cradled by Colored Races.
    C. The Conflict of Cultures.
    D. The Essence of the Missionary Problem.

X. THE NEMESIS OF WHITE IMPERIALISM.

    A. Passing the Peak.
    B. What the War Revealed to the Colored Races.
    C. The Dialectics of Imperialism.
    D. Belshazzar's Feast.

Epilogue: Caliban Considers.

Figure 17.5. "World Problems of Race: Syllabus, Dr. Hubert H. Harrison, Instructor," brochure, July 8–September 9, 1926, page 4. This fourth page of the 1926 Institute for Social Study's "World Problems of Race: Syllabus" lists the last six topics in Hubert Harrison's course as "China and the Powers," "Japan: The Frankenstein of European Imperialism," "The Revolt of Islam," "Cultural and Religious Aspects of Race," "The Nemesis of White Imperialism," and an "Epilogue" entitled "Caliban Considers." *Source:* Hubert H. Harrison Papers, Box 16, Folder 46, and Box 13, Folders 5–6, Rare Book and Manuscript Library, Columbia University Library. See https://dlc.library .columbia.edu/catalog/cul:m905qftw32.

awakening, and its menace. The ninth week treated "Cultural and Religious Aspects of Race," addressed the question "how old is civilization?" and focused on how civilization was "cradled by colored races" and discussed the conflict of cultures. The tenth session was simply entitled "Epilogue: Caliban Considers."[59]

Around July 8 Harrison prepared a typescript on "World Problems of Race," which summarized his Thursday evening lectures at the Urban League Building. His discussion of "Race and Its Treatment in Science and History" focused on the "rise of the modern concept of race." He pointed out that

> the King James' version of the Bible (which is the only one known to most of us), does not contain the word "race" in our modern sense of a breed of people. It uses the word only in the sense of a speed contest. And that goes to show that as late as 1611 our modern idea of race had not yet arisen, or had not found expression in the English language.
>
> The corresponding classical notion was expressed in Latin as *stirps*, but that was strictly biologic in meaning and would be expressed today as "stock" or "breed". True, the Greeks did set themselves on one side with all the rest of the world on the other as "barbarians", but so did the Jews; and even the Negroid South Africans call themselves "Bantu" (i.e. the people), setting the Hottentots and Bushmen on the other side of the line of division. Only in the germ did such terms resemble our full-fledged modern implication of superiority and inferiority as inherent in certain subdivisions of the human species. For that is the very essence of the modern concept of race.[60]

Harrison thought "it might interest Negroes to know that the word "slave" was originally the race name of a white people, the "Slave or Slavonians who were once Europe's slaves in the gross" and that "the Latin word for slave was *servus*—'serfs', 'Servians' and 'Serbians' are simply corruptions and evasions which serve to show that the earliest forms of slavery in Europe had nothing at all to do with Negroes." This, Harrison thought, would "prove serviceable to those who have to meet the argument that Negroes have always been the world's slaves and white men the world's masters." Harrison explained that "the conception now prevailing that white people are superior and darker people inferior arose as the mental reflex of a social fact . . . —the military and political dominations exercised by European whites over the darker people who as late as the fourteenth century had been superior to them." This did not happen at once "but spread as Europeans gradually appropriated the mariner's compass and gunpowder, two things invented by the Chinese and transmitted by the dark-skinned Moslems of Africa and Asia." The countries that faced on the sea, Italy, Spain, Portugal, "first made victorious use of these inventions for discovery and domination," and in their languages "we find the earliest expressions in which, as in a matrix, the modern ideas of race first became fixed."[61]

That these ideas were "reflexes of successful domination can be seen in such facts as the following: European nations which, like Russia, Austria, Greece and Switzerland, have exercised no domination over dark peoples, are lacking in race-prejudice based on skin-color; while those who have exercised such dominion have it in plenty." Further, those countries "in which dominion was mitigated by social intercourse in their own lands, like the Spanish, Portuguese and Italians, eventually lost most of the traces of that race-prejudice which buttresses the prevailing conceptions of race." On the other hand, "those colonial Europeans who have lived in Africa, Asia and America as overlords to dark people have more race-prejudice than the stay-at-home classes of their own people, and Southerners in America who have, historically, dominated over Negroes are the ones in whom race-prejudice ripens most thoroughly."[62]

On the subject of "Science and Race-Prejudice" Harrison wrote that since scientists are human and their "minds are colored by their social surroundings," it was "natural, therefore, that what we call science (being the product of men's minds) should reflect the concepts and ideas which saturate the scientists." This was "especially . . . true of the sciences that deal with the subject of race: biology, psychology, sociology and anthropology—physical and social," in whose findings "the personal element plays a great part." That was "why the racial pronouncements of American and British anthropologists, sociologists, psychologists and biologists" were "worth so little, as science, where Negroes are concerned." In those cases "the man behind the 'science' is too frequently full of racial 'fixations,'" and "Sir Harry Johnston, Dr. Madison Grant, [Herbert] Spencer and [George R.] Gliddon, Nathaniel S. Shaler and Amos Bean are some convincing illustrations of this truth."[63]

The army intelligence test results had been used as "'scientific' proofs of white superiority and Negro inferiority; since the I.Q.'s of Negroes, it is said, were lower than those of whites." "But," noted Harrison, "since these tests showed also that black men of Massachusetts, Pennsylvania and Ohio had higher I.Q.'s than the white men of Alabama, Mississippi and Tennessee," it seemed that "'intelligence'" was "a product of good schools, libraries and reading matter rather than of 'race traits and tendencies.'" Harrison concluded, "the FACTS of social science do not support the doctrines of racial superiority and inferiority, as the man-in-the-street can see by reading Dr. [George A.] Dorsey's *Why We Behave Like Human Beings*," but it would "be necessary for Negroes to grow their own scientists before they can be sure of 'science.'"[64]

Harrison next discussed "Race and History," arguing that Negroes must similarly grow their own historians and noting that "in the greatest book of the age [*The Decline of the West*], Oswald Spengler, a learned German, points out that white historians make history revolve around the fixed point of the white race, and he knocks the props from under this comforting habit." Though "civilization" was "certainly more than twenty-five thousand years old," it was "only during the last tenth of that period" that "white nations played any noticeable part therein." Formerly, "when the past was yet unexplored, it was easy to begin history with the Greeks, the first whites to be civilized (by the Egyptians, as stated by Herodotus, Plato, Aristotle, Pythagoras and Diodorus [Siculus])," but it was now "necessary to pretend that the ancient Ethiopians (whose very name means 'black-faced') and Egyptians were 'white' as well as the black Fulani, since otherwise geometry, architecture, astronomy, medicine, iron-smelting and religion would have to be credited to people who would be forced in our country to ride in 'Jim Crow' cars." Harrison concluded, "Thus 'history' plays pander to race-prejudice, and many Negro college graduates accept the results with complacence."[65]

———

On June 18, 1926, V. F. Calverton wrote to Harrison. The *Modern Quarterly: A Journal of Radical Opinion* was an independent Marxist periodical, initially nonsectarian in its pages, edited by the entrepreneurial and wide-ranging Calverton. It described itself as "Socialist," though tied to no party, and emphasized that it sought to be entirely rational in pursuit of revolutionary culturism. It consciously distanced itself from the *New Republic* and *The Nation*, which it referred to as liberal, not radical.[66]

In his letter Calverton asked that Harrison forgive his delay in responding to his "extraordinary and cordial letter of a month or so ago." Calverton had read the article Harrison submitted several times and believed it "to be a work that should undoubtedly be printed." He was not sure that *Modern Quarterly* could use it, since they were pressed with material, though it might be usable in the fall. He asked Harrison if he knew any possible subscribers to the *Modern Quarterly* and commented on his "pleasant memories" of their "contact with the Sunrise Club." *Modern Quarterly* apparently decided to use Harrison's piece because its managing editor, Eileen Hood, wrote to him on August 26 and said they would "make special haste" to get him fifty copies of the current issue by September 9. She asked him to take the names and addresses of his students to whom he intended to give or sell the copies.[67]

The issue Hood referred to was the September–December 1926 *Modern Quarterly*, which included Harrison's "The Real Negro Problem." The article, which he had largely developed as far back as 1911 during his Socialist Party days, began:

The African slave-trade was born of the desire of certain Europeans to acquire wealth without working. It was to fill the need for a cheap labor supply in developing new territory that Negro slaves were first brought to the western world by the Spanish, Dutch, and English during the sixteenth and seventeenth centuries. Contact of white with black was thus established on the basis of the economic subjection of the one to the other. This subjection extended to every sphere of life, physical, mental and social. Out of this contact there arose certain definite relations and consequent problems of adjustment. It is the sum of these relations which we (rightly or wrongly) describe as the Negro Problem.

"Unfortunately," when people spoke of "the Negro Problem" they carried "a certain mental attitude derived from the original meaning of the word, Problem," which involved "the idea of solution . . . by thinking." Those who "think loosely" assumed the "solution" would be "by thinking," and society was accordingly "pestered with this, that, and the other 'solution' of the Negro Problem." Harrison emphasized, however, it was "well to bear in mind that a race problem is always the sum of the relations between two or more races in a state of friction." With this understanding these relations were "not to be explained on the basis of the thinking or feeling of either party." "They must be interpreted . . . in terms of human relations and in the order in which human relations are established: (1) economic, (2) social, (3) political and (4) civic." Accordingly, "a knowledge of the historical conditions under which these relations developed" was "of the greatest value in understanding the problem."[68]

Harrison then moved to consider "the conditions under which the relations between the black and white races were established in America." He described how in the period of colonization "the land of America was granted by European kings to certain gentlemen who had no intention of working with the hands," which "was the only method of extracting the wealth which was the object of their ownership." "It was necessary," he argued, "to obtain a supply of those persons who could do this work for them; and to insure this, it was imperative that these persons should not own land themselves: they must be a permanently landless class; since it was unthinkable, then as now, that one should work the land of others for a part of the fruits if he could work his own land for all the fruits." This began "the process of establishing such a class" in America. Then:

After the adventurous servants of the King of Spain had starved and flogged and murdered all the natives of Santo Domingo and the adjacent islands, they felt the necessity of a fresh supply of people who could be made to work and produce wealth for them. Out of this was born the African slave trade, with which the Spanish supplied their need for cheap labor power in the colonies in the West Indies and South America. Brazil, in the seventeenth century, was the great slave mart of the New World and the Dutch of New Netherlands bought their slaves direct from Brazil or "captured" them from the Spanish slave ships. In fact, the first cargo of Negro slaves brought to Jamestown in 1619 had been so "captured." Not that they were the first slaves of North America. Under Spanish rule, the Indians of Florida and California had been enslaved, and under English rule white men, women and children from Ireland had been sold into American slavery as a result of [Oliver] Cromwell's Irish campaigns. And many of the English working class condemned to penal servitude shared the same fate.

In fact both slavery and the selling of their offsprings have been standing features of the Anglo-Saxon's social system until a few hundred years ago.[69]

Harrison then quoted *The Evolution of States*, by J. M. Robertson, who wrote that in the fourteenth century "of what trade the 'free' Anglo-Saxons did conduct the most important branch seems to have been the slave-trade," and in the words of a student of his, Frederick Seebohm, English economic history "begins with the serfdom of the masses of the rural population under Saxon rule—a serfdom from which it has taken a thousand years of English economic evolution to set them free." Harrison continues citing Robertson's sources, including the popular historian Sharon Turner, who wrote that "there can be no doubt that nearly three-fourths of the Anglo-Saxon population were in a state of slavery." To substantiate this Robertson and Harrison cite J. M. Kemble, J. F. Morgan, Rev. Geoffrey Hill, Prof. Ashley, F. W. Maitland, Bishop Stubbs, J. R. Green, and Paul G. Vinogradoff "to the same effect." Harrison also quotes Green: "At the time of Henry II's accession Ireland was full of Englishmen who had been kidnapped and sold into slavery. . . . A hundred years later than Dunstan the wealth of English nobles was sometimes said to spring *from breeding slaves for the market*" (italics Harrison's). The "'market' was for concubines and prostitutes as well as for laborers," and Edward Gibbon, according to Harrison, "justifiably infers (chap. 38) that the children of the Roman slave market of the days of Gregory the Great's *non Angli sed Angeli* [not Angles but Angels] were sold into slavery by their parents." "From the first to the last age," he maintains, "the Anglo-Saxons persisted in this unnatural practice." Thus, conclude both Robertson and Harrison, "under Saxon, Danish and Norman laws alike, a slave trade persisted for centuries."[70]

It was, said Harrison, "natural, therefore, that under Anglo-Saxon civilization the first attempt to solve the problem of cheap labor-supply should have resulted in the slavery of weaker peoples." In the territory that became the United States, "the first attempt was made to enslave the Indians. But hard work was death to them, and it became necessary to import white people from Europe for that purpose. All through the colonial period this importation continued with its consequent effects on the social and political life of the colonies." In fact, "the first Fugitive Slave Law," the "Massachusetts Act of 1630 'Respecting Masters, Servants and Laborers,'" was "framed, not in the South, but in the North, and was made not for black but for white laborers." Harrison thought that a "reading of this one act would destroy all those pretty illusions about 'our fathers and Freedom' which we get from the school histories." He explained:

> Side by side with the economic subjection of white men there grew up the economic subjection of black men, and for the same reason. These were of alien blood—and cheaper. The African slave trade outgrew the European slave trade, although the latter continued, in a lessening degree, down to the third or fourth decade of the nineteenth century. Negroes were brought here to work, to be exploited: and they were allowed no illusions as to the reason for their being here. Those white men who owned the land brought them here to extract the wealth which was in the land. The white aristocrat did not buy black slaves because he had a special hatred or contempt for anything black, nor because he believed that Negroes were inferior to white people. On the contrary he bought them precisely because, as working cattle, they were superior to whites and Indians alike.
>
> Being of alien blood, these black people were outside of the social and political system to which they were introduced and, quite naturally, beyond the range of such sympathies as helped to soften the hard brutalities of the system. They were, from the beginning, more ruthlessly exploited than the white workers. Thus they had their place made for them—at the bottom.

Harrison stated it was "a sociological law that whenever a certain social arrangement is beneficial to any class in a society, the class soon develops the psychology of its own advantage and creates unconsciously the ethics which will justify that social arrangement." Thus, "Men to whom the vicarious labor of slaves meant culture and refinement, wealth, leisure and education, naturally came—without any self-deception, to see that slavery was right." He cited the professor Achille Loria to the effect that "there is an economic basis to moral transformations in any society which is built on vicarious production."[71]

Harrison turned "to the resulting conditions of the slaves" who "were at the bottom, the most brutally exploited and, therefore, the most despised section of the laboring class." He maintained it was a consequence of the previously stated law

> that those who are exploited must needs be despised by those who exploit them. This mental attitude of the superior class (which makes the laws of that

society in which it is dominant) will naturally find its expression in those actions by which they establish their relations to the inferior class. And when ever anyone is kicked it is usually the man farthest down who gets it, because he is most contiguous to the foot.

Thus, "the Negro having been given a place at the bottom in the economic life of the nation, came to occupy naturally the place at the bottom in the nation's thinking."[72]

Harrison said "the nation advisedly" because "the dominant ideas of any society which is already divided into classes are as a rule the ideas preservative of the existing arrangements." But, since those arrangements included "a class on top, the dominant ideas will generally coincide with the interests of that class." The "ethics of its own advantage" are "diffused by that class throughout that society" and "will be, if [the] need arise[s], imposed upon the other classes, since every ruling class has always controlled the public instruments for the diffusion of ideas." It was "in this way" that "the slave-holding section of the dominant class in America first diffused its own necessary contempt for the Negro among the other sections of the ruling class, and the ideas of this class as a whole became through the agency of press, pulpit and platform, the ideas of 'the American People' on the Negro."[73]

It was "curious and interesting to note how the Southern attitude toward the Negro changed with the changing industrial system." When "wasteful agricultural methods of chattel slavery had exhausted the soil of the South and no new land loomed up on the horizon of the system, slavery began to decay." Planters of that section "settled down into the patriarchal type of family relations with the slaves, who were then simply a means of keeping the master's hands free from the contamination of work and not a means of ever-increasing profits. Slavery was then in a fair way to die of its own weight." But the invention of Whitney's cotton gin "enabled one man to do the work of three hundred," and "cotton came to the front as the chief agricultural staple in America" while "the black slave became a source of increasing revenue as a fertilizer of capital." "The idyllic relations of the preceding forty years came to a sudden end," "increased profits demanded increased exploitation and the ethics of advantage dictated the despising of the Negro."[74]

Harrison then explained how:

To the credit of our common human nature, it was found necessary to reconcile the public mind to the system of slavery. This was effected by building up the belief that the slaves were not really human; that they belonged to a different order of beings. Of course, this belief could not be rigidly adhered to, inasmuch as the slave would often reveal qualities almost human, such as fidelity, courage, intelligence and the power to procreate. This latter quality was very serviceable to the slave-owner. He could gratify his carnal desires with the slave woman while he sold for cash the children which were his and hers. And whenever the system was most profitable, the belief that the slave was not human was strongest. This belief dies hard, and, before it finally vanished, assumed many curious forms. In the early part of the nineteenth century defenders of American slavery argued that the Negro was a beast. Later they conceded that he was a man of an inferior sort, consigned to slavery by God as the only human condition that was good for him. Then, when the freed blacks began to produce men of mark and to lift themselves far above the slave level, it was argued that certain craniological peculiarities would prevent them from assimilating the learning and culture of Europe. Finally, when they gave such evidences of that assimilation as even their enemies could not deny, it was suddenly discovered that this is a white man's country.

One broad, general implication of this belief seems to be the denial of social, political and economic justice to all people not white. Since this is a white man's country, all other occupants of it must be pariahs subsisting on sufferance, and the future of civilization imperatively demands that their status as "inferiors" shall be fixed and determined for them by the "superior" caste.[75]

Meanwhile, as "the system of industrial production known as the machine system developed in the north" the "factory proletariat . . . could fertilize capital more rapidly and cheaply than the slaves," and this "form of production (and its products) came into competition with the slave system." The "tremendous conflict reflected itself upon the political field as a struggle for the restriction of slavery within its original bounds," as manifested in "the Louisiana Purchase, the annexation of Texas, the Missouri Compromise, the Dred Scott Decision, [and] the Kansas-Nebraska Bill"—all of which were "political episodes in the competition between the two main sections of the dominant class." In that conflict "each used the army, the navy, the executive, the courts and the legislature to strengthen its own position."[76]

Then, "when the business interests of the north had definitely captured the powers of government in the general election of 1860, the southerners seceded because they knew too well the technique of governmental power." They sought "a government which would be a [HH handwrites "the exclusive" in his typed manuscript draft] political reflex of their own economic dominance." To Harrison it was clear "now why the Northern statesmen like Lincoln insisted that preservation of the Union was the paramount issue in the struggle and not freedom of the slaves." Lincoln even "punished those officers of the army who in the early days of the war dared to act upon the contrary assumption." None of the arguments "of [Horace] Greeley, Conway and Governor Andrews could make any change in his attitude." It was not "until he saw that it was expedient 'as a war measure'" that Lincoln issued "the *Emancipation Proclamation* which brought 180,000 Negro soldiers into the Northern army and left half of the slaves in their chains."[77]

While "emancipation gave to the Negroes a new economic status—the status of free wage-laborers, competing with other wage-laborers for work," it meant that those "who had worked to create wealth for others were now turned loose without wealth or land to shift for themselves in a world already hostile to them." Yet "the mental attitude of the white south had been shaped by three centuries of slavery and was hard to get rid of." Since "it was difficult for them to think of black labor under any form but that of slavery . . . they naturally turned to compulsion as the proper mode of obtaining work for their former slaves." "This attitude was well expressed in the Black Codes of the Southern states during the fall and winter of 1865–66."[78]

When "the end of the hostilities gave them a free hand at home they began to give legislative expression to the new conditions" and "framed new constitutions and laws." "But," since "the Negro had no privilege of voting," there was "no guarantee that justice should be done him was exacted." The "new constitutions were formed, the legislatures met, laws were made, senators and representatives to Congress were chosen; but the Negro was not only not admitted to any participation in the government." These "new legislatures shocked the Northern sense of justice by the cruel and revengeful laws which they enacted"—by the "barbarity of the most odious slave-code." Then, "before the resentment of the national legislature had taken form, the Ku Klux Klan, the Knights of the White Camelias, the Society of the Pale Faces, and other bands of organized representatives of culture" began "to do their bloody work of terrorizing Negroes into economic and social subjection"—"all this before any steps had been taken to extend the suffrage to Negroes."[79]

As "the northerners investigated these conditions they met with such fierce and unreasoning hostility on the part of the South that they found it necessary to arm the Negro with the ballot in his own defense." Yet "professional southerners like Tom Dixon, Tom Watson, Ben Tillman, [James] Vardaman and [Coleman Livingston] Blease pretend to their ignorant or forgetful countrymen that the present attitude of the South was caused in the first instance by a reaction against 'Negro domination,' social and political, which the North had forced upon it." In fact, "subsequent developments" could not be explained "by those amiable enthusiasts who see in the 'freedom' of Negroes an act of genuine humanitarianism on the part of the North." In addition, "after the Northern business-men had secured the government—and their thousands of miles of railroad-grants—they promptly dropped the mask of humanitarian hypocrisy, and left the Negroes to shift for themselves." Harrison explained:

> During the disputed count of the [Rutherford B.] Hayes–[Samuel J.] Tilden electoral contest in 1877 a deal was arranged by which the Northerners agreed to withdraw the army which protected the Negroes' newly-granted franchise in the South, on condition that the Southerners concede the [presidential] election to Hayes. The new industrial order wanted above all things to retain control of the government which it had captured during the war, and upon the altar of this necessity it sacrificed the Negro in the south, just as Lincoln had done in the early days of the war. From that time the suppression of the Negro vote, the growth of "Jim Crow" legislation, lynching and segregation have continued with the continuing consent of Republican congressmen presidents and supreme courts. And through it all, certain Negro "leaders" [HH crosses out "like Booker T. Washington" and inserts "of the subservient type" in his typescript of the article] have found it very much worth their while to administer anodynes both to the Negro and the Nation, to reconcile the one to a bastard democracy and the other to a mutilated manhood.[80]

Harrison thought it important to trace "the nature of the economic changes which have given certain new and malignant features to the relations between black and white in America." The "effect upon the free laborers of the sudden influx of black competitors in the labor-market; the consequent attitude of the labor-unions; the political and social reflex of all this, with the vestiges of the old, re-developing under the new conditions"—all these were "parts of the problem."

Thus, Harrison argued, "In its broad, general aspects, the Negro problem is a problem of social adjustment. How can the white American and the black American adjust themselves satisfactorily to the presence of each other?" When the question was stated in this form, it was "clear that both sides must be heard from." "But, so far, it has been assumed that the proper adjustment must be wholly in the hands of one party to that adjustment," and this was "not equitable." The "resultant friction has sprung from this one-sided view of the matter, so that in the white man's mind, the Negro Problem presents itself in this form: 'How should I fix the status of the black man to my own satisfaction?'" Harrison then quoted the Rev. Quincy Ewing, himself a Southerner, writing on *The Heart of the Race Problem*, who expressed the crux of the matter in these words:

The foundation of it, true or false, is the white man's conviction that the Negro, as a race and as an individual, is his inferior; not human in the sense that he is human: not entitled to the exercise of human rights in the sense that he is entitled to the exercise of them. The problem itself, the essence of it, the heart of it, is the white man's determination to make good this conviction, coupled with constant anxiety lest by some means he should fail to make it good. The race problem, in other words, is not that the Negro is what he is in relation to the white man—the white man's inferior—but this, rather: How to keep him what he is in relation to the white man; how to prevent his never achieving or becoming that which would justify the belief on his part, or on the part of other people, that he and the white man stand on common human ground.[81]

While he was writing on and delivering lectures on "World Problems of Race" for the Institute for Social Study, Harrison continued to work with other organizations as well.

18

Lafayette Theatre Strike, *Nigger Heaven*, and Garvey Divorce (June–December 1926)

In the latter part of 1926 Harrison continued his involvement with the International Colored Unity League (ICUL), the Institute for Social Study (ISS), the American Negro Labor Congress (ANLC), and the National Urban League (NUL). He also continued to seek speaking engagements, to write reviews, and to agitate on Harlem street corners. He wrote critical pieces related to Carl Van Vechten's new novel *Nigger Heaven* and seemed, for a while, to draw close to the communist Workers Party. In September, however, workers at the Lafayette Theatre went on strike; one result of that conflict was that Harrison distanced himself from the communists. His stated reasons for this concerned white supremacy and Harrison's determination not to sacrifice "Negro" people's interests. Toward the end of the year he was also drawn into the divorce trial between Marcus and Amy Ashwood Garvey.

On July 28 he delivered a talk on the "New Americanism" before 150 business and professional men of the Bronx Rotary Club in an activity chaired by Professor Alexander Haring, of NYU. According to the *Amsterdam News* "Dr." Harrison's "remarkable appeal for better race relations" was "loudly cheered," and he "was greeted with thunderous applause when he insisted that 'the Negro is the touchstone of all our democratic pretensions in America, of the sincerity of our religious professions and the quality of our humanity.'" The powerful touchstone metaphor was one Harrison had used as early as 1911, while he was with the Socialist Party.[1]

In addressing his theme Harrison discussed "the great experiment in democracy" that was "going on" in "our America" and was "unique in the history of the world." In America there were "heirs of all the ages," assembled "through three centuries from the ends of all the earth," and Harrison predicted that "the great American experiment" would "determine . . . whether we can make out of the welter of races and nations one people, one culture, one democracy." While this would be a "hard task," he believed it could be done, based "on the known facts of the present and the past." The simple fact that "the Negro was successfully struggling toward the light" called "for commendation" by "all white Americans," since "the general advance of the nation" was "made up of the continued progress of each and every part."[2]

Harrison then offered that "the fathers have eaten sour grapes and the children's teeth are set on edge" but indicated this was merely "the old Hebrew statement [in Jeremiah 31:29 and Ezekiel 18:2] of the doctrine of social consequences." Its truth was "tested in the history of our common country," when "the founders of our democracy denied the implications of their own doctrine when they compromised with slavery and cast out of the Declaration of Independence the clause in which Thomas Jefferson condemned that institution." They "paltered with evil," and "their children paid for it with five million warring soldiers, a million casualties, hundreds of millions of dollars and a hatred between the sections which is but imperfectly disguised today." The question of the day for both races was "whether we will get together now or bequeath to our great grand-children the legacy of embittered race relations." The "common sense of America," Harrison argued, could "have but a single answer."[3]

The same day as his Rotary Club talk, Wilbur K. Thomas, executive secretary of the American Friends Service Committee (AFSC), wrote to him that he had spoken with William Pickens recently and it was suggested that "the time had come when there should be a very distinct peace movement among the colored people." As far as Thomas knew, there was "no out and out peace organization sponsored by Negroes," although there were "a few" individuals who were "members of some of the peace societies." Thomas did not believe "fighting and killing" to be "an indigenous part of Negro character"—rather, he thought "the true Negro" held "a non-combative pacifist view." He therefore asked "whether or not the time has come when some sort of an out and out peace movement can be inaugurated among the Negroes."[4]

Thomas acknowledged that in recent years there had been "a decided effort on the part of many leading Negroes to win favor by appealing to the war records of Negroes" and that efforts "to establish a peace movement among the Negroes" might "hinder the recognition of patriotic service of the Negro race." Though he sympathized with and understood that point of view, he nevertheless felt very strongly that "the Negro" would do "much more for the benefit of the rest of the world by standing for the highest and best things in the very beginning." This included showing that "Military service" was "not necessarily the highest type of patriotism." Thomas asked Harrison: "Aren't there those among you, who in spite of all difficulties . . . [are] willing to sponsor an out and out peace organization that, eventually if not now, can be in cooperation with similar organizations of white people, but solely controlled by Negro people?" At Pickens's suggestion Thomas sent similar letters to a few other interested people. Thomas recommended "there should be no publicity given to the matter at the present time."[5]

Harrison did not respond to Thomas's letter, and on October 7 Thomas wrote again, noting the lack of response, and pointing out that "[Chandler] Owen, [Leslie Pinckney?] Hill, [Lovett] Fort-Whit[e]man, and [Frank] Crosswaith are interested." Thomas followed up on November 2 and indicated that although Harrison had still not responded to the subject of a Peace Movement, he was planning a conference on November 30 and wanted Harrison's ideas. The aim of the conference was "not to segregate but to develop close collaboration between Negro and white."[6]

Harrison eventually did attend a "Conference to Discuss Peace Along Interracial Lines," which was held at the AFSC headquarters in Philadelphia, on November 30 and December 1, 1926, and he submitted a detailed outline for future work. On December 20 Thomas sent Harrison the seven-page "Findings" of the conference, thanked him for his participation, and indicated that he would convene a new committee. Eight days later Thomas wrote that the Peace Section had considered Harrison's idea about the *Voice*, liked it, but couldn't fund it. He would bring the plan before the Interracial Committee.[7]

In August 1926 Harrison had a personal experience that merited mention in his diary "with Mrs. Elsie St. John with whom I study French." This may have been the same Elsie that appeared in Harrison's correspondence in 1922. On August 21 she "collapsed on the floor, became hysterical, wept and laughed by turns and had to be put to bed." Her friend, Mrs. Ethel Thomas, was called on the phone and came over, but "the little soiree" planned for the evening "had to be cancelled." Mrs. Thomas sent Harrison "down to Miss Grace Campbell to keep her and her cousin, Mrs. Hamilton, from coming up" while she "phoned the other expected guests and headed them off." Harrison "donned an apron improvised from a towel and was washing dishes" when Mrs. Thomas came in. He also dusted chairs he brought up from the floor below, dusted furniture, and was helping prepare for the guests when he "first learned that Mrs. St. John was sick." Harrison and Mrs. Thomas stayed until one in the morning playing cards and helping their friend "through the worst of her troubles." "R Ptdvmbuvt tvn semel atque iterum [I kissed again and again]."[8]

During the summer William Pickens wrote a June 10, 1926, letter to Harrison via the 135th Street Library, asking for the names and addresses (including

Harrison's) of prospective reviewers for his new book of "220 after dinner stories," *American Aesop—Humor of the Negro, the Irishman, the Jew, and Others.* On August 16 Pickens wrote, "I wanted to show you a little 'squib' I wrote on that 'evolution talk,'—but you will see it in the papers, & in the Associated Negro Press."[9]

Pickens's article, "Evolution Is Discussed on Harlem Streets," appeared in the *New York News* of August 28 and is probably the foremost piece comparing Harrison to Socrates. Pickens wrote "the Age of Pericles and Socrates in Ancient Athens had nothing on the present age of Harlem in New York." He described "coming out of the 'movies' between 137th street and 138th street on Seventh avenue" and seeing "one of the biggest street corner audiences that we have ever met in this block, which is famous for street-corner lectures." The "subject was 'Evolution,'" and the "run of the street" audience was "fixed on a blackman who stood on a ladder-platform, with his back to the avenue and the passing busses and his face to the audience which blocked the spacious sidewalk." He spoke on "the theory of evolution, and its illustration in different lines of material and biological development,—the Darwinian science of the evolution of life, and the Marxian philosophy of the evolution of capitalism,—and a possible development from capitalism to a state of communism." Pickens had previously heard "many poor lectures indoors, including those of my own," and he "seldom tarr[ied] at a street-corner talk." But, catching wind of the subject, he "wanted to see what a random Harlem audience would do at such a lecture,—with autos, two story buses and clanging fire engines passing." Pickens, who had won prizes for his oratory at Yale, in a powerful testimony to Harrison's oratorical skills, described what he saw:

> Not in my life have I seen a more attentive audience at a lecture on a subject of this magnitude. How much were they "getting?" Their faces were certainly fixed on the speaker, who was Hubert H. Harrison. In half an hour none of those who were near enough to hear well, left, and none seemed to lose attention. And it was not funny—they were not laughing. The only time when there seemed to be smiles and bits of merriment was when the speaker fell to discussing certain theological dogmas and some hard-boiled religious creeds in the light of evolutionary science. I noticed that when he bore down on the fixed, immovable and unprogressive science of the pulpit, the people laughed.
>
> And some one was selling books among this street audience,—[Charles Darwin's] *The Descent of Man* and other such texts![10]

Pickens asked why would people "supposed to be uninclined to attend indoor sermons and lectures" listen "to a street talk on what is [proverbially] supposed to be a 'dry subject'?" He then offered insightful comments on the power and importance of soapbox orators (of which Harrison was a pioneer and extraordinary example):

> The street talk was virile and unconventional. Most of the indoor kind are platitudinous, artificial and lack courage. A fellow who is burdened with the weight of a church, a school, a lyceum or some other institution, is afraid to say some of the things which Harrison said boldly on this street-corner. The indoor talks are generally limited, muzzled, tongue-tied. This street talk was unchained, free, even daring.
>
> Perhaps, like Socrates, we must pursue truth on the street-corners and in the highways, and seek the Beautiful and the Good in the mob among the outcasts.[11]

Soon after this laudatory piece by Pickens, Harrison's first review of Carl Van Vechten's *Nigger Heaven* appeared in the September 1 *Amsterdam News* under the title "Homo Africanus Harlemi." Harrison considered Van Vechten's book a "breach of the peace" by an author "well and favorably known to Harlem's new and nocturnal aristocracy of 'brains' and booze," and he found it "strange" that "one of the professional experts on the Negro" would select a title that gave "such offence to all self-respecting Negroes." Van Vechten, however, had been "wined and dined by the seekers after salvation by publicity, by the pundits of 'advancement' and by the white pen-pushers who manufacture retail prominence for the smart snotties of the New Renaissance—Negro type, Model 1926." Because of such ties, Harrison suspected that *Nigger Heaven*— "the title and the theme"—would "be highly appreciated by Van Vechten's dusky hosts—and hostesses—over whose bottles he imbibed the conception of Harlem" his book "exhibited."[12]

Harrison's "main concern" was "not with the book's title but with its theme and treatment." He noted, however, that "as far back as 1923, in more than one review in *The New York World*," he had "warned 'our young writers' that if they persisted in neglecting the rich human and literary values which lie all around them they would be estopped from crying out loud when white writers dished up these viands spiced with the sauces of their own mental distortions." Now, he observed, "Mr. Van Vechten has done it!" Harrison considered *Nigger Heaven* an "'atmosphere' story of Harlem, flanked by tone-sketches and garnished with a vicious 'nigger dialect' whose sole source" must have been "the author's mind at 4 a.m. after supping—and something else." Harrison had "lived nineteen years in Harlem, roamed all its streets unchaperoned, and been at home with all its varied human types," and he assured all, unequivocally, that "Van Vechten's dialect doesn't exist up here." He had "never heard a Negro say 'leab'" or

"Ah doan perzackly recerlex' duh name." It was clear that "V. V." was "young"—he thought "that 'the berries' is Negro" ("it came up from the Jewish East Side") and so on. In addition, "some of the words in the 'Glossary of Negro Words and Phrases'" were "filthy to the last degree."[13]

The actual story of *Nigger Heaven* was "not easy to summarize" because the book contained "so much else besides the story in it." The author set out "to paint Negro Harlem society," and he first focused on "an impossible figure of a ruttish female who goes out to buy a pimp." After this "false start" the story moves "among the leisure class Harlemites," a "love-story" develops "with a spoilt rah-rah boy and a sweet little girl as protagonists," the male is cursed "with a college 'education' and an itch to write," and finally he suffers "the rotten results of his own waywardness and asinine incompetence." From the first page to the last "one brilliant quality of Van Vechten spills itself over this book, as it does in *The Blind Bow Boy*," writes Harrison. "He can describe furniture and its accessories, female clothes and fripperies with all the ecstatic abandon of a maiden lady at a wedding and the self-satisfaction of a man-milliner toying with a pink powder-puff." Harrison didn't think Van Vechten had an "equal among men" in that domain.[14]

Harrison knew that Van Vechten could write because *The Blind Bow Boy*, his novel of luxurious New York and Long Island, combined character and atmosphere, vice and refinement, in an organized literary presentation. "But" this "piece of cheap shoddy" contained "neither atmosphere, depth nor character." Harrison surmised that "in the last four chapters" Van Vechten became "painfully aware" he was "turning out superficial trash" and tried "to compensate," but "even that" failed.[15]

Harrison went on "to find a few good things to say." He thought Van Vechten's novel demonstrated "the present worthlessness of what passes for colored 'society' in Harlem"—its "cheap and tawdry assumptions of aristocracy, its reeking but camouflaged color prejudice and its collective crab-barrel tactics." It served as "a sort of argument-by-example."[16]

"One thing" Van Vechten had achieved was "to throw the fear of *Nigger Heaven* into 'the whole crowd . . . who hover around in Harlem dreaming that they are writing 'Negro' literature, because Van Vechten's kind has coddled them at pink-tea and literary contests." Harrison hoped that "this brutal and bungling book [would] serve as a spur to make them take the leap over the wall of weakness with which they are surrounded and write (with the virile power of Walter White), of the actual lives of actual Negroes in this Harlem, which has been suffering for six years from blasé neurotics whose Caucasian culture has petered out and who come to this corner of Manhattan for pungent doses of unreality, such as we get in *Nigger Heaven*." He thought that the book's selling price of $2.50 was "a pretty stiff price to pay for piffle."[17]

Van Vechten apparently read Harrison's "vivid report" and sent a copy to his friend James Weldon Johnson on September 7. Johnson replied he was "amused" by the review, in which he thought Harrison wasn't reviewing the book but unconsciously reviewing people in Harlem he didn't like.[18]

On September 1, 1926, (Dave?) Louis Thompson wrote to "My dear Harri[son]" of his "delight" and "relish" over the article in the current *Amsterdam News* "entitled 'Homo Africanus Harlemi' (whatever that is)." Thompson added, "As an Grator and Debater you are conceded to be by all who know you (and their name is Legion) in 'Class A1,' but, book-reviewing, owing to your extensive reading, intensive study and profound scholarship, is, in my poor opinion, your forte, 'par-excellent.'" He applauded the paragraph that began "Yet I am not one of those who believe" and added that "you showed up in no uncertain light, the accused folly and hypocrisy of the so-called social set up here who 'thou among us, are not of us.'" He hoped Harrison would soon write more for the *Amsterdam News*.[19] William Pickens wrote similarly to Harrison on September 24 that he "read carefully and with much good humor your review of Van Vechten's nasty book." He thought he "did the thing *justice*" and provided "the best word that has been spoken on that book,—in both courage and literary understanding."[20]

Around August 1927 Harrison also handwrote a review of Van Vechten's *Nigger Heaven* for broadcast on the radio station WGL on August 16. Van Vechten had brought his book out about a year earlier and "professed to give to the white outer-world the opportunity of a peep into the life of Negro Harlem." It sold well and in that sense "was a decided success." Since it "had its day," Harrison sought to provide the radio-audience "some critical consideration of its merits and demerits" (while running "the evident risk of stimulating an ephemeral interest in it").[21]

"'Nigger Heaven' was the name given first to the galleries of white churches" where "Negroes were herded together for worship," as they would later be herded "in the balconies of theaters, for enjoyment." Van Vechten's use of the phrase appeared "predicated on a different basis which would make it a cross between a Fool's Paradise and something worse." Harrison noted that the book's prologue tried to furnish an explanation of its title, but that effort turned "to rubbish" when a footnote to page 26 pointed out "that while Negroes may use the objectionable word among themselves, 'its employment by a white person is always fiercely resented.'" This showed that Van Vechten "knew what he was doing when he selected the title."[22]

Harrison next described how Van Vechten began his story "among the leisure class Harlemites," developed "a love-story with a spoilt rah-rah boy and a sweet little girl as protagonist," cursed him "with a college 'education' and an itch to write," and locked him "in the rotten results of his own wardness and asinine incompetence." It was thus, not so much the story as the "'atmosphere,' flanked by tone-sketches and garnished with a vicious Negro dialect," that "arrests attention." Van Vechten played "the literary game" of a "fictional Negro dialect" when he put "into the mouths of his Negro characters of the lower sort a jargon such as never was [heard] on land or sea." Harrison also repeated comments from his previous review about Van Vechten's "brilliant quality" of writing, particularly in his description of furniture. Harrison still maintained, however, that *Nigger Heaven* was "cheap" and "shoddy" and had "neither atmosphere, depth nor character." Its characters were "jerked by wires" that were "painfully visible," and "as literature—as art," it was "putrid."[23]

Shortly after his first review of Van Vechten's book Harrison noted several more personal events in his diary. On Monday, September 13, 1926, Hubert and Lin's last child, their son Billy, began school at Public School 139 on West 140th Street. He was assigned to Ms. Douglass's 1A class, and on the first day he was escorted by his mother and father. Hubert noted that "eleven years ago our first (Frances) began her school career at P.S. 119—and now our last (Bill) begins his."[24]

Ten days later, Harrison attended the funeral of his friend John I. Lewis and "delivered his eulogium." Lewis, secretary of the ICUL, "was stricken with heart-failure on Tuesday morning [September 21] on his way to work and left a wife and three daughters—the eldest was 4 years old last May and the youngest was only four months old." In attendance were (Abner?) Berry, Domingo, Charles C. Seifert, Madame Marie B. Houston, and Mr. and Mrs. Hodge Kirnon.[25]

On Labor Day, Monday September 6, 1926, the Black motion picture operators at the Lafayette Theatre at Seventh Avenue and 132nd Street failed to show up for work, delaying the performance from 1:15 to 2:00 p.m. That night at 9 p.m. they started picketing on Seventh Avenue near the theater, and Local 306 of the Motion Picture Machine Operators Union publicly took the position "that the Negro operators be given the same scale of wages as the white operators in union houses." A union representative said the union was backing the Black operators "because they believe that the colored workers are entitled to the same consideration as the whites." The representative also said that the "better theatres"—the Franklin, Lincoln, Renaissance, Roosevelt, Douglas, and Odeon—were all unionized; "that Negroes were employed" at the Renaissance, Roosevelt, Lincoln, and Douglas; and that colored operators were "being placed in the other theatres as fast as they qualify." The "white" members of the union were reportedly "incensed because of the forced withdrawal of two colored operators from the Lafayette Theatre" who were members of the union "seeking to secure the same scale of wages as paid in the other theatres."[26]

Frank Crosswaith, the Virgin Islands–born socialist and executive secretary of the Trade Union Committee for Organizing Negro Workers (TUCNW), had previously explained that the nine "Negro" motion picture operators in Harlem were not full union members but had affiliated with Local 306 as an auxiliary. For years they had sought to join the union, but "race prejudice stepped in between them and a union card each time." The TUCNW was established on May 23, 1925, by "Negro" and "white" trade unionists and aimed to "be similar in character to the Women's Trade Union League and the United Hebrew Trades." Its "sole purpose" was "the organizing of Negroes into the American Federation of Labor" through direct organizing and educational work.[27] It received funding from the American Fund for Public Service (AFPS, or Garland Fund), a charity set up to aid liberal and radical causes.[28]

On Friday evening, September 17, as the Lafayette strike continued, Richard B. Moore, secretary of the New York council of the ANLC, secretary of the HEF, and director of the ISS, was arrested on the corner of 138th Street and Seventh Avenue on a charge made by the manager of the Lafayette Theatre, Leo Burt. Moore had participated actively for a decade in social movements in Harlem, and he and Harrison, with whom he had spoken several times during the summer, were holding what the *Amsterdam News* described as "a lawful and orderly meeting" when his rights were "ruthlessly abridged." After Moore opened the meeting and spoke for ten minutes on general economic topics, denounced the policy of the Lafayette of paying sub-union wages to movie operators, and advocated that the community support the colored moving picture operators in their struggle for union wages and conditions, a police car reportedly drove up on the sidewalk into the group of fifty or sixty listeners. Moore was arrested and brought to the police station, where he was at first charged with contempt of court for violating an injunction against speaking and agitating for the organization of employees in the vicinity of the theater. The charge was changed later to disorderly conduct and was made by the theater manager. Moore argued that he was holding a perfectly legal and orderly meeting, that he knew of no injunction he could in any way be held to have violated, and that he was exercising his constitutional rights as a citizen. An adjournment was granted, a hearing date set for Friday September 24, and Moore was released in the custody of his attorney as the International Labor Defense got involved in his defense.[29]

In response to the developing conflict Leo Brecher, the Lafayette Theatre's owner, issued a September 22 statement to the *Amsterdam News* in which he explained that he had operated the Lafayette since June 8, 1925, and that every person employed there, with the exception of the manager, "was colored," making it the only theater in New York that had "exclusively colored workers." He added that the salaries at the Lafayette were higher than at union workplaces and that of the 4,500 licensed motion picture operators "only slightly more than a dozen colored operators had such licenses and no colored operators outside of colored districts did." He claimed that the "colored workers" had all been nonunion because the union had refused, up until six months ago, when it lifted its color bar, to accept them as members.[30]

On September 24 William Pickens, who was drawing closer to the ANLC and had recently written several articles for the Workers Party's *Daily Worker*, wrote to Harrison to ask about the Sunrise Club, where he had been asked to speak about Edwin C. Walker. He added that he had learned at a meeting the night before of Moore's arrest and wanted to know, "Where are the Negro papers?" He described the theater management's actions as "outrageous" and regretted that he would be unable to attend an upcoming meeting.[31]

The referred-to meeting was probably the Saturday afternoon, September 26, Liberty Hall meeting organized to protest Moore's arrest. It was sponsored by the American Civil Liberties Union (ACLU), the League for Industrial Democracy (LID), the NAACP, and the BSC and was chaired by Moore. During the meeting Moore claimed that his rights had been abridged when his free speech was denied, and he reportedly added, "The emancipation of the negro may have been made with the Civil War . . . but we are not free yet. Harlem, the mecca of the new negro, is being governed by the politicians, and not the working class, as we are supposed to believe."[32]

Harrison, representing the ICUL, also spoke at the meeting and said that he had called for "Negro" policemen for Harlem since 1916. "If we can hold out with our votes until our demands are met, we can demand negro captains for Harlem and receive equal rights with our white brothers from other departments of the city such as health." He proposed that a temporary committee be appointed pending formation of a permanent one and that their demands be presented to city officials. The temporary committee that was formed consisted of Grace P. Campbell, Williana J. Burroughs, George A. Weston, Walter T. Brandon, Harrison, Crosswaith, and Moore.[33]

On September 29, the *Amsterdam News* printed a statement from the "Colored Motion Picture Operators," which claimed that Crosswaith, "a colored official of the A.F. of L.," had advised them to make application for membership to the Motion Picture Operators' Union, Local 306, AFL, and they "were accepted and granted all rights and privileges." They added that "Colored operators employed by the Lafayette were always made to work 11 hours a day, a seven day week." The union favored "a day off in every week, in accordance with the most enlightened social laws of the nation," but "the Lafayette thinks this too good for the colored employees."[34]

That same issue of the *Amsterdam News* also reprinted a highly optimistic letter from Cyril V. Briggs, who was active with the ANLC and the Workers

Party and who was doing publicity work for the striking Passaic, New Jersey, textile workers. The letter, written on September 25, took the position that the "labor unions are increasingly opening up" to "Negro" workers "as the American labor movement gains knowledge and experience in the struggle and goes about rectifying its former mistakes." Briggs maintained, "Organized labor is beginning to realize that the interests of all workers—black and white—are inextricably interwoven and can never be separated. Bars that were formerly raised against us have been lowered by the force of economic conditions and the growing influence of the left-wing element within the unions." In addition, "The reactionary leadership that formerly kept the ranks of the workers divided in the face of the united front of the bosses is fast fading from the scene." Under such conditions, added Briggs, "the Negro workers should take full advantage of the changing spirit of the labor movement. We cannot longer afford to [be] the parasites in the sense that while being beneficiaries in every sense of the victories of organized labor we yet had no part in its struggles. . . . A united front of the workers against the united front of the bosses is the sole salvation of the workers. Organize!"[35]

In general, as the author Harold Cruse points out, "Briggs was far more optimistic about black and white labor possibilities than the facts of the Passaic textile strike revealed." Passaic was "the first big labor action the Communist left wing initiated in the 1920s," and, within a few months, "the Communists, on orders from Moscow's decisions of the Sixth Comintern Meeting of 1926, disowned their own strike, pulled out and turned the whole business over to the American Federation of Labor's United Textile Workers." In terms of the Lafayette Theatre struggle, Cruse notes that the AFL Motion Picture Operators' local, "after accepting the Negro operators under pressure, put them into separate Harlem locals."[36]

On Sunday, October 3, a "large and enthusiastic crowd of Negroes, workers and liberals filled Liberty Hall" for "a United Mass Demonstration to protest against the abridgement of the civil liberties and economic rights of the citizens of Harlem." The meeting was called by the ANLC to protest Moore's arrest. Participating organizations included the National Equal Rights League (NERL), the UNIA, the ICUL, the Negro Foreign Born Citizens Alliance, the African League, the BSCP, the International Labor Defense (ILD), and the ACLU.[37]

A "Dear Friend" letter signed by Williana J. Burroughs and dated October 4 was sent in the name of the "Joint Defense Committee of the Harlem Educational Forum[,] Institute For Social Study[, and] American Negro Labor Congress" and stated its purpose was "to protect the economic rights and civil liberties of the people of Harlem by securing adequate defense and effective action in support of Richard B. Moore who was unlawfully and wantonly arrested while championing these rights by the manager of the Lafayette Theatre." The joint committee, located at 200 West 135th Street, Room 211, listed E. Elliot Rawlins as chair; Williana J. Burroughs as secretary; Grace P. Campbell as treasurer; and W. A. Domingo, Otto E. Huiswood, Leroy Coles Jr., and Lennie L. George as members. Noticeably missing from the letterhead were Harrison, Willis Huggins, Louise Jackson, Mabel Byrd, F. Eugene Corbie, Peter D. Codrington, and N. E. White, of the ISS. The letter discussed "the arbitrary arrest" of Moore, describing it as "a blow at our most fundamental human rights and liberties." It advocated "equal economic rights for our people" and called on people to "defend these rights of free speech and equal opportunity which are basic to all advancement." Despite such support, Moore was found guilty and his sentence suspended.[38]

————

The October 6 *Amsterdam News* included Harrison's major piece on the Lafayette Theatre strike, entitled "As Harrison Sees It." In it Harrison offered his "own" account of the matter, for which he was "prepared to receive some hard knocks." He said that he got involved in the struggle when he "heard that trouble was brewing between the management of the theatre and the Negro motion-picture operators." At that time he was told "that it was a question of wages and working conditions in which the employees were being refused the rate of wages and the working conditions established by their union." As he explained: "That appealed to me, and I at once notified some of the colored operators who worked at other movie houses in Harlem that when the storm broke I should like to render them some assistance and that they could count upon my support." Thus, when the strike started Harrison was "prepared to lay aside . . . [his] usual activities and speak on behalf of the men." But, from the first, he added,

I made it quite clear that, unlike Abraham Lincoln, my prime object was not to save the union but "to free the slaves." For my long previous acquaintance with the American Federation of Labor did not predispose me to be friendly to its unions. Their policy seemed so constructed that, whereas the white worker could consider his fight for bread to be directed solely against the capitalist, the black worker was opposed by the general run of white working men, who kept him out of their unions for the most part and yet called him "scab" for getting their jobs at the only time when those jobs were available to him. My attitude on this has been maintained consistently since 1917, when Samuel Gompers assumed at Carnegie Hall, in the face of Colonel [Theodore] Roosevelt, responsibility for the East St. Louis riots on the ground of an alleged necessity for the white unionists to defend their jobs by murder against the Negro workers whom they had shut out of their unions—as Negroes. . . . My contention during the early part of the present strike of ONLY TWO MEN was that, in defense of the men and in vindication of the rights of Negroes in Harlem to get good work and good wages I would join hands with old Nick himself as long as I believed that he stood with them. That is still my contention.[39]

When the strike started Harrison publicly expressed his view and based his comments "on the allegations made" to him "both by the white union men who came to Harlem and by some of the colored ones." Their "main allegations were that (1) The Lafayette management had thrown out their Negro operators because they had joined the union and had installed white 'scabs' in their place; (2) That all the other movie houses in Negro Harlem were employing colored movie operators; [and] (3) That Mr. [Frank] Schiffman, general manager of the Brecher group of theatres, had declared that he would never give to colored men such a high wage as sixty dollars a week," which, Harrison was told, "was the union scale of wages for movie operators." Believing that "all these allegations were true," Harrison spoke two nights on Seventh Avenue at 132nd and 133rd Streets on behalf of the strikers and their union. He believed what he had been told and defended his actions. This was done, however, "WITHOUT FURTHER INQUIRY," because he had never claimed to be "an impartial investigator at that stage"; rather, he "was an advocate with a brief for one side only."[40]

Harrison's second meeting "was broken up by the police who declared that it was against the mandate of the court," which, they claimed, "had issued an injunction." He hadn't seen the injunction and proceeded to finish his talk at another location. This "precipitated a fight for the freedom of speech and lawful assemblage," a fight that was "still raging." Harrison thought it important to separate the free-speech case "from the case of the union versus the Lafayette." He believed the free-speech fight "to be well worth my support," but his opinion of the union struggle had "certainly undergone revision."[41]

He then explained how his thinking had changed on that matter after the "suspension of public speaking on the strikers' behalf" and after "a chance conversation in the local station house with Mr. [Leo] Burt, manager of the Lafayette," which afforded him "the time and the opportunity to INVESTIGATE" some of his earlier premises. Harrison reviewed back files of the *Amsterdam News* and said he "learned that down to a few months ago the union had bitterly opposed the admission of Negroes, and when it admitted them (after the threat had been made to organize a school for motion picture operators, produce a crowd of colored operators and swarm over the dikes by 'scabbing'), the union had refused to let them attend its meetings." Instead, the union "offered them the insulting proposal to let them meet by themselves in Harlem—with a white union official to be sent up to supervise their Jim Crow meeting." All of this was to be done "despite the fact that each colored unionist was required to pay [a] $200 entrance fee and the same dues as the white unionists." These facts "were corroborated" at the free-speech meeting at Liberty Hall on Sunday, September 19, by Frank Crosswaith, "who had organized the colored movie operators."[42]

These new facts caused Harrison to pause, and then, when he "learned further that all the B[r]echer houses except one were non-union, yet the white unionists had called no strikes in those houses WHERE WHITE MEN ONLY HAD ALWAYS WORKED AND WERE STILL WORKING," it seemed "that there was something fishy about their claim that they had the Negro workers' interests at heart." To Harrison "it appeared that they were sacrificing those interests by forcing the fight up here in order to secure a victory somewhere else." He then "learned from Mr. Sims, one of the two strikers, that the Lafayette management was willing to grant the union scale of wages, and most, or even all of the union conditions, and that, in fact, this scale had always prevailed at the Lafayette Theatre." He also learned "that the union officials would not accept such an easy surrender, but wanted a surrender all along the line (of the five other houses) as a condition precedent to calling off the strike at the Lafayette."[43]

After learning this, Harrison "passed out of the picture as a union sympathizer" because, as he stated earlier, "my primary object was to 'free the slaves' and not 'to save the union.'" Since the workers "were conceded freedom (i.e., union scale of wages and union conditions)" he "saw no reason" to "wage war for the union—this or any other." Harrison frankly admitted

with full realization of its import—that if I had to choose between a group of white men who had fired out the white union operators from their theatre when they took it over to make way for two Harlem Negro operators, and another group of white men, who (until they were forced to do otherwise) denied these boys and all other Negro operators a chance to secure decent wages and conditions—if as I say, I had to choose between these two groups of white men I would unhesitatingly choose the former.[44]

Harrison next examined the situation of the white union operators in Harlem, and, as he explained, "the worse was yet to come." He went to see Schiffman at the Lafayette to get his version, and, in the course of their talk, Schiffman "hinted very broadly" that Harrison "had been given much falsehood." When he told Harrison "that the statement that all the other movie houses in Harlem had Negro operators was untrue," Harrison "'called his hand'" and was invited to "go and see." They went to the Odeon on 145th Street, where he was informed "that the three movie operators employed there were white, and had always been." Harrison "climbed upstairs, looked into the projection room, and found a white man operating the machine." He next went to the Roosevelt "and found that, while they used a colored operator when the white one is out to dinner and off duty, the job was held down by the white operator." At the Lincoln, on West 135th Street, there were two colored "relief men," but the operator was white and had been there for a long time.[45]

Harrison then turned from advocate to mediator. He "could no longer advocate the entire cause of those who had . . . misrepresented such fundamental facts" to him but, "for the sake of the colored boys and the colored community," he "stayed in the game, trying to secure a conference between the two parties and an amicable adjustment, if that were possible." On "last Monday night" (September 20) he "secured the consent of the union's secretary (he said he was) and business agent to hold a conference between them and Messrs. Schiffman and Burt, with myself and either Mr. Romeo Dougherty [of the *Amsterdam News*] or another gentleman as mediators." Harrison told the union man that he was "one of the public." They met in front of the Lafayette to confer with Schiffman and Burt at 2 p.m. Then, when he met the union people on Tuesday (September 21) in front of the theater, "they hardly knew" him and claimed "that they didn't even know that there was to be any conference at 2:00." As Harrison left and walked down the street, he "met Mr. Johnson, a colored movie operator ('relief man')," who told him that after Harrison had left the previous night "they had a talk lasting nearly an hour with Schiffman, and they decided that the conference was not necessary." Harrison said he had no idea why the union officials had pretended they didn't know of their own agreement with him to enter the conference, and he decided to wash his hands of the union.[46]

He also decided it wasn't for him "to advise the colored boys," but he did "risk the prophecy that, after they have served their 'friends' turn, these 'friends' will do to them as they did before the sudden burst of friendship." While they might disagree with him "on their 'friends' good intentions," he thought "a record of facts stares them unblinkingly in the face." The decision was theirs, however, not his.[47]

Harrison, however, hadn't told all in his *Amsterdam News* letter. In his diary of September 22 he wrote that on that day (several days after learning about the discrimination against the "Negro" workers by the "white" union), his eldest daughter "Frances [age sixteen] began to work in the Lafayette Theater on 7th Ave. as assistant in the office and messenger." He added that he was "able to get her the job through my relations, recently developed, with Mr. Burt the manager and Mr. Schiffman the general manager—growing out of the strife of the Union picture projectors (2) in which I was first involved on the Union side. Now, however, I am on the managers' side."[48]

————

On November 17 the *Amsterdam News* printed a November 11 letter from Schiffman addressed to its columnist, Romeo Dougherty. Schiffman said that articles in the last issue of the paper referring to him and to the Lafayette prompted him to write. He said he held "no brief for Hubert Harrison" and emphasized that he "took the stump in an effort to arouse the community against the Lafayette Theatre." Schiffman, however, thought "it highly significant" that Harrison "publicly acknowledged" that he "spoke against the Lafayette without having first learned both sides of the issue" and that after he learned the theater's side and "investigated the truth or falsity of the statements made . . . by the union officials and by the theatre management," he felt it his "duty to publicly state the result" of his investigation, which was, "in effect," that he "considered the actions of the union wrong, and that the theatre had done everything within its power to be fair to employees." Schiffman said his "first contact" with Harrison "was when he accepted an invitation to come to my home and discuss the operators' difficulties." Schiffman then added, "the world has altogether too few men blessed with the thinking power, the education, the fair-mindedness, the culture which Hubert Harrison possesses."[49]

A second article, in the November 17 *Amsterdam News*, by Edgar M. Grey, was a scorching attack on Schiffman and a more veiled critique of Harrison. Grey had worked with Harrison in the Liberty League and the ICUL and was a man whom Harrison, according to his son William, didn't trust much. Grey attacked Schiffman for his letter, saying that it was "a marvel at sophistry." In particular, "Schiffman waited until he was about to close his letter before he mentioned the real reason for his annoyance—the strike which is being conducted by the union at his theatre." In addition, Schiffman tells us that he "holds no brief" for Harrison and recognized the "good common sense American" wisdom "that he who pays the piper also calls the tune." Grey added that Schiffman "over-reached himself" when he said his first acquaintance with Harrison was when Harrison accepted an invitation to go to his home "to discuss the difficulties of the operators." Grey asked: "Why has a man to go to the home of the chief of one side or another to discuss the affairs of another side?" He added, "In no case will a perfectly neutral person permit the place of such discussion to be suggested or to be under the control or keeping of any of the aggrieved parties." Grey recognized the intellectual gifts of Harrison but asked: "What has Mr. Schiffman done to utilize the brain of so able a man, whom he says in his letter is so learned and so well admired by him?" He added, "We do not know, but we believe that there must even be a clerkship that Mr. Harrison might fill creditably in the office of his friend and benefactor, Mr. Schiffman." He had not yet heard of "anything substantial that Mr. Schiffman has done for the good and learned Mr. Harrison."[50]

Some seven months later, in the May 1927 *Voice of the Negro*, Harrison noted that "the remarkable strike of the Two Moving Picture Operators at the Lafayette is still going on" but that "the theatre is still packed to capacity—not only every night, but every day at matinees." At the Renaissance the screen program was "always preceded by the display of the motion picture operators' union emblem" and the statement that the motion picture machine was operated by a union member; that theater, too, was "filled to capacity each day." Harrison concluded that it seemed "that neither the friendship nor the enmity of the union" had "any box-office effects."[51]

Harold Cruse in his *The Crisis of the Negro Intellectual* gives great importance to the Lafayette Theatre struggle, emphasizes the public positions taken, and notes "the sharp division within the Harlem radicals" over "how the Negro should organize along economic lines." He argues that as the struggle progressed "Harrison took up the cudgels for the Negro operators, but in a different way" than Briggs. Harrison "wanted to assist the operators in getting a fair and better deal with the Harlem theaters but was *against* their joining an AFL local because of the union's long standing, anti-Negro bias." Then, as "he learned that the operators had been required to pay the two hundred dollar initiating fee, but had been barred from attending regular union meetings downtown, he backed off with the statement: 'Unlike Abraham Lincoln, my prime objective was not to save the union but to free the slaves.'" According to Cruse, "Harrison concluded that the Negro operators had been used by the AFL."[52]

Cruse contrasted the positions of Briggs and Harrison with that of the Garveyites and suggested "sharper insight into the leadership deficiencies of Harlem during the Lafayette Theatre episode can be gleaned from an examination of how the Garvey nationalists reacted to the issue." He concludes that their "strictly hands-off position" revealed that "their . . . movement was not really attuned to the internal peculiarities of the Negro-white situation in the United States." They saw the solution to the problem "outside the system—namely, in Africa." Thus writes Cruse, in 1926, the "character of the Garvey movement served to hide the fact that the movement was not facing the hard realities in a scientific way—either at home or in Africa." When

during the Lafayette Theatre strike none other than Garvey's first wife, Mrs. Amy Ashwood-Garvey, brought her own musical comedy on to the Lafayette stage (on November 1, 1926), for a limited engagement . . . the timing of the appearance of this musical by a leading nationalist, showed that as far as the Lafayette strike was concerned, the nationalists were sorely lacking in the virtues of political unity concerning issues closer at hand than the distant shores of Africa.[53]

Cruse felt "the enmity between the Garveyites and the Communist leftwing," especially "Briggs and Moore, the leftwing critics of Garvey, [who] had already taken over agitational priorities in the Lafayette strike," had a lot to do with the Garveyite position. But this was "further complicated" by Harrison's criticism of the AFL unions. Soon it was also "revealed that Harrison had been in contact with Garvey's first wife Amy Ashwood Garvey who's [sic] play opened at the Lafayette in November and whose 'sensational divorce case,' with charges of adultery on both sides, made the front pages of the Harlem press in December." During the court proceedings it was revealed that "Harrison was ghostwriting Mrs. Amy *Ashwood*-Garvey's story of her life with Marcus Garvey, to be titled 'The Rise and Fall of Marcus Garvey.'" He adds that "the scandal strengthened the anti-Garveyites cabal" among the radicals.[54]

On October 6, 1926, in addition to its coverage of the Lafayette Theatre struggle, the *Amsterdam News* announced that "Dr." Harrison, "staff lecturer of the Board of Education," had opened a new fall and winter series of lectures at 200 West 135th Street, Room 212, on Saturday, October 2. The lectures were under the auspices of the Citizens Educational Committee, composed of Dr. E. Elliot Rawlins, Melville Charlton, Arthur A. Schomburg, William H. Davis, William Pickens, and Romeo L. Dougherty. Each month in rotation would be a lecture on four topics: "The Trend of the Times," "Literary Lights of Yesterday and Today," "Popular Science," and "Race Problems and History"; admission was twenty-five cents.[55]

The opening lecture was on "Civilization's Black Beginnings" and was a talk in popular form on the historical research and scientific exploration done by Egyptologists and others. On Saturday night, October 9, Harrison was scheduled to lecture on "A Reply to *Nigger Heaven*," in what was predicted to be "a sizzling summary of the Blasé Neurotics who make Harlem their happy hunting ground with some interesting side lights on our intellectual aristocracy of brains and booze." A second printed handout added that the talk would devastatingly treat "the so-called 'Literary' Set in Harlem." His October 16 talk was to be on "Who Is Who in Humanity" and would discuss "the racial inferiority argument in the light of science and history." The October 23 lecture would treat "Three Literary Giants"—H. G. Wells, George Bernard Shaw, and Anatole France. There would be a twenty-five-cents admission at each talk.[56]

On October 8, after Harrison openly changed sides on the Lafayette Theatre struggle, he received a letter from William Pickens about the printed

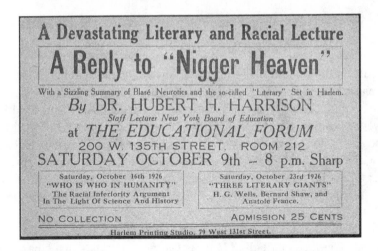

Figure 18.1. Reply to "Nigger Heaven," October 9, 1926, broadside. Promotional broadside for Hubert Harrison's October 9, 1926, lecture on Carl Van Vechten's *Nigger Heaven* and related reviews. On Saturday night, October 9, 1926, Hubert Harrison was scheduled to lecture on "A Reply to *Nigger Heaven*," in what was predicted to be "a sizzling summary of the Blasé Neurotics who make Harlem their happy hunting ground with some interesting side lights on our intellectual aristocracy of brains and booze." A second printed handout added that the talk would devastatingly treat "the so-called 'Literary' Set in Harlem." *Source:* Hubert H. Harrison Papers, Box 16, Folder 38, Rare Book and Manuscript Library, Columbia University. See https://dlc.library .columbia.edu/catalog/cul:j9kd51c6zf.

matter he had sent (probably the first lecture series circular). Pickens wrote: "Of course, I am one of the admirers of your talks on the streets, and indoors and in other places," and "I think you will do a great deal of good by them." However, he "never" liked "to serve as a dead member of any committee, and usually try to do what I can in a bona fide way, when the opportunity offers." If he had been asked before printing his name as a committee member, he would "doubtless have told you not to do so but to let me serve in ways in which I can serve the cause." He trusted that his "name will do no harm to the cause" and wished Harrison "Best wishes" for his lectures.[57]

During the first week of November 1926 Harrison noted in his diary that his eldest daughter, seventeen-year-old-Frances (who had been working in the theater since early in the Lafayette strike) ran away and then "came back!" Then, on Tuesday night, November 16, she left for Pittsburgh, "in charge of Irvin C. Miller, to begin her career on the stage in his show 'Desires Of 1927' at $30 a week." (Among Miller's previous theatrical efforts were *Broadway Rastus* in 1922, *Liza* in 1922, and *Dinah* in 1923.) That same night Hubert "gave [his fifteen-year-old daughter] Alice the severest beating of her life; first, for staying out all the afternoon and lying, saying that she had gone to a basket-ball game at the Parish House of the Abyssinian Baptist Church." When he went over to verify this, the director, Mr. Young, told him that there had been no game and showed him where the girls were practicing, sans Alice. When Hubert "upbraided her on her return she started to carry on," screaming at him "at the top of her voice." When he seized her "she began yelling for the police and demanded that [her younger sister, fourteen-year-old] Ada go for one." Hubert's wife, Lin, "held the door open so that all the neighbors" on the floor, "when they came to their doors, could see and hear, what was going on." Without letting go of Alice, Hubert "asked her mother repeatedly to shut the door; but she planted herself in the doorway and wouldn't." He "pushed the door shut, locked her out," and, in his words, "pounded Alice into submission." He then "had to dress and leave for the Renaissance Casino where the Virgin Islands Congressional Council was giving its dance" and where he "was engaged to speak in explanation of the stereoptican pictures of Africa and the Virgin Islands which preceded the dance." Harrison received $10 from Casper Holstein, president of the council, for his presentation. He had several dances, and the dance lasted till three in the morning. He noted: "This dance is degen-erating more and more into a tribade's annual: for about a third or more of the dancers on the floor are made up of female couples. The homo-sexual ten-dency is very strongly pronounced among Virgin Islands' women."[58]

On October 4, 1926, Wendell Phillips Dabney, the author and publisher of *Cincinnati's Colored Citizens: Historical Sociological and Biological* (1926) and owner and editor of the weekly *Union* (since 1905), wrote to Harrison and said he had sent him an autographed copy of his book. Dabney asked Harrison for a brief autobiographical sketch, since he deserved "to be better known in our section." He noted that the "Intelligentsia of our race incline more to such works as *Nigger Heaven*" and suggested that Harrison compare Mary White Oving-ton's review of that with the one she did of his book. He said he would look Har-rison up on his return to New York and asked him to do the same if he visited Cincinnati. Dabney again wrote to Harrison eleven days later, saying, "I knew not the magnitude of the savant till I received your material." He also sent a copy of Ovington's review and urged Harrison to see James Weldon Johnson's review. He told him that "Cincinnati is dastardly bad for lectures, our people here fall only for wine, women, and song" but said he would "try to arrange dates for Cincinnati, Columbus, Cleveland, Chicago."[59]

Around November 13, probably prompted in part by Dabney, Harrison wrote "*Nigger Heaven* —A Review of the Reviewers," an article that appeared in the *Amsterdam News* of November 24. He explained that his September 1 review of

Nigger Heaven seemed "to have released the rush of Negro writers and set the pace for the expressions of critical (and other) condemnation of that book," which he "had prophetically described as a 'breach of the peace.'" It had "also provoked Mr. Van Vechten's Negro friends to fly to his relief." Harrison claimed he would "have been genuinely surprised" if his "estimate of the book had proved to be the only estimate." He therefore set out "to summarize the critical output of its friends and foes without feeling any special animus against the former or any special friendship for the latter." He tried "not to falsify," since his "main motive" was "to shed some light on the character and quality of the numerous critical and pseudo-critical comments on the book" and "to assess their merit in the light of reason and the sociologic background on which alone literature and literary judgments must rest their claims to validity." He made "clear at the outset" that "in the face of much fog that has been raised," "in my review I did not base my unfavorable opinion of *Nigger Heaven* on the popular ground that it doesn't present the Negro in favorable light. I have always repudiated that point of view, and I do so now. It is no part of the critic's right to dictate to the creative artist what aspects of life he should select for representation."[60] He then explained that he had "condemned Van Vechten's book as a poor specimen of literary craftsmanship and on the further ground that it is a viciously false picture of the life it pretends to depict. Had its characters been more than mere lay figures, "lacking the breath of life," he would "have praised it for that—no matter how it might have 'shown up' Harlem Negro society." And, indeed, so far as it did that very thing—in spots—Harrison "gave it a modicum of commanding commendation."[61]

In presenting his "summary of the opinions" Harrison "pass[ed] over—for obvious reasons"—those that "appeared exclusively in the white press," though he considered "two by way of examples." Heywood Broun, "a 'columnist,' not a critic," in his review "guaranteed the artistic, literary and sociological merits of the book." His "naive, emotional reactions" had not yet provided "any recognized critical value to his pontifical pronouncements and, except as evidences of friendship, or back-scratching, they remain[ed] critically out of court." Harry Hansen, in the *New York World*, offered a "validation of Van Vechten's book," which was "a curious contradiction in terms." Toward the end of the review he admitted "that he himself is unacquainted with Negro Harlem, the theme of the book," yet he stated that "after reading Carl Van Vechten one has the impression that other writers have merely scratched the surface." Elsewhere he praised its "'scientific' accuracy." Clearly, "the one statement cancels the other." What Hansen's words suggested "is that, critically, one measure is used for white men's work dealing with white men and another for any man's work dealing with Negroes; and in such cases some white critics are not above surrendering themselves to 'the emotions of a cult' and endorsing something bizarre and 'exotic' just because it falls in with the present ephemeral jazz idea of what 'the Negro' is." Harrison added, "As I have shown elsewhere, [this] is largely a conventionalized expression of their own inner need for a new evocation and argues, as [Oswald] Spengler somewhere shows, the final exhaustion of the artistic impulse with-in the white race."[62]

Before "properly consider[ing] the colored critics of the book" he thought it "necessary to note Miss [Mary White] Ovington's furtive release on *Nigger Heaven*," for which he was "indebted to an Ohio editor [Wendell P. Dabney?] after trying unsuccessfully for two weeks to find it in New York." As "expected," Miss Ovington sang "soprano to the charming tenor and baritone in her cultural corner." In reality, she furnished "the materials for one of the strongest indictments against the book." She said she couldn't tell "how good this picture is," and "by 'good'" she meant "accurate." But that put her "out of court as a validator on the sociologic side." Her first paragraph was "apologetic," as when she wrote, "'The colored reader who is not familiar with Van Vechten's other novels may think that in *Nigger Heaven* the colored man is given a rotten deal.'" Since "ninety-nine per cent of the probable colored readers of the book are presumptively 'not familiar with Van Vechten's other novels' Miss Ovington's words suggest and imply that the book, as read, produces the impression in the Negro readers' minds that 'the colored man is given a rotten deal' in its pages." This view, wrote Harrison, "is hers—not mine." She went on to say that the book was "largely" concerned "with the Negro's 'sensual life.'" She then cited "the very books" to which Harrison had directed attention in his review of September 1 and insisted "that they are even more devoted to the sensual life than this one is." In this way she "established for the authors a definite addiction to the painting of 'sensual life,' to dirt and disrepute." Again, "the indictment is hers," and she also admitted Harrison's "charge of unreality in the characters and atmosphere of the book without seeming to be aware of how much she is admitting." "This novelist," Ovington added, "loves the tale that seems unreal and impossible, repugnant to common-sense," and she described Van Vechten as "this modernist who likes to draw the impossible." Miss Ovington "'boosts' the book, and in her closing sentence she advises to 'look in on the place,' i.e. *Nigger Heaven*"—which reminded Harrison "of Mr. James Weldon Johnson's closing sentence," which also recommended "that we read *Nigger Heaven*." In sum, Harrison thought Miss Ovington's critique suggested was "she had been conscripted into a species of defensive warfare for which she has neither aptitude nor inclination."[63]

In discussing James Weldon Johnson's review in the October issue of *Opportunity*, Harrison wrote that he "flies to the defence of his friend's imperiled prestige with a vigor which dispenses with both discretion and the facts." Using "the disdainful dogmatism of a Brahmin pundit he coolly assures . . . that 'the story comprehends nearly every phase of life in the Negro metropolis.'" Harrison replied, "but it's—not true." In the last sentence of his "duty-to-a-friend," Johnson writes: "'This reviewer would suggest reading the book before discussing it.'" Harrison "wished that he had taken his own advice more seriously" because if one "reads the book in any other than the mood of a propagandist or a back-scratcher" it would be clear "that it doesn't even touch such vital and obtrusive phases of life in the Negro metropolis as the churches and their influence, politics, the labor movement, the lodges and fraternalism, economic penetration by whites, the lodger evil, prostitution, organized superstition, or the newspapers." Harrison was "not saying that these things should be in such a novel, but their absence proves that the Brahmin's ponderous dogmatism was not dictated by anything remotely related to the truth." Johnson also said that "Van Vechten is the only white novelist I can now think of who has not viewed the Negro as a type, who has not treated the race as a unit, either good or bad." Harrison found this "exasperating" and not to be the case, citing Mark Twain, Joseph Conrad, [Sarah G.] Millin, T. S. Stribling, H. A. Shands, Gertrude Sanborn, and Paul Kester, "to mention only a few."[64]

Harrison next described how "most of the dubious commendation of *Nigger Heaven*" was "from a certain group of 'guardians of the gate,'" who offered a "flood of raucous rhetoric, inept opinion and juvenile sentimentalities." Yet "not one of these 'guardians'" had "ever known enough of either literary art or criticism to recognize unaided any product of genius from their own race, or any other, when they first met it face to face." He emphasized: "From Dunbar to Countée Cullen, from James Edwin Campbell to Claude McKay, [Langston] Hughes and [Jean] Toomer—good, bad or indifferent—every Negro of real or alleged merit in literature or any other art has had to be first pointed out by white critical opinion before these hounds of spring could bay upon the trail." This was "symptomatic of the critical worthlessness of these 'guardians of the gate,'" who were "so conscious of their own utter incompetence in this respect" that they would "gladly resign the risks of opinionizing on Negro literature every week into the hands of a white spinster who godmothers their group." Harrison considered this "a shameful fact" and "challenge[d] them to maintain any denial of it."[65]

Harrison noted that "Ovington's characterization of *Nigger Heaven* as 'so largely concerned with the Negro's sensual life' and of its author as largely addicted to dirt characterizations" coincided "with those made by writers in the *New York Age, New York News, Chicago Defender, Pittsburgh Courier* and *Heebie Jeebies*." It was, therefore, "with a sense of shock" that one read "Johnson's description of the same book as a 'scheme for the interpretation of Negro life in America that opens up a new world for colored writers.'" Curiously, Johnson was "the only one writing on the book" to offer "an explicit defence of its title," and on this matter Harrison reminded readers that "Van Vechten went out of his way to introduce one single footnote," which expressly told readers "that, while the word 'nigger' is often used among Negroes, it is by them considered the deadliest insult when used by a white man." Clearly, writes Harrison, "Van Vechten knew just what he was doing when he used the title—and he took pains to serve notice on the Negro boobs that he knew." All of this made "Mr. Johnson's labored defence of the title . . . 'sort of queer.'"[66]

The Courier's comments, "in sheer quantity and persistence, surpassed those of every other newspaper." One, by Harry B. Webber, took "much the same ground" that Harrison had taken in the *Amsterdam News* and "drew attention to the fact" that Harrison "had for many years been prophesying exactly what happened, viz.: that if Negro writers continued to ignore the masses of human material available in Harlem and elsewhere, some white writer would come along and utilize them in ways of which Negroes might not approve." Taken altogether, "the collective reactions to Van Vechten's book" were, to Harrison, "indicative of a keen appreciation of the relation which literature bears to life," and "even those who took the wrong turning on the road to knowledge were found resting their commendations and condemnations upon this relationship."[67]

———

In December 1926 Harrison was drawn into the Garvey divorce case. Amy Ashwood and Marcus Garvey had been married on Christmas Day, 1919, shortly after Amy reportedly saved Marcus's life. The marriage was said to be "a reward," but troubles soon developed. In August 1922 she sued Marcus for absolute divorce, alleging his adultery with Amy Jacques. The original defense was an absolute divorce obtained by Marcus in Missouri in 1921. He then married Amy Jacques in Maryland in July 1922. After a period of inaction and while Marcus Garvey was in the Atlanta Prison, his attorneys, Kohn and Nagler, in March 1926, hired private detectives to learn something of plaintiff Amy Ashwood's habits. Her apartment (at 666 St. Nicholas Avenue) was raided by members of the detective team of Herbert S. Boulin (former federal agent P-138) on April 8, 1926. Boulin had previously befriended Marcus Garvey while informing on him and his movement. The *Inter-State Tattler* reported that Amy Ashwood was trapped nude in her apartment with a lover named Joseph Frazier (a Columbia University graduate). Based on allegations the court allowed Marcus to put in a counterclaim, in which he also sought a divorce from Amy Ashwood Garvey. His lawyers asked for Amy Ashwood to be deported on moral turpitude charges. A large number of witnesses were eventually scheduled to testify in the trial; Amy Ashwood Garvey was represented by the attorney Oscar Garrett, of 2303 Seventh Avenue, in Harlem.[68]

The case went to trial on December 7, 1926, before the Hon. Peter A. Hatting, justice of the Supreme Court, New York County, at Trial Term Part IV, at the County Courthouse, Borough of Manhattan. Attorney Garrett "easily proved" that Marcus and Amy Jacques lived together at 133 West 129th Street and that he "held her out as his wife." Mrs. O'Meally, who once lived with them as a roomer, testified that on innumerable occasions she saw them retire at night and come out of the same room together in the morning. Mr. Kohn, "by failing to set up the Missouri divorce and the alleged subsequent marriage of Miss Jacques and the defendant in the state of Maryland[,] tacitly admitted that the relationship, if the jury believed the witnesses produced in behalf of the plaintiff, was adulterous."[69]

The question concerning adultery by Amy Ashwood Garvey on April 8 with Joseph Frazier "was full of drama and excitement." Mrs. Garvey said "that on the night of the raid she was suffering from some illness peculiar to women and which would make the act of which she was accused repulsive and against nature." She claimed "that all of the evening she was in bed discussing different phases of 'The Rise and Fall of Marcus Garvey,' a book which she claimed to be writing." The discussion reportedly focused on "the moral effect" of chapter 2, "Romantic Foreshadowings of Marcus Garvey." Mrs. Garvey said she worked until 2:30 a.m., when she invited Mr. Cox and Mr. Frazier, two men she was working with, "to spend the night in order that she might have assistance at hand if during the night her fears were realized and she needed a doctor." Cox allegedly declined to stay, while Frazier accepted and reclined on a divan in the sitting room. Both Mrs. Garvey and Frazier asserted that it was in this room that the party entering the apartment that morning found the man and dragged him into the bedroom, throwing him on the bed. Under cross-examination, Mrs. Garvey admitted "that she did not write the entire book, but had outside assistance" and that "she could not tell the meaning of certain words and phrases, nor could she recall the source of certain familiar poetic quotations contained in the book." On redirect examination Garret elicited that what Mrs. Garvey meant by writing the book was that "she furnished data to a person hired by the week to put this into final shape." She maintained, however, "that she herself wrote the entire chapter on the 'Romantic Foreshadowings of Marcus Garvey.'"[70]

Then, "in order to show that Amy Ashwood Garvey did not write any part of the book and that Frazier had therefore no motive, as far as the book was concerned, to be in the apartment on the night in question," Harrison was put on the stand on Thursday morning. He had been subpoenaed to give evidence and testify by the defendant Marcus Garvey's attorneys Kohn and Nagler. He described himself "as Mrs. Garvey's 'literary ghost,'" by which he meant "one who writes a book and submerges the true author's identity and allows another party to appear as the author." He testified that "only five chapters of the book had been completed and these were all done by him, including the second chapter. He maintained that he was hired at the rate of $30 per week of three evenings." Harrison was described as "a self-assured witness, suave and extremely literary in his answers." He "was certain that he had not been paid to testify in the case, that he had never been approached in the matter and had never been offered money to testify, but that on the contrary he was unaware of being called in as a witness until a few days before, when he was served with a subpoena from the court." Harrison's alleged "discomfiture came when on cross examination a letter which he sent to Mrs. Garvey, undated, unsigned, but in a handwriting which he was forced to admit was his own, was put in evidence showing that a man and a lawyer had offered him $100 to testify at the trial." Realizing that "the letter had disturbed the weight of his testimony, Dr. Harrison reached into his brief case and handed a batch of letters to Attorney Kohn, who on redirect examination offered one of them into evidence." Justice Hatting ruled it admissible over the objection and exception of Garrett. (This was the February 24, 1925, letter quoted in chapter 16.)[71]

The witnesses to prove Mrs. Garvey's adultery were the *Negro World* reporter Harold G. Baltow, who didn't write a news story of the raid, though he claimed he went along as a representative of the press; Mr. and Mrs. Edward O'Garo, who went because her husband could give a good account of where he was going at 2:30 in the morning; Henry Morales; and Marcellus Strong, "all of whom were shown to have an interest in the outcome of the action by virtue of being ardent followers of Mr. Garvey." The private detective Herbert S. Boulin, hired by the attorney Kohn, took the stand as a rebuttal witness and testified that none of the persons accompanying him on the raid were his paid operatives.[72]

After the defendants closed their cases each attorney was permitted a half hour to sum up evidence before the case went to jury at 4:25 p.m. Thursday. Harrison told Justice Hatting he feared being "attacked by an adherent of Mrs. Garvey," and a court officer escorted him to the subway. After a three-day trial, on December 10, the jury found both Garveys "guilty of misconduct (adultery)." The *Amsterdam News* reported that the two questions submitted to the jury were "Did Marcus Garvey at divers times after August, 1922, commit adultery at 133 West 129th street with a woman known as Amy Jacques?" and "Did Amy Ashwood Garvey commit adultery with a man known as Joseph Frazier on April 8, 1926, at 666 St. Nicholas avenue?" and "both questions were answered in the affirmative." Justice Hatting denied motions by attorneys for each party to set aside the verdict. The action was scheduled to go to another justice for a judgment based on the verdict, and the *New York Times* added that the "custom in such cases is to dismiss the complaint."[73]

The special finding of the jury that both parties were guilty of adultery did not technically settle the case. As a matrimonial action it could be tried in equity before a judge without a jury, or either party could request a trial by jury. The request was made in this case and the issues framed for the jury to answer according to its belief on the evidence produced. Since the jury found them both guilty by an affirmative answer to the questions submitted to it, the case was sent back to the equity side of Special Term, where the court would pass on the right of either party to a divorce. By consent the attorneys for all parties adjourned the equity case, which was on the calendar for Monday. It was expected that the action would be discontinued in order to avoid the embarrassment of having the court refuse relief to either side.[74]

As the trial ended, Amy Ashwood Garvey was traveling with "Hey, Hey." The *Amsterdam News* said that the verdict would recognize Mrs. Amy Jacques Garvey as the legal wife of Marcus Garvey until the court sets aside the Missouri divorce. In contrast, the December 18 *Pittsburgh Courier* reported it was thought "that the State of New York still recognizes the first Mrs. Garvey (Amy Ashwood Garvey) as Mrs. Garvey's legal wife."[75]

The *Courier* described "an amusing, if unfortunate, sidelight of the trial" to be "the position in which Dr. Hubert H. Harrison found himself when a passionate love letter was read into the record which was said to be a letter from Mrs. Garvey No. 1 to Dr. Harrison," saying that "she loved him alone and as soon as she got enough money she would establish a love-nest and the 2 of them would lead the Negro race." When Harrison saw a *Courier* reporter on Sunday, December 12, he said he "had been grossly misrepresented, as the letter read into the record was not addressed to him, neither was it signed by Mrs. Garvey." He said it "was not addressed to anyone" and "was signed 'Adje,' a short African word meaning 'big sister.'"

Harrison added, "The impression got out that I offered the letter to the court but I did not. I did present two letters, one Mrs. Garvey wrote me showing she had paid me $30 on account for writing her book ('The Rise and Fall of Marcus Garvey') and asking me to come to work on the book on a certain afternoon and another showing she accepted my proposition for writing the entire book." He noted that he "did not know anything about the case until a few weeks ago," when he "was summoned to court to testify," and that he "wrote the book and not Frazier, as Mrs. Garvey's side was tying to claim." Harrison explained: "I did write the book and not Frazier, and I produced two letters to prove Mrs. Garvey (No. 1) hired me for that purpose." He then added: "I have very frankly said before I didn't care which side won, and I don't now, but Mrs. Garvey never wrote me any love letters, nor did I write her any. I have in my possession both the original script manuscripts of the book, as well as the original typed manuscript."[76]

On January 2, 1927, the *Pittsburgh Courier* published Harrison's letter to the editor written on December 20. He praised "as an example of fair and honest news reporting" the *Courier*'s "account of the recent Garvey trial in New York." He added,

> The sensational version of one outstanding feature of that trial which was given by the white newspapers of this city was a deliberate misrepresenta-tion designed to furnish something spectacular. This was, of course, to be expected from them. But I was genuinely surprised to see that the most influ-ential Harlem newspaper [the *Amsterdam News*] did me the same injustice, despite the fact that its editor was in possession of a letter from me, setting forth the essential facts.[77]

He then explained, "As your correspondent noted, the letter, which was described as 'spicy,' was never addressed to me" and was "merely identified . . . as being in the plaintiff's handwriting." "Unfortunately," he added, "the plain-tiff's lawyers were so completely flabbergasted when it was read that they neglected to ask me the obvious question whether it was sent to me. It was not within my competence to tell what hadn't been asked." The two letters he had presented "as having been addressed to me, were additional proofs that I—not Mrs. Garvey or Mr. Joseph Frazier—was the writer of the book for which for eight months they have been taking the credit."

"The other letter," however, "was a different thing," and the paragraph in the *Amsterdam News* "which said that the letter introduced by the plaintiff declared that a hundred dollars was offered to its writer for his testimony was a malicious falsehood, which I can only account for on the ground that that paper's able court reporter was not on the job and it was induced to take its ver-sion from a fledgling clerk in the office of the plaintiff's counsel." Harrison added that an examination of the *Courier* had "demonstrated again that a news-paper's own reporter, free from both malice and favoritism, is a more depend-able source of news than any other." He predicted that "the maintenance of that policy is bound to yield worth while results in the growing popularity and prestige."[78]

On October 29, Michael Gold, editor of the *New Masses*, a new monthly, wrote to Harrison and told him to "Go ahead and do Vandercook if you can get the book."

The *New Masses,* as its title suggests, was to be modeled after the "old" *Masses,* though in fact it was less open to wide-ranging articles and tended to be closer to the labor policies of the Communist Party. Gold, in his letter, was undoubtedly referring to John W. Vandercook's recently published *Tom-Tom,* a description of life in the interior of Dutch Guiana. Gold also asked Harrison to "please try to get the review of two books I am sending you within ten days if possible."[79]

One of the books that Harrison may have been given to review was *The History of Witchcraft and Demonology,* by Montague Summers. His December 1926 handwritten review argued that Father Summers's book was "bound to damage the prestige of the series of learned works in which it appears." It "lacked the imprimatur of a bishop," and "its seven chapters with their flavor of medieval monasticism might appropriately be labeled 'Essays of Ecclesiastical Psychology.'" Summers spoke "with the pedantic assurance of the priesthood when the priesthood had prestige," and he "airily" preempted "the regions of sociology and psychology as his especial preserve."

Harrison thought "the readers of the *New Masses* should be interested in a concrete application of the principle of economic determinism to academic vagaries of historical interpretation," and this was "the sole excuse for introducing them to Father Summers and his book." Though Summers was "a studious and learned man," his book demonstrated "that learning does not always produce intelligence." Harrison described his "study of the records of witch trials" as one that showed him to be "narrow, dogmatic and bigoted." In contrast to "the large liberalism of [Alfred-Firmin] Loisy, [Hughes-Félicité-Robert de] Lammenais and [Jean-Baptiste-Henri] Lacordaire in the France of the 19th century and of Archbishop [John] Ireland in America," Harrison wondered "what it is that keeps English Catholics so delightfully backward and absurd" and noted that Summers seemed "firmly convinced of the truth of the allegations on which witch-hunts were based."[80]

On Sunday, December 5, Harrison wrote in his diary that his six-year-old son William had assured him "with all the calm seriousness of a sage, that 'this world is only a dream' and the people in it only dream that they are alive and doing things." He had "announced the same thesis on four or five previous occasions, the first being that of the death of Rudolph Valentino, the movie-actor." At that time he asked "whether the people thought that Valentino was really and truly dead." His explanation was "that both V's life and death were only incidents in a dream." Harrison commented, "I wonder!" On Tuesday, December 28, Billy again articulated his "dream theory."[81]

———

Dan Ecker, general secretary of the New York University YMCA, wrote to Harrison on November 24 that he was wanted to come for "Lobby Talks" on

"International Affairs, Politics, etc." and that the course would pay more than Ecker's. If Harrison started with these talks Ecker thought the other associations in the city might engage him. He was writing to a friend in "Church Men's Clubs" in order to secure speaking dates and asked what price Harrison required. In his postscript he added that he was still thinking of the college course of lectures. On December 10 Ecker again wrote to Harrison and enclosed a list of eleven questions sent to him by the previous year's "Y" president, Oliver C. Eckel, of Mt. Vernon. The Mt. Vernon "Y" was having a discussion on the admittance of Negroes to the "Y" for physical privileges, and Ecker asked Harrison to contact Eckel regarding the questions. He also appended the list from the Mt. Vernon "Y" men's meeting of December 18. It asked questions such as "Are Negroes less clean and less sanitary than whites?" "Is it true that Negroes displace whites in whatever neighborhood they enter because they are unclean?" "Does the Negro lack the ambition to work?"[82]

One of the persons impressed by Harrison was Robert Lawrence McKibbin, who wrote to him on December 13: "You have taught me much. One of the lessons I need to learn is true humility and in you I have seen one who truly is humble, and thus great." McKibbin confessed his own weakness—his lack of the courage of his convictions in the face of the world. He explained, "Seated with you where you were known and your accomplishments appreciated, I had pleasure in basking in your reflected glory. But in the open street, where ignorant whites [?] passed, I feared public opinion, and was uneasy. To my shame and sorrow I confess it." He then added that "the great work I hope to do is ever growing clearer in my brain." He suggested that Harrison visit the Rosicrucian Fellowship study center at 321 West 135th Street, where most of the members were "colored." By stopping there Harrison would "find much aid in finding the path, again."[83]

On December 20 Ecker wrote to Harrison that he had "read some startling documents but none so startling as the McKibbin letter." Ecker added that he had spoken to Dean Bouton, of NYU, about Harrison speaking in the university chapel on a day set aside for a secular service and wanted to know if Harrison would accept. Also, Mr. Hungerford, secretary of the NYC Bureau of Information, had asked him to ask Harrison whether he would "go on the air" with a series of topics. He also added, in a possible reference to the Garvey divorce trial, "I do hope your troubles are waning, it seems a shame to have you so worried by such unfortunate events." He concluded, "I thoroly enjoyed 'Side Lights on Negro Soldiers.'"[84]

As the winter of 1926–27 progressed Harrison once again faced a situation of no steady employment as he sought to point the way forward.

19

The *Pittsburgh Courier* and the *Voice of the Negro*
(January–April 1927)

Harrison began 1927 trying to make a living from his writings and lectures. As always, this proved difficult. He also made yet another determined effort to start a monthly publication, the *Voice of the Negro*, which was to serve as an organ for the International Colored Unity League. With Garvey now deported, Harrison attempted to offer some of the political and intellectual leadership he thought was needed.

The January 1927 *West Indian Statesman* contained Harrison's first published article of the year, a review of *Black Haiti*, by Blair Niles (a pseudonym for Mary Blair Rice). He judged it a "glorious book" that would "live to become a classic" and do for the Black republic what "on a grander scale" Mary Kingsley "did for black West Africa." Ms. Niles's "seeing eye" and "understanding mind" combined "to produce a work of conspicuous merit," and its fifteen chapters of sketches, impressions, description, history, biography, and travel resulted in fine "literature."[1]

Niles's opening chapter demonstrated how "Haytians 'spoof' white visitors" who come with "the fixed notion that the people are cannibals and savages." While many Haitians practice Voodoo and Obeah, Harrison pointed out that this was largely "restricted to the peasantry of the interior" and that these superstitions were matched in the United States by those featuring "new Messiahs," "spiritualist seances," and cults fearing the number thirteen. There was much more to Haiti than Voodoo, however, and in Port au Prince, Gonaives, and other large cities there flourished "an educated, refined and well-bred Hayti, conversant with a culture, social and intellectual, far in advance of that of Negro

America." It included "outstanding poets" like Oswald Durand, "historians and scholars like [Thomas] Madiou [Fils] and the Baron [Pompée Valentin] de Vastey of the past, and Leger [Jacques Nicolas Léger] and [Dr. J. C.] Dorsainvil of the present." Niles depicted both "Haytis with a sympathetic understanding marvelous in an outsider" and with a deftness that seemed casual.[2]

Harrison considered Niles particularly adept at unfolding "the long panorama" of Haitian history. Her story was replete with discussion of "Toussaint [L'Ouverture], [Henri] Christophe, [Jean-Jacques] Dessalines," and others, and she explained that "to the Haytians" their heroes are not stuffed figures "but men—Africans of extraordinary personality." In this way Niles makes history "live again." Finally, Harrison was impressed by Niles's objectivity, feeling, and wisdom. Her treatment of the decade-old American occupation of Haiti was "neither partisan nor opponent." Her feeling was evidenced in "enthusiastic sketches of the Haytian peasant women in their regal independence," in "the pathos and poignancy" used to describe the last phases of L'Ouverture's life, and in "the genial humanism with which she treats [Oswald] Durand." Her "warm wisdom" periodically "flashes out to thrill and illuminate, as when she compares white France with Black Hayti and says that, 'In the bringing together of these two elements each has intensified the racial quality of the other . . . the mingling of France with Africa was like giving to Africa a drink of champagne; with the result that the personality of Hayti is singularly vital.'" She contrasts this with the United States, where she feels "the Anglo-Saxon influence to some extent denatured the African," and with the Spanish-American countries, where "a certain austerity in the conquerors subdues the Negro."[3]

While the Niles review was circulating, Harrison booked several "Y" talks. On January 2, 1927, Oliver C. Eckel, of the Mt. Vernon "Y" Men's Club, wrote to him expressing concern on learning that he had been ill and indicating that members of his men's club were eager to hear Harrison speak again, possibly on January 22. He also sent a list of questions about popular misconceptions drawn from the groups' previous discussion (the same list that Dan Ecker, general secretary of the NYU YMCA, had previously sent). On January 11, Eckel wrote and asked if Harrison would speak on "The Negro Problem," a proposal that fit well with Harrison's schedule: he had completed a typed, twenty-two-page version of "The Real Negro Problem," which was essentially the same as his *Modern Quarterly* piece and was probably used for his lecture.[4]

Charles Brook, secretary for religious education of the Central Branch of the Brooklyn and Queens YMCA, wrote to Harrison on January 14 that Arthur L. Comither, executive secretary of the Carlton Avenue (Brooklyn) Y, and Dan Ecker, of the NYU Y, wanted to meet him and discuss having him lecture at their evening forums for $15 per lecture. Harrison was also invited by the YMCA and YWCA to spend "Negro History Week" in Lynchburg, Virginia. Ecker proposed that he lecture on "Race History" to an interracial committee and to college students of both sexes and races and that he discuss "The Negro and History" with social workers, society folk, and "cultured colored people of both sexes." Such activities, before racially mixed audiences in Lynchburg, were a bold step for the Y.[5]

Harrison accepted the Virginia offer and spoke before packed houses at Lynchburg's largest African American church on "The Black Man in History and Civilization"; at the recently opened, racially segregated Dunbar High School (where the poet Anne Spencer worked as librarian) on "The Inner Light"; and at the Baptist Seminary and College, to Black students and townspeople on "Who's Who in Humanity; or, The Racial Inferiority Argument in the Light of Science and Humanity." His lectures were reportedly well received, and J. T. Harris, executive secretary of the YMCA, wrote that they "excited an interest in the history of our Race," which would "be sure to have a most wholesome reaction." Harrison, in turn, declared that "the Colored people of Lynchburg, Va., are not only the most hospitable in the South, they are the most fortunately placed in relation to the whites, who treat them for the most part like people, rather than like Colored people." In Lynchburg, "both colored and white" were "exceptionally friendly and hospitable," and with such an attitude "spreading throughout the South," Harrison saw "a bright era ahead for all." He planned to return in April.[6]

———

When Harrison arrived back in New York he lectured at two "white institutions": the Bronx Union YMCA, where he led a weekly discussion group; and the Central Y of Brooklyn, "the largest white Y.M.C.A. in the world," where he spoke before "an exceptional crowd in size and interest." The secretary from the Bronx Union described his lecture as "an education in itself." The March 22 Y talk on "Culture and Civilization" was part of a series of lectures "on subjects other than race" that Harrison planned. At the end of that talk he was asked, "Doctor, where did you get your education?" He reportedly tapped his forehead as he descended from the platform and answered wearily, "'Right here, gentlemen, right here.'" He later explained that to him it was "the POSSESSION of knowledge that counts rather than the PLACE where the knowledge was acquired."[7]

Arthur L. Comither wrote to Harrison on March 11 that he "enjoyed" his address and that "many Caucasian hearers marveled at your encyclopedic mind, your ability to digress and return and reingorve [reinvigor] each idea in a way all your own must have given them a new slant on the ability of men of our group." Comither also thought Harrison's "answers to questions were superb, especially the one on 'Intermarriage.'" When leaving, he spoke with three men who wanted to know if he would do a return engagement. Comither felt "the meeting did much for bringing a better relation between the two groups" and asked for a copy of the *Embryo of the Voice of the Negro*, Harrison's new publication, which was passed out at the meeting.[8]

In those first few months of 1927 Harrison also spoke at a lyceum in Harlem, at the Sunrise Club, at a birthday dinner on Lenox Hill, at a gentleman's club on Long Island, at a New York institution of learning, and at a community church forum in Bay Shore, Long Island. In addition, he delivered lectures on Saturday nights at the 135th Street Library on "China," "Mexico," "Garveyism," "Dunbar," "Radicals," "Superiority," "The Virgin Islands," "Booker Washington," and "Contemporary Negro Authors." Audiences regularly packed the auditorium and "banded themselves into an organization responsible for the [new] publication" (the *Voice of the Negro*) and for the new forum of the International Colored Unity League. The new forum was taken over from the Board of Education, "at the suggestion of the local Librarian," when the board's "cutting off of its funds forced it to surrender more than nine-tenths of its lecture forums."[9]

Two additional places where Harrison spoke during this period were at Jewish men's clubs. On March 15, the attorney Arthur Hutter, writing on behalf of the Men's Club of Temple Israel of Far Rockaway, suggested that of three possible Harrison lecture topics, "Do We Need a Censorship" would prove most interesting. The club wanted Harrison to speak on April 4. Because it would be their first meeting of this kind, he asked him to "please send a few of the matters you plan to discuss" so the group could be "prepared to express their opinions pro or con in advance." He added, "Many are not accustomed to an open forum." Harrison's second talk on the related theme of "Should We Have Censorship?" was at the Jewish Men's Club of Temple Israel, in Lawrence, Long Island. He was received "enthusiastically," and the talk so impressed Joseph Zanda, the director of the club, that he sent Harrison an inscribed copy of *The Holy Scriptures* in "appreciation of an interesting and instructive evening." Later in the year Hutter would write to Harrison again, asking him to speak in Far Rockaway on December 5 on "Companionate Marriage."[10]

On Saturday morning, January 29, at about 4 a.m., Harrison recorded in his diary how he just returned from a party at Bob Douglas's place at 135 West 138th Street. The St. Kitts–born Douglas coached the Harlem "Rens" (the "New York Renaissance Big Five" basketball team), was a staunch supporter of progressive causes, and was a very popular figure in the Harlem community. Douglas and Mel Charlton (Hubert's long-time friend) had gone to Harrison's apartment after 10 p.m. on Friday to get him for a party at Bob's. While there, Douglas looked over Harrison's books and especially admired William Winter's *Life of David Belasco*, in which was pasted an inscribed note from Belasco to Harrison dated April 2, 1926. While Douglas went to get other people for the party, Charlton and Harrison went down Seventh Avenue to Gall Hutchinson's booze shop for a pint of whiskey, then to Nan Davis's hairdressing parlor to see Nan, and then to Douglas's house, where they had a "glorious time." Hubert met some old friends, including Mrs. Pearl Hankinson, Abbie Mitchell and her husband, the singer Alexander Gatewood, Hall Johnson, Bob Douglas's "sister," and "young Professor X and his 'boy-friend.'" He also "Danced attendance on Mrs. Sadie Brooks Humphries . . . fat, beautiful & brown," and met the attorney William McBurney, Mrs. Rose Williams (an actress), and Miss Bullard, who was "ravishingly gowned and very beautiful, [and] a teacher in P.S. 136." At the party "there was no drunkenness, nor any approach thereto," but everyone had "one high old time."[11]

On February 28 Harrison attended a testimonial banquet in honor of the Rev. John Wesley Johnson BD, given by Mr. and Mrs. Isaac Newton Brathwaite at St. Cyprian's Church, 169–175 West Sixty-Third Street. The activity was sponsored by the Sons and Daughters of Barbados. Clarence Crichlow (of the Crichlow-Brathwaite Shorthand School) was secretary of the organization, and the mortician H. Adolph Howell the honorary chairman of the charity fund committee. "Dr." Harrison, whose mother was from Barbados, was an honored guest, along with the Rev. James W. Brown DD, of Mother Zion AME Church, and Mr. Fred R. Moore, publisher of the *New York Age*.[12]

During 1927 Harrison had a number of important articles and reviews published in the *Pittsburgh Courier*. The *Courier*, under the editorship of Robert L. Vann, was probably the most widely read Black newspaper in America, and it provided an opportunity for Harrison to express his views and receive remuneration for his work.[13]

In "Du Bois a West Indian: . . . Prejudice Growing Less and Co-Operation More," in the January 29 issue, Harrison offered a brief and insightful overview of aspects of West Indian immigration. He pointed out that "the mingling of West Indian with American Negro has been highly beneficial to Harlem—and to America at large" and offered an explanation as to why West Indian immigrants were becoming Americanized and naturalized "despite the Garvey movement."[14]

Harrison began by emphasizing that "the destinies of the Negro-American and the Negro West Indians have been tangled and twisted together from the very beginning in this Western world." Examples he cited included Columbus's travel in the West Indies long before "anybody discovered America"; African slaves being imported into the West Indian islands, from which the practice spread to the colonies on the mainland; the fact that "the West Indies Negro" was "an earlier product of Christian civilization than the American Negro"; and the steady flow of contact back and forth including the "black Santo Domingo regiment" that saved "the white American patriots at the siege of Savannah in our Revolutionary War" and "the hundreds of black American colonists who have settled in Hayti and elsewhere, and have been absorbed into the general West Indian population." He also described how individual West Indians "often played a great part in the drama of Negro development here in America." Examples included the Jamaica-born John Brown Russwurm, editor of *Freedom's Journal*, "the first Negro newspaper" in America; Alexander Hamilton, "who 'passed for white' successfully after coming to America [from St. Croix] and became one of the Fathers of the country"; Denmark Vesey, "a Danish West Indian Negro who, although a freeman and property holder, risked and lost freedom, property and his life itself in a slave rebellion which he had organized in Charleston, S.C., in 1822"; and, "more recently," "at least one President of the United States" in whom "West Indian Negro blood has flowed."[15]

On the specifics of the migration, Harrison noted that of the forty thousand West Indians in the United States 70 percent were in New York City, and that concentration "resulted in intensifying the strains and problems of adjustment." He detailed a history of West Indies–born/U.S.-born relations, which "changed and developed with the kinds and quantity of social control and effective cooperation":

In the first period of West Indian immigration, when those who came here were mainly students and scholars seeking wider fields of usefulness, the Negroes of America drew from these some of their first and most favorable estimates of West Indian character, it was taken for granted that every West Indian immigrant was a paragon of intelligence and a man of birth and breeding. Then came the slump in West Indian sugar, caused by German and American competition and the impoverished islands began to decant upon the mainland their working population, laborers, mechanics, peasants, ambitious enough to be discontented with conditions at home and eager to improve their lot by seeking success in the land of Uncle Sam. At first they furnished the elevator operators, bellboys and porters, maids and washerwomen of upper Manhattan almost exclusively, with a few tradesmen and skilled workers thrusting themselves forward into better positions and breaking the trail for the Negro-Americans to follow. But during the last two decades they have won their way in New York as business men, lawyers, doctors, school teachers, musicians and journalists.[16]

He called attention to "the only Negro patron of art and letters in New York," his friend Casper Holstein, "a Negro from [St. Croix in] the Virgin Islands," and pointed out

> the significant fact that almost every important development originating in Negro Harlem—from the Negro Manhood Movement to political representation in public office, from collecting Negro books to speaking on the streets, from demanding Federal control over lynching to agitation for Negroes on the police force—every one of these has either been fathered by West Indians or can count them among its originators.[17]

"Of course," added Harrison, it had "not always been easy sledding for the West Indian." There had been "some prejudice," but it was "worn so thin by 1917 that in the political campaign of that year West Indian and American Negroes were pulling together like two horses in a team, working for the election of James C. Thomas, Jr., to the Aldermanic Board and for the principals [sic] of elective representation which has since been accepted by all political parties in Negro Harlem." He stressed that

> it was the Liberty League under whose banner the West Indian and American Negroes first cooperated on anything like a large scale; although in St. Mark's and St. Benedict's lyceums in West 53rd street they effected literary combination some years before and in the Equity Congress such stalwarts as Captain Blount, Prof. [David E.] Tobias and Louis Leavelle could always count upon their support in that great movement which gave birth to the "Fighting Fifteenth" [which became known as the "Harlem Hellfighters" during World War I].[18]

It was Harrison's "firm belief that, between the ordinary Negro American who lives by working and the ordinary West Indian in America there is not the least prejudice in the world." The reason was that "the working Negro American" lives by "work from the white man" and figures "the white man has work enough for both." To "the Negro American who lives on prestige," however, it was "a matter of life and death that the Negro masses should look up to him with reverence for the superiority vested in him by virtue of something called 'education.'" When this person met a similarly situated West Indian, it was often someone furnished "with a more thorough and competent intellectual equipment than race-prejudiced America has given to the Negro-American." Under such conditions Harrison felt that prejudices took shape, but "these prejudices seem[ed] restricted to the intelligentsia on both sides." He was speaking "of course, of the men," since "the cause of the West Indian woman" was one he would "not touch upon just now."[19]

West Indian men, however, were "marrying Negro-American women in ever-increasing numbers and rearing children who are American Negroes." These children were "indistinguishable from other Negro-Americans," and Harrison cited as "well-known Negro-Americans of West Indian ancestry" Du Bois, Charles W. Anderson, George E. Wibecan (the past grand trustee and past grand exalted ruler of the Elks), and the poet William Stanley Braithwaite. In contrast to "general belief," he added, British West Indians were "becoming naturalized Negro Americans at a fairly rapid rate," and "whether naturalized or not" they were becoming "Americanized—even despite the Garvey movement." They were exchanging cultural gifts with Negro America, and, Harrison felt, "if the West Indian brings to the market a certain outspoken and downright courage, he gains there a certain flexibility and tact which is necessary both for survival and success in the American atmosphere." He predicted: "When the years bring their harvest it will be found that the mingling of West Indian with American Negro has been highly beneficial to Harlem—and to America at large."[20]

A *Pittsburgh Courier* editorial the following week on "The International New York Negro" commented on Harrison's article and called attention to "the unusual composition of the Negro population in New York City," where "two-thirds" of the "foreign-born Negro population" of the United States lived. It noted that when they were "thrown in contact with the native-born citizens of their own color," a friction, attributable to "lack of understanding," was "bound to arise." Nevertheless, the *Courier* felt "cordial relations" currently existed and that differences were being ironed out by "time" and by "the outside forces to which both foreign and native Negroes are subjected." The "West Indian-South American Negroes" had come "to appreciate the difficulties that have confronted the Aframericans and the tact with which they have met them," and the American Negroes had "learned to value the spirit and contributions of their foreign brethren."[21]

In the February 12 *Pittsburgh Courier* book review "Dr." Harrison reviewed *The Negro in American Life*, by Jerome Dowd, which he had reviewed previously in *Opportunity* in October 1926. In January he had submitted two reviews, including a review of Dowd's book, to the *New Masses*. Its editor, Egmont Arens, wrote back to him that they had "delayed decision" on his reviews "to give the various editors opportunity to pass on them." He told Harrison they felt he was "meeting Professor Dowd's prejudice with a prejudice" of his own and that the "review would gain in strength if that were not so patent."[22]

In his *Courier* review Harrison described Dowd as "a scholarly writer on sociological subjects" who belonged "to that small but increasing group of white
men who, because of the dearth of scholarship among Negro-Americans," were
"getting themselves accepted as primary authorities on the more scientific
aspects of Negro history, life and thought." He noted that Dowd had already
written "two worthwhile volumes on 'The Negro Races' (of Africa)" and "constructed a striking picture of African life and customs, from scores of books
written exclusively by whites." In "dealing with the Negro nearer home," however, Dowd, "using a zoning system of his own," denied much "which he had
previously conceded" to Africans, "whose civilization he [had] declared to be
the equal, and in many respects the superior, of any way of life that is to be found
anywhere in the world."[23]

Overall, Harrison considered the book "a solid and meaty volume, full of facts
gleaned from a variety of sources" as well as "prejudices stubborn and ineradi-
cable, native to the author's mind." He knew "of no single volume written by a
white American which furnished such a comprehensive conspectus of the facts
of race-relationship in present day America," though "the author's outlook,
interpretations and conclusions" were "so widely at variance not only with the
facts but with the elementary principles of logic" that one was "moved to wonder what might be the nature of the psychic instrument with which white authors
in America do their thinking on the subject of the Negro."[24]

As an example of Dowd's "irrationalities" Harrison cited his statement that
he could "'find no ground' for believing that the Caucasian and the Negro will
ever amalgamate when they co-exist in large numbers." Dowd said this, wrote
Harrison, despite the fact that "by 1910 the number of mulattos in the United
States had risen to more than two millions." This absolutely demonstrated to
Harrison "that the men of the white race exhibit no repugnance to the most
intimate kind of intermingling with the women of the Negro race." In a second
example, Dowd wrote that "among the human races," as "among animals in general," the "pairing of the sexes is governed by consciousness of kind which
insures the blending of nearly related types only." Harrison, wondered where
mulattoes fit with this "'consciousness of kind.'" In a third example, Dowd wrote
that "civil equality or any other kind of equality between races as unlike as the
white and black, and mingled as they are in the same territory," was "a dream
which can never be realized." Though he made this statement, Dowd also called
"white supremacy" a "relic of barbarism which should be eliminated by the
progress of civilization." To Harrison, "hash-house thinking of this sort" made
people "realize the truth of the statement that HOMO SAP, doesn't need the
two extra syllables to serve him as a description."[25]

In his concluding remarks, Harrison stated that Dowd "was born, and bred
a southerner," and it was apparent that he was "still unable to transcend the

bias of his training—when he deals with the American Negro." His bias "determines his selection of materials in many instances," including his decision to quote General Robert Lee Bullard "on the Negro's war record" and to entirely ignore Charles H. Williams's *Sidelights on Negro Soldiers* and Kathryn M. Johnson and Addie W. Hunton's *Two Colored Women with the A.E.F.* These books, "with their poignant presentation of facts," disclosed "the organized race-prejudice of Bullard and other army officials against Negro soldiers in France." Nevertheless, if the reader eschewed Dowd's opinions and "follow[ed] the facts alone," *The Negro in American Life* offered "a serviceable organization of its subject matter."[26]

Harrison's review of *In Barbary*, by Colonel E. Alexander Powell, also appeared in the February 12 *Courier*. He described Powell, a traveler and author of perhaps half a dozen books, as one who "validates European imperialism in the out-of-the-way places of the earth." This particular volume offered both "a record of travel and a mine of historical, social and archaeologic information about Morocco, Algeria, Tunis and Tripoli." Though Powell's "memory slips" and "sometimes his defense of French imperialism and its methods savor too much of the inspired propaganda," Harrison found the book to be "of surprising merit as a living, moving picture of North Africa and its peoples." It was well written and contained "facts enough to satisfy the thirst of the average American for knowledge about sheik land" that was "more dependable than that furnished by the movies." This last comment likely referred to popular movies like those of the matinee idol Rudolph Valentino, who starred in *The Sheik* (1921) and *The Son of the Sheik* (1926).[27]

The *Pittsburgh Courier* of March 12 contained the thought-provoking Harrison article "No Negro Literary Renaissance," which the editor quickly pointed out did not necessarily reflect the *Courier's* views. The paper was "simply trying to arouse helpful and constructive discussion, out of which may grow a practical and sound program for our younger writers." It gave assurance that "equal space" would be given "to any literary critic qualified to reply to this article."[28]

Harrison began "No Negro Literary Renaissance" by poking fun at those "'genuinely interested' in the Negro," the "intelligentsia (the 'g' is hard as in 'get')," and the "'new' Negroes." He wondered if they knew who wrote such works of fiction as "*The American Cavalryman* [Henry F. Downing], *The Leopard's Claw* [George W. Ellis], *Veiled Aristocrats* [Gertrude Sanborn], or *The Vengeance of the Gods* [William Pickens]." While he assumed they had read *Nigger Heaven*, he wondered if they had read *Veiled Aristocrats*, "wherein a white author does try to hold your race up." He chided those who might not know Alrutheus Ambush Taylor, "that fine sonnet on 'The Mulatto,'" William H. Ferris's book

Sidelights on Negro Soldiers, Two Colored Women With the A.E.F., or "that immortal poem by the Baltimore poet entitled 'Lenox Avenue.'" If they weren't familiar with these, then Harrison asked, "what do you mean when you talk about a Negro literary renaissance?"[29]

Harrison took the position that

> the matter of a Negro literary renaissance is like that of the snakes of Ireland—there isn't any. Those who think that there is are usually people who are blissfully ignorant of the stream of literary and artistic products which have flowed uninterruptedly from Negro writers from 1850 to the present. If you ask them about the historical works of Major Wilson, George [Washington] Williams, William C. Neill, William Wells Brown, Rufus L. Perry, Atticus G. Haygood; the essays of T. Thomas Fortune, the fictional writings of Negroes from Frances E. Watkins [Harper] to Pauline Hopkins, [Paul Laurence] Dunbar and [Charles Waddell] Chesnutt, they stammer and evade to cover up their confusion.[30]

He wasn't just speaking of "casual colored people." A prime example was W. E. B. Du Bois, who, in 1905, while a professor at Atlanta University, "was hailed by black and white people as pre-eminently the 'scholar' of the race." That year he published under the auspices of Atlanta University *A Select Bibliography of the Negro American*, which was meant to be authoritative yet did not mention Charles W. Chesnutt, "the greatest Negro-American novelist." Chesnutt had already published *The Conjure Woman, The Wife of His Youth, The House Behind the Cedars*, and *The Marrow of Tradition*.[31]

To Harrison this was "nothing unusual for Mr. Du Bois." In the February 1927 *Crisis* Du Bois listed in "The Looking Glass" an "unusual article by a black West Indian author [Harrison] in a white magazine called *The Modern Quarterly*—but he studiously refrains from mentioning the writer's name, although it was and is perfectly well known to him." Harrison charged that Du Bois recently did "something similar" to George Schuyler and the "significant thing" was that this was "not peculiar to Mr. Du Bois" but was "a common trait of all our 'guardians of the gate'" who "blissfully wait until some white person stumbles on him (as was the case with Dunbar, William Lonsdale Brown, Charles Gilpin and Countée Cullen) before they venture to acknowledge him." This practice led "each such casual discoverer" to think "that the stream of Negro literary production bubbled up at the precise point that he discovered it."[32]

Harrison predicted that "so long as through the . . . narrowness . . . of such people the white man (who doesn't know our literary history) remains our only vendor of values in Negro writings, so long will we be cursed with jejune Jazz artists who must have managed to hop over both [Robert] Burns and Dunbar in their wild gyrations." He went on: "If the hysteria of the uneducated kiddies with which we are being deluged at this time is poetry, then the writings of [John] Milton, [John] Keats, [James Russell] Lowell, Dunbar, [Walter Everette] Hawkins and Claude McKay must be something else."[33]

Harrison next noted that, as he prepared his article, he had learned that "one of these kiddies who has perpetrated two books of alleged 'poems' is engaged in studying at school, for the first time, Milton's *Paradise Lost*." This was a reference to Langston Hughes, and Harrison asked: how "can we get literature from those who haven't lived, who haven't even read?" He said that "Chicago, Pittsburgh and even Charleston have begun to sneer at" the Van Vechten matter and then put forth the view that

> the Negro has something to give to American literature; but that something will follow the line of *The Chipwoman's Fortune* rather than those of *Salome* or *Lulu Belle*. In scholarship it will build on [Benjamin G.] Brawley, [Alrutheus Ambush] Taylor, [William A.] Sinclair, [John Wesley] Cromwell and [Carter G.] Woodson—that is, something more solid than the mere knowledge of their names! It will see in McKay and [Lucian B.] Watkins the only capable poets of our race today—as Dunbar was two decades ago—and will recognize in Countée Cullen (who is NOT a minister's son!) the one youngster marked out by Nature for a poet, with a fine development ahead of him rather than adequate achievement behind him. It will discover the virile short stories of William Pickens and the reason why no white critic praises them. It will pounce on the early work of Kelly Miller and Du Bois (before the one began to talk twaddle in print and the other to imitate himself, like an ancient but animated dowager). But in that day the Negro writer will be going for his authority on race-values, not to Mr. [Edward Byron] Reuter (who lists Kelly Miller as a mulatto!) nor to Mr. [Melville J.] Herskovits (who in a review of [Percy Amaury] Talbot's recent work on Nigeria shows a woeful ignorance of that author's earlier studies), but to the place where he should go—to the broad bosom of his own people.[34]

John P. Davis, a Harvard Law School student, accepted the *Courier*'s invitation and replied to Harrison in the issue of April 2. He opened with the observation that the *Courier*'s disclaimer had saved the paper but had "not saved the author, Doctor (of what?) Hubert H. Harrison" from "the serious charge of charlatanism." In sum, after pointed personal attacks, Davis suggested that Harrison's "best interests were served if he were to stick to street-corners and soap boxes and teaching economics to white people rather than do the difficult thing of posing as a literary critic."[35]

In addition to Davis's public criticism, Du Bois was working behind the scenes. On June 6, 1927, he wrote to E. Franklin Frazier,

for some time I have been wanting to get some information from you, but I keep forgetting it. Hubert H. Harrison, Harlem demagogue, has been claiming for some years past that he has a Doctorate in Philosophy from the University of Copenhagen. He is a man in his early 40's and was born in the Virgin Islands. I want to find out if his claim is true. I am particularly sure it is not, but how can I ascertain the facts?[36]

Frazier responded on June 8 that he had heard that Harrison "claimed to have received a Doctorate of Philosophy from the University of Copenhagen." However, "During the few times I have been in his presence he has carefully avoided talking about the matter." Frazier offered to write to Professor Jens Waring, at the University of Copenhagen, or indicated that Du Bois might want to do so. Frazier added, "I think that I recall Professor [Harold M.?] Westergaard saying that no Negro had received his doctorate from the University."[37]

Olaf Waage, a secretary, on behalf of D. Warming, wrote to Du Bois on July 12 that there was no indication that anyone by the name of Hubert Harrison received a doctorate from or matriculated at the University of Copenhagen since 1901, although any statement about the doctorate and/or attendance could not be made with "complete certainty."[38]

———

It does not appear that Harrison ever responded to Davis's article or knew of Du Bois's investigation. By the time Davis's article appeared Harrison was fully involved in his main political and literary efforts of 1927: the development of the International Colored Unity League and its organ, the *Voice of the Negro*. An inaugural, four-page publication, the *Embryo of the Voice of the Negro*, appeared in February, and it was "attended to" by Harrison at 513 Lenox Avenue. Distribution centered in New York, though there was an exchange list, which was probably used by both the *Embryo* and the subsequent *Voice of the Negro* and included fifty papers, of which thirteen were foreign and the rest spread out across the United States.[39]

Harrison explained that the four-page paper was "an Embryo," something "not yet big enough to be born," but that the four-page midget would grow into the *Voice of the Negro*. Behind the *Embryo* was a group of people who met at the public library every Saturday night and also met two Sundays a month at the Coachmen's Union Hall at 252 West 138th Street. These were "just ordinary people, the kind from whom came [Paul Laurence] Dunbar, [Frederick] Douglass, [Booker T.] Washington and Roland Hayes." They were trying to

Figure 19.1. The Embryo of the Voice of the Negro 1, no. 1 (February 1927), front cover. This issue of the organ of the International Colored Unity League, edited by Hubert H. Harrison, provides a brief history of the Harlem People's Forum since 1916, discusses the need for such a magazine, and offers some insights "On Reading Negro Books." *Source:* Hubert H. Harrison Papers, Box 17, Folder 10, Rare Book and Manuscript Library, Columbia University Library.

raise a thousand dollars to start the *Voice of the Negro* magazine, which would be "the Mouthpiece" of "a Movement toward Race Pride, Aspiration, Achievement and Co-Operation, in Harlem and elsewhere."[40]

The magazine, which was scheduled to begin at twelve pages and grow into thirty-two in three months, would include the principles of the ICUL. It would also discuss new matters, including plans for an "independent inquiry into the Virgin Islands situation" and a subsequent meeting between the Virgin Island Congressional Council's officers and the leaders in the islands, which was intended "to show up the rotten hypocrisy with which white politicians are fooling our people." Harrison urged people who wanted to support the *Embryo* to send a donation or bring it on a Saturday night. The names of contributors—"Those Who Put Their Racial Faith Into Deeds"—would be listed.[41]

On the front page of the *Embryo* Harrison explained that the paper wasn't an "'exclusive' family organ of a bunch of back-scratching aristocrats," "a poorly-paid echo of white people of means," or "a red-eyed radical pendant to the poor whites' labor-movement." It would not be "fourteen months late in finding out that a great Negro has passed away" and wouldn't "'kid' the Negro race into believing that when the 'Little Boys' (and girls) Brigade, shake their rattles, we are producing 'Negro Literature.'" It would, however, critically discover "a budding Chas. Gilpin, Claude McKay or Florence Mills BEFORE white people pass the news to it." It would "give THE GREAT TOILING MASSES a chance to understand what LIFE means" and "steer clear of Petty Spite and Narrow Prejudice and leave a thrill of Inspiration in the soul of every reader—every month." It also would "speak with the authority of knowledge about what's going on in Africa, India, China, Mexico, Nicaragua, Hayti, the Virgin Islands, and wherever people of color are striving and doing things." Finally, it would "nail the flag of RACIAL SELF-ASSERTION RACE PRIDE and AMBITION to its masthead."[42]

A second front-page article described the Harlem People's Forum, originally organized in 1916 by Harrison, as "Harlem's First and Foremost Forum." At the time it was founded Harlem Blacks "gathered to discuss only two topics: Religion and politics," but this forum "not only discussed sociology, economics, the drama, literature, history and science—it preached the propaganda of RACE when no one else had courage or initiative enough to do so." It was "the earliest promoter of the study of Negro history in Harlem and many hundreds and thousands of Harlemites drew their earliest inspiration from it." It had gone through "many ups and downs," but Harrison's faith and persistence remained undaunted, and the forum was now bringing out the *Embryo*. Both the forum and the *Voice of the Negro* were "Organs of A MOVEMENT" that aimed to "shake Jim-Crow, Lynching and Disfranchisement to their very foundations and rally the Hearts of Twelve Million Negroes" who were "longing for Light and Leading."[43]

In the *Embryo* Harrison prepared a special article on the ICUL. He began with his often-used explanation that "a race problem is the sum of the differences between two or more races in a state of friction" and that its solution "must be worked out or fought out by forces more complex than those of mere logic and argument." In light of this he judged that "the Negro problem in America" was "not insoluble: no human social problem ever was." The task was "grim but hopeful," and while the problem was "primarily of the white man's making," it was "the colored man [who] must do most of that work." This wasn't necessarily fair, but the "Negro" was "mainly concerned," since it involved "his health, education, morals, progress" and "very existence." The way to proceed was first "by organizing," which involved a cohesion and solidarity whose great binding force was "LOVE: love of race, love for one another, a blood-is-thicker-than-water policy, racial support and self-support, racial respect and self respect." Every lynching-bee and Jim Crow car taught the need to "stand by each other; one for all and all for one, in matters of money, mind, politics and religion," in order "to survive and succeed." Harrison emphasized that "we must organize to do work . . . where we are"—"in Boston or Bridgetown, Jamaica or Georgia," and "the old advice [made popular by Booker T. Washington in his September 18, 1895 'Atlanta Compromise' address] is still valuable: 'Cast down your buckets where you are!'"[44]

Harrison also explained that "the new nationwide organization," the ICUL, had sprung up to address the race problem, and an important part of "the program of this New Negro organization or race-loving men and women" was

> to stop Negroes from hating one another and Negro leaders from attacking each other; to mobilize all that energy against lynching, disfranchisement and Jim Crow; to use the ballot of the Northern Negro to secure such enforcement of the Constitution as will put the ballot into the hands of the Southern Negro, by which means-to-power he will be able to safeguard his own life, property and the future of his children; to encourage our people to buy, to own and to use property in town and country, building up by cooperative action such economic structures as will enable them to stand on their own legs and keep the dollars of the race; to co-operate with the Negro church, lodge and other organizations that are already doing good work and to help them to do better.[45]

As with all of Harrison's publications, there was a "Poems for the People" section, which included a poem entitled "The Negro" and a poem by Andy Razaf entitled "A New Year's Prayer," which hoped for a nobler, cleaner press that would speak the truth.[46] The *Embryo* also listed Harrison's upcoming special lecture, "What Good Is the West Indian?" at the Coachmen's Union Hall, on Sunday, March 13, at 2:45 p.m. In addition it offered a schedule for his upcoming 8:15 p.m. Saturday lectures for the ICUL's Educational Forum at the 135th Street Library: "Garveyism Versus Americanism: Has the Negro Any Future in America?" (February 26), "Are White Radicals Sincere?" (March 5),

"A Night with Paul Laurence Dunbar" (March 12), and "Is the Negro the Superior Race?—The Testimony of Science and History" (March 19).[47]

In "The World in Embryo" Harrison offered comments on international events. He suggested that the Chinese had learned "from the Christian Powers of Europe" a very significant lesson: "that the only sure way to get a square deal from them is to act the very opposite of Christian." He noted that the Rif (guerilla) leader Abd-El-Krim was safe on the island of Réunion (where he had been exiled to by the French) and that, though neither France nor Spain was "having easy sledding in Morocco," the League of Nations had "never once opened its mouth in condemnation of this piece of public piracy that smells to all the world." In terms of the Virgin Islanders, Harrison offered his sympathies, for they were "still under the heel of the Navy" and "victims of cheap politics and bunco-steering politicians in Congress." As regards "the natives of the Dutch East Indies," they were "raising Cain," and Dutch soldiers and marines were being rushed there while "perspiring publicists" blamed it on "our whiskered friend Bolshevism from Russia," not believing that "Dark people . . . [could] want to rule themselves and run out their foreign rulers."[48]

In "Facts and Comments" Harrison discussed domestic matters. He commented that the "COLORED INTELLIGENTSIA and GUARDIANS OF THE GATE" were not "brainy enough to discover that *Turbott Wolfe* by William Plomer is as deadly a piece of propaganda against Negroes as is *Nigger Heaven*," with the only difference being that Plomer's book was "really good art at the same time." He also commented on a caption of a picture in Du Bois's *Crisis* that seemingly moved Nigeria hundreds of miles and placed it on the Gold Coast of Africa. Finally, he mentioned that "Brother Van Vechten" had "turned down his little play-fellows of the *Crisis* and declared that *Opportunity* is the one and only greatest Negro Magazine." Harrison suggested that this might be related to the fact that "it was in *Opportunity* that brother [James Weldon] Johnson boosted the sale of brother Van Vechten's dirty book."[49]

The *Embryo* contained two Harrison reprints from 1924 *Boston Chronicle* articles. On the front page was "On Reading Negro Books," and on the second page was his "Lincoln and Douglass."[50] In the *Embryo* Harrison offered "Things Worth Remembering" and "Books You Will Like to Know." In the first section he mentioned Edgar Grey's "Racial Self Contempt" in the February 16 *Amsterdam News*, William M. Kelly "spanking" Langston Hughes in the February 9 *Amsterdam News*, Harrison's public library lecture on "Lincoln and Liberty: Fact Versus Fiction," and Lucien White's "remarkable editorial" in the February 5 *New York Age* on "Thomas Paine for Abolition." Among the books worth knowing were *Black Haiti*, by Blair Niles; *Tom-Tom*, by John Vandercock; *The Negro in American Life*, by Willis J. King; and *Digging for Lost African Gods*, by Count de Prorok.[51]

The *Embryo* also reprinted an article from the *Amsterdam News* of February 14 on Harrison's Saturday night forum at the 135th Street Library, in which he "declared that during the Civil War it was not the nation that saved the Negro, but the Negro that saved the nation." In it he drew on his numerous previous talks and articles that discussed Lincoln and key statements he had made, Frederick Douglass, the Thirteenth Amendment, and related topics, and he again emphasized that Douglass "meant more to Negroes than Lincoln" and that future generations would recognize that fact.[52]

In the February *Embryo of the Voice of the Negro* Harrison reprinted "Population, Immigration and the Negro," which he had published in the April 19, 1924, *Boston Chronicle*.[53] A final article in the *Embryo* was a brief piece on "Harlem's Liberal Church." For readers who had "intellectually and ethically outgrown the fundamental doctrines of orthodox churches" but still believed "in the religious value of a modern liberal church," there was an option. They could attend Rev. Ethelred Brown's Harlem Community Church at 149 West 136th Street.[54]

On Friday, March 25, at 9 p.m., a testimonial dinner of one hundred people was held for "Dr. Harrison" at Craig's Restaurant, 102 West 130th Street. Cyril G. Wallace, of 653 Lenox Avenue, handled ticket sales, and the ICUL's new magazine, the *Voice of the Negro*, was available. The event was to demonstrate "the appreciation of Harlem's New Negroes for the one who first taught them what The New Negro was."[55]

The after-dinner tribute to Harrison was delivered as "a piece of inter-racial courtesy and personal friendship" by the multitalented James Phillips, who had acted in *The Student Prince*, sang regularly on the radio station WEAF, and sculpted. Phillips emphasized that he was there because he was "interested in Dr. Harrison as an individual and an intelligent man." He described Harrison as "one of the standing proofs that your race can produce an intellect worthy of the respect of any race" and added that when he read *When Africa Awakes* he found "a truly dynamic mind" with both "academic learning" and "punch." Phillips "heartily commended Harrison "for dedicating his unusual talents to the service of his race" and described how Harrison saw "his own personal development as inseparably linked with the development of his race and of humanity at large." He stressed that "with his unusual gifts" Harrison could "wield a tremendous influence not only over the minds of his own people, but also over the minds of my people—as he is already doing." Phillips called upon Harrison "to use his great prowess to save his people from slavishly imitating the present prevailing narrow ideals of white society."[56]

After the testimonial "Dr." Harrison continued his lecture schedule for the Educational Forum of the ICUL. His "lay-sermons and addresses expounding the Gospel of the New Negro in the Trend of the Times" were held Saturday evenings at 8:15 p.m. at the 135th Street Library. His spring schedule included "Virgin Islanders: Citizens, Subjects, Aliens?" (March 26); "Seeking Our Own Salvation" (April 2); "Booker Washington: A Great Negro Statesman" (April 9); "Should Negroes Fight for the U.S.A.?" (April 16); and "Negro Poets—From Dunbar Down to Hughes" (April 23). Harrison was also scheduled to deliver a special Sunday lecture, "Is There Any Cure for Lynching?" on April 10, at 3 p.m., at the Coachman's Union League Hall.[57]

In April 1927, after one issue of the *Embryo*, the ICUL came out with its monthly magazine, the *Voice of the Negro*, which was "to serve as the organ of the Unity Movement." In its "Program and Principles" the ICUL explained that the magazine would "be always free from condemnation of other Negro movements; full of the spirit of helpful uplift and co-operation and replete with information about what is taking place in every quarter of the colored world." It would "strive to educate racial sentiment and guide it in channels of usefulness and co-operation, give publicity to all those who are achieving the things that will bring inspiration to others, and bring forward some of those struggling geniuses of our race who languish for lack of opportunity." The first issue was eight pages, sold for ten cents, and contained international and domestic news and commentary, race-conscious editorials, and "Poems for the People." The ICUL hoped to expand to twelve pages with the next issue and apologized "for the omission of many things—like the list of donors."[58]

The international commentary column on the first page, entitled "The Wider World: A Bird's-Eye View," opened up discussing "THE BIGGEST JOKE of the year," which was that the press was saying that President (Louis) Borno of Haiti had "refused to let Senator [William H.] King of Utah land on those shores." Harrison explained that, as "everybody knows, poor Borno isn't permitted by our State and Navy departments to wipe his own nose," it was clear that it was "they and not Borno" who were "barring Senator King from Hayti for his criticisms—not of Hayti—but of [the] joint careers there of the State and Navy departments."[59]

In "The Wider World" Harrison also discussed the Rev. Reginald G. Barrow case, China, Japan, Nicaragua, and Italy's movements in Africa. The Barrow case was settled in the U.S. District Court in New York on March 11, when Judge John C. Knox "sustained the writ of habeas corpus" and "discharged Barrow." The Navy Department, which was in charge of the Virgin Islands, had deported Barrow and his family from St. Croix. He came to the United States to study and preach and was ordained a bishop of the African Orthodox Church. The court decision meant that he couldn't be forced out of the United States "by those who ran him out of the Virgin Islands."[60]

Regarding China and Japan, Harrison explained that on March 15, "under the guise of a gathering of tax-payers," the British "surrendered Hankow to the Chinese," who "had taken it several weeks before and had been running it for a month." Though Britain "saved face," the damage was done "to white prestige in China." Shanghai would ultimately be returned, "after which the whole group of grabbed 'concessions,'" including "Hong Kong and Wei Hai Wei," would "follow suit." Japan, meanwhile, had purchased 172 airplanes, including sixty large bombers, from France, at a cost of 7 million dollars, while "The American Government," according to the *New York Times*, was "an interested observer."[61]

On Nicaragua, Harrison commented that in newspapers "the Nicaraguans are NOT colored people," yet "on the screen, however, they are just what those who have been in Central America and seen them, know them to be." He speculated "perhaps that fact is the foundation of most of their troubles." Harrison also wrote that Secretary of State Frank Kellogg and President Calvin Coolidge "had both assured us that [Juan Bautista] Sacasa's soldiers in Nicaragua had been armed with Mexican guns, furnished by the Mexican Government." Then, "when Secretary Kellogg's official representative, Stokely Morgan, chief of the Latin-American division of the State Department, appeared before the Senate Foreign Relations Committee on February 24 and 25th," he said that "most of the arms used by the Liberals [were] from Russian rifles, made in the United States in 1915 and 1916 for the Russian Army."[62]

Italy drew Harrison's final comments in this section. After fighting all winter Italy had "completed her conquest of Somaliland." All centers of revolt were crushed, and the sultan had been forced to flee into British territory. Harrison portentously commented, "Things begin to look black for Abyssinia." (In 1935 Italy would invade Abyssinia/Ethiopia.)[63]

The first issue of the *Voice of the Negro* had three important reprint articles. In "The Trend of the Times in the World of Color" Harrison printed "Wanted—A World Outlook," which was a reprint of "Our International Consciousness," from the January 12, 1924, *Boston Chronicle*. He also printed "Race Consciousness," which had appeared in the March 15, 1924, *Boston Chronicle*. These two pieces broadly shaped the direction of the *Voice of the Negro*. The final reprint article was "Hayti Finds a Friend," the review of Blair Niles's book *Black Hayti*, which had appeared in the January 1927 *West Indian Statesman*.[64]

In "Rockefeller and the Reds," on page 3 of the April *Voice of the Negro*, Harrison explained that "Rockefeller" was "a symbol for the capitalist system of production under which Negroes as well as whites have managed to make such progress as there is," while "Reds" was a symbol "of radical and revolutionary theorists [especially communists] who are impatient of progress, distrustful of reason and eager to try new things." There was also "a real personal Rockefeller and real personal 'reds.'" Harrison then suggested "that the world grows better bit by bit" and "receives more genuine help in that process from John D. Rockefeller than from all the reds in America." He critically added, "The professional 'red' is generally a parasite upon the process of production" who "doesn't do anything himself and won't let anyone else do anything," and "the bent of his genius is generally along the lines of obstruction and destruction."[65]

To "Negroes," the "Red" "comes blowing about the necessity for teaming up with our 'white brothers of the working class' against the 'boorjwahzee' or the hated capitalist in the great 'class war.'" Of course, added Harrison, "everyone above the level of a moron knows that we Negroes have never taken one single step away from the white workers: it is they, on the contrary who turn their backs upon us, who have refused and do refuse to let us live with them, eat with them, work with them, or even organize with them." Therefore, he emphasized, "if our 'red' friend were sincere he would preach his great sermons on solidarity, not to us but to them. The splendid doctrine that 'the lion shall lie down with the lamb,' is not denied by the lamb; but the fellow to whom it should be preached is the lion—not the lamb."[66]

Harrison added that while both Rockefeller and the "reds" had their symbolic "henchmen among us," what was surprising was "the fact that while the black 'red' serves a white master and thinks that is noble, he will take the label of 'Uncle Tom' off his own knob and placidly pin it on the back of any Negro who prefers Rockefeller to the 'reds.'" He noted that "Both the 'reds' among us and the 'Rockefellerites' are agreed on one thing, viz; that we Negroes ought to make friends of some white people. No well-paid colored 'red' can deny this without losing his graft. No 'red' at all can deny it without losing his 'principle.'"[67]

Harrison argued, however, that "surely any 'red' white or black, must concede that if the Negroes of America are to make friends with ANY whites, they must be guided in this matter by consideration of utility and advantage: in plain English, they must team up (on the 'reds' own principle) with those whites from whom they get most." It seemed to him "that IF NEGROES NEED TO MAKE FRIENDS OF WHITE PEOPLE, it is much more to the interests of America to make friends of those white people from whom they stand to gain something." It was "a matter of the record" that more was obtained "from friend capitalist than from the other fellow." When the black worker went out "to face a cruel world in search of work and wages, his first and fiercest antagonist TODAY is not the White Capitalist, but the Poor White Worker." "Why then should either white or black 'reds' expect us Negroes to have a monopoly of the world's supply of altruism?" For Harrison: "as between Rockefeller and the 'red'—personal or symbolic—we much prefer Rockefeller, and on the simple materialistic, Marxian and common-sensible ground that in THE PAST we have got more, IN THE PRESENT, we are getting more, and IN THE FUTURE, we are likely to continue to get more, from that side than from the other. Now, let the fight go on!"[68]

In some miscellaneous handwritten notes on "The Red Record of Radicalism" Harrison indicated he had discussed their theory in *When Africa Awakes* (pages 81–82) and their tactics in discussions of Theresa Malkiel versus Debs and in comments on the "Conservative Sixes and Radical Half-Dozens," including "The Gold Dust Twins and a Negro Section of Socialism."

In discussing "The Negro and the Reds" Harrison mentioned how "they took credit for an upsurge due to race," as for example in *The Messenger* and the Lusk Committee reports. He then asked, "From which kinds of white has the Negro most to gain?" and "What good has Revolution ever done to the common man?"[69]

The centerpiece of the first issue of the *Voice of the Negro* in April was the "Program and Principles of the International Colored Unity League." It was a more detailed elaboration of the "Program" than that reported on in the June 7, 1924, *Christian Science Monitor*, which was written about by Harrison in the June 21, 1924, *Boston Chronicle*. Drafted by Harrison, the introduction to the "Program and Principles" explained that

> the New Negro has come forward, neither to whine, to wheedle, nor to make petitions or vain demands; but to take his future in his own hands and mold his own destiny by mobilizing his manhood and his money, his resources of head, hand and heart. . . . he is seeking his own salvation by consolidating in his own hands and under his own control those forces for racial uplift and security, which are already his, to the end that he may thereby win the things he wants: political equality, social justice, civic opportunity and economic power.[70]

The "Program and Principles" emphasized that the ICUL "was organized" to be "the instrument" by which its "general objects" were carried out. It would "serve the interests of the great masses of our people, and anyone who sincerely desires, to devote his abilities to them will find his opportunity within its ranks." It held out "the hand of fellowship and brotherhood to all those of Negro blood, however diverse their purposes, provided those purposes be good," and its energies were to be spent against "those evil conditions created by race-prejudice." The ICUL would not criticize "other Negroes who are fighting in their own way for the uplift of the race." It would seek "to bring

Negroes together in social and spiritual concord, and to secure ultimately by their co-operation a homeland in America where Negroes can remove the stigma of alleged inferiority by demonstrating to the rest of the nation that they are as capable of democratic self-government under American institutions as any other racial element in this country of ours."[71]

In its quest for political equality the "Program and Principles" made clear that "the Negro in America will achieve neither political self-respect nor political power until he undertakes his own political thinking and uses the votes which he has in the North to secure the vote for his brother in the South." It held that "the doctrine of "RACE FIRST!" is the only one which promises political action by organized Negro voters along the lines of their sadly-neglected group interests." Accordingly, "the political program of the Unity League" was "to unite the political power of the Negro around these three points: (1) Representation in Congress and in State and Municipal legislatures, (2) Utilizing the balance of power in doubtful states, irrespective of previous party affiliations, (3) Enforcement of the 14th and 15th amendments to the Constitution." By doing this "the Northern Negro" could use "political power to get the ballot into the hands of the Southern Negro, and thus put the political power of the Negro all over the nation on a footing of permanent security." In addition, "the immediate program must include an attack upon 'Lily White-ism' by demanding the reduction of representation in the national conventions of political parties to the basis of votes actually cast in national elections."[72]

In seeking economic power, collective action was emphasized and centered on the premise that "We Negroes must finance the foundations of our own future and use our available wealth." The "Program and Principles" put out a call

> to . . . [buy] agricultural land in the neighborhood of those cities where we live in large numbers,
>
> To feed ourselves by raising meat, poultry, eggs, milk, vegetables and other farm-products co-operatively for sale to ourselves at rock-bottom prices . . .
>
> To maintain our own co-operative groceries and butcher-shops in those sections of cities where we live, and to serve them from our own farms by means of our own trucks.
>
> To encourage property-owning in the suburbs of large cities that we may not always be paying our earnings away in high priced city apartments.
>
> To erect our own apartment houses, halls and casinos in our own neighborhoods, so that our rents shall return into the race's pockets in the form of profits which may give employment to our architects, engineers, artists, business men and workers.

And ultimately, to link up the Negro farmer on the land, North and South with the selling centers in the cities . . . thus keeping the cycle of Negro industry and commerce as far as possible within the Negro's control.[73]

In its quest for social justice, and indicative of a more broadly unitary approach by Harrison (who had long encouraged questioning and criticizing religious dogma), the ICUL aimed "to foster the elements of racial strength and co-operation already existing in the Negro Church, which has done more for the education and spiritual uplift of the masses than any other agency in the race." The ICUL would also strive "to work in friendly and active co-operation" with "the great secret and fraternal organizations" whose benevolent work demonstrated "how great and practical a thing is self-help"; the "Negro newspapers," both national and local (another departure—from Harrison's criticism of the press); and "Negro school teachers," who "have faithfully contributed both light and leading." To all these institutions the ICUL would render assistance.[74]

The ICUL also aimed to champion "the spirit of Youth." It emphasized that the younger generation was "struggling to express itself in national and international concerns, [and] to bring hope, ambition and human aspiration into the orbit of public affairs." The ICUL was accordingly planning a "first National Congress" at which they would "arrange to maintain scholarships in the best Northern schools for deserving Negro boys and girls from Southern states." It also would "strive to unite the Negro, North and South, in an effective attack on all 'Jim Crow' laws." It aimed to "force the repeal of them by political, economic and educational pressure" and "to put an end, once and for all, to lynch-law and mob-violence, not by vain petitions but by effective means." It also sought "to secure justice and absolute equality before the law and at the polls in every state."[75]

The most innovative aspect of the ICUL's program was its call for "a Negro Homeland in America." This was in stark contrast to Garvey's proposal for a homeland in Africa. The "Program and Principles" declared:

America is ours and we are hers. This is the foundation principle of all our racial strivings. . . . It is on that principle that we urge as a final solution of the graver aspects of the American race-problem the setting up of a state, or states, in the Union as a homeland for the American Negro, where we can work out the ultimate economic and racial salvation as a part of the American people. Any Negroes, so desiring, could continue to dwell in any state in the Union as at present, under such conditions as such states may see fit to maintain; while the Negro state would serve as a conduit to drain off Negroes from those states where they are denied a square deal. There the

Negro's aspiration to be as great as other men can flower and bear fruit; there Negroes can become governors, generals, judges, United States senators and Congressmen, without being hampered by political tricksters and fair-weather promisers.[76]

The ICUL program contained "ill will to no one" and carried to the Negro "the gospel of salvation by his own works by faith in himself and his future." To spread this gospel the League planned to engage in an education campaign and send speakers "to tour the country North and South, establishing branches securing members, raising funds and making friends." The League's monthly magazine, the *Voice of the Negro*, was "to serve as the organ of the Unity Movement." The magazine would "be always free from condemnation of other Negro movements; full of the spirit of helpful uplift and co-operation and replete with information about what is taking place in every quarter of the colored world." It would "strive to educate racial sentiment and guide it in channels of usefulness and co-operation, give publicity to all those who are achieving the things that will bring inspiration to others, and bring forward some of those struggling geniuses of our race who languish for lack of opportunity."[77]

The "Program and Principles" were followed by a membership application for the ICUL. Harrison initially had five hundred cards printed. They simply said, "The undersigned subscribes to the Program and principles of the International Colored Unity League and hereby enrolls himself as a member." The membership fee was one dollar.[78]

On the last page of the first issue was an appeal to the reader, "whether White or Black." It asked to "help us to make the next number bigger, help us to expand to full magazine size and to 32 pages." Pointing to "the vast amount of good we could then do," it commented, "the forces of mischief are well subsidized; why not help to support something like this?" Donations were to be sent to Harrison at 513 Lenox Avenue.[79]

———

In May the second issue of the *Voice of the Negro*, now subtitled "A Magazine of Inspiration," appeared, with page numbering running from 9–16. The first article appeared on page 9 and articles and/or poems on pages 9–15. On the inside front cover was an advertisement for a spring dance to be given by the ICUL for the benefit of the *Voice of the Negro*, on Saturday evening, May 14, at 149 West 136th Street, with music performed by Herman Wallace's Dance Orchestra. Another advertisement was for the Fourth Annual Organdie and Bandanna Dance of the Virgin Islands' Congressional Council, at the Renaissance Casino, on Thursday evening, June 9, from 9 p.m. to 3 a.m. For an admission price of $1 one could listen to Herman Wallace's Dance Orchestra and Jacob Williams's Syncopators. The VICC was also planning a Picnic and Outing for May 30 at Loeffler's Park, Westchester. The American and West Indian Ladies were also having an Organdie Dance and Reception for 60 cents on Thursday evening, May 19, at the Imperial Elks' Auditorium, 160 West 129th Street, with music provided by Herman Wallace's Jazz Orchestra.[80]

In "The Wider World: A Birds Eye View" Harrison opened by discussing the crisis in China. Domestically, it was marked by "the military success of the People's Army surging up from the South under the leadership of Chiang Kai Shek and inflicting defeat after defeat upon the troops of [the warlord] Chang Tso Lin," the "simultaneous smoking out of Communist plotters against China's peace and security by both Chiang and Chang," and Chang's "vigorous defiance of the Russian-controlled wing of the People's Party." Internationally, there was "the clearing out of foreign gun-boats for a thousand miles down the Yangtse river"; the "'evacuating' (which means throwing out) of Western missionaries and civilians from the entire Yangtse valley region"; the "gathering of the armed forces of England, America, France and Italy at and near the international settlements at Shanghai"; and "Japan's suggestive refusal to join the Western powers in attempting to bully distracted China." Harrison commented: "It begins to look as if these colored people in eastern Asia do intend to run their own affairs."[81]

Harrison also noted that the Oolagah, Indian Territory (later Oklahoma)–born actor Will Rogers, "under a thin disguise of humor," had "become our authentic national commentator and critic." In the *New York Times* (for whom he was a syndicated columnist) Rogers predicted that in the upcoming Chicago election "the side with the most machine guns will win." He then added, "We send marines to Nicaragua to tell them how to run an election and send missionaries to China. No wonder we are funny to the rest of the world."[82]

In his discussion of South Africa Harrison commented, "The whites first took away the Negroes' land, compelled them to work for whites and established the pass-system." These actions failed "to keep them from rising and increasing in number," so "the Color-Bar Bill was passed at the last session of the legislature"—again "with no better results." Legislation before the current session included "a Union Native Council bill and a Representation of Natives in Parliament bill, the latter designed to rob the natives of Cape Colony of the franchise and the former to substitute a plaything parliament FOR NEGROES, which, it is supposed will satisfy the aspirations of the 'educated natives and colored people.'" There was also "the Colored Persons' Rights bill and the Native Land Act Amendment bill." Harrison did not think these measures would "dam the dikes," and he pointed out that fifty years earlier Anthony Trollope had declared that "South Africa is a country of black men—and not of white men.

It has been so; it is so; and it will be so." With some irony he added, "The white man's drive against manifest destiny goes on in South Africa."[83]

In his commentary Harrison also discussed how "a wrathful 'red,' white in color and frothing at the mouth, deluged us with insults and offensive epithets at the forum meeting at which *The Voice of the Negro* made its bow to the public." The "plain, hard common-sense of 'Rockefeller And The Reds' had acted on him like a purge." Harrison emphasized that "the principle of this magazine is 'RACE FIRST'—not 'CLASS FIRST'; and we will continue to write and say the things which will benefit the Negro Race, whether we please the 'radicals' of the Class War or not." The forum "was organized to bring INSPIRATION to Negroes and the only propaganda welcome there is propaganda for Racial Uplift and Advancement" whether or not that pleased "our 'Red' friends."[84]

In "The Wider World" Harrison also wrote, "Harlem is inferior to Chicago." He cited the fact that it had no bank, while Chicago had three; it had "no Negro business—Chicago has many streets full of Negro business"; and it had no life insurance companies, while "Chicago's Negroes not only organized and perfected several life insurance companies, but one of them has reached out and annexed New York as a business colony of Chicago."[85]

In "Knowledge or College" Harrison spoke about the exchange after his talk on "Culture and Civilization" at the Brooklyn Y. He used it to make the point that as "Negroes" in America grew "more intelligent and better informed every day," the danger remained that many would "substitute 'going to college' for 'getting some knowledge.'" To Harrison, "far too many degree dunces" were "complacently and contemptuously turned out every year by some of the white Colleges like Columbia, Yale and Harvard." He wryly added, "They would only circulate among Negroes, anyway."[86]

Harrison then discussed a recent *Amsterdam News* article that showed the results of a questionnaire seeking to find out "how many of our people today are conscious of the accomplishments of famous Negro men and women." The questions were submitted in person to thirty-two "Negroes" in Brooklyn, including three ministers, twelve "students," a newspaper editor, a college professor, a magazine editor, one journalist, etc. The only person to answer all the questions correctly was a black West Indian bishop, the next highest score was earned by a machinist. The students "fell down hard." To Harrison it looked as if "we will be forced to do what they used to do in the Danish West Indies before Uncle Sam took them over—find out whether our men and women KNOW rather than whether they WENT to college."[87]

In "The Gift of Gab" Harrison indicated that he had plans for a nationwide tour on behalf of the ICUL. He discussed his recent lectures in Lynchburg, Virginia, and the New York metropolitan area and hoped "that, in the interest of the 'I.C.U.L.,'" he might "exercise it in the near future through all of the 48 states."[88] A column entitled "Fashion's Fancy," by "Cécile," may have been written by Harrison, whose mother's name was "Cecilia." The article focused on the "definite rules which the well-dressed woman will follow to attain distinction." In each column "Fashion's Fancy" aimed to discuss briefly "the trend of the new mode." The first column emphasized that "simplicity still continues to be the keynote for the spring months."[89]

In "The Theatre in Tabloid" Harrison commented that Paul Green's *In Abraham's Bosom,* which had gone from the Provincetown Playhouse to Broadway's Garrick Theatre before it closed, though not a great play, was "an attempt—futile for the most part—to present without bias a typical Negro situation from Southern life." Its "seven incoherent scenes" showed that Green hadn't "learned the technique of play-writing." Both Abbie Mitchell and Rose McClendon "had their styles cramped effectively until the last scene," and Frank Wilson, who performed the role on Broadway, "won well deserved encomiums."[90]

During the previous month Harrison had seen "some good comedy" at the Lafayette Theatre, including Irving C. Miller's *Gay Harlem,* which was "one of the most interesting hits." Miss Elizabeth Smith "was an outstanding figure" and promised "to match [the legendary] Aida Walker in the days to come." Harrison added that though the Lafayette Theatre strike continued, the theater was still "packed to capacity," day and night, and "neither the friendship nor the enmity of the union has any box-office effects."[91]

In the second issue Harrison also reprinted the "Program and Principles of the International Colored Unity League" from the April issue.[92] Under "Poems for the People" were included "Ebon Maid and Girl of Mine," by Lucian B. Watkins; "If Christ Came Back," by Harrison's old friend Andy Razaf; and "The Dawn," by May Wong.[93]

In "What-Ho Aframerican!" Harrison wrote that at the Quaker meeting house in Philadelphia, "where a group of white and black and colored people had gathered to discuss the problems of peace and war," the chairman introduced the last speaker, a young "white" man, who said, "although it may surprise most of you, I believe I am more African than anyone in this room because I was born and bred in Africa." Harrison commented, "Here was a genuine 'Aframerican'—for he was an American citizen of African extraction. BUT HE WAS CAUCASIAN! And I wondered at the fatuity of those who coined the silly word as a substitute for NEGRO."[94]

An advertisement for *When Africa Awakes: The "Inside Story" of the Stirrings and Strivings of the New Negro in the Western World* indicated that there were only three hundred copies left. It described the book as "an exposition of the new point of view evolved during the Great War and coming daily into greater prominence since that time." It added, "So far, this point of view has not been fully presented by the Negro himself," though "White men like Seligmann,

Sandburg and Kerlin have tried to interpret it—to the white world." Harrison's book "presented directly that which they tried to interpret from the outside." The advertisement also quoted from *The Freeman*, which said the book was "deserving of reproduction in some source-book of materials on the race problem," and from Hodge Kirnon, in the *Negro World*, who wrote:

> It is to Dr. Harrison that the credit must go of being the first apostle of the New Negro as well as the first active interpreter and exponent of his ideas and attitude. He not only caught the glimpse and heard the rumbles of the rising wave of the New Negro, but he assisted in molding these ideals into their most effective channels.
>
> The book was available in paper for 55 cents from the office of the *Voice of the Negro* at 513 Lenox Avenue.[95]

One other advertisement of note concerned the Virgin Island Congressional Council, which was described as "an Organization unselfish in purpose, patriotic in principle, fearless in its devotion to democracy." The VICC had "kept the home-fires burning for Virgin Islanders at home and on the Mainland—with propaganda, publicity, co-operation and self help," and it was "the clearing house for civil rights in the Virgin Islands." Meetings were held on the first and third Sunday of each month at Lafayette Hall, with Casper Holstein as President.[96]

The *Voice of the Negro* lasted two issues and ended in May 1927. No specific reason has been found for its demise, though finances undoubtedly played a large part. Harrison had no money himself, he had no major organizational support, and he had no known rich benefactors. His desire to do a nationwide tour for the ICUL may have been another factor. Ill health may have also been a major factor. Toward the end of 1926 he took ill; he believed he was suffering from appendicitis, an inflammation of the vermiform appendix. He seemed to recover after consulting a physician and being told his illness was not serious. However, by September 1927 he was so sick that he was forced to spend some time in Bellevue, New York City's oldest public hospital. Within a few months he would have an "appendicitis" attack that led to his hospitalization and then, very quickly, to his death.[97]

20

Last Months and Death
(May–December 1927)

In the last months of his life Hubert Harrison spent considerable time thinking, writing, and speaking about matters related to "Race." Around May 28, 1927, he prepared a handwritten outline for "World Problems of Race," a summer college course to be held at the Urban League Building, 204 West 136th Street. The course was described as a "Ten-Week Course in the racial aspects of World History, Imperialism in Africa, Asia and America, the Black Man's contributions to civilization, and the present racial unrest." The course was offered under the auspices of the "Educational Forum of the International Colored Unity League," those interested could contact Cyril Wallace of 653 Lenox Avenue, and its outline read:

1. Race and its Reactions in History and Science.
2. The Black Man in History and Civilization.
3. The White Race's Rise to Power and Privilege.
4. The Partition of Africa.
5. Race and Color Problems in America and the West Indies.
6. The Brown Bridge of Britain's Empire—From Egypt to India.
7. China and the Power.
8. Soviet Russia: Its Bearing on White Rulership over Darker Races.
9. The League of Nations and the Future of the Darker Races.
10. The Collapse of the Caucasian: A Forecast.

In his diary of July 1 Harrison wrote, "Began my lecture course on 'World Problems of Race' (2nd Season) at the Urban League Hall. Had about ten or twelve persons."[1]

Later in the year, on November 12, 1927, a "Dr. Beck" wrote to Harrison regarding his proposed lecture series on race.[2] This was probably a reference to a series of talks on "Race and the Social Sciences" for which Harrison had two pages of notes:

1. *Race and the Social Sciences.*
   A. Race-Concepts: New and Old.
   B. Popular Illusions About Race and Race-Theories.
   C. The Racial Explanations of Human Culture: [John Stuart] Mill to [John Mackinnon] Robertson.
2. *Rise of the Modern Concept of Race.*
   A. Classical Notions of Race.
   B. Rise of Modern Idea of Race—By Contact & Conquest.
   C. The Present Prevailing Notion.
3. *Science and Race*
   A. The Pseudo-Darwinian Theory.
   B. The Measurement of Skulls.
   C. The Measurement of "Intelligence."
   D. Johns Hopkins To The Rescue.
4. *Race and History.*
   A. Historic Beginnings in Myth.
   B. Recent Archaeologic Revisions.
   C. The Racial History of Early Man.
   D. Bueckle [Henry Thomas Buckle], [James Henry] Breasted and [Albert] Churchward:
5. *Superior and Inferior Races.*
   A. Two Peeps Into Early History.
      I. Early English vs. Ripe Roman.
      II. Early Greeks & Egyptians of 700 B.C.
   B. The Explicit Theory of Culture Stages.
   C. Advanced & Retarded Peoples.
   D. Civilization Banks—Reserve.[3]

While he was preparing his handwritten outlines on "World Problems of Race" Harrison was also publishing important writings in the *Pittsburgh Courier*. His insightful May 28 "Cabaret School of Negro Writers Does Not Represent One-Tenth of Race" opened by explaining that "ten years ago" the word "cabaret" was regarded as "a Frenchified term for a 'dive.'" At that time "no respectable young woman would . . . be found in one—even with an escort." Conditions had changed, however, and "our most respectable 'advancement' organizations" now held "their 'benefits' and other entertainments in these places." Since no change had "come over the character of the cabaret," he proceeded to look for the explanation "change in the attitude of society—colored and white—toward the cabaret itself and what goes on there."[4]

One significant fact was "that Negro society, especially in its upper reaches," took "its standards of value ready-made from white society." "Changes of taste, amusements and ideals" in "white society" were "reflected more or less faithfully in the practices of Negro people." Considering the history of "Negroes" in America, such a relationship seemed "perfectly natural," although "some of its by-products," like the cabaret, were "rather bizarre." A second fact of significance was that great cities like New York, Chicago, and St. Louis influenced rural areas, dominated the life of the nation, and fixed, "sometimes arbitrarily, the cultural standards for all the people." The products of "Tin-Pan Alley" (the New York City district where much popular music was published) were widely and "rapidly diffused thanks to the modern means of rapid communication." The printed copies of hit songs, traveling vaudevillians, phonograph records, and radio broadcasting and the "'sweet magnolias,' 'ole black mammy,' 'brown-skin baby' and 'red hot mama' of a score of Jew boys in 'the roaring forties' of Broadway" could "readily and rapidly ruin the spontaneous artistic impulses of millions of people, and enthrone in their simple souls artforms" that bore "no necessary relation to their own lives."[5]

Harrison noted that "art as related to life" was "dying ... among the white race, as [Oswald] Spengler" and others had insisted. "Pictorially," the white race was "seeking salvation among 'primitives,' from the South seas to the Congo forests, as witness [Pablo] Picasso, [Henri] Matisse, [Paul] Gauguin, [Vincent] Van Gogh and even Winold Reiss [who would illustrate Alain Locke's *The New Negro*]." They went "to China for card games, to Old Egypt for dress designs, to the orient for their 'new' religions and to the Negro 'down South' or in Harlem cabarets for the zip, pep and verve needed to make their literature and art stand up." To Harrison, "the really funny feature in all this" was "that the black brother" remained "unconscious of the fact that he is giving creative inspiration to the whites when he starts in to imitate from them their imitation of him."[6]

This imitative behavior was to Harrison the essence of what to others was the art of the "New Negro." He explained that "when these whites seeking local (and other) color, first 'discovered' the Negro they came to Harlem," with "certain 'fixations' about the Negro in their minds, the most basic of which was the characteristic American one that he existed to furnish entertainment to others." Then, "whatever about him was quaint, queer, odd, bizarre and different was seized upon as the essential ... the 'real' Negro, the thing for which white editors, publishers and readers had been waiting all these years."[7]

The "earliest and easiest point of contact for these discoverers of 'The New Negro' was the cabaret," where "they could find not only a great variety of 'types' as conceived by them," but, "under the influence of post-war gin and Volstead whisk[e]y, they could revel in an 'atmosphere' which was to them 'realistic' and redolent of the 'genuine' Negro." Then, "as soon as the resultant 'stuff' began to sell, the colored cognoscenti, Harlem's high intelligentsia, flocked to the new centers of cultural exposition like a swarm of bees." In addition, "in order that they might 'get in on the graft' and sell their 'stuff' downtown," they "laid themselves out to attain the imitation which is the most fruitful form of flattery."[8]

In the process, "their doors were opened to the official expositors, they competed for the honor of entertaining them and shepherded their guests about Harlem with the air of exclusive proprietors." Then, "having attached themselves to the new cultural apostles in the capacity of kite-tails, they had to follow where these led." As "cabaret parties became the order of the night, the colored cognoscenti soon learned to see with the eyes of the angels whom they were entertaining." Thus, "the grotesque antics of bibulous baboons furnished the esthetic principles upon which a 'new' art for the New Negro was predicated," and this extended "from portrait painting and magazine illustrations to fiction and poetry."[9]

These developments "didn't 'catch on' in the Negro newspapers," but "the larger 'race' magazines, deriving their prestige wholly or in part from the white world, cheerfully transformed themselves into official vehicles for the exposition of these new principles." In these magazines "grotesque caricatures of the Negro appeared monthly on the covers and in the pages." Extremely young poets "were seduced by the opportunity for self-advertising into contributing alleged poems in which many lines consisted of one word each, and rhythm, cadence and idea were conspicuous by their absence. The riot was on." In prose it was similar, thus "genuine masters like John Matheus and the real critics like Frank Horne . . . could hardly be heard for the babel of callow cackling," and many "who began with sound artistic impulse but weak wills, like Zora Neale Hurston and Helene Johnson[,] were soon swimming with the tide of tenth-rate marketeers, nibbling at the fleshpots of Egypt, and headed for oblivion." While this happened, "the blowers of the ebony flutes" were "happy in the moment in their own fools' paradise constructed of such literary materials as have floated up out of the cabaret."[10]

"The Cabaret School of Negro Literature" was "apt to be a bit brash in its handling of language," and it had already "acquired some reputation for coarse vulgarity and indelicate expression"—which was another "trait imitated from its Greenwich Village godfathers." Both groups often mistook "the language of the gutter for the language of the common people." A "raft of vulgar and suggestive songs and indecent vaudeville acts" were "tending to identify Negroness with nastiness and giving the whole race a bad name." Nevertheless, it was "a poor defense to hide behind the claim of representing the humbler elements of society," for several reasons. First, "the real representation of these elements" was "still left to white writers," who attempted it with "artistic seriousness," writers such as Thomas S. Stribling, Eugene O'Neill, Paul Green, Mrs. Julia Peterkin, and Du Bose Heyward, or "humorously," such as Octavus Roy Cohen. Second, "the outstanding literary figures that have come up from these [humbler] elements—like [John] Bunyan, [Robert] Burns, Gerald Massey, Dunbar and McKay—have not been notorious for vulgarity of that, or any other sort."[11]

On the whole, Harrison judged that "the influence of the cabaret . . . has not been quite wholesome for Negro 'literature.'" Ninety percent "of Negro life" was "still unrepresented by the artists of the Cabaret School" and was "still waiting for those" with "gumption and courage enough to eschew the namby-pamby colored Brahmins and the seductions of the midnight maniacs from downtown." That opportunity, he stressed, was "still open for true creative artists from the younger generation of Negroes."[12]

––––––––––

Harrison followed "The Cabaret School" with another *Pittsburgh Courier* feature, which was a response to the Jamaica-born Arnold Mahew Wendell Malliet, who was now residing in Harlem, on West 129th Street. Malliet had founded the *British West Indian Review* in 1923, and in the July 2, 1927, *Courier* he wrote an article emphasizing the strong race prejudice in the United States as compared to Jamaica. It was the first in a series of articles he would write on "Why I Cannot Become Americanized." His series ran until August 13 and centered on a theme he developed in the July 9 issue—that he "came to the U.S. [in September 1917] with high hopes but found race prejudice barring him at every turn."[13]

In the final installment in his series Malliet argued: "So long as the dominating race philosophy of America remains what it is, so long will I refuse to become Americanized." He argued that "for a colored foreigner to become Americanized he must accept some very damaging falsehoods, believe many half-truths, and uphold some dangerous ideas which have degraded his race in the eyes of humanity." Specifically, Americanization demanded "wholesale acceptance of the prevailing ideas of American life," and Malliet thought it "unthinkable that a colored man born outside of the United States of America could enter the country and assimilate American ideas, customs, etc." and "take unto himself the characteristics of white Americans without possessing a mind morbidly obtuse to a proper appreciation of the eternal principles of Justice, Liberty and Fraternity." He emphasized that he was not discussing the question of naturalization, for a person could "become naturalized without being in sympathy with the institutions of, the country or desiring to assimilate American ideas, customs or characteristics." This was consistent with the fact, "generally known," that "most immigrants who become citizens do so for materialistic reasons."[14]

Toward the end of his article Malliet paid his respects to his "scholarly friend, Dr. Hubert H. Harrison," and pointed out that when he consented to write on the subject he did not intend to "open up a controversy." He again stressed that "Americanization" had a totally different meaning from "Naturalization," which was not the subject of the discussion. He also conceded "the economic and educational opportunities offered by America are far greater than those to be enjoyed in the West Indies" and were "sufficient to induce West Indians to come to America." Malliet also wanted it "clearly understood" that he "advocate[d] the most friendly relationship between West Indians and Afro-Americans" and "believe[d] that whatever the attitude of West Indians may be on Americanization they owe it to the welfare of the race to co-operate to the fullest extent with their colored American cousins in their fight for Liberty, Justice and Equality."[15]

On August 13 the *Courier* editors commented that they regretted ending the "historically significant . . . fair-minded and high-minded discussion of so delicate a problem" by Malliet, whose "very sane point of view" and "ability to express himself so forcefully in the beautiful English style" was "not often equaled in American periodicals." They considered "Malliet's prose" to be "the best that has been specially written for and made its original appearance in any Negro newspaper in America" and thought they had achieved their "aim" of providing "an intelligent yet vigorous approach to a delicate problem." They also announced, as they had when Malliet's series was set to begin, that "Dr." Harrison would reply to "Why I Cannot Become Americanized" with "Why I Became Americanized." They did not know how long it would take for Harrison to frame his reply, but they imagined it would be "before Christmas," and they would announce his article a week in advance.[16]

Harrison's response to Malliet appeared on October 22, 1927, less than two months before his unexpected death. He explained that he received his "first intimation" that the *Pittsburgh Courier* had "matched" him with Malliet in the July 23 issue and that in the August 27 issue he learned Malliet's series had ended on August 13. Such background helped prove his "innocence of any evil intent." Though his own "controversial make-up" was admittedly "very highly developed," Harrison explained that he still liked "to pick my own fights." Accordingly, he would not engage "in any controversy with Mr. Malliet," whose "friendly presentation of the points at issue between him and American 'civilization'" would be left by Harrison "to some of those remaining writers for *The Courier* who detest West Indians on principle." Instead, Harrison planned to seize the present "good opportunity to put in evidence that 'clannishness' so often ascribed to us, and to suggest that West Indians may be too 'canny' (not 'clanny') to stage a dog-fight for the enjoyment of the spectators." He therefore confined himself to a brief article presenting "the opposite point of view."[17]

To begin, Harrison wondered whether he was "a West Indian at all," since "Mr. Malliet and most Americans" seemed to "assume that a West Indian is a 'Britisher,' owing allegiance to a British King, and chock-full of British culture," though, in fact, there were "Spanish, French, Dutch, Danish and (now American[)] West Indians." Harrison said he had "never been British," was "born Danish," and was "now twice an American; first by my own free choice and next by Uncle Sam's purchase of the Danish islands." After leaving "those islands, finally, at the age of 17," he had "lived in New York for 27 years," and as he grew "into manhood" in New York, he became in the course of time "the kind of American which I am at present." In those twenty-seven years he had encountered "all sorts of Americans," including "white people who have the usual 'cracker' attitude of the British white man in South Africa, smooth white hypocrites like the British white man in Jamaica who pretend and patronize, and white men without a trace of race-prejudice." He had also met "Negroes who are fawning docile and slavish, Negroes who 'draw the color line,' and Negroes who are manly as Mr. Malliet." He had "to contend against black, white and colored people" for his "place in the sun," and he "often . . . found the whites eager to extend me welcome and recognition where Negroes [were] not."

> I have watched American race prejudice fluctuate in its incidence; [have] seen lynchings decrease, and inter-racial committees increase even in the South, have observed the multiplication of social contacts between black and white people from North Carolina to New York, from Atlanta to Chicago; have seen the strivings of black men—and women, too—from bootblacks to bankers, from coal-heavers, to college presidents; and, after looking the whole scene over, I am more in love with America than with any other place on earth.[18]

Harrison then described why he so loved America:

> I have found here the full measure of manhood not in a nice, fat place prepared for me, but in the opportunity to battle for any place. And although I cannot be President of the United States, I can be what men of my race have been and may be again, Senator, Congressmen, Registrar of the Treasury, Assistant Attorney-General or Minister to Hayti or Liberia. Lawyer, doctor, dentist, teacher, legislator, financier—all these are open to me and to my children, if we care to strive for them, and the future opens before us. And in the

meanwhile we are participants in the greatest democratic experiment that the world has ever seen. It is not the American of today that fascinates me, but the American which is evolving out of it. The "cracker" may yelp as much as he pleases, but his descendants and mine will make the future America; they will either live together in peace and prosperity or their conflicts will crack both democracy and America wide open in the presence of the enemies of both. Personally, I bet on democracy—and that's why I prefer to be here.[19]

Harrison next discussed why he was an "American psychologically":

I am so far American psychologically that the mere thought of being a *subject* (however kindly treated) of *belonging* to any human being, be he King or Emperor really fills me with disgust. I like to play my part when voters are being registered and enrolled, to go to the polls on Election Day with the consciousness that my vote is the equal of any other man's in determining the issues of an election and the policies of government. I realize, of course, that there are limitations—just as the magazine called *The Jamaica Critic* informs me that there are for black men in Jamaica, just as there are for the black people in St. Kitts who are not free either to organize a labor-union or run a newspaper of their own, just as there are for the millions of underpaid, downtrodden black people in South Africa. But I realize that, like the white people of England four-fifths of whom were slaves (serfs) down to the 18th century, I and these darker millions must take our places in the rising ranks of color and carry on as we have been doing, striving for, and achieving by our struggles, an increasing measure of the world's respect and consideration. We will not expect anything to be given to us, but mean to fight for what we want.[20]

Next, Harrison described the "baser elements in American life." He recognized the handicaps of "ignorance, stupidity and cowardice" as well as "our own inferiority complex and the snobbishness of some of our own people." But "these handicaps also exist in Jamaica and elsewhere," and he doubted "that remaining a West Indian would remove them anywhere from my path." Further, "as a purely sporting proposition," he recognized that "I make my living among these people, that, in some sense, I eat their bread; I partake of their spiritual nourishment such as books and free libraries, free schools, museums, parks, public gardens and recreations." If these things were "good enough" to "enjoy," they were "good enough" to "join in preserving" and to assist in "the fight against lynching, Jim-Crow, segregation, bad leadership and stupidity." He reasoned, "Becoming an American doesn't commit me to the upholding of these baser elements in American life."[21]

Figure 20.1. Irene Louise "Lin" Horton Harrison (December 28, 1879–May 28, 1962). Hubert Harrison's wife was believed to have been born in Antigua, British West Indies. Her parents may have lived in Antigua, possibly spent time in Puerto Rico, and may have been from Demerara, British Guiana. She married Hubert Harrison on April 17, 1909. At times over the course of their eighteen-year marriage Hubert lived apart from Lin and their children. Over the years, the Harrison family was often at the edge of poverty, and Lin worked as a seamstress. *Source:* Hubert H. Harrison Papers, Box 15, Folder 17, Rare Book and Manuscript Library, Columbia University Library. See https://dlc.library.columbia.edu/catalog/cul:g1jwstqm9k.

In a forceful paragraph Harrison then explained why he became "Americanized" and, in so doing, offered insights on how central the struggle for equality was to his radical internationalism:

So I became Americanized (whatever that may mean), I became an American, because I was eager to be counted in the fight wherever I happened to be, to bear the burden and heat of the day in helping to make conditions better in this great land for the children who will come after me. And although I am not SATISFIED with American conditions as they now are, I realize that in these days of change and unrest I would not have been satisfied anywhere else. In China I would be fighting against foreign domination, in Egypt, India, South Africa or West Africa I would be fighting against the British oligarchs, in Jamaica against the sinister repression of black people practiced by both whites and mulattoes, and in the Dutch, French or American West Indies against crackerism, stupidity or cowardice.[22]

In addition, Harrison wryly concluded, "when America gets ready to buy the West Indian islands of any European Power the inhabitants, as people who are OWNED, are not going to have any final voice in determining their destiny." They would have no more say "than the Porto Ricans or Virgin Islanders had."[23]

This was Harrison's penultimate published article before his death and it offered a deep and reflective view of his feelings toward "America"—his chosen land of citizenship.

———

Harrison's social activities, some of which were recorded in his diary along with other matters, were somewhat diminished during his last six months, perhaps because of the chronic appendicitis he had developed. He noted that in the last week of June his second daughter, Alice (age sixteen), had graduated from PS 136, the Harriet Beecher Stowe Junior High School at 136th Street and Edgecombe Avenue, after having completed her first high-school year. His youngest daughter, Ilva (age twelve), who was exceptionally bright, had taken and passed the competitive examination for admission to the very selective Hunter College High School. She and a young dancer, Anise Boyer, "were the only two colored girls from that school who were successful—with two white girls." Ilva also stood first on the promotion list and had the highest French score of all the eighth graders, and Hubert wrote a poem for her. Shortly after this, on Friday morning, July 1, he recorded in his diary that he had returned home at 5 a.m., after having "a glorious time" with Mel Charlton and Olive Hopkins (the soprano for the Mt. Olivet Baptist Church).[24]

On August 17, John Louis Hill, the editor-in-chief of Court-Astoria Publishers, wrote to him asking for a complete story of his life and work to be used in a forthcoming "Notable Negroes in America," which was to provide information on the "life and work of the really outstanding members of the colored race."[25] Later that month, on Tuesday, August 30, he noted in his diary "after four days of incessant rains it hailed yesterday for about five minutes," a downpour that he assumed "broke up the Sacco-Vanzetti demonstration." His

Figure 20.2. Ilva Henrietta Harrison (August 14, 1914–August 7, 1933). Ilva was the youngest daughter of Hubert and Irene Louise Horton Harrison. She was exceptionally bright, took and passed the competitive examination for admission to the very selective Hunter College High School, and did well as a student at Hunter College (where she majored in English). In the period between her father's death in December 1927 and her own death from tuberculosis in 1933 she was able to obtain work at the 135th Street Public Library. *Source:* Hubert H. Harrison Papers, Box 15, Folder 16, Rare Book and Manuscript Library, Columbia University Library. See https://dlc.library.columbia.edu/catalog/cul:j9kd51c6zd.

reference was to one of the many protest activities held in the wake of the August 23 state execution of the Italian anarchists Nicola Sacco and Bartolomeo Vanzetti. Sacco and Vanzetti had been charged with murder and robbery related to a 1920 payroll robbery in South Braintree, Massachusetts, and their case was widely viewed as a political frame-up against working-class radical activists.[26]

On September 16, Dr. Frank Laszlo wrote to Harrison from Budapest, Hungary, and said he was glad to receive his letter of August 29. He added that his friend Bela Scrank [Schrank?] had sent him Harrison's *Negro and the Nation*. During the previous winter he had given a lecture on the same problem. Laszlo's standpoint was that

> the awakening of the colonial races is a part of the labor movement, even the principal part because the white imperialism has his point of Achilles in the colonies. Therefore is the race problem the greatest problem of the world. It must be solved permanently and then the white proletariat can be freed. The European workers' movement can not have any success before the coloured races receive their freedom. Not only the white proletariat but the whole *white* race has a sole enemy and that is: the white imperialism. Therefore the aim of all races is common: down with the white imperialism. On it depends Europe's future or perish.

Laszlo added that his conception was "against all imperialistic or semi-imperialistic conceptions of Pan-Europe or United States of Europe" and that he was interested in the Fourth Pan African Congress but the September *Crisis* had said "not a word about it." He asked Harrison to help him "keep in touch with developments of the Negro movement" and hoped to hear from him soon.[27]

Harrison, up until his death, continued his usually fruitless search for steady employment, and on September 17 he again took the Post Office Department's clerk-carrier examination. He needed at least 60 on the "General tests" in order to count other scores, and an overall rating of 70 was required to be eligible. He received his very high score of 98, on December 8, only nine days before his death.[28]

———

Drusilla Dunjee Houston, founder of the Oklahoma Vocational Institute of Fine Arts and Crafts, wrote to Harrison on October 3 and said that she was "working at getting out another 1000 copies" of her book *Wonderful Ethiopians*. She detailed her plans for "a great magazine," for which she wanted Harrison to do "an educational feature as chief writer." She thought he could not put himself "before the public as someone else could," and she wanted to develop "a great magazine in content not size" that would "truly put forth the voice of the Negro." She had "stacks of manuscripts" and imagined Harrison did too. Her idea was "to make it the size of the former *Crisis*, about 16 pages, and to make it another *Nation*." The magazine "would interpret the intelligence of the Negro, our true social duty, [and] new world thought along any helpful line." She felt Oklahoma "would support such a magazine," and "it could be sent free to Congressmen," it could advertise her book and "amply repay" her, "it could advertise a Lecture Bureau" that would bring Harrison "before the nation," and "it could put Miss [Helene?] Johnson out with her shelf of books." She asked Harrison to "hold these ideas" and not to "mention them lest someone takes them and runs them into the ground." She also mentioned that she had been offered the position of dean of the state university and would "probably take it because I need money."[29]

Houston was very impressed by Harrison, and according to her biographer, Peggy Brooks-Bertram, felt a kindred spirit with him. She sent a poem to the Associated Negro Press, which touched on her friendship with Harrison (though not mentioning him by name) and was published in the October 22, 1927, *Baltimore Afro-American*. Entitled "True Friends," it read in part:

> I care not for the shake of hand,
> The kindly speech or costly gift;
> That come when I have gained a stand.
> The man I value, helps me lift
> The weight of care, he heeds my call
> And hears me when I'm small.[30]

By early October 1927 Harrison was apparently undergoing some health difficulties, and on October 5 Charles Brook of the Brooklyn and Queens YMCA, Central Branch, wrote to him expressing concern over his recent illness and indicating that a list of seven proposed lecture subjects that he had sent were acceptable. Brook added that Frank Goodman of the New York Federation of Churches might be able to arrange talks for Harrison in churches. He subsequently confirmed Harrison's upcoming lecture schedule as November 6, "African Life and Customs"; November 22, "Can We Disarm?"; November 29, "Rudyard Kipling in Prose and Verse"; December 6, "Japan, Friend or Menace?"; and December 13, "Some Trends and Tendencies of Our Civilization." Then, on November 25, Brook informed Harrison he had also recommended him to the Brooklyn Federation of Churches.[31] According to a tribute to Harrison that appeared in December, the Men's Forum of the Brooklyn Central YMCA was crowded on Tuesday nights for Harrison's lectures, and "an increasing number" came "to appreciate not only his breath of knowledge, but his simple human qualities." His talks "covered a wide range of subjects and he had something to say worth listening to on every subject."[32]

Arthur Hutter wrote to Harrison on November 22, 1927, that he had been called by the president of the Men's Club of Temple Israel of Far Rockaway on short notice to arrange for a speaker. "Knowing how enthusiastically" Harrison's "last effort at the Club was received" Hutter hoped to reach him before he made an engagement for the night of December 5. He suggested Harrison speak on "Companionate Marriage," which had been discussed in Judge Lindsey's book and was opposed by Rabbi Stephen Wise the previous Sunday at Carnegie Hall. He mentioned this because Rabbi Wise frequently spoke at the club, and "criticisms of his criticisms would tend to make the meeting more interesting."[33]

Another invitation to speak was sent to Harrison by a member of the Independent Colored Political Club of New Rochelle on November 29. They wanted him to appear as orator at their January 1 Emancipation Day Celebration at New Rochelle Junior High School. Harrison was also lecturing at the 135th Street Y and was scheduled there on December 25, 1927, and on January 1, 1928, to speak on "Soviet Russia and the Darker Races" and "The Yellow Peril."[34]

While Harrison was delivering his series of talks, on November 18, 1927, President Calvin Coolidge commuted "at once" the remainder of Marcus Garvey's prison sentence, with the understanding that he would be deported. Eight days later Garvey was released to the custody of the immigration service. He finally left the United States on December 2, 1927, pursuant to Section 19 of the February 5, 1917, "Act to Regulate the Immigration of Aliens to, and the Residence of Aliens in, the United States." That legislation allowed for the expulsion of aliens for crimes "involving moral turpitude," which included mail fraud. Garvey's departure from the United States came fifteen days before Harrison's unexpected death.[35]

————

J. A. Rogers wrote to Harrison from Paris on November 26 that he had received his letter that day. He was "so glad to get it" that he was "answering right away." He mentioned that his "very good friend," Felix Valzi, editor of the *Review of Nations*, in Geneva, was on his way to America, and he wanted Harrison "to get in touch with him right away," since Valzi was "an important man in European affairs, knowing almost everyone 'who is who.'" Rogers had mentioned Harrison to him. Rogers also mentioned that he had "just finished an article on Islam, Christianity and the Negro" for Valzi, who then asked him "to review all Negro books or books on the Negro, worthwhile for his magazine." Rogers told Harrison that he had "since been thinking" that the latter assignment was better suited for him, "as I do not know of anyone so well informed on the subject as you"—an appraisal Rogers wanted Harrison to share with Valzi. Rogers said he also had written to Ernestine Rose to arrange a meeting for Valzi and stressed to Harrison, "He is a very fine, sincere and quite approachable man so don't fail to write him."[36]

Rogers then told Harrison that he was "Glad very glad to hear that you are at last taking your light not only from under a bushel but a cave. Hope you'll keep up the good work as you have the capacity to be known as one of the biggest men in New York City." Rogers said that he would "certainly make a copy of the article" that Harrison "so kindly sent" and planned to return it c/o Kelley at the *Amsterdam News* in order "to economize on postage." It was six cents from Paris: "To me a struggling journalist, and a Negro at that, that means something."[37]

Rogers "couldn't help a smile" as he remembered a previous Harrison statement to the effect that he was glad that Rogers had the opportunity to travel. To that Rogers responded:

Well I believe in being a good soldier but sometimes I can't help thinking that it was a hell of a chance. I am not going to complain because I know your lot is harder than mine. I, at least, am alive, while you have your hands full. But sometimes I am going to write the inside story of my truth and tell of the financial difficulties I have had and that on top of my illness, or rather two illnesses. In the meantime I am telling you this confidentially: up to the present the *Courier* on which I depended has sent me only $25. In the meantime just ask [Floyd] Calvin on the sly why I have discontinued my articles, and hear what he says. More than once if it were not for kind friends here I'd be *fontu* [I'd waste away].[38]

Rogers mentioned that he was "working hard on a private romance," which accounted for his "remaining" in Paris. He added, "If I do not get into another field and continue to write on the Negro I see my finish in the poorhouse." Working in Europe he felt there was "indeed a chance." He asked that Hubert give his "warmest regards to all the family including Billy. Remember me also to the 'Madame' [Harrison] and tell her that if I don't write often it is because I am working hard at my writing." Rogers said he would try to send Harrison some pictures, extended his "warmest regards to all the friends," and again reminded him to write to Valzi.[39]

In a separate letter included with that of November 26, Rogers asked Harrison to help him sell his book *From "Superman" to Man*. With the money from a new edition Rogers, who admitted to being "a poor salesman," hoped "to get out a classic one next time." He sent Harrison his last twenty-five copies and asked him "to take so many and pay the printer"—and to "*be sure to send me the money, and in the time promised.*"[40]

On November 30, Harrison's article "Harlem's Neglected Opportunities: Twin Source of Gin and Genius, Poetry and Pajama Parties" appeared in the *Amsterdam News*. It was his last published article before his death. He began by offering the opinion that Harlem didn't quite match Durham, Nashville, or Chicago "in seizing the opportunities presented to it." He then followed with the obser-vation that "unpleasant truths are always distasteful, even though, like purga-tives, they may leave the system better." As an example he cited the "hornet's nest the late Dr. [Booker T.] Washington raised when, in an effort to lift the level of ministerial efficiency, he castigated 'those who had more perspiration than inspiration, and more lung power than brain power.'" Though Washing-ton meant well, his critics didn't agree, yet, "because of his brave words, good has come, and today there is in the Negro ministry a larger percentage of men like William Lloyd Imes of New York and Everett Daniels of Detroit." Based on his observation and reasoning, Harrison felt that "the journalist, like every other commentator on contemporary life, must risk telling the truth sometime, even in New York—in the none too certain hope that good will come thereof."[41]

Harrison wrote, "Ever since the literary gents from Greenwich Village 'dis-covered' Harlem as the twin-source of gin and genius, poetry and pajama par-ties, the spotlight of publicity has been playing on it." But just as the theater spotlight often showed objects in false colors, so it was "with Negro Harlem," which was "something of a cross between Hells Half Acre and a Fool's Para-dise." Harlem, to Harrison, was "a modern community facing modern problems, and in it the germs of a modern social intelligence" were "afloat on the abyss—as elsewhere." Some of its aspects were "promising," others "depressing," and in a future article he planned to speak "of Harlem's splendid promise." In this arti-cle, however, he sought to confine himself "to those features that are 'not so good' in the hope that we may bend our moral muscle to the task of collective self-improvement."[42]

Harrison observed that "the modern Harlemite lives in one of the most beautiful sections of New York, with spacious avenues, splendid apartments, wonderful theatres and all the social accessories that minister to comfort, self-respect and luxury." Yet in the days immediately preceding the recent Elks' convention, the lack of hotels in Harlem was "primarily responsible for the fact that hundreds of Negro Elks" stayed "in certain large hotels downtown which will not ordinarily receive Negroes." In this situation "white people made more money off the Elks' Convention than colored people did." This "was by no means the fault of the Elks' entertainment committee"; rather, it was "due to general conditions in Harlem," which "indict us all equally."[43]

Another "curious feature of Harlem life" was that "the managers of such large-scale enterprises as exist in Harlem, the heads of the big social service institutions and most of the prominent leaders, have come from other cities—many of them quite recently." This was "due in part to the fact that Harlem, like the rest of New York," was "largely populated by people who were born elsewhere." One reason for this non–New York leadership was "the manifest mutual envy, jealousy and hatred existing among Negroes and Negro groups in Harlem." Harrison noted how he had heard it said "in places as far apart as Chicago and Lynchburg, that 'Harlem Negroes hate each other harder than any other Negroes in the country.'"[44]

He used this as his starting point to address the problem of pulling the community together. He commented that "the first duty which any community owes to itself is that of social cohesion," and in that respect Harlem was "still neglecting one of its greatest opportunities." There was a "general belief" that Harlemites were "backward in this respect," and while in part this was attributable to "the inevitable social consequences of metropolitan life," it didn't seem as bad in Chicago. Others had blamed "the diversity of origins of the Harlem population"; Harrison, however, offered his "own idea of the matter"—his "law of social pressure":

> As I see it, any population as marked as the Negro obeys the law of social pressure in its formative stage. The convergent pressure from outside tends to make its units stick together, while the removal of that pressure makes them fly apart. . . .
>
> Now, despite all our talk, the cities of New York and Boston are those in which the least pressure of prejudice is put upon the Negro masses. And those cities are precisely the ones in which the Negro, by himself, has accomplished least. The complete deduction is one which I would rather not draw. But many Harlemites have drawn it themselves.[45]

Harrison next criticized the educational opportunities that were being wasted. The "white man of New York offers to the Negro child as good an education as that offered the white child—and it is a free gift. Grammar school, high school and college are absolutely free. Evening schools and evening colleges are the same." Then, "when the Negro's free college course is completed, he can start teaching in any school in the city." Harrison noted that "six of my friends are teaching in high schools that I would call 'white,' but there are neither white nor black schools in New York—only public schools." Harrison then asked, "What does the young Harlem Negro do with this wealth of opportunity?" He answered, "You can see him on any summer's night out on the sidewalk gyrating and contorting himself like a pet monkey, doing the 'Charleston' or the 'black bottom.' The Jew overflows City College, while the Harlem Negro in whose very mouth the building is situated, musters about twenty-five or thirty." As a glaring example of wasted opportunity Harrison described how the Board of Education had recently started enrolling students for an evening high school at PS 139 on West 140th Street. The minimum required was five hundred; they enrolled only 197 and had to close down the school.[46]

Similarly, when the Public Library recently acquired the Schomburg Collection, "Harlem's interest in it was so great" that Harrison claimed he took "a white man from Hungary [Dr. Lazlo?]" there to talk "because we would not be disturbed by anyone!" In order to draw people to the library, the librarian had newspapers, which many go to read, transferred there. Harrison did "pay a tribute to the young Negro women of Harlem" who "use the library," "read and study," and "go to high school in far greater numbers than the young men," though, he cautioned, what that promised for the future wasn't "pleasant to contemplate." Regarding music, Harrison noted that "every Sunday afternoon, from November to May," Professor Baldwin furnished an organ recital "attended by thousands of music lovers from all over the city." It was "entirely free" and "within easy walking distance," yet "one never finds ten Negroes at any time."[47]

Economically, Harrison considered "Negro Harlem" a washout. Reprising comments he had made in his *Voice of the Negro* article "The Wider World," in a business sense it was "peculiar," and for all its "bluff and bluster" Harlem had "no Negro bank," while Chicago had three. "Negro business" in Harlem still walked "on crutches," while in Chicago there were "many streets full of Negro businesses." Similarly, New York had "no life insurance companies," while "Chicago's Negro not only organized and perfected several," but one of them "reached out and annexed New York as a business colony of Chicago." This banking situation was "symbolic of the general economic situation," in which "millions of Negro dollars" were "lent out by the white bank to white business men to perfect the strangle-hold of white business on the pockets of the community." Harrison stressed that "until a Negro bank arises in Harlem," the "thrift of Harlemites" would be "a means of harnessing them more hopelessly to the chariot wheels of white business." Meanwhile, "local attempts to organize large-scale businesses" would "generally end in failure," and "in the long list of Harlem's neglected opportunities" there was "not one as tragic as this one of Negro business." Yet "while productive business" struggled "under such handicaps," the "business that panders to ephemeral pleasure" flourished. There were "poolrooms," "night clubs," "cabarets," "dance halls," "the numbers," and "Italian rum shops"—all of which made money "for their proprietors."[48]

Harrison next addressed the issue of a civic sense. He suggested, "It behooves us to give over bragging about things that were not contributed by us and get down to brass tacks." He considered "the small army" of homeowners "our best civic asset," though Brooklyn was far superior in that respect. The "development of a civic sense" was "a duty which devolves upon the entire community," and to make this point Harrison discussed "the beauty of Harlem's two main avenues, Seventh and Lenox." Their beauty was "largely the product of the trees," but city officials began to chop those trees down in 1923, and "not a word of protest" came from rent-payer or homeowner organizations. "If there existed in Harlem even an embryonic civic consciousness such a thing would have been challenged long ago." Yet, he predicted, it was "out of the development of a civic consciousness, of each citizen's organic relationship to the community and the community's responsibility for each citizen, that the Greater Harlem will arise." This "newer Harlem" would not "neglect the opportunities" at hand that challenged its members to "rise to the level" of the community's "social needs."[49]

After his 1926 illness and his September 1927 hospitalization Harrison was stricken with an appendicitis attack on December 7, 1927. His private physician, Dr. Leo Fitz Nearon, diagnosed his condition as chronic appendicitis and recommended an operation. Harrison decided to be operated upon to secure permanent relief, and in the week after the attack he was visited by numerous friends and acquaintances to whom he had told that he would go into the hospital. He entered Bellevue Hospital on Tuesday, December 13, and on Thursday at 11:15 a.m. Dr. Maurice E. Marlow, the house surgeon at Bellevue, performed the operation. Harrison recovered from the ether that was administered, though his condition remained serious, but he was apparently well enough on Friday that his wife, Lin, and several close friends, whom he recognized, were permitted to see him. On Friday he seemed to improve, but that evening he took a turn for the worse. At some point that day he gave Lin his wedding ring and wrote her a note asking her to "Please keep this ring safe for me until I come out of the hospital." He never came out. On Saturday complications arose that produced paralysis of the intestines, and death followed. What probably happened was that his appendix had ruptured, causing widespread infection. Hubert Harrison died Saturday night, December 17, at 7 p.m., in his private ward. Dr. Marlow officially listed the cause of death as "chronic appendicitis (appendectomy)." Hubert's daughter Aida said that the family was told that their father had died of peritonitis, which she suspects may have been tuberculosis related.[50]

Edgar Grey, writing on "Why Great Negroes Die Young" in the *New York News* of December 31, 1927, suggested a deeper cause of death. Calling him "the mightiest brain of the race" and describing him as a man constantly "fighting for his right to recognition," Grey claimed that Harrison was "permitted by the Negroes to talk, talk all night, burning up his energies." He added that in fifteen years of street talking Harrison received nothing, and the honors he did receive "were given him by those who had nothing to give . . . the pennies of the poor, but knowledge-hungry . . . and they had little." The "big Negro newspapers and business houses, schools and other organizations who had positions allowed themselves to be so hateful that they would not hire him." According to Grey, he "died for his convictions, but he died at 44, starved, underpaid, abused, hated by jealous men who feared the force of his mind and the immensity of his information." Grey concluded "Great Negroes" such as Harrison "will all die young until the race learns to value them as the men and women who shall form the foundation of the race's greatness."[51]

Harrison's body was laid in state at Albert T. Saunders Funeral Parlor, 106 West 136th Street, from Monday afternoon, December 19, to Wednesday afternoon, December 21. On the afternoon of the nineteenth at 3:30 p.m. the sculptress Augusta Savage made a death mask of him, to be the basis for a life-sized bust. The funeral services were held on December 21, at 8 p.m., at Mother AME Zion Church, on West 138th Street, where the Rev. Dr. J. W. Brown, pastor, officiated and the Rev. R. M. Bolden of the First Emanuel Church assisted. Casper Holstein was in charge of funeral arrangements and was assisted by Grey. Pallbearers included Richard B. Moore, Charles Seifert, Arthur Schomburg, Anselmo Jackson, Philip Levy, George Young, William T. R. Richardson (from St. Mark's Lyceum), and O. Simmons. Over one thousand people attended. The burial took place at Woodlawn Cemetery at Webster Avenue and 233rd Street in the Bronx, on Thursday morning, December 22, at 11 a.m. His remains rested "upon a slumber couch of mulberry crushed plush, beneath a crushed brocaded satin coverlet," and he was "buried in a silver mounted casket." The funeral expenses of $867 were paid by Casper Holstein; H. A. Howell was the undertaker.[52]

At the funeral service Rev. Brown stated: "Poverty and adversity in the life of this man only fired his spirit and his thirst for knowledge." His life set "a fine example for every aspiring and ambitious young man of his race." The journalist Grey described him as the "most complicated character," the "most brilliant writer," and the possessor of "the mightiest intellect that has sprung from our group." Richard B. Moore, secretary of the ANLC, referred to Harrison as the "Black Socrates" and "the pioneer of the Negro intellectual renaissance," which made Harlem "the mecca of Negro intellectual culture." Moore then quoted from Paul Laurence Dunbar, that "minorities, since time began, have shown the better side of man" and urged that all "assuage our grief in the glorious knowledge that he lived well." Arthur A. Schomburg, with great historical perspective, reminisced about Harrison's early days at St. Benedict's Lyceum and (knowing how immensely popular he was in his day) added, "He came ahead of his time." Among others in attendance were three "white" socialists, two "white" communists, and various intellectual, professional, and social leaders in the community, including William Pickens.[53]

Figure 20.3. Aida M. Harrison. Aida grew up with her three sisters and one brother in the stimulating Harrison home environment, where the pursuit of learning and knowledge was stressed. She excelled in the New York City public school system and graduated from City College at age nineteen. She obtained employment as a social worker and did work with the American Negro Theatre. In the 1940s Aida M. Harrison Richardson became a New York City public school teacher and later became an assistant principal before retiring in 1972. (In later life Aida preferred Aida Mae over Aida May.) *Source:* Hubert H. Harrison Papers, Box 15, Folder 4, Rare Book and Manuscript Library, Columbia University Library. See: https://dlc.library.columbia.edu/catalog/cul:02v6wwq12h. Aida's granddaughter Yvette-Harrison Richardson Hudson helped with the identification of this photo.

Figure 20.4. Casper Holstein (December 17, 1876?–April 1944). Born Egbert Joseph in Christiansted, St. Croix, Holstein immigrated to Harlem in 1884, served as president of the Virgin Islands Congressional Council, was in charge of and paid for Hubert Harrison's funeral arrangements, and described Harrison as "a mountain of inspiration not only to the Negro people but to the people of the Virgin Islands." In early 1924 Harrison became a founder and executive committee member of the Virgin Islands Committee. The VIC was led by its chairman, Rothschild (Polly) Francis, the editor of *The Emancipator,* which was published by the Working People's Committee of St. Thomas. The aim of the VIC was to secure measures that would promote the economic and political reconstruction of the Virgin Islands. *Source:* Schomburg Center for Research in Black Culture, Photographs and Prints Division, New York Public Library Digital Collections.

Harrison was survived by his widow, Lin, and their five children: Frances Marion, 18; Alice Genevieve, 16; Aida May, 15; Ilva Henrietta, 13, and William Alexander, 7. Other surviving relatives listed in the press included his niece, Mrs. C. Phillips of 270 West 143rd Street; his sister, Mrs. May Francis of 562 Morris Avenue, the Bronx; and a brother, Wilford Harrison, of Brooklyn.[54]

Even in death Harrison continued to struggle for a better world. The December 31, 1927, *Pittsburgh Courier* posthumously included his "last article." Quite fittingly it was "World Problems of Race," based on the typescript he had prepared around July 8, 1926, when he was teaching his "World Problems of Race" course in Harlem. The *Courier* headlined the important article "Dr. Harrison's Last Article: 'World Problems of Race': Writer Said Both Science and History Try to Rob Negro of Past Heritage; 'Ancient Egyptians' Called White Lest Negroes Get Credit for Medicine, Geometry, Religion and Architecture." It "was given to the Special feature Editor before Dr. Harrison was taken ill" and "was to have been a series." The *Courier* extended "to Dr. Harrison's family and relatives its deepest sympathy in their bereavement," adding, "The Race loses a stalwart champion in Dr. Harrison."[55]

Epilogue

After his death, Harrison's wife, Lin, received a number of noteworthy condolences, which were preserved.

The journalist Cleveland G. Allen wrote that Hubert Harrison "made a lasting contribution to the race, and was one of the great factors that helped to preserve the glorious history of the Negro. He was the Socrates of his day, and one of the Prophets of his age."[1]

Casper Holstein, president of the VICC, commented: "Hubert Harrison was a mountain of inspiration not only to the Negro people but to the people of the Virgin Islands. . . . Words fail to express how deeply he will be missed by us, and we know that in his death yourself and children have experienced a great loss." Holstein added, "Therefore we of the Virgin Islands' Congressional Council . . . voted to present you and the children One Hundred Dollars ($100.00)."[2]

Frank R. Crosswaith, special organizer of the Brotherhood of Sleeping Car Porters, wrote:

> My family and my colleagues in the work of organizing the Pullman porters join me in this expression of heart felt sympathy at the loss of your husband and father and our esteemed friend and comrade, Dr. Hubert H. Harrison.
>
> In a moment of such intense sorrow as is ours, words of condolence lose half their meaning; nevertheless, you who are Dr. Harrison's immediate family and who have been privileged to share his friendship, will find much pride and deep satisfaction . . . in the fact that he played his part nobly and left an indelible mark of pioneer service engraved in the hearts of his countrymen and all other men who knew him.

Of Dr. Hubert H. Harrison it truly can be said that neither . . . time nor the music of years can blot out the militantly constructive and invaluable educational service he rendered to the cause of race manhood and social justice. The story of the New Negro's fascinating fight for a man's place in our time, is the story of Hubert H. Harrison. And when the impartial historian writes the history of the black man's bid for a square deal, he will be building, with the written word a monument to Dr. Harrison which will stand for all time as a symbol of inspiration to the men and women of the Negro race as they move forward to positions of power, prestige and pride.

We share your grief. The race shares it also.[3]

A. Philip Randolph, general organizer of the BSCP, described Harrison as "our comrade and co-fighter for race justice" who "has made an enduring and valuable contribution to the life of the Negro of New York in particular, and the world in general."[4]

Mabel D. Keaton, an RN at the New York Tuberculosis and Health Association, Inc., described "the utter loss that Harlem has sustained through the death of your husband" and emphasized that "Harlem has lost a land mark, the Negro, a fearless champion of their cause. His method of fighting was different to most people, it was through information and education which was a worthwhile way."[5]

On January 8, 1928, J. A. Rogers sent a condolence letter to Mrs. Harrison, telling her, "Nothing will ever be able to express my great sorrow."[6]

A number of published Harrison obituaries and tributes are enlightening. One of the most powerful and insightful was entitled "Literary Genius of Hubert Harrison," by Oscar J. Benson in the December 24 *New York News*. Benson began:

There is a class of men in every generation whose knowledge is not hoarded: whose intellect is practical; and whose services are unlimited in the community in which they live, and naturally no one knows of their community without knowing of them. To this class of preceptors Hubert Harrison belongs.

Literary men of this class are seldom honored by posterity. . . . Like the plain "old uncle" Socrates they go about teaching here and there, their audiences are vast, and they are always in popular demand for their subject matters are of such material as to interest most anyone. . . . Hubert Harrison was of this type. But he was more. He was original. He spoke . . . what he thought. He was bookish, but not of the sort classed as a bookworm; yet he went through a greater quantity of books every day than most men of his time. . . . When he grabbed a book he knew just what parts to digest, what passages to mark, what dogma to criticize and whether any book was worth a second reading. I once asked him to give me a proximity of the number of books he read in one day and he shocked me by saying perhaps five or six.[7]

On Harrison's contributions, Benson offered:

[Hubert Harrison] . . . instituted a new school of social thought, packed a new forum, dignified the soap-box orator; blocked Lenox and Seventh Avenue traffic; sent humble men to libraries and book stores; sent them about to day and night schools; taught Negroes to think for themselves; taught them that in spite of all the handicaps of slavery and propaganda of anthropologists and sociologists, who said that the Negro was an imitator, that no one knew what the Negro could do until he tried. . . . Harrison struggled to break the Negro away from other sources and think alone.[8]

Benson elaborated further:

His doctrine of self-reliance, of self-respect, of confidence in yourself and in your race; his researching; bringing upon the public highway, in the lecture-room and before the Board of Education scholarly conclusions of men of mark, his reflection upon modern topics and his comments upon the modern action of world leaders, made his services of latent value in the community in which he lived; if not unparalleled with the history of the Negro. No man ever held the attention of such large crowds upon the public highway in Harlem, nor with their addresses made such an active impression upon the minds of intelligent men. His language was beautiful, for it was characterized with simplicity and was evidently absorbed by simple folks. He hated verbosity, envy, jealously, prejudice, but had sympathy for ignorance. He had no time to hate men for his life was busy and stimulating. He was one of the few men who could "keep his head when all about were losing theirs and blaming it on him." He kept close to the ground, his habits plain; his manner dignified without arrogance; and his tongue free from gossip.[9]

On a more personal level, Benson wrote:

He loved children, the poor, the common folks; those who were victims of circumstances. He longed to see Harlem more peaceful, more serene, more intellectual. He made great men his teachers, but not his masters. He was always willing to help or encourage a young writer or speaker. He saw the present condition of the Negro but anticipated a brighter future. Like most literary men he was misunderstood, misquoted and his doctrines misused, but "to be great is to be misunderstood."

His biography no man can write, unless it be culled from the influence his teachings had upon the lives of others.[10]

Drawing from Benson's insight, other Harrison's contemporaries further suggest his importance and influence in their tributes. In the *New York News* of December 31, Harrison's long-time friend the poet Andy Razaf offered a moving tribute, "Hubert H. Harrison Dead!" which ended:

> What a great loss to thy Race!
> Who is here to fill thy place?
> Who will match thy common sense;
> Knowledge, wit and eloquence?
> The world has lost no brighter star
> A sterling soul has gone afar;
> Whose work on earth was nobly done—
> Farewell, HUBERT HARRISON[11]

Another long-time friend and activist, Hodge Kirnon, offered "Hubert Harrison: An Appreciation" in the December 31 *Negro World*. Kirnon explained that Harrison "took pains with whatever he planned to do in his educational efforts to an extraordinary degree; yet he would often times say that he memorized assimilated and transposed his wide range of reading upon technical subjects into their simplest and most understandable forms with but little or no effort." He added that "unlike many of his contemporaries of lesser fame, he understood" the "inextricable relationship between the arts and philosophy," and his "discursive and discerning mind made it possible for him to appreciate and evaluate the drama, music and other forms of human expression, not only as the strivings of the mind in search of truth, but also as manifestations of the social characteristics of the age." He was thus "always able to catch glimpses of truth and of new ideas and to interpret them in both their ideological and practical aspects." Kirnon described how "Harrison spent a great deal of his time in reading a great number and variety of books, but he was able to preserve his intellectual individuality and hold his critical ability intact." He "was always the master, never the pedant," and "he always found time to do his own thinking." He "carried many social and philosophical problems in his mind for years, during which he would examine and probe them for hours; then he would shelve them for a short period, take them out again and again to be subjected to his rigid tests of critical inquiry, until he felt assured that he had reached some satisfactory solution." If no solution was forthcoming, Harrison "at least was made more aware of the difficulties and subtleties which surrounded such problems." Kirnon went on: "No trace of the Brahmin spirit was to be found in

Harrison. He lived with and amongst his people; not on the fringes of their social life. He taught the masses, and he drew much of his inspiration from them. He assisted in holding and directing the new spirit of the Negro and its accompanying ideals into their most effective channels. He consistently preached the idealization of black as an aesthetic ideal, and forever asked Negro men to emulate their women."[12]

Kirnon emphasized that Harrison was "a pioneer radical and racialist" and "the first Negro whose radicalism was comprehensive enough to include racialism, politics, theological criticism, sociology and education in a thoroughgoing and scientific manner." In his practice "Harrison lectured before more well informed and critical audiences than any other Negro in America upon such subjects as Socialism, anthropology, Negro history and contemporary historical events especially in their relations to the darker races." Stylistically, "his fine scorn and irony were anathema to those who carelessly or ignorantly challenged him without good reason." He was also "the possessor of an exceptionally remarkable and fertile mind, and his great and accurate knowledge upon almost every vital subject was an astonishment to even his most cultivated hearers." In conclusion Kirnon offered: "None will deny except those who envied him that Hubert Harrison has made an indelible stamp upon the intellectual life of the Negro," and "every one of us owes him a lasting debt of gratitude."[13]

A December 31 *New York News* obituary stated: "Tens of thousands of New Yorkers will miss the philosophy of the most brilliant street orator that this Metropolis has produced in the last generation." Harrison's "oratory was with him not only a pleasure, but a duty through which he felt impelled to serve his race and the country of his adoption." His soul "knew neither black nor white; neither race or religion," and "if the universal man has been created more genuinely in our day, we have not seen him." Harrison's "great fund of philosophy, his ready wit, his melodious measured utterances disarmed all those who came to scoff and turned them into his admiring pupils." He served as "a potent and living example to the countless thousands of Caucasians who have heard him in the last twenty-five years of the potential equality of the black man." He was

the harbinger of good-will and a better understanding between the races. Like Mohammed who went to the mountains when the mountains would not come to Mohammed, Harrison carried his mighty disarmament of prejudice to his fellow white citizens. Greater service than this no colored man can render. None has there been who have so intensively and effectively rendered that service in this great metropolis. His was not the policy of compromise or apology for his race. He did not go like many a Southern educator, hat in hand, to beg alms for his race from the financial and industrial magnates. . . .

He preached the brotherhood of man and the common basis of all the problems of all the races of mankind. It was therein that Hubert Harrison served nobly his day and generation. That was his contribution to his race's progress. Truly his death was Harlem's sorrow, but his race's loss.[14]

The *Amsterdam News*, in addition to a front-page piece on Harrison's funeral, contained an obituary entitled "Hubert Harrison," which read:

Harlem has lost one of its most stimulating personalities. Orator, scholar, critic, Hubert H. Harrison was known to thousands, black and white. He educated himself by sheer industry, reading five books a day, yet his mind was fresh and unjaded. He was scholarly enough to be chosen as a lecturer by the Board of Education and unconventional enough in his ideas to be one of the main speakers of the Socialist party. His mind was always moving; he deserted Christianity for atheism. . . . He was a teacher, an editor and a book reviewer for the daily papers. Through it all, he did Harlem a great service.[15]

The obituary went on:

The most widely read man in Harlem, he took his learning to the great mass of the people. One of the most familiar sights of Harlem was Hubert Harrison on a soapbox on Seventh avenue. Using none of the tricks of the street fakir, he drew hundreds of hearers by the force of his ideas and passed his erudition on to them. In this way he reached and influenced thousands of people who never read a book.[16]

The *Amsterdam News* obituary emphasized:

In his street speeches he spoke to the Negro in a language that the Negro could understand. He decried the slavish imitation of other races, he told the Negro to think for himself, he glorified in the beauty of the Negro woman, he proclaimed that the Negroes had within them a mighty spring of power and called upon them to release it, he used his scholarship to expose the countless fallacies of the white race about the Negro and itself. . . . Like most original thinkers, he stood alone. He belonged to none of the uplift organizations because he refused to be fettered by any policy but his own, which was to dig out the truth and proclaim it on the highway without fear. He could have had a smug income if he had been more deferential to the powers that be, the powers that want a Negro leader to go so far and no further. But, like Socrates, he bowed to nobody, and that was his strength.[17]

The *Chicago Defender* wrote, "For nearly a score of years, Dr. Harrison has been a picturesque figure in Harlem. It will be remembered how night after night, when the weather would permit, hundreds and hundreds of persons would crowd around the soap box on which he would make vigorous appeals for the Race to seek economic freedom." The *New York News* said, in a lengthy article, that "a palpable gloom hung over all of Harlem on Sunday when it was announced that Dr. Hubert Harrison was dead. For all colored Harlem realized that the mightiest brain in its midst was stilled—stilled by the cold and creeping hand of death."[18]

A December 24 article in the *New York Age* described Harrison as "one of Harlem's noted figures, known to thousands by sight through his public speaking from street corners on a wide range of scientific, philosophical and social questions" and said his death was "a shock to the entire community."[19]

"Vale! Dr. Harrison," an obituary by the Men's Forum of the Brooklyn Central YMCA, was dated December 30, 1927. It opened:

The many friends and admirers of Dr. Hubert H. Harrison were greatly saddened at his death. . . . Rarely has a foyer lecturer at Central so readily made an appeal to the minds and hearts of his hearers as this negro from the Danish West Indies. His audiences every Tuesday night were crowded with an increasing number who came to appreciate not only his breath of knowledge, but his simple human qualities. His discourses covered a wide range of subjects and he had something to say worth listening to on every subject.

The tribute went on:

His loss to Central is great. His loss to his own people, the colored race, is even greater. He labored with simple faith in order that his people might be delivered from the thraldom of race prejudice. Nobly did he live and his memory in death will be one that we shall always cherish and honor. . . . We grieve his loss, but have faith to believe that out of his life will arise a clearer recognition of the rights of the race of which he was such a distinguished member.[20]

On December 31, 1927, the *Pittsburgh Courier*, in addition to publishing "Dr. Harrison's Last Article: on 'World Problems of Race,'"[21] published an accompanying tribute, "Hubert H. Harrison!" The tribute stated that "in the death of Dr. Hubert H. Harrison, the well known writer and lecturer, the race lost a valuable asset." Harrison was "an amazingly well read man with an ability to present in simple language the most difficult subjects." As a literary critic he "wrote for some of the leading newspapers and periodicals long years before the present Negro vogue set in, and . . . in the field of literature . . . his opinions were most valuable." He conducted forums in Harlem, was a lecturer for the Board of Education, and "only this year he was employed by Columbia University as a lecturer on Contemporary Civilization." It was "a revelation to see Hubert Harrison, mounted on his street-corner ladder and surrounded by a crowd of several hundred Negroes, discussing philosophy, psychology, economics, literature, astronomy or the drama, and holding his audience spellbound."[22]

The *Pittsburgh Courier* added that Harrison "was one of that small band of intellectuals residing in Harlem that did so much to stimulate thinking among the masses of Negroes and thus contributed so much to the intellectual ferment notable in that section." Further, "while intelligent white people throughout the country have just recently been awakened to the necessity of adult education, it has been going on for over 15 years among the Negroes in New York, and in that work Dr. Harrison more than played his part." Harrison's "achievements should prove an inspiration to many young Negroes, for, despite the handicap of poverty, he became one of the most learned men of his day and was able to teach the wide masses of his race how to appreciate and enjoy all the finer things of life, to glance back over the whole history of mankind, and to look forward "as far as thought can reach."[23]

Around January 1928 Hodge Kirnon wrote a letter to the editor of the *Truth Seeker* and pointed out that

> in the passing of Hubert H. Harrison . . . the Freethought Movement in New
> York has sustained a great loss. . . . Harrison was one of the ablest exponents
> of Rationalism in the city, and was the first and foremost negro in the cause
> of Freethought. His scintillating wit, irony, profundity and wide range of
> knowledge attracted thousands of persons during his many years of outdoor
> and indoor lecture work.

Kirnon noted that Harrison "contributed articles to the *Truth Seeker* when he first connected himself with Freethought activities, and in the Golden Jubilee Number of the *Truth Seeker* published on Sept. 1, 1923, his picture with favorable comments was featured." Kirnon added, "In 1915, Mr. Harrison delivered a course of lectures on the Natural History of Religion at the Modern School, New York" and later on "accorded the honor of 'adjunct professor' of Comparative Religion." Harrison "was well known for his liberal and radical views on economics, sociology and religion" and was "one of the most brilliant of negro writers." Kirnon added that on February 11, 1911, the *Truth Seeker* had described him as "a Negro who has the reputation of being the most scholarly representative of his race in America.'"[24]

Williana Jones Burroughs, writing under the pseudonym Mary Adams in the May 1, 1928, *Daily Worker*, paid particular attention to the "persistent efforts" by Harrison and others in teaching that "Negroes . . . have a rich history of revolt."[25]

———

One important letter to the editor published in the February 17 *New York News* raises troubling points regarding the historical neglect of Harrison's life and contributions. That letter, by Hodge Kirnon, stated that "a subject of popular discussion among thoughtful people" was the "reason for the absence of any mention of the late Hubert Harrison in the columns of the three leading Negro monthly periodicals in this country." Specifically, "[Randolph's] *The Messenger* —'a journal of scientific radicalism'" had "not a word to say concerning the death of the first and ablest Negro exponent of scientific radicalism." Similarly, "[Du Bois's] *Crisis*—A Record of the Darker Races" lamented the passing of the boxer "Tiger" Flowers but failed "to record the services of a man who was a lecturer for the Board of Education, and of whom [NAACP field director] William Pickens says 'can speak more easily, effectively and interestingly on a greater variety of subjects than any other man I have met, even in the great Universities.'" Finally, "[the Urban League's] *Opportunity*—'a Journal of Negro Life'" was "equally silent over the demise of an acknowledged first rate thinker— one who gave liberally to the intellectual life of the Negro, [who had done major publicity work for their Sustaining Fund Campaign,] and whose writings have appeared in that journal." Kirnon concluded, "There is something wrong somewhere," and the "concerted silence is ominous."[26]

———

On May 5, 1928, Rev. Ethelred Brown sent a letter to Mrs. Harrison about renaming the Harlem Community Church he ministered at 149 West 136th Street in honor of (the freethinking) Hubert H. Harrison (whose April 27 birthday had just passed).[27] The Harlem Community Church was officially renamed the Hubert Harrison Memorial Church at a service on May 6. The resolution was moved by Frank Poret (Poree?), seconded by Hodge Kirnon, warmly supported by other speakers, and unanimously passed by a standing vote.[28]

A flyer stated that "The Hubert Harrison Memorial Church" was both "A Temple and A Forum" that aimed to be "a modern church" and "a cultural center worthy of the man whose name it bears and whose memory it will perpetuate."[29]

On June 5 Rev. Brown wrote to Mrs. Harrison that members of a church committee "have set out to raise [a] fund of $500, one half of which will provide a scholarship for a daughter, and the other half will be shared between you and

Figure E.1. Egbert Ethelred Brown (July 11, 1875–February 17, 1956). The Jamaica-born Brown was an ordained Unitarian minister who in 1920 founded the Harlem Community Church. On May 5, 1928, Rev. Ethelred Brown sent a letter to Mrs. Harrison about renaming the Harlem Community Church he ministered at 136th Street in honor of the deceased, freethinking Hubert Harrison (whose April 27 birthday had just passed). The Harlem Community Church was officially renamed the Hubert Harrison Memorial Church at a service on May 6, 1928. The resolution, seconded by Hodge Kirnon, passed unanimously. A flyer stated that the Hubert Harrison Memorial Church was both "A Temple and A Forum" that aimed to be "a modern church" and "a cultural center worthy of the man whose name it bears and whose memory it will perpetuate." On June 5, 1928, Rev. Brown wrote to Mrs. Harrison that members of a church committee "have set out to raise fund of $500, one half of which will provide a scholarship for a daughter, and the other half will be shared between you and the purchase of two engraved pictures of Dr. Harrison," one of which was "to be presented to the 135th Street Library and the other [to] the church." The *Amsterdam News* of September 10, 1930, announced that a "life-like portrait of the late Hubert Harrison, which was presented by the Hubert Harrison Memorial Committee to the 135th street branch of the Public Library at a special service held at the Hubert Harrison Memorial Church, is now hanging on the main floor of the library." The "officials of the library—central and local—in accepting the gift of the committee, wrote in high terms of the invaluable service rendered by Dr. Harrison in popularizing the library and in helping to make it the institution it now is in Harlem." A "similar picture was presented at the same time to the church at 149 West 136th street, where it now hangs." *Source:* Public domain.

the purchase of two engraved pictures of Dr. Harrison," one of which was "to be presented to the 135th Street Library and the other [to] the church."[30]

Then, on Sunday afternoon June 17, 1928, "A Memorial Meeting as a Tribute to the Late Dr. Hubert Harrison" was scheduled for the auditorium of the 135th Street Public Library. A flyer announcing the event read: "Dr. Hubert Harrison for many years gave unstintingly to the people of this city from the accumulated fund of his vast and profound knowledge, and thus in great measure helped to develop the cultural Harlem of to-day. Let the community therefore arise as a unit and pay its tribute to the man who was indeed its intellectual benefactor." "Tribute-Bearers" for the event were to include Edgar Grey, Hodge Kirnon, Richard B. Moore, William Pickens, W. A. Domingo, Dr. E. Elliot Rawlins, Rabbi A. Josiah Ford, Miss A. E. Hendrickson, and Miss Ernestine Rose. Participating artists were to include Mrs. Eulalie Domingo (pianist) and Mr. J. E. Phillips (vocalist), and the Choir of Congregation Beth B'Nai Abraham was scheduled to render an anthem. An orchestra would open the proceedings. Rev. Brown would preside, and financial proceeds were to aid in the "Harrison Memorial Fund."[31] At that meeting a 1926 edition of *The Universal Ethiopian Hymnal*, edited by Arnold J. Ford, which Harrison's family would preserve in his papers, was used.[32]

Meetings continued throughout 1928. As the first anniversary of Harrison's death approached, the *American Recorder* of December 8, 1928, announced that a "Memorial for the "Late Hubert Harrison" was scheduled for December 9. "Harrison, whose lectures on the avenues, in halls or whatever platforms he occupied used to thrill thousands of both races, has not been forgotten," and "those who were interested in the great work he had done . . . decided to rename the church at 149 West 136th street in his honor." Similar to what Reverend Brown had written on June 5, it pointed out that a "memorial committee was also formed to raise a fund, of which his daughter was to receive $250 as a scholarship and his widow $200. The remainder was to secure two portraits, lifesize, of the deceased for the church." It was hoped that the goal of the entire amount to be raised would be reached at the time of the meeting.[33]

Meetings continued in 1929, and Ethelred Brown wrote an August 26, 1929, letter to Mrs. Harrison about the Hubert Harrison Memorial Church, a photo of Harrison, and plans for a first-class propaganda pamphlet.[34] Around the second anniversary of Harrison's death, a December 22, 1929, memorial service at the church included Hodge Kirnon offering a select reading from Harrison and Ernestine Rose accepting Harrison's portrait for the 135th Street Public Library.[35]

The *Amsterdam News* of September 10, 1930, announced that a "life-like portrait of the late Hubert Harrison, which was presented by the Hubert Harrison

Figure E.2. "A Memorial Meeting as A Tribute to the Late Dr. Hubert Harrison, June 17, 1928," broadside notice. This flyer for "A Memorial Meeting Tribute to Hubert Harrison" on June 17, 1928, listed "Tribute-Bearers" as Edgar Grey, Hodge Kirnon, Richard B. Moore, William Pickens, W. A. Domingo, Dr. E. Elliot Rawlins, Rabbi A. Josiah Ford, Miss A. E. Hendrickson, and Miss Ernestine Rose, with Mrs. Eulalie Domingo (pianist), Mr. J. E. Phillips (vocalist), and the Choir of Congregation Beth B'Nai Abraham scheduled to be participating artists. *Source:* Hubert H. Harrison Papers, Box 16, Folder 30, Rare Book and Manuscript Library, Columbia University Library. See https://dlc.library.columbia.edu/catalog/cul:pzgmsbcdq0.

Memorial Committee to the 135th street branch of the Public Library at a special service held at the Hubert Harrison Memorial Church, is now hanging on the main floor of the library." The "officials of the library—central and local—in accepting the gift of the committee, wrote in high terms of the invaluable service rendered by Dr. Harrison in popularizing the library and in helping to make

His Death; Harlem's Sorrow; Race's Loss

Died Dec 17th 7/p.m.
New York News Dec 24th 1927.

HUBERT H. HARRISON,—Scholar, Orator, Writer.

Figure E.3. Hubert Harrison standing with cane, *New York News*, December 31, 1927. This photo of Harrison was accompanied by the heading "His Death; Harlem's Sorrow; Race's Loss" in the *New York News*, December 31, 1927. An accompanying obituary, "The Death of Hubert Harrison," in that issue of the paper stated that "tens of thousands of New Yorkers will miss the philosophy of the most brilliant street orator that this Metropolis has produced in the last generation." Harrison's "oratory was with him not only a pleasure, but a duty through which he felt impelled to serve his race and the country of his adoption." His soul "knew neither black nor white; neither race or religion," and "if the universal man has been created more genuinely in our day, we have not seen him." The *News* added that Harrison's "great fund of philosophy, his ready wit, his melodious measured utterances disarmed all those who came to scoff and turned them into his admiring pupils." He served as "a potent and living example to the countless thousands of Caucasians who have heard him in the last twenty-five years of the potential equality of the black man." He was "the harbinger of good-will and a better understanding between the races. Like Mohammed who went to the mountains when the mountains would not come to Mohammed, Harrison carried his mighty disarmament of prejudice to his fellow white citizens. Greater service than this no colored man can render. None has there been who have so intensively and effectively rendered that service in this great metropolis. His was not the policy of compromise or apology for his race. He did not go like many a Southern educator, hat in hand, to beg alms for his race from the financial and industrial magnates." Rather, "He preached the brotherhood of man and the common basis of all the problems of all the races of mankind. It was therein that Hubert Harrison served nobly his day and generation. That was his contribution to his race's progress. Truly his death was Harlem's sorrow, but his race's loss." *Source: New York News*, December 31, 1927.

it the institution it now is in Harlem." A "similar picture was presented at the same time to the church at 149 West 136th street, where it now hangs."[36]

After nine years of regular meetings, including yearly meetings in which the anniversary of Harrison's death was commemorated, the Hubert Harrison Memorial Church changed its name to the Harlem Unitarian Church at its May 2, 1937, meeting.[37]

———————

Hubert Harrison was born in St. Croix, Danish West Indies, of a Barbadian immigrant, plantation-working mother and a born-enslaved Crucian father. He lived in poverty on Estate Concordia and in the Water Gut section of Christiansted before coming to New York and living in an area that included some of the meanest tenements in New York City (in the West Sixties) and then in the most densely populated section of Harlem.

Harrison opposed the white supremacy and class injustice that he encountered after coming to New York. He understood white supremacy to be central to capitalist rule in the United States and to have broad a broad effect internationally. He deemed it a priority to work at developing an enlightened race consciousness, racial solidarity, and radical internationalism among "Negro" people—especially the "common people"—in struggles for "political equality" (particularly in employment and voting), against white supremacy, and for radical social change. He understood African Americans to be "the touchstone of the modern democratic idea"; emphasized that "while the color line exists," the "cant of democracy" can be used as a "camouflage" that is "intended as dust in the eyes of white voters"; and, perhaps most importantly, believed that true democracy and equality for African Americans implies "a revolution . . . startling even to think of."

While living his life in poverty he made remarkable contributions: as the leading Black activist in the Socialist Party and in the Freethought Movement; as the founder of the Liberty League, the militant New Negro Movement, and the International Colored Unity League; as the editor of *The Voice*, *New Negro*, *Negro World*, and *Voice of the Negro*; and as a pioneering soapbox orator and Board of Education and freelance educator.

He was described as "perhaps the foremost Aframerican intellect of his time," and his brilliance is evident in his writings and talks on democracy and equality, race, class, capitalism, imperialism, race consciousness, racial solidarity, "the common people," internationalism, the First World War, Black women, Black history, Black leadership, lynching, armed self-defense, the Ku Klux Klan, world history, ancient history, Africa and the Caribbean, the Virgin Islands, India, China, Christianity, Islam, Booker T. Washington, W. E. B. Du Bois, Marcus Garvey, J. A. Rogers, Claude McKay, Frederick Douglass,

Abraham Lincoln, Woodrow Wilson, Republicans, Democrats, the Single Tax party, the Socialist Party, the Communist Party, the "Harlem Renaissance," poetry, literature, and the theater.

With the completion of this two-volume biography of Hubert Harrison, "the father of Harlem radicalism," it is hoped that his extraordinary life of activism and his brilliant writing and thinking will increasingly be made available—and be of use—to current and future generations.

Figure E.4. Hubert Harrison gravesite marker. On December 23, 2014, eighty-seven years after his December 17, 1927, death, a beautiful jet-black slant marker with etching was placed on the gravesite of Hubert H. Harrison—the "intellectual giant" known as the "Father of Harlem Radicalism." The marker includes words based on the poem "Hubert H. Harrison" written by Andy Razaf, the unofficial poet laureate of the militant New Negro Movement. The gravesite is located at Plot—Salvia; Range—13; Grave—100, Woodlawn Cemetery, 517 East 233rd Street, the Bronx. The gravesite marker was obtained after people desirous of preserving the memory of Hubert Harrison began to organize for that purpose. Ilva Harrison, granddaughter of Hubert Harrison, selected, paid for, and chose the image and wording on the marker. *Source:* Lisa Troiano, Dominick DeNigris Monuments, Bronx, New York.

Acknowledgments

Volume 1 of this biography's preface and acknowledgments (xiii–xx) provided background and thanked many people who offered assistance related to my research and writing on Hubert Harrison. Those people are incorporated in these acknowledgments. Since that time, additional support for my writing and research has come from those who offered reviews and comments, those who helped to arrange Harrison presentations at which I was able to get important feedback, those who provided new assistance in my research, and those who provided important "subvention" contributions to Columbia University Press. For an independent historian all of these forms of assistance are extremely important.

Among those who offered reviews and comments are Sean Ahern, Christopher Ake, Kwasi Akyeampong, Abayomi Azikwe, Amiri Baraka, Colin Benjamin, Alberto Benvenuti, Maria Bibbs, Herb Boyd, Gene Bruskin, Vanessa Bush, Carole Boyce Davies, Emily Jane Dawson, Lloyd Dev, Peter Dimock, Bruce A. Dixon, Ibn Melvin Drakeford, Brent Hayes Edwards, Gwen Edwards, Shelley Ettinger, Bill Fletcher Jr., Rhone Fraser, Wayne Glasker, Larry A. Greene, Stephanie Hanlon, LaShawn Harris, Jonathan M. Hansen, Winston James, Kevin "Rashid" Johnson, Sterling Johnson, Brian Jones, Peniel E. Joseph, Yuri Kochiyama, Clarence Lang, David Levering Lewis, Rudolph Lewis, Charles L. Lumpkins, Manning Marable, Scott McLemee, Bret McCabe, Patty McCormick, E. Ethelbert Miller, Wilson J. Moses, Peter Moore, Gary Okihiro, Ken Olende, Bryan D. Palmer, Elena Pajaro Peres, Christopher Phelps, Lavelle Porter, Felicia Pride, Arnold Rampersad, David Roediger, Allen Ruff, Genevieve Ryan, Natty Mark Samuels, David Slavin, James Smethurst, Joyce Moore

Turner, George Tyson, Susan Van Gelder, Cornel West, Mat Witt, Komozi Woodard, John Woodford, and Dave Zirin.

Among those who helped to arrange Harrison presentations are Ann Marie Adams, Sean Ahern, Muhammad Ahmad (Maxwell Stanford Jr.), Kali Ahset-Amen, Simone A. James Alexander, Marva Allen, Radwa Ali, Milton Allimadi, David Allocco, Isa Anate, Lynne Anderson, Melissa Anyiwo, Sam Anderson, Thabiti Asukile, David Bacon, Nellie Bailey, Kazembe Balagun, Marc Barnhill, Kevin Barrett, Marcia Bayne-Smith, Claudrena Harold, John Bekken, Colin Benjamin, Vladimir Bonhomme, George Britt, Jamilla Brathwaite, Michael Braun, Nobel Bratton, Ed Buckner, Sarah Buie, Randall K. Burkett, Cornelius Bynum, J. Amos Caley, Doug Canton, Greg Carr, Campbell Ras Soup Carter, Linda M. Carter, Bob Carson, Mauro Camporeale, William C. Carlotti, Joel Chaffee, David Christian, Anthony Clarke, Charles Coleman, Valerie Combie, Mary Lynn Cramer, Tracy Crawford, Steve Cushmore, Russell Dale, Chenzira Davis-Kahina, Dana-ain Davis, Kathy Davis, Peaches Davis, Timur Davis, Wartyna L. Davis, Patrick Delices, Lloyd Dev, Bill DiFazio, Keianna Dixon, Michael De Dora, Casey Doyle, Sonia Jacobs Dow, Leo Downes, Jim Draegar, Ora Horton Drayton, John Elrick, Jeff Farias, Peter Filardo, John Flanders, Laura Flanders, Donna Fleming, Ian C. Fletcher, Glenn Ford, Ian Forrest, James Fugate, Kwame A. Mark Freeman, Margery Freeman, Morris Garner, Henry Louis Gates Jr., Sally Gellert, Etienne A. Gibbs, Lisa Gillingham, Eddie Goldman, Michael Gomez, Edmund W. Gordon, John E. Gore, Janice Graham, Trust Graham, Vera Ingrid Grant, Doug Enaa Greene, J. Everett Green, Ousmane Power Greene, Taqiyya Haden, Chrystena Hahn, Hugh Hamilton, Larry Hamm, Angela Harden, Fredrik Harris, Larry Hartenian, Michael G. Haskins, Bill Henning, Doug Henwood, Evelyn M. Hershey, Evelyn Brooks Higginbotham, Robert A. Hill, James Hoban, Courtney Hodock, John Hollingsworth, Gloria Hughes, Francis Abiola Irele, Jahi Issa, Jocelyn Jackson, Lawrence P. Jackson, Sandra Jackson, Karl Jagbandhansingh, Linda A. Jenkins, Anthony P. Johnson, Buzz Johnson, Ellsworth Johnson-Bey, Karen Johnson, Charles Jones, Mimi Jones, Trevor Jones, Dedon Kamathi, Nati Kamau-Natak, Richard Kearney, Eva Keith, Brian Kelly, Margaret Kimberley, Shannon King, Carol J. Kraemer, Umang Kumar, Edgar Lake, Michael Lardner, Mirna Lascano, Brooke Lehman, Utrice Leid, Naeemah Legair, Mary Anne Lenk, Nelson Lichtenstein, Erol Maitland, Ravi Malhotra, Amalia Mallard, Jason L. Mallory, Eric Mann, Abayomi Manrique, Stella Marrs, Marlowe Mason, Guirdex Masse, Phillip Maysles, Eric Maywar, Ali McBride, Sol McCants, Cynthia McKinney, Darlene McKight, Polly McLean, Laura McSpedon, Liz Mestres, Tony Monteiro, Mario Moorhead, Mark Naison, Ken Nash, Michael Nash, Navi Nasr, Amilcar Navarro, Immanuel Ness, Fred Nguyen, Nathaniel Norment Jr., Peggy Norris, Naji Mujahid, Yusuf Nurrudin, Emeka Nwadiora, Sally O'Brien, Peter Olney, Brendan O'Malley,

Bryan D. Palmer, Greg Pason, Chad Pearson, Paul Malachi Penchalapadu, Ruth Percy, Eugene "Doc" Petersen, Adrienne Petty, Marc Pessin, Pamela Pinnock, Steven Pitts, Lou Pizzitola, Ousmane Power-Greene, Tasha Prosper, Karla Rab, Joe Ramsey, Donna Rauch, Laurice Reynolds, Jimmy Richardson, Leonard Richardson, Jean Ross, Mary Roebuck, Mimi Rosenberg, Randy Rosenbeg, Allen Ruff, Michael T. Ryan, Angelica M. Santomauro, Daa'iya L. Sanusi, Arlene Scala, Lance Selfa, Malik Sekou, Damina Shahidi, Justin D. Shannahan, Stephen R. Shalom, Sibanye, Julie Siestreem April Simpson, Laura Sjalaj, Peter Soter, Ann Sparanese, Marc Steiner, Chris Stevenson, Susan Stewart, Shelley Stokes-Hammond, David Strachan, Kahli-Ahset Strayhorn, Tracie Strahan, Debby Strong, Mark Sylvester, Clarence Taylor, Karen D. Taylor, Jeanne Theoharis, Judy Thompson, Mark Thompson, Christopher Tinson, Muriel Tillinghast, Gary Glennell Toms, Max Uhlenbeck, Martha Urbiel, Dan Veach, Kimberly Veal, Tony Van Der Meer, Meredith Walters, Roland Washington, Charles Welch, John Wessell-McKoy, Bernard White, Robert White, Jocelyn E. Whitehead, Kate Wilgruber, Valerie Wilhite, Charles Williams, Dana Williams, Erika Williams, Jolivette Williams, Francille Rusan Wilson, Joe Wilson, Sean Wilson, Stella Winston, Stan Woodard, David Yazbeck, Steve Yothment, Steve Zeltzer, and Michael Zweig.

Among those who offered new research assistance (and in some cases other special assistance) are Linnea M. Anderson, Lene Asp, Terese Austin, Joellen ElBashir, Peggy Brooks Bertram, Roderick Bradford, Alan Bown, Sonia Casiano, Russell Christopher, Rob Cox, Tara C. Craig, Tracey Curley, Wyatt Day, Elizabeth Dunn, David Edgecombe, Martha Foley, John Gartrell, Carl Ginsbug, Heidi Heller, Anton Heins, Robert A. Hill, Emily Holmes, Ron Jackson, Timothy V. Johnson, Thai Jones, Gloria Joseph, Amber Elise Junipher, Cheryl C. King, Kwasi Konadu, Jennifer B. Lee, Paul Levy, Haley J. Maynard, Eric Mortensen, Patrick Raftery, Michael Ryan, Meredith A. Self, Susan Slovin, Daniel Tisdale, Nora Tossounian, Gina Troiano, Donna Mussenden Van Der Zee, Lauren Miller Walsh, Genevieve Whitaker, and Syl Woolford.

Among those who helped in "subvention" efforts are Sean Ahern, Chris and Diane Ake, Joe Berry, Peter Bohmer, Gene Bruskin, Melvin Drakeford, Steve Early, Debra Giblin, Elizbeth Gitt Charitable Foundation, the Peggy and Yale Gordon Center for Performing Arts, Dr. Edmund W. Gordon, Becky and Perri Hom, Alene Jackson, Vivek Jain, Jane Latour, Chenzira Kahina, Garret and Kathy Keizer, John Kerrick, Jane Latour, Leigh Lockwood, Michael Mery, Tracy Mott, Jessica Gordon Nembhard, Marc Pessin, Rockland Community Foundation, Dorothy Salem, Julie Siestreem, David Slavin, Michael Spiegel, Muriel Tillinghast, and Sharon Tipton.

A very special thanks is extended to my editors Stephen Wesley and Christian P. Winting, to my copy editor Robert Fellman and production editor Michael

Haskell, and to Alanna Duncan and Marielle Poss of Columbia University Press for supporting this work, appreciating Harrison's importance, and thoughtfully and skillfully working with me on such a major project.

To my wife, Becky Hom, and to my daughter, Perri Lin Hom, go my deepest and most special thanks and love. They have been enormously supportive and their freely and frequently offered "suggestions" have sustained this project while recognizing its importance. Without Becky's love, support, and encouragement and Perri's love, Harrison-like critical independence, and professional expertise, this project would never have been the joyous labor that it has been.

If there are any people that I have inadvertently omitted in these acknowledgments, I apologize, and I thank you.

Abbreviations

ACABA
Foner, Philip S., and Herbert Shapiro, eds. *American Communism and Black Americans: A Documentary History.* Vol. 1: *A Documentary History, 1919–1929.* Vol. 2: *A Documentary History, 1930–1934.* Philadelphia: Temple University Press, 1987, 1991.

ANB
Garraty, John A., and Mark C. Carnes, eds. *American National Biography.* 24 vols. New York: Oxford University Press, 1999.

ASABA
Foner, Philip S. *American Socialism and Black Americans: From the Age of Jackson to World War II.* Westport, CT: Greenwood, 1977.

B
Box

BF
Bureau File, Investigative Case Files of the Bureau of Investigation, 1908–1922, Records Group 65, Records of the Federal Bureau of Investigation, National Archives, Washington, DC.

BI
Bureau of Investigation

BWA
Hine, Darlene Clark, Elsa Barkley Brown, and Rosalyn Terborg-Penn, eds. *Black Women in America: An Historical Encyclopedia.* 2 vols. Brooklyn, NY: Carlson, 1993.

DANB
Logan, Rayford W., and Michael R. Winston, eds. *Dictionary of American Negro Biography.* New York: Norton, 1982.

DHNPUS	Aptheker, Herbert, ed. *A Documentary History of the Negro People in the United States.* Secaucus, NJ: Citadel, 1977.
DNA	National Archives, Washington, DC.
DoJ	Department of Justice
EAL	Buhle, Mari Jo, Paul Buhle, and Dan Georgakas. *Encyclopedia of the American Left.* Urbana: University of Illinois Press, 1990.
ENY	Jackson, Kenneth T., ed. *Encyclopedia of New York City.* New Haven, CT: Yale University Press, 1995.
F	Folder
FB	Flat Box
FSAA	Kornweibel, Theodore, Jr. *Federal Surveillance of Afro-Americans (1917–1925): The First World War, the Red Scare, and the Garvey Movement.* Lanham, MD: University Publications of America: 1986. 25 microfilm reels.
GP	Hill, Robert A., ed. *The Marcus Garvey and Universal Negro Improvement Association Papers.* 13 vols. Vols. 1–10: Berkeley: University of California Press, 1983–2006. Vols. 11–13: Durham, NC: Duke University Press, 2011–2016.
HATB	James, Winston. *Holding Aloft the Banner of Ethiopia: Caribbean Radicalism in Early Twentieth-Century America.* New York: Verso, 1998.
HD	HHH Diary. HP, B9, F1, including vol. 1, *September 18, 1907–August 8, 1923*; and vol. 2, *November 1, 1923–August 30, 1927*, HPDLC.
HH (HHH)	Hubert Harrison (Hubert H. Harrison)
HHVHR	Perry, Jeffrey B. *Hubert Harrison: The Voice of Harlem Radicalism, 1883–1918.* New York: Columbia University Press, 2008.
Hill, ed., *The Crusader*	*The Crusader.* Published by Cyril V. Briggs; facsimile ed., ed. and intro. Robert A. Hill, 3 vols. New York, 1987.
HP	Hubert H. Harrison Papers, 1893–1927, Columbia University Rare Book and Manuscript Library, New York. Finding

aid: https://findingaids.library.columbia.edu/ead/nnc-rb
/ldpd_6134799.

HPDLC

Hubert H. Harrison Papers, Columbia Digital Library Collections (Columbia University Libraries). https://dlc.library
.columbia.edu/sites/hubert_h_harrison.

HR

A Hubert Harrison Reader. Ed. and intro. Jeffrey B. Perry.
Middletown, CT: Wesleyan University Press, 2001.

JBP

Jeffrey B. Perry

JBPP

Jeffrey B. Perry Papers in possession of author

Kaiser Index

The Kaiser Index to Black Resources, 1948–1986. 5 vols.
From the Schomburg Center for Research in Black Culture
of the New York Public Library. Brooklyn: Carlson, 1992.

LOC

Library of Congress

LSAG

L. S. Alexander Gumby collection of Negroiana, 1800–1981,
Columbia University Rare Book and Manuscript Library.

MG

Marcus Garvey

MI

Military Intelligence

MID

Military Intelligence Division Records, Record Group 165,
National Archives, Washington, DC.

NAW

James, Edward T., ed., Janet Wilson James, assoc. ed., and
Paul S. Boyer, asst. ed. *Notable American Women, 1607–
1950: A Biographical Dictionary.* 3 Vols. Cambridge, MA:
Belknap Press of Harvard University Press, 1971, 1974.

NandN

Harrison, Hubert H. *The Negro and the Nation.* New York:
Cosmo-Advocate Publishing Co., 1917

NYC

New York City

NYHR

New York Supreme Court, Hall of Records, New York

OG

"Old German"

RCAH

Foner, Eric, and John Garraty, eds. *The Reader's Companion
to American History.* Boston: Houghton Mifflin, 1991.

RF	Martin, Tony. *Race First: The Ideological and Organizational Struggles of Marcus Garvey and the Universal Negro Improvement Association.* New Marcus Garvey Library 8. Westport, CT: Greenwood, 1976.
RG	Record Group
RR	Senate of the State of New York. *Revolutionary Radicalism: Its History, Purpose, and Tactics.* 2 parts of 2 vols. each. Albany, NY, 1920.
ScrAftermath	HHH Scrapbook. *Aftermath of the Great War 1918–1919.* Vol. 1: *Political: The Rising Tide of Color and "The Lesser Breeds."* Hubert H. Harrison Papers, Box 10, Folder 2, Rare Book and Manuscript Library, Columbia University.
ScrEarlyWr	HHH Scrapbook. *Early Writings of Hubert H. Harrison: Mainly in "The Truth Seeker," "The New York Call" "The International Socialist Review" "The Voice" and "The New Negro." Also "Zukunfdt," "The Colonies Magazine," and "The Medical Review of Reviews."* Hubert H. Harrison Papers, Box 13, Folders 1–2, Rare Book and Manuscript Library, Columbia University.
ScrMAM1	HHH Scrapbook. *Mainly About Me.* Vol. 1: *The Radical and Racial Phase. Newspaper Clippings & Other Items Relating to Hubert H. Harrison, 8/11/12* [November 8, 1912]. Hubert H. Harrison Papers, Flat Box 740, Rare Book and Manuscript Library, Columbia University.
ScrMAM2	*"M.A.M."* [*Mainly About Me*]. Vol. 2: *The Upward Climb. Hubert H. Harrison, Public Notices, Records and References.* Hubert H. Harrison Papers, Flat Box 740, Rare Book and Manuscript Library, Columbia University.
ScrPN	HHH Scrapbook. *Public Notices, Records and References.* Vol. 2: *The Upward Climb Scrapbook, 1 April 1903–2 April 1927* [Loose clippings and pasted into book; contains articles about Marcus Garvey trial. Continues *Mainly About Me*, vol. 1]. Hubert H. Harrison Papers, Box 13, Folder 5; Hubert H. Harrison Papers, Flat Box 740, Rare Book and Manuscript Library, Columbia University.
ScrWr	HHH Scrapbook. *Writings of Hubert Harrison Contributed to the Negro World Jan 1920 to Feb 1922: Major Pieces—Book Reviews, Editorial Contributions, Minor Pieces, Book Reviews, Editorial, Contributions, Verses, Etc., Duplicates* [unpasted]. *Writings Hubert Harrison Contributed to Negro*

World Scrapbook, 1918–10 October 1926 [Loose clippings and clippings pasted in book. Note: "most of the formal editorial ('leaders') of 1920 will be found reproduced in my 2nd book. 'When Africa Awakes'—H.H.]. Hubert H. Harrison Papers, Box 13, Folder 7, Rare Book and Manuscript Library, Columbia University.

SP   Socialist Party

SP, LNY   Socialist Party, Local New York, Papers, Tamiment Library, New York University.

WAA   Harrison, Hubert H. *When Africa Awakes: The "Inside Story" of the Stirrings and Strivings of the New Negro in the Western World*. New York: Porro Press, 1920; new exp. ed., ed. and intro. Jeffrey B. Perry. New York: Diasporic Africa Press, 2015.

WBD   *Webster's Biographical Dictionary*. Springfield, MA: G&C Webster, 1943.

WC   *The World* Collection, Butler Library, Columbia University.

WEBD   Lewis, David Levering, *W. E. B. Du Bois*, vol. 1: *Biography of a Race, 1868–1919*; vol. 2: *The Fight for Equality and the American Century, 1919–1963*. New York: Henry Holt, 1993, 2000.

WEBDB   William Edward Burghardt Du Bois

WEBDBP   William Edward Burghardt Du Bois Papers. Special Collections and University Archives, University of Massachusetts Libraries, Amherst. https://credo.library.umass.edu/view/collection/mums312.

WGMC   Rogers, Joel A. *World's Great Men of Color*. 2 vols. New York: J. A. Rogers, 1946–1947.

WNBD   *Webster's New Biographical Dictionary*. Springfield, MA: Merriam-Webster, 1988.

WNUD   *Webster's New Universal Unabridged Dictionary*. New York: Barnes & Noble, 1989.

WWCA   Yenser, Thomas, ed. *Who's Who in Colored America: A Biographical Dictionary of Notable Living Persons of African Descent in America, 1938–1939–1940*. 2nd ed. Brooklyn, NY: T. Yenser, 1940.

Notes

Introduction

1. *HHVHR*, 4–5; Joyce Moore Turner, *Caribbean Crusaders and the Harlem Renaissance* (Urbana: University of Illinois Press, 2005), 19; and Richard B. Moore, "Africa Conscious Harlem," *Freedomways* 3, no. 3 (Summer 1963): 320.

2. Joel A. Rogers, "Hubert Harrison: Intellectual Giant and Free-Lance Educator (1883–1927)," in *WGMC*, 2:611.

3. On Harrison being called the "Father of Harlem Radicalism" by Randolph and others, see Jervis Anderson, *A. Philip Randolph: A Biographical Portrait* (New York: Harcourt, Brace, Jovanovich, 1973), 79–80; Roi Ottley and William J. Weatherby, eds., *The Negro in New York: An Informal Social History* (New York: New York Public Library, 1967), 223; Warren J. Halliburton with Ernest Kaiser, *Harlem: A History of Broken Dreams* (Garden City, NY: Doubleday, 1974), 45; Helen C. Camp, "Harrison, Hubert Henry (April 27, 1883–December 17, 1917)," in *American Reformers: An H. W. Wilson Biographical Dictionary*, ed. Alden Whitman (Bronx, NY: H. W. Wilson, 1985), 406–7; Robert Hill, "On Collectors, Their Contributions to the Documentation of the Black Past," in *Black Bibliophiles and Collectors: Preservers of Black History*, ed. Elinor Des Verney Sinnette, W. Paul Coates, and Thomas C. Battle (Washington, DC: Howard University Press, 1990), 47–56, esp. 47; JBP, "Hubert Henry Harrison, 'The Father of Harlem Radicalism': The Early Years—1883 Through the Founding of the Liberty League and *The Voice* in 1917" (Ph.D. diss., Columbia University, 1986), 27n2; JBP, "Hubert Henry Harrison," in *Encyclopedia of African American Culture and History* (New York: Macmillan, 1995), 1230–31; *HATB*; *HR*, 2; and *WAA*, vi. The title "Father of Harlem Radicalism" takes on greater significance when one realizes that during and after the First World War Harlem symbolized the international center of radical Black activity. See Moore, "Africa Conscious Harlem," 320; and Seth M. Scheiner, *Negro Mecca: A History of the Negro in New York, 1865–1920* (New York, 1965), 8–9. Cary D. Wintz, *Black Culture and the Harlem Renaissance* (Houston, TX: Rice University Press, 1988), 1, 22, writes that in "the period between World War I and 1920" the "locus of black leadership shifted from

[Booker T. Washington's base in] Tuskegee [Alabama] to New York"; "Harlem, in short, was where the action was in black America in the decade following World War I." Claude McKay, *Harlem: Negro Metropolis* (1940; New York: Harcourt, Brace, Jovanovich, 1968), 16, points out how Harlem was a "magnet," and he describes it simply as "the Negro capital of the world."

4. Moore, "Africa Conscious Harlem," 320; *HATB*, 123.

5. *HHVHR*, 5. "Negro Question for Vol. I, Notes from Theodore Draper interview with W. A. Domingo, January 18, 1958 [New York, N.Y.]," 2, Theodore Draper Research Files, 1919–1990, Series 1: American Communism research files, 1915–1976; Subseries 1.3: American Communist Party (1919–1929), 1915–1968, B21, F20, Manuscript, Archives, and Rare Book Library, Robert W. Woodruff Library, Emory University, Atlanta, Georgia. On Harrison as the "New Negro ideological mentor," see Robert A. Hill, "Introduction: Racial and Radical: Cyril V. Briggs, *The Crusader* Magazine, and the African Blood Brotherhood, 1918–1922," in Cyril V. Briggs, ed., *The Crusader*, a facsimile of the periodical edited with a new introduction and index by Robert A. Hill (New York: Garland, 1987), 3 vols., 1:xv. J. A. Rogers writes, "The Garvey Movement and the *Messenger* Group, the first racial, the second economic in doctrine . . . both were fructified by the spirit and teaching of Harrison." *WGMC*, 2:615. Harrison also made a "profound contribution to the Caribbean radical tradition in the United States" as the historian Winston James (*HATB*, 123) points out.

6. *HHVHR*, 5, 8; *HR*, 294. On Malcolm's parents, see, for example, Ted Vincent, "The Garveyite Parents of Malcolm X," *Black Scholar* 20 (March/April 1989): 10–13.

7. HD, September 18, 1907. A list of Harrison's scrapbooks in Boxes 11–13 and Flat Box 740 of the Hubert H. Harrison Papers, 1883–1927, at Columbia University's Rare Book and Manuscript Library can be found in the Hubert H. Harrison Papers Finding Aid at https://findingaids.library.columbia.edu/ead/nnc-rb/ldpd_6134799/dsc/4.

8. HD, September 18, 1907.

9. HH, "The Meditations of Mustapha: A Soul in Search of Itself," *Negro World*, c. October 23, 1920; and *HR*, 260–62, quotation on 262.

10. Eugene O'Neill to HH, June 9, 1921, HP, B3, F5.

11. *WGMC*, 2:616.

12. "Lament Dream of Dr. Hubert Harrison," *Amsterdam News*, December 28, 1927, 1.

1. Return to Harlem and Resurrection of *The Voice*
(July–December 1918)

1. *HHVHR*, 110–12, 440n73; New York State Archives, Albany, NY; *State Population Census Schedules, 1915*; Election District 22; Assembly District 21; City: NY; County: NY; 31; County Clerk, NY County, Extract of State Census for June 1, 1915, No. 6747, for HHH, 231 W. 134th Street, A.D. 21, E.D. 22, Page 31, 32; 1920 Federal Census, *Manhattan Assembly District 13, NY, NY*; Roll: T625_1209; Page 1B; Enumeration District 972; Image 804; and Aida Harrison Richardson and William Harrison, interview with JBP, NYC, August 4, 1983, possession of JBP. Laura Forrester was listed as living with the Harrison family in the 1915 NYC and the 1920 federal censuses. She was listed with Charles and Williana Jones Burroughs in the 1910 federal census. On Charles Burroughs, see *HHVHR*, 73, 84–85, 89–91, 94, 100, 252, 361, 315, 437–38n45; on Williana

Jones Burroughs, see *HHVHR*, 2, 90–94, 100, 110, 437–38n5, 533; and on Laura Forrester (c. 1865–1923), see *HHVHR*, 89–90, 252, 270–71, 435n20, and Aida Harrison Richardson, interview with JBP, NYC, July 10, 1991, possession of JBP. In 1961 Charles Gordon Burroughs, the son of Charles and Williana Jones Burroughs, cofounded the DuSable Museum of African American History in Chicago with his wife, Margaret Taylor Goss Burroughs. See Kenan Heise, "Charles G. Burroughs, Teacher, Co-Founder of Du Sable [*sic*] Museum," *Chicago Tribune*, March 14, 1994; and Carola Burroughs to JBP, July 22, 2019.

2. *HHVHR*, 157, 169–70, 172, 175, 189–92, 194, 206–9, and 222–30.

3. *HHVHR*, 6–8, 141–219, 222–34, 471–2n18. On Harrison's labor organizing in the period around the Liberty Congress, see *HHVHR*, 513nn10–11; "Pullman Men to Organize," *Chicago Defender*, June 29, 1918, 3; "Pullman Employees Hold Great Mass Meeting," *Washington Bee*, June 29, 1918, 1; "Negro Workers Get Impetus to Organize in Labor Unions," *New York Call*, June 24, 1918; in *The Black Worker: A Documentary History from Colonial Times to the Present*, vol. 5: *The Negro Worker from 1900 to 1919*, ed. Philip S. Foner and Ronald L. Lewis (Philadelphia: Temple University Press, 1980), 443; "The Town Crier: 'Workers in War Time and Why They Should Combine,'" announcement of an address by "Hubert Harrison, colored organizer of New York, before the meetings of the Women Wage Earners Association, 704, T. St., NW, on June 30, 1918," *Washington Post*, June 29, 1918, 9; HP, FB740; and "A General Membership Meeting of the International Federation of Workers in the Hotel, Restaurant, Club and Catering Industry to be held at the Headquarters, 218 N. 13th Street (Philadelphia), Thursday, May 23rd, at 9. P.M., Nightworkers at 1 A.M.," flier, HP, FB740.

4. *HHVHR*, 8–9.

5. *HHVHR*, 9, 378–92.

6. *HHVHR*, 8, 407n28; *HR*, 5, 416n26; *WAA*, esp. vi–xi, xv–xvin14, xxiii–xxvi, 10, 39–40, 53, 155–56, 176–77, 211.

7. *HHVHR*, 2, 4–5, 8–9, 295–6, 337–39, 364; *WAA*, vi–viii, xv, xxiii–xv.

8. *HHVHR*, 5, 285–92, 381, 408n33; *WAA*, vii, xxii, xxiv, 12, 157. Particularly noteworthy is the fact that, in response to the white supremacist "pogrom" (Harrison's word) on the East St. Louis, Illinois, "Negro" community and attacks on the "Negro" community in the San Juan Hill section of New York City, Harrison led a mass protest rally attended by a thousand people in Harlem, which urged armed self-defense in the face of such attacks. East St. Louis is located twelve miles from Ferguson, Missouri, which on August 9, 2014, was the site of the fatal shooting of Michael Brown by a "white" police officer—an event followed by a series of related mass protests around the country, including in New York City. On Harrison's describing East St. Louis as a "pogrom," see HH, "The East St. Louis Horror," *The Voice*, July 4, 1917, in *New Negro* 4, no. 1 (September 1919): 8; *HR*, 93–95, quotation on 94; and *WAA*, 14–16, 155–56, quotation on 14. See also *HHVHR*, 282–86, 297–301; and "Urges Negroes to Get Arms: Liberty League President Advises His Race to 'Defend Their Lives,'" *New York Times*, July 5, 1917.

9. Jervis Anderson, *A. Philip Randolph: A Biographical Portrait* (New York: Harcourt, Brace, Jovanovich, 1973), 79–80; and Roi Ottley and William J. Weatherby, eds., *The Negro in New York: An Informal Social History* (New York: New York Public Library, 1967), 223.

10. On the Liberty Congress, see *HHVHR*, 378–83. On Joel E. Spingarn's pro-war stance, his appointment as a major in Military Intelligence, his advocacy of segregated camps, and his efforts to undermine the Liberty Congress, see *HHVHR*, 355, 373–78;

Ernest Allen Jr., "'Close Ranks': Major Joel E. Spingarn and the Two Souls of W. E. B. Du Bois," *Contributions in Black Studies* 3 (1979–1980): 25–38, esp. 26, 27, 33–35; Roy Talbert Jr., *Negative Intelligence: The Army and the American Left, 1917–1941* (Jackson: University Press of Mississippi, 1991), 119–27; and B. Joyce Ross, *J. E. Spingarn and the Rise of the NAACP, 1911–1939* (New York: Atheneum, 1972), 3–13, esp. 3–5, 84–102. Stephen G. Tomkins, "In 1917, Spy Target Was Black America," *Commercial Appeal* (Memphis), March 21, 1993, notes "Spingarn and black agent, Lt. T. Montgomery Gregory ran a small unit of undercover agents according to intelligence documents." Mark Ellis, *Race War and Surveillance: African Americans and the United States Government During World War I* (Bloomington: Indiana University Press, 2001), 146, writes: "Early in June 1918, he [Spingarn] secured approval for the formation of a subsection of MI-4 to do special work on 'Negro subversion.' He found himself a separate office in the business area of Washington and began identifying eligible black army officers to staff the projected Negro subversion subsection. He was assisted by Lt. T. Montgomery Gregory, a Howard University instructor." India Artis (NAACP/*Crisis Magazine*), to JBP, July 23, 2015, copy in possession of author, indicates that Joel E. Spingarn was chairman of the board of directors of the NAACP from January 1914 through January 6, 1919. On the Spingarn Medal, see http://www.naacp.org/awards/spingarn-medal/.

11. *HHVHR*, 384, 516–17nn49–50; J. G. C. Corcoran, Report of June 29, 1918, "In re: Harrison: Liberty Alleged Connections with Rich Anarchists," BF, OG 369936, RG 65, DNA, Reel 12, *FSAA*. See also Corcoran, Report of July 18, 1918, "In Re: Liberty Congress," BF, OG 369936 (and DNA, RG 65, R 687, OG 272751); and Richard B. Moore, "Hubert Harrison (1883–1927)," in *DANB*.

12. *HHVHR*, 366, 369–72, 374, 411–12n2, and 513n12; "Cession of Danish West Indies," House of Representatives, 64th Congress, 2d Session, Report No. 1505, Article 6, 9; and William W. Boyer, *America's Virgin Islands: A History of Human Rights and Wrongs* (Durham, NC: Carolina Academic Press, 1983), 136–37. Harrison became a citizen through naturalization in September 1922. On Harrison's draft registration, see HH, Registration Card, Serial Number 2795, Order Number 4744, Division Number 144, Registrar's Report 31-9-144-C, Manhattan City, NY, September 12 1918, original in U.S. Selective Service System, World War I Selective Service System Draft Registration Card, 1917–1918, DNA, M1509, 4582 rolls. In the 1915 New York State census, Harrison was listed as a U.S. citizen. On the Selective Service Act of May 18, 1917, see http://www.legisworks.org/congress/65/publaw-12.pdf; http://legisworks.org/sal/40/stats/STATUTE-40-Pg76.pdf. On the Espionage Act of June 15, 1917, which was originally found in Title 50 of the U.S. Code (War) but is now found under Title 18, Crime, see http://www.legisworks.org/congress/65/publaw-24.pdf. On the "Sedition Act" of May 16, 1918 (amendments of the Espionage Act of 1917), see http://www.legisworks.org/congress/65/publaw-150.pdf; and U.S. Code, Title 18, Part 1, Chapter 37, #792, at https://www.law.cornell.edu/uscode/text/18/792. On the outbreaks in Harlem and Harrison's being a member of the vigilance committee, see "Big Get Together Movement in Thirty-Eighth Precinct," *Chicago Defender*, September 14, 1918, 5.

13. HH, "The (New) *Voice*," *The Voice*, July 11, 1918, 4, MID, 10218-18-1; "Announcement," *New Negro* 3 (August 1919): 3, HP, B17, F8. See also from *The Voice*, July 11, 1918: [HH,] "The Resurrection of *The Voice*," 4; and "*The Voice*: A Newspaper for the New Negro," masthead, 1. On the closing of *The Voice* see ScrPN, HP, B13, F5–6, which reads, "From July, 1917, to April 1919," he [HH] "was editor of *The Voice*, a racial paper which

he founded." In *WAA*, 8, Harrison wrote: "*The Voice* failed in March 1919; but in the meanwhile it had managed to make an indelible impression."

14. *The Crusader Magazine*, edited by Cyril V. Briggs, in its inaugural issue spoke favorably of Harrison's "rejuvenated and resurrected *Voice*." See "Digest of Views: Democracy Now, or Later?" *Crusader* 1, no. 1 (September 1918): 13–14. On the labor organizing, see this chapter, note 3, and the announcement "Shall the White and Colored Workers Unite for Higher Pay? A Lecture on the Present Conditions in the Hotel and Restaurant Industry by Hubert Harrison, Editor 'The New York Voice' Organizer of the Hotel and Restaurant Workers Chairman of the Colored Liberty Congress Will Be Given at the Headquarters Building Workers in the Hotel and Restaurant Industry 1008 Pennsylvania Ave., N.W. [Washington, DC], Friday July 5, [1918] 8:30 P.M.," in ScrMAM1, HP, FB740.

15. [HH,] "The Voice Is Coming Out to Stay!" leaflet (c. July 4, 1918), HP, B16, F14; [HH,] "To Newsdealers," *The Voice*, July 11, 1918, 1, MID 10218-18-1; [HH,] "The Resurrection of *The Voice*"; [HH,] "To Our People in Washington, D.C.," *The Voice*, July 11, 1918, 1; and Monroe N. Work, *Negro Year Book: An Annual Encyclopedia of the Negro, 1921–22* (Tuskegee, AL: Tuskegee Institute, 1922), 380; and *HHVHR*, 378–81. In HH, "Two Negro Radicalisms," *New Negro*, n.s. 4 (October 1919): 4–5, Harrison writes that Garvey "holds up to the Negro masses those things which bloom in their hearts— racialism, race-consciousness, racial solidarity—things taught first in 1917 by *THE VOICE* and The Liberty League. That is the secret of his success so far." This article was reprinted with revisions and minus the second- and third-last paragraphs as "The Negro's Own Radicalism," *WAA*, 76–79. The missing paragraphs can be found in "Supplemental Notes to the Text," *WAA*, 180–81, and the quotation about "race consciousness" and "racial solidarity" can be found on 181. The historian Tony Martin explains that within a decade of 1919, "the southern United States was the most thoroughly UNIA-organized area in the world." See *RF*, 15–16.

16. "Certificate of Incorporation of The Race Publishing Company, Inc.," December 10, 1917, filed December 24, 1917, Office of the Secretary of State, State of New York, Albany, no. 10366, book 658, 905; "Equity Congress Assails Paper," *New York Age*, July 20, 1911, 1; "Colored Democrats Revolt Against Wood," *New York Age* , November 19, 1914, 1; "Hughes Lost by One Vote," *New York Age*, November 26, 1914, 1. On Charles T. Magill, see "Republic'ns [*sic*] Feast on 'Douglass Birthday,'" *Baltimore Afro-American*, February 25, 1928, 5. On Flourney, see "Pullman Porters Organize," *Chicago Defender*, June 29, 1918, 3. On the Equity Congress, see Arthur Browne, *One Righteous Man: Samuel Battle and the Shattering of the Color Line in New York City* (Boston: Beacon, 2015), 80.

17. [HH,] "*The Voice* Is Coming Out to Stay!"; [HH,] "The Resurrection of the *Voice*"; [HH,] "To Our People in Washington, D.C.," *The Voice*, July 11, 1918, 1; [HH,] "The (New) Voice"; and "Lee, Canada," in *Who's Who in Colored America: An Illustrated Biographical Directory of Notable Living Persons of African Descent in the United States*, 7th ed., ed. G. James Fleming and Christian E. Burckel (Yonkers, NY: Christian E. Burckel, 1950), 334. Canada Lee was born Leonard Lionel Cornelius Canegata. On the lay historian Rufus L. Perry, see Rufus Lewis Perry, *The Cushite, or, The Descendants of Ham* (Springfield, MA: Willey & Company, 1893). Harrison discusses the importance of building race unity from bottom up in HH, "The Right Way to Unity," *Boston Chronicle*, May 10, 1924; *HR*, 402–4.

18. [HH,] "*The Voice* Is Coming Out to Stay!"; [HH,] "The Resurrection of *The Voice*"; and *HHVHR*, 392–93. The leaflet announcing the resurrection of *The Voice* was printed by Alpha Press, of 260 Grand Street. Emmett Scott may have used his close relationship with the *New York Age* to get that paper to pressure William H. Willis of Beehive Printing to change its weekly printing schedule so as to adversely affect and eventually silence Harrison's militant *Voice* in 1917. For more on Scott, Willis, Beehive Printing, and the cessation of publication of *The Voice* in 1917, see *HHVHR*, 329. For the July 11, 1918, issue of *The Voice*, see Major W. H. Loving, to Chief Military Branch, "Subject: Newspaper Articles," July 15, 1918, MID, 10218-18-185-2, roll 3.

19. "*The Voice* Is Coming Out to Stay!" See the following from *The Voice*, July 11, 1918: [HH,] "The Resurrection of *The Voice*"; [HH,] "The (New) Voice"; "*The Voice*: A Newspaper for the New Negro," masthead, 1; [HH,] "To Newsdealers," 1; "In Memoriam 13," 4. *Chicago Defender*, "*The Voice* Appears Again," July 27, 1918, 4, wished Harrison "success." See also HH, "Houston vs. Waco," *The Voice*, August 28, 1917, HP, B4, F72, in *HR*, 95–97; and *HHVHR*, 322–23, 358, 500n117.

20. [HH,] "To Newsdealers"; [HH,] "Advertising Talks"; and [HH,] "The (New) Voice." Harrison also spoke of "Negro Womanhood" and sometimes spoke of "Manhood" including men and women in an inclusionary sense. I have not come across examples of Cyril Briggs, founder of the African Blood Brotherhood, speaking of an African Blood Sisterhood.

21. See [HH,] "The New Policies for the New Negro," *The Voice*, September 4, 1917, HP, B5, F35; and HH, "The New Politics for the New Negro," *WAA*, 39–40. Hill points out that "Literally, *sinn fein* means 'ourselves alone' or 'we ourselves.'" See *GP*, 1:lxxin116, 2:621n1.

22. On the Liberty Congress's petition, see "Petition to the House of Representatives of the United States of America," presented by the Hon. Frederick H. Gillett of Massachusetts, in the House of Representatives, Saturday, June 29, 1918 (Congressional Record), *The Voice*, July 11, 1918, 1, 2, 4; *Boston Guardian*, July 6, 1918, 1, 4; *Congressional Record*, June 29, 1918; and *DHNPUS*, 3:215–18. This petition is distinct from "The Liberty League's Petition to the House of Representatives of the United States, July 4, 1917," in *WAA*, 12–13. Also from page 1 of the July 11, 1918, issue of *The Voice*, see "Negro Heads French Commission"; "Negroes Asking for Foretaste of Democracy"; [HH,] "To Our People in Washington, D.C."; "White Men Wage War to Evade Draft"; "Negro Methodist Leaders Want to Unite"; and "Church Membership Increases."

23. "Inspector Ryan Arrested by West Indian Inn-Keeper," *The Voice*, July 11, 1918, 1, 2; "A Negro Intern at Bellevue Hospital," *The Voice*, July 11, 1918, 1. By 1925, according to David Levering Lewis, *When Harlem Was in Vogue* (1979; New York: Oxford University Press, 1981), 216, "five Afro-American physicians" were "permanent staff members" at Harlem Hospital; "there was a new school for nurses"; and there were plans "to send scores of interns to the hospital."

24. [Advertisement], "Tonight's the Night! At St. Marks Hall *The Voice* Jubilation Meeting Come Here First 8:30 P.M."; [Advertisement], "Harlem People's Forum Hubert Harrison, Lecturer Lectures Every Sunday 8:30 P.M. At Lafayette Lodge Rooms 165 W. 131st This Sunday Our Professional Friends The 'N.A.A.C.P.' National Association for the Acceptance of Color Proscription By Hubert Harrison Admission Free"; and Andrea Razafkeriefo, "The Voice": all from *The Voice*, July 11, 1918, 1. Raz's poem can be found in *HHVHR*, 393. Another Raz poem entitled "Hubert H. Harrison" was published in *Crusader* 1, no. 5 (December 1918): 17. On Andreamentania Paul Razafinkeriefo (Andy

Razaf, 1895–1973), see Barry Singer, *Black and Blue: The Life and Lyrics of Andy Razaf* (New York: Schirmer, 1992); "Andy Razaf's Mother Visits on the Coast," *Chicago Defender*, September 25, 1942, 19; "Composer and Lyricist Andy Razaf Dies at 77," *Los Angeles Times*, February 4, 1973; Stephen Holden, "A Lot of Songs from an Unsung Lyricist," *New York Times*, February 8, 1989; "Nephew of African Queen," *Pittsburgh Courier*, April 2, 1927, sec. 2, 1; and "Andy Razaf Papers: Biographical/Historical Information," NYPL, http://archives.nypl.org/scm/20766. See also Sinclair Wilberforce, "Harrison Delivers Inspiring Lecture at the Harlem People's Forum," *The Voice*, July 1 [August], 1918. See also [HH,] "Our Professional 'Friends,'" *The Voice*, November 7, 1917, rpt. with deletions in *WAA*, 55–60, with background commentary on 171–75, rpt. in *HR*, 143–47; and *HHVHR*, 354–55, 358. On the founding of the Liberty League, see *HHVHR*, 281–327, esp. 282–85. Harrison referred to the NAACP as the "National Association for the Advancement of Certain People" and as the "National Association for the Acceptance of Color Proscription": HH, "Why Is the Red Cross," *The Voice*, July 18, 1918, *WAA*, 27–29. On this topic see also *HR*, 356, 510n89. The NAACP did not have a Black "chairman" until Dr. Louis T. Wright in 1934. Preceding him were William English Walling, Charles Edward Russell, Oswald Garrison Villard, William English Walling, Joel E. Spingarn, and Mary White Ovington. See *NAACP: Celebrating a Century, 100 Years in Pictures* (Layton, UT: Gibbs Smith, 2009), 430.

25. [HH,] "The Resurrection of *The Voice*," 4; [HH,] "The (New) Voice"; [HH,] "Negro Policemen," *The Voice*, July 11, 1918, 4; and [HH,] "Is Democracy Unpatriotic?" *The Voice*, July 11, 1918, 4, HP, B5, F41; rpt. in *The Voice*, August 1, 1918, 4; and in *WAA*, 25–27.

26. [HH,] "Negro Policemen," *The Voice*, July 11, 1918, 4. Samuel Battle was the first Black police officer in Manhattan (1911) and in Harlem (1913). Robert Holmes, who became a NYC police officer in 1913 and was assigned to Harlem in 1917 (as its second Black police officer), was fatally shot while on duty in Harlem on August 6, 1917. See Browne, *One Righteous Man*, 75, 95–96, 116–17; and "Patrolman Holmes Is Buried with High Police Honors," *New York Age*, August 16, 1917, 1. James Lardner and Thomas Reppetto, *NYPD: A City and Its Police* (New York: Henry Holt, 2000), 241, offers the 1916 statistics.

27. The quotation is from *The Voice* (c. July 18, 1918) and was in "Police Brutality in Harlem," *Crusader* 1, no. 2 (October 1918): 14. Also included in this *Crusader* article was a reprint of a poem on police brutality by Razafkeriefo entitled "To Certain Policemen," which had appeared in *The Voice*.

28. From *The Voice*, July 11, 1918, see "Red Cross Reluctantly Lets Down the Bars," 4; "The Colored Woman Nurse" (rpt. from *New York World*), 2; and "Red Cross to Ease Anxious Hearts," 2. See also Darlene Clark Hine, "The Call That Never Came: Black Women Nurses and World War I; and Historical Note," *Indiana Military History Journal* (January 1983): 23–27.

29. HH, "The Negro and the War," *WAA*, 25.

30. [HH,] "Is Democracy Unpatriotic?"

31. [HH,] "Is Democracy Unpatriotic?" 4. President Woodrow Wilson, on April 2, 1917, went before a joint session of Congress seeking a declaration of war against Germany, stating: "We are fighting for the things which we have always carried nearest to our hearts—for democracy, for the right of those who submit to authority to have a voice in their own governments, for the rights and liberties of small nations, for a universal dominion of right by such a concert of free peoples as shall bring peace and safety to all nations and make the world itself at last free." See "Making the World 'Safe for

Democracy,'" *History Matters*, http://historymatters.gmu.edu/d/4943/; *HHVHR*, 299–300; and *WAA*, 160–61.

32. [HH,] "The Negro and the War," 25.

33. [HH,] "The Negro and the War," 25, 160; *HR*, 201–2; *HHVHR*, 366. On May 10, 1920, Congress passed legislation providing for the deportation of aliens convicted under the amended Espionage Act of 1917. The 1917 act was restricted to the period the United States was at war, and the 1918 amendments to the Espionage Act were repealed by a joint resolution of Congress on March 3, 1921. On the Espionage and Sedition Acts, see *GP*, 1:341n2, 453–54n1. Debs was charged with sedition for urging resistance to the military draft in a speech delivered on June 16, 1918, in Canton, Ohio. See "Debs, Socialist Chief Arrested on U.S. Warrant," *Chicago Tribune*, July 1, 1918; and "Debs Arrested," *New York Times*, July 1, 1918. On Harrison campaigning for Debs, see *HHVHR*, 191–95.

34. From *The Voice*, July 11, 1918, see "In the Crow's Nest," 3; "Doing Our Bit," 3; "Panama Correspondent" [HH,] "News from Panama," 2; a sports section, 3; Olive Bruce Miller, "Inspiration" [poem], 3; and poems by Razafkeriefo, including "To Certain Policemen," 3. See also "Yung Chen" [pseud. for HH], "Real Estate News from Siam," *The Voice*, September 4, 1917, HP, B6, F3; and "Gunga Din" [pseud. for HH], "The Black Man's Burden: A Reply to Rudyard Kipling," *Colored American Review* 1, no. 4 (December 1915): 3; rpt. as HH, "The Black Man's Burden (a Reply to Rudyard Kipling)," *WAA*, 145–46, 206.

35. "Democracy Now or Later? Well-Known Colored Editor, Field Secretary of Major Spingarn's National Association, Urges Negroes to 'Cry Aloud and Spare Not,'" *The Voice*, July 11, 1918, 2; rpt. from James Weldon Johnson, "What the Negro Is Doing for Himself," *Liberator* 1, no. 4 (June 1918): 29–31, https://www.marxists.org/history/usa/culture/pubs/liberator/1918/04/v1n04-jun-1918-liberator.pdf. *The Liberator* 1, no. 2 (April 2, 1918): 42, had an announcement on Harrison's *The Negro and the Nation*, which read: "A candid and uncompromising presentation of the situation of the Negro in America, by a Negro who thinks clearly and fearlessly and writes convincingly. The essay 'On a Certain Conservatism in Negroes,' is particularly refreshing as well as illuminating." https://www.marxists.org/history/usa/culture/pubs/liberator/1918/02/v1n02-apr-1918-liberator.pdf.

36. Anselmo Jackson, "The Awakening of the Masses," *The Voice*, July 11, 1918, 2. On Anselmo Jackson (1896–August 1964), see *GP*, 1:282n3. The contributing "dollars" and "supporting the policy of segregation" comments would apply in the case of Joel E. Spingarn. On Spingarn supporting segregated camps, see *WEBD*, 1:528–30; and on Spingarn contributing dollars (in 1916 and 1917), see Ellis, *Race War and Surveillance*, 142; and (in 1926) Ross, *J. E. Spingarn*, 64.

37. From *The Voice*, July 11, 1918, see "How Negroes Feel About Freedom," 4. According to Monroe N. Work, *Negro Year Book, 1918–1919* (Tuskegee, AL: The Negro Year Book Publishing Company, 1919), 45; and *GP*, 3:204n8, African Americans contributed an estimated $225 million to the war efforts by purchasing war savings stamps and Liberty bonds. The article "W.S.S. Drive Ends," *Chicago Defender*, September 21, 1918, 5, 'mentioned Harrison's involvement in a war savings stamps program the previous week. The article "Negro Editor Sells $1100 in War Stamps," *New York Tribune*, September 5, 1918, 3, states that Harrison, "to equip the various negro regiments now being formed," sold $1,100 worth of War Savings Stamps at the "Liberty Bell" in City Hall Park in New York on September 4, 1918. Harrison was also listed as a speaker at the Fourth Liberty Loan Drive in Harlem in "Fourth Liberty Loan Drive Going Big in

Harlem," *Chicago Defender*, October 12, 1918, 4. Judith Stein, *The World of Marcus Garvey: Race and Class in Modern Society* (Baton Rouge: Louisiana State University Press, 1986), 69, points out that many Black leaders encouraged the sale of war bonds and that for many wage workers this was a first introduction to paper wealth. All of this eventually facilitated the sale of BSL stock. Robert A. Hill notes that "Garvey's 'Liberty Loan Selling Plan' was modeled on the U.S. government's World War I Liberty Loan drive to which black Americans had contributed generously." See *GP*, 1:456n1. A "Buy Bonds" editorial in Cyril V. Briggs's *Crusader* 1, no. 2 (October 1918): 7, urged readers to buy Liberty Bonds because they were "the safest investment in the world" and to help "our brave boys" "over there" and "back them up in their struggle against Prussianism" and "make possible their early return."

38. From *The Voice*, July 11, 1918, see "War Department Against All Discrimination," 3; "An Appeal to the 12 Million Negroes of the United States," 2; "To the Patriotic Lady Across the Way," 2; "Sergeant Johnson, 'Hero', Tells Own Story," 3.

39. [HH,] "Read! Read! Read!" *The Voice*, July 18, 1918. See also [HH,] "Reading for Knowledge," July 1918, *WAA*, 123–26.

40. [HH,] "Read! Read! Read!"

41. HH, "Education and the Race," *WAA*, 123.

42. HH, "The Problems of Leadership," *WAA*, 54–55.

43. [HH,] "The Descent of Du Bois" [July 17, 1918], *The Voice*, July 25, 1918, *WAA*, 66–70, esp. 66. For the dating of Harrison's article, see *WAA*, 54, and for a fuller discussion of the article and events surrounding it, see *HHVHR*, 385–92, esp. 385–87; and *HR*, 170–72. For more background to Du Bois seeking a captaincy in MI while writing "Close Ranks," see *WEBD*, 1:555–60, 2:254, 470; and Allen, "'Close Ranks,'" 26. Note: in *HR* and *HHVHR* the title of the article is listed as "The Decent of Dr. Du Bois"—it should be "The Descent of Du Bois."

44. [HH,] "The Descent of Du Bois," *WAA*, 66–67. The statement issued by the War Department and Committee on Public Information emanated from the Colored Editors' Conference, which met in Washington, DC, June 19–21, 1918, in order to minimize the impact of the upcoming Liberty Congress. It stated, "We believe that today that justifiable grievances of the Colored people are producing not disloyalty, but an amount of unrest and bitterness which even the best efforts of their leaders may not be able always to guide." See "Newspaper Men and Leaders in Important Conference: Discuss Ways to Best Help Nation Win the War," *Chicago Defender*, July 6, 1918, 4. On the Colored Editors' Conference, see *HHVHR*, 373–78.

45. Mark Ellis, "'Closing Ranks' and 'Seeking Honors': W. E. B. Du Bois in World War I," *Journal of American History* 79, no. 1 (June 1992): 96–124, esp. 115–18, 124, states that Harrison's "charges were well founded," that Du Bois's actions and positions "led in the eyes of Harrison and others to the decline of Du Bois as the pre-eminent race leader in the post–Booker T. Washington era," and that "Harrison was the leading proponent of this view." Harrison "also used these events to offer suggestive comments on autonomous Black leadership and the response of both the government and the white left to such leadership." See *HHVHR*, 385–91; Ellis, *Race War and Surveillance*, 152, 159–81. The Aptheker quotation is found in *Writings and Periodicals Edited by W. E. B. Du Bois: Selections from* The Crisis, ed. Herbert Aptheker, vol. 1: *1911–1925* (Millwood, NY: Kraus-Thomson Organization, 1982), 159n.

46. [HH,] "Is Democracy Unpatriotic?," 4. On Joel E. Spingarn see this chapter, notes 9 and 10; and *HHVHR*, 355–66, 373–78; on the Liberty Congress, see *HHVHR*, 380–85.

47. HH, "The Problems of Leadership," *WAA*, 54–55.

48. [HH,] [re "Vesey St. Liberals"], n.d., HP, Writings; HH, ["White People"], n.d., HP, B6, F59, HPDLC.

49. HH, "When the Blind Lead," *WAA*, 70–73, 178, esp. 71–73; and HH, "The Problems of Leadership," *WAA*, 54–55. On Du Bois's failure to get the captaincy, see *HHVHR*, 392.

50. [HH,] "Close Ranks," *The Voice*, August 1, 1918, rpt. from *The Voice*, July 25, 1918; [masthead], *The Voice*, August 1, 1918, 2; [Woodrow Wilson,] "'The American Spirit Speaks,'" *The Voice*, August 1, 1918; and Woodrow Wilson, "Mob Action," from the Committee on Public Information," MID 10218-154, DNA, available as "President Woodrow Wilson's proclamation of July 26, 1918, denouncing lynching," http://www .amistadresource.org/documents/document_07_06_030_wilson.pdf. See also Anselmo Jackson, "Facts and Phrases," *The Voice*, August 1, 1918; "Dr. Du Bois' Defense," *Crusader* 1, no. 2 (October 1918): 13; *HHVHR*, 391–92; and *WEBD*, 1:552–60, esp. 560.

51. [HH,] "Note on the Foregoing," *The Voice*, August 1, 1918.

52. [HH,] "To Old Subscribers," *The Voice*, August 1, 1918. Unfortunately, though a complete copy of the July 11, 1918, issue of *The Voice* has been preserved, the only other complete issue located is that of October 31, 1917, on Microfilm R 903 Reel 3. See HH, "Introductory," *WAA*, 8; and ScrPN2, HP, B13, F5–6.

53. Wilberforce, "Harrison Delivers Inspiring Lecture at the Harlem People's Forum." In *The Voice*, c. 1918, Harrison wrote a poem, "Listen!" that discussed his going into a place of business and being attended to by "A Lady Of African Extraction" whom he treated cordially. She, however, paid more attention to an ill-kept white man who grinned and leered at her. After she smiled back, Harrison questioned "Whether our women Want respect Or White Men?" See [HH,] "Listen," *The Voice*, c. 1918, ScrWr, HP, B13, F7.

54. HD, September 16, 1918; HD, September 16, 1918. See "Minutes of Executive Committee," March 27 and September 18, 1918, SP, LNY, Reel 2639, SP Minutes, 1900–1936, Collection VI:5; and see *HHVHR*, 367–69, 512n6.

55. HD, March 27 and September 16, 1918; Report of the Joint Legislative Committee Investigating Seditious Activities, Filed April 24, 1920, in *RR*, 1:613–18; Theodore Draper, *The Roots of American Communism* (New York: Viking, 1957), 92–94; *ASABA*, 273; David A. Shannon, *The Socialist Party of America* (New York: Macmillan, 1955), 82–103, 119–20; William Z. Foster, *History of the Communist Party of the United States* (New York: International Publishers, 1952), 130; and Anthony Bimba, *History of the American Working Class* (1927; New York: International Publishers, 1934), 261. On Harrison leaving the SP in the spring of 1914, see *HHVHR*, 220. The historian David M. Kennedy writes that at the SP's St. Louis Convention of April 7, 1917, the party stated that the previous day's declaration of war was "a crime against the people of the United States" and urged "vigorous resistance." Kennedy notes "the party therefore stood, in the spring of 1917, as the largest center of organized opposition to American participation in the war." David M. Kennedy, *Over Here: The First World War and American Society* (New York: Oxford University Press 1980), 26–27, 35.

56. Kennedy points out that though pro-war socialists "were a small minority within the party," their ranks included many "prominent radical theorists and publicists," including Charles Edward Russell, Upton Sinclair, A. M. Simons, Allen Benson, William English Walling, Rose Pastor Stokes, W. J. Ghent, Robert Hunter, and John Spargo, all of whom "dissociated themselves from the manifesto issued by the convention, and declared

their support of the war effort." In early 1917, Rabbi Stephen Wise also broke ranks and declared support for the war. Kennedy, *Over Here*, 26–27, 35.

57. J. M. Robertson, *The Evolution of States: An Introduction to English Politics* (New York: n.p., 1913), 72, states "that it may be the last card of Conservatism to play off the war spirit against the reform spirit." In his copy Harrison then writes, "perhaps this was one of the conscious imperatives of the Great War—on both sides."

58. The reviewing stand for the February 17, 1919, parade was on Lenox Avenue between 133rd and 135th Streets. See "The Mayor's Committee of Welcome to Home-Coming Troops . . . February 17, 1919," Ticket, HP, FB740; "Mayor's Committee of Welcome to Home-Coming Troops," ribbon, HP, B14, F3; "Mayor of the City of New York Certificate of Membership on the Mayor's Committee of Welcome to Home-Coming Troops 1918–1919 to Hubert Harrison. . . . , Signed John F. Hylan, Mayor" (c. 1919), HP, FB740, HPDLC; *GP*, 9:136n3.

59. "National War Savings Committee of the United States Government . . . Committee of Greater New York Token of Appreciation," n.d., HP, FB740; and "Certificate of Membership, the Mayor's Committee of Welcome, 1918–1919." Dr. George E. Haynes, director of negro economics for the Department of Labor, on July 4, 1918, in an address said: "Do not forget that any person, black or white, who does not work hard, who lags in any way, who fails to buy a Liberty bond or a War Savings stamp, if he can, is against his country and is, therefore, our bitter enemy." See Scheiber and Scheiber, "The Wilson Administration and the Wartime Mobilization of Black-Americans, 1917–1918," *Labor History* 10, no. 3 (Summer 1969): 448–49. Word, ed., *Negro Year Book, 1918–1919*, 45–50, 91, estimated that Black Americans support of Liberty Loan, Liberty Bond, and Thrift Stamp drives amounted to more than $225 million. See also *GP*, 1:456n1. One notable labor activist who bought and promoted war bonds and later tried to downplay the fact was the socialist, syndicalist, and future communist leader William Z. Foster. See Investigation of Strike in Steel Industries: Hearings before the Committee on Education and Labor, U.S. Senate, 66th Congress, 1st Session (Washington, DC, 1919), 398–99, 423, cited in Draper, *The Roots of American Communism*, 445.

60. *HHVHR*, 367–68; "Negro Workers Get Impetus to Organize," *New York Call*, June 24, 1918; HD, September 16, 1918; Marsha Hurst Hiller, "Race Politics in New York City, 1890–1930" (PhD diss., Columbia University, 1972), 285–86, 289; and Edward R. Lewinson, *Black Politics in New York City* (New York: Twayne, 1974), 59. The lawyer John Clifford Hawkins (1879–?) was elected assemblyman in the New York state legislature in 1918 and reelected in 1919 and 1920, serving until 1921. See Thomas Yenser, ed., *Who's Who in Colored America: A Biographical Dictionary of Notable Living Persons of African Descent in America 1938–1939–1940*, 2nd ed. (Brooklyn: T. Yenser, 1940), 238–39.

61. HD, September 16, 1918; Work, ed., *Negro Year Book, 1918–1919*, 95, 120; Foner, *American Socialism and Black Americans*, 284–85; "Reverdy Ransom for Congress," *New York Independent*, August 24, 1918, 4, MID-10218-217; "Seat in Congress Sought by Negro," *Christian Science Monitor*, c. 1918, MID-10218-106; and *HHVHR*, 368–69.

62. "Digest of Views," *Crusader* 1, no. 1 (September 1918): 13, and "Roll of Honor," 23. See also Hill, "Introduction" to Briggs, ed., *The Crusader*, 1:v–lxvii, esp. xvii. In Cyril V. Briggs to Theodore Draper, March 17, 1958, B31, Envelope, "NEGRO Cyril V. Briggs," Theodore Draper Papers, Hoover Institution Archives, Palo Alto, CA. Briggs still referred to Harrison as his friend, thirty years after Harrison's death.

63. Andrea Razafkeriefo, "Hubert H. Harrison," *Crusader* 1, no. 4 (December 1918): 17. The poem is in *HHVHR*, 394. On December 23, 2014, a beautiful jet-black slant marker

with etching was placed on the previously unmarked gravesite of Harrison. The marker, purchased by Harrison's granddaughter Ilva Harrison, features words derived from Raz's poem, including "Speaker, Editor and Sage" and the phrase "What a Change Thy Work Has Wrought." The gravesite is at: Plot Salvia, Range 13, Grave 100, Woodlawn Cemetery, 517 E. 233rd St., Bronx, NY.

64. J. G. C. Corcoran, Report of July 18, 1918, "In Re: Liberty Congress," BF, OG 369936, RG 65, DNA, Reel 12, *FSAA*.

65. J. G. C. Corcoran, Report of August 30, 1918, "In Re: Liberty Congress," BF, OG 369936, RG 65, DNA, Reel 12, *FSAA*.

66. Herbert Parsons, Major U.S. Army, War Department, MID, "Memorandum re Moens," August 20, 1917, File MID 10218-2, DNA, *FSAA*, Reel 19.

67. Corcoran, Report of August 30, 1918.

68. J. G. C. Corcoran, Report of September 7, 1918, "In re: Liberty Congress," BF, OG 369936, RG 65, DNA, Reel 12, *FSAA*.

69. J. G. C. Corcoran, Reports of September 14 and October 18, 1918, "In Re: Liberty Congress," BF, OG 369936, RG 65, DNA, Reel 12, *FSAA*.

70. Corcoran, Report of October 23, 1918.

71. "The Case of Herman M. Bernelot-Moens," *Issues of To-Day*, February 11, 1922, 417; "Moens, Mystery Man," *Washington Post*, May 30, 1919; and "Twenty-Four Joy Riders Face Trial. Hollander Is Indicted Also on Immoral Picture Charge," *Washington Post*, November 1, 1918.

72. HD, April 9, 1919; "The Alleged and the Real Moens' Case," *Messenger*, July 1919; Constance McLaughlin Green, *The Secret City: A History of Race Relations in the Nation's Capital* (Princeton, NJ: Princeton University Press, 1967), 189, 201. Du Bois had invited Columbia University professor Franz Boas to a 1905 Atlanta University conference, "The Negro Physique." Aware that Boas had a penchant for measuring people, Du Bois offered to provide him with Black student subjects if Columbia would cover travel expenses. See Carl Degler, *In Search of Human Nature: The Decline and Revival of Darwinism in American Social Thought* (New York: Oxford University Press, 1991), 76.

73. HD, February 4–5, 1919. On Loving, see Ellis, *Race War and Surveillance*, 57–59, 176, 184–85; *GP* 1:327n1; and Roger D. Cunningham, "'The Loving Touch': Walter H. Loving's Five Decades of Military Music," *Army History* (Summer 2007): 4–25. For more on Loving's contact with Harrison, see *HHVHR*, 386–90.

74. HD, November 11, 1918. That evening Harrison recorded that he was "disappointed" "for the very last time" by "Bee," with whom he was having an affair.

75. HD, November 13, 1918. Harrison also commented, "The judgment of the middle of this century will decide that William The Last of Germany deserved the pity rather than the hatred of his contemporaries."

76. HD, November 13, 1918.

77. *WAA*, 162; *HR*, 209–10; Cashman,*w*; *GP*, 1:304n1.

78. HH, "The Negro at the Peace Congress," *The Voice*[?], c. December 1918, *WAA*, 30–32, 162. See also HH, "Africa at the Peace Table," *The Voice*, December 26, 1918, HP, B13, F1–2; rpt. as "Africa and the Peace," *WAA*, 32–35, 162–63; HH, "They Shall Not Pass," 35–36; Ellis, *Race War and Surveillance*, 193–95. At a UNIA mass meeting held on December 2, 1918, at the Palace Casino and presided over by Garvey, delegates chosen to represent "the negroes at the Versailles conference" included Randolph, Ida Wells Barnett, and Cadet (as interpreter). Only Cadet made the trip. See BI Special Agent D. Davidson, Report, "IN RE: MARCUS GARVEY, Negro Agitator," December 5,

1918, *GP*, 1:305–7, 1:404. On March 26, 1919, according to the *Negro World*, a meeting of "3,000 of the representatives of the 400,000,000 of the race" at the Mother Zion AME Church, "denounced the reactionary leader, W. E. B. Du Bois, and upheld Eliezer Cadet." Owen presided and Garvey, Amy Ashwood, Domingo, Randolph, and Professor Allan Whaley spoke. ["Synopsis of UNIA Meeting"], *Negro World*, March 29, 1919, *GP*, 1:392–93.

79. See HH, "The Negro at the Peace Congress."

80. HH, "Africa at the Peace Table." In Harrison's copy of an unidentified article from the *Literary Digest*, March 29, 1918, ScrAftermath, HP, B10, F2, 18, the *Greenville Piedmont* is quoted that "the easiest way to see what a man is fighting for is to see what he demands after he wins." To this Harrison writes, "Amen!"

81. HH, "Africa at the Peace Table." Winston James, *HATB*, 129, perceptively points out that "one of the most distinctive features of Harrison's political thought, compared to that of his black radical (socialist and black nationalist) contemporaries and his black nationalist predecessors of the nineteenth century, was his confidence in and humility before the peoples and cultures of Africa. Much of his time was spent in the study of the continent's history and culture. . . . In Harrison's outlook there is none of the arrogant New World 'civilizationism' that one finds, for instance, in Garvey's pronouncements; none of the 'civilizing the backward tribes of Africa,' as Garvey and the UNIA had aimed and promised to do. For Harrison, Africa was primarily a teacher; not a primitive unschooled child in need of 'civilization' and instruction." Robert A. Hill notes that Du Bois actively campaigned for a system of international administration of former German colonies in Africa. His "Memoranda on the Future of Africa," presented on November 11, 1918, to the NAACP board of directors called for a large Central African state built from former German colonies, Portuguese Africa, and the Belgian Congo. The Pan-African Congress, however, called only for international protection or oversight, not international administration. *GP*, 1:393n3; "The Future of Africa," *Crisis* 17 (June 1919): 119–20.

82. [HH,] "Goodwill Toward Men," *The Voice*, December 26, 1918, HP, B13, F1–2, *HR*, 257–58. See also "Negro and Wife Lynched," *New York Times*, May 20, 1918; *HR*, 257; *GP*, 1:515n5; Walter White, "The Work of a Mob," *Crisis* 16 (September 1918): 221–23, in Aptheker, *DHNPUS*, 3:327–32; "The Mary Turner Project," http://www.maryturner .org/.

83. [HH,] "Goodwill Toward Men," 258.

84. Regarding the "ludicrous lackey" phrase, Moton was quoted in the *Chautauqua Daily* in 1918 saying: "I am glad that my people were brought over here as slaves, for we were placed beside the strongest race that the world has yet produced, the Anglo-Saxon race." See A. J. Williams-Myers, "Chautauqua (New York) and the Use and Abuse of Selective Memory," *African Americans in New York Life and History* 18, no. 2 (July 1994): 51; citing Theodore Morrison, *Chautauqua: A Center for Education, Religion, and the Arts in America* (New York, 1963), 96.

85. HH, "'They Shall Not Pass!'" *The Voice*, January 30, 1919, HP, B13, F7; *WAA*, 35–36; Ellis, *Race War and Surveillance*, 195.

86. HH, "'They Shall Not Pass,'" 35–36.

87. HH, "A Hint of 'Our Reward,'" c. early 1919, *WAA*, 29–30; Reuben Gold Thwaites and Calvin Noyes Kendall, *A History of the United States for Grammar Schools* (1912; 1918; Boston: Houghton Mifflin, 1920); Emmett J. Scott, *Scott's Official History of the American Negro in the World War* (Chicago: Homewood, c. 1919).

2. Political Activities in Washington and Virginia
(January–July 1919)

1. Major W. H. Loving, P.C. [Philippine Constabulary], to Director, MID, "Subject: Spirit of Unrest Among Negroes," December 23, 1918, MID 10218-274-1, Reel 20, *FSAA*. On Harrison's describing East St. Louis as a "pogrom," see chapter 1, note 8.

2. Loving to Director of MID, "Subject: Activities Among Negroes in District of Columbia," January 5, 1919, *GP*, 1:338; "Records of Mass Meetings Held in Different Cities During the Month of January, 1919, and Names of Speakers Who Delivered Addresses" (c. January 31, 1919), *GP*, 1:364–66, which accompanied Loving to Director, MID, "Subject: Report of mass meeting during January, 1919," February 17, 1919, *GP*, 1:363–67. Col. John M. Dunn, acting director of MI, forwarded a copy of this report to William E. Allen, acting chief of the BI on February 21, 1919. See *GP*, 1:363n1.

3. "Come Let Us Reason Together Thrift Race of the World (Incorporated) Race and Labor Consolidation Conference in the Young Men's Christian Association 1816 Twelfth Street, Washington, D.C. January 1, 2 and 3, 1919," handout, c. January 1, 1919, MID 10218-261-25. Bryant had been involved in a swindle scheme in Florida in 1910. See "President Bryant of 'Thrift Race' Movement Sentenced," *Philadelphia Tribune*, December 25, 1920, 1, 2. See also Loving to Director of MI, January 5, 1919, *GP*, 1:338.

4. Loving to Director of MI, January 29, 1919, "Subject: Rev. George Frazier Miller of Brooklyn, N.Y. and Hubert H. Harrison of New York City Before the Bethel Literary Society of this City." See also *HHVHR*, 283–84, 289, 299; and "Will Demand Negro Rights: Sick and Tired of Asking them of Wilson, Says Orator in Faneuil Hall; Points to Case of Ireland," *Boston Herald*, June 14, 1917, 9. On Harrison's calls for armed self-defense see *HR*, 93–94; *HHVHR*, 282–86, 297–301; *WAA*, 14–16, 155–56; and "Urges Negroes to Get Arms: Liberty League President Advises His Race to 'Defend Their Lives,'" *New York Times*, July 5, 1917.

5. HH, "A Cure for the Ku-Klux," *The Voice*, January 30, 1919, ScrEarlyWr, HP, B13, F2 and 7; and in *WAA*, 36–38.

6. HH, "A Cure for the Ku Klux."

7. HH, "A Cure for the Ku Klux." The actual lines from *Childe Harold*, canto 2, stanza 76, read: "Hereditary bondsmen! know ye not, / Who would be free, themselves must strike the blow?"

8. *GP*, 1:338–39.

9. HH, "To the Young Men of My Race," [*The Voice* (?), January 1919], *WAA*, 91–95, quotations on 92, notes 186–87; *HR*, 175–77.

10. HH, "To the Young Men of My Race," 93. Baal, a God of the Canaanites, was considered a false god by the Jews.

11. HH, "To the Young Men of My Race," 93–94. See also Paul Laurence Dunbar, *The Complete Poems*, intro. W. D. Howells (1895; New York: Dodd, Mead, & Co., 1913), 75.

12. HH, "To the Young Men of My Race," 94–95.

13. HD, February 4–5, February 9, March 2–3, 1919. On Marie C. James, see "Noted Singer Stirs Audience: Miss James' Recital Aids Wilberforce College Fund; Credit to Alma Mater," *Afro-American*, May 21, 1910, 7; and "Music and Art," *Crisis* 2, no. 4 (February 1916): 163.

14. HD, February 4–5, 1919; HP, B2, F17–18. See Louise Bryant, *Six Red Months in Russia: An Observer's Account of Russia Before and During the Proletarian Dictatorship* (New York: George H. Doran Co., 1918); Albert Rhys Williams, *Soviet Russia: An Address*

(Chicago: Charles H. Kerr and Co., 1919) [copy of his February 19, 1919, address in Chicago]; Albert Rhys Williams, *Lenin: The Man and His Work* (New York: Scott and Seltzer, 1919); and John Reed, *Ten Days That Shook the World* (1919).

15. HD, February 4–5, 1919; HP, B2, F17–18; *HHVHR*, 132–34, 373–78, 392. Hubert's daughter Aida said that her mother had saved more letters from her father (than those originally given by Aida to this author). Notes from a telephone conversation between Aida Harrison Richardson and JBP, December 9, 1999, possession of JBP.

16. HD, February 4–5, 1919; *HHVHR*, 132–34, 373–78, 392.

17. HD, February 13, 1919. On Nellie Quander, see Alpha Kappa Alpha Sorority Inc., "Centennial Celebration," 2008, http://hustorage.wrlc.org/disk1/AKA/resources.html.

18. HD, February 14, 1919.

19. Maj. W. H. Loving to the Director, MI, February 17, 1919, *GP*, 1:363–64.

20. On Rev. Charles Martin, see Hill, ed., *Crusader*, 1:lviiin133; and the tribute by Adelaide Smith Casely Hayford in Adelaide M. Cromwell, *An African Victorian Feminist: The Life and Times of Adelaide Smith Casely Hayford, 1868–1960* (London: Frank Cass & Co., 1986), 134.

21. "Virgin Islanders Denounce Autocratic Administration in Their Home: Form Solid Organization to Aid Their People to Drive Out Crackerism—Want Civil Government and Removal of U.S. Marines," *Negro World* 2, no. 7 (March 29, 1919): 4; "Virgin Islands Commission Is Back with Data," *Chicago Defender*, February 23, 1924. Later in the year the Totten and Hendrickson served as selected delegates to a proposed December conference with people of the islands to discuss conditions there. At a meeting in the fall of 1919 Totten outlined organizational plans, spoke on the need for race solidarity in the islands, and stated that the League should not only serve as a watchdog for the islands but that it must go further and "eventually lift them from the yoke of the white man." A report was also read detailing the great "Welcome Home" reception for the Hon. Rothschild Francis, a prominent civil rights activist from St. Thomas. See "Negro Agitation," November 7, 1919, MID 10218-261-50, 10. On November 4, 1919, Totten issued an appeal asserting that the Virgin Islands had been shamefully neglected by the United States and asked U.S. citizens for aid on behalf of the five thousand inhabitants of the three islands reportedly near destitution as a result of the reaction after the war. See Isaac Dookhan, "The Search for Identity: The Political Aspirations and Frustrations of Virgin Islanders Under the United States Administration, 1917–1927," *Journal of Caribbean History* 12 (1979): 1–34, esp. 15.

22. "Virgin Islanders Denounce Autocratic Administration in Their Home."

23. HD, March 2–3, 1919; "The Religion of West Africa," advertisement for Woman's Home and Foreign Missionary Society, Washington, DC, February 27, 1919, ScrMAM2, HP, FB740.

24. [HH,] [Notes on Marcus Garvey], HD, March 2–3, 1919.

25. [HH,] [Notes on Marcus Garvey], HD, March 2–3, 1919.

26. [HH,] [Notes on Marcus Garvey], HD, March 2–3, 1919; "League of Nations and the Darker Races," *Howard University Record* 13, no. 3 (March 1919). In his copy of B. L. Putnam Weale (pseud. for Bertram Lenox Simpson), *The Conflict of Colour: The Threatened Upheaval Throughout the World* (New York: Macmillan, 1910), HP, B26, on 102, Harrison writes that the weakening of the white race "has increased since the First Great War 1914–18. And this despite the League of Nations, which represents the effort of white Europe to achieve a racial solidarity in face of the threatening fact."

27. HD, March 22, 1919; "Dr. Gordon to Fill Lyceum Dates," *Lyceum News* 8, no. 5 (December 1917): 13.

28. HD, March 22, 1919. On the leadership of Du Bois in relation to the masses, for example, see Clarence G. Contee, "Du Bois, the NAACP, and the Pan-African Congress of 1919," *Journal of Negro History* 57, no. 1 (January 1972): 13–28, 28, which cites Nannie H. Burroughs to James Weldon Johnson, July 21, 1921, Records of the NAACP, B C-158, LOC. In that correspondence Burroughs writes that Du Bois was too egotistical to be a leader of the masses. Contee adds, "Du Bois knew that his leadership was not one of demagoguery, but one of intellectuality." On this subject see also Du Bois's revealing self-evaluation on how he "never was, nor ever will be, personally popular" and how his leadership was "solely of ideas": W. E. B. Du Bois, *Dusk of Dawn: An Essay Toward an Autobiography of a Race Concept* (1940; New York: Schocken, 1968), 303.

29. HD, March 22, 1919.

30. HD, March 22, 1919.

31. HD, March 22, 1919; Judson MacLaury, U.S. Department of Labor History, "The Federal Government and Negro Worker Under President Woodrow Wilson," paper delivered at the Society for History in the Federal Government annual meeting, Washington, DC, March 16, 2000, https://www.dol.gov/general/aboutdol/history /shfgpr00.

32. HD, March 22, 1919.

33. HD, March 22, 1919.

34. See 1919 letters of recommendation from Rev. W. C. Brown (March 31), HP, B1, F16; William Gordon (April 23), HP, B1, F60; Dr. John Alex Morgan (April 21), HP, B2, F76; W. E. Lew (April 1919), HP, B2, F61; B. T. Johnson (April 1), HP, B2, F52; and J. Bond (April 7), HP, B1, F6.

35. "Negro History You Should Know," Washington, DC, March 25, 1919, in HH, ScrMAM1, HP, FB 740; "Negroes Urged to Strive: Dr. Hubert Harrison Warns Against Imitating White People," *Washington Post*, March 26, 1919; HD, March 25, 1919.

36. HD, March 25 and July 6, 1919; HH, "Introductory," *WAA*, 5–8. See also "Dignity of the Flag Upheld: Lecturer Fined for Displaying Ensigns of 10 by 16 Inches," *New York Globe*, July 31, 1923, ScrMAM2, HP, B3, F5–6, which says, "From July, 1917, to April 1919, he [HH] was editor of *The Voice*, a racial paper which he founded." On Harrison speaking in New York, see "Urges Negroes to Use Force," *Boston Herald*, July 28, 1919, MID 10218-130-13; and HD, April 9, 1919.

37. HD, March 25 and April 9, 1919. See also HH, "The Meditations of Mustapha: A Soul in Search of Itself," *Negro World*, c. October 23, 1920, HP, B5, F18; Photo of HH and two others, March 1919, HP, B15, F14; HH, "To My Wife and Sweetheart From her Husband and Lover," postcard, March 31, 1919, HP, B19, F13.

38. "Noted African Traveler in Town to Lecture," *Richmond News-Leader*, ScrMAM2, HP, FB740.

39. HD, April 25 and November 13, 1919. On Scott's role in Harrison's postal firing, see *HHVHR*, 131–34. On Harrison not becoming editor of an Urban League–related publication around 1915, see *HHVHR*, 246–48.

40. "Hubert Harrison, Speaker: Speaking Tomorrow," *Richmond News-Leader*, April 29, 1919; and advertisement re: Harrison talk on "Negro History and Negro Education," Richmond, VA, April 30, 1919, both in HP, FB740.

41. HD, April 25 and July 6, 1919; "Harlem Briefs," *Chicago Defender*, August 2, 1919, 3; "Urges Negroes to Use Force."

42. Major W. H. Loving to Director of MI, Washington, DC, Subject "Final Report on Negro Subversion," August 6, 1919, MID 10218-361-1. British Intelligence also picked up Loving's report and recirculated it as a special report on "Unrest Among Negroes." See Directorate of Intelligence (London) of the British Home Office, Special Report no. 10, "Unrest Among the Negroes," October 7, 1919, in W. F. Elkins, "'Unrest Among Negroes': A British Document of 1919," *Science & Society* (Winter 1968): esp. 68, 74, 77–78. See also Theodore Kornweibel Jr., *"Seeing Red": Federal Campaigns Against Black Militancy, 1919–1925* (Bloomington: Indiana University Press, 1998), 56.

43. Loving, to Director of MI, August 6, 1919. On Harrison's "broad-learning," David Levering Lewis, *When Harlem Was in Vogue* (1979; New York: Oxford University Press, 1981), 104, describes him as "omniscient."

44. HD, April 9, 1919; Constance McLaughlin Green, *The Secret City: A History of Race Relations in the Nation's Capital* (Princeton, NJ: Princeton University Press, 1967), 189.

45. HD, April 9, 1919; "The Alleged and the Real Moens' Case," *Messenger* 7, no. 7 (July 1919): 28–31, quotation on 30; Green, *The Secret City*, 189, 201. See also F. Godwin to Intelligence Officer, General Engineering Depot, War Department, Washington, DC, "Subject: Prof. Moens Case" (Previously reported), June 14, 1918, Reel 9140-2222-35, Reel 22, *FSAA*; and esp. J. G. C. Corcoran, Report of August 30, 1918, "In re: Liberty Congress," BF, OG 369936, RG 65, DNA, Reel 12, *FSAA*. Du Bois, it should be noted, had invited Columbia professor Franz Boas to a 1905 Atlanta University conference on "The Negro Physique." Aware that Boas had a penchant for measuring people, Du Bois offered to provide him with Black student subjects if Columbia would cover travel expenses. See Carl Degler, *In Search of Human Nature: The Decline and Revival of Darwinism in American Social Thought* (New York: Oxford University Press, 1991), 76.

46. "The Case of Herman M. Bernelot-Moens," *Issues of To-Day*, February 11, 1922, 417–18, copy in War Department File 9140-222 57x58-25, DNA, Reel 22, *FSAA*. "Moens, Mystery Man," *Washington Post*, May 30, 1919, 1; "Fake Scientist Convicted," *Washington Eagle*, April 2, 1919, 1; "The Moens Case," editorial, *Washington Bee*, April 5, 1919; "Moens Found Guilty," *Washington Bee*, April 15, 1919; "Prof. Moens: How He Was Entertained and by Whom," *Washington Bee*, April 15, 1919; and "Art Study Gets Moens in Prison," *Washington Post*, April 18, 1919.

47. "The Case of Herman M. Bernelot-Moens," 418.

48. "The Case of Herman M. Bernelot-Moens," 417; "Moens, Mystery Man"; "Fake Scientist Convicted"; "The Moens Case"; "Moens Found Guilty"; "Prof. Moens"; and "Art Study Gets Moens in Prison."

49. HD, April 9, 1919; "The Alleged and the Real Moens Case," *Messenger*, July 1919. See also Parents' League, April 1919 Notice of a Mass Meeting (to be held June 24, 1919), enclosed in letter from R. C. Tanner to WEBDB, http://credo.library.umass.edu/view/full/mums312-b015-i381.

50. Herman M. Bernelot Moens (article written by HH), "Three Black Bands," *Medical Review of Reviews* (December 1919): 719–23, quotation on 723; Harrison identifies himself as the author in his copy of the article on 722, HP, B13, F1 and 2. See also Herman M. Bernelot Moens, "The Intermixture of Races," *Medical Review of Reviews* (September 1919); and articles by R. W. Shufeldt in the April and October 1919 issues.

51. Green, *The Secret City*, 189; and Moens (HH), "Three Black Bands," 723. In November 1918 Dr. R. W. Shufeldt, then a major in the U.S. Army and an official at the Army Medical Museum, reportedly called the legation of the Netherlands, Washington,

DC, and said, "The way in which they treat your countryman is a disgrace to the United States." "The Case of Herman M. Bernelot-Moens," 417–18. "Comstockian" refers to the policies of censorship of obscene and immoral materials defined by Anthony Comstock (1844–1915), postal inspector and major force behind the founding of the New York Society for the Suppression of Vice. See Robert D. Cross, "Anthony Comstock," in *ANB*, esp. 5:308.

52. Moens (HH), "Three Black Bands," 720; Moens, "The Intermixture of Races."

53. Moens (HH), "Three Black Bands," 722. The Bull Durham tobacco bull was related to the "national pastime" and appeared in many early twentieth-century baseball parks. Michael Gartner, "Words," in *The Fireside Book of Baseball*, ed. Charles Einstein (New York: Simon and Schuster, 1956), suggests that the term "bullpen" was related to the fact that pitchers would often warm up in the shade of advertisements for Bull Durham tobacco on outfield fences in many parks. See also Richard Bruce Nugent, *Gay Rebel of the Harlem Renaissance*, ed. Thomas H. Wirth (Durham, NC: Duke University Press, 2002), 149.

54. Moens (HH), "Three Black Bands," 722. *Matinée de septembre* was completed by the forty-three-year-old French painter Paul Chabas in 1912.

55. HH, "Scientific Radical Liars: What Randolph and Owen Know (?) About Anthropology and Sociology: Prof Boas and Col. Snyder vs. the Editors of the Messenger, The Evidence in the Case," a portion of an article by Harrison in the *Chicago Enterprise*, *Negro World*, May 8, 1920, 10.

56. HH, "Scientific Radical Liars," 10.

57. HH, "Scientific Radical Liars," 10. There is no indication that Moens had an academic PhD or that he was a professor at any university. See Jan Voogd, "Research Briefing no. 1: Herman Marie Bernelot Moens," https://janvoogd.wordpress.com/tag/herman-marie-bernelot-moens/.

58. HH, "Scientific Radical Liars."

59. HH, "Scientific Radical Liars."

60. "The Case of Herman M. Bernelot-Moens," 418; "Moens Scandal Case to Come Up Soon in Capitol," *New York News*, April 1, 1920, 1; Theodore Kornweibel Jr. *"Investigate Everything": Federal Efforts to Compel Black Loyalty During World War I* (Bloomington: University of Indiana Press, 2002), 222–23.

3. *New Negro* Editor and Agitator (July–December 1919)

1. HH, "Announcement," *New Negro* 3 (August 1919): 3; and *New Negro*, n.s., 4, no. 1 (September 1919): 1, 3, HP, B17, F8, HPDLC. For Harrison's comments on *The Nation*, see [HH,] "The Nature of It," *New Negro*, n.s., 4, no. 1 (September 1919): 1, HP, B17, F8.

2. See Alexander Trachtenberg, ed., *The American Labor Year Book, 1919–1920* (New York: Rand School of Social Science, 1920), 168–72; Anthony Bimba, *The History of the American Working Class* (1927; New York: International Publishers, 1934), 268, 274, 276; Jeremy Brecher, *Strike!* (1972; San Francisco: Straight Arrow, 1973), 134; Robert Asher, "1919 Strike Wave," in *EAL*, 532–33; Selig Perlman and Philip Taft, *History of Labor in the United States, 1896–1932* (New York: The MacMillan Company, 1935), 4:433; William Z. Foster, *The Great Steel Strike and Its Lessons* (New York: B. W. Huebsch, 1920), 2, 170, 191; Judith Stein, *The World of Marcus Garvey: Race and Class in Modern Society* (Baton Rouge: Louisiana State University Press, 1986), 54; Arthur I. Waskow, *From Race*

Riot to Sit-In, 1919 and the 1960s: A Study in the Connections Between Conflict and Violence (Garden City, NY: Doubleday, 1966), 4, 6–8; and Robert K. Murray, *Red Scare: A Study in National Hysteria, 1919–1920* (Minneapolis: University of Minnesota Press, 1955), 7–9, 61, 111–12.

3. Waskow, *From Race Riot to Sit-In*, 9–10, 12, 38, 41–42, 104, 109, 145, quotation on 9; *DHNPUS*, 3:271–72; "Omaha Scene of Latest Mob Exploit," *New York Age*, October 4, 1919, 1, 2; "Race Troubles Reported from Many States," *New York Age*, October 11, 1919, 1, 2; James Weldon Johnson, *Along This Way: The Autobiography of James Weldon Johnson* (New York: Viking, 1933), 341; Jane Lang Scheiber and Harry N. Scheiber, "The Wilson Administration and the Wartime Mobilization of Black-Americans, 1917–1918," *Labor History* 10, no. 3 (Summer 1969): 433–58, esp. 457; Jessie Parkhurst Guzman, *Negro Year Book 1947: A Review of Events Affecting Negro Life, 1941–1946* (Tuskegee, AL: Department of Records and Research, Tuskegee Institute, 1947), 307; and *GP*, 2:98n3. On the rise in lynching, see Stein, *The World of Marcus Garvey*, 55. See also *ACABA*, 1:4, 2:359; Mark Ellis, "J. Edgar Hoover and the 'Red Summer' of 1919," *Journal of American Studies* 28, no. 1 (April 1994), 39–59, 51; William M. Tuttle Jr., *Race Riot: Chicago in the Red Summer of 1919* (1970; New York: Atheneum, 1975), 16.

4. Tuttle, *Race Riot*, 13–14. The Chicago Commission on Race Relations in its report found that "the general belief among Negroes is that resistance to violence is justified." Commission on Race Relations, "The Negro in Chicago: A Race Riot," in *Blacks in White America Since 1865: Issues and Interpretations*, ed. Robert C. Twombly (New York: David McKay Co., 1971), 203–23, esp. 223. November 1919 also saw Palmer raids, the witch-hunting Lusk Committee, and the founding of the U.S. Communist Party (actually two distinct parties).

5. John Hope Franklin, *From Slavery to Freedom: A History of Negro Americans*, 4th ed. (New York: Knopf, 1974), 357.

6. Waskow, *From Race Riot to Sit-In*, 21–37, esp. 23, 25, 27, 37; "Race Riot at Capital [*sic*]," *New York Age*, July 26, 1919, 1; Lloyd M. Abernethy, "The Washington Race War of July, 1919," *Maryland Historical Quarterly* 58 (December 1963): 309–24. See also *GP*, 1:473n3; and Peter Perl, "Race Riot of 1919 Gave Glimpse of Future Struggles," *Washington Post*, March 1, 1999, 1, which adds that "the Washington riot of 1919 was distinguished by strong, organized and armed black resistance, foreshadowing the civil rights struggles later in the century"; longtime *Post* reporter Chalmers Roberts called the paper's coverage "shamefully irresponsible."

7. Waskow, *From Race Riot to Sit-In*, 38–104, 38, 41, 42, 47; Bruce Kellner, ed., *The Harlem Renaissance: A Historical Dictionary for the Era* (New York: Methuen, 1987), 303; "Chicago Is in the Grip of Serious Race Riots," *New York Age*, August 2, 1919, 1; "Union Labor Leaders Foment Trouble in Chicago," *New York Age*, August 16, 1919, 1, 2; Ellis, "J. Edgar Hoover and the 'Red Summer' of 1919," 45. William M. Tuttle, "Labor Conflict and Racial Violence: The Black Worker in Chicago, 1894–1919," *Labor History* (Summer 1969): 408–32, esp. 408; *GP*, 1:473n4; and Robert Kerlin, *Voice of the Negro* (E. P. Dutton & Co., 1920; New York: Arno, 1968). Harrison's figure on the Chicago riots can be found in [HH,] "'Suppressing' Race Riots," *New Negro*, October 1919, 6. The Chicago Federation of Labor, which represented 500,000 workers, was described by William Z. Foster as one of "the most progressive central labor unions in the United States." At its August 3, 1919, meeting it acknowledged attempts were made "to blame the race riots on labor, saying that labor is probably the cause of the riots."

It countered "labor has done everything in the Stock yards and held out its hand to the Negro and established organizations and invited the Negroes into the white man's unions." Overall, the attitudes and practices of the labor movement, including one of "the most progressive central labor unions" speaking of "white man's unions," undoubtedly inflamed the situation. See Phil Bart, *Working Class Unity: The Role of Communists in the Chicago Federation of Labor, 1919–1923* (New York: New Outlook, 1975), 5, 11.

8. Waskow, *From Race Riot to Sit-In*, 188–89; Murray, *Red Scare*, 67–78; *GP*, 1:406n1; Patrick S. Washburn, *A Question of Sedition: The Federal Government's Investigation of the Black Press During World War II* (New York: Oxford, 1986), 25.

9. See from ScrAfter ("The Aftermath of the Great War"), HP, B10, F2: "Danger Peace Conference May Fail, Mr. Simond Says," *Literary Digest*, March 29, 1919, 21; "Bolshevism Sweeps Fast Over Europe," *New York American*, November 14, 1918 (on which Harrison writes "Game Opens"); "Germans Dread Future: Great Precautions to Prevent Anarchy in Demobilization," *New York Times*, November 22, 1918; and "Romanian Troops Refuse to Fight the Bolsheviki," "Poland, Rumania and Jugoslavs Fear Bolshevik Invasion," "Red Tide Stirs Paris," and "Spartacans Ask Bolsheviki to Start Invasion April 1 to Insure New Revolution," all from the *Washington Post*, March 26, 1919.

10. Waskow, *From Race Riot to Sit-In*, 188–89; Robert A. Bowen, "Radicalism and Sedition Among the Negroes as Reflected in Their Publications," July 2, 1919, case file OG ["Old German"] 359561, Record Group 65, BI, DNA; and Letter from Attorney General [A. Mitchell Palmer], transmitting in response to a Senate Resolution of October 17, 1919, A Report on the Activities of the Bureau of Investigation of the Department of Justice, Against Persons Advising Anarchy, Sedition, and the Forcible Overthrow of the Government, *Investigation Activities of the Department of Justice*, 66th Congress, 1st sess., 1919, Senate Documents, Vol. 12, No. 153, November 17, 1919, "Introduction to Exhibit 10," "Radicalism and Sedition Among the Negroes as Reflected in Their Publications," 162; Theodore Kornweibel Jr., *"Seeing Red": Federal Campaigns Against Black Militancy, 1919–1925* (Bloomington: Indiana University Press, 1998), xi, 22; Ellis, "J. Edgar Hoover and the 'Red Summer' of 1919," 53.

11. Waskow, *From Race Riot to Sit-In*, 188–89; "Radicalism and Sedition Among the Negroes as Reflected in Their Publications," 162; "Report of the Department of Justice on Sedition Among Negroes," *New York Age*, December 26, 1919, 4; and Ellis, "J. Edgar Hoover and the 'Red Summer' of 1919," 43, 59, where Ellis concludes, "In Hoover's mind, radical black organization for constitutional rights still endangered the American social order, and carried with it the threat of external subversion." Kornweibel, *"Seeing Red,"* xii–xiii, notes that Hoover's role "cannot be overestimated" and that in spearheading the BI's antiradical crusade in 1919, "he fixated on the belief that racial militants were seeking to break down social barriers separating blacks from whites, and that they were inspired by communists or were the pawns of communists. These notions became embedded in the FBI and its director." Kornweibel notes the "great irony" in the fact that "Palmer, Hoover, and their peers, like bulls facing a toreador, were also 'seeing red'" (xiv).

12. *Investigation Activities of the Department of Justice*, 66th Congress, 1st sess., 1919, Senate Documents, Vol. 12, No. 153, November 17, 1919, 184–85, 166–67; [HH,] "A Prophetic 'Voice': The Cause of the Negro's New Attitude Towards Race Riots," *New Negro*, September 1919, 8–9, HP, B17, F8; Kornweibel, *"Seeing Red,"* 60; and Andrea Razafkeriefo, "The Village Lynch-Smith (with Apologies to Longfellow)" [poem], *New*

Negro, September 1919, 12. Mark Ellis concludes that "the report was nonsense. . . . Bowen made no effort to understand the sense of betrayal blacks felt after the War for Democracy and failed to recognize the wide range of black viewpoints." Ellis, "J. Edgar Hoover and the 'Red Summer' of 1919," points out (46–47) that another critic of Hoover's analysis was Attorney General Palmer, who said the causes of the Washington and Chicago riots were "due solely to local conditions and were not inspired by Bolshevik and other radical propaganda." He adds (52) that Hoover was forced to back off his original position, and by October 18 he wrote that while "direct causes" were "purely local," it was "no doubt true that a secondary cause of the trouble was due to propaganda of a radical nature."

13. "Radicalism and Sedition," cited in Hill, "Introduction," in Briggs, ed., *Crusader* (Facsimile) 1:xxiii; Waskow, *From Race Riot to Sit-In*, 208. The nadir refers to a post-Reconstruction low period in race relations in the United States.

14. [HH,] "As the Currents Flow," *New Negro*, August 1919, 3. Harrison explained that the "white" press had reprinted a paragraph from the *New York World* that maintained "the Negro American has entered a new epoch in the history of his country." He added that it had "been too long the practice of the Southern Negro victims to beg and plead for mercy at the hands of a sordid mob." He also wondered why they didn't "arm themselves preparatory for self-defence" and reasoned "If they are to die at the hands of a 'legalized' mob, then it is up to them to sell their lives as dearly as possible." In this way the "white man" would be "made to take his own medicine" and "learn to appreciate its disagreeable and disgusting flavor."

15. Stein, *The World of Marcus Garvey*, 57–60.

16. *New Negro*, August 1919, 1, HP, B17, F8, HPDLC. See the *New York Age* series that ran early in 1920 including: "New Negro—What Is He?" editorial, January 24, 1920, 4; "Symposium on 'New Negro—What Is He?'" February 7, 1920, 1, 2; and "Symposium on 'New Negro—What Is He?'" February 28, 1920, 1, 2.

17. *New Negro*, August 1919, 1, HP, B17, F8, HPDLC.

18. See *New Negro*, September 1919, 1 HP, B17, F8; and [HH,] "Our Little Library," 16. The *New Negro* of August 1919, 1–3, incorrectly described Harrison as "The man who first coined the phrase 'The New Negro.'" For background on *The Clarion*, see *HHVHR*, 318–20, 331. The phrase "New Negro" was used at least as early as 1895. See August Meier, "The Social and Intellectual Origins of the New Negro," in *Negro Thought in America, 1880–1915* (1963; Ann Arbor: University of Michigan Press, 1987), 256–78, esp. 258. It also appeared in 1916 in William Pickens, *The New Negro, His Political and Civil Status and Related Issues* (New York: Neale Publishing Co., 1916). *New Negro* 2, no. 3 (April 15, 1918), says it was published semimonthly by "August Valentine Bernier, editor-proprietor, 118 West 134th Street, New York City, Beatrice Ione Wade, travelling Saleswoman and Agent, Contributing Editors John Edward Bruce 'Grit,' Alexander Rahming, Andrea Razafkeriefo, Wm. H. Scott," and is found in BF, OG 311587, RG 65, DNA, Washington, DC, *FSAA*, Reel 11. In *New Negro* (formerly *The Clarion*) 1, no. 6 (December 15, 1917): 14, Bernier was listed as proprietor and business manager, Gertrude Mille-Faide as managing editor, and Frank Billups as advertising manager. Domingo, Rahming, Scott, and Razafkeriefo were listed as contributing editors.

19. "Announcement," *New Negro*, August 1919, 3; [HH,] "The Need for It," *New Negro*, September 1919, 1.

20. [HH,] "The Nature of It," *New Negro*, September 1919, 1, HP, B17, F8, HPDLC. Before Harrison developed his news commentary columns, *New Negro* 3, no. 7

(August 1919), included "Contemporaneous Predictions: Culled for the *Clarion* from Liberal and Radical Press" (particularly *The Nation*), by Semper Fidelis (HH) on 6 and articles from *The Nation* on the League of Nations and disarmament and on President Wilson in Nicaragua, Santo Domingo, and Haiti. See also Domingo Rivera, "The Substance and the Shadow," 7; "Pres. Wilson's 1918 Labor Day Speech," 4; [HH?], "N.A.A.C. Condemns Mob Violence," 4; and HH, "Our Larger Duty," 5–6, rpt. in *WAA*, 100–4, with notes at 189–91. Harrison, an early supporter of Bolshevism among Black Americans, also published "A Bolshevist Solution of the Problem of High Rents—Decree of the Hungarian Soviet Government—March 27th, 1919," *New Negro* 4, no. 2 (October 1919): 7.

21. [HH,] "The Nature of It." When the *New Negro* appeared under Harrison's editorship both the BI and British MI took immediate notice. Charles J. Scully, BI agent and chief of the Radical Department, in his report of September 17, 1919, enclosed a copy of the report of Lt. Col. Norman H. C. Thwaites. Scully described Harrison as "a well educated, dangerous radical Negro" who had an article in the September *Clarion* [*New Negro*], which described how "'By virtue of its control[,] England rules and robs India.'" He noted that the issue of *The Clarion* announced the reappearance of the *New Negro* on September 1, with Harrison as editor and with the stated purpose being to develop the *New Negro* "as an organ of the international consciousness of the darker races, especially of the negro race." Thwaites also mentioned being in possession of the October issue of the *New Negro*, and he extracted from three articles, "Will the White Race Destroy Itself?," "Two Negro Radicalisms," and "The White War and the Colored Races." See Charles J. S. Scully, Report of September 17, 1919, Enclosing Report of Col. [N.] H. C. Thwaites of British Provost Marshall's Office, August 29, 1919, "Negro Agitators," BF, OG 3057[?], RG 65, DNA, Reel 8, *FSAA*.

22. [HH,] "As the Currents Flow," *New Negro*, August 1919, 3.

23. [HH,] "The World This Month," *New Negro*, September 1919, 2, 3, 11, esp. 2.

24. [HH,] "The World This Month," *New Negro*, September 1919, quotation on 2; HH, "The Negro at the Peace Congress" (probably first published in *The Voice*, c. December 1918), *WAA*, 30–32. Both Du Bois and Trotter went to the conference, despite difficulty in securing passage. Trotter was denied official recognition as a National Race Congress delegate though he did provide the French public with some leaflets on African Americans. See *GP*, 2:167n4; Stephen R. Fox, *The Guardian of Boston: William Monroe Trotter* (New York: Atheneum, 1971), 223–30. An International League of Darker Peoples founded on January 2, 1919, at a conference at the Lewaro-on-the-Hudson villa of Madame C. J. Walker, aimed to organize "Negro" delegates in a united front for the Paris Peace Conference. Proposals drafted by A. Philip Randolph were adopted for submission to the peace conference, and officers were chosen including Rev. Adam Clayton Powell, president; Isaac B. Allen, first vice president; Lewis G. Jordan, second vice president; Madame C. J. Walker, treasurer; Randolph, secretary; and Gladys Flynn, assistant secretary. In March, both Powell and Walker publicly resigned. See *GP*, 1:345nn1–2; *New York Age*, March 15, 1919; DNA, RG 65, files OG 258421, OG 377483; RG 165, file 10218-296.

25. [HH,] "The World This Month," *New Negro*, October 1919, 2–3, quotation on 2, HP, B17, F8, HPDLC. Regarding the former German colonies in Africa, the Paris Peace Conference awarded mandates for South-West Africa (now known as Namibia) to South Africa; for Togoland and the Cameroons (both of them partitioned) to France and Great Britain; and for the remaining portion of German East Africa to Belgium. See *GP*, 2:52n3, 1:290n12 (on the three types of mandates).

26. [HH,] "The World This Month," *New Negro*, October 1919, 2–3.

27. [HH,] "The World This Month," *New Negro*, October 1919, 2–3.

28. [HH,] "The World This Month," *New Negro*, October 1919, 2. In his "Farewell Address" of September 17, 1796, George Washington said "Tis our true policy to steer clear of permanent alliances with any portion of the foreign world." John Bartlett, ed., *Familiar Quotations: A Collection of Passages, Phrases, and Proverbs Traced to Their Sources in Ancient and Modern Literature*, 11th ed., rev. and exp. (Garden City, NY: Garden City Pub. Co., 1944), 268.

29. [HH,] "The World This Month," *New Negro*, October 1919, 3.

30. [HH,] "The World This Month," *New Negro*, October 1919, 3; *GP*, 1:473n6. On Sir Roger David Casement (1864–1916), see *GP*, 1:473n6, 5:800n8; *WNBD*, 179; Brian Inglis, *Roger Casement* (London: Holder and Stoughton, 1973), 13–107, 169–219; and Adam Hochschild, *King Leopold's Ghost: A Story of Greed, Terror, and Heroism in Colonial Africa* (Boston: Houghton Mifflin, 1998), 195–208, 267–68, 284–87.

31. [HH,] "The World This Month," *New Negro*, October 1919, 3.

32. See HH, ScrwrNW, HP, B13, F7. On the style of the editorials, see HD, March 17, 1920.

33. HH, "Our Larger Duty," *New Negro*, August 1919, 5–6. Also in HH, ScrEarlyWr, HP, B13, F1–2, in *WAA*, 100–4, quotation on 100–1. See also "Announcement," *New Negro*, August 1919, 3; WEBDB, *To the Nations of the World, Address of the Pan-African Conference* (London, 1900); WEBDB, *The Souls of Black Folk* (Chicago: A. C. McClurg & Co., 1903); *GP*, 2:69n7.

34. HH, "Our Larger Duty," *WAA*, 101.

35. HH, "Our Larger Duty," 102–3. In his copy of Lothrop Stoddard, *The Rising Tide of Color: Against White World-Supremacy* (1920; New York, Scribner, 1922), HP, B25, http://www.gutenberg.org/ebooks/37408, Harrison wrote on 9: "what welds them into this solidarity of sentiment is the solidarity of suffering—under the white man's foot." He added on 12, regarding the change in attitude, "It first started in the 1890s when Abyssinia defeated Italy. The start was thus made in Africa." The Swadeshi movement in India encouraged domestic production and the boycott of foreign goods.

36. HH, "Our Larger Duty," *WAA*, 103.

37. HH, "Negro Culture and the Negro College," *New Negro*, September 1919, 4–5, ScrEarlyWr, HP, B13, F1–2; rpt. with deletions as "H.H." [HH], "The Racial Roots of Culture," *Negro World*, July 31, 1920, 2; and as "The Racial Roots of Culture," *WAA*, 129–31.

38. Harrison, in his copy of Jerome Dowd, *The Negro Races: A Sociological Study* (New York: The Macmillan Company; London: Macmillan & Co., Ltd., 1907), HP, Box 21, criticizes Ratzel's sociology, which, according to Dowd, attributed "the gradual mixture of Fetallah with Negro blood" for "tending . . . to drag down the higher race, undermine its spirit and cause the States which it had formed to dissolve and disappear in the ocean of Negro disintegration and timidity." Harrison writes, "Ratzel's sociology is here at fault. For real reasons of any such decline of national culture cf. [John M.] Robertson's *The Evolution of States*." See Harrison's personal copy, with his comments, of J. M. Robertson, *The Evolution of States: An Introduction to English Politics* (New York: G. Putnam's Sons, 1913), HP, B24.

39. Joseph Ephraim Casely Hayford (1866–1930) was a journalist and political commentator considered "the principal West African political figure of his day." Born at Cape Coast, Ghana, he was educated there and in Sierra Leone before coming under the

influence of Edward Wilmot Blyden. From 1903 until his death, he published the *Gold Coast Leader*, "the leading journal of West African nationalism during this period." The author of *Ethiopia Unbound: Studies in Race Emancipation* (London: C. M. Philips, 1911) "played an important role in developing the ideology of West African nationalism." See *GP*, 1:350n1.

40. HH, "Negro Culture and the Negro College," 4. Many of these titles are mentioned in Richard B. Moore, "Africa Conscious Harlem," *Freedomways*, Summer 1963, 316–17.

41. HH, "Negro Culture and the Negro College," 4, 5. This mention of the Baptist Seminary and College at Lynchburg appeared in the original article but not in the 1920 reprint in *WAA*.

42. [HH,] "Two Negro Radicalisms," *New Negro*, n.s., 4 (October 1919), 4–5, HP, B13, F1–2; rpt. with revisions and without the second and third to last paragraphs as HH, "The Negro's Own Radicalism," *WAA*, 76–79.

43. [HH,] "Two Negro Radicalisms," 4–5. Wilson Jeremiah Moses, *The Golden Age of Black Nationalism, 1850–1925* (New York: Oxford University Press, 1978), 248, considers Harrison "guilty of exaggeration," since there "had been currents of black radicalism in America before the turn of the century." Moses adds, however, "there is an element of truth in what Harrison said, because certainly the 1920s did witness a growing diversity of opinion within the black community, and much of the opinion was radical."

44. [HH,] "Two Negro Radicalisms," 5. See, for example, "Negroes of World Prey of Agitators," *New York Times*, August 24, 1919, 1; and "I.W.W. Urge Revolt by Negro Mill Men," *New York Sun*, October 8, 1919.

45. See Roy Talbert Jr., *Negative Intelligence: The Army and the American Left, 1917–1941* (Jackson: University Press of Mississippi, 1991), 26n17; and *The Truth About the Lusk Committee*, Report Prepared by the Legislative Committee of the People's Freedom Union (New York: The Nation Press, Inc.), 4, 8–9.

46. [HH,] "Two Negro Radicalisms," 5.

47. [HH,] "Two Negro Radicalisms," 5.

48. [HH,] "Two Negro Radicalisms," 5. In this passage Harrison seems to foreshadow Martin Luther King Jr.'s "I Have a Dream" Address at the August 28, 1963, March on Washington for Jobs and Freedom, where King says: "In a sense we've come to our nation's capital to cash a check. This note was a promise that all men, yes, black men as well as white men . . . would be guaranteed the unalienable rights of life, liberty, and the pursuit of happiness. It is obvious today that America has defaulted on this promissory note insofar as her citizens of color are concerned. . . . Instead of honoring this sacred obligation, America has given the Negro people a bad check, a check which has come back marked insufficient funds." https://kinginstitute.stanford.edu/king-papers/documents/i-have-dream-address-delivered-march-washington-jobs-and-freedom.

49. [HH,] "Two Negro Radicalisms," 5. For this missing paragraph, see *WAA*, 180–81.

50. [HH,] "Two Negro Radicalisms," 5. For this missing paragraph, see *WAA*, 181.

51. [HH,] "Two Negro Radicalisms," 5.

52. See "Majority Report on Immigration," in SP, *National Convention of the Socialist Party Held at Indianapolis, IN, May 12 to 18, 1912*, stenographic report by Wilson E. McDermut, assisted by Charles W. Phillips, ed. John Spargo (Chicago: The Socialist

Party, 1912), 209–211; HH, "Race Prejudice—II," *New York Call*, December 4, 1911, 6, in *HR*, 55–57; HH, "Seeking a Way Out," *Boston Chronicle*, May 31, 1924, HP, B6, F43.

53. [HH,] "The White War and the Colored Races" [1918], *New Negro*, October 1919, 8–10; in *Negro World*, February 1920, HP, B13, F1–2; in *HR*, 203–8; and in *WAA*, 116–22, esp. 116. See also HH, "The White War and the Colored Races," n.d., HP, B6, F61, HPDLC. In a June 24, 1920, letter to T. Lothrop Stoddard (HP, B2, F19), Harrison wrote: "I am also enclosing a copy of an article on THE WHITE WAR AND THE COLORED RACES, written in 1918 and reprinted in the *Negro World* in February of this year. The substance of it had been previously delivered in Wall St. and Washington Heights, Madison Square and other places, in-doors and out to white audiences during 1915 and 1916." In *WAA*, 141, Harrison says that he wrote "The White World and the Colored Races" in 1917. In that case he may have actually been referring to the article "The White War and the Colored World," which was published on August 14, 1917, in *The Voice*. HP, B6, F62. See also HH, "The White War and the Colored World," HD, B6, F62, HPDLC; *HR*, 202–3; *WAA*, 96–98, 187–88; and *HHVHR*, 230–32, 266–69, 473n32.

54. Barbara Foley, *Spectres of 1919: Class and Nation in the Making of the New Negro* (Urbana: University of Illinois Press), 225, 290–91n30; and Linnea M. Anderson, Archivist, Social Welfare History Archives, Elmer L. Andersen Library, University of Minnesota, to JBP, December 31, 2015 (regarding undated memo mentioning Harrison's article on "The White Man's War" for the proposed Alain Locke–edited *Survey Graphic* issue on "Harlem: Mecca of the New Negro"), in Survey Associates Records, B94, F710 (Locke Files). Foley comments, "Perhaps Harrison's 'radical indictment' of 'capitalism'—a word that would not make it into the *Survey Graphic*," was "too much" for it to be included in that issue (225). See also *Survey Graphic* 6, no. 5 (March 1925), rpt. by Black Classic Press, 1981, https://web.archive.org/web/20080509055127 /http://etext.lib.virginia.edu/harlem/contents.html; and Alain Locke, ed., *The New Negro: An Interpretation* (New York: Albert & Charles Boni, 1925); rpt. as Alain Locke, ed., *The New Negro: An Interpretation*, with a new preface by Robert Hayden (New York: Atheneum, 1980); and rpt. as Alain Locke, ed., *The New Negro: Voices of the Harlem Renaissance*, intro. Arnold Rampersad (New York: Simon & Schuster, 1992).

55. [HH,] "The Problems of Leadership," *WAA*, 55. At a late fall 1919 meeting, the National Executive Committee of the SP called for the preparation of literature on the race question. This was a response to a recommendation passed by the emergency convention of the party held earlier in Chicago. The party secretary was instructed "to get in touch with the editors of the 'Messenger', a radical paper published in New York City, and have them submit manuscript for a leaflet on the race question." While the Socialists ignored Harrison's article, the more independent *Crusader*, edited by Cyril Briggs, called attention to the October *New Negro*. See "Negro Agitation," November 7, 1919, MID 10218-261-50, 13.

56. [HH,] "The White War and the Colored Races," [1918], *in New Negro*, October 1919, 8–10, quotation on 8; rpt. in *Negro World*, February 1920; and in *WAA*, 116–22, esp. 116. In his personal copy of Weale, *The Conflict of Colour*, Harrison writes that the secrets of supremacy "are found to be not *Race* but *Power*."

57. [HH,] "The White War and the Colored Races," *WAA*, 115–22, 116–17. The subheading appears on 116. See also Tigran H. Poyachean, *Armenia: The Case for a Forgotten Genocide* (Westwood, NJ: Educational Book Crafters, 1972), 1–15, 102–36.

58. [HH,] "The White War and the Colored Races," 8–9; *WAA*, 118. See also WEBDB, "The Roots of War," *Atlantic Monthly* 115 (May 1915): 707–14, which argued that the

war was a product of inter-European rivalries in Africa over the past few decades. Sir Henry Hamilton (Harry) Johnston claimed that the Germans desired "to wrest rich Morocco from French control, to take the French Congo from France, and the Portuguese Congo from Portugal, [and] to secure from Belgium the richest and most extensive tract of alluvial goldfields as yet discovered," that of trans-Zambesian Africa. See Roland Oliver, *Sir Harry Johnston and the Scramble for Africa* (New York: St. Martin's, 1958); and *GP*, 4:191n4.

59. [HH,] "The White War and the Colored Races," 9; *WAA*, 118–19. The General Robert Clive–led victory over a Bengal army in 1757 at Plassy, eighty miles north of Calcutta, led to the establishment of British rule in India.

60. [HH,] "The White War and the Colored Races," 9; *WAA*, 119–20. Montmarte, Seven Dials, and the Bowery were rough, lower-class sections of Paris, London, and New York, respectively.

61. [HH,] "The White War and the Colored Races," 9–10; *WAA*, 120–21.

62. [HH,] "The White War and the Colored Races," 10; *WAA*, 121.

63. [HH,] "The White War and the Colored Races," 10; *WAA*, 121–22.

64. [HH,] "The White War and the Colored Races," 10; *WAA*, 122.

65. [HH,] "The Women of Our Race," *New Negro*, October 1919, 6–7; also in *HR*, 105–6; and *WAA*, 89–91, 186.

66. [HH,] "The Women of Our Race," 6–7; *HR*, 105–6; *WAA*, 89–91.

67. Itambo Asong [HH], "The West African Woman, I," *New Negro*, September 1919, 10–11. The article found in HH, ScrEarlyWr, HP, B13, F1–2, indicates that Harrison was its author. A short piece, "Why Snake Has Neither Hands nor Feet," attributed to Itambo Asong of Oban, appears in Percy Anaury Talbot (of the Nigerian Political Service), *In the Shadow of the Bush* (London: William Heinemann, 1912), 376–77.

68. Asong [HH,] "The West African Woman, I," 10. See also Frederick Starr, *Liberia: Description, History, Problems* (Chicago: Frederick Starr, 1913), http://www.gutenberg.org/files/54542/54542-h/54542-h.htm; and George W. Ellis, *Negro Culture in West Africa* (New York: The Neale Pub. Co., 1914), https://archive.org/details/negrocultureinwe017267mbp. Hubert's daughter Aida recalled her father giving the Ellis book to his children. Richardson and Harrison, interview with JBP, August 4, 1983.

69. Asong [HH], "The West African Woman, I," 10.

70. Asong [HH], "The West African Woman, I," 10–11.

71. Asong [HH], "The West African Woman, I," 11.

72. [HH,] "The Need for It," *New Negro*, September 1919, 1.

73. G. McLean Ogle, "The Labor Unions in British Guiana," *New Negro*, August 1919, 10–11; "The New Spirit in Trinidad," *New Negro*, August 1919; rpt. from *Trinidad Literary Magazine*, [June 1919], 11, 16; [HH,] "Anxious Over Morocco in Africa!" *New Negro*, August 1919, 13.

74. "John Bull's Judge Lynch," *New Negro*, September 1919, 6–7; "John Bull," "Black Men's White Wives" (1913), *John Bull* [?], rpt. in *New Negro*, September 1919, 11; and [HH,] "The Fruits of Civilization," *New Negro*, and introduction; Arnold White, "West Ham and West Africa" (rpt. from *The Referee*), *New Negro*, September 1919, 15. "John Bull" was the name given to the English people and the typical Englishman. It was also the name of a nationalist and (during World War I) rabidly patriotic weekly founded by Horatio William Bottomley (1860–1933). Bottomley, an editor, publisher, and member of Parliament from 1906 to 1912 and 1918 to 1922, was convicted of fraud in 1922 and imprisoned for five years. See *GP*, 4:227n1, 5:431n3; *WNBD*, 127; *New York Times*, May 27,

1933; and "Bottomley Guilty of £150,000 Fraud; Gets 7-Year Term," *New York Times,* May 30, 1922.

75. Kobina Sekyi [William Esuman-Gwira Sekyi], "Education in West Africa," *New Negro,* October 1919, 11–12 (continued in November issue). William Esuman-Gwira Sekyi (Kobina Sekyi, 1892–1956), born at Cape Coast, was a lawyer, politician, and cultural nationalist critic of colonial rule who rejected both European names and European dress. See *GP,* 1:l. 51; 9:366–67n1; and Imanuel Geiss, *The Pan-African Movement,* trans. Ann Keep (1968; London: Africana Pub. Co., 1974), 274–75.

76. [HH,] "The World This Month," *New Negro,* September 1919, 3. See also Dookhan, "The Search for Identity," *Journal of Caribbean History* (1979): 1–34.

77. [HH,] "The World This Month," *New Negro,* October 1919, 2–4, esp. 4. For aspects of the history of the St. Croix Labor Union, see George F. Tyson, ed., *Searching for Truth and Justice: The Writings of Ralph D. de Chabert, 1915–1922* (Christiansted, St. Croix: Antilles Press, 2009). On D. Hamilton Jackson, see *GP,* 11:611–12n2; and for Jackson's paper, *The Herald,* see http://www.dloc.com/AA00040758/00002?search=hamilton +=jackson.

78. "A Danish Mass Meeting," *New York Age,* May 27, 1915, 8; "Danish West Indians Form Big Organization," *New York Age,* June 10, 1915, 7.

79. [HH,] "The World This Month," *New Negro,* September 1919, 3. Rothschild "Polly" Francis (1891–1963) was a self-educated activist, labor leader, journalist, Colonial Council member, and leading opponent of the U.S. Navy's occupation of the Virgin Islands. He traveled to the United States in 1920 as "the American representative of the Negro Workers of the Virgin Islands" and as a member of the Virgin Island Protective Association (VIPA). In New York he utilized the Socialist Party's *New York Call* to inform readers about the "hardships suffered under United States rule by the inhabitants of the island" and to seek funds for a printing press to take to the Virgin Islands to start a radical paper. His efforts were supported by the Virgin Islands Protective League. On May 21, 1921, Francis started *The Emancipator* in St. Thomas, and in early 1924 he served as chairman of the Virgin Islands Committee (VIC), of which Harrison was a founder and executive committee member. The VIC aimed to secure measures that would promote the economic and political reconstruction of the Virgin Islands and called on the U.S. Congress to grant a democratic form of government to the islands, to remove trade and commerce restrictions, and to grant full citizenship to Virgin Islanders residing in the United States. See Daisy Holder Lafond, "Rothschild Francis," in African Studies Club [of the Virgin Islands], *1991 Historical Calendar;* Leon A. Mawson, *Persecuted and Prosecuted* (New York: Vantage, 1987); Agent P-138 (Herbert S. Boulin), Report, September 7, 1920, BF OG258421, RG 65, DNA, Reel 11, *FSAA;* U.S. DOJ, Radical Division, Washington, DC, "General Intelligence Bulletin for September 25th, 1920," no. 30, File 10110-1683-46-328X, DNA, Reel 22, *FSAA;* Rothschild Francis, "Economic Conditions in St. Thomas, V.I., U.S.A.," *Messenger* 2, no. 9 (September 1919): 27–28; and Dookhan, "Search for Identity," *Journal of Caribbean History* (1979): 11–12, 16–17.

80. Francis, "Economic Conditions in St. Thomas, V.I., U.S.A.," 27–28; Eugene Kinckle Jones, "Negro Migration in New York State," *Opportunity* 4, no. 37 (January 1926): 7–11, esp. 7. Totten outlined the organization's plans at a meeting. A report of a "Welcome Home" reception given to Francis was also read, and the organization issued a November 4 appeal on behalf of the islands' inhabitants, who had been near destitution since the war. See "Negro Agitation," November 7, 1919; and J. G. Tucker, Special Report, September 25, 1920, RG 65, Reel 617, OG 208369.

81. Sir Rabindranath Tagore, "The Situation in India," *New Negro*, September 1919, 7. Sudarshan Kapur, *Raising Up: The African-American Encounter with Gandhi* (Boston: Beacon, 1992), 184n6, cites a Michael Winston interview, which points out "many African-Americans hung photographs of Tagore [1861–1941] in their homes even before they heard of Mahatma Gandhi" because they "were drawn to the Indian poet for 'the lyricism of his poetry,'" out of "a sense of solidarity and pride," and because "he was the first nonwhite to win the Nobel Prize for Literature." See also *WNBD*, 967–68.

82. Sayid Muhammad Berghash [HH], "Britain in India," *New Negro*, September 1919, 9–10. This article appears in HP, B13, F1–2, and Harrison writes alongside the author's byline "Pseudonym of H.H.H.," indicating that he was the author. On Barghash-ibn-Sa'id (c. 1834–1888), see *WNBD*, 75; Thomas Pakenham, *The Scramble for Africa: White Man's Conquest of the Dark Continent from 1876 to 1912* (New York: Avon, 1991), 286–99.

83. Berghash [HH], "Britain in India," 9. The article added that under this new law, "a copy of Edmund Burke's speeches on the trial of Warren Hastings, found on the person of a young Hindu student has sufficed to send him to the Andaman islands for 12 years!" Harrison's note about the Rowlatt Acts is in his copy of Stoddard, *The Rising Tide of Color*, 81.

84. Berghash [HH], "Britain in India," 10.

85. [HH,] [re India], *New Negro* 4, no. 2 (October 1919): 12.

86. Among articles in the *New Negro* of August 1919 were "Washington, Not Moscow" (rpt. from the *New Republic*), 14; "No Self-Determination for Egypt" (rpt. from *The Crime Against Russia*), 14; and "Equal Opportunity for Negroes," 15 (rpt. from *New York World*, c. July 31). This last piece was a letter from M. Diamond, of Brooklyn, who wrote that "The Negro Problem must be solved by humane treatment" and that the colored man "must demand" this. Harrison wrote, "Readers: please note the word DEMAND written by a white man for the Negro, while reactionary Negro papers in Harlem and elsewhere are telling us to beg and plead, that time, the great cure-all will bring us relief." Other articles included "The Flame of Democracy," 15 (rpt. from *Milwaukee Leader*); "Alabama Breaks Precedents," 15 (rpt. from *New York Times*); [HH,] "Abyssinian Prince Left, Insulted," 15–16; and [HH,] "Mr. Trotter at Palace Casino," 16. Yet other pieces included "The Shame of It All," 17 (an editorial from *Memphis Press*, July 20), for which the writer got ten days in prison; an advertisement for "The Clarion Readers Free Business Directory," 18; "Clarion Readers' Free Directory," 19; and an advertisement for the Clarion Publishing Association, 93 Washington Street, New York City (Care of Merchant's Press), Third Floor, August Valentine Bernier, Manager, 20.

87. [HH], "*The Nation*, the *New York Times*, and the *Washington Post*," *New Negro*, August 1919, 14. Other August articles on "race riots" included "The North Disgraced," 12, rpt. from *New York Globe*, "An Aftermath of War," 12, rpt. from *New York Call*, July 30; "Race Riots Tragically Emphasize a Vital National Duty," 13, rpt. from *Evening Mail*, July 30; "A Local Cotem on the Race Riots" (rpt. from *Amsterdam News*), 14–15; and John E. Bruce, "The Race Riots," 9.

88. [HH,] "A Prophetic 'Voice': The Cause of the Negro's New Attitude Toward Race Riots," *New Negro*, September 1919, 8, HP, B13, F1–2; and HH, "The East St. Louis Horror," *Voice*, July 4, 1917, HP, B4; rpt. in *New Negro*, September 1919, 8; and in *WAA*, 14–16.

89. [HH,] "'Suppressing' Race Riots," *New Negro*, October 1919, 6.

90. [HH,] "'Suppressing' Race Riots," 6.

91. [HH,] "The World This Month," *New Negro*, October 1919, 2–4, esp. 3–4.

92. [HH,] "The World This Month," 2, 3, 11, esp. 3.

93. [HH,] "The World This Month," 2, 3, 11, esp. 3; *Official Bulletin*, June 29, 1918.

94. [HH,] "The World This Month," *New Negro*, September 1919, 2, 3, 11.

95. [HH,] "In the Melting Pot," *New Negro*, September 1919, 14; and Alain LeRoy Locke, ed. Jeffrey C. Stewart, *Race Contacts and Inter-Racial Relations: Lectures on the Theory and Practice of Race* (1916; Washington, DC: Howard University Press, 1992). Harrison often wondered whether indolence was one of Professor Locke's gifts, but after several visits decided it wasn't. Alain LeRoy Locke (1885–1954) was a philosopher, educator, and critic who graduated magna cum laude from Harvard College and then attended Oxford's Hertford College as a Rhodes Scholar. Beginning in 1912 he taught at Howard University (except for 1925 through 1928), until his retirement in 1953. See Michael R. Winston, "Alain Leroy Locke," *DANB*, 398–404; and Jeffrey C. Stewart, *The New Negro: The Life of Alain Locke* (New York: Oxford University Press, 2018).

96. [HH,] "In the Melting Pot," *New Negro*, September 1919, 14.

97. [HH,] "The World This Month," *New Negro*, September 1919, 2, 3, 11, quotations at 2. See, for example, Ratzel, *History of Mankind*; and Augustin Hacquard, *Monographie de Tombouctou* (Paris, 1900). Pocahontas (born "Matoaka," c. 1595–1617) was an Indian princess and favored daughter of the Powhatan chief. She reportedly saved John Smith's life in 1608 and married John Rolfe in 1614. See *WNBD*, 806.

98. [HH,] "America's Backward Race," *New Negro*, September 1919, 5–6, quotation at 5.

99. [HH,] "America's Backward Race," 5–6. In his copy of Stoddard, *The Rising Tide of Color*, 120, Harrison notes that in "Chicago and the Southern Anglo-Saxon states" the "murder *rate* is 22 times higher than that of France & England."

100. [HH,] "America's Backward Race," 5–6.

101. "The Taster" (pseudonym for HH), "In the Melting Pot," *New Negro*, September 1919, 14–15, esp. 14.

102. "The Taster" [HH], "In the Melting Pot"; "Our Negro Settlements," *New York Sun*, January [or June] 15, 1911. See also "Mobs with Pistols and Ropes Rush Asbury Park Jail," *New York World*, November 15, 1910, HP-Sc 28; and *HHVHR*, 150, 451–52n24.

103. "The Taster" [HH], "In the Melting Pot," *New Negro*, October 1919, 14. See also "Enemies of Democracy," *New York Times*, June 30, 1919, 10.

104. "The Taster" [HH], "In the Melting Pot," *New Negro*, October 1919, 14–15.

105. "The Taster" [HH], "In the Melting Pot." In a separate article, [HH,] "That Dear Mr. Wilson," *New Negro*, October 1919, 15, Harrison again quoted the president: "We will fight for the things we have held nearest our hearts—for democracy—for the right of those who submit to authority to have a voice in their own government."

106. [HH,] "Poems for the People," *New Negro*, September 1919, 12–13, includes Andrea Razafkeriefo, "The Village Lynch-Smith (with Apologies to Longfellow)," 12; James Russell Lowell, "Sixty Years After," 12; and Adolph Wolff, "To a Negro Belle," 13. The September 1919 issue on 13 includes four additional poems by Razafkeriefo— "'Democracy,'" "God's Own," "Anima Anceps," and "Household Hints." The August 1919 issue includes poems on 17 by Tom Harris, "The Down Trodden Race"; and Ernest Sylvester, "Forward." James Russell Lowell (1819–1891) was an American poet, essayist, and diplomat whose bitter satires on Southern slaveholders include the *Biglow Papers* (named after Hosea Biglow, a pseudonym of Lowell; collected 1848, second series 1867). See *WNBD*, 623–24; and *WNUD*, 146. On Adolf Wolff (1883–1944), see Francis N.

Naumann and Paul Avrich, "Adolph Wolff: "Poet, Sculptor, and Revolutionist, but Mostly Revolutionist," *Art Bulletin* 67, no. 3 (September 1985): 486–500.

107. HH, "Sonnet to a Sick Friend" (poem), *New Negro*, September 1919, 13.

108. "Poems for the People" includes [HH,] "The Black Man's Burden (a Reply to Rudyard Kipling)"; and Andrea Razafkeriefo, "Prayer of the Lowly"; both in *New Negro*, October 1919, 13. The poem, originally written by Harrison under the pseudonym Gunga Din, in the *Colored American Review* 1, no. 1 (December 1915): 3 (later rpt. in *WAA*, 145–46; and in *HR*, 389–91), is discussed in *HHVHR*, 261–62, 484–85n98. See also Rudyard Kipling, "The White Man's Burden: The United States and the Philippine Islands," *New York Sun*, February 5, 1899; and *McClure's Magazine* (February 1899); Jay G. Robinson to the Editor, "The Black Man's Burden," *New York Times*, September 20, 1925, BR26, HP-Scr Mainly About Me: Radical and Racial Phase, FB740; and Louella D. Everett to the Editor, "The Black Man's Burden," *New York Times*, September 20, 1925, BR 26, HP, MAM2, FB740.

109. [HH,] "Our Little Library," *New Negro* 4, no. 1 (September 1919): 16.

110. [HH,] "Our Little Library," 16.

111. [HH,] "Books of the Month," *New Negro* 4, no. 1 (September 1919): 15–16.

112. [HH,] "Books of the Month," 16. Lala Lapjat Rai (1865–1928) was a prolific writer and forceful opponent of British rule in India who founded the Hindu reformist movement Arya Samaj, which spearheaded the Punjab's nationalist awakening. Rai was the first important leader of the Indian freedom movement to develop ties with African Americans. In 1917 Rai founded the Indian Home Rule League of America and the journal *Young India*. See Lala Lapjat Rai, *Young India: An Interpretation and a History of the Nationalist Movement from Within* (New York: B. W. Huebsch, 1916); Sudarshan Kapur, *Raising Up a Prophet: The African-American Encounter with Gandhi* (Boston: Beacon, 1992), 14–15; and Stanley A. Wolpert, *A New History of India* (New York: Oxford University Press, 1982), 277.

113. Ignacio Sanchez [HH], "Our Book Review ('The Negro in History and Civilization' a Review of J. A. Rogers *From Superman to Man*)," *New Negro*, October 1919, 15–16; rpt. as HH, "Our Book Review by Hubert Harrison: The Negro in History and Civilization: *From Superman to Man* by J. A. Rogers," *Negro World* 8 (July 31, 1920): 8; copy in "Writings" of HH scrapbook, HP, B13, F7. In the copy in his scrapbook, next to the byline Harrison writes, "Pseudonym of H.H.H." See also HH, "The Negro in History and Civilization (*From Superman to Man*, by J. A. Rogers)," in *WAA*, 135–36; J. A. Rogers to HH, undated letter included in Rogers's letter of November 26, 1927, HP-Co; and J. A. Rogers, *From Superman to Man* (Chicago; J. A. Rogers, 1917; New York: Helga M. Rogers, 1971, 1986; Middletown, CT: Wesleyan University Press, 2014). Ignacio Sanchez was probably derived from Ignatius Sancho (1729–1780), a formerly enslaved African who became an outstanding composer, musician, artist, playwright, and pamphleteer in England. According to Richard B. Moore, *The Letters of Ignatius Sancho* was sold in George Young's "Book Exchange" at 135 W. 135th Street. Richard B. Moore, "Africa Conscious Harlem," *Freedomways*, Summer 1963, 315–34, esp. 315–16; *Kaiser Index*, 4:261; Ignatius Sancho, *The Life of Ignatius Sancho, an African* (London, 1784); Arthur A. Schomburg, "West Indian Composers and Musicians," *Opportunity* 4, no. 47 (November 1926): 353; and Monroe Work, *Bibliography of the Negro in Africa and America* (1928; New York: Octagon, 1965), 475.

114. J. A. Rogers to HH, n.d. [1921], HP-Misc; Rogers, *From "Superman" to Man*, dust jacket; Tony Martin, *Literary Garveyism: Garvey, Black Arts, and the Harlem*

Renaissance (Dover, MA: Majority, 1983), 100; and *HR*, 447n12. Joel Augustus Rogers (1880–1966) was born in Negril, Jamaica. After coming to the United States he worked as a Pullman porter while pursuing a career as a journalist and historian of Black history, biography, and "race relations." His first book, *From Superman to Man* (1917), attacked white supremacist assumptions of Black inferiority, and it, like his *As Nature Leads: An Informal Discussion of the Reasons Why Negro and Caucasian Are Mixing in Spite of Opposition* (1919, J. A. Rogers; Baltimore, MD: Black Classic, 1987), was self-published. In the 1920s Rogers wrote a weekly column for the *Pittsburgh Courier*, served as contributing editor to the *Chicago Enterprise*, and was subeditor of Garvey's short-lived *Daily Negro Times* (1922). He also wrote occasional pieces for the *Negro World*. In 1924 he started a series of biographical sketches on Black historical figures, which he completed in 1947 as the two-volume *World's Great Men of Color*. That two-volume work includes an extremely laudatory and insightful portrait of Harrison (2:611–19). In 1925 he went to Europe as a correspondent, writing on life in Europe and the rise of fascism, and in 1926 he interviewed Garvey in prison for the *Amsterdam News*. He covered Italy's 1935–1936 invasion of Ethiopia and his interview with Emperor Haile Selassie, the symbol of resistance to Italian fascism, drew much attention. According to Robert A. Hill, "Rogers was critical of Garvey's leadership, and in 1922 he attended at least one meeting of the anti-Garvey group, the Friends of Negro Freedom," and in 1947 he labeled the Garvey movement "racial fascism" and compared Garvey to Mussolini and Hitler. See *GP*, 5:5–6n2; W. Burghardt Turner, "Joel Augustus Rogers: An Afro-American Historian," *Negro History Bulletin* 35, no. 2 (February 1972): 34–38; W. Burghardt Turner, "Joel Augustus Rogers: Portrait of an Afro-American Historian," *Black Scholar* 6, no. 5 (January–February 1975): 32–39; Rayford W. Logan, "J[oel] A[ugustus] Rogers," *DANB*, 531–32; *KI* 4:244–45; *HR*, 309–10; *WGMC* 2:432–42; Thabiti Asukile, "The Harlem Friendship of Joel Augustus Rogers (1880–1966) and Hubert Henry Harrison (1883–1927)," *African Americans in New York Life and History* 34, no. 2 (2010): 54–75; Thabiti Asukile, "Joel A. Rogers' Race Vindication: A Chicago Pullman Porter & the Making of From "Superman" to Man (1917)," *Western Journal of Black Studies* 35, no. 4 (2011): 281–93; Augustus Low and Virgil Clift, *Encyclopedia of Black America*; *Negro World*, May 7, 1921, January 7 and June 17, 1922, August 22 and December 12, 1925, November 3, 1928, June 16, 1932; *Pittsburgh Courier*, April 9, 1966; *Amsterdam News*, April 2, 1966; *New York Times*, April 27, 1966; and *HR*, 299, 447n10.

115. Sanchez [HH], "Our Book Review," *New Negro*, October 1919, 15.

116. Sanchez [HH], "Our Book Review," 16.

117. J. A. Rogers, "A Few Words of Praise," *New Negro*, October 1919, 12.

118. "Worth While Publications," *Crusader* 2, no. 3 (November 1919): 11.

119. See *GP*, 1:286n1, 2:19n2; and Murray, *Red Scare*, 251.

120. HD, September 30, 1919.

121. HD, October 1, 1919.

122. John C. Hawkins to Sup't of Buildings, Board of Education, New York City, October 1, 1919, HP-Co.

123. [HH,] "Introduction" [to a book], November 1, 1919, handwritten 1–3, 5, 6, quotation at 1; followed by [HH,] "The Attitude of the American Press Toward the American Negro," November 1, 1919, handwritten, 6, 7, 12, 17, 18, quotation at 1, HP, B5, F55, HPDLC.

124. [HH,] "Introduction," November 1, 1919, 2.

125. [HH,] "Introduction," 2–3. William Mitford (1744–1827) wrote a *History of Greece* (1784–1810), which was long popular until replaced by George Grote's (1794–1871) *History of Greece*, 10 vols. (1846–1856; 1888). See *WNBD*, 427, 693.

126. [HH,] "Introduction," 3, 5, 6.

127. [HH,] "Introduction," 5, 6.

128. [HH,] "The Attitude of the American Press," 6, 7, 12.

4. Reshaping the *Negro World* and Comments on Garvey
(December 1919–May 1920)

1. HD, March 17, 1920; [HH,] [Notes on Marcus Garvey], n.d., HD; *GP*, 1:559, 6:262n1; Robert A. Hill, ed., and Barbara Bair, associate ed., *Marcus Garvey: Life & Lessons; A Centennial Companion to the Marcus Garvey and Universal Negro Improvement Papers* (Berkeley: University of California Press, 1987), 371, 424; Stationery of Pioneer Development Corporation, c. 1919, in HP, B5, F52. Joyce Moore Turner, "Richard B. Moore and His Works," in *Richard B. Moore, Caribbean Militant in Harlem, Collected Writings 1920–1972*, ed. W. Burghardt Turner and Joyce Moore Turner (Bloomington: Indiana University Press, 1988), 25, 29, indicates that Moore was involved with a Pioneer Co-Operative Society, which conducted a grocery and delicatessen on the Rochdale Co-Operative Plan and used southern and West Indian products. On Conway's friendship with HH, see HD, March 1 and November 23, 1908.

2. "Sacrifice and Success the Theme at Liberty Hall" [Report of UNIA Meeting February 29, 1920]," *Negro World*, March 6, 1920, *GP*, 2:230–37, quotation at 236.

3. *RF*, 91, 92, 98.

4. "Sacrifice and Success the Theme at Liberty Hall," *Negro World*, March 6, 1920, *GP*, 2:236.

5. HH, "Two Negro Radicalisms," *New Negro* 4, no. 2 (October 1919): 4–5; William H. Ferris, "Garvey and the Black Star Line," *Favorite Magazine*, July 1920, *GP*, 2:471–73, esp. 472. See Monroe N. Work, *Negro Year Book: An Annual Encyclopedia of the Negro, 1921–22* (Tuskegee, AL: Tuskegee Institute, 1922), 53–63 (on racial consciousness), 73–83 (on race riots). On "capitalist imperialism" and "the dogma of the color line" see HH, "'Democracy' in America," *Negro World*, October 8, 1921, 3, *HR*, 283. See also Cyril Briggs, "Our Approach to the Garveyites," *Harlem Liberator*, September 23, 1933, *GP*, 7:561–62, 561; and see *GP*, 2:98n4.

6. *GP*, 1:cxiv, lix–lxii; "Hodge Kirnon Analyzes the Garvey Movement," *Negro World*, January 28, 1922, 7; "A Word Regarding Titles," *Negro World*, April 30, 1921. See also *RF*, 6, on Garvey's founding of the Universal Negro Improvement and Conservation Association and African Communities (Imperial) League. For "The General Objects" of the organization, including "civilizing the backward tribes of Africa," see *Philosophy and Opinions of Marcus Garvey*, 2 vols., ed. Amy Jacques-Garvey, intro. Hollis R. Lynch (1925; New York: Atheneum, 1971), 2:38; and *GP*, 1:lix. In 1925 Garvey stated: "It is because we have studied history that we of the Universal Negro Improvement Association have started toward empire." See *GP*, 1:lii, which cites "Building Empires," *Negro World*, October 3, 1925, 1.

7. James, *HATB*, 129; and HH, "Africa at the Peace Table, *Voice*, December 26, 1918, rpt. as "Africa and the Peace," *WAA*, 33–35, esp. 34; and as "Africa at the Peace Table," *HR*, 210–12, esp. 212.

8. HH, "'Democracy' in America," *Negro World*, October 8, 1921, 3, *HR*, 283.

9. HH, "Wanted—A Colored International," *Negro World*, May 28, 1921, *HR*, 226.

10. *GP*, 1:xxxvii–xxxviii, lxv, 2:72–78, esp. 73; and *Black Man: A Monthly Magazine of Negro Thought and Opinion* 1 (August–September 1935), 14.

11. *HHVHR*, 30–34, 414–18; *HR*, 317. Neville A. T. Hall, *Slave Society in the Danish West Indies: St. Thomas, St. John, and St. Croix*, ed. B. W. Higman (Baltimore, MD: Johns Hopkins University Press, 1992), 160, describes the "incipient class formation" through systematic promotion of "coloreds" into intermediate positions.

12. *HHVHR*, 63–64; and HH, "A Negro on Lynching," *New York Times*, June 28, 1903. See also Claude McKay, "A Negro Poet and His Poems," *Pearson's Magazine*, September 1918, 275, cited in *HR*, 32. Consistent with Harrison's use of the word "shock," Theodore W. Allen, *The Invention of the White Race*, 2 vols.; vol. 1: *Racial Oppression and Social Control*; vol. 2: *The Origin of Racial Oppression in Anglo-America* (New York: Verso, 1994, 1997), 1:113, writes that early twentieth-century Caribbean immigrants to the United States "experienced the 'cultural shock' of the transition from the class-based 'tri-partite social order' with its African-Caribbean 'colored' intermediate stratum, to the white-supremacist social order in the United States." Harrison and McKay, like many other Caribbean immigrants coming from the "tri-partite social order" at home, would lead quite active and radical lives after encountering the virulent white supremacy in the United States. The historian Winston James emphasizes "the prominence and often pre-eminence of Caribbean immigrants" in American radicalism. See *HR*, 51, 427n84; and James, *HATB*, 1.

13. *GP*, 1:lxvi, lxvii; *RF*, 7.

14. *GP*, 1:lxvi–lxviii; *Black Man: A Monthly Magazine of Negro Thought and Opinion*, December 1933, 5–6.

15. *HHVHR*, 332–39, esp. 337–38.

16. *RF*, 13. The June 23, 1919, BSL Certificate of Incorporation was signed by Garvey, Edgar M. Grey, Richard E. Warner, George W. Tobias, and Janie Jenkins. See *GP*, 1:441–44.

17. "Bureau of Investigation Report," c. October 14, 1919, *GP*, 2:72–79; and see Judith Stein, *The World of Marcus Garvey: Race and Class in Modern Society* (Baton Rouge: Louisiana State University Press, 1986), 36.

18. Edward O'Toole (of the *New York World*) Memorandum to [Isaac D. White, head of the *World's* Bureau of Accuracy and Fair Play], June 30, 1919, *WC*, in *GP*, 1:451–2; *GP*, 2:411n120.

19. *GP*, 1:431n2; *Negro World*, June 19, 1920.

20. "District Attorney Sinks 'The Black Star Line,'" *New York World*, June 19, 1919, *GP*, 1:431.

21. "Bureau of Investigation Report," c. October 14, 1919, *GP*, 2:72–79, esp. 76–77. See also *GP*, 1:411n1.

22. *GP*, 1:211–12n3, 444n2, 462–63, 2:xxxi, 147n1; and "Marcus Garvey Defies His Enemies," *Negro World*, August 2, 1919, *GP*, 1:471–72; and see *GP*, 7:980.

23. *GP*, 1:211–12n3, 444n2, 462–63, 2:xxxi, 147n1. Richard E. Warner, statement, to Thomas Mahoney, July 18, 1919, DNA, RG 165, File 10218-373/4, *GP*, 1:463–65. See also *GP*, 1:444n2, 1:471–72.

24. See *The Messenger*, September 2, 1919, 3; and *GP*, 7:979. In 1925 Domingo wrote: "I edited the paper [*Negro World*] for about eleven months. During that time Mr. Garvey became dissatisfied because I did not boost his ideas, so he used the front page of

814 | 4. Reshaping the *Negro World*

the paper for a signed article setting forth his personal propaganda. So much at variance were our views on the character of his propaganda that he had me 'tried' before the executive committee of the UNIA, for writing editorials not in keeping with the programme he had outlined. I convinced the nine persons who composed the committee that I had not violated the terms of my engagement and they gave me a sustaining verdict. This happened a little after Mr. Garvey had launched his idea of the Black Star Line [June 23, 1919]. Prior to this he had asked me to write editorials and speak on the street corners in support of the project, and I refused because I believed the undertaking unsound economically. A few weeks after my 'trial,' I sent him my resignation." W. A. Domingo to editor, "Mr. W. A. Domingo's Connection with the UNIA," *Gleaner*, June 15, 1925, *GP*, 2:40n1.

25. *RF*, 58–59, citing "The Policy of the *Messenger* on West Indians and American Negroes—W. A. Domingo vs. Chandler Owen," *Messenger*, March 1923, 639. In August 1920 a few hundred Garveyites attacked a big-tent meeting on 138th Street led by the Reverend Adam Clayton Powell Sr., at which Reverend Charles S. Morris, of Norfolk, Virginia, presented a sermon that rejected Garvey's African program. *RF*, 59. Phineas Taylor Barnum (1810–1891) was a showman known for promoting his hoaxes.

26. "Two Negro Crooks Use Office of Deputy District Attorney Kilroe to Save Themselves from Jail," *Negro World*, August 2, 1919, *GP*, 1:474–75.

27. *GP*, 1:31–32, 474–76, esp. 476nn1–2; 2:xlix, 5–7; People v. Garvey, no. 126535, Ct. Spec. Sessions, N.Y. County Ct., August 9, 1920; "Negro Editor Arrested," *New York World*, August 6, 1919; "Negro Editor Is Arraigned in Criminal Libel Case," *New York World*, August 29, 1919.

28. *GP*, 2:32n4, 52n7, 60n1; People of the State of Illinois v. Marcus Garvey, no. 258703, in DNA, RG 65, 198940-106.

29. Jas. O. Peyronnina, "Bureau of Investigation Report" [from Chicago], October 5 and October 6, 1919, *GP*, 2:56–58, 58–60. See also "District Attorney Swan Now Handling Garvey Case," *Chicago Defender*, September 6, 1919; "Attorney Bares N.Y. Editor's Plot," *Chicago Defender*, September 20, 1919; "Law Is Still on Mark Garvey's Trail," *Chicago Defender*, September 27, 1919; "Brundage 'Sinks' Black Star Line," *Chicago Defender*, October 4, 1919; *GP*, 2:31–32, 62n1, 349–71.

30. *GP*, 2:xlix, 239–41.

31. Robert A. Hill, "'The Foremost Radical Among His Race': Marcus Garvey and the Black Scare, 1918–1921," *Prologue: The Journal of the National Archives* 16, no. 1 (Winter 1984): 214–31, quotation at 221; and Theodore Kornweibel Jr., *"Seeing Red": Federal Campaigns Against Black Militancy, 1919–1925* (Bloomington: Indiana University Press, 1998), 5, 15; and Lanier Winslow, Department of State, Washington, to Frank Burke, Esquire, BI, DOJ, August 15, 1919.

32. L. Lamar Winslow, Department of State, to Frank Burke, BI, August 13, 1919, OG 258421, DNA, Reel 11, *FSAA*; Robert Stewart, Assistant Attorney General, to William Bauchop Wilson, Secretary of Labor, August 15, 1919, and the accompanying anonymous letter dated August 11, 1919, *GP*, 1:482–85.

33. See M. J. Davis, "Bureau of Investigation Report," August 22, 1919, *GP*, 1:494–96.

34. J. E[dgar] Hoover, DOJ, BI, Memorandum for Mr. Ridgely, October 11, 1919, *GP*, 2:72.

35. "Bureau of Investigation Report," c. October 14, 1919.

36. "Race First!" editorial, *Negro World*, July 26, 1919, *GP*, 1:468–69. The editorial was reprinted in *Negro World*, April 10, 1920, with this explanation: "This week we are

reproducing an editorial written on July 26th last year by Mr. W. A. Domingo, at present editor of *The Emancipator*, under the caption, 'Race First!' It makes quite interesting reading. Comment of our own is unnecessary. Each reader may furnish his own. H.[ubert] H.[arrison]." Interestingly, Tony Martin quotes from the July 26, 1919, editorial, attributes it (incorrectly) to Marcus Garvey, and names his book on Garvey *Race First*. See *RF*, 22, 37n1, 317, where he describes Harrison as a believer in "Race First." This and the earlier quotation from Domingo are the key references in the book to this phrase, yet he attributes it to Garvey and uses it as the title of his book.

37. HH, "Patronize Your Own," *Negro World*, May 1, 1920; rpt. in *WAA*, 87–89, quotation at 87; and *HR*, 111–12. See also [HH,] "What It Stands For," rpt. in *The Voice*, September 19, 1917, rpt. from "Declaration of Principles of the Liberty League of Negro Americans," *Clarion*, September 1, 1917, 1–2. *The Clarion*, another publication by Liberty League members, whose platform was that of the Liberty League, in its issue of September 1, 1917, 8, listed August A. Bernier as "Proprietor" and Lovett Fort Whiteman as "Collaborator." Harrison's "Introductory," *WAA*, 8, explains, "the AFRICA of the title is to be taken in its racial rather than its geographical sense." See also HH, "The New Policies for the New Negro," *The Voice*, September 4, 1917; rpt. as HH, "The New Politics for the New Negro," in *WAA*, 39–40, 165; and see *HHVHR*, 249–50.

38. See HH, "The New Politics for the New Negro," 40. The Harrison-influenced *Clarion* of August 15, 1917, also ran the article "Negroes First, Last and Always." In *GP*, 1:470n1, Robert A. Hill comments, "Harrison would make use of the slogan ['Race First!'] in *When Africa Awakes*" to support his criticisms of the Socialists. Hill also mentions Wilson's "America First" speech as well as Sinn Fein.

39. See *WGMC* (1947 ed.) 2:615; and *GP*, 1:470n1.

40. The *Yarmouth* was never completely paid for, and after several disastrous voyages it was later sold (as partial payment in a settlement) at public auction in December 1921 for $1,625. *GP*, 2:xxxi.

41. MG, Editorial Letter, rpt. from Garvey v. United States, no. 8317, Ct App., 2d Cir., February 2, 1925, government exhibit no. 25, in *GP*, 2:26–27.

42. [HH,] "Two Negro Radicalisms," *New Negro*, October 1919, 4–5, HP, B13, F1–2; rpt. with revisions and without the second- and third-last paragraphs as HH, "The Negro's Own Radicalism," in *WAA*, 76–79. See *WAA*, 180. For Harrison's mention, several months later, of Owen, Randolph, Domingo, and Briggs as the Socialists' "chief militant representatives among us," see HH, "An Open Letter to the Socialist Party of New York City," *Negro World*, May 8, 1920, 2. The mention of these four by name was omitted in August 1920 when Harrison reprinted this article in *WAA*, 184.

43. HH, "Two Negro Radicalisms," 5. For the quoted passage, See also *WAA*, 181.

44. "Negro Agitation," October 20, 1919, DNA, RG 65, file OG 3057, Roll 304 6. See also *GP*, 2:83–85, esp. 84, 167n4, 329n10, 330n12, and 5:58–114.

45. One George Tyler (1880?–1919) was arrested and while in police custody and returning to his third-floor cell reportedly "abruptly turned, leaped over the railing, and fractured his skull, an injury that proved fatal." See *GP*, 2:79n5; *Philadelphia Tribune*, October 18, 1919; *New York Times*, October 17, 1919.

46. *GP*, 2:xxxi–xxxii. "Garvey Shot in Row Over Money," *Chicago Defender*, October 18, 1919, LSAG, File 32-74; "Negro Agitation," November 7, 1919, MID 10218-261-50; "Report of UNIA Meeting" [from *Negro World*, October 25, 1919], *GP*, 2:xxxi–xxxii, 100–5, esp. 100; HH, "Marcus Garvey at the Bar of U.S. Justice," Associated Negro Press, c. July 1923—3 pages of a Harrison manuscript on this article are in HP, B5,

F16; and this article also appeared as HHar (Special Correspondent Associated Negro Press, New York, NY), "New York Writer Analyzes Garvey Case: Compares Provisional President with O'NEILL's 'Emperor Jones,' Made Famous by Charles Gilpin," *Kansas City Call*, July 5, 1923, copy provided to JBP by Robert A. Hill; and "Negro Agitation," October 20, 1919, OG 3057, Roll 304 6. BSL records indicate 11,182 shares were sold in October 1919, compared to 5,530 in September. See Stein, *The World of Marcus Garvey*, 80, citing "Monthly Summary of Shares of Stock Issued . . ." Garvey v. USA, 2648.

47. See "Negro Agitation," section on "Hubert Harrison and the 'New Negro,'" October 20, 1919, enclosure included in Major H. A. Strauss, US War Department, MI, to Director of MI (Attention Lieut. Colonel Wrisley Brown), "Report on Negro Subversion," October 31, 1919, MID 10218-364-10, which also appears as the "Negro Agitation" section in "Hubert Harrison and the 'New Negro,'" October 20, 1919, MID 10218-364-12, rpt. in part in *GP*, 2:83–85, esp. 85. See also George F. Lamb, Division Superintendent, DOJ, BI, New York City, to Frank Burke, Assistant Director and Chief, BI, DOJ, Washington, DC, "Attention Mr. Hoover: In Re: Radical Negro Activities," October 31, 1919, BF, OG 359413, RG 65, DNA, Reel 11, *FSAA*; and Colonel Thwaites of British MI, "Report on Negro Agitation," enclosure to a letter from George F. Lamb to Frank Burke, October 31, 1919, DNA, RG 65, OG 3057. Hill (*GP*, 2:85) lists the speaker as "Robert [*Hubert*] Har[r]ison" (while a difficult-to-read copy of the original document appears to read "Hubert Harrison"). There is no indication that Hubert Harrison had an agreement with Marcus Garvey to speak on behalf of the "Black Star Line" or "Back to Africa Movement" at that time. *GP*, 2:85n2. The report "also quoted a lengthy section from a Harrison article in the October issue [of the *New Negro*], 'Two Negro Radicalisms.'" Two important paragraphs that were only available in part in the MID report and that Hill does not reprint at all were the following:

> This Race Consciousness takes many forms, some negative, others positive. On the one hand we balk at Jim Crow, object to educational starvation, refuse to accept goodwill for good deeds, and scornfully reject our conservative leaders. On the other hand, we are seeking racial independence in business and reaching out into new fields of endeavor. One of the most taking enterprises at present is the Black Star Line, a steamship enterprise being floated by Mr. Marcus Garvey of New York. Garvey's project (whatever may be its ultimate fate) has attracted tens of thousands of Negroes. Where Negro "radicals" of the type known to white radicals can scarce get a handful of people, Garvey fills the largest halls and the Negro people rain money on him. This is not to be explained by the argument of "superior brains," for this man's education and intelligence are markedly inferior to those of the brilliant "radicals" whose "internationalism" is drawn from other than racial sources. But this man holds up to the Negro masses those things which bloom in their hearts—racialism, race-consciousness, racial solidarity—*things taught first in 1917 by THE VOICE and The Liberty League. That is the secret of his success so far.*

> All over this land and in the West Indies Negroes are responding to the call of the battle against the white man's Color Line. *And, so long as this remains, the international dogma of the white race, so long will the new Negro war against it. This is the very Ethiopianism which England has been combatting from Cairo to the Cape.*

The words in italics in these two paragraphs were in Harrison's original October 1919 *New Negro* article but were replaced by ellipses and interestingly did not appear in the Military Intelligence Report. See *WAA*, 180–81. The first of these two paragraphs will also be discussed in chapter 5 of this volume.

48. "Negro Agitation," October 20, 1919, MID 10218-364-12, in RG 165; "Report of UNIA Meeting" (from *Negro World*, October 25, 1919), *GP*, 2:100–5, esp. 100, quotation at 103. HH, "Marcus Garvey at the Bar of U.S. Justice"; HH, "New York Writer Analyzes Garvey Case"; "Negro Agitation," November 7, 1919, MID 10218-261-50; "Ten Thousand Negroes Try to Get Into Liberty Hall [October 19]," *Negro World*, October 25, 1919, *GP*, 2:100–4.

49. "Stirring Speech Delivered by Hon. Marcus Garvey in the South [Report of UNIA Meeting, Newport News, October 25, 1919]," *Negro World*, November 1, 1919, *GP*, 2:112–20.

50. MG, [editorial letter from Newport News, October 29, 1919,] *Negro World*, November 1, 1919, *GP*, 2:121–22, quotation at 121. Anselmo Jackson indicates that beginning in 1916, "the followers of Harrison responding to his demand that a New Negro Manhood Movement among Negroes be organized formed the Liberty League . . . prior to Garvey." See *HR*, 338.

51. *GP*, 2:127; Doris Henry, Intelligence Report of Meeting at Madison Square Garden, October 30, 1919, N, LC, part 1, B4, investigative file 1, in *GP*, 2:133–34. On Harrison's Liberty League's tricolor flag, see *HHVHR*, 292–93, 461n33, 489n30.

52. *GP*, 2:98n4; Derek H. Aldcroft, *From Versailles to Wall Street: 1919–1929*, 2nd ed. (Berkeley: University of California Press, 1977), 55–77; and Stein, *The World of Marcus Garvey*, 72.

53. *GP*, 2:xxxii–xxxiii.

54. Stein, *The World of Marcus Garvey*, 69.

55. Stein, *The World of Marcus Garvey*, 69–70, citing, among other sources, *New York Age*, January 10, 1920, and May 28, 1921.

56. The *Messenger* had urged Blacks to buy five-dollar Liberty bonds to support the magazine, while supporters of the imprisoned Black IWW leader Ben Fletcher sold Liberty bonds to help free him. Stein, *The World of Marcus Garvey*, 71.

57. [WAR Department Office of MI], to Director of MI, Subject: Negro Subversion, November 19, 1919, MID 10218-261-51, has enclosed a flyer: "Join the Universal Negro Improvement Association and African Community League Read Our 7 Points"; and HH, "Our Civic Corner," *New York News*, September 2, 1915, HP, B5, F4. On Harrison's use of the passage from the Banks poem "What I Live For," see *HHVHR*, 256, 480–81n45, 492n47.

58. HD, March 17, 1920; [HH,] [Notes on Marcus Garvey], n.d., HD. See also "Connections with the Garvey Movement, March 17 and 8, 1920," *HR*, 182–88.

59. HD, March 17, 1920; [HH,] [Notes on MG], n.d., HD. Garvey eventually did start a short-lived Booker T. Washington University at 3–13 West 136th Street in 1922 and then in September 1926 acquired the Smallwood Corey Institute in Claremont, Virginia, which contained sixty-six acres and several buildings and was renamed Liberty University. See *Negro World*, September 2, 1922; *GP*, 4:939–40, 942n1, 6:xli; and Hill and Bair, eds., *Marcus Garvey: Life & Lessons*, xlvii. In 1922 the UNIA *Constitution and Book of Laws* called for a "University of the UNIA" (General Laws, art. 31, sec. 2). See *GP*, 4:916n1.

60. HD, March 17, 1920; [HH,] [Notes on MG], n.d., HD. Amy Ashwood Garvey (1897–1969) married Marcus Garvey on Christmas Day 1919, but the marriage was soon

in difficulty. On March 6, 1920, Marcus separated from Amy and sought an annulment. On June 10 Amy claimed Marcus abandoned her, and on July 15 Marcus claimed that he left her and sued for an annulment. Because of adverse reactions to publicity from her disclosures, he withdrew his suit. Marcus obtained a divorce on July 5, 1922, in Missouri, and later that month married his secretary, Amy Jacques. See *GP*, 1:74n2, 2:xlix, 79n5, 79–80, 103–4, 408–9n2, 7:738n1, 904n1; Amy Ashwood Garvey, "Portrait of a Liberator," [New York, n. d.], AAG; Tony Martin, "Amy Ashwood Garvey," *BWA*, 1:481–82; Marcus Garvey v. Amy Ashwood Garvey, no. 24028, NYHR, July 15, 1920; Gerald Fraser, "Widow of Marcus Garvey, 'Black Moses,' Revisits Harlem," *New York Times*, August 17, 1968, 29; and Stein, *The World of Marcus Garvey*, 26n6, 32n19.

61. HD, March 17, 1920; [HH,] [Notes on Marcus Garvey], n.d., HD.

62. HD, March 17, 1920; [HH,] [Notes on Marcus Garvey], n.d., HD. On Edward David Smith-Green (1888–1969), see *GP*, 1:227n4, 2:407n1, 5:717n1, 9:356n3; Hill and Bair, eds., *Marcus Garvey: Life & Lessons*, 427; "Sec. Black Star Line Is Shot," *Gleaner*, December 13, 1919, in *GP*, 2:167–68.

63. HH, "At the Back of the Black Man's Mind," n.d. [November 1922?], HP, B4, F12, *HR*, 277–82.

64. HH, "Plans for a Negro College," January, February 1920, HD; and see HP, B5, F52.

65. HD, January 26, 1920. Included in Harrison's diary were articles entitled "Joe Rinn Seeks Go with Oliver Lodge," unidentified newspaper, January 27, 1920; "Raises Bid for Spirit Proofs," *New York Evening Post*, January 28, 1920; and "Defies Lodge to Produce a Spirit," *New York World*, January 28, 1920. On Harrison and Rinn, see also *HHVHR*, 116–17, 441–2n6, 442n7. See also "Offers $5,000 Gift for a Real Spirit," *New York Times*, January 28, 1920, 4.

66. HH, "Lincoln and Liberty: Fact Versus Fiction, A Lecture delivered at Liberty Hall Before the UNIA Feb 10, 1920," Lecture Notes, HP, B5, F12, HPDLC. Unfortunately, missing from HH, ScrWrNW, HP, B13, F7, were *Negro World* articles from February 7, 14, 21, and 28, 1920. When he spoke on conditions in Liberia, Harrison reportedly said "it is up to our people of this and other countries of color to help these people adjust to their conditions." See Report of Special Agent "WW" [William A. Bailey], February 26, "In Re: Negro Radical Activities," February 17, 1920, *GP*, 2:217–18, quotation at 218. "WW" was the code name of William A. Bailey, a Black special employee of the BI who reported on the Garvey movement and on the ABB. See *GP*, 2:170n1; J. M. Fowler to Frank Burke, February 20, 1920, DNA, RG 65, file OG 267600.

67. HH, "Lincoln and Liberty: Fact Versus Fiction," lecture notes, c. February 10, 1920. See Dinitia Smith and Nicholas Wade, "DNA Test Finds Evidence of Jefferson Child by Slave," *New York Times*, November 1, 1998; "Monticello's Other Children," *New York Times*, November 8, 1998; and Nicholas Wade, "Descendants of Slave's Son Contend That His Father Was George Washington," *New York Times*, July 7, 1999.

68. HH, "Lincoln and Liberty: Fact Versus Fiction," lecture notes, c. February 10, 1920. During the Civil War "Negro" soldiers were to fight for ten dollars per month and have three dollars deducted for clothing allowance; "white" soldiers got extra money for clothing. The "Negro" soldiers refused pay until they received an equal amount. When the Massachusetts legislature offered to pay the money owed the "Negro" soldiers of Massachusetts's 54th and 55th Regiments, they refused, insisting that they wanted equality of treatment. A ruling by the U.S. attorney general in 1864 finally opened the way to equal pay. See John Davis, ed., *The American Negro Reference Book* (1966;

Englewood Cliffs: Prentice-Hall, 1986), 608. On Crittenden, see *WAA*, 169–71; and chapter 6, note 68, in this volume.

69. HH, "Lincoln and Liberty: Fact Versus Fiction," lecture notes, c. February 10, 1920. On Abraham Lincoln's quotes, see Mary Maclean, ed., *Letters and Addresses of Abraham Lincoln* (New York: Trow, 1903; New York: A. Wessels Co., 1907), HP, Bo; also available at https://catalog.hathitrust.org/Record/000567921. Harrison obtained his copy of this book in 1908, marked it up considerably, and kept it for the remainder of his life. See, for example, 116–120, quotation at 119; 188–199, quotation at 197–98; 243–49, 363; 291–92; 303–5. On André Calliou, see *DANB*, 86–87.

70. HD, February 15, 1920.

71. HD, March 1, 1920.

72. HD, March 17, 1920; [HH,] [Notes on MG], n.d., HD. The interpolation in square brackets is Harrison's—here he used brackets instead of parentheses.

73. HD, March 17, 1920; [HH,] [Notes on MG], n.d., HD. In his scrapbook on *Negro World* writings Harrison listed the issues of the paper that were missing from his collection. They included those of January 17, 24, 31, February 7, 14, 21, 28, April 3, 10, 24, May 15, 29, June 19 July 31, August 21, 28, October 23, and November 20. See HP, ScrWrNW, B13, F7. In the 1920 Census enumerated on January 7, 1920, Harrison was listed as "Editor Negro World." See U.S. Department of Commerce, Bureau of the Census, "Fourteenth Census of the United States: 1920—Population," New York City, Enumeration District 972, Sheet 1, line 87.

74. See HD, March 17, 1920; [HH,] [Notes on MG], n.d., HD; "Statement of Hubert Harrison. In re: U.S. vs. Black Star Line, Inc. Post Office Building, New York, Jan. 16, 1922," 1. Stenographic minutes by M. J. Davis. Interview conducted by Mr. O. B. Williamson (Postal Inspector). Marcus Garvey: F.B.I. Investigation File, Microfilm rpt,. Scholarly Resources Inc., Wilmington, DE; in *GP*, 4:424–27. In this document Harrison indicated that he served as editor of the *Negro World* until November 1920, after which he became "Associate editor," "one of the contributing editors." Harrison also said "between January, 1920 and November, 1921 [1920?], when I gave up the editorship." Harrison's name appeared as "Associate Editor" of the *Negro World* on the masthead from c. March 6, 1920, to c. December 25, 1920. His name also appeared as "Contributing Editor" of the *Negro World* on the masthead from c. January 1, 1921, to c. September 9, 1922, and Robert A. Hill also lists Harrison as contributing editor from January 1, 1921, to c. September 9, 1922. See *GP*, 7:972–73.

75. [HH,] [Notes on Marcus Garvey], n.d., HD. A British MI report of February 10, 1920, *GP*, 2:205–210, quotation at 209, sent to the New York office of U.S. MI stated Harrison, who was the "former editor of the Clarion and New Negro (defunct) is now associate Editor of the Negro World." It also stated he was "in charge of the West India[n] News section of the paper."

76. Copies existing from that period: May 8; June 19 and 26; July 3, 17, and 31; and August 14 and 21. Almost two years later, in the *Negro World* of February 4, 1922, Harrison wrote that "In a recent confab with Mr. Marcus Garvey, the Managing Editor of the Negro World, it came out that the M[anaging]. E[ditor]. would like to see a resumption of that section of the N.W. which we created in 1920—the 'West Indian News Notes.' We have, therefore, promised him to start the news notes again soon. But, of course, it will not be possible to make them as elaborate as 1920—the difference in scope corresponding to the difference between Editor and Contributing Editor. But we will do the best we can under the circumstances, and trust that those who want to keep in touch

with the drift and current of events in that interesting corner of the world will enjoy our summaries and comments." See HH, "West Indian News Notes to Be Resumed," "With the Contributing Editor Column," *Negro World*, February 4, 1922, 6.

77. HD, March 17, 1920.

78. HD, March 17, 1920.

79. HD, March 17, 1920; William H. Ferris, *The African Abroad, or, His Evolution in Western Civilization, Tracing His Development Under Caucasian Milieu* (The Tuttle, Morehouse & Taylor Press, 1913; New Haven, 1968), https://catalog.hathitrust.org/Record/001131081.

80. HD, March 17, 1920.

81. HD, March 17, 1920. Around January 7, 1920, Professor Buck was secretary general of the UNIA. *GP*, 2:181. Garvey announced in the *Negro World* of March 13, 1920, that B. C. Buck and Fred D. Powell "are no longer involved with the above named corporation [the BSL]." See "Important Notice," *Negro World*, March 13, 1920, in *GP*, 2:261. H. M. Mickens was an AME minister from Waterbury, Connecticut, and secretary-general of the UNIA between B. C. Buck and J. D. Brooks. *GP*, 2:221n1. Gillard worked with one of the Baptist churches in New York City. See Report by Special Agent WW, February 17, 1920, *GP*, 2:217–18.

82. HD, March 17, 1920.

83. HD, March 17, 1920.

84. HD, March 17, 1920. For background on Capt. Joshua Cockburn (1877–1942), see *GP*, 1:515n3, 2:157–58, 161–62, 211n5; and Hill and Bair, eds., *Marcus Garvey: Life & Lessons*, 370.

85. HD, March 17, 1920.

86. Tony Martin, *Literary Garveyism: Garvey, Black Arts, and the Harlem Renaissance* (Dover, MA: Majority, 1983), 5, esp. "Poetry for the People," 43–90.

87. Martin, *Literary Garveyism*, 5, esp. "Poetry for the People," 43–90, 43.

88. Martin, *Literary Garveyism*, 5, esp. "Poetry for the People," 43–90, 11.

89. HH, "On a Certain Condescension in White Publishers" (Part I), *Negro World*, March 4, 1922, 7, HP, B13, F7; in *HR*, 293–95. See also Martin, *Literary Garveyism*, 93.

90. HH, "On a Certain Condescension in White Publishers" (Part II), *Negro World*, March 11, 1922; and Martin, *Literary Garveyism*, 91, 93, which points out that Mary White Ovington wrote a "Book Chat" column in the *Negro World* in 1921 and 1922.

91. HH, "On a Certain Condescension in White Publishers" (Part I), *HR*, 294.

92. Martin, *Literary Garveyism*, 27, writes: "Perhaps it might be an appreciation of René Maran's prize winning novel *Batouala*; or it might be an attack on the writings of T. S. Stribling, white author of the 1921 novel, *Birthright*, or a discussion of art and propaganda—such was the stuff that many a *Negro World* editorial was made of." Interestingly, each of the examples Martin used referred to subjects written about by Harrison.

93. HH, "Introductory," *WAA*, 8; HH, "Statement of Hubert Harrison: 'In re: U.S. vs. Black Star Line, Inc.,' Jan. 16, 1922," *GP*, 4:424; and Frederick G. Detweiler, *The Negro Press in the United States* (Chicago: University of Chicago Press, 1922), 1, 7. Robert A. Hill does not credit the editorship to Harrison but refers to it as "superbly" done. See *GP*, 1:242. Martin, *Race First*, 92, writes: "The most important of Garvey's papers and possibly his single greatest propaganda device was the *Negro World*." Lynward F. Coles, "To the Editor," August 6, 1920, *Crusader* 3, no. 2 (October 1920): 25–26, on 25, commented that the *Negro World* under the editorship of Harrison and Ferris was "very well

edited." He knew that Harrison was "a close student of political economy, psychology, and history" and felt that those who knew him were "not surprised at his complimentary editorials." He was, however, "surprised to know of his connection with the U.N.I.A. and A.C.L." Garvey explained, "from 1919–1920, the Organization [UNIA] flared forth in all its mighty ways." (MG), "The Next Move!" *The Blackman* 1, no. 6 (November 1934): 1. On the UNIA's "gigantic proportions," see HH, "An Open Letter to the Socialist Party of New York City," *Negro World*, May 8, 1920, 2. Herbert J. Seligmann, director of publicity for the NAACP and author of *The Negro Faces America*, considered the *Negro World* to be "the chiefest of all . . . Garvey's means for effecting his ends." Herbert J. Seligmann, "Negro Conquest," *World Magazine*, December 4, 1921, *GP*, 4:239–44, quotation at 241.

94. "WW" [Special Agent William A. Bailey], report, "In re: Negro Radical Activities," [April 3, 1920], *GP*, 2:280–83, quotation at 281.

95. Martin, *Literary Garveyism*, ix–xi, 115. Martin adds that "Harrison was a self taught man who was accepted as an equal in the community of scholars" and was, in a sense a "renaissance" person—one of "broad learning and culture for whom literature and the arts" were "as much a part of . . . everyday existence as were race uplift and politics"—he "attained to a level of artistic, scholarly and political interest which was quite remarkable."

96. Martin, *Literary Garveyism*, 25–26, adds that the paper's "emphasis was clearly on fostering a mass interest in literature and the arts."

97. Bruce only became a columnist for the *Negro World* in May 1920, after Harrison became principal editor. *GP*, 1:200n2. Bruce was listed as contributing editor of the *Negro World* on the masthead from c. January 1921 to August 9, 1924. See *GP*, 7:979.

98. See Claude McKay, *A Long Way from Home: An Autobiography*, intro. St. Clair Drake (1937; New York: Harcourt, Brace, & World, 1970), 41–42, 67; and Wayne F. Cooper, *Claude McKay: Rebel Sojourner in the Harlem Renaissance, a Biography* (Baton Rouge: Louisiana State University Press, 1987), 107–10. Tony Martin notes that at least several of McKay's early *Negro World* articles were "commissioned" by Harrison, "McKay's first friend among the Harlem intellectuals." To Martin, such examples demonstrated that "leading *Negro World* literary figures" like Harrison "were very much a part of the wider Harlem literary community." Martin, *Literary Garveyism*, 32, 101, 132.

99. *GP*, 2:xlix.

100. On February 29, 1920, at Liberty Hall, "Raz," "whose poems have recently been appearing in the columns of The Negro World," rendered two songs—"Garvey! Hats Off to Garvey!" and "U.N.I.A.," which "raised the roof." See "Sacrifice and Success the Theme at Liberty Hall," *Negro World*, March 6, 1920, *GP*, 2:230–37. On Watkins, see Lucian B. Watkins to HH, April 13, 1920, HP-Co.

101. HH, "Introductory," in *WAA*, 8; HH, "Statement of Hubert Harrison: 'In re: U.S. vs. Black Star Line, Inc.,'" June 16, 1922, *GP*, 4:424–27; and Detweiler, *Negro Press*, 1, 7. On *Negro World* circulation figures, see *GP*, 2:352; Ferris, "Garvey and the Black Star Line," *GP*, 2:472; HH, "Marcus Garvey at the Bar of United States Justice"; and Raymond Sheldon, assistant chief of staff for MI to director, MID, letter, January 21, 1921. On Harrison's radical influence, see Bruce to HH, January 12, 1921, re: Harrison's "An Economic Suggestion to the UNIA"; Draper interview with Domingo, January 18, 1958; "A Walking Encyclopedia," *Negro World*, September 4, 1920, HP, Sc, 33; HH to Lothrop Stoddard, August 21, 1920, HP, B2, F19, where Harrison explains that his function at the *Negro World* was "to give a little tone" in order "to balance Garvey's Megalomania." On the paper's expansion to ten pages, which occurred as the rival *Emancipator* ceased

publication, see *Negro World*, May 1, 1920. Around June 19, 1920, Garvey wrote that the "present circulation" of the *Negro World* is 50,000 copies (though at the time the libel was published [c. September 19–20, 1919], its circulation was about 10,000 or 15,000). Its big increase clearly came during the period of Harrison's managing editorship. See "Black Star Line Vindicated by White American Jury," *Negro World*, June 19, 1920, *GP*, 2:349–71, esp. 352, 357. In an August 18, 1920, interview Garvey also claimed that the *Negro World* circulation was 50,000. See Charles Mowbry White, Interview with MG, August 18, 1920, National Civic Federation Papers, New York Public Library, New York City, "The Negro," B152, in *GP*, 2:602–4.

102. Martin, *Literary Garveyism*, 156.

103. "Statement of Hubert Harrison 'In re: U.S. vs. Black Star Line, Inc.,'" January 16, 1922, 1, *GP*, 4:424. See also Work, *Negro Year Book, 1921–1922*, 53–63, 73–83; HH, "Marcus Garvey at the Bar of United States Justice"; *GP*, 1:xlviii–xlix; "Negro 'Napoleon' Counts on a Loyal Million to Aid Him," *New York World*, c. January 14, 1922. On money from the BSL being used to pay for space in the *Negro World*, see Garvey's response to Direct Examination in the Black Star Line vs. *Chicago Defender* in *Negro World*, June 19, 1920, *GP*, 2:351, 356, esp. 358.

104. Ferris, "Garvey and the Black Star Line," *GP*, 2:471–73, adds, in his early days in the United States, Garvey "did not create any stir until he set down his stakes in New York," where he "first . . . addressed the Liberty League, which was founded by Mr. Hubert H. Harrison, former editor of the 'Voice.'"

105. J. S. Patterson to the Editor, "Praises *Negro World*," *Negro World*, June 26, 1920, 2.

106. HD, March 17 and May 24, 1920; [HH], [Notes on Marcus Garvey], n.d., HD. The night after Garvey spoke to Harrison, BI Special Agent "WW" (William A. Bailey) heard Harrison speak on February 17 at a UNIA meeting in New York "on the conditions in Liberia." Harrison reportedly said "that it 'is up to our people of this and other countries of color to help these people to adjust to their conditions there.'" See "WW," report, "In re: Negro Radical Activities" (February 26, 1920), DNA, *GP*, 2:216–21, quotations at 217–18. See also MG, "Black Star Line and Universal Negro Improvement Association Planning to Repatriate to Liberia Between 500,000 and 1,000,000 Negroes in 1921," *Negro World*, January 1, 1921, *GP*, 3:114–15, quotation at 314; and see John E. Bruce's January 1918 comments on Garvey, where he concludes that unlike the "good military strategist," "wise statesman, and shrewd politicians" who "always conceal more than they reveal," "Garvey *tells all* and so we have his number." "You wont do Mr Garvey too *muchee talkee*," he adds. John E. Bruce, [Statement re Marcus Garvey], c. January 1918, John Edward Bruce Papers, SCRBC, *GP*, 1:235–36.

107. HD, March 17 and May 24, 1920; [HH,] [Notes on MG], HD.

108. HD, March 17 and 18 and May 24, 1920.

109. HD, March 17 and 18 and May 24, 1920.

110. HD, March 17 and 18 and May 24, 1920.

111. John E. Bruce to C. D. B. King, April 5, 1920, HP-Co, also in John Edward Bruce Papers, B2 Ms. 4. Charles Dunbar Burgess King (1877–1961) was born in Monrovia and became president in 1920. In August 1919 he visited the United States seeking a $5 million government loan to pay Liberian debts to European bankers. His visit ended in failure, and he was monitored by the BI. See *GP*, 2:4n1; "Unrest Among the Negroes," special report no. 10, October 7, 1919, 10, DNA, RG 59, file 882.51/1259; *New York Times*, September 5, 1961.

112. John E. Bruce to Judge J. J. Dossen, April 5, 1920, John E. Bruce Papers, Schomburg Center for Research in Black Culture, New York Public Library.

113. F. Wilcum Ellegor to My Dear Mr. Johnson re HH, April 15, 1920, HP-Co; and Wilcum Ellegor to Johnson [re HH], April 15, 1920 [n.b. second letter of this date.], HP, B1, F49. See also Hill and Bair, eds., *Marcus Garvey: Life & Lessons*, 382–83, 398–99. Gabriel M. Johnson (b. 1871), born into a politically powerful Americo-Liberian family, served as a UNIA potentate at the time of the August 1920 convention. Johnson opposed a loan from the U.S. government, preferring a private loan from the UNIA. The United States proposed and called for "Americans to be appointed as the 'native' commissioners in order to ensure reform in Liberia's 'native' policy." This provision challenged Johnson's influence in recruiting Liberian labor, and he lost his bid for reelection as mayor of Monrovia in December 1921. See *GP*, 2:430–31n2; DNA, RG 165, file 10218-364-167; and Hill and Bair, eds., *Marcus Garvey: Life & Lessons*, 398–99.

114. "Report of UNIA Meeting," *Negro World*, May 1, 1920, *GP*, 2:305–320. [HH,] "The Attitude of the American Press Toward the American Negro," November 1, 1919, 1–2, discusses the "dispersion."

115. "Report of UNIA Meeting," *Negro World*, May 1, 1920. The reference to going downtown possibly referred to the location of New York City's passport office, where both Harrison and J. W. H. Eason sought passports to go to Liberia for the UNIA in April and May 1920. The BI instructed the State Department's Passports Division to deny them passports on grounds of the radical nature of the plans. See DNA, RG 65, file OG 185161, May 7, 1920; and *GP*, 2:320n21.

116. "Report of UNIA Meeting," *Negro World*, May 1, 1920. See Gustave Spiller, ed., *Papers on Inter-racial Problems Communicated to the First Universal Races Congress Held at the University of London, July 26–29, 1911* (London, 1911), esp. 364; *GP*, 2:320n22; and WEBDB, *The Autobiography of W. E. B. Du Bois* (New York: International Publishers, 1968), 262–63.

117. HD, May 24, 1920. Harrison added in his diary comments on "Pin-headed preachers' gab-fest middle of May—No Passports Pryce's Remonstrance Garvey's Answer." [HH,] [Notes on MG], n.d., HD.

118. Frank Burke, assistant director and chief of the BI to Charles Brelsford Welsh, acting chief, Passport Division, Department of State, May 7, 1920, *GP*, 2:336. George F. Ruch (1898–1938) was a special agent of the BI (June 1918–July 1924) and then appointed assistant director (January 1925) when J. Edgar Hoover was appointed director. See *GP*, 2:22n3.

119. HD, May 24, 1920. See also *GP*, 1:224n1, 2:188.

120. HD, May 24, 1920. See *HHVHR*, 282–85, regarding the June 12 (not May 12) date.

121. HD, May 24, 1920. A remarkably similar appraisal, done three-and-one-half years later by the Rev. E. Ethelred Brown, said of Garvey: "In the first place he is bombastic, conceited and arrogant. These qualities are too painfully obvious to call for further comment. Secondly, he has no regard whatever for exactness of statement and cares nothing for the character and reputation of other men. He lives in an atmosphere of exaggerations and falsehoods. He tells you of 50000 delegates at a Convention attended by 200, and he makes it impossible by his exaggeration [for anyone] to know when his figures are true or near true or absolutely false. As to the reputation and character of men, almost every man who has left his association has been branded a thief and a liar and worse. He has prostituted the high uses of a newspaper to his own

unscrupulous ends. And he has not changed. . . . Thirdly, Marcus Garvey cannot work with men. He gets on splendidly with tools but any man who dares to be a man becomes his enemy and is forthwith dismissed from his presence. On two succeeding conventions he has brought about the dismissal of men whom he himself at the preceding convention presented for election as efficient loyal and honorable. They were too efficient too loyal too honorable to continue to be his tools, his phonograph—and they went. Fourthly—he is a mean shifter of responsibilities. He claims all the honor and disowns all the blame." See Rev. E. Ethelred Brown, "Garvey-istic Devotion," sermon, August 12, 1923, E. Ethelred Brown Papers, Schomburg Center for Research in Black Culture, New York Public Library, *GP*, 5:423–31, esp. 423–24, 429–30, quotation at 430.

122. Dowd, *The Negro Races: A Sociological Study*, 246–47, HP, B21.

123. HD, May 24, 1920. *Negro World*, July 31, 1920, 2, would mention that Smith-Green was no longer associated with BSL.

124. HD, May 24, 1920. In four issues of the *Cleveland Gazette* in October 1923, Hugh Mulzac explained "Why the Black Star Line Failed." First, "the management in the New York office was incompetent"; second, "the ships were worthless"; and third, "they were used mostly for propaganda." Regarding "the mystery ship," the "Phyllis Wheatley," he added: "There never was any ship by that name, nor was there any by the name of Frederick Douglass or Antonio Maceo. The hulks, Yarmouth, Kanawha, and Shadyside, were all the boats the Black Star Line Co. ever owned and it is almost a libel of the word 'boat' to call any one of them that." See Hugh Mulzac, "Why the Black Star Line Failed," *Cleveland Gazette*, October 6, 13, 20, 27, 1923, *GP*, 5:472–78.

5. Debate with *The Emancipator* (March–April 1920)

1. [HH], [Notes on Marcus Garvey], HD, B9, F3; *WAA*, 74–75, 179–80; "H.H." [HH], "'Just Suppose' a Riddle for 'Scientific Radical' Liars, with Apologies to C. OW.," *Negro World*, April 10, 1920, HP, B13, F7. See also *RF*, 317; and Theodore G. Vincent, *Black Power and the Garvey Movement* (Berkeley, CA: Ramparts, 1971), 7.

2. Owen apparently became so disillusioned with socialist radicalism that by 1923 he moved to Chicago, edited the *Chicago Bee*, and became involved with the Republican Party. See *GP*, 5:231n1; Theodore Kornweibel Jr., "Owen, Chandler (1889–1967)," in *DANB*, 476–77, esp. 476; and JBP, "Owen, Chandler," in *Encyclopedia of the Great Black Migration*, 3 vols., ed. Steven A. Reich (Westport, CT: Greenwood, 2006), 2:645–47. On the threats against Owen in which Garvey warned he "could not be responsible for anything that might happen," including "a hand off or a leg off or a broken head," see Special Employee Andrew M. Battle, Report, September 8, 1922, *GP*, 5:7–8. Theodore Kornweibel Jr., *No Crystal Stair: Black Life and the Messenger* (Westport, CT: Greenwood, 1975), 57, discusses Owen's brother Toussaint, a highly skilled tailor, and socialist-led garment unions.

3. *Emancipator*, April 3, 1920, 4; "Our Reason for Being," 4, *Emancipator*, March 13, 1920; *GP*, 2:40n2, xlix; DNA, RG 165, file 10218-264/7; and *WAA*, 182–83. Vincent, *Black Power and the Garvey Movement*, 74, claims that "Harrison and Briggs were friends for many years" and that they supported each other with the *Colored American Review* and the Liberty League. He cites interviews with Harry Haywood and Richard B. Moore on 278n68.

4. *GP*, 2:40, 284n1, 288n1; BSL v. New Negro Publishing Co., NYHR, case no. 8242, March 25, 1920.

5. HH, "Race First vs. Class First," *New Negro*, n.s., 4 (October 1919): 4–5, rpt. with supplemental notes in *WAA*, 79–82, 181–83; and H.H., "An Open Letter to the Socialist Party of New York City," originally published in *Negro World* 8 (May 8, 1920): 2; rpt. in *HR*, 113–16, esp. 115; rpt. with deletions and supplemental notes in *WAA*, 82–86, 183–85, esp. 184.

6. "Race First!" *Crusader* 2, no. 7 (March 1920): 8–9, quotation at 9. In June 1920, Briggs's ABB suggested "for the guidance of members and the race in general" that they "adopt the policy of race first" and "encourage the Universal Negro Improvement Association as the biggest thing so far effected in surface movements." "The African Blood Brotherhood," *Crusader* 2, no. 10 (June 1920): 22. The BI agent J. G. Tucker mentioned *The Crusader*'s "Race First" appeal in his report of March 13, and his report of June 19 referred to the June 1920 *Crusader*, which claimed that the ABB had over one thousand members, though, very significantly, Tucker thought the actual number was more like fifteen. See Special Report of J. G. Tucker, March 13 and June 19, 1920, RG 65, Reel 616, OG 208369.

7. HH, "An Open Letter to the Socialist Party of New York City," *Negro World* 8 (May 8, 1920): 2; rpt. with omissions in *WAA*, 82–86; and in *HR*, 113–16. See especially *HR*, 115; and the note in *WAA*, 184, which include the original sentence that mentions Briggs and was omitted in the August 1920 *WAA* reprinting. See Hill, "Introduction," in Hill, ed., *The Crusader*, 1:v–lxvii, esp. xxviii; "The African Blood Brotherhood," *Crusader* 2, no. 10 (June 1920): 22; "Negro First!" *Crusader* 2, no. 2 (October 1919): 9; "Race First," *Crusader* 2, no. 7, 8–9; and Andrea Razafkeriefo's critical "Race First," *Crusader* 6, no. 1 (whole no. 42): 26.

8. *GP*, 2:288–89n2.

9. "An Era of 'Wild-Cat' Business Promotions," *Emancipator*, March 13, 1920, 4. The first issue announced that beginning the following week it would publish "the complete" Department of Justice report "on radicalism among Negroes" and emphasized the report was "no easy task," since "crackers in government" were "not anxious to spread radicalism" that advertised the efforts of "Hubert Harrison, Marcus Garvey, Chandler Owen . . . [William] Colson . . . [W. A.] Domingo, [and A. Philip] Randolph." See "A Startling Disclosure Next Week," *Emancipator*, March 13, 1920, 4.

10. Incog, "The Potentate Flounders in the Deep of Diplomacy: Empire Building in Harlem," *Emancipator*, March 27, 1920, 4. On Chief Alfred Charles Sam, see *GP*, 1:485n3, 536–47.

11. "A Startling Disclosure Next Week," *Emancipator*, March 13, 1920, 4. See also from *Emancipator*, March 20, 1920: "Gov't Scores Negro Radicals: Suppressed Report Condemns Fearless, Negro Agitators," 1; Declare Yourself," 3; "Bubbles," 4; "The Weekly Message of the Satanic Majesty, Potentate," by "Mephistophense Potentate" (Mephistopheles is a demon in German folklore), 4; William Bridges, editor of *The Challenge*, to the editors (including Domingo), "An Appreciation," 4; and "Our News Policy," 3.

12. "The Potentate Flounders," 4.

13. Anselmo Jackson, "An Analysis of the Black Star Line," *Emancipator*, March 27, 1920, 2, *GP*, 2:271–72. The installments of April 3, 10, 17, and 24 by Jackson appear in *GP*, 2:272–79. See also "Account by W. A. Domingo of Marcus Garvey's St. Mark's Church Hall Lecture," New York, n.d., in *GP*, 1:190–92, esp. 191.

14. Jackson, "An Analysis of the Black Star Line," *GP*, 2:271–72.

15. HH, "Race First Versus Class First," *Negro World*, March 27, 1920; rpt. in *WAA*, 79–82, 181–83, quotations at 80; and *HR*, 107–9.

16. HH, "Race First Versus Class First," *Negro World*, March 27, 1920; *WAA*, 79–80.

17. HH, "Race First Versus Class First," *Negro World*, March 27, 1920; *WAA*, 80.

18. HH, "Race First Versus Class First," *Negro World*, March 27, 1920; *WAA*, 81–82.

19. HH, "Race First Versus Class First," *Negro World*, March 27, 1920; *WAA*, 81–82; and "Majority Report on Immigration," in SP, *National Convention of the Socialist Party Held at Indianapolis, IN, May 12 to 18, 1912*, 209–11. See also *HHVHR*, 186–89.

20. HH, "Race First Versus Class First," *WAA*, 81–82. Harrison's editorial appealed to the BSL agent G. S. Johnson, who, at a UNIA meeting on March 28, responded to *The Emancipator* attacks by saying the UNIA had "a man who knew every principle of Socialism in the person of Mr. Harris[on] of the *Negro World*." See Comments by G. S. Johnson in "Report by Special Agent WW," March 28, 1920, DNA, RG 65, file OG 258421.

21. See *Emancipator*, April 3, 1920, 1; and Anselmo Jackson, "Analysis of the Black Star Line," part 2, *Emancipator*, April 3, 1920; in *GP*, 2:272–74, quotations at 272–73.

22. *Emancipator*, April 3, 1920, 1, 2.

23. "Before and After," *Emancipator*, April 3, 1920, 3. See also HH, "The Negro's Own Radicalism," originally published as HH, "Two Negro Radicalisms," *New Negro*, n.s., 4 (October 1919): 4–5, rpt. with revisions and minus the second and third last paragraphs as "The Negro's Own Radicalism" in *WAA*, 76–79, 180–81, and also possibly rpt. with the missing paragraphs in *Negro World*, March 27, 1920.

24. "Opinion of Owen & Randolph Editors of the 'Messenger,'" *Emancipator*, April 3, 1920, 4; *GP*, 2:40, 284n1, 288n1; and BSL v. New Negro Publishing Co., NYHR, case no. 8242, March 25, 1920.

25. "Opinion of Owen & Randolph Editors of the 'Messenger,'" 4.

26. "Race First Versus Class First," *Emancipator*, April 3, 1920, 4.

27. "Race First Versus Class First."

28. "Race First Versus Class First."

29. "Race First Versus Class First."

30. HH, "Just Crabs," *Negro World*, April 3, 1920; rpt. in *WAA*, 73–74, 179–80; and in *HR*, 109–11. In 1923 Garvey wrote: "Having had the wrong education as a start in his racial career, the negro has become his own greatest enemy. Most of the trouble I have had in advancing the cause of the race has come from negroes. Booker Washington aptly described the race in one of his lectures by stating that we were like crabs in a barrel, that none would allow the other to climb over, but on any such attempt all would continue to pull back into the barrel the one crab that would make the effort to climb out." See Garvey, "The Negro's Greatest Enemy," *Current History* 18, no. 6 (September 1923): 951–57, in Marcus Garvey, *Philosophy and Opinions of Marcus Garvey*, 2 vols., ed. Amy Jacques-Garvey, intro. Hollis R. Lynch (1925; New York: Atheneum, 1971), 1:133; and in *GP*, 1:3–12. On February 18, 1995, at a Newark, New Jersey, conference on "Booker T. Washington and Modern Black Leadership Revisited" sponsored by the New Jersey Historical Commission, Professor Louis R. Harlan, a biographer of Booker T. Washington, informed JBP that he had heard that Washington told "crab stories" and that though he couldn't cite a specific instance at the time he thought they might be referred to in the published papers of Claude G. Bowers, who transcribed Washington speeches in his youth. Harrison thought this "Just Crabs" article was important in defending "the principles of the New Negro Manhood Movement." See *WAA*, 55, 179–82; *HR*, 109–11; and HH, "Connections with the Garvey Movement," HD, March 17 and

18, 1920. Another staple in the social philosophy of Booker T. Washington was that "no man can keep another man down in the ditch without staying down in the ditch with him." See Dr. G. Lake Imes, *The Philosophies of Booker T. Washington* (Tuskegee, AL: Tuskegee Institute, 1941), 10.

31. HH, "Just Crabs," in *WAA*, 73–74; "H.H." [HH], "'Just Suppose' a Riddle for 'Scientific Radical' Liars, with Apologies to C. OW.," *Negro World*, April 10, 1920.

32. HH, "Just Crabs," 73–74.

33. HH, "The Problems of Leadership," in *WAA*, 54–55; and HH, "A Tender Point," in *WAA*, 54–55, quotation at 55.

34. HH, "Just Crabs," in *WAA*, 75. Randolph and Owen referred to *The Messenger* as "the only journal of scientific radicalism in the world published by Negroes." See HH, "Scientific Radical Liars: What Randolph and Owen Know (?) About Anthropology and Sociology: "Prof Boas and Col. Snyder vs. the Editors of the Messenger; The Evidence in the Case," HH, (portion of an article), *Chicago Enterprise*, in *Negro World*, May 8, 1920, 10.

35. HH, "Just Crabs," in *WAA*, 75.

36. "H.H." [HH], "The Lion and the Lamb," *Negro World*, April 3, 1920, HP, B13, F7.

37. "H.H." [HH], "The Lion and the Lamb."

38. "H.H." [HH], "The Lion and the Lamb."

39. HH, "The Crab Barrel," *Negro World*, April 3, 1920, HP, B13, F7. (These verses began on April 3 and appeared on April 10 and 17 as continuations.)

40. HH, "The Crab Barrel."

41. HH, "The Crab Barrel." Agent P-138 in his report of September 7, 1920, DNA RG65, OG 329359, *GP*, 2:7, claimed Garvey considered Domingo "the most spiteful man he had ever met."

42. "'H.H.' Challenged," *Emancipator* 1, no. 5 (April 10, 1920): 2; and HD, March 17–18, 1920, and May 24, 1920 (on "Garvey's Character").

43. Cyril V. Briggs, "*Yarmouth* Granted Change of Registry Since Oct. 2, 1919," *Emancipator*, April 10, 1920; *GP*, 2:286–89. Hill says on 289n3 that "prostituted literati" alluded to Harrison.

44. "H.H." [HH], "'Just Suppose' a Riddle for 'Scientific Radical' Liars, with Apologies to C. OW.," *Negro World*, April 10, 1920, HP, B13, F7.

45. "H.H." [HH], "'Just Suppose' a Riddle for 'Scientific Radical' Liars."

46. "H.H." [HH], "'Just Suppose' a Riddle for 'Scientific Radical' Liars." Chandler Owen was enrolled in the Columbia University Law School in 1917, but he did not graduate. See *Columbia University Alumni Register, 1754–1931, Compiled by the Committee on General Catalogue* (New York: Columbia University Press, 1932), 663, https://babel.hathitrust.org/cgi/pt?id=ucl.b4525470;view=1up;seq=9.

47. HD, May 24, 1920. See *HHVHR*, 282–85, regarding the June 12 (not May 12) date.

48. "H.H." [HH], "'Just Suppose' a Riddle for 'Scientific Radical' Liars." Harrison's "Scientific Radical Liars: What Randolph and Owen Know (?) About Anthropology and Sociology; Prof Boas and Col. Snyder vs. the Editors of the Messenger; The Evidence in the Case," *Negro World*, May 8, 10, offered a portion of his article from the *Chicago Enterprise*. It presented quotations defending Moens from Colonel H. D. Snyder, the U.S. Army's Chief Medical Officer in Panama, and from Professor Franz Boas of Columbia University and compared these opinions "with the bumptious cocksureness of the two ignoramuses [Owen and Randolph] who have bluffed themselves (and others) into believing that they know something of 'sociology or economics, of biology or

anthropology.'" Harrison sarcastically concluded "most of us ordinary mortals feel it necessary to have facts to back up the opinions that we scatter broadcast, but 'scientific radicals' are able to dispense with them."

49. "H.H." [HH], "'Just Suppose' a Riddle for 'Scientific Radical' Liars." Virgin Islands–born Harold Eustace Simmlkjaer (c. 1890–1956) was active politically with the Independent Political Council of Harlem (Randolph's and Owen's organization) and with Ferdinand Q. Morton's UCD, wrote the pamphlet *The Scientific Side of the Negro Problem* in 1921, and had the lead role in the "Negro-cast" performance of O'Neill's *The Dreamy Kid* at the Provincetown Playhouse in New York on October 31, 1919. See "H. E. Simmelkjaer, 66, A Political Leader," *New York Times*, June 26, 1958, 28; and James Weldon Johnson, "From Black Manhattan," in *The Harlem Renaissance*, ed. Harold Bloom (Philadelphia: Chelsea House, 2004), 149–59, esp. 152.

50. "H.H." [HH], "'Just Suppose' a Riddle for 'Scientific Radical' Liars."

51. "H.H." [HH], "'Just Suppose' a Riddle for 'Scientific Radical' Liars."

52. "H.H." [HH], "'Just Suppose' a Riddle for 'Scientific Radical' Liars"; and William Harrison, "Research Notes on Life of Hubert Harrison," c. 1951, HP, B8, F12, esp. "Interview with Momma," February 10, 1951, re: "Sexless Twins." See also HH, [Notes re "The Red Record of Radicalism"], [c. 1927], HP, B6, F7, where Harrison referred to Owen and Randolph as "The Gold Dust Twins."

53. HH, "The Crab Barrel (part II)," April 10, 1920, HP, B13, F7.

54. [HH], "The Crab-Barrel Brigade," *Negro World*, April 17, 1920, HP, B13, F7 (a cut-off letter to the editor on the back of a "Press-Titution" article). Damon and Pythias in classical mythology were two young friends whose extreme loyalty was manifest by Damon's willingness to offer his life for a pledge that Pythias, who had incurred the wrath of Dionysius, would return to settle his affairs. When Pythias returns, Dionysius, because of their true love and friendship for each other, lets them both go free. Baron Richard von Krafft-Ebing (1840–1902) was a German physician, neurologist, and professor who studied sexual "pathology" and "deviance" and whose principal work was *Psychopathia Sexualis* (1886), a collection of case histories, many dealing with male homosexuality.

55. [HH], "The Crab-Barrel Brigade," *Negro World*, April 17, 1920.

56. Anselmo R. Jackson, "An Analysis of the Black Star Line" [part 4], *Emancipator*, April 17, 1920, 2; *GP*, 2:276–78. The April 17 issue also mentioned that Otto Huiswoud and Edgar M. Grey spoke at the People's Educational Forum.

57. "Discard Ambition and Ignorance," *Emancipator*, April 17, 1920, 3. The "Mr. Hyde" refers to a person with a dual character, as in Robert Louis Stevenson's *Strange Case of Dr. Jekyll and Mr. Hyde* (1886).

58. "Character Assassination Must Stop!" *Emancipator*, April 17, 1920, 4.

59. "Character Assassination Must Stop!"

60. (A. Philip Randolph and Chandler Owen,) "Opinion of Randolph & Owen Editors of the 'Messenger': Supposing—with Apologies to the Ha Ha Editor," *Emancipator*, April 17, 1920, 4.

61. "Opinion of Randolph & Owen," 4.

62. "Opinion of Randolph & Owen," 4. The *Yarmouth* and the *Shadyside* were the BSL's first and second ships.

63. "Opinion of Randolph & Owen," 4.

64. Cyril V. Briggs, "Now for the Dirty Work," *Emancipator*, April 24, 1920, 3.

65. Regarding the threat on Domingo, see the report of Agent P-138, September 4, 1920, DNA, RG 65, file OG 329359, *GP*, 2:6.

66. HH, "'Patronize Your Own,'" *Negro World*, May 1, 1920, 2; rpt. in *WAA*, 87–89; and in *HR*, 111–13.

67. HH, "'Patronize Your Own.'"

68. H.H. [HH], "An Open Letter to the Socialist Party of New York City," *Negro World*, 8 (May 8, 1920), 2; rpt. with deletions in *WAA*, 82–86, 183–85; and in *HR*, 113–16; H.H. [HH], "Is an Answer Impossible?" *Negro World*, May 8, 1920, 2; [HH,] "Scientific Radical Liars: What Randolph and Owen Know (?) About Anthropology and Sociology: Prof. Boas and Col. Snyder vs. the Editors of the Messenger," *Negro World*, May 8, 1920, 2; and "Hagar" (probably HH), to the editor, "Negroes Should Be Taught Pride of Race," *Negro World*, May 8, 1920, 3. "Aunt Hagar" and "Aunt Hagar's chillum" were slang in the African American community for African Americans. See Steven Watson, *The Harlem Renaissance: Hub of African-American Culture, 1920–1930* (New York: Pantheon, 1995), 47. *Hagar* (Boston: Houghton Mifflin, 1913) was also the title of a semiautobiographical feminist novel written by Mary Johnston.

69. H.H. [HH], "Is an Answer Impossible?" 2. The quoted passage was from HH, "Race First Versus Class First," *Negro World*, March 27, 1920; rpt. in *WAA*, 79–82, quotation at 81–82.

70. H.H., "Is an Answer Impossible?" 2. The original article was "Majority Report on Immigration," in Socialist Party, *National Convention of the Socialist Party Held at Indianapolis, IN, May 12 to 18, 1912*, 209–11.

71. H.H., "An Open Letter to the Socialist Party of New York City," 2; rpt. in *WAA*, 82–83; and in *HR*, 113–14. See also *HHVHR*, 345–48.

72. H.H., "An Open Letter to the Socialist Party of New York City," *WAA*, 84; *HR*, 114.

73. H.H., "An Open Letter to the Socialist Party of New York City," *WAA*, esp. 85, where the sentence is missing, and 184, where the missing sentence is discussed. See also *HR*, 115, where the missing sentence appears.

74. H.H., "An Open Letter to the Socialist Party of New York City," *HR*, 115; and HH, "Race First Versus Class First," *Negro World*, March 27, 1920; rpt. in *WAA*, 79–82, esp. 81–82, where the quotation appears; and HH, "Race First Versus Class First," *Negro World*, March 27, 1920; rpt. in *HR*, 107–9, esp. 109, where the quotation appears.

75. H.H., "An Open Letter to the Socialist Party of New York City," 2; *WAA*, 185–86; *HR*, 116.

76. H.H., "An Open Letter to the Socialist Party of New York City," 2; *WAA*, 186; *HR*, 116. See also James, *HATB*, 128.

6. Early *Negro World* Writings (January–July 1920)

1. HH, "The Problems of Leadership," in *WAA*, 54–55.

2. HH, "When the Blind Lead," *Negro World*, c. February 1920; rpt. in *WAA*, 70–73, quotation at 70; and in *HR*, 173–74; [WEBDB], "Leadership," *Crisis* 19, no. 4 (February 1920): 173; and [WEBDB], "Close Ranks," *Crisis* 16, no. 3 (July 1918): 111.

3. WEBDB, "Leadership," 173; and HH, "When the Blind Lead," *WAA*, quotation at 70–71.

4. See HH, "When the Blind Lead," 71–72, 178n; and *HHVHR*, 384–91. The criticism of Emmett Scott may refer to Du Bois's "Our Success and Failure," which charged that Scott was "concealing fatal knowledge" of white supremacist U.S. wartime policies. According to Du Bois's biographer David Levering Lewis, this attack led to a "furious controversy in the black press, with significant segments of the NAACP membership siding with Booker T. Washington's former secretary [Scott] against what was seen as the editor's [Du Bois's] pitiless, unfair reproach." See WEBDB, "Our Success and Our Failure," *Crisis* 18, no. 3 (July 1919): 127–30, quotation at 129; and in *Writings and Periodicals Edited by W. E. B. Du Bois: Selections from* The Crisis, ed. Herbert Aptheker, vol. 1: *1911–1925* (Millwood, NY: Kraus-Thomson Organization, 1982), 1:234–37, quotation at 236. See also *W. E. B. Du Bois*, 1:574. Scott had helped Du Bois apply for a captaincy in the MI Branch of the War Department after Du Bois wrote to him that "the subject of my lectures . . . [has been] first, that it is absolutely necessary for the emancipation and uplift of the colored races that Germany be thoroughly beaten in the present conflict." See WEBDB to Emmett Scott, April 24, 1918, DNA, File MID 10218-129, Reel 19, *FSAA*.

5. HH, "When the Blind Lead," in *WAA*, 72–73.

6. HH, "An Open Letter to the Young Men of My Race," *Negro World*, April 17, 1920; rpt. in *WAA*, 91–95; and in *HR*, 175–77; originally in *The Voice*, c. January 1919. See chapter 2 in this volume. Harrison's "Open Letter" caught the eye of BI agent J. G. Tucker, who, in his report of April 17, mentioned it and described Harrison as "a well-known Negro Radical" and "one of the associate editors" of the *Negro World*. The Department of Justice's Radical Division quoted from the letter and said it "would unquestionably tend to incite race hatred." See Tucker, Report, April 17, 1920; U.S. DOJ, Radical Division, Washington, DC, "Confidential Bulletin of Radical Activities," Week ending April 17, 1920, File 10110-1683, DNA, Reel 22, *FSAA*.

7. Granville H. Martin to Editor [HH] of *Negro World*, "The U.N.I.A. and Politics," May 9, 1920, in *Negro World*, June 5, 1920, HP, B13, F7; and "The Opposition to Booker T. Washington," *Literary Digest* 27, no. 7, whole no. 695 (August 15, 1903): 187.

8. HH, response to letter by Granville H. Martin, "The U.N.I.A. and Politics," *Negro World*, June 5, 1920, in HH, ScrWrNW, HP, B13, F7. Robert A. Hill writes that Garvey eschewed politics and had a "static view of political abstinence." See *GP*, 1:lix, lxvi.

9. HH, "The U.N.I.A. and Politics."

10. HH, "The U.N.I.A. and Politics." On the SP in the South, see *HHVHR*, 7, 144, 149. On May 22 Harrison offered a few remarks at Liberty Hall on "The New Negro and Politics." An undercover BI agent attended and reported that Harrison "spoke of the resolute determination of the New Negro to stick to his race, despite what was said to discourage him." Harrison reportedly "claimed that the Negro of today had complete faith in himself as a race and that the day of politicians hiding their true characters behind the photograph of Abraham Lincoln and deceiving the people, was a thing of the past." Agent P-135, Report of May 27, 1920, 1920, BF OG238421, RG 65, DNA, Reel 11, *FSAA*.

11. "H.H." [HH], "A Negro for President," *Negro World*, June 19, 1920, 2; rpt. in *WAA*, 44–46; and in *HR*, 147–49, quotation at 148. For publication information more accurate than the June 1920 publication date on *WAA*, 46, see *WAA*, 167. See MG, (editorial letter,) *Negro World*, June 21, 1919, in *GP*, 1:429–31, esp. 431n2; and see *Negro World*, June 19, 1920. George Edwin Taylor (1857–1925), a "Negro," had run for president in 1904 on the ticket of the National Negro Liberty Party. See Bruce L. Mouser, *For Labor, Race,*

and Liberty: George Edwin Taylor, His Historic Run for the White House, and the Making of Independent Black Politics (Madison: University of Wisconsin Press, 2012).

12. "H.H.," "A Negro for President," 2; *WAA*, 44–45; *HR*, 148. Interestingly, Harrison's friend J. A. Rogers would later write that as many as five presidents (Thomas Jefferson, Andrew Jackson, Abraham Lincoln, Warren G. Harding, and Calvin Coolidge) may have had "Negro blood." See J. A. Rogers, *The Five Negro Presidents: According to What White People Said They Were* (St. Petersburg, 1965).

13. "H.H.," "A Negro for President," 2; *WAA*, 45–46; *HR*, 149.

14. "H.H.," "A Negro for President," *WAA*, 46; *HR*, 149.

15. "H.H." [HH], "*The Crisis* Asleep," *Negro World*, June 19, 1920, 2; "English Rule in Africa," *Crisis* 20, no. 2 (June 1920): 96; and *GP*, 2:212n12.

16. "H.H.," "*The Crisis* Asleep," 2; and Michael L. Conniff, *Black Labor on a White Canal: Panama, 1904–1981* (Pittsburgh, PA: University of Pittsburgh Press, 1985), 31–36, 52–61.

17. [HH,] "Shillady Resigns," *Negro World*, June 19, 1920, 2, HP, B13, F7; rpt. in *WAA*, 60–61; and in *HR*, 177–78. There was no author named with the original article, which was written by HH and incorrectly identified in *WAA*, 61, as being published in July 1920. On John R. Shillady (1875–1943), see *GP*, 5:158–59n5, 442n5; Theodore Kornweibel Jr., *"Seeing Red": Federal Campaigns Against Black Militancy, 1919–1925* (Bloomington: Indiana University Press, 1998), 69; *Crisis* 15, no. 5 (March 1918): 219; *New York Times*, September 7, 1943; and John R. Shillady, "Resignation," *Crisis* 20, no. 2 (June 1920): 72.

18. [HH,] "Shillady Resigns," *WAA*, 60.

19. [HH,] "Shillady Resigns," *WAA*, 60–61.

20. "H.H." [HH], "The Crisis Asleep," 2; Claude McKay, *A Long Way from Home*, ed. Gene Andrew Jarrett (1937; New Brunswick, NJ: Rutgers University Press, 2007), 113–14. On Washington's involvement in Harrison's firing by the Post Office, see *HHVHR*, 132–34. Claude McKay (1889–1948) was a Jamaican-born poet and novelist sympathetic to the socialists and communists and who became a major literary figure in Harlem in the 1920s. See Wayne F. Cooper, *Claude McKay: Rebel Sojourner in the Harlem Renaissance, a Biography* (Baton Rouge: Louisiana State University Press, 1987); Wayne F. Cooper, *The Passion of Claude McKay* (New York: Schocken, 1973); *GP*, 2:21n2, 9:351n1; and *WNBD*, 636.

21. Elliott M. Rudwick, *W. E. B. Du Bois, Propagandist of the Negro Protest* (New York: Atheneum, 1969), 211–12; Peter M. Bergman, *The Chronological History of the Negro in America* (New York: Harper & Row, 1969), 399; William H. Ferris, response to Henry F. Downing, *Negro World*, June 19, 1920, 2. On the Spingarn Medal, see NAACP, "The Spingarn Medal," http://www.naacp.org/awards/spingarn-medal/.

22. Arthur Schomburg to "My Dear Mr. Harrison" and "H.H." [HH], to Arthur Schomburg, "The Spingarn Medal Again," *Negro World*, June 26, 1920, 2. For Ferris's comments on Schomburg's letter about Du Bois and the Spingarn Medal for 1919, see W. H. Ferris, letter, *Negro World*, July 3, 1920, 2. Imanuel Geiss, *The Pan-African Movement*, trans. Ann Keep (1968; London: Methuen, 1974), 176–98, discusses what is referred to as "The Pan-African Conference of 1900 and the first Pan-African Association." On 233, Geiss refers to the 1919 meeting as "The First Pan-African Congress."

23. HH, "The Problems of Leadership," 54. See also J. G. Tucker, Report, July 3, 1920, BF OG207369, RG 65, DNA, Reel 8 and Reel 10, *FSAA*, which says that the *Negro World*

"issue of the third instant" includes "'White Stool Pigeon Incites Chicago Race Riot' and 'Our White Friends' over the initials H. H. (HUBERT HARRISON)."

24. Grover Cleveland Redding (c. 1883–1921), also known as George Brown, Grover Redding, and George Reading, was born in Georgia and was a UNIA member in Chicago before helping organize the Star Order of Ethiopia and the Ethiopian Mission to Abyssinia. He reportedly told his followers he was an Abyssinian prince and direct descendant of King Menelik and the Queen of Sheba and was financially supported by the Abyssinian government to gather "Negroes" for transport to Abyssinia. Redding was denounced in the *Negro World* after his arrest in Chicago. See *Chicago Defender*, January 15, 1921; and *Negro World*, February 19, 1921.

25. "White Stool Pigeon Incites Chicago Race Riot: 'Dr. Jonas' Proves to Be British Government Spy, Working Hand in Hand with Our Own Authorities—White Government Agent Goes Scot Free—His Dupes Pay the Penalty," *Negro World*, July 3, 1920, 1 (dateline "Chicago, June 23"); *GP* 2:388–89nn1–2; U.S. DOJ, Radical Division, Washington, DC, "Strictly Confidential: General Intelligence Bulletin," no. 48, April 30, 1921, File OG 374217, DNA, Reel 12, *FSAA*; and "Murder Charges Filed Against Five Negroes," *El Paso Herald*, June 25, 1920, 12.

26. R. D. Jonas (b. c. 1868), also known as "Rev. R. D. Jones," "Elder R. D. Jones," and "Prophet Jonas," was born Rupert Deveraux Griffith in Tredegar, Wales. In 1917 he was employed by U.S. MI as an informer on "Negro subversion." In January 1919 he offered his services to the BI in New York to inform on Black radicals. The British employed him as an informer, and he covered Black radicals such as Randolph and Owen. British MI paid him, and U.S. MI shared the information. Jonas's frequent reports on Black radical organizations in this period were, according to the historian Hill, "the single most important source on the subject." In 1920, in Chicago, he was held as a material witness against Redding, whose claim to be heir to Ethiopian royalty he had supported. See "R. D. Jonas," *GP*, 1:337n1, 1:402–5, esp. 405n1, 531–32, which contains the Hill quotation on "Jonas' frequent reports" being "the single most important source" on "the most significant black radical organizations in America," and 2:389n2.

27. "White Stool Pigeon Incites Chicago Race Riot," *Negro World*, July 3, 1920, 1; *GP* 2:388–89nn1–2. A piece entitled "Editorial Notes," probably prepared by Harrison, included discussion of the Chicago incident, in which the man who burned the flag was a "white" policeman and the man shot defending the flag was Black, concluding: "White men cannot and must not be permitted to lead Negroes in a movement like ours." "Editorial Notes," *Negro World*, July 3, 1920, 2.

28. "White Stool Pigeon Incites Chicago Race Riot"; *GP* 2:388–89nn1–2.

29. HH, "Our White Friends," *Negro World*, July 3, 1920, 2; cited in Federal Bureau of Investigation, United States Department of Justice, Washington, DC, RG 65 208369, Reel 617; in *WAA*, 61–63, esp. 61–62; and in *HR*, 180–82.

30. HH, "Our White Friends," 2; *WAA*, 61–62. Some writings related to the "blinkers of Anglo Saxon Civilization" concept found in *WAA*, 62, include the following: (1) "As long as the Color Line exists . . . the cant of Democracy is intended as dust in the eyes of white voters. . . . It furnishes bait for the clever statesmen." HH, "Our Larger Duty," *New Negro*, August 1919, 5–6, quotation at 5; rpt. in *WAA*, 100–4, where the quotation on 101 puts the word "Democracy" in quotation marks; (2) "It is only the Blindspot in the eyes of America, and its historians, that can overlook and misread so clean and encouraging a chapter of human struggle and human uplift [as Black Reconstruction]." WEBDB, *Black Reconstruction in America: An Essay Toward a History of the Part Which*

Black Folk Played in the Attempt to Reconstruct Democracy in America, 1860–1880 (1935; New York: Atheneum, 1971), 577. (3) Theodore W. Allen: "All the while their white blindspot prevents them from seeing what we are talking about is . . . the 'white question,' the white question of questions—the *centrality* of the problem of white supremacy and the white-skin privilege which have historically frustrated the struggle for democracy, progress and socialism in the US." In J. H. Kagin (pseud. for Noel Ignatin [Ignatiev] and Ted [Theodore W.] Allen), "White Blindspot" (1967); and M. (reference to "Molly Pitcher," pseud. for TWA) to Dear J. H. (Kagin), "A Letter of Support," in J. H. Kagin, *White Blindspot* (Osawatomie Associates, 1967), rpt. along with Ted (Theodore W.) Allen, "Can White ~~Workers~~ Radicals Be Radicalized?" (c. 1968–1969), as Noel Ignatin (Ignatiev) and Ted (Theodore W.) Allen, *White Blindspot & Can White ~~Workers~~ Radicals Be Radicalized?* (Detroit: Radical Education Project; New York: NYC Revolutionary Youth Movement, 1969), 10. See JBP, "The Developing Conjuncture and Some Insights from Hubert Harrison and Theodore W. Allen on the Centrality of the Fight Against White Supremacy," *Cultural Logic*, July 2010 [2012]: 9n9, https://www.jef freybperry.net/attachments/Perry.pdf.

31. HH, "Our White Friends," 2; *WAA*, 62–63; and "Chicago Riot Result of a Radical Plot," *Boston Globe*, June 21, 1920.

32. HH, "Our White Friends," 2; *WAA*, 63.

33. "H.H." [HH], "A Tender Point," *Negro World*, July 3, 1920, 2; rpt. in *WAA*, 63–66, quotations at 63–64; and in *HR*, 178–80.

34. "H.H." [HH], "A Tender Point," *Negro World*, July 3, 1920, 2; *WAA*, 64.

35. "H.H." [HH], "A Tender Point," *Negro World*, July 3, 1920, 2; *WAA*, 64–65.

36. "H.H." [HH], "A Tender Point," *Negro World*, July 3, 1920, 2; *WAA*, 65–66.

37. "H.H." [HH], "A Tender Point," *Negro World*, July 3, 1920, 2; *WAA*, 66. Samuel Ringgold Ward (1817–1866?) was a leading abolitionist and worker on the Underground Railroad in the nineteenth century. See Louis Filler, "Samuel Ringgold Ward," *DANB*, 631–32.

38. HH, "When the Tail Wags the Dog," *Negro World*, c. July 1920, 2; rpt. in *WAA*, 46–48, quotations at 47 and notes 167–68; and in *HR*, 154–55.

39. HH, "When the Tail Wags the Dog," 2; *WAA*, 48. Roscoe Conkling Simmons was related to Booker T. Washington and prominently involved with Republican Party politics.

40. HH, "The Grand Old Party," *Negro World*, July 1920, which is dated and identified in *WAA*, 49–53, quotations at 49, 52; and in *HR*, 151–54.

41. *HR*, 129; *HHVHR*, 101–3, 269.

42. *GP*, 1:lix, lxvi, lxviii; *Gleaner*, September 23, 1915; and "Negroes Determined to Do for Themselves in Africa, What White People Have Done in Europe and Elsewhere," *Negro World*, October 22, 1921, 2.

43. HH, "The Grand Old Party," 49–50; *HR*, 152.

44. HH, "The Grand Old Party," 49.

45. HH, "The Grand Old Party," 50. See also *HR*, 129–36, 151; *HHVHR*, 101–3, 269; and *WAA*, 169–71; James G. Blaine, *Twenty Years of Congress: From Lincoln to Garfield, with a Review of the Events That Led to the Political Revolution of 1860*, 2 vols. (Norwich, CT: Henry Bill Pub Co., 1884–1886), 1:260–63, 282; and Martin Duberman, *Charles Francis Adams, 1807–1886* (Stanford, CA: Stanford University Press, 1960), esp. 227–28, 230, 238–39, and the chapter "The Secession Crisis and the Committee of Thirty-Three," 223–58. Regarding the Crittenden resolutions that the Joint Committee "had

taken over," see John J. Crittenden, "Joint Resolution Proposing Certain Amendments to the Constitution of the United States," Bills and Resolutions, Senate, 36th Congress, 2nd Sess., December 18, 1860; reproduced at Library of Congress, *American Memory, A Century of Lawmaking for a New Nation: U.S. Congressional Documents and Debates, 1774–1875,* http://avalon.law.yale.edu/19th_century/critten.asp. Regarding the Corwin Amendment, which passed both Houses of Congress, see Christopher A. Bryant, "Stopping Time: The Pro-Slavery and 'Irrevocable' Thirteenth Amendment" (2003), University of Cincinnati College of Law Scholarship, Faculty Articles and Other Publications, Paper 63, esp. 514–16, http://scholarship.law.uc.edu/fac_pubs/63. See Abraham Lincoln's First Inaugural Address, March 4, 1861, final version, 7, where he comments, regarding the proposed resolution, "I have no objection to its being made express, and irrevocable." Abraham Lincoln Papers at the Library of Congress, transcribed and annotated by the Lincoln Studies Center, Knox College, Galesburg, IL, http://memory.loc.gov/cgi-bin/query/r?ammem/mal:@field%28DOCID+@lit%28d077 3800%29%29.

46. HH, "The Grand Old Party," in *WAA*, 50–52.

47. HH, "The Grand Old Party," in *WAA*, 53. See also HH, "Lincoln and Liberty: Fact Versus Fiction," in 4 parts: *Negro World*, March 5, 1921, 8; March 12, 1921, 8; March 19, 1921, 7; and March 26, 1921, 7; HP B13, F7; rpt. in *HR*, 130–36.

48. [HH,] "Curbing the Gouging Landlords," *Negro World*, April 17, 1920, HP, B13, F7.

49. "H.H." [HH], "A 'Cheap' Administration," *Negro World*, May 29, 1920, HP, B13, F7.

50. "H.H." [HH], "A 'Cheap' Administration."

51. (Negro Postal Clerks) Thos. E. Ghoufison College Sta.; H. M. Cornelius, Sta. L.; Julius A. Thomas GPO; C. E. Cyril GPO (?) D. T. Treagle, Sta. L., to HH, c. June 1920, HP, B3, F2.

52. HH, "Lynching: Its Cause and Cure," *Negro World*, June 26, 1920, 2; rpt. in *WAA*, 22–24, quotations at 22–23. This is incorrectly listed in *WAA* as being published in July 1920. For the correct date, see J. G. Tucker, Report, June 26, 1920, BF OG 208369, RG 65, DNA, Reel 10, *FSAA*, which states: "New York radical Negro weekly, in its issue of June 26th, under the caption 'Lynching, Its Cause and Cure,' over the initials H.H." See also John R. Shillady, Secretary, to the Chairman and the Board of Directors (of the NAACP), "A Resignation," *Crisis* 20, no. 2 (June 1920): 72.

53. See "Duluth Lynchings Online Resource: Historical Documents Relating to the Tragic Events of June 15, 1920," Minnesota Historical Society, St. Paul, https://www .mnhs.org/duluthlynchings.

54. HH, "Lynching: Its Cause and Cure," 2; *WAA*, 23; "Three Indicted for Lynchings by Duluth Mob," 1; "Trio Indicted in Duluth as Negro Slayers," 1; "3 Are Indicted in Duluth Lynchings," 4; "Three More are Indicted in Duluth Lynchings," 6.

55. HH, "Lynching: Its Cause and Cure," 2; *WAA*, 23.

56. HH, "Lynching: Its Cause and Cure," 2; *WAA*, 23–24.

57. HH to Stoddard, June 24, 1920; HH, "The New International," *Negro World*, May 15, 1920, based on FBI Report of J. G. Tucker, May 15, 1920, RG 65 OG 208369, Reel 616, 22. An article entitled "A New International" from which the quotations are taken was rpt. in *WAA*, 111–13, quotations at 112–13. This same article was rpt. as "H.H." [HH], "A New International," *Negro World*, August 14, 1920, 2. This article was a partial basis for but should not be confused with Harrison's subsequent, very important article HH,

"Wanted—A Colored International," *Negro World*, May 28, 1921, HP, B13, F7. See U.S. DOJ, Radical Division, Washington, DC, "Weekly Bulletin," no. 17, week ending May 15, 1920, File OG 374217, DNA, Reel 12, *FSAA*; and J. G. Tucker, Report, May 20, 1920, BF OG207369, RG 65, DNA, Reel 8, also Reel 10, *FSAA*, both of which cite "THE NEW INTERNATIONAL," in the issue of May 15.

58. HH, "The New International," *Negro World*, May 15, 1920; rpt. in *WAA*, 112–13.

59. HH, "The New International." In his copy of Weale, *The Conflict of Colour*, Harrison writes that the secrets of supremacy "are found to be not *Race* but *Power*."

60. HH, "The New International," *WAA*, 112–13. Article 22 of the League of Nations covenant, which was signed as part of the Treaty of Versailles on May 7, 1919, established three classes of mandates. Class A mandates were provisionally recognized until able to survive on their own; class B mandates were directly administered by the mandatory power; and class C mandates were administered under laws of the mandatory country as territories. The League of Nations came into official existence on January 10, 1920. See *GP*, 1:289–90n12, 9:219n2.

61. See W. F. Elkins, "Suppression of the Negro World in the British West Indies," *Science & Society* 35, no. 3 (Fall 1971): 344–47. Harrison claimed to have been "credibly informed" that Sam Duncan had written "to the governors of the various British West Indian islands, resulting in the outlawing of the *Negro World* in those islands." See HD, May 24, 1920. See also *GP*, 2:xlix, li.

62. HH, "Bolshevism in Barbados," probably from *Negro World*, c. February 1920; rpt. in *WAA*, 110–11.

63. HH, "Help Wanted for Hayti," probably from *Negro World*, c. January 24, 1920; rpt. in *WAA*, 104–5, quotation at 104; and in *HR*, 234–36. The date of this article has been corrected from *HR* and *WAA*.

64. HH, "Help Wanted for Hayti," 104–5.

65. HH, "The Cracker in the Caribbean," probably from *Negro World*, c. 1920; rpt. in *WAA*, 105–8, quotations at 105–6; and in *HR*, 236–38. The U.S. Marines and Navy occupied Santo Domingo in 1916 and again in December 1920. After being severely criticized for occupying Santo Domingo, President Wilson agreed to withdraw U.S. forces. This was not done, however, until 1922, when a new, provisional government was established and election plans announced. See *GP*, 4:776n5. The United States occupied Haiti from 1915 to 1934. Great Britain, France, Belgium, and Italy demanded annexation and partition among themselves of Germany's former colonies in Africa. See *GP*, 1:361n2.

66. HH, "The Cracker in the Caribbean," *WAA*, 106. The activities of the Wilson administration in Haiti drew national attention after the Democratic vice presidential nominee, and former assistant secretary of the Navy, Franklin Delano Roosevelt, in a campaign statement declared: "You know I have had something to do with the running of a couple of little republics. The facts are that I wrote Haiti's Constitution myself, and, if I do say it, I think it is a pretty good Constitution." He was referring to the constitution written under the U.S. Navy occupation. In a campaign speech, the Republican presidential nominee, Warren G. Harding, spoke of the "rape of Haiti" and charged that "thousands of natives have been killed by American marines." This greatly fueled opposition to the occupation. See Hans Schmidt, *The United States Occupation of Haiti, 1915–1934* (New Brunswick, NJ: Rutgers University Press, 1971), 118.

67. HH, "The Cracker in the Caribbean," *WAA*, 106–7.

68. HH, "The Cracker in the Caribbean," 107.

69. HH, "The Cracker in the Caribbean," 107–8. Harrison wryly ended: "If we were now appealing directly to the white men of America we might dwell upon the moral aspects of the question. But we must leave that to others."

70. "L. F. Bowler" (possibly HH) to the editor of the *Evening Sun* (from *New York Evening Sun*, June 18, 1920), "Getting Excited and Nervous: Bulala-Gwai; Has Scientific Crime Brought Into Use Death Snuff of Africa?," rpt. in *Negro World*, July 3, 1920, 2. This article mentions the "When Africa Awakes" concept. A Michael Gold article in the *New York World* of August 23, 1920, discussed Garvey and the UNIA convention and quoted from the article ("Getting Excited and Nervous") about Bulala Gwai and "When Africa Awakes." Gold's article, entitled "When Africa Awakes" (the name of Harrison's just-completed book), talks of reading the editorial in the *Negro World* (Harrison was the principal editor) that "boasted of 'Bulala Gwai' a deadly natural poison used by the black medicine men in the jungle," which "can be and will be called in requisition when *Africa Awakes*, to drive the invaders from her soil." See also "The Purple-Robe Champion of 'Africa for the Africans,'" *Literary Digest*, September 4, 1920, 61. Harrison was always selling books, and according to his daughter Aida, one of the things she never fully understood was her father's selling of "Coofu" (special oils). The journalist Eric Walrond mentions how one could hear street vendors selling "Coofu medicine compounded from the best African herbs." See Richardson and Harrison, interview with JBP, August 4, 1983; Eric Walrond, "The Black City," *Messenger*, January 1924, in *Speech and Power: The African-American Essay and Its Cultural Content from Polemics to Pulpit*, 2 vols., ed. Gerald Early (Hopewell, NJ: Echo, 1992–1993), 1:51–54.

71. HH, "U-Need-a-Biscuit," *Negro World*, July 17, 1920, 2; rpt. as HH, "U-Need-a-Biscuit," in *WAA*, 98–100, quotations at 98–99; and in *HR*, 149–51. See also OG 208369, Reel 616. Starting in 1902, "Uneeda Biscuit" was a nationally advertised and sold soda cracker of the National Biscuit Company and its successors. David Stivers, Archivist, the Nabisco Company, Parsippany, New Jersey, telephone interview with JBP, January 9, 1995. J. G. Tucker, Report, July 17, 1920, BF OG207369, RG 65, DNA, Reel 10, *FSAA*, stated that in the *Negro World* "of the 17th instant," the editorial "U Needa Biscuit" appeared "over the initials H. H. (HUBERT HARRISON)."

72. HH, "U-Need-a-Biscuit," 2; *WAA*, 99–100.

73. HH, "U-Need-a-Biscuit," *WAA*, 100.

74. Leonard Brathwaithe to the editor, "A Word of Praise," *Negro World*, July 31, 1920, 2.

75. HH, "When Might Makes Right," probably from *Negro World*, c. 1920; in *WAA*, 108–10, quotations at 108–9; and in *HR*, 215–16.

76. HH, "When Might Makes Right," *WAA*, 109.

77. HH, "When Might Makes Right," *WAA*, 109–10.

78. HH, "Education and the Race," in *WAA*, 126–28, quotations at 126–27 (and reference to it as an editorial on 123); and in *HR*, 122–24.

79. HH, "Education and the Race," *WAA*, 127.

80. HH, "Education and the Race," *WAA*, 127–28. When Harrison died one of the books he still retained was Frederick Soddy, *Matter and Energy* (New York: Henry Holt, 1912). Frederick Soddy (1877–1956) was an English chemist who did research in radioactivity, investigated isotopes, and won the Nobel Prize for chemistry in 1921. See *WNBD*, 929.

81. HH, "Education and the Race," 128.

82. "Hagar" (possibly HH) to the editor, "Negroes Should Be Taught Pride of Race," April 17, 1920, *Negro World*, May 8, 1920, 3; rpt. in Tony Martin, comp. and ed., *African Fundamentalism: A Literary and Cultural Anthology of Garvey's Harlem Renaissance* (Dover, MA: Majority, 1991), 10. On Hagar, see Genesis 16:11–12; and Steven Watson, *The Harlem Renaissance: Hub of African-American Culture, 1920–1930* (New York: Pantheon, 1995), 47.

83. "Hagar" [possibly HH] to the editor, *Negro World*, May 8, 1920, 3; and "Editor's note" that follows.

84. "H.H." [HH], "The Racial Roots of Culture," *Negro World*, July 31, 1920, 2; rpt. in *WAA*, 129–31; and in *HR*, 120–22. "The Racial Roots of Culture" appeared in *New Negro* 4, no. 1 (September 1919): 4–5, as "Negro Culture and the Negro College," HP, B13, F1–2, but the article in the *Negro World* is slightly shortened. See also chapter 3 in this volume.

85. McKay, *A Long Way from Home*, 41–42. McKay fondly described Harrison as "very black," "compact of figure," with a "head [that] resembled an African replica of Socrates." He wrote that he knew "for a time" that Harrison was "the black hope of the Socialists" and that he "spoke precisely and clearly, with fine intelligence and masses of facts." On Mr. "Gray," see 35–37.

86. McKay, *A Long Way from Home*, 36, 38, 41–42, 67.

87. McKay, *A Long Way from Home*, 42, 67. Tony Martin describes at least several of McKay's early *Negro World* articles as "commissioned" by Harrison, whom he describes as "McKay's first friend among the Harlem intellectuals." To Martin, such examples demonstrated that "leading *Negro World* literary figures" like Harrison "were very much a part of the wider Harlem literary community." See Tony Martin, *Literary Garveyism: Garvey, Black Arts, and the Harlem Renaissance* (Dover, MA: Majority, 1983), 32, 132.

88. Claude McKay to Editor [MG], *Negro World* [given to HH], December 17, 1919, HP, B2, F66. In the *Negro World* of June 26, 1920, appeared a letter by "Africanus" (probably McKay) and two articles on Wales, probably also by McKay. See "Africanus" to the Editor, "White Women and Negroes in England," *Negro World*, June 26, 1920, 8; "Race-Rioting in Wales" and "White Women Sells Herself to Negro on Contract," *Negro World*, June 26, 1920, 10.

89. McKay to Editor, *Negro World*, December 17, 1919; McKay, *A Long Way from Home*, 67.

90. McKay to Editor, *Negro World*, December 17, 1919, closed: "Yours for an awakened Negro race."

91. HH to Mr. (Lucian B.) Watkins, January 2, 1920, HP, B2, F20, HPDLC; Lucian B. Watkins to HH, April 8, 1920; W. E. Reid to Lucian B. Watkins, September 11, 1919, and January 15, 1920, all in HP, B2, F20; George Hutchinson, *The Harlem Renaissance in Black and White* (Cambridge, MA: Harvard University Press, 1996), 514n55; and Martin, *Literary Garveyism*, 66. Lucian B. Watkins (1879–1921) was born in Chesterfield, Virginia, and died from his war wounds on February 1, 1921. His poetry is found in *Voices of Solitude* (1907); James Weldon Johnson, ed., *The Book of Negro American Poetry* (New York: Harcourt Brace and Co., 1922); and Robert Kerlin, *Negro Poets and Their Poems* (Washington, DC: Associated Publisher, Inc., 1923). See also Robert Kerlin, *The Voice of the Negro: 1919* (New York: E. P. Dutton, c. 1920), 183, 188.

92. HH to the Cornhill Company, April 9, 1920, HP, B2, F6, HPDLC.

93. HH to Lucian B. Watkins, April 9, 1920, B2, F20.

94. W. E. Reid to Lucian B. Watkins, April 9, 1920.

95. Lucian B. Watkins to HH, April 13, 1920, HP, B2, F20.

96. W. E. Reid, Cornhill Company, to HH, April 15, 1920, HP, B3, F18.

97. Walter Everette Hawkins, *Chords and Discords* (Boston, 1920). In his copy in HP, B22, Harrison wrote, "Return to AR [Andrea Razafkeriefko]." HH, "A Volume of Verse: *Chords and Discords* by Walter Everette Hawkins," *Negro World*, June 5, 1920, HP, B13, F7. "Parnassian" refers to poetry in general and more specifically to a nineteenth-century school of French poets characterized by belief in art for art's sake and emphasis on metrical form.

98. On February 29, 1920, at Liberty Hall "Raz," "whose poems have recently been appearing in the columns of The Negro World," rendered two songs, "Garvey! Hats Off to Garvey!" and "U.N.I.A.," which reportedly "raised the roof." The "words were skillfully put together and the music was inspiring." See "Sacrifice and Success the Theme at Liberty Hall (Report of UNIA Meeting February 29, 1920)," *Negro World*, March 6, 1920, *GP*, 2:230–37; and Martin, *Literary Garveyism*, 32, 132–33.

99. HH, "On a Certain Condescension in White Publishers" [Part I], *Negro World*, March 4, 1922, 7, HP, B13, F7; in *HR*, 293–95, quotations at 294; and in Martin, *African Fundamentalism*, 21–24.

100. HH, "On a Certain Condescension in White Publishers (Concluded)," *Negro World*, March 11, 1922, HP, B13, F7, in *HR*, 295–96, quotation at 296. Scott McLemee, "Harrison Redux: The Resurrection of a Pioneering Cultural Journalist," *Columbia Journalism Review*, May 6, 2009, https://archives.cjr.org/critical_eye/harrison_redux.php.

101. "H.H." [HH], "Press-Titution: By Upton Sinclair," *Negro World*, April 17, 1920, HP, B13, F7.

102. HH, "The Negro Year Book, 1918–1919: Edited by Monroe N. Work," *Negro World*, April 17, 1920, HP, B13, F7, *HR*, 322–23. Monroe Nathan Work (1866–1945) became head of the Tuskegee Institute's Division of Records and Research in 1908. See Monroe N. Work, comp., *A Bibliography of the Negro in Africa and America* (1928; New York: Argosy-Antiquarian Ltd., 1965); *Negro Year Book and Annual Encyclopedia of the Negro 1912* (Tuskegee Institute, Alabama: Monroe N. Work, 1913); Dorothy B. Porter, "Monroe Nathan Work," *DANB*, 667–68; *GP*, 2:509n5; and *Kaiser Index*, 5:396.

103. HH, "*Darkwater*," *Negro World*, April 17, 1920, HP, B13, F7; in *WAA*, 137–40, quotation at 137; and in *HR*, 319–22. See also WEBDB, *Darkwater: Voices from Within the Veil* (New York: Harcourt, Brace, and Co., 1920), https://www.gutenberg.org/files /15210/15210-h/15210-h.htm.

104. HH, "*Darkwater*," *WAA*, 137.

105. HH, "*Darkwater*," 137–38.

106. HH, "*Darkwater*," 138. Harrison avoided use of the word "gotten." See HH," "Gotten Is Rotten," *Negro World*, January 15, 1921, HP, B13, F7; and chapter 9, n2.

107. HH, "*Darkwater*," *WAA*, 138–39.

108. HH, "*Darkwater*," *WAA*, 139.

109. HH, "*Darkwater*," *WAA*, 139–40.

110. HH, "*Darkwater*," 140. Interestingly, Harrison's appraisal of Du Bois's strength in some ways anticipated comments by Arnold Rampersad, who wrote that Du Bois's "greatest gift was poetic in nature" and that "his scholarship, propaganda, and political activism drew their ultimate power from his essentially poetic vision of human experience and from his equally poetic reverence for the word." See *WAA*, 203–4; *HR*, 448n18; and Arnold Rampersad, *The Art and Imagination of W. E. B. Du Bois* (1976; New York: Schocken, 1990), ix.

111. [HH,] "Our Little Library," *Negro World*, July 3 and July 17, 1920, 2. This article was undoubtedly written by Harrison, cf. [HH,] "Our Little Library," *New Negro* 4, no. 1 (September 1919): 16. See also [HH,] "Our Little Library," *Negro World*, August 21, 1920, 8. In the August 28 *Negro World* Harrison wrote, "Answers to Questions Concerning Books" and explained that "many letters" had been received about the prices of the books and the places where they could be obtained," and he answered for each book. He added that "those who want good books on science, history, religion and literature at very low prices should write to the Rationalist Press Association of London, England, and ask for their list of six-penny reprints," and he added that the "three books in the Negro list that can be most easily obtained are Nos. 17, 20 and 25." "H.H." [HH], "Answers to Questions Concerning Books," *Negro World*, August 28, 1920, 9, HP, B13, F7.

112. [HH,] "*As Nature Leads* by J. A. Rogers," "Our Book Review," *Negro World*, July 3, 1920, 8; H.H. [HH], "The Negro in History and Civilization: (*From Superman to Man* by J. A. Rogers)," "Our Book Review by Hubert Harrison," *Negro World*, July 31, 1920, 8, in HH, ScrWrNW, HP, B13, F7. This article was published earlier as Ignacio Sanchez [HH], "Our Book Review ('The Negro in History and Civilization' a Review of J. A. Rogers' *From Superman to Man*)," *New Negro* 4, no. 2 (October 1919): 15–16; and subsequently in *WAA*, 135–36; in *HR*, 299–301; and in Martin, *African Fundamentalism*, 142–43. See also Rogers, *As Nature Leads*; Rogers, *From "Superman" to Man*; and this volume, chapter 3.

113. [HH,] "*As Nature Leads*," 8.

114. [HH,] "*As Nature Leads*," 8. Harrison strongly objected to racial-inferiority arguments, and in his copy of Dowd, *The Negro Races*, in response to Dowd's arguing that there are "peculiarities of his [the Negro's] psychology, and acquired characteristics" that are "obstacles to infusing European civilization into the Negro" and "the unfavorable way in which he responds to civilization is due to a cause that is organic or anatomical," Harrison wrote, "This southern crap may pass as science in N.C. But it won't pass with men who study races & race-theories. Cf Robertson's *The Evolution of States*, Finot's *Race Prejudice*, Taylor's *Origin of the Aryans*, Darwin's *Descent of Man*, and the *patriotic* sprees of English, American and other whites in war-time."

115. [HH,] "*In Spite of the Handicap* by James D. Corrothers, D.D.," "Our Book Review," *Negro World*, July 10, 1920, HP, B13, F7.

116. [HH,] "*In Spite of the Handicap*."

117. "H.H." [HH], "The Seamy Side of White Christian Civilization: As Seen by a White Medicine Man," *Negro World*, July 24, 1920, HP, B13, F7.

118. "H.H." [HH], "The Seamy Side of White Christian Civilization."

119. "H.H." [HH], "The Seamy Side of White Christian Civilization," quoting John Roach Straton, *The Menace of Immorality in Church and State: Messages of Wrath and Judgment* (New York: George H. Doran, 1920), 31–89, esp. 80–86, https://archive.org/details/menaceofimmora00stra. Here, too, Harrison speaks of the "blindness of the average white man in another precursor to the 'white blindspot'" concept. See also August Forel, *The Sexual Question: A Scientific, Psychological, Hygienic, and Sociological Study for the Cultured Classes* (London: Rebman Limited, 1908), https://en.wikisource.org/wiki/The_Sexual_Question.

120. "H.H.," "The Seamy Side of White Christian Civilization," quoting Straton, *Menace of Immorality*, 49.

121. "H.H." [HH], "The Seamy Side of White Christian Civilization," quoting Straton, *Menace of Immorality*, 79–81.

122. HH, "Myth, Magic and Religion: A Study of Pagan Influences in the Religion of Islam," book review, *Negro World*, July 31, 1920, 8, HP, B13, F7; in Martin, *African Fundamentalism*, 161–62. See Samuel W. Swemer, *The Influence of Animism on Islam: An Account of Popular Superstitions* (London: Central Board of Missions and Society for Promoting Christian Knowledge; and New York: Macmillan, 1920), https://archive.org/details/animismonislam00zwemuoft/page/n8; https://www.answering-islam.org/Books/Zwemer/Animism/. See also some publications of Earnest Alfred Wallis Budge (1857–1934), https://www.gutenberg.org/ebooks/author/2338; William Robertson Smith (1848–1894), *Religion of the Semites* (New York, 1889); Mohammed ibn al-Shibli (d. AH 789), *Akam ul Mirjan fi Akham al Jann*; C. Meinhof, *Africanische Rechtsgebrüche* (Berlin, 1914), 162; and James George Frazer, *The Golden Bough: A Study in Magic and Religion*, 3rd ed., 12 vols. (New York: Macmillan, 1913–1917).

123. HH, "Myth, Magic and Religion," 8.

124. HH, "Myth, Magic and Religion," 8.

125. HH, "Myth, Magic and Religion," 8.

126. HH, "Our International Consciousness," in *WAA*, 96. In his copy of Stoddard, *The Rising Tide of Color: Against White World-Supremacy*, Harrison on 90 asks: "How often are the limits of a man's knowledge taken as the limits of things! Mr. Stoddard was blandly ignorant of the history of Negro Africa as given in Lady Lugard's book and the writings of Mr. Cooley, Dr. Henry Barth and others. To these I referred him later." On 100 he adds, "Mr. Stoddard mixed his terms for self-protection, I think. The ignorance of African national consciousness (or cultural) is refreshing—tho natural in a graduate of Harvard, black or white"; "he evidently thinks that none of them can read—newspapers & magazines."

127. "Stoddard, T[heodore] Lothrop," in *National Cyclopaedia of American Biography* (New York: James T. White & Co., 1955), 40:371; HH, "The Rising Tide of Color Against White World Supremacy, by Lothrop Stoddard," *Negro World*, May 29, 1920, HP, B13, F7; in *WAA*, 140–44, with notes on 204–5; and in *HR*, 305–9; and I. A. Newby, *Jim Crow's Defense: Anti-Negro Thought in America, 1900–1930* (Baton Rouge: Louisiana State University Press, 1965), 54–55.

128. "Stoddard, T(heodore) Lothrop," 40:371; Lothrop Stoddard to HH, June 17, 1920, HP, B2, F19; HH, "The Rising Tide of Color Against White World Supremacy," *Negro World*, May 29, 1920; rpt. in *WAA*, 140–41. See also Weale, *The Conflict of Colour*; T. Shirby Hodge, *The White Man's Burden: A Satirical Forecast* (Boston: Gorham, 1915); and Newby, *Jim Crow's Defense*, 54–55.

129. HH, "The Rising Tide of Color Against White World Supremacy," *WAA*, 141. It appears that Harrison is referring to HH, "The White War and the Colored World," *Voice*, August 14, 1917, HP B6, F21; in *WAA*, 96–98, 187–88; and in *HR*, 202–3, and should not be confused with the similar but longer HH, "The White World and the Colored Races" (1918), in *New Negro* 4, no. 2 (October 1919): 8–10; in *WAA*, 116–22; and in *HR*, 203–9.

130. HH, "The Rising Tide of Color Against White World Supremacy," *WAA*, 141–42. Madison Grant (1865–1937) gained fame for his *The Passing of the Great Race; or, The Racial Basis of European History* (1916; 4th rev. ed., New York: Charles C. Scribner's Sons, 1921). See *ENY*, 500; and Degler, *In Search of Human Nature*, 48; *GP*, 5:722n3; John Higham, *Strangers in the Land*, rev. ed. (New Brunswick, NJ: Rutgers University Press, 1988), 234–30.

131. HH, "The Rising Tide of Color Against White World Supremacy," *WAA*, 143.

132. HH, "The Rising Tide of Color," *WAA*, 143–44.

133. HH, "The Rising Tide of Color," *WAA*, 144.

134. Lothrop Stoddard to HH, June 17, 1920, HP, B2, F19; HH, "The Rising Tide of Color," *WAA*, 113–15, quotations at 113; rpt. in *HR*, 309–10. In the June 12, 1920, *Negro World* appeared an editorial, "The Rising Tide of Color," which speaks of "Race First" and of supporting UNIA, "the biggest thing erected so far in service movements." See FBI Report of J. G. Tucker, June 19, 1920, 25–26. William Randolph Hearst (1863–1951) owned the most powerful newspaper chain in the United States, one known for sensationalist reporting and bellicose nationalism. See *WNBD*, 457; *GP*, 1:289n5; and *ENY*, 140.

135. Stoddard to HH, June 17, 1920; HH, "The Rising Tide of Color," *WAA*, 113–14.

136. Harrison, "The Rising Tide of Color," *WAA*, 114–15.

137. Stoddard to HH, June 17, 1920; HH to Lothrop Stoddard, June 24, 1920, HP, B2, F19, HPDLC.

138. HH to Stoddard, June 24, 1920; and HH, "The White World and the Colored Races" [1918], rpt. in *New Negro* 4, no. 2 (October 1919): 8–10, and rpt. in *Negro World*, February 1920; and in *WAA*, 116–22.

139. HH to Lothrop Stoddard, July 14, 1920, HP, B2, F19, HPDLC.

140. Lothrop Stoddard to HH, July 20, 1920, HP, B2, F19.

141. Lothrop Stoddard to HH, August 4 and August 21, 1920, HP, B2, F19, HPDLC. Ernest Gruening (1887–1974) was hired by Oswald Garrison Villard to work for the *Nation*, where he became managing editor in 1920. He later worked for the U.S. Department of the Interior (1934–1939) and was elected as governor of Alaska (1939–1953) and U.S. senator (1953–1967). See *WNBD*, 428; Hutchinson, *The Harlem Renaissance in Black and White*, 212–13.

142. HH to Stoddard, August 21, 1920.

143. HH to Stoddard, August 21, 1920. *Tartuffe* was a comedy in five acts by Moliere first performed in 1664. It was published in book form in English as *The Impostor*.

144. Lothrop Stoddard to HH, August 25 and September 18, 1920, HP, B2, F19.

145. HH to Lothrop Stoddard, September 30, 1920, HP, B2, F19, HPDLC; and Lothrop Stoddard to HH, November 1, 1920, HP, B2, F19.

146. Stoddard to HH, November 1, 1920.

147. HH to Lothrop Stoddard, November 13, 1920, HP, B2, F19, HPDLC.

148. HH to Stoddard, November 13, 1920. See also William I. Thomas, *Sex and Society: Studies in the Social Psychology of Sex* (Chicago: University of Chicago Press, 1907).

149. HH to Stoddard, November 13, 1920. Jean-Jacques Dessalines (1758?–1806) was formerly enslaved, took part in the Haitian liberation struggle, was central to the establishment of the Republic of Haiti in 1804, and served as its first emperor (1804–1806). See *WGMC*, 2:475–79; *WNBD*, 278. No information on a "Club Dessalines" has been found.

150. HH, "West Indian News Notes," *Negro World*, July 17, 1920, 6; HH, "West Indian News Notes by Hubert H. Harrison," *Negro World*, July 3, 1920, 6; [HH,] "W. I. News Notes," *Negro World*, August 21, 1920, 6; and [HH,] "West Indian News Notes," *Negro World*, August 28, 1920, 7; and February 26, 1921, 9.

7. The 1920 UNIA Convention and Influence on Garvey
(August–November 1920)

1. HD, August 28, 1920, HP, B9, F1; *GP*, 2:xxxi–xxxiii; "Bureau of Investigation Summary of the Minutes of Black Star Line Board of Directors' Meetings, 14

November 1919—26 July 1920 (Excerpt)," *GP*, 2:684–86; and "Finances of the Black Star Line," *GP*, 2:687–91, esp. 688.

2. HD, August 28, 1920. On James Walker Hood Eason (1886–1923), see Robert A. Hill, ed., and Barbara Bair, associate ed., *Marcus Garvey: Life & Lessons; A Centennial Companion to the Marcus Garvey and Universal Negro Improvement Papers* (Berkeley: University of California Press, 1987), 381–82; *GP*, 1:515n2; and Randall K. Burkett, *Black Redemption: Churchmen Speak for the Garvey Movement* (Philadelphia: Temple University Press, 1978), 51–63.

3. HD, August 28, 1920. Herbert S. Boulin, Special Agent P-138, "Report on Negro Activities—Marcus Garvey," August 11, 1920, *GP*, 2:566–67, offered comments somewhat similar to those of Harrison.

4. HD, August 28, 1920. On McGuire, see *GP*, 2:508–9n1.

5. Willard T. Holmes to the Editor, "Radical Negro Orators," *New York Globe*, August 5, 1920, HP, B12, F4.

6. Special Agent P-138 (Boulin), "Report on Negro Activities—Marcus Garvey," August 9, 1920, *GP*, 2:565–66. Boulin, a former Pinkerton Detective from 1915 to 1920, was terminated as an undercover agent by Hoover in August 1921. See *GP*, 2:541n3, 3:730n1; and Theodore Kornweibel Jr., *"Seeing Red": Federal Campaigns Against Black Militancy, 1919–1925* (Bloomington: Indiana University Press, 1998), 63, 110–15.

7. "Retraction by Marcus Garvey," August 11, 1920, People of the State of New York v. Marcus Garvey, *GP*, 2:568–69.

8. [HH], [Notes on Marcus Garvey], HD, B9, F3. Though Harrison was probably unaware of it at the time, Grey was a chief source of information for the BI's "special undercover informant P-138" (Boulin), who advised Garvey to reach the settlement with Grey. Kornweibel, *"Seeing Red,"* 112. Some later Garvey litigation is referenced in *GP*, 5:219n 1.

9. *New York Age*, August 14, 1920; cited in *GP*, 2:597n2. See also William H. Ferris, "The Psychology of Robes and Pageants," *Negro World*, October 15, 1921, 4.

10. HD, August 31, 1920. On the "Declaration of Rights of the Negro Peoples of the World," see *GP*, 2:571–75. Boulin (P-138) reported that August 12 "was taken up in debating over one clause in the Bill of Rights, now known as the 'Declaration of Rights.'" The clause was: "That no Negro shall fight in the army of any alien, race without getting the consent of the leader of the Negro Race World, except in self defence." Rev. McGuire was one of four delegates who opposed this clause "on the grounds that it is against the international law" and "against the laws and constitution of the Nation." Garvey ruled his opponents out of order and told them to sit down twice. According to Boulin, Garvey "ruled with an iron hand" and instructed "his fanatics" on how to vote. See Special Agent P-138, ("Report on Negro Activities—Marcus Garvey"), August 12, 1920, *GP*, 2:569–70.

11. "Report by Special Agent P-138 . . . In Re: Negro Activities (Marcus Garvey), August 14, 1920," *GP*, 2:582; "Declaration of Right of the Negro Peoples of the World," August 13, 1920, *GP*, 2:571–78. It is possible that Harrison, who was a believer in African, not African American or Afro-Caribbean, leadership in Africa helped inject the slogan "Africa for the Africans" in the "Declaration." Robert A. Hill points out that "Hubert Harrison was also instrumental in popularizing the slogan ['Africa for the Africans'] before Garvey arrived" and notes that Edward Wilmot Blyden, whose work Harrison knew well, was an early proponent of the idea. See George Shepperson,

"Pan-Africanism and 'Pan-Africanism': Some Historical Notes," *Phylon* 23, no. 4 (Winter 1962): 346–58, esp. 350; *GP*, 4:66n4.

12. HD, August 31, 1920. On salaries for Garvey and Eason, see also Special Agent P-138, (Report "Negro Activities—Radical Matters"), August 21, 1920, *GP*, 2:612–13, 2:592. On Garvey's living quarters, see the photo in Jervis Anderson, *This Was Harlem: A Cultural Portrait, 1900–1950* (New York: Farrar Straus Giroux, 1982), photo facing p. 92.

13. HD, August 31, 1920. According to Hill, "Garvey repeatedly claimed the world-wide black population to be four hundred million." *GP*, 9:161n4. On the opening night of the UNIA convention Garvey spoke of sending a telegram to Eamon de Valera, from the convention "representing 400,000,000 Negroes of the world." See *GP*, 1:lxxiv, lxxivn126, 2:478. In July 1921 Garvey spoke of the "400 million Africans" worldwide "who have Negro blood coursing through their veins." See MG, "A Membership Appeal from Marcus Garvey to the Negro Citizens of New York" [July 1921], *GP*, 3:560. He mentions "the 400,000,000 Negroes of the world" again in MG, "Opening Speech of the Convention by Marcus Garvey," August 1, 1921, *Negro World*, August 6, 1921, *GP*, 3:576; and in MG to Warren G. Harding, telegram, August 1, 1921, *GP*, 3:585. Arthur Schomburg also criticized Garvey's claim to "control four hundred million followers." See James, *HATB*, 213.

14. Special Agent P-138, [Report "Negro Activities—Radical Matters,"] August 19, 1920, *GP*, 2:608.

15. HD, August 18, 1920. On Henrietta Vinton Davis (1860–1941), see Hill and Bair, *Marcus Garvey: Life & Lessons*, 375–76; *GP*, 1:419–20n2, 7:318n3; and William Seraile, "Henrietta Vinton Davis and the Garvey Movement," *African Americans in New York Life and History* 7, no. 2 (July 1983): 7–24.

16. HD, August 28, 1920.

17. "A Walking Encyclopedia," *Negro World*, September 4, 1920, HP, FB740. Elsewhere Harrison indicated he spoke on the "Lion and Dead Mule" on August 25. See *WNBD*, 631–32; *GP*, 9:626n8.

18. HD, August 28, 1920, and August 31, 1920.

19. HD, August 28, 1920, and August 31, 1920.

20. HD, August 31, 1920. The article in the UNIA constitution pertaining to "Speaker In Convention" appeared in the constitutions of 1918, 1920, and 1921 but was dropped in 1922. See *GP*, 4:1068n2.

21. HD, August 28, 1920. Hill was able to put together a list of 144 delegates "whose names appeared in accounts of the convention printed in the *Negro World*, the *Negro World Convention Bulletin*, and in the records of the Bureau of Investigation." The list, it should be noted, does not include Harrison. See *GP*, 2:682–83.

22. HD, August 31, 1920.

23. HD, September 4, 1920, and September 5, 1920. On James A. Jackson (b. 1878), see Kellner, *The Harlem Renaissance*, 190.

24. HD, August 31, 1920.

25. HD, September 4, 1920. Harrison adds that Mrs. Downing, "(the white wife of a colored man) an old friend of Mrs. Hayford," came by, and they discussed a recent "base article against her husband—and her" by John E. Bruce. Mrs. Hayford planned to go west the following week and return to New York by the end of the month.

26. HD, September 4 and September 5, 1920; *GP*, 2:525n5.

27. HD, September 6, 1920.

28. HD, September 6 and 17, 1920.

29. HD, August 31, 1920.

30. Elie Garcia's secret report detailed a litany of social ills and urged the UNIA to downplay its intentions of "enlightening the native tribes." See Elie Garcia, UNIA Commissioner to Liberia, to Marcus Garvey and the UNIA, August 1920 (part 1, post June 27, 1920), DJ-FBI, file 61-826-X20, *GP*, 2:660–72, esp. "Part 2. Notes," 666–72; and Martin, *RF*, 123, citing *Philosophy and Opinions of Marcus Garvey*, 2 vols., ed. Amy Jacques-Garvey, intro. Hollis R. Lynch (1925; New York: Atheneum, 1971), 2:399–405, 131, on the 1924 publishing of Garcia's secret report; and 148nn167–68, where part of its history is discussed, including its eventual publication in the *Amsterdam News*, September 10, 1924. On the July or August date, see Statement of Hubert Harrison, "In re: U.S. vs. Black Star Line, Inc.," January 16, 1922, 1; and *GP*, 4:425. For more on the history of the Garcia report, see Agent "800" [James Wormley Jones] to Mr. Geo[rge] F. Ruch, December 16, 1921, *GP*, 4:273–74.

31. The trip was headed by Elie Garcia, who remained in Liberia until mid-August 1920 and in October 1920 was made BSL secretary, a position he held until he was indicted, with Garvey and others, for mail fraud in early 1922. See *GP*, 2:120n1; Marcus Garvey v. United States, no. 8317, Ct. App., 2s Cir., February 2, 1925, 2022–2122; *Negro World*, January 27, 1923.

32. Agent "800" to Mr. Geo[rge] F. Ruch, December 16, 1921, *GP*, 4:273–74.

33. Garcia, UNIA Commissioner to Liberia, to MG and the UNIA, August 1920 [part 1, June 27, 1920], *GP*, 2:660–72, esp. 666–67.

34. Garcia, to MG and the UNIA, August 1920 [part 1, June 27, 1920], *GP*, 2:660–72.

35. See Martin, *RF*, 123.

36. Part 2 of Garcia's report on "Economical and Moral Conditions" did appear in 1925 in *Philosophy and Opinions of Marcus Garvey*, 2:399–405.

37. This list is taken from [HH], [Notes on Marcus Garvey], n.d., HD.

38. Brown, "Garvey-istic Devotion," 429–30, evaluated Garvey similarly: "In the first place he is bombastic, conceited and arrogant. These qualities are too painfully obvious to call for further comment."

39. Brown, "Garvey-istic Devotion," esp. 425, also considered Garvey "a coward President and a stubborn man—because of his cowardice to admit failure when failure was obvious, because of his remarkable stubbornness to [attempt to] carry through a scheme doomed for obvious reasons to failure from the [very] start." Nyasaland was a British protectorate and today is Malawi.

40. As examples of Garvey's lies Harrison cited "his circulars advertising the Madison Square Garden meeting asserted that 25,000 (Twenty-Five Thousand) delegates were present from all parts of the world whereas the official balloting . . . showed . . . 103 . . . the highest number cast for any office. Garvey himself, sole nominee also, received 92 votes for President-General. Yet, despite such facts, he is again declaring in circulars out today that there will be 20,000 delegates in the parade on Tuesday [August 31]." See HD, August 28, 1920. See also *GP*, 2:682–83, which lists 144 delegates. Harrison wrote that "Garvey has a great talent for lying. In 1920 when he attacked his first wife in Liberty Hall he said that if she had ever bought any houses he was absolutely ignorant of the transaction. But, on the stand, when shown a check of the B.S.L. for $5,000 made out to her and drawn and paid by him to

a real estate agent for the purchase of a house for her, he 'explained' that that was for a lien on the property. A check as a lien is a new thing in real estate deals." See HH, "Marcus Garvey at the Bar of United States Justice." Brown "Garvey-istic Devotion," esp. 429–30, evaluated Garvey similarly: "He [Garvey] has no regard whatever for exactness of statement and cares nothing for the character and reputation of other men. He lives in an atmosphere of exaggerations and falsehoods. He tells you of 50000 delegates at a Convention attended by 200, and he makes it impossible by his exaggeration [for anyone] to know when his figures are true or near true or absolutely false. As to the reputation and character of men, almost every man who has left his association has been branded a thief and a liar and worse. He has prostituted the high uses of a newspaper to his own unscrupulous ends. And he has not changed." Domingo called Garvey the "Biggest propagandist the world has ever seen" and added "Garvey and truth were just not on good terms." Theodore Draper interview with W. A. Domingo, January 18, [1958], 3, Theodore Draper Papers, Emory University, Atlanta, Georgia.

41. WEBDB, "The U.N.I.A.," *Crisis* 25, no. 3 (January 1923), 120–22; rpt. in *GP*, 5:208–12, cited the organization's published report of 1921 and the analysis of it, made first by Domingo in the *Crusader* and afterward corrected in minor detail by the *Crisis*. It also cited the suppressed report of 1922 that was ordered to be printed by the UNIA Congress but had not yet been issued until the *Crisis* printed it. He emphasized, "Garvey's claims of membership for the U.N.I.A. have been untrue and even fantastic." He ultimately concludes that "the U.N.I.A. has at present less than 18,000 active members." See WEBDB, "The U.N.I.A.," *Crisis* 25, no. 3 (January 1923), 120–22; rpt. in *GP*, 5:208–12.

42. On August 18, 1920, the MID requested information on Garvey. Then on August 21 in the *Negro World* appeared retractions on Kilroe, Grey, and Warner. See August 18, 1920, request for information on Garvey, MID 10218-261-53; *Negro World*, August 21, 1920, 1.

43. After Harrison left, the *Negro World* changed its policy on skin-lightening and hair-straightening product advertisements. See *Chicago Whip*, November 1923; *GP*, 5:xxxv–xxxvi.

44. According to Hill, "as early as 1914," Garvey "urged blacks to look around and take a leaf of the book of EXAMPLES set before you by our [white] friends and benefactors—our brothers of Salvation." He also "adopted the aristocratic titles, honorary degrees, and the assorted panoply of devices symbolizing the grandeur of Europe's achievements." See *GP*, 1:lii, which cites *Negro World*, June 21, 1919.

45. Robert W. Bagnall, "The Madness of Marcus Garvey," *Messenger*, 5, no. 3 (March 1923), 638–48, describes Garvey as a "paranoiac." Du Bois considered Garvey "dictatorial, domineering, inordinately vain and very suspicious." WEBDB, "Marcus Garvey," *Crisis* 2 (December 1920): 58–60.

46. Brown, "Garvey-istic Devotion," esp. 429–30, made a similar evaluation of Garvey, describing him as "a mean shifter of responsibilities," one who "claims all the honor and disowns all the blame." On Sam G. Kpakpa-Quartey, see *GP*, 2:167n3.

47. [HH], [Notes on Marcus Garvey], HD. Brown, "Garvey-istic Devotion," 429–30, observed that "Marcus Garvey cannot work with men. He gets on splendidly with tools but any man who dares to be a man becomes his enemy and is forthwith dismissed from his presence. On two succeeding conventions he has brought about the dismissal of men whom he himself at the preceding convention presented for election as efficient loyal and honorable. They were too efficient too loyal too honorable to continue to be his tools,

his phonograph—and they went." Du Bois used "dictatorial" and "very suspicious" to describe Garvey in WEBDB, "Marcus Garvey," 58–60.

48. Garvey's hero was said to be Napoleon, and Amy Ashwood Garvey spoke of him having a "Napoleonic complex." See *GP*, 1:liv. According to J. A. Rogers, "Garvey 'worshipped Napoleon.'" See *WGMC*, 2:415.

49. See HD, August 31, 1920.

50. Hill quotes a reporter concerning a later period that "nothing revealed Garvey's lack of political understanding more than the vicious attack which he made upon Emperor Haile Selassie of Ethiopia" at the time of that country's struggle for national independence against fascism. See *GP*, 7:664n1.

51. On Garvey's desire for a "Negro" nation in Africa at a later time, see "Marcus Garvey Lauds Bill Introduced in Mississippi Legislature by Senator [T. S.] McCallum That United States Secure by Treaty of Otherwise Sufficient Territory in Africa to Establish Negro Nation," *Negro World*, February 18, 1922; rpt. in *GP*, 4:496–504. Senator McCallum introduced a "concurrent resolution of the [Mississippi] Senate and House of Representatives memorializing the Congress of the United States to request the President to secure by treaty, negotiations or otherwise from our late war allies, sufficient territory on the continent of Africa to make a suitable and final home for the American negro and to use such part of our allied war debt as may be necessary to secure said concession." The resolution passed the Mississippi state senate on February 20, 1922, by 25 to 9 with 15 abstentions. The *Negro World* of March 18, 1922, published the resolution. See also *GP*, 9:xlix. For Garvey's view of Africa as a nation and potential empire published later, see MG, [Editorial letter,] *Negro World*, January 26, 1924; rpt. in *GP*, 5:536–47, quotation at 539, where he writes, "we are going to make our contribution through the building up of one of the greatest nations and empires in the world." It should be noted that WEBDB, "The Negro's Fatherland," *Survey*, November 10, 1917, argued for the creation of a "great free central African state" as a partial solution to the competing European claims in Africa.

52. I have not been able to locate this article.

53. HH, "The Negro at the Peace Congress," in *WAA*, 30–32, originally published as [HH,] "The Negro at the Peace Congress," [*Voice*? c. December 1918?]; HH, "Africa and the Peace," *Voice*, December 26, 1918; rpt. in *WAA*, 32–35, originally published as [HH,] "Africa at the Peace Table," *Voice*, December 26, 1918, in HP, B13, F1–2.

54. See chapter 16, note 2, in this volume.

55. HD, December 10, 1920. Trinidad-born Cyril A. Crichlow (1889–1965), official stenographer and reporter for the UNIA, traveled with Garvey and recorded his speeches for the *Negro World*. He was also a member of the executive council of the UNIA in 1921 and, in February 1921, was sent as resident secretary of the UNIA commission to Liberia, which was to start the UNIA's building and farming program. Garvey said Crichlow was "responsible for all our records and all data and reports pertaining to the interests of the [UNIA] in Liberia." See *GP*, 2:329n5; Hill and Bair, *Marcus Garvey: Life & Lessons*, 373; MG to Gabriel Johnson, February 1, 1921, DNA, RG 84; *Crisis* 20, no. 2 (June 1920): 104; Judith Stein, *The World of Marcus Garvey: Race and Class in Modern Society* (Baton Rouge: Louisiana State University Press, 1986), 100.

56. HD, December 10, 1920, and March 22, 1921.

57. HD, March 2, 1925.

58. HH, "A Difference of Opinion," "Editorial Notes," *Negro World*, August 7, 1920, in HH, ScrWrNW, HP, B13, F7.

59. HH, "A Difference of Opinion." On Joseph Ephraim Casely-Hayford (1866–1930), see *GP*, 1:350n1. On John Mensah Sarbah (1864–1910) of the Gold Coast see *Kaiser Index*, 4:163.

60. HH, "A Difference of Opinion."

61. [Dave?] Louis Thompson to HH, August 7, 1920, HP, B3, F44.

62. L. M. Meade to "Mr. Hubert Harrison, Editor of the *Negro World*," August 11, 1920; rpt. in "Negro and White in Africa: Discussion by Bruce Grit and His Critics," *Negro World*, August 21, 1920, 7.

63. Bruce "to Mr. Dear H. H.," in "Negro and White in Africa: Discussion by Bruce Grit and His Critics; Bruce Grit Replies," *Negro World*, August 21, 1920, 7.

64. "H.H." [HH], "A New International," *Negro World*, August 14, 1920, 2; rpt. in *WAA*, 111–13, n194–96; originally published as HH, "The New International," *Negro World*, May 15, 1920.

65. "H.H." [HH], "Our Political Power," *Negro World*, August 21, 1920, 2, HP, B13, F7; rpt. in *HR*, 155–57.

66. "H.H." [HH], "Our Political Power."

67. "H.H." [HH], "Our Political Power." Agent P-138 (Herbert S. Boulin) reported on a September 5 meeting of the VIPA; its participants included Miss Elizabeth Hendrickson, Mr. Tollman, and Rothschild Francis. See P-138, Report, September 7, 1920, BF OG258421, RG 65, DNA, Reel 11, *FSAA*. The U.S. Department of Justice, Radical Division, Washington, DC, "General Intelligence Bulletin For September 25th, 1920," no. 30, File 10110-1683-46-328X, DNA, Reel 22, *FSAA*, said that Francis, who claimed "to be the American representative of the Negro Workers of the Virgin Islands, and member of the Virgin Island p[P]rotective Association," was utilizing the *New York Call* to inform readers about "the alleged hardships suffered under United States rule by the inhabitants of the island." He was also seeking funds for printing-press materials to take to the Virgin Islands in order to establish a radical paper.

68. "H.H." [HH], "Our Political Power," 2.

69. [Hodge Kirnon], "Contemporary Comment: As to 'HH,'" *Negro World*, August 21, 1920; rpt. from the *Promoter*, in HH, ScrMAM1, HP, FB740.

70. [HH], "The Negro in Industry: *The Great Steel Strike* by William Z. Foster," *Negro World*, August 21, 1920, 2, HP, B13, F7, and FB740; rpt. in *HR*, 81–83.

71. [HH], "The Negro in Industry," 2; *HR*, 82; Foster, *The Great Steel Strike*, 207–8.

72. [HH], "The Negro in Industry," 2; *HR*, 83.

73. [HH], "The Negro in Industry," 2; *HR*, 83.

74. HH, "Introductory," in *WAA*, 8; HH, *NandN*, 7. Regarding Harrison's comment "as President Wilson so sincerely put it," see [HH,] "The Negro and the War," in *WAA*, 25. Thompson would be indicted along with Garvey, Elie Garcia, and George Tobias in February 1922 on mail-fraud charges, of which he was later acquitted. See Hill and Bair, *Marcus Garvey: Life & Lessons*, 430–31; and *GP*, 2:390n1.

75. HH, "On a Certain Condescension in White Publishers," [Part 1], *Negro World*, March 4, 1922, 7; rpt. in *HR*, 293–95, quotation on 294.

76. HH, "Introductory," in *WAA*, 5–6. On the title page the author was described as the "Author of *The Negro and the Nation*, *Lincoln and Liberty*, and Associate Editor of the *Negro World*."

77. HH, "Introductory," in *WAA*, 6–7. Both "H.H." [HH], "Getting Excited and Nervous," *Negro World*, July 3, 1920, 2; and L. F. Bowler [HH?] to *Evening Sun*, June 16, 1920, mention the "When Africa Awakes" concept.

78. See "H.H." [HH], "Getting Excited and Nervous," *Negro World*, July 3, 1920, 2; L. F. Bowler [HH?], to *Evening Sun*, June 16, 1920; and Hill and Bair, *Marcus Garvey: Life & Lessons*, 406. On Annie Turnbo-Malone (c. 1869?–1957), see *Inter-State Tattler*, December 30, 1927; and see the State Historical Society of Missouri, https://shsmo.org/historicmissourians/name/m/malone/.

79. HH, "Introductory," in *WAA*, 6–7; and David Levering Lewis, *When Harlem Was in Vogue* (1979; New York: Oxford University Press, 1981), 104. The journalist Herbert J. Seligmann (1891–1984) was director of publicity for the NAACP. See *GP*, 4:244n1.

80. HH, "Introductory," in *WAA*, 7–8. The title of the book may have been related to George Wells Parker, "When Africa Awakes" (poem), *Crusader* 1, no. 6 (February 1919): 26. See also Hill, ed., *Crusader*, 1:xx.

81. HH, "Personal Letters," *Negro World*, August 28, 1920, 1.

82. HH, "Personal Letters," *Negro World*, August 28, 1920, 1; HH to Thomas Wallace Swann, September 11, 1920, HP, B2, F24, HPDLC. Swann worked for several Black papers and magazines and was an officer of the International League of Darker Peoples in January 1919. See *GP*, 1:390n2.

83. HH to Swann, September 11, 1920; H.[odge] Kirnon, [Review of *WAA*], *Negro World*, September 11, 1920. Kirnon's *Promoter* is described very positively in "Another New Negro Magazine," *Negro World*, August 21, 1920, 1. A biographical sketch of Kirnon, "an early follower of Harrison" who believed American Blacks' fight was in the United States and that racial consciousness should "be developed alongside of class consciousness," is provided in *GP*, 5:4–5n1.

84. HH to Swann, September 11, 1920; Kirnon, [Review of *WAA*], *Negro World*, September 11, 1920.

85. Kirnon, [Review of *WAA*], *Negro World*, September 11, 1920.

86. HH to Copyright Office, Washington, DC, December 29, 1920 HP, B2, F5, HPDLC.

87. John E. Bruce to HH, January 12, 1921, HP, B1, F18.

88. [John E. Bruce,] "Newspaper Man Writes," *Kansas City Call*, January 8, 1921.

89. John E. Bruce, "Bruce Grit's Column," manuscript, handwritten, B5 Mss B-11 Ms. 21, John E. Bruce Papers, SCRB, n.d. (probably January 8, 1921). J. A. Rogers writes that Harrison "momentarily forgot names, but his memory was astounding. In his addresses he would reel off quotations from poets great and obscure, cite passages from Spencer, Darwin, Huxley, and other scientists and scholars without an error; in jokes and anecdotes he was to the point." See *WGMC*, 2:617.

90. Chester A. Scott to HH, February 13, 1921, HP, B3, F33.

91. *GP*, 3:770, which cites UNIA, *Constitution and Book of Laws*: "Rules and Regulations for Juveniles," as revised and amended in August 1921.

92. Lewis, *When Harlem Was in Vogue*, 104.

93. "Negroes Form New Party to Combat Republicans," *Negro World*, August 28, 1920, 10; [HH], "Negro Party Brands Bridges as a Faker," "Meant for issue of 10/30/20," *Negro World*, November 6, 1920, HP, B5, F31; in *GP*, 2:431n2.

94. "Negroes Form New Party," 10; [HH], "Negro Party Brands Bridges." Hill writes that the Liberty Party was formed in August 1920 by Harrison, Bridges, and Edgar Grey and was a continuation of Harrison's Liberty League. Harrison, in Harlem street meetings of the party, reportedly "urged blacks to arm themselves for future confrontations and to vote only for black candidates in the forthcoming elections." According to Hill, the "original call for a black president had been made by Bridges in an editorial in his *Challenge* magazine and had been officially endorsed by the *Negro World* in June 1920."

See *GP*, 3:254n2, where Hill also states that the Liberty Party was formed partly in response to the Tulsa race riot of May 1920. (The Tulsa "riot" actually occurred on May 31 and June 1, 1921.) In an October 1916 *Crisis* editorial Du Bois had discussed the need for a "Negro Party." Also, a National Liberty Party had convened in East St. Louis on July 6–7, 1904. George Edwin Taylor of Ottumwa, Iowa, was nominated as their presidential candidate, and J. Max Barber's early twentieth-century *Voice of the Negro* referred to him as "The Only Colored Man Ever Nominated for the Presidency." See Stephen John Williams, "A Black Standard-Bearer of a Black Party," *City Sun*, July 1–7, 1992, 3, 5. There was also an abolitionist Liberty Party in the 1840s that sought to do work within the electoral arena and had some offshoots surviving into the 1860s.

95. "Negroes Form New Party," *Negro World*, August 28, 1920, 10. The New York State Assembly suspended five Socialist members on January 7, 1920, on the charge of membership in the SP. See "Monthly Labor Review," *Advance*, February 6, 1920, 8.

96. J. G. Tucker, Report, September 4, 1920, BF OG208369, RG 65, DNA, Reel 10, *FSAA*.

97. P-138, Report, September 15, 1920, BF OG258421, RG 65, DNA, Reel 11, *FSAA*. Boulin added that Harrison was "once a prominent figure in the Socialist party" and was "now semi-attached to Garvey's *Negro World*."

98. J. G. Tucker, Special Report, September 25, 1920, RG 65 Reel 617 OG 208369; and P-138, Report, September 25, 1920, BF OG258421, RG 65, DNA, Reel 11, *FSAA*.

99. "Confidential Report, 9/30/20," [re Herman Marie Bernolet], File OG 369936, FSAA Reel 12.

100. P-138, Report, "In re: Negro Activities," October 6, 1920, BF OG258421, RG 65, DNA, Reel 11, *FSAA*.

101. P-138, Report, "Negro Radical Activities," October 14, 1920, BF OG258421, RG 65, DNA, Reel 11, *FSAA*.

102. J. G. Tucker, Report, 10-9-20, BF OG 208369-1, RG 65, DNA, Reel 10, *FSAA*; U.S. DOJ, Radical Division, Washington, DC, "General Intelligence Bulletin: Strictly Confidential," no. 32, October 9, 1920, File 10110-1683-48-328x, DNA, Reel 22, *FSAA*.

103. P-138, Report, "Negro Radical Activities," October 10, 1920, BF RG 65, DNA, Reel 7, *FSAA*. See also P-138, Report, "IN RE: NEGRO ACTIVITIES," January 7, 1921, BF BS 202600-667-3/4, DNA, Reel 7, *FSAA*. James Wormley Jones (1884–1958), confidential informant "800," was the BI's first African American special agent. He infiltrated the UNIA and the ABB and reported on those and other Black organizations. By June 1920 Jones was responsible for registering all incoming mail at UNIA headquarters. See *GP*, 2:203n4, 230n3; *Negro World*, March 13, 1920; *Negro World*, June 26, 1920.

104. [HH], "Negro Party Brands Bridges." Harrison indicates that "words oral or written" with Bridges would be a "futile exchange." HH to William Bridges, November 3, 1920, HP, B2, F26, HPDLC.

105. [HH], "Negro Party Brands Bridges"; Special Report of J. G. Tucker, October 16, 1920, 17; October 10, 1920; *GP*, 3:254n2.

106. William Bridges to the Editor, "Bridges Enters General Denial," *Negro World*, November 13, 1920.

107. William Bridges to the Editor, "Bridges Enters General Denial."

108. HH to Thomas Wallace Swann, November 9, 1920.

109. *GP*, 3:254n2.

110. "Colored Dots: 'The New Negro Eloquently Presented,'" *Petersburg Evening Progress*, October 26, 1920; "A Great Musical Program and Address," *Petersburg Evening*

Progress, October 28, 1920; and "Mass Meeting at Metropolitan Church," *Petersburg Evening Progress*, October 29, 1920, ScrMAM1, HP, FB740. Harrison mentions his trip to Petersburg in [HH], [Notes on Marcus Garvey], HD.

111. "Colored Dots"; "Dr. Harrison Delivers Inspiring Address," *Petersburg Evening Progress*, October 27, 1920, HP, ScrMAM1, HP, FB740. The October 27 talk was at a bazaar sponsored by women workers of Zion Baptist Church.

112. [Article re Harrison's fourth lecture in Petersburg], [*Petersburg Evening Progress*], October 29, 1920, HP, FB740; "Colored Dots"; "A Great Musical Program and Address"; and "Mass Meeting at Metropolitan Church."

113. "Who Is Hubert Harrison?" handout card, c. November 1920.

114. HH to "Dear Mr. St. Prix," November 22, 1920, in JBPP. For information on the Philadelphia UNIA, see *Negro World*, July 3, 1920, 4.

115. HH to "Dear Mr. St. Prix," November 22, 1920.

116. "All Philadelphia is Invited To A Rare Treat 'Heaven, Earth and Hell, Or a Race in Search of It's Soul' A Wonderful Satisfying Lecture By Dr. Hubert H. Harrison, D.S.C. . . . Author of 'The Negro and the Nation' 'The Black Man's Burden' 'When Africa Awakes,' etc.," at Women's Christian Alliance Hall, Sunday November 28, 1920, 2 PM, leaflet, c. November 28, 1920. See also [HH], [Notes on MG], HD.

117. Joseph St. Prix to HH, November 29, 1920, in JBPP; and *GP*, 2:645, 650n3.

118. HH to Joseph St. Prix, December 1, 1920, in JBPP.

119. HH to Joseph St. Prix, December 1, 1920.

120. HH to Joseph St. Prix, December 6, 1920, in JBPP.

121. HH to Joseph St. Prix, December 1, 1920.

122. "A Great Lecture For Friend and Foe Alike The 'Back To Africa' Movement By Hubert Harrison, Doctor of Civil Science," at Women's Christian Alliance Hall, Sunday December 12, 1920, leaflet, c. December 12, 1920; [HH], [Notes on MG], HD, B4, F61.

123. Harrison wrote to Jose Clarana in April 1921: "It is therefore necessary to point out that soon after the convention closed I ceased to be the editor of *The Negro World*—as had been prophesied before." See HH, "Addendum to the Above," *Negro World*, April 23, 1921, 5. See also [W. A. Domingo,] "Race First!" *Negro World*, July 26, 1919; rpt. in *GP*, 1:468–70; Ferris, "The Spectacular Career of Garvey," *Amsterdam News*, February 11, 1925; "Report of UNIA Meeting" [from *Negro World*, October 25, 1919]; rpt. in *GP*, 2:100–5, esp. 100; "Report of UNIA Meeting," *Negro World*, March 6, 1920; rpt. in *GP*, 2:236; *GP*, 1:211–12n3, 444n2, 529, 2:582; HH, "Marcus Garvey at the Bar of United States Justice" (where Harrison says circulation decreased to 3,000); Hill-Noble interview, aired November 20, 1983, 21; and HH to Lothrop Stoddard, August 21, 1920, which explains that "for ten months in 1920 he [Harrison] was editor-in-chief of Marcus Garvey's *Negro World*, from which he resigned because of differences of opinion with the owner." See also "Dignity of the Flag Upheld," *Globe*, July 31, 1923, ScrMAM1, HP, FB 740. Harrison's last *Negro World* article was on November 2, 1922. See [HH,] [Notes on MG], HD. On the factors in Garvey's decline, see, for example, Ernest Allen Jr., "Marcus Garvey and Booker T. Washington: Patters of Militancy and Accommodation" [draft], n.p., March 1978, 13, possession of author; and *GP*, 1:lxxviii–lxxxvi. In a matter of months after Harrison ceased being managing editor, the paper's circulation was cut in half, from 50,000 to 25,000. Special Agent P-138 [Boulin] in his "Report" on "Negro Activities," July 2, 1921, DNS, RG file BS 202600-667-63, *GP*, 3:506, says that associate editor of the *Negro World* Hudson Price told him on June 29, 1921, that "6 months ago [January 1921] the negro worlds circulation was only 25,000 copies."

124. On Washington's financing, see *DANB*, 634.

125. Monroe N. Work, *Negro Year Book: An Annual Encyclopedia of the Negro, 1921–22* (Tuskegee, AL: Tuskegee Institute, 1922), 53–63, 73–83; HH, "Marcus Garvey at the Bar of United States Justice," *GP*, 1:xlviii–xlix; "Negro 'Napoleon' Counts on a Loyal Million to Aid Him," *New York World*, c. January 14, 1922. On the uses of BSL monies for the *Negro World*, see "Brief for the United States, *Marcus Garvey v. United States*, U.S. Circuit Court of Appeals, Second Circuit," New York, c. December 10, 1924, *GP*, 6:49–66, esp. 50, which cites Marcus Garvey v. United States, no. 8317, Ct. App., 2d Cir., February 2, 1925, fol. 194ff. On Du Bois, Randolph, and Owens, see, for example, [HH], "The Lion and the Lamb," *Negro World*, April 3, 1920; "The Garland Fund," *Pittsburgh Courier*, October 16, 1926, in HP-Mi; "'Slush Fund' Aired: Prominent Men and Organizations Received 'Gifts' Totalling $62,405 of Dissipated Garland Millions," *Pittsburgh Courier*, October 9, 1926, 1, 2; "Applications Favorably Acted Upon"—I. Gifts: 1922–1927, Vol. 2 "Brotherhood of Sleeping Car Porters," [Garland Fund] American Fund for the Public Service, New York Public Library, New York, NY; Gifts 1928–1933, vol. 7, "Messenger," American Fund for the Public Service, New York Public Library; and, regarding Du Bois, "Miscellaneous Reports," 1922–1944, vol. 6; American Fund for the Public Service, New York Public Library; Andrew Buni, *Robert L. Vann of the "Pittsburgh Courier": Politics and Black Journalism* (Pittsburgh, PA: University of Pittsburgh Press, 1974), 148–49, which points out that James Weldon Johnson, the only Black director of the fund, had great influence.

126. [HH,] "The Lion and the Lamb," *Negro World*, April 3, 1920.

127. HH, "Just Crabs," *Negro World*, c. April 1920; rpt. in *WAA*, 73–75, esp. 74–75; HH, [Notes re "The Red Record of Radicalism"], [c. 1927], HP, B6, F7. See [Masthead], *Emancipator*, March 13, 1920, 4. "Just Crabs" was clearly a barb directed at the *Emancipator* group of Black socialists whom it referred to as "The Subsidized Sixth," in allusion to W. E. B. Du Bois's "Talented Tenth" concept and to their financial backing from the Socialist Party. See HH, "Race First Versus Class First," in *WAA*, 80. The originally autonomous ABB later merged all its locals with those of the Workers (Communist) Party–controlled American Negro Labor Congress. This was done under a directive of the all-"white" Parity Commission of the Workers (Communist) Party. See Workers (Communist) Party of America, *The Fourth National Convention of the Workers (Communist) Party, Report of the Central Executive Committee of the 4th National Convention, Held in Chicago, Illinois, August 21st to 30th, 1925* (Chicago, [1925]), 123, 165–66. Note that Du Bois faced similar financial problems with the *Horizon* and the Niagara Movement. See Elliott Rudwick, "W. E. B. Du Bois: Protagonist for Afro-American Protest," in *Black Leaders of the Twentieth Century*, ed. John Hope Franklin and August Meier (Urbana: University of Illinois Press, 1982), 63–84, quotation on 72.

128. "Discard Ambition and Ignorance," *Emancipator*, April 17, 1920, 3; William Harrison Interview with Simmons, February 23, [1951]; and M. K. Bunde, Memorandum for Col. [Parker] Hitt, February 14, 1921, DNA, RG 165, MID 10218-417-1.

129. "Momma" (Mrs. Irene Louise Horton Harrison) interview with William Harrison, (New York), February 10, 1951, HP, B8, F12; and "Addendum to the Above," *Negro World*, April 23, 1921, 5. Claude McKay tells of speaking with Harrison and other radicals at the *Liberator* and discussing how to make the Garvey movement more class conscious. Claude McKay, *A Long Way from Home*, ed. Gene Andrew Jarrett (1937; New Brunswick, NJ: Rutgers University Press, 2007), 67, 108–9. *GP*, 1:lix, lxvi.

130. "Hubert Harrison Dies Suddenly in Bellevue Hospital," *New York Age*, December 24, 1927, 2; "Dr. Harrison Dies After Operation," *Pittsburgh Courier*, December 24, 1927, 1; Hodge Kirnon, "As to 'H.H.,'" in HH, "Contemporary Comment," *Negro World*, August 21, 1920, 2. On Harrison's African lectures such as that on "Negro History and Its Place in Education," see, for example, Wilberforce, "Harrison Delivers Inspiring Lecture at Harlem People's Forum," *Voice*, August 1, 1918. See also HH, "Know Thyself," *Negro World*, April 16, 1921, 4; John Henrik Clarke, ed., *Marcus Garvey and the Vision of Africa* (New York: Vintage, 1974), 197.

131. HH, "Two Negro Radicalisms," *New Negro*, October 1919, 4–5; quotation in *WAA*, 180; and in *HR*, 104. A *Negro World* rpt. of this article is cited in "Before and After," *Emancipator*, April 3, 1920, 3. See also HH, "Some Reasons Why Such a Collection Is Necessary," [Notes], n.p., c. 1925, HP, B6, F28.

132. HH, "Marcus Garvey at the Bar of United States Justice," Associated Negro Press, c. July 1, 1923, 2–4; rpt. in *HR*, 184–99, esp. 196–97; rpt. as HH, "New York Writer Analyzes Garvey Case: Compares Provisional President with O'NEILL's 'Emperor Jones,' Made Famous by Charles Gilpin," *Kansas City Call*, July 5, 1923. On the BSL idea see Ferris, "The Spectacular Career of Garvey," *Amsterdam News*, February 11, 1925; "Calls Garvey Good Orator, Poor Businessman and Robber," *Amsterdam News*, May 30, 1923, esp. 6. On Charles Christopher Seifert (1880–1949), see *GP*, 1:226–27n3.

133. Kirnon, "As to 'H.H.'"; in HH, "Contemporary Comment," *Negro World*, August 21, 1920, 2. On Garvey, see *GP*, 1:lxvii, lix, lx, 25n5. The Reverend James W. H. Eason, the American Leader of the UNIA at Liberty Hall, declared: "One part [the key part] of that [UNIA] program intends to teach the Negroes of the world racial consciousness." In "U.N.I.A. Program Being Put Over: Thus Says American Leader in Telling Speech Before Overwhelming Audience in Liberty Hall," *Negro World*, August 27, 1921, 2. Garvey explained that the UNIA seeks to inculcate "race pride, and race consciousness in the mind and heart of every Negro." See MG, "A Membership Appeal from Marcus Garvey to the Negro Citizens of New York," [July 1921], DNA, RG 165, File 10218-261, *GP*, 3:560–64, quotation on 562.

134. *GP*, 1:xxxvii–xxxviii.

135. H.H. [HH], "The U.N.I.A.," *Negro World*, August 14, 1920, 2, HP, B6, F45; H.[odge] Kirnon, [Review of HH's *WAA*], *Negro World*, September 11, 1920; Crosswaith to Mrs. Hubert H. Harrison & Family, December 20, 1927, HP, B1, F36. Nathan I. Huggins, *Voices from the Harlem Renaissance* (New York: Oxford University Press, 1974), 8, writes: "The 'New Negro' was actually a creature of the pre-war years. If anything his radicalism was more sharply political in the early years of the war than it was to be in the 1920s."

136. [HH], "Race Consciousness," *Boston Chronicle*, March 15, 1924, HP, B6, F43; rpt. in *Voice of the Negro* 1, no. 1 (April 1927): 3–4; in *HR*, 116–17; HH, "Introductory," in *WAA*, 8; [HH], "The Need for It," *New Negro* 4, no. 1 (September 1919): 1; rpt. in *HR*, 101–2, on the need "of extending racial consciousness"; HH, "Some Reasons Why Such a Collection is Necessary," n.p., [c. 1925?], HP, B6, F28. See Ferris, "The Spectacular Career of Garvey," *Pittsburgh Courier*, February 11, 1925. Lester A. Walton, "Marcus Garvey: His Rise and Fall," *Chicago Defender*, April 4, 1925, 12, stated that Garvey said monetary losses "are insignificant compared with benefits accruing from the awakening of a race consciousness and the arousing of the proper appreciation of the Negro for his own." On Sherrill's comments, see *GP*, 1:lxxxix, which cites *Negro World*, August 25,

1923, 10. On "race consciousness" and Garvey, see also A. F. Elmes, "Garvey and Garveyism—An Estimate," *Opportunity* 3, no. 29 (May 1925): 139–41.

137. *GP*, 1:lix, lxvi.

138. *GP*, 1:lxx–lxxvii, quotation on lxx; and Hill and Bair, *Marcus Garvey: Life & Lessons*, 403. In the prepublication publicity for the Hill volumes the statement was made that "Ireland's Sinn Fein movement was the major ideological influence on Garvey after his arrival in the United States in 1916." University of California Press, "Special Charter Subscription Offer," 2. When Hill appeared on television in New York, the main center of activity for both Harrison and Garvey, he made absolutely no mention of the Sinn Fein or the Irish movement and made considerable mention of Harrison. This is a rather startling occurrence if the Irish struggle, and not Harrison, was, as Hill argues, the major ideological influence on Garvey's radicalism. See Robert A. Hill, "Television Interview with Gil Noble, Radio TV Reports, Inc., *Like It Is*, WABC-TV, November 20, 1983, 1:00 PM, New York," full text (New York: Radio TV Reports, Inc.), 17–18. It should also be noted that Hill did cite BI sources on the role of outside (Sinn Fein) agitators on Garvey and the Garvey movement. See *GP*, 1:lxxii, citing RG 65 BS 198940 "Marcus Garvey [Negro]." Such an argument has been standard white supremacist fare during the First World War (when it was "Sinn Fein" or "Bolshevist" agitators) through the latter part of the twentieth century, when "Communist" became the code word. "Communist agitators" was also the argument of the white supremacist regime that ruled South Africa. This argument seems premised on white supremacy and on the belief that Black people are unable to define and lead their own struggles. On Garvey's tricolor flag, see also *RF*, 42–43, 63n8.

139. *GP*, 1:lxv. The quote is from a Garvey speech of October 16, 1921, in *Negro World*, October 22, 1921; rpt. in *GP*, 4:119–22, quotation on 120.

140. HH, "What It Stands For," *Voice*, September 19, 1917; rpt. in *HR*, 89–92; [HH], "Is Democracy Unpatriotic?" *Voice*, July 11, 1918, 4; rpt. in *WAA*, 25–27, quotation on 27; and [Masthead], *Voice*, August 1, 1918, 1, HP-Wr; HH, *NandN*, 2. See also HH, "The U.N.I.A. and Politics," *Negro World*, June 5, 1920, HP-Sc, 33.

141. *GP*, 1:lxvi.

142. Kirnon, rpt. in Harrison, "As to 'H.H.,'" *Negro World*, August 21, 1920; [Announcement], *New Negro* 3, no. 7 (August 1919): 7; "Is There Any Cure for Lynching?" handout, c. March 25, 1927, HP-Mi; [HH], "Race Consciousness," *Voice of the Negro* 1, no. 1 (April 1927): 3–4; HH, "Introductory," in *WAA*, 8; [HH], "The Need for It," *New Negro* 4, no. 1 (September 1919), 1; "Liberty League of Negro-Americans: Africa First," Membership Card no. 1 issued to HH, September 2, 1917, HP, B14, F9.

143. *GP*, 1:lxx. Of interest is Cyril V. Briggs to the Editor, "Africa for the Africans," *New York Globe*, December 13, 1917, 12. Hill claims "Hubert Harrison was also instrumental in popularizing the slogan before Garvey arrived, but the 'Africa for the Africans' theme did not originate with him." Hill cites Joseph Booth's *Africa for the Africans* (1897) and Edward Wilmot Blyden as earlier users and Cyril V. Briggs as a later user. See *GP*, 4:66n4. See also Shepperson, "Pan-Africanism and 'Pan-Africanism,'" 350, which points out the slogan's "much earlier beginnings" and its use by Martin R. Delany, Edward Blyden ("who, in his writings and speeches in Africa, America, and England, did so much to popularize it"), Rev. Otis T. Tiffany, and Joseph Booth. While Harrison was editor of the *Negro World*, however, the paper ran "Negroes Should Enforce the Principle of Africa for the Africans at Home and Abroad," *Negro World*, August 21, 1920, 1.

144. "Up You Mighty Race" was a familiar Garvey slogan, quoted by Claude McKay, *Harlem: Negro Metropolis* (1940; New York: Harcourt, Brace, Jovanovich, 1968), 154. It is also the title of chapter 3 of a major study of Garvey and the UNIA. See Edmund David Cronon, *Black Moses: The Story of Marcus Garvey and the Universal Negro Improvement Association* (1955; Madison: University of Wisconsin Press, 1969), 39–72. "Race First," based on the use of that phrase in a Garvey *Negro World* article, is the title of another major study of Garvey and the UNIA. See *RF*, 63n1. On Harrison's phrases, see [Editorial, title missing], *Voice*, July 4, 1917; "Liberty League of Negro-Americans: Africa First," Membership Card no. 1 issued to Hubert H. Harrison, September 2, 1917; "From Caesar Drunk to Caesar Sober," *Voice*, August 7, 1917, HP, B4, F60; [HH], "New Policies for the New Negro," *Voice*, September 4, 1917, HP, B4, F35; rpt. as HH, "The New Politics for the New Negro," in *WAA*, 39–40. In the rpt. in *WAA* Harrison changed the title of the article to "The New Politics for the New Negro" and replaced "Africa first" with "Race First" in the fifth paragraph. In his "Introductory" to *WAA* he explains that "Africa First" was used "in its racial, rather than geographical sense." *WAA*, 8. In the *WAA* version of "The New Politics for the New Negro" Harrison, for emphasis, italicizes the last paragraph: *"The new Negro race in America will not achieve political self-respect until it is in a position to organize itself as a politically independent party and follow the example of the Irish Home Rulers. This is what will happen in American politics.*—September, 1917." Also, see the *Negro World* Editorial "Race First!," which begins: "Perhaps no phrase has done more to consolidate the sentiment of the Negroes of the world than that summed up in the two words: 'Negro First.' If we remember correctly the slogan was coined by the well-known lecturer and scholar, Hubert Harrison." [W. A. Domingo], "Race First!" *Negro World*, July 26, 1919; rpt. in *Negro World*, April 10, 1920; and in *GP*, 1:469–70. Hill says unequivocally that "Hubert H. Harrison was the originator of the 'race first' concept, which he said he derived from 'the American doctrine of 'Race First.'" Hill, "Introduction," *Crusader*, 5:lxvii, esp. lviin122, which quotes 3n.

145. *GP*, 1:lxxi, lxxin116.

146. HH, "New Policies for the New Negro," *Voice*, September 4, 1917.

147. *GP*, 1:lxxii, 472–3n1. Liberty Hall was the name the Irish Transport and General Workers' Union (ITGWU) gave to their Dublin headquarters in 1912. James Connolly (1868–1916), a radical socialist, described it as "the fortress of the militant working class of Ireland." At Liberty Hall, the Irish Brotherhood decided to proceed with the Easter Rising of 1916. The UNIA's Liberty Hall was at 120 West 138th Street (the southwest corner of Lenox Avenue and 138th Street), and the property was acquired from the Metropolitan Baptist Church. Many UNIA headquarters in other communities were subsequently named Liberty Hall. See *GP*, 1:472–73n1; *Workers' Republic*, April 8, 1916; rpt. in James Connolly, *Labour and Easterweek*, ed. Desmond Ryan (Dublin: The Sign of Three Candles, 1949), 175; Catherine O'Shannon, ed., *Fifty Years of Liberty Hall: The Golden Jubilee of the Irish Transport and General Workers Union, 1909–1959* (Dublin: ITGWU, 1959).

148. William Harrison Interview with Simmons, February 23, [1951]; *Clarion* 1, no. 2 (August 15, 1917); and William Harrison, "Research Notes on Life of Hubert H. Harrison," c. 1951, HP, B8, F12. When Harrison edited the *New Negro* the slogan on the masthead read: "Unity is Strength, Liberty is Life, Liberty Is Progress, Liberty is Prosperity." See *New Negro* 3, no. 7 (August 1919): 3.

149. *GP*, 1:lxxv, lxxvn128.

150. *GP*, 1:290; [HH], "Declaration of Principles [of the Liberty League], *Clarion*, September 1, 1917; rpt. as "What It Stands For," *Voice*, September 19, 1917; rpt. as "Declaration of Principles" [of the Liberty Leagues], in *HR*, 89–90; HH, "Marcus Garvey at the Bar of United States Justice."

151. Jackson, "An Analysis of the Black Star Line," *Emancipator*, March 27, 1920, 2.

8. Post-Convention Mediations, Writings, and Reviews (September–December 1920)

1. Truman Hughes Talley, "Marcus Garvey: The Negro Moses," *World's Work*, December 1920, 165, described Harrison as "a West Indian of varied but world-wide education" writing for the *Negro World*.

2. HH, "Meditations of Mustapha as translated by Hubert H. Harrison," "The Black Man's Burden," *Negro World*, September 20, 1920, HP, B13, F7. This "The Black Man's Burden" is not to be confused with previous articles by Harrison with that name (in two parts) in *International Socialist Review* 12, no. 10 (April 1912): 660–663; rpt. in *HR*, 62–67; and in *International Socialist Review* 12, no. 11 (May 1912): 762–64; rpt. with slight changes in *NandN*, 11–20; *HR*, 67–71. See also HH, "The Black Man's Burden: Proem to Part Two, undated: broadside," HPDLC.

3. HH, "Meditations of Mustapha as translated by Hubert H. Harrison," "The Black Man's Burden."

4. See Heinrich Barth, *Travels and Discoveries in North and Central Africa, etc.*, 5 vols. (London, 1857–1858); and Basil Davidson, *African Civilization Revisited: From Antiquity to Modern Times* (Trenton, NJ: Africa World Press, 1991), 388–89.

5. HH, "Meditations of Mustapha," "The Black Man's Burden."

6. [HH], "Meditation: Heroes and Hero-Worship, and the Heroic in Human History," *Negro World*, October 16, 1920, HH, ScrWrNW, HP, B13, F7; rpt. in *HR*, 258–60, quotation on 259. The Carlyle quotation is from *Sartor Resartus*, chap. 7, "Organic Filaments." In that document "reverence" is capitalized and "clodpole" (printed here) is "clodpoll." See *Sartor Resartus: The Life and Opinions of Herr Teufelsdrockh* (1831), http://www.gutenberg.org/files/1051/1051-h/1051-h.htm.

7. [HH], "Meditation: Heroes and Hero-Worship," 259.

8. [HH], "Meditation: Heroes and Hero-Worship," 260.

9. [HH,] "Lincoln and Douglass," *Embryo of the Voice of the Negro* 1, no. 1 (February 1927): 2, HP, B17, F10.

10. HH, "The Meditations of Mustapha: A Soul in Search of Itself," *Negro World*, c. October 23, 1920; rpt. in *HR*, 260–62, quotation on 261. In a handwritten version of this article with "Delivered at the Radical Forum" (crossed out by HH), Harrison writes: "The Meditation of last week on Hero-Worship was un-signed by an oversight." Harrison closed, "Next week: 'The Souls of Black Folk' [crossed out by HH] Next week: 'Peace on Earth,'" in HP, B5, F18. For Tennyson's *In Memoriam* (XCVI), see https://archive.org/stream/inmemoriambyalfr00tennuoft/inmemoriambyalfr00tennuoft_djvu.txt. See also HH, "The Meditations of Mustapha: A Soul in Search of Itself," n.d., typescript, HP, B5, F16, HPDLC.

11. HH, "The Meditations of Mustapha: A Soul in Search of Itself," 261–62.

12. HH, "The Meditations of Mustapha: A Soul in Search of Itself," 262.

13. HH, "The Meditations of Mustapha: 'Peace on Earth,'" *Negro World*, October 30, 1920, HP, B13, F7; WEBDB, "Credo," *Independent* 57 (October 6, 1904): 787, http://credo .library.umass.edu/view/full/mums312-b227-i010.

14. HH, "The Meditations of Mustapha: 'Peace on Earth.'"

15. HH, "The Meditations of Mustapha: 'Peace on Earth.'"

16. HH, "The Meditations of Mustapha: 'Peace on Earth.'"

17. HH, "The Meditations of Mustapha: 'Peace on Earth.'"

18. WEBDB to HH, November 10, 1920, HP, B1, F44; HH to WEBDB, November 18, 1920, HP, B2, F25, HPDRC.

19. [HH], "The Ku Klux Klan," *Negro World*, November 13, 1920, HP, B13, F7. This article is distinct from HH, "Ku Klux Klan in the Past," *Negro World* (September 24, 1921), HP, B13, F7; rpt. in *HR*, 267–70.

20. [HH], "The Ku Klux Klan."

21. [HH], "The Ku Klux Klan."

22. [HH], "The Ku Klux Klan."

23. [HH; no authorship is indicated in the *Negro World*, but in his scrapbook the article is identified as Harrison's], "The Line-Up on the Color Line," *Negro World*, December 4, 1920, HP, B13, F7; rpt. in *HR*, 216–19, quotations on 216.

24. [HH], "The Line-Up on the Color Line," *HR*, 216–17.

25. [HH], "The Line-Up on the Color Line," *HR*, 217.

26. [HH], "The Line-Up on the Color Line," *HR*, 217–18.

27. [HH], "The Line-Up on the Color Line," *HR*, 218

28. [HH], "The Line-Up on the Color Line," *HR*, 218.

29. [HH], "The Line-Up on the Color Line," *HR*, 218–19.

30. [HH], "The Line-Up on the Color Line," *HR*, 218–19.

31. H.H. [HH], "The Soul of a Sycophant. *Finding a Way Out* by Robert Russa Moton," "Our Book Review," *Negro World*, September 4, 1920, HP, B13, F7; and Robert Russa Moton, *Finding a Way Out: An Autobiography* (Garden City, NY: Doubleday, Page & Co., 1920). In 1998 the Robert Russa Moton Museum in Farmville, Virginia, was designated a National Historic Landmark.

32. H.H., "The Soul of a Sycophant."

33. H.H., "The New Negro as Seen by a White Man—*The Negro Faces America* by Herbert J. Seligmann," "Our Book Review," *Negro World*, September 4, 1920, HP, B13, F7; and Herbert J. Seligmann, *The Negro Faces America* (New York: Harpers & Brothers, 1920), https://catalog.hathitrust.org/Record/000338751.

34. H.H., "The New Negro as Seen by a White Man."

35. HH, "Our Newspaper Press: *The Voice of the Negro*, by Robert Kerlin," "Our Book Review," *Negro World*, September 4, 1920, HP, B13, F7; and Robert Kerlin, *The Voice of the Negro: 1919* (New York: Dutton, 1920), https://catalog.hathitrust.org/Record /000338416.

36. H.H. [HH], "The Superscientist," review of *The Place of Science in Modern Civilization and Other Essays* by Thorstein Veblen, *Negro World*, September 11, 1920, HP, B13, F7; rpt. in *HR*, 323–25, quotations on 323. The quotes cited from this article are based on Harrison's handwritten corrections on the printed version in HP.

37. H.H. [HH], "The Superscientist," in *HR*, 324.

38. H.H. [HH], "The Superscientist," 324–25.

39. H.H. [HH], "The Superscientist," 325.

40. HH, "Books About Africa," handwritten copy for *Negro World*, December 11, 1920, HP, B4, F21.

41. HH, "Books About Africa."

42. HH, "Books About Africa"; and Frederick Starr, *Liberia: Description, History, Problems* (Chicago: Frederick Starr, 1913), https://www.gutenberg.org/files/54542/54542-h/54542-h.htm.

43. HH, "Books About Africa," *Negro World*, December 11, 1920; and Gorge W. Ellis (1875–1919), *Negro Culture in West Africa: A Social Study of the Negro Group of the Vai-Speaking People* (New York: Neale, 1914), https://archive.org/details/negroculture inwe017267mbp. Harrison gave this book to his children.

44. HH, "Books About Africa," *Negro World*, December 11, 1920; and P. Amaury Talbot (1877–1945), *In the Shadow of the Bush* (London: Heinemann, 1912).

45. HH, "Books About Africa," *Negro World*, December 11, 1920; and Daniel Crawford, *Thinking Black: 22 Years Without a Break in the Long Grass of Central Africa* (London: Morgan & Scott, Ltd. 1914), https://archive.org/details/thinkingblack22y00craw rich/page/n12.

46. HH, "Books About Africa," *Negro World*, December 11, 1920; Arthur Conan Doyle, *The Crime of the Congo (Illustrated)* (Cork: Bookbaby, 1909), https://archive.org/stream/crimeofcongo00doyliala/crimeofcongo00doyliala_djvu.txt; and Edmund Dene Morel, *The Black Man's Burden: The White Man in Africa from the Fifteenth Century to World War I* (New York: B. W. Huebsch, 1920), https://archive.org/stream/blackmansbur den00moreuoft/blackmansburden00moreuoft_djvu.txt.

47. HH, "Books About Africa," *Negro World*, December 11, 1920; and Mungo Park, *Travels in the Interior of Africa* (London, 1799; New York: Arno, 1971). An 1893 edition is available at http://www.gutenberg.org/ebooks/5266. Basil Davidson writes similarly, "Park must have a leading place in any anthology of West African memoirs for the quality of his writing, the importance of what he had to say, and the initiating stimulus of what he did." Davidson, *African Civilization Revisited*, 361.

48. [HH], "On 'Civilizing' Africa," *Negro World*, December 18, 1920, HP, B13, F7.

49. [HH], "On 'Civilizing' Africa."

50. [HH], "On 'Civilizing' Africa." See Dowd, *The Negro Races*.

51. [HH], "On 'Civilizing' Africa"; and see E. A. Wallis Budge, *Osiris and the Egyptian Resurrection* (New York: G. P. Putnam's Sons, 1911), http://www.iapsop.com/ssoc/1911__budge__osiris_and_the_egyptian_resurrection.pdf.

52. [HH], "On 'Civilizing' Africa," *Negro World*, December 18, 1920.

53. HH, "The Black Man's Burden: A Review of *The Black Man's Burden* by E. D. Morel," *Negro World*, December 11, 1920; rpt. in *HR*, 326–30, based on c. November–December 11, 1920, combined handwritten and typed manuscript (including new lead paragraph) for review of *The Black Man's Burden* in HP, B13, F7. On November 7, 1920, Harrison wrote "The Black Man's Burden: Proem to Part Two." See [HH], "The Black Man's Burden: Proem to Part Two," 5 pp., handwritten and dated, November 7, 1920, HP, B4, F15. (This article is the same as one dated September 20, 1920, which is in HP, B13, F7.)

54. HH, "The Black Man's Burden: A Review," 326–30, quotations on 326.

55. HH, "The Black Man's Burden: A Review," 326–27.

56. HH, "The Black Man's Burden: A Review," 328.

57. HH, "The Black Man's Burden: A Review," 328.

58. HH, "The Black Man's Burden: A Review," 328–29.

59. HH, "The Black Man's Burden: A Review," 329–30.

60. HH, "The Black Man's Burden: A Review," 330.

61. HH, "Canary Cottage (A Dramatic Opinion)," *Negro World*, October 30, 1920, HP, B13, F7 (also a handwritten copy in HP, B4, F30); rpt. in *HR*, 377–78, quotations in *HR*, 377.

62. HH, "Canary Cottage," 377. The *bamboula* is a "gay and spirited dance" that originated on the Guinea coast, was especially popular in eighteenth-century St. Croix, St. Thomas, and Puerto Rico, and was opposed by the Roman Catholic Church. See Florence Lewisohn, *St. Croix Under Seven Flags* (Hollywood, FL: Dukane, 1970), 136.

63. HH, "Canary Cottage," 377–78.

64. HH, "Canary Cottage," 378.

65. HH, "Canary Cottage," 378.

66. [HH,] "Last Week at Lafayette," *Negro World*, November 13, 1920, HP, B13, F7.

67. [HH], "The Darktown Follies," *Negro World*, November 13, 1920.

68. [HH], "The Darktown Follies."

69. HH, "On the Stage: 'The Darktown Follies'; A Great Hit at the Lafayette," *New York Dispatch*, November 19, 1920, HP, B13, F7.

70. HH, "On the Stage: 'The Darktown Follies.'"

71. HH, "On the Stage: 'The Darktown Follies.'"

72. Globe Credit Union, Promissory Note Globe Credit Union, n.d. c 1920? HP, B4, F16, HPDLC. Cyril Wallace may have later driven a taxi and worked out of an insurance office on 125th Street near St. Nicholas Avenue. See William Harrison Notebook.

73. Unique Operating Company, Bill for "Mr. Herbert H. Harrison . . . ," per A. B. Crichlow, November 15, 1920, HP, B1, F35.

74. Berley & Co. Inc. Real Estate Sale & Management, to Mr. Hubert Harrison, February 16, 1921, HP-Mi. Three months later, however, Harrison wrote himself a note to "Go to L. L. Hall for Mail. Write & ask agents to put gas jets in living room & to supply chandelier in front room." See "Six Lectures on Sex and Sex Problems," May 14–June 18, 1921, by Hubert H. Harrison, Instructor in Embryology, at the Cosmopolitan College of Chiropractic, 240 West 138th Street, HP, B16, F39.

75. HH, "When You Want a Book Place Your Order with Hubert H. Harrison (513 Lenox Ave.) Book-Seller to the Reading Public of Harlem . . . ," c. 1921, HP, B13, F4; HH, "Class Book. An American History for Public Schools. 2. The Art of the Short Story page 5," c. 1920, HP, B4, F34.

9. Early 1921 *Negro World* Writings and Reviews
(January–April 1921)

1. [HH,] "On Praise: (From the Arabic of Abulfeda, Prince of Humah (in Syria), 1328. (Done into modern English by Hubert H. Harrison)," *Negro World*, January 1, 1921, HP, B13, F7, HPDLC; rpt. in *HR*, 263. Indication that Harrison was the author of this piece is suggested by [HH,] "The Crab Barrel," *Negro World*, April 3, 1920; see also chapter 5, note 41, in this volume. See also A. Razaf[in]keriefo to "Dear Friend Harrison," October 22, 1917; rpt. in *The Voice*, October 31, 1917, in which Raz writes that "satire" was a trait "second nature" to Harrison. Abu'l Fida was a famous writer on history, geography, and cosmography of Kurdish ancestry from Hama (in present-day Syria). On

Garvey, see HH, "Marcus Garvey at the Bar of U.S. Justice," also published as HH, "New York Writer Analyzes Garvey Case," *Kansas City Call*, July 5, 1923; James Weldon Johnson, *Black Manhattan* (1930; New York: Atheneum, 1970), 253; *WGMC*, 2:606; Ferris, "The Spectacular Career of Marcus Garvey," *Amsterdam News*, February 11, 1925; Nathan I. Huggins, *Harlem Renaissance* (New York: Oxford University Press, 1974), 42, 44, 46; *GP*, 1:xl, l, lv–lvii, xc, lviii.

2. HH to the Editor of the *New Review*, "Southern Socialists and the Ku Klux Klan," [n.p., c. 1914—1915]; rpt. in *HR*, 76–78; see *Negro World*, January 8, 1921, HP, B13, F7, where Harrison handwrote over the article: "An Unpublished letter of 1914 or 1915." It was probably sent in 1914. For background to this letter, see *HHVHR*, 214–15, 468n43–46. In his personal copy Harrison changed "gotten" to "got." HH, "Gotten Is Rotten," *Negro World*, January 15, 1921, HP, B13, F7, explained that in his previous week's column "the man who fingered my manuscript presumed to add 'ten' to one word, thus making 'gotten' where I had written 'got.'" Harrison made clear that "ever since I began public writing I have striven to be true to the standards of correct English," and "whether 'gotten' is written by Professor William James, Professor Du Bois or Mark Twain," it was "slovenly, slipshod and incorrect," and he would "never use it—except in mockery of someone else."

3. HH to the Editor of *New Review*, "Southern Socialists and the Ku Klux Klan"; and Walter L. Fleming, *Documentary History of Reconstruction: Political, Military, Social, Religious, Educational, & Industrial 1865 to the Present Time*, vol. 1 (Cleveland, OH: Arthur H. Clark Co., 1906), https://archive.org/details/documentaryhisto01inflem.

4. HH to the Editor of *New Review*, "Southern Socialists and the Ku Klux Klan"; *HHVHR*, 183; and Theresa Malkiel, "Socialists Despise Negroes in the South," *New York Call*, August 21, 1911, 3 (which had a Memphis dateline).

5. HH to the Editor of *New Review*, "Southern Socialists and the Ku Klux Klan."

6. [HH,] "Education and the U.N.I.A.," *Negro World*, January 8, 1921, HP, B13, F7.

7. [HH,] "Education and the U.N.I.A."

8. [HH,] "'Subject' vs. 'Citizen,'" *Negro World*, January 22, 1921, HP, B13, F7.

9. [HH,] "'Subject' vs. 'Citizen.'" J. Raymond Jones described how when he arrived in the United States from the Virgin Islands ("where only the elite could vote"), around the time of World War I, "the realization that anyone in New York 21 years old or over could vote was truly an eye-opening experience." See John C. Walter, *The Harlem Fox: J. Raymond Jones and Tammany, 1920–1970* (Albany: State University of New York Press, 1989), 35.

10. HH, "The New Conscience," *Negro World*, April 2, 1921, 7.

11. HH, "The New Conscience," 7.

12. On being "the only professional Negro book reviewer in captivity," see HH, "An Englishman Visits America: *The Soul of John Brown*—by Stephen Graham," *Negro World*, February 12, 1921, 7, HP, B13, F7; and HH to Clifford Smyth, February 23, 1923, HP, B2, F4. In May 1922 Harrison wrote in an unaddressed letter to an unidentified publication: "About five years ago I began in my weekly newspaper *The Voice*, a series of weekly book reviews and literary criticisms. These were afterwards transferred to *The New Negro* and later to *The Negro World*, a weekly newspaper with a circulation of more than fifty thousand. So I inaugurated what was the first (and up to a short time ago, the only) book-review section in any negro publication." See HH to the Editor, May 1922, HP, B2, F8, HPDLC.

13. [HH,] "The Negro Soldier in France: *Two Colored Women with the American Expeditionary Forces* by Addie W. Hunton and Kathryn M. Johnson, *The Brooklyn Eagle Press*

[1920]," *Negro World*, January 29, 1921, HP, B13, F7. See also https://catalog.hathitrust
.org/Record/100676523.

14. [HH,] "The Negro Soldier in France"; and Kingsley, *Travels in West Africa, Congo
Francais, Corisco, and Cameroons*. Herodotus reportedly said: "The Carthaginians also
tell us that they trade with a race of men who live in a part of Libya beyond the Pillars of
Heracles [later known as the Straits of Gibraltar]. On reaching this country, they unload
their goods, arrange them tidily along the beach, and then, returning to their boats, raise
a smoke. Seeing the smoke, the natives come down to the beach, place on the ground a
certain quality of gold in exchange for the goods, and go off again a distance. The Carthaginians then come ashore and take a look at the gold; and if they think it represents a fair
price for their wares they collect it and go away; if, on the other hand, it seems too little,
they go back aboard and wait; and the natives come and add to the gold until they are satisfied. There is perfect honesty on both sides." From A. de Selincourt, trans., *Herodotus: The
Histories* (London: Penguin, 1954); cited in Basil Davidson, *African Civilization Revisited:
From Antiquity to Modern Times* (Trenton, NJ: Africa World Press, 1991), 66.

15. [HH,] "The Negro Soldier in France."

16. [HH,] "The Negro Soldier in France."

17. "H.H." [HH], "An Englishman Visits America"; John Graham, *The Soul of John
Brown* (New York: Macmillan, 1920), https://archive.org/details/soulofjohnbrown00grah
/page/n5.

18. "H.H.," "An Englishman Visits America." Mr. "White" may have been Walter Francis White (1893–1955) of the NAACP.

19. "H.H.," "An Englishman Visits America."

20. "H.H.," "An Englishman Visits America."

21. "H.H.," "An Englishman Visits America."

22. "H.H.," "An Englishman Visits America."

23. "H.H.," "An Englishman Visits America."

24. "H.H." [HH], "Africa as She Is: *Africa, Slave or Free?* by John H. Harris," *Negro
World*, February 19, 1921, 7, HP, B13, F7; John H. Harris, *Africa: Slave or Free?* (Student
Christian Movement, 1919; New York: E. P. Dutton, 1920; repr. New York: Negro Universities Press, a Division of Greenwood Publishing Corp., 1969), https://ia601403.us
.archive.org/30/items/africaslaveorfr00harrgoog/africaslaveorfr00harrgoog.pdf.

25. "H.H.," "Africa as She Is."

26. "H.H.," "Africa as She Is."

27. "H.H.," "Africa as She Is."

28. "H.H.," "Africa as She Is." The last quotation is said to be from Jesus's Sermon
on the Mount. See Matthew 7:5.

29. "H.H.," "Africa as She Is." In these insights Harrison's comments call to mind
the work of the Italian Marxist Antonio Gramsci (1891–1937), author of *Prison Notebooks*
(written between 1929 and 1935), who wrote on "hegemony."

30. "H.H.," "Africa as She Is." Sir Sydney Haldane Olivier wrote *The League of Nations
and Primitive Peoples* (London: Oxford University Press, 1918), *The Repartition of Africa*
(London, 1918), and *White Capital and Coloured Labour* (London: Independent Labour
Party, 1900).

31. "H.H.," "Africa as She Is"; Cornelius Howard Patton, *The Lure of Africa* (New York:
Missionary Education Movement, 1917).

32. "H.H.," "Africa as She Is." See also [HH,] "Who Built the Great Zimbabwe," n.p.,
#49, for *Negro World*, c. February 19, 1921, HP, B6, F63 (a review of a work by John H.

Harris), HPDLC; and "Black History Being Revised in Zimbabwe to Include the African Kingdom of Great Zimbabwe in the 14th Century," *New York Times*, October 17, 1982.

33. HH, "Another Negro Poet," *Negro World*, March 12, 1921, 8, HP, B13, F7; rpt. in *HR*, 391–92; Claude McKay, *Spring in New Hampshire and Other Poems* (London: Grant Richards, 1920), signed by author February 18, 1921, HP, B23, https://archive.org /stream/springinnewhamp00mckarich/springinnewhamp00mckarich_djvu.txt; and HH, "Poetry of Claude McKay," review of *Spring in New Hampshire and Other Poems* by Claude McKay, *Negro World*, May 21, 1921, HP, B5, F53; rpt. in *HR*, 393–94. On the poet Lucian B. Watkins (1879–1921), see *GP*, 13:66n5.

34. HH, "Another Negro Poet," 8.

35. "H.H.H.," "Poetry of Claude McKay," *Negro World*, May 21, 1921; rpt. in *HR*, 393–94, quotation on 393.

36. "H.H.H.," "Poetry of Claude McKay," 393; and see "If We Must Die," http://www .harlemshadows.org/if-we-must-die.html.

37. "H.H.H.," "Poetry of Claude McKay," *HR*, 393–94.

38. Claude McKay, *A Long Way from Home*, ed. Gene Andrew Jarrett (1937; New Brunswick, NJ: Rutgers University Press, 2007), 113–14.

39. Wayne F. Cooper, *The Passion of Claude McKay* (New York: Schocken, 1973), 145–47, esp. 146, cites McKay to James Ivy, May 20, 1928.

40. HD, March 19, 1921; *WGMC*, 2:616.

41. "H.H.H.," "The Real Woodrow Wilson," *Negro World*, April 9, 1921, HP, B13, F7. See also William Bayard Hale, *The Story of a Style* ["a psycho-analytic study of Woodrow Wilson"] (New York: B. W. Huebsch, 1920), https://archive.org/details/storyof style00hale.

42. "H.H.H.," "The Real Woodrow Wilson."

43. "H.H.H.," "The Real Woodrow Wilson."

44. "H.H.H.," "The Real Woodrow Wilson"; Hale, *The Story of a Style*, 6.

45. "H.H.H.," "The Real Woodrow Wilson."

46. "H.H.H.," "The Real Woodrow Wilson." See also Woodrow Wilson, Address at Memorial Hall, Columbus, Ohio, September 4, 1919, http://www.presidency.ucsb.edu /ws/index.php?pid=117361.

47. José Clarana to HH, "Woodrow Wilson and Hale," *Negro World*, April 16, 1921, 4. See also José Clarana, *Os Estados Unidos Pela Civilisacao dos Estados Unidos; Ensaios Politicos e Sociaes por José Clarana* (Rio de Janeiro: Officina Graficas do Jornal do Brasil, 1919).

48. Clarana to HH, "Woodrow Wilson and Hale."

49. Clarana to HH, "Woodrow Wilson and Hale."

50. HH, "With the Contributing Editor," *Negro World*, April 23, 1921, 5; and HH, "Addendum to the Above," *Negro World*, April 23, 1921, 5.

51. HH, "With the Contributing Editor," *Negro World*, April 30, 1921, 5. See also "A Word Regarding Titles" (not written by Harrison), *Negro World*, April 30, 1921, 2. On the Friends of Negro Freedom, see *GP*, 4:817n1, 856–58.

52. HH, "*The Mote and the Beam* [by Solomon T. Plaatje]" (a review of *The Mote and the Beam: An Epic on Sex Relationship 'Twixt White and Black in British South Africa*), 11 pages. "*Diane Tsa Seconna (Sechuana Proverbs)*," *Negro World*, April 23, 1921, 5, HP, B13, F7. The summer 1920 trip of Adelaide Casely-Hayford and her niece Kathleen Easmon to the United States was to visit schools and raise funds for a vocational school for girls. After a two-year lecture tour she returned to Africa and in 1923 opened a technical

and industrial school for girls in Freetown. See *GP*, 6:522n4; *Negro World*, August 14, 1920; and Adelaide M. Cromwell, *An African Victorian Feminist: The Life and Times of Adelaide Smith Casely Hayford, 1868–1960* (London: Frank Cass & Co., 1986), 104–35.

53. HH, *"The Mote and the Beam,"* 5; Solomon T. Plaatje, *Native Life in South Africa* (1914; fourth ed., July 1978), http://www.gutenberg.org/ebooks/1452; *GP*, 2:212–13n15, 7:271n10, 272n19.

54. HH, *"The Mote and the Beam,"* 5; and Rogers, *As Nature Leads.*

55. HH, *"The Mote and the Beam,"* 5.

56. HH, "South Africa Again: *Native Life in South Africa* by Sol Plaatje," *Negro World*, August 13, 1921, 11, HP, B13, F7.

57. On Scott Nearing (1883–1983), see Steve Sherman, "Scott Nearing," *EAL*, 512–13; Harvey Klehr, "Scott Nearing," in Bernard K. Johnpoll and Harvey Klehr, eds., *Biographical Dictionary of the American Left* (Westport, CT: Greenwood, 1986), 289–90; Scott Nearing, *The Conscience of a Radical* (Harborside, ME, 1965); and Scott Nearing, *The Making of a Radical: A Political Biography* (New York, 1972).

58. HH, "Imperialist America" (review of *The American Empire* by Scott Nearing), *Negro World*, April 30, 1921, 5, HP, B13, F7; rpt. in *HR*, 221–23, quotations on 221–22. See also HH, "'Imperialist America' *The American Empire* by Scott Nearing," typed article, n.d. [c. April 1921], HP, B5, F3, HPDLC; HD, April 6, 1921; and Scott Nearing, *The American Empire* (New York: Rand School of Social Science, 1921), http://library.umac .mo/ebooks/b28345721.pdf.

59. HH, "Imperialist America," 5; *HR*, 222.

60. HH, "Imperialist America," *HR*, 222–23; and James Oneal, *The Workers in American History* (1910; 3rd rev. ed., St. Louis, Missouri: The National Rip-Saw, 1912). The 1910 edition is available at http://webapp1.dlib.indiana.edu/inauthors/view?docId =VAC1311&brand=ia-books.

61. HH, "Imperialist America," 5; *HR*, 223; Nearing, *The American Empire*, 90–94.

62. HH, "Lincoln and Liberty—Fact Versus Fiction: Chapter One: Historical Fictions," *Negro World*, March 5, 1921, 8, HP, B13, Folder 7. See also Mary Maclean, ed., *Letters and Addresses of Abraham Lincoln* (New York: A. Wessels Company, 1907); *HHVHR*, 101–3; *HR*, 129–36; HH, "Lincoln and Liberty: Fact Versus Fiction," a lecture c. 1911; and "Negro Lecturer Attacks Lincoln" [re Harrison Lecture on Lincoln Not a Humanitarian or Friend Of Liberty, Fact Versus Fiction, Lecture for the Brooklyn Philosophical Association, at Long Island Business College], *New York Call*, February 11, 1912, both in HP, B5, F13.

63. HH, "Lincoln and Liberty," *Negro World*, March 5, 1921.

64. HH, "Lincoln and Liberty." See John Bach McMaster, *With the Fathers: Studies in the History of the United States* (1896).

65. HH, "Lincoln and Liberty," *Negro World*, March 5, 1921.

66. HH, "Lincoln and Liberty."

67. HH, "Lincoln and Liberty."

68. HH, "Lincoln and Liberty."

69. HH, "Lincoln and Liberty: Fact Versus Fiction; Chapter Two. Lincoln Not an Abolitionist, Republicans Opposed Abolitionist Doctrine," *Negro World*, March 12, 1921, 8, HP, B13, F7; rpt. in *HR*, 130–33, quotations on 130–31.

70. HH, "Lincoln and Liberty: Chapter Two," 131, which cites MacLean, ed. *Letters and Addresses of Abraham Lincoln*, 118.

71. HH, "Lincoln and Liberty: Chapter Two," 131–32, which is based on MacLean, ed., *Letters and Addresses of Abraham Lincoln.*

72. HH, "Lincoln and Liberty," *Negro World*, March 12, 1921; *HR*, 133.

73. HH, "'Lincoln and Liberty' Fact vs Fiction: Chapter Three. Lincoln and Republican Party Favor Perpetual Slavery" . . . "To Save the Union—Not to Free the Slaves," *Negro World*, March 19, 1921, 7, HP, 13, F7; rpt. in *HR*, 133–36, quotations on 133.

74. HH, "'Lincoln and Liberty': Chapter Three." Thomas Corwin (b. 1794, Kentucky; d. 1865) served as member of the U.S. House (1831–1840, 1859–1861), senator from Ohio, and chair of the Congressional Committee of Thirty-Three (1861), which sought compromise on the secession crisis. See *WNBD*, 236. In HH, "The Grand Old Party," *Negro World* (July 1920); rpt. in *WAA*, 49–53, 168–71; and *HR*, 151–54, after making his extremely important point about the desire for political control, and after citing this historical record, Harrison concludes that "the Republican party's only interest in the Negro is to get his vote for nothing" (*WAA*, 52; *HR*, 153).

75. HH, "'Lincoln and Liberty': Chapter Three," *HR*, quotations on 135.

76. HH, "'Lincoln and Liberty': Chapter Three."

77. "H.H.H." [HH], "A Crooked Deal for the Black Patriot" [chapter 4 of "Lincoln and Liberty"], *Negro World*, March 26, 1921, 7, HP, B13, F7.

78. "H.H.H." [HH], "A Crooked Deal for the Black Patriot."

79. "H.H.H." [HH], "A Crooked Deal for the Black Patriot." On André Callioux (1820–1863), see C. Peter Ripley, "André Callioux," *DANB*, 86–87.

80. "H.H.H." [HH], "A Crooked Deal for the Black Patriot"; and Abraham Lincoln to Charles D. Robinson, August 17, 1865, in *Collected Works of Abraham Lincoln*, https://quod.lib.umich.edu/l/lincoln/lincoln7/1:1100?rgn=div1;view=fulltext. The bracketed corrections are based on Lincoln's original letter.

81. "H.H.H." [HH], "A Crooked Deal for the Black Patriot."

82. "H.H.H." [HH], "A Crooked Deal for the Black Patriot."

83. Addie Sisco, "The Lincoln Articles Appreciated," *Negro World*, April 9, 1921, 7. In the *Negro World* of April 16, Harrison wrote that he had sent four papers and a letter to Sisco in Chicago but they were returned because of a bad address. See HH, "Address Wanted," *Negro World*, April 16, 1921, 4.

84. [HH,] "Jottings: Pictures at the Lafayette," *Negro World*, February 12, 1921, 7, HP, B13, F7. Around February 16, 1921, Harrison wrote some "Review Notes" in which he jotted "This is the New History: food, dress, living condition, mortality rates, etc." See HH, "Review Notes," c. February 16, 1921, HP-Mi, B12, F8–9.

85. [HH,] "Are Negro Actors White," *Negro World*, March 12, 1921, 8, HP, B13, F7; rpt. in *Crusader* 4, no. 2, whole no. 32 (April 1921): 25.

86. [HH,] "Are Negro Actors White."

87. [HH,] "Are Negro Actors White."

88. [HH,] "Are Negro Actors White"; poem by Andrea Razafkeriefo, "Two Whites at the Show," *Crusader* 1, no. 7 (March 1919): 7; rpt. in *Crusader* 4, no. 2, whole no. 32 (April 1921): 25.

89. HH, "Take Notice," *Negro World*, March 26, 1921, 7; HH, "Lost Somewhere in Harlem," *Negro World*, April 9, 1921, 7.

90. HD, April 13 and April 15, 1921. C. E. Rappollee (or Rev. Whitehead), Despatching Secretary, to Henry M. Hough, Governor, St. Thomas, Virgin Islands of the United States, "Report on activities of one D. Hamilton Jackson," February 10, 1923, General

Records of the Department of State, RG 59, 811S.00/37, Reel 18, *FSAA*, wrote that Jackson "became linked up with two or three negro socialists here" and in 1920 "he went to the States and entered Hampton Institute." According to Wilm. Jensen, Acting Judge of District Court, Virgin Islands, to Hon. J. J. Gaffney, Government Secretary, St. Thomas, "Confidential," February 10, 1923, RG 59, 811S.00/37, Reel 18, *FSAA*, "Jackson is brother-in-law to Casper Holstein, and it is said that all the poisonous articles published in the Negro World by Holstein are inspired by Jackson."

91. HH, "Know Thyself," *Negro World*, April 16, 1921, 4, HP, B13, F7; and *GP*, 2:203n4.

10. The Liberty League, Tulsa, and Mid-1921 Writings
(May–September 1921)

1. *GP*, 3:xxxiii–xxxiv. U.S. DOJ, Radical Division, Washington, DC, "Strictly Confidential: General Intelligence Bulletin," for week ending May 7, 1921, no. 49, File OG 374217, DNA, Reel 12, *FSAA*, reads: "For nearly two years his newspaper ran with a deficit and only recently has begun to pay for itself. The deficit was made from the Black Star Line and was charged up as advertisement." Then "about one year ago the printing bill was $1,000 per week, meaning a deficit of $300 per week. At that time they were printing 50,000." The distribution "has been reduced to 35,000," and, "with the reduction in the price of the paper now pays for itself with a slight margin of profit," with sales amounting "to $1000 or $1200 per week."

2. *GP*, 3:xxxiii–xxxiv; P-138, Report, June 8, 1921, DNA, RG 65, Reel 7, file BS 202600-667-49.

3. *GP*, 3:xxxiv, liv–lvii.

4. *GP*, 3:xxxv–xxxvi.

5. HD, April 7 and 13, 1921; *GP*, 2:508–9n1, 4:998n1.

6. M. K. Bunde, "Memorandum for Lt. Col. [Parker] Hitt, "Subject: Negro Activities," February 14, 1921, DNA, MID, 10218-417-1, Roll 117 encl., also in Reel 21, *FSAA*.

7. "The Program of the American Arm of the Communist International: Program of the United Communist Party," section entitled "Negro Problem," *Toiler* no. 158 (February 12, 1921): 2.

8. J. G. Tucker, Special Agent, "Special Report," May 7, 1921, Bureau File BS 202600-1628, RG 65, DNA, Reel 7, *FSAA*.

9. Claude McKay, *A Long Way from Home*, ed. Gene Andrew Jarrett (1937; New Brunswick, NJ: Rutgers University Press, 2007), 41–42, 67.

10. See *GP*, 5:741n1; M. Bird, "Robert Minor (1884–1952)," *EAL*, 475; and Robert Minor Papers, 1907–1952, NNC, RBML, http://www.columbia.edu/cu/lweb/archival/collections/ldpd_4079112/.

11. McKay, *A Long Way From Home*, 89. McKay thought the idea for the meeting with Minor came from Harrison, but Hill thinks this "improbable." He finds it "more plausible that "it was Briggs." See Hill, *Crusader*, lxiin178.

12. "P-138," Report "In Re: Negro Activities (AFRICAN BLOOD BROTHERHOOD and attempts of Communists to influence same)," July 13, 1921, Bu Sec 202600-2031-7 Roll 941 and Reel 7, *FSAA*; *ACABA*, 1:3. Boulin added in his report that neither Moore, Reid, McKay, Domingo, nor Briggs were citizens, but Grey was. See also *GP*, 3:681–82n1. Stokes's offer led U.S. MI to seek more information on Harrison, and on June 23 the Second Corps Area (New York City) of the MID filed a report that held that Grey

reportedly said that Harrison had refused money from the CP and that the ABB had taken it. This offer was reportedly made about the end of May 1921 at a meeting held in Greenwich Village. Harrison wanted an all-Negro organization. See Report of F-155, July 10, 1921, RG 65 Bu Sec 202600-2031. See also "Claude McKay with the Liberator," *Crusader* 4, no. 2, whole no. 32 (April 1921): 21; Hill, "Introduction," in Hill, ed., *The Crusader*, 1:v–lxvii, esp. xl; and *GP*, 1:525. On Boulin ("P-138"), see *GP*, 3:730n1.

13. HH, "Wanted—A Colored International," *Negro World*, May 28, 1921, HP, B13, F7; rpt. in *HR*, 223–28.

14. HH, "Wanted—A Colored International," esp. *HR*, 223–24.

15. HH, "Wanted—A Colored International," *HR*, 225.

16. On the "touchstone" quote, see HH, "The Negro and Socialism: 1: The Negro Problem Stated," *New York Call*, November 28, 1911, 6; rpt. in *HR*, 54.

17. HH, "Wanted—A Colored International," *HR*, 225.

18. HH, "Wanted—A Colored International," *HR*, 225–26.

19. HH, "Wanted—A Colored International," *HR*, 226–27.

20. HH, "Wanted—A Colored International," *HR*, 227.

21. HH, "Wanted—A Colored International," *HR*, 227.

22. HH, "Wanted—A Colored International," *HR*, 227–28.

23. "Negroes Meet Today to Seek Tulsa Redress: Hubert Harrison of Colored Liberty League Wires Oklahoma Gov. to Punish Responsible Whites," *New York Call*, June 5, 1921, 1, 2. The "Purpose of the League," rpt. from *New York Call*, June 5, in *Negro World*, June 25 1921, 6.

24. "Negroes Meet Today to Seek Tulsa Redress," 1, 2.

25. "Negroes Meet Today to Seek Tulsa Redress," 1–2.

26. "85 Whites and Negroes Die in Tulsa Riots as 3,000 Armed Men Battle in Streets," *New York Times*, June 2, 1921. On Tulsa, see Scott Ellsworth, *Death in a Promised Land: The Tulsa Race Riot of 1921* (Baton Rouge: Louisiana State University Press, 1982), esp. 61–67; R. Halliburton, "The Tulsa Race War of 1921," *Journal of Black Studies* 2, no. 3 (March 197), 333–76; "The Race War in Tulsa, Okla.," *Negro World*, July 9, 1921, 6; "Home Guards Set Fire to Buildings While Airplanes Dropped Bombs on Homes in Negro District in Tulsa," *Negro World*, June 18, 1921, 1; "Tulsa Negroes Homes Fired; 175 Die in Riot," *Chicago Daily News*, June 1, 1921, RG 59, DNA, Reel 18, *FSAA* (including nine "whites"); Sam Howe Verhovek, "75 Years Later, Tulsa Confronts Its Race Riot," *New York Times*, May 31, 1996; and "Oklahoma Clears Black in Deadly 1921 Race Riot," *New York Times*, October 26, 1996.

27. "Negroes Meet Today to Seek Tulsa Redress," 1–2, quotes 1.

28. J. G. Tucker, Special Agent, "Special Report," June 11, 1921, BF, BS 20260-1628-?, RG 65, DNA, Reel 7, *FSAA*. See also Herbert Shapiro, *White Violence and Black Response: From Reconstruction to Montgomery* (Amherst: University of Massachusetts Press, 1988), 159, which cites the *Baltimore Afro-American*, June 10, 1921.

29. MID, General Staff, Negative Branch, Washington, DC, "Confidential Weekly Situation Survey," no. 179, for week ending June 8, 1921, RG 59, File 504-69, DNA, Reel 12, *FSAA*.

30. "Bad Advice to Colored Men: To Carry Weapons Provokes Their Use," *New York Evening Journal*, June 5, 1921, HH VF SCRBC [*Negro World*, June 18, 1921, 7]; and Ellsworth, *Death in a Promised Land*, 48.

31. HH to the editor of the *New York Times*, "Negroes and Self-Defense," June 6, 1921, in *Negro World*, June 18, 1921, HP, B13, F7; "Urges Negroes to Get Arms: Liberty League

President Advises His Race to 'Defend Their Lives,'" *New York Times*, June 6, 1921. J. T. Flournoy, [BI] Special Agent, Monthly General Intelligence Report of May 15 to June 16, 1921, BF, BS 202600, RG 65, DNA, Reel 6, *FSAA*, included the June 6 article in the *New York Times* in his "Monthly General Intelligence Report," noting that the "Secretary of the Belgian Ambassador here" submitted the clipping in which "negroes in New York were urged to arm by Hubert H. Harrison."

32. HH to the editor of the *New York World*, "Negroes and Self-Defense," in *Negro World*, June 18, 1921, HP, B13, F7. The Liberty League address was listed as 513 Lenox Avenue, c/o Porro Press.

33. P-138, Report, June 8, 1921. On Harrison selling *WAA* at mass meetings in Harlem while Garvey was away, see *GP*, 4:14n3.

34. P-138, Report, June 8, 1921.

35. P-138, Report, June 8, 1921; Ernest Allen Jr., "The New Negro, 1910–1922: Explorations in Identity and Social Consciousness, 1910–1922," in *1915, the Cultural Moment: The New Politics, the New Woman, the New Psychology, the New Art, and the New Theatre in America*, ed. Adele Heller and Lois Rudnick (New Brunswick, NJ: Rutgers University Press, 1991), 48–68, esp. 67n46.

36. P-138, Report, June 11, 1921 File BS 20260-667-22A, DNA, Reel 7, *FSAA*.

37. J. G. Tucker, Special Agent, "Special Report," June 11, 1921.

38. J. E. H. [James Edgar Hoover], "Memorandum for Mr. Ruch," June 13, 1921, BF, BS 202600-2155, RG 65, DNA, Roll 941, Reel 17, *FSAA*. On Jones, see *GP*, 2:203n4, 230n3.

39. P-138, Report, June 23, 1921, File BS 202600-667-?, DNA, RG 65, Reel 7, *FSAA*; P-138, Report "In Re: Hubert H. Harrison—Negro Activities," June 22, 1921 and June 16, 1921, Bu Sec 202600-2031 Roll 941.

40. P-138, Report, June 24, 1921, File 202600-667-39, DNA, Reel 7, *FSAA*.

41. HH, "With the Contributing Editor," *Negro World*, June 18, 1921, 7.

42. HH, "With the Contributing Editor."

43. HH, "With the Contributing Editor"; followed by the two editorials, "Bad Advice to Negroes [*World*, June 6, 1921]," "Bad Advice to Colored Men [*NYEJ*, June 6, 1921]"; "Negroes and Self Defense" (first Harrison's letter to *New York Times*, June 6, 1921, then Harrison's letter to the *New York World*, June 6, 1921).

44. HH, "With the Contributing Editor," *Negro World*, June 18, 1921.

45. U.S. House of Representatives, 67th Cong., 1st sess., Hearing Before the Committee on the Judiciary Constitutionality of a Federal Antilynching Law, Statement of Hon. Merrill Moores, Member of Congress, Serial 10, Part 1, June 18, 1921 (Washington: GPO, 1921), in RG 60, 158260-145, Reel 14, *FSAA*.

46. Parker Hitt to Director, MID, Washington, DC, "SUBJECT: Negro Activities," June 23, 1921, MID 10218-424-1, Roll 7.

47. T. M. Reddy, Acting Division Superintendent, DOJ, BI, 10 Park Row, New York, to Chief, BI, DOJ, Washington, DC, "Attention: Mr. J. E. Hoover," June 26[?], 1921, 202600-667-162, DNA, Reel 7, *FSAA*, enclosure, "Special Weekly Report on Radical Activities in Greater New York for the period ending June 25, 1921," 19.

48. [Lewis J. Baley] Chief, BI, DOJ, Washington, DC, to T. M. Reddy, Esq., Acting Division Superintendent, DOJ, BI, New York, July 1, 1921, BS File 202600-2155-2, DNA, RG 65, Roll 941, *FSAA*, Reel 7. Harrison was again identified as "Herbert H. Harrison."

49. W. R. Palmera, Special Agent, BI, Report, "In Re: Hubert H. Harrison, Negro Activities," July 8, 1921, File 202600-2155-3, DNA, Roll 941, Reel 7, *FSAA*. Luther Harris Evans, *The Virgin Islands: From Naval Base to New Deal* (1945; Westport, CT:

Greenwood, 1975), 61–64, esp. 63, explains that Virgin Islanders living abroad retained Danish citizenship and did not obtain U.S. citizenship when the United States purchased the Virgin Islands.

50. W. R. Palmera, Special Agent, BI, Report, "In Re: Hubert H. Harrison, Negro Activities," July 13, 1921, File 202600-2155-5, DNA, Reel 7, *FSAA*. Though Palmera said the letter from Miller was attached, the actual copy of the letter has "No letter attached 7/16/21" handwritten and initialed on it. W. R. Palmera, Special Agent, "Report Re Hubert H. Harrison—Negro Activities," July 16, 1921, Bu Sec 202600-2155, Roll 941.

51. P-138, Report, "IN RE: NEGRO ACTIVITIES," July 11, 1921, File BS 202600-667-?, DNA, Reel 7, *FSAA*.

52. *GP*: 3:xxxiv, 5:114n6; "P-138," Report "In Re: "Negro Activities (AFRICAN BLOOD BROTHERHOOD and attempts of Communists to influence same)," July 13, 1921, Bu Sec 202600-2031-7, Roll 941; Chief to Frank I. O'Connell, Esq., July 14, 1921, Bu Sec 202600-2155; Lewis J. Baley, Chief, BI, DOJ, Washington, DC, to Frank X. O'Donnell, Esq., July 14, 1921, Bu Sec File 202600-2155-4, DNA, Roll 941 and RG 65 Reel 7, *FSAA*.

53. W. R. Palmera, Special Agent, BI, Report, "Re: HUBERT H. HARRISON, Negro Activities," July 14, 1921, File 202600-2155-6 enc., DNA, Reel 7, *FSAA*; and DNA, Roll 941.

54. P-138, Report, "IN RE: NEGRO ACTIVITIES," July 19, 1921, File BS 202600-2031-?, DNA, Reel 7, *FSAA*.

55. C. J. Scully, Acting Division Superintendent, to Lewis J. Baley, Esq., Chief, BI, DOJ, Washington, DC, "ATTENTION J. E. HOOVER, ESQ.," "Re: HUBERT H. HAR-RISON," July 16, 1921, BS File 202600-2155-6, DNA, RG 65 Reel 7, *FSAA*.

56. P-138, Report, "RE: NEGRO ACTIVITIES," July 20?, 1921, File BS 202600-667, DNA, Reel 7, *FSAA*.

57. P-138, Report, "IN RE: HUBERT H. HARRISON (NEGRO ACTIVITIES)," July 26[?], 1921, File BS 202600-2155-?, DNA, Reel 7, *FSAA*.

58. P-138, Report "In Re: Hubert H. Harrison—Negro Activities," July 25, 1921, Bu Sec 202600-2155, Roll 941; P-138, Report "In Re: Hubert H. Harrison—Negro Activities," July 28, 1921, Bu Sec 202600-2155-8, Roll 941 and Reel 7, *FSAA*. Garvey, meanwhile, was planning an August UNIA convention. See "50,000 Negro Delegates to Parade in New York," *Negro World*, July 30, 1921, 1.

59. Lewis J. Baley, Chief, BI, DOJ, Washington, DC, to Frank I. O'Donnel, B241, City Hall Station, New York City, July 25[?], 1921, DNA, RG 65 Reel 7, *FSAA*.

60. *GP*, 3:lvi, 465; and Cyril A. Crichlow, Resident Secretary, to Hon. MG, President General, UNIA, "Subject: Resignation," c. June 24, 1921, File 10216-261-74, DNA, Reel 20, *FSAA*.

61. *GP*, 3:xxxiii, 9. See also "Introduction," *GP*, 3:xxxiii–xxxvii.

62. L. B. Weeks, acting chief of staff for MI, Report to the Director, MID, September 3, 1921, "Subject: Negro Situation in New York and Jersey City, DNA RG 165, MID 10218-261-76, *GP*, 4:12–13.

63. *GP*, 3:xxxvi–xxxvii. See, for instance, the August 27 ABB handout "To New Negroes Who Really Seek Liberation: To the Delegates of the Second Negro International Convention and the Negro Race in General." The *Negro World* talked of the Bolshevist ABB being forced out of the UNIA convention in *Negro World*, September 3, 1921.

64. U.S. DOJ, Radical Division, Washington, DC, "Strictly Confidential: General Intelligence Bulletin," for week ending August 6, 1921, no. 63, File OG 374217, DNA, Reel 12, *FSAA*. An August 8 report by Agent M. J. Davis provided similar information. See

P-138, Report "In Re: Hubert H. Harrison—Negro Activities," August 8, 1921, Bu Sec 202600-2155, Roll 941; and Reel 7, *FSAA*.

65. M. J. Davis, Special Report [section Re: Hubert H. Harrison], 8, August 8, 1921, Bu Sec 202600-33, Roll 941.

66. HD, April 15, 1921; P-138, Report, August 19, 1921, File BS 202600-667-79, DNA, Reel 7, *FSAA*.

67. P-138, Report, "RE: NEGRO ACTIVITIES," August 22, 1921, File BS 202600-2155-12, DNA, Reel 7, *FSAA*; 202600-667-82, RG 65, BOI, NA; Theodore Kornwei-bel Jr., *"Seeing Red": Federal Campaigns Against Black Militancy, 1919–1925* (Bloomington: Indiana University Press, 1998), 143, 211n8.

68. P-138, Report, "RE: "H. H. HARRISON, LIBERTY LEAGUE," August 25, 1921, File Bu Sec 202600-2155, Roll 941; and DNA, Reel 7, *FSAA*.

69. P-138, Report, "RE: NEGRO ACTIVITIES," August 31, 1921, File BS 202600-667-79, DNA, Reel 7, *FSAA*. Stokes spoke before the UNIA convention on August 19, 1921. See *GP*, 3:675–81.

70. Edward J. Brennan, Acting Division Superintendent, DOJ, BI, New York, to William J. Burns, Director, BI, DOJ, Washington, DC, "Attention: Intelligence Division," August 27, 1921, Bureau File BS 202600-2155, RG 65, DNA, Reel 17, *FSAA*.

71. [HH], "Why Books?" *Negro World*, August 27, 1921, HP, B13, F7.

72. J. Edgar Hoover, "Special Assistant to the Attorney General," to William L. Hurley, Esq., of the Department of State, Washington, DC, September 2, 1921, with enclosed copy report by Frank B. Faulhaber, Special Agent, New York, "IN RE: MARCUS GARVEY," August 30, 1921, *GP*, 3:715–18.

73. See Confidential Informant 800 to George F. Ruch, September 4, 1921, DJ-FBI, 61-826, *GP*, 4:22–23.

74. L. B. Weeks, Acting Chief of Staff for MI, Report to the Director, MID, September 3, 1921, "Subject: Negro Situation in New York and Jersey City," *GP*, 4:12–13. On Harrison's mass meetings in Harlem (while Garvey was away in 1921) at which he sold *WAA*, see *GP*, 4:14n3.

75. C. B. Valentine (Cyril Briggs), "The Negro Convention," *Toiler*, October 1, 1921, 13–14.

76. *GP*, 3:xxxvi–xxxvii. C. Valentine (Briggs), "The Negro Convention," *Toiler*, October 1, 1921, 13–14, strongly criticized Garveyism.

77. HH, "The Harlem Hospital," *Negro World*, May 7, 1921, 5, HP, B13, F7.

78. HH, "The Harlem Hospital," 5.

79. "Liberty League Demands for New York City," August 1921, HP, B5, F10, HPDLC.

80. HH, "The Racial Roots of Education," *Negro World*, May 7, 1921, HP, B13, F7.

81. HH, "The Racial Roots of Education."

82. "People's Educational Forum," *New York Dispatch*, May 27, 1921, 1.

83. "H.H.H." [HH], "Stupidity and the N.A.A.C.P.," *Negro World*, May 14, 1921, HP, B13, F7 and B6, Fo33, which contains a note.

84. "H.H.H.," "Stupidity and the N.A.A.C.P."

85. HD, April 13, 1921.

86. Edwin Duke per H.H.H., "What's in a Name: An Open Letter from a White Man to the People Who Have No Home (Name)," *Negro World*, July 16, 1921.

87. HH, "As to the Name Negro," *Negro World*, August 6, 1921, 4. John E. Bruce also wrote an article on Gordon in *Negro World*, July 30, 1921, in *GP*, 3:559–60. See also Bernardo Ruiz Suarez, *The Color Question in the Two Americas*, trans. John Crosby Gordon

(New York: Hunt, 1922). The referred-to June 1919 article may have been W. A. Domingo, "What Are We, Negroes or Colored People?" *Messenger*, May–June 1919, 20–23.

88. [HH,] "An Apology," *Negro World*, August 13, 1921, 11, HP, B13, F7.

89. "H.H." [HH], "The Negro and the Census," *Negro World*, August 27, 1921, HP, B13, F7. See also *GP*, 4:1024n1.

90. "H.H.," "The Negro and the Census." For a later article, which argues that in the United States "Census Making Is, Above All, a Political Process" to support white supremacy, see Theodore W. Allen, "'Race' and 'Ethnicity': History and the 2000 Census," *Cultural Logic* 3, nos. 1–2 (Fall 1999), http://www.jeffreybperry.net/attachments /allen_race_and_ethnicity.pdf.

91. [HH,] "A Unique Negro," *Negro World*, September 3, 1921, 5, HP, B4, F66; and "Select Society for Research: Unique Plan to Trace the History of the Race," *Lexington* (Kentucky) *Standard*, October 21, 1911, 1. See also [HH,] "An Explanation," *Negro World*, September 10, 1921, HP, ScrWrNW, B13, F7.

92. [HH,] "A Unique Negro."

93. [HH,] "A Unique Negro."

94. "H.H.," "Hands Across the Sea," *Negro World*, September 10, 1921, HP, B4, F65; and *Negro World*, October 9, 1921, HP, B13, F7; rpt. in *HR*, 238–39; and HH, "Imperialist America: *The American Empire* by Scott Nearing," *Negro World*, April 30, 1921, 5; rpt. in *HR*, 221–23, quotations on 221–22.

95. "H.H.," "Hands Across the Sea," 239. See "U.S. Troops Attack Haitian Girls [ages six to twelve]," *Chicago Defender*, May 15, 1920, 1; and Hans Schmidt, *The United States Occupation of Haiti, 1915–1934* (New Brunswick, NJ: Rutgers University Press, 1971).

96. "H.H.," "Hands Across the Sea," 239.

97. HH, "Ku Klux Klan in the Past," *Negro World*, September 24, 1921, HP, B13, F7; rpt. in *HR*, 267–70, quotations on 267–68; Kenneth T. Jackson, *The Ku Klux Klan in the City, 1915–1930* (New York: Oxford University Press, 1967), 11; and *GP*, 4:715n2, 1089n2.

98. HH, "Ku Klux Klan in the Past," *HR*, 268.

99. HH, "Ku Klux Klan in the Past," *HR*, 268–69.

100. HH, "Ku Klux Klan in the Past," *HR*, 269.

101. HH, "Ku Klux Klan in the Past," *HR*, 268–69. In 1915 the KKK was revived under the leadership of William J. Simmons, the son of a leader of the original Klan founded in Pulaski, Tennessee. See *GP*, 2:230n2.

102. HH, "Ku Klux Klan in the Past," *HR*, 270.

103. HH, "Ku Klux Klan in the Past," *HR*, 270.

104. "H.H." [HH], [Review of Algernon Sidney Crapsy's *The Ways of the Gods*,] *The Freeman*, May 4, 1921 [top part missing], HP, B6, F51.

105. "H.H." [HH], "The Caucasian Canker in South Africa: The Real South Africa by Ambrose Pratt," *Negro World*, May 14, 1921, HP, B13, F7; rpt. in *HR*, 330–34, quotations on 330–31. See also Ambrose Pratt, *The Real South Africa* (Indianapolis, IN: Bobbs-Merrill, 1912), https://archive.org/details/realsouthafrica00pratiala.

106. "H.H.," "The Caucasian Canker in South Africa," 331.

107. "H.H.," "The Caucasian Canker in South Africa," 331–32.

108. "H.H.," "The Caucasian Canker in South Africa," 332–33.

109. "H.H.," "The Caucasian Canker in South Africa," 333–34.

110. "H.H.," "The Caucasian Canker in South Africa," 334.

111. HH, "First Principles," *Negro World*, July 16, 1921, 7, HP, B13, F7. See also Herbert Spencer, *First Principles* (London: Williams and Norgate, 1863), http://www.gutenberg.org/files/55046/55046-h/55046-h.htm.

112. HH, "First Principles."

113. HH, "First Principles." In his scrapbook Harrison crossed out his entire last paragraph.

114. [HH,] "Germany, England and the African," *Negro World*, July 23, 1921, HP, B13, F7; Sir Hugh Clifford, *German Colonies: A Plea for the Native Races* (London: J. Murray, 1918), https://archive.org/details/germancoloniespl00clifuoft/page/n3; Hans Georg von Doering, *Colonies and Calumnies: A Reply to Sir. H. Clifford's "German Colonies"* (Germany: Walter de Gruyter, 1919); Ajax (pseudonym), *France's Black Militarism: Sidelights on the French Colonial System: A Future Menace to World Peace* (Berlin: Dietrich Reimer, 1919); and George Bernard Shaw, *Man of Destiny* (1898), https://www.gutenberg.org/files/4024/4024-h/4024-h.htm.

115. [HH,] "Germany, England and the African."

116. [HH,] "Germany, England and the African."

117. [HH,] "Germany, England and the African."

118. [HH,] "Germany, England and the African."

119. [HH,] "Germany, England and the African."

120. "L.M.M." to the editor, "Mr. Harrison Commended," July 22, 1921, in *Negro World*, July 27, 1921, 5.

121. HH, "American Slavery Past and Present," *Negro World*, August 13, 1921, 11, HP, B13, F7. See also William A. Sinclair, *The Aftermath of Slavery: A Study of the Condition and Environment of the American Negro* (Boston: Small, Maynard & Co., 1905), https://archive.org/details/aftermathofslave00sinc/page/n7. Scylla (a rock) and Charybdis (a whirlpool), both in the Strait of Medina, off Sicily, are considered two perilous alternatives, neither of which can be avoided without encountering the other.

122. HH, "American Slavery Past and Present."

123. HH, "American Slavery Past and Present."

124. HH, "American Slavery Past and Present."

125. [HH], "Why Books?" *Negro World*, August 27, 1921, HP, B13, F7.

126. [HH], "Why Books?"

127. See Eugene O'Neill, *The Emperor Jones* (Cincinnati, OH: Steward Kidd Company, 1921), https://archive.org/details/emperorjones00onei/page/n7; and *The Emperor Jones; Diff'rent; The Straw* (1921; New York: Boni and Liveright, [1923]), HP, B24; and *WNBD*, 753.

128. Logan and Winston, *Dictionary of American Negro Biography*, 261; *GP*, 7:243–44n4.

129. HH, "The Emperor Jones," *Negro World*, June 4, 1921, 6 (also typed copy, "The Emperor Jones," by HH, which is part of a longer article that appeared in *Negro World* of June 4, 1921), HP, B4, F52; and HH, "The Emperor Jones," June 4, 1921, HPDLC; rpt. in *HR*, 378–83; William Bridges to the Editor, *Negro World*, March 26, 1921, 2; *Negro World*, February 26, 1921; *Times* (London), November 14, 1923 and September 11, 1925; and *GP*, 7:243–44n4, which cites Eugene O'Neill to Abdias do Nascimento, December 6, 1944, qtd. in Carl N. Degler, *Neither Black nor White: Slavery and Race Relations in Brazil and the United States* (New York: Macmillan, 1971), 181.

130. HH, "The Emperor Jones," 380. Robert A. Hill similarly treats it as a "psychological study." See *GP*, 7:243–44n4.

131. HH, "The Emperor Jones," 380–81.

132. HH, "The Emperor Jones," 381.

133. HH, "The Emperor Jones," 381–82.

134. HH, "The Emperor Jones," 382.

135. HH, "The Emperor Jones," 382.

136. HH, "The Emperor Jones," 382–83.

137. Eugene O'Neill to HH, June 9, 1921, HP, B3, F5. On the Black Theater and the general desire for idealized types, see Theodore Kornweibel Jr., *No Crystal Stair: Black Life and the Messenger* (Westport, CT: Greenwood, 1975); and Theodore Kornweibel Jr., "Theophilius Lewis and the Theater of the Harlem Renaissance," in *The Harlem Renaissance Remembered: Essays Edited with a Memoir by Arna Bontemps*, ed. Arna Wendell Bontemps (New York: Dodd, Mead, 1972), 171–89.

138. *Negro World*, July 30, 1921; quoted in Tony Martin, *Literary Garveyism: Garvey, Black Arts, and the Harlem Renaissance* (Dover, MA: Majority, 1983), 11–12.

139. Charles S. Johnson refers to Garvey as "the 'Emperor Jones of Finance.'" See Charles S. Johnson, "After Garvey—What?" *Opportunity* 1, no. 8 (August 1923): 231–33, esp. 231. See also O'Neill to HH, June 9, 1921. Several paragraphs that Harrison wrote were omitted from the *Negro World* article. Martin, *Literary Garveyism*, 161 (citing Johnson, *Black Manhattan*, 256), writes: "It was inevitable that someone would sooner or later compare Garvey to the buffoonish Emperor Jones. James Weldon Johnson of the NAACP obliged. As far as he was concerned, the Emperor Jones was but a modest fool compared to Garvey. Within a brief ten years, Johnson argued, 'a Black West Indian, here in the United States, in the twentieth century, had actually played an imperial role such as Eugene O'Neill never imagined in his *Emperor Jones*.'" For the view that Emperor Jones was based on W. H. Ellis, an African American from Texas whom O'Neill met in Mexico, see *Negro History Bulletin* 24 (May 1961): 183–84.

140. HH, "Marcus Garvey at the Bar of United States Justice," 2–4.

141. H. L. Mencken to HH, July 10, [1921], HP, B3, F71. In his copy of Stoddard, *The Rising Tide of Color*, on 111, after Stoddard writes "Basques are primordially *colored*!" Harrison writes "Really now! Nordic Spaniards are a bit steep, what?" On 112 he adds that "Stoddard—who hasn't been there insists that they are 'pure white' and had become steadily more Nordic! 'Oh what a tangled web we weave/When first we practice to deceive—ourselves!'" On 113 Harrison writes, "I wonder just how he would explain *Brazil* and *Argentina*. The Romans and Egyptians must have been Nordic then! Putting it plainly, once for all, on this Nordic non-sense Mr. Stoddard is a solemn ass." Then on 164 he states, "In the struggle for survival the Nordics proved the least fit."

142. H. L. Mencken to HH, July 19, [1921] and January 11, [1922], HP, B3, F71.

143. HH to Fred R. Moore, n.d., HP, B2, F12.

144. HH to Lothrop Stoddard, May 20, 1921, HP, B2, F19. See also *GP*, 2:463n3. Hill points out that Garveyites apparently read his book with interest, and many were heartened by his prediction of an end to white supremacy. See also Emory J. Tolbert, "Outpost Garveyism and the UNIA Rank and File," *Journal of Black Studies* 5, no. 3 (March 1975): 240–41.

145. HH to Lothrop Stoddard, July 1, 1921 (written June 19, 1921), 1 p., multiple pages only have 1, other page[s] missing, HP, B2, F19, HPDLC; and T. Shirby Hodge (pseudonym of Roger S. Tracy), *The White Man's Burden: A Satirical Forecast* (Boston: Gorham, 1915).

146. HH to Lothrop Stoddard, July 15, 1921, HP, B2, F19.

147. J. Williams to HH, May 8, 1921, HP, B3, F53.

148. Williams to HH, November 6, 1921.

11. *Negro World* Writings and Reviews (September 1921–April 1922)

1. "H.H.H." [HH], "Letter to the Editor," *Negro World*, October 1, 1921, HP, B13, F7.

2. HH, "'Democracy' in America," *Negro World*, October 8, 1921, 3; rpt. in *HR*, 282–86, esp. 283; and HH, "Wanted—A Colored International," *Negro World*, May 28, 1921; rpt. in *HR*, 223–28 (referenced paragraphs on 224 and chapter 8 in this volume).

3. See HH, "Introductory," in *WAA*, 5; [HH,] "Our Larger Duty," *New Negro* 3, no. 7 (August 1919), 5, HP, B3, F1–2; rpt. in *WAA*, 100–4; and *HR*, 99–101; HH, "Superior to Whom?" *BC*, May 3, 1924, HP, B6, F43; [HH,] "Two Negro Radicalisms," *New Negro* 4, no. 2 (October 1919), 4–5; rpt. in *HR*, 102–5, and rpt. with revisions and minus the second and third last paragraphs as "The Negro's Own Radicalism" in *WAA*, 76–79, quotation on 78; and Wilfred D. Samuels, *Five Afro-Caribbean Voices in American Culture, 1917–1929* (Boulder, CO: Belmont, 1977), 16.

4. HH, "'Democracy' in America," 283–84; and see this volume, chapter 9.

5. HH, "'Democracy' in America," 285–86.

6. HH, "The Negro and the Health and Tenement House Departments," *Negro World*, November 26, 1921, HP, B13, F7, which cites New York City, Department of Health, "Infant Mortality Among the Colored Population," *Weekly Bulletin*, n.s., 10, no. 45 (November 1921).

7. HH, "The Negro and the Health and Tenement House Departments."

8. HH, "The Negro and High Rents," *Negro World*, March 4, 1922, HP, B13, F7; and *GP*, 6:81n2.

9. HH, "The Theory and Practice of International Relations Among Negro-Americans," *Negro World*, October 22, 1921, 6, HP, B13, F7. Nathan I. Huggins, *Voices from the Harlem Renaissance* (New York: Oxford University Press, 1974), 6, writes: "World War I was all-important to the consciousness of the 'New Negro': The war dislodged blacks throughout the world—blacks from the various imperial systems were called to serve the war effort. They were, thus, pulled out of their various traditional contexts and introduced to a world-view that had been previously available to only a few of them. They became conscious of one another."

10. HH, "The Theory and Practice of International Relations Among Negro-Americans." Regarding "not" being inserted in the article, see HH, "The Brown Man Leads the Way," *Negro World*, October 29, 1921, 8, HP, B13, F7. Answers to the quiz are in HH, "That Questionnaire," *Negro World*, November 5, 1921, HP, B13, F7.

11. HH, "That Questionnaire," *Negro World*, November 5, 1921, 8. The Rowlatt Committee was established in 1917 "to investigate revolutionary conspiracies." The Rowlatt Bills were enacted in early 1919, and there was wide-ranging opposition to the acts, particularly after Mahatma Gandhi organized a *hartal* (or work stoppage) that became known throughout India and marked his emergence as a national leader. See Judith M. Brown, *Modern India: The Origins of Asian Democracy*, 2nd ed. (New York: Oxford University Press, 1994), 203.

12. HH, "The Washington Conference," *Negro World*, November 19, 1921, 4, HP, B13, F7; rpt. in *HR*, 229–31; *GP*, 3:633n2, 4:190n3, 227n2, 776n4; and Thomas H. Buckley,

The United States and the Washington Conference, 1921–1922 (Knoxville: University of Tennessee Press, 1970), vii, 3–19, 63–74, 76, 172, 185–90.

13. HH, "The Washington Conference," 229; *GP*, 3:633n2, 4:190n3; Buckley, *The United States and the Washington Conference*, 70–74, 185–190; William Roger Louis, *British Strategy in the Far East, 1919–1939* (Oxford: Oxford University Press, 1971), 14, 79–108.

14. HH, "The Washington Conference," 229.

15. HH, "The Washington Conference," 229–30.

16. HH, "The Washington Conference," 230. See also Buckley, *The United States and the Washington Conference*, 49–50.

17. HH, "The Washington Conference," 230–31; and "Scoffs at Arms Parley: Dutch Trade Union Head Doubts If Its Purpose Is Earnest," *New York Times*, October 20, 1921, 16. In his copy of Weale, *The Conflict of Colour*, 106, where Weale discusses Japan's role in Asia, Harrison writes: "Could white men realize that colored men read and ponder their writings such chapters as this would hardly ever be printed. But, thank Heaven, they think that they write only for each other's eyes!"

18. HH, "The Washington Conference, 230–31; and H. G. Wells, *The Salvaging of Civilization* (New York: Macmillan, 1921).

19. [HH,] "Four Live Lectures on the Question of the Hour: The Washington Peace Conference by Mr. Hubert Harrison," printed handout, c. November 27, 1921, HP-Mi, B16, F17, HPDLC.

20. [HH,] "Notes [re] Disarmament and the Darker Races: Outline of Portion of Chapter Eleven," handwritten notes, c. December 1921, HP, B4, F43. See also *GP*, 4:339n4; Immanuel C. Y. Hsü, *The Rise of Modern China* (New York: Oxford University Press, 1970), 532–33.

21. HH, "Disarmament and the Darker Races," December 4, 1921 [?]; "H.H.," "Disarmament and the Darker Races," *Negro World*, December 31, 1921, 6. See HP, B4, F43–45 and B13, F7; and "Hira Lal Ganesha" [HH], "Disarmament and the Darker Races," c. December 1921, HPDLC. See also *HR*, 232. Ganesha is a major Hindu deity also respected by many Buddhists.

22. HH, "Disarmament and the Darker Races," December 4, 1921 [?].

23. HH, "Disarmament and the Darker Races"; in *HR*, 233.

24. HH, "Disarmament and the Darker Races," *Negro World*, December 31, 1921, 6; in *HR*, 232.

25. HH, "Disarmament and the Darker Races," *HR*, 232–33.

26. HH, "Disarmament and the Darker Races," *HR*, 233; and Stephen Bonsal, "Critical Problems of the Disarmament Conference," *Current History: A Monthly Magazine of the New York Times* 15, no. 1 (October 1921): 1–10.

27. HH, "Disarmament and the Darker Races," 234.

28. HH, "The Tragedy of Motherhood: *Rachel: A Play in Three Acts* by Angelina W. Grimké—The Cornhill Company, Boston, 1920," *Negro World*, October 15, 1921, 8, HP, B13, F7.

29. HH, "The Tragedy of Motherhood."

30. HH, "The Tragedy of Motherhood."

31. HH, "Africa Here and There" [review of *Wings of Oppression*, *Night Drums*, and *African Adventure*], *Negro World*, November 12, 1921, 3, HP, B13, F7. On *An African Adventure*, see https://www.gutenberg.org/files/25569/25569-h/25569-h.htm#title.

32. HH, "Africa Here and There."

33. HH, "Africa Here and There."

34. HH, "Africa Here and There"; and Arthur Conan Doyle, *The Crime of the Congo* (New York: Doubleday, Page & Co., c. 1909).

35. HH, "The Southern Black—as Seen by the Eye of Fiction" [review of *Highly Colored*, by Octavus Roy Cohen], *Negro World*, December 10, 1921, 8, HP, B13, F7. Octavus Roy Cohen (1891–1959) wrote some 1,100 short stories, sixty books, six plays, and reams of radio material, including some for the *Amos and Andy* radio shows of 1945–1946. Among his early writings were *Polished Ebony* (1919) and *Highly Colored* (New York: Dodd, Mead & Co., 1921), https://catalog.hathitrust.org/Record/003521630. See Robert L. Gale, "Octavus Roy Cohen," *ANB*, 5:165–66; and Kellner, ed., *The Harlem Renaissance*, 75–76.

36. HH, "The Southern Black."

37. HH, "The Southern Black."

38. "H.H." [HH], "Frederick Palmer, *The Folly of Nations*," book review, *Negro World*, January 21, 1922, 7, HP, B13, F7; and Frederick Palmer, *The Folly of Nations* (New York: Dodd, Mead, 1921), https://archive.org/details/follynationspar00palmgoog/page/n8. Claudius, king of Denmark, says: "Diseases desperate grown / By desperate appliances are reliev'd, / or not at all," in *Hamlet*, 4:3, l. 9.

39. HH, "*The Story of Mankind* by Hendrik Van Loon," *Negro World*, February 18, 1922, 5; rpt. in *HR*, 362–63; and Hendrik Van Loon, *The Story of Mankind* (New York: Boni and Liveright, 1921), https://www.gutenberg.org/files/754/754-h/754-h.htm.

40. HH, "A Good Word for the Stage," *Negro World*, March 4, 1922, HP, B13, F7.

41. HH, "On a Certain Condescension in White Publishers" (part 1), *Negro World*, March 4, 1922, 7, HP, B13, F7; rpt. in *HR*, both parts 1 and 2, 293–96, quotations on 294; Tony Martin, *Literary Garveyism: Garvey, Black Arts, and the Harlem Renaissance* (Dover, MA: Majority, 1983), 91–92; and Thadious M. Davis, "Jesse Redmon Fauset," in *BWA*, 1:411–16.

42. HH, "On a Certain Condescension in White Publishers" (part 1), 294–95.

43. HH, "On a Certain Condescension in White Publishers" (part 1), 295.

44. HH, "On a Certain Condescension in White Publishers (Concluded)," *Negro World*, March 11, 1922, 7, HP, B13, F7; rpt. in *HR*, 295–96, quotations on 295; Stoddard, *The Rising Tide of Color Against White World Supremacy*; T. Lothrop Stoddard, *The New World of Islam* (New York: Charles Scribner's Sons, 1921) https://archive.org/details/newworldislam01stodgoog/page/n6; and John Graham, *The Soul of John Brown* (New York: Macmillan, 1920), 33–34.

45. HH, "On a Certain Condescension in White Publishers (Concluded)," 295–96. For his advice on book reviewing, see chapter 6 in this volume, text before note 111.

46. T. Lothrop Stoddard to HH, August 1, 1921 and October 27, 1921, HP, B2, F19.

47. HH, "The Brown Man Leads the Way: A Review of *The New World of Islam* by Lothrop Stoddard," *Negro World*, October 29, 1921, 8, and November 5, 1921, 5, HP, B13, F7; rpt. in *HR*, 310–19, quotations on 311. See also Stoddard, *The New World of Islam*; and Lothrop Stoddard, *The French Revolution in San Domingo* (Boston: Houghton Mifflin, 1914), https://archive.org/details/frenchrevolutio00stodgoog/page/n4.

48. HH, "The Brown Man Leads the Way," in *HR*, 311.

49. HH, "The Brown Man Leads the Way," 312.

50. HH, "The Brown Man Leads the Way," 312.

51. HH, "The Brown Man Leads the Way," 312–13.

52. HH, "The Brown Man Leads the Way," 313.

53. HH, "The Brown Man Leads the Way," 313–14.

54. HH, "The Brown Man Leads the Way," 314. In his last years Harrison was teaching himself Arabic and reading the Koran. See Richardson and Harrison, interview with JBP, August 4, 1983.

55. HH, "The Brown Man Leads the Way," 314–15. *Weltpolitik*, the German for "world politics," was the title of several Harrison scrapbooks.

56. HH, "The Brown Man Leads the Way," 315. On the Islamic awakening in former colonies, see also *GP*, 9:257–58n14.

57. HH, "The Brown Man Leads the Way," 316.

58. HH, "The Brown Man Leads the Way," 316.

59. HH, "The Brown Man Leads the Way," 316–17.

60. HH, "The Brown Man Leads the Way," 317. The Bahai faith is a form of Babism, started in 1863 by Hussain Ali, or Bahullah. It has a mystical quality, reflects attitudes of the Islamic Shia sect, and emphasizes tolerance and belief in the worth of all religions.

61. HH, "The Brown Man Leads the Way, (Concluding Part)," 317; and HH, "The Theory and the Practice of International Relations Among Negro-Americans," *Negro World* 11 (October 22): 6, HP, B13, F7.

62. HH, "The Brown Man Leads the Way, (Concluding Part)," 317–18.

63. HH, "The Brown Man Leads the Way, (Concluding Part)," 318.

64. HH, "The Brown Man Leads the Way, (Concluding Part)," 318–19.

65. Lothrop Stoddard to HH, November 5, 1921, HP, B2, F19.

66. Lothrop Stoddard to HH, November 5, 1921.

67. Lothrop Stoddard to HH, December 16, 1921, HP, B2, F19.

68. Lothrop Stoddard to HH, April 28, 1922, HP, B2, F19; and Lothrop Stoddard, *The Revolt Against Civilization: The Menace of the Under-Man* (New York: C. Scribner's Sons, 1922).

69. Asukile, "The Harlem Friendship of Joel Augustus Rogers (1880–1966) and Hubert Henry Harrison (1883–1927)," *African Americans in New York Life and History* 34, no. 2 (2010): 54–75.

70. J. A. Rogers to HH, n.d. [c. 1921?], multi page [only have 4], HP, B3, F24.

71. J. A. Rogers, *From "Superman" to Man* (Chicago: Goodspeed, 1917). Harrison's comments are on the dust jacket of the New York, Helga M. Rogers, 1971, rpt. ed. See also Martin, *Literary Garveyism*, 100.

72. "H.H." [HH], "White People Versus Negroes: Being the Story of A Great Book [*From 'Superman' to Man*, by J. A. Rogers]," *Negro World*, January 7, 1922, 10, HP, B13, F7; rpt. in *HR*, 301–5, quotations on 301–2. See also Ignacio Sanchez [HH], "Our Book Review" ["The Negro in History and Civilization," a Review of J. A. Rogers, *From 'Superman' to Man*], *New Negro*, October 1919, 15–16, HP, B13, F1–2; HH, "The Negro in History and Civilization: (*From 'Superman' to Man by J. A. Rogers*)," "Our Book Review by Hubert Harrison," *Negro World*, July 31, 1920, 8; rpt. in *WAA*, 135–36; and in *HR*, 301–5.

73. "H.H." [HH], "White People Versus Negroes," *HR*, 302.

74. "H.H." [HH], "White People Versus Negroes," 302–3.

75. "H.H." [HH], "White People Versus Negroes," 303.

76. "H.H." [HH], "White People Versus Negroes," 303–4.

77. "H.H." [HH], "White People Versus Negroes," 304.

78. "H.H." [HH], "White People Versus Negroes," 304. Willis Jefferson King (1886–1976) wrote *The Negro in American History* (New York: Methodist Book Concern, 1926), a copy of which is contained in HP, B23.

79. "H.H." [HH], "White People Versus Negroes," 304–5.

80. J. A. Rogers, "An Open Letter to Arthur Brisbane," *Negro World*, February 4, 1922, 6, HP, B6, F53.

81. Rogers, "An Open Letter to Arthur Brisbane." For Harding on "inescapable difference," see "Address of the President of the United States at the Celebration of the Semicentennial of the Founding of the City of Birmingham, Alabama" (Washington, DC, 1921), 7, https://archive.org/details/addressofpreside00hard. See also Gustave Spiller, ed., *Papers on Inter-Racial Problems Communicated to the First Universal Races Congress Held at the University of London July 26–29, 1911*; and Jean Finot, *Race Prejudice*, ed. Florence Wade-Evans (New York: E. Dutton, 1906), HP, B22.

82. HH, ["Harrison Replies,"] *Negro World*, February 11, 1922, 5.

83. HH, ["Harrison Replies"], 5.

84. HH, "West Indian News Notes to Be Resumed," *Negro World*, February 4, 1922, 6, HP, B6, F53; HH, "West Indian News Notes," *Negro World*, March 25, 1922, 12.

85. HH, "West Indian News Notes to Be Resumed."

86. *Negro World*, April 1, 1922, 4.

87. "Frances Dearborn" [HH], "The Black Tide Turns in Politics," HP, B8, F6; and *HR*, 158.

88. "Frances Dearborn" [HH], "The Black Tide Turns in Politics," *HR*, 158.

89. "Frances Dearborn" [HH], "The Black Tide Turns in Politics," *HR*, 158–59.

90. "Frances Dearborn" [HH], "The Black Tide Turns in Politics," *HR*, 159.

91. "Frances Dearborn" [HH], "The Black Tide Turns in Politics," *HR*, 159–60.

92. "Frances Dearborn" [HH], "The Black Tide Turns in Politics," *HR*, 160.

93. "Frances Dearborn" [HH], "The Black Tide Turns in Politics," *HR*, 161.

94. "Frances Dearborn" [HH], "The Black Tide Turns in Politics," *HR*.

95. HH, "Aphorisms and Reflections," begun December 20, 1921, HD, HP, B9, F1; Edward Gibbon, *The Memoirs of The Life of Edward Gibbon* (London: Methuen, 1900), 97–98, 122. A footnote refers to *A New Method of Making Common-Place Books Written by the Late Learned Mr. John Lock[e]*, translated from the French (London, 1706). To support his view, Harrison referred to Samuel Johnson in *The Idler* 74 and to the Scottish lawyer and biographer James Boswell's *Johnson*.

96. HH, "Aphorisms and Reflections," begun December 20, 1921, HD. Joseph De Veuster (1840–1889), "Father Damien," served on the leper colony Molokai I, where he contracted leprosy in 1884 and refused a cure because he wanted to remain on the island.

12. The Period of Garvey's Arrest (October 1921–March 1922)

1. *GP*, 4:xxxi.

2. Harrison appeared as "Contributing Editor" of the *Negro World* on the masthead from c. January 1, 1921, to c. September 9, 1922, though Hill lists him as contributing editor until c. March 25, 1922. See *GP*, 7:972.

3. Edward J. Brennan to William Burns, director, BI, September 1, 1921, *GP*, 4:1, includes Madarikan Deniyi, "African Redemption Fund Is Fraud Negroes in America Are Warned to Beware of Fakers," September 1, 1921 *GP*, 4:1–2. On Deniyi, see *GP*, 9:143, 12:108–9n1; and HH, "The Prince of Cheese, undated: autograph manuscript notes," HP, 5, F57, HPDLC.

4. *GP*, 4:xxxi–xxxii; and *New York Times*, October 27, 1921. See "Race, and the Rights of Man," *Freeman* 4, no. 80 (September 21, 1921): 29–30, HP-Scr. D; HH, "Our White Friends," *Negro World*, July 3, 1920, 2; rpt. in *WAA*, 61–63, quotation on 63, where Harrison uses the phrase "the white men who desire to be 'Our Professional Friends,'" not "Our Professional White Friends"; and HH, "A Tender Point," *WAA*, 63–66, quotation on 65.

5. See *Negro World*, November 5, 1921, *GP*, 4:141–51, quotations on 142, 145; Richard B. Sherman, *The Republican Party and Black America from McKinley to Hoover, 1896–1933* (Charlottesville: University of Virginia Press, 1973), 148–49; and "Address of the President of the United States at the Celebration of the Semicentennial of the Founding of the City of Birmingham, Alabama" (Washington, DC, 1921), 9, https://archive.org/details/addressofpreside00hard.

6. On the meeting with the Klan, see Marcus Garvey to chairman, Liberty Hall, Cable, June 25, 1922, in *Negro World*, July 1, 1922, *GP*, 4:679.

7. In 1921 the Communist Party was illegal (and functioned underground), and the Workers Party was established as its legal "front" (and functioned publicly). Both parties continued in existence until April 11, 1923, when the CP sent a letter to the WP reading in part: "The Communist Party of America at its Third National Convention, held in New York City on April 7 . . . went on record unanimously as recognizing the fact that the Workers Party of America, of which members of the Communist party of America were a component part, has developed into a Communist Party." It continued, "The Convention therefore, decided by unanimous vote to dissolve the Communist Party of America, leaving the Workers Party of America, which is already fraternally affiliated with the Communist International as the only organization carrying on the struggle for Communist principles in the United States. The Workers Party of America is authorized, when it deems it desirable, to adopt the name 'Communist Party of America.'" Robert J. Alexander, "Splinter Groups in American Radical Politics," *Social Research* 20, no. 3 (Autumn 1953): 294; from *International Press Correspondence*, May 30, 1923.

8. Briggs claimed to have joined the CP "before the Palmer raids" (November 7, 1919, and January 2, 1920). See Hill, ed., *Crusader*, I:xxiv; and Cyril Briggs to Theodor Draper, March 17, 1958, Hoover Institution Archives, Stanford University, Stanford, CA, B31, http://www.marxisthistory.org/history/usa/groups/abb/1958/0317-briggs-todraper.pdf.

9. The Communist Party's October 1, 1921, *Toiler*, under its new manager "A. B. Martin" (future party head Jay Lovestone), carried C. B. Valentine (Briggs), "The Negro Convention," *Toiler*, October 1, 1921, 13–14, which explained that the ABB criticized Garveyism, which was described as "a shrewd mixture of racialism, religion and nationalistic fanaticism . . . [with] roots in the past oppression of the negro. . . . Garveyism looks at every white face as 'per se' an enemy. Herein lies one of the chief reasons for the bitter opposition it has met from the class-conscious negro worker."

10. "Speech by Marcus Garvey" (September 4, 1921), *Negro World*, September 10, 1921, *GP*, 4:23–27.

11. *GP*, 4:xvi, xvii, xxxii, 9:317n1. In early 1922 the BSL disbanded.

12. "Some Escrow!" *Crusader* 5, no. 2 (October 1921): 29.

13. "Mr. Garvey's Place Is in the United States" and "The U.N.I.A. Financial Reports," both in *Crusader* 5, no. 2 (October 1921): 11.

14. W. A. Domingo, "Figures Never Lie, BUT Liars Do Figure," *Crusader* 5, no. 2, whole no. 36 (October 1921): 13–14, *GP*, 4:153–55; and, from the same issue, see

"Garvey Shows His Hand," 23–24; and "Briggs Says Garvey Lies," 25. See also "Black Star Line Has No Ships," *Savannah Tribune*, November 2, 1922, from Crusader News Service, October 30, 1922, *GP*, 5:115–16.

15. MG, "Notice: To All Divisions and Members of the Universal Negro Improvement Association," *Negro World*, October 15, 1921, 5; *GP*, 4:566; *RF*, 131, 148n167, citing *Amsterdam News*, September 10, 1924; *GP*, 2:203n4, 230n3.

16. "800" to George F. Ruch, October 18, 1921, *GP*, 4:125; Cyril V. Briggs to MG, August 15, 1921, rpt. as "Garvey Turns Informer," *Crusader* 5, no. 3 (November 1921): 1, *GP*, 3:667–68. On Garvey presenting the letter to Justice Renaud, see *GP*, 3:668n1. The Briggs letter invited Garvey "to a conference on those major questions in the work for African liberation in which both yourself and I, and our respective organizations are intensely interested."

17. ("Statement of District Attorney Edward Swann"), "The People of New York v. Marcus Garvey," October 26, 1921, NYHR, docket 8315, City Magistrates' Court of the City of New York, Twelfth District, *GP*, 4:135–36.

18. *Amsterdam News*, October 26, 1921, *GP*, 4:137–38.

19. "800" to George F. Ruch, October 25, 1921, *GP*, 4:130–31. On Ruch's friendship with Hoover see Athan G. Theoharis and John Stuart Cox, *The Boss: J. Edgar Hoover and the Great American Inquisition* (Philadelphia, 1988), 97; and Theodore Kornweibel Jr., *"Seeing Red": Federal Campaigns Against Black Militancy, 1919–1925* (Bloomington: Indiana University Press, 1998), 103. Burns served as chief of the BI (1921–1924) and had a reputation as a strong anticommunist. See Graham Adams Jr., "William John Burns," *ANB*, 4:27–28; *WNBD*, 154, 360; *GP*, 3:729n1, 9:162n1; and Kornweibel, *"Seeing Red,"* 5.

20. *Colored Eagle*, October 1921; and Edmund D. Cronon, *Black Moses: The Story of Marcus Garvey and the Universal Negro Improvement Association* (Madison: University of Wisconsin Press, 1955), 96–97.

21. *RF*, 241; Bishop McGuire, "Why I Left the U.N.I.A." and "Why I Joined the A.B.B.," *Crusader* 5, no. 4, whole no. 40 (December 1921): 1. On Gordon, the former UNIA national leader from Los Angeles, see *GP*, 2:562n1, 4:195, 9:305n12. Gordon and McGuire later rejoined the UNIA.

22. George F. Ruch to J. Edgar Hoover, November 5, 1921, *GP*, 4:163.

23. "Extra! 'S. S. Phyllis Wheatley' a Garvey Myth, 'To Take in Negroes, No Doubt,'" *Crusader* 5, no. 3, whole no. 39 (November 1921): 1, 25; and C. Valentine (Briggs), "Garvey Turns Informer," *Crusader* 5, no. 3 (November 1921): 8, *GP*, 4:229–30.

24. Ruch to Hoover, November 5, 1921.

25. W. W. Grimes to J. Edgar Hoover, "Memorandum," November 5, 1921, *GP*, 4:164.

26. Mortimer J. Davis, Report, November 18, 1921; and *GP*, 4:197–98.

27. Davis, Report, November 18, 1921; and "800" (Jones) to George F. Ruch, November 16, 1921, *GP*, 4:191–92. Davis also reported that there was "nothing" in the BI files "indicating that the Black Star Line has ever owned such a ship as the 'Phyllis Wheatley.'" There were, however, "many statements made by the officials of the Line, and in the 'Negro World' which would lead to the belief that they did not own a ship by that name." Advertisements had even appeared in the paper "offering to take freight and passengers on the 'Phyllis Wheatley' to Africa." Jones told Ruch that Garvey would have "more to rave about," since he had put Briggs in touch with Crichlow, who was planning to write articles "exposing Garvey and his whole scheme in Liberia." Jones did this "anonymously," by writing to Briggs that he could get all the dope on Garvey's African scheme from Crichlow. Briggs then made arrangements with Crichlow for the articles.

28. *Amsterdam News*, November 16, 1921, in *GP*, 4:191.

29. J. Edgar Hoover to George F. Ruch, November 17, 1921, *GP*, 4:196. See also *GP*, 3:721n1. Matthews added that Special Agent Edward Anderson, of the New York office, had spoken with someone (possibly Edgar Grey) in New York who claimed "the government was in possession of information that a bribe of $5,000 had been passed in connection with the obtaining of Garvey's visa."

30. "800" to George F. Ruch, November 25, 1921, *GP*, 4:217–18. Jones reported to Ruch on November 18 on Garvey's suit, on a Crichlow suit against Garvey scheduled for November 21, and on the fact that Crichlow told him he had forwarded his report to the State Department. Crichlow sought $1,237 in back pay and reimbursement of expenses from his return trip from Africa. On January 26, 1922, a New York court awarded him $700, but not the full amount, because illness had prevented him from performing all his duties. "800" to George F. Ruch, November 18, 1921, *GP*, 4:200–1; see also 4:lii, 9:225n1.

31. "800" to Ruch, November 25, 1921. Jones offered the opinion that if Garvey was "closely watched" on his next trip, "he could be gotten for violation of the Mann Act."

32. "800" to George F. Ruch, November 26, 1921, *GP*, 4:219–20.

33. "Case of Briggs vs. Garvey . . . ," *Negro World*, December 3, 1921, 3; rpt. in *Crusader* 6, no. 1 (January–February 1922): 1; and in *GP*, 4:231.

34. "Garvey Arrests Brooks, Charging Theft of Black Star Line Funds, and Cyril Briggs for Criminal Libel," *New York News*, December 3, 1921, *GP*, 4:231.

35. William J. Burns to Rush D. Simmons, Chief Inspector, POD, December 7, 1921, *GP*, 4:231.

36. Mortimer J. Davis, Report, December 8, 1921, *GP*, 4:197–98.

37. "800" to Mr. Geo(rge) F. Ruch, December 14, 1921, *GP*, 4:271–73.

38. "800" to Mr. Geo(rge) F. Ruch, December 14, 1921, *GP*, 4:271–73.

39. Agent "800" to Mr. Geo[rge] F. Ruch, December 16, 1921. On Garcia's August 1920 report on conditions in Liberia, see *Philosophy and Opinions of Marcus Garvey*, 2 vols., ed. Amy Jacques-Garvey, intro. Hollis R. Lynch (1925; New York: Atheneum, 1971), 2:399–405; and see *RF*, 123, 131 (on the 1924 publishing of Garcia's secret report), and 148nn167–68, where part of its history is discussed, including its eventual publication in the *Amsterdam News*, September 10, 1924. On Crichlow's report, see Cyril A. Crichlow, UNIA resident secretary, to Marcus Garvey, June 24, 1921, *GP*, 9:11–39; Cyril A. Crichlow, "What I Know About Liberia [Part I]," *Crusader* 5, no. 4, whole no. 40 (December 1921): 20–23; and "What I Know About Liberia [Part II]," *Crusader* 6, no. 1, whole no. 42 (January–February 1922): 18–23; and reference to his report of April 12, 1920, in *GP*, 9:16, 287–92. (That was the last issue of *The Crusader*.) See also, in the *Crusader* of January–February 1922, Cyril A. Crichlow, "A Simple Statement in Three Parts: Including Some Most Illuminative Documents as to Garvey's Intrigues Against Liberia, and Liberian Opposition to Garveyism," 23–26; "Marcus Garvey Arrested," 5; "Crusader Warned Its Readers Against Marcus Garvey," 5; and "The Workers Party, Marcus Garvey and the Negro," 15–16; and see also *GP*, 9:292–304.

40. "800" to Ruch, December 16, 1921.

41. "800" to Mr. Geo[rge] F. Ruch, December 19, 1921, *GP*, 4:298–99; "African Blood Brotherhood Meeting Breaks Up in Disorder," UNIA publicity circular, enclosed with Confidential Informant "800" to George F. Ruch, December 19, 1921, *GP*, 4:299–301; "African Blood Brotherhood Meeting Breaks Up in Disorder," *Negro World*, December 24, 1921, 3.

42. Mortimer J. Davis, Report, December 21, 1921, *GP*, 4:306–7.

43. Davis, Report, December 21, 1921, *GP*, 4:306–7.

44. "800" to Mr. Geo[rge] F. Ruch, December 24, 1921, *GP*, 4:307.

45. "800" to Mr. Geo F. Ruch, January 7, 1921 [1922], *GP*, 4:330–32. Thomas may have been James C. Thomas Jr. (1889–1958), a young attorney who spoke at the June 12, 1917, founding meeting of the Liberty League and was an assistant U.S. DA for the Southern District of New York (1921–1926). See *GP*, 1:10; and *HHVHR*, 285.

46. "800," to Ruch, January 7, 1921 [1922].

47. "800" to Mortimer J. Davis, Report, January 14, 1922, *GP*, 4:355–62, esp. 355–56.

48. "Complaint Against Marcus Garvey," United States of America vs. Marcus Garvey Complaint: Violation 215 U.S.C.C., Southern District of New York, January 12, 1922, *GP*, 4:340–42. See also "In African Ship Line Activities: 'Provisional President' of Dark Continent Charged with Fraud in Sale of 'Ghost' Steamer Tickets," *New York Tribune*, January 13, 1922; "3,000 Negroes Yell Loyalty to Garvey," *New York Herald*, January 14, 1922; "Garvey, Financier and 'Sir President of Africa,' Is Held: Harlem's Wizard of Black Star Line and Colonization Scheme Is Given $2,500 Bail," *New York World*, January 13, 1922, 1, 6, a portion of which is rpt. in *GP*, 4:352–53; *New York World*, January 13, 1922; "Negro 'Napoleon' Counts on a Loyal Million to Aid Him," *New York World*, January 14, 1922; "Africa's 'President' Held on U.S. Charge," *New York Herald*, c. January 15, 1922, all in FOIPA-HHH.

49. Edward W. Knappman, ed., *Great American Trials* (Detroit: Gale Research, 1994), 304; *RF*, 191.

50. *RF*, 192.

51. Oliver B. Williamson, to Rush D. Simmons, January 18, 1922, *GP*, 4:361; "In African Ship Line Activities," *New York Tribune*, January 13, 1922; "Complaint Against Marcus Garvey," *GP*, 4:340–42. See also *GP*, 4:xxxii, 9:317n1.

52. "Garvey, Financier and 'Sir President' of Africa Is Held," *New York World*, January 13, 1922, 1, 6. A complete copy of this article is found in James K. Hall, Chief, FOIAPA Section, Records Management Division, to JBP, September 10, 1984, in response to an FOIPA request concerning HHH from 1905–1933, in possession of JBP. In "800" to George F. Ruch, January 22, 1922, *GP*, 4: 443–44, on 443, reference is made to Harrison possibly writing articles for the *New York World* on Garvey under the name "Spewak." Samuel Spewack (1899–1971) was born in the Ukraine, immigrated to New York, and began work for the *New York World* c. 1918–1919. See Dorothy L. Swerdlove, "Samuel Spewack and Bella Spewack," *ANB*, 20:468–70; *GP*, 4:442n4, 443; *New York Times*, October 15, 1971. Reference is made to Harrison providing "Spewak" materials in "Report made by Mortimer J. Davis, for period 1/18/22, made on 1/21/22," in *GP*, 4:439–41. Other articles on the arrest include "3,000 Negroes Yell Loyalty to Garvey," *New York Herald*, January 14, 1922; "Garvey Acclaimed as 'Prince of Men' by 1,000 Backers: 'Provisional President of Africa' Wildly Cheered During Address Denying Accusations; New Negro Knows the Use of Machine Gun, He Says; Blue-Clad, Sword Clanking Militia Parade Aisles Under Red, Green and Black Flag," *New York World*, January 14, 1922, in *GP*, 4:353–54; "Africa's President Held on U.S. Charge: Garvey, Black Star Line Promoter, Accused of Misuse of Mails," *New York Herald*, c. January 14, 1922.

53. "Garvey, Financier and 'Sir President' of Africa Is Held," *New York World*, January 13, 1922, 1, 6. No mention was made of the Yarmouth, the maiden ship of the line, which was laid up. BSL advertisements claimed to offer "A line of steamships to run between America, Africa, the West Indies, Canada, South and Central America,

carrying freight and passengers"; that "untold possibilities for the race" would be opened; and that its stock, which sold for $5 a share, was "sold only to Negroes." Garvey emphasized that the BSL "presents to every black man, woman and child the opportunity to climb the great ladder of industrial and commercial progress" and encouraged "Every colored man, woman and child should buy stocks in this corporation."

54. "Negro 'Napoleon' Counts on a Loyal Million to Aid Him," *New York World*, January 14, 1922, in JBP's FOIA/PA request on "Hubert Henry Harrison" (#235,055). This article may have been written or significantly influenced by Harrison. See also "Garvey Acclaimed as 'Prince of Men' by 1,000 Backers," *New York World*, January 14, 1922, *GP*, 4:353–54.

55. "Negro 'Napoleon' Counts on a Loyal Million to Aid Him"; "Garvey Acclaimed as 'Prince of Men' by 1,000 Backers." The report made by Mortimer J. Davis on January 21, 1922, in *GP*, 4:439–41, indicates that the interviewer that Garvey spoke to was "Spewak" and (on 441) that a "series of book your passage ads were now in the hands of Mr. Spewak of the New York World."

56. HH to J. O. H. Cosgrave, editor of the *Sunday World*, November 13, 1921, HP, B2, F16, HPDLC. See also "800" to George F. Ruch, January 22, 1922, *GP*, 4:443–44, esp. 443. Herbert J. Seligman, "Negro Conquest: Marcus Garvey, . . . Is Inflaming the Heart of the Oppressed Black Man," *World Magazine*, December 4, 1921, *GP*, 4:239–44, on 242, refers to Garvey's financial claims published in the *Negro World* of August 13, 1921, including an "extraordinary item" of $46,555.20 spent on "purchasing the 'good will' of the weekly newspaper, the *Negro World*." This article may have drawn on materials that Harrison left with the *Sunday World* editor Cosgrave on November 13, 1921.

57. "Report made by Mortimer J. Davis, January 18, 1922, New York City, in re: Black Star Line, Inc., Marcus Garvey, et al., Vio. Sec. 215, U.S.C.C., Using the Mails to Defraud," 1, *GP*, 4:382. Frederick Augustus Toote (1895–1951?) served as president of the Philadelphia branch of the UNIA and was on the Board of Directors of the BSL. See Robert A. Hill, ed., and Barbara Bair, associate ed., *Marcus Garvey: Life & Lessons; A Centennial Companion to the Marcus Garvey and Universal Negro Improvement Papers* (Berkeley: University of California Press, 1987), 432–43; *GP*, 2:371n9.

58. Statement of Capt. J. W. Jones, January 13, 192[2], *GP*, 4:410–15.

59. Statement of Jones, January 13, 192[2],

60. "Statement of Elie Garcia," January 13, 192[2], enclosure with Mortimer J. Davis, Report, January 18, 1922, 1921, *GP*, 4:390–404, quotation on 400.

61. "Statement of Orlando M. Thompson," January 13, 192[2], enclosure with Mortimer J. Davis, Report, January 18, 1922, *GP*, 4:382–89, quotations on 387.

62. "Statement of James D. Brooks," January 13, 192[2], enclosure with Davis, Report, January 18, 1922, *GP*, 4:382–89, 405, quotation on 407.

63. Mortimer J. Davis, Report, January 14, 1922, *GP*, 4:355–62, esp. 355–56. Hill writes, "Briggs probably joined the Workers party as early as May 1921." See *GP*, 1:525.

64. Agent "800" to Mr. Geo F. Ruch, January 17, 1922; Kornweibel, *"Seeing Red,"* 122–23; Witold S. Sworakowski, "The Communist International," in *World Communism, a Handbook: 1918–1965*, ed. Witold Sworakowski (Stanford, CA: Hoover Institution Press, 1973), 78–92, esp. 80. Davis described the amended Thompson testimony as a "matter of self-protection." See "Report by Special Agent Mortimer J. Davis: U.S. vs. Black Star Line, Inc., Vio. Sec. 215, U.S.C.C. (Using Mails to Defraud)," March 8, 1922, *GP*, 4:541.

65. "Statement of Hubert Harrison 'In re: U.S. vs. Black Star Line, Inc.,'" Post Office Building, New York, January 16, 1922, stenographic minutes by M. J. Davis. Interview

conducted by Mr. O. B. Williamson (Postal Inspector). Marcus Garvey: FBI Investigation File, Microfilm rpt., Scholarly Resources Inc., Wilmington, DE, in *GP*, 4:424–27, quotations on 424. Harrison indicated that he lived at 570 Lenox Avenue.

66. "Statement of Hubert Harrison, 'In re: U.S. vs. Black Star Line, Inc.,'" *GP*, 4:424–25.

67. "Statement of Hubert Harrison, 'In re: U.S. vs. Black Star Line, Inc.,'" 4:425.

68. "Statement of Hubert Harrison, 'In re: U.S. vs. Black Star Line, Inc.,'" 4:425.

69. "Statement of Hubert Harrison, 'In re: U.S. vs. Black Star Line, Inc.,'" 4:425–26.

70. "Statement of Hubert Harrison, 'In re: U.S. vs. Black Star Line, Inc.,'" 4:426.

71. "Statement of Hubert Harrison, 'In re: U.S. vs. Black Star Line, Inc.,'" 426. Copies of the photograph and circular are in *GP*, 9:323. The BSL first promised a ship for the African trade on November 1, 1919, and Garvey set various dates for its sailing before settling on February 28, 1920. Instead of such a ship, the *Kenawha* (Kanawha) and the *"Shady Side"* were bought, though the BSL was in no shape to make either purchase and by the summer of 1920 had a deficit of over $250,000 and rising operating losses. Nevertheless, Garvey promised dividends at the end of the financial year, and over $100,000 worth of stock was sold from July to December 1920. Garvey's so-called fourth boat, supposedly for the African trade, was the phantom *Phyllis Wheatley*, and throughout 1920 and 1921 he promised it would sail. On October 16 he set the date as January 1921, and on February 17, 1921, a doctored photograph of the alleged *Phyllis Wheatley* appeared in the *Negro World*. Garvey never actually took a step to get the ship, and only after he left for the West Indies in February 1921 did a vice president of the BSL make a frantic, belated, and unsuccessful effort to arrange a purchase. Sailings were advertised and passengers and freight booked on the various BSL ships, and passages continued to be sold even after Garvey's return in July 1921. See Brief for the United States, Marcus Garvey v. United States, U.S. Circuit Court of Appeals, Second Circuit, December 10, 1924, *GP*, 6:49–66.

72. "Statement of Hubert Harrison, 'In re: U.S. vs. Black Star Line, Inc.,'" *GP*, 4:426.

73. "Statement of Hubert Harrison, 'In re: U.S. vs. Black Star Line, Inc.,'" *GP*, 4:426.

74. "Report made by Mortimer J. Davis, for period 1/18/22, made on 1/21/22, New York City, In re: Black Star Line, Inc., Marcus Garvey, et al.," 1, in *GP*, 4:439–42, esp. 439. A copy of this report was "furnished to P.O. Inspector Williamson for his information." On Crichlow's report, see note 40 in this chapter. On Crichlow's suit against Garvey, see "800" to George F. Ruch, November 18, 1921, *GP*, 4:200–1.

75. "Report made by Mortimer J. Davis, for period 1/18/22," *GP*, 4:439–40.

76. Harrison's memoranda were included in "Report made by Mortimer J. Davis, for period 1/18/22," *GP*, 4:440–41.

77. Harrison's memoranda, *GP*, 4:440.

78. Harrison's memoranda included in "Report made by Mortimer J. Davis, for period 1/18/22," *GP*, 4:440.

79. Harrison's memoranda, *GP*, 4:440–41. "Summary Report of the Books and Records of the Black Star Line and UNIA by Thomas P. Merrilees, Expert Bank Accountant," October 27, 1922, *GP*, 5:58–114, writes (on 112) that the UNIA Executive Council on July 20, 1921, decided "that the New York local turn over to the Parent Body all monies due her for Construction Loan, that the Parent Body in turn buy out the interest in the 'Negro World' held by the New York Local." Offsetting entries were then made in Cash Received and Cash Disbursed books on July 27, though "the Parent Body did not deposit the check to their credit or issue another of like amount." Then in their Statement of

Assets four days later they said their net worth was $82,390.13, which included $60,000 from "the good will of the Negro [W]orld." Thus, their net worth was increased $60,000 by *Negro World* "good will," and that "good will" itself had "an appreciation of $13,444.80 in four days ownership."

80. "Report made by Mortimer J. Davis for period 1/18/22," 2–3, HH memoranda, *GP*, 4:441. A copy of this report was "furnished to P.O. Inspector Williamson for his information." See *GP*, 1:456n1, 3:xxxiv, 4:xxxi, 9:327n8. On March 28, 1921, Agent James E. Amos reported that Bishop George McGuire, the former UNIA chaplain general, told him he had bought $1,000 in stock in the BSL and that he "was forced to buy stock as all officials of the company were—money for same being taken from his salary each month." See *GP*, 4:622n3.

81. Harrison memoranda, *GP*, 4:441; and see Elie Garcia, UNIA Commissioner to Liberia, to MG and the UNIA, August 1920 [part 1, June 27, 1920], *GP*, 2:660–72, esp. 671.

82. "Report made by Mortimer J. Davis, for period 1/18/22," *GP*, 4:441. "Negro 'Napoleon' Counts on a Loyal Million to Aid Him," *New York World*, January 14, 1922; "Garvey Acclaimed as 'Prince of Men' by 1,000 Backers," *New York World*, January 15, 1922, *GP*, 4:353–54. The "UNIA Auditor General's Report," *Negro World*, August 20, 1921, *GP*, 3:620–27, esp. 621–22, discusses what Harrison said.

83. The "Paris" family became prominent in Harlem's Black Jewish community, then moved to Ethiopia in 1930, and, after Arnold Ford's death in 1935, Eudora Paris assumed the leadership of the Afro-American immigrant community in Ethiopia. See *GP*, 4:441–2n3; William R. Scott, "A Study of Afro-American and Ethiopian Relations, 1896–1941," PhD diss., Princeton University, 1971, 121–33; Andrew M. Battle, Special Employee, Report, April 27, 1923, for period of April 20 to 27, 1923, "Re: Negro Radical Activities," *GP*, 5:29–31. On Harrison's "Parris" relatives, see *HHVHR*, 37. It should also be noted that a girl, Ann Rebecca (possibly Carmelita Maria), was born to James Paris and Emily Perry at Mt. Pleasant on June 14, 1893. James Paris was a laborer. On these relations, see Baptism of "Ann Rebecca," September 16, 1893, "Baptisms Solemnized During the Years March 3, 1883–October 21, 1899," 193, St. John's Episcopal Church, Christiansted, St. Croix, USVI, Eliza Samuel, age four, was confirmed on March 23, 1911, and Emily Parris (later Allen) was confirmed in 1896 at St. John's Church. See Confirmation of "Eliza Samuel" and "Emily Parris," "Confirmations for 1880–1912," SJEC. In U.S. Department of Commerce, Bureau of the Census, "Census of the Virgin Islands of the United States: 1917," St. Croix, Northside Quarter, Sheet 11, Enumeration District 36, line 47–49, which was enumerated on January 9, 1918, Carmelita Parris, 25, was married to John Philips, 38, a fisherman who owned his own business (boat?), and they had an adopted six-year-old son, Herbert A. Percy. They lived on Estate William.

84. HD, March 17, 1920; *GP*, 1:515n3, 2:211n5; *Negro World*, July 31, 1920, 2; Capt. Joshua Cockburn to Marcus Garvey, Sagua, La Grande [Cuba], December 2 and 5, 1919, NFRC, Marcus Garvey case file exhibits, C-33-688, FRC 539-440, *GP*, 2:157–58, 161–62; UNIA Press Release, "African Blood Brotherhood Meeting Breaks Up in Disorder," December 19, 1921, *GP*, 4:299–301, esp. 301; "800" to George F. Ruch, December 19, 1921, DJ-FBI, file 61-826-X15; "Affidavit of James E. Amos," July 17, 1923, *GP*, 5:402–3.

85. *GP*, 1:227n4, 2:407n1, 5:717n1, 9:356n3. "Sec. Black Star Line Is Shot: Edmund Smith-Green, Receives Bullet Wound," *Gleaner*, December 13, 1919, *GP*, 2:167–68; *Negro World*, July 31, 1920; Edward Anderson, "Marcus Garvey—Alleged Violation of the Mann Act, August 31, 1921," *GP*, 3:720–21; (Report by Special Agent) "P-138" [Herbert S.

Boulin], "Marcus Garvey—Alleged Violation Mann Act, August 31, 1921," *GP*, 3:722–23; (Report by Special Agent) F. B. Faulhaber, "In Re: Marcus Garvey; Alleged Violation Mann White Slave Act, August 31, 1921," *GP*, 3:723–25.

86. *GP*, 2:329n5; UNIA Press Release, "African Blood Brotherhood Meeting Breaks Up in Disorder," December 19, 1921, *GP*, 4:299–301, esp. 301; "800" to George F. Ruch, December 19, 1921, DJ-FBI, file 61-826-X15; "African Blood Brotherhood Meeting Breaks Up in Disorder," *Negro World*, December 24, 1921, 3; "800" to George F. Ruch, November 26, 1921, *GP*, 4:219–20; "Report Made by Mortimer J. Davis, for Period 1/18/22"; "800" to George F. Ruch, November 18, 1921, *GP*, 4:200–1; Cyril A. Crichlow, UNIA Resident Secretary, to MG, June 24, 1921, *GP*, 9:11–39.

87. Kornweibel, *"Seeing Red,"* 126.

88. Mortimer J. Davis, Special Agent, US DOJ, "Received from Hubert H. Harrison for use of U.S. DOJ collections of clippings to the papers as follows . . . ," October 3, 1922. HP-Mi and copy in possession of JBP. On the naturalization see HH, Certificate of Naturalization #1806138, vol. 172, number 42659, September 26, 1922, FOIA/PA Request no. NYC840409.

89. HH, "Marcus Garvey at the Bar of United States Justice," Associated Negro Press, July 1, 1923, 2–4, HP, B5, F16, HPDLC; and *HR*, 194–99. See also HH, "New York Writer Analyzes Garvey Case: Compares Provisional President with O'Neill's 'Emperor Jones,' Made Famous by Charles Gilpin," *Kansas City Star*, July 5, 1923.

90. HH, "Marcus Garvey at the Bar of United States Justice."

91. HH, "Marcus Garvey at the Bar of United States Justice."

92. HH, "Marcus Garvey at the Bar of United States Justice."

93. "Report made by Mortimer J. Davis, for period 1/18/22, made on 1/21/22, New York City, In re: Black Star Line, Inc., Marcus Garvey, et al.," 2–3.

94. HD, August 28, 1920; [HH,] [Notes on MG,] HD, May 24, 1920.

95. "Article in the *Baltimore Afro-American*," August 25, 1922, *GP*, 4:999; Marcus Garvey v. New York Times, no. 30753, NY State Supreme Court; Garvey v. *Amsterdam News*, September 1922 (served on John E. Robinson, managing editor). Also, the Garvey divorce case and adultery charges included a subpoena in February, and the court action commenced in August 1922. See *GP*, 2:168–69n1, 9:39n2.

96. "800" to Mr. Geo[rge] F. Ruch [special agent of the BI], January 22, 1922, *GP*, 4:443–44. See also "Negro 'Napoleon' Counts on a Loyal Million to Aid Him," *New York World*, January 14, 1922. This article may have been written by Harrison.

97. "800" to Ruch, January 22, 1922.

98. "Statement of Orlando Thompson," provided to Mortimer J. Davis, Special Agent, James Amos, Special Agent, and F. J. Kilmartin, Stenographer, February 21, 1922, included with "Report by Special Agent Mortimer J. Davis: U.S. vs. Black Star Line, Inc., Vio. Sec. 215, U.S.C.C. (Using Mails to Defraud)," March 8, 1922, *GP*, 4:546–54.

99. "Report by Special Agent Mortimer J. Davis," March 8, 1922, *GP*, 4:541.

100. "Report by Special Agent Mortimer J. Davis," *GP*, 4:542.

101. "Enclosure [re: Gwendolyn Campbell, in charge of the stenographic force in Garvey's office] in Report by Special Agent Mortimer J. Davis," March 8, 1922, *GP*, 4:558–60. Campbell worked as Garvey's private secretary in Jamaica in 1914. *GP*, 9:39n3.

102. WEBD to D. J. Steyne-Parve, Consul General for the Netherlands, New York, c. April 1922, MU, WEBDB(P), reel 10, frame 1276, in *GP*, 4:623–24.

103. "Marcus Garvey, 'Back to Africa' Leader, Given Severe Rebuke by Justice Panken" [unidentified newspaper article possibly from *Harlem Home News*, April 26, 1922], *GP*, 4:620–22.

104. "Marcus Garvey . . . Given Severe Rebuke by Justice Panken," *GP*, 4:620–22.

105. "Marcus Garvey . . . Given Severe Rebuke by Justice Panken."

106. E. Ethelred Brown, "Garveyism, a Dispassionate, Unprejudiced Appraisement," *Jamaica Times*, May 20, 1922, *GP*, 4:635–39.

107. E. Ethelred Brown, "Garvey-istic Devotion," sermon, August 12, 1923, NN-SC, E. Ethelred Brown Papers, in *GP*, 5:423–31, esp. 423–25. Horatio William Bottomley (1860–1933) was an English newspaper editor and folk hero and founder of the influential weekly *John Bull*. He served as an MP (1906–1912, 1918–1922) and was a rabid patriot and nationalist during World War I. In 1922 he was convicted of fraud. See *New York Times*, May 27, 1933; Alan Hyman, *The Rise and Fall of Horatio Bottomley* (London: Cassell and Co., 1972); *GP*, 5:431n3; "Bottomley Guilty of £150,000 Fraud; Gets 7-Year Term," *New York Times*, May 30, 1922.

108. Charles S. Johnson, "After Garvey—What?" *Opportunity* 1, no. 8 (August 1923): 231–33. On Charles Ponzi (1878, 1879, or 1883–1949), see *New York Times*, January 19, 1949; Donald H. Dunn, *Ponzi! The Boston Swindler* (New York: McGraw-Hill, 1975), x, 243; *GP*, 5:431n2; "Charles Ponzi, a Pyramid of Postage," *New York Times*, December 7, 1986; and Mark Sullivan, *Our Times: The United States, 1920–1925*, vol. 6: *The Twenties* (New York: Charles Scribner's Sons, 1935), 541–42.

109. *GP*, 5:431n2, 9:661n7.

110. Marcus Garvey to chairman, Liberty Hall, Cable, June 25, 1922; rpt. in *Negro World*, July 1, 1922, *GP*, 4:679, which in a footnote cites Jackson, *The Ku Klux Klan in the City*, 12–13, 16; and Alexander, *The Ku Klux Klan in the Southwest*, 8–11, 36–38. The interview was not published. Walter White of the NAACP tried to obtain a copy and, in so doing, wrote to the New York attorney Lewis R. Gravis about "a memorandum of the interview held at Atlanta some time ago between Marcus Garvey and Edward Young Clarke. The sense of this interview was an agreement whereby Garvey was to be allowed to come into the South to sell stock to Negroes in his various enterprises, particularly the Black Star Line[,] with the protection and sanction of the Ku Klux Klan[,] while in return Garvey was to seek to break up organizations among Negroes opposed to the Klan, and particularly the National Association for the Advancement of Colored People." See Walter White to Lewis R. Travis, August 28, 1924, DLC, NAACP, in *GP*, 4:680n2.

111. *GP*, 4:xxxii–xxxiv.

112. *GP*, 4:817n2, 5:xxxiii, 9:556n2, citing *Literary Digest* 74, no. 18 (August 19, 1922). On the "Garvey Must Go" campaign of 1922 and the hand sent to Randolph, see *RF*, 322–24.

113. "Garvey Denounced at Negro Meeting: Police Quiet Audience as Speakers Assail 'Provisional President of Africa' Called Ally of Ku Klux Klan [P]rofessor Pickens Advises Race to Get Along with Whites in This Country," *New York Times*, August 7, 1922, *GP*, 4:816–17, 817n1; *Messenger* 4, no. 8 (August 1922): 474.

114. "Garvey a Crook or Liar! Charges A. P. Randolph: Adherents of 'Potentate' Make Numerous Interruptions at Friends of Negro Freedom Meeting Many Are Ejected; Socialist Candidate Urges Colored People Ally Themselves with Working-Class Movement," *New York Call*, August 14, 1922, *GP*, 4:857–58.

115. "Workers Party Convention Picks List of Candidates" and "Harlem West Side Branch, N.Y., in Action," both in *Toiler*, August 5, 1922, 5.

116. "Here Is Proposed Program for Workers Party. It Will Be Presented to Convention Dec. 25th," *Toiler*, December 2, 1922, 1, 4; Claude McKay, *The Negroes in America*, trans. from the Russian, ed. by Alan L. McLeod, trans. by Robert J. Weiner (1923; Port Washington, NY: National University Publications, 1979), 37.

117. *Baltimore Afro-American*, August 25, 1922, in *GP*, 4:999n1. See also *GP*, 5:219n1.

118. James E. Amos, Report, August 6, 1922, for the period of August 30 to September 6, 1922, *GP*, 5:6–7. On Eason's new organization, see Andrew M. Battle, Special Employee, Report, October 2, 1922, for period of September 21 to 24, 1922, "In Re: U.S. vs. Marcus Garvey Et AL Negro Radical Activities," *GP*, 5:29–31. On threats to kill Grey and Warren, see the BI report. See *GP*, 4:566. James E. Amos (1879–1953) was an African American bodyguard to President Theodore Roosevelt who in 1921 joined the BI as a special agent after having worked for the William J. Burns Detective Agency. Garvey accused Amos of conspiring with Domingo and others to encourage lawsuits against him and the UNIA. See *GP*, 4:525n1; *Kaiser Index*, 1:164; *New York Times*, December 29, 1953; "G-Man for 26 Years," *Ebony* 2, no. 11 (October 1947): 9–13; *Baltimore Afro-American*, January 16, 1954, 14; *Amsterdam News*, January 2, 1954, 4; Curt Gentry, *J. Edgar Hoover: The Man and His Secrets* (New York: Norton, 1991), 280.

119. HH to Ferdinand Q. Morton, November 19, 1921, HP, B2, F11.

120. HD, April 6, 1921. On Wednesday, April 13, 1921, Harrison wrote in his diary: "Tonight I give my second lesson (lecture) in Embryology at the Chiropractic College." See also "Six Lectures on Sex and Sex Problems," May 14–June 18, 1921, by Hubert H. Harrison, Instructor in Embryology, at the Cosmopolitan College of Chiropractic, in the College Building, 240 West 138th Street, HP, B13, F5–6. As late as 1980 there were reportedly only sixty-three Black professional chiropractors in the United States, out of nearly 25,000. See *Kaiser Index*, 1:471, which cites *Jet*, September 11, 1980.

121. Blanche Wylie Welzmiller to HH, August 4, 1921, HP, B3, F50.

122. HD, April 15, September 17, and October 17, 1921.

123. HH to John F. Hylan, September 12, 1921 [rpt. from an unidentified newspaper article entitled "(Hubert?) Harrison Answers Alderman Harris"], HP, B4, F74.

124. HH to Hylan, September 12, 1921. Such partisan politics undoubtedly drew Harrison some support in Democratic circles. He would later write that he was "a member of the speakers committee of Tammany hall" and of the "Mayor's Committee on Reception of Distinguished Guests." See HH to Arthur Hilliard, October 27, 1925, HP, B2, F2. Harrison says the year was 1921. The National Prohibition Act, commonly called the Volstead Act, passed on October 28, 1919 (overcoming President Woodrow Wilson's October 27, 1919, veto), provided for enforcement of the recently ratified Eighteenth Amendment, forbade the manufacture and sale of beverages with alcoholic content greater than 0.5 percent, and imposed fines and prison terms on violators. The Eighteenth Amendment was repealed by the Twenty-First Amendment on February 20, 1933. *RCAH*, 871–75, 1122.

125. HH to Ferdinand Q. Morton, November 19, 1921, HP, B2, F11, HPDLC.

126. Ernest R. Crandall to HH, October 14, 1921, HP, B2, F10.

127. Van Wyck Brooks to HH, October 20, 1921, HP, B1, F12.

128. John C. Hawkins to Dr. Ernest L. Crandall, October 24, 1921, HP, B2, F36; HH to Martin J. Healy, December 7, 1921, HP, B2, F21, HPDLC. On November 14 Crandall wrote to Harrison and said he "had not yet received a recommendation" from Morton. This letter was somehow delayed, however, and Harrison did not receive it till May 1922.

See Ernest R. Crandall to HH, November 14, 1921 (Harrison writes "rec'd May 1922" in corner), HP, B1, F31.

129. John E. Robinson to HH, October 20, 1921, HP, B3, F22. The *Amsterdam News* may have been the paper that published Harrison's open letter to Hylan.

130. HH to Morton, November 19, 1921.

131. Van Wyck Brooks to HH, November 25, 1921, HP, B1, F12.

132. HH to Healy, December 7, 1921; John C. Walter, *The Harlem Fox: J. Raymond Jones and Tammany, 1920–1970* (Albany: State University of New York Press, 1989), 4, 34–35; Edward R. Lewinson, *Black Politics in New York City* (New York: Twayne, 1974), 64.

133. HH to Healy, December 7, 1921; and John T. Carroll to the Editor, *New York Globe*, October 12, 1914.

134. Max Eastman to HH, n.d. (on *Liberator* stationery naming Floyd Dell, Claude McKay, and Mike Gold as editors, therefore probably c. 1921), HP, B1, F45. *The Liberator* was first published in 1918 under the editor Max Eastman and was a successor to *The Masses*, which was banned from the mails in August 1917 for its opposition to the war. It ceased publication in 1924. Its tradition was later continued by the *New Masses*, which began in 1926. See *ACABA*, 1:4.

135. Claude McKay, *A Long Way from Home*, ed. Gene Andrew Jarrett (1937; New Brunswick, NJ: Rutgers University Press, 2007), 118; HD, October 26, 1921. Crystal Eastman (1881–1928) served as managing editor of *The Liberator* from 1917–1921. Allen F. Davis, "Crystal Eastman," in *NAW*, 1:543–45.

136. "Harlem Social Notes," *Negro World*, November 19, 1921, 4. On Duse Mohammed Ali, see "Foreign Affairs," *Negro World*, March 25, 1922, 4.

137. Glenn Frank to HH, January 13, 1922, HP, B1, F55; T. S. Stribling, *Birthright, a Novel* (New York: Century, 1921).

138. HH, "Chiropractic—Good and Bad," *Negro World*, December 10, 1921, *HP*, B13, F7.

139. HH, "Chiropractic—Good and Bad."

140. J. Freeman Otto to Sir William Ferris," "Dr. J. F. Otto of College of Chiropractic, Replies to Hubert H. Harrison," *Negro World*, December 31, 1921, 6.

141. T. Benedict Furniss to HH, December 13 and December 21, 1921, HP, B1, F56.

142. "Students Reply to Article," *Negro World*, December 24, 1921, 10, HP, B13, F7.

143. "H.H." [HH], "Safety First," *Negro World*, December 24, 1921, 10. See Cosmopolitan College of Chiropractic Catalogue, 1921–22, HP, ScrMAM2, FB740, which contains a photo of Professor Harrison, B.Sc. Harrison would also at times be referred to as a D.Sc.

144. "H.H.," "Safety First."

145. "H.H.," "Safety First."

146. HH, "'Finale,'" *Negro World*, December 31, 1921, 3, HP, B13, F7.

147. "H.H." [HH], "'Put Up or Shut Up!'" *Negro World*, January 21, 1922, 7, HP, B13, F7.

148. Louis S. Siegfried to HH, March 1, 1922, HP, B3, F37; Benedict Furniss to HH, March 4, 1922, HP, B1, F56.

149. T. Benedict Furniss, "In Defense of Chiropractic," *Negro World*, March 11, 1922.

150. HP, B9, F2 and B19, F17.

151. Elsie to HH, [Letter #9,] February 20, 1922, HP, B19, F17. *Snappy Stories* was edited by Lauren Mackall at 9 East Fortieth Street, New York City. See *The Editor: The Journal of Information for Literary Workers* 57, no. 4 (April 29, 1922): 2.

152. Elsie to HH, (incomplete), c. February 1922, HP, B19, F17.

153. HH to Elsie, [Letter #4,] February 8, 1922 and [Letter #5,] February 13, 1922, both in HP, B19, F18, HPDLC.

154. HH, "Drifting" (poem), handwritten, February 1922, HP, B4, F48, HPDLC.

13. Lecturer, Book Reviewer, and Citizenship (March 1922–June 1923)

1. "Board of Education the City of New York Borough of Manhattan Public Lectures Great Hall of Cooper Institute Wednesday evenings, Trend of the Times, Saturday Evenings, Miscellaneous Subjects March and April, 1922 . . . Saturday March 4 Dr. Hubert H. Harrison 'The Brother in Black,'" HP, FB40; HD, June 3, 1923. For some previous speakers at the Great Hall, see https://cooper.edu/admissions/facts.

2. M. F. Ruiz to HH, March 6, 1922, HP, B3, F29.

3. Ernest Crandall to M. F. River [Ruiz], March 16, 1922, HP, B1, F32; and M. F. Ruiz to Dr. HH, March 18, 1922, HP, B3, F29.

4. HH to Dr. Ernest Crandall, March 17, 1922, HP, B2, F10, HPDLC. In his books, Harrison retained Tennyson's *Gems from Tennyson*, with illustrations by W. J. Hennessy [et al.] (Boston: Ticknor and Fields, 1866), HP, B25, which, as noted in the book, he gave to his daughter Ilva on February 15, 1924. See also HH, "The Greatest American Writer: notes regarding Mark Twain," January 26, 1924, HP, B4, F64, HPDLC.

5. M. F. Ruiz to Dr. Ernest L. Crandall, March 19, 1922, HP, B3, F28; and to HH, March 21, 1922, HP, B3, F29.

6. Ernest Crandall to HH, March 27, 1922, HP, B1, F31.

7. HH, "Bridging the Gulf of Color," c. April 1922, handwritten, HP, B4, F23; rpt. in *HR*, 273–77. For dating this piece, see Crandall to HH, April 22, 1922, HP, B1, F31.

8. HH, "Bridging the Gulf of Color."

9. HH, "Bridging the Gulf of Color." Harrison is probably referring to the lesson of the fox and the goat from the fifth-century BCE Aesop's *Fables*. In his scrapbooks Harrison critically divided existing "Negro American" leadership into two broad categories: "The Subservients" and "The Protestants." Chief among Harrison's "subservients" was Booker T. Washington. See *HHVHR*, 122–23, 445nn26–27; and HP-Sc 5, *The Negro American*, vol. 8: *The Negro Factions: 1. The Protestants. 2. The Subservients*, HP, B12, F6.

10. HH, "Bridging the Gulf of Color."

11. HH, "Bridging the Gulf of Color."

12. HH, "Bridging the Gulf of Color."

13. HH, "Bridging the Gulf of Color." Harrison is referring to his Radical Forum lecture series that began in 1914. See *HHVHR*, 225–26.

14. HH, "Bridging the Gulf of Color."

15. H. E. Miller to HH, May 23, 1922, HP, B2, F73. On May 31 Miller again wrote Harrison that they had received his letter of May 27, which indicated Harrison was preparing his speech. They were eager "to see this talk," asked him to send it soon, and hoped he would enjoy his broadcasting experience. See Miller to HH, May 31, 1922, HP, B2, F73.

16. Ernest R. Crandall to HH, November 14, 1921 (Harrison writes "rec'd May 1922" in corner), HP, B1, F31.

17. Summons for Hubert H. Harrison et al. vs. Global Credit Union, Municipal Court of the City of New York, Borough of Manhattan, May 8, 1922, HP, B14, F16, HPDLC.

18. George A. Dame to HH, March 16, 1922, HP, B1, F41; Margaret Williamson to HH, June 14, 1922, HP, B3, F54; EJP, Rand McNally & Co., to HH, June 23, 1922, HP, B3, F15; Monroe N. Work to HH, July 20, 1922, HP, B3, F56; HD, November 2, 1922.

19. Martin J. Healy to Hon. Richard E. Enright, April 5, 1922, HP, B2, F37.

20. Certificate [April 13, 1922] from Police Commissioner Enright, described in Chief Naturalization Examiner, "MEMORANDUM re Mr. Harrison, 2270-42659," July 27, 1922 FOIA/PA Request no. NYC840409.

21. HH, "Of *White and Black*: A Negro Reviewer's Judgment on Shands's Novel of Texas Life," *New York World*, April 27, 1922, HP, B5, F53; and Hubert Anthony Shands, *White and Black* (New York: Harcourt, Brace, 1922), https://archive.org/details /whiteblack00shaniala/page/n5.

22. HH, "Of *White and Black*."

23. HH, "Of *White and Black*."

24. HH, "Of *White and Black*."

25. "A St. Croix Creole" [HH] to the Editor, "Dumb St. Croix [written May 7, 1922]," *New York Evening Post*, May 15, 1922, 6, HP, B2, F8; rpt. in *HR*, 240–41. On Harrison's mention of his former, highly esteemed teacher in St. Croix (probably Wilford Jackson, father of D. Hamilton Jackson), see Romeo L. Dougherty, "D. Hamilton Jackson," *West End News* (Frederiksted, St. Croix), March 29, 1915, 3–4; and see George F. Tyson, ed., *Searching for Truth and Justice: The Writings of Ralph D. de Chabert, 1915–1922* (Christiansted, St. Croix: Antilles Press, 2009).

26. "A St. Croix Creole" [HH] to the editor, "Dumb St. Croix." See also *Negro World*, June 13, 1922, regarding the May 15, 1922, letter of protest related to the Virgin Islands rally of May 10, at which Harrison spoke. Harrison would become a naturalized U.S. citizen on September 26, 1922.

27. HH, "*Harlem Shadows*: Comments by a Writer of His Race on the Poems of Claude McKay," *New York World*, May 21, 1922, HP, B4, F67; and Claude McKay, *Harlem Shadows: The Poems of Claude McKay* (New York: Harcourt, Brace, 1922), https://archive.org /details/harlemshadows00mcka/page/n3.

28. HH, "*Harlem Shadows*."

29. HH, "*Harlem Shadows*."

30. HH, "Negro Church History: A Book of It Badly Marred by Neglect of the Race Foundation" [a review of *The History of the Negro Church*, by Carter G. Woodson (Washington, DC: Associated Publishers, 1921)], *New York World*, July 23, 1922, HP, B5, F29; rpt. in *HR*, 339–40.

31. HH, "M. Maran's *Batouala*, a French-African Tale: Work of a Negro Novelist as It Impresses a Negro Reviewer—Prize Story of a Land That Has Known the Abuses of Civilization"; "A Review by Hubert H. Harrison," *New York World*, August 20, 1922, HP, B5, F22; rpt. in *HR*, 334–36; and René Maran, *Batouala* (New York: Thomas Seltzer, 1922). Ernest Hemingway from the *Toronto Star* of March 25, 1922, and *The Crisis* 24, no. 5 (September 1922): 218–19, 231, are cited in Chidi Ikonné, *From Du Bois to Van Vechten: The Early New Negro Literature, 1903–1926* (Westport, CT: Greenwood, 1981), 6, 38nn18–19. Tony Martin, *Literary Garveyism: Garvey, Black Arts, and the Harlem Renaissance* (Dover, MA: Majority, 1983), 94–99, 98, notes that Harrison referred to "Maran's bill of indictment against the barbarous brutality of French rule."

32. HH, "M. Maran's *Batouala*," *HR*, 334.

33. HH, "M. Maran's *Batouala*," *HR*, 335.

34. HH, "M. Maran's *Batouala*," *HR*, 335.

35. HH, "M. Maran's *Batouala*," *HR*, 335–36.

36. "Rene Maran Gets Little Money from Sale of Book," *Chicago Defender*, April 5, 1923, HP, ScrPN2, B13, F5–6.

37. HH, [*Early Civilization: An Introduction to Anthropology*, by A. A. Goldenweiser, a review,] *Negro World*, September 9, 1922, 4.

38. HH, Declaration of Intention, Supreme Ct. County of New York, June 22, 1915; and HH, Petition for Naturalization #42659, June 22, 1922, both from FOIA/PA Request no. NYC840409, in possession of JBP (hereafter HHFOIA). In the 1920 census it was incorrectly reported that Hubert was naturalized in 1913. See U.S. Department of Commerce—Bureau of the Census, "Fourteenth Census of the United States: 1920—Population," New York City, Enumeration District 972, Sheet 1, line 87. Line 88 reported that Lin was naturalized but gave no date.

39. HH, Petition for Naturalization, June 22, 1922; and HH to War Department, June 23, 1922, cited in HH to Naturalization Examiner, July 5, 1922, HHFOIA.

40. Robert C. Davis to Naturalization Examiner, NYC, re Hubert Henry Harrison, July 1, 1922, HHFOIA.

41. HH to Naturalization Examiner, July 5, 1922, HHFOIA. Harrison's confusion as to the status of Virgin Islanders was well founded. William Boyer writes that "Virgin Islanders [unequivocally] assumed that the [1917] transfer of the Islands conferred on them American citizenship." They were soon disabused of this view when Acting Secretary of State Frank L. Polk wrote to Senator William S. Kenyon on March 9, 1920, explaining that the State Department was issuing passports "to inhabitants of the Virgin Islands entitled to the protection of the government, but have not the civil and political status of citizens of the United States." See William W. Boyer, *America's Virgin Islands: A History of Human Rights and Wrongs* (Durham, NC: Carolina Academic Press, 1983), 136–38, esp. 137, which cites Waldo Evans, *The Virgin Islands, a General Report by the Governor* (Washington, DC: Navy Department, 1928), 62, for the Polk quotation.

42. Commissioner of Naturalization: Your 2270-P-42659; Hubert Henry Harrison, July 26, 1922, HHFOIA.

43. "Brief Slip U.S. Department of Labor Naturalization Service New York File No. 2270-42659 In re Hubert Henry Harrison," July 26, 1922, HHFOIA.

44. Chief Naturalization Examiner, "MEMORANDUM re Mr. Harrison, 2270-42659," July 27, 1922.

45. Chief Naturalization Examiner to Police Commissioner, Police Headquarters, New York, N.Y., re 2270-42659 [HJ], July 28, 1922, HHFOIA.

46. Robert C. Davis to Commissioner of Naturalization, U.S. Department of Labor, Washington, DC, August 8, 1922, HHFOIA.

47. Acting Chief Naturalization Examiner to Commissioner of Naturalization re Your 2270-P-42659 (HH); August 21, 1922, HHFOIA.

48. HH to Mayor John F. Hylan, "Hubert Harrison Answers Alderman Harris," September 12 [15?], 1922. This is a reprint from a probable *New York Age* article entitled "[Hubert?] Harrison Answers Alderman Harris."

49. HH, Certificate of Naturalization #1806138, Vol. 172, Number 42659, September 26, 1922, HHFOIA; Correspondence and Flag from NY Chapter Colonial Dames to HH, September 26, 1922, HP, B15, F29; HD, September 26, 1922; J. A. Rogers, *The Real Facts About Ethiopia* (1936; Baltimore: Black Classics, 1982), 3.

50. Mortimer J. Davis, Special Agent, US DOJ, "Received from Hubert H. Harrison for use of U.S. Department of Justice collections of clippings to the papers as follows . . . ,"

October 3, 1922; Commissioner of Naturalization to HH, re 2270-P-42659, 1st ultimo, October 4, 1922, HHFOIA; HD, October 5, 1922.

51. HD, October 14, 1922. In Harrison's papers also appeared some handwritten notes entitled "Caliban Considers: Notes & Citations," which quoted from James Russell Lowell's "Stanzas on Freedom": "They are slaves who dare [will] not choose / Hatred, scoffing and abuse, / Rather than in silence shrink / From the truth they needs must think, / They are slaves who dare not be / In the right with two or three." HH, "Caliban Considers: Notes & Citations," c. July 1923, HP, B4, F26; and James Russell Lowell, "Freedom," https://www.bartleby.com/71/0411.html. Caliban was a deformed native in Shakespeare's *Tempest*. Around July 1923 Harrison wrote: "At end of 22 chap. 1 of Caliban Considers by [?]" on two printed pages on "Race Values and Race Destinies." See HH, [miscellaneous writings,] c. July 1923, HP, B4, F26. In his copy of Stoddard, *The Rising Tide of Color*, Harrison writes: "Note that in his chapters on the Yellows and the Browns the author quotes from yellow and Brown sources their own opinions of what is before them. But in his chapter on Black Africa he thinks it unnecessary to examine a single book, newspaper or magazine from Black Africa. This has been typical of white men when dealing with black.—as I point out in the Introduction to 'Caliban Considers[.]' And of course, it reduces all their lucubrations to so much subjective piffle."

52. HD, October 14, 1922. Van Veen's friend who knew people at the lecture bureaus was most probably James F. Morton Jr. See "James F. Morton, Museum Curator, Fatally Injured," *Paterson Evening News*, October 7, 1941, 1, 2; James F. Morton, "How to Encourage a Race to Rise," letter, *New York Times Saturday Review of Books*, June 11, 1910, HP-Sc 6, 20. Morton indicated he lectured for "the New York Board of Education" in James F. Morton to the Editor, *Loyal Citizen Sovereignty* 1, no. 2 (November 1922): 9.

53. HD, November 2, 1922. See also Patrick Edward Dove, *The Theory of Human Progression*, abr. Julia A. Kellog (New York: Isaac H. Blanchard, 1910) https://archive.org/details/progressiontheory00doverich.

54. "The Single Taxers' Opportunity: The Earth Is the Birthright of All Mankind! The Rent of Land Belongs to the People—Hubert Harrison will address the Forum on Saturday—December 2nd [1922] 8:30 p.m. Subject: The Single-Taxers' Opportunity," c. December 2, 1922, HP, ScrMOM2, FB740.

55. HD, October 20, 1922; John C. Walter, *The Harlem Fox: J. Raymond Jones and Tammany, 1920–1970* (Albany: State University of New York Press, 1989), 34–35; Edward R. Lewinson, *Black Politics in New York City* (New York: Twayne, 1974), 64. J. Raymond Jones (1899–1991) was born in Charlotte Amalie, St. Thomas, Dutch West Indies, and came to New York during the war. In 1920 he founded the Carver Democratic Club in Harlem and became an important Tammany politician, heading that organization from 1964 to 1967. See Walter, *The Harlem Fox*; Sam Roberts, "The Harlem Fox: When Tammany Spelled Power," *New York Times*, March 20, 1989; Lewinson, *Black Politics in New York City*, 19–20, 90–102, 123–34, 144–60; and C. Gerald Fraser, "J. Raymond Jones, Harlem Kingmaker, Dies at 91," *New York Times*, June 11, 1991.

56. HD, November 2, 1922.

57. Henri W. Shields to HH, November 11, 1922, HP, B3, F36; Dr. Royal S. Copeland to HH, December 27, 1922, HP, B1, F28.

58. *Loyal Citizen Sovereignty* 1, no. 1 (October 1922): 1–2, 4. Page 4 of that first issue contained an article urging to "Keep Church and State Separate." On James F. Morton Jr., see *HHVHR*, 118.

59. *Loyal Citizen Sovereignty* 1, no. 2 (November 1922): 6; HH to the Editor, *Loyal Citizen Sovereignty* 1, no. 2 (November 1922): 9.

60. James F. Morton to the Editor, *Loyal Citizen Sovereignty* 1, no. 2 (November 1922): 9.

61. J. Winfield Scott to HH, November 17, 1922, HP, B3, F34.

62. *Loyal Citizen Sovereignty* 1, no. 3 (December 1922): 1, 6; 2, no. 1 (January 1923): 6.

63. HD, August 18, September 19, and July 14, 1922. During the summer Harrison had noted in his scrapbook across the article "Girls' Camp Differs Others, from Others," *New York Star*, August 4, 1922, that "wide-spread homosexualism among high school girls is humorously disposed of."

64. HD, September 19, 1922.

65. "'Garvey Must Go' Negroes Declare," *New York Times*, September 11, 1922, 19; *GP*, 3:xxxiii, 4:679–80, 5:9–11.

66. *GP*, 5:li, 11n2; *New York Age*, October 21, 1922; *Negro World*, October 6, 1923; J. A. Rogers, "Additional Facts on Marcus Garvey and His Trial for Using the Mails to Defraud," Negroes of New York, Writers Program, New York, 1939, NN-Sc. Special Agent Joseph G. Tucker, September 30, 1922, DJ-FBI, file 61-189, reported that volume 1, number 1, of Garvey's daily appeared on September 25 and was published by the Negro Times Publishing Co. See also *GP*, 5:31n2, 5:57n2, where Hill writes: "To date, no issues of the *Daily Negro Times* have been found." On the paper's closing see *New York Star*, October 26, 1922. After the paper closed, Fortune worked for the *Negro World*. See also *Messenger* 4, no. 12 (December 1922): 546–47; *GP*, 4:891n4.

67. HH, "*The Day of Faith*: by Arthur Sommers Roche; Little Brown & Company," *Daily Negro Times*, September 25, 1922, HP, B4, F19.

68. HD, September 6, 1922.

69. HD, October 5 and 20 and November 2, 1922. On Edwin C. Walker (1849–1931), see *HHVHR*, 116–17.

70. HD, September 29, 1922.

71. HD, September 30, 1922. In addition to the missing "Weltpolotik" scrapbook three other Harrison "Weltpolotik" scrapbooks have been located and are in the possession of JBP. They include: Weltpolotik (vol. 1) Newspaper Clippings 1921–1922—The Far East, The Middle East, The Near East 45 (including Egypt), Africa, Europe, Latin America, and the U.S.A.; Welt-Politik (vol. 3): Magazine Articles—[Lausanne ?] . . . Conference (1922–23), Africa Morocco (1925), General Mexico & Latin America; and Welt-Politik (vol. 4): A Series of Clippings 1925 -1926—Europe (Miscellaneous, England, France, Italy, The Balkans, General), The Near East (Insurgent Syria, The Mosul Dispute, General), The Middle East (The Saklatvala Case, General), The Far East (Japan, China, General), Africa (The Moroccan War), General, The Rising Tide.

72. HD, September 30, 1922.

73. HD, September 30, 1922.

74. HD, October 5, 1922.

75. J. Krassny to the editor, "Satyricon of Petronius," *New York Times*, October 22, 1922. See Petronius, *The Satyricon*, trans. and intro. William Arrowsmith (New York: New American Library, 1959), esp. v–xviii; and *The Satyricon of Petronius Arbiter*, https://www.gutenberg.org/files/5225/5225-h/5225-h.htm. In 1842 Congress enacted the first federal law prohibiting the importation of indecent prints and paintings, and in 1865 it forbade domestic mailing of obscene material. The Mail Fraud Statute of 1873 extended to envelopes and postcards, and the Comstock Act of 1873 prohibited selling or advertising through the mails any obscene literature and items "for the prevention of contraception."

Versions of the Comstock law, which similarly aimed at social control, were developed in twenty-two states. See Beverly A. Brown, "American Smut: A Historical Perspective on Obscenity Laws," *U.S. Postal Inspection Service Bulletin*, September 1994, 33–36; Bruce Shapiro, "From Comstockery to Helmsmanship," *Nation*, October 1, 1990, 335–37.

76. Ernestine Rose to HH, September 14, 1922, HP, B3, F26. Ernestine Rose (1880–1961) was on the staff of the New York Public Library from 1905 until 1942 and was well known for her work (beginning June 1920) in the creation and development of the 135th Street Branch (later the Countée Cullen Regional Branch and the Schomburg Collection). She helped in developing the library as an "active, integral part of the community, with a special educational and social function." See *NYPL Staff News*, April 6, 1961, 45; Martha Foley, assistant archivist, NYPL, to author, December 13, 1996; Robert Sink, archivist, NYPL, interview with JBP, December 16, 1996; "Harlem Library to Have Negro Workers Soon: Ernestine Rose Succeeds Miss Cohen as Librarian," *Negro World*, June 19, 1920, 1; and Ernestine Rose, "A Librarian in Harlem," *Opportunity* 1, no. 7 (July 1923): 206–7, 220.

77. HH to the Editor, "Satyricon of Petronius," *New York Times*, October 22, 1922, 116, HP, B6, F16; rpt. in *HR*, 364–65.

78. Floyd Calvin to HH, December 13, 1922, HP, B1, F21.

79. HD, June 3, 1923; "Public Lecture Service October–December 1922 New York Public Library 103 West 135th St. Manhattan Saturdays Literary Lights of Yesterday Today and Tomorrow by Dr. Hubert H. Harrison," handout, c. October 1922, HP, B16, F8. Dr. Crandall even asked him to suggest someone to fill the position of local superintendent of the 135th Street Library at his lectures. At the bottom of Crandall's letter Harrison wrote: "Miss Florence Lee Thomas, Percy Green or his Lady Teacher, Jas. S. Watson, Mrs. Rosalie Scott McClendon, Fannie B. Rhone, [and] Dr. Murray"; these may have been people he considered recommending. See Ernest R. Crandall to HH, October 6, 1922, HP, B1, F31, and HH's handwritten comments.

80. HD, June 3, 1923; Ernest L. Crandall to HH, November 6, 1922, HP, B1, F31.

81. HH, "At the Back of the Black Man's Mind," n.d. [prob. November 1922], HP, B4, F12; rpt. in *HR*, 277–82, quotations on 277–78. See also HH, "At the Back of the Black Man's Mind," unpublished article submitted to the *New Republic*, November 1922?, HPDLC. In Robert Littell to HH, April 27, 1923, HP, B2, F64, Littell asked forgiveness for his "long delay with your manuscripts." Harrison handwrote on his copy of the letter, "After 6 mos. received back manuscripts of 'The Back of the Black Man's Mind' and 'Bridging the Gulf of Color'—both sent only at Littell's request."

82. HH, "At the Back of the Black Man's Mind," *HR*, 278.

83. HH, "At the Back of the Black Man's Mind," *HR*, 278–79.

84. HH, "At the Back of the Black Man's Mind," *HR*, 279.

85. HH, "At the Back of the Black Man's Mind," *HR*, 279–80.

86. HH, "At the Back of the Black Man's Mind," *HR*, 280.

87. HH, "At the Back of the Black Man's Mind," *HR*, 280–81.

88. HH, "At the Back of the Black Man's Mind," *HR*, 281; and "Frances Dearborn" [HH], "The Black Tide Turns in Politics," *HR*, 158–59.

89. HH, "At the Back of the Black Man's Mind," *HR*, 281–82. Boanerges was the surname said to be given by Jesus to James and John, and a "Boanerges" is a vigorous orator. See *WNUD*, 163; Mark 3:17.

90. [New York Board of Ed,] "Public Lecture Service January and February 1923 Public School 89 Lenox Ave.–134th and 135th Sts. Sundays 'Trend of the Times,'" c.

January 6, 1923, HP, ScrPN2, B13, F5–6, which indicates the Board of Ed Lecture Bureau was headed by George J. Ryan, president, and included, among others, Crandall, director of lectures; and Wendell M. Thomas, assistant director of lectures. The lectures were free, and schoolchildren were admitted if accompanied by parents or teachers. See HD, June 3, 1923; "Dr. Hubert Harrison to Deliver Lectures in Harlem for the Board of Education," *Harlem Home News*, January 31, 1923, HP, B16, F8. The *Chicago Defender* claimed "there are but eight of these ['Trend of the Times'] lecturers, all of whom are classed as speakers of unusual intelligence." See "Race Wins Honor When Harrison Speaks Mar. 10," *Chicago Defender*, March 10, 1923, HP, ScrPN2.

91. "The Independent Lecture Committee,' handout, c. January 6, 1923, HP, ScrPN2.

92. "Dr. Hubert Harrison to Deliver Lectures in Harlem," *Harlem Home News*, January 31, 1923.

93. "Dr. Hubert Harrison to Deliver Lectures in Harlem"; "135th St. (Harlem) Library Notes," *Negro World*, February 3, 1923, HP, ScrPN2.

94. William Pickens to HH, n.d. [c. February 5, 1923], HP, B3, F9—see Ernest R. Crandall to William Pickens, February 19, 1923, HP, B1, F34. Pickens added, "Any community of 500 colored people could have a good forum."

95. William Pickens, "Hubert Harrison Philosopher of Harlem," *Amsterdam News*, February 7, 1923, 12, HP, ScrPN2.

96. Pickens, "Hubert Harrison Philosopher of Harlem."

97. Pickens, "Hubert Harrison Philosopher of Harlem."

98. Crandall to Pickens, February 19, 1923. Pickens appended a copy of his note to Crandall along with William Pickens to HH, handwritten note c. February 19, 1923, HP, B3, F9.

99. HH, "Potentate and Poet: These the Main Figures of 'The Penitent,' Novel of Old Russia [by Edna Worthley Underwood] (Houghton-Mifflin)," *New York World*, December 10, 1922; Edna Worthley Underwood, *The Penitent* (Boston: Houghton, Mifflin, 1922), https://archive.org/details/penitent00underich/page/n9.

100. [HH,] "*Nigger*. By Clement Wood," *New York Tribune*, December 11, 1922, HP, B5, F36; Clement Wood, *Nigger: A Novel* (New York: E. P. Dutton & Co., 1922), https://babel.hathitrust.org/cgi/pt?id=emu.10002308967;view=1up;seq=8.

101. [HH,] "*Nigger*. By Clement Wood."

102. HD, November 2 and 23, 1922.

103. "The Annual Celebration of the Emancipation Proclamation," leaflet, c. January 1, 1923, HP, ScrPN2; HH, [notes re] "Declaration of Indep.," January 1, 1923, HP, ScrPN2.

104. HH, "Negro's Part in History" [review of Carter G. Woodson, *The Negro in Our History* (Washington, D.C.: Associated Publishers, 1922), https://archive.org/details/negrohistory00woodrich/page/n5], *New York Tribune*, January 7, 1923, HP, B5, F33.

14. The KKK, Garvey's Conviction, Speaking, Virgin Islands, and Reviews (1923)

1. *GP*, 4:715n2, 1089n2; Kenneth T. Jackson, *The Ku Klux Klan in the City, 1915–1930* (New York: Oxford University Press, 1967), 3–7, 11–13; U.S. Congress, House Committee on Rules, *Hearings on the Ku Klux Klan*, 67th Cong., 1st sess., 1921.

2. See in HP, B13, F5–6, the following: "Ku Klux Klan Members Quiz Negro Who Denounces Klan: Dr. Harrison, Noted Lecturer Replies by Challenge to Public Debate: Klan Side Presented; but Speakers Refuse to Disclose Identity—Lecturer Draws Greatest Applause," *Paterson Morning Times*, January 8, 1923, 1, 2; "Negro Lecturer Debates Klan with Self-Identified Klansman: Dr. Hubert H. Harrison, Danish West Indian Native, Issues Challenge as Police Stand Guard, to Discuss on Public Platform the Subject 'Resolved, That the Ku Klux Klan is a Menace to American Liberty,'" *Paterson Morning Call*, January 8, 1923, 1, 2; "Dr. Harrison Repeats Defi to the Klan: Is Anxious to Debate; West Indian Colored Dominie Challenges Entire K.K.K. to Meet on Platform and Discuss the Issue," *Paterson Evening News*, January 11, 1923; and "Debate May Be Staged, Negro Vs. Ku Klux Klan: K.K.K. Is Challenged; Dr. Harrison Lashes Klan as Unpatriotic and Foe of American Ideals," *Paterson Evening News*, January 8, 1923, 1, 12. See also Marc Mappen, "Jerseyana," *New York Times*, November 11, 1990.

3. "Ku Klux Klan Members Quiz Negro," 1, 2; "Negro Lecturer Debates Klan," 1, 2; "Dr. Harrison Repeats Defi"; and "Debate May Be Staged," 1, 12. For more on the KKK in Paterson, see *Negro World*, April 22, 1922, 2; and David M. Chalmers, *Hooded Americanism: The History of the Ku Klux Klan* (Durham, NC: Duke University Press, 1987), 243. On May 7, 1925, Harrison received a copy of Jean Finot's *Race Prejudice*, HP-B22. On 310–11 he wrote Finot argues "The science of inequality is emphatically a science of White people. It is they who have invented it and set it going, who have maintained, cherished and propagated it, thanks to *their* observations and *their* deductions. Deeming themselves greater than men of other colours, they have elevated into superior qualities all the traits which are peculiar to themselves, commencing with the whiteness of the skin and the pliancy of the hair." Harrison commented, "not so, its source is always sociologic rather than intellectual." Then he added, "—sociologic relations to the peoples whom they rule over." On 299 he added, "Could he have known the *facts* as given in Blaine & Schurz he would have realized that the ex-rebels forced the North to give the Negro the ballot since the whites refused to take the oath of allegiance in numbers sufficient to furnish reconstruction governments and had as early as *1865* organized lawless terrorist organizations."

4. "Ku Klux Klan Members Quiz Negro," 1.

5. "Negro Lecturer Heckled by Klan Sympathizers: Crowd Cheers Speaker When He Answers Dozen Annoyers in Paterson Hall," *New York World*, January 8, 1923; "Debate May Be Staged," 1, 12; "Ku Klux Klan Members Quiz Negro," 1, 2; "Dr. Harrison Repeats Defi"; and "Negro Lecturer Debates Klan," 1, 2. Arthur H. Bell (1891–1973) was a Bloomfield, New Jersey, attorney who served as grand dragon of the Knights of the KKK in the 1920s and 1930s; on August 18, 1940, he arranged a joint rally of the KKK and the German-American Bund in New Jersey. Michael Newton and Judy Ann Newton, *The Ku Klux Klan: An Encyclopedia* (New York: Garland, 1991), 45.

6. "Dr. Harrison Repeats Defi."

7. Arthur E. Bestor to HH, February 10, 1923, HP, B1, F3. Over the years Chautauqua featured many prominent Southern white supremacists, including the author Thomas Dixon Jr., Mississippi senator James K. Vardaman, and South Carolina senator Benjamin R. Tillman. See A. J. Williams-Myers, "Chautauqua (New York) and the Use and Abuse of Selective Memory," *African Americans in New York Life and History* 18, no. 2 (July 1994): esp. 48–49, 51–52.

8. HH to Clifford Smyth, International Book Review, February 23, 1923, HP, B2, F4, HPDLC. Harrison enclosed "leaflets of the Board of Education that you may see that I

work for them regularly as an oral critic of literature." See, for example, "Dr. Hubert Harrison to Deliver Lectures in Harlem for the Board of Education," *Harlem Home News*, January 31, 1923, HP, B13, F5–6. When he died Harrison still had in his personal library John Macy's *The Spirit of American Literature* (New York: Boni and Liveright, 1913), HP, B23.

9. Margaret Normil to HH, April 17, 1923, HP, B3, F4; Marguerite Brown to HH, January 2, 1925, HP, B1, F15; and Robert E. Ely to HH, April 18, 1923, HP, B1, F50.

10. HH, "Memoranda" [on "The Control of Negro Sentiment" and "What I Think I Can Do"], handwritten notes, c. March 1923, HP, B5, F20, HPDLC. For background to Harrison's article, see Abram L. Harris, "The Negro Problem as Viewed by Negro Leaders," *Current History* 18, no. 3 (June 1923): 410–18; *GP*, 4:1015n3; and Frederick G. Detweiler, *The Negro Press in the United States* (Chicago: University of Chicago Press, 1922), 28–30.

11. "Race Wins Honor When Harrison Speaks Mar. 10," *Chicago Defender*, March 10, 1923, HP, B13, F5–6; HD, June 3, 1923; and Handout for HH Talk on "The Brother in Black," at New York City, City Hall, March 10, 1923, HP, B13, F5–6.

12. M. F. Ruiz to HH, March 19 and 27, 1923, HP, B3, F29; Ernest Crandall to M. F. River [Ruiz], March 26, 1923, HP, B1, F32. Ruiz wanted to show Harrison Crandall's reply so Harrison could "best judge whether or not" Crandall's assertion that he was used at what Crandall referred to as "'white centres' such as yiddish and Italians" was true.

13. "Literary Lights of Yesterday and Today" "Trend of the Times" Public Lecture Service of the New York City Board of Education, New York Public Library [135th Street], March 7–April 28, 1923, HP, ScrPN2, HPDLC; HD, June 3, 1923.

14. HD, June 3 and 27, 1923.

15. HD, June 3, 1923; John Keracher to Phil[ip Kerr] April 19, 1923. Thanks to Franklin Rosemont of the Charles H. Kerr Publishing Company for this correspondence and for pointing out Philip was no relation to Charles H.

16. Ernest Crandall to HH, June 4, 1923, HP, B1, F31. Crandall explained that the sketch would be "brief" and that he did not want it to have "anything that your people would take exception to."

17. HD, June 21, 1923; HH, "The Negro and the Nation," handwritten, unpublished ["An address by Dr. Hubert H. Harrison of the Lecture Bureau of Dept. of Education, New York City, Thurs., June 21st 1923—By Radio Broadcasting of America Telephone and Telegraph Co., June 21, 1923,"], HP, B5, F28, HPDLC; rpt. in *HR*, 286–90. WEAF, a subsidiary of AT&T, began broadcasting August 16, 1922, at 463 West Street, and on October 14, 1924, it moved to a new studio at 195 Broadway. See *ENY*, 973, 1248.

18. HD, June 21, 1923; HH, "The Negro and the Nation," *HR*, 286–87.

19. HH, "The Negro and the Nation," *HR*, 287.

20. HH, "The Negro and the Nation," *HR*, 287–88. In the text quoted Harrison adds: "It was Abraham Lincoln who told us that years ago, so still it must be said, 'The judgments of the Lord are true and righteous altogether.'" The quote is from Lincoln's Second Inaugural Address, March 4, 1865.

21. HH, "The Negro and the Nation," *HR*, 288; *GP*, 9:136–37nn3, 5; Arthur E. Barbeau and Florette Henri, *The Unknown Soldiers: Black American Troops in World War I* (Philadelphia: Temple University Press, 1974), 72–81, 111–13. For Lincoln to Charles D. Robinson, August 17, 1864, see https://lincolnscivilwar.wordpress.com/2014/08/17/to

-charles-d-robinson/. See also HH, "A Crooked Deal," *Negro World*, March 26, 921, 7; see chapter 9 in this volume.

22. HH, "The Negro and the Nation," *HR*, 288.

23. HH, "The Negro and the Nation," *HR*, 288–89.

24. HH, "The Negro and the Nation," *HR*, 289. Harrison is referring to the Jeannes Foundation (aka Negro Rural Schools Fund), the Phelps Stokes Fund, and the Carnegie Foundation for the Advancement of Teaching.

25. HH, "The Negro and the Nation," *HR*, 289–90.

26. HH, "The Negro and the Nation," *HR*, 290.

27. Handout re HH talk for the Sunrise Club on "The Ku Klux Klan Past and Present," March 19, 1923, and April 3, 1923, HP, B13, F5–6. The dinner cost $1.50, including tips.

28. HD, March 23, 1923; and "Sunrise Club Dining Society Notices, thirtieth Season, 1922–1923," HP, B16, F42, HPDLC. Later in the year, on June 18, 1923, J. A. Rogers, while in New York, gave Harrison a copy of his book *The Ku Klux Klan Spirit* (New York: Messenger Pub. Co., 1923), HP, B19, F12, in which he wrote—*"A mon ami, H.H.H. avec beaucoup, beaucoup de remerciements pour tous ses effort et sep. interests en moi et nes ouvrages* [To my friend, H.H.H. with much, much gratitude for all your effort and interest in me and my works]."

29. HD, April 3, 1923, where Harrison adds that, on Saturday, March 31, at the luncheon of the New York Public Lecturers' Association, he heard Dr. Crandall; Dr. Thomas J. Walsh, "of Fordham University"; Professor William B. Otis, "the most outspoken reactionary" that he had met; and "old Mr. Carney, an amiable bore," who held him "in friendly esteem." After his arrest and conviction Garvey intensified antisocialist pronouncements and praised Benito Mussolini and the Italian fascist movement. See *GP*, 5:xxxv.

30. Vera Simonton to HH, April 3, [1923?], HP, B3, F38.

31. HH, "Post Multos Annos," notes, April 14, 1923, HP, B5, F55, HPDLC.

32. HD, April 30, 1923.

33. HD, April 30, 1923.

34. HD, April 30, 1923.

35. HD, May 1 and 31, 1923, citing W. E. H. Lecky's biographical introduction to Thomas Carlyle, *The French Revolution: A History* (New York: Appleton, 1900), 1:xiv, xvi.

36. HD, July 2, 1923, citing John Fiske in *The Discovery of America* (1892), 2:441n.

37. *RF*, 58–59, citing "The Policy of the *Messenger* on West Indians and American Negroes—W. A. Domingo vs. Chandler Owen," *Messenger* (March 1923): 639. See *New York Age*, August 28, 1920; and *GP*, 5:117n1.

38. *GP*, 5:8n1; *New York World*, September 6, 1922; *New York Times*, September 6, 1922; *New York Age*, September 9, 1922; *Negro World*, September 23, 1922; *Messenger* 4, no. 10 (October 1922): 499. On the "Garvey Must Go" campaign of 1922 and the hand sent to Randolph, see *RF*, 322–24.

39. See *RF*, 59, citing WEBDB, "A Lunatic or a Traitor," *Crisis*, no. 28 (May 1924): 9.

40. Special Employee Andrew M. Battle, Report, September 8, 1922, *GP*, 5:7–8.

41. Special Agent James E. Amos, [Re: U.S. vs. Marcus Garvey et al.] Report, September 6, 1922, *GP*, 5:6.

42. "'Garvey Must Go' Negroes Declare: Three Harlem Mass Meetings Hear Leader of Improvement Association Criticized," *New York Times*, September 11, 1922; *GP*, 3:xxxiii; 4:679–80; 5:xxxiii, li, 9–11. Around this time Norris and Eason, whom Garvey

had impeached during the 1922 convention, were forming a competing organization, the Universal Negro Alliance.

43. "Dr. Eason, Former Garveyite, Makes Exposures of UNIA," *New York Age*, October 14, 1922, *GP*, 5:48–50.

44. Special Agent James E. Amos, Report, October 19, 1922, *GP*, 5:54–5. See also Theodore Kornweibel Jr., *"Seeing Red": Federal Campaigns Against Black Militancy, 1919–1925* (Bloomington: Indiana University Press, 1998), 62. See *GP*, 4:818n2.

45. "Summary Report of the Books and Records of the Black Star Line and UNIA by Thomas P. Merrilees, Expert Bank Accountant," October 27, 1922, *GP*, 5:58–114, quotation on 101; *GP*, 5:114n3.

46. "Black Star Line Has No Ships," *Savannah Tribune*, November 2, 1922, rpt. from Crusader News Agency, October 30, 1922, *GP*, 5:115–16.

47. MG to William Phillips, November 9, 1922, *GP*, 5:133.

48. "Negro Preacher Is Shot in Back: Eason Tells Police He's a Witness Against Marcus Garvey," *New Orleans Times-Picayune*, January 2, 1923, *GP*, 5:161–62; Harry D. Gulley, Bureau Agent, Report, "U.S. vs. MARCUS GARVEY ET AL (Negro Radicals): Using Mails to Defraud; Probable Conspiracy to Kill Govt. Witness," "Attention Mr. Hoover," January 16, 1923, *GP*, 5:174–80, quotation on 176. See also "Garvey Sympathizers Murder Former Leader: Assassins Kill Rev. J. W. H. Eason," *Amsterdam News*, January 10, 1923; "Report by Special Agent Mortimer J. Davis," January 6, 1923, in re: U.S. vs. Marcus Garvey, et al., Vio. Sec. 215, USCC (Using Mails to Defraud)," *GP*, 5:165–69; and *GP*, 5:lii, 170–72, 174–202, 230–32, 242–46, 263–66, 273–276, 298–300.

49. Report of Special Agent H. D. Gulley, April 10, 1923, DJ-FBI file 61; cited in *GP*, 5:300n2; *GP*, 5:xxxiii–iv, lii, lvi, 108n1, 180n1, 411n3, 202n1; *Chicago Defender*, August 16, 1924; *Negro World*, August 9, 1924; *Amsterdam News*, January 10, 1923; *New York Times*, January 31, 1923, 2; Special Agent James E. Amos, Report, January 17, 1923, *GP*, 5:182–87, including enclosure of draft letter by Chandler Owen et al.

50. Davis, Report, January 6, 1923, *GP*, 5:166–68, 169n1; "Report by Special Agent James Amos, January 13, 1923, DJ-FBI, file 61.

51. "The Murder of Dr. Eason," editorial, *New York News*, January 10, 1923, found in DJ-FBI, file 61, *GP*, 5:170–71. On January 12, while awaiting trial, Garvey had Elie Garcia arrested for petty larceny. UNIA leaders including William H. Ferris increasingly distanced themselves from Garvey, and many UNIA leaders now decided to give the government confidential statements. *GP*, 5:lii. Garvey removed the UNIA officials E. L. Gaines (international organizer), Rudolph Smith (third vice president), G. O. Marke (supreme deputy), and Henrietta Vinton Davis (fourth vice president) in June 1923. In July, Vernal Williams resigned as UNIA attorney, and between June and September William H. Ferris resigned as *Negro World* literary editor. The August 1923 UNIA convention was cancelled.

52. Andrew M. Battle [Special Employee], Report, [January 13, 1923], DJ-FBI, file-61, *GP*, 5:174. See also *GP*, 3:694nn6–7.

53. Andrew M. Battle [Special Employee], Report, [January 16, 1923], DJ-FBI, file-61, GP, 5:181, which on 181–82n1 adds, "On January 20 the *Negro World* launched a defense fund for the two defendants" (citing *Negro World*, January 20, 1923). For Ulysses S. Poston's criticism of Garvey, see *GP*, 9:635–36n2.

54. Pickens et al. to Daugherty, January 15, 1923, *GP*, 5:182–87. See also *GP*, 5:xxxiv, lii, 9:56n2; Amos, Report, January 17, 1923.

55. Special Agent James E. Amos, Report, January 17, 1923, *GP*, 5:182–87, including enclosure of draft letter by Chandler Owen et al. The "American vs. West Indian" theme was apparent in the "Garvey Must Go" campaign, especially in the *Messenger. GP*, 5:217n2. Domingo countered these views in W. A. Domingo, "Open Forum," *Messenger* 5, no. 3 (March 1923): 639–45, which criticized Owen and led to Domingo's quitting the staff. See Theodore Kornweibel Jr., *No Crystal Stair: Black Life and the Messenger* (Westport, CT: Greenwood, 1975), 133–75; and *GP*, 1:260, 2:678.

56. Amos, Report, January 17, 1923; and Owen et al., letter.

57. Amos, Report, January 17, 1923; and Owen et al., letter.

58. Mortimer J. Davis and James E. Amos, Report, January 23, 1923, *GP*, 5:196, 358n30.

59. Andrew M. Battle [Special Employee], Report, January 26, 1923, *GP*, 5:197.

60. *GP*, 5:199n1; J. E. Hoover, to the Director, January 27, 1923, DJ-FBI, file 61.

61. *GP*, 5:200n1; "Report of Special Agent Harry D. Gulley," February 8, 1923, DJ-FBI, file 61. *GP*, 5:180n4.

62. Mortimer Davis Report of February 1, 1923, GP, 4:473–74. The NAACP, ABB, and Friends of Negro Freedom were cited as organizations that fight against the UNIA "Enemy Organizations That Fight Underhand Against Great Movement" *Negro World*, January 27, 1923, 1.

63. Mortimer J. Davis, Report, February 14, 1923, *GP*, 5:243–45. See also *GP* 4:804n2, 5:879; and Robert A. Hill, ed., and Barbara Bair, associate ed., *Marcus Garvey: Life & Lessons; A Centennial Companion to the Marcus Garvey and Universal Negro Improvement Papers* (Berkeley: University of California Press, 1987), 414–15.

64. *GP*, 5:lii, 231n2, 246n1, citing Agent Wilcox to William J. Burns, February 21, 1923, DJ-FBI, file 61. Bureau Agent Gulley in a June 25 report wrote: "C. F. Dyer stated . . . Ramus, from the first time that he met him, always stated that he was going to get DR. EASON." See Harry D. Gulley, Bureau Agent, Report, "Attention Mr. Hoover," June 25, 1923, *GP*, 5:380–81.

65. *GP*, 5:300n1; Reports by Special Agent Mortimer J. Davis, April 11 and 27, 1923, DJ-FBI, file 61.

66. Andrew M. Battle [Special Employee], Report, [April 27, 1923], *GP*, 5:293–94.

67. Battle [Special Employee], Report, [April 27, 1923], *GP*, 5:293–94. After a five-day retrial, a jury would unanimously acquit Dyer and Shakespeare on August 8, 1924. They were declared innocent and freed. The *Negro World* praised the reversal; the *Chicago Defender* called it "the most flagrant case of miscarried justice in the history of the local bar." *GP*, 5:300n1.

68. Mortimer J. Davis, Report, May 10, 1923, *GP*, 5:298–300.

69. *GP*, 5:liii.

70. Davis, Report, May 25, 1923; see *GP*, 3:48–9n.; and "Affidavit of James E. Amos," July 17, 1923, *GP*, 5:402–3.

71. *GP*, 5:373, 382–83n4, 384, 6:59, 66n4, 357n7. See "Writ of Error of Marcus Garvey, Marcus Garvey v. United States, U.S. Circuit Court of Appeals, Second Circuit, New York, October 18, 1924," which cites Marcus Garvey v. United States, no. 8317, Ct. App. 2d Cir., February 2, 1925, 11, in *GP*, 6:14–31. There were others besides Dancy who complained. See DJ-FBI, file 61; and *GP*, 3:607n1, 5:382–83n4.

72. *GP*, 5:liii, 300nn1–2, 382–83n4, 6:59, 66n4; Writ of Error of Marcus Garvey, Marcus Garvey v. United States, U.S. Circuit Court of Appeals, Second Circuit, October 18, 1924; Brief for the United States, Marcus Garvey v. United States, U.S. Circuit Court of

Appeals, Second Circuit, December 10, 1924, in *GP*, 6:49–66, quotation on 49; Marcus Garvey v. United States, no. 8317, Ct. App. 2d Cir., February 2, 1925, 11, in *GP*, 6:14–31. In *GP*, 6:66n4, Hill explains: "The guilty verdict was based upon the third count of the *first* indictment, number C 31/37 of 17 February 1922. In the official trial transcript, however, the verdict was erroneously recorded as based upon 'Count 3 of the 2nd Indictment c. 33–688,' a reference to the indictment of 22 January 1923" (*Marcus Garvey v. United States*, no. 8317, Ct. App., 2d Cir., 2 February 1925, 16). *GP*, 5:382–83n4.

73. *GP*, 5:500nn1– 2. Jamaica's prime minister Edward Seaga requested a full pardon for Garvey from President Ronald Reagan in October 1983; the request was endorsed by Senator Jesse Helms, who lauded Garvey's "dream of black achievement, of black participation in the free enterprise system, and of black leadership throughout the world." Congressman Charles Rangel of New York presented House Resolution no. 84 to the House Subcommittee on Criminal Justice on July 28, 1987. The bill reads, "Expressing the sense of the Congress that the mail fraud charges brought against Marcus Garvey by the federal government were not substantiated and that his conviction on those charges was unjust and unwarranted." *GP*, 7:608n3, *Congressional Record* 98th Cong. 1st sess., pt. S:14, 110–14, esp. 111; *New York Times*, October 18, 1983.

74. HD, June 21, 1923. For Robert A. Hill on the trial, see *GP*, 5:382–83n4. Cronon, *Black Moses*, 117, writes that "the *Negro World* asserted that his [Mack's] charge to the jury was 'a masterpiece of fairness and impartiality'" and that "the Garvey *Negro Times* [before the sentencing] reported in banner headline, Judge Mack charges the jury in an able and impartial way," and announced, "Garvey, man of destiny, calmly awaits verdict." Cronon, 249n31, cites the *Chicago Defender*, June 30, 1923; and *Negro Times*, June 18, 1923.

75. Nahum Daniel Brascher to HH, July 3, 1923, HP, B1, F8; HH, "Marcus Garvey at the Bar of United States Justice," in *HR*, 196–97. For important Harrison diary writings on Garvey, see "24-5-20[;] 17-3-1920 & following 25 pages[;] and also 10-12-1920 re Crichlow $100 a day." This is based on his entry in HD, after August 8, 1923.

76. HH, "Marcus Garvey at the Bar of United States Justice," *HR*, 195.

77. HH, "Marcus Garvey at the Bar of United States Justice," *HR*, 195–96.

78. HH, "Marcus Garvey at the Bar of United States Justice," *HR*, 196.

79. HH, "Marcus Garvey at the Bar of United States Justice," *HR*, 196. *RF*, 160–61, explains that the ship was advertised "'on or about' March 27 and later 'on or about April 25'" and that some $8,900 was collected from bookings. The money was mixed with other funds and was never refunded. Du Bois concurred on the fairness of the trial. He wrote: "No Negro in America ever had a fairer and more patient trial than Marcus Garvey. He convicted himself by his own admissions, his swaggering monkey-shiens in the court room with monocle and long tailed coat and his insults to the judge and the prosecuting attorney." WEBDB, "A Lunatic or a Traitor," *Crisis* 27, no. 7 (May 1924): 8–9; rpt. in *GP*, 5:583–84.

80. HH, "Marcus Garvey at the Bar of United States Justice," *HR*, 196–97.

81. HH, "Marcus Garvey at the Bar of United States Justice," *HR*, 197.

82. HH, "Marcus Garvey at the Bar of United States Justice," *HR*, 197–98. Charles S. Johnson, "After Garvey—What?" *Opportunity* 1, no. 8 (August 1923): 231–33, 232, writes similarly: "Obviously there was evidence of even greater guilt than could be established by witnesses. The specific count on which he was convicted was that of selling stock in the Black Star Line after it had become and was known to him to be insolvent."

According to J. A. Rogers, Garvey told him in an interview in London: "I am going to say now what I have refrained from saying in America because of the harm it might have done in places like Harlem. I wish to say, emphatically, that the Negro must beware of the Jew. The Jew is no friend of the Negro, though the Negro has been taught to believe that." Rogers says Garvey went on: "When they wanted to get me, they had a Jewish judge try me, and a Jewish prosecutor (Mattuck). I would have been freed but two Jews on the jury held out against me ten hours and succeeded in convicting me, whereupon the Jewish judge gave me the maximum penalty." See *Philadelphia Tribune*, September 27, 1928; quoted in J. A. Rogers, "Additional Facts on Marcus Garvey and His Trial for Using the Mails to Defraud," Negroes of New York Writers Program, New York, 1939, NN-Sc, in *GP*, 6:367n3.

83. HH, "Marcus Garvey at the Bar of United States Justice," 198.

84. HH, "Marcus Garvey at the Bar of United States Justice," 198.

85. HH, "Marcus Garvey at the Bar of United States Justice," 198–99. On Isaac Newton Braithwaite, see *GP*, 2:580n17; and Hill and Bair, *Marcus Garvey: Life & Lessons*, 364.

86. HH, "Marcus Garvey at the Bar of United States Justice," 199. *The Emperor Jones* theme was subsequently used by Robert Morse Lovett, "An Emperor Jones of Finance," *New Republic*, July 11, 1923; and Charles S. Johnson. In the August 1923 issue of *Opportunity*, perhaps influenced by Harrison, Johnson also referred to Garvey as "the 'Emperor Jones of Finance.'" See Johnson, "After Garvey—What?," 231–33, 231.

87. HH, "Marcus Garvey at the Bar of United States Justice," 199. Rev. E. Ethelred Brown, in his August 12, 1923, sermon on "Garvey-istic Devotion," described the affection of Garvey's followers as "affection for a person gone stark staring mad." E. Ethelred Brown, "Garvey-istic Devotion," sermon, August 12, 1923, NN-SC, E. Ethelred Brown Papers, in *GP*, 5:423–31, esp. 426–27. Interestingly, Colin Grant, *Negro with a Hat: The Rise and Fall of Marcus Garvey* (New York: Oxford University Press, 2008), 448, tells of Garvey's first wife, Amy Ashwood Garvey, seeing him in Hyde Park, London, in the last year of his life and describing how Marcus "caught sight of his former wife, and immediately 'drooping shoulders were straightened and he mounted the platform in the manner of the old Liberty Hall Days. He tried hard to recapture the power of those days, but alas it was too late. . . . He could no longer carry his listeners; even hecklers got the better of him."

88. HH, "Religion and Education, Reviews of *They Call Me Carpenter: A Tale of the Second Coming*, . . . and *The Goose Step: A Study of American Education*, . . . by Upton Sinclair," *Amsterdam News*, May 2, 1923, HP, B6, F9; Upton Sinclair, *They Call Me Carpenter: A Tale of the Second Coming* (New York: Boni and Liveright, 1922), https://archive.org/details/theycallmecarpe00sincgoog/page/n8; Upton Sinclair, *The Goose-Step: A Study of American Education* (Pasadena, CA: Upton Sinclair, 1923), https://archive.org/details/goosestepstudyof00sinc/page/n9. Harrison's papers contain an undated and apparently unpublished review of *Oil*. See HH, n.d., unpublished, "*Oil*—By Upton Sinclair," [a review] by Hubert Harrison, 2 pp., HP, B5, F44.

89. HH, "Religion and Education."

90. HH, "Religion and Education."

91. Robert Reiss to HH, May 9, 1923, HP-Co.

92. Ticket for Silver Jubilee Parade of the Municipal Departments Under the Auspices of Mayor's Committee on Celebration of the 25th Anniversary of the Greater City of New York Saturday, May 26, 1923; Ticket for Mayor's Committee on Celebration of 25th Anniversary of the Greater City of New York, June 16, 1923; and Announcement,

"Dr. H. H. Harrison [D. Sc.], Sigma Tau Sigma Guest of Honor May 29, *1923*," all at HP, B13, F5–6.

93. HD, June 3, 1923. Casper Alexander Joseph (1877–1944) was born in St. Croix and after moving to Brooklyn started using his mother's maiden name, Holstein. He became a Harlem political activist, philanthropist for Black causes, and a successful businessman. He was known as the "king of Policy" for the lucrative system of [illegal] betting on three-digit "numbers" he devised. He was particularly active around matters pertaining to the Virgin Islands and was the principal financial contributor to *Opportunity*'s prize contest. See George F. Tyson, ed., *Searching for Truth and Justice: The Writings of Ralph D. de Chabert, 1915–1922* (Christiansted, St. Croix: Antilles Press, 2009), xvi; Kellner, ed., *The Harlem Renaissance*, 171–72; Edgar M. Grey, "Is the Numbers an Evil in Harlem," *New York Daily News*, December 17, 1927; "Rich Negro Seized for $50,000 Ransom," *New York Times*, September 23, 1928; "Wealthy Negro Is Set Free by His Abductors," *New York Times*, September 24, 1928; Thomas J. Randall, "Policy 'King' Defies Graft Probers," *Daily Mirror*, December 23, 1930; and *Opportunity* 3, no. 1 (July 1925): 220; *Opportunity* 3, no. 34 (October 1925): 38–39; *Opportunity* 4, no. 46 (October 1926): 318; and *Opportunity* 5, no. 6 (June 1927): 179.

94. Menu and Seating Arrangements for "A Testimonial Dinner to Horace B. Liveright in recognition of his important part in the successful fight against the so-called 'Clean Books' bill at the Hotel Brevoort Thursday, June 14, 1923," HP, B13 F5–6; HD, June 21, 1923. In 1917 Liveright's book publishing company attracted Eugene O'Neill and other controversial authors and frequently had conflicts with the Society for the Suppression of Vice. Liveright wrote articles on censorship, and in 1924 the company waged a successful campaign against a proposed "clean books bill" in the state legislature. See *ENY*, 124. Rascoe described Liveright as "the St. George among publishers for his gallant single-handed triumph over the ... dragon of censorship."

95. Burton Rascoe, "A Bookman's Day Book—Thurs. 6/14/23," *New York Tribune*, June 24, 1923, HP, B13, F5–6. On Thursday, November 1, 1923, Harrison wrote in his diary: "Last night, the flush of work still on me, I began for H. L. Mencken's magazine an article on 'The Superior Anglo-Saxon' for which he had asked me sometime ago." He did several hundred words that day. HD, November 1, 1923.

96. Rascoe, "A Bookman's Day Book."

97. HH, "The Negro Actor on Broadway: A Critical Interpretation by a Negro Critic," *New York World*, June 4, 1923, HP, B5, F27, HPDLC, in *HR*, 383–87.

98. HH, "The Negro Actor on Broadway."

99. HH, "The Negro Actor on Broadway." Willis Richardson (1889–1977) was a playwright who worked as a clerk for the U.S. Bureau of Printing and Engraving from 1910 until his retirement in 1955. His most famous work was *The Chip Woman's Fortune*, performed in Harlem in 1923 by the Ethiopian Art Players. It moved to Broadway on May 15, where it was the first serious play by a Black writer to be performed on the "white stage." See Kellner, *Harlem Renaissance*, 72–73, 302; *Opportunity* 2, no. 22 (October 1924): 317.

100. HH, "The Negro Actor on Broadway."

101. HH, "The Negro Actor on Broadway."

102. HH, "The Negro Actor on Broadway."

103. HH, "Caliban in the Slums: *Goat Alley: A Play in Three Acts*," *New Republic*, July 18, 1923, 214, HP, B4, F27; Ernest Howard Culbertson, *Goat Alley: A Tragedy of Negro*

Life (Cincinnati, OH: Stewart Kidd Co., c. 1922), https://catalog.hathitrust.org/Record /006152895; and Johnson, *Black Manhattan*, 192.

104. HH, "Caliban in the Slums," 214.

105. HH, "Caliban in the Slums," 214.

106. "Dignity of the Flag Upheld: Lecturer Fined for Displaying Ensigns of 10 by 16 Inches," *New York Globe*, July 32, 1923, HP, B13, F5–6; Joseph G. Tucker, "Special Report of Radical Activities Covering Greater New York District," August 4, 1923, 61-23-240, FOIPA-HH.

107. HD, August 2, 1923.

108. HD, August 2, 1923. Six days later, on August 8, Aida's left foot "was run over" by an American Railway Express Company truck at 139th Street and Lenox Avenue. She was taken to Harlem Hospital, where X-rays showed no broken bones. See HD, August 8, 1923.

109. HH to Dr. Jacob Ross, October 10, 1923, HP, B2, F14, HPDLC.

110. HD, December 3, 1923.

111. HD, November 1, 1923, while living at 2484 Seventh Avenue. HH, "The Virgin Islands: A Colonial Problem," combined handwritten and typed manuscript sent to *The Nation*, before December 6, 1923, HP, B6, F48; rpt. in *HR*, 241–50. See Ireta Van Doren to HH, October 5, 1923, HP, B3, F46; Ernest H. Gruening to HH, November 25, 1922, HP, B1, F62; "*The Nation* announces its Complete Editorial Separation from the *New York Evening Post*," *Nation*, July 6, 1923, 1; Ashley L. Totten, "The Truth Neglected in the Virgin Islands," *Nation*, first part, July 1926, and second part, August 1926, in Tom Lutz and Susanna Ashton, eds., *These "Colored" United States* (New Brunswick, NJ: Rutgers University Press, 1996), 275–88.

112. HH, "The Virgin Islands," 241–42.

113. HH, "The Virgin Islands," 242–43. On Sir Henry Morgan (1635–1688), see Sherry, *Raiders and Rebels*, 60, 80.

114. HH, "The Virgin Islands," 243.

115. HH, "The Virgin Islands," 243–44.

116. HH, "The Virgin Islands," 244.

117. HH, "The Virgin Islands," 244–45.

118. HH, "The Virgin Islands," 244–45. For important additional information on the St. Croix Labor Union, see George F. Tyson, ed., *Searching for Truth and Justice: The Writings of Ralph D. Chabert, 1915–1922* (Christiansted, St. Croix, USVI: Antilles Press, 2009).

119. HH, "The Virgin Islands," 245.

120. HH, "The Virgin Islands," 245–46. Edwin Denby (1870–1929) served as U.S. secretary of the navy (1921–1924).

121. HH, "The Virgin Islands," 246.

122. HH, "The Virgin Islands," 246–47.

123. HH, "The Virgin Islands," 247.

124. HH, "The Virgin Islands," 247–48.

125. HH, "The Virgin Islands," 248.

126. HH, "The Virgin Islands," 249.

127. HH, "The Virgin Islands," 249; William W. Boyer, *America's Virgin Islands: A History of Human Rights and Wrongs* (Durham, NC: Carolina Academic Press, 1983), 130; Isaac Dookhan, "The Search for Identity," *Journal of Caribbean History* 21 (1979): 1–34, esp. 12, which says Jackson started the "most vociferously and persistently

anti-government" *Herald* in St. Croix on October 29, 1915, while Francis started the *Emancipator* in St. Thomas on May 21, 1921. Barrow was an editor of the *Herald*.

128. HH, "The Virgin Islands," 249.

129. HH, "The Virgin Islands," 249–50.

130. HH, "The Virgin Islands," 250.

131. Ernest Gruening to HH, December 6, 1923, and January 19, 1924, HP, B1, F62; Ashley L. Totten, "The Truth Neglected in the Virgin Islands," *Nation*, July and August 1926; in Lutz and Ashton, eds., *These "Colored" United States*, 275–88.

132. Boyer, *America's Virgin Islands*, 163.

133. HH, "The Partition of Africa: [Review of] *The Partition and Colonization of Africa* by Charles Lucas," *Nation*, September 5, 1923, HP, B5, F51; Charles Lucas, *The Partition and Colonization of Africa* (Oxford: Clarendon, 1922), https://archive.org/details /partitioncoloniz00lucauoft/page/n5.

134. HH, "Christian History: *A Short History of Christianity*, by Salomon Reinach," *Nation*, October 3, 1923, 358–59, HP, B4, F31; Salomon Reinach, *A Short History of Christianity* (New York: G. P. Putnam's Sons, 1922), https://catalog.hathitrust.org/Record /006582513.

135. HH, "The Real Negro Humor: Brought Out, Says a Writer of the Race, in Octavus Roy Cohen's Tales," *New York World*, October 23, 1923, HP, B6, F4; rpt. in *HR*, 337–39, quotations on 338; Octavus Roy Cohen, *Dark Days and Black Knights* (New York: Dodd, Mead, 1923). See also "The Creator of Florian Slappey: Octavus Roy Cohen," *New York Times*, January 14, 1923. Octavus Roy Cohen (1891–1959) was born in Charleston, South Carolina.

136. HH, "The Real Negro Humor," 338.

137. HH, "The Real Negro Humor," 338–39.

138. HH, "What A Profound Literary Scholar Thinks of Pickens' Book," Associated Negro Press, c. November 1923, HP, B6, F54, HPDLC; William Pickens, *Bursting Bonds: The Heir of Slaves*, enlarged ed. (Boston: Jordan & More, 1923), https://catalog.hathitrust .org/Record/008585478.

139. HH, "Black Bards of Yesterday and Today: by Hubert H. Harrison, *The Book of American Negro Poetry*, Selected and Edited by James Weldon Johnson," *National Star*, December 16, 1923, [bottom part missing], HP, B4, F13; rpt. in *HR*, 394–96, quotations on 395; James Weldon Johnson, ed., *The Book of American Negro Poetry* (New York, Harcourt, Brace & Co., 1922), http://www.gutenberg.org/ebooks/11986.

140. HH, "Black Bards of Yesterday and Today," *HR*, 395–96.

141. HH, "Black Bards of Yesterday and Today," *HR*, 396.

142. HH, "Black Bards of Yesterday and Today," *HR*, 396.

143. HH, [re Beer, *African Questions at the Paris Peace Conference* (New York, 1923), c. 1923,] HP, B5, F26, HPDLC. On German policies of segregation and white supremacy, see *GP*, 9:269n3. George Beer, *African Questions at the Paris Peace Conference: With Papers on Egypt, Mesopotamia, and the Colonial Settlement*, ed. Louis Herbert Gray (New York: Macmillan, 1923), https://catalog.hathitrust.org/Record/000488119.

144. Floyd Calvin, Extracts (written by HH) from Calvin's letter to HH, November 12, 1923, 5 (p. 3 missing), HP, B8, F3; and "Passing the First Half-Century Mark," *Truth Seeker* 50, no. 35 (September 1): 553–70. See also JBP, "Hubert Harrison: Pioneering African American Activist in the Freethought Movement," *Truth Seeker* (May–August 2017): 6–14, 44–46.

145. Calvin, Extracts (written by HH) from Calvin's letter to HH, November 12, 1923.

146. HH, "The League of Nations and the Present European Crisis," handwritten lecture notes [with theatre notes on back for lecture on November 18, 1911, at PS 89 for Bd. of Ed.], c. November 18, 1923, HP, B5, F8, HPDLC.

147. HH, "The League of Nations and the Present European Crisis." Marcus Garvey later expressed admiration for Hitler as a forceful nationalist and patriot who had brought "national salvation" and "control" to his country. In 1933 he wrote that Chancellor Hitler "cannot be mistaken for anything else than a patriot. He loves Germany and desires to see that country restored to its heretofore distinguished Imperial position." While he later recognized that "Hitler hates the Jew, he also hates the Negro," he also praised him and noted "the Germans want to keep their blood pure, just as we want to keep ours pure." Garvey went so far as to claim that "the race purity idea" was developed by "we Negroes of pride, long before Hitler discovered [it]." See Marcus Garvey, "Adolph [sic] Hitler," *Blackman* 1, no. 1 (December 1933): 1–2, 2–3, *GP*, 7:567; *Blackman* 1, no. 2 (January 1934): 13–14; *Blackman* 2, no. 3 (September–October 1936): 1–2; *GP*, 7:568n2.

148. HH, "The League of Nations and the Present European Crisis."

149. HH, [notes re Theater and Florence Mills], November 18, 1923, HP-Wr.

150. HD, December 2, 1923.

151. HD, December 2, 1923.

152. Charles S. Johnson to HH, December 8 and December 26, 1923, HP, B2, F53. Charles Spurgeon Johnson (1893–1956) became director of research and publicity for the National Urban League, edited the *Urban League Bulletin*, and, in 1923, founded the organization's *Opportunity* magazine to supplement, not compete with, *The Crisis* by focusing on Harlem's cultural activities. Langston Hughes considered him one of the three "midwives" of the Harlem renaissance (with Jessie Fauset and Alain Locke). Preston Valien and Bonita H. Valien, "Charles Spurgeon Johnson," in *DANB*, 347–49; Kellner, *Harlem Renaissance*, 192.

153. Phil A. Jones to HH, December 20, 1923; and January 4, 1924, HP, B2, F56.

15. *Boston Chronicle*, Board of Ed, and the *New Negro*
(January–June 1924)

1. Master Alcofribas [HH], "The Demi-Men" and "Flappers vs. Bachelors," *Tattler*, January 20 and 27, 1924, HP, B4, F57; and Steven Watson, *The Harlem Renaissance: Hub of African-American Culture, 1920–1930* (New York: Pantheon, 1995), 136. On François Rabelais (c. 1483–1553), see Donald M. Frame, *François Rabelais: A Study* (New York: Harcourt Brace Jovanovich, 1977), esp. xii–xv, 12, 14, 20, 22–24. One of the remaining books in Harrison's collection (obtained on September 14, 1927, and subsequently annotated) was Francois Rabelais, *The Works of Rabelais*, ed. and trans. Urquhart and Motteux, ill. Chalon (London: Published for the trade, [n.d.]), HP, B24.

2. Master Alcofribas [HH], "Over at Joe's," *Tattler*, February 3, 1924, HP, B4, F57. "Joe's" may have been "Joe Wood's Coconut Grove," in the basement of 253 West 125th Street, which was owned by the entrepreneur Leo Brecher and his partner, the former Lower East Side schoolteacher Frank Schiffman. The building, which had opened in 1913 as Hurtig and Seamon's Music Hall, later gained fame as Harlem's famed Apollo Theatre. David Hinckley, "Top of the World: The Apollo, 1934," *New York Daily News*, May 12, 1998.

3. Master Alcofribas [HH], "Over at Joe's."

4. Master Alcofribas [HH], "Over at Joe's."

5. Wendell K. Thomas to HH, January 16, 1924, HP, B3, F42.

6. HH, "The Rent and Housing Situation," handwritten notes for "Board of Education Lecture, Sunday Jan. 20th 1924—Hubert Harrison," c. January 20, 1924, HP, B6, F10, HPDLC.

7. HH, "What Should Be the Immigration Policy of the U.S.A.?" handwritten notes (for a lecture), February 17, 1924 (also November 30, 1924), HP, B6, F56, HPDLC.

8. HH, "What Should Be the Immigration Policy of the U.S.A.?"

9. HH, "What Should Be the Immigration Policy of the U.S.A.?"

10. "Shining Lights of Literature," March–April 1924 New York City Board of Education Public Lecture Series handout card, HP, B13, F5–6. See, for example, "Summing Up Shaw: notes from Board of Education lecture regarding George Bernard Shaw," April 26, 1924, HP, B6, F35, HPDLC.

11. HH, "The Record of the 68th Congress and Problems of the 69th," Handwritten notes for a lecture, March (1924?), HP, B6, F6, HPDLC. See also HH, "Committees Legislate," handwritten notes, c. 1924. Around March (1924?) Harrison also handwrote: "When younger I knew more than now / I knew everything / —All could be reduced to *one* / What does 'the juridical relations' / Express in *case* of *murder, perjury, drunkenness.*" HH, "When younger . . . ," handwritten notes, March (1924?). In that same period, Harrison also obtained a copy of John Moffatt Mecklin, *The Ku Klux Klan: A Study of the American Mind* (New York: Harcourt, Brace and Co., 1924).

12. HH, "The West Indian in the United States," handwritten notes [for a lecture], March 30, 1924, HP, B6, F52, HPDLC. On Wibecan, see *Who's Who in Colored America: A Biographical Dictionary of Notable Living Persons of Negro Descent in America, 1938–40*, ed. Thomas Yenser (Brooklyn, NY: Thomas Yenser, 1940), 561; and Edward R. Lewinson, *Black Politics in New York City* (New York: Twayne, 1974), 83–84.

13. The Permanent Committee of the Public Lecture Forum to Ernest Crandall, Letter re HH, Early Spring 1924, HP, B3, F7.

14. William Pickens to HH, n.d., [NB: p. 1 is missing,] HP, B3, F9.

15. Ernest Crandall to HH, May 20, 1924, HP, B3, F7.

16. Wendell K. Thomas to HH, October 6, 1924, HP, B3, F42.

17. HH, "History and Forecast of the Disarmament Movement," handwritten lecture notes by HH, November 16, 1924, HP, B4, F69, HPDLC.

18. HH, "History and Forecast of the Disarmament Movement."

19. HH, "History and Forecast of the Disarmament Movement."

20. Alfred Haughton to HH, December 21, 1923, and January 4, 1923[4], January 22, 1924, HP, B2, F35. The *Boston Chronicle*'s office was located in a four-story building at Northampton and Tremont Streets in Boston.

21. "Dr. Hubert Harrison," *Boston Chronicle*, January 26, 1924, HP, B13, F5–6. James Larkin (1876–1947) was born in Liverpool, England, to poor Irish Catholic parents. In 1893 he joined the socialist Independent Labor Party, was arrested several times for opposition to the Boer War, became involved in the 1905 dock strike, and in 1906 was elected general organizer for the National Union of Dock Workers. In 1908 he founded the Irish Transport and General Workers Union and was elected general secretary in 1910. Together with James Connolly, Larkin led the Irish Socialist Party. He also edited the *Irish Worker*. After traveling to the United States in 1914 he formed the James Connolly Socialist Club of New York, allied with John Reed in the left wing of the SP, and was a founding member of the Communist Labor Party. In 1920 Larkin

was convicted of criminal anarchy for which he served almost three years before receiving a pardon and being deported in 1923. See Harvey Klehr, "James Larkin," in Johnpoll and Klehr, eds., *Biographical Dictionary of the American Left*, 240–41; Branko Lazitch in collaboration with Milorad M. Drachovitch, *Biographical Dictionary of the Comintern*, new rev. and exp. ed. (Stanford, CA: Hoover Institution Press, 1986), 248–49; Solon De Leon, ed., in collaboration with Irma C. Hayssen and Grace Poole, *American Labor Who's Who* (New York: Hanford, 1925), 300–1; Bruce Nelson, *Irish Nationalists and the Making of the Irish Race* (Princeton, NJ: Princeton University Press, 2012), 47, 52, 255; Bertram D. Wolfe, *Strange Communists I Have Known* (New York: Stein and Day, 1965), 52–71.

22. HH, "Our International Consciousness," *Boston Chronicle*, January 12, 1924 [?], HP, B6, F43.

23. Jessie Redmon Fauset (April 27, 1882–April 30, 1960), the first Black woman to graduate from Cornell University, was a writer and poet who served as literary editor of the *Crisis* from 1919 to 1926. She attended the Second Pan-African Congress in London, Brussels, and Paris. See Jessie Fauset, "Impressions of the Second Pan African Congress," *Crisis* 23, no. 1 (November 1921): 12–18, https://www.marxists.org/history/usa/workers/civil-rights/crisis/1100-crisis-v23n01-w133.pdf; and "What Europe Thought of the Pan-African Conference," *Crisis* 23, no. 2 (December 1921): 60–68, https://www.marxists.org/history/usa/workers/civil-rights/crisis/1200-crisis-v23n02-w134.pdf; Arthur Davis, "Jessie [Redmon] Fauset," *DANB*, 219–20; *GP*, 9:166n4, citing Kellner, ed., *Harlem Renaissance*, 120–21; and *ENY*, 393.

24. HH, "Our International Consciousness." "*Bantu* peoples" is used as a general label for the three hundred to six hundred ethnic groups in Africa who speak Bantu languages. They inhabit a geographical area stretching east and southward from central Africa across the African Great Lakes region down to southern Africa.

25. HH, "Our International Consciousness."

26. HH, "Our International Consciousness." Harrison kept organized clippings on many of these topics in his three surviving "Weltpolitik" scrapbooks from the 1921–1926 period. See chapter 13, note 76, in this volume.

27. HH, "Our International Consciousness."

28. HH, "The World We Live In," *Boston Chronicle*, January 19, 1924, HP, B6, F43.

29. HH, "The World We Live In."

30. HH, "'English as She Is Spoke,'" *Boston Chronicle*, January 26, 1924, HP, B6, F43.

31. HH, "'English as She Is Spoke.'"

32. HH, "'English as She Is Spoke.'" Among books he cited were *The New Testament of Our Lord and Savior Jesus Christ* (New York: American Bible Society, 1891), which he obtained on November 5, 1914, HP, B20; and the "Last book read by Hubert Harrison 9/24/27 in Bellevue Hospital": Sir George Otto Trevelyan, *The Life and Letters of Lord Macaulay*, vol. 1 (New York, 1909), HP, B23.

33. HH, "Science and Race Prejudice," *Boston Chronicle*, February 2, 1924, HP, B6, F43. In his personal copy of Dowd, *The Negro Races*, after Dowd on 86 offers a lengthy paragraph purporting to explain "the face features . . . of the Negro" Harrison writes: "*Quote* entire passage as example of the weird superstitions with which American scholars approach the scientific problem of race."

34. HH, "Science and Race Prejudice."

35. HH, "Science and Race Prejudice."

36. HH, "Science and Race Prejudice."

37. HH, "The Newspaper and Social Service," *Boston Chronicle*, February 9, 1924, HP, B6, F43.

38. HH, "The Newspaper and Social Service."

39. HH, "The Newspaper and Social Service."

40. HH, "The Newspaper and Social Service."

41. "'Lincoln & Liberty' Lecture by Dr. Hubert H. Harrison Graduate of Copenhagen, Denmark, Historian; 3 Years lecturer of New York Board of Education; Soldier, And Globe Trotter, Ford Hall, Lincoln's Birthday, February 12 Under Auspices of *Boston Chronicle*," *Boston Chronicle*, c. February 2, 1924, HP, B6, F43, was advertised with a quote from Professor Kendrick Shedd, of the University of Rochester. See also "Plan for Crowds at Ford Hall," *Boston Chronicle*, February 2, 1924, HP, B6, F43; Alfred Haughton to HH, February 4, 1924, HP, B2, F35; "Colored Soldiers Refused Half Pay: Dr. Harrison Honors Lincoln but Points Out Expedients Adopted by Emancipator. Lauds Frederick Douglass," *Boston Chronicle*, February 16, 1924, 1, 3, HP, B6, F43; and "Scholar Likes Lincoln," *Christian Science Monitor*, February 13, 1924, HP, B13, F5–6. Arthur H. Moore, chairman of the Boston Urban League, presided.

42. "Lincoln & Liberty," *Boston Chronicle*, c. February 2, 1924; "Plan for Crowds at Ford Hall"; Haughton to HH, February 4, 1924; "Colored Soldiers Refused Half Pay"; and "Scholar Likes Lincoln."

43. "Colored Soldiers Refused Half Pay."

44. "Colored Soldiers Refused Half Pay," 3; "Black Fighter Won Civil War for the Union: Statement Made by Colored Lecturer in Address on Lincoln," *Haverhill* (MA) *Evening Gazette*, February 15, 1924, HP, B12, F8–9.

45. "Black Fighter Won Civil War for the Union."

46. "Black Fighter Won Civil War for the Union."

47. "Black Fighter Won Civil War for the Union."

48. William Pickens to HH, February 20, 1924, HP, B3, F9; and William Pickens, *American Aesop: Negro and Other Humor* (New York: Jordan and Moore, 1926).

49. Alfred Tennyson, *Gems From Tennyson*, ill. W. J. Hennessy [et al.] (Boston: Ticknor and Fields, 1866), HP, B25, has written comments by HH on 16, 90.

50. HH, "Lincoln and Douglass," *Boston Chronicle*, February 16, 1924, HP, B6, F43.

51. HH, "Lincoln and Douglass."

52. HH, "Lincoln and Douglass."

53. HH, "Education out of School," *Boston Chronicle*, February 23, 1924, HP, B6, F43; rpt. in *HR*, 125–26, quotation on 125.

54. HH, "Education out of School," 125–26.

55. HH, "Education out of School," 126.

56. HH, "Education out of School," 126. George W. Stocking Jr., in discussing two of Harrison's preferred authors, Henry Thomas Buckle and Herbert Spencer, suggests that "standing outside the normal process by which intellectual traditions are transmitted, the autodidact may embody the spirit of his age in an unusually direct way." See George W. Stocking Jr., *Victorian Anthropology* (New York: Free Press, 1987), 112.

57. HH, "A Few Books," *Boston Chronicle*, March 1, 1924, HP, B6, F43. In his copy of Stoddard, *The Rising Tide of Color*, Harrison on 148 writes: "It seems then that a new explanatory formula for power and progress is necessary. And that formula is given by a genuine historical scholar in John M. Robertson's 'The Evolution of States' (1913) 152."

58. HH, "A Few Books," *Boston Chronicle*, March 1, 1924. On a later effort "to supply literature on the Negro adapted to the home and the school," see Carter G. Woodson to

HH, May 6 1927, HP, B3, F55. On May 17, 1927, Harrison received Carter Godwin Wood-son, *The Negro in Our History* (Washington, DC: Associated Publishers, 1927), HP, B26.

59. HH, "A Few Books," *Boston Chronicle*, March 1, 1924.

60. HH, "Race Consciousness," *Boston Chronicle*, March 15, 1924, HP, B6, F43; rpt. in *HR*, 116–17.

61. HH, "Race Consciousness," *HR*, 116–17.

62. HH, "The Feet of the Young Men," *Boston Chronicle*, March 22, 1924, HP, B6, F43.

63. HH, "The Negro-American Speaks," *Boston Chronicle*, March 29, 1924, HP, B6, F43.

64. HH, "The Negro-American Speaks."

65. HH, "Opening the Doors," *Boston Chronicle*, April 5, 1924, HP, B6, F43. Cooper Union (for the Advancement of Science and Art), a private, tuition-free college at Astor Place in Manhattan, was founded by Peter Cooper in 1859 "to provide a free education to gifted students from the working class." Abraham Lincoln spoke at its Great Hall on February 27, 1860. See *ENY*, 279, 282–83; Herbert Mitgang, "Cooper Union's Past Is on Exhibit," *New York Times*, June 15, 1987; The Great Hall of the Cooper Union at Cooper Square, "Fall Program for 1986," possession of JBP.

66. HH, "Opening the Doors." A similar liberating experience was had by the historian Nathan Huggins at the University of California, Berkeley, where he found that "I could float my ideas out there on a bluebook under the name of Nathan Huggins, and nobody knew whether I was a good guy or a bad guy." See Lawrence W. Levine, "The Historical Odyssey of Nathan Irvin Huggins," in Nathan Irvin Huggins, *Revelations: American History, American Myths*, ed. Brenda Smith Huggins (New York: Oxford University Pres, 1995), 5.

67. HH, "Opening the Doors."

68. HH, "Population, Immigration, and the Negro," *Boston Chronicle*, April 19, 1924, HP, B6, F43.

69. HH, "Population, Immigration, and the Negro."

70. HH, "'Superior'—to Whom," *Boston Chronicle*, May 3, 1924, HP, B6, F43. See also HH, "Unintelligent Intelligence Tests," *New Leader* 1, no. 42 (November 1, 1924): 8, HP, B12, F8–9.

71. HH, "The Right Way to Unity," *Boston Chronicle*, May 10, 1924, HP, B6, F43; rpt. in *HR*, 402–4.

72. HH, "The Right Way to Unity," *HR*, 403–4.

73. *HHVHR*, 125–26, 446n35. See also WEBDB, "Talented Tenth," in Booker T. Washington et al., *The Negro Problem: A Series of Articles by Representative American Negroes of Today* (New York: James Pott, 1903), 33–75, quotations on 42, 75. Martin Luther King Jr.'s early assessment of Du Bois's "Talented Tenth" concept, as expressed in his *Stride Toward Freedom*, was, according to David Levering Lewis, "W. E. B. Du Bois and the Dilemma of Race," *Prologue* 27, no. 1 (Spring 1995): 43, that it was "a tactic for an aristocratic elite who would themselves be benefited while leaving behind the 'untalented' 90 per cent."

74. WEBDB, *Dusk of Dawn: An Essay Toward an Autobiography of a Race Concept* (1940; New York: Schocken, 1968), 216–17; and Nathan I. Huggins, *Harlem Renaissance* (New York: Oxford University Press, 1971), 5.

75. HH, "The Common People," *Boston Chronicle*, May 17, 1924, HP, B6, F43; rpt. in *HR*, 404–5.

76. HH, "The Common People," *HR*, 404–5.

77. HH, "Seeking a Way Out," *Boston Chronicle*, May 31, 1924, HP, B6, F43. In his 1895 Atlanta Exposition Address Booker T. Washington advised southern Blacks to "cast down your buckets where you are," and he advised southern whites to similarly "cast down your buckets" and utilize available southern Black labor. See Louis R. Harlan and Raymond W. Smock, eds., *The Booker T. Washington Papers*, 13 vols. (Urbana: University of Illinois Press, 1972–1984), 3:584–85.

78. HH, "On Reading Negro Books," *Boston Chronicle*, June 7, 1924, HP, B6, F43. On "Ode to Ethiopia," see Paul Laurence Dunbar, *The Complete Poems*, intro. W. D. Howells (1895; New York: Dodd, Mead, & Co., 1913), 16.

79. HH, "On Reading Negro Books." Harrison made handwritten corrections to the last lines in his papers.

80. HH, "In Case of War—What?," *Boston Chronicle*, June 14, 1924, HP, B6, F43.

81. HH, "In Case of War—What?"

82. HH, "The Roots of Power," *Boston Chronicle*, June 21, 1924, HP, B6, F43; rpt. in *HR*, 405–6.

83. HH, "The Roots of Power," *HR*, 406.

84. HH, "How to End Lynching," *Boston Chronicle*, June 28, HP, B6, F43; in *HR*, 270–71.

85. HH, "How to End Lynching," *HR*, 271.

86. Charles S. Johnson to HH, March 13, 1924, HP, B2, F53. On the coming-out party see also Jervis Anderson, *This Was Harlem: A Cultural Portrait, 1900–1950* (New York: Farrar Straus Giroux, 1982), 200–3, 204–7; and Chidi Ikonné, *From Du Bois to Van Vechten: The Early New Negro Literature, 1903–1926* (Westport, CT: Greenwood, 1981), 92–93.

87. Jeffrey C. Stewart, *The New Negro: The Life of Alain Locke* (New York: Oxford University Press, 2018), 408–9, 894nn1–3.

88. Stewart, *The New Negro*, 434–35; and A. L. (Alain Leroy Locke) to Mr. [Paul] Kellogg, c. April 5, 1924, in Locke Files, B94, F710.

89. Alain Locke to "Mr. [Paul] Kellogg," April 16, 1924, in Locke Files, B94, F710.

90. PUK [Paul Kellogg] to GS [Gertrude Springer], memo, April 30, 1924, Locke Files, B94, F710. Linnea M. Anderson, archivist, Social Welfare History Archives, University of Minnesota, to JBP, December 31, 2015, writes that GS "is probably Gertrude Springer."

91. Outline of "The *Survey Graphic* Harlem Issue," n.d., in Locke Files, B94, F710. Linnea M. Anderson writes, regarding the three-page memo, "Yes, it appears to have been written and submitted by Locke, I am not certain whether it was included in the memo to GS, who is probably Gertrude Springer." Anderson notes, "Kellogg states that it was shared with 'staff' whereas Locke refers to 'board,'" and adds, "I would assume Kellogg's understanding of who saw it is more accurate." Anderson to JBP, December 31, 2015, re undated memo mentioning Hubert Harrison's article on "The White Man's War," in the proposed *Survey Graphic* issue on "The New Negro," Locke Files, B94, F710.

92. PUK [Paul Kellogg] to Mr. [Alain Leroy] Locke, May 10, 1924, Locke Files, B94, F710.

93. Barbara H. Foley, *Spectres of 1919: Class and Nation in the Making of the New Negro* (Urbana: University of Illinois Press, 2003), 225, 290–91n30. *Survey Graphic* 6, no. 5 (March 1925); and Alain Locke, *The New Negro: An Interpretation* (New York: Albert & Charles Boni, 1926).

94. HH, "The White World and the Colored Races," [1918], *in New Negro* 4, no. 2 (October 1919): 8–10; rpt. in *Negro World* (February 1920) and in *WAA*, quotations on

116 and 122. In a June 24, 1920, letter to T. Lothrop Stoddard (HP, B2, F19), Harrison wrote: "I am also enclosing a copy of an article on THE WHITE WAR AND THE COLORED RACES, written in 1918 and rpt. in the *Negro World* in February of this year. The substance of it had been previously delivered in Wall St. and Washington Heights, Madison Square and other places, in-doors and out to white audiences during 1915 and 1916." On *WAA*, 141, Harrison says that he first wrote "The White World and the Colored Races" in 1917. In that case he may have actually been referring to the article "The White World and the Colored World," which was published on August 14, 1917, in *The Voice*. See *WAA*, 96–98.

16. ICUL, Midwest Tour, Board of Ed, NYPL, and 1925
(March 1924–December 1925)

1. HD, March 23, 1924.

2. "Dr. Harris(on) Candidate for Congress on Socialist (Single Tax) Ticket," *Chicago Defender*, June 7, 1924, HP, B13, F5–6; "Wants State for Negroes: Unity League Launches a National Movement for Political, Economic and Spiritual Co-operation; Dr. Hubert Harrison Touring U.S. In Its Interest," *Boston Chronicle*, June 21, 1924, 10, HP, B13, F5–6; "Negroes Plan New American State: International Colored Unity League Organizing Branches to Further Project," *Christian Science Monitor*, June 7, 1924, 5B, HP, B13, F5–6; "Separate Colored State Urged by Harrison," *New York News*, August 2, 1924; "Separate State for Negroes Urged," *Baltimore Afro-American*, August 8, 1924, HP, B13, F5–6; "Lecturer Proposes Independent State for Negro Citizens," *Pittsburgh Courier*, August 30, 1924; "Wants Exclusive Negro Territory in U.S.," *New York World*, August 3, 1924, HP, B13, F5–6; and Joseph G. Tucker, "Special Report of Radical Activities in the Greater New York District for Period Week Ending July 26, 1924," File 61-23-297, U.S. DOJ, FBI, Washington, D.C. Garvey, in his call for "Africa for the Africans," argued for a separate state in Africa. See *GP*, 4:32, 42n5, which cites "Garvey Plan for Colored State Repudiated by U.S. Delegates," *New York Tribune*, September 6, 1921. Hill claims "Hubert Harrison was also instrumental in popularizing the slogan ['Africa for the Africans'] before Garvey arrived, but the 'Africa for the Africans' theme did not originate with him." Hill cites Joseph Booth's *Africa for the Africans* (1897) and Edward Wilmot Blyden as earlier users and Cyril V. Briggs as a later user. See *GP*, 4:66n4. See also George Shepperson, "Pan-Africanism and 'Pan-Africanism': Some Historical Notes," *Phylon* 4 (Winter 1962): 350.

3. Theodore Draper, *American Communism and Soviet Russia: The Formative Period* (New York: Viking, 1960), 350. On the general acceptance of Draper's view, see Leslie G. Carr, "The Origins of the Communist Party's Theory of Black Self-Determination: Draper vs. Haywood," *Insurgent Sociologist* 10, no. 3 (Winter 1981): 35–49, esp. 36. See also William Eric Perkins, "Black Nation," *EAL*, 95. Of note is the fact that six years earlier, around the time of the Liberty Congress, Max Freudenheim, an Austrian living in the Bronx, was arrested under the Espionage Act, indicted by a federal grand jury, and charged with evading the draft and being engaged in German propaganda. Freudenheim claimed that "Germany loves the negro race, and that in the event of their [the Germans] winning the war they would give the race certain of the states for their own and let them [the negroes] have a Government of their own." See "Held for Disloyal Talk in Black Belt," *New York Star*, May 23, 1918; "Kaiser Loved Negroes, Said Indicted Austrian," *New York Evening Star*, June 29, 1918; "Seize German Here for Luring Negroes:

Freudenheim Promised Them Certain States for Their Own . . . Also Talks of a Kingdom," *New York Times*, June 30, 1918; all found in File 21645, DNA, *FSAA*, Reel 23.

4. Claude McKay, *The Negroes in America*, ed. Alan L. McLeod, trans. Robert J. Winter (1923; Port Washington, NY: Kennikat, 1979), 11.

5. F. W. B. Coleman, legation of the United States of America, Riga, Latvia, despatch no. 3967, 2, and enclosure no. 3984, 9, to Secretary of State Charles Evans Hughes, August 10, 1926, DNA, RG 59, 861.00B/431, Microfilm Publication M316, Reel 64, frames 0974–0991.

6. Bernardo Ruiz Suarez, *The Color Question in Two Americas*, trans. John Crosby Gordon (New York: Hunt, 1922), HP, https://archive.org/details/colorquestiontwo 00ruizrich/page/n9. See esp. 38–41, 50–53, 56–60, 62–66.

7. In [HH,] "'Subject,' vs. 'Citizen,'" *Negro World*, January 22, 1921, HHHP-Sc, 33, Harrison wrote that "Negro people in the Northern United States are citizens, while they are subjects in the Southern United States, the West Indies and the British possessions." He stressed, "A subject, is in its strict sense, a person who owes allegiance to a government, its laws and officials without having as a right, the power to make or remake that government or those lands," while citizens have "in theory, at least, the power to change their mistakes and their laws to suit their needs."

8. "Negroes Plan New American State"; "Dr. Harris(on) Candidate for Congress on Socialist (Single Tax) Ticket"; "Wants State for Negroes." In contrast, Garvey cited examples of Jewish unity and Zionism as models for African nationalism. At Liberty Hall in 1922 he asked, "If the Jews can have Palestine, why not the Negroes another Palestine in Africa?" See *GP*, 6:41n1; *Negro World*, August 8, 1922.

9. "Negroes Plan New American State"; "Dr. Harris(on) Candidate for Congress on Socialist (Single Tax) Ticket"; and "Wants State for Negroes."

10. "Negroes Plan New American State," which incorrectly said that Harrison had been to Africa twice. He never traveled to Africa. Also "Dr. Harris(on) Candidate for Congress on Socialist (Single Tax) Ticket" and "Wants State for Negroes," The March 17, 1924, *New York World* ran the headline "Garvey Proclaims Negroes' Right to Self Government." The article said that Garvey, before six thousand people in Madison Square Garden, demanded "Africa for the Africans." He also explained that his commission to obtain concessions of African land from the Portuguese government and the Liberian government had been successful. He then circulated a repatriation petition to President Coolidge and made a collection. See "Garvey Proclaims Negroes' Right to Self Government," *New York World*, March 17, 1924, *GP*, 5:572–73.

11. "Negroes Plan New American State"; "Dr. Harris(on) Candidate for Congress on Socialist (Single Tax) Ticket"; and "Wants State for Negroes."

12. "Dr. Harris(on) Candidate for Congress on Socialist (Single Tax) Ticket."

13. "Wants State for Negroes."

14. "Dr. Harris(on) Candidate for Congress on Socialist (Single Tax) Ticket"; "Wants State for Negroes"; "Negroes Plan New American State." In his personal copy of Walter Lippman, *A Preface to Politics* (1913; New York: Henry Holt, 1917), HP, B23, Harrison wrote on an introductory page, "But why substitute the reformer for the politician? It is he who finds his golden opportunity in the popular indifference to politics, and the reformer is not one tenth as significant as the politician."

15. HD, March 23, 1924; "Dr. Harris(on) Candidate for Congress on Socialist (Single Tax) Ticket"; "League of Women for Community Service: 558 Massachusetts Ave" (re HH), *Boston Chronicle*, June 21, 1924, HP, B13, F5–6; "Wants State for Negroes." On

the League of Women for Community Service, see Ena L. Farley, "League of Women for Community Service, Boston," in *BWA*, 705–6; and Ena L. Farley, "Caring and Sharing Since World War I: The League of Women for Community Service—A Black Volunteer Organization in Boston," in *Black Women in American History: The Twentieth Century*, 4 vols., ed. Darlene Clark Hine (Brooklyn, NY: Carlson, 1990), 1:317–28; rpt. from *Umoja: A Scholarly Journal of Black Studies* 1, no. 2 (Summer 1977): 2–12. J. A. Jackson (for A.N.R.), "Round About New York" (re HH), June 21, 1924, HP, ScrMAM2, FB740, notes that Rogers had recently finished an article on the history of jazz for *Survey*.

16. "Dr. Harris(on) Candidate for Congress on Socialist (Single Tax) Ticket."

17. Joseph G. Tucker, "Special Report of Radical Activities Covering Greater New York District, Period Ending July 5, 1924," August 4, 1924, included with Edward J. Brennan, Special Agent in Charge, BI, New York, to Director, BI, Washington, "Attention: J. E. Hoover, Esq. RE: Special Report of Radical Activities Covering Greater New York District . . . NY File # R-100," August 7, 1924, 61-23-294, FOIPA-HH. Joseph G. Tucker, "Special Report of Radical Activities," July 26, 1924; and Joseph G. Tucker, "Special Report of Radical Activities In the Greater New York District," August 4, 1923, included in F. X. O'Donnell, Acting Special Agent in Charge, BI, New York, to Director, BO, Washington, "RE: Special Report of Radical Activities Covering Greater New York District, Period." NY File # R-100," August 9, 1924, 61-23-299, FOIPA-HH.

18. Eugene O'Neill to HH, March 15 and October 12, 1924, HP, B3, F5; HH, handwritten comment on letter from Eugene O'Neill to HH, October 12, 1924.

19. Eugene O'Neill to HH, January 10, 1925, HP, B3, F5; Eugene G. O'Neill, *The Emperor Jones; Diff'rent; The Straw* (1921; New York: Boni and Liveright, [1923]), HP, B24.

20. Mayor's Committee on Celebration of the Twenty-Fifth Anniversary of the Greater City of New York ticket to the New York Silver Jubilee Motion Picture Carnegie Hall Seventh Avenue at Fifty-Seventh Street Monday Evening—March 31st 1924; and "The City of New York The Mayor's Committee on Reception to Distinguished Guests Cordially Invites You to be Present On the Occasion of the Presentation by His Excellency Baron De Cartier De Marchienna," Invitation to HH, May 20, 1924, both in HP, B13, F5–6; and "Members of the Mayor's Committee. May 26, 1924," Municipal Archives, City of New York, John F. Hylan Papers, "Mayor's Committee on Reception to Distinguished Guests—General—1924," B#331. In 2014 the monument was installed along Battery Place.

21. Isaac Dookhan, "The Search for Identity," *Journal of Caribbean History* 12 (1979): 1–34, esp. 16–17, citing Casper Holstein to Bailey, August 11, 1925, in ACLU files for 1925; News Release, February 29, 1924, Rothschild Francis: To Virgin Islanders Resident in the United States, March 20, 1924, and enclosed Notice of Mass Meeting; and "A Memorandum in Support of Legislation Introduced Into Congress," February 1924, all in ACLU files for 1924.

22. "3,000 Hear Report on Virgin Isles," *Chicago Defender*, May 3, 1924, 1; and Dookhan, "The Search for Identity," 15.

23. "Virgin Island Societies Stage Huge Mass Meeting in Renaissance Casino: Attendance of Over 3,000 Hear Dr. Charles E. Mitchell of Richmond and Dr. Hubert Harrison Tell of Conditions, There," *Emancipator* (St. Thomas), May 12, 1924, 1. Problems continued on the islands, and later in the year Holstein wrote a letter to the *New York World* thanking the paper for a "splendid" December 14 editorial and outlining issues that "Virgin Islanders had been agitating around for years and were likely discussed at

the April 27 meeting." See Casper Holstein to the editor, "The Virgin Islands," *New York World*, December 22, 1924, HP-Mi.

24. HD, May 12, 1924.

25. HD, May 22, 1924. Billingsgate is a fish market in London known for the crudity of language used in its stalls.

26. HD, 26 May 1924; The Sunrise Club, "The Terrific Tempest in the Theologic Tea-Pot, The Warfare Between Modernists and Fundamentalists as Seen From the Side-lines, The opening speaker is Dr. Hubert Harrison," May 26, 1924, brochure, HP, B13, F5-6, HPDLC.

27. Mrs. [?] J. Rigo to HH, May 27, 1924, HP, B3, F21.

28. "Dinner in Honor of Dr. Hubert H. Harrison Craig's Dining Room New York, N.Y.," Program, May 31, 1924, HP, B13, F5-6; "Dr. Harrison Banqueted," *Boston Chronicle*, June 7, 1924, HP, B13, F5-6; J. A. Jackson (for A.N.R.), "Round About New York," unidentified newspaper clip, June 21, 1924, HP, B13, F5-6; HD, May 26, 1924; and HD, June 1, 1924, where Harrison observed that the "white" assistants of the 135th Street Library were in attendance though "oddly enough, not a single one of the six colored assistants was present."

29. Moore, "Hubert Henry Harrison," *DANB*, 293.

30. *WGMC*, 2:617.

31. "Dr. Harrison Banqueted"; HD, June 1, 1924.

32. "Dinner in Honor of Dr. Hubert H. Harrison," Program, May 31, 1924; "Dr. Harrison Banqueted"; HD, June 1, 1924.

33. Henri Shields to Mrs. Elizabeth Davis, May 22, 1924, HP, B3, F35; and John C. Walter, *The Harlem Fox: J. Raymond Jones and Tammany, 1920–1970* (Albany: State University of New York Press, 1989), 58.

34. Ernestine Rose to Mrs. Elizabeth Davis, May 29, 1924, HP, B3, F26; and Ernestine Rose to My Dear Mr. [HH], May 29, 1924, HP, B3, F27.

35. HD, June 1, 1924.

36. Eubie Blake (per H. Brill [?]) to HH, June 23, 1924, HP, B2, F39.

37. Chas. S. Gilpin to "To Whom it may concern" [re HH], June 30, 1924, HP, B1, F58.

38. HH, "A History of Democracy" (review of *The Irresistible Movement of Democracy*, by John Simpson Penman), *Nation*, July 16, 1924, 78.

39. G. Victor Cools to HH, August 11, 1924, HP, B1, F27; HD, September 24, 1924. See Bernard A. Weisberger, "Robert M. La Follette," *EAL*, 634–35. Pickens, Du Bois, and James Weldon Johnson supported La Follette. See Sherman, *The Republican Party and Black America*, 206n22, 210. See also *GP*, 5:650n1.

40. *GP*, 5:675–76n5.

41. HD, August 15 and 19, 1924.

42. HD, August 15 and 19, 1924; Dookhan, "The Search for Identity," esp. 8 and 15, which points out that VICC president Casper Holstein was the brother-in-law of D. Hamilton Jackson.

43. HD, August 27, 1924. Lucille Campbell Green Randolph (1883–1963) was born in Virginia, moved to New York, started a beauty parlor, married Asa Philip Randolph, and served as the principal financial supporter of *The Messenger* in its earliest days. See Peter Wallenstein, "Lucille Campbell Green Randolph," *BWA*, 2:961–62.

44. HD, August 27, 1924.

45. HD, August 27 and 28, 1924. On "Bug House Square" see Franklin Rosemont, ed., *From Bughouse Square to the Beat Generation: Selected Writings of Slim Brundage*,

Founder & Janitor of the College of Complexes (Chicago: Charles H. Kerr, n.d.); and Franklin Rosemont, introduction to Frank O. Beck, *Hobohemia: Emma Goldman, Lucy Parsons, Ben Reitman & Other Agitators & Outsiders in 1920/30s Chicago* (Chicago: Charles H. Kerr, 2000), 5–28, esp. 19.

46. HD, September 24, 1924.

47. HH, "City of Success," (Oklahoma City) *Black Dispatch* (for the Associated Negro Press), September 19, 1924, HP, B4, F32. The same article appeared as HH, "City of Success," (Indianapolis) *Freeman* (for the Associated Negro Press), September 20, 1924, HP, B4, F33.

48. HH, "City of Success." By 1922 Chicago had three "Negro" aldermen, Oscar DePriest, Louis Anderson, and Robert R. Jackson. There were no "Negroes" in the U.S. Congress between George H. White of North Carolina, who retired in 1901, and the 1928 election of DePriest, who was the first African American member of Congress elected from a northern state. He was elected three times. On DePriest see *GP*, 5:159n4, 547n5; and Robert E. Martin, "Oscar Stanton DePriest," in *DANB*, 173–74. In contrast, Cary D. Wintz, *Black Culture and the Harlem Renaissance* (Houston, TX: Rice University Press, 1988), 25: "The most significant problem that confronted Harlem was the failure to establish a viable black middle class there. While Harlem attracted a significant number of Black intellectuals, writers, and poets in the 1920s, and it became the home of a large number of black churches, newspapers, and civil rights organizations, it housed relatively few black businesses."

49. HH, "City of Success."

50. HH, "City of Success."

51. HD, September 24, 1924. In "Indianapolis, Ind.," *Pittsburgh Courier*, September 26, 1924, (newspaper clipping re HH lectures), ScrMAM, HP, FB740, the *Courier* mentioned Harrison was speaking in Indianapolis for two weeks and had already given some fine points on education.

52. HD, October 17, 1924; "Two Colored Men Speak At Court House: . . . Speakers Were Rev. Charles Sumner Williams and Dr. Herbert Harrison," *Vincennes Sun*, October 16, 1924, HP-Mi.

53. HD, October 17, 1924; "Mass Meeting of Colored Citizens of Floyd County, at the Court House, New Albany, Ind. Friday Night, Oct. 17, 1924 at 8 o'clock Dr. Huber [sic] Harrison Staff Lecturer of New York Board of Education, and Candidate for Congress in the 21st New York District," leaflet, c. October 17, 1924 (re Harrison for Indpt. Voters' League), HP, B16, F29, HPDLC; and HD, October 16 and 18, 1924.

54. "Speaker Explodes 'Silent Cal' Myth at Meeting Here: Harrison Declares G.O.P. Has Left Negro, Not Negro G.O.P.," *Evansville* (Indiana) *Courier*, October 22, 1924, HP-Mi; "Tidrington's Home Town Comes Thru," (Indianapolis?), October 24, 1924, HP-Mi; "Colored Orators Close Campaign in the County: New York Orator Charges the G.O.P. Has Greatly Neglected His People," (Marion, Indiana) *Leader Tribune* [?], November 1, 1924, HP-Mi; and "Advice to Colored Voters!" flyer, c. 1924 (re Harrison lecture and the 1924 Indianapolis Democratic and Republican Candidates, noted as Klansmen), HP, ScrMAM2, FB740. On the Klan in 1924, see *GP*, 5:675–76n2. Jackson, *The Ku Klux Klan in the City, 1915–1930*, 144, writes: "From 1922 to 1925, Indianapolis was the unrivalled bastion of the Invisible Empire in Mid-America."

55. "Colored Orators Close Campaign in the County"; "G.O.P. Singing, 'We Ain't a Goin' to Steal No More,' Says Colored Orator," (Marion, Indiana) *Leader Tribune*,

November 2, 1924, HP, ScrMAM2, FB740. See also *GP*, 5:687n1, citing Sherman, *The Republican Party and Black America*, 113–23.

56. "G.O.P. Singing, 'We Ain't a Goin' to Steal No More.'"

57. "G.O.P. Singing, 'We Ain't a Goin' to Steal No More.'"

58. *RCAH*, 343; Jackson, *The Ku Klux Klan in the City*, 156.

59. Mildred Chatfield Smith to HH, September 5, 1924, HP-Co; [Mildred Chatfield Smith], [Form Letter], n.d., HP, B3, F39.

60. Walter White to HH, September 15, 1924, HP, B3, F52.

61. "Colored Voters: Can You Forget?" c. November 2, 1924, leaflet of Royal H. Weller, HP, B16, F12.

62. Walter Yust to HH, December 18, 1924, HP, B3, F57.

63. HD, January 11, 1925.

64. R. Irving Johnson to HH, February 10, 21, 24, 1925, HP, B2, F54. On *Reflexus*, see *Black World/Negro Digest* (February 1973): 88.

65. R. Irving Johnson to HH, March 5, 1925, B2, F54. Annie Malone (c. 1875–post 1930) was president of Poro College, in St. Louis, which trained women for sales and technical work. She developed the "Poro system" of beauty products for door-to-door sale. Her efforts made her a millionaire. See Robert A. Hill, ed., and Barbara Bair, associate ed., *Marcus Garvey: Life & Lessons; A Centennial Companion to the Marcus Garvey and Universal Negro Improvement Papers* (Berkeley: University of California Press, 1987), 406.

66. "[Chicago] *Defender* Also Parts With Roscoe Simmons," *Amsterdam News*, April 29, 1925, 1, 2, HP, B12, F8–9, loose. Elmer A. Carter, "E. Simms Campbell—Caricaturist," *Opportunity* 10, no. 3 (March 1932): 82, indicates that only one issue of *Reflexus* was published. That issue was April 1925. On 55 of that issue was a notice of a forthcoming article, "Civilization's Black Beginnings," by Dr. Hubert Harrison, which was described as "a marvelous historical outline dug from the great libraries of the world showing that black men were first to develop the early arts of civilization and culture." Special thanks to Joellen El Bashir, curator, Moorland-Spingarn Research Center, Howard University, for providing a copy of this rare issue. See also "Defender's Shake Up Reveals 'Graft Ring,'" *Pittsburgh Courier*, May 2, 1925.

67. C. Spencer to HH, March 18, 1925, B3, F40; and "Civilization's Black Beginnings," *Chicago Defender*, May 9, 1925.

68. Allan Nevins, editor, *The Sun*, to HH, HP, B3, F3. Also c. February 14, 1925, Harrison hand wrote a page number 2 re "Garveyesque locution" and other matters (on the back of a letter from *The Sun* to HH postmarked February 14, 1925). See HP, B3, F3.

69. HH, "The Voice of the Negro" Reviews of *The Everlasting Stain*, by Kelly Miller, and *The Negro in South Carolina During the Reconstruction*, by Alrutheus Ambush Taylor, *New York Star?*, c. February 14, 1925, HP, B6, F49. For dating, see "Garveyesque locution," 2. Alrutheus Ambush Taylor (1883–1954) published *The Negro in South Carolina During the Reconstruction* (https://babel.hathitrust.org/cgi/pt?id=mdp.39015013 251320;view=1up;seq=4) in 1924 while he was working on his PhD.

70. HH, "The Voice of the Negro" Reviews.

71. HH, "The Voice of the Negro" Reviews.

72. HH, "The Voice of the Negro" Reviews. Harrison wrote: "It seems obvious, however, that no real meaning can be seen in this volume of the sudden, wide-spread defiance of law and order by openly armed citizens until one knows what the rest of the South was doing. The national organization of K.K. rebels had planned what happened and the local adherents in the State were carrying out the major tactics of a campaign decided

on outside the state. But of this nothing is given in the book before us—which is a 'closed study' of what happened in the S. of S.C. alone between 1865 and 1878." See [HH], re "Garveyesque locution," 2; and John Moffatt Mecklin, *The Ku Klux Klan: A Study of the American Mind* (LaVergne, TN: Kessinger, 1963). See also HH, "Sample Reviews" (notes), unpublished, c. March 3, 1925, HP, B6, F14.

73. Ernest R. Crandall to HH, February 21, March 7, 1925, HP, B1, F33. No schedule was found.

74. HH, "The United States Air Service," March 14, 1925, HP, B6, F46, HPDLC.

75. [HH?,] "Miscegenation and the Rhinelander Case," newspaper source unidentifiable with crossouts by HH, c. 1925, HP, B5, F21, and HP, B18, F2. On the Rhinelander case, see J. A. Rogers, *Sex and Race: A History of White, Negro, and Indian Miscegenation in the Two Americas* (1942; New York, Helga M. Rogers, 1979), 2:346–48. Of special interest on "miscegenation" are the three volumes of *Sex and Race* by Harrison's friend Rogers.

76. [HH?,] "Miscegenation and the Rhinelander Case." Definitions of "race" have varied throughout U.S. history. See, for example, Allen, *The Invention of the White Race*, 1:27–28, 272n10.

77. *GP*, 6:xxxvi–xxxvii; 87–88, second n1; report by Special Agent James E. Amos, February 6, 1925, DJ-FBI.

78. *Amsterdam News*, February 11, 1925; Marcus Garvey v. Amy [Ashwood] Garvey, New York Supreme Court, February 1, 1921, case 24028, NNHR; and *GP*, 6:104–105n2.

79. Subpoena of HH in Garvey vs. Garvey divorce trial, December 3, 1926, HP-B14, F17; "Garvey Divorce Trial Starts," *New York Times*, December 8, 1926, 20; "Letter in Garvey Suit: A Writer Says He Got Affectionate Note from Negro Leader's Wife," *New York Times*, December 10, 1926, 21; "Jury Finds Both Garveys Guilty of Misconduct," *Amsterdam News*, December 15, 1926, 1, 2.

80. HD, March 1, 1925.

81. HD, March 2, 1925. Lester A. Walton, "Marcus Garvey: His Rise and Fall," *Chicago Defender*, April 4, 1924, 1, 12, HP-Mi, described how in his "first year" in the United States "Garvey led a from hand-to-mouth existence," he "joined Hubert Harrison's Liberty league," and his UNIA "saw its best days between 1919 and 1921." Amy Ashwood Garvey to President Calvin Coolidge, July 26, 1925, WNRC, RG 204, file 42-793, *GP*, 6:212–13, on 213, mentions she was writing a book on "The rise and fall of Marcus Garvey." On 6:213n1, Hill indicates that Amy Ashwood Garvey wrote "various drafts of an account of her life with Garvey and the founding of the UNIA; however, these memoirs were never published. In April 1926 she claimed that men broke into her home and stole a section of an early manuscript, which she called 'The Rise and Fall of Marcus Garvey.' He cites Amy Ashwood Garvey, "Portrait of a Liberator," Amy Ashwood Garvey Papers; and *New York Times*, April 12, 1926. Elsewhere he cites a reference from chapter 3 45, chapter 4 76, chapter 7 2b and 2c, and chapter 11 22–23 of that work. See *GP*, 6:197n12, 7:583n1, 700n7. See also Amy Ashwood Garvey, "The Rise and Fall of Marcus Garvey," Robert A. Hill Collection, 1890–2014, Rubenstein Library, Duke University, BRE3; Hill and Bair, *Marcus Garvey: Life & Lessons*, 359, citing *New York Amsterdam News*, November 3 and 10, 1926, September 21, 1940; and Amy Ashwood Garvey, "Portrait of a Liberator" [1969], Amy Ashwood Garvey papers, Lionel Yard Collection, New York.

82. HD, March 2, 1925. Harrison later added next to that entry: "But Mrs. G. is such a wildly romantic liar." Delos Johnson, a reporter for the *Pittsburgh Courier*, later wrote that when Amy Ashwood brought the "sex problem" into an interview, it was "safe to

conclude that their [Marcus's and Amy Ashwood's] difference was primarily founded on this question rather than that of the policy of the great movement that had been their joint consecrated work." When she was asked by the press, "What is the trouble between you and Garvey," Amy Ashwood replied in part: "Some people may wonder what is the cause of so long and bitter a fight, extending over a period of years, between Marcus Garvey and I. Back of it all . . . we were not mated. Garvey knew nothing about sex life. . . . He lacked the ability to hold my love." Delos Johnson, "Highlights of Career of Marcus Garvey as Told in Pictures and by Courier Artist: . . . Amy Ashwood Garvey, Consumed by Fires of Vengeance, Tells of Lack of Sex Appeal of U.N.I.A. Leader . . . ," *Pittsburgh Courier*, January 8, 1927.

83. HD, March 5, 1925.

84. Augusta Fells Savage (1892–1962) was born in Florida and studied at Cooper Institute (1921–1924). In 1923 she was admitted to the Fontainebleau School of Fine Arts Summer School for American Architects, Painters, and Sculptors and was denied admission when two "white" Alabama girls who had won similar scholarships explained they could not travel with "a colored girl." In 1924 various Black activists supported efforts to enable her to study at the Academy of Fine Arts in Rome, Italy. That effort failed too, for lack of money, since money that Savage earned from her work in a laundry was being sent to Florida to her paralyzed father and other fundraising efforts fell short. She was an extraordinarily talented sculptress and an activist in political causes who fought against racism, sexism, and discrimination; suffered extreme personal hardships; and eventually stopped her artistic work. Her works include a number of subject studies, including ones of Du Bois, Garvey, Harrison, and a young Harlem youth whose bronze 1929 study she titled *Gamin*. See Deirdre Bibby, "Augusta Savage," *BWA*, 2:1011–13, esp. 1012; Elton C. Fax, "Augusta Savage," in Logan and Winston, *Dictionary of American Negro Biography*, 542–43; Kellner, ed., *Harlem Renaissance*, 315–16; *Kaiser Index*, 4:163; Jessie Carney Smith, "Augusta Savage," in *Notable Black American Women*, ed. Jessie Carney Smith (Detroit: Gale Research, 1992), 979–83; Cleveland G. Allen, "Miss Augusta Savage," *Opportunity* 1, no. 6 (June 1923): 25; Augusta Savage, "Augusta Savage: An Autobiography," *Crisis* 36 (August 1929): 269; and Gary A. Reynolds and Beryl J. Wright, *Against the Odds: African-American Artists and the Harmon Foundation* (Newark, NJ: Newark Museum Association, 1989), 252–54.

85. Sunrise Club, "Sunrise Club Dining Society Notices, thirty-second Season, 1924–1925," includes Announcement, "'High-Brows,' 'Low Brows,' and Bell-Wethers—The Psychography of the Social Crazy-Horse," HH lecture, March 30, 1925, HP, B16, F42, HPDLC.

86. F. D. Bluford to HH, April 14, 1925, HP, B1, F5; "Civilization's Black Beginnings," *Chicago Defender*, May 9, 1925.

87. Jean Blackwell Hutson, "The Schomburg Center for Research in Black Culture," in *Black Bibliophiles and Collectors: Preservers of Black History*, ed. Elinor Des Verney Sinette, W. Paul Coates, and Thomas C. Battle (Washington, DC: Moorland-Spingarn Research Center, 1982), 69–80, 69. Catherine B. Allen Latimer was appointed an assistant at the NYPL, 135th Street branch, in 1920, the first African American so appointed. In 1926 she was appointed assistant branch reference librarian in charge of the Division of Negro Literature and History of the 135th Street branch of the NYPL. See "Catherine A. Latimer (1895?–1948)," in *Notable Black American Women*, ed. Jessie Carney Smith (Detroit: Gale Research, Inc., 1992), 657–58; *Who's Who in Colored America, 1938–40*, 323; *Kaiser Index*, 5 vols.; Kellner, ed., *Harlem Renaissance*, 215; "Four Colored Girls

Chosen by New York Public Library," *New York Age*, August 7, 1920, 5; "Library to Preserve Historical Records," *Chicago Whip*, March 27, 1925, SC-Micro Reel 7, SCRBC.

88. Ernestine Rose to HH, n.d. [c. March 11, 1925?], HP, B3, F27.

89. Jean Blackwell Hutson, "The Schomburg Collection," in John Henrik Clarke, *Harlem: A Community in Transition* (New York: Citadel, 1964); and also in *Freedomways* (1964). See also Elinor des Verney Sinette, *Arthur Alfonso Schomburg, Black Bibliophile & Curator: A Biography* (Detroit: New York Public Library and Wayne State University Press, 1989), 132–35; "Library to Preserve Historical Records."

90. "New Exhibition Is Opened at 135th St. Public Library," *Harlem Home News*, May 13, 1925, Schomburg SC Micro R-707, Reel 6, Harlem Vol. 1. See also Sinnette, *Arthur Alfonso Schomburg*, 135; David Levering Lewis, *When Harlem Was in Vogue* (1979; New York: Oxford University Press, 1981), 105. Franklin Ferguson Hopper (1878–1950) was instrumental in securing funds from the Carnegie Corporation of New York for the purchase of the Arthur Schomburg Collection. See *Bulletin of the New York Public Library* 54 (1950): 613; Harry Miller Lydenberg, "Franklin Ferguson Hopper, 1878–1950," *Bulletin of the New York Public Library* 55 (1951): 159–61. I am indebted to Martha Foley, assistant archivist, NYPL, to JBP, December 13, 1996, for this information.

91. See "Report of the Director," *Bulletin of the New York Public Library* 29 (1925): 227–28; and Foley to JBP, December 13, 1996.

92. [HH,] "Some Reasons Why Such a Collection Is Necessary" [c. April 1925?], unpublished, HP, B6, F28, HPDLC.

93. [HH,] "Some Reasons Why Such a Collection Is Necessary."

94. [HH,] "One Decade of Harlem's Mental Growth," [c. 1925?], HP-Wr. Young's Book Exchange was "wedged into a narrow store in West 135th Street" and by 1921 contained, according to the *New York Times*, "the largest collection of books by and about the negro race that has been assembled anywhere and which is open to the public." It was run by "George Young, a tall negro with a gentle voice and pleasant face" who started the exchange around 1915 with six books. He "believed that there ought to be a place where people could go to get books about the negro, and books written by the negro himself." He was always interested in literary work and "belonged to the St. Mark's Lyceum." In six years "Young's collection has grown to 8,000 to 10,000 books by and pertaining to negroes." See "Pullman Porter Now a Bookseller," *New York Times*, October [21?], 1921, SCRBC, SC Micro R-707, Reel 6 Harlem Vol. 1.

95. *Bulletin of the New York Public Library* 30 (1926): 157–58; and Foley to JBP, December 13, 1996. On May 25, 1926, the NYPL acquired the Arthur A. Schomburg collection of Negro literature and art through a $10,000 purchase by the Carnegie Foundation. The collection consisted of "several thousand books, rare print, autographs and manuscripts" and was "to be housed temporarily in the 135th Street Branch Library." It contained "virtually every important book written by or about the Negro in the United States and a number of volumes on the same subject in French, German, Assyrian, Latin and Spanish." Additions were to be made from time to time. See "Negro Books and Art Given Public Library: Schomburg Collection, Including Rare Prints, Acquired Through Carnegie Foundation," *New York World*, May 26, 1926, HP, Clippings, B12, F8–9; "Schomburg Negro Library Sold," *Amsterdam News*, May 26, 1926, HP, Clippings, B12, F8–9; Hutson, "The Schomburg Center for Research in Black Culture," 69–80, esp. 69.

96. Melvin J. Chisum to HH, August 11, 1925, with HH addendum at bottom, HP, B1, F24. Chisum, a confidant of Emmett Scott, had infiltrated both William Monroe

Trotter's Boston Suffrage League and Trotter's and Du Bois's Niagara Movement for Booker T. Washington. William F. Moggleston, "Booker T. Washington," *ANB*.

97. U.S. Poston, Letter of Introduction re [HH], August 27, 1925, HP, B3, F12. Walter, *The Harlem Fox*, 3–4, 46, points out that the Five Cent Fare Club, whose leadership was mostly West Indian and southern African Americans, grew in opposition to the United Colored Democracy, headed mostly by northern African Americans. It "died immediately after the Hylan—[Jimmy] Walker campaign" (of 1925). Walter (37) also points out that Poston was UNIA minister of labor and industry and controlled many UNIA business ventures.

98. A. L. Schwartz to HH, September 21, 1925, HP, B3, F32.

99. HH to Arthur Hillard, October 27, 1925, HP, B2, F2, HPDLC. On Healy's club, see Walter, *The Harlem Fox*, 4.

100. HH, "Class Book [1920 crossed out-JP]," "*An American History For Public Schools*, 2, The Art of the Short Story, page 5," c. March 1925–March 1926, HP, B4, F34. See also HH, "Class Book: An American History for Public Schools; The Art of the Short Story, 1920–1926: autograph manuscript draft (unpublished)," Manuscript, 1920–1926, HPDLC.

101. HH, "The Art of the Short Story, page 5," c. November 1925–March 1926.

102. HH, "Class Book [1920 crossed out-JP]," "*An American History For Public Schools*, 2, The Art of the Short Story, page 5," c. November 1925–March 1926.

103. HH, "Class Book [1920 crossed out-JP]," "*An American History For Public Schools*, 2, The Art of the Short Story, page 5," c. November 1925–March 1926. For some undated Harrison notes on books by Blaine and Elson, see "Lincoln and Liberty: research notes from books by Blaine (vol. 1, chap. 12; 20 years) and Elson (History of U.S.)," HP, B5, F13, HPDLC.

17. NYC Talks, Workers School, and *Modern Quarterly* (January–September 1926)

1. HD, January 3, 1926; "Today," *New York Times*, February 7, 1926, 2, HP-Mi.

2. "H.H.H.," "Is the Housing Problem Still with Us?" (Notes for a Board of Education Lecture), January 23, 1926, HP, B5, F6, HPDLC; and *Literary Digest*, April 4, 1925, 15.

3. "H.H.H.," "Is the Housing Problem Still with Us?"

4. [HH?], "The Love-Letters of Sappho and Phaon: A Peep(k) into the Privacy of a [Modern—crossed out] Royal Romance as transcribed by Elbert Harborn [HH]. New York: Boni and Liveright 1926," on ICUL stationery, c. January 19, 1926, HP, B7, F21.

5. [HH?], "The Love-Letters of Sappho and Phaon."

6. "New Virgin Islands Report," *Amsterdam News*, February 10, 1926, "Virgin Islanders See New Day in Citizenship Grant," *Chicago Defender*, February 26, 1927, both in 1927, HP, Clippings, B12, F8–9. William W. Boyer, *America's Virgin Islands: A History of Human Rights and Wrongs* (Durham, NC: Carolina Academic Press, 1983), 144–45, writes that Ashley L. Totten and Casper Holstein were "rival leaders" among Virgin Island immigrants in New York and that Dookhan, "The Search for Identity," *Journal of Caribbean History* 12 (May 1979): 16–20, "provides a fairly complete account of the political activities of the . . . various Virgin Islands' organizations in the United States during the period 1917–1927." In April 1926 the Associated Press reported that Rothschild

Francis, editor of *The Emancipator* and "a strong critic of the present system of government of the Virgin Islands," had been "convicted and sentenced to prison for one year on a charge of embezzlement." He planned to appeal. "Negro Editor Convicted: Virgin Islands Agitator Is Found Guilty of Embezzlement," [?], April 22, 1926, HP-Clippings.

7. HD, March 5, 1926.

8. Clarence Darrow to HH, March 13, 1926, HP, B1, F40; Kellner, ed., *The Harlem Renaissance*, 315–16.

9. Walter White to Miss Augusta Savage, March 15, 1926, HP, B3, F51. On Savage, see chapter 16, note 84, in this volume.

10. Letter, from 1230 Druid Hill [Avenue], Baltimore, Md., to Miss [Augusta] Savage, March 18, 1926, HP, B3, F58. The writer was possibly Laura Frances Dickerson Wheatley, a 1917 Morgan College graduate. See *Morgan College Bulletin* 10, no. 1 (January 1918).

11. Edgar M. Grey to HH, February 6, 1926, HP, B1, F61.

12. Stationery of the ICUL, c. 1926, HP, B16, F23, HPDLC.

13. "Bishop Brown Finds US in Revolution," *New York Times*, February 23, 1926. *Voice of the Negro* was also the name of the monthly edited by Jesse Max Barber from January 1904 through October 1907, which in November 1906 changed its name to *The Voice*. See *DANB*, 27.

14. "Colored League Head to Talk at Heights: Dr. Hubert H. Harrison to Speak Before Social Problems Club Tomorrow at Noon," *NYU Daily News*, March 10, 1926, HP-Mi; and "Dr. Harrison Addresses Social Problems Club," *NYU Daily News*, March 12, 1926, 4.

15. "Negro Scholar Receives Remarkable Tribute at New York University," *Amsterdam News*, April 7, 1926, 9.

16. Dan H. Ecker to HH, March 26, 1926, HP, B1, F47; and "Dr. Harrison to Talk at Social Problems Club," *NYU Daily News*, April 8, 1926, 3.

17. "Dr. Harrison Berates Activity of the Politician," *NYU Daily News*, April 9, 1926 [?], HP, MAN2, FB740.

18. "Negro Scholar Receives Remarkable Tribute at New York University," 9; Dan H. Ecker to HH, March 26, 1926; Fred L. Kriete to HH, March 30, April 8, 1926, HP, B2, F59; "Racial Problems Expert to Talk: Dr. Harrison Will Discuss 'Science and Race Prejudice' at W.S.C. Playhouse," *NYU Daily News*, April 12, 1926, 4, HP, B18, F3–4.

19. "Speaker Calls Race Prejudice 'Complex,'" *NYU Daily News*, April 14, 1926.

20. "Negro Traitors I Have Known," announcement re HH lecture, March 21, 1926, HP, B16, F31, HPDLC; "Harlem Forum Reopens," c. April 13, 1926, Schomburg SC Micro R-707, Reel 6, Harlem Vol. 1; and "Is the White Race Doomed?" Sunrise Club notice (re HH lecture), March 29, 1926, HP, B16, F42, HPDLC.

21. "Harlem Forum Reopens"; "Is the White Race Doomed?"

22. "Harlem Forum Reopens."

23. "Hubert Harrison Tendered Dinner," *Amsterdam News*, May 26, 1926, HP, B13, F5–6; "Negro Scholar Receives Remarkable Tribute at New York University," 9.

24. Eliza Buckner Marquess to Cyril Wallace, March 25, 1926, HP, B2, F69.

25. "Communist Boring Into Negro Labor: . . . Ten Young Negroes Are Sent to Moscow Under Soviet 'Scholarships' to Study Bolshevism," *New York Times*, January 17, 1926; Ernest Allen Jr., "American Negro Labor Congress," *EAL*, 27–28. See also *Negro Champion*, June 1926.

26. Lovett Fort-Whiteman to HH, April 1, 1926, and n.d. (probably April 2, 1926), HP, B1, F53.

27. Fort-Whiteman to HH, April 1, 1926.

28. "Soviet Wants Negroes in All Trade Unions: Bolshevist Leader Urges Reds to Insist on their Inclusion, Especially Here," *New York Times*, April 2, 1926, HP, B18, F3–4.

29. "Hubert Harrison, Negro Scholar, Joins Ranks of A.N.L.C. Workers: Staff Lecturer of the N.Y. Board of Education to Make Speaking Tour of A.N.L.C. Locals in the East in Interest of Labor Organization Among Negro Workers," *Negro Champion*, June 1926, 2; "Negro Scholar Receives Remarkable Tribute at N.Y. University," *Negro Champion*, June 1926, 3; rpt. from the *Amsterdam News*; "Hubert Harrison to Lecture at N.Y.U.," *Amsterdam News*, c. September 29, 1926, listed in HP, B18, F3–4 as October 1926. Among others moving toward the communists in the late 1920s were William Pickens and W. E. B. Du Bois. See "Du Bois Visits the Soviet Union," *Daily Worker*, November 23, 1926; and William Pickens, "The Second World Congress Against Imperialism" (1929), Tamiment Institute, NYU, Manuscript File, "William Pickens."

30. "Official Bulletin Workers School Workers Party of America, District No. 2, 108 East 14th Street, New York City," c. April 1, 1925. See also *GP*, 5:751n2; and Marv Gettleman, "Workers Schools," *EAL*, 853–55.

31. The Workers School, "Training for the Class Struggle," Announcement of Courses 1926–1927, c. October 11, 1926, Tamiment Workers School Vertical File F#4. The Communist Party was already seriously split by internal factions, and Ella G. Wolfe, a ranking party member (who, along with her husband, Bertram, the director of the Workers School, were both in the Lovestone camp), said that "Harrison was a Fosterite—he was a Communist." From JBP interview with Ella G. Wolfe, March 12, 1981, Hoover Institution, Palo Alto, California. Since her memory of Harrison was not clear, it is questionable how accurate her recollection was.

32. James H. Hubert to HH, May 8, 1926, HP, B2, F46.

33. Ernest R. Crandall to HH, June 11, 1926, HP, B1, F31.

34. *WGMC*, 2:618.

35. "Engaged by Urban League," *Chicago Defender*, June 19, 1926, HP, B18, F3–4. During the summer of 1926 the weather remained abnormally cold. On Saturday, June 5, Harrison wore his thick winter underwear and heavy winter overcoat because the weather was so cold it would have been "proper for early March." On Friday and Saturday, August 20–21, there was "early winter weather, low temperature, drizzles, [and] rains," and Harrison "put off" his "summer underwear (B.V.D.'s)"; some women had "either put on their Fall overcoats or gone into what they call 'tailored suits.'" HD, June 5, 1926, and August 21, 1926.

36. HH, "The Significance of 'Lulu Belle,'" *Opportunity*, July 1926, 228–29, quotations on 228. Ridgeley Torrence's three plays were "The Rider of Dreams," "Granny Maumee," and "Simon the Cyrenian." Harrison mentioned Torrence's plays from 1912 or 1913. James Weldon Johnson writes that on April 5, 1917, the Coloured Player at the Garden Theatre in Madison Square Garden performed these plays, initiating "a new era" in "the entire history of the Negro in the American theater." James Weldon Johnson, *Black Manhattan* (1930; New York: Arno, 1968), 175; cited in Ikonné, *From Du Bois to Van Vechten*, 15, 41nn47–48. David Belasco (July 24, 1853–May 14, 1931) was a producer and director, and his Belasco Theatre at 111 West Forty-Fourth Street was built in 1906. *ENY*, 98–99.

37. HH, "The Significance of 'Lulu Belle,'" 228–29. Johnson, *Black Manhattan*, 205, writes that the play had a "cast of sixty or more persons, above three-fourths of who were colored."

38. HH, "The Significance of 'Lulu Belle,'" 228–29.

39. HH, "The Significance of 'Lulu Belle,'" 229.

40. HH, "The Significance of 'Lulu Belle,'" 229.

41. HH, "The Significance of 'Lulu Belle,'" 229.

42. HH, "The Significance of 'Lulu Belle,'" 229.

43. James H. Hubert to HH, July 17, 1926, HP, B2, F46.

44. HH, "About Things Theatrical: The Significance of 'Lulu Belle,'" *Amsterdam News*, July 28, 1926, 9. See also HH, "The Significance of 'Lulu Belle,'" 228–29. The Urban League's executive secretary, Eugene Kinckle Jones, wrote to Harrison on August 3 and expressed appreciation for his efforts "in the Urban League Sustaining Fund Campaign." He had not had a chance to talk with James H. Hubert concerning a conversation he had with Harrison and thought he would wait till September (since Hubert was on vacation and he would soon be leaving on vacation) before attempting to answer Harrison's letter of July 31. See Eugene Kinckle Jones to HH, August 3, 1926, HP, B2, F55.

45. HH, "About Things Theatrical: The Significance of 'Lulu Belle.'"

46. HH, "Review of *Digging for Lost African Gods*, by Byron Khun de Prorok, F.R. G.S. Officer d'Academie," *Opportunity*, August 1926, 259, HP, B4, F42; and Byron Khun de Prorok, *Digging for Lost African Gods: The Record of Five Years Archeological Excavation in North Africa* (New York: G. P. Putnam's Sons, 1926), https://archive.org/details/diggingforlostaf009795mbp/page/n10. On September 4, 1927, Harrison obtained Frederick Soddy, *Matter and Energy* (New York: Henry Holt and Co., 1912), and subsequently wrote annotations in it. See also "The Doheny Expedition to Hava Supai Canyon," Library of the American Museum of Ethnology and Sociology, Harvard University (received June 11, 1926), http://www.bearfabrique.org/Catastrophism/sauropods/supai.html.

47. HH, "Review of *Digging for Lost African Gods*," 259.

48. HH, "Review of *Digging for Lost African Gods*,"

49. HH, "*The Negro in American Life*—by Willis J. King," *Opportunity*, October 1926, 325–26. On June 22, 1926, Harrison received Willis J. King, *The Negro in American Life, an Elective Course for Young People on Christian Race Relationships* (New York: Methodist Book Concern 1926), part of the World Friendship Series of books. See HP, B23. On 85 Harrison writes, "Only modern wars—and not all of *them*," commenting on King's statement that "practically all the wars of history have had the economic basis as their *raison d'etre*." On 89, regarding race riots, King writes "the white workman, feeling that his back was against the wall . . ." Harrison responds, "But how could this be when there were both higher wages & more work?" On 92, King writes that the AFL "has from its beginning declared a policy of no discrimination on the basis of race." Harrison responded, "This is not true. And has practiced the opposite."

50. HH, "*The Negro in American Life*," 325–26.

51. HH, "*The Negro in American Life*."

52. "Hubert Harrison to Lecture at N.Y.U.," *Amsterdam News*, October 13, 1926, 9.

53. "Dr. Harrison Lectures on China Today at 'Y,'" *NYU Daily News*, October 14, 1926, HP, B13, F5–6. "Harrison Delivers Lecture on China: Initial Talk at Heights 'Y' Heard by Large Audience," *NYU Daily News*, October 15, 1926, 2, HP, B13, F5–6.

54. "Harrison Delivers Lecture on China," 2; "'China's Challenge to the Powers': Hubert Harrison Lecture Subject Before N.Y.U. Students," *Amsterdam News*, October 20, 1926, 9.

55. "World Problems of Race: Syllabus, Dr. Hubert H. Harrison, Instructor," brochure, July–September 1926, HP, B16, F46 and B3, F5–6; and HH, "World Problems of Race: syllabus, 8 July–9 September 1926," HP, B16, F46, HPDLC.

56. On Willis Nathaniel Huggins (1886–1940), see *GP*, 7:777–78n2, 945n1; *New York Times*, July 19, 1941; Donald Franklin Joyce, *Gatekeepers of Culture: Black-Owned Book Publishing in the United Stats, 1817–1981* (Westport, CT: Greenwood, 1983), 33; and John Henrik Clarke, *Africans at the Crossroads: Notes for an African World Revolution* (Trenton, NJ: Africa World Press, 1991), 239–40, 326, 369–71.

57. "World Problems of Race: Syllabus, Dr. Hubert H. Harrison, Instructor," "Epilogue: Caliban Considers," brochure, July–September 1926. A photo of those in attendance at the September 9 lecture in the "World Problems of Race" series can be found at HP, B15, F3, HPDLC; and in *HR*, 398.

58. "World Problems of Race: Syllabus," "Epilogue: Caliban Considers." Caliban is the beastlike slave of Prospero in Shakespeare's *The Tempest*. *Webster's New Unabridged Universal Dictionary*, 210, adds that Caliban "represents a person of uneducable, bestial, and malevolent characteristics, esp. one who is deformed."

59. "World Problems of Race: Syllabus," "Epilogue: Caliban Considers." In his copy of Weale, *The Conflict of Colour*, on 39, Harrison writes "Note carefully: the seeds of culture were obtained from the North African Moslem's *first* by those Europeans who were in closest contact with them—and later by others." Harrison apparently also spoke on India at NYU, and the school paper reported, "Dr. Harrison's address on 'India's Challenge to the Powers', was enlightening, authentic, and imposing." *WGMC*, 2:618.

60. HH, "World Problems of Race," typescript, c. July 8, 1926, HP, B6, F65, HPDLC. This is essentially the same as HH, "World Problems of Race," *Pittsburgh Courier*, December 31, 1927, which was billed as Harrison's "Last Article." On the subject of the post–King James Bible development of the "white race" in the Anglo-American plantation colonies, see Theodore W. Allen, *The Invention of the White Race*, 2 vols., intro. and notes by JBP, vol. 1: *Racial Oppression and Social Control*, and vol. 2: *The Origin of Racial Oppression in Anglo-America* (1994, 1997; New York: Verso, 2012).

61. HH, "World Problems of Race," c. July 8, 1926.

62. HH, "World Problems of Race."

63. HH, "World Problems of Race."

64. HH, "World Problems of Race"; George A. Dorsey, *Why We Behave Like Human Beings* (New York: Harper and Brothers, 1925), HP, B21, received February 13, 1926. See also https://archive.org/details/whywebehavelikeh00dors_0.

65. HH, "World Problems of Race," c. July 8, 1926. He closed by stating that his next article would be on "Civilization's Black Beginnings." In his copy of Stoddard, *The Rising Tide of Color*, Harrison, on page 100, notes, "Some correspondence which the author had with me may have corrected this idea. At least I offered some bibliographic aids—at his suggestion—and it may be that he now finds this thesis difficult to maintain, in the face of the evidence" regarding the Black race never showing real constructive power. On page 101 he writes, "he means in the last 20 centuries." But, "see Herodotus for a similar comment by Egyptians on the whites and Cicero's letter to Atticus for an even lower estimate of Anglo-Saxons by a Roman." "And Mr. S. was not at all acquainted with 'the whole of history'—certainly not with African history." "All this 'never, never, never' of triumphant ignorance is highly reminiscent of Gertrude's 'The lady doth protest too much!'" "Mark that he includes *the Nile* and so gives his case away. He cannot now argue that the Egyptians were white." In addition, "they gave the world (according to the

ipissima verba [the very words] of Herodotus, Aristotle, Plato, Diodorus Siculus) the alphabet, paper, monotheism, geometry and astronomy. See also the ponderous tomes of Albert Churchward and the Abbie Thomas Moneeux [Molyneux?] also Dr. E. Zeller: 'Pre-Socratic Philosophy' and Prof. Albert Weber: 'History of Philosophy'—But then these men are only—scholars!"

66. Eileen Hood to HH, August 26, 1926, HP, B2, F43; *The Modern Quarterly* (February–April l926), HP-Bo; V. F. Calverton to HH, June 18, 1926, HP, B1, F20. See Art Casciato, "V. F. Calverton," *Biographical Dictionary of the American Left*, 61–63; Alan M. Wald, "Victor Francis Calverton," *ANB*, 4:252–53; Paul Buhle, "Modern Quarterly/Modern Monthly," *EAL*, 482–83; Hutchinson, *The Harlem Renaissance*, 279; V. F. Calverton, "The New Negro," *Daily Worker*, April 23, 1927, 3.

67. Hood to HH, August 26, 1926; *Modern Quarterly* (February–April l926), HP, B17, F7; Calverton to HH, June 18, 1926.

68. HH, "The Real Negro Problem," *Modern Quarterly* 3, no. 4 (September–December 1926): 314–21, quotations on 314–15. When published, the page layout for page 319 was placed on page 320 and the layout for page 320 was placed on page 319. In HP, B6, F5, HPDLC, is a lengthy edited typescript by Harrison of twenty-two pages, undated but probably edited from around 1926–1927. The first ten pages are HH, "The Real Negro Problem: I. The Why of the Matter," and pages 11–22 are "The Black Man's Burden [crossed out] II: The What of It." The first ten pages are extremely similar to the *Modern Quarterly* article. This *Modern Quarterly* article is based in part on HH, "The Negro and Socialism I: The Negro Problem Stated," *New York Call*, November 28, 1911, 6; and HH, "The Real Negro Problem," *NandN*, 1917, 30–40. See also Oliver C. Eckel to HH, January 11, 1927.

69. HH, "The Real Negro Problem," 315–16.

70. HH, "The Real Negro Problem," 316. In his copy of the Robertson book Harrison adds, "The Anglo-Saxons or English and Americans seem to have had slavery in their blood for some time." See Robertson, *The Evolution of States*, 374, https://archive.org /details/evolutionstates00robegoog.

71. HH, "The Real Negro Problem," 316–17.

72. HH, "The Real Negro Problem," 317, 319.

73. HH, "The Real Negro Problem," 319.

74. HH, "The Real Negro Problem," 319.

75. HH, "The Real Negro Problem," 318, 319.

76. HH, "The Real Negro Problem," 318.

77. HH, "The Real Negro Problem," 318.

78. HH, "The Real Negro Problem," 318, 320.

79. HH, "The Real Negro Problem," 320.

80. HH, "The Real Negro Problem," 320–21.

81. HH, "The Real Negro Problem," 321.

18. Lafayette Theatre Strike, *Nigger Heaven*, and Garvey Divorce
(June–December 1926)

1. "Hubert Harrison Addresses Bronx Rotary Club on 'New Americanism': Board of Education Lecturer Is Guest of Successful Uptown Business and Professional Men— Loudly Cheered," *Amsterdam News*, July 28, 1926, 9. On the "Negro as the touchstone

of the modern democratic idea" see HH, "The Negro and Socialism, I—The Negro Problem Stated," *New York Call*, November 28, 1911, 6; rpt. in *HR*, 52–55, quotation on 54.

2. "Hubert Harrison Addresses Bronx Rotary Club on 'New Americanism.'"

3. "Hubert Harrison Addresses Bronx Rotary Club on 'New Americanism.'"

4. American Friends Service Committee to HH, July 28, 1926, [multiple pages only have 1], HP, B3, F43. On Thomas see Mary Hoxie Jones, *Swords Into Ploughshares: An Account of the American Friends Service Committee, 1917–1937* (1937; Westport, CT: Greenwood, 1971), 20.

5. American Friends Service Committee to HH, July 28, 1926.

6. Wilbur K. Thomas to HH, October 7 and November 2, 1926, HP, B3, F43.

7. Wilbur K. Thomas to HH, December 20 and 28, 1926, B3, F43; "Findings of the Conference to Discuss Peace Along Interracial Lines Held at American Friends Service Committee Headquarters . . . Philadelphia Nov. 30 and Dec. 1, 1926," December 20, 1926, HP, B8, F1. On the American Friends Service Committee's "Interracial Service Section," see Jones, *Swords Into Ploughshares*, 131.

8. HD, August 21, 1926.

9. William Pickens to HH, June 10 and August 16, 1926, HP, B3, F9. A typed manuscript for the Associated Negro Press is in HP, B8, F19.

10. William Pickens, "Evolution Is Discussed on Harlem Streets," *New York News*, August 28, 1926, HH microfiche, Schomburg Center, NYPL.

11. Pickens, "Evolution Is Discussed on Harlem Streets."

12. HH, "Homo Africanus Harlemi: *Nigger Heaven*, by Carl Van Vechten," *Amsterdam News*, September 1, 1926, 20, HP, B4, F71; and Carl Van Vechten, *Nigger Heaven* (New York: Knopf, 1926). The quotes are based on HH's corrections. See also *GP*, 7:244nn5–6; and Nathan I. Huggins, *Voices from the Harlem Renaissance* (New York: Oxford University Press, 1974), 6, 93–118. For a discussion of Van Vechten's book and reaction to it see Robert F. Worth, "*Nigger Heaven* and the Harlem Renaissance," *African American Review* 29, no. 3 (Fall 1995): 461–73, esp. 473. L. M. Hussey, "Homo Africanus," *American Mercury* 4 (1925): 86–87, writes that African Americans had learned to survive by wearing the mask and playing the role of "good nigger." See George Hutchinson, *The Harlem Renaissance in Black and White* (Cambridge, MA: Harvard University Press, 1996), 331.

13. HH, "Homo Africanus Harlemi."

14. HH, "Homo Africanus Harlemi." See also *GP*, 7:244n5.

15. HH, "Homo Africanus Harlemi."

16. HH, "Homo Africanus Harlemi."

17. HH, "Homo Africanus Harlemi."

18. Carlo V. V. [Carl Van Vechten] to James Weldon Johnson, September 7, 1926, in Bruce Kellner, ed., *"Keep A-Inchin' Along": Selected Writings of Carl Van Vechten About Black Art and Letters* (Westport, CT: Greenwood, 1979), 253–54, which cites the Carl Van Vechten Collection, Manuscript and Archives Division, NYPL.

19. [Dave?] Louis Thompson to HH, September 1, 1926, HP, B3, F44.

20. William Pickens to HH, September 24, 1926, HP, B3, F9.

21. HH, "*Nigger Heaven* [by Carl Van Vechten] A Review (On Radio W. G. L.)," c. August 1927, HP, B5, F37, HPDLC, where it is dated September 1927. For the 1927 dating see *Chicago Defender*, August 13, 1927, 11, for reference to this radio talk on August 16. WGL started on January 1, 1927, in New York. It became WADA, 1280 AM; it was originally 1020 AM.

22. HH, "*Nigger Heaven* . . . A Review (On Radio W.G.L.)."

23. HH, "*Nigger Heaven*." Harrison added that "while 9/10 of Harlem's Negroes do speak a distressingly bad version of our English tongue—like most other Americans—they do not speak like the Scarlet Creeper, the Bolito King nor any other of Mr. Van Vechten's lower-class-characters."

24. HD, September 13, 1926.

25. HD, September 23, 1926.

26. "Lafayette Owner Issues Statement of His Stand in Present Harlem Fight," *Amsterdam News*, September 22, 1926, 10; "Lafayette Theatre Picketed" *Amsterdam News*, September 15, 1926, 1.

27. Frank Crosswaith, "Open Letter," May 4, 1925, AFPS AFAU I. Gifts, 1922–1927 Vol. 14 F5, "Trade Union Committee For Organizing Negro Workers," "Report in Full Covering Activities From June 1, 1925 to December 31, 1925." Other officers of the TUCNW were Thomas Curtis, chairman, and Gertrude E.(lise) [née Johnson] McDougald [Ayer] (aka Elise Johnson McDougald), vice chair. They received a gift of $500. Their financial support was mostly "white," and out of the $3,174 they collected in 1925, only two $5 contributions came from Black people.

28. Charles Garland, of Massachusetts, set up the AFPS (Garland Fund) in 1922 with $1,674,000 inherited from his stockbroker father. He "stipulated that the money be given to liberal or radical sources that COULD GET NO ASSISTANCE FROM OTHER SOURCES." In practice, according to the *Pittsburgh Courier*, however, "the white liberals and radicals got over $1,600,000 while the black liberals and radicals got only a little over $62,000." The NAACP received $34,918.30, the *Messenger* $3,850, the Brooklyn Urban League $2,000, the TUCNW $1,934, the BSCP $11,200, and the NUL $1,000. There was "an apparent bond of friendship" between the AFPS board and the NAACP, as manifested by a June 19, 1923, gift of $15,000 to move into and pay rent on its "expensive and palatial offices on Fifth avenue at Fourteenth street." In addition, Du Bois received $5,000 for a "study of Negro education in South Carolina." On October 16, 1926, the *Pittsburgh Courier* stated that the fortune of Charles Garland was "all gone." See "Garland's Gift of $800,000 to Public Fund Confirmed," *Pittsburgh Courier*, July 24, 1922, 1; "'Slush Fund' Aired," *Pittsburgh Courier*, October 9, 1926; "The Garland Fund," *Pittsburgh Courier*, October 16, 1926; and Andrew Buni, *Robert L. Vann of the "Pittsburgh Courier": Politics and Black Journalism* (Pittsburgh, PA: University of Pittsburgh Press, 1974), 148–49, which points out that James Weldon Johnson, the only Black director of the fund, had great influence.

29. "Speaker Nabbed by Police on Harlem Corner: Richard Moore Hauled Off Box," *Amsterdam News*, September 27, 1926, 4; "Negro Leader Arrested for Union Speech," *Daily Worker*, September 30, 1926, 5; "Negroes Begin Move for More Recognition: Committee Will Demand More Police Captains and Health Protection Like Whites," *New York Times*, September 27, 1926; "Big Crowd at Harlem Meeting," *Pittsburgh Courier*, October 9, 1926.

30. "Lafayette Owner Issues Statement . . . ," *Amsterdam News*, September 22, 1926, 10.

31. Pickens to HH, September 24, 1926. See, for example, William Pickens, "'Color Line' Aids the Boss to Detriment of the Workers," *Daily Worker*, September 15, 1926, 4.

32. "Negroes Begin Move for More Recognition." The BSCP was officially founded in 1925 on a program of fighting for a 240-working-hour month and improved work conditions. Randolph was the leading spokesperson, and *The Messenger* was used to put

forth its aims. See Bruce Kellner, ed., *The Harlem Renaissance: A Historical Dictionary for the Era* (New York: Methuen, 1987), 54.

33. "Negroes Begin Move for More Recognition." On July 17, 1983, the *New York Times* reported that "more than 10 percent of the force is black. The police department said there are seven blacks holding the rank of captains and above, compared with 399 whites in these positions." See Sam Roberts, "House Panel Is Set to Hear Charges of Police Brutality to City's Blacks," *New York Times*, July 17, 1983. On Harrison demanding "Negro" police officers in Harlem see *HHVHR*, 5, 311, 341; and HH, "Prejudice Growing Less and Co-Operation More, Says Student of Question," *Pittsburgh Courier*, January 29, 1927, II, 7; and in *HR*, 250–53, esp. 252.

34. "Colored Motion Picture Tenders Issue Statement," *Amsterdam News*, September 29, 1926, 10.

35. Cyril V. Briggs, "Former Editor Writes in From New Jersey," letter to the editor, September 25, 1926; rpt. in *Amsterdam News*, September 29, 1926.

36. On the separate locals see also Harold Cruse, *The Crisis of the Negro Intellectual: From Its Origins to the Present* (New York: William Morrow, 1967), 76, which cites Sterling D. Spero and Abram L. Harris, *The Black Worker: The Negro and the Labor Movement* (1931; New York: Atheneum, 1972), 348.

37. "Big Crowd at Harlem Meeting," *Pittsburgh Courier*, October 9, 1926.

38. "Joint Defense Committee of the Harlem Educational Forum, Institute for Social Study, American Negro Labor Congress" to "Dear Friend," October 4, 1926, HP-Co; and "Richard Moore Found Guilty," *Amsterdam News*, October 6, 1926, 1.

39. HH, "As Harrison Sees It," *Amsterdam News*, October 6, 1926, 11. Harrison adds that "this attitude will be found fully justified" in *WAA*, 20–22. Also see HH, "The Trouble at the Lafayette," *Empire State Gazette*, October 10, 1926, clipping, HP, ScrMAM2, which was the same as the October 6, 1926, *Amsterdam News* article, except that the last paragraph was missing. The *Amsterdam News* of October 6 reported that the Lafayette's general manager, Schiffman, offered to put union men in the Lafayette and that Tom Johnson, the chief operator at the Roosevelt, said that "Negro Operators Will Not Be Made the Goat." Meanwhile, Black musicians were called out at the Lafayette and "white" musicians were to be called out at another Brecher theater, the Plaza. See "Schiffman Offers to Put Union Men in Lafayette," *Amsterdam News*, October 6, 1926.

40. HH, "As Harrison Sees It."

41. HH, "As Harrison Sees It."

42. HH, "As Harrison Sees It."

43. HH, "As Harrison Sees It."

44. HH, "As Harrison Sees It."

45. HH, "As Harrison Sees It."

46. HH, "As Harrison Sees It." (Romeo) Lionel Dougherty (c. 1885–1944), from St. Thomas, wrote for the *Amsterdam News* for twenty-five years, beginning in the 1920s. "Romeo Dougherty, Vet Negro Sports and Drama Critic Dies," *New York Age*, December 15, 1944; and Kellner, *Harlem Renaissance*, 103.

47. HH, "As Harrison Sees It."

48. HD, September 22, 1926.

49. Frank Schiffman, "Letter from Mr. Schiffman," *Amsterdam News*, November 17, 1926.

50. Edgar M. Grey, "The Drama Puts in Strong Defense Via Versatile Pen," *Amsterdam News*, November 17, 1926.

51. [HH], "The Theatre in Tabloid," *Voice of the Negro* 1, no. 2 (May 1927): 12, HP, B17, F10.

52. Cruse, *The Crisis of the Negro Intellectual*, 77, cites *Amsterdam News*, October 6, 1926, 11, and November 17, 1926, 11. There is no indication that Cruse knew about Schiffman's hiring of Harrison's daughter. See also the November 10, 1926, *Daily Worker* article "Discrimination Against Negro Workers Must Be Stopped," which discusses the American Federation of Musicians and was a rpt. from the *Pittsburgh Courier*. Briggs last mention of Harrison in the Communist Party press was in Cyril V. Briggs, "The Decline of the Garvey Movement," *Communist* 10, no. 6 (June 1931): n2.

53. Cruse, *The Crisis of the Negro Intellectual*, 81–82. See also "George McClennon of the 'Laughing Clarinet' to Star in 'Hey Hey!': Will Furnish the Spice of the Program in Mrs. Garvey's New Play, Which Comes to the Lafayette Monday," *Amsterdam News*, November 3, 1926, 10.

54. Cruse, *The Crisis of the Negro Intellectual*, 82–83. Cruse focused on the "West Indian" element of the radicals and Garveyites. On October 20 the *Amsterdam News* announced that Amy Ashwood Garvey, the first wife of Marcus Garvey, would make her debut as a producer of a musical comedy called *Hey! Hey!* on Monday, November 1. It added that her "ability as a writer" could "be judged to a great extent by her biography of 'The Rise and Fall of Marcus Garvey' [which Harrison had also worked on], which has not been released for public distribution" and which "only eminent critics and publishers have had the opportunity to read." It added, "If their opinions are to be regarded with any consideration, she has a definite style." On November 10 the *Amsterdam News* declared "Mme. Garvey's Show a Hit at the Lafayette." The title of the play was "'HEY! HEY! HE'S IN THE JAILHOUSE NOW'" and it was described as "a burlesque on the life of Marcus Garvey." The leading character was named "Morco Garbo." Garbo is described as "a seeker of beautiful women" who is "never satisfied without a harem" and who spends his time "attempting to confidence those with whom he comes in contact." See "African President's Former Wife to Present Musical Comedy," *Amsterdam News*, October 20, 1926; "Mme. Garvey's Show a Hit at the Lafayette," *Amsterdam News*, November 10, 1926; Delos Johnson, "Highlights of Career of Marcus Garvey," *Pittsburgh Courier*, January 8, 1927. See also *GP*, 2:78n3, which cites "Amy Ashwood Garvey, Portrait of a Liberator" [unpublished MS].

55. "Dr. Hubert Harrison Opens Lecture Series," *Amsterdam News*, October 6, 1926, HP, VF SC.

56. "Dr. Hubert Harrison Opens Lecture Series"; HH, "A Reply to 'Nigger Heaven,'" (re 3 lectures by HH for Educational Forum on October 9, 16, and 23), printed handout, c. October 9, 1926, HP, B16, F38, HPDLC. Also c. October 16, 1926, there was another printed handout "A Reply to 'Nigger Heaven'" (re 2 lectures by HH for Educational Forum on October 16 and 23 by HH). In his copy of Stoddard, *The Rising Tide of Color*, on 126, Harrison writes: "The Negro produced iron-smelting and wheeled vehicles, and if we include in that term the black Egyptians, they gave Greece the alphabet, geometry, paper, religion, sculpture and architecture."

57. William Pickens to HH, October 8, 1926, HP, B3, F9.

58. HD, November 16, 1926. On suggestions of lesbian relations in the writings of the Virgin Island–born Nella Larsen see David L. Blackmore, "'That Unreasonable Restless Feeling,' The Homosexual Subtexts of Nella Larsen's *Passing*," *African American Review* 26, no. 3 (1992): 475–84.

59. W[endell] P. Dabney to HH, October 4 and 15, 1926, HP, B1, F38. Wendell Phillips Dabney (1865–1953) owned, edited, and managed *The Union*, Cincinnati's Black weekly, from 1905 until 1953. He also was the first president of the Cincinnati branch of the NAACP and author of *Cincinnati's Colored Citizens* (1926). See William David Smith, "Wendell Phillips Dabney," *DANB*, 154–55; *GP*, 5:599n2; *Kaiser Index*, vol. 2; and Tom Lutz and Susanna Ashton, eds., *These "Colored" United States* (New Brunswick, NJ: Rutgers University Press, 1996), 218.

60. HH, "*Nigger Heaven*—a Review of the Reviewers" (c. November 13, 1926), *Amsterdam News*, November 24, 1926; rpt. in *HR*, 344–51, quotations on 344.

61. HH, "*Nigger Heaven*—a Review of the Reviewers," 344–45.

62. HH, "*Nigger Heaven*—a Review of the Reviewers," 345.

63. HH, "*Nigger Heaven*—a Review of the Reviewers," 345–46.

64. HH, "*Nigger Heaven*—a Review of the Reviewers," 346–47; and James Weldon Johnson, "Romance and Tragedy in Harlem—a Review," *Opportunity* 4, no. 46 (October 1926): 316. Harrison has some handwritten notes of a review of Gertrude (née Liebson) Millin's *God's Stepchildren* (1924) in HP, B6, F29, HPDLC.

65. HH, "*Nigger Heaven*—a Review of the Reviewers," 347.

66. HH, "*Nigger Heaven*—a Review of the Reviewers," 348; and Johnson, "Romance and Tragedy in Harlem—a Review," 316. For more on the debate around the use of the term "nigger" and for further support for Harrison's position that Van Vechten knew what he was doing in using the term, see Chidi Ikonné, *From Du Bois to Van Vechten: The Early New Negro Literature, 1903–1926* (Westport, CT: Greenwood, 1981), 31–32, 44.

67. HH, "*Nigger Heaven*—a Review of the Reviewers," 350–51.

68. "Sordid Divorce Trial to Be Heard Here Soon: U.N.I.A. Potentate's First Wife's Suit On; Celebrated Garvey Divorce Case Now On Trial . . . ," *Amsterdam News*, December 8, 1926; "Mrs. Garvey No. 1 Wife of the Provisional President of Africa Trapped in Her Apartment Nude with Lover by Boulin's Operators," *Inter-State Tattler*, April 16, 1926, HP-clipping; "Wife No. 1 Bares Fall of Marcus Garvey," *New York Evening Journal*, April 16, 1926, HP, clippings, B18, F3–4 (which also discusses her book); "United States Asked by Garvey Attorney to Exile Raided Wife on Moral Turpitude Grounds," *New York News*, April 17, 1926, HP, clippings, B18, F3–4; "Jury Finds Both Garveys Guilty of Misconduct: Divorce Trial Starts Crammed Full of Drama"; "'Spicy' Letter to Dr. Harrison Read; Writing of the Book 'Rise and Fall of Marcus Garvey'—Authorship in Question," *Amsterdam News*, December 15, 1926; and Delos Johnson, "Highlights of Career of Marcus Garvey," *Pittsburgh Courier*, January 8, 1927.

69. Subpoena of HH in Garvey vs. Garvey divorce trial, December 3, 1926, HP-Scr D, B14, F7; "Garvey Divorce Trial Starts," *New York Times*, December 8, 1926, 20; "Letter in Garvey Suit: A Writer Says He Got Affectionate Note from Negro Leader's Wife," *New York Times*, December 10, 1926; "Jury Finds Both Garveys Guilty of Misconduct," 1, 2.

70. "Jury Finds Both Garveys Guilty of Misconduct," 1, 2. The *New York Times* reported that Mrs. Garvey claimed she had merely employed Harrison to aid her in writing *The Life and Times of Marcus Garvey*. See "Garvey Divorce Trial Starts," 20; "Letter in Garvey Suit," 21.

71. Subpoena of HH in Garvey vs. Garvey divorce trial, December 3, 1926; "Garvey Divorce Trial Starts," 20; "Letter in Garvey Suit," 21; "Jury Finds Both Garveys Guilty of Misconduct"; Johnson, "Highlights of Career of Marcus Garvey," *Pittsburgh Courier*, January 8, 1927.

72. "Jury Finds Both Garveys Guilty of Misconduct."

73. "Jury Finds Both Garveys Guilty of Misconduct"; "Both the Garveys Guilty: Dismissal of Divorce Case Likely to Follow Jury's Verdict," *New York Times*, December 11, 1926; Subpoena of HH in Garvey vs. Garvey divorce trial, December 3, 1926, HP-Scrapbook, B14, F17; "Garvey Divorce Trial Starts," *New York Times*, December 8, 1926; "Letter in Garvey Suit," *New York Times*, December 10, 1926.

74. "Jury Finds Both Garveys Guilty of Misconduct."

75. "Jury Finds Both Garveys Guilty of Misconduct"; "Both Garveys Found Guilty, H. H. Harrison Denies Mrs. Garvey Wrote Him 'Love Note,'" *Pittsburgh Courier*, December 18, 1926, HP, SceMAM2, FB740. (Neither the original script manuscripts nor the original typed manuscript were found in the Harrison Papers.)

76. "Both Garveys Found Guilty, H. H. Harrison Denies Mrs. Garvey Wrote Him 'Love Note.'"

77. HH, "Letter to the Editor," December 20, 1926, in *Pittsburgh Courier*, January 2, 1927, HP, ScrMAM2, FB740.

78. HH, "Letter to the Editor," December 20, 1926.

79. Michael Gold to HH, October 29, 1926, HP-Co. Michael Gold (1893–1967, born Itzok Isaac Granich), wrote for *The Call* and *The Masses* before editing *The Liberator*, coediting the *New Masses* and writing a regular column for the *Daily Worker*. See Gerald Sorin, "Michael Gold," in *ANB*, 9:175–76; and John W. Vandercook, *Tom-Tom* (New York: Harper & Brothers, 1926).

80. HH, "A Modern Medicine Man," handwritten, for *New Masses*, December 1926, HP, B5, F24, HPDLC; HH, "Review Notes on *The History of Witchcraft and Demonology* by Montague Summers," HD, B6, F16, HPDLC; and Montague Summers, *A History of Witchcraft and Demonology* (New York: Knopf, 1926).

81. HD, December 5 and 28, 1926.

82. Dan H. Ecker to HH, November 24 and December 10, 1926, HP, B1, F47.

83. Robert Lawrence McKibbin to HH, December 13, 1926, HP, B2, F67.

84. Dan H. Ecker to HH, December 20, 1926, HP, B1, F47.

19. The *Pittsburgh Courier* and the *Voice of the Negro*
(January–April 1927)

1. Blair Niles, *Black Haiti: A Biography of Africa's Eldest Daughter* (New York: G. P. Putnam's Sons, 1926), HP, B24, obtained by HH on August 21, 1926; and see https://digitalcollections.nypl.org/items/510d47df-e2f8-a3d9-e040-e00a18064a99. Blair Niles was a pseudonym for Mary Blair Rice (1880–1959); HH, "Hayti Finds a Friend: *Black Hayti—a Biography of Africa's Eldest Daughter*," *West Indian Statesman*, January 27, 1927; rpt. in *Voice of the Negro* 1, no. 1 (April 1927): 6, HP, B17, F10, http://www.columbia.edu/itc/english/edwards/RBML_TVOTN_Vol_1_No_1_April_1927.pdf; rpt. in *HR*, 366–68, quotations on 366–67. Basil Davidson, *African Civilization Revisited: From Antiquity to Modern Times* (Trenton, NJ: Africa World Press, 1991), 412–13, also writes favorably of Kingsley.

2. HH, "Hayti Finds a Friend," *HR*, 367.

3. HH, "Hayti Finds a Friend," *HR*, 367–68.

4. Oliver C. Eckel to HH, January 2, 11, 18, 1927, HP, B1, F46; HH, "The Real Negro Problem," c. January 11, 1927, typescript in HP, B6, F5; HH, "The Real Negro Problem, *Modern Quarterly* 3, no. 4 (September–December 1926): 314–21, HP, B23.

5. Charles Brook to HH, January 14, 1927, HP, B1, F10; HH, "Says Races Do Well in Lynchburg: New Yorker Sees Era of Co-operation," *Chicago Defender*, March 26, 1927, HP, B6, F17.

6. HH, "Says Races Do Well in Lynchburg"; [HH,] "The Gift of Gab," *Voice of the Negro* 1, no. 2 (May 1927): 10–11, http://www.columbia.edu/itc/english/edwards/RBML _TVOTN_Vol_1_No_2_May_1927.pdf.

7. HH, "Says Races Do Well in Lynchburg"; [HH,] "Knowledge or College," *Voice of the Negro* 1, no. 2 (May 1927): 10; A. L. Comither to HH March 11, 1927, HP, B1, F26; and [HH,] "The Gift of Gab," 10–11.

8. Comither to HH March 11, 1927; and [HH], "The Gift of Gab," 10–11.

9. "Says Races Do Well in Lynchburg"; [HH,] "Knowledge or College," 10; and [HH,] "The Gift of Gab," 10–11. On March 11, 1927, Harrison paid $3 cash on a bill of $4 for five hundred ICUL membership cards, which were printed by the *New York Age*. See ICUL, "Bill for Membership Cards," HP, B14, No 8, HPDLC, Item 155.

10. Arthur Hutter to HH, March 15 and November 22, 1927, HP, B2, F48. *The Holy Scriptures: According to the Masoretic Text: A New Translation with the Aid of Previous Versions and with Constant Consultation of Jewish Authorities* (Philadelphia: Jewish Publication Society of America, 1917), HP, B20.

11. HD, January 29, 1927; David Belasco to HH, April 2, 1926; in David Belasco, *The Merchant of Venice: A Comedy by William Shakespeare as Arranged for the Contemporary Stage* (New York, privately printed; 1922), inside cover, HP, B25. See also William Winter, *Life of David Belasco* (New York: Moffat, Yard, 1918), https://catalog.hathitrust.org /Record/001374191.

12. Mr. and Mrs. I. Newton Brathwaite, "Testimonial Banquet in Honor of Rev. John Wesley Johnson, B.D., St. Cyprian's Church, 169–175 West 63rd Street," February 28, 1927, HP, B16, F43, HPDLC.

13. *GP*, 2:403n1; Andrew Buni, *Robert L. Vann of the "Pittsburgh Courier": Politics and Black Journalism* (Pittsburgh, PA: University of Pittsburgh Press, 1974), 108, 136–41.

14. HH, "Du Bois a West Indian, Declares Dr. H. H. Harrison: Prejudice Growing Less and Co-Operation More," *Pittsburgh Courier*, January 29, 1927.

15. HH, "Du Bois a West Indian." The president Harrison referred to was probably Warren G. Harding. See J. A. Rogers, *The Five Negro Presidents: According to What White People Said They Were* (St. Petersburg, FL: Helga M. Rogers, 1965), 11–13.

16. HH, "Du Bois a West Indian."

17. HH, "Du Bois a West Indian."

18. HH, "Du Bois a West Indian." New York's "Fighting Fifteenth" National Guard infantry regiment, founded in 1916, was composed of Black enlisted soldiers and Black and "white" officers and became the U.S. Army's 369th Infantry Regiment during World War I. It was known as the "Harlem Hellfighters."

19. HH, "Du Bois a West Indian."

20. HH, "Du Bois a West Indian."

21. "The International New York Negro," *Pittsburgh Courier*, February 5, 1927.

22. HH, "*The Negro in American Life*—by Jerome Dowd," *Pittsburgh Courier*, February 12, 1927, HP, B4, F18; Egmont Arens to HH, January 14, 1927, HP, B1, F2. The second review was probably the one that later appeared as HH, "*In Barbary* by E. Alexander Powell," *Pittsburgh Courier*, February 12, 1927.

23. HH, "*The Negro in American Life*—by Jerome Dowd." Harrison also maintained that Dowd's work furnished justification for John Vandercock's claim in *Tom-Tom* "that

the 'fathers of the race had and still possess blessed secrets, wonderful lores and great philosophies that rank the jungle Negro's civilization as the equal, and in many respects the superior, of any way of life that is to be found anywhere in the world.'"

24. HH, "*The Negro in American Life*—by Jerome Dowd."

25. HH, "*The Negro in American Life*—by Jerome Dowd." Harrison called "consciousness of kind" a "facile phrase," which he attributed to "Professor [Franklin H.] Giddings" and said was "utilized by professor Dowd to stop the gaps in his thinking." See chapter 14 in this volume and HD, April 30, 1923, on "Homo Sap."

26. HH, "*The Negro in American Life.*"

27. HH, "*In Barbary,*" *Pittsburgh Courier,* February 12, 1927; *WNBD*, 1014.

28. HH, "No Negro Literary Renaissance," *Pittsburgh Courier,* March 12, 1927, HP, B5, F38; rpt. in *HR*, 351–54. For other critics of the Renaissance, see the chapter "The Black Intelligentsia: Critics," in Cary D. Wintz, *Black Culture and the Harlem Renaissance* (Houston, TX: Rice University Press, 1988), 130–53, 248n3. See also the important article Ousmane Kirumu Power-Greene, "No Negro Renaissance: Hubert H. Harrison and the Role of the New Negro Literary Critic," in *The Harlem Renaissance Revisited: Politics, Arts, and Letters*, ed. Jeffrey O. G. Ogbar (Baltimore, MD: Johns Hopkins University Press, 2010), 20–30.

29. HH, "No Negro Literary Renaissance," 352. Chidi Ikonné, *From Du Bois to Van Vechten: The Early New Negro Literature, 1903–1926* (Westport, CT: Greenwood, 1981), xi, argues somewhat similarly that "the Literary Awakening was only a moment in a long but continued development of racial pride and self-confidence in literature."

30. HH, "No Negro Literary Renaissance," 352.

31. HH, "No Negro Literary Renaissance," 352.

32. HH, "No Negro Literary Renaissance," 352–53.

33. HH, "No Negro Literary Renaissance," 353.

34. HH, "No Negro Literary Renaissance," 353–54.

35. John P. Davis, "An Answer to Dr. Hubert Harrison's Article," *Pittsburgh Courier,* April 2, 1927.

36. WEBDB to Edward Franklin Frazier, June 6, 1927, WEBDBP, Ms 312.

37. E. Franklin Frazier to WEBDB, June 8, 1927, WEBDBP, Ms 312.

38. Olaf Waage, secretary, on behalf of D. Warming (University of Copenhagen), to WEBDB, June 6, 1927, WEBDBP, Ms 312. There is no indication that Harrison ever studied or lived in Copenhagen.

39. HH, *The Embryo of the Voice of the Negro: A Magazine Struggling to Be Born* 1, no. 1 (February 1927): HP, B17, F10, http://www.columbia.edu/itc/english/edwards/RBML_TVOTN_Vol_1_No_1_Feb_1927.pdf. The "Exchange List" included the *Birmingham Reporter; Fraternal Visitor,* Mobile, AL; Monroe Work; *Denver Star; Howard University Record; Zion Observer,* Jacksonville, FL; *Savannah Tribune; Atlanta Independent;* Associated Negro Press; *Chicago Whip; Chicago Ideal; New Era,* Shreveport, LA; *National Defender,* Gary, IN; *Freeman,* Indianapolis, IN; *Plain Dealer,* Indianapolis, IN; *The Ledger,* Indianapolis, IN; *Saturday News,* Hopkinsville, KY; *Black Dispatch,* Oklahoma City, OK; *Cleveland Gazette; The Recorder,* Cincinnati, OH; *Portland Times; Philadelphia American; The Courier; Houston Observer; Dallas Express; Western World Reporter,* Memphis, TN; *Southern Workman,* Hampton, VA; *Journal & Guide,* Norfolk, VA; *The Herald,* Norfolk, VA; *The Star,* Newport News, VA; *Boston Press,* Martinsburg, WV; *The Call,* Kansas City, MO; *Afro-American; Christian Recorder,* Baltimore, Philadelphia?; *Boston Guardian; Monitor,* Omaha, NE; *Monitor,* Boston; *New Jersey Observer,* Newark, NJ; *The Freeman,*

New York City; *Young India*, New York City; *Gold Coast Leader*, Gold Coast, West Africa; *Liberian News*, Monrovia; *Agricultural World*, Monrovia; *Saturday Magazine*, Freetown, Sierra Leone; *Guardian*, Freetown; *Echo*, Freetown; *The International*, Johannesburg, South Africa; *Lagos Standard*; *Lagos Weekly Record*; *Barbados Times*; *Daily Gleaner*; *Dispatch*, Ancon, Canal Zone; *Belize Independent*; and *Oriental Economist*, Tokyo. See [HH,] "Exchange List," c. 1927, HP, B4, F55, HPDLC.

40. HH, "What's It All About?" *Embryo of the Voice of the Negro* 1, no. 1 (February, 1927): 2.

41. HH, "What's It All About?" 2. Financial contributors for February included Murray Tavernier, Verner Tavernier, H. Eustace Williams, the Unity League, Mrs. Mabel Keaton, Julius Thomas, "A Roman Catholic Priest," Elijah Schmidt, Clarence Smith, and John Neckles. See in *Embryo of the Voice of the Negro* 1, no. 1 (February 1927): [HH,] "Those Who Put Their Faith Into Deeds," 2; and [HH,] "Facts and Comments," 3.

42. [HH,] "What This Race Really Needs Is a Good Magazine," *Embryo of the Voice of the Negro* 1, no. 1 (February, 1927): 1.

43. [HH,] "Harlem's First and Foremost Forum," *Embryo of the Voice of the Negro* 1, no. 1 (February 1927): 1.

44. [HH,] "The I.C.U.L.," *Embryo of the Voice of the Negro* 1, no. 1 (February 1927): 2.

45. [HH,] "The I.C.U.L."

46. "The Negro," *Embryo of the Voice of the Negro* 1, no. 1 (February 1927): 3; Andrea Razaf, "A New Year's Prayer," *Embryo of the Voice of the Negro* 1, no. 1 (February 1927): 1.

47. "[Advertisement (re HH lectures for the Educational Forum of the International Colored Unity League)]," *Embryo of the Voice of the Negro* 1, no. 1 (February, 1927): 4.

48. [HH,] "The World in Embryo," *Embryo of the Voice of the Negro* 1, no. 1 (February 1927): 3.

49. [HH,] "Facts and Comments," *Embryo of the Voice of the Negro* 1, no. 1 (February, 1927): 3.

50. [HH,] "On Reading Negro Books," *Embryo of the Voice of the Negro* 1, no. 1 (February 1927): 1, 3; rpt. from *Boston Chronicle*, June 7, 1924, *HR*, 365–66; and [HH,] "Lincoln and Douglass," *Embryo of the Voice of the Negro* 1, no. 1 (February, 1927): 2; rpt. from *Boston Chronicle*, February 16, 1924.

51. [HH,] "Things Worth Remembering," *Embryo of the Voice of the Negro* 1, no. 1 (February 1927): 3; [HH,] "Books You Will Like to Know," *Embryo of the Voice of the Negro* 1, no. 1 (February 1927): 3.

52. [HH,] "'Negro Saved Nation' in 1861," *Embryo of the Voice of the Negro* 1, no. 1 (February 1927): 3–4, quotations on 3. See also *Amsterdam News*, February 14, 1927, 3; Abraham Lincoln, "Unfinished draft of letter to C. D. Robinson," August 17, 1864, in Maclean, ed., *Letters and Addresses of Abraham Lincoln*, 303–5; HH, "The Negro and the Nation," handwritten, unpublished, c. June 21, 1923; and in *HR*, 286–87; HH, "A Crooked Deal," *Negro World*, March 26, 1921; and [HH,] "'Negro Saved Nation' in 1861," 3–4.

53. [HH,] "Population, Immigration and the Negro," *Embryo of the Voice of the Negro* 1, no. 1 (February 1927): 4; rpt. from *Boston Chronicle*, April 19, 1924. On the same page Harrison rpt. from the Preston News Service the article "North Carolina Man Says He Is Father of 42," *Embryo of the Voice of the Negro* 1, no. 1 (February 1927): 4.

54. [HH,] "Harlem's Liberal Church," *Embryo of the Voice of the Negro* 1, no. 1 (February 1927): 4. The Harlem Community Church was Unitarian and started in 1920 with young West Indians attracted to its progressive activities. Included among its charter members were Black socialists and sympathizers such as Grace Campbell, Frank Crosswaith, W. A. Domingo, and Richard B. Moore, as well as Garveyites. See *GP*, 5:431n1.

Egbert Ethelred Brown (c. 1875–1964) was born in Jamaica and was ordained a Unitarian minister in the United States in 1912. In 1920 Brown founded the Harlem Community Church at 149 West 136th Street, and in 1928 the church's name was changed to the Hubert Harrison Memorial Church. "Biography," Brown, (Egbert Ethelred) Papers, 1908–1965, SCRBC, NYPL.

55. "Is There Any Cure for Lynching?" Special Sunday Lecture, April 10, 3 p.m., Coachman's Union League Hall, 252 W. 139th St. [by HH], printed handout, c. March 25, 1927, HP, B16, F14 (including announcement of "Special Sunday lecture, Sunday, April 10, . . . 'Is There Any Cure for Lynching?'"); and ICUL, "The Educational Forum of The International Colored Unity League and Is There Any Cure for Lynching, circa 25 March 1927," broadside, c. March 25, 1927, HPDLC.

56. "Is There Any Cure for Lynching?" [printed handout], c. March 25, 1927; James Phillips (transcribed by HH), "From a Well-Wisher," c. March 25, 1927, HP, B4, F59; James Phillips, "Dr. Harrison—a Tribute," c. March 25, 1927, HP, B4, F59, HPDLC.

57. "Is There Any Cure for Lynching?" (printed handout), c. March 25, 1927; "Says Races Do Well in Lynchburg," *Chicago Defender*, March 26, 1927.

58. [HH,] "Program and Principles of the International Colored Unity League," *Voice of the Negro* 1, no. 1 (April 1927): 4–6; *Voice of the Negro* 1, no. 2 (May 1927): 12–13, *HR*, 399–402. The first issue also had advertisements from the Lafayette and Renaissance Theatres, attorney H. Eustace Williams, Dr. Kaplan of 531 Lenox Avenue, Silver Furniture of 525 Lenox Avenue, the Virgin Islands Congressional Council, and a joint advertisement from *Who's Who in Colored America* and *Voice of the Negro*.

59. [HH,] "The Wider World: A Bird's-Eye View," *Voice of the Negro* 1, no. 1 (April 1927): 1.

60. [HH,] "The Wider World: A Bird's-Eye View."

61. [HH,] "The Wider World: A Bird's-Eye View." Chinese nationalists boycotted British goods and students waged protests in 1925, in July 1926 Chiang Kai-shek began his northern campaign, and in late 1926/early 1927 Britain agreed to concessions and the Chinese ended the boycott. Chiang set up a new conservative government at Nanking in April 1927 and promptly purged communists and Russians from Hankow before temporarily retiring. At the same time, landless peasants under the leadership of Mao Tse-tung and Chu-the started to seize land in Fukien and Kiangsi and challenged the Nanking government. Chiang would come out of retirement to lead a second northern campaign in April 1928. See *GP*, 7:138n3.

62. [HH,] "The Wider World: A Bird's-Eye View."

63. [HH,] "The Wider World: A Bird's-Eye View." "Abyssinia" was the name used for Ethiopia, outside of Africa, until the middle of the twentieth century. The word is related to an Arab word, "habesh" ("mixed breed"), and refers to the Habeshat people who settled in coastal northeastern Africa around the seventh century BCE.

64. HH, "The Trend of the Times in the World of Color: Wanted—a World Outlook," *Voice of the Negro* 1, no. 1 (April 1927): 2; rpt. from HH, "Our International Consciousness," *Boston Chronicle*, January 12, 1924; [HH,] "Race Consciousness," *Voice of the Negro* 1, no. 1 (April 1927): 3; rpt. from [HH,] "Race Consciousness," *Boston Chronicle*, March 15, 1924, *HR*, 116–17; and HH, "Hayti Finds a Friend: *Black Hayti—a Biography of Africa's Eldest Daughter*," *Voice of the Negro* 1, no. 1 (April 1927): 7; rpt. from *West Indian Statesman*, January 1927, *HR*, 366–68.

65. HH, "Rockefeller and the 'Reds,'" *Voice of the Negro* 1, no. 1 (April 1927): 3.

66. HH, "Rockefeller and the 'Reds.'"

67. HH, "Rockefeller and the 'Reds.'"

68. HH, "Rockefeller and the 'Reds.'"

69. [HH,] "The Red Record of Radicalism" [parts 1 through 3 missing], c. March–April 1927, HP, B6, F7, HPDLC. Around April 1927.

70. [HH,] "Program and Principles of the International Colored Unity League," *Voice of the Negro* 1, no. 1 (April 1927): 4–6, quotation on 4; rpt. in *HR*, 399–402, quotation on 399–400. Harrison outlined this program in "Negroes Plan New American State: International Colored Unity League Organizing Branches to Further Project," *Christian Science Monitor*, June 7, 1924, HP, MaM2, FB740; and "Wants States for Negroes: Unity League Launches National Movement for Political, Economic, and Spiritual Co-Operation; Dr. Hubert Harrison Touring U.S. in Its Interest," *Boston Chronicle*, June 21, 1924, HP, B6, F43.

71. [HH,] "Program and Principles," 400.

72. [HH,] "Program and Principles," 400.

73. [HH,] "Program and Principles," 400–1.

74. [HH,] "Program and Principles," 401.

75. [HH,] "Program and Principles," 401–2.

76. [HH,] "Program and Principles," 402.

77. [HH,] "Program and Principles," 402.

78. [Membership Subscription of ICUL], *Voice of the Negro* 1, no. 1 (April 1927): 6; Bill from the *New York Age* to HH of the ICUL, March 11, 1927, HP-Mi.

79. [HH,] "Will You Help?" *Voice of the Negro* 1, no. 1 (April 1927): 8.

80. *Voice of the Negro* 1, no. 2 (May 1927). Another advertisement encouraged people to "dance away the dull cares of life" with Herman Wallace's Jazzers for 30 cents. See [Advertisement re Spring Dance of the ICUL for the benefit of the *Voice of the Negro*], c. 14 May 1927, printed handout, HP, B16, F40, HPDLC.

81. HH, "The Wider World: A Birds Eye View," *Voice of the Negro* 1, no. 2 (May 1927): 9.

82. HH, "The Wider World: A Birds Eye View."

83. HH, "The Wider World: A Birds Eye View." The concept of "Manifest Destiny" was used in the middle and later nineteenth century to argue that it was the ("white") United States' destiny to expand its influence in the Americas. Harrison applied similar logic to (Black) South Africa.

84. HH, "The Wider World: A Birds Eye View."

85. HH, "The Wider World: A Birds Eye View."

86. [HH,] "Knowledge or College," *Voice of the Negro* 1, no. 2 (May 1927): 10.

87. [HH,] "Knowledge or College."

88. [HH,] "The Gift of Gab," *Voice of the Negro* 1, no. 2 (May 1927): 10–11.

89. "Cécile" [HH], "Fashion's Fancy," *Voice of the Negro* 1, no. 2 (May 1927): 11.

90. [HH,] "The Theatre in Tabloid," *Voice of the Negro* 1, no. 2 (May 1927): 12.

91. [HH,] "The Theatre in Tabloid," 12.

92. [HH,] "Program and Principles of the International Colored Unity League," *Voice of the Negro* 1, no. 2 (May 1927): numbering runs 12–13.

93. "Poems for the People," *Voice of the Negro* 1, no. 2 (May 1927): 14–15, which includes Andy Razal [Razaf], "If Christ Came Back," 14; and May Wong, "The Dawn," 15.

94. [HH,] "What-Ho Aframerican!" *Voice of the Negro* 1, no. 2 (May 1927): 14.

95. [HH,] "Only 300 Copies Left of When Africa Awakes," *Voice of the Negro* 1, no. 2 (May 1927): 15.

96. *Voice of the Negro* 1, no. 2 (May 1927): 16. Other advertisements included those from Silver Furniture, the Lafayette Theatre, Dr. Kaplan (eyesight specialist), and H. R. George & Company (Incorporated), Investment Bankers. *Voice of the Negro* 1, no. 2 (May 1927): 16. The Lafayette advertisement may have been placed by Frank Schiffman.

97. "Harlem Scholar Succumbs After 'Minor' Operation: Came to America in 1900 from St. Croix, Virgin Islands, Where He Was Born—Unusual Ability Forced Recognition Here," *Amsterdam News*, December 21, 1927, 1, 4; "Hubert Harrison Dies Suddenly in Bellevue Hospital: Complications Following Operation Brings Death," *New York Age*, December 24, 1927, 2. The last book read by Hubert Harrison, on September 24, 1927, in Bellevue Hospital, was Baron Thomas Babington Macaulay, *The Life and Letters of Lord Macaulay*, vol. 1, ed. the Right Hon. Sir George Otto Trevelyan, Bart., enlarged and complete ed., including Macaulay's marginal notes (New York and London: Harper & Brothers, 1909), in HP, B23. "The Honor Roll" listed those who "made it possible . . . to hear The VOICE again" and included, among others, "The Rev. Charles Martin, D.D., $5; The Violet Social Club of the American West-Indian Ladies Aid, $5; and Miss Elizabeth Hendrickson, $2." "The Honor Roll," *Voice of the Negro* 1, no. 2 (May 1927): 14.

20. Last Months and Death (May–December 1927)

1. HH, "'World Problems of Race,' by Dr. Hubert H. Harrison," 4 pp., n.d. (probably c. May 28, 1927), handwritten HP; and HD, July 1, 1927; "World Problems of Race: Syllabus," pamphlet (HH instructor), July 8, 1926–September 9, 1926, in HP, B16, F46, and SCRMAM2, HP, B13, F5–6.

2. Dr. Beck to HH, November 12, 1927, HP, B2, F3. On November 12 Harrison wrote a second letter to Dr. Beck from memory with five lectures proposed. See HH to Dr. Beck, re "Lecture Series," November 12, 1927, HP, B2, F3, HPDLC.

3. HH, "Race and the Social Sciences," notes, n.d. (probably c. November 12, 1927), HP, B6, F1, HPDLC; and Beck to HH, November 12, 1927. See also Albert Churchward, *The Origin and Evolution of Primitive Man* (London: George Allen & Company, Ltd., 1912).

4. HH, "Cabaret School of Negro Writers Does Not Represent One-Tenth of Race," *Pittsburgh Courier*, May 28 1927, HP, B4, F24. See also HH, "The Cabaret School, 1927: clippings," HPDLC, item 31.

5. HH, "Cabaret School of Negro Writers."

6. HH, "Cabaret School of Negro Writers."

7. HH, "Cabaret School of Negro Writers."

8. HH, "Cabaret School of Negro Writers." Wallace Thurman wrote that patronage in the famous Harlem cabarets was "almost 95 percent white." See Wallace Thurman, "Harlem Facets," *World Tomorrow* 10, no. 11 (November 1927): 466; cited in Chidi Ikonné, *From Du Bois to Van Vechten: The Early New Negro Literature, 1903–1926* (Westport, CT: Greenwood, 1981), 7, 40n25.

9. HH, "Cabaret School of Negro Writers"

10. HH, "Cabaret School of Negro Writers."

11. HH, "Cabaret School of Negro Writers."

12. HH, "Cabaret School of Negro Writers."

13. See A. M. Wendell Malliet, "Continuing Fight on American Prejudice, Shows Better Conditions at Home," *Pittsburgh Courier*, July 2, 1927; "West Indian Tells 'Why I

Cannot Become Americanized,'" *Pittsburgh Courier*, July 9, 1927; and "Malliet Closes Still Crying 'I Cannot Become Americanized,'" *Pittsburgh Courier*, August 13, 1927.

14. Malliet, "I Cannot Become Americanized."

15. Malliet, "I Cannot Become Americanized."

16. Malliet, "Continuing Fight on American Prejudice, Shows Better Conditions at Home"; and Malliet, "I Cannot Become Americanized," *Pittsburgh Courier*, August 13, 1927.

17. HH, "Hubert Harrison Answers Malliet: Replies to Malliet Saying He Did Freely What Other Islanders May Be Forced To: Likes America Because Country Is Democratic; Has 'Fighting Chance' Here Which Is Denied 'Subjects' in Crown Countries," *Pittsburgh Courier*, October 22, 1927.

18. HH, "Hubert Harrison Answers Malliet."

19. HH, "Hubert Harrison Answers Malliet." Harrison's son William Harrison became a lawyer, and his daughter Aida Harrison Richardson was a New York City public school teacher and then a public school principal. Richardson and Harrison, interview with JBP, August 4, 1983.

20. HH, "Hubert Harrison Answers Malliet." *HATB*, 73–74, points out: "It is somewhat paradoxical, too, but nevertheless true, that in New York, and other northern cities such as Boston and Philadelphia, Caribbeans, at least those from the British Caribbean—enjoyed a level of freedom for political association and protest that they did not enjoy in the islands."

21. HH, "Hubert Harrison Answers Malliet."

22. HH, "Hubert Harrison Answers Malliet."

23. HH, "Hubert Harrison Answers Malliet."

24. HD, July 1, 1927; [HH,] "Poem for Miss Ilva Henrietta Harrison," c. 1927, HP, B8, F11. After Hubert's death Leana Jackson sent a condolence letter to Irene Harrison in which she compared Ilva to her father—smart, witty, and literary. Leana Jackson to Mrs. Harrison, December 27, 1927, HP, B2, F51.

25. John Louis Hill to HH, August 17, 1927, HP, FB740.

26. HD, August 30, 1927.

27. Dr. Frank Laszlo to HH, September 16, 1927, HP, B2, F60.

28. United States Post Office Department, Hubert H. Harrison Test Score, Clerk-Carrier Examination taken on September 17, 1927, and received December 8, 1927, HP, B14, F15, HPDLC. Harrison, of 646 Lenox Avenue, scored 34 on sorting and 64 on following instructions; his total was 328.

29. Drusilla Dunjee Houston to HH, October 3, 1927, HP, B2, F44. On Drusilla Dunjee Houston (1876–1941), see Drusilla Dunjee Houston, *Wonderful Ethiopians of the Ancient Cushite Empire* (Oklahoma City, 1926; Baltimore, MD: Black Classic Press, 1985), including W. Paul Coates, "Drusilla Dunjee Houston: An Introductory Note About the Author and Her Work," i–iv; and James S. Spady, "Drusilla D. Houston: A Umum Commentary, A Search and Personal Notes," v–viii.

30. Drusilla Dunjee Houston, "True Friends" (for the ANP), *Baltimore Afro-American*, October 22, 1927. Peggy Brooks-Bertram indicated she believed this poem was about Harrison in a phone call followed by a letter, on May 9, 2016. Peggy Brooks-Bertram to JBP, May 9, 2016, possession of JBP.

31. Charles Brook to HH, October 5, November 10, and November 25, 1927, HP, B1, F10.

32. "Vale! Dr. Harrison," Obituary by Men's Forum, Brooklyn Central YMCA, December 30, 1927, HP-Co; John Leslie Platz to HH, December 1927, HP, B3, F11.

33. Arthur Hutter to HH, November 22, 1927, HP, B2, F48.

34. Illegible [Independent Colored Political Club member] to HH, November 29, 1927, HP, B2, F49; Louis B. Bryan, "Brief History of Life and Work of Hubert Harrison," Federal Writers' Project, April 20, 1937, HP-Mi.

35. *GP*, 6:608n1. Garvey was deported to Jamaica from New Orleans.

36. J. A. Rogers to HH, November 26, 1927, HP, B3, F23.

37. Rogers to HH, November 26, 1927. Rogers's comment may be an allusion to Luke 11:33: "No one, after lighting a lamp, puts it away in a cellar nor under a basket, but on the lampstand, so that those who enter may see the light" (New American Standard).

38. Rogers to HH, November 26 1927.

39. Rogers to HH, November 26, 1927. Rogers ended with the postscript: "Remember me especially to Domingo when you see him."

40. J. A. Rogers to HH, undated letter included in Rogers's letter of November 26, 1927, HP-Co.

41. HH, "Harlem's Neglected Opportunities: Twin Source of Gin and Genius, Poetry and Pajama Parties," *Amsterdam News*, November 30, 1927, HP, B4, F68; rpt. in *HR*, 357–62, quotations on 358. William Lloyd Imes (1889–1986) was a minister in Plainfield, New Jersey; Philadelphia; and at St. James Presbyterian Church in New York (1925–1943). See Bruce Kellner, ed., *The Harlem Renaissance: A Historical Dictionary for the Era* (New York: Methuen, 1987), 183; and William Lloyd Imes Papers, Special Collections Research Center, Syracuse University, Syracuse, NY.

42. HH, "Harlem's Neglected Opportunities," 358.

43. HH, "Harlem's Neglected Opportunities," 358–59.

44. HH, "Harlem's Neglected Opportunities," 359.

45. HH, "Harlem's Neglected Opportunities," 359–60.

46. HH, "Harlem's Neglected Opportunities," 360.

47. HH, "Harlem's Neglected Opportunities," 360–61. Harrison may be referring to Donald Baldwin Sr., father of James Baldwin, who played the organ at Trinity Presbyterian Church.

48. HH, "Harlem's Neglected Opportunities," 361.

49. HH, "Harlem's Neglected Opportunities," 361–62.

50. "Harlem Scholar Succumbs After 'Minor' Operation." This article includes a biography, obituary, and photo. See also Charles Brook to HH, October 5, 1927, HP, B1, F10; "Hubert Harrison Dies Suddenly in Bellevue Hospital"; Hubert H. Harrison Standard Certificate of Death, December 17, 1927, Department of Health of the City of New York, Bureau of Records, Register no. 28066, Bellevue Hospital, December 17, 1927; "Dr. Harrison Dies After Operation," *Pittsburgh Courier*, December 24, 1927, HP-Mi; Oscar J. Benson, "Literary Genius of Hubert Harrison," *New York News*, December 24, 1927, SCRBC, NYPL, vertical file (microfilm); "Dr. H. H. Harrison, Noted Colored Lecturer, Dies," *(Survey) Graphic*, December 20, 1927; "Obituary: Hubert H. Harrison," *New York World*, December 18, 1927; "Garvey Aid and Author Passes Away: Hubert H. Harrison Dies in New York," *Chicago Defender*, December 24, 1927, SCRBC, NYPL, vertical file (microfilm) "Hubert Harrison"; and HH, note to Lin (Irene Louise Horton Harrison), c. December 16, 1927, HP, B2, F17, HPDLC. Dr. Peter Wong, of Jersey City, strongly suggests that the actual cause of death was probably peritonitis, a complication resulting from his surgery for chronic appendicitis. Dr. Peter Wong, interviews with JBP, New York City, August 1, 1993, and November 20, 1999.

51. Edgar M. Grey, "Why Great Negroes Die Young," *New York News*, December 31, 1927. An indication of Harrison's work schedule is provided in an undated note he wrote for Edgar Grey in which he says he was up till 6 a.m. and would be getting up again at noon. See HH to Edgar [M.] Gray [Grey], undated, HPDLC. Grey added: "The black man" in the United States "cannot advance a step farther than the white man permits without placing in jeopardy the lease of his life." The "colored man . . . must undergo greater struggles than a white man." He "must come from nothing without assistance by the driving force of his own personality and genius to be recognized by white folks before his own race will recognize him as worth-while." Consequently, "when the Negro arrives at the point of white men's, and resultantly, his race's recognition, he has burnt up more energy than would have been for the average ten white men who reach the top." Grey cited the examples of Bert Williams, George Walker, Paul Laurence Dunbar, Joe Gans, Joe Walcott, Darkey Taylor, Jack Johnson, Florence Mills, and Tiger Flowers.

52. "Harlem Scholar Succumbs After 'Minor' Operation"; "Hubert Harrison Dies Suddenly in Bellevue Hospital"; Benson, "Literary Genius of Hubert Harrison"; "Lament Dream of Dr. Hubert Harrison," *Amsterdam News*, December 28, 1927; Standard Certificate of Death, HH, December 17, 1927; "Dr. H. H. Harrison, Noted Colored Lecturer, Dies." Funeral Arrangements for Hubert. H. Harrison, Receipt, December 31, 1927, HP, B14, F5, HPDLC. J. Lister to Mrs. Hubert H. Harrison, December 23, 1927, HP, B3, F31. Albert T. Saunders Funeral Home, funeral arrangements bill, December 31, 1927. On April 17, 1945, Albert T. Saunders sent a card concerning the grave of Harrison at Woodlawn Cemetery, Lot 130, Sec. 74, Grave 25, HP, B14, F13, HPDLC. Also buried in Harrison's subsequently shared gravesite is Daniel Joseph, a stepnephew of Casper Holstein. The St. Croix historian George F. Tyson explains that Daniel Joseph's mother was Mary Ann Miller and his father was, with "a high degree of certainty," Richard Joseph. Richard Joseph's "father was Albert Johannes Joseph, who [also] fathered Casper Holstein with Emily/Emiline Elizabeth Holstein." George W. Tyson to JBP, July 21, 2016.

53. "Lament Dream of Dr. Hubert Harrison."

54. Standard Certificate of Death, HH, December 17, 1927; "Harlem Scholar Succumbs After 'Minor' Operation"; "Hubert Harrison Dies Suddenly in Bellevue Hospital"; and "[Call Harrison's Death Bellevue Atrocity: His Death; Harlem's Sorrow; Race's Loss] Celebrated Harlem Mass Leader Dies After Operation," *New York News*, December 24, 1927, SCRBC, NYPL vertical file (microfilm), "Hubert Harrison." "Celebrated Harlem Mass Leader Dies After Operation."

55. HH, "Dr. Harrison's Last Article: 'World Problems of Race': Writer Said Both Science and History Try to Rob Negro of Past Heritage; 'Ancient Egyptians' Called White Lest Negroes Get Credit for Medicine, Geometry, Religion and Architecture," *Pittsburgh Courier*, December 31, 1927. This was a reprint of HH, "World Problems of Race," typescript, c. July 8, 1926.

Epilogue

1. Cleveland G. Allen to Mrs. Hubert H. Harrison, December 18, 1927, HP, B1, F1.

2. Casper Holstein, president of VICC, to Mrs. Harrison, December 18, 1927, HP, B2, F41. See also Casper Holstein to [Mrs. Hubert H. Harrison?], calling card signed, [December 1927?], HP, B2, F42.

3. Frank R. Crosswaith, special organizer, Brotherhood of Sleeping Car Porters, to Mrs. Hubert H. Harrison & Family, December 20, 1927. The letterhead of the organization listed: "A. Philip Randolph, General Organizer; W. H. Des Verney, Assistant General Organizer; A. L. Totten, Assistant General Organizer; Roy Lancaster, Secretary-Treasurer; Frank R. Crosswaith, Special Organizer; and S. E. Grain, Field Representative." Geraldo Guirty, *"Sixtonian": Vignettes 'bout "Amalia"* (New York: Vintage, 1991), 78, writes: "Deeply impressed by the messages and oratory of Harrison, Crosswaith was inspired to join the Socialist Party. Harrison gave the eager Crucian the party's address on East 19th Street. The next day he used his lunch hour to visit the socialist office . . . [and] he was given his membership card."

4. A. Philip Randolph, general organizer, Brotherhood of Sleeping Car Porters, to Mrs. Hubert H. Harrison, December 21, 1927, HP, B3, F16.

5. Mabel D. Keaton to Mrs. HHH, typed letter signed, December 20, 1927, HP, B2, F57. The New York Tuberculosis and Health Association, located at 202 West 136th Street, included Harry I. Hopkins, director; E. Eliot Rawlins MD; Miss Ernestine Rose; James H. Hubert; and others.

6. J.A. Rogers to Mrs. Hubert H. Harrison, January 8, 1928, HP, B3, F25.

7. Benson, "Literary Genius of Hubert Harrison."

8. Benson, "Literary Genius of Hubert Harrison." Lester A. Walton, "Street Speaker Heralds Spring in Harlem: Negro Orators Resume Soap-Box Talks on Various Topics," *New York World*, March 25, 1928, added: "Hubert Harrison was in a class by himself as a street speaker. He was well read, could talk interestingly on many subjects and . . . always was able to gather about him a large number of hearers whenever he spoke in Harlem. Usually he discussed some important phase of the race question. He invariably ended by telling of some valuable books or pamphlets which he offered for sale."

9. Benson, "Literary Genius of Hubert Harrison."

10. Benson, "Literary Genius of Hubert Harrison."

11. Andy Razaf, "Hubert H. Harrison Dead!" *New York News*, December 31, 1927, HP-Mi. This poem was based on his 1918 poem "Hubert H. Harrison," *Crusader* 1, no. 4 (December 1918): 17. The first four stanzas, but not the last three, of this poem were rpt. in *HHVHR*, 394.

12. Hodge Kirnon, "Hubert Harrison: An Appreciation," *Negro World*, December 31, 1927, Schomburg Center for Research in Black Culture, New York Public Library, vertical file (microfilm), "Hubert Harrison."

13. Kirnon, "Hubert Harrison: An Appreciation."

14. "The Death of Hubert Harrison," *New York News*, December 31, 1927, Schomburg Center for Research in Black Culture, New York Public Library, vertical file (microfilm), "Hubert Harrison."

15. "Hubert Harrison," *Amsterdam News*, December 28, 1927, 16. The front-page article in the *Amsterdam News* of December 28, 1927, was on Harrison. See "Lament Dream of Dr. Hubert Harrison." The Hubert Harrison obituary also appeared in the *Boston Chronicle* of December 31, 1927 [?]. Schomburg Center for Research in Black Culture, New York Public Library, vertical file (microfilm), "Hubert Harrison." In addition, see "Noted Educator Laid to Rest at Woodlawn—Impressive but Simple Services at Zion," *New York News*, December 31, 1927; "Dr. Harrison Dies After Operation" (dated New York, December 22), *Pittsburgh Courier*, December 24, 1927.

16. "Hubert Harrison," *Amsterdam News*, December 28, 1927, 16.

17. "Hubert Harrison," *Amsterdam News*, December 28, 1927, 16.

18. "Garvey Aid and Author Passes Away," 2, "Celebrated Harlem Mass Leader Dies After Operation."

19. "Hubert Harrison Dies Suddenly in Bellevue Hospital."

20. "Vale! Dr. Harrison."

21. HH, "Dr. Harrison's Last Article," 5. See also May 28, 1926, and July 8, 1926, typescripts discussed in chapter 17.

22. "Hubert H. Harrison!" *Pittsburgh Courier*, December 31, 1927.

23. "Hubert H. Harrison!" *Pittsburgh Courier*, December 31, 1927.

24. Hodge Kirnon to the Editor, "Hubert H. Harrison," *Truth Seeker*, c. January 1928.

25. See Mary Adams [Williana Jones Burroughs], "Record of Revolts in Negro Workers' Past," *Daily Worker*, May 1, 1928.

26. Hodge Kirnon, letter to the Editor, *New York News*, February 17, 1928, HP-Co.

27. Egbert Ethelred Brown, 428 St. Nicholas Avenue, New York City, letter to Mrs. Harrison, re renaming church in honor of HHH, May 5, 1928, HP, B1, F14.

28. Egbert Ethelred Brown, minister, Hubert H. Harrison Memorial Church, to Mrs. Hubert H. Harrison, May 12, 1928, HP, B1, F14. "Harlem Community Church Renamed in Honor of the Late Hubert Harrison," *New York Age*, May 12, 1928; and Ethelred Brown, "A Brief History of the Harlem Unitarian Church," September 11, 1949, 12 pp., esp. 6–7, https://www.meadville.edu/files/resources/brief-history-of-harlem-unitarian-church.pdf.

29. Hubert Harrison Memorial Church, flyer, c. May 20, 1928, HP, B16, F21, HPDLC.

30. Ethelred Brown letter to Mrs. Harrison, Hubert Harrison Memorial Church. June 5, 1928.

31. "He Served Us in Life . . . A Memorial Meeting to Honor the Late Hubert Harrison," June 17, 1928, flyer, HP, B16, F30, HPDLC.

32. Arnold J. Ford, ed., *The Universal Ethiopian Hymnal* (1918; New York: Beth B'nai Abraham Publishing Co., 1926), HP, B19, F4.

33. "Memorial: Late Hubert Harrison Noted Educator and Lecturer," *American Recorder* 1, no. 1 (December 8, 1928): 2.

34. Ethelred Brown letter to Mrs. Harrison, August 26, 1929.

35. Hubert Harrison Memorial Church, December 22, 1929, Memorial Service, Hodge Kirnon Select Reading from Harrison.

36. "Hubert Harrison's Portrait in Library," *Amsterdam News*, September 10, 1930. Neither of these portraits has been located.

37. "Unitarians Make Bow in Harlem: Hubert H. Harrison Memorial Church Changes Name," *Amsterdam News*, May 8, 1937, 13. In death, as in life, Hubert Harrison's views generated controversy and debate. Over twelve years after the 1937 renaming of the Hubert Harrison Memorial Church to its original name as the Harlem Community Church, Rev. Brown stated that "a grave and serious mistake" had been made originally "by changing the name of 'The Harlem Community Church' to 'The Hubert Harrison Memorial Church.'" Brown explained that the church had hoped to draw "to its support a fair proportion of the students of his [Harrison's] 'Outdoor University'" and that "on the contrary, many of those students," the "radicals," had "protested against the naming of the church after Harrison in the face of his known agnostic position." In addition, there were also protests against the naming "on the part of the conservatives," and "for nine years we bore the name of a man who in his lifetime showed no real interest in our work." Ethelred Brown, "A Brief History of the Harlem Unitarian Church," September 11, 1949, pp. 7–8, Unitarian Universalist Association Archives, 24 Farnsworth Street, Boston, MA, 02210.

Index

HH refers to Hubert Harrison